# INVESTMENTS

## *Second Canadian Edition*

**Zvi Bodie**
*Boston University*

**Alex Kane**
*University of California, San Diego*

**Alan J. Marcus**
*Boston University*

**Stylianos Perrakis**
*University of Ottawa*

**Peter J. Ryan**
*University of Ottawa*

Represented in Canada by:
*McGraw-Hill Ryerson Limited*

**IRWIN**

Toronto • Chicago • New York • Auckland • Bogotá
Caracas • Lisbon • London • Madrid • Mexico • Milan
New Delhi • San Juan • Singapore • Sydney • Tokyo

*McGraw-Hill*
*A Division of The **McGraw·Hill** Companies*

INVESTMENTS



This book was printed on acid-free paper.

1 2 3 4 5 6 7 8 9 0 DOC DOC 9 0 9 8 7 6

ISBN 0-256-19522-6

Editor-in-chief: *Dave Ward*
Senior sponsoring editor: *Evelyn Veitch*
Developmental editor: *Elke Price*
Marketing manager: *Gary Bennett*
Project supervisor: *Margaret Rathke*
Senior production supervisor: *Laurie Sander*
Senior designer: *Crispin Prebys*
Prepress Buyer: *Jon Christopher*
Compositor: *Shepard Poorman Communications Corp.*
Typeface: *10/12 Times Roman*
Printer: *R. R. Donnelley & Sons Company*

Library of Congress Catalog Card Number 96-61051

http://www.mhcollege.com

# To the Student

## "Why Are Textbook Prices So High?"

This is, by far, the most frequently asked question heard in the college publishing industry. There are many factors that influence the price of your new textbook. Here are just a few:

### Author Royalties

Authors are paid based on a percentage of new book sales and do not receive royalties on the sale of a used book. They also are deprived of their rightful royalties when their books are illegally photocopied.

### The Cost of Instructor Support Materials

Your instructor may be making use of teaching supplements, many of which are provided by the publisher. Teaching supplements include videos, colour transparencies, instructor's manuals, software, computerized testing materials, and more. These supplements are designed as part of a learning package to enhance your educational experience.

### Developmental Costs

These costs are associated with the extensive development of your textbook. Expenses include permissions fees, manuscript review costs, artwork, typesetting, printing and binding costs, and more.

### Marketing Costs

Instructors need to be made aware of new textbooks. Marketing costs include academic conventions, remuneration of the publisher's representatives, promotional advertizing pieces, and the provision of instructor's examination copies.

### Bookstore Markups

In order to stay in business, your local bookstore must cover its costs. A textbook is a commodity, just like any other item your bookstore may sell, and bookstores are the most effective way to get the textbook from the publisher to you.

## Publisher Profits

In order to continue to supply students with quality textbooks, publishers must make a profit to stay in business. Like the authors, publishers do not receive any compensation from the sale of a used book or the illegal photocopying of their textbooks.

We at Irwin/McGraw-Hill Ryerson Limited hope you will find this information useful and that it addresses some of your concerns. We also thank you for your purchase of this new textbook.

McGraw-Hill Ryerson Limited
College Division
300 Water Street
Whitby, Ontario L1N 9B6

# About the Authors

## Zvi Bodie

*Boston University*

Zvi Bodie is Professor of Finance and Economics at the Boston University School of Management. He is the director of Boston University's Chartered Financial Analysts Examination Review Program and has served as consultant to many private and governmental organizations. Professor Bodie is a research associate of the National Bureau of Economic Research, where he was director of the NBER Project on Financial Aspects of the U.S. Pension System, and he is a member of the Pension Research Council of The Wharton School. He is widely published in leading professional journals, and his previous books include *Pensions in the U.S. Economy, Issues in Pension Economics,* and *Financial Aspects of the U.S. Pension System*.

## Alex Kane

*University of California, San Diego*

Alex Kane is Professor of Finance and Economics at the University of California, San Diego, and is a fellow of the National Bureau of Economic Research in the Financial Markets and Monetary Economics Group. The author of many articles published in finance and management journals, Professor Kane has research interests in the areas of capital market theory, corporate finance, and portfolio management.

## Alan J. Marcus

*Boston University*

Alan Marcus is Associate Professor of Finance at Boston University. He is a research fellow of the National Bureau of Economic Research, where he participates in the Financial Markets and Monetary Economics Group. He also took part in the NBER project on pension economics. Professor Marcus has been a research fellow of the Center for the Study of Futures Markets at Columbia University. His main research interests are futures and options markets, and he has published more than 20 articles in these and related areas. Professor Marcus is currently a member of the Financial Research department at Freddie Mac, the Federal Home Loan Mortgage Corporation.

## Stylianos Perrakis
*University of Ottawa*

Stylianos Perrakis is Professor of Finance and Economics, with a joint appointment at the Faculty of Administration and the Department of Economics of the University of Ottawa. Professor Perrakis is the author of many articles published in leading academic and professional journals in economics and finance, especially in the areas of industrial organization, corporate finance, and option pricing. He has served as a consultant to many private and governmental organizations, including the Institute of Canadian Bankers and the World Bank. He is also the author of *Canadian Industrial Organisation* and has taught as a visiting professor in universities in Switzerland, France, and the United States.

## Peter J. Ryan
*University of Ottawa*

Peter Ryan is Associate Professor of Finance at the University of Ottawa. His research interests include both contingent claims in general and the incentive effects of financial claims in corporate structures. His articles on the subject of options and financial instruments have been published in a number of international journals in finance and management science.

# Foreword

Along with the explosive growth in world financial markets has come an interaction between scholarly theory and day-to-day business practice that is unprecedented in the history of economics. Not only are the tools of modern finance the accepted modes of analysis for sophisticated investors and traders, they are also the sources of many of the new products that are dramatically altering the financial markets. For the teacher of investments, however, the excitement and relevance of the field are matched by its dangers. A teacher must carefully craft a course for the student that balances the ever-changing and often unsettled background of scholarly theories against the temptation to titillate with the latest fad to hit the securities markets. The only way to teach successfully in such a minefield is to take a firm grasp of what is truly fundamental and to utilize what is happening in the financial markets to illustrate the workings of these fundamentals. *Investments* accomplishes that difficult task with consummate skill.

*Investments* sensibly begins with an overview that lays out the workings of the securities markets in a thorough but lively fashion. After the student has been exposed to the institutional structure of the securities markets, the fundamental intuitions of the trade-off between return and risk and the role of information are developed and used to clarify the workings of the markets. The major asset-pricing models are all treated with a commendable clarity that should make teaching them a pleasure.

A central theme of the book is the investor's perspective on using securities to form portfolios. The fine treatments of the stock and fixed-income markets further this theme with their emphasis on the empirical properties of these markets, and derivative securities such as options and futures become natural topics from the perspective of how they fit into investor portfolios. A careful distinction is drawn between passive and active investment management, and this distinction is used to great advantage to deal with such troublesome matters as the reconciliation of the efficient market hypotheses with active management. As with all the material, a clear presentation of the theory is accompanied by a rich matrix of institutional material within which it is applied.

Students and teachers will welcome this thoroughly modern and well executed treatment of investments. I believe that it will become the central text in the field.

***Stephen A. Ross***

# Preface

In teaching and practice, the field of investments has experienced many changes over the last two decades. This is due in part to an abundance of newly designed securities, in part to the creation of new trading strategies that would have been impossible without concurrent advances in computer technology, and in part to rapid advances in the theory of investments that have come out of the academic community. In no other field, perhaps, is the transmission of theory to real-world practice as rapid as is now commonplace in the financial industry. These developments place new burdens on practitioners and teachers of investments far beyond what was required only a short while ago.

*Investments* is intended primarily as a textbook for courses in investment analysis. Its guiding principle has been to present the material in a framework that is organized by a central core of consistent fundamental principles. Every attempt was made to strip away unnecessary mathematical and technical detail, and to provide the intuition that may guide students and practitioners as they confront new ideas and challenges in their professional lives.

The primary goal of this text is to present material of practical value, but all five co-authors are active researchers in the science of financial economics and find virtually all of the material in this book to be of great intellectual interest. Fortunately, we think, there is no contradiction in the field of investments between the pursuit of truth and the pursuit of wealth. Quite the opposite. The capital asset pricing model, the arbitrage pricing model, the efficient markets hypothesis, the option-pricing model, and the other centerpieces of modern financial research are as much intellectually satisfying subjects of scientific inquiry as they are of immense practical importance for the sophisticated investor.

Since 1983, the three U.S. authors have participated in an annual review program in Boston for candidates from all over the world preparing for the Chartered Financial Analyst examinations. The book has benefited from this CFA experience in two ways. First, the text has incorporated much of the content of the readings and other study materials in the official CFA curriculum. As a result, the book includes some material not found in most other investments texts. Second, we have included questions from CFA examinations in the end-of-chapter problem sets throughout the book. The number of CFA questions has been greatly expanded in this edition.

## Realistic Presentation of Modern Portfolio Theory

The exposition of modern portfolio theory in this text differs from its presentation in all other major investments texts in that we develop the basic model starting with a risk-free asset, such as a Treasury bill, and a single risky asset, such as a common stock mutual fund.[1] Not until later are other risky assets added. Other texts develop the model by first assuming that the investor has to choose from two risky assets; only later do they introduce the possibility of investing in a risk-free asset. Ultimately both approaches reach the same end point, which is a model in which there are many risky assets in addition to a risk-free asset.

We think our approach is better for two important reasons. First, it corresponds to the actual procedure that most individual investors follow. Typically, one starts with all of one's money invested in a bank account and only then considers how much to invest in something riskier that may offer the prospect of a higher expected return. The next logical step is to consider the addition of other risky assets, such as real estate or gold, which requires determining whether the benefits of such increased diversification are worth the additional transaction costs involved in including them in one's portfolio.

The second advantage of our approach is that it vastly simplifies exposition of the mathematics for deriving the menu of risk-return combinations open to the investor. Portfolio optimization techniques are mathematically complex, ultimately requiring a computer. Anything that can help to simplify their presentation should thus be welcome. In short, we believe our approach is both more realistic and analytically simpler than the conventional one.

## Changes in the Second Canadian Edition

In this second edition we have introduced substantial changes from the first Canadian and the U.S. editions. These result from efforts to streamline the presentation, as textbooks inevitably tend to grow beyond manageable lengths with the additon of recent developments. Our intent was to limit material to what is likely to be needed in investments and portfolio theory courses, while providing sufficient depth in important topics and indicating the extensions to more advanced concepts. Some re-ordering of topics has occurred, as we have tried to respond to the reactions of various reviewers and past users of the text.

This Canadian edition is both an adaptation of the U.S. text for a Canadian audience and an extension of the material to incorporate several topics of specific Canadian interest. The adaptation has changed the presentation and examples of the basic material with respect to currency, macroeconomic environment, tax rates and legislation, and other legal and institutional features of the Canadian econ-

[1] We define and discuss mutual funds in Chapter 4. For now it is sufficient to know that a common stock mutual fund is a diversified portfolio of stocks in which an investor can invest as much money as desired.

omy. Thus, the first four chapters include a description of the markets, instruments, and institutions that are specific to the Canadian environment, as well as a summary description of the same concepts in the U.S. context.

The inclusion of the U.S. material was motivated by several factors. First, much of the investment activity by Canadian investors takes place in U.S. markets, implying that Canadian investment professionals cannot afford to ignore the situation south of their country's border. Second, not only does the U.S. market set the standards for most of the financial innovation and research in Canada, but it also paces many of the economic developments that underlie the performance of the Canadian financial system.

Nevertheless, several Canadian financial aspects are unique and deserve more extended coverage in their theoretical and empirical aspects. What follows is a summary of major additions and innovations in the seven parts of this edition; however, we cannot mention in this brief preface all the differences from the former editions.

## Part I: Introduction

This section in the second Canadian edition has been reorganized by shortening the first chapter and moving details to Chapters 3 and 4. The fourth chapter includes material on individual and institutional concerns that had previously been in the eighth part, as well as details of taxation and mutual funds. This chapter serves to provide students with motivation for many of the complex analyses and strategies that follow, introducing many concepts in general terms. Chapter 3 has been repackaged to include an explanation of market structure and to remove the mutual fund section.

## Part II: Portfolio Theory

The introductory material on concepts and issues has been moved from the first section and combined with the theoretical concepts of utility, risk aversion, and portfolio construction as well as an introduction to interest and interest rates. Chapters 6 and 7 are essentially unchanged, except for the addition of a section on asset allocation from Chapter 24 of the previous edition; this serves to illustrate the process for individuals as detailed in the chapter.

## Part III: Equilibrium in Capital Markets

In Chapter 8, material on the multifactor CAPM that previously appeared in the appendix has been compressed and added as a subsection in section 2 of the chapter. In addition, a new section has been added to explain how the CAPM can be extended to account for the costs of liquidity. The remaining chapters are largely unchanged, except for the addition of more recent data. Coverage of international diversification has been moved to Part IV.

## Part IV: Active Portfolio Management

Chapter 11 is an updated version of the former Chapter 12 and includes extensive new evidence on anomalies in both Canada and the United States. The following chapter is an amalgamation of the former separate chapters on active management and performance measurement. This avoids the problems that result from presenting either theory before practical insights or practical techniques without theoretical basis, as well as the repetition that separate treatment entails. We have tried to present a logical path through the subject by starting with the active manager's objective and the problem of measurement under active management, followed by the conventional theory of evaluation and an analysis of the measures used. The next step is to identify and evaluate the two subjects of timing and selectivity; this leads to the practice of asset allocation and the attribution of performance to different decisions in the process. Finally, the general issue of performance evaluation is examined by way of reporting and results. The last chapter on international investing has been moved to this part and re-ordered somewhat, with an additional subsection discussing the techniques available for international diversification.

## Part V: Fixed-Income Securities

There is a significant revision to Chapter 14 (formerly Chapter 15) in this edition. The first section introduces the various types of bond instruments, followed by a discussion of the risk of default and bond indentures. The material on bond prices and yields has been expanded and the topic of realized compound yield to maturity has been advanced from the following chapter. The chapter on term structure also has been expanded to relate more to bond pricing and forward rates; the subject of measurement of the term structure has been amplified, and the bootstrapping method has been outlined. In the final chapter in this part, the first section has been expanded to present more motivation for managing interest rate risk, and bond duration has been given a complete section.

## Part VI: Equities

Chapter 17, on security analysis, has undergone significant re-packaging to shorten the presentation of less critical material. The first section presents balance sheet valuation and incorporates the discussion of intrinsic versus market valuation. Dividend discount models are presented much more briefly, with details of derivation moved to the appendix. Earnings, growth, and P/E analysis are integrated and now are followed by a new section contrasting the growth and value investing approaches. The following sections are similar to the first edition, with some expansion of the industry analysis portion. The contingent claims approach to valuation has been moved to the appendix. Chapters 18 and 19 have only minor changes, consisting of the removal of the material on value investing, the relocation of the Graham approach in Chapter 17, and the inclusion of additional academic evidence on the validity of these approaches of financial statement and technical analysis.

## Part VII: Derivative Assets

Chapter 20 has been reorganized to include a description of options and option-like securities and now includes trading strategies and innovations; there is a new subsection on exotic options, while valuation has been moved to the following chapter, now entitled Option Valuation. This chapter contains most material from the old introductory chapter on elementary bounds and option-pricing models. The chapter on futures has been updated and enhanced. The material in Chapter 23 can be expected to change with each new edition. The most recent important developments in investment research will be presented in Chapter 23 so as to keep the reader abreast of new directions. In this edition we discuss the significance of stochastic volatility of asset returns, some challenges to the classical CAPM pricing of assets, and the effect of differential borrowing and lending rates on option pricing.

## Part VIII: Players and Strategies

This part has been eliminated with material moved to earlier chapters. This decision was made both to condense the book and to make the material available to readers where it is more likely to be read.

## Acknowledgments

As Canadian authors, we first would like to express our gratitude to Professors Bodie, Kane, and Marcus for their production of what we recognized to be an outstanding text in its original form. Also, we are grateful for their agreement to join in our production of a Canadian edition. In addition, a large number of reviewers read both the first and the revised editions of the American text. Of these, coincidentally, Jean Masson is now our colleague and has contributed information used in our version. All of these persons deserve thanks for their particular insights. We also would like to note the extensive contributions and comments of our Canadian reviewers; almost all of their suggestions were incorporated into the final draft, as they led to clarifications and more effective presentations. These reviewers were:

| | |
|---|---|
| Steve Beveridge | University of Alberta |
| Francis Boabang | Saint Mary's University |
| Alex Faseruk | Memorial University |
| Larbi Hammami | McGill University |
| I.G. Morgan | Queen's University |
| Eben Otuteye | University of New Brunswick |

| | |
|---|---|
| Alam Shamsul | University of Lethbridge |
| Harry Turtle | University of Manitoba |
| Brian Warrack | Wilfrid Laurier University |

A great quantity of material and information was contributed by Gilles Gagne of Nesbitt Burns over the course of the writing of the text. Other institutions giving considerable support were ScotiaMcLeod and the Export Development Corporation. For granting permission to include many of their examination questions in the text, we are grateful to the Institute of Chartered Financial Analysts.

Many of the tables and graphs have been compiled from information provided through the cooperation of Statistics Canada. Readers wishing further information may obtain copies of related publications by mail from Publications Sales, Statistics Canada, Ottawa, Ontario K1A 0T6. Copies also may be obtained by calling 613-951-7277 or calling toll-free, 800-267-6677. Readers also may facsimile their orders by dialing 613-951-1584.

Much of the work of obtaining data, locating articles, and reproducing and collating manuscript chapters was performed by Danny Perrakis; we are happy to acknowledge his assistance.

Much credit also is due to the development and production team at Irwin: our special thanks go to Rod Banister, Publisher; Evelyn Veitch, Sponsoring Editor; Elke Price, Developmental Editor; Becky Dodson, Project Editor; and the rest of the development team.

***Stylianos Perrakis***
***Peter J. Ryan***

# Brief Contents

# Contents

# Prologue

**THIS IS A BOOK ABOUT INVESTING IN SECURITIES SUCH AS STOCKS, BONDS, OPTIONS, AND FUTURES CONTRACTS.** It is intended to provide an understanding of how to analyze these securities, how to determine whether they are appropriate for inclusion in your **investment portfolio**[1] (the set of securities you choose to hold), and how to buy and sell them.

We can usefully divide the process of investing, both in theory and in practice, into two parts: security analysis and portfolio management. **Security analysis** is the attempt to determine whether an individual security is correctly valued in the marketplace; that is, it is the search for mispriced securities. **Portfolio management** is the process of combining securities into a portfolio tailored to the investor's preferences and needs, monitoring that portfolio, and evaluating its performance. This book is intended to provide a thorough treatment of both parts of the investment process.

This book is designed first and foremost to impart knowledge of practical value to anyone interested in becoming an investment professional or a sophisticated private investor. It provides a lot of institutional detail, but of necessity it also contains a lot of theory. It is impossible to be a sophisticated investor or investment professional today without a sound basis in valuation theory, modern portfolio theory, and option pricing theory at the level presented in the following chapters.

---

[1] Throughout this text key terms are denoted in boldface, summarized at the end of each chapter, and defined in the Glossary.

# THE MAIN THEMES OF INVESTMENTS

## The Risk-Return Trade-off

One simple strategy for an investor to pursue is to keep all of his or her money invested in a bank account. This strategy has a number of advantages. It is safe, and it requires no expertise and little effort on the part of the investor.

However, if an investor is willing to consider the possibility of taking on some risk, there is the potential reward of higher expected returns. A considerable part of this book is devoted to exploring the nature of this **risk-return trade-off** and the principles of rational portfolio choice associated with it. The approach we present is known as **modern portfolio theory (MPT).**

The main organizing principle of MPT is **efficient diversification.** The basic idea is that any investor who is averse to risk, that is, who requires a higher expected return in order to increase exposure to risk, will be made better off by reorganizing the portfolio so as to increase its expected return without taking on additional risk.

In this book we devote considerable space to explaining the principles of efficient diversification and applying them to the issue of **asset allocation.** Asset allocation is the choice of how much to invest in each of the broad asset classes—stocks, bonds, cash, real estate, foreign securities, *derivative securities,*[2] gold, and possibly others to achieve the best portfolio given the investor's objectives and constraints.

## Active vs. Passive Management

We define **passive management** as a strategy of holding a well-diversified portfolio of generic security types without attempting to outperform other investors through superior market forecasting or superior ability to find mispriced securities. Depending on the approach used to find the best portfolio mix, passive management can be quite sophisticated. Indeed, as we show in our exposition of the asset allocation decision, efficient diversification can be a rather complex process, requiring many inputs and the aid of a computer.

**Active management** can take two forms: market timing and security selection. The most popular kind of **market timing** is trying to time the stock market, increasing one's commitment to stocks when one is "bullish" (when one thinks the market will do relatively well), and moving out of stocks when one is "bearish." But market timing is potentially just as profitable in the markets for fixed-income securities, where the name of the game is forecasting interest rates. Successful market timing, whether in the market for stocks or for bonds, requires superior forecasting ability.

---

[2] Derivative securities include options and futures contracts. They are described briefly in Chapter 2 and then discussed in much greater detail in Part VII.

**Security selection** is the attempt to find mispriced securities and to improve one's risk-return trade-off by concentrating on such securities. Security selection can involve both buying those securities believed to be underpriced and selling those believed to be overpriced. Successful security selection requires the sacrifice of some amount of diversification.

There is a large body of empirical evidence to support a theory called the **efficient markets hypothesis (EMH),** which among other things says that active management of both types should not be expected to work for very long. The basic reasoning behind the EMH is that in a competitive financial environment successful trading strategies tend to "self-destruct." Bargains may exist for brief periods, but with so many talented, highly paid analysts scouring the markets for them, by the time you or I "discover" them, they are no longer bargains.

To be sure, there are some extremely successful investors, but according to the EMH one can account for some or all of them on the basis of luck rather than skill. And even if their success in the past derived from skill at finding some extraordinary bargains, the EMH would say that their chances to continue to find more in the future are slight. Even the legendary Benjamin Graham,[3] the father of modern security analysis and the teacher of some of today's investment giants, has said that the job of finding true bargains has become difficult if not impossible in today's competitive environment. In part, this situation is testimony to the success Graham and his followers have had in teaching the principles of fundamental analysis.

Our view is that markets are nearly efficient. Nevertheless, even in this competitive environment profit opportunities may exist for especially diligent and creative investors. This idea motivates our treatment of active portfolio management in Part IV.

## Equilibrium Pricing Relationships

A fascinating feature of financial markets, and one that is not at all apparent to the untrained observer, is that the prices of securities must often have a specific relationship to each other, because if the relationships are violated market forces will come into play to restore them. Financial economists refer to these as *equilibrium pricing relationships,* and in this text we explain them in detail.

Perhaps the most important of these relationships is well known and accepted in both academic and professional circles. It is known as the principle of **arbitrage.** Arbitrage is the act of buying an asset at one price and simultaneously selling it or its equivalent at a higher price. If you can buy Seagram's stock over-the-counter (OTC) for $40 per share and sell it on the Toronto Stock Exchange (TSE) for $40.50, you can make a risk-free, instantaneous arbitrage profit of 50 cents per share.

[3] We will have much more to say about Graham and his ideas about investing in Chapter 17.

Pure arbitrage opportunities of this sort are very rare, because it requires only the participation of a few arbitrageurs to eliminate the price differential. The increased demand for Seagram's by arbitrageurs buying on the OTC market would drive the price above $40, and the increased supply on the TSE would drive the price down, until the stock would reach a single price in both markets. To academics, the *single price law* or **law of one price** is the fundamental concept in establishing market prices. Stated simply, this principle ensures that equivalent securities or bundles of securities are priced so that risk-free arbitrage is not possible.

Practitioners and academics may often disagree about the right way to characterize equilibrium yield and price relationships, but almost everyone would agree that the law of one price holds almost all of the time in the securities markets. Our example is a simplified illustration of arbitrage and the activity of arbitrageurs that ignores complications such as transaction costs; usually arbitrage opportunities involve not one security but combinations of them. "Financial engineers" create new securities and price them by applying the law of one price to the future cash flows generated by them, by comparison to the cash flows of combinations of existing securities.

Of the remaining relationships, some of the best known, are the following:

1. The security market line (expected return-beta) relationship.
2. The put-call parity relationship.
3. The Black-Scholes option pricing model.
4. The spot-futures parity relationship.
5. The international interest rate parity relationship.

These relationships are more than just intellectually pleasing theoretical constructs. In most cases if they are violated, the first investors to discover the violation have opportunities for large profits with little or no risk. For example, the recent practice of *program trading* is primarily a systematic method of profiting from violations of equilibrium pricing relationships in the market for the Standard & Poor's 500 stock-index futures contract.

A well-trained investment professional must not only be aware of these equilibrium relationships, but also must understand why they exist and how to profit from any violation of them. We have tried to provide the basis for this knowledge throughout the book, as well as in the specific chapters in which these relationships are presented and explained.

## The Use of Options and Futures Contracts in Implementing Investment Strategy

In today's securities markets, there are a variety of ways sophisticated investors can tailor the set of possible investment outcomes to their specific knowledge or preferences regarding security returns. The emergence of markets for so-called derivative securities such as options and futures contracts has made it possible to implement strategies unheard of only a few short years ago. Perhaps in no other area of investments is the recent business school graduate at a greater advantage over the investment veteran who studied investments several years ago.

Probably the most well known of these strategies is *portfolio insurance.* There are a variety of ways an investor can combine stocks and/or bonds with derivative securities to eliminate the possibility of loss of principal while preserving much of the upside potential of an investment in the stock market. These securities and strategies are here to stay. The investment professional must understand and master them if he or she is to avoid technological obsolescence.

In our chapters on derivative securities we explain in some detail and with a minimum of mathematics the use of options and futures in implementing portfolio insurance and other investment strategies.

## Text Organization

The text has seven parts, which are fairly independent and may be studied in a variety of sequences. Part I is introductory and contains much institutional material. Part II contains the core of modern portfolio theory as it relates to optimal portfolio selection. Part III contains the core of modern portfolio theory as it relates to the equilibrium structure of expected rates of return on risky assets. It builds on the material in Part II and therefore must be preceded by it.

Part IV is devoted to active portfolio management and performance measurement. It has as a prerequisite the material on MPT in Part II. Part V, which is on the analysis and valuation of fixed-income securities, is the first of three parts on security valuation. Part VI is devoted to equity securities. Part VII covers derivative assets such as options, futures contracts, and convertible securities.

### Canadian and U.S. Content

The main object of our study is the Canadian investment environment. Thus, whenever we refer to unspecified securities, financial markets, or investment professionals, it should be implicitly understood that we refer to Canadian ones. Likewise, we have tried to report extensively on the main Canadian studies on each topic.

Nonetheless, this book is addressed to the problems of Canadian investors. It cannot, therefore, ignore the fact that much Canadian investing takes place abroad, especially in the United States. Accordingly, we have covered in detail all relevant U.S. features of every topic discussed in this book. This is particularly true for those topics where significant differences exist between Canada and the United States, or where there are no Canadian counterparts. As we shall see, the existence of an investment opportunity in the United States can also frequently serve the needs of Canadian investors and, thus, precludes the establishment of a comparable opportunity in Canada.

## Other Features

A unique feature is the inclusion of self-test questions and problems within the following chapters. These Concept Checks are designed to provide the student with a means for determining whether he or she has understood the preceding material and for reinforcing that understanding. Detailed solutions to all Concept Checks are provided at the end of the book.

These in-chapter questions may be used in a variety of ways. They may be skipped altogether in a first reading of the chapter with no loss in continuity. They can then be done with any degree of diligence and intensity upon the second reading. Finally, they can serve as models for solving the end-of-chapter problems.

The end-of-chapter problems progress from the simple to the complex. We strongly believe that practice in solving problems is a critical part of learning investments, so we have provided many opportunities. Many are taken from past (U.S.) chartered financial analyst examinations and therefore represent the kinds of questions that professionals in the field believe are relevant to the "real world."

# The Investments Field and Career Opportunities

As with any other field of scientific inquiry, the theory of investments is constantly changing and, we believe, advancing. In that sense we too are always learning something new. What makes it especially exciting is that the lag between discovery and application in investments is extraordinarily short. For example, the Black-Scholes option pricing formula and the dynamic hedging strategy that is its mainspring were developed in 1973.[4] Just a few years later practitioners were busy applying it on the Chicago Board Options Exchange.

Far from being an exception, the example of the Black-Scholes formula has become the paradigm for the relationship between the academic and applied worlds in investments. Indeed, Fischer Black himself is an example of this development, moving from a professorship at MIT's Sloan School of Management to a full partnership in the investment banking firm of Goldman Sachs.

We believe that the filed of investments offers great opportunities for careers that are both fascinating and lucrative, but the competition is fierce. A mastery of the material in this text will, we hope, give you a competitive advantage.

[4] See Fischer Black and M. Scholes, "The Pricing of Options and Corporate Liabilities," *Journal of Political Economy,* May–June 1973.

## Key Terms

Investment portfolio
Security analysis
Portfolio management
Risk-return trade-off
Modern portfolio theory
Efficient diversification
Asset allocation
Passive management
Active management
Market timing
Security selection
Efficient markets hypothesis
Arbitrage
Law of one price

*Part I*

# Introduction

*Chapter 1*

# The Investment Environment

**EVEN A CURSORY GLANCE AT THE FINANCIAL PAGES OF DAILY NEWSPAPERS REVEALS A BEWILDERING COLLECTION OF SECURITIES, MARKETS, AND FINANCIAL INSTITUTIONS.** Although it may appear chaotic, the financial environment is not so: there is rhyme and reason behind the array of instruments and markets. The central message we want to convey in this chapter is that financial markets and institutions evolve in response to the desires, technologies, and regulatory constraints of the investors in the economy. In fact, we could *predict* the general shape of the investment environment (if not the design of particular securities) if we knew nothing more than these desires, technologies, and constraints.

Competition and liquidity are major factors of the investment environment, and their interplay helps to define the resultant structure. If government regulations do not prohibit competition, then more attractive instruments and markets will draw both capital and companies seeking capital away from their illiquid counterparts. We see the impact of this in Canadian markets, where many innovative instruments available in the United States do not have Canadian equivalents; insufficient liquidity in Canada either precludes the establishment of markets or has caused their demise. Competition implies that these U.S. instruments are available to Canadian investors; thus, a presentation of both U.S. instruments and available Canadian equivalents is necessary for a complete appreciation of the environment.

This chapter provides a broad overview of the investment environment. We begin by describing the purpose of investing and examining the difference between financial investment and real investment. We then proceed to the four sectors of the financial environment: household, business, government, and foreign. We see how many features of the investment environment are natural responses of profit-seeking firms and individuals to opportunities created by the demands of these sectors, and we examine the driving forces behind financial innovation. Next, we discuss current trends in financial markets. We conclude the chapter with a discussion of the issue of ownership and control of the corporation.

## 1.1 The Investment Objective

The reader of a book on investments presumably has a good idea of what the objective of investing is—making a return on capital. This broad statement, however, encompasses a range of possibilities for the kind of return expected, from a safe, guaranteed percentage each year to a chance at a quick and large profit. (In the investment world, phrases such as *preservation of capital* and *speculation* may be used to describe these objectives.) Different kinds of investors will be attracted to strategies from the very conservative to the very risky, and at times to combinations of them, based on their future needs; how much, how safely, and how quickly they want their return on capital, together with their personal tolerances for risk, will dictate the kinds of investments they are likely to make at different stages of their lives. In Chapter 4, we address these concerns more specifically, but for now we need only explain the interplay between investors' desires and the requirements that users of capital have.

Investment choices must be linked directly to the question of the timing of consumption. An investor chooses to exchange current consumption for later wealth available for future consumption. This reflects current needs and the anticipation of future needs. In theory, the choice will be made so as to maximize the utility for consumption over the investor's lifetime. The choice also must respect the riskiness of certain types of investments and its effect on necessary consumption in the near future.

The participants in the financial system are divided between those who have a surplus of capital for their present needs and those who have a deficit of capital. Generally, the former group comprises individuals and the latter, corporations and governments. In order to obtain capital, those with a deficit must issue securities, which are bought by those with excess funds. The types of securities or financial instruments will be defined formally in the following chapter, but we can begin by talking about stocks and bonds, issued by private corporations. While the bonds are notes which acknowledge indebtedness and specify the terms of repayment, stocks are instruments that convey ownership rights to their holders with no guarantee of any fixed, or even positive, return. Stocks enable investors to participate in business activities while being protected from the major deficiencies of individual ownership or partnership. They are relatively liquid, enabling the investor to extract the true value of the shares fairly quickly, and they offer limited liability, so that the greatest loss to be suffered is the investment itself, in the case of a catastrophe in the business.

Investors are a very diverse group. Some of them are content with a fixed return if the principal is guaranteed; these investors usually place funds in a savings account. Others are looking for opportunities to double their investment in a matter of days. Neither of these extremes is of much interest to the subject of this book; some might label these individuals as "hoarders" or "speculators" rather than investors. There is a place, however, for both of these behaviours within the overall investment plan of an investor, provided this is part of a portfolio of investments. At times, cash may be held in a safe form with virtually no return, while highly risky investments offering extravagant returns also can be justified.

Similarly, corporations and governments have different characteristics. Some may need capital for a short period with an almost certain return to be derived in the normal course of business. Others may need funds for risky business projects, with uncertain payoff schedules and levels. The first kind are likely to finance with short-term instruments, while the latter will need to issue shares in their companies.

The issuing of new shares by corporations points to an area of misunderstanding for the novice investor. He expects to buy shares at one price and profit by reselling them at a higher price; or perhaps there is a loss involved. But who sells and repurchases the shares from the investor? Contrary to mistaken belief, it is not the corporation itself that is buying and selling; it is other investors. The activity reported in the financial news refers to the resale of existing shares between investors, and rarely to the issuance, or even repurchase, of shares by the originating corporations. This resale market, or exchange, is significant in the area of corporate finance for various reasons, but the major importance of the exchange is to establish a fair market valuation of the shares. This ultimately becomes relevant to the corporation when it needs to issue new shares at a fair price, which only occurs when it needs to raise new capital.

## Real Investment versus Financial Investment

What we have been discussing so far is **financial investment,** that is, the investment by individuals in stocks and bonds of corporations. For the most part, this occurs as investors enter the securities markets and exchange cash for the financial instruments. Since the cash is exchanged between investors and no new capital reaches the corporations, no **real investment** occurs as a result of this activity. Real investment only occurs when a corporation takes capital and invests it in productive assets; this may come about as a result of reinvested profits, but major real investment requires the issuance of new debt or equity instruments.

Real investment is channeled into **real assets,** which determine the productive capacity of the economy. These real assets are the land, buildings, machines, and knowledge necessary to produce goods, together with the workers and their skills in operating those resources. In contrast to real assets are **financial assets,** such as stocks or bonds. These assets, per se, do not represent a society's wealth. Shares of stock are no more than sheets of paper; they do not directly contribute to the productive capacity of the economy. Instead, financial assets contribute to the productive capacity of the economy *indirectly,* because they allow for separation of the ownership and management of the firm and facilitate the transfer of funds to enterprises with attractive investment opportunities. Financial assets certainly contribute to the wealth of the individuals or firms holding them, because they are *claims* to the income generated by real assets or claims on income from the government.

When the real assets used by a firm ultimately generate income, that income is allocated to investors according to their ownership of financial assets, or securities, issued by the firm. Bondholders, for example, are entitled to a flow of income based on the interest rate and par value of the bond. Equity holders or stockholders are entitled to any residual income after bondholders and other creditors are paid. In this way the values of financial assets are derived from and depend on the values of the underlying real assets of the firm.

Real assets are income-generating assets, whereas financial assets define the allocation of income or wealth among investors. Individuals can choose between consuming their current endowments of wealth today and investing for the future. When they invest for the future, they may choose to hold financial assets. The money a firm receives when it issues securities (sells them to investors) is used to purchase real assets. Ultimately, then, the returns on a financial asset come from the income produced by the real assets that are financed by the issuance of the security. In this way, it is useful to view financial assets as the means by which individuals hold their claims on real assets in well-developed economies. Most of us cannot personally own a bank, but we can hold shares of the Royal Bank or the Bank of Nova Scotia, which provide us with income derived from providing banking services.

An operational distinction between real and financial assets involves the balance sheets of individuals and firms in the economy. Real assets appear only on the asset side of the balance sheet. In contrast, financial assets always appear on both sides of balance sheets. Your financial claim on a firm is an asset, but the firm's issuance of that claim is the firm's liability. When we aggregate over all balance sheets, financial assets will cancel out, leaving only the sum of real assets as the net wealth of the aggregate economy.

Another way of distinguishing between financial and real assets is to note that financial assets are created *and destroyed* in the ordinary course of doing business. For example, when a loan is paid off, both the creditor's claim (a financial asset) and the debtor's obligation (a financial liability) cease to exist. In contrast, real assets are destroyed only by accident or by wearing out over time.

**CONCEPT CHECK** Question 1. Are the following assets real or financial?

*a.* Patents
*b.* Lease obligations
*c.* Customer good will
*d.* A college education
*e.* A $5 bill

## 1.2 CLIENTS OF THE FINANCIAL SYSTEM

We start our analysis with a broad view of the major clients that place demands on the financial system. By considering the needs of these clients and the risks they face, we can gain considerable insight into why organizations and institutions have evolved as they have.

The traditional classification of the investment clientele identifies three sectors: household, corporate, and government. This classification is convenient, although it has problems in allocating not-for-profit agencies, among others. It also is deficient in a financial sense for Canada, since it excludes the position of the foreign sector. Consequently, we identify the net position of investment in foreign assets against holdings by foreign investors as the fourth sector.

### The Household Sector

Households constantly make economic decisions that affect their present and future cash flows, but we will consider most of these decisions as already made and focus on financial decisions specifically, selecting the financial assets that households desire to hold.

Even this limited focus, however, leaves a broad range of issues to consider. Most households are potentially interested in a wide array of assets, and the assets that are attractive can vary considerably depending on each household's economic situation. Even a limited consideration of taxes and risk preferences can lead to widely varying asset demands.

Taxes lead to varying asset demands because people in different tax brackets "transform" before-tax income into after-tax income at different rates. For example, income from dividends and capital gains is taxed at a lower rate than interest income. High tax-bracket investors naturally will seek securities that generate income from capital gains and dividends, compared with low tax-bracket investors, who may prefer fully taxable interest-bearing instruments. A desire to minimize taxes also leads to demand for portfolios of such securities. In other words, differential tax status creates "tax clienteles" that in turn give rise to demand for a range of assets with a variety of tax implications.

Risk considerations also create demand for a diverse set of investment alternatives. At an obvious level, differences in risk tolerance create demand for assets with a variety of risk-return combinations. Diverse investment demands arise from individual hedging requirements, that is, needs to offset particular risks. For example, a resident of Toronto planning to retire in Vancouver in 15 years might search for instruments whose values are tied to real estate valuation in Vancouver. A real estate limited partnership, as described in Chapter 4, with a portfolio based in B.C., might serve that end.

Risk motives also lead to demand for ways that investors can easily diversify their portfolios and even out their risk exposure. We will see that these diversification motives inevitably give rise to mutual funds that offer small individual investors the ability to invest in a wide range of stocks, bonds, precious metals, and virtually all other financial instruments.

## The Business Sector

Whereas household financial decisions are concerned with how to invest money, businesses typically need to raise money to finance their investments in real assets: plant, equipment, technological know-how, and so forth. Table 1.1 presents balance sheets of Canadian private corporations and government enterprises as a whole for 1993. The heavy concentration on tangible assets is obvious. Broadly

**Table 1.1** Balance Sheet of Nonfinancial Canadian Corporations, 1993 (Private, Public)

| Assets | $ Billion | % Total | Liabilities and Net Worth | $ Billion | % Total |
|---|---|---|---|---|---|
| **TANGIBLE ASSETS** | | | **LIABILITIES** | | |
| Residential structures | 102 | 7 | Finance and other short-term paper | 40 | 2.7 |
| Nonresidential structures | 404 | 27.6 | Trade payables | 109 | 7.5 |
| Machinery and equipment | 201 | 13.7 | Bank loans | 101 | 6.9 |
| Inventories | 106 | 7.2 | Other loans | 49 | 3.3 |
| Land | 161 | 11 | Bonds and mortgages | 267 | 18.2 |
| Total tangibles | 974 | 66.6 | Corporate claims | 596 | 40.7 |
| | | | Other | 66 | 4.5 |
| **FINANCIAL ASSETS** | | | Total liabilities | 1227 | 83.9 |
| Deposits and cash | 76 | 5.2 | | | |
| Consumer credit | 2 | 0.1 | | | |
| Trade receivables | 119 | 8.1 | | | |
| Short-term debt securities | 29 | 2 | | | |
| Mortgages and long-term debt securities | 15 | 1 | | | |
| Corporate claims | 171 | 11.7 | | | |
| Equity and foreign investments | 9 | 0.6 | | | |
| Other | 70 | 4.8 | | | |
| Total financial assets | 490 | 33.5 | Net worth | 236 | 16.1 |
| Total | 1463 | 100 | | 1463 | 100 |

Reproduced by authority of the Minister of Industry, 1996, *Statistics Canada, Balance Sheet Accounts,* cat. #13-214, 1993, table 3.

speaking, there are two ways for private businesses to raise money—they can borrow it, either from banks or directly from households by issuing bonds, or they can "take in new partners" by issuing stocks, which are ownership shares in the firm. Public enterprises can, in addition, also obtain money from the government budget, which is financed through taxes.

Businesses issuing securities to the public have several objectives. First, they want to get the best price possible for their securities. Second, they want to market the issues to the public at the lowest possible cost. Hence, businesses might want to farm out the marketing of their securities to firms that specialize in such security issuance, because it is unlikely that any single firm is in the market often enough to justify a full-time security issuance division. The process of issuing securities requires immense effort. The security issue must be brought to the attention of the public. Buyers then must subscribe to the issue, and records of subscriptions and deposits must be kept. The allocation of the security to each buyer must be determined, and subscribers finally must exchange money for the securities. These activities clearly call for specialists. The complexities of security issuance have been the catalyst for creation of an investment banking industry catering to business demands. The lowest-cost securities to issue are simple instruments that may not match the household sector's demand; transforming simple instruments to match householders' needs is the role of yet other financial intermediaries.

## The Government Sector

Like businesses, governments often need to finance their expenditures by borrowing. Unlike businesses, governments cannot sell equity shares; they are restricted to borrowing to raise funds when tax revenues are not sufficient to cover expenditures. The federal government also can print money, of course, but this source of funds is limited by its inflationary implications, and so most national governments usually try to avoid excessive use of the printing press.

Governments have a special advantage in borrowing money because their taxing power makes them very creditworthy and therefore able to borrow at the lowest rates. The financial component of the consolidated balance sheet of all levels of government is presented in Table 1.2. Notice that the major liabilities are government securities. The federal government has special powers not available to the other levels, through its control over the Bank of Canada. The latter is the main institution responsible for Canada's monetary policy. This policy is a major determinant of Canada's economic performance, including output growth, price level, and interest rates.

A second, special role of the government is to regulate the financial environment. This is fulfilled in Canada by both federal and provincial governments, resulting in a fragmented regulatory system. Since trading in Canadian financial markets often transcends interprovincial borders, the fragmentation of the regulatory system has at times created inefficiencies and problems of law enforcement.

**Table 1.2** Financial Assets and Liabilities of Canadian Governments, 1993

| Assets | $ Billion | % Total | Liabilities | $ Billion | % Total |
|---|---|---|---|---|---|
| Deposits and currency | 13 | 4.1 | Currency and reports | 3 | 0.4 |
| Trade receivables | 4 | 1.3 | Payables and loans | 38 | 5 |
| Loans | 16 | 5.1 | Short-term paper | 193 | 25.6 |
| Short-term paper | 15 | 4.8 | Federal, provincial, municipal, and other bonds | 476 | 63 |
| Mortgages | 4 | 1.3 | Life insurance and pensions | 1 | 0.1 |
| Federal, provincial, municipal, and other bonds | 83 | 26.4 | Government enterprise claims | 7 | 0.9 |
| Government enterprise claims | 118 | 37.6 | Other | 38 | 5 |
| Equity and foreign investments | 13 | 4.1 | | | |
| Other | 47 | 15 | | | |
| Total | 314 | 100 | Total | 755 | 100 |

Reproduced by authority of the Minister of Industry, 1996, *Statistics Canada, Balance Sheet Accounts,* cat. # 13-214, 1993, table 3.

**Table 1.3** Foreign Sector Balance Sheet, 1994

| | Assets ($ billion) | Liabilities ($ billion) | Net Canadian Holdings ($ billion) |
|---|---|---|---|
| United States | 148.1 | 306.2 | (158.1) |
| United Kingdom | 26.3 | 72.0 | (45.7) |
| Rest of E.C. | 23.9 | 74.3 | (50.3) |
| European Community | 50.2 | 146.3 | (96.0) |
| Japan | 7.6 | 60.7 | (53.1) |
| Rest of the world | 90.0 | 124.4 | (34.5) |
| Total | 295.9 | 637.6 | (341.7) |

Reproduced by authority of the Minister of Industry, 1996, *Statistics Canada, Canada's International Investment Position,* cat. #67-202, 1994, table 1.

Some government regulations are relatively innocuous. For example, the Ontario Securities Commission is responsible for disclosure laws that are designed to enforce truthfulness in various financial transactions that take place in that province. Other types of government intervention in the financial markets, however, have been more controversial. For instance, both federal and provincial governments have instituted programs to encourage investment in certain sectors. Programs to stimulate resource development, research, and small business creation (as in Ontario and Quebec) have led to inefficient investment, as the focus on tax reduction has overshadowed the need for determining good investment prospects.

## The Foreign Sector

As revealed by Table 1.3, showing the foreign sector balance sheet, the Canadian position is highly negative, reflecting the importance of foreign investors in the Canadian economy. For instance, Canadian investors hold $50.2 billion of E.C.

assets, while European investors hold $146.3 billion, for a net negative balance of $96 billion. As divided here, Canada is a net debtor with respect to every foreign group. The large numbers indicate a need for the creation of financial instruments that will protect against foreign exchange risk for both Canadian and foreign investors; the market has responded by offering a large number of investment alternatives.

## 1.3 The Response to Clientele Demands

When enough clients demand and are willing to pay for a service, it is likely in a capitalistic economy that a profit-seeking supplier will find a way to provide and charge for that service. This is the mechanism that leads to the diversity of financial markets. Let us consider the market responses to the disparate demands of the three sectors.

### Financial Intermediation

Direct investment in businesses that need to finance real investments is intrinsically difficult for most households, small as they are. Thus **financial intermediaries,** such as banks, investment companies, insurance companies, and credit unions have naturally evolved to bring the two sectors together. Financial intermediaries sell their own liabilities to raise funds that are used to purchase liabilities of other corporations.

For example, a bank raises funds by borrowing (taking in deposits) and lending that money to other borrowers. The spread between the rates paid to depositors and the rates charged to borrowers is the source of the bank's profit, earned as a reward for the convenience and cost savings that it provides both types of clients. The problem of matching lenders with borrowers is solved when each comes independently to the common intermediary. Thus, the problem of coordination creates a market niche for the bank as an intermediary.

Financial intermediaries are distinguished from other businesses in that both their assets and their liabilities are overwhelmingly financial. As we have seen in Table 1.2, the balance sheets of financial institutions include very small amounts of tangible assets. Now compare Table 1.4 with Table 1.1, the balance sheet of the nonfinancial corporate sector. The contrast arises precisely because intermediaries simply move funds from one sector to another.

Other examples of financial intermediaries are investment companies, insurance companies, and credit unions. All these firms offer similar advantages, in addition to playing a middleman role. First, by pooling the resources of many small investors, they are able to lend considerable sums to large borrowers. Second, by lending to many borrowers, intermediaries achieve significant diversification, meaning they can accept loans that individually might be risky. Third, intermediaries build expertise through the volume of business they do. One indi-

**Table 1.4** Balance Sheet of Financial Institutions, 1993

| Assets | $ Billion | % Total | Liabilities and Net Worth | $ Billion | % Total |
|---|---|---|---|---|---|
| **TANGIBLE ASSETS** | | | **LIABILITIES** | | |
| Equipment and structures | 47 | 2.8 | Deposits | 646 | 38.2 |
| Land | 11 | 0.7 | Loans | 31 | 1.8 |
| Total tangibles | 58 | 3.4 | Money market securities | 14 | 0.8 |
| | | | Bonds and mortgages | 59 | 3.5 |
| **Financial Assets** | | | Life insurance | 424 | 25.1 |
| Deposits and cash | 64 | 3.8 | Corporate claims | 375 | 22.2 |
| Consumer credit | 102 | 6 | Other | 134 | 7.9 |
| Loans | 202 | 12 | Total liabilities | 1,683 | 99.6 |
| Money market securities | 137 | 8.1 | | | |
| Mortgages and long-term debt securities | 660 | 39.1 | | | |
| Corporate equity and foreign investments | 353 | 20.9 | | | |
| Other | 113 | 6.7 | | | |
| Total financial assets | 1,633 | 96.6 | Net worth | 7 | 0.4 |
| Total | 1,690 | 100 | | 1,690 | 100 |

Reproduced by authority of the Minister of Industry, 1996, *Statistics Canada, Balance Sheet Accounts,* cat. #13-214, 1993, table 3.

vidual trying to borrow or lend directly would have much less specialized knowledge of how to structure and execute the transaction with another party.

**Mutual funds** are the result of the "smallness problem," as most household portfolios are not large enough to be spread among a wide variety of securities. It is very expensive in terms of brokerage fees to purchase one or two shares of many different firms, and it clearly is more economical for stocks and bonds to be purchased and sold in large blocks.

Economies of scale also explain the proliferation of analytic services available to investors. Newsletters, databases, and brokerage house research services all exploit the fact that the expense of collecting information is best borne by having a few agents engage in research to be sold to a large client base. This set-up arises naturally. Investors clearly want information, but with only small portfolios to manage, they do not find it economical to incur the expense of collecting it. Hence, a profit opportunity emerges: A firm can perform this service for many clients and charge for it.

## Investment Banking and Brokerage Services

Just as economies of scale and specialization create profit opportunities for financial intermediaries, so too do these economies create niches for firms that perform specialized services for businesses. We said before that firms raise much of their capital by selling securities such as stocks and bonds to the public. Because these firms do not do so frequently, however, investment banking firms that specialize in such activities are able to offer their services at a cost below that of running an in-house security issuance division.

Investment bankers or, as they are known in Canada, **investment dealers,** such as ScotiaMcLeod, RBC Dominion, or Nesbitt-Burns, advise the issuing firm on the prices it can charge for the securities issued, market conditions, appropriate interest rates, and so forth. Ultimately, the investment banking firm handles the marketing of the security issue to the public.

These same investment dealers also are involved in the retail business of trading for clients on the stock exchanges, although some may identify different niches for their emphasis. As part of the service of advising customers of investment opportunities, large stock brokers have extensive in-house analysis departments. This merging of the two sides of the securities industry gives rise to two problems. In order to serve their corporate clients, the investment bankers may not divulge the impending issue to the trading public; furthermore, keeping that corporate business involves not giving advice that would tend to lower the share price. This leads to the creation of an artificial barrier within the securities firm between the brokerage and investment banking departments; on the other hand, that barrier is breached to the extent that negative forecasts by the analysis department are likely to be softened. As an alternative, information and analysis may be carried out by independent firms, to avoid public distrust of the dealers' recommendations. In parallel, there is a growing volume of trading executed by discount brokers who have no analysis departments and offer investment advice provided by the independents for a fee, if at all. The absorption of most securities dealers by the chartered banks, who must satisfy the other financing needs of the same corporate clients, results in yet another internal barrier.

Investment dealers also can help firms design securities with special, desirable properties. As an example of this practice, consider a pharmaceutical company undertaking a risky research and development (R&D) project for a new drug. It needs to raise money for research costs and realizes that if the research is successful the company will need to build a new manufacturing plant requiring still more financing. To deal with this contingency, the investment dealer might design a bond-with-warrant issue. (A *warrant* is a security giving its holder the option to purchase stock from the firm at a specified price up until the warrant's expiration date.) The bonds and warrants are issued, and the research commences. If the research is eventually successful, the stock price will increase, the warrant holders will find it advantageous to exercise their options to purchase additional shares, and as they purchase those shares, additional funds will flow to the firm precisely as they are needed to finance the new manufacturing plant. The design of the financing scheme lets the firm avoid two separate security offerings and saves the considerable costs of the second offering. The exercise of the warrants provides additional financing at no additional flotation costs.

## Financial Engineering

The bond-with-warrant issue for the pharmaceutical company is an example of **financial engineering.** The company's need for initial and contingent financing led to a creative packaging of securities that met the particular needs of the firm.

The investment diversity desired by households, however, is far greater than most businesses have a desire to satisfy. Most firms find it simpler to issue "plain vanilla" securities, leaving exotic variants to others who specialize in financial markets. This, of course, creates a profit opportunity for innovative security design and repackaging that investment dealers are only too happy to fill.

Consider the astonishing changes in the mortgage markets since 1970, when mortgage **pass-through securities** were first introduced in the United States by the Government National Mortgage Association (GNMA, or Ginnie Mae). In Canada, these same instruments became available as National Housing Act (NHA) mortgage-backed securities (MBSs); this occurred in 1986, when the government took direct action to improve the liquidity of the mortgage market. The NHA MBS represents an undivided interest in a relatively homogeneous pool of residential mortgages insured and guaranteed by the Canada Mortgage and Housing Corporation (CMHC). MBS holders receive prorated shares of all the principal and interest payments made on the underlying mortgage pool.[1]

Mortgage-backed securities were a tremendous innovation in mortgage markets. The *securitization* of mortgages meant that mortgages could be traded just like other securities in national financial markets. Availability of funds no longer depended on local credit conditions; with mortgage pass-throughs trading in national markets, mortgage funds could flow from any region to wherever demand was greatest.

The next round of innovation began when it became apparent that investors might be interested in mortgage-backed securities with different effective times to maturity. Thus was born the *collateralized mortgage obligation* (CMO), for which an active market exists in the United States but not in Canada. The CMO meets the demand for mortgage-backed securities with a range of maturities by dividing the overall pool into a series of classes, called *tranches*.[2]

Although these securities are relatively complex, the message here is that security demand elicited a market response. The waves of product development in the last two decades are responses to perceived profit opportunities created by as-yet unsatisfied demands for securities with particular risk, return, tax, and timing attributes. As the investment banking industry becomes even more sophisticated, security creation and customization become more routine. Most new securities are created by dismantling and rebundling more basic securities. A Wall

---

[1] For example, the pool might total $10 million of 12 percent, 30-year amortization, 5-year term mortgages. The rights to the cash flows could then be sold as 500 units, each worth $20,000. Each unit holder would then receive 1/500 of all monthly interest and principal payments made on the pool. The banks that originated the mortgages continue to service them, but no longer own the mortgage investments; these have been passed through to the MBS holders.

[2] The so-called fast-pay tranche receives all the principal payments made on the entire mortgage pool until the total investment of the investors in the tranche is repaid. In the meantime, investors in the other tranches receive only interest on their investment. In this way the fast-pay tranche is retired first and is the shortest-term mortgage-backed security. The next tranche then receives all of the principal payments until it is retired, and so on, until the slow-pay tranche, the longest-term class, finally receives payback of principal after all other tranches have been retired.

Street joke asks how many investment bankers it takes to sell a light bulb. The answer is 100—one to break the bulb and 99 to sell off the individual fragments.

This discussion leads to the notion of primitive versus derivative securities. A **primitive security** offers returns based only on the status of the issuer, who is generally a corporation or government. For example, corporate bonds make stipulated interest payments depending only on the solvency of the issuing firm. Dividends paid to stockholders depend as well on the board of directors' assessment of the firm's financial position. In contrast, **derivative securities** yield returns that depend on additional factors pertaining to the prices of other assets. For example, the payoff to stock options depends on the price of the underlying stock and not on the financial conditions of the writer (issuer) of the option. In our mortgage examples, the derivative mortgage-backed securities offer payouts that depend on the original mortgages, which are the primitive securities. **Swaps,** by which firms arrange to exchange loan payments, have rapidly grown to prominence among derivative instruments. Much of the innovation in security design may be viewed as the continual creation of new types of derivative securities from the available set of primitive securities.

Derivatives have become an integral part of the investment environment. The primary role of derivatives is to hedge risks, but they also are used to take highly speculative positions. Through the misunderstanding of complex derivatives and their correct use, however, firms may be increasing their exposure to risk when they believe that they are hedging. In the 1990s, spectacular examples such as the $157 million loss of Procter & Gamble on interest-rate derivatives and the $700 million loss in Piper Jaffray Companies' fixed income portfolio were probably cases of misunderstanding about hedging; the bankruptcy of Barings, on the other hand, was due to the uncontrolled speculation of one of its traders, Nick Leeson. Despite these losses, derivatives play a legitimate role in the financial system and in portfolio management.

**CONCEPT CHECK**

Question 2. If you take out a car loan, is the loan a primitive security or a derivative security?

Question 3. Explain how a car loan from a bank creates both financial assets and financial liabilities.

## Response to Taxation and Regulation

We have seen that much financial innovation and security creation may be viewed as a natural market response to unfulfilled investor needs. Another driving force behind innovation is the ongoing game played between governments and investors regarding taxation and regulation. Many financial innovations are direct responses to government attempts either to regulate or to tax investments of various sorts.

The money market industry developed as a result of earlier U.S. banking regulations that capped interest rates on bank deposits. These caps on domestic rates, and the requirement for reserve deposits against domestic bank accounts, also led to the creation of U.S. dollar-denominated time deposits in foreign accounts, popularly known as *Eurodollar accounts.* The market for Eurodollars and other Eurocurrencies (referring to accounts in major currencies held outside the particular country) has experienced phenomenal growth since then, even though the motivating U.S. regulations have been changed.[3]

Another innovation largely attributable to tax avoidance motives is the long-term deep discount, or zero-coupon, bond. These bonds pay little or no interest, instead providing most or all of the return to investors through a redemption price that is higher than the initial sales price. Corporations were allowed, under U.S. tax regulations, to impute an implied interest expense based on this built-in price appreciation. Originally, the technique for imputing tax-deductible interest expenses was excessively advantageous to corporations, resulting in a large number of issues of these bonds; ultimately, the interest imputation procedures were amended, and the issue of zeroes for tax purposes ended.

Meanwhile, however, the financial markets had discovered that zeroes were useful ways to lock in a long-term investment return. When the supply of primitive zero-coupon bonds ended, financial innovators created derivative zeroes by purchasing Government of Canada bonds, "stripping" off the coupons, and selling them separately as zeroes. The major Canadian investment dealers combined to institutionalize these stripped bonds by selling claims against a pool of government bonds under the name of Sentinels. Various instruments with catchy names such as *Cougars, TIGRS,* and *LYONS* were issued by other financial institutions; *LYONS* is the acronym for Merrill Lynch's liquid-yield option notes, which are zero-coupon convertible bonds for corporate issuers.

Another tax-induced innovation is the **split share.** With lower tax rates for capital gains than dividends, high tax-bracket investors prefer growth to income while tax-exempt investors prefer the opposite. Rather than choosing stocks that offer these characteristics, investors can buy shares in reliable high-yielding but growing industries, such as communications and banking, that have been split into *income* and *capital* shares. Essentially, the income portion returns the original investment plus a stream of dividends, while the capital portion pays the capital gain since the creation of the split share. The underlying shares are bought by the financial engineer, who splits them into the two components and issues these against the original holding for a span of several years. Examples of these include shares in Bell Canada Enterprises, the major chartered banks, and even a portfolio of these same banks.

Most examples of innovative instruments are responses to U.S. tax or regulatory restrictions, reflecting the dominance of the U.S. financial markets. Eurobonds and financial futures are products that have left behind their U.S. origins and become international, now serving a far more diverse purpose than escaping U.S. taxes or regulations. The process continues as unanticipated financial innovations

[3] Regulation Q arose from the financial collapse in the U.S. at the time of the Great Depression and lasted until 1980.

**Table 1.5** Innovative Instruments Managed by Merrill Lynch in 1991 for Canadian Issuers

| Issuer | Size of Issue ($ millions) | Type of Instrument (yield) | Maturity | Characteristic |
|---|---|---|---|---|
| Ontario Hydro | $1,250 (Cdn) | Global bonds (10⅞%) | 1996 | First global debt offering by a Canadian issuer |
| Rogers Communications | $718.75 (US) | LYONS (variable) | 2001 | First LYONS offering by a Canadian issuer and first debt offering under the Multijurisdictional Disclosure System |
| Hydro-Quebec | $900 (US) | Debentures (9.4%) | 2021 | Largest Yankee debt offering by a Canadian issuer |
| Rogers Cantel Mobile | $460 (US) | Senior secured guaranteed notes (10¾%) | 2001 | Largest noninvestment grade offering by a Canadian company |
| Ontario Hydro | $3,990 (Cdn) | Zero-coupon global bonds (discounted) | 1992–2031 | First global offering of zero-coupon debt by a Canadian issuer |
| PanCanadian Petroleum | $300 (US) | Medium-term notes (by term) | 1992–2021 | First cross-border medium-term note program under the Multijurisdictional Disclosure System |

are created to evade the government's efforts to obtain fiscal revenues; as the government reacts to these innovations, even more instruments are designed.

Table 1.5 summarizes an advertisement by Merrill Lynch of announcements of innovative instruments issued through them and other investment dealers. These include LYONS and zero-coupon bonds, as well as other securities that we will describe later.

## 1.4 Current Trends

We have recently observed three trends in the contemporary investment environment:

1. Globalization.
2. Issuing derivative securities.
3. Securitization and credit enhancement.

Each is a logical consequence of the demand and supply forces that give rise to specialized markets and instruments. Although the smaller-sized Canadian financial system has not fostered the growth of the last and more recent of these developments, globalization always has been a feature of Canadian investment and derivative securities have become quite common in Canada.

### Globalization

If a wider array of investment choices can improve welfare, why should we limit ourselves to purely domestic assets? **Globalization** requires efficient communication technology and the dismantling of regulatory constraints. These tendencies in worldwide investment environments have encouraged international investing in recent years. An obvious but often overlooked opportunity for international investing comes from the purchase of shares of Canadian multinational companies, such as Inco or Northern Telecom. The overseas sales, purchasing, and production of such firms already provides a significant degree of international diversification. Even mid-size firms probably have a fair amount of foreign exposure, particularly through U.S. sales.

Canadian investors can invest in mutual funds specifically designed to hold shares in foreign assets. The most common of these hold either purely U.S. or internationally diversified portfolios. More recently, we have seen mutual funds devoted to single countries, or to specific geographical areas, such as Southeast Asia or Latin America. Canadians can also take advantage of foreign investment opportunities in a number of ways:

1. Purchase of foreign securities (several U.S. firms and a small number of overseas companies), which are cross-listed on Canadian stock markets.
2. Purchase of U.S. securities on U.S. exchanges through Canadian brokers.
3. Purchase of overseas firms whose shares are listed on U.S. exchanges, or for which American Depository Receipts (ADRs) exist; ADRs are U.S.-traded securities representing claims to shares of non-American companies.

Purchasing foreign securities on Canadian exchanges is no more difficult than purchasing Canadian shares. The investor must, however, take care to distinguish foreign firms' securities from those issued by closely held Canadian subsidiaries of foreign parent firms.

It should be noted that the investment implications of holding foreign securities may be significantly different from those of domestic firms. Even U.S. securities traded on the Toronto Stock Exchange (TSE) expose their holders to exchange rate risk. Holding U.S. ADRs implies a double exposure to such risk: between foreign currency and U.S. dollars, and between U.S. and Canadian dollars.

Globalization is a major factor in the raising of capital by Canadian corporations and government issuers. Issues and instruments now are described as global when they simultaneously appear domestically and in foreign markets; portions of the total issue are allocated to different markets and, in the case of equities, may be denominated in both the Canadian dollar and the currency of the other market, where the shares will continue to trade quoted in that currency. For example, Magna International offered shares under the Multijurisdictional Disclosure System at $16.50 Canadian and $14.60 U.S.; two global bond issues were reported in Table 1.5.

The federal and provincial governments, their agencies, and larger Canadian corporations have long been engaged in issuing debt or equity instruments in foreign markets, and, in particular, debt denominated in foreign currencies. Foreign currencies expose the issuer to foreign exchange risk. For example, a deutsche mark bond becomes expensive if the mark appreciates against the dollar; this may be controlled, however, if the issuer takes steps to hedge against currency fluctuations or even uses the bond to offset foreign currency receipts.

The Export Development Corporation (EDC) has been especially active in issuing innovative instruments. Figure 1.1 shows an instance where EDC issued a bond denominated in the European currency unit, known as the ECU. Canadian or other investors purchasing this bond will be protected against depreciation of their domestic currency with respect to the basket of European currencies still used in the European Common Market.

A common opportunity is for investors to receive payments in U.S. dollars from securities issued by Canadian firms. In some cases, such as Moore Corp. (the largest business forms company in the world), the bulk of the income is generated in the United States or abroad, and financial results are presented in U.S. dollars; Moore can be bought on the TSE or the NYSE in the corresponding currency. Alternatively, several Canadian banks, such as the Royal Bank, issue preferred shares paying dividends eligible for the dividend tax credit but denominated in U.S. dollars and traded on the TSE. In both these cases, purchase of the U.S. dollar securities provides a hedge against Canadian dollar depreciation against the U.S. dollar.

## Issuing Derivative Securities

Derivative securities may be relatively simple instruments, such as warrants or options on a single company's stock, or they may be quite complicated—taking their value from a number of underlying instruments. Effectively, the foreign-denominated securities mentioned above are derivatives because their value depends on the exchange rate. Canadian issuers can appeal to the wishes of investors to have their investment returns depend on more than the financial results of companies operating in the Canadian economy.

Once again, EDC provides some interesting examples of derivative securities. Figure 1.2 describes EDC's issue of a dual currency bond with payment in either Australian dollars or Japanese yen, at the option of the holder. These obviously will have appeal to Australian and Japanese investors; however, they also provide an opportunity to Canadian or other investors to speculate on the appreciation of either of the currencies against the dollar. Figure 1.3 reproduces the cover page of the prospectus for PINs, or protected index notes. Each PIN on issue cost $10 in U.S. dollars and promised, at the option of the holder, to repay the $10 upon maturity after five-and-a-half years, or, at any time up to maturity, an amount based on the value of the S&P 500[4] relative to its value at issue. The holder is guaranteed a minimum repayment of the initial investment without interest but also can participate in any appreciation in the U.S. equity market—in both cases speculating on the exchange rate.

Creative security design often calls for **bundling** primitive and derivative securities into one composite security. The long-established example of this is the

---

[4] The S&P 500 is a stock market index based on the value of the 500 largest firms in the United States; see the discussion in Chapter 2.

**Figure 1.1**
Globalization: A bond issue denominated in European Currency Units.

OFFERING CIRCULAR

# ECU 200,000,000

**Export Development Corporation**

**(An agent of Her Majesty in right of Canada)**

**Société pour l'expansion des exportations**

**(Mandataire de Sa Majesté du chef du Canada)**

**9 per cent. Notes due 21st January, 1994**

---

**Issue Price: 100.925 per cent.**

---

Principal of and interest on the Notes will be paid without deduction for or on account of Canadian taxes to the extent set out under "Description of the Notes — Taxation". Interest on the Notes is payable annually on 21st January in each year commencing on 21st January, 1993.

The Notes will mature on 21st January, 1994. The Notes are not redeemable prior to maturity except that Export Development Corporation ("EDC" or the "Issuer") may redeem all (but not some only) of the Notes in the event that Canadian taxes are imposed as set out herein. See "Description of the Notes — Redemption".

Application has been made to list the Notes on the Luxembourg Stock Exchange (the "Exchange").

The Notes will be represented initially by a temporary global Note in bearer form (the "Temporary Global Note"), without interest coupons, which will be deposited with a common depositary on behalf of Morgan Guaranty Trust Company of New York, Brussels Office, as Operator of the Euroclear System ("Euroclear") and Centrale de Livraison de Valeurs Mobilières S.A. ("CEDEL S.A.") on or about 21st January, 1992 (the "Closing Date"). Interests in the Temporary Global Note will be exchangeable for interests in a semi-permanent global Note in bearer form (the "Semi-Permanent Global Note") not earlier than the date which is 40 days after the Closing Date, upon certification as to non-United States beneficial ownership. The Semi-Permanent Global Note will be exchangeable for definitive Notes as soon as reasonably practicable after notice in writing requiring such exchange has been given by the relevant Accountholder (as defined herein) but in any event within 30 days of the date of such notice.

---

**UBS Phillips & Drew Securities Limited**

**Banque Bruxelles Lambert S.A.** — **BNP Capital Markets Limited**
**Credit Suisse First Boston Limited** — **Deutsche Bank Capital Markets Limited**

**ABN AMRO BANK N.V.** — **Banque Generale du Luxembourg S.A.**
**Barclays de Zoete Wedd Limited** — **Daiwa Europe Limited**
**Dresdner Bank Aktiengesellschaft** — **Generale Bank**
**Istituto Bancario San Paolo di Torino S.P.A.** — **Kredietbank N.V.**
**Merrill Lynch International Limited** — **Norinchukin International PLC**
**Paribas Capital Markets Group** — **Swiss Bank Corporation**
**Swiss Volksbank** — **Wood Gundy Inc.**

The date of this Offering Circular is 15th January, 1992

**Figure 1.2**
Derivative securities: A dual-currency bond issue.

*This announcement appears as a matter of record only.* *September, 1990*

# Export Development Corporation

## ¥20,000,000,000

## Dual Currency
## Japanese Yen/Australian Dollar
## Bonds—First Series (1990)

**Issue Price: 99.3% Coupon Rate: 8.0% (A$335.75)**
**Maturity Date: September 5, 2000**

**Daiwa Securities Co. Ltd.**

**The Nikko Securities Co., Ltd.** **The Nomura Securities Co., Ltd.** **Yamaichi Securities Company, Limited**

**New Japan Securities Co., Ltd.**

**KOKUSAI Securities Co., Ltd.** **The Nippon Kangyo Kakumaru Securities Co., Ltd.**

**Sanyo Securities Co., Ltd.** **Universal Securities Co., Ltd.**

**Cosmo Securities Co., Ltd.** **Dai-ichi Securities Co., Ltd.** **Marusan Securities Co., Ltd.**

**Okasan Securities Co., Ltd.** **Taiheiyo Securities Co., Ltd.** **Tokyo Securities Co., Ltd.**

**Toyo Securities Co., Ltd.** **Wako Securities Co., Ltd.** **Yamatane Securities Co., Ltd.**

**Figure 1.3**
Derivative securities: Prospectus for a minimum-return index investment.

**Offering Circular dated June 25, 1991**

*This Offering Circular constitutes a public offering of these securities only in those jurisdictions where they may be lawfully offered for sale. No securities commission nor similar authority in Canada has in any way passed upon the merits of the securities offered hereunder and any representation to the contrary is an offence.*

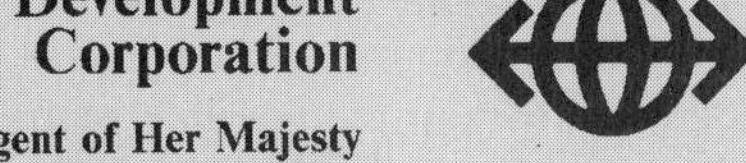

**Export Development Corporation**

**(An agent of Her Majesty in right of Canada)**

**Société pour l'expansion des exportations**

**(Mandataire de Sa Majesté du chef du Canada)**

**U.S.$75,000,000**

**S&P 500® Protected Index Notes Due 1997 ("PINS")**

The S&P 500 Protected Index Notes Due 1997 (the "Notes") offered hereby will mature on January 3, 1997 (the "Stated Maturity"). The Notes may not be called for redemption by Export Development Corporation ("EDC") prior to Stated Maturity. Each Note will have a principal amount of U.S.$10 and all payments with respect to the Notes will be denominated in U.S. dollars. At Stated Maturity, a holder of each Note (a "Holder") will receive in respect of each Note held by such Holder the greater of (A) U.S.$10 or (B) the Repurchase Price which will be computed by reference to the Standard & Poor's 500 Composite Stock Price Index (the "S&P 500 Index"). The repurchase price of each Note (the "Repurchase Price") will equal U.S.$10 multiplied by the Spot S&P Index (as hereinafter defined) for the applicable Valuation Date (as hereinafter defined) divided by the Strike S&P Index (as hereinafter defined) (rounded down to the nearest cent). The Strike S&P Index will equal 105% of the Initial S&P Index (as hereinafter defined). No interest will be paid on the Notes, except to the extent that the Repurchase Price exceeds U.S.$10 upon exercise of the Repurchase Option or at Stated Maturity. The Repurchase Price will not exceed U.S.$10 unless the S&P 500 Index increases to a level greater than the Strike S&P Index. Prior to 10:00 a.m. on the sixteenth Business Day immediately preceding the Stated Maturity, a Holder will have the option (the "Repurchase Option") to require EDC to repurchase any Notes held by such Holder at the Repurchase Price. If a Holder exercises the Repurchase Option prior to January 3, 1992, the amount payable to the Holder will be equal to 95% of the Repurchase Price.

The valuation and payment of the Repurchase Price may be postponed as a result of a Market Disruption Event (as hereinafter defined). In such event the Holder will receive the Repurchase Price determined as of a later date, except that Notes tendered for repurchase that become subject to such postponed valuation and payment will not be repurchased if the Holder elects in the Repurchase Notice that the Note Agent withdraw the Repurchase Notice (a "Withdrawal Election") in the event of a Market Disruption Event (as hereinafter defined).

**PRICE: U.S.$10.00 per Note**

**Minimum Subscription: 100 Notes**

| | Price to the Public (1)(2) | Agents' Commission | Proceeds to EDC (3) |
|---|---|---|---|
| Per Note | U.S.$10.00 | U.S.$0.30 | U.S.$9.70 |
| Total Offering (4) | U.S.$75,000,000 | U.S.$2,250,000 | U.S.$72,750,000 |

Notes:

(1) The subscription price has been determined by negotiation between EDC and the Agents (as hereinafter defined).

(2) On June 24, 1991, the Canadian dollar purchase price of each Note would have been C$11.43 based on the noon exchange rate of C$1.1427 for each U.S.$1.00.

(3) The expenses of the issue of approximately C$350,000 are being borne by the Issuer and the Agents.

(4) EDC has granted to the Agents an overallotment option, exercisable from time to time up to the Date of Closing (as hereinafter defined) with the concurrence of EDC, to distribute an additional 1,000,000 Notes on the same terms and conditions as the other Notes offered hereby. To the extent such option is exercised, the Agents will offer to the public such additional Notes at the price shown above.

**Investment in the Notes is speculative and a Holder may sustain a substantial loss of its investment if such Holder elects to exercise the Repurchase Option and the Notes are repurchased prior to Stated Maturity. Since the return to a Holder on exercise of the Repurchase Option or at Stated Maturity is determined solely by reference to the S&P 500 Index, the Notes are not suitable for persons unfamiliar with the risks of investing in equity securities. (See "Risk Factors".) In order for a Holder to avoid a loss of principal on the Notes, the level of the S&P 500 Index must increase to the Breakeven Point (as hereinafter defined) or the Notes must be held to Stated Maturity. (See "Description of Notes — Breakeven Point" and "Description of the Notes — Repurchase Price".) The Notes will constitute direct unsecured obligations of EDC and, as such, will constitute direct obligations of Her Majesty in right of Canada. (See "Description of the Notes — Status".)**

The Repurchase Option will be exercisable on any Business Day (as hereinafter defined) after the Date of Closing and will expire at 10:00 a.m. on the sixteenth Business Day immediately preceding the Stated Maturity of the Notes. Any Holder who does not exercise the Repurchase Option will receive in respect of each Note held by such Holder the greater of (A) U.S.$10 or (B) the Repurchase Price, at the Stated Maturity. The Repurchase Option may not be exercised by or on behalf of any Holder in respect of fewer than 100 Notes or integral multiples thereof. (See "Description of the Notes — Repurchase Option".)

convertible preferred share or bond, by which the holder has the right to exchange the convertible for a number of common shares in the company; this usually is done when the converted value is higher than the value of the original instrument as a fixed-income security. PINs can be considered as an example of bundling.

Quite often, creating a security that appears to be attractive requires the **unbundling** of an asset. An example is given by the strip bonds such as Sentinels—the composite bond cash flow of regular interest payments and principal is unbundled into single payments. Other examples of unbundling were given in the discussion on financial innovation in Section 1.3. Both CMOs and the bank capital shares permit investors to concentrate on the payment stream, and its risk, which appeal to their particular interests.

**CONCEPT CHECK** Question 4. How can tax motives contribute to the desire for unbundling?

## Securitization and Credit Enhancement

Until recently, financial intermediaries served to channel funds from national capital markets to smaller local ones. **Securitization,** however, now allows borrowers to enter capital markets directly, as discussed in the context of the securitization of the mortgage market.

In contrast to the long-term MBS market, short-term loans are also securitized by investment bankers. The major asset-backed securities are issued for credit card debt, automobile loans, home equity loans, and student loans. In these cases, the regular payments made by the borrowers to the original grantors of the credit are passed through to the holders of the securities. The security for the paper is the underlying pool of loans and the security associated with them. The pooling and issuing by the investment banker makes these illiquid small instruments negotiable; the process enables the borrower (the original holder of the paper) to enjoy the use of the funds, while the lenders receive a superior return on those funds.

In the past, a corporation that was not in the best of financial conditions would be able to obtain loans only through commercial banks. The banks' credit departments scrutinized each customer. A business shopping around for a loan might be sized up simultaneously by several different banks. Today, the credit-hungry corporation can arrange for **credit enhancement.** It engages an insurance company to put its credit behind the corporation's, for a fee. The firm can then float a bond of "enhanced" credit rating directly to the public. Figure 1.4 shows an example of credit enhancement in a joint financial venture between the Rockefeller Group and Aetna Casualty and Surety. The Rockefeller Group is a privately held corporation and thus is exempt from a large part of typical disclosure rules. It cannot issue publicly traded bonds at reasonably low yields without revealing information to the public that it wishes to keep private. Instead, it purchases Aetna's backing. Aetna can perform its own credit analysis, keeping the information revealed confidential.

**Figure 1.4**
Aetna's credit enhancement of the Rockefeller Group's bond.

Offering Circular

# $100,000,000

## Rockefeller Group International Finance N.V.

13¼% Notes Due 1989

*Unconditionally Guaranteed as to Payment of Principal and Interest by*

## Rockefeller Group, Inc.

*and under a Surety Bond Issued by*

## The Ætna Casualty and Surety Company

**Issue Price 99¾%**

Principal of, premium, if any, and interest on the Notes will be payable without deduction for, or on account of, United States or Netherlands Antilles withholding taxes, all as set forth herein. Interest will be payable annually on June 21, commencing in 1985.

The Notes will mature on June 21, 1989. The Notes are redeemable (i) as a whole or from time to time in part, on or after June 21, 1987 at a redemption price equal to 101¼% of the principal amount of the Notes if made prior to June 21, 1988 and 100½% of the principal amount of the Notes if made on or after June 21, 1988, plus, in each case, accrued interest to the date fixed for redemption, and (ii) as a whole at any time in the event of certain developments involving United States or Netherlands Antilles withholding taxes, at their principal amount plus accrued interest to the date fixed for redemption. See "Description of the Notes". The Notes may also be redeemed as a whole, at a redemption price equal to their principal amount plus accrued interest to the date fixed for redemption, at the option of The Ætna Casualty and Surety Company ("Ætna") upon the occurrence of certain events. See "Description of the Surety Bond".

The Notes will be unconditionally guaranteed as to the payment of principal, premium, if any, and interest and certain other amounts by Rockefeller Group, Inc. As a private corporation, Rockefeller Group, Inc., does not disclose financial information to the public. Accordingly, arrangements have been made for payments of principal of, premium, if any, and interest on, and certain other amounts with respect to, the Notes to be guaranteed under a Surety Bond issued by Ætna. See "Description of the Notes" and "Description of the Surety Bond".

Application has been made to list the Notes on the Luxembourg Stock Exchange.

The Notes have not been registered under the United States Securities Act of 1933 and may not be offered or sold, directly or indirectly, in the United States of America, or its territories or possessions or to citizens, nationals or residents thereof, except as set forth herein. See "Underwriting".

A temporary global Note without interest coupons in the amount of $100,000,000 will be delivered to a depositary in London for the account of participants in Euro-clear and CEDEL S.A. on or about June 21, 1984 and will be exchangeable for definitive Notes not earlier than 90 days after the completion of the distribution upon certification that such Notes are not beneficially owned by United States citizens, nationals or residents, as set forth herein. Interest on the Notes will not be payable until issuance of the definitive Notes. See "Description of the Notes—Denominaton and Transfer".

MORGAN GUARANTY LTD

AMRO INTERNATIONAL LIMITED
CHASE MANHATTAN LIMITED
CREDIT SUISSE FIRST BOSTON LIMITED
DEUTSCHE BANK AKTIENGESELLSCHAFT
DRESDNER BANK AKTIENGESELLSCHAFT
ENSKILDA SECURITIES
SKANDINAVISKA ENSKILDA LIMITED
LEHMAN BROTHERS INTERNATIONAL
SHEARSON LEHMAN/AMERICAN EXPRESS INC
SAMUEL MONTAGU & CO. LIMITED
ORION ROYAL BANK LIMITED
SOCIÉTÉ GÉNÉRALE
SOCIÉTÉ GÉNÉRALE DE BANQUE S.A.
SWISS BANK CORPORATION INTERNATIONAL LIMITED
UNION BANK OF SWITZERLAND (SECURITIES) LIMITED
S. G. WARBURG & CO. LTD.

**May 25, 1984**

## 1.5 Corporate Control and Concentration

As the legal owners of the corporation, a firm's shareholders have the right to expect that it will be managed so as to maximize the value of their holdings. Considerable attention has been paid recently to battles for the control of corporations that are the target of takeover attempts and to those corporations whose executives appear to be earning exorbitant salaries. In Canada there is also the question of whose hands are directing the corporations that control so much of the national assets and employment.

The issue of corporate control is significant because so much shareholder wealth is at stake. The size of modern corporations and the risk imposed by complex technological changes mean a large amount of wealth is endangered. Management poses two threats in this environment. First, incompetent managers may be very expensive to shareholders (and to corporate employees, who also are stakeholders). Second, management's control of pecuniary rewards and other perquisites comes directly from the pockets of shareholders. This creates a conflict between management and shareholders, which is called the **agency problem.** A great deal of financial theory is dedicated to the analysis of this problem. Corporate executives are probably the best-compensated professionals in the nation, which is fine as long as shareholders are happy. After all, competition itself should ensure that managerial resource compensation is allocated as efficiently as any production factor in the economy.

The control structure of a standard, publicly traded firm is modeled on a democratic arrangement. Its main features are, in theory, as follows:

1. No one has to own shares. Willing investors buy shares, satisfied shareholders can buy more, and unsatisfied shareholders can unload the stock at any time.
2. Management has to disclose to the public a great deal of information, which is audited by independent experts.
3. Important decisions of management must be approved by voting in shareholder meetings.
4. The normal rule is one share/one vote, but the law also allows multiple-voting shares;[5] thus, shareholder voting power is proportional to the shareholder's stake in the corporation. (Absentee shareholders can vote by proxy.)
5. Corporate management, from the president down, is subject to control by the board of directors led by the chairman. Individual directors are elected by shareholders, who can unseat directors in any meeting. Shareholder meetings can be called by shareholders, as well as by management. One annual meeting is mandatory.

Given such a system, what can go wrong? If management is unsatisfactory, the board, in principle, will oust it. If the board members are not on their toes, share-

---

[5] See the discussion of restricted shares in Chapter 2.

holders will oust them. In the end, if all works as intended, the corporation will be run by management that executes the (aggregate) will of the shareholders.

Currently, shareholders are informed, in the announcement of the annual meeting, as to how management is compensated. Also they are given a comparative view of the performance of the company under its management. In addition, there is a statement of policy about compensation, usually expressing the view that, in order to attract the best management, the board believes in a compensation level in the top half of comparable managerial salaries (a difficult objective for all firms to achieve simultaneously). When perquisites and incentive options are added to the basic salary, the aggregate compensation for senior executives often constitutes a significant proportion of the net income of the firm. It is no wonder that for large companies, compensation packages draw a lot of public attention, particularly when corporate results are unimpressive.

When we have large corporations and many diversified investors, control is very dispersed. In many cases, even the largest shareholder holds less than 2 percent of the shares. Management, as a whole, through executive stock options and compensation shares, may become an important shareholder. By and by, one may find that management controls the board, rather than vice versa. One counterbalance that is showing some signs of effectiveness is the holding of blocks of shares by institutional investors, such as mutual funds. These often, either alone or in collaboration, can exert sufficient influence to direct the management in the shareholders' favour.

What about proxy fights to wrest control of the firm from current management? Evidence shows that the cost of an average proxy fight is in the millions of dollars. Shareholders who attempt such a fight have to use their own funds. Management that defends against it uses corporate coffers in addition to already existing communication channels to shareholders at large. Little wonder that few such attempts are made. When they are, 75 percent fail. Dissidents win some seats on the board of directors in a majority of cases, but seldom enough to assume control of the company. Ousting the management of a large corporation is a modern-day version of David's battle with Goliath.

In fact, shareholders' greatest protection is the hunger and might of other businesses. How does this sword of Damocles work? A bad management team, whether incompetent or excessively greedy, presumably causes the firm's shares to sell at a price that reflects its poor performance. Now imagine the management of one business observing another that is underperforming. All it has to do is acquire the underperforming business, fire current management, put in place its own (presumably better) people, and the stock price should reflect its expectations of improved performance. The acquiring firm might therefore be willing to bid up the price of shares of the target firm by as much as 50 percent to acquire it. In the process, the economy gets rid of one bad management team and becomes more efficient.

Just the threat of this mechanism ought to keep management on its toes. However, give management the ability to engage in expensive takeover defenses (at shareholder expense, of course), and its vulnerability is limited. The danger of antitakeover regulation that allows poor managers to protect their positions is clear.

What about the arguments that takeovers lead to shutdowns and unemployment, and that funds for takeovers are diverted from productive resources? A firm that takes over another one must believe that it can improve operations. If it pays a premium for the acquisition, the acquiring firm must believe it can create additional value to justify the purchase price. Potential efficiency gains might therefore be expected to be an impetus for mergers and acquisitions. Of course, one might argue that some acquisitions are motivated more by tax motives than true economic efficiency, but this seems more a reason to modify tax law than intrude in the market for corporate control.

The argument that takeover funds are diverted from productive uses is without merit. After all, the money that is paid by the acquirer to the target firm's shareholders does not disappear; it is reinvested in financial markets. If shareholders had needed the money for food, they would have sold their shares in the first place. In the end, the displacement of bad management ought to bring in, if anything, more investment funds in this newly created opportunity.

In Canada, there is added concern about corporate control. Canadian corporate assets are controlled by individuals and families, by conglomerates, by financial institutions, and even by the government to a significant degree. A 1985 count showed 32 family empires (such as the Bronfmans and the Westons) and 5 publicly held conglomerates (such as Bell Canada and Canadian Pacific) controlling approximately one-third of the nonfinancial assets in Canada. Comparable U.S. statistics show that one-third share of assets to be controlled by the 100 largest corporations, with very few of those effectively controlled by individuals (such as the control of Ford Motors by the Ford family).

More precise Canadian statistics from 1985 indicate that 33.5 percent of nonfinancial assets and 31.5 percent of profits were controlled by 25 corporations owned by foreign firms (e.g., Imperial Esso owned by Exxon), the federal government, and Canadian corporations. The latter 11 corporations actually controlled 11.3 percent of assets and 7.3 percent of profits.[6]

The structure of control is through holding companies. The prime example is that of the Edper Bronfman network, the now partially publicly owned creation of a branch of the Bronfman family. This corporation owns controlling interests in other corporations that hold others in a bewildering entanglement, down to the final levels where products and services are sold and physical assets exist. The holdings might be as small as 10 percent or complete, but generally the debt and equity of small investors is used to leverage the initial capital in Edper. This enables the management of Edper to direct the resources of dozens of companies ranging across natural resources (forest products and mining), financial services (investments, insurance, and banking), and real estate.

---

[6] Edward G. Grabb, "Who Owns Canada? Concentration of Ownership and the Distribution of Economic Assets 1975–1985," *Journal of Canadian Studies* 25, no. 2 (Summer 1990), pp. 72–93.

Why is this **concentration** of control a matter of concern? Leaving aside the political question of the desirability of government ownership, the major corporations in Canada are controlled by a minute number of individuals or by foreign corporations (controlled obviously by foreigners). Should the interests of Canadians as a whole diverge from those of the owners of the significant factors of production for the nation, there is no remedy besides government intervention. Such a possibility does not exist for the United States economy.[7]

## SUMMARY

**1.** Investors select investments that will provide them with the kind of returns that will suit their needs and preferences. Their investment opportunities correspond to the need for funds by corporations and governments. The after-tax returns that accompany the various types of financial instruments guide investors' choices.

**2.** Real investment creates real assets that are used to produce the goods and services created by an economy. Financial investment is in financial assets, which are claims to the income generated by real assets. Securities are financial assets. Financial assets are part of an investor's wealth, but not part of national wealth. Instead, financial assets determine how the "national pie" is split up among investors.

**3.** The financial environment is composed of four sectors: household, business, government, and foreign. Households decide on investing their funds. Businesses and government, in contrast, typically need to raise funds.

**4.** The diverse task and risk preferences of households create a demand for a wide variety of securities. In contrast, businesses typically find it more efficient to offer relatively uniform forms of securities. This conflict gives rise to an industry that creates complex derivative securities from primitive ones.

**5.** The smallness of households leads to a market niche for financial intermediaries, mutual funds, and investment companies. Economies of scale and specialization are factors supporting the investment banking industry.

**6.** Three recent trends in the financial environment are globalization, issuing derivative securities (especially by bundling and unbundling), and securitization and credit enhancement.

**7.** Stockholders own the corporation and, in principle, can oust an unsatisfactory management team. In practice, ouster may be difficult because of the advantage that management has in proxy fights. The threat of takeover helps keep management doing its best for the firm.

**8.** The Canadian economy is characterized by an extreme degree of concentration of equity holdings, with effective control of one-third of all nonfinancial assets by a small number of corporations and family empires.

---

[7] A different problem arises in Japan, where banks and industrial conglomerates own each other in complicated arrangements that involve both business and financial dealings.

## Key Terms

Financial investment
Real investment
Real assets
Financial assets
Financial intermediaries
Mutual funds
Investment dealers
Financial engineering
Pass-through security
Primitive security
Derivative security
Swaps
Split share
Globalization
Bundling
Unbundling
Securitization
Credit enhancement
Agency problem
Concentration

## Selected Readings

*An excellent discussion of financial innovation may be found in:*

Miller, Merton H. "Financial Innovation: The Last Twenty Years and the Next." *Journal of Financial and Quantitative Analysis* 21 (December 1986), pp. 459–471.

*Detailed discussions of a variety of financial markets and market structures are provided in:*

Garbade, Kenneth D. *Securities Markets.* New York: McGraw-Hill, 1982.

Wood, John H.; and Norm L. Wood. *Financial Markets.* San Diego: Harcourt Brace Jovanovich, 1985.

*Several trends in the capital market are discussed in:*

*Recent Innovations in International Banking.* Basel: Bank for International Settlements, 1986.

*The subject of Canadian corporate control is discussed in:*

Eckbo, Espen B. "Mergers and the Market for Corporate Control: The Canadian Evidence." *Canadian Journal of Economics* 19 (May 1986), pp. 236–260.

*A broad range of nontechnical articles on the subject of investing in Canada and by Canadians appear quarterly in the* Canadian Investment Review (CIR). *These articles usually are organized by themes. Some examples of interest to our discussion would be:*

"Market Innovation in Canada." *CIR* 3, no. 2 (Fall 1990).

"Investment Perspectives on Ethics, Ownership and Control." *CIR* 4, no. 2 (Fall 1991).

Poapst, James V. "Households as Financial Managers: An Assessment." *CIR* 2, no. 2 (Fall 1989).

Halpern, Paul; and Frederick Heath. "Canada's Securities Investment Universe: The Size of It." *CIR* 2, no. 2 (Fall 1989).

## Problems

1. Suppose you discover a treasure chest of $10 billion in cash.
   *a.* Is this a real or financial asset?
   *b.* Is society any richer for the discovery?
   *c.* Are you wealthier?

   *d.* Can you reconcile your answers to (b) and (c)? Is anyone worse off as a result of the discovery?

2. Lanni Products is a start-up computer software development firm. It currently owns computer equipment worth $30,000 and has cash on hand of $20,000 contributed by Lanni's owners. For each of the following transactions, identify the real and/or financial assets that trade hands. Are any financial assets created or destroyed in the transaction?
   *a.* Lanni takes out a bank loan. It receives $50,000 in cash and signs a note promising to pay back the loan over three years.
   *b.* Lanni uses the cash from the bank plus $15,000 of its own funds to finance the development of new financial planning software.
   *c.* Lanni sells the software product to Microsoft, which will market it to the public under its own name. Lanni accepts payment in the form of 1,500 shares of Microsoft stock.
   *d.* Lanni sells the shares of Microsoft stock for $80 per share and uses part of the proceeds to pay off the bank loan.
3. Reconsider Lanni Products from problem (2).
   *a.* Prepare Lanni's balance sheet just after it gets the bank loan. What is the ratio of real assets to financial assets?
   *b.* Prepare the balance sheet after Lanni spends the $65,000 to develop the financial planning software product [see problem 2(b)]. What is the ratio of real assets to financial assets?
   *c.* Prepare the balance sheet after Lanni accepts payment of shares from Microsoft. What is the ratio of real assets to financial assets?
4. Examine the balance sheet of the financial sector (Table 1.4). What is the ratio of tangible assets to total assets? What is that ratio for nonfinancial firms? Why should this difference be expected?
5. In the 1960s, the U.S. government instituted a 30 percent withholding tax on interest payments on bonds sold in the United States to overseas investors. (The tax has since been repealed.) What connection does this have to the contemporaneous growth of the huge Eurobond market, where U.S. firms issue dollar-denominated bonds overseas?
6. Why would you expect securitization to take place only in highly developed capital markets?
7. Suppose that you are an executive of Ford Motor Canada and that a large share of your potential income is derived from year-end bonuses that depend on your firm's annual profits.
   *a.* Would purchase of Ford Canada's stock be an effective hedging strategy for the executive who is worried about the uncertainty surrounding his or her bonus?
   *b.* Would purchase of Toyota stock be an effective hedging strategy?
8. Consider again the Ford executive in problem (7). In light of the fact that the design of the annual bonus exposes the executive to risk that he or she would like to shed, why doesn't Ford instead pay the executive a fixed salary that doesn't entail this uncertainty?

**9.** What is the relationship between securitization and the role of financial intermediaries in the economy? What happens to financial intermediaries as securitization progresses?

**10.** Although we stated that real assets comprise the true productive capacity of an economy, it is hard to conceive of a modern economy without well-developed financial markets and security types. How would the productive capacity of the Canadian economy be affected if there were no markets in which one could trade financial assets?

**11.** Why does it make sense that the first futures markets introduced in 19th-century America were for trades in agricultural products? For example, why did we not see instead futures markets for goods such as paper or pencils?

**12.** Financial engineering has been disparaged as nothing more than paper shuffling. Critics argue that resources that go to *rearranging* wealth (that is, bundling and unbundling financial assets) might better be spent on *creating* wealth (that is, creating real assets). Evaluate this criticism. Are there any benefits realized by creating an array of derivative securities from various primary securities?

*Chapter* 2

# Markets and Instruments

**THIS CHAPTER COVERS A RANGE OF FINANCIAL SECURITIES AND THE MARKETS IN WHICH THEY TRADE.** Our goal is to introduce you to the features of various security types. This foundation will be necessary to understand the more analytic material that follows in later chapters.

We refer to the traditional classification of securities into money market instruments or capital market instruments. The **money market** includes short-term, marketable, liquid, low-risk debt securities. Money market instruments sometimes are called *cash equivalents* because of their safety and liquidity. **Capital markets,** in contrast, include longer-term and riskier securities. Securities in the capital market are much more diverse than those found within the money market. For this reason, we will subdivide the capital market into four segments. Accordingly, this chapter contains a discussion of five markets overall: the money market, longer-term fixed income capital markets, equity markets, and the two so-called derivative markets—options and futures markets.

## 2.1 THE MONEY MARKET

The money market is a subsector of the fixed income market. It consists of very short-term debt securities that usually are highly marketable. Many of these securities trade in large denominations and so are out of reach of individual investors. Money market funds, however, are easily accessible to small investors. These mutual funds pool the resources of many investors and purchase a wide variety of money market securities on their behalf.

**Figure 2.1**
Rates on money market securities.

From *The Globe and Mail,* June 3, 1995. Reprinted by permission.

# Money Rates

**ADMINISTERED RATES**

| | |
|---|---|
| Bank of Canada | 7.64% |
| Canadian prime | 9.00% |

**MONEY MARKET RATES**
(for transactions of $1-million or more)

| | |
|---|---|
| 3-mo. T-bill(when-issued) | 7.12% |
| 1-month treasury bills | 7.30% |
| 2-month treasury bills | 7.24% |
| 3-month treasury bills | 7.13% |
| 6-month treasury bills | 7.00% |
| 1-year treasury bills | 6.96% |
| 10-year Canada bonds | 7.72% |
| 30-year Canada bonds | 8.14% |
| 1-month banker's accept. | 7.40% |
| 2-month banker's accept. | 7.38% |
| 3-month banker's accept. | 7.23% |
| Commercial Paper (R-1 Low) | |
| 1-month | 7.40% |
| 2-month | 7.35% |
| 3-month | 7.25% |
| Call money | 7.50% |

**Supplied by Dow Jones Telerate Canada**

**UNITED STATES**

NEW YORK (AP) — Money rates for Friday as reported by Dow Jones Telerate:

Telerate interest rate index: 5.740

Prime Rate: 9.00
Discount Rate: 5.25
Broker call loan rate: 7.75
Federal funds market rate:
High 6.00, low 6.00, last 6.00
Dealers commercial paper:
30-180 days: 5.88-5.59

Commercial paper by finance company: 30-270 days: 5.84-5.41

Bankers acceptances dealer indications: 30 days, 5.87; 60 days, 5.75; 90 days, 5.70; 120 days, 5.60; 150 days, 5.54; 180 days, 5.48

Certificates of Deposit Primary: 30 days, 4.86; 90 days, 5.13; 180 days, 5.17

Certificates of Deposit by dealer: 30 days, 5.91; 60 days, 5.83; 90 days, 5.77; 120 days, 5.72; 150 days, 5.69; 180 days, 5.68

Eurodollar rates: Overnight, 6.00-6.125; 1 month, 5.93750-6.00; 3 months, 5.8125-5.875; 6 months, 5.6875-5.75; 1 year, 5.5625-6.625

London Interbank Offered Rate: 3 months, 6.00; 6 months, 5.875; 1 year, 5.875

Treasury Bill auction results: average discount rate: 3-month as of May 30: 5.64; 6-month as of May 30: 5.61; 52-week as of May 25: 5.54

Treasury Bill, annualized rate on weekly average basis, yield adjusted for constant maturity, 1-year, as of May 30: 5.92

Treasury Bill market rate, 1-year: 5.21-5.19

Treasury Bond market rate, 30-year 6.52

**Table 2.1** Components of the Money Market, 1994

| | $ Billions |
|---|---|
| Canada bills | 4,547 |
| Provincial securities | 158 |
| Canadian banker's acceptances | 625 |
| Corporate and finance paper | 670 |
| Bank, trust & mortgage company paper | 570 |
| Other | 37 |
| **Total money market trading** | **6,607** |

Data from Investment Dealers Association of Canada *Capital Market Statistics Report.* Reprinted by permission.

Figure 2.1 is a reprint of a money rates listing from *The Globe and Mail.* It includes the various instruments of the money market that we will describe in detail. Table 2.1 lists total trading volume in 1994 of the major instruments of the money market.

## Treasury Bills

*Treasury bills* (T-bills) are the most marketable of all Canadian money market instruments. T-bills represent the simplest form of borrowing: the government raises money by selling bills to the public. Investors buy the bills at a discount from the stated maturity value. At the bill's maturity, the holder receives from the government a payment equal to the face value of the bill. The difference between the purchase price and ultimate maturity value constitutes the investor's earnings.

T-bills with initial maturities of 3, 6, and 12 months are issued weekly. Sales are conducted via auction, at which chartered banks and authorized dealers can submit only *competitive* bids. A competitive bid is an order for a given quantity of bills at a specific offered price. The order is filled only if the bid is high enough relative to other bids to be accepted. By contrast, a noncompetitive bid is an unconditional offer to purchase at the average price of the successful competitive bids; such bids can be submitted only for bonds. The government rank-orders bids by offering price and accepts bids in order of descending price until the entire issue is absorbed. Competitive bidders face two dangers: they may bid too high and overpay for the bills, or they may bid too low and be shut out of the auction.

T-bills are purchased primarily by chartered banks, by the Bank of Canada (as part of its monetary policy), and by individuals who obtain them on the secondary market from a government securities dealer. T-bills are highly liquid; that is, they are easily converted to cash and sold at low transaction cost with not much price risk. Unlike most other money market instruments, which sell in minimum denominations of \$100,000, T-bills are offered in denominations of \$1,000, \$5,000, \$25,000, \$100,000 and \$1 million.

**T-Bill Yields.** T-bill yields are not quoted in the financial pages as effective annual rates of return. Instead, the **bond equivalent yield** is used. To illustrate this method, consider a \$10,000 par value T-bill sold at \$9,600 with a maturity of a half year, or 182 days. With the bond equivalent yield method, the bill's discount from par value, which here equals \$400, is "annualized" based on a 365-day year. The \$400 discount is annualized as

$$\$400 \times (365/182) = \$802.20$$

The result is divided by the \$9,600 purchase price to obtain a bond equivalent yield of 8.356 percent per year. Rather than report T-bill prices, the financial pages report these bond equivalent yields.

The bond equivalent yield is not an accurate measure of the effective annual rate of return. To see this, note that the half-year holding period return on the bill is 4.17 percent: the \$9,600 investment provides \$400 in earnings, and 400/9,600 = .0417. The compound interest-annualized rate of return, or **effective annual yield,** is therefore

$$(1.0417)^2 - 1 = .0851 = 8.51\%$$

We can highlight the source of the discrepancy between the bond equivalent yield and the effective annual yield by examining the bond equivalent yield formula:

$$r_{\text{BEY}} = \frac{10{,}000 - P}{P} \times \frac{365}{n} \tag{2.1}$$

where $P$ is the bond price, $n$ is the maturity of the bill in days, and $r_{\text{BEY}}$ is the bond equivalent yield. The bond equivalent formula thus takes the bill's discount from par as a fraction of price and then annualizes by the factor $365/n$. The annualization techniques uses simple interest rather than compound interest. Multiplication by $365/n$ does not account for the ability to earn interest on interest, which is the essence of compounding. The discrepancy is, therefore, greater for a 91-day bill and disappears for a one-year bill.

The quoted yields for U.S. T-bills use a formula similar to that in equation 2.1, with a 360-day year and the par value of 10,000 in the denominator instead of $P$. The resulting yield is known as the **bank discount yield.** As a result, the quoted U.S. rate for the example would have been 7.912 percent. Part of the difference in yields between Canadian and U.S. bills can thus be attributed to the method of quoting yields. A convenient formula relating the bond equivalent yield to the bank discount yield is

$$r_{\text{BEY}} = \frac{365 \times d}{360 - (d \times n)}$$

where $d$ is the discount yield. Suppose $d = .07912$; then

$$r_{\text{BEY}} = \frac{365 \times .07912}{360 - (.07912 \times 61)} = .08356$$

the previously derived yield. Hence, in this case, about 0.4 percentage points of the differential between Canadian and U.S. quoted yields stem from the method of calculation.

In Figure 2.1, the money market listings include Treasury bills for closing prices on June 2, 1995. Three-month T-bills show a bond equivalent yield of 7.13 percent. To determine a bill's true market price, we must solve equation 2.1 for $P$. Rearranging equation 2.1, we obtain

$$P = 10{,}000/[1 + r_{\text{BEY}} \times (n/365)] \tag{2.2}$$

Equation 2.2 in effect first "deannualizes" the bond equivalent yield to obtain the actual proportional interest rate, then discounts the par value of \$10,000 to obtain the T-bill's sale price. In the case at hand, $n = 91$ days, and the yield is 7.13 percent for the bill, so that the price is

$$\$10{,}000/[1 + .0713 \times (91/365)] = \$9{,}825.34$$

---

**CONCEPT CHECK** Question 1. Find the price of the six-month bill from Figure 2.1.

---

The bond equivalent yield is the bill's yield over its life, assuming that it is purchased for the auction bid price and annualized using simple interest techniques. Note that this yield uses a simple interest procedure to annualize, also known as *annual percentage rate* (APR), and so there are problems in comparing yields on bills with different maturities. Nevertheless, yields on most securities with less than a year to maturity are annualized using a simple interest approach.

Finally, the effective annual yield on the quoted bill based on the market price, \$9,825.34, is 7.32 percent. The bond's 91-day return equals (10,000 − \$9,825.34), or 1.7776 percent. Annualizing this return, we obtain $(1.017776)^{91/365} = 1.0732$, implying an effective annual interest rate of 7.32 percent.

## Certificates of Deposit and Bearer Deposit Notes

A *certificate of deposit* (CD), is a time deposit with a chartered bank. Time deposits may not be withdrawn on demand. The bank pays interest and principal to the depositor only at the end of the fixed term of the deposit. Similar time deposits offered by trust companies are known as *guaranteed investment certificates* (GICs).

Although both CDs and GICs are nontransferable in Canada, some bank time deposits issued in denominations greater than \$100,000 are negotiable; that is, they can be sold to another investor if the owner needs to cash in the deposit before its maturity date. In Canada these marketable CDs are known as *bearer deposit notes* (BDN). By contrast, a CD in the United States is a marketable instrument, similar to BDNs. Recently, some trust companies also have issued transferable GICs. CDs and GICs are treated as bank deposits by the Canada Deposit Insurance Corporation (CDIC), so they are insured for up to \$60,000 in the event of a bank insolvency.

## Commercial Paper

Large, well-known companies often issue their own short-term unsecured debt notes rather than borrow directly from banks. These notes are called *commercial paper.* Very often, commercial paper is backed by a bank line of credit, which gives the borrower access to cash that can be used (if needed) to pay off the paper at maturity. Commercial paper maturities range up to one year; longer maturities would require registration under the Ontario Securities Act and so are almost never issued. Most often, commercial paper is issued with maturities of less than one or two months and minimum denominations of \$50,000. Therefore, small investors can invest in commercial paper only indirectly, via money market mutual funds.

Commercial paper is considered to be a fairly safe asset, because a firm's condition presumably can be monitored and predicted over a term as short as one month. Many firms issue commercial paper intending to roll it over at maturity, that is, issue new paper to obtain the funds necessary to retire the old paper. If in the meantime there are doubts raised about their creditworthiness, then the borrowers may be forced to turn to other, more expensive, sources of financing. For instance, in March 1992, Olympia and York was forced to retire its outstanding commercial paper several weeks before it became insolvent.

If lenders become complacent about a firm's prospects and grant rollovers heedlessly, they can suffer big losses. When Penn Central defaulted in the United States in 1970, it had $82 million of commercial paper outstanding. However, very few such defaults on commercial paper have been observed in the past 40 years.

## Bankers' Acceptances

A *bankers' acceptance* starts as an order to a bank by a bank's customer to pay a sum of money at a future date, typically within six months. At this stage, it is similar to a postdated check. When the bank endorses the order for payment as "accepted," it assumes responsibility for ultimate payment to the holder of the acceptance. At this point, the acceptance may be traded in secondary markets like any other claim on the bank. Bankers' acceptances are considered very safe assets because traders can substitute the bank's credit standing for their own. They are used widely in foreign trade where the creditworthiness of one trader is unknown to the trading partner. Acceptances sell at a discount from the face value of the payment order, just as T-bills sell at a discount from par value.

## Eurodollars

*Eurodollars* are U.S. dollar-denominated deposits at foreign banks or foreign branches of American banks. By locating outside the United States, these banks escape regulation by the Federal Reserve Board. Despite the tag "Euro," these accounts need not be in European banks, although that is where the practice of accepting dollar-denominated deposits outside the United States began.

Most Eurodollar deposits are for large sums, and most are time deposits of less than six months' maturity. A variation on the Eurodollar time deposit is the Eurodollar certificate of deposit. A Eurodollar CD resembles a U.S. domestic bank CD, except that it is the liability of a non-U.S. branch of a bank (typically a London branch). The advantage of Eurodollar CDs over Eurodollar time deposits is that the holder can sell the asset to realize its cash value before maturity. Eurodollar CDs are considered less liquid and riskier than U.S. domestic CDs, however, and thus offer higher yields. Firms also issue Eurodollar bonds, which are dollar-denominated bonds in Europe, although bonds are not a money market investment because of their long maturities.

All of the above instruments—time deposits, CDs, and bonds—also exist denominated in all major currencies; these are labelled Eurocurrency instruments when located outside the country of currency. When issued in Canadian dollar denominations then they are referred to as *Euro-Canadian* dollars; these constitute a minor portion of the Eurocurrency market, which is dominated by Eurodollar trading.

## Repos and Reverses

Dealers in government securities use *repurchase agreements* (also called *repos* or *RPs*) as a form of short-term, usually overnight, borrowing. The dealer sells government securities to an investor on an overnight basis, with an agreement to buy back those securities the next day at a slightly higher price. The increase in the price is the overnight interest. The dealer thus takes out a one-day loan from the investor, and the securities serve as collateral.

A *term repo* is essentially an identical transaction, except that the term of the implicit loan can be 30 days or more. Repos are considered very safe in terms of credit risk because the loans are backed by the government securities. A *reverse repo* is the mirror image of a repo. Here, the dealer finds an investor holding government securities and buys them, agreeing to sell them back at a specified higher price on a future date.

The U.S. repo market was upset by several failures of government security dealers in 1985. In these cases the dealers had entered into the typical repo arrangements with investors, pledging government securities as collateral. The investors did not take physical possession of the securities as they could have under the purchase and resale arrangement. Some of the dealers, unfortunately, fraudulently pledged the same securities as collateral in different repos; when the dealers went under, the investors found that they could not collect the securities that they had "purchased" in the first phase of the repo transaction. In the wake of the scandal, repo rates for nonprimary dealers increased, whereas rates for some well-capitalized firms fell as investors became more sensitive to credit risk.[1] Investors can best protect themselves by taking delivery of the securities, either directly or through an agent such as a bank custodian.

## Brokers' Calls

Individuals who buy stocks on margin borrow part of the funds to pay for the stocks from their broker. The broker in turn may borrow the funds from a bank, agreeing to repay the bank immediately (on call) if the bank requests it. Chartered banks make such call loans to investment firms that use them to finance their inventory of securities. The rate paid on these loans is usually closely related to the rate on short-term T-bills.

## The LIBOR Market

The **London Interbank Offered Rate** (LIBOR) is the rate at which large banks in London are willing to lend money among themselves. This rate has become the premier short-term interest rate quoted in the European money market, and it

[1] Stephen A. Lumpkin, "Repurchase and Reverse Repurchase Agreements," in T. Cook and T. Rowe (editors), *Instruments of the Money Market* (Richmond, Va.: Federal Reserve Bank of Richmond, 1986).

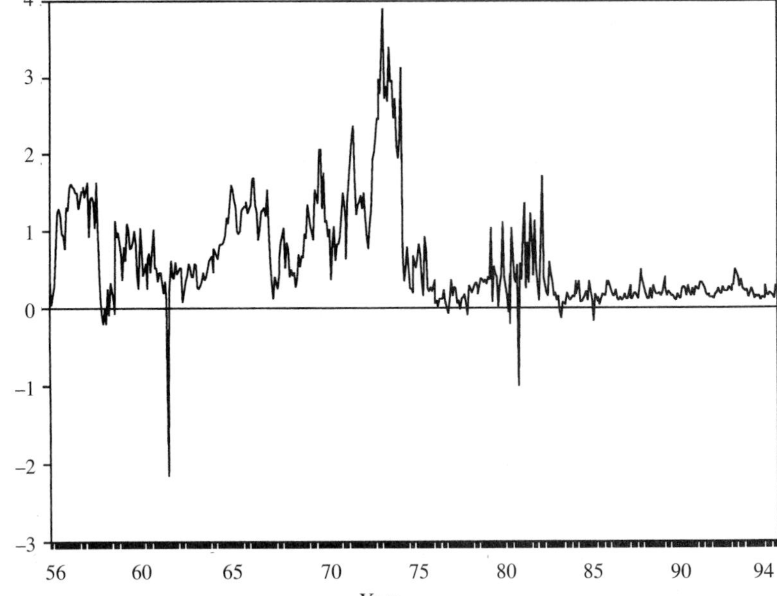


**Figure 2.2**
The spread between short-term corporate paper and T-bill rates.

Constructed from data from *ScotiaMcLeod's Handbook of Canadian Debt Market Indices,* 1957–1994, February 1995. Used by permission of Scotia Capital Markets Fixed Income Research.

serves as a reference rate for a wide range of transactions. For example, a corporation might borrow at a rate equal to LIBOR plus 2 percent.

## Yields on Money Market Instruments

Although most money market securities are of low risk, they are not risk-free. For example, as we noted earlier, the U.S. commercial paper market was rocked by the Penn Central bankruptcy, which precipitated a default on $82 million of commercial paper. Money market investors in that country became more sensitive to creditworthiness after this episode, and the yield spread between low- and high-quality paper widened.

The securities of the money market do promise yields greater than those on default-free T-bills, at least in part because of greater relative riskiness. In addition, many investors require more liquidity; thus they will accept lower yields on securities such as T-bills that can be quickly and cheaply sold for cash. Figure 2.2 shows that commercial paper, for example, has consistently paid a risk premium over T-bills of approximately equal maturity. Moreover, that risk premium increased with economic crises, such as the energy price shocks associated with the two OPEC disturbances, even though it has been lower overall in more recent years, as compared to earlier periods.

## 2.2 THE FIXED-INCOME CAPITAL MARKET

The fixed-income capital market is composed of longer-term borrowing instruments than those that trade in the money market. This market includes Government of Canada bonds, provincial and municipal bonds, corporate bonds, and mortgage securities. Bonds can be *callable* during a given period; this feature allows the issuer to redeem the bond at par value, or at a stated premium prior to maturity.

### Government of Canada Bonds

The Canadian government borrows funds in large part by selling both nonmarketable and marketable debt securities. The nonmarketable securities are known as *Canada Savings Bonds* (CSB); they are issued each year on November 1st, generally for a seven-year term. Although these bonds are nontransferable, they are perfectly liquid, since they can be cashed any time prior to maturity at face value plus accrued interest. Because of this latter feature, the valuation of CSBs is quite complex and transcends the level of this text.

*Government of Canada Bonds* or simply *Canada Bonds* are longer-term marketable debt securities issued by the Canadian federal government. These bonds have varying maturities at issue date, ranging up to 40 years. They are considered part of the money market when their term becomes less than three years. Canada bonds are generally noncallable and make semiannual coupon payments that are set at a competitive level designed to ensure their issue at or near par value.

Figure 2.3 is a listing of actively traded Canada bonds as they appear in *The Globe and Mail*. Under the Government of Canada section, note the bond (*arrow*) that matures in June 2001. The coupon income, or interest, paid by the bond is 9.75 percent of par value, meaning that for a $1,000 face value bond, $97.50 in annual interest payments will be made in two semiannual installments of $48.75 each. In the trading of a security, bid and ask prices are quoted; these represent, respectively, the price at which an investor can sell or buy the asset. These prices are not shown separately in this listing, but their average is given as 110.784, denoting a percentage of par value. Thus, the price shown should be interpreted as 110.784 percent of par, or $1,107.84 for a $1,000 face value bond. This price increased by $9.22 from the previous day's closing price, or $.922 per $100 of par value. Finally, the yield to maturity on the bond is 7.473 percent.

The **yield to maturity** reported in the financial pages is calculated by determining the semiannual yield and then doubling it, rather than compounding it for two half-year periods. This use of a simple interest technique to annualize means that the yield is quoted on an annual percentage rate (APR) basis, rather than as an effective annual yield. The APR method in this context is also called the *bond equivalent yield.* From Figure 2.3 we can see that the yields on Government of Canada bonds are generally rising with term to maturity; this is not true uniformly, due to the different coupons of bonds with similar maturities. Listings for callable bonds trading at a premium (selling above par value) show the yield

**Figure 2.3**
Canadian bonds.
From *The Globe and Mail,* June 14, 1995. Reprinted by permission.

# Canadian Bonds

## Provided by RBC Dominion Securities

**Selected quotations, with changes since the previous day, on actively traded bond issues. Yields are calculated to full maturity, unless marked C to indicate callable date. Price is the midpoint between final bid and ask quotations June 13, 1995.**

| Issuer | Coupon | Maturity | Price | Yield | $ Chg |
|---|---|---|---|---|---|
| **GOVERNMENT OF CANADA** | | | | | |
| CANADA | 7.75 | 15 SEP 96 | 101.165 | 6.749 | +0.320 |
| CANADA | 8.00 | 15 MAR 97 | 102.025 | 6.744 | +0.380 |
| CANADA | 7.50 | 1 JUL 97 | 101.185 | 6.866 | +0.420 |
| CANADA | 6.25 | 1 FEB 98 | 98.255 | 6.983 | +0.500 |
| CANADA | 6.50 | 1 SEP 98 | 98.365 | 7.074 | +0.600 |
| CANADA | 5.75 | 1 MAR 99 | 95.325 | 7.205 | +0.670 |
| CANADA | 7.75 | 1 SEP 99 | 101.715 | 7.265 | +0.760 |
| CANADA | 9.25 | 1 DEC 99 | 107.299 | 7.301 | +0.766 |
| CANADA | 8.50 | 1 MAR 00 | 104.725 | 7.292 | +0.800 |
| → CANADA | 9.75 | 1 JUN 01 | 110.784 | 7.473 | +0.922 |
| CANADA | 9.50 | 1 OCT 01 | 109.825 | 7.508 | +0.950 |
| CANADA | 9.75 | 1 DEC 01 | 111.300 | 7.509 | +0.985 |
| CANADA | 8.50 | 1 APR 02 | 104.780 | 7.583 | +0.905 |
| CANADA | 7.25 | 1 JUN 03 | 97.308 | 7.708 | +0.846 |
| CANADA | 7.50 | 1 DEC 03 | 98.413 | 7.759 | +0.863 |
| CANADA | 10.25 | 1 FEB 04 | 115.287 | 7.781 | +0.957 |
| CANADA | 6.50 | 1 JUN 04 | 91.650 | 7.813 | +0.850 |
| CANADA | 9.00 | 1 DEC 04 | 107.768 | 7.822 | +0.965 |
| CANADA | 8.75 | 1 DEC 05 | 106.379 | 7.844 | +1.025 |
| CANADA | 10.00 | 1 JUN 08 | 115.726 | 8.025 | +0.755 |
| CANADA | 9.50 | 1 JUN 10 | 112.216 | 8.078 | +0.807 |
| CANADA | 9.00 | 1 MAR 11 | 107.874 | 8.103 | +0.805 |
| CANADA | 10.25 | 15 MAR 14 | 120.224 | 8.128 | +0.928 |
| CANADA | 9.75 | 1 JUN 21 | 116.385 | 8.214 | +1.020 |
| CANADA | 8.00 | 1 JUN 23 | 97.550 | 8.225 | +0.900 |
| CANADA | 9.00 | 1 JUN 25 | 108.568 | 8.225 | +1.004 |
| CMHC | 8.80 | 1 MAR 00 | 105.400 | 7.416 | +0.800 |
| REAL RETURNS | 4.25 | 1 DEC 21 | 97.575 | 4.406 | +0.900 |
| **PROVINCIAL** | | | | | |
| ALBERTA | 7.00 | 20 AUG 97 | 100.047 | 6.970 | +0.422 |
| ALBERTA | 8.50 | 1 SEP 99 | 104.064 | 7.355 | +0.767 |
| ALBERTA | 6.38 | 1 JUN 04 | 89.921 | 7.970 | +0.834 |
| B C | 7.00 | 9 JUN 99 | 98.918 | 7.318 | +0.711 |
| B C | 9.00 | 9 JAN 02 | 106.206 | 7.773 | +0.935 |
| B C | 9.00 | 21 JUN 04 | 106.124 | 8.032 | +0.926 |
| B C | 8.50 | 23 AUG 13 | 100.890 | 8.401 | +0.850 |
| B C | 8.00 | 8 SEP 23 | 94.595 | 8.506 | +0.920 |
| HYDRO QUEBEC | 9.25 | 2 DEC 96 | 103.125 | 6.961 | +0.350 |
| HYDRO QUEBEC | 10.88 | 25 JUL 01 | 113.235 | 8.083 | +0.940 |
| HYDRO QUEBEC | 11.00 | 15 AUG 20 | 119.075 | 9.061 | +0.700 |
| HYDRO QUEBEC | 9.63 | 15 JUL 22 | 105.425 | 9.082 | +0.650 |
| MANITOBA | 6.75 | 24 AUG 95 | 99.935 | 6.950 | NC |
| MANITOBA | 7.00 | 19 APR 99 | 98.567 | 7.431 | +0.688 |
| MANITOBA | 7.88 | 7 APR 03 | 99.165 | 8.018 | +0.886 |
| MANITOBA | 10.50 | 5 MAR 31 | 121.240 | 8.580 | +1.190 |
| NEW BRUNSWIC | 7.00 | 17 MAR 98 | 99.575 | 7.167 | +0.500 |
| NEW BRUNSWIC | 8.38 | 26 AUG 02 | 102.550 | 7.900 | +0.900 |
| NEW BRUNSWIC | 8.50 | 28 JUN 13 | 99.325 | 8.574 | +0.700 |
| NEWFOUNDLAND | 10.13 | 22 NOV 14 | 108.625 | 9.165 | +0.800 |
| NOVA SCOTIA | 9.60 | 30 JAN 22 | 107.625 | 8.849 | +0.900 |
| ONTARIO HYD | 10.88 | 8 JAN 96 | 102.000 | 7.154 | NC |
| ONTARIO HYD | 7.25 | 31 MAR 98 | 100.024 | 7.234 | +0.529 |
| ONTARIO HYD | 9.63 | 3 AUG 99 | 107.362 | 7.515 | +0.766 |
| ONTARIO HYD | 8.63 | 6 FEB 02 | 103.451 | 7.943 | +0.924 |
| ONTARIO HYD | 9.00 | 24 JUN 02 | 105.478 | 7.966 | +0.920 |
| ONTARIO | 8.75 | 16 APR 97 | 102.847 | 7.057 | +0.376 |
| ONTARIO | 9.00 | 15 SEP 04 | 105.055 | 8.206 | +0.930 |
| ONTARIO | 7.50 | 7 FEB 24 | 87.295 | 8.711 | +0.840 |
| P E I | 9.75 | 30 APR 02 | 108.425 | 8.122 | +0.900 |
| P E I | 11.00 | 19 SEP 11 | 119.200 | 8.760 | +0.800 |
| QUEBEC | 8.00 | 30 MAR 98 | 101.585 | 7.354 | +0.530 |
| QUEBEC | 10.25 | 7 APR 98 | 107.175 | 7.367 | +0.550 |
| QUEBEC | 10.25 | 15 OCT 01 | 110.300 | 8.132 | +0.900 |
| QUEBEC | 9.38 | 16 JAN 23 | 102.835 | 9.092 | +0.620 |
| SASKATCHEWAN | 9.88 | 6 JUL 99 | 108.066 | 7.527 | +0.756 |
| SASKATCHEWAN | 9.50 | 16 AUG 04 | 107.962 | 8.242 | +0.939 |
| SASKATCHEWAN | 9.60 | 4 FEB 22 | 108.910 | 8.731 | +0.990 |
| TORONTO -MET | 10.38 | 4 SEP 01 | 111.575 | 7.973 | +0.950 |
| **CORPORATE** | | | | | |
| AGT LIMITED ← | 9.50 | 24 AUG 04 | 108.000 | 8.238 | +0.875 |
| AVCO FIN | 8.75 | 15 MAR 00 | 104.000 | 7.722 | +0.750 |
| BELL CANADA | 9.20 | 1 JUN 99 | 105.625 | 7.529 | +0.750 |
| BELL CANADA | 9.50 | 15 JUN 02 | 107.875 | 8.008 | +0.875 |
| BELL CANADA | 9.70 | 15 DEC 32 | 109.625 | 8.817 | +0.875 |
| BC TELEPHONE | 9.65 | 8 APR 22 | 108.875 | 8.782 | +0.875 |
| CDN IMP BANK | 7.10 | 10 MAR 04 | 93.375 | 8.173 | +0.875 |
| CDN IMP BANK | 9.65 | 31 OCT 14 | 107.750 | 8.807 | +0.750 |
| CDN UTIL | 8.43 | 1 JUN 05 | 101.750 | 8.169 | +1.000 |
| CDN UTIL | 9.40 | 1 MAY 23 | 106.875 | 8.737 | +0.625 |
| IMASCO LTD | 8.38 | 23 JUN 03 | 100.875 | 8.223 | +0.875 |
| INTERPRV PIP | 8.20 | 15 FEB 24 | 93.500 | 8.824 | +0.875 |
| MOLSON BREW | 8.20 | 11 MAR 03 | 99.750 | 8.241 | +0.875 |
| NVA SCOT PWR | 9.75 | 2 AUG 19 | 108.500 | 8.887 | +0.875 |
| NOVA GAS | 8.30 | 15 JUL 03 | 100.375 | 8.234 | +0.875 |
| NOVA GAS | 9.90 | 16 DEC 24 | 110.500 | 8.889 | +1.000 |
| PANCDN PETE | 8.75 | 9 NOV 05 | 103.500 | 8.240 | +0.875 |
| ROYAL BANK | 10.50 | 1 MAR 02 | 112.875 | 7.980 | +1.000 |
| TALISMAN | 9.45 | 22 DEC 99 | 106.250 | 7.782 | +0.750 |
| TALISMAN | 9.80 | 22 DEC 04 | 108.375 | 8.499 | +0.875 |
| THOMSON CORP | 9.15 | 6 JUL 04 | 105.125 | 8.331 | +0.875 |
| TRANSCDA PIP | 9.45 | 20 MAR 18 | 105.500 | 8.880 | +0.750 |
| UNION GAS | 9.75 | 13 DEC 04 | 109.000 | 8.358 | +1.000 |
| WSTCOAST ENE | 9.50 | 10 JAN 00 | 106.875 | 7.684 | +0.875 |
| WSTCOAST ENE | 9.70 | 15 NOV 04 | 108.750 | 8.338 | +1.000 |
| WSTCOAST ENE | 9.90 | 10 JAN 20 | 110.000 | 8.891 | +0.875 |

**MAPLE LEAF WARRANTS**

| Underlying Issue | Type | Expiry | Strike | Price | $ Chg |
|---|---|---|---|---|---|
| CAN 9.00 DEC 04 | C | 14 FEB 96 | 101.800 | 6.185 | +0.750 |

## ScotiaMcLeod Indexes

| Index | Close | % chg | Yield | Chg | 52 wk High | 52 wk Low |
|---|---|---|---|---|---|---|
| Short | 245.62 | 0.56 | 7.150 | -0.22 | 245.79 | 215.83 |
| Mid | 267.75 | 0.83 | 7.804 | -0.16 | 269.25 | 223.77 |
| Long | 286.86 | 0.80 | 8.373 | -0.09 | 289.52 | 232.20 |
| Universe | 267.89 | 0.72 | 7.695 | -0.17 | 269.15 | 226.21 |

## Benchmarks

| Issuer | Coupon | Maturity | Price | Yield | $ chg |
|---|---|---|---|---|---|
| U.S. Treasury | 7 5/8 | Feb/25 | 113 23/32 | 6.57 | +1 28/32 |
| British gilt | 8.5 | Oct/05 | 103 19/32 | 7.97 | +1 1/32 |
| German | 6.875 | May/05 | 101.15 | 6.71 | +0.81 |
| Japan #174 | 4.5 | Jun/05 | 112.50 | 2.885 | +0.20 |

calculated to the first call date, while for discount bonds the yield is calculated to the redemption date. (No such callable bonds appear in Figure 2.3.)

---

**Concept Check** Question 2. Why does it make sense to calculate yields on discount bonds to maturity and yields on premium bonds to the first call date?

---

## Provincial and Municipal Bonds

Figure 2.3 shows a representative sample of bonds issued by provincial governments and by provincial Crown Corporations; the latter are generally guaranteed by the corresponding provincial government. One municipal bond, Metro Toronto, also appears in the listings. All these bonds are similar in their characteristics to federal government issues, with a variety of maturities and coupon rates, and are available to investors at any given time. These securities are considered extremely safe assets, even though not as safe as comparable Government of Canada bonds. Consequently, a small yield spread can be observed in Figure 2.3 between Government of Canada bonds and provincial bonds, as well as between the bonds of the various provinces. For instance, bonds maturing in 2004 yield 7.813 percent for Canada's, 8.206 percent for Ontario's, and 8.032 percent for British Columbia's.

U.S. municipal bonds are exempt from federal income tax and from state and local tax in the issuing state. Hence, the quoted yield is an after-tax yield, which should be compared with after-tax yields on other bonds. This explains why the quoted yields on municipals are lower than the quoted (before-tax) yields on other comparable bonds. Since the tax advantage is not available to Canadian investors, U.S. municipal bonds generally would not be attractive to them.

## Corporate Bonds

Corporate bonds enable private firms to borrow money directly from the public. These bonds are similar in structure to government issues—they typically pay semiannual coupons over their lives and return the face value to the bondholder at maturity. However, they differ most importantly from government bonds in degree of risk. Default risk is a real consideration in the purchase of corporate bonds, and Chapter 14 discusses this issue in considerable detail. For now, we distinguish only among *secured bonds,* which have specific collateral backing them in the event of firm bankruptcy, unsecured bonds called *debentures,* which have no collateral, and *subordinated debentures,* which have a lower priority claim to the firm's assets in the event of bankruptcy. Referring to Figure 2.3 again, we see an AGT Limited bond maturing in 2004 (*arrow*) and paying a coupon of 9.50 percent; its yield of 8.238 percent compares with the above-mentioned government bonds with yields ranging from 7.813 percent to 8.206 percent.

Corporate bonds usually come with options attached. *Callable bonds* give the firm the option to repurchase the bond from the holder at a stipulated call price. *Retractable* and *extendible bonds* give the holder the option, respectively, to redeem the bonds earlier and later than the stated maturity date. *Convertible bonds* give the bondholder the option to convert each bond into a stipulated number of shares of stock. These options are treated in more detail in Chapter 14.

## Mortgages and Mortgage-Backed Securities

An investments text of 20 years ago probably would not include a section on mortgage loans, since at that time investors could not invest in them. Now, because of the explosion in mortgage-backed securities, almost anyone can invest in a portfolio of mortgage loans, and these securities have become a major component of a fixed-income market.

Home mortgages usually are written with a long-term (25- to 30-year maturity) amortization of the principal. Until the 1970s, almost all such mortgages had a fixed interest rate over the life of the loan, with equal fixed monthly payments. Since then these so-called conventional mortgages have become renewable at one- to five-year intervals, at which point their interest rates may be renegotiated. More recently, a diverse set of alternative mortgage designs has been developed.

Fixed-rate mortgages pose difficulties to banks in years of increasing interest rates because of the mismatching of the maturities of assets and liabilities. Banks commonly issue short-term liabilities (the deposits of their customers) and hold long-term assets such as fixed-rate mortgages. Hence, they suffer losses when interest rates increase: The rates they pay on deposits increase while their mortgage income remains fixed. The five-year renewal period helps to alleviate this problem.

A relatively recent introduction is the *adjustable rate mortgage.* These mortgages require the borrower to pay an interest rate that varies with some measure of the current market interest rate. For example, the interest rate might be set at two points above the current rate on one-year Treasury bills and might be adjusted once a year. Often, a contract sets a limit, or cap, on the maximum size of an interest rate change within a year and over the life of the contract. The adjustable rate contract shifts the risk of fluctuations in interest rates from the lender to the borrower.

Because of the shifting of interest rate risk to their customers, banks are willing to offer lower rates on adjustable rate mortgages than on conventional fixed-rate mortgages. This proved to be a great inducement to borrowers during a period of high interest rates in the early 1980s. As interest rates fell, however, conventional mortgages appeared to regain popularity.

A *mortgage-backed security* (MBS) is either an ownership claim in a pool of mortgages or an obligation that is secured by such a pool. These claims represent securitization of mortgage loans. Mortgage lenders originate loans and then sell packages of these loans in the secondary market. Specifically, they sell their claim to the cash inflows from the mortgages as those loans are paid off. The mortgage originator continues to service the loan, collecting principal and interest payments, and passes these payments along to the purchaser of the mortgage. For this reason, these mortgage-backed securities are called *pass-throughs.* Like the adjustable rate mortgages, they were designed to deal with the mismatching of maturities of bank assets and liabilities. Mortgage-backed pass-through securities were first introduced in Canada by the Canada Mortgage and Housing Corporation (CMHC, a federal Crown Corporation) in 1987. CMHC pass-throughs carry a federal government guarantee under the National Housing Act (NHA), which insures the timely payment of principal and interest. Thus, the cash flow can be considered risk-free even if individual borrowers default on their mortgages. This guarantee increases the marketability of the pass-through. Therefore, investors can buy or sell NHA MBSs like any other bond.

Although pass-through securities often guarantee payment of interest and principal, they do not guarantee the rate of return. Holders of mortgage pass-throughs therefore can be severely disappointed in their returns in years when interest rates drop significantly. This is because homeowners usually have an option to prepay, or pay ahead of schedule, the remaining principal outstanding on their mortgages. This right is essentially an option held by the borrower to "call back" the loan for the remaining principal balance, quite analogous to the option held by government or corporate issuers of callable bonds. The prepayment option gives the borrower the right to buy back the loan at the outstanding principal amount rather than at the present discounted value of the *scheduled* remaining payments. The exercise of this option usually requires the payment of a penalty or bonus by the borrower, which also is passed through to the MBS investors; prepayments also may occur due to the sale of the underlying property. When interest rates fall, causing the present value of the scheduled mortgage payments to increase, the borrower may choose to take out a new loan at today's lower interest rate and use the proceeds of the loan to prepay or retire the outstanding mortgage. This refinancing may disappoint pass-through investors, who are liable to "receive a call" just when they might have anticipated capital gains from interest rate declines. Figure 2.4 is a recent listing from *The Globe and Mail* of both prepayable and nonprepayable MBSs.

**Figure 2.4** Mortgage-backed securities.

From *The Globe and Mail,* June 12, 1995. Reprinted by permission.

## Mortgage-Backed Securities

Mortgage-backed securities are investments in pools of residential mortgages guaranteed by the Canadian government under the National Housing Act. This representative list of actively traded pools is provided by Wood Gundy Inc. and shows the gross bid price for transactions of at least $1-million at Friday's close. The list is divided between open mortgages that are prepayable, and are likely to produce accelerated return of principal, and closed mortgages, on which unscheduled principal payments are not permitted. Indicated yields assume no prepayments. All MBS are priced to their weighted average maturity date.

### Prepayable

| Pool | Issuer | Maturity | Coupon | Price | Yield |
|---|---|---|---|---|---|
| 96404645 | Shoppers | Jan.97 | 8.250 | 100.71613 | 7.59 |
| 96405642 | Canada Trust | Jul.97 | 7.750 | 100.19092 | 7.61 |
| 96407176 | London Life | Jan.96 | 7.250 | 99.58049 | 7.60 |
| 96407549 | SunLife Trust | Jan.98 | 7.875 | 100.25201 | 7.68 |
| 96407978 | Mackenzie | Apr.98 | 7.375 | 99.04404 | 7.74 |
| 96410170 | FirstLine | May.99 | 6.250 | 95.25057 | 7.94 |
| 96411004 | MUTUAL | Oct.99 | 8.750 | 102.17220 | 7.95 |
| 96411178 | CIBC | Oct.99 | 8.875 | 102.53290 | 7.96 |
| 96411582 | Household | Jun.00 | 8.100 | 99.70861 | 8.05 |
| 96500194 | Sec Home | Jul.98 | 7.125 | 98.10583 | 7.86 |

### Nonprepayable

| Pool | Issuer | Maturity | Coupon | Price | Yield |
|---|---|---|---|---|---|
| 99001752 | Maritime Life | Mar.96 | 9.000 | 100.64050 | 7.35 |
| 99003139 | Royal Bank | Jan.97 | 7.875 | 100.45989 | 7.34 |
| 99003915 | CIBC | Sep.97 | 7.000 | 98.98133 | 7.39 |
| 99004640 | CIBC | Mar.03 | 8.250 | 100.60343 | 8.07 |
| 99004657 | Met. Trust | Feb.98 | 7.500 | 99.77996 | 7.47 |
| 99005308 | Met. Trust | Jul.00 | 7.625 | 98.97034 | 7.81 |
| 99005597 | FirstLine | Aug.98 | 6.625 | 97.23163 | 7.55 |
| 99005928 | CIBC | Jan.97 | 4.750 | 96.06456 | 7.34 |
| 99006397 | TD BANK | Sep.99 | 8.625 | 102.77706 | 7.73 |
| 99006678 | Bk Of Montre | Dec.00 | 8.000 | 100.36016 | 7.84 |

## 2.3 Equity Securities

### Common Stock as Ownership Shares

*Common stocks,* also known as *equity securities* or *equities,* represent ownership shares in a corporation. Each share of common stock entitles its owner to one vote on any matters of corporate governance that are put to a vote at the corporation's annual meeting, as well as to a share in the financial benefits of ownership.

The corporation is controlled by a board of directors elected by the shareholders. The board, which meets only a few times each year, selects managers who actually run the corporation on a day-to-day basis. Managers have the authority to make most business decisions without the board's specific approval. The board's mandate is overseeing the management to ensure that it acts in the best interests of shareholders. The members of the board are elected at the annual meeting. Shareholders who do not attend the annual meeting can vote by *proxy,* empowering another party to vote in their name. Management usually solicits the proxies of shareholders and normally gets a vast majority of these proxy votes. Occasionally, however, a group of shareholders intent on unseating the current management or altering its policies will wage a proxy fight to gain the voting rights of shareholders not attending the annual meeting. Thus, although management usually has considerable discretion to run the firm as it sees fit—without daily scrutiny from the equityholders who actually own the firm—both scrutiny from the board and the possibility of a proxy fight serve as checks on management's jurisdiction.

Another related check on management's discretion is the possibility of a corporate takeover. In these episodes, an outside investor who believes that the firm is mismanaged will attempt to acquire the firm. Usually, this is accomplished with a *tender offer,* which is an offer made to purchase, at a stipulated price (usually substantially above the current market price), some or all of the shares held by the current stockholders. If the tender is successful, the acquiring investor purchases enough shares to obtain control of the firm and can replace the existing management.

Several Canadian firms have at times issued a special type of common stock (**restricted shares**) that has no voting rights, or only restricted voting rights, but otherwise participates fully in the financial benefits of share ownership. For instance, a company may issue two classes of shares, only one of which has the right to vote; alternatively, the senior class may have five votes and the subordinate class only one vote per share. Such shares accounted for about 15 percent of the market on the Toronto Stock Exchange at the end of 1989. They were issued by firms that wanted to expand without diluting the holdings of a controlling group. Occasionally, restricted shares were issued to comply with regulatory requirements, such as those restricting foreign ownership in Canadian broadcasting.

Restricted shares sometimes carry different (generally higher) financial benefits for their holders than regular common stock. Otherwise, the loss of the right to vote should be reflected in a lower market value for restricted than for ordinary shares; this loss is the market value of the right to vote. Restricted shareholders also have some legal protection in case of tender offers. Several studies have examined this value of the voting rights, as well as other implications of restricted shares.[2]

The common stock of most large corporations can be bought or sold freely on one or more stock exchanges. A corporation whose stock is not publicly traded is said to be *closely held.* In most closely held corporations, the owners of the firm also take an active role in its management. Takeovers, therefore, are generally not an issue.

Thus, although there is substantial separation of the ownership and the control of large corporations, there are at least some implicit controls on management that tend to force it to act in the interests of the shareholders.

## Characteristics of Common Stock

The two most important characteristics of common stock as an investment are its **residual claim** and **limited liability** features.

Residual claim means that stockholders are the last in line of all those who have a claim on the assets and income of the corporation. In a liquidation of the firm's assets, the shareholders have a claim to what is left after all other claimants, such as the tax authorities, employees, suppliers, bondholders, and other creditors, have been paid. For a firm not in liquidation, shareholders have claim to the part of operating income left over after interest and taxes have been paid. Management either can pay this residual as cash dividends to shareholders or reinvest it in the business to increase the value of the shares.

Limited liability means that the greatest amount shareholders can lose in event of failure of the corporation is their original investment. Unlike owners of unincorporated businesses, whose creditors can lay claim to the personal assets of the owner (e.g., house, car, furniture), corporate shareholders may at worst have worthless stock. They are not personally liable for the firm's obligations.

---

[2] See, for instance, Vijay Jog and Allan Riding, "Price Effects of Dual-Class Shares," *Financial Analysts Journal,* January/February 1986, and "Market Reactions of Return, Risk, and Liquidity to the Creation of Restricted Voting Shares," *Canadian Journal of Administrative Sciences* 6, no. 1 (March 1989); Elizabeth Maynes, Chris Robinson, and Alan White, "How Much Is a Share Vote Worth?" *Canadian Investment Review* 3, no. 1 (Spring 1990); Chris Robinson and Alan White, "Empirical Evidence on the Relative Valuation of Voting and Restricted Voting Shares," *Canadian Journal of Administrative Sciences* 7, no. 4 (December 1990); and Elizabeth Maynes, "Evidence on the Value of a Stock Exchange Listing," *Canadian Journal of Administrative Sciences* 8, no. 3 (September 1991). There are also non-Canadian studies on restricted shares; see, for instance, M. Partch, "The Creation of a Class of Limited Voting Common Stock and Shareholder Wealth," *Journal of Financial Economics* 18, no. 2 (June 1987).

**Concept Check**

Question 3.

*a.* If you buy 100 shares of Alcan stock, to what are you entitled?

*b.* What is the most money you can make on this investment over the next year?

*c.* If you pay $50 per share, what is the most money you could lose over the year?

## Stock Market Listings

Figure 2.5 is a partial listing from *The Globe and Mail* weekly report of stocks traded on the Toronto Stock Exchange. The TSE is one of several Canadian markets in which investors may buy or sell shares of stock. We will examine these markets in detail in Chapter 3.

To interpret the information provided for each traded stock, consider the two listings for Canadian Tire, Cdn Tire and Cdn Tir nv (arrows). These two shares are otherwise identical, except that the second or class A listing has no voting rights; for this reason, its quoted prices are somewhat lower than those of Cdn Tire, with the difference representing the value of the voting privilege. For the class A shares, the first two columns provide the highest and lowest price at which the stock has traded in the last 52 weeks, 14¼ and 10, respectively. The 0.40 figure following the name means that the dividend payout to its shareholders in each class over the last quarter was $0.40 per share on an annual basis. Thus, Canadian Tire class A stock, which is selling at 13⅝ (the last recorded, or *close* price, in the seventh column), has a dividend yield of 0.40/13.625 = .0293, or 2.93 percent; this is higher than the yield on the voting shares, 2.60 percent of the price of 15⅜. A cursory analysis of the stock listings shows that dividend yields vary widely among firms. It is important to recognize that high-yield dividend stocks are not necessarily better investments than low-yield stocks. Total return to an investor comes from dividends and **capital gains,** or appreciation in the value of the stock. Low-yield dividend firms presumably offer greater prospects for capital gains, or investors would not be willing to hold the low-yield firms in their portfolios.

The share profit, or earnings per share, represents the corporate earnings for the last four quarters divided by the number of shares outstanding. P-E ratio, or **price-earnings ratio,** is the ratio of the closing stock price to last year's earnings per share. The P-E ratio tells us how much stock purchasers must pay per dollar of earnings that the firm generates for each share. The P-E ratio also varies widely across firms. Where neither dividend yield nor P-E ratio are reported in Figure 2.5, the firms have zero dividends, or zero or negative earnings. We shall have much to say about P-E ratios in Chapter 18.

The sales column shows that 585,100 shares of the stock were traded in the week ending June 2, 1995. Shares commonly are traded in **board lots** of 100 shares each; however, a board lot consists of 1,000 shares for stocks selling below

**Figure 2.5**

Stock market listings.

From *The Globe and Mail*, June 3, 1995. Reprinted by permission.

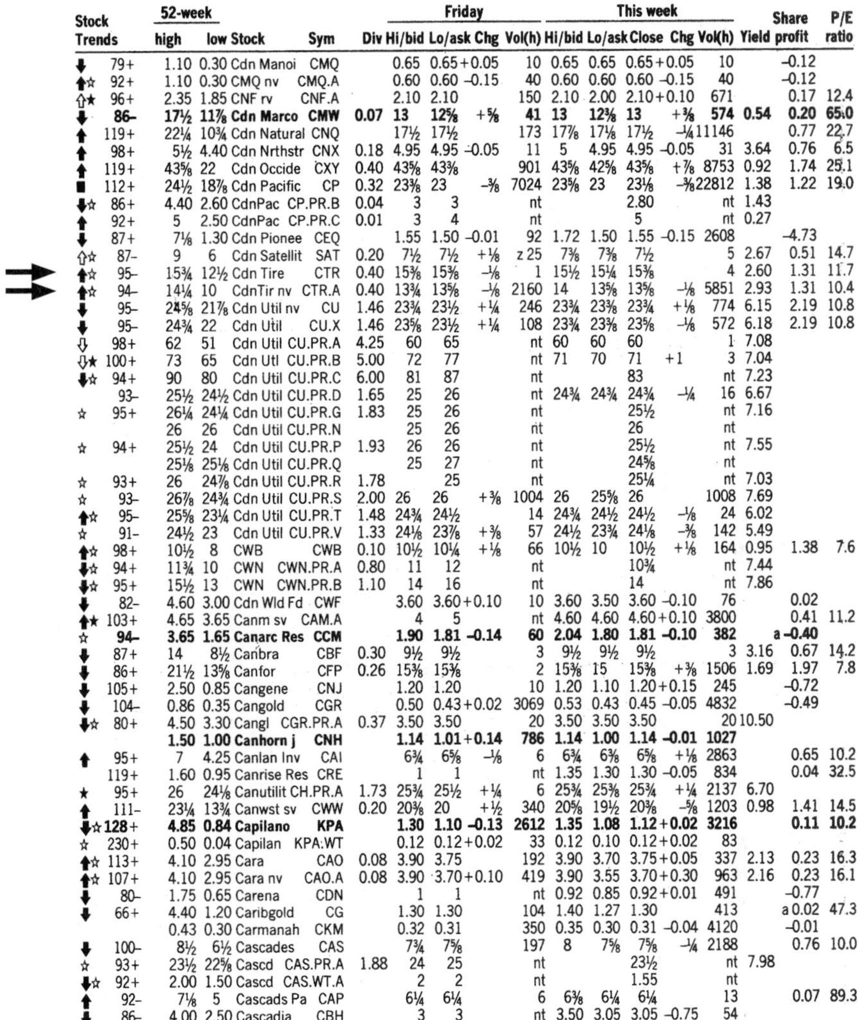

| Stock | 52-week | | | | | Friday | | | | This week | | | | | | Share | P/E |
|---|---|---|---|---|---|---|---|---|---|---|---|---|---|---|---|---|---|
| Trends | high | low | Stock | Sym | Div | Hi/bid | Lo/ask | Chg | Vol(h) | Hi/bid | Lo/ask | Close | Chg | Vol(h) | Yield | profit | ratio |
| ↓ 79+ | 1.10 | 0.30 | Cdn Manoi | CMQ | | 0.65 | 0.65 | +0.05 | 10 | 0.65 | 0.65 | 0.65 | +0.05 | 10 | | −0.12 | |
| ↑☆ 92+ | 1.10 | 0.30 | CMQ nv | CMQ.A | | 0.60 | 0.60 | −0.15 | 40 | 0.60 | 0.60 | 0.60 | −0.15 | 40 | | −0.12 | |
| ⇧★ 96+ | 2.35 | 1.85 | CNF rv | CNF.A | | 2.10 | 2.10 | | 150 | 2.10 | 2.00 | 2.10 | +0.10 | 671 | | 0.17 | 12.4 |
| **↓ 86−** | **17½** | **11⅞** | **Cdn Marco** | **CMW** | **0.07** | **13** | **12⅝** | **+⅝** | **41** | **13** | **12⅜** | **13** | **+⅜** | **574** | **0.54** | **0.20** | **65.0** |
| ↑ 119+ | 22¼ | 10¾ | Cdn Natural | CNQ | | 17½ | 17½ | | 173 | 17⅞ | 17⅛ | 17½ | −¼ | 11146 | | 0.77 | 22.7 |
| ↑ 98+ | 5½ | 4.40 | Cdn Nrthstr | CNX | 0.18 | 4.95 | 4.95 | −0.05 | 11 | 5 | 4.95 | 4.95 | −0.05 | 31 | 3.64 | 0.76 | 6.5 |
| ↑ 119+ | 43⅝ | 22 | Cdn Occide | CXY | 0.40 | 43⅝ | 43⅜ | | 901 | 43⅝ | 42⅝ | 43⅝ | +⅞ | 8753 | 0.92 | 1.74 | 25.1 |
| ■ 112+ | 24½ | 18⅞ | Cdn Pacific | CP | 0.32 | 23⅜ | 23 | −⅜ | 7024 | 23⅝ | 23 | 23⅛ | −⅜ | 22812 | 1.38 | 1.22 | 19.0 |
| ↓☆ 86+ | 4.40 | 2.60 | CdnPac | CP.PR.B | 0.04 | 3 | 3 | | nt | | | 2.80 | | nt | 1.43 | | |
| ↑ 92+ | 5 | 2.50 | CdnPac | CP.PR.C | 0.01 | 3 | 4 | | nt | | | 5 | | nt | 0.27 | | |
| ↓ 87+ | 7⅛ | 1.30 | Cdn Pionee | CEQ | | 1.55 | 1.50 | −0.01 | 92 | 1.72 | 1.50 | 1.55 | −0.15 | 2608 | | −4.73 | |
| ⇧☆ 87− | 9 | 6 | Cdn Satellit | SAT | 0.20 | 7½ | 7½ | +⅛ | z 25 | 7⅜ | 7⅜ | 7½ | | 5 | 2.67 | 0.51 | 14.7 |
| ↑☆ 95− | 15¾ | 12½ | Cdn Tire | CTR | 0.40 | 15⅜ | 15⅜ | −⅛ | 1 | 15½ | 15¼ | 15⅜ | | 4 | 2.60 | 1.31 | 11.7 |
| ↑☆ 94− | 14¼ | 10 | CdnTir nv | CTR.A | 0.40 | 13¾ | 13⅝ | −⅛ | 2160 | 14 | 13⅝ | 13⅝ | −⅛ | 5851 | 2.93 | 1.31 | 10.4 |
| ↓ 95− | 24⅝ | 21⅞ | Cdn Util nv | CU | 1.46 | 23¾ | 23½ | +¼ | 246 | 23¾ | 23⅜ | 23¾ | +⅛ | 774 | 6.15 | 2.19 | 10.8 |
| ↓ 95− | 24¾ | 22 | Cdn Util | CU.X | 1.46 | 23⅝ | 23½ | +¼ | 108 | 23¾ | 23⅜ | 23⅝ | −⅛ | 572 | 6.18 | 2.19 | 10.8 |
| ⇩ 98+ | 62 | 51 | Cdn Util | CU.PR.A | 4.25 | 60 | 65 | | nt | 60 | 60 | 60 | | 1 | 7.08 | | |
| ⇩★ 100+ | 73 | 65 | Cdn Utl | CU.PR.B | 5.00 | 72 | 77 | | nt | 71 | 70 | 71 | +1 | 3 | 7.04 | | |
| ↓☆ 94+ | 90 | 80 | Cdn Util | CU.PR.C | 6.00 | 81 | 87 | | nt | | | 83 | | nt | 7.23 | | |
| 93− | 25½ | 24½ | Cdn Util | CU.PR.D | 1.65 | 25 | 26 | | nt | 24¾ | 24¾ | 24¾ | −¼ | 16 | 6.67 | | |
| ☆ 95+ | 26¼ | 24¼ | Cdn Util | CU.PR.G | 1.83 | 25 | 26 | | nt | | | 25½ | | nt | 7.16 | | |
| | 26 | 26 | Cdn Util | CU.PR.N | | 25 | 26 | | nt | | | 26 | | nt | | | |
| ☆ 94+ | 25½ | 24 | Cdn Util | CU.PR.P | 1.93 | 26 | 26 | | nt | | | 25½ | | nt | 7.55 | | |
| | 25⅛ | 25⅛ | Cdn Util | CU.PR.Q | | 25 | 27 | | nt | | | 24⅝ | | nt | | | |
| ☆ 93+ | 26 | 24⅞ | Cdn Util | CU.PR.R | 1.78 | | 25 | | nt | | | 25¼ | | nt | 7.03 | | |
| ☆ 93− | 26⅞ | 24¾ | Cdn Util | CU.PR.S | 2.00 | 26 | 26 | +⅜ | 1004 | 26 | 25⅝ | 26 | | 1008 | 7.69 | | |
| ↑☆ 95− | 25⅝ | 23¼ | Cdn Util | CU.PR.T | 1.48 | 24¾ | 24½ | | 14 | 24¾ | 24½ | 24½ | −⅛ | 24 | 6.02 | | |
| ☆ 91− | 24½ | 23 | Cdn Util | CU.PR.V | 1.33 | 24⅛ | 23⅞ | +⅜ | 57 | 24½ | 23¾ | 24⅛ | −⅜ | 142 | 5.49 | | |
| ↑☆ 98+ | 10½ | 8 | CWB | CWB | 0.10 | 10½ | 10¼ | +⅛ | 66 | 10½ | 10 | 10½ | +⅛ | 164 | 0.95 | 1.38 | 7.6 |
| ↓☆ 94+ | 11¾ | 10 | CWN | CWN.PR.A | 0.80 | 11 | 12 | | nt | | | 10¾ | | nt | 7.44 | | |
| ↓☆ 95+ | 15½ | 13 | CWN | CWN.PR.B | 1.10 | 14 | 16 | | nt | | | 14 | | nt | 7.86 | | |
| ↓ 82− | 4.60 | 3.00 | Cdn Wld Fd | CWF | | 3.60 | 3.60 | +0.10 | 10 | 3.60 | 3.50 | 3.60 | −0.10 | 76 | | 0.02 | |
| ↑★ 103+ | 4.65 | 3.65 | Canm sv | CAM.A | | 4 | 5 | | nt | 4.60 | 4.60 | 4.60 | +0.10 | 3800 | | 0.41 | 11.2 |
| ☆ **94−** | **3.65** | **1.65** | **Canarc Res** | **CCM** | | **1.90** | **1.81** | **−0.14** | **60** | **2.04** | **1.80** | **1.81** | **−0.10** | **382** | | **a −0.40** | |
| ↓ 87+ | 14 | 8½ | Canbra | CBF | 0.30 | 9½ | 9½ | | 3 | 9½ | 9½ | 9½ | | 3 | 3.16 | 0.67 | 14.2 |
| ↓ 86+ | 21½ | 13⅝ | Canfor | CFP | 0.26 | 15⅜ | 15⅜ | | 2 | 15⅜ | 15 | 15⅜ | +⅜ | 1506 | 1.69 | 1.97 | 7.8 |
| ↓ 105+ | 2.50 | 0.85 | Cangene | CNJ | | 1.20 | 1.20 | | 10 | 1.20 | 1.10 | 1.20 | +0.15 | 245 | | −0.72 | |
| ↓ 104− | 0.86 | 0.35 | Cangold | CGR | | 0.50 | 0.43 | +0.02 | 3069 | 0.53 | 0.43 | 0.45 | −0.05 | 4832 | | −0.49 | |
| ↓☆ 80+ | 4.50 | 3.30 | Cangl | CGR.PR.A | 0.37 | 3.50 | 3.50 | | 20 | 3.50 | 3.50 | 3.50 | | 20 | 10.50 | | |
| | **1.50** | **1.00** | **Canhorn j** | **CNH** | | **1.14** | **1.01** | **+0.14** | **786** | **1.14** | **1.00** | **1.14** | **−0.01** | **1027** | | | |
| ↑ 95+ | 7 | 4.25 | Canlan Inv | CAI | | 6¾ | 6⅝ | −⅛ | 6 | 6¾ | 6⅜ | 6⅝ | +⅛ | 2863 | | 0.65 | 10.2 |
| 119+ | 1.60 | 0.95 | Canrise Res | CRE | | 1 | 1 | | nt | 1.35 | 1.30 | 1.30 | −0.05 | 834 | | 0.04 | 32.5 |
| ★ 95+ | 26 | 24⅛ | Canutilit | CH.PR.A | 1.73 | 25¾ | 25½ | +¼ | 6 | 25¾ | 25⅜ | 25¾ | +¼ | 2137 | 6.70 | | |
| ↑ 111− | 23¼ | 13¾ | Canwst sv | CWW | 0.20 | 20⅜ | 20 | +½ | 340 | 20⅝ | 19½ | 20⅜ | −⅝ | 1203 | 0.98 | 1.41 | 14.5 |
| ↓☆ **128+** | **4.85** | **0.84** | **Capilano** | **KPA** | | **1.30** | **1.10** | **−0.13** | **2612** | **1.35** | **1.08** | **1.12** | **+0.02** | **3216** | | **0.11** | **10.2** |
| ☆ 230+ | 0.50 | 0.04 | Capilan | KPA.WT | | 0.12 | 0.12 | +0.02 | 33 | 0.12 | 0.10 | 0.12 | +0.02 | 83 | | | |
| ↑☆ 113+ | 4.10 | 2.95 | Cara | CAO | 0.08 | 3.90 | 3.75 | | 192 | 3.90 | 3.70 | 3.75 | +0.05 | 337 | 2.13 | 0.23 | 16.3 |
| ↑☆ 107+ | 4.10 | 2.95 | Cara nv | CAO.A | 0.08 | 3.90 | 3.70 | +0.10 | 419 | 3.90 | 3.55 | 3.70 | +0.30 | 963 | 2.16 | 0.23 | 16.1 |
| ↓ 80− | 1.75 | 0.65 | Carena | CDN | | 1 | 1 | | nt | 0.92 | 0.85 | 0.92 | +0.01 | 491 | | −0.77 | |
| ↓ 66+ | 4.40 | 1.20 | Caribgold | CG | | 1.30 | 1.30 | | 104 | 1.40 | 1.27 | 1.30 | | 413 | | a 0.02 | 47.3 |
| | 0.43 | 0.30 | Carmanah | CKM | | 0.32 | 0.31 | | 350 | 0.35 | 0.30 | 0.31 | −0.04 | 4120 | | −0.01 | |
| ↓ 100− | 8½ | 6½ | Cascades | CAS | | 7¾ | 7⅝ | | 197 | 8 | 7⅝ | 7⅝ | −¼ | 2188 | | 0.76 | 10.0 |
| ☆ 93+ | 23½ | 22⅝ | Cascd | CAS.PR.A | 1.88 | 24 | 25 | | nt | | | 23½ | | nt | 7.98 | | |
| ↓☆ 92+ | 2.00 | 1.50 | Cascd | CAS.WT.A | | 2 | 2 | | nt | | | 1.55 | | nt | | | |
| ↑ 92− | 7⅛ | 5 | Cascads Pa | CAP | | 6¼ | 6¼ | | 6 | 6⅜ | 6¼ | 6¼ | | 13 | | 0.07 | 89.3 |
| ↓ 86− | 4.00 | 2.50 | Cascadia | CBH | | 3 | 3 | | nt | 3.50 | 3.05 | 3.05 | −0.75 | 54 | | | |

$5, while it falls to 25 shares for stocks above $100. Investors who wish to trade in smaller odd lots can expect to pay higher commissions to their stock brokers, although many brokers are not charging an odd-lot differential in order to attract the small investor. The commission structure actually makes trading in a small number of higher-priced stocks (say 25 shares at $120) cheaper on a percentage basis than the same value of a low-priced stock (say 1,000 shares at $3). The highest price and lowest price per share at which the stock traded in that week were 14 and 13⅝, respectively. The last, or closing, price of 13⅝ was down ⅛ from the closing price of the previous week.

### Preferred Stock

*Preferred stock* has features similar to both equity and debt. Like a bond, it promises to pay to its holder fixed dividends each year. In this sense, preferred stock is similar to an infinite-maturity bond, that is, a perpetuity. It also resembles a bond in that it does not convey voting power regarding the management of the firm. Preferred stock is an equity investment, however, in the sense that failure to pay the dividend does not precipitate corporate bankruptcy. Instead, preferred dividends are usually *cumulative;* that is, unpaid dividends cumulate and must be paid in full before any dividends may be paid to holders of common stock.

Preferred stock also differs from bonds in terms of its tax treatment for the firm. Because preferred stock payments are treated as dividends rather than interest, they are not tax-deductible expenses for the firm. This disadvantage is offset somewhat by the fact that corporations may exclude dividends received from domestic corporations in the computation of their taxable income. Preferred stocks, therefore, make desirable fixed-income investments for some corporations. Similarly, preferred dividends are taxed like common dividends for individual investors, which confers them a higher after-tax yield than bonds with the same pretax yield. Hence, even though they rank after bonds in the event of corporate bankruptcy, preferred stocks generally sell at lower yields than do corporate bonds.

Preferred stock is issued in variations similar to those of corporate bonds. It can be callable by the issuing firm, in which case it is said to be *redeemable.* It also can be convertible into common stock at some specified conversion ratio. A firm often issues different series of preferreds, with different dividends, over time. For example, in Figure 2.5, there are 12 different issues of Canadian Utilities preferreds (Cdn Util), in addition to two classes of common. A recent innovation in the market is adjustable rate preferred stock, which, similar to adjustable rate mortgages, ties the dividend rate to current market interest rates.

## 2.4 Stock and Bond Market Indices

### Stock Market Indices

The daily performance of the Dow Jones Industrial Average and the Toronto Stock Exchange (TSE) Composite Index are staple portions of the Canadian evening news report. Although these indices are, respectively, the best-known measures of the performances of the U.S. and Canadian stock markets, they are only two of several indicators of stock market performance in the two countries. Other indices are computed and published daily. In addition, several indices of bond market performance are widely available.

The ever-increasing role of international trade and investments has made indices of foreign financial markets part of the general news. Thus, foreign stock exchange indices, such as the Nikkei Average of Tokyo and the Financial Times Index of London, are fast becoming household names.

**Dow Jones Averages.** The Dow Jones Industrial Average of 30 large blue-chip corporations has been computed since 1896. Its long history probably accounts for its preeminence in the public mind. (The average covered only 20 stocks until 1928.) The Dow is a **price-weighted average,** which means that it is computed by adding the prices of the 30 companies and dividing by a divisor.

Originally, the divisor was simply 20 when 20 stocks were included in the index; thus, the index was no more than the average price of the 20 stocks. This makes the index performance a measure of the performance of a particular portfolio strategy that buys one share of each firm in the index. Therefore, the weight of each firm in the index is proportional to the share price rather than the total outstanding market value of the shares. For example, if shares of firm XYZ sell for $100 each and it has 1 million shares outstanding, while shares of firm ABC sell for $25 each but there are 20 million shares outstanding, the "Dow portfolio" would have four times as much invested in XYZ as in ABC ($100 compared with $25) despite the fact that ABC is a more prominent firm in the market (with a $500 million market value of equity versus only $100 million for XYZ).

Table 2.2 illustrates this point. Suppose that ABC increases by 20 percent, from $25 to $30, while XYZ increases by only 10 percent, from $100 to $110. The return on a price-weighted average of the two stocks would come to only 12 percent, whereas the combined market value of the two stocks actually increases by more than 18 percent. Because of its lower price, the superior performance of ABC relative to XYZ has a smaller effect on the price-weighted average than it does on the actual combined value of the stocks.

**CONCEPT CHECK** Question 4. Suppose that shares of XYZ increase in price to $110 while shares of ABC fall to $20. Find the percentage change in the price-weighted average of these two stocks. Compare that to the percentage change in their combined market value.

As stocks are added to or dropped from the average, or stocks split over time, the Dow divisor is continually adjusted to leave the average unaffected by the change. For example, if XYZ were to split two for one, and its share price were

**Table 2.2** Price-Weighted Returns

| Stock | Initial Price | Final Price | Shares (million) | Initial Value of Outstanding Stock ($ million) | Final Value of Outstanding Stock ($ million) |
|---|---|---|---|---|---|
| ABC | 25 | 30 | 20 | 500 | 600 |
| XYZ | 100 | 110 | 1 | 100 | 110 |
| Average | 62.5 | 70 | | **Total market value 600** | **710** |

Increase in average price = 12% = 70/62.5 − 1
Increase in market value = 18.3% = 710/660 − 1

**Table 2.3** Price-Weighted Returns after a Stock Split

| Stock | Initial Price | Final Price | Shares (million) | Initial Value of Outstanding Stock ($ million) | Final Value of Outstanding Stock ($ million) |
|---|---|---|---|---|---|
| ABC | 25 | 30 | 20 | 500 | 600 |
| XYZ | 50 | 55 | 2 | 100 | 110 |
| Index value | $\frac{75}{1.20} = 62.5$ | $\frac{85}{1.2} = 70.83$ | | | |
| Market value | | | | 600 | 710 |

therefore to fall to $50, we would not want the average to fall, because that would incorrectly indicate a fall in the general level of market prices. Following a split, the divisor must be reduced to a value that leaves the average unaffected by the split. Table 2.3 illustrates this point. The initial share price of XYZ, which was $100 in Table 2.2, falls to $50 if the stock splits at the beginning of the period. Notice that the number of shares outstanding doubles, leaving the market value of total shares unaffected. The divisor, $d$, which originally was 2.0 when the two-stock average was initiated, must be reset to a value that leaves the average unchanged. Because the sum of the post-split stock price is 75 and the pre-split average price was 62.5, we calculate the new value of $d$ by solving $75/d = 62.5$. The value of $d$ therefore falls from its original value of 2.0 to $75/62.5 = 1.20$, and the initial value of the average is indeed unaffected by the split: $75/1.20 = 62.5$. At period end, shares of ABC will sell for $30, while shares of XYZ will sell for $55, representing the same 10 percent return it was assumed to earn in Table 2.2. The new value of the price-weighted average is $(30 + 55)/1.20 = 70.83$, and the rate of return on the average is $70.83/62.5 - 1 = .133$, or 13.3 percent. Notice that this return is greater than that calculated in Table 2.2. The relative weight of XYZ, which is the poorer-performing stock, is lower after the split because its price is lower; the performance of the average therefore improves. This example illustrates again that the implicit weighting scheme of a price-weighted average is somewhat arbitrary, being determined by the prices rather than the outstanding market values of the shares in the average.

In the same way that the divisor is updated for stock splits, if one firm is dropped from the average and another firm with a different price is added, the divisor has to be updated to leave the average unchanged by the substitution. By now, the advisor for the Down Jones Industrial Average has fallen to a value of about .75.

Dow Jones & Company also computes a Transportation Average of 20 airline, trucking, and railroad stocks; a Public Utility Average of 15 electric and natural gas utilities; and a Composite Average combining the 65 firms of the three separate averages. Each is a price-weighted average, and thus over-weights the performance of high-priced stocks.

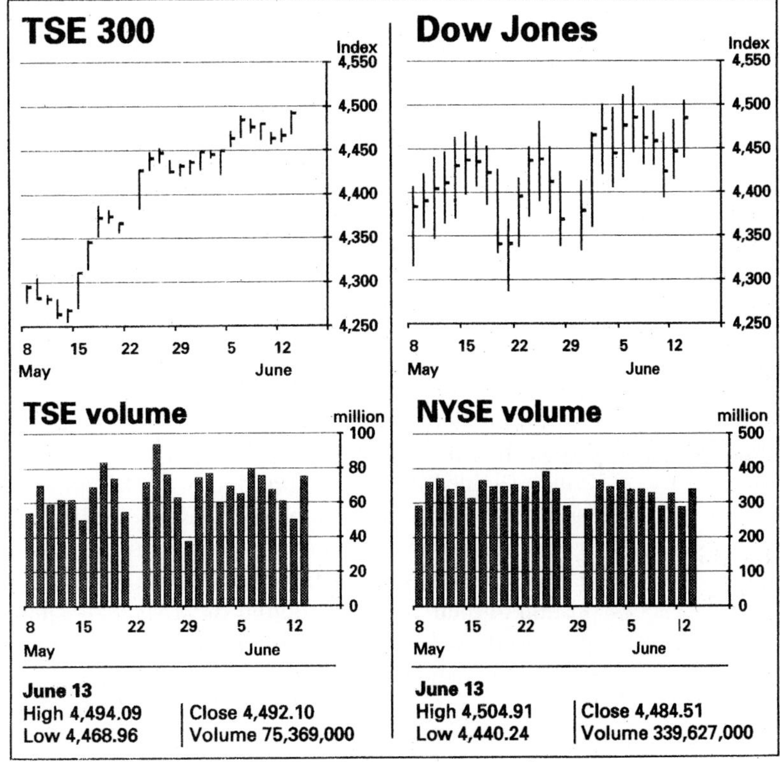


**Figure 2.6**
TSE 300 Indices and Dow Jones Averages.
From *The Globe and Mail,* June 14, 1995. Reprinted by permission.

Figure 2.6 reproduces some of the data reported on the TSE Index and the Dow Jones Industrial Average from *The Globe and Mail.* The bars show the range of values assumed by the average on each day. The small boxes indicate the highs, lows, and closing averages of both exchanges.

**Toronto Stock Exchange Indices.** The TSE 300 Composite Index is Canada's best-known stock market indicator. It contains the 300 largest securities (in terms of market value) traded on the TSE, regardless of industry group, but excluding *control blocks* composed of more than 20 percent of outstanding shares. Besides being more broadly based than the Dow, it differs also in being a **market value-weighted index.** In the case of the firms XYZ and ABC that we mentioned above, the TSE 300 would give ABC five times the weight given to XYZ because the market value of its outstanding equity is five times larger. The TSE 300 is computed by calculating the total market value of the 300 stocks in the index and the total market value of those stocks on the previous day of trading, always excluding the control blocks. The percentage increase in the total market value from one day to the next represents the increase in the index. The rate of return of the index therefore equals the rate of return that would be earned by an investor holding a portfolio of all 300 stocks in the index in proportion to their market value, except that the index does not reflect cash dividends paid out by those stocks.

To illustrate, look again at Table 2.2. If the initial level of a market value-weighted index of stocks ABC and XYZ were set equal to an arbitrarily chosen starting value such as 100, the index value at year-end would be $100 \times (710/600) = 118.3$. The increase in the index reflects the 18.3 percent return earned on a portfolio consisting of those two stocks held in proportion to outstanding market values.

Note also from Tables 2.2 and 2.3 that market value-weighted indices are unaffected by stock splits. The total market value of outstanding XYZ stock increases from $100 million to $110 million regardless of the stock split, thereby rendering the split irrelevant to the performance of the index.

A nice feature of both market value-weighted and price-weighted indices is that they reflect the returns to buy-and-hold portfolio strategies. If one were to buy each share in the index in proportion to its outstanding market value, the value-weighted index would perfectly track capital gains on the underlying portfolio. Similarly, a price-weighted index tracks the returns on a portfolio composed of an equal number of shares in each firm.

Investors today can purchase shares in mutual funds that hold shares in proportion to their representation in the TSE 300. These **index funds** yield a return equal to that of the TSE 300 index and so provide a low-cost passive investment strategy for equity investors.

The Toronto Stock Exchange also computes two other indices, the TSE 35[3] and the TSE 100; as well, it presents several stock indices based on narrow industry groupings, such as the Oil and Gas Index and the High Technology Index. The Montreal Stock Exchange computes the 25-stock Canadian Market Portfolio Index and several industry stock indices. The Vancouver Stock Exchange calculates its own VSE Index, based on the low-capitalization stocks traded there. Figure 2.7 reproduces a listing from *The Globe and Mail* of the performance of industry group and subgroup stock indices from the TSE.

The TSE 35 was introduced in 1987 and is aimed especially at the trading of derivative products, such as index options and futures (see Section 2.5). The 35 firms whose stocks are represented in the index are some of the largest and most actively traded Canadian firms. The TSE 35 is a modified market value-weighted index, with a ceiling of 10 percent placed on any one stock so that it doesn't dominate the index. All major industry groupings in the TSE 300 are also represented in the TSE 35, with the exception of Real Estate.

The TSE 100 is another value-weighted index, introduced in 1993. Like the TSE 35, it is composed of stocks drawn from the largest firms in the TSE 300 group.[4] It represents an intermediate benchmark, geared toward those investors

[3] The TSE 35 is also known as the Toronto 35 or T 35 index.

[4] The stocks left over in the TSE 300 after the removal of the TSE 100 firms form what is known as the TSE 200 index. Unlike the other two indices, the TSE 200 is not always given in the daily quotes in the financial press.

**Figure 2.7**
Canadian stock indices.
From the *Globe and Mail,* June 3, 1995. Reprinted by permission.

# Canadian Indexes

## Toronto Stock Exchange

| 52-week high | 52-week low | Index | Open | High | Low | Close | Chg | % Chg | Vol (100s) | Div yield | Avg P/E | Tot. Ret. |
|---|---|---|---|---|---|---|---|---|---|---|---|---|
| 4452.06 | 3935.66 | TSE 300 | 4422.48 | 4449.80 | 4422.48 | 4449.80 | +4.19 | +0.1 | 432886 | 2.31 | 15.49 | 8744.75 |
| 236.19 | 198.63 | TSE 35 | 234.19 | 235.19 | 233.06 | 235.15 | +0.02 | +0.0 | 200769 | 2.83 | 15.57 | 377.76 |
| 270.74 | 235.95 | TSE 100 | 268.52 | 270.15 | 267.63 | 270.12 | +0.55 | +0.2 | 340853 | 2.52 | 14.91 | 282.66 |
| 269.74 | 236.09 | TSE 200 | 268.65 | 269.05 | 267.77 | 268.02 | −1.01 | −0.4 | 92033 | 1.42 | 18.65 | 275.19 |

## TSE 300 Subgroups

| Index | High | Low | Close | Chg | Vol |
|---|---|---|---|---|---|
| Metals & minerals | 4317.75 | 4280.97 | 4308.26 | −6.75 | 2217171 |
| Integrated mines | 4408.19 | 4371.55 | 4395.13 | −3.76 | 1689363 |
| Mining | 2386.74 | 2357.05 | 2380.35 | −9.75 | 527808 |
| Gold & Prec Mtls | 10418.50 | 10269.44 | 10309.43 | −123.16 | 2820960 |
| Oil and gas | 4599.67 | 4583.38 | 4598.23 | −7.64 | 3634133 |
| Integrated Oils | 4785.82 | 4757.17 | 4777.17 | −6.40 | 788274 |
| Oil & gas prdcr | 4639.52 | 4624.74 | 4639.41 | −7.74 | 2580856 |
| Oil & gas services | 727.12 | 722.88 | 723.85 | −3.27 | 265003 |
| Paper & forest | 5008.93 | 4951.69 | 5008.93 | +30.74 | 4257284 |
| Consumer products | 7160.58 | 7025.23 | 7160.58 | +103.16 | 5526427 |
| Food processing | 5306.98 | 5273.68 | 5306.98 | −11.11 | 71509 |
| Tobacco | 13227.49 | 12911.42 | 13227.49 | +189.64 | 389649 |
| Distilleries | 10444.16 | 10137.67 | 10444.16 | +244.95 | 1227697 |
| Breweries/bev | 5015.58 | 4968.69 | 5015.58 | +57.36 | 3678214 |
| Household goods | 1493.04 | 1466.94 | 1468.58 | −19.89 | 101739 |
| Biotech/pharm | 642.00 | 628.96 | 628.96 | −5.35 | 57619 |
| Industrial products | 2883.85 | 2831.56 | 2871.15 | +10.56 | 7912933 |
| Steel | 1091.51 | 1080.33 | 1081.45 | −5.41 | 1039944 |
| Fabricating & eng | 3454.53 | 3434.01 | 3444.27 | −3.50 | 905245 |
| Transport equip | 27332.16 | 26804.41 | 27124.27 | +117.20 | 283220 |
| Tech hardware | 7390.80 | 7211.71 | 7336.28 | +8.78 | 1464691 |
| Building material | 4684.65 | 4604.02 | 4604.02 | −80.63 | 24600 |
| Chem & fertilizer | 4399.50 | 4283.36 | 4370.56 | +31.39 | 3399010 |
| Bus serv | 1721.23 | 1688.13 | 1721.23 | +9.89 | 158450 |
| Tech software | 1405.63 | 1394.23 | 1405.41 | +5.89 | 205310 |
| Autos & parts | 9091.70 | 8778.29 | 8997.60 | +140.33 | 432463 |
| Real estate & const | 1742.08 | 1725.26 | 1725.26 | −8.59 | 47693 |
| Transport & envir | 4923.18 | 4862.51 | 4888.13 | −44.36 | 1749671 |
| Pipelines | 3818.01 | 3776.35 | 3776.35 | −38.42 | 461101 |
| Utilities | 3326.59 | 3311.13 | 3318.04 | +2.97 | 2041321 |
| Telephone utils | 3173.23 | 3155.64 | 3161.90 | −0.21 | 1490926 |
| Gas & Electrical | 3592.34 | 3568.34 | 3585.39 | +15.40 | 550395 |
| Comm & media | 8178.71 | 8105.31 | 8152.88 | −29.48 | 1956544 |
| Broadcasting | 4493.01 | 4464.26 | 4464.26 | −14.45 | 318790 |
| Cable & ent | 18316.30 | 18102.34 | 18274.84 | +169.75 | 937797 |
| Publishing | 8636.12 | 8561.47 | 8606.93 | −85.60 | 699957 |
| Merchandising | 3873.47 | 3849.15 | 3873.47 | +15.10 | 1033053 |
| Wholesale | 5505.42 | 5461.28 | 5505.42 | +44.14 | 30011 |
| Food stores | 6970.26 | 6916.13 | 6945.42 | −4.82 | 67776 |
| Dept stores | 1061.22 | 1052.65 | 1061.22 | +4.29 | 38048 |
| Specialty stores | 1363.05 | 1352.43 | 1358.31 | −8.34 | 515085 |
| Hospitality | 58145.18 | 57165.73 | 58145.18 | +892.16 | 382163 |
| Financial services | 3358.78 | 3320.57 | 3358.78 | +29.86 | 8699914 |
| Banks & trusts | 3730.23 | 3681.60 | 3730.23 | +38.03 | 8173334 |
| Invest co & fund | 6697.42 | 6642.87 | 6657.50 | −36.31 | 384997 |
| Insurance | 3360.08 | 3354.92 | 3360.08 | +5.16 | 4450 |
| Fin mangmt cos | 1109.00 | 1095.40 | 1106.60 | +6.72 | 137133 |
| Conglomerates | 5286.68 | 5231.62 | 5250.70 | −53.69 | 930377 |

## TSE 100 subgroups

| Index | High | Low | Close | Chg | Vol |
|---|---|---|---|---|---|
| Consumer | 260.32 | 256.01 | 260.32 | +2.83 | 6936622 |
| Industrial | 293.39 | 288.83 | 292.30 | +0.06 | 8589559 |
| Interest Sensitive | 257.53 | 254.56 | 257.26 | +1.27 | 10583661 |
| Resource | 274.80 | 273.21 | 274.34 | −0.76 | 7975428 |

## The day's TSE 300

The TSE 300 composite index through the day yesterday, showing the change each hour from the previous day's close:

| | | | | | |
|---|---|---|---|---|---|
| 9:45 a.m. | 4422.48 | −23.13 | 1 p.m. | 4444.27 | −1.34 |
| 10 a.m. | 4428.96 | −16.65 | 2 p.m. | 4446.23 | +0.62 |
| 11 a.m. | 4436.67 | −8.94 | 3 p.m. | 4447.01 | +1.40 |
| Noon | 4437.07 | −8.54 | 4 p.m. | 4449.80 | +4.19 |

## Montreal Stock Exchange

| 52-week high | 52-week low | Index | Open | High | Low | Close | Chg | % Chg | Vol (100s) | Div yield | Avg P/E |
|---|---|---|---|---|---|---|---|---|---|---|---|
| 2196.69 | 1706.52 | Mkt portfolio | 2173.36 | 2189.58 | 2173.36 | 2187.20 | −3.17 | −0.1 | 198678 | 2.67 | 16.57 |
| 2595.39 | 2136.01 | Banking | 2550.94 | 2589.04 | 2550.94 | 2589.04 | +27.52 | +1.1 | 94235 | 4.26 | 9.13 |
| 3117.83 | 2329.69 | Forest prod | 3009.27 | 3030.98 | 3009.27 | 3030.98 | +8.68 | +0.3 | 6762 | 1.78 | 10.95 |
| 2172.25 | 1413.50 | Industrial prod | 2128.06 | 2151.53 | 2128.06 | 2147.39 | −6.91 | −0.3 | 29499 | 1.52 | 14.55 |
| 2977.46 | 2479.94 | Mining | 2830.38 | 2838.05 | 2822.70 | 2827.82 | −14.07 | −0.5 | 44068 | 1.10 | 22.93 |
| 1761.44 | 1372.17 | Oil & gas | 1741.46 | 1751.64 | 1741.46 | 1749.38 | −1.50 | −0.1 | 14605 | 2.02 | 23.94 |
| 2021.71 | 1806.53 | Utilities | 1908.88 | 1917.51 | 1907.65 | 1911.35 | −1.23 | −0.1 | 24360 | 5.61 | 12.69 |

## Vancouver

| 52-week high | 52-week low | Index | Open | High | Low | Close | Chg | % Chg | Vol |
|---|---|---|---|---|---|---|---|---|---|
| 1049.48 | 690.00 | Composite | 802.40 | 809.07 | 801.33 | 809.07 | +6.67 | +0.8 | 32634285 |
| 930.69 | 638.41 | Comm/Industrial | 649.95 | 653.87 | 648.45 | 653.58 | +3.63 | +0.6 | 1046183 |
| 1722.40 | 1073.34 | Resource | 1310.30 | 1330.89 | 1302.70 | 1329.29 | +18.99 | +1.4 | 2317061 |
| 809.12 | 528.81 | Venture | | | | 631.69 | +4.89 | +0.8 | 29086551 |

**Table 2.4** TSE 300 vs. TSE 35 vs. TSE 100 vs. TSE 200 Relative Weights as of March 31, 1995

| | TSE 300 | TSE 35 | TSE 100 | TSE 200 | 300/35 Over/Under Weighting (%) | 300/100 Over/Under Weighting (%) | 300/200 Over/Under Weighting (%) |
|---|---|---|---|---|---|---|---|
| **GROUPS** | | | | | | | |
| Metals & minerals | 8.04% | 9.55% | 9.59% | 1.28% | −1.51% | −1.55% | 6.76% |
| Gold & precious minerals | 11.49 | 11.62 | 11.29 | 12.33 | −0.13 | 0.20 | −0.84 |
| Oil & gas | 11.32 | 9.88 | 9.07 | 21.23 | 1.44 | 2.25 | −9.91 |
| Paper & forest products | 5.38 | 2.61 | 4.29 | 10.14 | 2.77 | 1.09 | −4.76 |
| Consumer products | 7.47 | 10.75 | 7.72 | 6.40 | −3.28 | −0.25 | 1.07 |
| Industrial products | 15.77 | 13.05 | 16.03 | 14.63 | 2.72 | −0.26 | 1.14 |
| Real estate | 0.29 | 0.00 | 0.00 | 1.55 | 0.29 | 0.29 | −1.26 |
| Transportation/ environmental services | 1.76 | 1.48 | 1.57 | 2.59 | 0.28 | 0.19 | −0.83 |
| Pipelines | 2.24 | 1.44 | 2.75 | 0.00 | 0.80 | −0.51 | 2.24 |
| Utilities | 9.29 | 10.60 | 9.90 | 6.63 | −1.31 | −0.61 | 2.66 |
| Communications & media | 3.77 | 5.09 | 3.27 | 5.97 | −1.32 | 0.50 | −2.20 |
| Merchandizing | 3.72 | 2.22 | 2.88 | 6.37 | 1.50 | 0.84 | −2.65 |
| Financial services | 15.33 | 16.79 | 16.86 | 9.67 | −1.46 | −1.53 | 5.66 |
| Conglomerates | 4.13 | 4.92 | 4.79 | 1.23 | −0.79 | −0.66 | 2.90 |
| **SECTORS** | | | | | | | |
| Resource | 36.23% | 33.66% | 34.24% | 44.98% | 2.57% | 1.99% | −8.75% |
| Consumer | 14.96 | 18.06 | 13.87 | 18.73 | −3.10 | 1.09 | −3.77 |
| Industrial | 21.66 | 19.45 | 22.38 | 18.44 | 2.21 | −0.72 | 3.22 |
| Interest sensitive | 27.15 | 28.83 | 29.51 | 17.85 | −1.68 | −2.36 | 9.30 |

who feel that the TSE 300 contains too many relatively illiquid stocks, while the TSE 35 has too few stocks to be really representative. There also are some derivative products (options and futures) on the TSE 100. Table 2.4 compares the relative weights of the industry groups in the TSE 300, TSE 200, TSE 100, and TSE 35 indices.

The TIP (Toronto 35 Index Participation) is a derivative product based on the TSE 35. It is sold in units representing participation in a trust created by the TSE. The trust holds a portfolio of the stocks in the TSE 35, which is designed to trace accurately the performance of that index. TIPs are listed like common shares, which pay dividends and can be bought on margin. They allow small investors to hold a diversified portfolio of senior Canadian firms representing most sectors of the Canadian economy. Effectively, TIPs are like a mutual fund without the management fee.

**CONCEPT CHECK**

Question 5. Reconsider the stock of firms XYZ and ABC from question 4. Calculate the percentage change in the market value-weighted index. Compare that to the rate of return of a portfolio that holds $500 of ABC stock for every $100 of XYZ stock, that is, an index portfolio.

**Figure 2.8**
Performance of U.S. stock indices.
From the *Globe and Mail*, May 4, 1996. Reprinted by permission.

# U.S. Indexes

## New York Stock Exchange

| 52-week high | 52-week low | Index | Open | High | Low | Close | Chg | % Chg | Vol (100s) |
|---|---|---|---|---|---|---|---|---|---|
| 5689.74 | 4340.64 | DJ Industrials | 5514.52 | 5555.71 | 5439.74 | 5478.03 | -20.24 | -0.4 | 388775 |
| 2221.06 | 1621.31 | DJ Transport | 2195.47 | 2211.55 | 2165.26 | 2179.88 | -12.91 | -0.6 | 49450 |
| 234.00 | 194.11 | DJ Utilities | 208.36 | 209.12 | 204.86 | 205.56 | -2.10 | -1.0 | 59178 |
| 1847.58 | 1427.19 | DJ 65 Composite | 1808.43 | 1821.11 | 1783.16 | 1794.83 | -9.23 | -0.5 | 497403 |
| 109.77 | 93.56 | DJ 20 Bond | 101.57 | 101.57 | 101.57 | 101.57 | -0.22 | -0.2 | |
| 638.41 | 347.56 | S&P 100 | 620.05 | 625.06 | 616.68 | 618.06 | -1.99 | -0.3 | |
| 238.13 | 135.12 | S&P 400 MidCap | 234.66 | 236.79 | 234.66 | 235.07 | +0.41 | +0.2 | |
| 663.03 | 624.21 | S&P 500 | 643.39 | 648.38 | 640.24 | 641.63 | -1.75 | -0.3 | |
| 68.62 | 62.53 | S&P Financial | 63.60 | 64.09 | 63.21 | 63.27 | -0.33 | -0.5 | |
| 780.73 | 741.03 | S&P Industrials | 766.06 | 772.14 | 762.51 | 764.41 | -1.63 | -0.2 | |
| 531.58 | 490.27 | S&P Transport | 522.82 | 523.54 | 514.33 | 517.18 | -5.64 | -1.1 | |
| 205.00 | 182.82 | S&P Utilities | 188.13 | 189.89 | 187.42 | 187.61 | -0.52 | -0.3 | |

## New York

| Index | High | Low | Close | Chg | % Chg |
|---|---|---|---|---|---|
| NYSE Composite | 348.32 | 344.83 | 345.40 | -0.81 | -0.2 |
| NYSE Financial | 284.26 | 281.40 | 281.57 | -0.91 | -0.3 |
| NYSE Industrial | 444.39 | 439.85 | 440.70 | -0.95 | -0.2 |
| NYSE Transport | 332.88 | 328.43 | 329.83 | -2.62 | -0.8 |
| NYSE Utilities | 245.72 | 243.24 | 243.57 | -0.33 | -0.1 |

## American

| Index | High | Low | Close | Chg | % Chg |
|---|---|---|---|---|---|
| Amer Biotech | 150.86 | 147.52 | 148.26 | +0.36 | +0.2 |
| Amex markt valu | 591.06 | 587.96 | 589.69 | +0.72 | +0.1 |
| Institutional | 669.79 | 660.20 | 661.65 | -2.02 | -0.3 |
| Japan Index | 220.21 | 220.21 | 220.21 | | |
| Major market | 575.39 | 567.05 | 569.20 | -1.84 | -0.3 |
| Oil and gas | 337.21 | 333.92 | 334.83 | -1.74 | -0.5 |

## Nasdaq

| Index | High | Low | Close | Chg | % Chg |
|---|---|---|---|---|---|
| Nasdaq composite | 1193.63 | 1178.32 | 1184.60 | +6.27 | +0.5 |
| NNM Composite | 534.58 | 527.63 | 530.42 | +2.79 | +0.5 |
| NNM Industrial | 457.98 | 454.54 | 456.04 | +3.41 | +0.8 |

## New York Odd Lots

**Odd-lot trades made Thursday through the New York Stock Exchange:**

Customer purchases.1,308,820 Short sales....176,733
Other sales ................1,617,358 Total sales 1,794,091

**Other U.S. Market Value Indices.** Standard & Poor's publishes the widely used S&P composite 500 stock index, a 500 stock industrial index, as well as transportation, utility, and financial stock indices. The New York Stock Exchange publishes a market value-weighted composite index of all NYSE-listed stocks, in addition to sub-indices for industrial, utility, transportation, and financial stocks. The American Stock Exchange, or AMEX, also computes a market value-weighted index of its stocks. These indices are even more broadly based than the S&P 500. The National Association of Securities Dealers publishes an index of nearly 3,000 OTC firms using the NASDAQ quotation service.

The ultimate equity index so far computed is the Wilshire 5,000 index of the market value of all NYSE and AMEX stocks plus actively traded OTC stocks. Figure 2.8 reproduces a listing from *The Globe and Mail* of stock index performance.

**Equally Weighted Indices.** Market performance sometimes is measured by an equally weighted average of the returns of each stock in an index. Such an averaging technique, by placing equal weight on each return, corresponds to an implicit portfolio strategy that places equal dollar values on each stock. This is in contrast to both price weighting (which requires equal numbers of shares of each stock) and market value weighting (which requires investments in proportion to outstanding value). The Montreal Exchange's Canadian Market Portfolio index and the Value Line index in the United States are examples of equally weighted indices.

Unlike price- or market value-weighted indices, equally weighted indices do not correspond to buy-and-hold portfolio strategies. Suppose that you start with equal dollar investments in the two stocks of Table 2.2, ABC and XYZ. Because ABC increases in value by 20 percent over the year while XYZ increases by only 10 percent, your portfolio no longer is equally weighted; it is now more heavily invested in ABC. To reset the portfolio to equal weights, you would need to rebalance: either sell off some ABC stock and/or purchase more XYZ stock. Such rebalancing would be necessary to align the return on your portfolio with that on the equally weighted index.

## Foreign and International Stock Market Indices

Development in financial markets worldwide includes the construction of indexes for these markets. The popular indexes are broader than the Dow Jones average and most are value weighted.

The most important are the Nikkei, FTSE (pronounced "footsie"), and DAX. The Nikkei 225 is a price-weighted average of the largest Tokyo Stock Exchange (TSE) stocks. The Nikkei 300 is a value-weighted index. FTSE is published by the *Financial Times* of London and is a value-weighted index of 100 of the largest London Stock Exchange corporations. The DAX index is the premier German stock index. Figure 2.9 shows the list of foreign stock exchange indices published by the *Financial Post.* More details on international indices are provided in Chapter 13.

## Bond Market Indicators

Just as stock market indices provide guidance concerning the performance of the overall stock market, bond market indicators measure the performance of various categories of bonds. ScotiaMcLeod publishes the main Canadian bond market indices, while in the United States the three most well-known groups of indices are those of Merrill Lynch, Lehman Brothers, and Salomon Brothers. Table 2.5 lists some of the indices compiled by ScotiaMcLeod, as well as their average values in 1994.

The indices all are computed monthly, and all measure total returns as the sum of capital gains plus interest income derived from the bonds during the month. Any intra-month cash distributions received from the bonds are assumed to be reinvested weekly during the month back into the bond market.

The major problem with these indices is that true rates of return on many bonds are difficult to compute because the infrequency with which the bonds trade make reliable up-to-date prices difficult to obtain. In practice, prices often

**Figure 2.9**

Listing of Foreign Stock Market Indices.

From the *Financial Post,* May 31, 1996. Reprinted by permission.

## International Indexes

| — 52 week — high | low | | Close | Net chg | % chg |
|---|---|---|---|---|---|
| **Japan** | | | | | |
| 22282.05 | 14485.41 | Nikkei | 21886.35 | -135.15 | -0.61 |
| 1718.00 | 1193.16 | Tokyo Topix | 1673.41 | -7.45 | -0.44 |
| **Britain** | | | | | |
| 2885.20 | 2467.90 | FT Ordinaries | 2790.30 | -16.60 | -0.59 |
| 3857.10 | 3282.70 | FT SE 100 | 3746.70 | -29.00 | -0.77 |
| 2059.14 | 1733.40 | FT 500 | 2007.51 | -11.50 | -0.57 |
| 2268.20 | 1611.88 | FT Act. All Share | 1884.42 | -11.87 | -0.63 |
| **Germany** | | | | | |
| 904.93 | 765.61 | FAZ Aktien | 891.72 | -9.83 | -1.09 |
| 2601.90 | 2203.70 | Commerzbank | 2562.90 | -25.30 | -0.98 |
| 2570.78 | 2083.93 | DAX Aktien | 2527.31 | -24.14 | -0.95 |
| **Australia** | | | | | |
| 2300.80 | 1961.10 | All Ordinaries | 2253.30 | -10.90 | -0.48 |
| 3454.40 | 2949.90 | All Industrials | 3310.40 | -13.90 | -0.42 |
| 1058.50 | 851.90 | Metals & Minerals | 1073.20 | -3.10 | -0.29 |
| **Hong Kong** | | | | | |
| 11594.99 | 8895.82 | Hang Seng Bank | 11157.07 | -43.49 | -0.39 |
| **Taiwan** | | | | | |
| 6182.70 | 4503.37 | Taiwan Weighted | 5892.92 | 16.49 | 0.28 |
| **China** | | | | | |
| 173.43 | 105.34 | Shenzhen Composite | 158.08 | -2.73 | -1.70 |
| 776.13 | 516.46 | Shanghai Composite | 636.36 | -14.19 | -2.18 |
| **Indonesia** | | | | | |
| n.a. | n.a. | JKSE Index | 617.24 | -5.24 | -0.84 |
| **Philippines** | | | | | |
| 3286.30 | 2196.48 | PHS Composite | 3286.30 | 1.24 | 0.04 |
| **Singapore** | | | | | |
| 2493.71 | 2053.23 | Straits Times | 2332.91 | -1.51 | -0.06 |
| **Thailand** | | | | | |
| n.a. | n.a. | SET Index | 1311.91 | 9.71 | 0.75 |
| **France** | | | | | |
| 2146.79 | 1721.14 | CAC 40 | 2108.44 | -8.66 | -0.41 |
| **Italy** | | | | | |
| 674.10 | 0.00 | Banca Commercial | 669.14 | -0.67 | -0.10 |
| **Switzerland** | | | | | |
| 1259.89 | 973.46 | Swiss Bank Corp. | 1211.97 | -7.04 | -0.58 |
| **Netherlands** | | | | | |
| 383.60 | 287.10 | CBS Gen. All Share | 380.80 | -1.40 | -0.37 |
| **Belgium** | | | | | |
| 9477.27 | 7544.66 | Brussels General | 9345.46 | -78.57 | -0.83 |
| **Sweden** | | | | | |
| 2005.50 | 1588.00 | Affarsvarlden | 1957.60 | -19.00 | -0.96 |
| **Spain** | | | | | |
| 365.01 | 290.11 | Madrid Exchange | 361.71 | -2.43 | -0.67 |
| **South Africa** | | | | | |
| n.a. | n.a. | Johannesburg All Share | 6250.80 | -16.70 | -0.27 |
| **Mexico** | | | | | |
| 3352.88 | 1958.82 | General IPC | 3260.86 | -18.62 | -0.57 |
| **Argentina** | | | | | |
| 567.42 | 375.89 | BUSE Merval | 603.79 | 4.47 | 0.74 |
| **Brazil** | | | | | |
| 57108 | 35370 | BRSP Bovespa | 56878 | 620.74 | 1.10 |
| **Venezuela** | | | | | |
| n.a. | n.a. | CCS Bursatil | 4476.88 | 7.20 | 0.16 |
| **Chile** | | | | | |
| 111.66 | 92.33 | Santiago IPSA | 96.89 | 0.16 | 0.17 |
| **India** | | | | | |
| 3869.87 | 2826.08 | Bombay BSE Sensex | 3700.62 | -39.83 | -1.06 |
| **Turkey** | | | | | |
| n.a. | n.a. | IST Composite | 61941.86 | 1527.05* | 2.53 |
| **Malaysia** | | | | | |
| n.a. | n.a. | KLSE Composite | 1141.07 | 3.12 | 0.27 |

**Table 2.5** ScotiaMcLeod's Long-Term Bond Index, 1994

| Index | Yield | Price | Value |
|---|---|---|---|
| All governments | 8.89 | 108.46 | 251.46 |
| Canada | 8.67 | 109.21 | 248.7 |
| Provincials | 9.3 | 106.73 | 255.66 |
| Municipals | 9.36 | 107.35 | 262.6 |
| All corporates | 9.48 | 107.34 | 253.73 |
| AA | 9.28 | 108.40 | 255.03 |
| A | 9.52 | 111.18 | 263.39 |
| BBB | 11.69 | 102.23 | 254.09 |
| Overall | 8.97 | 108.51 | 252.00 |

Modified from *ScotiaMcLeod's Handbook of Canadian Debt Market Indices* 1957–1994, February 1995. Used by permission of Scotia Capital Markets Fixed Income Research.

must be estimated from bond valuation models. These "matrix" prices may differ substantially from true market values.

## 2.5 Derivative Markets

One of the most significant developments in financial markets in recent years has been the growth of futures and options markets. These instruments provide payoffs that depend on the values of other assets, such as commodity prices, bond and stock prices, or market index values. For this reason, these instruments sometimes are called **derivative assets,** or **contingent claims.** Their values derive from or are contingent on the values of other assets.

### Options

A *call option* gives its holder the right to purchase an asset for a specified price, called the *exercise* or *strike price,* on or before a specified expiration date. For example, a February call option on Alcan Aluminum stock with an exercise price of $40 entitles its owner to purchase Alcan stock for a price of $40 at any time up to and including the expiration date in February. Each option contract is for the purchase of 100 shares. However, quotations are made on a per-share basis. The holder of the call need not exercise the option; it will be profitable to exercise only if the market value of the asset that may be purchased exceeds the exercise price.

When the market price exceeds the exercise price, the option holder may "call away" the asset for the exercise price and reap a profit equal to the difference between the stock price and the exercise price. Otherwise, the option will be left unexercised. If not exercised before the expiration date of the contract, the option simply expires and no longer has value. Calls therefore provide greater profits when stock prices increase and thus represent bullish investment vehicles.

In contrast, a *put option* gives its holder the right to sell an asset for a specified exercise price on or before a specified expiration date. A February put on Alcan with an exercise price of $40 thus entitles its owner to sell Alcan stock ("put the stock") to the put writer at a price of $40 at any time before expiration in February, even if the market price of Alcan is lower than $40. Whereas profits on call options increase when the asset increases in value, profits on put options increase when the asset value falls. The put is exercised only if its holder can deliver an asset worth less than the exercise price in return for the exercise price.

Figure 2.10 gives listed stock option quotations from *The Globe and Mail.* The quotations cover Montreal, Toronto, and Vancouver option trading. The third option listed in Trans Canada Options[5] is for shares of Air Canada. The number on the same line as the company name indicates that the closing (C) price for Air Canada stock was $5½ per share. The total number of all option contracts on Air Canada traded the previous day is given next. Options were traded on Air Canada with exercise prices of $5, $6, and $7. (Options with other exercise prices might exist but were not traded the previous day.) These values, the exercise price or strike price, are given in the second column of numbers, after the expiration month.

The next three columns of numbers provide the bid, ask, and last trade prices of call options on Air Canada shares with expiration dates of July, October, and January. The prices of call options decrease in successive rows for a given expiration date, corresponding to progressively higher exercise prices. This makes sense, because the right to purchase a share at a given exercise price is worth less as the exercise price increases. For example, with an exercise price of $5, the January call lists for $1.15 per share, whereas the option to purchase the stock for an exercise price of $6 is worth only $0.65. The exercise price indicates the range of prices at which the stock has traded during the life of the option; thus, we see that Air Canada has had a price near $5 in the last six months. The last two columns give an indication of the liquidity of the option as they record the volume traded and the "open interest," which refers to the total number of contracts outstanding in that option.

Put options, with various strike prices and times to maturity, are denoted with a p next to the exercise price. Put prices, of course, increase with the exercise price. The right to sell a share of Air Canada at a price of $6 is less valuable than the right to sell it at $7.

Most options have relatively short expiration dates, that is, less than one year. For some firms, however, there is a class of options called LEAPS (for long-term equity anticipation shares) with much longer expiration dates, of two to three years at issue. In 1995, LEAPS for several large Canadian companies, such as Biochem and Laidlaw, were trading on Trans Canada Options, although none of them traded on the date shown in Figure 2.10.

---

[5] Trans Canada Options was renamed The Canadian Derivatives Clearing Corporation as of 1996.

**Figure 2.10**
Trans Canada options market listings.

From *The Globe and Mail*, June 3, 1995. Reprinted by permission.

# Trans Canada Options

Trading yesterday in Trans Canada Options, which combine Montreal, Toronto and Vancouver option trading. P is a Put.

**Five most active TCO option classes**

| | Volume | Op Int |
|---|---|---|
| Seagram | 1524 | 12924 |
| Repap | 1000 | 2393 |
| Labatt John | 902 | 10677 |
| TSE 35 | 878 | 14349 |
| Royal Oak | 715 | 5482 |

| Stock Series | | Close Bid | Ask | Last | Total Vol Vol | Tot Op Int Op Int |
|---|---|---|---|---|---|---|
| **Abitibi-Price** | | | **$22⅝** | | **85** | **6873** |
| Jun95 | $20 | 2.75 | 3.00 | 2.50 | 20 | 874 |
| Jul95 | $22 | 1.35 | 1.55 | 1.05 | 10 | 947 |
| | $24 | 0.35 | 0.55 | 0.35 | 10 | 70 |
| Aug95 | $24 | 0.60 | 0.80 | 0.65 | 10 | 20 |
| Sep95 | $24 | 0.90 | 1.10 | 1.00 | 35 | 40 |
| **Agnico Eagl** | | | **$17½** | | **10** | **1782** |
| Sep95 | $18 | 1.25 | 1.40 | 1.40 | 10 | 278 |
| **Air Canada** | | | **$5½** | | **210** | **28157** |
| Jul95 | $6 | 0.10 | 0.15 | 0.15 | 20 | 3512 |
| Oct95 | $6 | 0.40 | 0.50 | 0.40 | 40 | 1865 |
| | $7 | 0.15 | 0.20 | 0.20 | 30 | 7026 |
| Jan96 | $5 | 1.05 | 1.15 | 1.15 | 20 | 20 |
| | $6 | 0.60 | 0.70 | 0.65 | 50 | 679 |
| | $6 p | 0.60 | 0.70 | 0.60 | 30 | 110 |
| | $7 p | 1.40 | 1.55 | 1.45 | 20 | 50 |
| **Alcan** | | | **$40¼** | | **35** | **8365** |
| Jun95 | $40 p | 0.60 | 0.75 | 0.80 | 25 | 75 |
| Jan96 | $42½ | 2.65 | 2.70 | 2.70 | 10 | 25 |
| **BCE** | | | **$43** | | **307** | **4662** |
| Jun95 | $42½ | 0.60 | 0.85 | 0.75 | 10 | 11 |
| | $42½p | 0.30 | 0.50 | 0.35 | 80 | 452 |
| Aug95 | $42½p | 0.60 | 0.70 | 0.65 | 12 | 787 |
| Nov95 | $42½p | 0.95 | 1.10 | 1.00 | 5 | 213 |
| | $45 p | 2.55 | 2.80 | 2.55 | 200 | 220 |
| **Bank of Mtl** | | | **$29⅜** | | **166** | **4867** |
| 95 | $27 | 2.35 | 2.60 | 2.55 | 70 | 598 |
| Jul95 | $26 | 3.35 | 3.60 | 3.30 | 3 | 256 |
| | $29 | 0.70 | 0.85 | 0.75 | 30 | 64 |
| Oct95 | $27 | 2.70 | 2.80 | 2.20 | 20 | 48 |
| | $28 | 1.80 | 2.00 | 1.55 | 40 | 361 |
| | $29 | 1.10 | 1.30 | 1.10 | 5 | 41 |
| | $29 p | 0.65 | 0.80 | 0.65 | 6 | 0 |
| Jan96 | $28 | 2.00 | 2.25 | 2.05 | 4 | 504 |
| | $29 p | 0.85 | 1.05 | 1.05 | 6 | 0 |
| | $30 | 0.85 | 1.05 | 1.00 | 40 | 294 |
| Jan97 | $28 | 2.85 | 3.20 | 3.00 | 12 | 313 |
| **Bank of NS** | | | **$29⅝** | | **170** | **7791** |
| 95 | $24 | 5½ | 5⅞ | 5½ | 15 | 5 |
| Jul95 | $26 | 3.55 | 3.80 | 3.40 | 10 | 49 |
| | $29 | 0.80 | 1.05 | 0.75 | 40 | 1023 |
| Oct95 | $29 | 1.20 | 1.30 | 1.25 | 10 | 59 |
| Jan96 | $25 | 4.55 | 4.65 | 4.60 | 70 | 2528 |
| | $30 | 1.05 | 1.30 | 1.00 | 15 | 421 |
| Jan97 | $25 | 5½ | 6 | 5⅜ | 3 | 101 |
| | $30 | 2.45 | 2.95 | 2.90 | 22 | 211 |
| **Barrick Gld** | | | **$34⅜** | | **57** | **29558** |
| Jun95 | $32½ | 2.00 | 2.25 | 1.85 | 20 | 91 |
| | $35 | 0.50 | 0.65 | 0.70 | 10 | 580 |
| Jul95 | $32½ | 2.70 | 2.90 | 2.90 | 7 | 6208 |
| Oct95 | $35 | 2.55 | 2.75 | 2.75 | 5 | 574 |
| | $37½ | 1.50 | 1.70 | 1.50 | 15 | 938 |
| **Biochem Phar** | | | **$24¾** | | **50** | **22905** |
| Jun95 | $26 | 0.35 | 0.60 | 0.55 | 10 | 101 |
| Jul95 | $26 | 1.10 | 1.35 | 1.55 | 30 | 175 |
| Jan97 | $26 | 5⅝ | 6⅛ | 6⅜ | 10 | 29 |
| **Biomira** | | | **$3.15** | | **40** | **120** |
| Jun95 | $5 p | 1.80 | 2.05 | 2.05 | 20 | 90 |
| Dec95 | $5 p | 1.85 | 2.10 | 1.95 | 20 | 20 |
| **Bombr** | | | **$30⅝** | | **118** | **6435** |
| Jul95 | $24 | 6½ | 6⅞ | 6½ | 10 | 99 |
| | $27 | 3.75 | 4.00 | 4.00 | 30 | 150 |
| | $31 | 0.80 | 1.05 | 1.05 | 10 | 125 |
| Jan96 | $20 | 10½ | 10⅞ | 10⅝ | 4 | 529 |
| | $22 | 8½ | 8⅞ | 8⅝ | 30 | 143 |
| | $28 | 4.15 | 4.40 | 4.60 | 34 | 219 |
| **Bombrdr** | | | **$30⅝** | | **71** | **876** |
| Jan97 | $28 | 6¼ | 6¾ | 6½ | 60 | 183 |
| | $30 | 5⅜ | 5⅞ | 5⅝ | 10 | 77 |
| | $34 | 3.30 | 3.70 | 3.30 | 1 | 73 |
| **Cdn Bd 2001** | | | **$110.10** | | **28** | **355** |
| Jun95 | $90 | 17.30 | 20.40 | 20.34 | 12 | 40 |
| Sep95 | $107 | 3.05 | 3.30 | 3.25 | 16 | 17 |
| **Cdn Bd 2021** | | | **$117.30** | | **118** | **446** |
| Jun95 | $90 | 27.00 | 27.60 | 27.79 | 17 | 0 |
| | $114 | 3.25 | 3.50 | 3.55 | 22 | 32 |
| | $116 | 1.45 | 1.70 | 1.85 | 8 | 8 |
| | $116p | 0.40 | 0.65 | 0.30 | 18 | 2 |
| Jul95 | $118 | 1.10 | 1.35 | 1.35 | 24 | 0 |
| Sep95 | $110p | 0.20 | 0.45 | 0.35 | 10 | 39 |
| | $116p | 1.75 | 2.00 | 1.90 | 5 | 4 |
| | $118 | 1.70 | 1.95 | 2.00 | 4 | 0 |
| | $118p | 2.75 | 3.00 | 2.80 | 10 | 0 |
| **Cdn Bd 2011** | | | **$108.65** | | **100** | **1416** |
| Jun95 | $90 | 18.35 | 18.95 | 18.89 | 31 | 0 |
| | $104 | 4.50 | 4.80 | 4.65 | 7 | 58 |
| | $106 | 2.55 | 2.80 | 2.85 | 7 | 32 |
| | $108 | 0.90 | 1.15 | 1.00 | 3 | 35 |
| | $108p | 0.45 | 0.70 | 0.45 | 22 | 22 |
| Jul95 | $108p | 1.10 | 1.35 | 1.10 | 8 | 31 |
| Sep95 | $106 | 3.20 | 3.45 | 3.40 | 6 | 88 |
| | $108 | 2.00 | 2.25 | 2.10 | 3 | 8 |
| | $108p | 1.80 | 2.05 | 2.00 | 13 | 10 |
| **CIBC** | | | **$32⅛** | | **404** | **4547** |
| Jun95 | $32 | 0.40 | 0.65 | 0.25 | 80 | 80 |
| | $33 | 0.10 | 0.30 | 0.25 | 30 | 38 |
| | $33 p | 0.75 | 0.85 | 1.25 | 84 | 536 |
| Sep95 | $32 p | 0.75 | 0.90 | 1.00 | 70 | 125 |
| | $35 | 0.20 | 0.40 | 0.35 | 10 | 329 |
| | $35 p | 2.90 | 3.15 | 3.00 | 20 | 65 |
| Dec95 | $32 p | 1.00 | 1.20 | 1.20 | 10 | 70 |
| | $33 p | 1.45 | 1.65 | 1.55 | 20 | 20 |
| | $35 p | 2.95 | 3.20 | 3.45 | 10 | 30 |
| Jan96 | $35 | 0.70 | 0.95 | 0.85 | 14 | 277 |
| Jan97 | $30 | 5 | 5¼ | 5⅛ | 30 | 235 |
| | $30 p | 1.10 | 1.15 | 1.10 | 21 | 43 |
| | $35 | 2.10 | 2.35 | 2.35 | 5 | 71 |
| **Cdn Natural** | | | **$17½** | | **30** | **2364** |
| Jul95 | $16 p | 0.02 | 0.20 | 0.10 | 30 | 110 |
| **Cascades** | | | **$7¾** | | **20** | **8517** |
| Oct95 | $8 | 0.50 | 0.65 | 0.60 | 10 | 140 |
| **Corel** | | | **$21⅝** | | **65** | **3874** |
| 95 | $22½ | 0.75 | 1.00 | 0.75 | 20 | 918 |
| Jun95 | $22½ | 0.20 | 0.25 | 0.20 | 30 | 90 |
| Jul95 | $20 | 2.15 | 2.25 | 2.20 | 25 | 841 |
| | $20 p | 0.35 | 0.50 | 0.35 | 10 | 223 |
| **Cott** | | | **$14** | | **435** | **6993** |
| Jun95 | $12 | 1.85 | 2.05 | 1.80 | 20 | 707 |
| | $12 p | 0.02 | 0.10 | 0.05 | 160 | 938 |
| | $14 | 0.35 | 0.50 | 0.35 | 75 | 1060 |
| | $14 p | 0.50 | 0.60 | 0.55 | 7 | 455 |
| Jul95 | $14 | 0.80 | 0.95 | 0.75 | 10 | 243 |
| Aug95 | $14 | 1.20 | 1.40 | 1.10 | 5 | 203 |
| | $14 p | 1.10 | 1.30 | 1.05 | 6 | 20 |
| | $16 | 0.45 | 0.60 | 0.40 | 10 | 100 |
| Sep95 | $12 | 2.60 | 2.70 | 2.65 | 10 | 193 |
| | $12 p | 0.40 | 0.55 | 0.55 | 15 | 499 |
| | $14 | 1.45 | 1.65 | 1.60 | 50 | 733 |
| | $16 | 0.65 | 0.80 | 0.65 | 47 | 582 |
| | $16 p | 2.50 | 2.75 | 2.55 | 20 | 0 |
| **Delrina** | | | **$16¼** | | **293** | **4967** |
| Jun95 | $17½ | 0.20 | 0.35 | 0.30 | 14 | 553 |
| | $17½p | 1.55 | 1.80 | 1.75 | 30 | 394 |
| Jul95 | $17½p | 1.70 | 1.95 | 1.70 | 30 | 96 |
| Sep95 | $15 p | 0.95 | 1.00 | 1.00 | 10 | 213 |
| | $17½p | 2.20 | 2.70 | 2.15 | 40 | 594 |
| | $22½ | 0.35 | 0.60 | 0.50 | 9 | 195 |
| Dec95 | $12½p | 0.40 | 0.55 | 0.55 | 10 | 160 |
| | $15 | 3.30 | 3.80 | 3.30 | 5 | 79 |
| | $15 p | 1.35 | 1.60 | 1.35 | 100 | 478 |
| | $17½ | 2.20 | 2.70 | 2.20 | 15 | 200 |
| | $17½p | 2.50 | 2.60 | 2.60 | 30 | 192 |
| **Dofasco Inc** | | | **$18½** | | **20** | **3904** |
| Jun95 | $19 p | 0.70 | 0.95 | 0.75 | 20 | 265 |
| **Domtar Inc** | | | **$12¾** | | **35** | **1821** |
| Nov95 | $13 | 1.25 | 1.50 | 1.40 | 35 | 248 |
| **Gulf Cda** | | | **$5⅜** | | **30** | **1112** |
| Sep95 | $4 | 1.35 | 1.60 | 1.60 | 30 | 30 |
| **Imperial Oil** | | | **$52¾** | | **100** | **1315** |
| Jul95 | $55 | 0.65 | 0.90 | 0.70 | 100 | 100 |
| **Inco** | | | **$34⅝** | | **180** | **5742** |
| Jun95 | $32½p | 0.06 | 0.15 | 0.15 | 60 | 108 |
| | $35 p | 0.80 | 0.85 | 0.85 | 20 | 300 |
| Jul95 | $35 | 1.20 | 1.35 | 1.20 | 40 | 74 |
| | $37½ | 0.35 | 0.40 | 0.50 | 60 | 366 |
| **Labatt John** | | | **$25½** | | **902** | **10677** |
| Aug95 | $22 | 3.55 | 3.80 | 3.70 | 250 | 631 |
| | $23 | 2.65 | 2.90 | 2.90 | 121 | 921 |
| | $24 | 1.95 | 2.20 | 2.15 | 50 | 351 |
| | $24 p | 0.50 | 0.60 | 0.50 | 20 | 50 |
| | $25 | 1.20 | 1.30 | 1.10 | 240 | 1419 |
| | $26 | 0.80 | 0.85 | 0.75 | 220 | 320 |
| Nov95 | $25 | 1.40 | 1.65 | 1.35 | 1 | 161 |
| **Laidlaw** | | | **$12⅝** | | **40** | **4928** |
| Jan96 | $6 | 6⅜ | 6¾ | 6½ | 10 | 756 |
| Jan97 | $8 | 5⅛ | 5⅝ | 5⅝ | 30 | 17 |
| **Loewen Gp** | | | **$46¾** | | **32** | **806** |
| Sep95 | $40 | 6¾ | 7 | 6¾ | 20 | 44 |
| | $45 | 2.85 | 3.10 | 3.10 | 10 | 34 |
| Dec95 | $45 p | 1.65 | 1.90 | 1.90 | 2 | 2 |
| **MacBlo** | | | **$19⅛** | | **16** | **2265** |
| Jul95 | $18 | 1.30 | 1.45 | 1.30 | 6 | 194 |
| Jan96 | $20 | 1.05 | 1.10 | 1.20 | 10 | 76 |
| **Magna** | | | **$54¾** | | **49** | **1607** |
| Jul95 | $55 | 2.15 | 2.40 | 1.80 | 2 | 2 |
| Aug95 | $50 p | 1.00 | 1.25 | 1.40 | 10 | 58 |
| | $52½ | 4.00 | 4.50 | 3.60 | 10 | 54 |
| | $55 | 2.65 | 3.15 | 2.15 | 5 | 217 |
| | $57½ | 1.90 | 2.15 | 1.90 | 12 | 126 |
| Nov95 | $55 | 4.30 | 4.80 | 4.00 | 10 | 43 |
| **Methanex** | | | **$11⅞** | | **558** | **13520** |
| Jun95 | $12 | 0.25 | 0.40 | 0.25 | 25 | 103 |
| | $12 | 0.25 | 0.40 | 0.25 | 25 | 103 |
| | $13 p | 1.10 | 1.30 | 1.50 | 20 | 230 |
| | $13 p | 1.10 | 1.30 | 1.50 | 20 | 230 |
| Jul95 | $11 p | 0.20 | 0.35 | 0.25 | 20 | 200 |
| | $11 p | 0.20 | 0.35 | 0.25 | 20 | 200 |
| | $12 p | 0.55 | 0.70 | 0.45 | 20 | 40 |
| | $12 p | 0.55 | 0.70 | 0.45 | 20 | 40 |
| Sep95 | $12 | 1.00 | 1.20 | 1.15 | 25 | 199 |
| | $12 | 1.00 | 1.20 | 1.15 | 25 | 199 |
| | $13 | 0.60 | 0.75 | 0.65 | 14 | 222 |
| | $13 | 0.60 | 0.75 | 0.65 | 14 | 222 |
| | $14 | 0.30 | 0.45 | 0.40 | 10 | 89 |
| | $14 | 0.30 | 0.45 | 0.40 | 10 | 89 |
| | $18 | 0.02 | 0.15 | 0.15 | 10 | 120 |
| | $18 | 0.02 | 0.15 | 0.15 | 10 | 120 |
| Dec95 | $12 | 1.45 | 1.65 | 1.65 | 15 | 130 |
| | $12 | 1.45 | 1.65 | 1.65 | 15 | 130 |
| | $13 | 1.00 | 1.25 | 1.05 | 120 | 200 |
| | $13 | 1.00 | 1.25 | 1.05 | 120 | 200 |
| **Midln Wlwy** | | | **$9⅜** | | **30** | **1701** |
| Jun95 | $7 | 2.35 | 2.55 | 2.20 | 15 | 131 |
| Sep95 | $7 | 2.40 | 2.65 | 2.35 | 10 | 80 |
| Dec95 | $10 | 0.60 | 0.75 | 0.65 | 5 | 84 |
| **Mitel** | | | **$6⅝** | | **45** | **9100** |
| Sep95 | $7 | 0.45 | 0.55 | 0.45 | 37 | 1705 |
| Dec95 | $7 | 0.75 | 0.80 | 0.75 | 8 | 597 |
| **National Bnk** | | | **$10¼** | | **40** | **5759** |
| Oct95 | $10 | 0.60 | 0.85 | 0.85 | 30 | 293 |
| | $11 | 0.15 | 0.40 | 0.15 | 10 | 36 |
| **Newbridge** | | | **$50½** | | **321** | **3912** |
| Jun95 | $42½ | 8 | 8½ | 8⅜ | 10 | 52 |
| | $45 | 5⅝ | 6⅛ | 5 | 5 | 223 |
| | $45 p | 0.20 | 0.30 | 0.25 | 20 | 240 |
| | $47½ | 3.55 | 3.90 | 3.65 | 35 | 484 |
| | $47½p | 0.40 | 0.50 | 0.70 | 5 | 186 |
| | $50 | 1.90 | 2.15 | 1.80 | 25 | 418 |
| | $50 p | 1.40 | 1.45 | 1.40 | 17 | 67 |
| | $52½ | 0.85 | 1.00 | 0.80 | 30 | 64 |
| | $55 | 0.25 | 0.40 | 0.30 | 20 | 110 |
| | $57½ | 0.05 | 0.15 | 0.15 | 21 | 71 |
| | $60 | 0.01 | 0.10 | 0.10 | 2 | 81 |
| Jul95 | $45 p | 0.75 | 0.90 | 1.05 | 20 | 90 |
| | $47½p | 1.45 | 1.70 | 1.55 | 40 | 40 |
| | $50 | 3.35 | 3.70 | 2.70 | 3 | 77 |
| Sep95 | $45 p | 1.65 | 1.90 | 1.90 | 14 | 79 |
| | $50 | 5 | 5¼ | 4.95 | 20 | 94 |
| | $50 p | 3.60 | 3.95 | 4.00 | 10 | 15 |
| | $52½ | 3.85 | 4.20 | 3.75 | 15 | 51 |
| | $55 | 2.90 | 3.15 | 3.10 | 5 | 263 |
| | $57½ | 2.15 | 2.40 | 2.10 | 4 | 55 |
| **Nortel** | | | **$51¾** | | **65** | **8238** |
| Jun95 | $50 | 1.95 | 2.20 | 2.10 | 10 | 507 |
| | $52½ | 0.65 | 0.70 | 0.65 | 20 | 321 |
| | $52½p | 1.20 | 1.35 | 1.20 | 5 | 45 |
| Jul95 | $57½ | 0.20 | 0.30 | 0.25 | 27 | 77 |
| Jan97 | $40 | 16⅛ | 16⅝ | 16⅝ | 1 | 74 |
| | $45 p | 1.45 | 1.70 | 1.65 | 2 | 16 |
| **Nova** | | | **$12** | | **45** | **10019** |
| Jul95 | $12 | 0.40 | 0.45 | 0.45 | 25 | 807 |
| Jan97 | $13 | 1.80 | 1.95 | 1.80 | 20 | 854 |
| **Pegasus Gl** | | | **$16⅛** | | **12** | **778** |
| Aug95 | $17 | 0.95 | 1.15 | 1.10 | 12 | 25 |
| **Petro-Cda** | | | **$13** | | **17** | **1966** |
| Sep95 | $12 | 1.20 | 1.40 | 1.30 | 7 | 206 |
| Dec95 | $12 | 1.45 | 1.70 | 1.60 | 10 | 66 |
| **Placer Dom** | | | **$34½** | | **2** | **18552** |
| Jan98 | $30 p | 2.30 | 3.30 | 2.30 | 1 | 1 |
| **Ranger Oil** | | | **$8⅜** | | **20** | **1277** |
| Oct95 | $9 | 0.45 | 0.65 | 0.50 | 20 | 174 |
| **Repap** | | | **$10⅜** | | **1000** | **2393** |
| Aug95 | $11 | 0.45 | 0.65 | 0.50 | 1000 | 2230 |
| **Rgr Cm** | | | **$15¾** | | **20** | **4943** |
| Oct95 | $15 p | 0.45 | 0.55 | 0.50 | 20 | 125 |
| **Royal Bank** | | | **$30⅝** | | **69** | **7705** |
| Jul95 | $30 | 1.00 | 1.15 | 0.90 | 3 | 926 |
| Oct95 | $30 | 1.55 | 1.65 | 1.40 | 6 | 614 |
| Jan96 | $25 | 5⅝ | 5⅞ | 5¾ | 10 | 479 |
| | $30 | 2.00 | 2.50 | 1.95 | 15 | 1928 |
| Jan97 | $30 | 3.20 | 3.60 | 3.20 | 3 | 271 |
| | $35 | 1.35 | 1.60 | 1.35 | 32 | 232 |
| **Royal Oak** | | | **$4.20** | | **715** | **5482** |
| Sep95 | $4 | 0.65 | 0.80 | 0.75 | 300 | 827 |
| | $4 p | 0.25 | 0.35 | 0.30 | 80 | 210 |
| Dec95 | $4 | 1.00 | 1.10 | 1.00 | 280 | 970 |
| | $4 p | 0.40 | 0.50 | 0.40 | 40 | 220 |
| | $5 | 0.55 | 0.65 | 0.60 | 15 | 417 |
| **SHL System** | | | **$8¾** | | **20** | **4163** |
| Jul95 | $9 | 0.40 | 0.60 | 0.45 | 10 | 70 |
| Sep95 | $10 | 0.50 | 0.60 | 0.55 | 10 | 796 |
| **Seagram** | | | **$42** | | **1524** | **12924** |
| Jun95 | $40 | 1.95 | 2.05 | 1.85 | 9 | 114 |
| Jul95 | $37½ | 4.75 | 5 | 4.85 | 6 | 639 |
| | $40 | 2.55 | 2.70 | 2.60 | 86 | 254 |
| | $40 p | 0.40 | 0.65 | 0.70 | 10 | 87 |
| | $42½ | 1.05 | 1.10 | 1.05 | 81 | 405 |
| | $45 | 0.35 | 0.60 | 0.30 | 3 | 175 |
| Oct95 | $35 p | 0.30 | 0.45 | 0.30 | 500 | 111 |
| | $42½ | 2.30 | 2.55 | 2.40 | 32 | 18 |
| Jan96 | $30 | 12⅛ | 12⅝ | 11½ | 5 | 15[illegible] |
| | $40 | 4.25 | 4.75 | 3.95 | 10 | 15[illegible] |
| Jan97 | $35 | 10⅝ | 11⅛ | 10 | 10 | 4[illegible] |
| | $45 | 4.25 | 4.75 | 3.95 | 10 | 9[illegible] |
| **Stone-Consol** | | | **$19¾** | | **2** | **40** |
| Oct95 | $17 | 3.10 | 3.60 | 3.30 | 2 | 20 |
| **TSE 100** | | | **$270.12** | | **50** | **534** |
| Jun95 | $265 | 4.95 | 5¼ | 4.85 | 5 | 16 |
| | $265 | 4.95 | 5¼ | 4.85 | 5 | 16 |
| | $270 | 1.70 | 1.95 | 1.85 | 20 | 25 |
| | $270 | 1.70 | 1.95 | 1.85 | 20 | 25 |
| **TSE 35** | | | **$235.15** | | **878** | **14349** |
| Jun95 | $220p | | 0.20 | 0.10 | 20 | 366 |
| | $225p | | 0.20 | 0.25 | 10 | 1265 |
| | $227½p | 0.15 | 0.35 | 0.40 | 5 | 206 |
| | $230 | 4.95 | 5½ | 5⅝ | 45 | 462 |
| | $230p | 0.55 | 0.65 | 0.55 | 80 | 400 |
| | $232½ | 3.10 | 3.40 | 3.55 | 102 | 269 |
| | $232½p | 1.00 | 1.15 | 1.10 | 37 | 740 |
| | $235 | 1.55 | 1.75 | 1.85 | 215 | 572 |
| | $235p | 1.85 | 2.05 | 2.15 | 45 | 352 |
| | $237½ | 0.65 | 0.85 | 0.85 | 155 | 330 |
| | $240 | 0.15 | 0.35 | 0.40 | 60 | 515 |
| Jul95 | $232½ | 5½ | 6 | 5 | 4 | 6 |
| | $232½p | 2.30 | 2.50 | 2.50 | 5 | 19 |
| | $240 | 1.85 | 2.05 | 1.95 | 30 | 96 |
| Sep95 | $225 | 13⅝ | 14⅛ | 14 | 10 | 341 |
| | $225p | 1.70 | 1.85 | 1.85 | 40 | 444 |
| | $230 | 10⅛ | 10⅝ | 9⅝ | 10 | 522 |
| | $235 | 6⅝ | 7⅛ | 6⅝ | 5 | 501 |
| **TVX Gold** | | | **$10** | | **50** | **7049** |
| Jun95 | $10 | 0.40 | 0.45 | 0.45 | 8 | 3108 |
| Jul95 | $10 p | 0.40 | 0.50 | 0.40 | 20 | 140 |
| Oct95 | $10 p | 0.50 | 0.65 | 0.55 | 12 | 22 |
| Jan96 | $9 p | 0.30 | 0.40 | 0.40 | 10 | 10 |
| **Talisman** | | | **$27¼** | | **10** | **1891** |
| Jun95 | $22 | 5⅛ | 5½ | 5¼ | 10 | 10 |
| **Tee-Comm** | | | **$8¾** | | **355** | **984** |
| Jun95 | $6 | 2.60 | 2.85 | 2.50 | 25 | 0 |
| | $9 | 0.20 | 0.35 | 0.30 | 20 | 30 |
| Jul95 | $6 | 2.65 | 2.90 | 2.75 | 50 | 0 |
| | $9 | 0.85 | 0.95 | 0.95 | 70 | 165 |
| Jan96 | $8 p | 0.90 | 1.05 | 0.95 | 40 | 40 |
| | $9 | 1.65 | 1.80 | 1.55 | 150 | 100 |
| **TD Bank** | | | **$20⅞** | | **222** | **6006** |
| Jun95 | $20 | 0.75 | 1.00 | 0.75 | 40 | 64 |
| Jul95 | $21 | 0.35 | 0.40 | 0.35 | 117 | 581 |
| Oct95 | $22 | 0.15 | 0.30 | 0.25 | 60 | 66 |
| Jan96 | $20 | 1.65 | 1.90 | 1.90 | 5 | 812 |
| **TCPL** | | | **$17⅞** | | **105** | **2609** |
| Aug95 | $19 | 0.10 | 0.25 | 0.20 | 100 | 677 |
| Nov95 | $18 | 0.80 | 1.00 | 0.90 | 5 | 41 |
| **WBB** | | | **$** | | **5** | **98** |
| Jan98 | $34 | 4.75 | 5¼ | 4.75 | 5 | 66 |
| **WTR** | | | **$** | | **2** | **2** |
| Jan98 | $16 p | 0.55 | 0.80 | 0.55 | 2 | 2 |
| **ZCB** | | | **$** | | **20** | **126** |
| Jan97 | $16 p | 1.30 | 1.70 | 1.35 | 10 | 0 |
| | $18 | 2.85 | 3.35 | 2.95 | 10 | 50 |
| **ZME** | | | **$** | | **15** | **117** |
| Jan97 | $12 | 2.75 | 3.25 | 3.30 | 15 | 32 |

**Total contract volume** 9765
**Total open interest** 375139

**CONCEPT CHECK** Question 6. What would be the profit or loss per share of stock to an investor who bought the September maturity CIBC call option with exercise price $35 on June 2, 1995, if the stock price at the expiration of the option was $37? What about a purchaser of the put option with the same exercise price and maturity?

## Futures Contracts

The *futures contract* calls for delivery of an asset or its cash value at a specified delivery or maturity date for an agreed-upon price, called the *futures price,* to be paid at contract maturity. The *long position* is held by the trader who commits to purchasing the commodity on the delivery date. The trader who takes the *short position* commits to delivering the commodity at contract maturity.

Figure 2.11 illustrates the listing of several futures contracts as they appear in *The Globe and Mail.* The listings include commodity futures traded on the Winnipeg Exchange, as well as bond futures, bond futures options, and stock index futures from the Montreal and Toronto Exchanges. The top line in boldface type gives the contract name and size. Thus, the first contract listed on the left is for the TSE 35 index, traded on the Toronto Stock Exchange. Each contract calls for delivery of 500 times the value of the TSE 35 stock price index.

The next two rows detail price data for contracts expiring on various dates. The September 1995 maturity contract's highest futures price during the day was 241.50, the lowest was 241, and the settlement price (a representative trading price during the last few minutes of trading) was 241.44. The settlement price rose by 2.62 from the previous trading day. The highest and lowest futures prices over the contract's life to date have been 240.20 and 228.04, respectively. Finally, open interest was 1822. Corresponding information is given for the other maturity date.

The trader holding the long position profits from price increases. Suppose that at expiration the TSE 35 index is at 245. The long position trader who entered the contract at the futures price of 241.50 on October 18 would pay the previously agreed-upon 241.50 for each unit of the index, which at contract maturity would be worth 245. Because each contract calls for delivery of $500 times the index, ignoring brokerage fees, the profit to the long position would equal $500 × (245 − 241.50) = $1,750. Conversely, the short position must deliver 500 times the value of the index for the previously agreed-upon futures price. The short position's loss equals the long position's profit.

In addition to futures contracts, there are also stock index options. Figure 2.10 shows several call and put option contracts, quoted on both the TSE 100 and the TSE 35 stock index. Index options differ from stock options because they are *cash settlement* options. If the value of the index rises above the exercise price, then the holder of a call option on the TSE 35 index receives, upon exercise, a cash amount equal to $500 times the difference between the stock index and exercise price. Conversely, the put option holder would exercise the option only when the index falls below the exercise price.

**Figure 2.11**
Canada futures and future options.

From the *Globe and Mail*, June 14, 1995. Reprinted by permission.

# Cdn. Futures & Options

## Toronto Futures Exchange

### Futures

| SeaHi | SeaLow | Mth. | Open | High | Low | Settle | Chg. | Opint |
|---|---|---|---|---|---|---|---|---|
| TSE 35 $500x, 0.02 pt = $10 | | | | | | | | |
| 238.10 | 222.20 | Jun95 | 237.00 | 238.70 | 236.50 | 238.70 | +2.64 | 2528 |
| 240.20 | 228.04 | Sep95 | 241.00 | 241.50 | 241.00 | 241.44 | +2.62 | 1822 |
| Est sales | | Prv Sales | Prv Open Int | | | | | Chg. |
| 2623 | | 841 | 4435 | | | | | +109 |
| TSE 100 $500x, 0.05 pt = $25 | | | | | | | | |
| 272.80 | 258.00 | Jun95 | | | | 273.10 | +2.50 | 130 |
| | | Sep95 | | | | 276.10 | +2.10 | 99 |
| Est sales | | Prv Sales | Prv Open Int | | | | | Chg. |
| 192 | | 0 | 229 | | | | | 'inch |

## Montreal Exchange

### Futures

| SeaHi | SeaLow | Mth. | Open | High | Low | Settle | Chg. | Opint |
|---|---|---|---|---|---|---|---|---|
| 3-month bankers' acceptances, $1M, pts. of 100% | | | | | | | | |
| 92.95 | 90.47 | Jun95 | 92.78 | 92.99 | 92.77 | 92.97 | +0.22 | 21395 |
| 93.53 | 90.42 | Sep95 | 93.20 | 93.53 | 93.18 | 93.51 | +0.36 | 29215 |
| 93.51 | 90.39 | Dec95 | 93.30 | 93.50 | 93.28 | 93.49 | +0.33 | 15447 |
| 93.46 | 89.95 | Mar96 | 93.24 | 93.42 | 93.22 | 93.38 | +0.27 | 16838 |
| 93.37 | 89.92 | Jun96 | 93.28 | 93.28 | 93.20 | 93.26 | +0.26 | 9678 |
| 93.30 | 90.17 | Sep96 | 93.09 | 93.15 | 93.09 | 93.15 | +0.23 | 5818 |
| 93.22 | 90.20 | Dec96 | 93.05 | 93.05 | 93.05 | 93.03 | +0.18 | 1617 |
| Est sales | | Prv Sales | Prv Open Int | | | | | Chg. |
| 17726 | | 6610 | 100654 | | | | | –544 |
| 1-month bankers' acceptances, $3M, pts. of 100% | | | | | | | | |
| 92.73 | 91.85 | Jun95 | | | | 92.83 | +0.15 | 55 |
| 92.84 | 92.52 | Jul95 | | | | 92.96 | +0.15 | 45 |
| 92.80 | 92.80 | Aug95 | | | | 93.06 | +0.15 | 10 |
| Est sales | | Prv Sales | Prv Open Int | | | | | Chg. |
| | | 50 | 110 | | | | | +25 |
| 10-year Cda bonds, $100K, pts of 100%, 1 pt = $10 | | | | | | | | |
| 109.05 | 99.70 | Jun95 | 106.85 | 107.12 | 106.85 | 107.59 | +0.87 | 2625 |
| 108.75 | 102.46 | Sep95 | 106.53 | 107.20 | 106.46 | 107.17 | +0.79 | 21376 |
| Est sales | | Prv Sales | Prv Open Int | | | | | Chg. |
| 3255 | | 3119 | 24001 | | | | | +627 |
| 5-year Cda bonds, $100K, pts of 100% | | | | | | | | |
| 106.31 | 104.89 | Sep95 | 105.70 | 105.77 | 105.57 | 105.77 | +0.69 | 1755 |
| Est sales | | Prv Sales | Prv Open Int | | | | | Chg. |
| 45 | | 36 | 1855 | | | | | +36 |

### Options

| Price | Calls | — | Last | Puts | — | Last |
|---|---|---|---|---|---|---|
| Canada bond futures, $100,000, pts. of 100% | | | | | | |
| | Jun | Jul | Aug | Jun | Jul | Aug |
| 103 | s | 4.17 | 4.17 | s | r | 0.01 |
| 104 | s | 3.17 | 3.34 | s | r | 0.22 |
| 105 | s | 2.17 | 2.57 | s | r | 0.43 |
| 106 | s | 1.15 | 1.90 | s | r | 0.75 |
| 107 | r | 0.33 | 1.34 | r | 0.16 | 1.17 |
| 108 | r | 0.58 | 0.89 | 0.85 | 1.41 | 1.71 |
| 109 | s | s | 0.55 | s | s | 2.35 |
| Prev. day calls vol | | 0 | Open int. | | | 61 |
| Prev. day puts vol | | 2 | Open int. | | | 124 |
| 3-mo. bankers' acceptances futures,$1M,pts of 100% | | | | | | |
| | Jun | Sep | Dec | Jun | Sep | Dec |
| 89.50 | 3.47 | 4.01 | 3.99 | r | r | 0.01 |
| 90.00 | 2.97 | 3.51 | 3.49 | r | r | 0.01 |
| 90.50 | 2.47 | 3.01 | 2.99 | r | r | 0.03 |
| 91.00 | 1.97 | 2.51 | 2.49 | r | 0.01 | 0.05 |
| 91.50 | 1.47 | 2.01 | 2.00 | r | 0.02 | 0.08 |
| 92.00 | 0.97 | 1.52 | 1.58 | r | 0.04 | 0.14 |
| 92.50 | 0.47 | 1.08 | 1.18 | r | 0.10 | 0.22 |
| 93.00 | 0.06 | 0.70 | 0.83 | 0.08 | 0.20 | 0.36 |
| 93.50 | r | 0.39 | 0.54 | 0.53 | 0.38 | 0.55 |
| Prev. day calls vol | | 40 | Open int. | | | 11524 |
| Prev. day puts vol | | 0 | Open int. | | | 7189 |

## Winnipeg Commodity Exchange

### Futures

| SeaHi | SeaLow | Mth. | Open | High | Low | Settle | Chg. | Opint |
|---|---|---|---|---|---|---|---|---|
| CANOLA 20 tonnes, can $/tonne | | | | | | | | |
| 483.0 | 31.0 | Jun95 | 402.0 | 404.5 | 402.0 | 404.0 | +7.2 | 153 |
| 459.5 | 362.0 | Aug95 | 415.5 | 421.0 | 415.5 | 419.6 | +4.9 | 8747 |
| 426.5 | 350.0 | Sep95 | 403.5 | 406.5 | 403.5 | 405.5 | +2.5 | 4119 |
| 425.5 | 119.5 | Nov95 | 397.0 | 400.2 | 397.0 | 400.0 | +2.5 | 20568 |
| 430.2 | 383.0 | Jan96 | 405.5 | 408.2 | 405.5 | 408.0 | +2.8 | 6347 |
| 423.9 | 390.0 | Mar96 | 413.0 | 414.0 | 412.3 | 414.0 | +3.0 | 2520 |
| Est sales | | Prv Sales | Prv Open Int | | | | | Chg. |
| | | 2639 | 42454 | | | | | +313 |
| FLAXSEED 20 tonnes, can $/tonne | | | | | | | | |
| 350.5 | 269.0 | Jul95 | 304.0 | 305.0 | 304.0 | 305.0 | +2.0 | 738 |
| 341.0 | 279.0 | Oct95 | 304.0 | 304.5 | 303.1 | 303.4 | +0.9 | 3158 |
| 340.0 | 282.5 | Dec95 | 306.0 | 306.5 | 305.1 | 305.5 | +1.0 | 2868 |
| Est sales | | Prv Sales | Prv Open Int | | | | | Chg. |
| | | 428 | 7211 | | | | | –92 |
| OATS 20 tonnes, can $/tonne | | | | | | | | |
| 139.0 | 106.5 | Jul95 | 132.0 | 132.3 | 131.3 | 131.5 | –1.2 | 732 |
| 139.5 | 109.8 | Oct95 | 129.0 | 129.6 | 128.8 | 129.0 | –0.8 | 1002 |
| 135.1 | 115.5 | Dec95 | 130.0 | 130.0 | 129.3 | 129.5 | –0.8 | 1311 |
| Est sales | | Prv Sales | Prv Open Int | | | | | Chg. |
| | | 66 | 3350 | | | | | –15 |
| RYE 20 tonnes, can $/tonne | | | | | | | | |
| 119.5 | 116.0 | Jul95 | | | | 116.0 | | 17 |
| 120.0 | 119.0 | Sep95 | | | | 120.0 | | 15 |
| Est sales | | Prv Sales | Prv Open Int | | | | | Chg. |
| | | 0 | 32 | | | | | |
| WESTERN BARLEY 20 tonnes,can $/tonne | | | | | | | | |
| 140.0 | 99.0 | Aug95 | 135.5 | 139.0 | 135.5 | 139.0 | +4.5 | 4327 |
| 126.5 | 111.6 | Nov95 | 124.0 | 127.0 | 124.0 | 126.3 | +2.4 | 3114 |
| 126.4 | 114.5 | Feb96 | 128.5 | 130.0 | 127.6 | 127.6 | +2.2 | 543 |
| 127.0 | 119.0 | May96 | 126.0 | 130.9 | 126.0 | 128.8 | +2.9 | 379 |
| Est sales | | Prv Sales | Prv Open Int | | | | | Chg. |
| | | 712 | 8363 | | | | | +3 |
| WHEAT 20 tonnes, can $/tonne | | | | | | | | |
| 173.8 | 101.0 | Jul95 | 173.5 | 174.8 | 173.5 | 174.8 | +1.1 | 3438 |
| 160.0 | 105.9 | Oct95 | 160.0 | 160.0 | 159.8 | 160.0 | +0.3 | 2721 |
| 159.0 | 134.5 | Dec95 | 158.5 | 158.5 | 158.1 | 158.5 | +0.4 | 2632 |
| 159.6 | 139.6 | Mar96 | 159.5 | 159.5 | 159.5 | 159.5 | | 927 |
| Est sales | | Prv Sales | Prv Open Int | | | | | Chg. |
| | | 385 | 9753 | | | | | +2 |

The right to purchase the asset at an agreed-upon price, as opposed to the obligation, distinguishes call options from long positions in futures contracts. A futures contract *obliges* the long position to purchase the asset at the futures price; the call option, in contrast, *conveys the right* to purchase the asset at the exercise price. The purchase will be made only if it yields a profit.

Clearly, a holder of a call has a better position than does the holder of a long position on a futures contract with a futures price equal to the option's exercise price. This advantage, of course, comes only at a price. Call options must be purchased; futures investments may be entered into without cost. The purchase price of an option is called the *premium*. It represents the compensation the holder of the call must pay for the ability to exercise the option only when it is profitable to do so. Similarly, the difference between a put option and a short futures position is the right, as opposed to the obligation, to sell an asset at an agreed-upon price.

### Other Derivative Assets: Warrants, Swaps, and Hybrid Securities

In addition to options and futures, there are other contingent claims traded in Canadian financial markets. We list briefly the most important of then, which will be discussed in more detail in Chapters 20–22.

*Warrants* are like call options, with the difference being that the holder receives the shares upon exercise from the firm that issued them, rather than from another investor. For this reason, unlike call options, the exercise of warrants increases the number of outstanding shares of a corporation and its capital, while diluting the equity of its stockholders. Warrants also trade on the regular stock exchanges and have much longer expiration dates than normal stock options.

A *swap* is an agreement between two parties to exchange a set of liabilities, like the obligation to pay a stream of future interest payments in a given currency and rate. For instance, in an interest rate swap, one party trades its fixed interest payments against the other party's payments at a rate that varies with a benchmark rate, like LIBOR. Swaps are brokered by intermediaries, and the terms of representative agreements are quoted in the over-the-counter market.

Last, some firms have issued instruments that are essentially a combination of a bond and a call option on a stock index. Most such instruments are traded in the over-the-counter market, but a couple of them trade on the TSE. The Protected Index Notes, or PINs, that we saw briefly in Chapter 1, are an example of the latter. We shall return to them in Chapter 20.

## Summary

**1.** Money market securities are very short-term debt obligations. They are usually highly marketable and have relatively low credit risk. Their low maturities and low credit risk ensure minimal capital gains or losses. These securities trade in large denominations but may be purchased indirectly through money market funds.

**2.** Much of the Canadian government borrowing is in the form of Canada bonds. These are coupon-paying bonds usually issued at or near par value. Canada bonds are similar in design to coupon-paying corporate bonds. Provincial governments and Crown Corporations also issue similar default-free coupon-paying bonds.

**3.** Mortgage pass-through securities are pools of mortgages sold in one package. Owners of pass-throughs receive all principal and interest payments made by the borrower. The bank that originally issued the mortgage merely services the mortgage, simply "passing through" the payments to the purchasers of the mortgage. The government guarantees the timely payment of interest and principal on mortgages pooled into these pass-through securities.

**4.** Common stock is an ownership share in a corporation. Each voting share entitles its owner to a vote on matters of corporate governance and to a prorated share of the dividends paid to shareholders. Restricted shares have a lower number of votes, or no right to vote. Stock, or equity, owners are the residual claimants on the income earned by the firm.

**5.** Preferred stock usually pays fixed dividends for the life of the firm; it is a perpetuity. A firm's failure to pay the dividend due on preferred stock, however, does not precipitate corporate bankruptcy. Instead, unpaid dividends simply cumulate. New varieties of preferred stock include convertible and adjustable-rate issues.

**6.** Many stock market indices measure the performance of the overall market in Canada and the United States. The Dow Jones Averages, the oldest and best-known indicators, are U.S. price-weighted indices. Today, many broad-based market value-weighted indices are computed daily. These include the main Canadian index, Toronto Stock Exchange's 300 stock index, as well as the U.S. Standard & Poor's 500 stock index, the NYSE and AMEX indices, the NASDAQ index, and the Wilshire 5000 index. The Montreal Exchange's Canadian Market Portfolio index and the Value Line index are equally weighted averages of individual firms' returns.

**7.** A call option is a right to purchase an asset at a stipulated exercise price on or before a maturity date. A put option is the right to sell an asset at some exercise price. Calls increase in value while puts decrease in value as the value of the underlying asset increases.

**8.** A futures contract is an obligation to buy or sell an asset at a stipulated futures price on a maturity date. The long position, which commits to purchasing, gains if the asset value increases, while the short position, which commits to delivering the asset, loses.

## Key Terms

Money market
Capital markets
Bond equivalent yield
Effective annual yield
Bank discount yield
London Interbank Offered Rate (LIBOR)
Yield to maturity
Restricted shares
Residual claim
Limited liability
Capital gains
Price-earnings ratio
Board lots
Price-weighted average
Market value-weighted index
Index funds
Derivative assets
Contingent claims

## Selected Readings

*The standard reference to the securities, terminology, and organization of the U.S. money market is:*

Stigum, Marcia. *The Money Market,* Homewood, Ill.: Dow Jones-Irwin, 1983.

*A good survey of a wide variety of U.S. financial markets and instruments is:*

Logue, Dennis E. (editor). *The WG&L Handbook of Financial Markets.* Cincinnati, Ohio: Warren, Gorham, & Lamont, 1995.

*The Canadian money market is described in:*

Sarpkaya, S. *The Money Market in Canada,* 4th ed. Toronto, Ont.: CCH Canadian, 1989.

*A reference to Canadian and international fixed-income instruments is the annual publication:*

*Guide to International Investing.* Toronto, Ont.: CCH Canadian.

*An extended coverage of restricted voting shares is in:*

Smith, Brian; and Ben Amoako-Adu. *Financing Canadian Corporations with Restricted Shares* (Monograph). London, Ont.: National Centre for Management Research and Development, University of Western Ontario, 1990.

*Institutional details of Canadian options markets are provided by:*

The prospectus of Trans Canada Options Inc., 1980.

*Institutional features of futures markets are provided by:*

Hore, John E. *Trading on Canadian Futures Markets,* 4th ed. Toronto, Ont.: The Canadian Securities Institute, 1989.

## Problems

The following multiple-choice problems are based on questions that have appeared in past CFA examinations.

**1.** *a.* Preferred stock:

i. Is actually a form of equity.
ii. Pays dividends not taxable to Canadian corporations.
iii. Is normally considered a fixed-income security.
iv. All of the above.

*b.* Straight preferred stock yields are usually lower than yields on straight bonds of the same quality because of:

i. Marketability
ii. Risk
iii. Taxation
iv. Call protection

**2.** The investment manager of a corporate pension fund has purchased a Treasury bill with 180 days to maturity at a price of $9,600 per $10,000 face value. The manager has computed the bank discount yield at 8 percent.

*a.* Calculate the bond equivalent yield for the Treasury bill. Show your calculations.

*b.* Briefly state two reasons why a Treasury bill's bond equivalent yield is always different from the discount yield.

**3.** A bill has a bank discount yield of 6.81 percent based on the ask price, and 6.90 percent based on the bid price. The maturity of the bill (already accounting for skip-day settlement) is 60 days. Find the bid and ask prices of the bill.

**4.** Reconsider the T-bill of problem 3. Calculate its bond equivalent yield and effective annual yield based on the ask price. Confirm that these yields exceed the discount yield.

**5.** The following questions deal with yields.

*a.* Which security offers a higher effective annual yield?

i. A three-month bill selling at $9,764.

ii. A six-month bill selling at $9,539.

*b.* Calculate the bond equivalent yield on each bill.

**6.** A U.S. Treasury bill with 90-day maturity sells at a bank discount yield of 3 percent.

*a.* What is the price of the bill?

*b.* What is the 90-day holding period return of the bill?

*c.* What is the bond equivalent yield of the bill?

*d.* What is the effective annual yield of the bill?

**7.** Find the after-tax return to a corporation that buys a share of preferred stock at $40, sells it at year-end at $40, and receives a $4 year-end dividend. The firm is in the 45 percent tax bracket.

**8.** Consider the three stocks in the following table. $P_t$ represents price at time $t$, and $Q_t$ represents shares outstanding at time $t$. Stock $C$ splits two for one in the last period.

| | $P_0$ | $Q_0$ | $P_1$ | $Q_1$ | $P_2$ | $Q_2$ |
|---|---|---|---|---|---|---|
| *A* | 90 | 100 | 95 | 100 | 95 | 100 |
| *B* | 50 | 200 | 45 | 200 | 45 | 200 |
| *C* | 100 | 200 | 110 | 200 | 55 | 400 |

*a.* Calculate the rate of return on a price-weighted index of the three stocks for the first period ($t = 0$ to $t = 1$).

*b.* What must happen to the divisor for the price-weighted index in year 2?

*c.* Calculate the price-weighted index for the second period ($t = 1$ to $t = 2$).

**9.** Using the data in problem 8, calculate the first period rates of return on the following indices of the three stocks:

*a.* A market value-weighted index.

*b.* An equally weighted index.

**10.** Which of the following securities should sell at a greater price?

*a.* A 10-year Canada bond with a 9 percent coupon rate versus a 10-year Canada bond with a 10 percent coupon rate.

*b.* A three-month maturity call option with an exercise price of $40 versus a three-month call on the same stock with an exercise price of $35.

*c.* A put option on a stock selling at $50, or a put option on another stock selling at $60 (all other relevant features of the stocks and options may be assumed to be identical).

*d.* A three-month T-bill with a discount yield of 6.1 percent versus a three-month bill with a discount yield of 6.2 percent.

**11.** Why do call options with exercise prices greater than the price of the underlying stock sell for positive prices?

**12.** Both a call and a put currently are traded on stock XYZ; both have strike prices of $50 and maturities of six months. What will be the profit to an investor who buys the call for $4 in the following stock price scenarios in six months?

*a.* $40

*b.* $45

*c.* $50

*d.* $55

*e.* $60

*f.* What will be the profit in each scenario to an investor who buys the put for $6?

**13.** Explain the difference between a put option and a short position in a futures contract.

**14.** Examine the first 25 stocks listed in the stock market listings for TSE stocks in your local newspaper. For how many of these stocks is the 52-week high price at least 50 percent greater than the 52-week low price? What do you conclude about the volatility of prices on individual stocks?

*Chapter 3*

# How Securities Are Traded

**THE BUYING AND SELLING OF SECURITIES IS, TO THE ORDINARY INVESTOR, A FAIRLY SIMPLE PROCEDURE.** A telephone call to the broker is all that is needed to place an order and cause a given number of shares or bonds to be traded. Behind the execution of that order, however, lies a complicated and efficient system; and even the statement of the order must follow one of a variety of forms, so that it will follow the investor's actual wishes. The creation or issuance of securities, and the subsequent exchange of them between investors, requires the participation of a large number of financial professionals, who are subject to precise regulations in their actions.

We examine in this chapter the institutional details and mechanics of making investments in securities. We see how firms issue securities in the primary market and then how investors trade in these securities in the secondary market. The secondary market is further specified, depending on the type and structure of the exchange where trading takes place. How the trading is handled varies with the type of exchange, but the details seen by the investor are similar. We explain the notion of trading using margin, in which security is provided for borrowed money or short sales. The cost of trading in securities is an important factor affecting returns, and it is related to the services provided to the investor. Finally, we present the subject of how securities markets are regulated by various bodies to protect the interests of investors by guaranteeing a degree of openness and fairness in trading.

## 3.1 How Firms Issue Securities

When firms need to raise capital they may choose to sell (or *float*) new securities. These new issues of stock, bonds, or other securities typically are marketed to the public by investment bankers in what is called the **primary market.** Purchase and sale of already issued securities among private investors take place in the **secondary market.**

There are two types of primary market issues of common stock. *Initial public offerings,* or *IPOs,* are stocks issued by a formerly privately owned company selling stock to the public for the first time. *Seasoned new issues* are offered by companies that already have floated equity. A sale by Canadian Pacific of new shares of stock, for example, would constitute a seasoned new issue. A *secondary offering* is a stock sale that has all the characteristics of a primary market issue but is in fact a secondary market transaction. Although the number is falling, many foreign multinational firms have Canadian subsidiaries, with a fraction of the total equity traded on Canadian exchanges and the remaining holding retained by the parent. When a parent company or any company that holds a significant interest in another firm chooses to sell all or a part of that holding, a secondary offering results. The shares then are sold to the general public as in a new equity issue; however, the parent firm receives the cash proceeds and no new shares are issued.

In the case of bonds we also distinguish between two types of primary market issues. A *public offering* is an issue of bonds sold to the general investing public that can then be traded on the secondary market. A *private placement* is an issue that is sold to a few institutional investors at most and generally held to maturity.

### Investment Bankers

Public offerings of both stocks and bonds typically are marketed via an **underwriting** by investment bankers, often known in Canada as *investment dealers.* In fact, more than one investment dealer usually markets the securities. A lead firm forms an *underwriting syndicate* of other investment dealers to share the responsibility for the stock issue.

The bankers advise the firm regarding the terms on which it should attempt to sell the securities. A preliminary registration statement describing the issue and the prospects of the company must be filed with the provincial securities commission in the provinces in which the securities will be offered for sale. This *preliminary prospectus* is known as a *red herring* because of a statement, printed in red, that the company is not attempting to sell the security before the registration is approved. When the statement is finalized and approved by the commission, it is called the **prospectus.** At this time, the price at which the securities will be offered to the public is announced.

There are two methods of underwriting a securities issue. In a *firm commitment* underwriting arrangement, the investment bankers purchase the securities from the issuing company and then resell them to the public. The issuing firm sells the securities to the underwriting syndicate for the public offering price less a spread that serves as compensation to the underwriters. In such an arrangement, the underwriters assume the full risk that the shares cannot in fact be sold to the public at the stipulated offering price. In the event that significant changes take place in market conditions, the underwriters can escape from the firm commitment, if a *market-out* clause exists. By contrast, in a *bought deal* the underwriter takes full responsibility for the issue under any circumstances.

An alternative to this arrangement is the *best-efforts* agreement. In this case, the investment banker agrees to help the firm sell the issue to the public but does not actually purchase the securities. The banker simply acts as an intermediary between the public and the firm and thus does not bear the risk of being unable to resell purchased securities at the offering price. The best-efforts procedure is more common for initial public offerings of common stock, for which the appropriate share price is less certain.

Corporations engage investment bankers either by negotiation or by competitive bidding. Negotiation is more common. Besides being compensated by the spread between the purchase and public offering prices, an investment banker may receive shares of common stock or other securities of the firm. In the case of competitive bidding, a firm may announce its intent to issue securities and then invite investment bankers to submit bids for the underwriting. Such a bidding process may reduce the cost of the issue; however, it might also bring fewer services from the investment banker. Many public utilities are required to solicit competitive bids from underwriters.

## Prompt Offering Prospectus

The Ontario Securities Commission (OSC) permits the preparation of a prospectus for a new issue, with only minor additions to available financial information. This information, filed annually with the OSC, contains virtually all required information for a prospectus. The approval of the supplementary material requires only a few days instead of weeks, thus allowing the prompt placement of the issue with the underwriters; this is known as the *prompt offering prospectus* (POP). This system reduces the underwriters' risk and makes bought deals more attractive. The sale to the public, however, still requires a full prospectus.

## Underpricing

Underwriters face a peculiar conflict of interest. On the one hand, acting in the best interest of the issuing firm, they should attempt to market securities to the public at the highest possible price, thereby maximizing the revenue realized from the offering. On the other hand, if they set the offering price higher than the public will pay, they will be unable to market the securities to customers. Underwriters left with unmarketable securities will be forced to sell them at a loss on the secondary market. Underwriters therefore must balance their own interests against those of their clients. The lower the public offering price, the less capital the firm raises, but the greater the chance that the securities can be sold at that price. Also, the lower the price, the less effort is needed to find investors to purchase the securities. If the offering is made at a low enough price, investors will beat down the doors of the underwriters to purchase the securities.

Observation of early trading in IPOs suggests that they are in many cases substantially underpriced—often by more than fifty percent—compared to what investors are willing to pay. Studies of IPO pricing in many countries consistently show that investors who purchase shares of an issue at the initial offering price and then resell the stock shortly after public trading begins (usually the first day to a few weeks later) earn substantial abnormal returns.[1] For example, one study reports average abnormal returns in the United States of 16 percent; in Canada of 9 percent; in the United Kingdom of 11 percent; in Japan of 32 percent; and in Germany of 21 percent.[2] Recognition of this underpricing causes IPOs to be commonly oversubscribed. Demand from the public at the offering price greatly exceeds the offering quantity; unfortunately, it is extremely difficult for small investors to obtain any shares as the best issues go primarily to institutions. Competitive bidding for an issue by underwriters is supposed to alleviate the underpricing problem, but negotiation between the issuer and the underwriter is far more common in Canada.

## 3.2 Where Securities Are Traded

Once securities have been issued to the public, investors may trade among themselves. This occurs in markets that have evolved to meet the needs of investors; consider what would happen if the organized markets did not exist. Investors seeking to sell would have to find potential buyers. To avoid a buyers' market, there would need to be a meeting place, which also would serve buyers who did not want to be at the mercy of sellers. Hence buyers and sellers would meet and bargain for satisfactory prices, or agents would undertake to match potential buyers and sellers; ideally, competition among agents would drive down their fees. Eventually, the meeting place would evolve into a financial market, as was the case for a pub called Lloyd's in London and a Manhattan curb on Wall Street. Without this evolution of the secondary market, the costs of selling shares would be extremely detrimental to the purchase of shares in the primary market; so an efficient secondary market, which determines a fair and accurate price and allows the relatively quick and cheap transfer of shares, is crucial to the raising of investment capital by businesses.

---

[1] Abnormal return measures the return on the investment net of the portion that can be attributed to general market movements. See the discussion of this concept in Chapter 12.

[2] Jay R. Ritter and Kathleen A. Weiss, "Going Public," *The New Palgrave Dictionary of Money and Finance,* 1992.

The markets that have evolved can be characterized as four types: direct search markets, brokered markets, dealer markets, and auction markets. The **direct search** market is what we have described above, where buyers and sellers must seek each other out directly. Such markets are characterized by sporadic participation and low-priced and nonstandard goods.

The next level of organization is a **brokered market.** If there is sufficient activity in trading a good, brokers can find it profitable to offer search services to buyers and sellers. Examples include the real estate market, as well as primary and secondary markets for security trading. Markets for large **block transactions** of shares have developed, since attempts to move them on the regular exchanges would cause major price movements; blocks are recorded as being "crossed" on the exchange by traders, who have located other large traders, even though the trade does not actually pass through the usual exchange process.

When trading activity in a particular type of asset increases, **dealer markets** arise. Here, dealers specialize in various commodities, purchase assets for their own inventory, and sell goods for a profit from their inventory. Dealers, unlike brokers, trade assets for their own accounts. The dealer's profit margin is the "bid-asked" spread, the difference between the price at which the dealer buys for and sells from inventory. Dealer markets save traders on search costs because market participants are easily able to look up the prices at which they can buy from or sell to dealers. Obviously, a fair amount of market activity is required before dealing in a market is an attractive source of income. The over-the-counter securities market is one example of a dealer market.

The most integrated market is an **auction market,** in which all transactors in a good converge at one place to bid on or offer a good. The New York Stock Exchange (NYSE) is an example of an auction market, as are all the major Canadian markets. An advantage of auction markets over dealer markets is that one need not search to find the best price for a good. If all participants converge, they can arrive at mutually agreeable prices and thus save the bid-asked spread. Continuous auction markets (as opposed to periodic auctions such as in the art world) require very heavy and frequent trading to cover the expense of maintaining the market. For this reason, larger exchanges set up listing requirements, which limit the shares traded on the exchange to those of firms in which sufficient trading interest is likely to exist.

---

**CONCEPT CHECK**

Question 1. Many assets trade in more than one type of market. What types of markets do the following trade in?

*a.* Used cars.
*b.* Paintings.
*c.* Rare coins.

---

## The Secondary Markets

There are five **stock exchanges** in Canada. Three of these, the Toronto Stock Exchange (TSE), the Montreal Exchange (ME), and the Vancouver Stock Exchange (VSE), are national in scope. The other two are regional exchanges, which list firms located in a particular geographic area (Manitoba and Alberta). There also are several exchanges for the trading of options and futures contracts, which we will discuss in the options and futures chapters.

The ME is the oldest organized securities market in Canada. It was officially granted a charter in 1874, when it was known under the name of "Montreal Stock Exchange." The TSE was formally incorporated in 1878. It became the largest Canadian financial market in the 1930s and remains so today (see the discussion below). Nonetheless, the ME has shown signs of increased activity in the last decade and has pioneered the introduction of many derivative products and other financial innovations (albeit not always successfully).

The VSE was incorporated in 1907. From the very beginning it specialized in small, resource-oriented firms, primarily in Western Canada. In recent years it has tried to diversify its activities and become more North American in scope. As for the Alberta and Winnipeg stock exchanges, they have remained regionally oriented in their activities, even though they were formed at about the same time as the VSE.

An exchange provides a facility for its members to trade securities, and only members of the exchange may trade there. Therefore memberships, or *seats,* on the exchange are valuable assets. The exchange member charges investors for executing trades on their behalf. This is the means by which brokerage firms operate. They own seats on exchanges and advertise their willingness to execute trades for customers for a fee. The commissions that can be earned through this activity determine the market value of a seat. Hence, the price of a seat is taken as an indicator of the buoyancy of the market. For instance, a seat on the New York Stock Exchange (NYSE), which sold for more than U.S. $1 million prior to the October 1987 crash, was worth only U.S. $625,000 by January 1988. The highest price of a seat on the TSE was $175,000 in 1991, but by 1996 it had fallen to $52,000.

The TSE is by far the largest Canadian exchange. The shares of approximately 1,150 firms trade there, and over 1,500 stock issues (common and preferred stock) are listed. Daily trading volume on the TSE regularly exceeds 25 million shares. Table 3.1 shows the value and the volume of market trading for securities listed on the five Canadian and six U.S. stock exchanges as of 1994.

From Table 3.1 you can see that the TSE accounts for about 82 percent of the value of shares traded on Canadian exchanges. The ME trades many of the same stocks as the TSE, but in much smaller volumes. The VSE is also national in scope; originally focused on resource stocks, it has recently expanded as a market for younger high-tech or other start-up companies. Regional exchanges provide a market for trading shares of local firms that do not meet the listing requirements

**Table 3.1** North American Stock Exchanges, 1994

| Exchange | Value of Securities Traded ($ million annually) | Percent of Total Canadian |
|---|---|---|
| New York | 3,454,345 | |
| Toronto | 182,202 | 81.8% |
| Chicago | 134,107 | |
| American | 82,354 | |
| Pacific | 79,093 | |
| Boston | 51,898 | |
| Philadelphia | 50,135 | |
| Montreal | 32,443 | 14.6 |
| Vancouver | 5,795 | 2.6 |
| Alberta | 2,227 | 1.0 |
| Winnipeg | 0.6 | 0 |
| | | 100.0% |

Data from *TSE Review,* May 1995. Reprinted by permission.

of the national exchanges. While the NYSE dominates North American trading, the TSE is the second highest in volume and third in value of trading. On a world-wide basis, the NYSE and Tokyo stock exchanges account for the vast majority of the value of trading, at 39 percent and 29 percent, respectively, in developed markets. The TSE is 10th in value of trading at barely two percent of the world total, while it is seventh in capitalization.[3]

The national exchanges are willing to list a stock (i.e., allow trading in that stock on the exchange) only if it meets certain criteria of size and stability. Table 3.2 gives the initial listing requirements of the TSE for industrial companies. Unlike the NYSE, the TSE has different requirements for the various kinds of companies. The next most important (after industrial) types of companies listed on the TSE include mining and energy companies; these are required to have both capital and either reserves of or potential for mineral production. These requirements ensure that a firm is of significant trading interest before the TSE will allocate facilities for it to be traded on the floor of the exchange. If a listed company suffers a decline and fails to meet the criteria in Table 3.2 (or those applicable), it may be delisted from the exchange.

Although most common and preferred stocks are traded on the exchanges, bonds are not. Corporate and all federal, provincial, and municipal government bonds are traded only over the counter.

[3] Many Canadian corporations also are listed on U.S. exchanges, a practice known as "interlisting." For a discussion of the benefits of interlisting, see Usha Mittoo, "How Canadian Companies Win by Interlisting Shares on U.S. Exchanges," *Canadian Investment Review,* Winter 1993/1994. See also Lorne Switzer, "The Benefits and Costs of Listing Canadian Stocks in U.S. Markets," *Corporate Structure, Finance and Operations* 4 (1986), pp. 141–56.

**Table 3.2** Minimum Listing Requirements for the TSE

| | |
|---|---|
| **FINANCIAL REQUIREMENTS** | |
| Pretax cash flow in last year | $ 200,000 |
| Average annual pretax cash flow in previous 2 years | $ 150,000 |
| Net tangible assets | $1,000,000 |
| Adequate working capital | |
| **PUBLIC DISTRIBUTION** | |
| Market value of publicly held stock | $ 350,000 |
| Shares publicly held | 200,000 |
| Number of holders of board lot or more | 200 |

Data from the Toronto Stock Exchange, 1986. Reprinted by permission.

## The Over-the-Counter Market

There are several hundred issues traded on the Canadian **over-the-counter market** (OTC) on a regular basis, and, in fact, any security may be traded there. The OTC market, however, is not a formal exchange; there are neither membership requirements for trading nor listing requirements for securities. In the OTC market, brokers registered with the provincial Securities Commission act as dealers in OTC securities. Security dealers quote prices at which they are willing to buy or sell securities. A broker can execute a trade by contacting a dealer listing an attractive quote.

The Canadian OTC market has developed similarly to that of the United States. Prior to automation, quotations of stock were recorded manually and published daily. The so-called pink sheets were the means by which dealers communicated their interest in trading at various prices. This was a cumbersome and inefficient technique, and published quotes were a full day out of date. In 1971, the U.S. National Association of Securities Dealers Automated Quotation system, or **NASDAQ,** began to offer immediate information on a computer-linked system of bid and asked prices for stocks offered by various dealers. The **bid price** is that at which a dealer is willing to purchase a security; the **asked price** is that at which the dealer will sell a security. The system allows a dealer who receives a buy or a sell order from an investor to examine all current quotes, call the dealer with the best quote, and execute a trade. The system has grown in importance by providing real competition to the NYSE and has now come to be known as the Nasdaq Stock Market. By 1995, the volume of trading was roughly equal to that on the NYSE, although the dollar volume was lower due to the lower-priced securities found on the Nasdaq. The Canadian OTC market, by contrast, is far less significant; often, stocks trading on the OTC market are the subject of manipulation by some small brokerage houses and promoters.

The Canadian Over-the-Counter Automated Trading System **(COATS)** was patterned after Nasdaq and introduced in 1986. In 1991, responsibility for the operation and regulation of COATS was transferred to the Canadian Dealing Network Inc. (CDN), a subsidiary of the TSE. To be quoted by the CDN system, a firm must satisfy a number of criteria, involving primarily the disclosure of financial information. Other conditions refer to the financial position of the issuer, the size of the public float, the number of public investors, and so on. Although no precise requirements are stated for each one of these criteria, they all are taken into account when the board of directors of CDN examines a firm's application to be included in the system. By contrast, Nasdaq sets minimum size requirements for several financial variables of a firm before it will allow it to become part of its network.

There are two levels of interaction with CDN. A *user* has access to the network in order to receive current market information (bids and offers) and statistics for the previous trading day. Such users are brokers who accept bid or asked prices in executing a trade on behalf of their clients; they also may act as principals for their own accounts. Information on any trade is automatically recorded by the system.

The higher level is for a user who has been approved as a *market-maker* in a CDN security. This grants access to the CDN system for listing bid and asked quotations. These market-makers must maintain inventories of a security and continually stand ready to buy these shares from or sell them to the public at the quoted bid and asked prices. They earn profits from the spread between the bid price and the asked price. These higher-level subscribers may enter the bid and asked prices at which they are willing to buy or sell stocks into the computer network and update these quotes as desired.

For bonds, the over-the-counter market is a loosely organized network of dealers linked together by a computer quotation system for a number of bellwether bonds. In practice, the corporate bond market often is quite "thin," in that there are few investors interested in trading a particular bond at any particular time. The bond market is subject to a type of liquidity risk, because it can be difficult to sell holdings quickly if the need arises.

## The Third and Fourth Markets

The **third market** refers to trading of exchange-listed securities on the OTC market. The development of this phenomenon followed its evolution in the United States. Until recently, members of an exchange were required to execute all their trades of exchange-listed securities on the exchange itself and to charge commissions according to a fixed schedule. This schedule was disadvantageous to large traders, who were prevented from realizing economies of scale on large trades. The restriction led brokerage firms that were not members of the NYSE, and so not bound by its rules, to establish trading in the OTC market on large NYSE-listed firms. These trades took place at lower commissions than would have been charged on the NYSE, and the third market grew dramatically until 1975, when commissions on all orders became negotiable in the United States. Negotiated commissions became a common practice in Canada after April 1983, together with the growing popularity of discount brokerage houses.

The **fourth market** refers to direct trading between investors in exchange-listed securities without benefit of a broker. Large institutions who wish to avoid brokerage fees altogether may engage in direct trading.

## Foreign Markets

An important development in trading is the cross-listing of major corporations on exchanges around the world. In particular, listing on the London and Tokyo Stock Exchanges (the latter also is referred to as the TSE) permits traders to trade virtually at any hour of the day, if so inclined. This has implications for valuation, as news can be received and traded upon immediately, leading to more pricing efficiency. The London exchange uses the computerized Stock Exchange Automated Quotations (SEAQ) system, which was based on Nasdaq and COATS. Although market orders are traded at the quoted prices, negotiated prices between the bid and asked prices can be set; securities firms can act as both brokers and dealers. The London regulations do not require the immediate identification of traders and offer the benefit of anonymity to traders wishing to move large quantities over time.

The TSE is divided into two sections, the first being for about 1,200 actively traded stocks, with the remaining 400 in the second section. The larger first section stocks are traded on the exchange floor, while the remaining stocks trade electronically. Floor trading is conducted similarly to the NYSE system of using specialists, but the "specialists" do not trade for their own accounts; they still are required to take actions to maintain an orderly market but basically confine their actions to matching limit and market orders.

## Derivatives Markets

Markets also exist in Canada for trading in options and futures. Unlike stocks, for which the primary markets exist to raise capital for the issuing firms, derivatives are created as contracts between investors; therefore, there is only a secondary market for them. Options are traded through the Canadian Derivatives Clearing Corporation, combining the Toronto, Montreal, and Vancouver exchanges. Commodity futures for agricultural products are traded on the Winnipeg Commodity Exchange; financial futures, in T-bills for example, trade on the Montreal Exchange. In addition, there are a number of options and futures that trade on U.S. or foreign exchanges. Because of the complexity of these derivatives, our discussion of these markets is given in Chapters 20 and 22. The mechanics of trading in derivatives are similar to stock trading, but there are far more complicated strategies. We describe these strategies in a later chapter.

## 3.3 Trading on Exchanges

Most of the material in this section applies to all securities traded on exchanges. Some of it, however, applies just to stocks, and in such cases we use the terms *stocks* or *shares.*

### The Participants

When an investor instructs a broker to buy or sell securities, a number of players must act to consummate the trade. We start our discussion of the mechanics of exchange trading with a brief description of the potential parties to a trade.

The investor places an order with a broker. The latter contacts a brokerage firm owning a seat on the exchange (a *commission broker*) to execute the order. *Floor traders* (also known as floor attorneys) are representatives of members of the exchange charged with executing the trades on behalf of their firms' clients.

**Registered traders** are floor traders entrusted with **market-making** in specific stocks. A registered trader, who is known as a *specialist* in the NYSE, is central to the trading process. Registered traders maintain a market in one or more listed securities. We will examine their role in detail shortly.

### Types of Orders

Investors may issue several types of orders to their brokers. *Market orders* are simple buy or sell orders that are to be executed immediately at current market prices. In contrast, investors can issue *limit orders,* whereby they specify prices at which they are willing to buy or sell a security. If the stock falls below the limit on a limit-buy order, then the trade is to be executed. If stock XYZ is selling at $45, for example, a limit-buy order may instruct the broker to buy the stock if and when the share price falls below $43. Correspondingly, a limit-sell order instructs the broker to sell as soon as the stock price goes above the specified limit. Orders also can be limited by a time period. Day orders, for example, expire at the close of the trading day. If it is not executed on that day, the order is canceled. *Open* or *good-till-canceled orders,* in contrast, remain in force for up to six months unless canceled by the customer.

*Stop-loss orders* are similar to limit orders in that the trade is not to be executed unless the stock hits a price limit. In this case however, the stock is to be sold if its price falls *below* a stipulated level. As the name suggests, the order lets the stock be sold to stop further losses from accumulating. Symmetrically, *stop-buy orders* specify that the stock should be bought when its price rises above a given limit. These trades often accompany short sales, and they are used to limit potential losses from the short position. Short sales are discussed in greater detail in Section 3.4.[4]

## The Execution of Trades

The registered trader, who is the central figure in the execution of trades, makes a market in the shares of one or more firms. Part of this task is simply mechanical. It involves maintaining a "book" listing all outstanding unexecuted limit orders entered by brokers on behalf of clients. Actually, the book is now a computer console. When limit orders can be executed at market prices, the registered trader sees to the trade; in this role, he or she merely acts as a facilitator. As buy and sell orders at mutually agreeable prices cross the trading desk, the market-maker matches the two parties to the trade.

The registered trader is required to use the highest outstanding offered purchase price and lowest outstanding offered selling price when matching trades. Therefore, this system results in an auction market—all buy orders and all sell orders come to one location, and the best bids "win" the trades.

The most interesting function of the market-maker is to maintain a "fair and orderly market" by dealing personally in the stock. In return for the exclusive right to make the market in a specific stock on the exchange, the registered trader is required to maintain an orderly market by buying and selling shares from inventory. Registered traders maintain bid and asked prices, within a maximum spread specified by TSE regulations, at which they are obligated to meet at least a limited amount of market orders. If market buy orders come in, the registered traders must sell shares from their own accounts at the maintained asked price; if sell orders come in, they must be willing to buy at the listed bid price.

Ordinarily, in an active market registered traders can cross buy and sell orders without direct participation on their own accounts. That is, the trader's own inventory need not be the primary means of order execution. However, sometimes the market-maker's bid and asked prices will be better than those offered by any other market participant. Therefore, at any point, the effective asked price in the market is the lower of either the registered trader's offered asked price or the lowest of the unfilled limit-sell orders. Similarly, the effective bid price is the highest of unfilled limit-buy orders or the trader's bid. These procedures ensure that the registered trader provides liquidity to the market.

By standing ready to trade at quoted bid and asked prices, the market-maker is exposed somewhat to exploitation by other traders. Large traders with ready access to late-breaking news will trade with market-makers only if the latters' quoted prices are temporarily out of line with assessments based on the traders' (possibly superior) information. Registered traders who cannot match the

---

[4] An excellent and comprehensive guide to more complex orders is given in *How to Invest in Canadian Securities*, issued by the Canadian Securities Institute.

information resources of large traders will be at a disadvantage when their quoted prices offer profit opportunities to more-informed traders.

You might wonder why market-makers do not protect their interests by setting a low bid price and a high asked price. A registered trader using that strategy would not suffer losses by maintaining a too-low asked price or a too-high bid price in a period of dramatic movements in the stock price. Traders who offer a narrow spread between the bid and the asked prices have little leeway for error and must constantly monitor market conditions to avoid offering other investors advantageous terms.

There are two reasons why large bid-asked spreads are not viable options for the market-maker. First, one source of his or her income is derived from frequent trading at the bid and asked prices, with the spread as a trading profit. A too-large spread would tend to discourage investors from trading, and the market-maker's business would dry up. Another reason registered traders cannot use large bid-asked spreads to protect their interests is that they are obligated to provide price continuity to the market.

To illustrate the principle of price continuity, suppose that the highest limit-buy order for a stock is $30, while the lowest limit-sell order is $32. When a market buy order comes in, it is matched to the best limit-sell at $32. A market sell order would be matched to the best limit-buy at $30. As market buys and sells come to the floor randomly, the stock price would fluctuate between $30 and $32. The exchange authorities would consider this excessive volatility, and the market-maker would be expected to step in with bid and/or asked prices in between these values to reduce the bid-asked spread to an acceptable level, such as ¼ or ½ point.

Registered traders earn income both from commissions for acting as brokers for orders and from the spread between the bid and asked prices at which they buy and sell securities. It also appears that their "book" of limit orders gives them unique knowledge about the probable direction of price movement over short periods of time. For example, suppose the market-maker sees that a stock now selling for $45 has limit-buy orders for over 100,000 shares at prices ranging from $44.50 to $44.75. This latent buying demand provides a cushion of support, because it is unlikely that enough sell pressure could come in during the next few hours to cause the price to drop below $44.50. If there are very few limit-sell orders above $45, some transient buying demand could raise the price substantially. The trader in such circumstances realizes that a position in the stock offers little downside risk and substantial upside potential. Such unique access to the trading intentions of other market participants seems to allow a market-maker to earn substantial profits on personal transactions.

Specific regulations of the TSE govern the registered traders' ability to profit from their superior information and their responsibility to maintain an orderly market. Such a market should respond to changes in information affecting the value of the stock by adjusting the price without excessive fluctuations. The trader achieves this result by making *stabilizing* trades. As defined by the TSE, a stabilizing trade is one in which a purchase (sale) is made at a price lower (higher)

**Table 3.3** Block Transactions on the Toronto Stock Exchange, 1995

| | Transactions | Value ($ billions) | Shares (millions) | Percent of TSE Volume |
|---|---|---|---|---|
| First quarter | 21,467 | $ 18.91 | 1,309 | 35.38% |
| Second quarter | 31,512 | 33.02 | 2,015 | 54.47 |
| Third quarter | 30,110 | 30.11 | 1,859 | 49.55 |
| Fourth quarter | 33,491 | 32.57 | 2,015 | 48.92 |
| **Year** | **116,580** | **$114.64** | **7,198** | **45.68%** |

Data from *TSE Review,* 1995. Reprinted by permission.

than the last price on an *uptick* (*downtick*); an uptick is an upward move in the share price. Registered traders are required to make a minimum 70–30 superiority of stabilizing over destabilizing trades, where the latter is defined as the reverse of a stabilizing trade.[5]

The effectiveness of the market-making system was challenged by the market crash of October 19, 1987, when NYSE stock prices fell about 25 percent on one day. In the face of overwhelming sell pressure, market-makers were called upon to purchase huge amounts of stock. In buying $486 million of stock on this single day, specialists suffered large losses, thereby eliminating much of their net worth. This precluded further share purchases by specialist firms and brought the stock market close to a halt. Since the crash, the NYSE has sharply increased the capital requirements for its specialist firms.

Moreover, in the wake of the market collapse, many specialists apparently decided not to sacrifice their own capital in a seemingly hopeless effort to shore up prices. Although specialists as a whole were net purchasers of stock, fully 30 percent of the specialists in a sample of large stocks were net sellers on October 19. These firms came under criticism for failing to live up to their mandate to attempt to support an orderly market.

## Block Sales

Institutional investors frequently trade blocks of several thousand shares of stock. Table 3.3 shows that *block transactions* of over 100,000 shares now account for almost half of all trading on the TSE; on the NYSE, block trading also represents about one half. Such transactions are often too large to be handled comfortably by registered traders, who do not wish to hold such large blocks of stock in their inventory.

In response to this problem, "block houses" have evolved in the United States to aid in the placement of block trades. Block houses are brokerage firms that help

[5] *Toronto Stock Exchange Member's Manual,* Division G, Part XIX, p. G19-3.

**Figure 3.1**
The daily block trading report.

From *The Globe and Mail,* September 1, 1996. Reprinted by permission.

# TSE blocks

**(Trades of 100,000 or more shares worth at least $1-million)**

| Stock | Sym | Buyer | Seller | Volume ('000s) | Price |
|---|---|---|---|---|---|
| Anderson | AXL | Midland | Midland | 111 | 13.80 |
| Barrick Gld | ABX | RBC Domi | RBC Domi | 100 | 37.05 |
| Barrick Gld | ABX | NesBurns | NesBurns | 129 | 37.00 |
| Bema j | BGO | 1st Marath | 1st Marath | 100 | 11.00 |
| Bema j | BGO | 1st Marath | 1st Marath | 100 | 11.00 |
| Bema j | BGO | 1st Marath | 1st Marath | 100 | 10.90 |
| Bema j | BGO | 1st Marath | 1st Marath | 100 | 10.85 |
| Bomb sv | BBD.B | Deutsche | Deutsche | 1000 | 19.20 |
| Bre-X Min | BXM | NesBurns | NesBurns | 100 | 24.40 |
| CAE | CAE | RBC Domi | RBC Domi | 100 | 10.55 |
| CIBC | CM | Gordon | Gordon | 140 | 45.80 |
| Cdn Natural | CNQ | RBC Domi | RBC Domi | 116 | 27.85 |
| CdnTir nv | CTR.A | CIBC Wood | CIBC Wood | 150 | 16.30 |
| C Eurocan | KEU | Griffiths | Griffiths | 200 | 6.50 |
| Domtar Inc | DTC | Newcrest | Newcrest | 100 | 11.10 |
| Edper | EPR.IR | Midland | Midland | 250 | 51.80 |
| Geomaqu | GEO | NesBurns | NesBurns | 1200 | 3.65 |
| Imasco | IMS | Scotia McL | Scotia McL | 100 | 26.95 |
| Imasco | IMS | Scotia McL | Scotia McL | 100 | 26.95 |
| Intl Fors sv | IFP.A | RBC Domi | RBC Domi | 100 | 11.40 |
| Jannock | JN | Deacon | Deacon | 120 | 14.50 |
| Laid nv | LDM.B | TD Securit | TD Securit | 200 | 13.00 |
| Loewen | LWN | Richardson | Richardson | 100 | 40.00 |
| Loew | LWN.PR.C | Richardson | Richardson | 147 | 30.45 |
| MacBlo | MB | Gordon | Gordon | 100 | 19.75 |
| Mytec Tech | MYT | RBC Domi | RBC Domi | 229 | 5.95 |
| National Bnk | NA | Levesque | Levesque | 100 | 11.50 |
| Newbridge | NNC | Newcrest | Newcrest | 106 | 78.95 |
| Richland | RLP.A | Goepel | Goepel | 376 | 4.25 |
| TIPS | TIP | RBC Domi | RBC Domi | 100 | 26.90 |
| TCPL | TRP | RBC Domi | RBC Domi | 125 | 22.00 |
| Westcoast Enr | W | RBC Domi | RBC Domi | 500 | 21.75 |
| Western Ga | WG | 1st Marath | 1st Marath | 150 | 6.75 |
| Western Ga | WG | 1st Marath | 1st Marath | 150 | 6.75 |

# ME blocks

**(Trades of 100,000 or more shares worth at least $1-million)**

| Stock | Sym | Buyer | Seller | Volume ('000s) | Price |
|---|---|---|---|---|---|
| Falconbridg | FL | Deutsche | Deutsche | 125 | 29.80 |
| Falconbridg | FL | RBC Dom | RBC Dom | 200 | 29.80 |
| Falconb | FL.IR.A | RBC Dom | RBC Dom | 150 | 20.40 |
| Falconb | FL.IR.A | Deutsche | Deutsche | 200 | 20.40 |
| Imasco | IMS | Richardson | Richardson | 164 | 27.00 |
| Midland Wlwy | MWI | CIBC Wood | CIBC Wood | 300 | 9.50 |
| Teleglobe | TGO | Levesque | Levesque | 150 | 23.95 |
| Theratech sv | TH.B | Levesque | Levesque | 789 | 4.00 |

# VSE blocks

**(Trades of 100,000 or more shares worth at least $1-million)**

| Stock | Sym | Buyer | Seller | Volume ('000s) | Price |
|---|---|---|---|---|---|
| Paramount V | PVF | Meridian | Meridian | 1300 | 2.35 |
| Paramount V | PVF | Meridian | Meridian | 500 | 2.45 |

to find potential buyers or sellers of large block trades. With the absorption of independent major broker firms by the chartered banks in Canada, blocks are still handled by most large brokerages. Figure 3.1 shows an example of the daily report on block trading activity on the three major exchanges. Gordon Capital is noted for its role as a block house on the TSE.

## Settlement

An order executed on the exchange must be settled within three working days. The purchaser must deliver the cash, and the seller must deliver the stock to the broker, who in turn delivers it to the buyer's broker. Transfer of the shares is made easier when the firm's clients keep their securities in *street name,* meaning that the broker holds the shares registered in the firm's own name on behalf of the client.

Settlement is simplified further by a clearinghouse. The trades of all exchange members are recorded each day, with members' transactions netted out, so that each member need only transfer or receive the net number of shares sold or bought that day. Each member settles only with the clearinghouse, instead of with each firm with whom trades were executed.

### Trading on the OTC Market

On the exchanges, all trading takes place through a registered trader. Trades on the OTC market, however, are negotiated directly through dealers. Each dealer maintains an inventory of selected securities. Dealers sell from their inventories at asked prices and buy for them at bid prices.

An investor wishing to purchase or sell shares engages a broker who tries to locate the dealer offering the best deal on the security. This contrasts with exchange trading, where all buy or sell orders are negotiated through the registered trader, who arranges for the best bids to get the trade. In the OTC market, brokers must search the offers of dealers directly to find the best trading opportunity. It has been noted that the NASDAQ system does not permit the entry of a customer's limit order placed with a broker to be seen by all other brokers; thus, shares may trade at a higher price than a limit-sell, without that order being filled. This deficiency and the high spreads that have been observed have caused NASDAQ to come under investigation.

Exchange trading is effectively conducted in an auction market, whereas OTC trading is conducted in a *dealer market.* The CDN system facilitates access for users in obtaining a full set of dealer bid and asked quotes provided by the approved market-makers. Because this system bypasses the registered trader system, OTC trades do not require a centralized trading floor, as do exchange-listed stocks. Dealers can be located anywhere, as long as they can communicate effectively with other buyers and sellers.

## 3.4 Trading with Margin

The concept of **margin** refers to the need for investors to provide security whenever they engage in a transaction in which the asset value of their accounts can fall beneath the value of the liabilities they have incurred. In this event, they—and failing them, their brokers—would be liable to pay the shortfall. This possibility arises if investors purchase shares without having the full purchase price available or if they short sell shares or derivative securities.

### Buying on Margin

Investors who purchase stocks on margin borrow part of the purchase price of the stock from their brokers. The brokers in turn borrow money from banks at the call money rate to finance these purchases and charge their clients that rate plus a service charge for the loan. All securities purchased on margin must be left with the brokerage firm in street name, because the securities are used as collateral for the loan.

The regulators of the various exchanges set limits on the extent to which stock purchases can be financed via margin loans. Currently, the margin is 30 percent for optionable stocks, meaning that, at most, 70 percent of the purchase price may be borrowed; however, on the TSE, ME, and Alberta Stock Exchange, this margin rises to as much as 100 percent on low-price stocks.

The margin is defined as the ratio of the net worth, or "equity value" of the account, to the market value of the securities. To demonstrate, suppose that the investor initially pays \$6,000 toward the purchase of \$10,000 worth of stock (100 shares at \$100 per share), borrowing the remaining \$4,000 from the broker. The account will have a balance sheet as follows:

| Assets | | Liabilities and Owner's Equity | |
|---|---|---|---|
| Value of stock | \$10,000 | Loan from broker | \$4,000 |
| | | Equity | \$6,000 |

The initial margin is:

$$\text{Margin ratio} = \frac{\text{Equity value}}{\text{Market value of assets}} = \frac{\text{Market value of assets} - \text{Loan}}{\text{Market value of assets}} \tag{3.1}$$

$$= \frac{\$10{,}000 - \$4{,}000}{\$10{,}000} = .6$$

If the stock's price declines to \$70 per share, the account balance becomes:

| Assets | | Liabilities and Owner's Equity | |
|---|---|---|---|
| Value of stock | \$7,000 | Loan from broker | \$4,000 |
| | | Equity | \$3,000 |

The equity in the account falls by the full decrease in the stock value, and the percentage margin is now \$3,000/\$7,000 = 43 percent.

If the stock value were to fall below \$4,000, equity would become negative, meaning that the value of the stock is no longer sufficient collateral to cover the loan from the broker. To guard against this possibility, the broker sets a *maintenance margin*. If the percentage margin falls below the maintenance level, the broker will issue a *margin call*, requiring the investor to add new cash or securities to the margin account. If the investor does not act, the broker may sell the securities from the account to pay off enough of the loan to restore the percentage margin to an acceptable level.

An example will show how the maintenance margin works. Suppose the maintenance margin is 30 percent. How far could the stock price fall before the investor would get a margin call? We use algebra to answer this question.

Let $P$ be the price of the stock. The value of the investor's 100 shares is then $100P$, and the equity in his or her account is $100P - \$4{,}000$. The percentage margin is therefore $(100P - \$4{,}000)/100P$. The price at which the percentage margin equals the maintenance margin of .3 is found by solving the equation:

$$\frac{100P - \$4{,}000}{100P} = .3$$

$$100P - \$4{,}000 = 30P$$

$$70P = \$4{,}000$$

$$P = \$57.14$$

If the price of the stock were to fall below $57.14 per share, the investor would get a margin call.

**CONCEPT CHECK** Question 2. If the maintenance margin in the above example were 40 percent, how far could the stock price fall before the investor would get a margin call?

Why do investors buy stock (or bonds) on margin? They do so when they wish to invest an amount greater than their own money alone would allow. Thus they can achieve greater upside potential, but they also expose themselves to greater downside risk.

To see how, let us suppose that an investor is bullish (optimistic) on Seagram's stock, which is currently selling at $100 per share. The investor has $10,000 to invest and expects Seagram's stock to go up in price by 30 percent during the next year. Ignoring any dividends, the expected rate of return would thus be 30 percent if the investor spent only $10,000 to buy 100 shares.

But now let us assume that the investor also borrows another $10,000 from the broker and invests it in Seagram's also. The total investment in Seagram's would thus be $20,000 (for 200 shares). Assuming an interest rate on the margin loan of 9 percent per year, what will be the investor's rate of return now (again ignoring dividends) if Seagram's stock does go up 30 percent by year's end?

The 200 shares will be worth $26,000. Paying off $10,900 of principal and interest on the margin loan leaves $15,100 ($26,000 − $10,900). The rate of return therefore will be

$$\frac{\$15{,}100 - \$10{,}000}{\$10{,}000} = 51\%$$

The investor has parlayed a 30 percent rise in the stock's price into a 51 percent rate of return on the $10,000 investment.

Doing so, however, magnifies the downside risk. Suppose that instead of going up by 30 percent the price of Seagram's stock goes down by 30 percent to $70 per share. In that case, the 200 shares will be worth $14,000, and the investor is left with $3,100 after paying off the $10,900 of principal and interest on the loan. The result is a disastrous rate of return:

$$\frac{\$3{,}100 - \$10{,}000}{\$10{,}000} = -69\%$$

**CONCEPT CHECK** Question 3. Suppose that in the previous example the investor borrows only $5,000 at the same interest rate of 9 percent per year. What will be the rate of return if the price of Seagram's stock goes up by 30 percent? If it goes down by 30 percent? If it remains unchanged?

## Short Sales

Typically, investors purchase shares in the expectation of a rising price and sell them later to close out the position. Occasionally, investors expect a share price to decline; to profit from this they must engage in a **short sale.** In this procedure, an investor borrows shares of stock from another investor through a broker and sells the shares. Later, the investor (the short seller) must repurchase the shares in the market in order to replace the shares that were borrowed. This is called *covering* the short position. If the stock price has fallen, the shares will be repurchased at a lower price than that at which they were initially sold, and the short seller reaps a profit. If the stock price rises, however, the short seller incurs a loss. Table 3.4 compares the cash flows of purchases and short sales.

Since the shares are borrowed through the brokerage house from an investor who has a long position in the stock, the short seller also risks that the borrowed stock will be sold by its owner; in this case, the short seller must repurchase and close the position, unless further stock can be borrowed. This may result in a loss

**Table 3.4** Cash Flows from Purchasing versus Short-Selling Shares of Stock

| Purchase of Stock | | |
|---|---|---|
| **Time** | **Action** | **Cash Flow** |
| 0 | Buy share | − Initial price |
| 1 | Receive dividend, sell share | Ending price + Dividend |

Profit = (Ending price + Dividend) − Initial price
Note: A negative cash flow implies a cash *outflow*.

| Short Sale of Stock | | |
|---|---|---|
| **Time** | **Action** | **Cash Flow** |
| 0 | Borrow share; sell it | Initial price |
| 1 | Repay dividend and buy share to replace the share originally borrowed | − (Ending price + Dividend) |

Profit = Initial price − (Ending price + Dividend)

at that time, even though the stock may subsequently fall; hence, the short seller's strategy is at the mercy of the lender's own investment decision.

Short sellers must not only return the shares but also give the lender any dividends paid on the shares during the period of the short sale, because the lender of the shares would have received the dividends directly from the firm had the shares not been lent.

Exchange rules permit short sales only after an *uptick,* that is, only when the last recorded change in the stock price is positive. This rule apparently is meant to prevent waves of speculation against the stock. In other words, the votes of "no confidence" in the stock that short sales represent may be entered only after a price increase.

Finally, exchange rules require that proceeds from a short sale must be kept on account with the broker. The short seller therefore cannot invest these funds to generate income. In addition, short sellers are required to post margin (which is essentially collateral) with the broker to ensure that the trader can cover any losses sustained should the stock price rise during the period of the short sale.[6]

To illustrate the actual mechanics of short selling, suppose that you are bearish (pessimistic) on Seagram's stock, and that its current market price is \$100 per share. You tell your broker to sell short 1,000 shares. The broker borrows 1,000 shares either from another customer's account or from another broker.

The \$100,000 cash proceeds from the short sale are credited to your account. Suppose the broker has a 50 percent margin requirement on short sales. This means that you must have other cash or securities in your account worth at least \$50,000 that can serve as margin (that is, collateral) on the short sale. Let us suppose that you have \$50,000 in Treasury bills. Your account with the broker after the short sale will then be:

| Assets | | Liabilities and Owner's Equity | |
|---|---|---|---|
| Cash | \$100,000 | Short position in Seagram's stock (1,000 shares owed) | \$100,000 |
| T-bills | \$ 50,000 | Equity | \$ 50,000 |

Your margin ratio is the equity in the account, \$50,000, divided by the current value of the borrowed shares, \$100,000. Initially,

$$\text{Margin ratio} = \frac{\text{Equity value}}{\text{Value of stock owed}}$$

$$= \frac{\text{Market value of assets} - \text{Value of stock owed}}{\text{Value of stock owed}} \tag{3.2}$$

$$= \frac{\$50{,}000}{\$150{,}000}$$

[6] We should note that although we have been describing a short sale of a stock, bonds also may be sold short.

If you are right, and Seagram's stock falls to $70 per share, you can close out your position at a profit. To cover the short sale, you buy 1,000 shares to replace the borrowed shares for $70,000. Because your account was credited by $100,000 at the time of the short sale, your profit is $30,000, which is the decline in share price times the number of shares sold short.

On the other hand, if the price of Seagram's rises while you are short, you may get a margin call. Suppose the broker's maintenance margin requirement is 30 percent for short sales, so that the equity in your account must be at least 30 percent of the value of your short position at all times. How far can the price of Seagram's rise before you get a margin call?

Let $P$ be the price of Seagram's stock; then the value of the shares you must repay is $1{,}000P$, and the equity in your account is $\$150{,}000 - 1{,}000P$. The critical value of $P$ for a margin ratio of 30 percent is

$$\frac{\text{Equity value}}{\text{Value of stock owed}} = \frac{\$150{,}000 - 1{,}000P}{1{,}000P} = .3$$

$$\$150{,}000 - 1{,}000P = 300P$$

$$P = \$115.38 \text{ per share}$$

If Seagram's stock should rise above $115.38 per share, you will get a margin call and you will have to either put up additional cash or cover your short position.

---

**CONCEPT CHECK** Question 4. If the short position maintenance margin in the preceding example were 40 percent, how far could the stock price rise before the investor would get a margin call?

---

Notice in our two margin examples that the balance sheets showed a progression from the assets including only the purchased stock to having T-bills, which were needed for margin for the short position. Those T-bills could have been included in the first balance sheet, if you happened to hold them in your account. The assets provided for margin purposes can earn a return within the account. The balance sheet could, and would normally, also include other stocks in your portfolio. It is the aggregate value of the account that goes into the margin calculation. Table 3.5 shows the balance sheet for a more complicated account, first at the time of opening the positions—a margin purchase of 500 shares of Seagram's at $100 and a short sale of 300 shares of Alcan at $40—in addition to other assets, and then at a later date; we ignore any dividends or interest payments and suppose that no cash is advanced at the time of the opening trades.

If the margin position had come from all purchases or all short sales, the calculations would have been simple extensions of equations 3.1 and 3.2, where we aggregate long positions for market value, short positions for value owed, and the loan amounts. When we have both long and short positions, we have to calculate

**Table 3.5** Illustration of a Margined Account

| Initial Account Position | | | |
|---|---|---|---|
| **Assets** | | **Liabilities** | |
| Cash | $ 12,000 | Alcan (300 @ $40) (short position) | $ 12,000 |
| T-bills | 30,000 | Broker loan (Seagram's) | 50,000 |
| Seagram's (500 @ $100) | 50,000 | Equity | 72,500 |
| CIBC (1,000 @ $30) | 30,000 | | $134,500 |
| Noranda (500 @ $25) | 12,500 | | |
| | $134,500 | | |

| Later Account Position | | | |
|---|---|---|---|
| **Assets** | | **Liabilities** | |
| Cash | $ 12,000 | Alcan (300 @ $50) (short position) | $ 15,000 |
| T-bills | 30,000 | Broker loan (Seagram's) | 50,000 |
| Seagram's (500 @ $102) | 51,000 | Equity | 71,000 |
| CIBC (1,000 @ $28) | 28,000 | | $136,000 |
| Noranda (500 @ $30) | 15,000 | | |
| | $136,000 | | |

the exposure of the account on both long and short sides and sum the requirements to protect against both. If the equity in the account is sufficient to cover both sides, then margin has been met. The initial margin requirement for the margin purchase alone in this account is found by considering the market value of the account before the effect of the short sale, or $122,500 when we remove the $12,000 short sale and cash proceeds; the equity value is found by subtracting the $50,000 loan, which we then divide by the market value of the securities held long, or $122,500, for a margin ratio of .59. The investor needs $50,000 to establish an initial margin of .5 and has $22,500 excess equity.

For the short position alone, we remove the effect of the margin purchase from the market value; so the investor has $84,500 less $12,000 as equity value, which is divided by the short value of $12,000 for a margin ratio of 6; but we have counted the same equity twice in arriving at the two satisfactory ratios. To cover the short sale margin requirement, the investor needs assets of $V$ where $(V - \$12,000)/\$12,000$ must equal .5 (the initial margin ratio); solving for $V$ yields $18,000 as the asset requirement. Separately, there is plenty of excess equity in the account, but combined, the investor needs $50,000 plus $18,000, or $68,000, equity in the account before making both the margin purchase and the short sale. There is an excess of only $4,500; if only $20,000 in T-bills were there, the investor would have needed to find another $5,500 to place on deposit.

In finding the amount of margin that the investor must provide, we have been using the following two formulas; for margin purchases, the market value of collateral required is

$$\text{Market value} = \text{Loan value}/(1 - \text{Margin ratio}) \qquad \textbf{(3.3)}$$

and for short sales, the value of collateral required is

$$\text{Market value} = \text{Short value} \times (1 + \text{Margin ratio}) \qquad \textbf{(3.4)}$$

Using these equations, we can see that at the later date, the account easily satisfies the maintenance margin requirement of \$50,000/(1 − .3) = \$71,429 for the purchase plus \$15,000 × (1 + .3) = \$19,500 for the short sale, summing to \$90,929 against assets of \$136,000.

**CONCEPT CHECK** Question 5. If at the later date in the preceding example the prices of Noranda and CIBC were the same as given but Seagram's had fallen to \$80, how high could Alcan stock rise before a margin call would result? If instead Alcan rose to \$60, how low could Seagram's fall before promoting a margin call?

## 3.5 TRADING COSTS

Part of the cost of trading is the explicit payment to the broker of a commission. The size of this commission depends mostly on the choice between a full-service or discount broker. *Full-service brokers* provide a variety of services. Besides carrying out the basic services of executing orders, holding securities for safekeeping, extending margin loans, and facilitating short sales, normally they also provide information and advice relating to investment alternatives. Full-service brokers usually are supported by a research staff that issues analyses and forecasts of general economic, industry, and company conditions and often makes specific buy or sell recommendations. Some customers take the ultimate leap of faith and allow a full-service broker to make buy and sell decisions for them by establishing a *discretionary account.* This step requires an unusual degree of trust on the part of the customer, because an unscrupulous broker can "churn" an account, that is, trade securities excessively in order to generate commissions.

*Discount brokers* are able to charge much lower commissions by restricting their services to execution of orders, holding securities for safekeeping, offering margin loans, and facilitating short sales. They provide the basic information of price quotations about indices and individual securities. The more comprehensive discounters also will offer analytical services of advice and software for an additional fee, these being provided by outside firms.

In recent years, discount brokerage services have become increasingly available, offered by both mutual fund management companies and chartered banks. With the chartered banks having bought up most of the independent full-service banks as well, we have banks such as the Royal Bank offering both full-service and discount brokerage subsidiaries to customers in an attempt to provide a full range of financial services. Customers are able to deposit cash with their banks, transfer it to pay for securities, and have interest and dividends either transferred back to their bank accounts or deposited in money market funds.

A recent development for discount services is for customers to handle their quotation and order requests by touch-tone telephone, using the listing codes for stocks, indices, and options. It can be a lengthy process to navigate the sequence, compared to a live broker; however, the further fee savings and immediate availability make this an attractive feature to many investors. The process is accelerated if handled through a computer and modem, especially in conjunction with a number of on-line data and analysis services that are offered.

In addition to the explicit cost of commissions, there is an implicit cost deriving primarily from the **bid-asked spread.** If the broker for a trade is actually the dealer in the security, instead of a commission, the fee for purchase or sale will come entirely in the form of the bid-asked spread. (In the case of bond trading, this is the usual procedure.) For most trades, the investor will have to pay the asked price or receive the bid and pay a commission to the broker.

We can look at the cost of buying or selling securities as having an explicit part—the broker's commission—and an implicit part—the dealer's bid-asked spread. Sometimes the broker is a dealer in the security being traded and will charge no commission but will collect the fee entirely in the form of the bid-asked spread. Another implicit cost of trading that some observers would distinguish is the price concession an investor may be forced to make for trading in any quantity that exceeds the quantity the dealer is willing to trade at the posted bid or asked price. Combining the spread and the price concession, full-service brokers may claim that they are able to achieve better execution on the major exchanges than their competition; that is, their higher explicit costs are offset by lower implicit costs.

The commission for trading common stocks is generally around 2 percent of the value of the transaction, but it can vary significantly. Previously, the schedule of commissions was fixed, but in today's environment of negotiated commissions there is substantial flexibility. On some trades, full-service brokers will offer even lower commissions than will discount brokers. In general, it pays the investor to shop around.

Total trading costs consisting of the commission, the dealer bid-asked spread, and the price concession can be substantial. According to one U.S. study, the round-trip costs (costs of purchase and resale) of trading large blocks of stocks of small companies can be as high as 30 percent.[7]

In most cases, however, costs of trades are far smaller. Because of the existence of negotiated commissions, the quoted rates are not representative of actual fees paid on larger orders. The commissions can be as low as .25 percent of the value

[7] T. F. Loeb, "Trading Cost: The Critical Link between Investment Information and Results," *Financial Analysis Journal,* May–June 1983.

# More Services for the Masses

**Comparing Discount Brokers**

| | TD Green Line | BM Investor Line | RB Action Direct | CIBC Investor's Edge | BNS Scotia Discount |
|---|---|---|---|---|---|
| Cost to buy 1,000 shares $20 Canadian stock* | $85 | $65 | $85 | $95 | $70 |
| Phone keypad price query and order entry | Yes | Yes | Yes | No | No |
| Direct PC link and order entry | Yes | Yes | No | No | No |
| Hours open | 24 hours | 24 hours | 24 hours | 8–8 M–F 9–5 Sat. | 8–5:30 M–F |
| Trade on non-North American markets | Yes | No | No | No | No |
| Fee to buy $25,000 full front-load mutual fund | 1% | 1% | 1% | 1% | 1% |

*Commission on this trade at a full-service broker: $454

**BY ANDREW ALLENTUCK**
**Special to The Globe and Mail**

Discount brokers have come a long way from being low-fee order execution services. Originally conceived as Bay Street's answer to fast food—cut rates for minimal service with no research and no advice—several now provide services distinct from those offered by full service brokers.

Discount brokerage services operated by Royal Bank of Canada (Action Direct), Bank of Montreal (InvestorLine) and Toronto-Dominion Bank (Green Line) are willing to take orders to buy or sell securities 24 hours a day, seven days a week.

- Royal Bank's Action Direct provides a keypad instruction system for those with touch-tone phones and nimble fingers; it can take orders or give stock quotes at any time through the phone's keypad.
- Toronto-Dominion's Green Line provides phone order entry and real-time market quotes and, for those with personal computers, account inquiries and order taking at any time of the day or night.
- Bank of Montreal's InvestorLine runs around the clock as well and provides, in addition to phone order taking and a PC-linked quote system, charting services that follow securities listed on major exchanges, graphs, and portfolio valuations as securities prices change.
- Discount brokerages operated by Canadian Imperial Bank of Commerce (Investor's Edge) and Bank of Nova Scotia (Scotia Discount Brokerage) do not currently offer on-line modem links. Senior managers of the firms suggest that such services are under review.

Investing substantial sums through keypads and keyboards is far from the traditional image of plush offices and cerebral stockbrokers giving advice to treasured clients. But, says Paul Bates, president of Green Line Investor Services Inc., "our clients choose us because they want speed and cheap trades and accuracy. In turn, we do not take inexperienced clients who need the advice of a full service broker."

*(Continued)*

Discount brokers do not encourage clients to form relationships with their order takers. Yet the formula of offering impersonal but inexpensive service is succeeding, the discount brokers say. Each of the services says it has thousands of clients. It would seem that rather than returning to the warm, fuzzy model of the traditional broker-client relationship, the discounters are moving to even less human forms of service through keypads and computers.

Following the lead of large U.S. discount brokers, who showed that knowledgeable investors wanted more trading for lower fees, Green Line eliminated the frills of brokering. In the mid-1980s it offered commissions lower than those of the full service brokers.

"We had access to brokers around the clock since 1984," Mr. Bates says. "The next step was the addition of trading via a client's computer. In the last year, we have enhanced this service. Now you can trade during the night on world exchanges that happen to be open—London, for example—in the small hours of the Canadian morning."

Discount brokers are less likely to take you out to lunch than a full service broker. But the fact that a client can, with the aid of a modem, get the last 45 days of account transactions or charting (a Bank of Montreal service), all at low or zero phone line charges, suggests that what separates full service from discount brokers—service—needs to be redefined.

The line separating full service from discount brokers is not clearcut. Discount brokers' relatively inexpensive service becomes more costly if a client orders extras. Discounters may charge to deliver a certificate, to issue cheques to clients, and for safekeeping of securities.

Need a records search done? There may be a charge, even though the cost of extras can seldom run the discounted fee up to the level charged by the full service broker. In the securities business, as in much of the rest of life, lunch isn't free.

Computer links to full service brokers have long been available to institutional clients. Fees at large brokers and mutual funds decline as sums involved increase. What discount brokers really do, says Peter Bacon, president of Bank of Montreal's InvestorLine, is to lower the level at which anyone can get a reduced trading fee. "They have, in this sense, democratized pricing," he says.

For the firms with keypad and keyboard order entry, automation is not quite complete. Discount brokers ensure that registered representatives who know exchange rules review all orders before they become trades.

The potential volume of orders that can be created by individuals ordering buys or sells in the middle of the night raises a question of whether all this activity may affect the orderliness of markets.

According to Tannis MacLaren, acting chief of compliance for the Ontario Securities Commission, discount brokers offering 24-hour service pose no regulatory problems.

"Every broker can take orders overnight," Ms. MacLaren says. "Somebody on a phone or a broker taking an order by modem does not make the trade any faster. If they were trading out of their own book [inventory] it would be more of a problem. It would affect liquidity and transparency [openness] and when material information is disclosed. But that is not the case."

Full service brokers can do some of what the keypad and keyboard-driven order entry systems do.

Off-hours order taking by full service brokers has always been possible, for one can call a registered representative's voice mail or home at any time. Full service brokers are often willing to discount their own services for large, active accounts.

Full service brokers have computer terminal links for institutional clients. In any event, for North American exchanges, trading only happens in normal business hours. Finally, the computer-driven order system is not quite that, for all orders pass by brokers who know and must comply with exchange rules.

One clear advantage computer-driven services have is at the edges of the time windows into foreign markets. In Vancouver, it's barely dawn when the Toronto and New York stock exchanges open; entering orders the night before makes sense for those with day jobs.

*Globe & Mail Report on Business,* July 26, 1994, p. B20. Reprinted by permission.

of stocks traded for large transactions made through discount houses. The accompanying box discusses comparative commissions and services of discount brokers.

There is one Canadian phenomenon that deserves mention at this point. A number of brokerage houses act as exclusive market-makers for low-capitalization stocks. Under such circumstances the stocks are extremely illiquid, with bid-asked spreads as high as 50 percent of the asked value. These stocks generally are thought to be poor investment prospects.

## 3.6 Regulation of Securities Markets

Trading in securities markets in Canada is regulated under a number of laws. Laws such as the federal Canada Business Corporations Act govern the conduct of business firms, while the various provincial Securities Acts regulate the trading of securities. Most legislation is at the provincial level, even though historically the first Canadian laws concerning securities were introduced at the federal level in the late 19th century. Provincial legislation in the Maritime Provinces followed shortly thereafter, while the Ontario Companies Act was established in 1907. The Ontario Securities Act, Canada's first provincial securities act, was passed in 1945, and has been revised repeatedly since that time. Other provinces generally have tended to follow Ontario's lead. Although the federal government doesn't have a Securities Act, portions of the Criminal Code of Canada are specifically directed to securities trading.

In addition to the laws, there also is considerable self-regulation in the financial services industry. It takes place via regulations governing membership in various associations of professionals participating in the industry. Thus, the Investment Dealers Association of Canada encompasses stock exchange members and bond dealers, while the Investment Funds Institute of Canada is the association of Canadian mutual funds. Self-regulation also occurs through the organized stock exchanges. (See the accompanying box for a discussion of the Canadian regulatory issue.

Provincial securities legislation exists in all Canadian provinces and territories, but provincial securities commissions exist only in six provinces, the five provinces with organized stock exchanges plus Saskatchewan. These commissions are responsible for administering and enforcing the provincial securities laws. The key purpose of these laws is to protect investors from fraud. They achieve this by controlling (through registration) the people participating in the financial services industry and by ensuring that investors have all material facts at their disposal in order to make their own investment decisions. The approval, however, by a securities commission of a prospectus or financial report does not mean that it views the security as a good investment. The commission cares only that the relevant facts are disclosed; investors make their own evaluations of the security's value.

Relevant facts are revealed for prospective investors when a primary issue takes place, through the prospectus. Investors also must be kept informed, on a

## Debalkanizing Canada's Securities Industry

BANFF, ALTA.—Up here in the Rockies, the Balkans and the problems tearing that unhappy region apart seem far away.

But as the Investment Dealers Association annual meeting got under way yesterday, it was no small irony that keynote speaker Paul Johnson, the British historian, talked about the Balkans as a dangerous place in a dangerous world that lacks leadership.

The irony here is that Canada's investors and investment dealers must exist in a balkanized Canadian securities system of 12 separate jurisdictions—one for each of the provinces and territories. The irony was further underscored when, immediately following Johnson's speech, delegates heard a panel discussion on "Interprovincial securities regulation—harmonization or disparity." It would have had a clearer ring to it if it were titled "harmonization or balkanization."

So what does all this have to do with you? Lots, if you're an investor or saver.

As the millennium approaches, the vanguard of the baby boom will be trudging into retirement territory—millions of them with billions to invest to insure their futures in an age when government pensions will become unreliable and increasingly inadequate.

The IDA, which has 115 members employing about 23,000 people in the securities industry, wants to be right at the centre of the action as the year 2000 and the boomer bulge present an unparalleled business opportunity. For the IDA, which stresses investor protection and capital markets efficiency above all, it would very likely be much more efficient, ahem profitable, to have a unified system—a single jurisdiction instead of 12 securities commissions mirroring the maddening jungle of interprovincial trade barriers.

That's not to say Canadian capital markets are deficient now. Joseph Oliver, who takes over from the retiring Charles Caty as IDA chief executive this week, says he will stack up Canada's capital-raising record against that of any other country. For its population size, Canada easily beats the U.S. for the amounts of equity it raises.

But Oliver, formally with First Marathon Securities Ltd in Toronto, acknowledges that the IDA has some battles to win before it cements its members' position as the country's preeminent providers of investment products and services.

He says the IDA has a good chance to savor a victory this fall when it probably will be recognized by the Ontario Securities Commission as a self-regulatory organization—along the lines of lawyers' and accountants' group.

Along the same lines, the IDA wants the stock exchanges, particularly the TSE, to recognize that IDA members can regulate themselves. Meantime, the exchanges should be able to see their way clear to allow IDA members to work within uniform national standards.

Yesterday's publication of the final report of the Task Force on Operational Efficiencies in the Administration of Securities Regulations is another step to debalkanizing securities jurisdictions. The report was commissioned by the Canadian Securities Administrators, the organization of the provincial and territorial regulators.

A Canadian Securities Commission is probably a long way off. Indeed, it may never happen. But the demand for a better, more efficient securities system has never been stronger.

If the country's securities regulators, working with the industry, can't move steadily and strongly to debalkanize the securities system they deserve a kick up the Dolomites.

William Hanley, "Debalkanizing Canada's Securities Industry," *The Financial Post*, June 27, 1995, p. 26. Reprinted by permission.

continuous basis, about all important changes to a company's status, such as changes in the control structure of the corporation, acquisitions or disposals of major assets, and proposed takeovers or mergers. Companies also must issue several financial reports on a quarterly basis and more complete reports annually.

Several problems are created by the fragmentation along provincial lines of the regulatory system for Canadian securities markets. Financial transactions in such markets may involve parties residing in different provinces; for instance, a group of Ontario investors purchases the shares of a Quebec company, traded on the TSE. Such a transaction would fall under the jurisdiction of two provinces' regulatory bodies, implying that it should simultaneously comply with the Quebec and Ontario regulatory regimes. Apart from the fact that this may create multiple (and costly) investigations of the same transaction, it also would generate uncertainty among the investors about the set of rules governing their investment.

Such problems are avoided in the United States, where the securities industry is regulated by national agencies. The most important of these is the Securities Exchange Commission (SEC), established by the 1934 Securities Exchange Act, to ensure the full disclosure of relevant information relating to the issue of new securities and the periodic release of financial information for secondary trading. The act also empowered the SEC to register and regulate securities exchanges, OTC trading, brokers, and dealers. It thus established the SEC as the administrative agency responsible for broad oversight of the securities markets. The SEC, however, shares oversight with other regulatory bodies. For example, the Commodity Futures Trading Commission (CFTC) regulates trading in futures markets, whereas the Federal Reserve Bank (the Fed) has broad responsibility for the health of the U.S. financial system. In this role, the Fed sets margin requirements on stocks and stock options and regulates bank lending to the securities markets' participants.

The Investment Dealers Association and the stock exchanges have established the Canadian Investor Protection Fund (CIPF) to protect investors from losses if their brokerage firms fail. Just as the Canadian Deposit Insurance Corporation provides federal protection to depositors against bank failure, the CIPF ensures that investors will receive the value of their accounts up to a maximum of $250,000. Securities held for their account in street name by the failed brokerage firm and cash balances up to a limit of $60,000 will be replaced by equivalent securities, or by their cash value. The CIPF is financed by levying an "insurance premium" on its participating, or member, brokerage firms.

The events surrounding the market crash of October, 1987, led U.S. regulatory agencies and the exchanges to consider ad hoc solutions to the volatility created by heavy trading in primary and derivative securities. The absence of a single regulatory body for stock, options, and futures markets was seen at first as a contributing problem, but eventually the reaction was to attempt to impede the downward, or even upward, spiral in prices on the different exchanges by introducing "circuit breakers" for the different exchanges. Large price changes, such as 50 points on the Dow Jones Industrial Average during the trading day, lead to the suspension of some normal trading possibilities, such as execution of index arbitrage strategies and program trading. As the price changes become more extreme, more and more practices are temporarily suspended. Less than ten years later, with the index more than double the 1987 value, the definition of a 50-point limit has been questioned. Whether these limits serve more to reduce investor anxieties or moderate volatility is debatable.

The regulatory response to the 1987 crash gives no evidence of attentive listening to the results of academic analyses of the phenomenon, which were numerous. Testimony was given by many experts, and researchers produced a large number of articles ranging from statistical analyses to more theoretical and conjectural discussions of the potential causes. The mechanical trading limitations are not consistent with what was recommended following rigorous investigation of trading patterns. Of the many studies of the event, two in particular can be cited as indicative of a different interpretation of the causes. Furbush[8] demonstrated that there was a significant association between price movements and program trading, particularly for index arbitrage; however, on the two days of the crash (October 19 and 20), program trading was not being used to exploit the volatility through index arbitrage. Kleidon and Whaley[9] investigated the integration of the markets for stocks and derivatives and found it insufficient. They argued for better mechanisms in trading to achieve the integration that would lead to better price efficiency; in particular, they found that circuit breakers would work in the opposite direction.

One of the important restrictions on trading involves *insider trading.* It is illegal for anyone to transact in securities to profit from **inside information,** that is, private information held by senior officers, directors, or major stockholders (with a direct or indirect interest of at least 10 percent of the voting shares) that has not yet been divulged to the public. The difficulty is that the definition of insiders can be ambiguous. Although it is obvious that the chief financial officer of a firm is an insider, it is less clear whether the firm's biggest supplier can be considered one as well. However, the supplier may deduce the firm's near-term prospects from significant changes in orders. This gives the supplier a unique form of private information, yet the supplier does not necessarily qualify as an insider. These ambiguities plague security analysts, whose job is to uncover as much information as possible concerning the firm's expected prospects. The distinction between legal private information and illegal inside information can be fuzzy.

The OSC requires officers, directors, and major stockholders of all publicly held firms to report all of their transactions in their firm's stock within 10 days of the end of the month of the transaction. A compendium of insider trades is published monthly in the OSC's insider trading bulletin, extracts of which are published promptly by *The Globe and Mail.* The idea is to inform the public of any implicit votes of confidence or no confidence made by insiders.

---

[8] D. Furbush, "Program Trading and Price Movement: Evidence from the October 1987 Market Crash," *Financial Management* 8, no. 3 (Autumn 1989), pp. 68–83.

[9] A. W. Kleidon and R. E. Whaley, "One Market? Stocks, Futures and Options During October 1987," *The Journal of Finance* 47 (1992), pp. 851–77.

Do insiders exploit their knowledge? The answer seems to be, to a limited degree, yes. Two forms of evidence support this conclusion. First, there is massive evidence of "leakage" of useful information to some traders before any public announcement of that information. For example, share prices of firms announcing dividend increases (which the market interprets as good news concerning the firm's prospects) commonly increase in value a few days *before* the public announcement of the increase.[10] Clearly, some investors are acting on the good news before it is released to the public. Similarly, share prices tend to increase a few days before the public announcement of above-trend earnings growth.[11] At the same time, share prices still rise substantially on the day of the public release of good news, indicating that insiders, or their associates, have not fully bid up the price of the stock to the level commensurate with that news.

The second sort of evidence on insider trading is based on returns earned on trades by insiders. Researchers have examined the SEC's summary of insider trading to measure the performance of insiders. Muelbroek[12] investigated the contention by previous researchers that insider trading actually improves market efficiency by accelerating the price adjustment process, through the examination of SEC information on illegal trading activity. She found there to be no doubt that insider trading causes significant price adjustment to occur in advance of the public release of information and gave some support to the view that this "victimless crime" is actually beneficial. A Canadian study by Baesel and Stein[13] investigated the abnormal return on stocks over the months following purchases or sales by insiders. They found that a simulated policy of buying a portfolio of stocks purchased by insiders yielded an abnormal return in the following eight months of about 3.8 percent. If the insiders were also directors of Canadian banks (presumed to be even better informed), the abnormal return persisted for 12 months and rose to 7.8 percent. In both cases, the major part of the gain occurred after publication of the insiders' actions. Insider sales, however, did not generate information leading to abnormal gains.

## SUMMARY

**1.** Firms issue securities to raise the capital necessary to finance their investments. Investment bankers market these securities to the public on the primary market. Investment bankers generally act as underwriters who purchase the secu-

[10] See, for example, J. Aharony and I. Swary, "Quarterly Dividend and Earnings Announcement and Stockholders' Return: An Empirical Analysis," *Journal of Finance* 35 (March 1980).

[11] See, for example, George Foster, Chris Olsen, and Terry Shevlin, "Earnings Releases, Anomalies, and the Behavior of Security Returns," *The Accounting Review,* October 1984.

[12] Lisa K. Muelbroek, "An Empirical Analysis of Illegal Insider Trading," *The Journal of Finance* 47, no. 5 (December 1992), pp. 1661–99.

[13] Jerome Baesel and Garry Stein, "The Value of Information: Inferences from the Profitability of Insider Trading," *Journal of Financial and Quantitative Analysis,* September 1979. See also Jean-Marc Suret and Elise Cormier, "Insiders and the Stock Market," *Canadian Investment Review* 3, no. 2 (Fall 1990).

rities from the firm and resell them to the public at a markup. Before the securities may be sold to the public, the firm must publish a securities commission-approved prospectus that provides information on the firm's prospects.

**2.** Issued securities are traded on the secondary market, that is, on organized stock exchanges. Securities also trade on the over-the-counter market and, for large traders, through direct negotiation. Only members of exchanges may trade on the exchange. Brokerage firms holding seats on the exchange sell their services to individuals, charging commissions for executing trades on their behalf. The TSE and ME have fairly strict listing requirements; the VSE is much less restrictive. The two regional exchanges provide listing opportunities for local firms who do not meet the requirements of the national exchanges.

**3.** Trading of common stocks in exchanges takes place through registered traders or market-makers; these act to maintain an orderly market in the shares of one or more firms, maintaining "books" of limit-buy and limit-sell orders and matching trades at mutually acceptable prices. Market-makers also will accept market orders by selling from or buying for their own inventory of stocks when an imbalance of buy and sell orders exists.

**4.** The over-the-counter market is not a formal exchange but an informal network of brokers and dealers who negotiate sales of securities. The CDN system provides on-line computer quotes offered by dealers in the stock. When an individual wishes to purchase or sell a share, the broker can search the listing of offered bid and asked prices, call the dealer who has the best quote, and execute the trade.

**5.** Block transactions are a fairly recent but fast-growing segment of the securities market, which currently accounts for over one third of trading volume. These trades often are too large to be handled readily by regular market-makers, and thus block houses have developed that specialize in these transactions, identifying potential trading partners for their clients.

**6.** Buying on margin means borrowing money from a broker in order to buy more securities. By buying securities on margin, an investor magnifies both the upside potential and the downside risk. If the equity in a margin account falls below the required maintenance level, the investor will get a margin call from the broker.

**7.** Short selling is the practice of selling securities that the seller does not own. The short seller borrows the securities sold through a broker and may be required to cover the short position at any time on demand. The cash proceeds of a short sale are always kept in escrow by the broker, and the broker usually requires that the short seller deposit additional cash or securities to serve as margin (collateral) for the short sale.

**8.** In addition to providing the basic services of executing buy and sell orders, holding securities for safekeeping, making margin loans, and facilitating short sales, full-service brokers offer investors information, advice, and even investment decisions. Discount brokers offer only the basic brokerage services but usually charge less.

**9.** Total trading costs consist of commissions, the dealer's bid-asked spread, and price concessions. These costs can represent as much as 30 percent of the value of the securities traded.

**10.** Securities trading is regulated by the provincial securities commissions, as well as by self-regulation of the exchanges and the dealer associations. Many of the important regulations have to do with full disclosure of relevant information concerning the securities in question. Insider trading rules also prohibit traders from attempting to profit from inside information.

## Key Terms

Primary market
Secondary market
Underwriting
Prospectus
Direct search
Brokered market
Block transactions
Dealer market
Auction market
Stock exchange
Over-the-counter market (OTC)
NASDAQ
Bid price
Asked price
CDN system (COATS)
Third market
Fourth market
Registered trader
Market-making
Margin
Short sale
Bid-asked spread
Inside information

## Selected Readings

*A good treatment of investment banking is found in:*

Smith, Clifford W. "Investment Banking and the Capital Acquisition Process." *Journal of Financial Economics* 15 (January–February 1986).

*An overview of securities markets is provided in:*

Garbade, Kenneth D. *Securities Markets.* New York: McGraw-Hill, 1982.

*The American specialist system is examined in:*

Stoll, Hans R. "The Stock Exchange Specialist System: An Economic Analysis." *Monograph Series in Finance and Economics,* Graduate School of Business Administration, New York University, 1985.

*An examination of market functioning during the October 1987 crash is:*

The Brady Commission Report, or formally, the *Report of the Presidential Task Force on Market Mechanisms.* Washington, D.C.: United States Government Printing Office, 1988.

*Material facts about listing and trading on Canadian markets are available in:*

*The Toronto Stock Exchange Fact Book,* published annually, and *The TSE Review,* published monthly. Produced by the Toronto Stock Exchange, Toronto, Ontario.

*Guide to International Investing* (annual). Don Mills, Ontario: CCH Canadian, 1991.

*An examination of the pros and cons of a national Canadian securities regulatory system is in:*

Daniels, Ronald. "How 'Broke' Is the System of Provincial Securities Regulation?" *Canadian Investment Review* 5, no. 1 (Spring 1992).

## Problems

1. FBN, Inc., has just sold 100,000 shares in an initial public offering. The underwriter's explicit fees were $70,000. The offering price for the shares was $50, but immediately upon issue the share price jumped to $53.
   *a.* What is your best guess as to the total cost to FBN of the equity issue?
   *b.* Is the entire cost of the underwriting a source of profit to the underwriters?
2. Suppose that you sell short 100 shares of Seagram's, now selling at $120 per share.
   *a.* What is your maximum possible loss?
   *b.* What happens to the maximum loss if you simultaneously place a stop-buy order at $128?
3. An expiring put will be exercised and the stock will be sold if the stock price is below the exercise price. A stop-loss order causes a stock sale when the stock price falls below some limit. Compare and contrast the two strategies of purchasing put options versus issuing a stop-loss order.
4. Compare call options and stop-buy orders.
5. Do you think it is possible to replace market-makers by a fully automated computerized trade-matching system?
6. Consider the following limit-order book of a specialist. The last trade in the stock took place at a price of $50.

| Limit-Buy Orders | | Limit-Sell Orders | |
|---|---|---|---|
| **Price ($)** | **Shares** | **Price ($)** | **Shares** |
| 49.75 | 500 | 50.25 | 100 |
| 49.50 | 800 | 51.50 | 100 |
| 49.25 | 500 | 54.75 | 300 |
| 49.00 | 200 | 58.25 | 100 |
| 48.50 | 600 | | |

   *a.* If a market-buy order for 100 shares comes in, at what price will it be filled?
   *b.* At what price would the next market-buy order be filled?
   *c.* If you were the specialist, would you desire to increase or decrease your inventory of this stock?
7. Consider the following data concerning the NYSE:

| Year | Average Daily Trading Volume (thousands of shares) | Annual High Price of an Exchange Membership* |
|---|---|---|
| 1988 | 161,461 | $820,000 |
| 1989 | 165,470 | 675,000 |
| 1990 | 156,777 | 430,000 |
| 1991 | 178,917 | 440,000 |
| 1992 | 202,266 | 600,000 |
| 1993 | 264,519 | 775,000 |

*Data from the New York Stock Exchange *Fact Book,* 1994.

*a.* What do you conclude about the short-run relationship between trading activity and the value of a seat?

*b.* Based on these data, what do you think has happened over the last six years to the average commission charged to traders?

**8.** You are bullish on BCE stock. The current market price is $50 per share, and you have $5,000 of your own to invest. You borrow an additional $5,000 from your broker at an interest rate of 8 percent per year and invest $10,000 in the stock.

*a.* What will be your rate of return if the price of BCE stock goes up by 10 percent during the next year? (Ignore the expected dividend.)

*b.* How far does the price of BCE stock have to fall for you to get a margin call if the maintenance margin is 30 percent?

**9.** You are bearish on BCE stock and decide to sell short 100 shares at the current market price of $50 per share.

*a.* How much in cash or securities must you put into your brokerage account if the broker's initial margin requirement is 50 percent of the value of the short position?

*b.* How high can the price of the stock go before you get a margin call if the maintenance margin is 30 percent of the value of the short position?

**10.** Call one full-service broker and one discount broker and find out the transaction costs of implementing the following strategies:

*a.* Buying 100 shares of Seagram's now and selling them six months from now.

*b.* Investing an equivalent amount in six-month at-the-money call options (calls with strike prices equal to their stock prices) on Seagram's stock now and selling them six months from now.

Questions 11, 14, and 15 are from the 1986 Level I CFA examination:**

**11.** If you place a stop-loss order to sell 100 shares of stock at $55 when the current price is $62, how much will you receive for each share if the price drops to $50?

*a.* $50.

*b.* $55.

*c.* $54⅞.

*d.* Cannot tell from the information given.

**12.** You've borrowed $20,000 on margin to buy shares in Disney, which is now selling at $80 per share. Your account starts at the initial margin requirement of 50 percent. The maintenance margin is 35 percent. Two days later, the stock price falls to $75 per share.

*a.* Will you receive a margin call?

---

** Reprinted with permission of AIMR. 

*b.* How low can the price of Disney shares fall before you receive a margin call?

**13.** On January 1, you sold short one round lot (that is, 100 shares) of Zenith stock at $14 per share. On March 1, a dividend of $2 per share was paid. On April 1, you covered the short sale by buying the stock at a price of $9 per share. You paid 50 cents per share in commissions for each transaction. What is the value of your account on April 1?

**14.** You wish to sell short 100 shares of XYZ Corporation stock. If the last two transactions were at $34\frac{1}{8}$ followed by $34\frac{1}{4}$, you only can sell short on the next transaction at a price of

*a.* $34\frac{1}{8}$ or higher

*b.* $34\frac{1}{4}$ or higher

*c.* $34\frac{1}{4}$ or lower

*d.* $34\frac{1}{8}$ or lower

**15.** Specialists on the New York Stock Exchange do all of the following *except:*

*a.* Act as dealers for their own accounts.

*b.* Execute limit orders.

*c.* Help provide liquidity to the marketplace.

*d.* Act as odd-lot dealers.

*Chapter 4*

# Individuals and Institutional Investors

**SO FAR, WE HAVE INTRODUCED WHY, WHERE, AND HOW INVESTORS IMPLEMENT DECISIONS TO MAKE CAPITAL INVESTMENTS IN THE FINANCIAL MARKETS.** In the following parts of the book, we will learn details of the theories and practices involved in those investment decisions. Investment is always dependent on desired consumption levels over the life cycle, and individuals attempt to reduce the uncertainty surrounding future consumption; they do this by hedging or insuring against the risks that confront them. As investors age, they devote an increasing amount of attention to guaranteeing a comfortable retirement income, rather than to improving current consumption.

The choices of individual investors can be made by directly using the concepts we shall develop or they can be left to professionals with far greater experience in the field. With that in mind, we shall look at two of the most important institutional players in the investment field: mutual funds serve investors' needs to increase their wealth and income for consumption as needed, while pension funds aim to provide investors with steady income upon retirement. The discussion provided here focuses on the actions that these institutions take in order to satisfy their clients' needs. Terms and concepts that will later be clarified are used here to illustrate how these aspects of investment are important to individual decisions and what are the implications of the relationship between individuals and institutions. Individuals have direct control over the choice between mutual funds that might manage their discretionary savings. In contrast, their employers make the decisions about which pension funds will manage their (involuntary) savings, deducted from their income. Tax considerations also affect the choice of investment vehicles and dictate the appropriate instruments to be used by professional managers. Investors often choose to shelter income and savings out of the desire to minimize the payment of unnecessary taxes.

This chapter relates the individual's investment needs to various institutions, including the tax system, as it describes the details of how these institutions function. At the same time, it provides a perspective on the environment that causes investment decisions to be made; in some of the topics, issues will be raised that will anticipate more formal development in the following chapters. Here, we will see how individuals respond to personal needs in choosing an investment strategy. We also will see how a number of institutional investors serve those individual needs and, as a result, are limited in the kinds of investment strategies that they employ. We conclude with a brief presentation of the Canadian tax system and how individuals respond to it in trying to maximize their after-tax income.

## 4.1 The Life Cycle and the Risk-Return Trade-Off

### Human Capital, Insurance, and Personal Assets

The first significant investment decision for most individuals concerns education, building up their human capital. The major asset most people have during their early working years is the earning power that draws on their human capital. In these circumstances, the risk of illness or injury is far greater than the risk associated with their financial wealth.

The most direct way of hedging human capital risk is to purchase insurance. Viewing the combination of your labour income and a disability insurance policy as a portfolio, the rate of return on this portfolio is less risky than the labour income by itself. Life insurance is a hedge against the complete loss of income as a result of the death of any of the family's income earners.

Insurance is not limited to covering loss of life and income, however; besides insuring personal assets and health, insurance can be used to accumulate retirement savings and do so in a way that has tax benefits. We shall illustrate this in more detail in Section 4.5, where we discuss tax deferral.

The first major economic asset acquired by most people is a personal residence. This is a financial investment that requires an evaluation of potential appreciation in residential values in light of rental expense. When we consider real estate investment as a diversifying alternative, it is important to recognize the degree of direct exposure from a personal residence; in many cases, a personal portfolio may be over-weighted in real estate.

The risk in this area is correlated to risk in human capital. Individuals are first exposed to the risk of a downturn in their employer's industry or factors affecting the firm itself. Should the individual lose his or her job, the necessity of moving, with associated expenses and the risk of housing prices, presents itself. Hence, the investment portfolio should attempt to diversify away from the industry sector and real estate, if the latter is over-weighted.

Other personal assets also can be considered. Art, jewelry, and cars may represent possibilities to individuals. Because of the illiquidity of these assets, however, investment should only be made if there is also a great degree of personal satisfaction associated with the objects.

## Saving for Retirement and the Assumption of Risk

People save and invest money to provide for future consumption and leave an estate. The primary aim of lifetime savings is to allow maintenance of the customary standard of living after retirement. Life expectancy, when one makes it to retirement at age 65, approaches 85 years, so the average retiree needs to prepare a 20-year nest egg and sufficient savings to cover unexpected health-care costs. Investment income also may increase the welfare of one's heirs, favourable charity, or both.

The leisure that investment income can be expected to produce depends on the degree of risk the household is willing to take with its investment portfolio. Empirical observation summarized in Table 4.1 indicates how a person's age and stage in the life cycle affects attitude toward risk.

The evidence in Table 4.1 supports the life-cycle view of investment behaviour. Questionnaires suggest that attitudes shift away from risk tolerance and toward risk aversion as investors near retirement age. With age, individuals lose the potential to recover from a disastrous investment performance. When they are young, investors can respond to a loss by working harder and saving more of their income. But as retirement approaches, investors realize there will be less time to recover. Hence, the shift to safe assets. See the accompanying box for some recent responses to the changing circumstances.

**Table 4.1** Amount of Risk That Investors Said They Were Willing to Take (by Age)

| | Under 35 | 35–54 | 55 and Over |
|---|---|---|---|
| No risk | 54% | 57% | 71% |
| A little risk | 30% | 30% | 21% |
| Some risk | 14% | 18% | 8% |
| A lot of risk | 2% | 1% | 1% |

From Market Facts, Inc., Chicago, Ill. Reprinted by permission.

## INVESTMENT SHIFTS TO SUIT LIFESTYLE

There's a new type of mutual fund in the United States that may come to Canada soon. Called lifestyle funds, these offer a strategy to vary the level of risk to match your own risk tolerance.

The funds—with names like LifePath (Wells Fargo & Co.), Lifestage (T. Rowe Price Associates Inc.), Generation (Aetna Life Insurance & Annuity Co.) and Life Solutions (State Street Global Advisors)—have proved popular with employers and their retirement plans. Some automatically change risk levels over time to reflect perceived changes in your lifestyle.

The theory is that you have a greater appetite for risk in your middle years, when you are starting to plan for retirement. As working years grow shorter, you shift into less volatile investments to reduce your exposure to market swings.

Fine-tuning your portfolio as you get older is something you can do yourself—and many people do. But others who find mutual funds a mystery might appreciate handing the job to a professional manager.

The only comparable products in Canada are asset allocation funds, which divide your money among different asset classes and shift the mix regularly. But the determining factor is changing market conditions, not your age or risk tolerance.

Asset allocation funds have been around only a few years and have shown mixed returns. The jury is still out on whether they are better than a balanced fund with a fixed mix.

"Old wine in new bottles," is how Stephen Gadsden describes asset allocation funds. He's the author of *Understanding Life Cycle Investing* (McGraw-Hill Ryerson, $19.99), a new book that tells Canadians how to invest in mutual funds with their age and risk tolerance in mind.

Mr. Gadsden, who runs a Fortune Financial Corp. mutual fund dealership in Richmond Hill, Ont., is a former academic with a master's degree in psychology. It's this background that led him to formulate a five-stage life cycle with the trademarked name of Active Investment Management (AIM).

The stages are:

- The early years, ages 20 to 30. You are launching a career and your income is relatively modest. In the midst of marriage, starting a family and buying a home, you gravitate to conservative investments such as term deposits and money market funds. You value liquidity and capital preservation, not growth.
- The aggressive years, ages 30 to 40. Your career has matured and you have more money for debt reduction or longer-term investments. You want above-average growth potential and you're willing to accept higher levels of risk. Liquidity is less important now, but tax savings are highly valued.
- The consolidation years, ages 40 to 50. You have experienced some success and started earning serious money. Your debts are getting whittled down and you are devoting more time to investing. The emphasis is on balance. You want security and income, without sacrificing aggressive growth.
- The preretirement years, ages 50 to 60. You have entered your peak earnings years and amassed some assets. In anticipation of retirement, you're starting to scale down your aggressive growth funds in favour of those that provide higher dividends, less volatility, and more liquidity.
- The retirement years, ages 60 and beyond. At the start of a new life, you hope to preserve your retirement assets and make them generate a constant, stable income. Although moving primarily into fixed-income securities, you keep a small component (about 20 percent) in common stocks or equity funds.

After identifying investments appropriate to your life stage, you can then integrate your personal fi-

*(Continued)*

nancial goals. For example, a 35-year-old man would focus on growth. But if he needs cash reserve for emergencies and liquidity for his teenaged children's education fund, he's better off varying the mix.

One of the toughest tasks for investors is to build a mutual fund portfolio that reflects who they are. This book tries to address this vexing question, which is often overlooked in other fund guides.

Ellen Roseman, *The Globe and Mail,* May 24, 1995, p. B9. Reprinted by permission.

**CONCEPT CHECK** Question 1.

*a.* Think about the financial circumstances of your closest relative in your parents' generation (preferably your parents' household, if you are fortunate enough to have them around). Write down the objectives and constraints for their investment decisions.

*b.* Now consider the financial situation of your closest relative who is in his or her 30s. Write down the objectives and constraints that would fit his or her investment decision.

*c.* How much of the difference between the two statements is due to the age of the investors?

## 4.2 MANAGEMENT BY INSTITUTIONS

Investors can be differentiated as individuals and institutions. A frequent lament is that individuals appear to be abandoning the markets to the institutions. As small investors, individuals are thought to provide liquidity to the market, which institutional portfolios are too large to do. Nevertheless, individuals provide the funds to the institutions to invest; although individuals have no immediate control over pension funds, mutual funds must respond by buying and selling as their investors add or withdraw cash. This process should still channel funds to the best investment opportunities.

Institutions must attempt to interpret and serve the requirements of households in making their investment decisions. Generally, the household sector equates to individuals, but occasionally there will be **personal trusts.**[1] The institutions that respond to household needs by investing in stock and bond markets include mutual funds, pension funds, endowment funds, and life insurance companies. Casualty insurance companies, like banks and trust companies, tend to have more

[1] These are established when an individual confers legal title to another person or institution (the trustee) to manage that property for one or more beneficiaries. The beneficiaries are of two types, essentially, those entitled to a life income and those entitled to the remaining principal upon death of the former. By definition of the objective of the trust, the options of the trustee are limited; the requirements have been made much clearer for the trustee than for individuals.

conservative investments, with shorter maturities, due to the nature of their cash payouts. Each of the institutions must tailor its policies to the needs of its clients and the regulations or circumstances guiding it. We shall examine how these respond accordingly, with particular attention to mutual funds and pension funds.

A formal process for making investment decisions has been established by the Association for Investment Management and Research (AIMR), established by the merger of the Financial Analysts Federation (FAF) with the Institute of Chartered Financial Analysts (ICFA). The idea is to subdivide the major steps (objectives, constraints, and policies) into concrete considerations of the various aspects, making the process more tractable. The standard format appears in Table 4.2, and we shall discuss the three parts of the process in turn.

## Institutions and Their Objectives

Portfolio objectives centre on the risk-return trade-off between the expected return the investors want (*return requirements* in the first column of Table 4.2) and how much risk they are willing to assume (*risk tolerance*). Investment managers must know the level of risk that can be tolerated in the pursuit of a better rate of return. Table 4.3 lists factors governing return requirements and risk attitudes for each of the seven major investor categories discussed.

For mutual funds, the objectives are spelled out precisely in the prospectus. Individuals and trustees can be guided by those statements, even if the objectives are not guaranteed to be met. A detailed discussion follows in the next section.

Pension funds usually are categorized as **defined contribution plans** or **defined benefit plans.** The former are, in effect, tax-deferred retirement savings accounts established by the firm in trust for its employees; the employees bear all the risk and receive all the return from the plans' assets. In the second form, which are predominate, the assets serve as collateral for the liabilities that the firm sponsoring the plan owes to the plan beneficiaries. The difference between the two is crucial to how the objective is defined and how the plan will be directed, as we see in Section 4.4.

**Endowment funds** are organizations chartered to use their money for specific nonprofit purposes. They are financed by gifts from one or more sponsors and are typically managed by educational, cultural, and charitable organizations or by independent foundations established solely to carry out the fund's specific purposes. Generally, the investment objectives of an endowment fund are to produce a steady flow of income subject to only a moderate degree of risk. Trustees of an endowment fund, however, can specify other objectives as dictated by the circumstances of the particular endowment fund.

Life insurance companies generally try to invest so as to hedge their liabilities, which are defined by the policies they write. Thus, there are as many objectives as there are distinct types of policies. Until a decade or so ago there were only two types of life insurance policies available for individuals: whole-life and term. A **whole-life insurance policy** combines a death benefit with a kind of savings plan that provides for a gradual buildup of cash value that the policyholder can

**Table 4.2** Determination of Portfolio Policies

| Objectives | Constraints | Policies |
|---|---|---|
| Return requirements | Liquidity | Asset allocation |
| Risk tolerance | Horizon | Diversification |
| | Regulations | Risk positioning |
| | Taxes | Tax positioning |
| | Unique needs | Income generation |

**Table 4.3** Matrix of Objectives

| Type of Investor | Return Requirement | Risk Tolerance |
|---|---|---|
| Individual and personal trusts | Life cycle (education, children, retirement) | Life cycle (younger: more risk tolerant) |
| Mutual funds | Variable | Variable |
| Pension funds | Assumed actuarial rate | Depends on proximity of payouts |
| Endowment funds | Determined by current income needs and need for asset growth to maintain real value | Generally conservative |
| Life insurance companies | Should exceed new money rate by sufficient margin to meet expenses and profit objectives; also actuarial rates important | Conservative |
| Nonlife insurance companies | No minimum | Conservative |
| Banks | Interest spread | Variable |

withdraw at a later point in life, usually at age 65. **Term insurance,** on the other hand, provides death benefits only, with no buildup of cash value.

The interest rate embedded in the schedule of cash value accumulation promised under a whole-life policy is a fixed rate; life insurance companies try to hedge this liability by investing in long-term bonds. Often, the insured individual has the right to borrow at a prespecified fixed interest rate against the cash value of the policy.

During the inflationary years of the 1970s and early 1980s, when many older whole-life policies carried contractual borrowing rates as low as 4 percent or 5 percent per year, policyholders borrowed heavily against the cash value to invest in money market mutual funds paying double-digit yields. Other actual and potential policyholders abandoned whole-life policies and took out term insurance, investing the difference in the premiums on their own.

In response to the public's change in tastes, the insurance industry came up with some new policy types, of which two are of particular interest to investors: **variable life** and **universal life.**[2] Under a variable life policy, the insured's premium buys a fixed death benefit plus a cash value that can be invested in a variety of mutual funds from which the policyholder can choose. With a universal life policy, policyholders can increase or reduce the premium or death benefit according to their changing needs. Furthermore, the interest rate on the cash value component changes with market interest rates. These two plans effectively unbundle the charges for insurance and savings. The great advantage of variable and universal life insurance policies is that earnings on the cash value are not taxed until the money is withdrawn.[3]

The life insurance industry also provides services or products in the pension area, these being the sale of annuities and pension fund management service. Prior to the introduction of the Registered Retirement Savings Plan (RRSP) for individual retirement planning, the monopolistic sale by insurance companies of annuities was a major source of income. The insurance industry must now compete with other financial intermediaries for the sale of RRSPs. The RRSP must, however, be collapsed into an annuity or a Registered Retirement Income Fund (RRIF); since RRIFs are less popular than annuities, which may only be offered by insurance companies, the industry has benefited from the wide adoption of RRSPs.

Since the cash flow characteristics of life insurance and pensions are quite similar, insurance companies have developed expertise in fund management that is transferable to the pension industry. One example of this is the **insured defined benefit pension.** A firm sponsoring a pension plan enters into a contractual agreement by which an insurance company assumes all liability for the benefits accrued under the plan. This guarantee is given in return for an annual premium based on the benefit formula and the number and characteristics of the employees covered by the plan.

## Constraints

Both households and institutional investors restrict their choice of investment assets. These restrictions arise from their specific circumstances. Identifying these restrictions/constraints will affect the choice of investment policy. Five common types of constraints are described below.

**Liquidity** is the ease (speed) with which an asset can be sold and still fetch a fair price. It is a relationship between the time dimension (how long will it take to dispose) and the price dimension (what discount from fair market price) of an investment asset.

---

[2] A third type was *adjustable life,* which enabled the policyholder to vary benefits and premiums according to his or her changing needs.

[3] Investment contracts with insurance features also may be protected against seizure in bankruptcy.

When an actual concrete measure of liquidity is necessary, one thinks of the discount when an immediate sale is unavoidable.[4] Cash and money market instruments, such as Treasury bills and commercial paper, where the bid-asked spread is a fraction of 1 percent, are the most liquid assets, and real estate is among the least liquid. Office buildings and manufacturing structures can easily be assessed a 50 percent liquidity discount.

Both individual and institutional investors must consider how likely they are to dispose of assets at short notice. From this likelihood, they establish the minimum level of liquid assets they want in the investment portfolio.

The **investment horizon** is the planned liquidation date of all or part of the investment; for example, it might be the time to fund college education or the retirement date for a wage earner. For a university endowment, an investment horizon could relate to the time needed to fund a major campus construction project. Horizon needs to be considered when investors choose between assets of various maturities, such as bonds, which pay off at specified future dates.

Only professional and institutional investors are constrained by *regulations.* First and foremost is the **prudent man** law. That is, professional investors who manage other people's money have a fiduciary responsibility to restrict investment to assets that would have been approved by a prudent investor. The law is purposefully nonspecific. Every professional investor must stand ready to defend an investment policy in a court of law, and interpretation may differ according to the standards of the times.

Also, specific regulations apply to various institutional investors. For instance, Canadian pension portfolios are limited to a 20 percent maximum holding of foreign assets, as are individual retirement portfolios. Similarly, provincial legislation governs mutual fund holdings, imposing a maximum on the percentage of ownership in a single corporation; this regulation keeps professional investors from getting involved in the actual management of corporations.

Tax consequences are central to investment decisions. The performance of any investment strategy should be measured by how much it yields in real, after-tax investment returns. For household and institutional investors who face significant tax rates, tax sheltering and deferral of tax obligations may be pivotal in their investment strategy.

## Unique Needs

Virtually every investor faces special circumstances. Imagine husband-and-wife aeronautical engineers holding high-paying jobs in the same aerospace corporation. The entire human capital of that household is tied to a single player in a

[4] In most cases, it is impossible to know the liquidity of an asset with certainty, before it is put up for sale. In dealer markets (described in Chapter 3), however, the liquidity of the traded assets can be observed from the bid-asked spread that is quoted by the dealers, that is, the difference between the "bid" quote (the lower price the dealer will pay the owner) and the "asked" quote (the higher price a buyer would have to pay the dealer).

**Table 4.4** Matrix of Constraints

| Type of Investor | Liquidity | Horizon | Regulatory | Taxes |
|---|---|---|---|---|
| Individuals and personal trusts | Variable | Life cycle | None | Variable |
| Mutual funds | Low | Short | Little | None |
| Pension funds | Young, low; mature, high | Long | Some (federal) | None |
| Endowment funds | Little | Long | Little | None |
| Life insurance companies | Low | Long | Complex | Yes |
| Nonlife insurance companies | High | Short | Little | Yes |
| Banks | Low | Short | Changing | Yes |

rather cyclical industry. This couple would need to hedge the risk (find investment assets that yield more when the risk materializes, thus partly insuring against the risk) of a deterioration in the economic well-being of the aerospace industry.

An example of a unique need for an institutional investor is a university whose trustees let the administration use only cash income from the endowment fund. This constraint would translate into a preference for high-dividend-paying assets.

Table 4.4 presents a summary of the importance of each of the general constraints to each of the seven types of investors.

## 4.3 Mutual Funds and Other Investment Companies

Throughout the 1980s and 1990s, investors have increasingly turned to mutual funds to make their decisions for them, and funds have mushroomed over that period in number, size, and variety. With over $200 billion of assets under management, mutual funds are a dominant force in the financial markets. What they choose to favour or reject will rise and fall in price accordingly, and prices will change rapidly if different companies concurrently reach the same decision. We shall examine here how these institutions work and perhaps what is the appeal that they hold for individual investors.

### Mutual Funds

Mutual funds are firms that manage pools of other people's money. Individuals buy shares of mutual funds, and the funds invest the money in certain specified types of assets (e.g., common stocks, tax-exempt bonds, and mortgages). The shares issued to the investors entitle them to a pro rata portion of the income generated by these assets.

Mutual funds perform several important functions for their shareholders:

1. *Record keeping and administration.* The funds prepare periodic status reports and reinvest dividends and interest.
2. *Diversification and divisibility.* By pooling their money, investment companies enable shareholders to hold fractional shares of many different securities. Funds can act as large investors even if any individual shareholder cannot, providing liquidity to investors in terms of their ability to increase or decrease their holdings, as desired.
3. *Professional management.* Many, but not all, mutual funds have full-time staffs of security analysts and portfolio managers who attempt to achieve superior investment results for their shareholders.
4. *Lower transaction costs.* By trading large blocks of securities, investment companies can achieve substantial savings on brokerage fees and commissions.
5. *Increased investment opportunities.* Investment companies enable investors to enter many markets that are inaccessible to them as individuals, such as foreign markets, indices, specific types of instruments, and specific sectors of the economy.

There are two types of mutual funds: **closed-end funds** and **open-end funds.** Open-end funds stand ready to redeem or issue shares at their net asset value (NAV), which is the market value of all securities held divided by the number of shares outstanding. The number of shares outstanding of an open-end fund changes daily, as investors buy new shares or redeem old ones. Closed-end funds do not redeem or issue shares at net asset value. Shares of closed-end funds are traded through brokers, as are other common stocks, and their price can therefore differ from NAV.[5]

The prices of closed-end funds are listed with other shares in the financial pages. Single-country funds in which capital is invested in a single foreign country, are generally closed-end. The NAV must be obtained from other sources offering specific information about funds; the majority of closed-end funds trade at a discount, typically of about 10 percent of NAV.

Many investors consider closed-end fund shares selling at a discount to their NAV to be a true bargain. Even if the market price never rises to the level of NAV, the dividend yield on an investment in the fund would exceed the dividend yield on the same securities held outside the fund. To see this, imagine a fund with a NAV of $10 per share and a market price of $9 that pays an annual dividend of $1 per share. Its dividend yield based on NAV is 10 percent per year, which is the yield obtainable by buying the securities directly. But the dividend yield to someone buying shares in the fund at $9 would be 11.11 percent per year.

The market price of open-end funds, on the other hand, cannot fall below NAV because these funds redeem shares at NAV. The price at which the fund can be bought or sold will differ from NAV, however, if the fund carries a load. Shares

[5] The divergence of the market price of a closed-end fund's shares from NAV constitutes a major puzzle, which has yet to be satisfactorily explained by finance theorists.

of a **load fund** are sold by security brokers, many insurance brokers, and others. A load is in effect a sales commission, usually from 3 percent to 8.5 percent of NAV, which is paid to the seller. More recently, the practice has arisen of charging the load upon redemption, if the fund is cashed in within less than five years. Thus, the load also serves to deter movement in and out of the fund.

Shares of a **no-load fund** are bought directly from the fund at NAV and carry no sales charge. The investment performance of no-load funds does not differ systematically from that of load funds, so it would seem that an investor who buys into a load fund is simply paying the retail price for an equivalent item readily available wholesale.

Figure 4.1 shows part of the listings for mutual funds published every weekday in *The Globe and Mail.* As explained, funds are identified as charging a front-end or redemption load, or none. Some are seen to be unavailable or closed; this indicates that the managers do not wish to pool further capital with that fund due to excessive size.

At the end of 1993, there were 826 open-end mutual funds with assets of close to $127 billion. Of these, 108 were money market funds with assets of almost $16,666 million. Table 4.5 gives a breakdown of the number of mutual funds and their assets by size and type of fund at the end of 1993.

## Management Companies and Mutual Fund Investment Policies

Management companies are firms that manage a family of mutual funds. They typically organize the funds and then collect a management fee for operating them. Some of the best-known management companies are AGF, Altamira, Guardian, and Investors; also, most major banks and trust companies direct a variety of funds. Each offers an array of open-end mutual funds with different investment policies. Table 4.6. lists the 12 largest mutual fund families and discusses some of their features.

Figure 4.1 also gives a listing of the funds offered by Altamira. Generally, the name of each fund describes its investment policy; thus, there are funds that are formed to provide income from dividends and/or interest, to pursue growth, to focus on industry sectors, or to focus on various geographical areas. Some funds have names that provide little indication as to their investment policies (such as the AltaFund); one must consult the fund prospectus for a clear definition in these cases.

Some funds are designed as candidates for an individual's whole investment portfolio. Such funds, which hold both equities and fixed-income securities, can be classified as *income* or *balanced funds.* Wiesenberger's manual,[6] which provides information on U.S. funds, comments that income funds "provide as liberal a current income from investments as possible," whereas balanced funds "minimize investment risks so far as this is possible without unduly sacrificing possibilities for long-term growth and current income."

[6] *Investment Companies, 1987,* Wiesenberger Investment Companies Services.

**Figure 4.1**
Canadian Mutual Funds

*The Globe and Mail,* Thursday, May 16, 1996. Reprinted by permission.

# Canadian Mutual Funds

## The Globe and Mail, Thursday, May 16, 1996

**Recent prices of investment funds supplied by Fundata Canada Inc. at 5:45 p.m. May 15. Prices reported by funds are the net asset value per share or unit last calculated and are for information purposes only. Confirmation of price should be obtained from the fund. Chg—penny change from last valuation; D—distributed by fund sponsor; G—redemption charge; I—distributed by independent dealers; L—sales charge; N—no sales charge; O—optional front—end or redemption charge; R—eligible for RRSPs; Z—not available for sale; m—minimum purchase of $150,000; u—U.S. currency; x—ex—dividend; (n)—not a member of IFIC; (Date following fund denotes last valuation).**

| Fund | Load | RSP | Dist | Val | Chg |
|---|---|---|---|---|---|
| **ABC FUNDS** | | | | | |
| mFully-Mgd 04/30 | N | R | D | 8.02 | — |
| mFund-Value 04/30 | N | R | D | 11.34 | — |
| **ACADIA INVESTMENT FUNDS** | | | | | |
| Balanced 05/14 | N | R | | 10.65 | +.03 |
| Bond 05/14 | N | R | | 10.43 | +.01 |
| Mortgage 05/14 | N | R | | 10.00 | unch |
| **ADMAX REGENT GROUP** | | | | | |
| A.Amer Sel Gth | O | | I | 5.39 | +.05 |
| A.Asset All | O | R | I | 13.31 | +.07 |
| A.Cdn Perf | O | R | I | 7.22 | +.03 |
| A.Cdn Sel Gth | O | R | I | 5.41 | +.03 |
| A.Glo Hlth | O | | I | 11.75 | +.06 |
| R.Dragon 888 | O | | I | 7.70 | -.03 |
| R.Europa | O | | I | 10.24 | +.02 |
| R.Intl | O | | I | 6.34 | -.02 |
| R.Korea | O | | I | 12.46 | -.07 |
| R.Nippon | O | | I | 12.73 | +.20 |
| R.Tiger | O | | I | 12.10 | -.10 |
| R.World Inc | O | R | I | 12.21 | +.01 |
| **AGF GROUP C$ SERIES A** | | | | | |
| Amer Grth | L | | I | 14.23 | -.04 |
| Asian Grth | L | | I | 16.25 | -.10 |
| Cdn Bond | L | R | I | 5.13 | +.02 |
| Cdn Equity | L | R | I | 14.02 | +.06 |
| Cdn Resources | L | R | I | 20.31 | +.17 |
| China Focus | L | | I | 7.54 | unch |
| Euro Growth | L | | I | 10.46 | -.04 |
| Germany | L | | I | 20.75 | +.12 |
| Glo GovtBond | L | | I | 10.38 | unch |
| Grth & Income | L | R | I | 18.86 | +.17 |
| Grth Equity | L | R | I | 24.17 | -.01 |
| High Income | L | R | I | 9.88 | -.02 |
| Intl ST Income | L | | I | 10.85 | -.01 |
| Japan | L | | I | 5.36 | +.07 |
| Resource Cap | L | R | I | 9.92 | +.07 |
| Special | L | | I | 12.76 | +.03 |
| Strategic Inc | L | R | I | 9.41 | unch |
| US Income | L | | I | 10.50 | -.01 |
| World Equity | L | | I | 6.53 | -.02 |
| **AGF GROUP C$ SERIES B** | | | | | |
| Amer Grth | G | | I | 14.10 | -.04 |
| Asian Grth | G | | I | 16.13 | -.09 |
| Cdn Bond | G | R | I | 5.12 | +.01 |
| Cdn Equity | G | R | I | 13.90 | +.06 |
| Cdn Resources | G | R | I | 20.17 | +.17 |
| China Focus | G | | I | 7.46 | -.01 |
| Euro Growth | G | | I | 10.36 | -.03 |
| Germany | G | | I | 20.60 | +.11 |
| Glo GovtBond | G | | I | 10.37 | unch |
| Grth & Income | G | R | I | 18.71 | +.17 |
| Grth Equity | G | R | I | 23.99 | -.01 |
| High Income | G | R | I | 9.87 | -.02 |
| Intl ST Income | G | | I | 10.72 | unch |
| Japan | G | | I | 5.32 | +.07 |
| Special | G | | I | 12.66 | +.03 |
| Strategic Inc | G | R | I | 9.41 | +.01 |
| US Income | G | | I | 10.51 | -.01 |
| World Equity | G | | I | 6.50 | -.02 |
| **AGF GROUP C$ SERIES C** | | | | | |
| Amer Grth | N | | I | 14.07 | -.04 |
| Asian Grth | N | | I | 16.16 | -.09 |
| Cdn Bond | N | R | I | 5.11 | +.01 |
| Cdn Equity | N | R | I | 13.90 | +.06 |
| Cdn Resources | N | R | I | 20.18 | +.17 |
| China Focus | N | | I | 7.45 | unch |
| Euro Growth | N | | I | 10.38 | -.03 |
| Germany | N | | I | 20.59 | +.11 |
| Glo GovtBond | N | | I | 10.35 | unch |
| Grth & Income | N | R | I | 18.68 | +.16 |
| Grth Equity | N | R | I | 23.94 | -.01 |
| High Income | N | R | I | 9.84 | -.02 |
| Intl ST Income | N | | I | 10.78 | unch |
| Japan | N | | I | 5.31 | +.06 |
| Special | N | | I | 12.66 | +.03 |
| Strategic Inc | N | R | I | 9.41 | +.01 |
| US Income | N | | I | 10.48 | -.01 |
| World Equity | N | | I | 6.50 | -.02 |
| **AGF GROUP U$ SERIES A** | | | | | |
| uAmer Grth | L | | I | 10.40 | -.01 |
| uAsian Grth | L | | I | 11.88 | -.05 |
| uChina Focus | L | | I | 5.51 | unch |
| uEuro Growth | L | | I | 7.65 | -.01 |
| uGermany | L | | I | 15.16 | +.10 |
| uGlo GovtBond | L | | I | 7.59 | +.01 |
| uIntl ST Income | L | | I | 7.93 | unch |
| uJapan | L | | I | 3.92 | +.06 |
| uSpecial | L | | I | 9.33 | +.04 |
| uUS Income | L | | I | 7.67 | unch |
| uWorld Equity | L | | I | 4.77 | -.01 |
| **AGF GROUP U$ SERIES B** | | | | | |
| uAmer Grth | G | | I | 10.30 | -.02 |
| uAsian Grth | G | | I | 11.79 | -.05 |
| uChina Focus | G | | I | 5.46 | +.01 |
| uEuro Growth | G | | I | 7.57 | -.01 |
| uGermany | G | | I | 15.05 | +.10 |
| uGlo GovtBond | G | | I | 7.58 | +.01 |
| uIntl ST Income | G | | I | 7.83 | +.01 |
| uJapan | G | | I | 3.89 | +.06 |
| uSpecial | G | | I | 9.26 | +.04 |
| uUS Income | G | | I | 7.68 | unch |
| uWorld Equity | G | | I | 4.75 | -.01 |
| **AGF GROUP U$ SERIES C** | | | | | |
| uAmer Grth | N | | I | 10.29 | -.01 |
| uAsian Grth | N | | I | 11.81 | -.05 |
| uChina Focus | N | | I | 5.44 | unch |
| uEuro Growth | N | | I | 7.58 | -.02 |
| uGermany | N | | I | 15.05 | +.10 |
| uGlo GovtBond | N | | I | 7.56 | +.01 |
| uIntl ST Income | N | | I | 7.88 | +.01 |
| uJapan | N | | I | 3.88 | +.05 |
| uSpecial | N | | I | 9.25 | +.03 |
| uUS Income | N | | I | 7.66 | unch |
| uWorld Equity | N | | I | 4.75 | -.01 |
| **AGF MANAGEMENT** | | | | | |
| Germany C$ M | O | | Z | 21.07 | +.11 |
| uGermany U$ M | O | | Z | 15.40 | +.10 |
| **AIC GROUP** | | | | | |
| Advantage | O | R | I | 34.48 | +.16 |
| Divers Cda | O | R | I | 15.09 | -.02 |
| Emerg Markets | O | | I | 8.94 | unch |
| Value | O | | I | 24.43 | +.07 |
| World Equity | O | | I | 11.27 | +.06 |
| **ALL-CANADIAN** | | | | | |
| Capital | L | R | I | 12.45 | -.01 |
| Compound | L | R | Z | 16.17 | -.02 |
| Consumer | L | R | I | 3.47 | unch |
| Resources | L | R | I | 4.57 | -.02 |
| **ALTAMIRA** | | | | | |
| AltaFund | N | R | I | 21.43 | +.06 |
| Asia Pacific | N | | I | 13.53 | -.06 |
| Balanced | N | R | I | 14.82 | unch |
| Bond | N | R | I | 13.25 | +.03 |
| Cap Growth | N | R | I | 15.36 | -.01 |
| Dividend | N | R | I | 2.73 | -.01 |
| Equity | N | R | I | 33.07 | +.04 |
| European Equ | N | | I | 12.68 | +.03 |
| Glo Bond | N | R | I | 10.37 | -.02 |
| Glo Discovery | N | | I | 4.50 | unch |
| Glo Diversified | N | | I | 14.21 | +.01 |
| Growth & Inc | N | R | I | 8.19 | -.01 |
| Hi Yield Bond | N | | I | 5.27 | -.01 |
| Income | N | R | I | 7.64 | +.02 |
| Japanese | N | | I | 4.61 | +.06 |
| Precious Metal | N | R | I | 9.33 | -.02 |
| Recovery | N | R | I | 12.16 | -.03 |
| Resource | N | R | I | 16.63 | +.03 |
| ST Global Inc | N | R | I | 11.94 | -.03 |
| ST Govt Bond | N | R | I | 5.45 | unch |
| Science & Tech | N | | I | 7.14 | +.05 |
| Select Amer | N | | I | 27.85 | +.10 |
| Special Gro | N | R | I | 18.77 | +.07 |
| US Larger Co | N | | I | 14.97 | +.01 |
| **AMI PRIVATE CAPITAL** | | | | | |
| Equity 05/13 | N | R | D | 15.22 | — |
| Income 05/13 | N | R | D | 9.90 | — |
| Optimix 05/13 | N | R | D | 13.49 | — |
| **A.P.P.Q.(n)** | | | | | |
| Balanced 05/10 | N | R | | 14.49 | — |
| **ASSOCIATE INVESTORS** | | | | | |
| Assoc Inv | N | R | D | 8.04 | +.02 |
| **ATLAS ASSET MGT: ATLAS** | | | | | |
| Am Advantage C$ | N | | I | 14.78 | -.07 |
| uAm Advantage U$ | N | | I | 10.80 | -.05 |
| Am EmergVal C$ | N | | I | 11.05 | unch |
| uAm EmergVal U$ | N | | I | 8.08 | +.01 |
| Am LrgCap Gr C$ | N | | I | 21.29 | +.05 |
| uAm LrgCap Gr U$ | N | | I | 15.56 | +.04 |
| Am LrgCapVal C$ | N | | I | 12.47 | +.01 |
| uAm LrgCapVal U$ | N | | I | 9.11 | +.01 |
| Am Opportun C$ | N | | I | 12.67 | +.04 |
| uAm Opportun U$ | N | | I | 9.26 | +.03 |
| Cdn Balanced | N | R | I | 11.49 | +.01 |
| Cdn Bond | N | R | I | 10.07 | +.02 |
| Cdn Diversified | N | R | I | 11.08 | unch |
| Cdn EmergGrth | N | R | I | 16.52 | +.12 |
| Cdn EmergVal | N | R | I | 11.93 | +.13 |
| Cdn HiYldBnd | N | R | I | 10.94 | +.01 |
| Cdn LrgCap Gth | N | R | I | 14.32 | +.05 |
| Cdn LrgCap Val | N | R | I | 11.55 | -.01 |
| Glo Equity | N | | I | 14.94 | unch |
| Mgd Futures C$ 05/14 | N | | I | 12.80 | +.05 |
| uMgd Futures U$ 05/14 | N | | I | 9.35 | +.03 |
| NAFTA | N | | I | 11.75 | -.03 |
| **ATLAS ASSET MGT: HERCULES** | | | | | |
| Em Mkt Debt | N | | I | 10.56 | +.04 |
| Euro Value | N | | I | 11.95 | +.05 |
| Glo Sh Term | N | | I | 10.12 | +.01 |
| Latin Amer | N | | I | 8.29 | unch |
| Pacific Basin | N | | I | 10.05 | unch |
| World Bond | N | R | I | 10.53 | unch |
| **AZURA POOLED FUNDS(n)** | | | | | |
| Balanced 05/09 | O | | I | 10.52 | — |
| Balanced RRSP 05/09 | O | R | I | 10.52 | — |
| Conservative 05/09 | O | | I | 10.25 | — |
| Growth 05/09 | O | | I | 10.97 | — |
| Growth RRSP 05/09 | O | | I | 11.09 | — |

Finally, an **index fund** tries to match the performance of a broad market index. For example, First Canadian Equity Index Fund is a no-load mutual fund that replicates the composition of the TSE 300 index, thus providing a relatively low-cost way for small investors to pursue a passive common stock investment strategy. (Altamira does not offer an index fund.)

**Table 4.5** Classification of Mutual Funds by Type (as of 4th quarter 1993)

| Type of Fund | Number of Funds* | Combined Assets ($ millions) | Percent of Total Assets |
|---|---|---|---|
| Canadian equity | 177 (157) | $ 27,939.1 | 22 |
| U.S. equity | 74 (63) | 4,420.2 | 3.5 |
| International equity | 118 (79) | 18,730.7 | 14.8 |
| Specialty equity | 36 (24) | 1,565 | 1.2 |
| Balanced | 125 (113) | 19,424.7 | 15.3 |
| Preferred dividends | 20 (19) | 3,694.2 | 2.9 |
| Bond | 129 (104) | 16,182.8 | 12.8 |
| Mortgage | 25 (22) | 16,191.3 | 12.8 |
| Bond and mortgage | 8 | 1,370.6 | 1.1 |
| Money market | 108 (102) | 16,665.7 | 13.4 |
| Real estate | 6 | 626.2 | 0.5 |
| Total | 826 (697) | $126,810.5 | 100 |

*Numbers in parentheses represent the funds for which data were available and whose assets were totaled in the next column.

Data from *Mutual Fund Sourcebook,* 1994. Reprinted by permission.

**Table 4.6** The Major Mutual Fund Families

| Family | Total Net Assets ($ millions)* | Number of Funds** | Range of Up-Front or Deferred Sales Charges (%) | Basic Switching Charges |
|---|---|---|---|---|
| AGF Group | 3,860.5 | 16 | 1–14.5 | 2% max |
| Altamira | 4,454.7 | 17 (13) | None | None |
| Bolton Tremblay | 1,084.2 | 13 (11) | 1–11 | 2% max |
| Dynamic Group | 1,574.9 | 15 (14) | 3–13.5 | 2% max |
| Global Strategy | 3,306 | 17 (15) | 9–14.6 | 9% max |
| Industrial Group | 7,355.2 | 15 | 1.5–10.5 | 2% max |
| Investors Group | 19,687.6 | 28 (26) | 1–6 | None |
| Templeton Group | 3,114.2 | 9 | 6–12 | 2% max |
| Toronto-Dominion | 5,055.6 | 25 (18) | None | None |
| Trimark Group | 5,155.8 | 10 (8) | 1–9 | 2% max |
| United Group | 1,071.6 | 12 | 2–14 | 2% max |

*As of fourth quarter 1993.
**Numbers in parentheses represent funds for which data were available and whose assets were used to calculate the previous column.

Data from *Mutual Fund Sourcebook,* 1994. Reprinted by permission.

## Choosing a Mutual Fund

When choosing a mutual fund, an individual investor should consider not only the fund's stated investment policy, but also its management fees and other expenses. There are three types of fees, which we discuss next.

**Front- and Back-End Load.** These fees are paid to cover commissions for selling agents and to deter rapid switching in and out of funds, which is detrimental to keeping the assets fully invested in long-term assets. The front-end load typically can be as high as 8 percent, so that a $1,000 investment only leaves $920 invested in a portfolio; discount brokers will often cut their commission to lower the load fee to the investor, and larger investments rapidly lead to a lower charge. Back-end loads leave the initial investment intact but usually charge 6 percent in the first year, falling by a percent per year, for redemptions; the load may apply to the initial or the final asset value. In addition, there are many no-load funds, which appear to have no poorer performance than their costly cousins.

**Operating Expenses.** These expenses refer to the costs incurred by the mutual fund in operating the portfolio, including administrative expenses and advisory fees paid to the investment manager. These expenses usually are expressed as a percent of total assets under management and may range from .2 to 2.5 percent. Funds may voluntarily lower the actual expenses charged to the portfolio if they are lower than specified by the prospectus.

**Other Charges.** Under U.S. regulations, these additional expenses are known as 12b-1 charges and refer to the use of fund assets to pay for distribution costs, such as advertising, promotional literature (for example, prospectuses), and broker commissions; the latter occurs if a formal load-fee is not charged.

The combination of operating expenses and other charges is expressed as a ratio of total assets and is then referred to as the **management expense ratio.** Comparative data on virtually all important aspects of Canadian mutual funds are available from various sources. For example, Portfolio Analytics Limited has prepared for the discount broker Green Line Investment Services a FundTrak disk. The disk, using the *Financial Post* database, gives information on over 300 funds (including U.S. and international funds). The data provided include performance, management expense ratios and load structures, characterization as to purpose, asset allocation, NAV, dividend payouts, and other relevant material. Similar material on U.S. mutual funds is available in annual volumes provided by Wiesenberger Investment Companies Services.

## Commingled Funds

*Commingled funds* are investment pools managed by financial and insurance companies, as well as by other funds managers for trust or retirement accounts that are too small to warrant managing on a separate basis; they also are used for portions of pension funds restricted to certain areas. A commingled fund is similar in form to an open-end mutual fund. Instead of shares, though, the fund offers units that are bought and sold at net asset value. The manager may offer an array of different commingled funds for trust or retirement accounts to choose from, for example, a money market fund, a bond fund, and a common stock fund. In certain cases, these funds may be formed as *unit investment trusts* as a means of avoiding realization of gains when assets are sold and the proceeds reinvested. The holding in the trust is not deemed to be realized, so that tax or other regulatory consequences can be avoided, but the composition of the portfolio can be adjusted to meet market conditions. (The concept of unit investment trust has another interpretation in the United States.)

### Real Estate Limited Partnerships and Mortgage Funds

A *real estate limited partnership* functions similarly to a closed-end mutual fund, using leverage to purchase real estate. Partnership units are sold to the public to raise equity capital, which is leveraged by borrowing from banks and issuing mortgages. *Mortgage funds* invest directly in mortgages by purchasing pass-through securities of different maturities; they tend to be managed by banks or trust companies. A limited partnership, by its very construction, pays no income taxes; all income or loss is recognized in the hands of its unit holders. The mortgage funds are treated as any other mutual fund, for tax purposes.

The equivalent U.S. institution occupies a significant niche in the market, responding to perceived inflation and interest rates. The real estate investment trust (REIT) can take the form of either an equity or a mortgage trust. REITs generally are established by banks, insurance companies, or mortgage companies, which then serve as investment managers to earn a fee.

## 4.4 Pension Funds

### Defined Contribution versus Defined Benefit Plans

Although employer pension programs vary in design, they usually are classified into two broad types: defined contribution and defined benefit. Under a *defined contribution* (DC) plan, each employee has an account into which the employer and the employee (in a contributory plan) make regular contributions. Benefit levels depend on the total contributions and investment earnings of the accumulation in the account.

In a *defined benefit* (DB) plan, the employee's pension benefit entitlement is determined by a formula that takes into account years of service for the employer and, in most cases, wage or salary. Many defined benefit formulas also take into account the CPP (Canada Pension Plan) benefit to which an employee is entitled. These are called "integrated" plans.

The DC arrangement is conceptually the simpler of the two. The employer, and sometimes also the employee, makes regular contributions into the employee's retirement account. The contributions usually are specified as a predetermined fraction of salary, although that fraction need not be constant over the course of a career.

Contributions from both parties are tax deductible, and investment income accrues tax-free. Often, the employee has some choice as to how the account is to be invested. In principle, contributions may be invested in any security, although in practice most plans limit investment options to various bond, stock, and money market funds. At retirement, the employee typically receives an annuity whose size depends on the accumulated value of the funds in the retirement account. The employee bears all the investment risk; the retirement account is by definition fully funded, and the firm has no obligation beyond making its periodic contribution.

A typical DB plan determines the employee's benefit as a function of both years of service and wage history. As a representative plan, consider one in which the employee receives retirement income equal to 1 percent of final salary multiplied by the number of years of service. Thus, an employee retiring after 40 years of service with a final salary of $15,000 per year would receive a retirement benefit of 40 percent of $15,000, or $6,000 per year.

The annuity promised to the employee is the employer's liability. The present value of this liability represents the amount of money that the employer must set aside today to fund the deferred annuity that commences upon the employee's retirement.

---

**CONCEPT CHECK** Question 2. An employee is 40 years old and has been working for the firm for 15 years. If normal retirement age is 65, the interest rate is 8 percent, and the employee's life expectancy is 80, what is the present value of the accrued pension benefit?

---

*Defined benefit pension funds* are pools of assets that serve as collateral for firms' pension liabilities. Traditionally, these funds have been viewed as separate from the corporation. Funding and asset allocation decisions are supposed to be made in the beneficiaries' best interests, regardless of the financial condition of the sponsoring corporation.

Beneficiaries presumably want corporate pension plans to be as well-funded as possible. Their preferences with regard to asset allocation policy, however, are less clear. If beneficiaries could not share in any windfall gains—if the defined benefit liabilities were really fixed in nominal terms—rationally, they would prefer that the funds be invested in the least risky assets. If beneficiaries had a claim on surplus assets, however, the optimal asset allocation could in principle include virtually any mix of stocks and bonds.

Another way to view the pension fund investment decision is as an integral part of overall corporate financial policy. Seen in this perspective, defined benefit liabilities are part and parcel of the firm's other fixed financial liabilities, and pension assets are part of the firm's assets. From this point of view, any plan surplus or deficit belongs to the firm's shareholders. The firm thus manages an extended balance sheet, which includes both its normal assets and liabilities and its pension assets and liabilities, in the best interests of *shareholders.*

The question of who should benefit from surpluses in pension funds, due partially to good performance in the market, has become a subject of much controversy since the end of the 1980s, as described in the accompanying box.

## Group Seeks To Save Pension Surplus

**BY JOHN PARTRIDGE**
**and MARGOT GIBB-CLARK**
**The Globe and Mail**

A small group of ex-Confederation Life Insurance Company employees is trying to marshal support to block the fallen company's liquidator from grabbing an estimated $50 million to $200 million in pension fund surpluses.

Both the pension funds and the surpluses were placed in the hands of a separate administrator, **Deloitte & Touche,** about two weeks ago by the Superintendent of Pensions for Ontario.

A spokesman for the employee group and its lawyer said that liquidator, **Peat Marwick Thorne Inc.,** has not yet indicated that it will go after the surplus.

However, they said precedents in other liquidations lead them to fear the firm may try to grab the extra millions to help pay off **Confederation Life's** creditors or give a break on employer pension contributions to companies that have been buying chunks of the insurer's business since the liquidation began August 15.

Peat Marwick spokesman Paul Costello could not be reached.

In a related development, some ex-employees who were laid off early this year said yesterday they are angry because the liquidator has canceled more generous severance arrangements they had reached with the company, cutting them back to statutory minimums.

A group of about 60 employees who were laid off in early February were informed by the liquidator in a registered letter dated August 26 that it is "unable to continue these [enhanced] payments." The final payment would be September 9, and group benefits coverage is to cease October 21, the letters said.

Some had negotiated deals under which, rather than a lump-sum severance payment, they were to continue to receive monthly pay cheques and benefits for a year or more, in some cases, as a bridge until their pensions kicked in.

"If I had known in February that I was going to get paid only until September 9, I would have planned my life accordingly and so would a lot of people," one former employee said bitterly. "But now they're just saying forget it."

On the pension front, a group calling itself the Former Confed Employees Association wrote to other former workers on August 31 asking for donations of $50 to help cover legal and other expenses it expects to incur in an anticipated battle with the liquidator over the surplus.

"We cannot overemphasize the importance of getting an organized claim against the assets of Confed," the group said in the letter, which was signed by Donald Woolridge, an ex-vice-president who retired from Confederation three years ago.

"The surpluses in the pension plans may be in the millions of dollars, and unless we take action now, our voice may go unheard, and the money lost."

Mr. Woolridge, 65, said in an interview that the group has hired Koskie & Minsky, a Toronto law firm.

The group cited recently amended regulations under the Ontario Pension Benefits Act. These prohibit companies from gaining access to a surplus without the written consent of two-thirds of the pensioners and others entitled to a pension but not yet at retirement age.

"So we must organize to present an effective voice on this issue," Mr. Woolridge wrote.

The group said its goal is to ensure that beneficiaries of the company's two registered pension plans—one for salaried employees, the other for field sales agents—receive all the money to which they are entitled and that Peat Marwick does not use any of the surplus for other purposes.

As well, the group said, it will seek to ensure the continuation of supplementary pensions—payable over and above the registered pensions—to which

*(Continued)*

some members of the association or their surviving spouses are entitled.

(Under federal regulations, the maximum annual pension for which companies can claim tax deductions on their contributions is about $60,000. For higher-earning employees, most of them executives, many companies, including Confederation, boost pension payments by setting up supplemental plans, usually financed out of cash flow rather than through a separate fund.)

The group added that it also will try to ensure that present and future Confederation retirees, and employees laid off since the liquidation began, continue to receive benefits such as group life, health and dental insurance and mortgage assistance from the liquidator.

"This has major, major implications as far as people's lives are concerned," Mr. Woolridge said from his Toronto home. "We are a significant group with rights and we want to protect them and make sure we get what we are legally entitled to."

So far, about 200 former Confederation employees of the approximately 1,000 who were sent the letter have sent in cheques. Further mailings are planned.

No current figures are available, but in its annual report for 1993, Confederation said the surplus of assets over obligations in the registered pensions plans was $88.6 million, up from $38.9 million a year earlier.

However, lawyer Susan Rowland of Koskie & Minsky said the final tally, depending on several factors, "could be anywhere from $50 million to $200 million."

Other pension experts said that although Peat Marwick may be able to win part of the surpluses to help pay off creditors, it will not be an easy fight.

Besides, the two-thirds approval rule, barriers could include the actual wording of the pension plan documents, how Confederation invested the pension money, and how the Ontario Pension Commission feels about the matter.

"A lot of these cases end up in court," said consulting actuary Dan McCaw, president of William M. Mercer Ltd. consultants.

The usual solution, he added, is splitting the surplus. "You'll have to give [employees] something to get it."

The outcome for Confederation's former employees will also depend on whether their plans were funded through an insurance contract or a trust, said pension lawyer David Vincent of Fasken Campbell Godfrey.

Trust laws are rigorous in protecting the beneficiaries of that trust—in pensions, the plan members, he said. So it would be more difficult for a liquidator to get surplus out of a trust than an insurance contract.

He added, however, that he would not be surprised if Confederation's plans are insurance contracts, for the simple reason that insurance companies often prefer to avoid dealing with outside trustees "because they see them as competitors."

The experts said members of Confederation's supplemental pension plans, meanwhile, are likely out of luck—because the plans are financed out of cash flow—and may have to make do with their pension entitlement under the registered plans.

*The Globe and Mail, Report on Business,* September 10, 1994, pp. B1, B14. Reprinted by permission.

The special tax status of pension funds creates the same incentive for both defined-contribution and defined-benefit plans to tilt their asset mix toward assets with the largest spread between pretax and after-tax rates of return. In a defined-contribution plan, because the participant bears all of the investment risk, the optimal asset mix also depends on the risk tolerance of the participant.

In defined-benefit plans, optimal investment policy may be different because the sponsor absorbs the investment risk. If the sponsor has to share some of the upside potential of the pension assets with plan participants, there is an incentive to eliminate all investment risk by investing in securities that match the promised benefits. If, for example, the plan sponsor has to pay $100 per year for the next five years, it can provide this stream of benefit payments by buying a set of five zero-coupon bonds each with a face value of $100 and maturing sequentially. By so doing, the sponsor eliminates the risk of a shortfall. This called **immunization** of the pension liability.

If the pension fund is overfunded, then a 100 percent fixed-income portfolio is no longer required to minimize the cost of the corporate pension guarantee. Management can invest surplus pension assets in equities, provided it reduces the proportion so invested when the market value of pension assets comes close to the value of the accumulated benefit obligation (ABO). Such an investment strategy is a type of portfolio insurance known as *contingent immunization.*

To understand how contingent immunization works, consider a simple version of it that makes use of a stop-loss order. Imagine that the ABO is $100 and that the fund has $120 of assets entirely invested in equities. The fund can protect itself against downside risk by maintaining a stop-loss order on all its equities at a price of $100. This means that should the price of the stocks fall to $100, the fund manager would liquidate all the stocks and immunize the ABO. A stop-loss order at $100 is not a perfect hedge because there is no guarantee that the sell order can be executed at a price of $100. The result of a series of stop-loss orders at prices starting well above $100 is even better protection against downside risk.

If the only goal guiding corporate pension policy were shareholder wealth maximization, it would be hard to understand why a financially sound pension sponsor would invest in equities at all. A policy of 100 percent bond investment would minimize the cost of guaranteeing the defined benefits.

In addition to the reasons given for a fully funded pension plan to invest only in fixed-income securities, there is a tax reason for doing so, too. The tax advantage of a pension fund stems from the ability of the sponsor to earn the pretax interest rate on pension investments. To maximize the value of this tax shelter, it is necessary to invest entirely in assets offering the highest pretax interest rate. Because capital gains on stocks can be deferred and dividends are taxed at a much lower rate than interest on bonds, corporate pension funds should invest entirely in taxable bonds and other fixed-income investments.

Yet we know that, in general, pension funds invest from 40 percent to 60 percent of their portfolios in equity securities. Even a casual perusal of the practitioner literature suggests that they do so for a variety of reasons—some right and some wrong. There are two possible correct reasons.

The first is that corporate management views the pension plan as a trust for the employees and manages fund assets as if it were a defined contribution plan. It believes that a successful policy of investment in equities might allow it to pay extra benefits to employees and is therefore worth taking the risk. As explained before, if the plan is overfunded, then the sponsor can invest in stocks and still minimize the cost of providing the benefit guarantee by pursuing a contingent immunization strategy.

The second possible correct reason is that management believes that through superior market timing and security selection it is possible to create value in excess of management fees and expenses. Many executives in nonfinancial corporations are used to creating value in excess of cost in their businesses. They assume that it also can be done in the area of portfolio management. Of course, if that is true, then one must ask why they do not do it on their corporate account rather than in the pension fund. That way, they could have their tax shelter "cake" and eat it, too. It is important to realize, however, that to accomplish this feat, the plan must beat the market, not merely match it.

### Pension Fund Appraisal

Institutions operating pension funds for their employees can assess the performance both of their funds and of the professional managers they hire for portions of the funds. Several organizations, the largest being SEI, will evaluate performance by comparing the realized returns to benchmarks based on selected categories such as long-term bonds, small-cap equities, or market indices. The overall performance over various time periods can be compared to results of other institutions in general or of a similar type, such as universities or hospitals.

If an institution has been using a number of managers for different purposes, or if it is considering a change to other potential managers, it can obtain information about the results they have obtained. Combining the realized returns with the variability of results over different periods will permit the identification of managers who will satisfy the objectives of the pension fund.

## 4.5 Taxation and Tax Sheltering

### The Canadian Tax System

Investment choice by individuals is a process of placing funds temporarily under the control of others in the hope of obtaining a future cash flow greater than the amount invested. Governments consider the increase in funds, or the return on investment, to be taxable, like earned income. For the investor, the return available after tax is what is relevant. Frequently, the tax payable may reflect the risk involved in the investment; hence, the government may encourage risky investments by exempting part, or even all, of their returns from income tax. In order to stimulate investment in certain areas or of certain types, the government may legislate particularly favourable tax treatment. Thus, tax policy is often (many would say always) a reflection of social policy.

In Canada, the three major characteristics of income tax that are relevant to investment are the treatment of interest, dividends, and capital gains. The receipt of interest is predictable and relatively certain (barring default by the borrower), leading the government to tax it as ordinary income. Since equity is more risky than debt for investors, but safer for corporations, equity investment is encouraged by offering a lower effective tax rate. Dividends being more assured than capital gains, we would expect a higher tax rate on dividends than on capital

**Table 4.7** Calculation of Tax Payable upon Forms of Investment Income

| Source | Interest | Dividend | Capital Gain |
|---|---|---|---|
| Income | 1,000 | 1,000 | 1,000 |
| Dividend gross-up (25%) | | 250 | |
| Capital gain exclusion (25%) | | | (250) |
| Taxable income | 1,000 | 1,250 | 750 |
| Federal tax (29%) | (290) | (362.50) | (217.50) |
| Dividend tax credit (13⅓%) | | 166.67 | |
| Basic federal tax | (290) | (195.83) | (217.50) |
| Ontario tax (58%) | (168.20) | (113.58) | (126.15) |
| Federal surtax (8%) | (23.20) | (15.67) | (17.40) |
| Ontario surtax (30%) | (50.46) | (34.07) | (37.84) |
| Total income tax | (531.86) | (359.15) | (398.89) |
| After-tax income | 468.14 | 640.85 | 601.11 |
| Retention ratio | 46.81% | 64.08% | 60.11% |

**Table 4.8** After-Tax Retention of Income from Interest, Dividends, and Capital Gains, 1994

| Province | Ontario | Quebec | British Columbia |
|---|---|---|---|
| Combined federal and provincial tax rate | 53.19% | 52.94% | 54.16% |
| **RETENTION RATE ON:** | | | |
| Interest | 46.81 | 47.06 | 45.84 |
| Dividends | 64.08 | 61.28 | 63.43 |
| Capital gains | 60.11 | 60.30 | 59.38 |

gains. Thus, the system rewards long-term equity investment for growth more than equity investment for dividend income, and in turn, dividend income more than interest income.

Although the system has changed extensively since the introduction of the capital gains tax in 1972, we now have a system which favours dividends through a complicated adjustment procedure and capital gains by exclusion of some of the gain from taxable income. Dividends are currently "grossed up" by increasing the actual amount by 25 percent and including this in taxable income; then a tax credit of 13⅓ percent of the grossed-up amount is granted against taxes due. Actual capital gains are reduced by 25 percent and then included in taxable income.

Table 4.7 illustrates the calculation of taxes and the after-tax return for an income of $1,000 from the three types of investment income: interest, dividends, and capital gains. As we see in Table 4.8, comparing the after-tax retention rates in Ontario, Quebec, and British Columbia, capital gains are currently taxed slightly more than are dividends, although the difference is minimal. The fact that capital gains can be accrued over a period of time, but are taxable only upon realization, causes their treatment to be more favourable, in reality.

Timing is an important detail in the effect of taxation. Generally, income is taxed in the year that it is received, although corporations may account for income on an accrual basis. Bond interest is then taxed when received, which is determined as the payment date by the issuer; similarly, dividends are taxed as of the payment date (not to be confused with the declaration or record dates). Capital gains are based on the years of purchase and sale; because of transfer delays, the date for tax purposes—the **settlement date**—is formally three business days after the actual trade date (this makes the days prior to Christmas an active period of trading, as annual gains and losses are established).

One exception to the actual receipt of cash occurs for so-called **zero-coupon bonds,** or **zeroes** (described in Section 1.3), and similarly for compound interest savings bonds. Although no actual interest is paid, interest is imputed from the increase in value over the life of the zero-coupon bond; similarly, the savings bonds' interest is not received until redemption. In both cases, the income tax is paid annually on the imputed interest, making these negative cash flow instruments. Note that the government is precluding the possibility of an investor claiming the increase in value of the zero, from its initial discounted value to its redemption value, as a capital gain to be taxed at the preferential rate.

Besides timing, location of the source of income is important. As international investments become more common, income from foreign sources is likely to become part of taxable income. It is fortunate that agreements between taxing authorities permit the recognition of foreign income tax as a credit against Canadian taxes, although only to the extent that that tax would have been charged under Canadian law. Note that it is the source of the income that causes a country to tax it first, that is, U.S.-source income will be taxed there. Capital gains on foreign assets, however, are taxable in Canada and generally are not taxable under the foreign tax regime.

The significance of the after-tax returns on different forms of investment is that the prices of financial assets are determined by the returns, on an after-tax basis, that are required by investors in recompense for the risks posed by the assets. Investment choices in response to tax policies must be made from the available set of instruments that are competitively priced to appeal to the investing public. As previously mentioned, occasionally governments may judge that the investment appeal of certain assets does not attract sufficient capital; in such cases, additional incentives may be offered to increase their appeal.

## Tax Deferral and Shelters

There are four important tax-sheltering options that can radically affect the optimal asset allocation for individual investors. The first is the tax-deferral option, which arises from the fact that you do not have to pay tax on a capital gain until you choose to realize the gain. The second and third options are similar; they are called tax-deferred retirement plans, such as the Registered Retirement Savings

Plan, and tax-deferred annuities, which are offered by life insurance companies. The fourth option is the class of investments known as tax shelters. We will discuss each of these options in more detail below.

A fundamental feature of the Income Tax Act is that tax on the capital gain of an asset is payable only when the asset is sold,[7] this is the **tax-deferral option.** The investor, therefore, can control the timing of the tax payment. From a tax perspective, this option makes stocks in general preferable to fixed-income securities.

To see this, compare Seagram's stock with a Seagram's bond. Suppose both offer an expected total return of 15 percent this year. The stock has a dividend yield of 5 percent and an expected appreciation in price of 10 percent, whereas the bond has an interest rate of 15 percent. The bond investor must pay tax on the bond's interest in the year it is earned, whereas the Seagram's stockholder pays tax only on the dividend and defers paying tax on the capital gain until the stock is sold.

Suppose the investor is investing $2,000 for five years and is in a 51 percent tax bracket. An investment in the bond will earn an after-tax return of 7.35 percent per year (.49 × 15 percent). The yield after taxes at the end of five years is

$$\$1{,}000 \times 1.0735^5 = \$1{,}424.64$$

For the stock, dividend yield after taxes will be 2.479 percent per year ([1. − (.51 × 1.25) + .1333] × 5 percent). Because no taxes are paid on the capital gain until year 5, the return before paying the capital gains tax is

$$\$1{,}000 \times (1 + .02479 + .10)^5 = 1{,}000(1.1245)^5 = \$1{,}800.35$$

In year 5, the capital gain is

$$\$1{,}800.35 - \$1{,}000(1.02479)^5 = 1{,}800.35 - 1{,}130.25 = \$670.10$$

Taxes due are $256.46, leaving $1,543.88, which is $119.24 more than the bond investment yields. Deferral of the capital gains tax allows the investment to compound at a faster rate until the tax is actually paid.

Note that the more of one's total return that is in the form of price appreciation, the greater the value of the tax-deferral option.

Recent years have seen the establishment of **tax-deferred retirement plans** in which investors can choose how to allocate assets. Such plans include self-directed RRSPs and employer-sponsored "tax-qualified" defined contribution plans. A feature they all have in common is that contributions and earnings are subject to neither federal nor provincial income tax until the individual withdraws them as benefits.

[7] The only exception to this rule occurs in futures investing, where National Revenue treats a gain as taxable in the year it occurs, regardless of whether the investor closes the position. Note also that on pure discount bonds, imputed interest is taxable, even though no interest payment is received until sale or maturity (making these very popular in RRSPs). Additionally, note that there are capital gains exemptions for principal residences and small businesses.

Typically, an individual may have some investment in the form of such qualified retirement accounts and some in the form of ordinary taxable accounts. The basic investment principle that applies is to keep whatever bonds you want to hold in the retirement account while placing equities in the ordinary account. You maximize the tax advantage of the retirement account by holding in it the security that is the least tax advantaged.

To see this point, consider the following example. Suppose Eloise has $200,000 of wealth, $100,000 of it in a tax-qualified retirement account. She has decided to invest half of her wealth in bonds and half in stocks, so she allocates half of her retirement account and half of her nonretirement funds to each. By doing this, Eloise is not maximizing her after-tax returns. She could reduce her tax bill with no change in before-tax returns simply by shifting her bonds into the retirement account and holding all her stocks outside the retirement account.

---

**CONCEPT CHECK** Question 3. Suppose Eloise earns a 10 percent per year rate of interest on bonds and 15 percent per year on stocks, all in the form of price appreciation. In five years she will withdraw all her funds and spend them. By how much will she increase her final accumulation if she shifts all bonds into the retirement account and holds all stocks outside the retirement account? She is in a 28 percent tax bracket.

---

**Deferred annuities** are essentially tax-sheltered accounts offered by life insurance companies. They combine the same kind of deferral of taxes available on RRSPs with the option of withdrawing one's funds in the form of a life annuity. Variable annuity contracts offer the additional advantage of mutual fund investing. One major difference between a RRSP and a variable annuity contract is that, whereas the amount one can contribute to a RRSP is tax deductible and extremely limited as to maximum amount, the amount one can contribute to a deferred annuity is unlimited, but not tax deductible.

The defining characteristic of a life annuity is that its payments continue as long as the recipient is alive, although virtually all deferred annuity contracts have several withdrawal options, including a lump sum of cash paid out at any time. You need not worry about running out of money before you die. Like CPP, therefore, life annuities offer longevity insurance and would seem to be an ideal asset for someone in the retirement years. Indeed, theory suggests that where there are no bequest motives, it would be optimal for people to invest heavily in actuarially fair life annuities.[8]

There are two types of life annuities, **fixed annuities** and **variable annuities.** A fixed annuity pays a fixed nominal sum of money per period (usually each

---

[8] For an elaboration of this point, see Laurence J. Kotlikoff and Avia Spivak, "The Family as an Incomplete Annuities Market," *Journal of Political Economy* 89 (April 1981).

month), whereas a variable annuity pays a periodic amount linked to the investment performance of some underlying portfolio.

In pricing annuities, insurance companies use **mortality tables** that show the probabilities that individuals of various ages will die within a year. These tables enable the insurer to compute with reasonable accuracy how many of a large number of people in a given age group will die in each future year. If it sells life annuities to a large group, the insurance company can estimate fairly accurately the amount of money it will have to pay in each future year to meet its obligations.

Variable annuities are structured so that the investment risk of the underlying asset portfolio is passed through to the recipient, much as shareholders bear the risk of a mutual fund. There are two stages in a variable annuity contract: an accumulation phase and a payout phase. During the *accumulation* phase, the investor contributes money periodically to one or more open-end mutual funds and accumulates shares. The second, or *payout,* stage usually starts at retirement, when the investor typically has several options, including the following:

1. Taking the market value of the shares in a lump-sum payment.
2. Receiving a fixed annuity until death.
3. Receiving a variable amount of money each period that is computed according to a certain procedure.

This procedure is best explained by the following example. Assume that, at retirement, John Shortlife has $100,000 accumulated in a variable annuity contract. The initial annuity payment is determined by setting an *assumed investment return* (AIR), 4 percent per year in this example, and an assumption about mortality probabilities. In Shortlife's case, we assume he will live for only three years after retirement and will receive three annual payments starting one year from now.

The benefit payment in each year, $B_t$, is given by the recursive formula

$$B_t = B_{t-1}[(1 + R_t)/(1 + \text{AIR})] \qquad \textbf{(4.1)}$$

where $R_t$ is the actual holding period return on the underlying portfolio in year $t$. In other words, each year the amount Shortlife receives equals the previous year's benefit multiplied by a factor that reflects the actual investment return compared with the assumed investment return. In our example, if the actual return equals 4 percent, the factor will be one, and this year's benefit will equal last year's. If $R_t$ is greater than 4 percent, the benefit will increase, and if $R_t$ is less than 4 percent, the benefit will decrease.

The starting benefit is found by computing a hypothetical constant payment with a present value of $100,000 using the 4 percent AIR to discount future values and multiplying it by the first year's performance factor. In our example, the hypothetical constant payment is $36,035.

The box on page 138 summarizes the computation and shows what the payment will be in each of three years if $R_t$ is 6 percent, then 2 percent, and finally 4 percent. The last column shows the balance in the fund after each payment.

This method guarantees that the initial $100,000 will be sufficient to pay all

## Illustration of a Variable Annuity

Starting accumulation = \$100,000
$R_t$ = Rate of return on underlying portfolio in year $t$
Assumes investment return (AIR) = 4 percent per year
$B_t$ = Benefit received at end of year $t$

$$= B_{t-1} \frac{1 + R_t}{1 + \text{AIR}}$$

$B_o$ = \$36,035. This is the hypothetical constant payment, which has a present value of \$100,000, using a discount rate of 4 percent per year.
$A_t$ = Remaining balance after $B_t$ is withdrawn

| $t$ | $R_t$ | $B_t$ | Remaining balance $= A_t = A_{t-1} \times (1 + R_t) - B_t$ |
|---|---|---|---|
| 0 | | | \$100,000 |
| 1 | 6% | 36,728 | 69,272 |
| 2 | 2% | 36,022 | 34,635 |
| 3 | 4% | 36,022 | 0 |

benefits due, regardless of what actual holding period returns turn out to be. In this way, the variable annuity contract passes all portfolio risk through to the annuitant.

By selecting an appropriate mix of underlying assets, such as stocks, bonds, and cash, an investor can create a stream of variable annuity payments with a wide variety of risk-return combinations. Naturally, the investor wants to select a combination that offers the highest expected level of payments for any specified level of risk.[9]

**Concept Check**

Question 4. Assume Victor is now 75 years old and is expected to live until age 80. He has \$100,000 in a variable annuity account. If the assumed investment return is 4 percent per year, what is the initial annuity payment? Suppose the annuity's asset base is the TSE 300 equity portfolio and its holding period return for the next five years is each of the following: 4 percent, 10 percent, −8 percent, 25 percent, and 0. How much would Victor receive each year? Verify that the insurance company would wind up using exactly \$100,000 to fund Victor's benefits.

[9] For an elaboration on possible combinations, see Zvi Bodie, "An Innovation for Stable Real Retirement Income," *Journal of Portfolio Management,* Fall 1980; and Zvi Bodie and James E. Pesando, "Retirement Annuity Design in an Inflationary Climate," Chapter 11 in Zvi Bodie and J. B. Shoven (editors), *Financial Aspects of the United States Pension Systems* (Chicago: University of Chicago Press, 1983).

Variable life insurance is another tax-deferred investment vehicle offered by the life insurance industry. A variable life insurance policy combines life insurance with the tax-deferred annuities described earlier.

To invest in this product, you pay either a single premium or a series of premiums. In each case there is a stated death benefit, and the policyholder can allocate the money invested to several portfolios, which generally include a money market fund, a bond fund, and at least one common stock fund. The allocation can be changed at any time.

A variable life policy has a cash surrender value equal to the investment base minus any surrender charges. Typically, there is a surrender charge (about 5 percent of the purchase payments) if you surrender the policy during the first several years, but not thereafter. At policy surrender, income taxes become due on all investment gains.

Variable life insurance policies offer a death benefit that is the greater of the stated face value or the market value of the investment base. In other words, the death benefit may rise with favourable investment performance, but it will not go below the guaranteed face value. Furthermore, the surviving beneficiary is not subject to income tax on the death benefit.

The policyholder can choose from a number of income options to convert the policy into a stream of income, either on surrender of the contract or as a partial withdrawal. In all cases, income taxes are payable on the part of any distribution representing investment gains.

The insured can gain access to the investment without having to pay income tax by borrowing against the cash surrender value. Policy loans of up to 90 percent of the cash value are available at any time at a contractually specified interest rate.

**Tax shelters** are investment opportunities under which most, if not all, of the investment can be deducted from ordinary income over a few years' horizon. These generally are structured as *limited partnerships* (LP) for the investors, with a general partner who is usually related to the sponsor of the shelter. The advantage of this arrangement is that there is only minimal risk of any further assessment of liability against the limited partners, while a share of LP expenses are deductible against income; if the structure involved a limited liability corporation, these expenses would *not* be deductible. Tax regulations allow the write-off of these expenses over three years, typically, with administrative expenses of setting up and selling the LP requiring five years to write off.

The consequences of entering into an LP include the generation of a cash flow of income from the business for the life of the LP, often 10 years or even much longer, against which the amortized expenses can be deducted for income tax purposes. If a partner wishes to sell his share, however, the adjusted cost basis is likely to be zero for the purpose of determining the taxable capital gain. Such a sale is further impeded by illiquidity in the (OTC) resale market, with large bid-ask spreads.

Shelters are created to raise capital to finance investment in various areas, including commercial real estate (such as Multiple Unit Residential Buildings, or

MURBs), filmmaking, and railroad boxcars. Two more popular forms have been the flow-through share programme of the 1980s and mutual fund LPs, currently in favour.

*Flow-through shares* were issued to allow mining and energy companies to pass through their exploration and resource depletion expenses to shareholders who would be able to use the deduction against income; the companies themselves usually did not have enough taxable income to make use of the expenses. Companies were able to raise significant amounts of capital to finance resource exploration and development in this way. The federal government originally encouraged this arrangement to increase activity and employment in the mining and energy sectors. As capital was squandered on marginal prospects, and tax revenues suffered from helping in the financing, the government greatly reduced the attractiveness of the shares by reducing the write-off allowances; this virtually killed the programme.

*Mutual fund LPs* raise capital to pay for the commissions paid to salespersons for back-end load funds. Since no front-end fee is collected, the fund managers do not have the cash to pay the commissions. In return for financing the commissions, partners are entitled to receive all the resulting back-end load fees, as well as a percentage of the regular management fees paid by mutual fund shareholders. This income is received for 10 or more years through the LP. The load income and management fee income tend to offset each other as fund performance varies. Ultimately, the after-tax cash flow is correlated with the performance of the underlying mutual fund; having much lower risk, it dominates direct investment in the fund.[10] Resale of the LPs is costly, with many investors trying to sell after the three-year write-off period; an attempt has been made to improve liquidity by consolidating the partnerships into a TSE-traded security.

The government's tax treatment of LPs, which delays the write-off allowances over a period of years, is arbitrary. Since the expense usually occurs shortly after the capital is raised, there is no rationale for disallowing an immediate deduction; the reason is to reduce the effect on tax revenues. If the tax treatment is made too punitive, however, the result will be to eliminate the LP as a viable financing mechanism. This would remove the opportunity from smaller investors, leaving it only to large investors able and willing to provide capital. Structured as a business, the investment can become a clear expense as incurred.

Many tax shelters, such as MURB investments, have turned out to have very poor results. Although taxes were saved originally, little of the after-tax investment was returned. Although early flow-through share partnerships were extremely profitable, the later ones resulted in investment in low-quality mining companies and yielded little payoff. The saving of taxes must be a secondary consideration to the overall profitability of the investment when choosing a shelter. Given the complexity of the tax consequences, the advice of a tax accountant, rather than that of the selling broker, is strongly recommended to prospective

---

[10] See Peter J. Ryan, "Gimme More Than Shelter," *Canadian Investment Review,* Fall 1995, pp. 22–27.

investors. That advice ought to include some appraisal of the investment prospects, as well as tax planning.

## SUMMARY

**1.** The life-cycle approach to the management of an individual's investment portfolio views the individual as passing through a series of stages, becoming more risk-averse in later years. The rationale underlying this approach is that as we age, we use up our human capital and have less time remaining to recoup possible portfolio losses through increased labour supply.

**2.** People buy life and disability insurance during their prime earning years to hedge against the risk associated with loss of their human capital, that is, their future earning power.

**3.** When discussing the principles of portfolio management, it is useful to distinguish among seven classes of investors:

*a.* Individual investors and personal trusts.
*b.* Mutual funds.
*c.* Pension funds.
*d.* Endowment funds.
*e.* Life insurance companies.
*f.* Nonlife insurance companies.
*g.* Banks.

In general, these groups have somewhat different investment objectives, constraints, and portfolio policies.

**4.** To some extent, most institutional investors seek to match the risk and return characteristics of their investment portfolios to the characteristics of their liabilities.

**5.** As an alternative to investing in securities through a broker, many individuals invest in mutual funds and other investment companies. Mutual funds free the individual from many of the administrative burdens of owning individual securities and offer the prospect of superior investment results. Mutual funds are classified according to whether they are open-end or closed-end, whether they are load or no-load, and by the type of securities in which they invest. Real estate limited partnerships are specialized investment companies that invest in real estate; mortgage funds invest in loans secured by real estate.

**6.** Pension plans are either defined contribution plans or defined benefit plans. Defined contribution plans are, in effect, retirement funds held in trust for the employee by the employer. The employees in such plans bear all the risk of the plan's assets and often have some choice in the allocation of those assets. Defined benefit plans give the employees a claim to a money-fixed annuity at retirement. The annuity level is determined by a formula that takes into account years of service and the employee's wage or salary history.

**7.** If the only goal guiding corporate pension policy were shareholder wealth maximization, it is hard to understand why a financially sound pension sponsor would invest in equities at all. A policy of 100 percent bond investment would both maximize the tax advantage of funding the pension plan and minimize the cost of guaranteeing the defined benefits.

**8.** The Canadian tax system is designed to make investment in equity more favourable than investment in debt, by offering a dividend tax credit and excluding some of the capital gains from taxation. Capital gains and dividends are taxed at approximately the same effective rate.

**9.** There are four ways to shelter investment income from federal income taxes. The first is by investing in assets whose returns take the form of appreciation in value, such as common stocks or real estate. As long as capital gains taxes are not paid until the asset is sold, the tax can be deferred indefinitely. The second way of tax sheltering is through investing in tax-deferred retirement plans, such as RRSPs. The general investment rule is to hold the least tax-advantaged assets in the plan and the most tax-advantaged assets outside of it. The third way of sheltering is to invest in the tax-advantaged products offered by the life insurance industry—tax-deferred annuities and variable and universal life insurance. They combine the flexibility of mutual fund investing with the tax advantages of tax deferral. Finally, there are investments in tax shelters, which finance investment in mutual funds, real estate, or other assets. Poor prospects with tax benefits make bad investments.

## Key Terms

Personal trusts
Defined contribution plans
Defined benefit plans
Endowment funds
Whole-life insurance policy
Term insurance
Variable life
Universal life
Insured defined benefit pension
Liquidity
Investment horizon
Prudent man
Closed-end funds
Open-end funds
Load fund
No-load fund
Index fund
Management expense ratio
Immunization
Settlement date
Zero-coupon bonds (zeroes)
Tax-deferral option
Tax-deferred retirement plans
Deferred annuities
Fixed annuities
Variable annuities
Mortality tables
Tax shelters

## Selected Readings

*For a collection of essays presenting the Institute of Chartered Financial Analysts' approach to portfolio management, see:*

Ambachtsheer, Keith P. "Strategic Approaches to Asset Allocation." *Asset Allocation for Institutional Portfolios,* The Institute of CFAs, 1988.

Maginn, John L.; and David L. Tuttle (editors). *Managing Investment Portfolios: A Dynamic Analysis,* 2d edition. Boston: Warren, Gorham, & Lamont, 1990.

*For a further discussion of the theory and evidence regarding the investment policies of corporate defined benefit pension plans, see:*

Bodie, Z. "Managing Pension and Retirement Assets: An International Perspective." *Journal of Financial Services Research,* December 1990.

Bodie, Z.; J. Light; R. Morck; and R. A. Taggart. "Corporate Pension Policy: An Empirical Investigation." *Financial Analysts Journal* 41, no. 5 (September–October 1985).

*A number of interesting articles appear under the collective theme "Investment Management: A New Look" in the special edition of: Canadian Investment Review* IV, no. 1 (Spring 1991).

## Problems

**1.** Your neighbour has heard that you have just successfully completed a course in investments and has come to seek your advice. She and her husband are both 50 years old. They have just finished making their last payments for their condominium and their children's college education and are planning for retirement. Until now, they have neither been able to set aside any savings for retirement, and so have not participated in their employers' voluntary tax-sheltered savings plan, nor have they opened RRSPs. Both of them work, and their combined after-tax income last year was $50,000. They are both in the 42 percent marginal tax bracket. They plan to retire at age 65 and would like to maintain the same standard of living in retirement as they enjoy now.

*a.* Devise a simple plan for them on the assumption of a combined CPP income of $10,000 per year. How much should they start saving? (Assume they will live to age 80, can shelter as much retirement savings as they want from tax, and will earn a zero real rate of return.)

*b.* Redo part (a) with the following changes:

i. The real interest rate is assumed to be 3 percent per year.

ii. Your neighbors are 40 years old instead of 50.

iii. The tax bracket after retirement drops to 15 percent.

*c.* What advice on investing their retirement savings would you give them? If they are very risk-averse, what would you advise?

The following problems are based on questions that appeared in past CFA examinations:*

**2.** (Level I) Several discussion meetings have provided the following information about one of your firm's new advisory clients, a charitable endowment fund recently created by means of a one-time $10,000,000 gift:

---

*Objectives*

- *Return requirement.* Planning is based on a minimum total return of 8 percent per year, including an initial current income component of $500,000 (5 percent on beginning capital). Realizing this current income target is the endowment fund's primary return goal. (See "Unique needs.")

*Constraints*

- *Time horizon.* Perpetuity, except for requirement to make an $8,500,000 cash distribution on June 30, 1998. (See "Unique needs.")
- *Liquidity needs.* None of a day-to-day nature until 1998. Income is distributed annually after year-end. (See "Unique needs.")
- *Tax considerations.* None; this endowment fund is exempt from taxes.
- *Legal and regulatory considerations.* Minimal, but the prudent man rule applies to all investment actions.
- *Unique needs, circumstances, and preferences.* The endowment fund must pay out to another tax-exempt entity the sum of $8,500,000 in cash on June 30, 1998. The assets remaining after this distribution will be retained by the fund in perpetuity. The endowment fund has adopted a "spending rule" requiring a first-year current income payout of $500,000; thereafter, the annual payout is to rise by 3 percent in real terms. Until 1998, annual income in excess of that required by the spending rule is to be reinvested; after 1998, the spending rate will be reset at 5 percent of the then-existing capital.

  With this information and information found in this chapter, do the following:

*a.* Formulate an appropriate investment policy statement for the endowment fund.
*b.* Identify and briefly explain three major ways in which your firm's initial asset allocation decisions for the endowment fund will be affected by the circumstances of the account.

**3.** (Level I) Your client says, "With the unrealized gains in my portfolio, I have almost saved enough money for my daughter to go to college in eight years, but educational costs keep going up." Based on this statement alone, which one of the following appears to be least important to your client's investment policy?
*a.* Time horizon
*b.* Purchasing power risk
*c.* Liquidity
*d.* Taxes

**4.** (Level I) The aspect least likely to be included in the portfolio management process is
*a.* Identifying an investor's objectives, constraints, and preferences.
*b.* Organizing the management process itself.
*c.* Implementing strategies regarding the choice of assets to be used.

*d.* Monitoring market conditions, relative values, and investor circumstances.

CFA **5.** (Level I) Investors in high marginal tax brackets probably would be least interested in a

*a.* Portfolio of diversified stocks
*b.* Tax-deferred retirement fund
*c.* Commodity pool
*d.* High-income bond fund

CFA **6.** (Level II) Sam Short, CFA, has recently joined the investment management firm of Green, Spence, and Smith (GSS). For several years, GSS has worked for a broad array of clients, including employee benefit plans, wealthy individuals, and charitable organizations. Also, the firm expresses expertise in managing stocks, bonds, cash reserves, real estate, venture capital, and international securities. To date, the firm has not utilized a formal asset allocation process but instead has relied on the individual wishes of clients or the particular preferences of its portfolio managers. Short recommends to GSS management that a formal asset allocation process would be beneficial and emphasizes that a large part of a portfolio's ultimate return depends on asset allocation. He is asked to take his conviction an additional step by making a proposal to executive management.

*a.* Recommend and justify an approach to asset allocation that could be used by GSS.
*b.* Apply the approach to a middle-aged, wealthy individual characterized as a fairly conservative investor (sometimes referred to as a "guardian investor").

CFA **7.** (Level II) You are a portfolio manager and senior executive vice president of Advisory Securities Selection, Inc. Your firm has been invited to meet with the Trustees of the Wood Museum Endowment Fund. Wood Museum is a privately endowed charitable institution that is dependent on the investment return from a \$25 million endowment fund to balance the budget. The treasurer of the museum recently has completed a budget that indicates a need for cash flow of \$3 million in 1992, \$3.2 million in 1993, and \$3.5 million in 1994 from the endowment fund to balance the budget in those years. At the present time, the entire endowment portfolio is invested in Treasury bills and money market funds because the trustees fear a financial crisis. The trustees do not anticipate any further capital contributions to the fund. The trustees are all successful business people, and they have been critical of the fund's previous investment advisors because they did not follow a logical decision-making process. In fact, several previous managers were dismissed because of their inability to communicate with the trustees and their preoccupation with the fund's relative performance rather than the cash flow needs. Advisory Securities Selection, Inc., has been contacted by the trustees because of its reputation for understanding and relating to its clients' needs. The trustees have asked you, as a prospective portfolio manager for the Wood Museum Endowment Fund, to prepare a written report in response to the following questions. Your report will be circulated to the trustees before the initial interview on June 15, 1991. Explain in detail how each of the following relates to the determination of either investor objectives or investor constraints that can be used to determine the portfolio policies for this three-year period for the Wood Museum Endowment Fund.

*a.* Liquidity requirements.
*b.* Return requirements.
*c.* Risk tolerance.
*d.* Time horizon.
*e.* Tax considerations.
*f.* Regulatory and legal considerations.
*g.* Unique needs and circumstances.

CFA

**8.** (Level III) Mrs. Mary Atkins, age 66, has been your firm's client for five years, since the death of her husband, Dr. Charles Atkins. Dr. Atkins had built a successful newspaper business that he sold two years before his death to Merit Enterprises, a publishing and broadcasting conglomerate, in exchange for Merit common stock. The Atkinses had no children, and their wills provide that upon their deaths the remaining assets shall be used to create a fund for the benefit of Good Samaritan Hospital, to be called the Atkins Endowment Fund. Good Samaritan is a 180-bed, not-for-profit hospital with an annual operating budget of $12.5 million. In the past, the hospital's operating revenues often have been sufficient to meet operating expenses and occasionally even generate a small surplus. In recent years, however, rising costs and declining occupancy rates have caused Good Samaritan to run a deficit. The operating deficit has averaged $300,000–$400,000 annually over the last several years. Existing endowment assets (i.e., excluding the Atkins estate) of $7.5 million currently generate approximately $375,000 of annual income, up from less than $200,000 five years ago. This increased income has been the result of somewhat higher interest rates, as well as a shift in asset mix toward more bonds. To offset operating deficits, the Good Samaritan board of governors has determined that the endowment's current income should be increased to approximately 6 percent of total assets (up from 5 percent currently). The hospital has not received any significant additions to its endowment assets in the past five years. Identify and describe an appropriate set of investment objectives and constraints for the Atkins Endowment Fund to be created after Mrs. Atkins' death.

**9.** (Level III) You have been named as investment advisor to a foundation established by Dr. Walter Jones with an original contribution consisting entirely of the common stock of Jomedco, Inc. Founded by Dr. Jones, Jomedco manufactures and markets medical devices invented by the doctor and collects royalties on other patented innovations. All of the shares that made up the initial contribution to the foundation were sold at a public offering of Jomedco common stock, and the $5 million proceeds will be delivered to the foundation within the next week. At the same time, Mrs. Jones will receive $5 million in proceeds from the sale of her stock in Jomedco. Dr. Jones' purpose in establishing the Jones Foundation was to "offset the effect of inflation on medical school tuition for the maximum number of worthy students." You are preparing for a meeting with the foundation's trustees to discuss investment policy and asset allocation.

*a.* Define and give examples that show the differences between an investment objective, an investment constraint, and an investment policy.

*b.* Identify and describe an appropriate set of investment objectives and investment constraints for the Jones Foundation.

*c.* Based on the investment objectives and investment constraints identified in part (*b*), prepare a comprehensive investment policy statement for the Jones Foundation to be recommended for adoption by the trustees.

**10.** John Oliver, formerly a senior partner of a large management consulting firm, has been elected president of Mid-South Trucking Company. He has contacted you, a portfolio manager for a large investment advisory firm, to discuss the company's defined-benefit pension plans. Upon assuming his duties, Oliver learned that Mid-South's pension plan was 100 percent in bonds, with a maximum maturity of 10 years. He believes that "a pension plan should be managed so as to maximize return within well-defined risk parameters," and "anyone can buy bonds and sit on them." Mr. Oliver has suggested that he meet with you, as an objective advisor, and the plan's actuary to discuss possible changes in plan asset mix. To aid you in preparing for the meeting, Mr. Oliver has provided the current portfolio (Table 4P.1). He also has provided the following information about the company and its pension plans.

*Company*

Mid-South is the eighth largest domestic trucking company, with annual revenues of $500 million. Revenues have grown about 8 percent per year over the past five years, with one down year. The company employs about 7,000 people, compared with 6,500 five years ago. The annual payroll is

**Table 4P.1** Current Portfolio

| | Cost | Market Value | Current Yield | Yield to Maturity |
|---|---|---|---|---|
| Short-term reserves | $ 10,000,000 | $ 10,000,000 | 5.8% | 5.8% |
| Notes, 90 days to 1 year | 25,000,000 | 25,500,000 | 6.5 | 6.4 |
| Notes, 1 to 5 years | 110,000,000 | 115,000,000 | 8.0 | 7.8 |
| Bonds, 5 to 10 years | 115,000,000 | 127,500,000 | 8.8 | 8.5 |
| **Total** | **$260,000,000** | **$278,000,000** | **8.1%** | **7.9%** |

about $300 million. The average age of the workforce is 43 years. Company profits last year were $20 million, compared with $12 million five years ago.

*Pension Plan*

Mid-South's pension plan is a defined-benefit plan that was established in 1965. The company annually contributes 7 percent of payroll to fund the plan. During the past 5 years, portfolio income has been used to meet payments for retirees, while company contributions have been available for investment. Although the plan is adequately funded on a current basis, unfunded past service liabilities are equal to 40 percent of plan assets. The liability is to be funded over the next 35 years. Plan assets are valued annually on a rolling four-year average for actuarial purposes.

Whereas FASB No. 87 requires an annual reassessment of the assumed rate of return, for purposes of this analysis, Mid-South's management, in consultation with the actuary, has decided to use an assumed annual rate of 7 percent. This compares with actual plan results that have averaged 10 percent per year over the past 20 years. Wages and salaries are assumed to increase 5 percent per year, identical with past company experience.

Before the meeting, you review your firm's investment projections, dated March 31, 1987. Your firm believes that continued prosperity is the most likely outlook for the next three to five years but has allowed for two alternatives: first, a return to high inflation; or second, a move into deflation/depression. The details of the projections are shown in Table 4P.2.

**Table 4P.2** Investment Projections

| Scenarios | Expected Annual Total Return (%) |
|---|---|
| **CONTINUED PROSPERITY (60% PROBABILITY)** | |
| Short-term reserves (Treasury bills) | 6.0 |
| Stocks (S&P 500 index) | 12.0 |
| Bonds (S&P high-grade bond index) | 8.0 |
| **HIGH-INFLATION SCENARIO (25% PROBABILITY)** | |
| Short-term reserves (Treasury bills) | 10.0 |
| Stocks (S&P 500 index) | 15.0 |
| Bonds (S&P high-grade bond index) | 3.0 |
| **DEFLATION/DEPRESSION SCENARIO (15% PROBABILITY)** | |
| Short-term reserves (Treasury bills) | 2.0 |
| Stocks (S&P 500 index) | −6.0 |
| Bonds (S&P high-grade bond index) | 12.0 |

*a*. Based on this information, create an investment policy statement for the Mid-South Trucking Company's pension plan. Based upon your policy statement and the expectations shown, recommend an appropriate asset allocation strategy for Mid-South Trucking Company's pension plan limited to the same asset classes shown. Justify your changes, if any, from the current portfolio. Your allocation must sum to 100 percent.

*b*. At the meeting, the actuary suggests that Mid-South consider terminating the defined-benefit plan, purchasing annuities for retirees and vested employees with the proceeds, and establishing a defined-contribution plan. The company would continue to contribute 7 percent of payroll to the defined-contribution plan.

Compare the key features of a defined-benefit plan and a defined-contribution plan. Assuming Mid-South were to adopt and retain responsibility for a defined-contribution plan, briefly explain any revisions to your asset allocation strategy developed in part (*a*) above. Again, your allocation must sum to 100 percent and be limited to the same asset classes shown.

CFA

**11.** You are Mr. R. J. Certain, a retired CFA, who formerly was the chief investment officer of a major investment management organization. Although you have over 30 years of experience in the investment business, you have kept up with the literature and developed a reputation for your knowledge and ability to blend modern portfolio theory and traditional portfolio methods.

The chairman of the board of Morgan Industries has asked you to serve as a consultant to him and the other members of the board of trustees of the company's pension fund. Since you are interested in developing a consulting practice and in keeping actively involved in the investment management business, you welcome the opportunity to develop a portfolio management decision-making process for Morgan Industries that you could apply to all types of investment portfolios.

Morgan Industries is a company in transition. Its long-established business, dating back to the early years of the century, is the production of steel. Since the 1960s, however, Morgan gradually has built a highly profitable stake in the domestic production of oil and gas.

Most of the company's 1982 sales of $4 billion were still derived from steel operations. Because Morgan occupies a relatively stable niche in a specialized segment of the steel industry, its losses on steel during the 1982 recession were moderate compared to industry experience. At the same time, profit margins for Morgan's oil and gas business remained satisfactory despite all the problems in the world oil market. This segment of the company's operations accounted for the entire 1982 net profit of $150 million. Even when steel operations recover, oil and gas operations are expected to contribute, on average, over half of Morgan's annual profits.

Based on the combination of the two segments of the company's operations, the overall cyclicality of company earnings appears to be approximately the same as that of the S&P 500. Several well-regarded security analysts, citing the outlook for recovery in steel operations, as well as further gains in oil and gas production, project earnings progress for Morgan over the next five years at about the same rate as for the S&P 500. Debt comprises about 35 percent of the long-term capital structure, and the beta (market risk) for the company's common stock is also about the same as for the S&P 500.

Morgan's defined-benefit pension plan covers 25,000 active employees, vested and unvested, and 15,000 retired employees, with the latter projected to exceed 20,000 in five years. The burden of pension liabilities is large because the steel industry has long been labour intensive and the company's current labour force in this area of operations is not as large as it was some years ago. Oil and gas operations, although growing at a significant rate, account for only 10 percent of the active plan participants and for even less of the retired beneficiaries.

Pension assets amounted to $1 billion of market value at the end of 1982. For the purpose of planning investment policy, the present value of the unfunded pension liability is calculated at $500 million. Although the company's outstanding debt is $600 million, it is clear that the unfunded pension liability adds significantly to the leverage in the capital structure.

Pension expenses charged to company income—and reflected in company contributions to the pension trust—were $80 million in 1982. The level of expenses, which are projected to rise with payroll, reflects current assumptions concerning inflation, the rate of return on pension assets, wage and salary increases, and benefits changes. If these assumptions were to prove completely correct, the current method of funding would amortize the unfunded pension liability over 20 years. Since assumptions are subject to change in the light of new information, they must be reviewed periodically. Revision by one percentage point in the assumed rate of investment return, for example, would require a current change in the level of pension expenses by $15 million before taxes, or about $7 million after taxes. The current actuarially assumed rate of return is 8.5 percent.

Pension investment policy, through its influence on pension expenses, unfunded pension liability, and the company's earnings progress, is a critical issue for Morgan's management. The chairman is strongly committed to the corporate goal of achieving a total investment return for shareholders superior to that of other large industrial companies. He recognizes that a more aggressive pension investment policy—if successful—would facilitate attainment of the corporate goal through a significant reduction in pension expenses and unfunded pension liability. He also worries, however, that a significant drop in the market value of the company's pension fund—now $1 billion—could result in a major setback in the company's growth strategy. Current pension investment policy is based on an asset mix of approximately 50 percent common stocks and 50 percent fixed-income securities.

The chairman is concerned about the overall investment management and direction of the pension fund and is very interested in your informed and objective evaluation.

What recommendations would you make to the chairman and why?

## Appendix 4A: The Black-Dewhurst Proposal

In 1981, Fischer Black and Moray Dewhurst created a stir among pension plan finance specialists by making a proposal that carried to a logical extreme the notion that a pension plan is a way to shelter investment income from corporate income taxes.[11] They claimed that, to maximize the value of a firm to its shareholders, a firm should fully fund its pension plan and invest the entire amount in bonds.

In this proposal, they recommend that a firm arbitrage taxes by substituting bonds for stocks in the pension fund. The simple form of the plan consists of four operations carried out at the same time:

1. Sell all equities, $\$X$, in the pension fund.
2. Purchase on pension account $\$X$ of bonds of the same risk as the firm's own bonds.
3. Issue new debt in an amount equal to $\$X$.
4. Invest $\$X$ in equities on corporate account.

The net effect of these operations will be that the firm will have more debt outstanding owed on corporate account and more bonds owned on pension account. The market value of the firm's own shares should thereby go up by as much as the corporate tax rate multiplied by the amount of new debt taken on in the manoeuvre.

The plan adds value because the firm earns close to the pretax rate of return on the bonds in the fund while paying the after-tax rate on the debt issued to support the procedure. Because the dividends from the common stock are not taxable and the tax on the capital gains can be deferred indefinitely by not selling appreciated stock, the effective tax rate on the equities held on corporate account will be very low. Thus, the after-tax return on the equities will not fall significantly if they are switched from pension account to corporate account. If all value accrues to the firm's shareholders, the effective corporate tax rate on equities is zero, and the stocks held on corporate account are equivalent to the stocks previously held by the pension fund, then the gain to shareholders has a present value of $\$TX$, where $T$ is the marginal corporate income tax rate faced by the firm.

[11] See Fischer Black and M. P. Dewhurst, "A New Investment Strategy for Pension Funds," *Journal of Portfolio Management,* Summer 1981.

**Table 4A.1** Hi-Tek Corp. Balance Sheets before Black-Dewhurst Manoeuvre

| Assets | | Liabilities and Owners' Equity | |
|---|---|---|---|
| **A. CORPORATE BALANCE SHEET ($ MILLION)** | | | |
| Current assets | $ 2 | Debt | $10 |
| Property, plant, and equipment | 48 | Owners' equity | 40 |
| **Total assets** | **$50** | **Total liabilities** | **$50** |
| **B. PENSION FUND BALANCE SHEET ($ MILLION)** | | | |
| Stocks | $10 | PV of accrued benefits | $10 |
| | | Fund balance | 0 |

**Table 4A.2** Hi-Tek Corp. Balance Sheets after Black-Dewhurst Manoeuvre

| Assets | | Liabilities and Owners' Equity | |
|---|---|---|---|
| **A. CORPORATE BALANCE SHEET ($ MILLION)** | | | |
| Current assets | $ 2 | Debt | $20 |
| Property, plant, and equipment | 48 | Owners' equity | 40 |
| Stocks | 10 | | |
| **Total assets** | **$60** | **Total liabilities** | **$60** |
| **B. PENSION FUND BALANCE SHEET ($ MILLION)** | | | |
| Bonds | $10 | PV of accrued benefits | $10 |
| | | Fund balance | 0 |

To clarify this proposal, let us take a specific example. The Hi-Tek Corporation is a relatively new company, with a young workforce and a fully funded defined-benefit pension plan. Hi-Tek's total corporate assets are worth $50 million, and its capital structure is 20 percent debt and 80 percent equity. Its pension assets consist entirely of a well-diversified portfolio of common stocks indexed to the TSE 300 and worth $10 million. The present value of its pension liabilities is $10 million. The corporate balance sheet is presented in Table 4A.1, part **A,** and the pension fund's balance sheet in Table 4A.1, part **B.**

Hi-Tek's treasurer, who is in charge of the pension fund, has read the Black-Dewhurst article and decides to implement the proposal. The pension fund sells its entire $10 million stock portfolio to the corporation and invests the proceeds in corporate bonds issued by other high-technology companies. The corporation pays for the stock by issuing $10 million of new bonds. The resulting new balance sheets are presented in Table 4A.2.

According to Black and Dewhurst, the result of these transactions should be an increase in the market value of owners' equity of as much as $10 million multiplied by the corporate tax rate, currently 40 percent. In other words, the market value of the outstanding shares of Hi-Tek's common stock should increase by $3.4 million.[12]

To see why, let $r$ be the interest rate on the debt. As a result of the previous four operations, the company now will be earning $r \times \$10$ million per year in interest on the bonds it bought on pension account and paying from its after-tax cash flow $(1 - T)r \times \$10$ million per year on the debt it issued on corporate account. The net cash flow to the firm will be $.34r \times \$10$ million per year, the tax saving on the interest. The present value of this saving in perpetuity is $3.4 million:

$$(.34r \times \$10 \text{ million})/r = \$3.4 \text{ million}$$

Note that even though Hi-Tek's debt ratio has increased from .2 to .3, the overall risk of the firm has not changed. If we accept the theory that the pension fund assets and liabilities belong to the shareholders, the risk of the assets does not change when the $10 million of stock in the pension fund is, in effect, transferred to a corporate account.

This plan implies that the company should increase its contributions to the pension fund up to the limits allowed by National Revenue. This is because for every dollar of assets added to the pension fund, invested in bonds, and supported by issuing new bonds, the tax saving increases by $rT$ per year and the PV of shareholders' equity increases by $\$T$. Thus, if $T$ is .34, shareholders' equity rises by $.34 for every dollar added to pension assets or for every dollar switched out of stocks into bonds.

[12] If the corporate tax rate on equities is greater than zero, the gain in shareholders' equity will be smaller than $3.4 million.

*Part II*

# Portfolio Theory

*Chapter* 5

# Concepts and Issues: Return, Risk, and Risk Aversion

**THIS CHAPTER INTRODUCES SOME KEY CONCEPTS AND ISSUES THAT ARE CENTRAL TO INFORMED INVESTMENT DECISION MAKING.** The material presented is basic to the development of portfolio theory in this and subsequent parts of the book.

The investment process consists of two broad tasks. One task is security and market analysis, by which we assess the risk and expected-return attributes of the entire set of possible investment vehicles. The second task is the formation of an optimal portfolio of assets. This task involves the determination of the best risk-return opportunities available from feasible investment portfolios and the choice of the best portfolio from that feasible set. This latter task is known as *portfolio theory.*

We start this chapter by presenting the basic components of the return of any financial asset: real and nominal interest rates and risk premiums on risky securities. Then, we review the historical record of rates of return on Treasury bills, bonds, and stocks. These elements are basic tools of the security analysis task, to which we return in later chapters.

The remainder of this chapter introduces three themes in portfolio theory, all centering on risk.

The first is the basic tenet that investors avoid risk and demand a reward for engaging in risky investments. The reward is taken as a risk premium, an expected rate of return higher than that available on alternative risk-free investments.

The second theme allows us to summarize and quantify investors' personal tradeoffs between portfolio risk and expected return. To do this we introduce the utility function, which assumes that investors can assign a welfare, or "utility," score to any investment portfolio depending on its risk and return.

Finally, the third fundamental principle is that we cannot evaluate the risk of an asset separate from the portfolio of which it is a part; that is, the proper way to measure the risk of an individual asset is to assess its impact on the volatility of the entire portfolio of investments. Taking this approach, we find that seemingly risky securities may be portfolio stabilizers and actually low-risk assets.

Appendix A to this chapter discusses continuous compounding. Appendix B describes the theory and practice of measuring portfolio risk by the variance or standard deviation of returns. We also discuss other potentially relevant characteristics of the probability distribution of portfolio returns, as well as the circumstances in which variance is sufficient to measure risk. Appendix C discusses the classical theory of risk aversion.

## 5.1 Determinants of the Level of Interest Rates

Interest rates and forecasts of their future values are among the most important inputs into an investment decision.

For example, suppose you have $10,000 in a savings account. The bank pays you a variable interest rate tied to some short-term reference rate such as the 30-day Treasury bill rate. You have the option of moving some or all of your money into a longer-term Guaranteed Investment Certificate (GIC) that offers a fixed rate over the term of the deposit.

Your decision depends critically on your outlook regarding interest rates. If you think rates will fall, you will want to lock in the current higher rates by investing in a relatively long-term GIC. If you expect rates to rise, you will want to postpone committing any funds to long-term GICs.

Forecasting interest rates is one of the most notoriously difficult parts of applied macroeconomics. Nonetheless, we do have a good understanding of the fundamental factors that determine the level of interest rates:

1. The supply of funds from savers, primarily households.
2. The demand for funds from businesses to be used to finance physical investments in plant, equipment, and inventories (real assets or capital formation).
3. The government's net supply and/or demand for funds as modified by actions of the monetary authority.

Before we elaborate on these forces and resultant interest rates, we need to distinguish real from nominal interest rates.

## Real and Nominal Rates of Interest

Suppose exactly one year ago you deposited \$1,000 in a one-year time deposit guaranteeing a rate of interest of 10 percent. You are about to collect \$1,100 in cash.

Is your \$100 return for real? That depends on what money can buy these days, relative to what you *could* buy a year ago. The consumer price index (CPI) measures purchasing power by averaging the prices of goods and services in the consumption basket of an average urban family of four. While this basket may not represent your particular consumption plan, suppose for now that it does.

Suppose the rate of inflation (percent change in the CPI, denoted by $i$) for the last year amounted to $i = 6$ percent. This tells you the purchasing power of money is reduced by 6 percent a year. The value of each dollar depreciates by 6 percent a year in terms of the goods it can buy. Therefore, part of your interest earnings are offset by the reduction in the purchasing power of the dollars you will receive at the end of the year. With a 10 percent interest rate, after you net out the 6 percent reduction in the purchasing power of money, you are left with a net increase in purchasing power of about 4 percent. Thus, we need to distinguish between a **nominal interest rate**—the growth rate of your money—and a **real interest rate**—the growth rate of your purchasing power. If we call $R$ the nominal rate, $r$ the real rate, and $i$ the inflation rate, then we conclude

$$r \approx R - i$$

In words, the real rate of interest is the nominal rate reduced by the loss of purchasing power resulting from inflation.

In fact, the exact relationship between the real and nominal interest rate is given by

$$1 + r = \frac{1 + R}{1 + i}$$

This is because the growth factor of your purchasing power, $1 + r$, equals the growth factor of your money, $1 + R$, divided by the new price level, that is, $1 + i$ times its value in the previous period. The exact relationship can be rearranged to

$$r = \frac{R - i}{1 + i}$$

which shows that the approximation rule overstates the real rate by the factor $1 + i$.

For example, if the interest rate on a one-year CD is 8 percent, and you expect inflation to be 5 percent over the coming year, then using the approximation formula, you expect the real rate to be $r = 8$ percent $-$ 5 percent $=$ 3 percent. Using the exact formula, the real rate is

$$r = \frac{.08 - .05}{1 + .05} = .0286,$$

or 2.86 percent. Therefore, the approximation rule overstates the expected real rate by only 0.14 percent (14 basis points). The approximation rule is more exact for small inflation rates and is perfectly exact for continuously compounded rates. We discuss further details in Appendix A of this chapter.

Before the decision to invest, you would realize that conventional investment certificates offer a guaranteed *nominal* rate of interest. Thus, you can only infer the expected real rate by subtracting your expectation of the rate of inflation.

It is always possible to calculate the real rate after the fact. The inflation rate is published by Statistics Canada (StatsCan). The future real rate, however, is unknown, and one has to rely on expectations. In other words, because future inflation is risky, the real rate of return is risky even if the nominal rate is risk free.

Until recently, we could not observe what the risk-free real rate of interest in the Canadian economy was. However, in late 1991, the Canadian government issued the so-called Real Return Bonds, or RRBs, which offer a guaranteed real rate of interest for a 30-year maturity. The RRBs pay a real coupon of 4.25 percent on a principal amount that is adjusted by the CPI. Hence, the actual nominal rate of interest earned by investors is the promised real rate plus the rate of inflation as measured by the proportional increase in the CPI. A similar innovation was introduced in early 1988 in the United States by the Franklin Savings and Loan Association of Ottawa, Kansas, but it did not find much success. The issuer has since gone under, and the instruments are no longer available to U.S. investors.

## The Equilibrium Real Rate of Interest

Three basic factors—supply, demand, and government actions—determine the *real* interest rate. The nominal interest rate, which is the rate we actually observe, is the real rate plus the expected rate of inflation. So a fourth factor affecting the interest rate is the expected rate of inflation.

Although there are many different interest rates economywide (as many as there are types of securities), economists frequently talk as if there were a single representative rate. We can use this abstraction to gain some insights into determining the real rate of interest if we consider the supply and demand curves for funds.

Figure 5.1 shows a downward-sloping demand curve and an upward-sloping supply curve. On the horizontal axis, we measure the quantity of funds, and on the vertical axis, we measure the real rate of interest.

The supply curve slopes up from left to right because the higher the real interest rate, the greater the supply of household savings. The assumption is that at higher real interest rates, households will choose to postpone some current consumption and set aside or invest more of their disposable income for future use.[1]

The demand curve slopes down from left to right because the lower the real interest rate, the more businesses will want to invest in physical capital. Assuming that businesses rank projects by the expected real return on invested capital, firms

---

[1] There is considerable disagreement among experts on the issue of whether household saving does go up in response to an increase in the real interest rate.

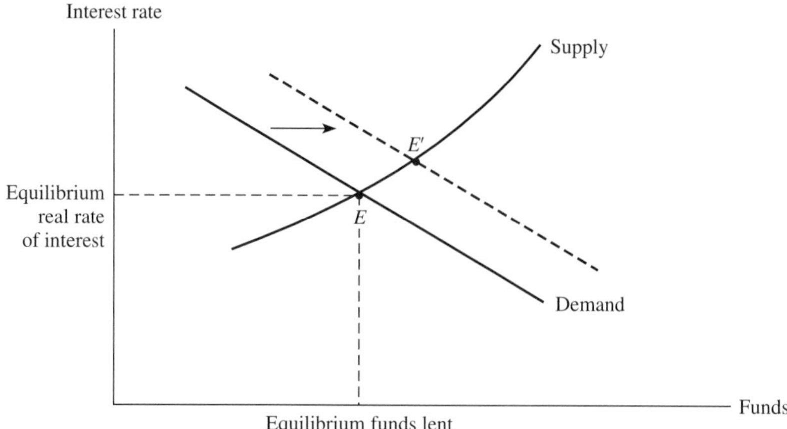


**Figure 5.1** Determination of the equilibrium real rate of interest.

will undertake more projects the lower the real interest rate on the funds needed to finance those projects.

Equilibrium is at the point of intersection of the supply and demand curves, point $E$ in Figure 5.1.

The government and the central bank (Bank of Canada) can shift these supply and demand curves either to the right or to the left through fiscal and monetary policies. For example, consider an increase in the government's budget deficit. This increases the government's borrowing demand and shifts the demand curve to the right, which causes the equilibrium real interest rate to rise to point $E'$. That is, a forecast that indicates higher than previously expected government borrowing increases expected future interest rates. The central bank can offset such a rise through an expansionary monetary policy, which will shift the supply curve to the right.

Thus, while the fundamental determinants of the real interest rate are the propensity of households to save and the expected productivity (or we could say profitability) of investment in physical capital, the real rate can be affected as well by government fiscal and monetary policies.

## The Equilibrium Nominal Rate of Interest

We've seen that the real rate of return of an asset is approximately equal to the nominal rate minus the inflation rate. Because investors should be concerned with their real returns—the increase in their purchasing power—we would expect that as the inflation rate increases, investors will demand higher nominal rates of return on their investments. This higher rate is necessary to maintain the expected real return offered by an investment.

Irving Fisher (1930) argued that the nominal rate ought to increase one for one with increases in the expected inflation rate. If we use the notation $E(i)$ to denote the current expectation of the inflation rate that will prevail over the coming period, then we can state the so-called Fisher equation formally as

$$R = r + E(i)$$

This relationship has been debated and empirically investigated. The equation implies that if real rates are reasonably stable, then increases in nominal rates ought to predict higher inflation rates. The results are mixed; while the data do not strongly support this relationship, nominal interest rates seem to predict inflation as well as alternative methods, in part because we are unable to forecast inflation well with any method.

One reason it is difficult to determine the empirical validity of the Fisher hypothesis that changes in nominal rates predict changes in future inflation rates is that the real rate also changes unpredictably over time. Nominal interest rates can be viewed as the sum of the required real rate on nominally risk-free assets, plus a "noisy" forecast of inflation.

In Part V, we discuss the relationship between short- and long-term interest rates. Longer rates incorporate forecasts for long-term inflation. For this reason alone, interest rates on bonds of different maturities may diverge. In addition, we will see that prices of long-term bonds are more volatile than those of short-term bonds. This implies that expected returns on long-term bonds may include a risk premium, so that the expected real rate offered by bonds of varying maturity also may vary.

**CONCEPT CHECK** Question 1.

*a.* Suppose the real interest rate is 3 percent per year and the expected inflation rate is 8 percent. What is the nominal interest rate?

*b.* Suppose the expected inflation rate rises to 10 percent, but the real rate is unchanged. What happens to the nominal interest rate?

## Bills and Inflation, 1957–1994

The Fisher equation predicts a close connection between inflation and the rate of return on T-bills. This is apparent in Figure 5.2, which plots both time series on the same set of axes. Both series tend to move together, which is consistent with our previous statement that expected inflation is a significant force determining the nominal rate of interest.[2]

[2] See Nabd T. Khoury and Guy McLeod, "The Relationship between the Canadian Treasury-Bill Rate and Expected Inflation in Canada and the United States," *Canadian Journal of Administrative Sciences,* 2, n. 1 (June 1985).

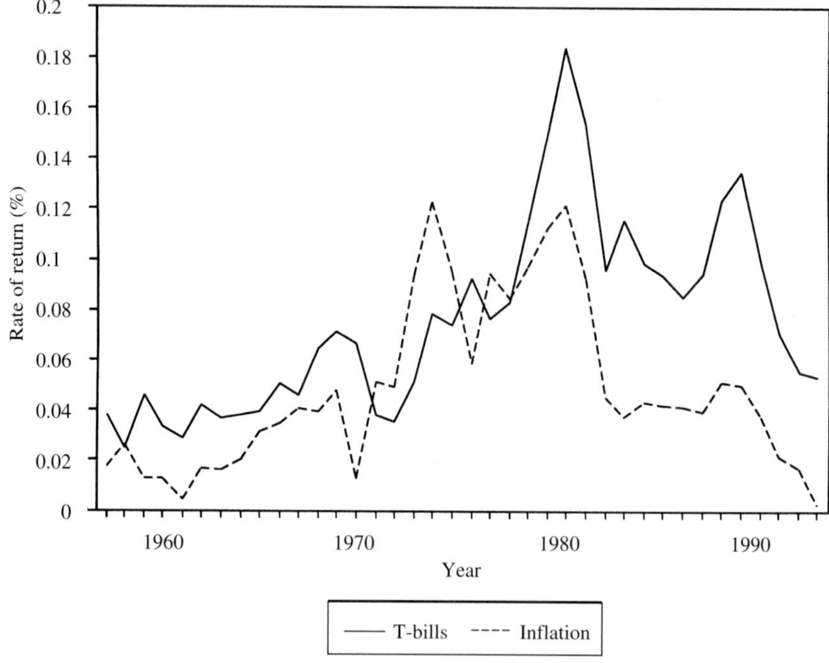


**Figure 5.2**
Rates of return, 1957–1994.

Data from ScotiaMcLeod's *Handbook of Canadian Debt Market Indices 1947–1994,* February 1995.

For a holding period of 30 days, the difference between actual and expected inflation is not large. The 30-day bill rate will adjust rapidly to changes in expected inflation induced by observed changes in actual inflation. It is not surprising that we see nominal rates on bills move roughly in tandem with inflation over time.

## 5.2 Risk and Risk Premiums

Risk means uncertainty about future rates of return. We can quantify that uncertainty using probability distributions.

For example, suppose you are considering investing some of your money, now all invested in a bank account, in a stock market index fund. The price of a share in the fund is currently \$100, and your *time horizon* is one year. You expect the cash dividend during the year to be \$4, so your expected *dividend yield* (i.e., dividends earned per dollar invested) is 4 percent.

Your total **holding-period return** (HPR) will depend on the price you expect to prevail one year from now. Suppose your best guess is that it will be \$110 per share. Then your *capital gain* will be \$10 and your HPR 14 percent. The definition of the holding period return in this context is capital gain income plus dividend income per dollar invested in the stock at the start of the period:

**Table 5.1** Probability Distribution of HPR on the Stock Market

| State of the Economy | Probability | Ending Price | HPR |
|---|---|---|---|
| Boom | .25 | $140 | 44% |
| Normal growth | .50 | 110 | 14 |
| Recession | .25 | 80 | −16 |

$$\text{HPR} = \frac{\text{Ending price of a share} - \text{Beginning price} + \text{Cash dividend}}{\text{Beginning price}}$$

In our case we have

$$\text{HPR} = \frac{\$110 - \$100 + \$4}{\$100} = .14, \text{ or } 14\%$$

This definition of the HPR assumes the dividend is paid at the end of the holding period. To the extent that dividends are received earlier, the HPR ignores reinvestment income between the receipt of the payment and the end of the holding period. Recall also that the percent return from dividends is called the dividend yield, and so the dividend yield plus the capital gains yield equals the HPR.

There is considerable uncertainty about the price of a share a year from now, however, so you cannot be sure about your eventual HPR. We can try to quantify our beliefs about the state of the economy and the stock market, however, in terms of three possible scenarios with probabilities as presented in Table 5.1.[3]

How can we evaluate this probability distribution? Throughout this book we will characterize probability distributions of rates of return in terms of their **expected** or **mean return,** $E(r)$, and their **standard deviation,** $\sigma$. The expected rate of return is a probability-weighted average of the rates of return in all scenarios. Calling $p(s)$ the probability of each scenario and $r(s)$ the HPR in each scenario, where scenarios are labeled or "indexed" by the variable $s$, we may write the expected return as:

$$E(r) = \sum_{s} p(s)r(s) \tag{5.1}$$

Applying this formula to the data in Table 5.1, we find that the expected rate of return on the index fund is:

$$E(r) = .25 \times 44\% + .5 \times 14\% + .25 \times (-16\%) = 14\%$$

In section 5.5 and in Appendix B, we argue that the standard deviation of the rate of return ($\sigma$) is a measure of risk. It is defined as the square root of the

[3] Chapters 5 through 7 rely on some basic results from elementary statistics. For a refresher, see the section titled "Quantitative Review" in the appendix at the end of the book.

**variance,** which in turn is defined as the expected value of the squared deviations from the expected return. The higher the volatility in outcomes, the higher will be the average value of these squared deviations. Therefore, variance and standard deviation measure the uncertainty of outcomes. Symbolically,

$$\sigma^2 = \sum_s p(s)\,[r(s) - E(r)]^2 \tag{5.2}$$

Therefore, in our example,

$$\sigma^2 = .25(44 - 14)^2 + .5(14 - 14)^2 + .25(-16 - 14)^2 = 450$$

and

$$\sigma = 21.21\%$$

Clearly, what would trouble potential investors in the index fund is the downside risk of a $-16$ percent rate of return, not the upside potential of a 44 percent rate of return. The standard deviation of the rate of return does not distinguish between these two; it treats both as deviations from the mean. As long as the probability distribution is more or less symmetric about the mean, however, $\sigma$ is an adequate measure of risk. In the special case where we can assume that the probability distribution is normal—represented by the well-known bell-shaped curve—$E(r)$ and $\sigma$ are perfectly adequate to characterize the distribution.

Getting back to the example, how much, if anything, should you invest in the index fund? First, you must ask how much of an expected reward is offered for the risk involved in investing money in stocks.

We measure the reward as the difference between the expected HPR on the index stock fund and the **risk-free rate,** that is, the rate you can earn by leaving money in risk-free assets such as T-bills, money market funds, or the bank. We call this difference the **risk premium** on common stocks. If the risk-free rate in the example is 6 percent per year, and the expected index fund return is 14 percent, then the risk premium on stocks is 8 percent per year. The difference between the actual rate of return on a risk-free asset and the risk-free rate is called **excess return.** Therefore, the risk premium is the expected excess return.

The degree to which investors are willing to commit funds to stocks depends on **risk aversion.** CFAs and financial analysts generally assume investors are risk averse in the sense that, if the risk premium were zero, people would not be willing to invest any money in stocks. In theory then, there must always be a positive risk premium on stocks in order to induce risk-averse investors to hold the existing supply of stocks instead of placing all their money in risk-free assets. We explore their theory more systematically further on in this chapter.

Although this simple scenario analysis illustrates the concepts behind the quantification of risk and return, you still may wonder how to get a more realistic estimate of $E(r)$ and $\sigma$ for common stocks and other types of securities. Here history has insights to offer.

## 5.3 The Historical Record

### Bills, Bonds, and Stocks: 1957–1994

The record of past rates of return is one possible source of information about risk premiums and standard deviations. We can estimate the historical risk premium by taking an average of the past differences between the HPRs on the asset type and the risk-free rate. Table 5.2 presents the annual HPRs on three asset classes for the period 1957–1994.

The first column shows the one-year HPR on a policy of "rolling-over" 91-day Treasury bills as they mature. Because this rate changes from month to month, it is risk-free only for a 91-day holding period. The second column presents the annual HPR an investor would have earned by investing in Canadian bonds with maturities higher than 10 years. The third column illustrates the HPR on the TSE 300 index of common stocks, which is a value-weighted stock portfolio of 300 of the largest corporations in Canada. (We discussed the TSE 300 stock index in Chapter 2.) Finally, the last column gives the annual inflation rate as measured by the rate of change in the consumer price index.

At the bottom of each column are five descriptive statistics. The first is the arithmetic mean or average HPR. For bills it is 7.57 percent, for bonds it is 8.39 percent, and for common stock it is 10.60 percent. These numbers imply an average risk premium of 0.82 percent per year on bonds and 3.03 percent on stocks (the average HPR less the risk-free rate of 7.57 percent).

The third statistic reported at the bottom of Table 5.2 is the standard deviation. The higher the standard deviation, the higher the variability of the HPR. This standard deviation is based on historical data rather than forecasts of *future* scenarios, as in equation 5.2. The formula for historical variance, however, is similar to equation 5.2. It is as follows:

$$\sigma^2 = \frac{n}{n-1} \sum_{t=1}^{n} \frac{(r_t - \bar{r})^2}{n} \qquad \textbf{(5.3)}$$

Here each year's outcome is taken as a possible scenario.[4] Deviations are simply taken from the historical average, $\bar{r}$, instead of the expected value $E(r)$. Each historical outcome is taken as equally likely, and given a "probability" of $1/n$.

Figure 5.3 gives a graphic representation of the relative variabilities of the annual HPR on the three different asset classes. We have plotted the three time series on the same set of axes. Clearly, the annual HPR on stocks is the most variable series. The standard deviation of stock returns has been 16.53 percent, compared to 10.71 percent for bonds and 3.87 percent for bills. Here is evidence

[4] We multiply by $n/(n-1)$ in equation 5.3 to eliminate statistical bias in the estimate of variance.

**Table 5.2** Rates of Return, 1957–1994

| Date | T-bill | LT Bond | Stock | CPI Change |
|---|---|---|---|---|
| 1957 | 0.03822 | 0.0794 | −0.20584 | 0.01794 |
| 1958 | 0.02507 | 0.01922 | 0.31247 | 0.02643 |
| 1959 | 0.0462 | −0.05072 | 0.04586 | 0.01288 |
| 1960 | 0.03312 | 0.12192 | 0.01782 | 0.01271 |
| 1961 | 0.02891 | 0.09158 | 0.32746 | 0.00418 |
| 1962 | 0.04215 | 0.05034 | −0.07094 | 0.01667 |
| 1963 | 0.03634 | 0.04579 | 0.15601 | 0.01639 |
| 1964 | 0.0379 | 0.06161 | 0.25433 | 0.02016 |
| 1965 | 0.03924 | 0.00048 | 0.06682 | 0.03162 |
| 1966 | 0.05034 | −0.01055 | −0.07067 | 0.03448 |
| 1967 | 0.04593 | −0.00484 | 0.18088 | 0.04074 |
| 1968 | 0.06444 | 0.02142 | 0.22445 | 0.03915 |
| 1969 | 0.07085 | −0.0286 | −0.00809 | 0.04795 |
| 1970 | 0.067 | 0.16389 | −0.03566 | 0.01307 |
| 1971 | 0.03807 | 0.1484 | 0.08008 | 0.05161 |
| 1972 | 0.03554 | 0.08113 | 0.27383 | 0.04908 |
| 1973 | 0.05111 | 0.01969 | 0.00274 | 0.09357 |
| 1974 | 0.0785 | −0.04529 | −0.25927 | 0.123 |
| 1975 | 0.07407 | 0.08022 | 0.18483 | 0.09524 |
| 1976 | 0.09265 | 0.23636 | 0.11022 | 0.0587 |
| 1977 | 0.07656 | 0.09036 | 0.10706 | 0.09446 |
| 1978 | 0.08336 | 0.04096 | 0.2972 | 0.08443 |
| 1979 | 0.11412 | −0.0283 | 0.4477 | 0.09689 |
| 1980 | 0.14974 | 0.02179 | 0.30134 | 0.11199 |
| 1981 | 0.18406 | −0.02086 | −0.10246 | 0.12199 |
| 1982 | 0.1542 | 0.45823 | 0.05541 | 0.09229 |
| 1983 | 0.09624 | 0.09609 | 0.35487 | 0.04514 |
| 1984 | 0.11587 | 0.16896 | −0.02393 | 0.03765 |
| 1985 | 0.09878 | 0.26679 | 0.25065 | 0.04376 |
| 1986 | 0.0933 | 0.1721 | 0.08954 | 0.04192 |
| 1987 | 0.08479 | 0.01766 | 0.05879 | 0.04122 |
| 1988 | 0.0941 | 0.11301 | 0.11081 | 0.03959 |
| 1989 | 0.12361 | 0.1517 | 0.21373 | 0.05168 |
| 1990 | 0.13484 | 0.04323 | −0.14798 | 0.05 |
| 1991 | 0.09833 | 0.25296 | 0.12015 | 0.03777 |
| 1992 | 0.07076 | 0.11568 | −0.01433 | 0.02136 |
| 1993 | 0.05509 | 0.22087 | 0.32548 | 0.01704 |
| 1994 | 0.05353 | −0.07387 | −0.00176 | 0.00229 |
| Mean | 0.07571 | 0.08392 | 0.10604 | 0.04834 |
| Variance | 0.0015 | 0.01148 | 0.02733 | 0.00113 |
| Standard | 0.0387 | 0.10713 | 0.16531 | 0.03367 |
| Minimum | 0.02507 | −0.07387 | −0.25927 | 0.00229 |
| Maximum | 0.18406 | 0.45823 | 0.4477 | 0.123 |

Data from *ScotiaMcLeod's Handbook of Canadian Debt Market Indices, 1947–1994.* Reprinted by permission.

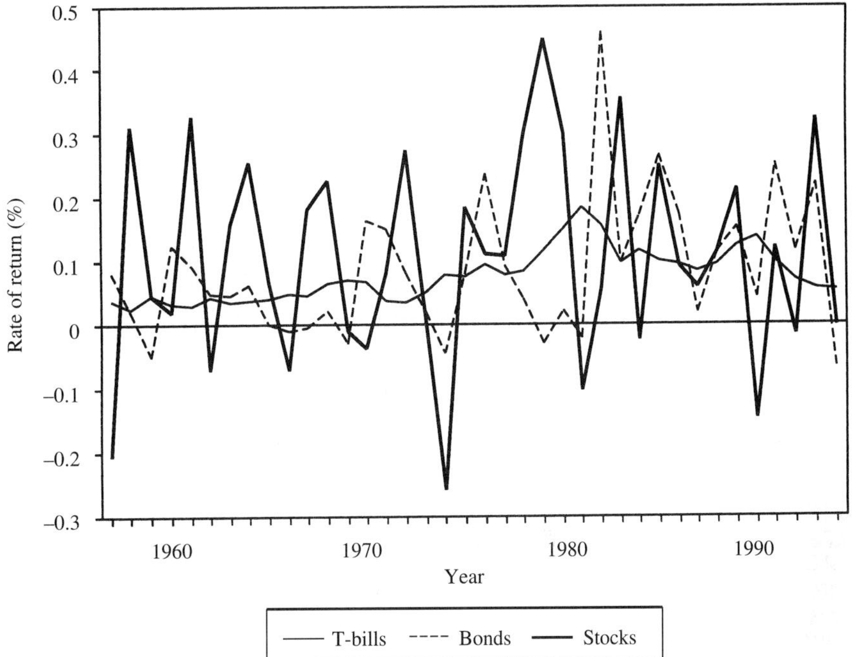


**Figure 5.3**

Rates of return on bills, bonds, and stocks, 1957–1994.

Data from *ScotiaMcLeod's Handbook of Canadian Debt Market Indices, 1947–1994,* February 1995. Used by permission of Scotia Capital Markets Fixed Income Research.

of the risk-return trade-off that characterizes security markets: The markets with the highest average returns also are the most volatile.

Comparable figures for U.S. stocks show that they have both a higher return and a higher risk than their Canadian counterparts. Thus, over the period 1926–1993, the average annual HPR for the 500 stocks that made the S&P 500 index was 12.31 percent, with a standard deviation of 20.46 percent. Similarly, a recent study by Roll[5] that used daily data covering the period April 1988–March 1991 gives average annual HPRs of 4.20 percent and 12.27 percent for Canada and the United States, with corresponding standard deviations of 9.97 percent and 14.37 percent. Part of the Canada–U.S. difference is due to the different industrial composition of their respective economies.

The other summary measures at the bottom of Table 5.2 show the highest and lowest annual HPR (the range) for each asset over the 33-year period. The size of this range is another possible measure of the relative riskiness of each asset class. It too confirms the ranking of stocks as the riskiest and bills as the least risky of the three asset classes.

---

[5] See R. Roll, "Industrial Structure and the Comparative Behavior of International Stock Market Indexes," *Journal of Finance* 47, no. 1 (March 1992).

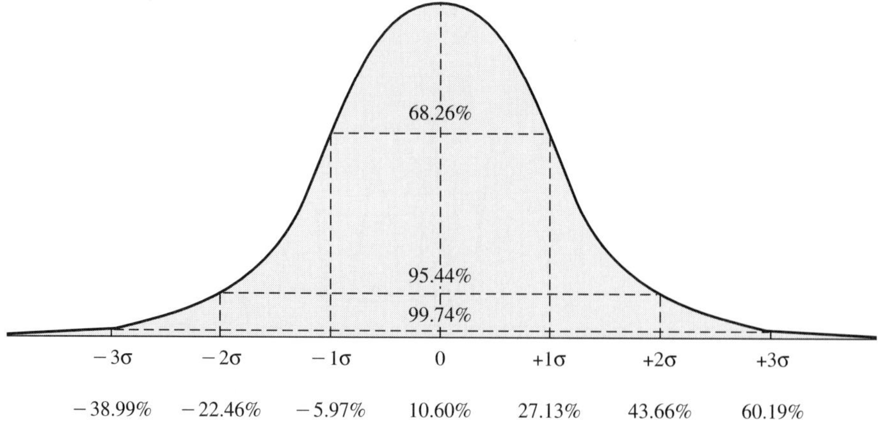


**Figure 5.4**
The normal distribution.

An all-stock portfolio with a standard deviation of 16.53 percent would constitute a very volatile investment. For example, if stock returns are normally distributed with that standard deviation and an expected rate of return of 10.60 percent (the historical average), then in roughly one year out of three, returns will be less than −5.97 percent (10.60 percent − 16.53 percent) or greater than 27.13 percent (10.60 percent + 16.53 percent).

Figure 5.4 is a graph of the normal curve with a mean of 10.60 percent and a standard deviation of 16.53 percent. The graph shows the theoretical probability of rates of return within various ranges given these parameters.

Panels A and B of Figure 5.5 present another view of the historical data, the actual frequency distribution of returns on various asset classes over the period 1957–1994. Notice the greater range of stock returns relative to bill or bond returns.

We should stress that variability of HPR in the past can be an unreliable guide to risk, at least in the case of the risk-free asset. For an investor with a holding period of one year, for example, a one-year T-bill is risk-free with a $\sigma$ of zero, despite the fact that the standard deviation of the one-year T-bill rate estimated from historical data is not zero.

Does the risk of the HPR on a financial asset reflect the risk of the cash flows from the real assets on which the financial assets are a claim? This is one of the most interesting and elusive questions in empirical finance. Ideally, the answer would be in the affirmative, reflecting prudent and competitive investment practices. So far, the evidence is inconclusive, as discussed in Chapter 11 on market efficiency.

The risk of cash flows of real assets reflects both *business risk* (profit fluctuations due to business conditions) and *financial risk* (increased profit fluctuations due to leverage). This reminds us that an all-stock portfolio represents claims on leveraged corporations. Most corporations carry some debt, the service of which

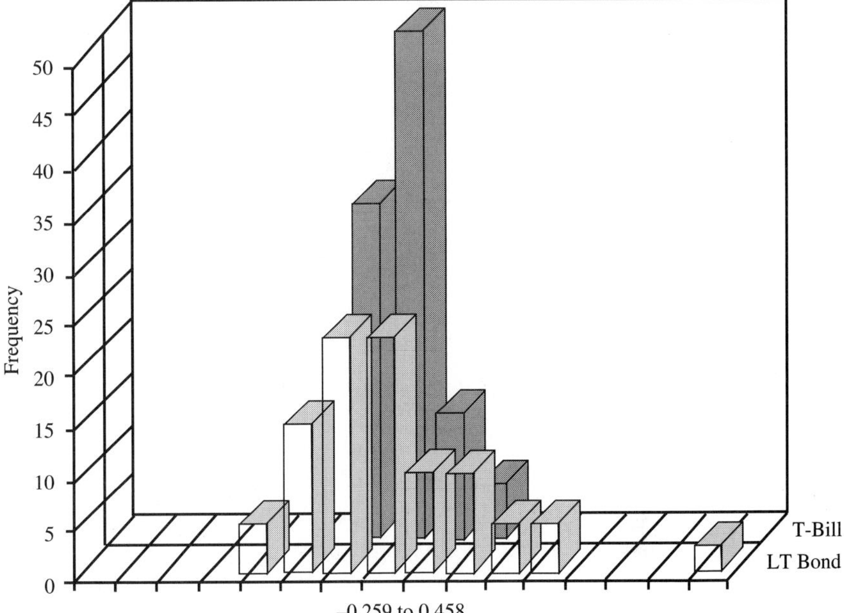


**Figure 5.5a**

Frequency distributions of the annual HPR on three asset classes: T-bills and Long-term bonds.

Data from *ScotiaMcLeod's Handbook of Canadian Debt Market Indices,* 1947–1994. Reprinted by permission.

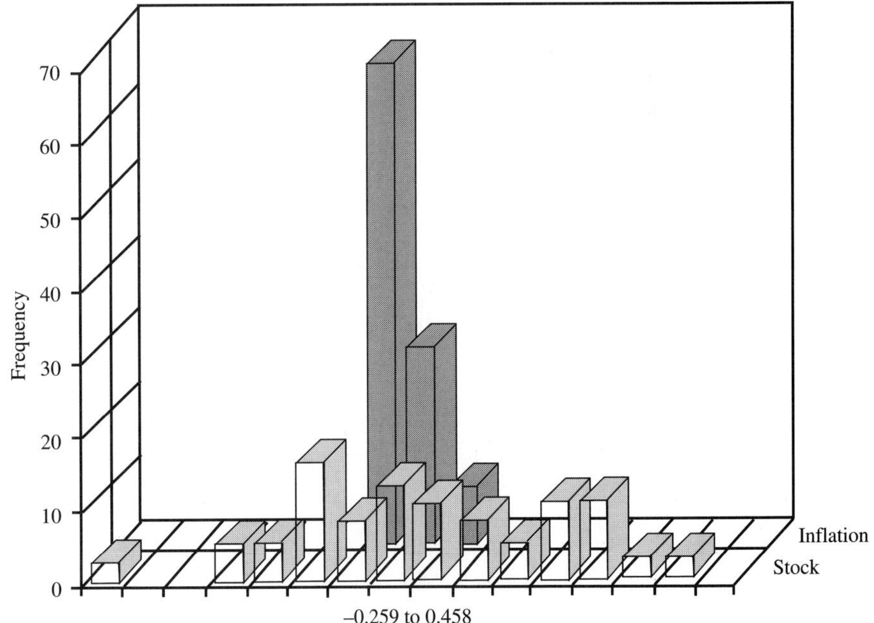


**Figure 5.5b**

Frequency distributions of the annual HPR on three asset classes: Stocks and Inflation.

Data from *ScotiaMcLeod's Handbook of Canadian Debt Market Indices,* 1947–1994. Reprinted by permission.

## INVESTING: WHAT TO BUY WHEN?

In making broad-scale investment decisions, investors may want to know how various types of investments have performed during booms, recessions, high inflation, and low inflation. The table below shows how 10 asset categories performed during representative years since World War II. But history rarely repeats itself, so historical performance is only a rough guide to the future.

**Average Annual Return on Investment***

| Investment | Recession | Boom | High Inflation | Low Inflation |
|---|---|---|---|---|
| Bonds (long-term government) | 17% | 4% | −1% | 8% |
| Commodity index | 1 | −6 | 15 | −5 |
| Diamonds (1-carat investment grade) | −4 | 8 | 79 | 15 |
| Gold† (bullion) | −8 | −9 | 105 | 19 |
| Private home | 4 | 6 | 6 | 5 |
| Real estate‡ (commercial) | 9 | 13 | 18 | 6 |
| Silver (bullion) | 3 | −6 | 94 | 4 |
| Stocks (blue chip) | 14 | 7 | −3 | 21 |
| Stocks (small growth-company) | 17 | 14 | 7 | 12 |
| Treasury bills (3-month) | 6 | 5 | 7 | 3 |

*In most cases, figures are computed as follows: Recession—average of performance during calendar years 1946, 1975, and 1982; boom—average of 1951, 1965, and 1984; high inflation—average of 1947, 1974, and 1980; low inflation—average of 1955, 1961, and 1986.

†Gold figures are based only on data since 1971 and may be less reliable than others.

‡Commercial real estate figures are based only on data since 1978 and may be less reliable than others.

Modified from *The Wall Street Journal,* November 13, 1987. Reprinted by permission of *The Wall Street Journal,* 

Sources: Commerce Dept.; Commodity Research Bureau; DeBeers Inc.; Diamond Registry; Dow Jones & Co.; Dun & Bradstreet; Handy & Harman; Ibbotson Associates; Charles Kroll (Diversified Investor's Forecast); Merrill Lynch; National Council of Real Estate Investment Fiduciaries; Frank B. Russell Co.; Shearson Lehman Bros.; T. Rowe Price New Horizons Fund.

is a fixed cost. Greater fixed cost makes profits riskier; thus, leverage increases equity risk.

**CONCEPT CHECK** Question 2. Compute the average excess return on stocks (over the T-bill rate) and its standard deviation for the years 1957–1968.

## 5.4 REAL VERSUS NOMINAL RISK

The distinction between the real and the nominal rate of return is crucial in making investment choices when investors are interested in the future purchasing power of their wealth. Thus, a Canada bond that offers a "risk-free" *nominal*

**Table 5.3** Purchasing Power of $1,000 20 Years from Now and 20-Year Real Annualized HPR

| Assumed Annual Rate of Inflation | Number of Dollars Required 20 Years from Now to Buy What $1 Buys Today | Purchasing Power of $1,000 to Be Received in 20 Years | Annualized Real HPR |
|---|---|---|---|
| 4% | $2.19 | $456.39 | 7.69% |
| 6 | 3.21 | 311.80 | 5.66 |
| 8 | 4.66 | 214.55 | 3.70 |
| 10 | 6.73 | 148.64 | 1.82 |
| 12 | 9.65 | 103.67 | |

Purchase price of bond is $103.67.
Nominal 20-year annualized HPR is 12% per year.
Purchasing power = $1,000/(1 + Inflation rate)$^{20}$.
Real HPR, $r$, is computed from the following relationship:

$$\begin{aligned} r &= (1 + R)/(1 + i) - 1 \\ &= 1.12/(1 + i) - 1 \end{aligned}$$

rate of return is not truly a risk-free investment—it does not guarantee the future purchasing power of its cash flow.

An example might be a bond that pays $1,000 on a date 20 years from now but nothing in the interim. While some people see such a zero-coupon bond as a convenient way for individuals to lock in attractive, risk-free, long-term interest rates (particularly in RRSP[6] accounts), the evidence in Table 5.3 is rather discouraging about the value of $1,000 in 20 years in terms of today's purchasing power.

Suppose the price of the bond is $103.67, giving a nominal rate of return of 12 percent per year (since $103.67 \times 1.12^{20} = 1{,}000$). We can compute the real annualized HPR for each inflation rate.

A revealing comparison is at a 12 percent rate of inflation. At that rate, Table 5.3 shows that the purchasing power of the $1,000 to be received in 20 years would be $103.67, or what was paid initially for the bond. The real HPR in these circumstances is zero. When the rate of inflation equals the nominal rate of interest, the price of goods increases just as fast as the money accumulated from the investment, and there is no growth in purchasing power.

At an inflation rate of only 4 percent per year, however, the purchasing power of $1,000 will be $456.39 in terms of today's prices; that is, the investment of $103.67 grows to a real value of $456.39, for a real 20-year annualized HPR of 7.69 percent per year.

Again looking at Table 5.3, you can see that an investor expecting an inflation rate of 8 percent per year anticipates a real annualized HPR of 3.70 percent. If

[6] Registered Retirement Savings Plan.

the actual rate of inflation turns out to be 10 percent per year, the resulting real HPR is only 1.82 percent per year. These differences show the important distinction between expected and actual inflation rates.

Even professional economic forecasters acknowledge that their inflation forecasts are hardly certain even for the next year, not to mention the next 20.

When you look at an asset from the perspective of its future purchasing power, you can see that an asset that is riskless in nominal terms can be very risky in real terms.

---

**CONCEPT CHECK** Question 3. Suppose the rate of inflation turns out to be 13 percent per year. What will be the real annualized 20-year HPR on the nominally risk-free bond?

---

We now turn to a more detailed exploration of our earlier statements, about investor risk aversion and the need for a risk premium to induce investors to hold stocks.

## 5.5 RISK AND RISK AVERSION

### Risk with Simple Prospects

The presence of risk means that more than one outcome is possible. A *simple prospect* is an investment opportunity in which a certain initial wealth is placed at risk, and there are only two possible outcomes. For the sake of simplicity, it is useful to begin our analysis and elucidate some basic concepts using simple prospects.

Take as an example initial wealth, $W$, of \$100,000, and assume two possible results. With a probability, $p$, of .6, the favourable outcome will occur, leading to final wealth, $W_1$, of \$150,000. Otherwise, with probability $1 - p = .4$, a less favourable outcome, $W_2 = \$80{,}000$, will occur. We can represent the simple prospect using an event tree:

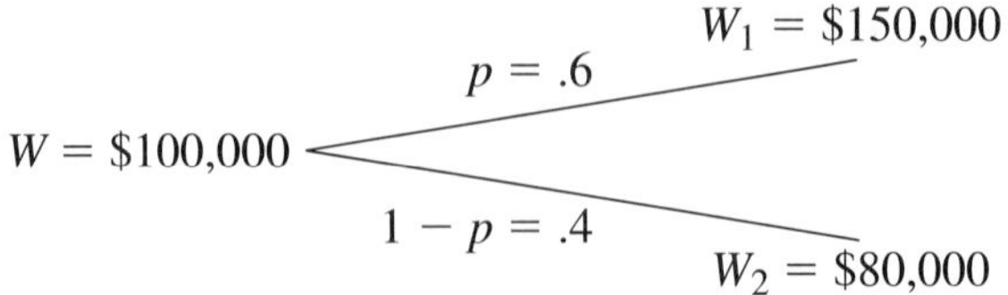


Suppose that an investor, Susan, is offered an investment portfolio with a payoff in one year that is described by such a simple prospect. How can she evaluate this portfolio?

First, she could try to summarize it using descriptive statistics. For instance, her mean or expected end-of-year wealth, denoted $E(W)$, is

$$\begin{aligned} E(W) &= pW_1 + (1 - p)W_2 \\ &= .6 \times 150{,}000 + .4 \times 80{,}000 \\ &= \$122{,}000 \end{aligned}$$

The expected profit on the \$100,000 investment portfolio is \$22,000: 122,000 − 100,000. The variance, $\sigma^2$, of the portfolio's payoff is calculated as the expected value of the squared deviations of each possible outcome from the mean:

$$\begin{aligned} \sigma^2 &= p[W_1 - E(W)]^2 + (1 - p)[W_2 - E(W)]^2 \\ &= .6(150{,}000 - 122{,}000)^2 + .4(80{,}000 - 122{,}000)^2 \\ &= 1{,}176{,}000{,}247 \end{aligned}$$

The standard deviation, $\sigma$, the square root of the variance, is therefore \$34,292.86.

Clearly, this is risky business: The standard deviation of the payoff is large, much larger than the expected profit of \$22,000. Whether the expected profit is large enough to justify such risk depends on the alternative portfolios.

Let us suppose Treasury bills are one alternative to Susan's risky portfolio. Suppose that at the time of the decision, a one-year T-bill offers a rate of return of 5 percent; \$100,000 can be invested to yield a sure profit of \$5,000. We can now draw Susan's decision tree:

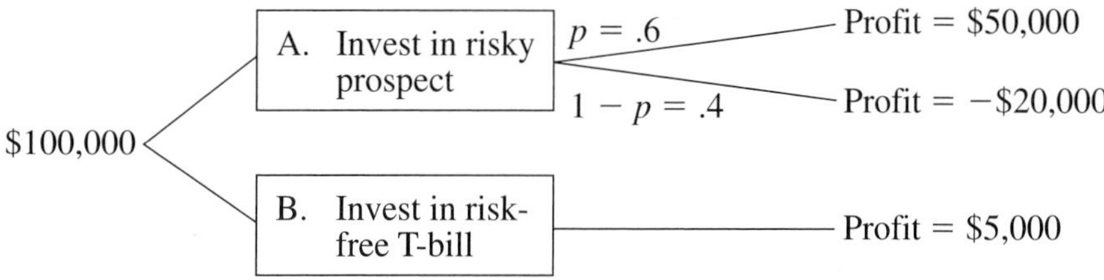


Earlier, we showed the expected profit on the portfolio to be \$22,000. Therefore, the expected marginal, or incremental, profit of the risky portfolio over investing in safe T-bills is

$$\$22{,}000 - \$5{,}000 = \$17{,}000$$

meaning that one can earn an expected risk premium of \$17,000 as compensation for the risk of the investment.

The question of whether a given risk premium provides adequate compensation for the investment's risk is age-old. Indeed, one of the central concerns of finance theory (and much of this text) is the measurement of risk and the determination of the risk premiums that investors can expect of risky assets in well-functioning capital markets.

---

**CONCEPT CHECK** Question 4. What is the risk premium of Susan's risky portfolio in terms of rate of return rather than dollars?

---

## Risk, Speculation, and Gambling

One definition of *speculation* is "the assumption of considerable business risk in obtaining commensurate gain." Although this definition is fine linguistically, it is useless without first specifying what is meant by "commensurate gain" and "considerable risk."

By *commensurate gain* we mean a positive expected profit beyond the risk-free alternative. This is the risk premium. In our example, the dollar risk premium is the profit net of the alternative, which is the sure T-bill profit. The risk premium is the incremental expected gain from taking on the risk. By *considerable risk* we mean that the risk is sufficient to affect the decision. An individual might reject a prospect that has a positive risk premium because the added gain is insufficient to make up for the risk involved.

To gamble is "to bet or wager on an uncertain outcome." If you compare this definition to that of speculation, you will see that the central difference is the lack of "good profit." Economically speaking, a gamble is the assumption of risk for no purpose but enjoyment of the risk itself, whereas speculation is undertaken because one perceives a favourable risk-return trade-off. To turn a gamble into a speculative prospect requires an adequate risk premium for compensation to risk-averse investors for the risks that they bear. Hence *risk aversion and speculation are not inconsistent.*

In some cases a gamble may appear to the participants as speculation. Suppose that two investors disagree sharply about the future exchange rate of the Canadian dollar against the British pound. They may choose to bet on the outcome. Suppose that Paul will pay Mary \$100 if the value of one pound exceeds \$2.00 one year from now, whereas Mary will pay Paul if the pound is worth less than \$2.00. There are only two relevant outcomes: (1) the pound will exceed \$2.00, or (2) it will fall below \$2.00. If both Paul and Mary agree on the probabilities of the two possible outcomes, and if neither party anticipates a loss, it must be that they assign $p = .5$ to each outcome. In that case the expected profit to both is zero and each has entered one side of a gambling prospect.

What is more likely, however, is that the bet results from differences in the probabilities that Paul and Mary assign to the outcome. Mary assigns it $p > .5$, whereas Paul's assessment is $p < .5$. They perceive, subjectively, two different prospects. Economists call this case of differing belief's *heterogeneous expectations.* In such cases investors on each side of a financial position see themselves as speculating rather than gambling.

Both Paul and Mary should be asking, "Why is the other willing to invest in the side of a risky prospect that I believe offers a negative expected profit?" The ideal way to resolve heterogeneous beliefs is for Paul and Mary to "merge their information," that is, for each party to verify that he or she possesses all relevant information and processes the information properly. Of course, the acquisition of information and the extensive communication that is required to eliminate all heterogeneity in expectations is costly, and thus, up to a point, heterogeneous expectations cannot be taken as irrational. If, however, Paul and

Mary enter such contracts frequently, they would recognize the information problem in one of two ways: Either they will realize that they are creating gambles when each wins half of the bets, or the consistent loser will admit that he or she has been betting on inferior forecasts.

---

**CONCEPT CHECK** Question 5. Assume that dollar-denominated T-bills in Canada and pound-denominated bills in the United Kingdom offer equal yields to maturity. Both are short-term assets, and both are free of default risk. Neither offers investors a risk premium. However, a Canadian investor who holds U.K. bills is subject to exchange rate risk since the pounds earned on the U.K. bills eventually will be exchanged for dollars at the future exchange rate. What expectation about future exchange rates would determine whether a Canadian investor who purchases U.K. bills is engaging in speculation or gambling?

---

## Risk Aversion and Utility Values

We have discussed risk with simple prospects and how risk premiums bear on speculation. A prospect that has a zero risk premium is called a *fair game.* Investors who are *risk averse* reject investment portfolios that are fair games or worse. Risk-averse investors are willing to consider only risk-free or speculative prospects. Loosely speaking, a risk-averse investor "penalizes" the expected rate of return of a risky portfolio by a certain percentage (or penalizes the expected profit by a dollar amount) to account for the risk involved. The greater the risk the investor perceives, the larger the penalization. (One might wonder why we assume risk aversion as fundamental. We believe that most investors accept this view from simple introspection, but we discuss the question more fully in Appendix C of this chapter.)

We can formalize this notion of a risk-penalty system. To do so, we will assume that each investor can assign a welfare, or **utility,** score to competing investment portfolios based on the expected return and risk of those portfolios. The utility score may be viewed as a means of ranking portfolios. Higher utility values are assigned to portfolios with more attractive risk-return profiles. Portfolios receive higher utility scores for higher expected returns and lower scores for higher volatility. Many particular "scoring" systems are legitimate. One reasonable function that is commonly employed by financial theorists assigns a portfolio with expected return $E(r)$ and variance of returns $\sigma^2$ the following utility score:

$$U = E(r) - \frac{1}{2}A\sigma^2 \qquad \textbf{(5.4)}$$

where $U$ is the utility value and $A$ is an index of the investor's aversion to taking on risk. (The factor of $\frac{1}{2}$ is a scaling convention that will simplify calculations in later chapters. It has no economic significance, and we could eliminate it simply by defining a "new" $A$ with half the value of the $A$ used here.)

Equation 5.4 is consistent with the notion that utility is enhanced by high expected returns and diminished by high risk. (Whether variance is an adequate measure of portfolio risk is discussed in Appendix B.) The extent to which variance lowers utility depends on *A*, the investor's degree of risk aversion. More risk-averse investors (who have the larger *A*s) penalize risky investments more severely. Investors choosing among competing investment portfolios will select the one providing the highest utility level.

Notice in equation 5.4 that the utility provided by a risk-free portfolio is simply the rate of return on the portfolio, since there is no penalization for risk. This provides us with a convenient benchmark for evaluating portfolios. For example, recall Susan's investment problem, choosing between a portfolio with expected return .22 (22 percent) and standard deviation $\sigma = .34$, and T-bills, providing a risk-free return of 5 percent. Although the risk premium on the risky portfolio is large, 17 percent, the risk of the project is so great that Susan does not need to be very risk averse to choose the safe all-bills strategy. Even for $A = 3$, a moderate risk-aversion parameter, equation 5.4 shows the risky portfolio's utility value as $.22 - \frac{1}{2} \times 3 \times .34^2 = .0466$, or 4.66 percent, which is slightly lower than the risk-free rate. In this case, Susan would reject the portfolio in favor of T-bills.

The downward adjustment of the expected return as a penalty for risk is $\frac{1}{2} \times 3 \times .34^2 = .1734$, or 17.34 percent. If Susan were less risk averse (more risk tolerant), for example with $A = 2$, she would adjust the expected rate of return downward by only 11.56 percent. In that case, the utility level of the portfolio would be 10.44 percent, higher than the risk-free rate, leading her to accept the prospect.

**CONCEPT CHECK**

Question 6. A portfolio has an expected rate of return of .20 and standard deviation of .20. Bills offer a sure rate of return of .07. Which investment alternative will be chosen by an investor whose $A = 4$? What if $A = 8$? *Note:* Treat the interest rates as decimals (for example, $E(r) = .20$, not 20 percent) to answer this question.

Because we can compare utility values to the rate offered on risk-free investments when choosing between a risky portfolio and a safe one, we may interpret a portfolio's utility value as its "certainty equivalent" rate of return to an investor. That is, the **certainty equivalent rate** of a portfolio is the rate that risk-free investments would need to offer with certainty to be considered equally attractive to the risky portfolio.

Now we can say that a portfolio is desirable only if its certainty equivalent return exceeds that of the risk-free alternative. A sufficiently risk-averse investor may assign any risky portfolio, even one with a positive risk premium, a certainty equivalent rate of return that is below the risk-free rate, which will cause the investor to reject the portfolio. At the same time, a less risk-averse (more risk-tolerant) investor will assign the same portfolio a certainty equivalent rate that exceeds the risk-free rate and thus will prefer the portfolio to the risk-free alter-

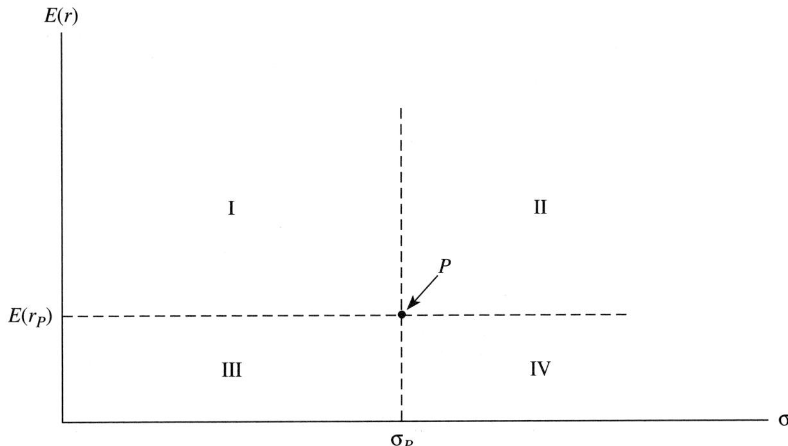


**Figure 5.6**
The trade-off between risk and return of a potential investment portfolio.

native. If the risk premium is zero or negative to begin with, any downward adjustment to utility only makes the portfolio look worse. Its certainty equivalent rate will be below that of the risk-free alternative for all risk-averse investors.

In contrast to risk-averse investors, **risk-neutral** investors judge risky prospects solely by their expected rates of return. The level of risk is irrelevant to the risk-neutral investor, meaning that there is no penalization for risk. For this investor, a portfolio's certainty equivalent rate is simply its expected rate of return.

A risk lover is willing to engage in fair games and gambles; this investor adjusts the expected return upward to take into account the "fun" of confronting the prospect's risk. Risk lovers always will take a fair game because their upward adjustment of utility for risk gives the fair game a certainty equivalent that exceeds the alternative of the risk-free investment.

We can depict the individual's trade-off between risk and return by plotting the characteristics of potential investment portfolios that the individual would view as equally attractive on a graph with axes measuring the expected value and standard deviation of portfolio returns. Figure 5.6 plots the characteristics of one portfolio.

Portfolio *P*, which has expected return $E(r_p)$ and standard deviation $\sigma_p$, is preferred by risk-averse investors to any portfolio in quadrant IV because it has an expected return equal to or greater than any portfolio in that quadrant and a standard deviation equal to or smaller than any portfolio in that quadrant. Conversely, any portfolio in quadrant I is preferable to portfolio *P* because its expected return is equal to or greater than *P*'s and its standard deviation is equal to or smaller than *P*'s.

This is the mean-standard deviation, or equivalently, **mean-variance (M-V) criterion.** It can be stated as *A* dominates *B* if

$$E(r_A) \geq E(r_B)$$

and

$$\sigma_A \leq \sigma_B$$

and at least one inequality is strict.

In the expected return–standard deviation graph, the preferred direction is northwest, because in this direction we simultaneously increase the expected return *and* decrease the variance of the rate of return. This means that any portfolio that lies northwest of $P$ is superior to $P$.

What can be said about the portfolios in quadrants II and III? Their desirability, compared with $P$, depends on the exact nature of the investor's risk aversion. Suppose an investor identifies all portfolios that are equally attractive as portfolio $P$. Starting at $P$, an increase in standard deviation lowers utility; it must be compensated for by an increase in expected return. Thus, point $Q$ is equally desirable to this investor as $P$. Investors will be equally attracted to portfolios with high risk and high expected returns compared with other portfolios with lower risk but lower expected returns.

These equally preferred portfolios will lie on a curve in the mean-standard deviation graph that connects all portfolio points with the same utility value (Figure 5.7). This is called the **indifference curve.**

To determine some of the points that appear on the indifference curve, examine the utility values of several possible portfolios for an investor with $A = 4$, presented in Table 5.4. Note that each portfolio offers identical utility, since the high-return portfolios also have high risk. Although in practice the exact indifference curves of various investors cannot be known, this analysis can take us a long way in determining appropriate principles for portfolio selection strategy.

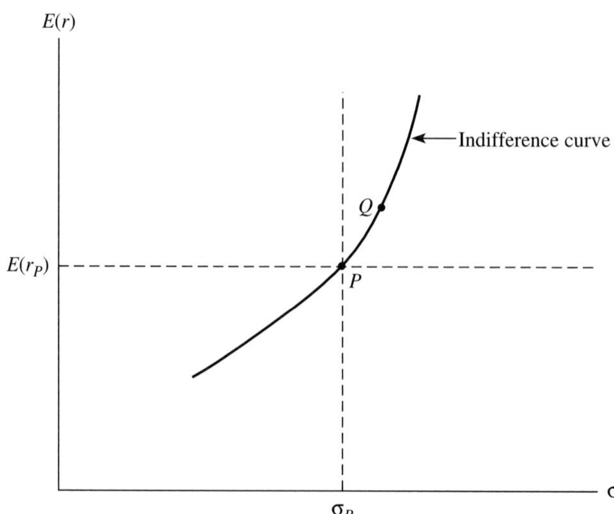


**Figure 5.7**
The indifference curve.

**Table 5.4** Utility Values of Possible Portfolios

| Expected Return, $E(r)$ | Standard Deviation, $\sigma$ | Utility = $E(r) - \frac{1}{2}A\sigma^2$ |
|---|---|---|
| .10 | .200 | $.10 - .5 \times 4 \times .04 = .02$ |
| .15 | .255 | $.15 - .5 \times 4 \times .065 = .02$ |
| .20 | .300 | $.20 - .5 \times 4 \times .09 = .02$ |
| .25 | .339 | $.25 - .5 \times 4 \times .115 = .02$ |

**CONCEPT CHECK** Question 7.

*a.* How will the indifference curve of a less risk-averse investor compare to the indifference curve drawn in Figure 5.7?

*b.* Draw both indifference curves passing through point *P.*

## 5.6 PORTFOLIO RISK

### Asset Risk versus Portfolio Risk

We have focused so far on the return and risk of an individual's overall investment portfolio. Such portfolios are composed of diverse types of assets. In addition to their direct investment in financial markets, investors have stakes in pension funds, life insurance policies with savings components, homes, and, not least, the earning power of their skills (human capital).

The riskiness of an asset cannot be judged in isolation from an investor's entire portfolio of assets. Sometimes, adding a seemingly risky asset to a portfolio actually reduces the risk of the portfolio as a whole. Investing in an asset in order to reduce the overall risk of a portfolio is called **hedging.**

The most direct example of hedging is an insurance contract, which is a legal arrangement transferring a specific risk from the insured to the insurer for a specified cost (the insurance premium). Suppose you own a $100,000 house and have a total net worth of $300,000. There is a small possibility that your house will burn to the ground within the coming year. If it does, your net wealth will be reduced by $100,000. If it does not, your wealth remains unchanged (independent of any income from this and other investments, which we shall ignore to simplify the example).

Say your probability assessment of the event "the house will burn to the ground during the coming year" is 0.002. Your expected loss (0.002 × $100,000 = $200) is small in terms of your overall wealth. On the other hand, a fire would reduce your wealth by a full one-third.

An insurance contract to cover this risk might cost $220, a price that exceeds the expected loss and thereby provides expected profit to the insurer. If we evaluate the payoff to the insurance contract in isolation, insurance looks like a risky security.

Not only is the expected profit of the policy negative (−$20), and the expected rate of return negative (−20/220 = −9.09 percent), but the risk also seems to be substantial. The standard deviation of the policy's payoff is identical to that of the uninsured house. You receive either $100,000 (with probability 0.002) or nothing (with probability 0.998), a payoff structure that might remind you of a lottery.

Does this mean only risk lovers should purchase insurance? Clearly not. Instead, the example illustrates the fallacy of evaluating the risk of an asset (the insurance contract) separately from the other assets owned by the investor.

Consider the insured house as a *portfolio* that includes the insurance contract and the house.

| Portfolio Component | Value if No Fire | Value if Fire |
|---|---|---|
| House | $100,000 | 0 |
| Insurance contract | 0 | $100,000 |

The payoff of the entire portfolio, house plus policy, in the two outcomes is identical and equal to $100,000 because the house is insured for its precise value, and the insurance kicks in only when the value of the house goes to zero (in the event of a fire). Thus, the portfolio's overall risk has been reduced to zero.

Insurance contracts are obvious hedging vehicles. In many contexts, financial markets offer similar, although perhaps less direct, hedging opportunities. For example, consider two firms, one producing suntan lotion, the other producing umbrellas. The shareholders of each firm face weather risk of an opposite nature. A rainy summer lowers the return on the suntan-lotion firm but raises it on the umbrella firm. Shares of the umbrella firm act as "weather insurance" for the suntan-lotion firm shareholders in precisely the same way that fire insurance policies insure houses. When the lotion firm does poorly (bad weather), the "insurance" asset (umbrella shares) provides a high payoff that offsets the loss.

Another means to control portfolio risk is **diversification,** by which we mean that investments are made in a wide variety of assets so that the exposure to the risk of any particular security is limited. By placing one's eggs in many baskets, overall portfolio risk actually may be less than the risk of any component security considered in isolation.

To examine these effects more precisely, and to lay a foundation for the mathematical properties that will be used in coming chapters, we will consider an example with less than perfect hedging opportunities, and in the process review the statistics underlying portfolio risk and return characteristics.

## A Review of Portfolio Mathematics

Consider the problem of Humanex, a nonprofit organization deriving most of its income from the return of its endowment. Years ago, the founders of Best Candy willed a large block of Best Candy stock to Humanex with the provision that Humanex may never sell it. This block of shares now comprises 50 percent of Humanex's endowment. Humanex has free choice as to where to invest the remainder of its portfolio.[7]

The value of Best Candy stock is sensitive to the price of sugar. In years when the Caribbean sugar crop fails, the price of sugar rises significantly and Best Candy suffers considerable losses. We can describe the fortunes of Best Candy stock using the following scenario analysis:

| | Normal Year for Sugar | | Abnormal Year |
|---|---|---|---|
| | Bullish Stock Market | Bearish Stock Market | Sugar Crisis |
| Probability | .5 | .3 | .2 |
| Rate of return | .25 | .10 | −.25 |

To summarize these three possible outcomes using conventional statistics, we review some of the key roles governing the properties of risky assets and portfolios.

*Rule 1.* The mean or *expected return* of an asset is a probability-weighted average of its return in all scenarios. Calling $Pr(s)$ the probability of scenario $s$ and $r(s)$ the return in scenario $s$, we may write the expected return, $E(r)$, as

$$E(r) = \sum_s Pr(s)r(s) \tag{5.5}$$

Applying this formula to the case at hand, with three possible scenarios, we find that the expected rate of return of Best Candy's stock is

$$\begin{aligned} E(r_{\text{Best}}) &= .5 \times .25 + .3 \times .10 + .2(-.25) \\ &= .105 \\ &= 10.5\% \end{aligned}$$

*Rule 2.* The *variance* of an asset's returns is the expected value of the squared deviations from the expected return. Symbolically,

$$\sigma^2 = \sum_s Pr(s)[r(s) - E(r)]^2 \tag{5.6}$$

[7] The portfolio restriction is admittedly unrealistic. We use this example only to illustrate the various strategies that might be used to control risk and to review some useful results from statistics.

Therefore, in our example

$$\sigma^2_{\text{Best}} = .5(.25 - .105)^2 + .3(.10 - .105)^2 + .2(-.25 - .105)^2$$
$$= .035725$$

The *standard deviation* of Best's return, which is the square root of the variance, is $\sqrt{.035725} = .189$, or 18.9 percent.

Humanex has 50 percent of its endowment in Best's stock. To reduce the risk of the overall portfolio, it could invest the remainder in T-bills, which yield a sure rate of return of 5 percent. To derive the return of the overall portfolio, we apply rule 3:

*Rule 3.* The rate of return on a portfolio is a weighted average of the rates of return of each asset comprising the portfolio, with portfolio proportions as weights. This implies that the *expected* rate of return on a portfolio is a weighted average of the *expected* rate of return on each component asset.

In this case, the portfolio proportions in each asset are .5, and the portfolio's expected rate of return is

$$\begin{aligned} E(r_{\text{Humanex}}) &= .5E(r_{\text{Best}}) + .5r_{\text{Bills}} \\ &= .5 \times .105 + .5 \times .05 \\ &= .0775 \\ &= 7.75\% \end{aligned}$$

The standard deviation of the portfolio may be derived from the following:

*Rule 4.* When a risky asset is combined with a risk-free asset, the portfolio standard deviation equals the risky asset's standard deviation multiplied by the portfolio proportion invested in the asset.

In this case, the Humanex portfolio is 50 percent invested in Best stock and 50 percent invested in risk-free bills. Therefore

$$\begin{aligned} \sigma_{\text{Humanex}} &= .5\sigma_{\text{Best}} \\ &= .5 \times .189 \\ &= .0945 \\ &= 9.45\% \end{aligned}$$

By reducing its exposure to the risk of Best by half, Humanex reduces its portfolio standard deviation by half. The cost of this risk reduction, however, is a reduction in expected return. The expected rate of return on Best stock is 10.5 percent. The expected return on the one-half T-bill portfolio is 7.75 percent. This makes the risk premiums over the 5 percent rate on risk-free bills 5.5 percent for Best stock and 2.75 percent for the half T-bill portfolio. By reducing the share of Best stock in the portfolio by one half, Humanex reduces its portfolio risk premium by one half, from 5.5 percent to 2.75 percent.

In an effort to improve the contribution of the endowment to the operating budget, Humanex's trustees hire Sally, a recent MBA, as a consultant. Investigating the sugar and candy industry, Sally discovers, not surprisingly, that during years of sugar crisis in the Caribbean basin, SugarBeet, a Canadian sugar refiner that uses beets as raw material, reaps unusual profits and its stock price soars. A scenario analysis of SugarBeet's stock looks like this:

| | Normal Year for Sugar | | Abnormal Year |
|---|---|---|---|
| | Bullish Stock Market | Bearish Stock Market | Sugar Crisis |
| Probability | .5 | .3 | .2 |
| Rate of return | .01 | −.05 | .35 |

The expected rate of return on SugarBeet's stock is 6 percent, and its standard deviation is 14.73 percent. Thus, SugarBeet is almost as volatile as Best, yet its expected return is only a notch better than the T-bill rate. This cursory analysis makes SugarBeet appear to be an unattractive investment. For Humanex, however, the stock holds great promise.

SugarBeet offers excellent hedging potential for holders of Best stock because its return is highest precisely when Best's return is lowest—during a Caribbean sugar crisis. Consider Humanex's portfolio when it splits its investment evenly between Best and SugarBeet. The rate of return for each scenario is the simple average of the rates on Best and SugarBeet because the portfolio is split evenly between the two stocks (see rule 3).

| | Normal Year for Sugar | | Abnormal Year |
|---|---|---|---|
| | Bullish Stock Market | Bearish Stock Market | Sugar Crisis |
| Probability | .5 | .3 | .2 |
| Rate of return | .13 | .025 | .05 |

The expected rate of return on Humanex's hedged portfolio is .0825, with a standard deviation of 0.483, or 4.83 percent.

Sally now summarizes the reward and risk of the three alternatives:

| Portfolio | Expected Return | Standard Deviation |
|---|---|---|
| All in Best Candy | .105 | .1890 |
| Half in T-bills | .0775 | .0945 |
| Half in SugarBeet | .0825 | .0483 |

The numbers speak for themselves. The hedge portfolio including SugarBeet clearly dominates the simple risk-reduction strategy of investing in safe T-bills. It has higher expected return *and* lower standard deviation than the one-half T-bill portfolio. The point is that, despite SugarBeet's large standard deviation of return, it is a risk reducer for some investors—in this case, those holding Best stock.

The risk of the individual assets in the portfolio must be measured in the context of the effect of their return on overall portfolio variability. This example demonstrates that assets with returns that are inversely associated with the initial risky position are the most powerful risk reducers.

---

**CONCEPT CHECK** Question 8. Suppose that the stock market offers an expected rate of return of 20 percent, with a standard deviation of 15 percent. Gold has an expected rate of return of 18 percent, with a standard deviation of 17 percent. In view of the market's higher expected return and lower uncertainty, will anyone choose to hold gold in a portfolio?

---

To quantify the hedging or diversification potential of an asset, we use the concepts of covariance and correlation. The **covariance** measures how much the returns on two risky assets move in tandem. A positive covariance means that asset returns move together. A negative covariance means that they vary inversely, as in the case of Best and SugarBeet.

To measure covariance, we look at return "surprises" or deviations from expected value in each scenario. Consider the product of each stock's deviation from expected return in a particular scenario:

$$[r_{\text{Best}} - E(r_{\text{Best}})][r_{\text{Beet}} - E(r_{\text{Beet}})]$$

This product will be positive if the returns of the two stocks move together across scenarios, that is, if both returns exceed their expectations or both fall short of those expectations in the scenario in question. On the other hand, if one stock's return exceeds its expected value when the other's falls short, the product will be negative. Thus, a good measure of how much the returns move together is the *expected value* of this product across all scenarios, which is defined as the covariance:

$$\text{Cov}(r_{\text{Best}}, r_{\text{Beet}}) = \sum_{s} Pr(s)\,[r_{\text{Best}}(s) - E(r_{\text{Best}})][r_{\text{Beet}}(s) - E(r_{\text{Beet}})] \qquad \textbf{(5.7)}$$

In this example, with $E(r_{\text{Best}}) = .105$ and $E(r_{\text{Beet}}) = .06$ and with returns in each scenario summarized as follows, we find the covariance from a simple application of equation 5.7.

| | Normal Year for Sugar | | Abnormal Year |
|---|---|---|---|
| | Bullish Stock Market | Bearish Stock Market | Sugar Crisis |
| Probability | .5 | .3 | .2 |
| **Stock** | | | |
| Best Candy | .25 | .10 | −.25 |
| SugarBeet | .01 | −.05 | .35 |

The covariance between the two stocks is:

$$\begin{aligned}\text{Cov}(r_{\text{Best}}, r_{\text{Beet}}) &= .5(.25 - .105)(.01 - .06) \\ &\quad + .3(.10 - .105)(-.05 - .06) + .2(-.25 - .105)(.35 - .06) \\ &= -.02405\end{aligned}$$

The negative covariance confirms the hedging quality of SugarBeet stock relative to Best Candy. SugarBeet's returns move inversely with Best's.

An easier statistic to interpret than the covariance is the **correlation coefficient,** which scales the covariance to a value between $-1$ (perfect negative correlation) and $+1$ (perfect positive correlation). The correlation coefficient between two variables equals their covariance divided by the product of the standard deviations. Denoting the correlation by the Greek letter $\rho$, we find that

$$\begin{aligned}\rho(\text{Best, SugarBeet}) &= \frac{\text{Cov}[r_{\text{Best}}, r_{\text{SugarBeet}}]}{\sigma_{\text{Best}}\sigma_{\text{SugarBeet}}} \\ &= \frac{-.0240}{.189 \times .1473} \\ &= -.86\end{aligned} \tag{5.8}$$

This large negative correlation (close to $-1$) confirms the strong tendency of Best and SugarBeet stocks to move inversely, or "out of phase" with one another.

The impact of the covariance of asset returns on portfolio risk is apparent in the following formula for portfolio variance.

*Rule 5.* When two risky assets with variances $\sigma_1^2$ and $\sigma_2^2$, respectively, are combined into a portfolio with portfolio weights $w_1$ and $w_2$, respectively, the portfolio variance $\sigma_P^2$ is given by

$$\sigma_P^2 = w_1^2\sigma_1^2 + w_2^2\sigma_2^2 + 2w_1w_2\text{Cov}(r_1,r_2)$$

In this example, with equal weights in Best and SugarBeet, $w_1 = w_2 = .5$, and with $\sigma_{\text{Best}} = .189$, $\sigma_{\text{Beet}} = .1473$, and Cov $(r_{\text{Best}}, r_{\text{Beet}}) = -.02405$, we find that

$$\sigma_P^2 = .5^2 \times .189^2 + .5^2 \times .1473^2 + 2 \times .5 \times .5\,(-.02405) = .00233$$

or that $\sigma_P = \sqrt{.00233} = .0483$, precisely the same answer for the standard deviation of the returns on the hedged portfolio that we derived directly from the scenario analysis.

Rule 5 for portfolio variance highlights the effect of covariance on portfolio risk. A positive covariance increases portfolio variance, and a negative covariance acts to reduce portfolio variance. This makes sense because returns on negatively correlated assets tend to be offsetting, which stabilizes portfolio returns.

Basically, hedging involves the purchase of a risky asset that is negatively correlated with the existing portfolio. This negative correlation makes the volatility of the hedge asset a risk-reducing feature. A hedge strategy is a powerful alternative to the simple risk-reduction strategy of including a risk-free asset in the portfolio.

In later chapters we will see that, in a rational equilibrium, hedge assets must offer relatively low expected rates of return. The perfect hedge, an insurance contract, is by design perfectly negatively correlated with a specified risk. As one would expect in a "no free lunch" world, the insurance premium reduces the portfolio's expected rate of return.

---

**CONCEPT CHECK** Question 9. Suppose that the distribution of SugarBeet stock is as follows:

| Bullish Stock Market | Bearish Stock Market | Sugar Crisis |
|---|---|---|
| .07 | −.05 | .20 |

*a.* What would be its correlation with Best?
*b.* Is SugarBeet stock a useful hedge asset now?
*c.* Calculate the portfolio rate of return in each scenario and the standard deviation of the portfolio from the scenario returns. Then evaluate $\sigma_P$ using rule 5.
*d.* Are the two methods of computing portfolio standard deviation consistent?

---

## SUMMARY

**1.** The economy's equilibrium level of real interest rates depends on the willingness of households to save (as reflected in the supply curve of funds) and the expected profitability of business investment in plant, equipment, and inventories, as reflected in the demand curve for funds. It also depends on government fiscal and monetary policy.

**2.** In Canada, investors can invest in securities offering a guaranteed nominal rate of interest. Their real rate of return depends on the actual rate of inflation. A recently marketed issue of Canada bonds offers a guaranteed real rate of return.

**3.** The equilibrium expected rate of return on any security is the sum of the risk-free rate and a security-specific risk premium.

**4.** Investors face a trade-off between risk and expected return. Historical data confirms our intuition that assets with low degrees of risk provide lower returns on average than do those of higher risk.

**5.** Assets with guaranteed nominal interest rates are risky in real terms because the future inflation rate is uncertain.

**6.** Speculation is the undertaking of a risky investment for its risk premium. The risk premium has to be large enough to compensate a risk-averse investor for the risk of the investment.

**7.** A fair game is a risky prospect that has a zero-risk premium. It will not be undertaken by a risk-averse investor.

**8.** Investors' preferences toward the expected return and volatility of a portfolio may be expressed by a utility function that is higher for higher expected returns and lower for higher portfolio variances. More risk-averse investors will apply greater penalties for risk. We can describe these preferences graphically using indifference curves.

**9.** The desirability of a risky portfolio to a risk-averse investor may be summarized by the certainty equivalent value of the portfolio. The certainty equivalent rate of return is a value that, if it is received with certainty, would yield the same utility as the risky portfolio.

**10.** Hedging is the purchase of a risky asset to reduce the risk of a portfolio. The negative correlation between the hedge asset and the initial portfolio turns the volatility of the hedge asset into a risk-*reducing* feature. When a hedge asset is perfectly negatively correlated with the initial portfolio, it serves as a perfect hedge and works like an insurance contract on the portfolio.

## Key Terms

Nominal interest rate
Real interest rate
Holding-period return (HPR)
Expected return
Mean return
Standard deviation
Variance
Risk-free rate
Risk premium
Excess return
Risk aversion
Utility
Certainty equivalent rate
Risk–neutral
Risk lover
Mean-variance (M-V) criterion
Indifference curve
Hedging
Diversification
Covariance
Correlation coefficient

## Selected Readings

*A classic work on risk and risk aversion is:*

Arrow, Kenneth. *Essays in the Theory of Risk Bearing.* Amsterdam: North Holland, 1971.

*Some good statistics texts with business applications are:*

Levy, Haim; and Moshe, Ben-Horim. *Statistics: Decisions and Applications in Business and Economics.* New York: Random House, 1984.

Wonnacott, Thomas H.; and Ronald J. Wonnacott. *Introductory Statistics for Business and Economics.* New York: John Wiley & Sons, 1984.

*The classic article on the determination of the level of interest rates is:*

Fisher, Irving. *The Theory of Interest: As Determined by Impatience to Spend Income and Opportunity to Invest It.* New York: Augustus M. Kelley, Publishers, 1965 (originally published in 1930).

*The first Canadian study on bond returns was:*

Khoury, Nabil T. "Historical Return Distributions of Investments in Canadian Bonds: 1950–1976." *Journal of Business Administration* 12, no. 1 (Fall 1980).

*Historical returns on a variety of Canadian instruments, updated on an ongoing basis, are found in the following publications:*

*Scotia McLeod's Handbook of Canadian Debt Market Indices 1947–1994.* ScotiaMcLeod, February 1995.

Hatch, James E.; and Robert W. White. *Canadian Stocks, Bonds, Bills and Inflation.* Charlottesville, Va.: The Financial Analysts Research Foundation, 1988.

## Problems

1. You have $5,000 to invest for the next year and are considering the following three alternatives:
   *a.* A money market fund with an average maturity of 30 days offering a current yield of 6 percent per year.
   *b.* A one-year savings deposit at a bank offering an interest rate of 7.5 percent.
   *c.* A 20-year Canada bond offering a yield to maturity of 9 percent per year.
   *d.* What role does your forecast of future interest rates play in your decision?
2. Use Figure 5.1 in this chapter to analyze the effect of the following on the level of real interest rates:
   *a.* Businesses become more optimistic about future demand for their products and decide to increase their capital spending.
   *b.* Households are induced to save more because of increased uncertainty about their future Canada Pension Plan benefits.
   *c.* The Bank of Canada undertakes open-market sales of Canada Treasury securities to reduce the supply of money.
3. You are considering the choice between investing $50,000 in a conventional one-year bank GIC offering an interest rate of 8 percent and a one-year inflation-plus GIC offering 3 percent per year plus the rate of inflation.
   *a.* Which is the safer investment?
   *b.* Which offers the higher expected return?
   *c.* If you expect the rate of inflation to be 4 percent over the next year, which is the better investment? Why?
   *d.* If we observe a risk-free nominal interest rate of 8 percent per year and a risk-free real rate of 3 percent, can we infer that the market's expected rate of inflation is 5 percent per year?
4. Suppose that you revise your expectations regarding the stock market (which were summarized in Table 5.1 in the chapter) as follows:

| State of the Economy | Probability | Ending Price ($) | HPR (%) |
|---|---|---|---|
| Boom | .3 | 140 | 44 |
| Normal growth | .4 | 110 | 14 |
| Recession | .3 | 80 | −16 |

   Use equations 5.1 and 5.2 to compute the mean and standard deviation of the HPR on stocks. Compare your revised parameters with your previous ones.
5. Derive the probability distribution of the one-year holding period return on a 30-year Canada bond with a 9 percent coupon if it is currently selling at par and the probability distribution of its yield to maturity (YTM) a year from now is as follows:

| State of the Economy | Probability | YTM (%) |
|---|---|---|
| Boom | .25 | 12.0 |
| Normal growth | .50 | 9.0 |
| Recession | .25 | 7.5 |

For simplicity, assume that the entire 9 percent coupon is paid at the end of the year rather than every six months.

**6.** Using the historical risk premiums as your guide, if the current risk-free interest rate is 8 percent, what is your estimate of the expected annual HPR on the TSE 300 stock portfolio?

**7.** Compute the means and standard deviations of the annual holding period returns listed in Table 5.2 of the chapter using only the last 19 years, 1976–1994. How do they compare with these same statistics computed from data for the period 1957–1976? Which do you think are the most relevant statistics to use for projecting into the future?

**8.** During a period of severe inflation, a bond offered a nominal HPR of 80 percent per year. The inflation rate was 70 percent per year.
*a.* What was the real HPR on the bond over the year?
*b.* Compare this real HPR to the approximation $R = r - i$.

**9.** You own a house worth $250,000 and intend to insure it fully against fire for the next year. Suppose that the probability of its burning to the ground during the year is .001 and that an insurance policy covering the full value costs $500. Consider the insurance policy as a security.
*a.* What is its expected holding period return?
*b.* What is the standard deviation of its HPR?
*c.* Is the policy a risky asset? Why?

Use the following expectations on stocks *X* and *Y* to answer problems 10 through 12 (round to the nearest percent).

| | Bear Market | Normal Market | Bull Market |
|---|---|---|---|
| Probability | 0.2 | 0.5 | 0.3 |
| Stock *X* | −20% | 18% | 50% |
| Stock *Y* | −15% | 20% | 10% |

**10.** What is the expected return for stocks *X* and *Y*?

| | Stock *X* | Stock *Y* |
|---|---|---|
| *a.* | 18% | 5% |
| *b.* | 18% | 12% |
| *c.* | 20% | 11% |
| *d.* | 20% | 10% |

**11.** What is the standard deviation of returns on stocks *X* and *Y*?

| | Stock *X* | Stock *Y* |
|---|---|---|
| *a.* | 15% | 26% |
| *b.* | 20% | 4% |
| *c.* | 24% | 13% |
| *d.* | 28% | 8% |

**12.** Assume you invest your $10,000 portfolio in $9,000 of stock *X* and $1,000 of stock *Y*. What is the expected return on your portfolio?
*a.* 18%
*b.* 19%
*c.* 20%
*d.* 23%

**13.** Given $100,000 to invest, what is the expected risk premium in dollars of investing in equities versus risk-free T-bills based on the following table?

| Action | Probability | Expected Return |
|---|---|---|
| Invest in equities | .6 | $50,000 |
| | .4 | −$30,000 |
| Invest in risk-free T-bills | 1.0 | $ 5,000 |

*a.* $13,000
*b.* $15,000
*c.* $18,000
*d.* $20,000

**14.** Based on the scenarios below, what is the expected return for a portfolio with the following return profile?

| | Market Condition | | |
|---|---|---|---|
| | Bear | Normal | Bull |
| Probability | .2 | .3 | .5 |
| Rate of return | −25% | 10% | 24% |

*a.* 4%
*b.* 10%
*c.* 20%
*d.* 25%

**15.** You are faced with the probability distribution of the holding period return on the stock market index fund given in Table 5.1 of the chapter. Suppose the price of a put option on a share of the index fund with an exercise price of $110 and a maturity of one year is $12.
*a.* What is the probability distribution of the HPR on the put option?

*b.* What is the probability distribution of the HPR on a portfolio consisting of one share of the index fund and a put option?
*c.* In what sense does buying the put option constitute a purchase of insurance in this case?
*d.* Explain why the market price of the put option cannot be less than \$10 as long as the market price of the underlying stock is \$100.

**16.** Take as given the conditions described in the previous problem, and suppose that the risk-free interest rate is 6 percent per year. You are contemplating investing \$114/1.06 in a one-year CD and simultaneously buying a call option on the stock market index fund with an exercise price of \$110 and a maturity of one year.
*a.* What is the probability distribution of your dollar return at the end of the year?
*b.* What must be the market price of the call option, and why?

**17.** Consider a risky portfolio. The end-of-year cash flow derived from the portfolio will be either \$50,000 or \$150,000 with equal probabilities of .5. The alternative risk-free investment in T-bills pays 5 percent per year.
*a.* If you require a risk premium of 10 percent, how much will you be willing to pay for the portfolio?
*b.* Suppose that the portfolio can be purchased for the amount you found in (a). What will be the expected rate of return on the portfolio?
*c.* Now suppose that you require a risk premium of 15 percent. What is the price that you will be willing to pay?
*d.* Comparing your answers to (a) and (c), what do you conclude about the relationship between the required risk premium on a portfolio and the price at which the portfolio will sell?

**18.** Consider a portfolio that offers an expected rate of return of 10 percent and a standard deviation of 15 percent. T-bills offer a risk-free 8 percent rate of return. What is the maximum level of risk aversion for which the risky portfolio is still preferred to bills?

**19.** Draw the indifference curve in the expected return–standard deviation plane corresponding to a utility level of .05 for an investor with a risk aversion coefficient of 3. *Hint:* Choose several possible standard deviations, ranging from .05 to .25, and find the expected rates of return providing a utility level of .05. Then plot the expected return–standard deviation points so derived.

**20.** Using the same instructions supplied in problem 19, now draw the indifference curve corresponding to a utility level of .04 for an investor with risk aversion coefficient $A = 4$. Comparing your answers to problems 19 and 20, what do you conclude?

**21.** Draw an indifference curve for a risk-neutral investor providing a utility level of .05.

**22.** What must be true about the sign of the risk aversion coefficient, $A$, for a risk lover? Draw the indifference curve for a utility level of .05 for a risk lover.

Use the following data in answering problems 23, 24, and 25.

**Utility Formula Data**

| Investment | Expected Return $E(r)$ | Standard Deviation ($\sigma$) |
|---|---|---|
| 1 | 12% | 30% |
| 2 | 15 | 50 |
| 3 | 21 | 16 |
| 4 | 24 | 21 |

$$U = E(r) - \tfrac{1}{2}A\sigma^2 \text{ where } A = 4.0$$

**23.** Based on the utility formula above, which investment would you select if you were risk averse?
*a.* 1
*b.* 2
*c.* 3
*d.* 4

**24.** Based on the utility formula above, which investment would you select if you were risk neutral?
*a.* 1
*b.* 2
*c.* 3
*d.* 4

**25.** The variable ($A$) in the utility formula represents the:
*a.* Investor's return requirement.
*b.* Investor's aversion to risk.
*c.* Certainty-equivalent rate of the portfolio.
*d.* Preference for one unit of return per four units of risk.

Consider the historical data of Table 5.2, showing that the average annual rate of return on the TSE 300 portfolio over the past 38 years has averaged about 3.0 percent more than the Treasury bill return and that the TSE 300 standard deviation has been about 16.5 percent per year. Assume that these values are representative of investors' expectations for future performance and that the current T-bill rate is 7 percent. Use these values to answer problems 26 to 28.

**26.** Calculate the expected return and variance of portfolios invested in T-bills and the TSE 300 index with weights as follows:

| $W_{bills}$ | $W_{market}$ |
|---|---|
| 0 | 1.0 |
| 0.2 | 0.8 |
| 0.4 | 0.6 |
| 0.6 | 0.4 |
| 0.8 | 0.2 |
| 1.0 | 0 |

**27.** Calculate the utility levels of each portfolio of problem 26 for an investor with $A = 3$. What do you conclude?

**28.** Repeat problem 27 for an investor with $A = 5$. What do you conclude?

Reconsider the Best and SugarBeet stock market hedging example in the text, but assume for problems 29 to 31 that the probability distribution of the rate of return on SugarBeet stock is as follows:

| | Bullish Stock Market | Bearish Stock Market | Sugar Crisis |
|---|---|---|---|
| Probability | .5 | .3 | .2 |
| Rate of return | .10 | −.05 | .20 |

**29.** If Humanex's portfolio is half Best stock and half SugarBeet, what are its expected return and standard deviation? Calculate the standard deviation from the portfolio returns in each scenario.

**30.** What is the covariance between Best and SugarBeet?

**31.** Calculate the portfolio standard deviation using rule 5 and show that the result is consistent with your answer to problem 29.

## Appendix 5A: Continuous Compounding

Suppose your money earns interest at an annual nominal percentage rate (APR) of 6 percent per year compounded semiannually. What is your *effective* annual rate of return, accounting for compound interest?

We find the answer by first computing the per (compounding) period rate, 3 percent per half year, and then computing the future value (FV) at the end of the year per dollar invested at the beginning of the year. In this example, we get

$$\text{EV} = (1.03)^2 = 1.0609$$

The effective annual rate ($R_{\text{EFF}}$ is just this number minus 1.0).

$$R_{\text{EFF}} = 1.0609 - 1 = .0609 = 6.09\% \text{ per year}$$

The general formula for the effective annual rate is:

$$R_{\text{EFF}} = \left(1 + \frac{\text{APR}}{n}\right)^n - 1$$

where APR is the annual percentage rate, and $n$ is the number of compounding periods per year. Table 5A.1 presents the effective annual rates corresponding to an annual percentage rate of 6 percent per year for different compounding frequencies.

As the compounding frequency increases, $(1 + \text{APR}/n)^n$ gets closer and closer to $e^{\text{APR}}$ where $e$ is the number 2.71828 (rounded off to the fifth decimal place). In our example, $e^{.06} = 1.0618365$. Therefore, if interest is continuously compounded, $R_{\text{EFF}} = .0618365$, or 6.18365 percent per year.

**Table 5A.1** Effective Annual Rates for an APR of 6 percent

| Compounding Frequency | $n$ | $R_{EFF}$(%) |
|---|---|---|
| Annually | 1 | 6.00000 |
| Semiannually | 2 | 6.09000 |
| Quarterly | 4 | 6.13636 |
| Monthly | 12 | 6.16778 |
| Weekly | 52 | 6.17998 |
| Daily | 365 | 6.18313 |

Using continuously compounded rates simplifies the algebraic relationship between real and nominal rates of return. To see how, let us compute the real rate of return first using annual compounding and then using continuous compounding. Assume the nominal interest rate is 6 percent per year compounded annually and the rate of inflation is 4 percent per year compounded annually. Using the relationship

$$\text{Real rate} = \frac{1 + \text{Nominal rate}}{1 + \text{Inflation rate}} - 1$$

$$r = \frac{(1 + R)}{(1 + i)} - 1 = \frac{R - i}{1 + i}$$

we find that the effective annual real rate is

$$r = 1.06/1.04 - 1 = .01923 = 1.923\% \text{ per year}$$

With continuous compounding, the relationship becomes

$$e^r = e^R/e^i = e^{R - i}$$

Taking the natural logarithm we get

$$r = R - i$$
$$\text{Real rate} = \text{Nominal rate} - \text{Inflation rate}$$

all expressed as annual, continuously compounded percentage rates.

Thus, if we assume a nominal interest rate of 6 percent per year compounded continuously and an inflation rate of 4 percent per year compounded continuously, the real rate is 2 percent per year compounded continuously.

To pay a fair interest rate to a depositor, the compounding frequency must be at least equal to the frequency of deposits and withdrawals. Only when you compound at least as frequently as transactions in an account can you assure that each dollar will earn the full interest due for the exact duration it has been in the account. These days, on-line computing for deposits is feasible, so one expects the frequency of compounding to grow until the use of continuous or at least daily compounding becomes the norm.

# Appendix 5B: A Defense of Mean-Variance Analysis

## Describing Probability Distributions

The axiom of risk aversion needs little defense. So far, however, our treatment of risk has been limiting in that it took the variance (or equivalently, the standard deviation) of portfolio returns as an adequate risk measure. In situations in which variance alone is not adequate to measure risk, this assumption is potentially restrictive. Here, we provide some justification for mean-variance analysis.

The basic question is how one can best describe the uncertainty of portfolio rates of return. In principle, one could list all possible outcomes for the portfolio over a given period. If each outcome results in a payoff such as a dollar profit or rate of return, then this payoff value is the *random variable* in question. A list assigning a probability to all possible values of the random variable is called the probability distribution of the random variable.

The reward for holding a portfolio typically is measured by the expected rate of return across all possible scenarios, which equals

$$E(r) = \sum_{s=1}^{n} Pr(s)r_s$$

where $s = 1, \ldots, n$ are the possible outcomes or scenarios, $r_s$ is the rate of return for outcome $s$, and $Pr(s)$ is the probability associated with it.

Actually, the expected value or mean is not the only candidate for the central value of a probability distribution. Other candidates are the median and the mode.

The median is defined as the outcome value that exceeds the outcome values for half the population and is exceeded by the other half. Whereas the expected rate of return is a weighted average of the outcomes, the weights being the probabilities, the median is based on the rank order of the outcomes and takes into account only the order of the outcome values rather than the values themselves.

The median differs significantly from the mean in cases where the expected value is dominated by extreme values. One example is the income (or wealth) distribution in a population. A relatively small number of households command a disproportionate share of total income (and wealth). The mean income is "pulled up" by these extreme values, which makes it nonrepresentative. The median is free of this effect, since it equals the income level that is exceeded by half the population, regardless of by how much.

Finally, a third candidate for the measure of central value is the mode, which is the most likely value of the distribution or the outcome with the highest probability. However, the expected value is by far the most widely used measure of central or average tendency.

We now turn to the characterization of the risk implied by the nature of the probability distribution of returns. In general, it is impossible to quantify risk by a single number. We can, however, describe the probabilities and magnitudes of the possible deviations from the mean, or the "surprises," in a concise fashion, to illuminate the risk-return trade-off. The easiest way to accomplish this is to answer a set of questions in order of their informational value and to stop at the point where additional questions would not affect our notion of the risk-return trade-off.

The first question is, "What is a typical deviation from the expected value?" A natural answer would be, "The expected deviation from the expected value is ______." Unfortunately, this answer is meaningless because it is necessarily zero: Positive deviations from the mean are offset exactly by negative deviations.

There are two ways of getting around this problem. The first is to use the expected *absolute* value of the deviation. This is known as MAD (mean absolute deviation), which is given by

$$\sum_{s=1}^{n} Pr(s) \times \text{Absolute value}[r_s - E(r)]$$

The second is to use the expected *squared* deviation from the expected, or mean, value, which is simply the variance of the probability distribution

$$\sigma^2 = \sum_{s=1}^{n} Pr(s)\,[r_s - E(r)]^2$$

Note that the unit of measurement of the variance is percent squared. To return to our original units, we compute the standard deviation as the square root of the variance, which is measured in percentage terms, as is the expected value.

The variance also is called the *second central moment* around the mean, with the expected return itself being the first moment. Although the variance measures the average squared deviation from the expected value, it does not provide a full description of risk. To see why, consider the two probability distributions for rates of return on a portfolio, in Figure 5B.1.

*A* and *B* are probability distributions with identical expected values and variances. The graphs show that the variances are identical because probability distribution *B* is the mirror image of *A*.

What is the principal difference between *A* and *B*? *A* is characterized by more likely but small losses and less likely but extreme gains. This pattern is reversed in *B*. The difference is important. When we talk about risk, we really mean "*bad* surprises." The bad surprises in *A*, although they are more likely, are small (and limited) in magnitude. The bad surprises in *B* could be extreme, indeed unbounded. A risk-averse investor will prefer *A* to *B* on these grounds; hence, it is worthwhile to quantify this characteristic. They asymmetry of the distribution is called *skewness,* which we measure by the *third central moment,* given by

$$M_3 = \sum_{s=1}^{n} Pr(s)\,[r_s - E(r)]^3$$

Cubing the deviations from expected value preserves their signs, which allows us to distinguish good from bad surprises. Because this procedure gives greater

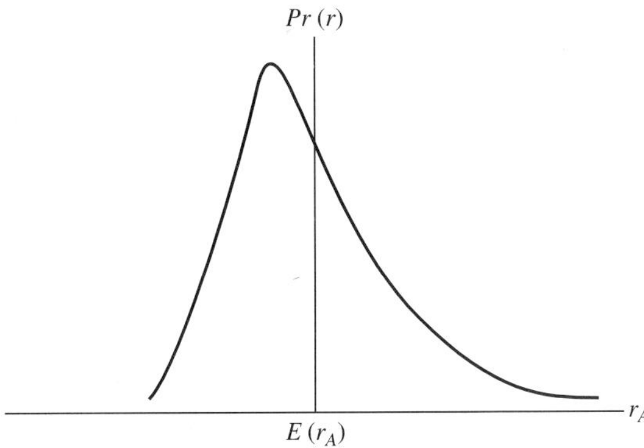


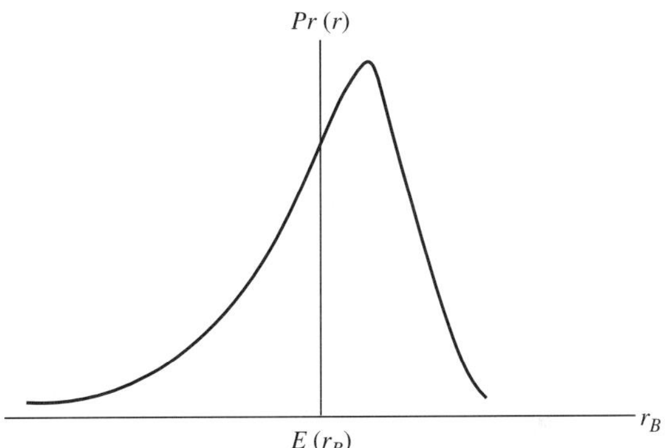


**Figure 5B.1**
Skewed probability distributions for rates of return on a portfolio.

weight to larger deviations, it causes the "long tail" of the distribution to dominate the measure of skewness. Thus, the skewness of the distribution will be positive for a right-skewed distribution such as *A* and negative for a left-skewed distribution such as *B*. The asymmetry is a relevant characteristic, although it is not as important as the magnitude of the standard deviation.

To summarize, the first moment (expected value) represents the expected reward. The second and higher central moments characterize the uncertainty of the reward. All the even moments (variance, $M_4$, and so on) represent the likelihood of extreme values. Larger values for these moments indicate greater uncertainty. The odd moments ($M_3$, $M_5$, and so on) represent measures of asymmetry. Positive numbers are associated with positive skewness and hence are desirable.

We can characterize the risk aversion of any investor by the preference scheme that the investor assigns to the various moments of the distribution. In other words, we can write the utility value derived from the probability distribution as

$$U = E(r) - b_0\sigma^2 + b_1M_3 - b_2M_4 + b_3M_5 - \ldots$$

where the importance of the terms lessens as we proceed to higher moments. Notice that the "good" (odd) moments have positive coefficients, whereas the "bad" (even) moments have minus signs in front of the coefficients.

How many moments are needed to describe the investor's assessment of the probability distribution adequately? Samuelson's "Fundamental Approximation Theorem of Portfolio Analysis in Terms of Means, Variances, and Higher Moments"[8] proves that in many important circumstances:

1. The importance of all moments beyond the variance is much smaller than that of the expected value and variance. In other words, disregarding moments higher than the variance will not affect portfolio choice.
2. The variance is as important as the mean to investor welfare.

Samuelson's proof is the major theoretical justification for mean-variance analysis. Under the conditions of this proof, mean and variance are equally important, and we can overlook all other moments without harm.

The major assumption that Samuelson makes to arrive at this conclusion concerns the "compactness" of the distribution of stock returns. The distribution of the rate of return on a portfolio is said to be compact if the risk can be controlled by the investor. Practically speaking, we test for compactness of the distribution by posing a question: Will the risk of my position in the portfolio decline if I hold it for a shorter period, or will the risk approach zero if I hold the risky portfolio for only an instant? If the answer is yes, then the distribution is compact.

In general, compactness may be seen as being equivalent to continuity of stock prices. If stock prices do not take sudden jumps, then the uncertainty of stock returns over smaller and smaller time periods decreases. Under these circumstances, investors who can rebalance their portfolios frequently will act so as to make higher moments of the stock return distribution so small as to be unimportant. It is not that skewness, for example, does not matter in principle. It is, instead, that the actions of investors in frequently revising their portfolios will limit higher moments to negligible levels.

Continuity or compactness is not, however, an innocuous assumption. Portfolio revisions entail transaction costs, meaning that rebalancing must of necessity be somewhat limited and that skewness and other higher moments cannot be ignored entirely. Compactness also rules out such phenomena as the major stock price jumps that occur in response to takeover attempts. It also rules out such dramatic events as the 25 percent one-day decline of the stock market on October 19, 1987. Except for these relatively unusual events, however, mean-variance analysis is adequate. In most cases, if the portfolio may be revised frequently, we need to worry about the mean and variance only.

---

[8] Paul A. Samuelson, "The Fundamental Approximation Theorem of Portfolio Analysis in Terms of Means, Variances, and Higher Moments," *Review of Economic Studies*, 37, 1970.

Portfolio theory, for the most part, is built on the assumption that the conditions for mean-variance (or mean-standard deviation) analysis are satisfied. Accordingly, we typically ignore higher moments.

**CONCEPT CHECK** Question 5B.1. How does the simultaneous popularity of both lotteries and insurance policies confirm the notion that individuals prefer positive to negative skewness of portfolio returns?

## Normal and Lognormal Distributions

Modern portfolio theory, for the most part, assumes that asset returns are normally distributed. This is a convenient assumption because the normal distribution can be described completely by its mean and variance, which provides another justification for mean-variance analysis. The argument has been that, even if individual asset returns are not exactly normal, the distribution of returns of a large portfolio will resemble a normal distribution quite closely.

The data support this argument. Table 5B.1 shows summaries of the results of one-year investments in many portfolio selected randomly from NYSE stocks. The portfolios are listed in order of increasing degrees of diversification; that is, the numbers of stocks in each portfolio same are 1, 8, 32, and 128. The percentiles of the distribution of returns for each portfolio are compared to what one would have expected from portfolios identical in mean and variance but drawn from a normal distribution.

**Table 5B.1** Frequency Distributions of Rates of Return from a One-Year Investment in Randomly Selected Portfolios from NYSE-Listed Stocks

| | $N = 1$ | | $N = 8$ | | $N = 32$ | | $N = 128$ | |
|---|---|---|---|---|---|---|---|---|
| **Statistic** | **Observed** | **Normal** | **Observed** | **Normal** | **Observed** | **Normal** | **Observed** | **Normal** |
| Minimum | −71.1 | NA | −12.4 | NA | 6.5 | NA | 16.4 | NA |
| 5th centile | −14.4 | −39.2 | 8.1 | 4.6 | 17.4 | 16.7 | 22.7 | 22.6 |
| 20th centile | −.5 | −6.3 | 16.3 | 16.1 | 22.2 | 22.3 | 25.3 | 25.3 |
| 50th centile | 19.6 | 28.2 | 26.4 | 28.2 | 27.8 | 28.2 | 28.1 | 28.2 |
| 70th centile | 38.7 | 49.7 | 33.8 | 35.7 | 31.6 | 32.9 | 30.0 | 30.0 |
| 95th centile | 96.3 | 95.6 | 54.3 | 51.8 | 40.9 | 39.9 | 34.1 | 33.8 |
| Maximum | 442.6 | NA | 136.7 | NA | 73.7 | NA | 43.1 | NA |
| Mean | 28.2 | 28.2 | 28.2 | 28.2 | 28.2 | 28.2 | 28.2 | 28.2 |
| Standard deviation | 41.0 | 41.0 | 14.4 | 14.4 | 7.1 | 7.1 | 3.4 | 3.4 |
| Skewness ($M_3$) | 255.4 | 0.0 | 88.7 | 0.0 | 44.5 | 0.0 | 17.7 | 0.0 |
| Sample size | 1,227 | — | 131,072 | — | 32,768 | — | 16,384 | — |

From Lawrence Fisher and James H. Lorie, "Some Studies of Variability of Returns on Investments in Common Stocks," *Journal of Business*, 43 (April 1970); published by the University of Chicago. Reprinted by permission.

Looking first at the single stock portfolios ($N = 1$), the departure of the return distribution from normality is significant. The mean of the sample is 28.2 percent, and the standard deviation is 41.0 percent. In the case of a normal distribution with the same mean and standard deviation, we would expect the fifth percentile stock to lose 39.2 percent, but the fifth percentile stock actually lost 14.4 percent. In addition, while the normal distribution's mean coincides with its median, the actual sample median of the single stock was 19.6 percent, far below the sample mean of 28.2 percent.

In contrast, the returns of the 128-stock portfolios are virtually identical in distribution to the hypothetical normally distributed portfolio. The normal distribution therefore is a pretty good working assumption for well-diversified portfolios. How large a portfolio must be for this result to take hold depends on how far the distribution of the individual stocks is from normality. It appears that a portfolio typically must include at least 32 stocks for the one-year return to be close to normally distributed.

There remain theoretical objections to the assumption that individual stock returns are normally distributed. Given that a stock price cannot be negative, the normal distribution cannot be truly representative of the behavior of a holding period rate of return because it allows for any outcome, including the whole range of negative prices. Specifically, rates of return lower than $-100$ percent are theoretically impossible because they imply the possibility of negative security prices. The failure of the normal distribution to rule out such outcomes must be viewed as a shortcoming.

An alternative assumption is that the continuously compounded annual rate of return is normally distributed. If we call this rate $r$ and we call the effective annual rate $r_e$, then $r_e = e^r - 1$, and since $e^r$ can never be negative, the smallest possible value for $r_e$ is $-1$ or $-100$ percent. Thus, this assumption nicely rules out the troublesome possibility of negative prices while still conveying the advantages of working with normal distributions.

Under this assumption, the distribution of $r_e$ will be *lognormal.* This distribution is depicted in Figure 5B.2.

For *short* holding periods, that is, where $t$ is small, the approximation of $r_e(t) = e^{rt} - 1$ by $rt$ is quite accurate and the normal distribution provides a good approximation to the lognormal. With $rt$ normally distributed, the effective annual return over short time periods may be taken as approximately normally distributed.

For short holding periods, therefore, the mean and standard deviation of the effective holding period returns are proportional to the mean and standard deviation of the annual, continuously compounded rate of return on the stock and to the time interval.

Therefore, if the standard deviation of the annual continuously compounded rate of return on a stock is 40 percent ($\sigma = .40$), then the variance of the holding period return for one month, for example, is for all practical purposes

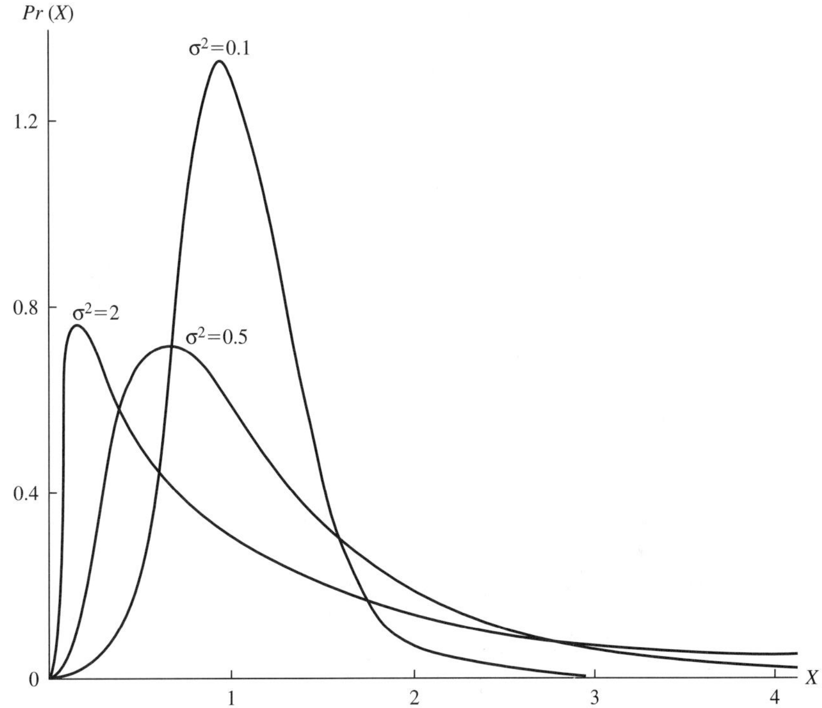


**Figure 5B.2**
The lognormal distribution for three values of $\sigma^2$.

$$\sigma^2(\text{monthly}) = \frac{\sigma^2}{12} = \frac{.16}{12} = .0133$$

and the standard deviation is $\sqrt{.0133} = .1155$.

To illustrate this principle, suppose that the Dow Jones Industrials went up one day by 50 points from 3,200 to 3,250. Is this a "large" move? Looking at annual, continuously compounded rates on the Dow Jones portfolio, we find that the annual standard deviation historically has been about 27 percent. Under the assumption that the return on the Dow Jones portfolio is lognormally distributed and that returns between successive subperiods are uncorrelated, the one-day distribution has a standard deviation (based on 250 trading days per year) of

$$\begin{aligned}\sigma(\text{day}) &= \sigma(\text{year})\sqrt{1/250} \\ &= \frac{.27}{\sqrt{250}} \\ &= .0171 \\ &= 1.71\% \text{ per day}\end{aligned}$$

Applying this to the opening level of the Dow Jones on that trading day, 3,200, we find that the daily standard deviation of the Dow Jones index is 3,200 × .0171 = 54.7 points per day.

Since the daily rate on the Dow Jones portfolio is approximately normal, we know that in one day out of three, the Dow Jones will move (from a starting level of 3,200) by more than 54 points either way. Thus, a move of 50 points is hardly an unusual event.

---

**CONCEPT CHECK** Question 5B.2. Look again at Table 5B.1. Are you surprised that the minimum rates of return are less negative for more diversified portfolios? Is your explanation consistent with the behaviour of the sample's maximum rates of return?

---

### Summary: Appendix 5B

**1.** The probability distribution of the rate of return can be characterized by its moments. The reward from taking the risk is measured by the first moment, which is the mean of the return distribution. Higher moments characterize the risk. Even moments provide information on the likelihood of extreme values, and odd moments provide information on the asymmetry of the distribution.

**2.** Investors' risk preferences can be characterized by their preferences for the various moments of the distribution. The fundamental approximation theorem shows that when portfolios are revised often enough, and prices are continuous, the desirability of a portfolio can be measured by its mean and variance alone.

**3.** The rates of return on well-diversified portfolios for holding periods that are not too long can be approximated by a normal distribution. For short holding periods (up to one month), the normal distribution is a good approximation for the lognormal.

### Problem: Appendix 5B

1. The Smartstock investment consulting group prepared the following scenario analysis for the end-of-year dividend and stock price of Klink Inc., which is selling now at $12 per share:

| | | End-of-Year | |
|---|---|---|---|
| Scenario | Probability | Dividend ($) | Price ($) |
| 1 | .10 | 0 | 0 |
| 2 | .20 | .25 | 2.00 |
| 3 | .40 | .40 | 14.00 |
| 4 | .25 | .60 | 20.00 |
| 5 | .05 | .85 | 30.00 |

Compute the rate of return for each scenario and

*a.* The mean, median, and mode.

*b.* The standard deviation and the mean absolute deviation.

*c.* The first moment and the second and third moments around the mean. Is the probability distribution of Klink stock positively skewed?

## APPENDIX 5C: RISK AVERSION AND EXPECTED UTILITY

We digress here to examine the rationale behind our contention that investors are risk averse. Recognition of risk aversion as central in investment decisions goes back at least to 1738. Daniel Bernoulli, one of a famous Swiss family of distinguished mathematicians, spent the years 1725 through 1733 in St. Petersburg, where he analyzed the following coin-toss game. To enter the game one pays an entry fee. Thereafter, a coin is tossed until the *first* head appears. The number of tails, denoted by $n$, that appears until the first head is tossed is used to compute the payoff, $\$R$, to the participant, as

$$\$R(n) = 2^n$$

The probability of no tails before the first head ($n = 0$) is ½ and the corresponding payoff is $2^0 = \$1$. The probability of one tail and then heads ($n = 1$) is ½ × ½ with payoff $2^1 = \$2$, the probability of two tails and then heads ($n = 2$) is ½ × ½ × ½, and so forth.

The following table illustrates the probabilities and payoffs for various outcomes:

| Tails | Probability | Payoff = $\$R(n)$ | Probability × Payoff |
|---|---|---|---|
| 0 | ½ | $1 | $1/2 |
| 1 | ¼ | $2 | $1/2 |
| 2 | ⅛ | $4 | $1/2 |
| 3 | 1/16 | $8 | $1/2 |
| • | • | • | • |
| • | • | • | • |
| $n$ | $(½)^{n+1}$ | $\$2^n$ | $1/2 |

The expected payoff is therefore

$$E(R) = \sum_{n=0}^{\infty} Pr(n)R(n)$$

$$= ½ + ½ + \ldots$$

$$= \infty$$

This game is called the "St. Petersburg Paradox." Although the expected payoff is infinite, participants obviously will be willing to purchase tickets to play the game only at a finite, and possible quite modest, entry fee.

Bernoulli resolved the paradox by noting that investors do not assign the same value per dollar to all payoffs. Specifically, the greater their wealth, the less their "appreciation" for each extra dollar. We can make this insight mathematically precise by assigning a welfare or utility value to any level of investor wealth. Our utility function should increase as wealth is higher, but each extra dollar of wealth should increase utility by progressively smaller amounts.[9] (Modern economists would say that investors exhibit "decreasing marginal utility" from an additional payoff dollar.) One particular function that assigns a subjective value to the investor from a payoff of $\$R$, which has a smaller value per dollar the greater the payoff, is the function $\log(R)$. If this function measures utility values of wealth, the subjective utility value of the game is indeed finite.[10] The certain wealth level necessary to yield this utility value is \$2.38, because $\log(2.38) = .866$. Hence the certainty equivalent value of the risky payoff is \$2.38, which is the maximum amount that this investor will pay to play the game.

Von Neumann and Morgenstern adapted this approach to investment theory in a complete axiomatic system in 1946. Avoiding unnecessary technical detail, we restrict ourselves here to an intuitive exposition of the rationale for risk aversion.

Imagine two individuals who are identical twins, except that one of them is less fortunate than the other. Peter has only \$1,000 to his name while Paul has a net worth of \$200,000. How many hours of work would each twin be willing to offer to earn one extra dollar? It is likely that Peter (the poor twin) has more essential uses for the extra money than does Paul. Therefore, Peter will offer more hours. In other words, Peter derives a greater personal welfare or assigns a greater "utility" value to the 1,000 1st dollar than Paul does to the 200,000 1st.

Figure 5C.1 depicts graphically the relationship between wealth and the utility value of wealth that is consistent with this notion of decreasing marginal utility.

Individuals have different rates of decrease in their marginal utility of wealth. What is constant is the *principle* that per-dollar utility decreases with wealth. Functions that exhibit the property of decreasing per-unit value as the number of units grows are called concave. A simple example is the log function, familiar from high school mathematics. Of course, a log function will not fit all investors, but it is consistent with the risk aversion that we assume for all investors.

Now consider the following simple prospect:

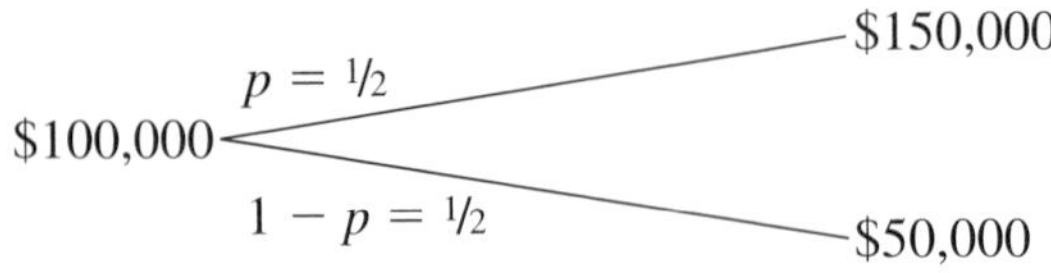


[9] This utility function is similar in spirit to the one that assigns a satisfaction level to portfolios with given risk-and-return attributes. However, the utility function here refers not to investors' satisfaction with alternative portfolio choices but only to the subjective welfare they derive from different levels of wealth.

[10] If we substitute the "utility" value, $\log(R)$, for the dollar payoff, $R$, to obtain an expected utility value of the game (rather than expected dollar value), we have, calling $V(R)$ the expected utility,

$$V(R) = \sum_{n=0}^{\infty} Pr(n) \log[R(n)] = \sum_{n=0}^{\infty} (\tfrac{1}{2})^{n+1} \log(2^n) \propto 0.866$$

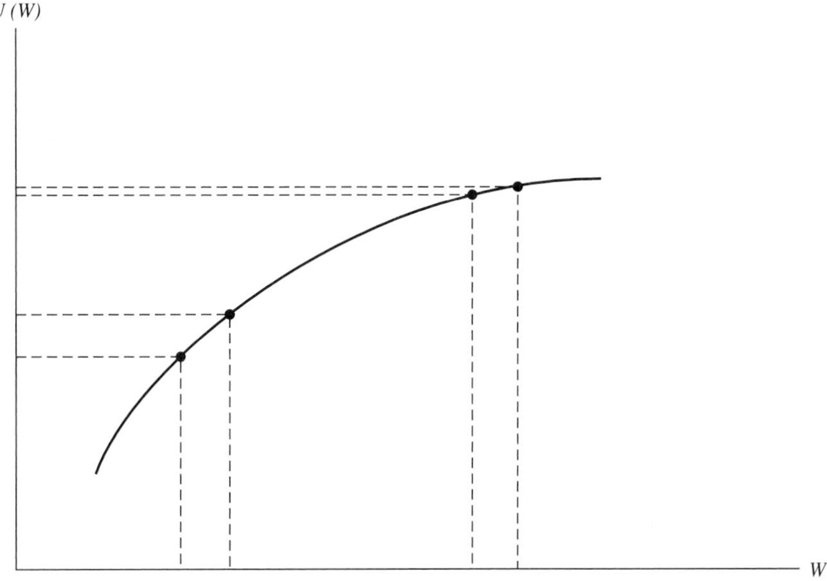


**Figure 5C.1**
Utility of wealth with a log utility function.

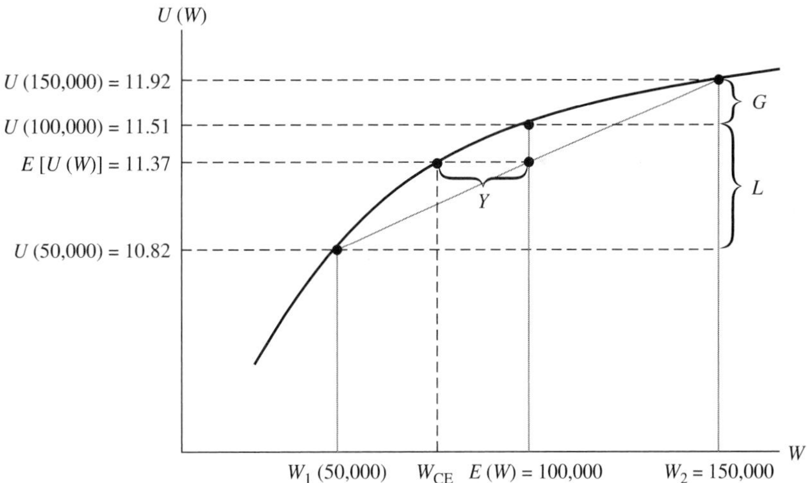


**Figure 5C.2**
Fair games and expected utility.

This is a fair game in that the expected profit is zero. Suppose, however, that the curve in Figure 5C.1 represents the investor's utility value of wealth, assuming a log utility function. Figure 5C.2 shows this curve with the numerical values marked.

Figure 5C.2 shows that the loss in utility from losing \$50,000 exceeds the gain from winning \$50,000. Consider the gain first. With probability $p = .5$, wealth goes from \$100,000 to \$150,000. Using the log utility function, utility goes from log(100,000) = 11.51 to log(150,000) = 11.92, the distance $G$ on the graph. This gain is $G = 11.92 - 11.51 = .41$. In expected utility terms, then, the gain is $pG = .5 \times .41 = .21$.

Now consider the possibility of coming up on the short end of the prospect. In that case, wealth goes from \$100,000 to \$50,000. The loss in utility, the distance $L$ on the graph, is $L = \log(100{,}000) - \log(50.000) = 11.51 - 10.82 = .69$. Thus the loss in expected utility terms is $(1 - p)L = .5 \times .69 = .35$, which exceeds the gain in expected utility from the possibility of winning the game.

We compute the expected utility from the risky prospect as follows:

$$\begin{aligned} E[U(W)] &= pU(W_1) + (1 - p)U(W_2) \\ &= \tfrac{1}{2}\log(50{,}000) + \tfrac{1}{2}\log(150{,}000) \\ &= 11.37 \end{aligned}$$

If the prospect is rejected, the utility value of the (sure) \$100,000 is log(100,000) = 11.51, which is greater than that of the fair game (11.37). Hence the risk-averse investor will reject the fair game.

Using a specific investor utility function (such as the log utility) allows us to compute the certainty equivalent value of the risky prospect to a given investor, Mary Smith. This is the amount that, if received with certainty, the investor would consider equally attractive as the risky prospect.

If log utility describes the investor's preferences toward wealth outcomes, then Figure 5C.2 also can tell us what is, for Smith, the dollar value of the prospect. We ask, "What sure level of wealth has a utility value of 11.37 (which equals the expected utility from the prospect)?" A horizontal line drawn at the level 11.37 intersects the utility curve at the level of wealth $W_{CE}$. This means that

$$\log(W_{CE}) = 11.37$$

which implies that

$$\begin{aligned} W_{CE} &= e^{11.37} \\ &= \$86{,}681.86 \end{aligned}$$

$W_{CE}$ is therefore the certainty equivalent of the prospect. The distance $Y$ in Figure 5C.2 is the penalty, or the downward adjustment, to the expected profit that is attributable to the risk of the prospect:

$$\begin{aligned} Y &= E(W) - W_{CE} \\ &= \$100{,}000 - \$86{,}681.86 \\ &= \$13{,}318.14 \end{aligned}$$

Smith views \$86,681.86 for certain as being equal in utility value as \$100,000 at risk. Therefore, she would be indifferent between the two.

---

**CONCEPT CHECK** Question 5C.1. Suppose the utility function is $U(W) = \sqrt{W}$.

*a*. What is the utility level at wealth levels \$50,000 and \$150,000?

*b*. What is expected utility if $p$ still equals .5?

*c.* What is the certainty equivalent of the risky prospect?
*d.* Does this utility function also display risk aversion?
*e.* Does this utility function display more or less risk aversion than the log utility function?

---

Does revealed behaviour of investors demonstrate risk aversion? Looking at prices and past rates of return in financial markets, we can answer with a resounding "yes." With remarkable consistency, riskier bonds are sold at lower prices than are safer ones with otherwise similar characteristics. Riskier stocks also have provided higher average rates of return over long periods of time than less risky assets such as T-bills. For example, over the 1957–1994 period, the average rate of return on the TSE 300 portfolio exceeded the T-bill return by about 3.0 percent per year.

It is abundantly clear from financial data that the average, or representative, investor exhibits substantial risk aversion. For readers who recognize that financial assets are priced to compensate for risk by providing a risk premium and at the same time feel the urge for some gambling, we have a constructive recommendation: Direct your gambling desire to investment in financial markets. As Von Neumann once said, "The stock market is a casino with the odds in your favour." A small risk-seeking investor may provide all the excitement you want with a positive expected return to boot!

**Problems: Appendix 5C**

1. Suppose that your wealth is $250,000. You buy a $200,000 house and invest the remainder in a risk-free asset paying an annual interest rate of 6 percent. There is a probability of .001 that your house will burn to the ground and its value be reduced to zero. With a log utility of end-of-year wealth, how much would you be willing to pay for insurance (at the beginning of the year)? (Assume that, if the house does not burn down, its end-of-year value still will be $200,000.)
2. If the cost of insuring your house is $1 per $1,000 of value, what will be the certainty equivalent of your end-of-year wealth if you insure your house at:
   *a.* ½ its value?
   *b.* Its full value?
   *c.* 1½ times its value?

*Chapter 6*

# Capital Allocation between the Risky Asset and the Risk-Free Asset

**PORTFOLIO MANAGERS SEEK TO ACHIEVE THE BEST POSSIBLE TRADE-OFF BETWEEN RISK AND RETURN.** A top-down analysis of their strategies starts with the broadest decisions concerning portfolio composition and progresses to ever-finer details about the exact make-up of the portfolio.

For example, the **capital allocation decision** refers to the proportion of the overall portfolio that the investor chooses to place in safe but low-return money market securities versus risky but higher-return securities like stocks. Given the fraction of funds apportioned to risky investments, the investor next makes an **asset allocation decision,** which describes the distribution of risky investments across broad asset classes like stocks, bonds, real estate, foreign assets, and so on. Finally, the **security selection decision** describes the choice of which particular securities to hold within each asset class.

The top-down analysis of portfolio construction has much to recommend it. Most institutional investors follow a top-down approach. Capital allocation and asset allocation decisions will be made at a high organizational level, with the choice of the specific securities to hold within each asset class delegated to particular portfolio managers. Individual investors typically follow a less structured approach to investment management, but they too typically give priority to broader allocation issues. For example, an individual's first decision is usually how much of his or her wealth must be left in a safe bank or money market account. The box on pages 209–210 describes asset allocation for the individual.

## ASSET ALLOCATION WORKS ONCE CONFUSION CLEARED

### Greater Return at Less Risk Is Possible with Right Strategy

"Asset allocation"—an overused, misused, confused term.

Ever since Harry Markowitz won a Nobel Prize in 1990 for his work on diversification in an investment portfolio, asset allocation has been a buzzword of the financial community.

Once of interest only to pension plan managers, its appeal now is recognized by mutual fund and investment dealers. The result is a proliferation of products and services for the small investor.

Does it work? Yes, unequivocally.

However, because there is so much misinformation about asset allocation and what it can do, you can easily conclude otherwise.

Critics routinely make two mistakes: They focus on investment return and equate asset allocation with computer-driven market timing.

Return on investment is obviously important and many asset allocation services do rely on computer models. Nevertheless, the fundamental goal of asset allocation is to reduce risk in a portfolio.

The objective is lower volatility for a targeted rate of return—or higher return for a given level of risk.

If we define asset allocation as the distribution of investments among various asset classes, the first question is, "What should be included in the mix?"

Typically, the answer will be cash, bonds and stocks, and, perhaps, some real estate. Some investors may add limited partnerships, options, collectibles, and other personal favourites.

Once this decision is made, the next question is, "How much of each asset should be in the portfolio?" The answer is crucial to long-term performance.

A study of 91 large U.S. pension plans looked at three determinants of investment performance—asset allocation, market timing and security selection—to see which had the greatest impact. The conclusion? Over 90 percent of a portfolio's performance can be attributed to how the money was apportioned among cash, bonds, and stocks.

By far, asset allocation outweighed the contribution of market timing and security selection.

How do you make the asset mix decision? Basically, there are two approaches, frequently known as strategic and tactical.

At the strategic level, your own risk tolerance and personal objectives influence the choices.

What is your investment time horizon? One year, 5, 10, 25 years? For most investors, it is much longer than typically assumed, because it should also include the period after retirement.

Do you have cash or income needs? How much volatility can you bear? These kinds of considerations should drive your decision.

Tactical asset allocation is an attempt to change the asset mix, within the overall strategic guidelines, if you feel the ability exists to predict which way the markets are headed.

Using the tactical approach, a particular asset class would be overweighted or underweighted to improve overall portfolio return or minimize the downside. Market timing and sector rotation are examples of tactical asset allocation.

The research of Harry Markowitz, along with fellow Nobel Prize winner Bill Sharpe, is commonly referred to as Modern Portfolio Theory. MPT is the statistical foundation for asset allocation. It suggests that combining assets with different performance characteristics into a portfolio will increase total return or decrease volatility.

The key to this "magic of diversification" lies in the fact that all investment assets do not go up and down at the same rate or the same time. If you hold assets that do not correlate with each other, the increases in one can offset losses in another.

It is possible to quantify the expected outcome of

*(Continued)*

such a combination by considering historical returns, volatility and cross-correlations of various alternatives. This takes some work but a good financial planner or investment adviser should be able to help. There are also software packages that can do the job.

If you do not want to be so involved in the decision making, a number of mutual fund companies—such as AGF, Royal Trust and the 20/20 Group—offer products or services that use sophisticated computer models to carry out the tactical moves.

The disadvantage is that you are abdicating the strategic and tactical decisions. However, if the professional managers' discipline can reduce volatility or increase return beyond what you can achieve alone, that may be a reasonable trade-off.

Regardless of who makes the decisions, it is important to keep in mind that asset allocation is more a risk management technique than anything else. At any moment in time, the diversified portfolio will, by definition, be underperforming the asset class that is currently capturing the headlines.

In the long run, however, this modern-day version of diversification will deliver more return with less risk.

By George Hartman, *The Globe and Mail,* August 20, 1992. Reprinted by permission of the author. George Hartman is author of the book, *Risk Is a Four-Letter Word.*

This chapter treats the broadest investment decision: capital allocation between risk-free assets versus the risky portion of the portfolio. We will take the composition of the risky portfolio as given and refer to it as "the" **risky asset.** In Chapter 7 we will examine how the composition of the risky portfolio may best be determined. For now, however, we start our top-down journey by asking how an investor decides how much to invest in the risky versus the risk-free asset.

This capital allocation problem may be solved in two stages. First, we determine the risk-return trade-off encountered when choosing between the risky and risk-free assets. Then we show how risk aversion determines the optimal mix of the two assets. This analysis leads us to examine so-called passive strategies, which call for allocation of the portfolio between a (risk-free) money market fund and an index fund of common stocks.

## 6.1 Capital Allocation Across Risky and Risk-Free Portfolios

History shows us that long-term bonds have been riskier investments than investments in Treasury bills and that stock investments have been riskier still. On the other hand, the riskier investments have offered higher average returns. Investors, of course, do not make all-or-nothing choices from these investment classes. They can and do construct their portfolios using securities from all asset classes. Some of the portfolio may be in risk-free Treasury bills, and some in high-risk stocks.

The most straightforward way to control the risk of the portfolio is through the fraction of the portfolio invested in Treasury bills and other safe money market securities versus risky assets. This *capital allocation decision* is an example of an *asset allocation* choice—a choice among broad investment classes, rather than among the specific securities within each asset class. Most investment professionals consider asset allocation to be the most important part of portfolio construction. Therefore, we start our discussion of the risk-return trade-off available to investors by examining the most basic asset allocation choice: the choice of how much of the portfolio to place in risk-free money market securities versus in other risky asset classes.

We will denote the investor's portfolio of risky assets as *P*, and the risk-free asset as *F*. We will assume for the sake of illustration that the risky component of the investor's overall portfolio is comprised of two mutual funds: one invested in stocks and the other invested in long-term bonds. For now, we take the composition of the risky portfolio as given and focus only on the allocation between it and risk-free securities. In the next chapter, we turn to asset allocation and security selection across risky assets.

Throughout this chapter we will consider investors holding a risky portfolio, called *P*, and some risk-free securities such as T-bills. When we shift wealth from the risky portfolio to the risk-free asset, we do not change the relative proportions of the various risky assets within the risky portfolio. Rather, we reduce the relative weight of the risky portfolio as a whole in favour of risk-free assets.

For example, assume that the total market value of an initial portfolio is \$300,000, of which \$90,000 is invested in the Ready Asset money market fund, a risk-free asset for practical purposes. The remaining \$210,000 is invested in risky equity securities—\$113,400 in Seagram's (VO) and \$96,600 in Canadian Tire (CT). The VO and CT holding is "the" risky portfolio, 54 percent in VO and 46 percent in CT:

$$\text{VO:} \quad w_1 = \frac{113{,}400}{210{,}000} = .54$$

$$\text{CT:} \quad w_2 = \frac{96{,}600}{210{,}000} = .46$$

The weight of the risky portfolio, *P*, in the **complete portfolio,** including risk-free investments, is denoted by $y$:

$$y = \frac{210{,}000}{300{,}000} = .7 \text{ (Risky assets)}$$

$$1 - y = \frac{90{,}000}{300{,}000} = .3 \text{ (Risk-free assets)}$$

The weights of each stock in the complete portfolio are as follows:

$$\text{VO:} \quad \frac{\$113{,}400}{\$300{,}000} = .378$$

$$\text{CT:} \quad \frac{\$96{,}600}{\$300{,}000} = .322$$

$$\text{Risky portfolio} \quad = .700$$

The risky portfolio is 70 percent of the complete portfolio.

Suppose that the owner of this portfolio wishes to decrease risk by reducing the allocation to the risky portfolio from $y = .7$ to $y = .56$. The risky portfolio would total only \$168,000 (.56 × \$300,000 = \$168,000), requiring the sale of \$42,000 of the original \$210,000 risky holdings, with the proceeds used to purchase more shares in Ready Asset (the money market fund). Total holdings in the risk-free asset will increase to 300,000 (1 − .56) = \$132,000, or the original holdings plus the new contribution to the money market fund:

$$\$90{,}000 + \$42{,}000 = \$132{,}000$$

The key point, however, is that we leave the proportions of each stock in the risky portfolio unchanged. Because the weights of VO and CT in the risky portfolio are .54 and .46, respectively, we sell .54 × \$42,000 = \$22,680 of VO and .46 × \$42,000 = \$19,320 of CT. After the sale, the proportions of each share in the risky portfolio are in fact unchanged:

$$\text{VO:} \quad w_1 = \frac{113{,}400 - 22{,}680}{210{,}000 - 42{,}000} = .54$$

$$\text{CT:} \quad w_2 = \frac{96{,}600 - 19{,}320}{210{,}000 - 42{,}000} = .46$$

Rather than thinking of our risky holdings as VO and CT stock separately, we may view our holdings as if they were in a single fund that holds VO and CT in fixed proportions. In this sense we treat the risky fund as a single risky asset, that asset being a particular bundle of securities. As we shift in and out of safe assets, we simply alter our holdings of that bundle of securities commensurately.

Given this assumption, we now can turn to the desirability of reducing risk by changing the risky/risk-free asset mix, that is, reducing risk by decreasing the proportion $y$. As long as we do not alter the weights of each stock within the risky portfolio, the probability distribution of the rate of return on the risky portfolio remains unchanged by the asset reallocation. What will change is the probability distribution of the rate of return on the complete portfolio that consists of the risky asset and the risk-free asset.

---

**CONCEPT CHECK** Question 1. What will be the dollar value of your position in VO and its proportion in your overall portfolio if you decide to hold 50 percent of your investment budget in Ready Asset?

---

## 6.2 The Risk-Free Asset

By virtue of its power to tax and control the money supply, only the government can issue default-free bonds. Actually, the default-free guarantee by itself is not sufficient to make the bonds risk-free in real terms. The only risk-free asset in real terms would be a perfectly price-indexed bond. Moreover, a default-free perfectly indexed bond offers a guaranteed real rate to an investor only if the maturity of the bond is identical to the investor's desired holding period. Even indexed bonds are subject to interest rate risk, because real interest rates change unpredictably through time. When future real rates are uncertain, so is the future price of perfectly indexed bonds.

Nevertheless, it is common practice to view Treasury bills as "the" **risk-free asset.** Their short-term nature makes their values insensitive to interest rate fluctuations. Indeed, an investor can lock in a short-term nominal return by buying a bill and holding it to maturity. The inflation uncertainty over the course of a few weeks, or even months, is negligible compared with the uncertainty of stock market returns.

In practice, most investors use a broader range of money market instruments as a risk-free asset. All the money market instruments are virtually free of interest rate risk because of their short maturities and are fairly safe in terms of default or credit risk.

Most money market funds hold, for the most part, three types of securities: Treasury bills, bearer deposit notes (BDNs), and commercial paper (CP), differing slightly in their default risk. The yields to maturity on BDNs and CP for identical maturity, for example, are always slightly higher than those of T-bills. The pattern of this yield spread for short-term high-quality commercial paper is shown in Figure 6.1

Money market funds have changed their relative holdings of these securities over time, but by and large, T-bills make up only about 15 percent of their portfolios. Nevertheless, the risk of such blue-chip short-term investments as BDNs and CP is minuscule compared with that of most other assets, such as long-term corporate bonds, common stocks, or real estate. Hence, we treat money market funds as the most easily accessible risk-free asset for most investors.

The notion of a risk-free asset seems straightforward, but nevertheless is the source of surprising amounts of confusion. Consider for example, the nearby box, which touts the possibility of stock market-like returns without the risk. The article argues that long-term bonds can provide returns approximately three-quarters that of stocks with negligible risk. This analysis is faulty for several reasons.

First, the investment instruments suggested in the article are by no means risk free. Interest rate fluctuations can impart uncertainty to the value of these securities at any time before their maturity dates. In fact, as we saw in Figure 5.3 of Chapter 5, the volatility of the rates of return on these long-term fixed-income securities historically has been quite high.

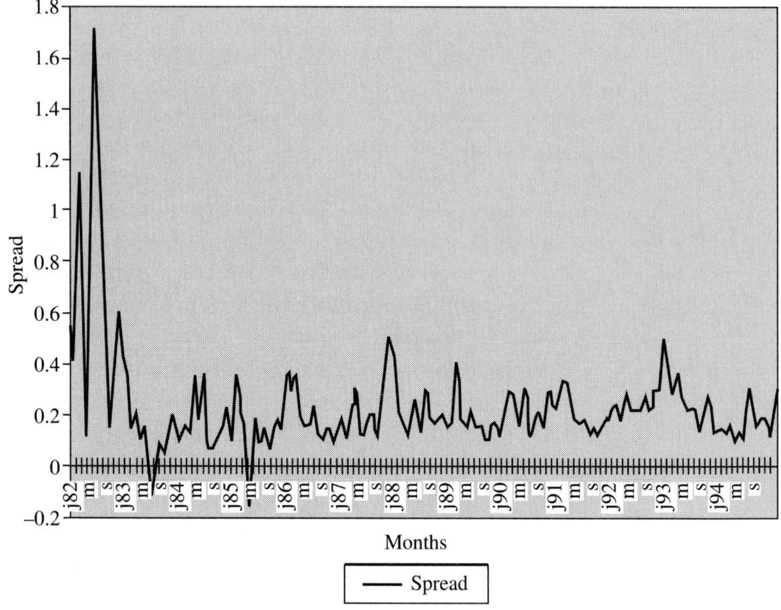


**Figure 6.1** The pattern of the yield spread for high-quality corporate paper versus 3-month Treasury bills.

Second, we have argued that the risk premium is properly viewed as an incremental rate of return above the risk-free rate. As the rates available on high-quality short-term instruments rise, so should the expected rate on riskier assets, if their risk premiums are to be preserved. When the article cites the long-term historical return on stocks as about 10 percent and notes that fixed income securities are now providing yields almost that high, it ignores the fact that the expected rate of return of the stock market might well have risen along with the rates available on these securities.

Finally, the article seems to imply that locking in a nominally risk-free rate for 5 or 10 years avoids risk. But, as Robert A. Clarfeld, who is quoted in the article, points out, a fixed nominal return leaves you exposed to opportunity-cost risk, since it is possible that available rates of return might continue to rise, leaving behind a portfolio with fixed payments.

## 6.3 Portfolios of One Risky Asset and One Risk-Free Asset

In this section, we examine the risk-return combinations available to investors. This is the "technological" part of asset allocation; it deals with only the opportunities available to investors given the features of the broad asset markets in which they can invest. In the next section, we will address the "personal" part of the problem—the specific individual's choice of the best risk-return combination from the set of feasible combinations.

## LOCK IN STOCK-MARKET RETURNS, WHILE AVOIDING THE RISK

Are interest rates rising? Is inflation going up? Are stocks riskier than bonds?

Who cares.

Bulls, bears and nervous Nellies can feel the turmoil in the markets and lock in yields near 8%—and maybe higher—for the next 5 or 10 years.

How? By investing in municipal bonds, Treasury notes, zero-coupon Treasury bonds, and even some bank certificates of deposit. Rising interest rates have pushed returns on these investments into the 8% range, tax-adjusted, as long as you don't touch the money early.

"It's an uncertain world, but by locking in an 8% return, you know pretty much what you're going to get at the end of the period," says Jim Floyd, senior analyst at the Leuthold Group, an institutional-investment consulting group in Minneapolis.

What's more, that 8% return will probably be pretty close to how stocks will perform, with a sliver of risk. Research by Leuthold suggests that although the long-term historical return on stocks is 10%, the return during the next decade is likely to be closer to 8%.

If you can lock in 75% of the historical return of the stock market with zippo risk, what's stopping you?" asks James Wilson, a financial planner in Columbia, S.C.

Financial advisers caution, though, that you shouldn't overdo it. Although it may be prudent to anchor a portion of your holdings into a low-risk, fairly certain return, it's still wise to keep some money in the stock market.

"You want to participate in any upside should the market continue to perform," says Robert A. Clarfeld, a New York financial planner and accountant. He also cautions that inflation could heat up, eating up the value of an 8% return.

**Safe Yields Now and Then**

| | Today | Beginning 1994 |
|---|---|---|
| Municipal bonds* | 11.8% | 10.3% |
| Treasury notes† | 7.8 | 5.2 |
| Treasury strips‡ | 8.1 | 7.0 |
| Bank CDs§ | 7.7 | 5.4 |

*Taxable-equivalent yield on Bond Buyer municipal-bond index for investors in 36% federal tax bracket
†Five-year Treasury notes
‡Twenty-year zero-coupon Treasury bonds
§Highest-yield five-year bank certificate of deposit as quoted by BanxQuote Money Markets

By Ellen E. Schultz, "Your Money Matters." *The Wall Street Journal*, December 14, 1994. Reprinted by permission.

Suppose that the investor already has decided on the composition of the optimal risky portfolio. The investment proportions in all the available risky assets are known. Now the final concern is with the proportion of the investment budget, $y$, to be allocated to the risky portfolio, $P$. The remaining proportion, $1 - y$, is to be invested in the risk-free asset, $F$.

Denote the risky rate of return by $r_P$ and denote the expected rate of return on $P$ by $E(r_P)$ and its standard deviation by $\sigma_P$. The rate of return on the risk-free asset is denoted as $r_f$. In the numerical example we assume that $E(r_P) = 15$ percent, $\sigma_P = 22$ percent, and that the risk-free rate is $r_f = 7$ percent. Thus, the risk premium on the risky asset is $E(r_P) - r_f = 8$ percent.

With a proportion $y$ in the risky portfolio and $1 - y$ in the risk-free asset, the rate of return on the *complete* portfolio, denoted $C$, is $r_C$ where

$$r_C = yr_P + (1 - y)r_f$$

Taking the expectation of this portfolio's rate of return,

$$\begin{aligned} E(r_C) &= yE(r_P) + (1 - y)r_f \\ &= r_f + y[E(r_P) - r_f] \\ &= .07 + y(.15 - .07) \end{aligned} \tag{6.1}$$

This result is easily interpreted. The base rate of return for any portfolio is the risk-free rate. In addition, the portfolio is *expected* to earn a risk premium that depends on the risk premium of the risky portfolio, $E(r_P) - r_f$, and the investor's exposure to the risky asset, denoted by $y$. Investors are assumed to be risk averse and thus unwilling to take on a risky position without a positive risk premium.

As we noted in Chapter 5, when we combine a risky asset and a risk-free asset in a portfolio, the standard deviation of that portfolio is the standard deviation of the risky asset multiplied by the weight of the risky asset in that portfolio. In our case, the complete portfolio consists of the risky asset and the risk-free asset. Since the standard deviation of the risky portfolio is $\sigma_P = .22$,

$$\begin{aligned} \sigma_C &= y\sigma_P \\ &= .22y \end{aligned} \tag{6.2}$$

which makes sense because the standard deviation of the portfolio is proportional to both the standard deviation of the risky asset and the proportion invested in it. In sum, the rate of return of the complete portfolio will have expected return $E(r_C) = r_f + y[E(r_P) - r_f] = .07 + .08y$ and standard deviation $\sigma_C = .22y$.

The next step is to plot the portfolio characteristics (as a function of $y$) in the expected return–standard deviation plane. This is done in Figure 6.2. The expected return–standard deviation combination for the risk-free asset, $F$, appears on the vertical axis because the standard deviation is zero. The risky asset, $P$, is plotted with a standard deviation, $\sigma_P = .22$, and expected return of .15. If an investor chooses to invest solely in the risky asset, then $y = 1.0$, and the resulting portfolio is $P$. If the chosen position is $y = 0$, then $1 - y = 1.0$, and the resulting portfolio is the risk-free portfolio $F$.

What about the more interesting midrange portfolios where $y$ lies between zero and 1? These portfolios will graph on the straight line connecting points $F$ and $P$. The slope of that line is simply $[E(r_P) - r_f]/\sigma_P$ (or rise/run), in this case .08/.22.

The conclusion is straightforward. Increasing the fraction of the overall portfolio invested in the risky asset increases the expected return by the risk premium of equation 6.1, which is .08. It also increases portfolio standard deviation according to equation 6.2 at the rate of .22. The extra return per extra risk is thus .08/.22 = .36.

To derive the exact equation for the straight line between $F$ and $P$, we rearrange equation 6.2 to find that $y = \sigma_C/\sigma_P$, and substitute for $y$ in equation 6.1 to de-

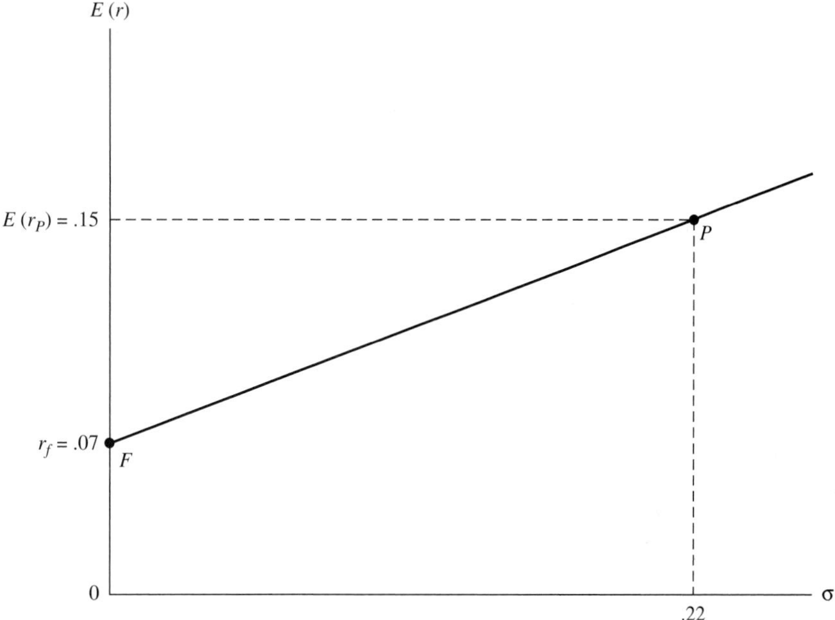


**Figure 6.2**
Expected return–standard deviation combinations.

scribe the expected return–standard deviation trade-off:

$$
\begin{aligned}
E[r_C(y)] &= r_f + y[E(r_P) - r_f] \\
&= r_f + \frac{\sigma_C}{.22}[E(_P) - r_f] \\
&= .07 + \frac{.08}{.22}\sigma_C
\end{aligned}
$$

Thus, the expected return of the portfolio as a function of its standard deviation is a straight line, with intercept $r_f$ and slope as follows:

$$
\begin{aligned}
S &= \frac{E(r_P) - r_f}{\sigma_P} \\
&= \frac{.08}{.22}
\end{aligned}
$$

Figure 6.3 graphs the *investment opportunity set,* which is the set of feasible expected return and standard deviation pairs of all portfolios resulting from different values of $y$. The graph is a straight line originating at $r_f$ and going through the point labeled $P$.

This straight line is called the **capital allocation line** (CAL). It depicts all the risk-return combinations available to investors. The slope of the CAL, $S$, equals the increase in the expected return of the chosen portfolio per unit of additional

**Figure 6.3**
The investment opportunity set with a risky asset and a risk-free asset.

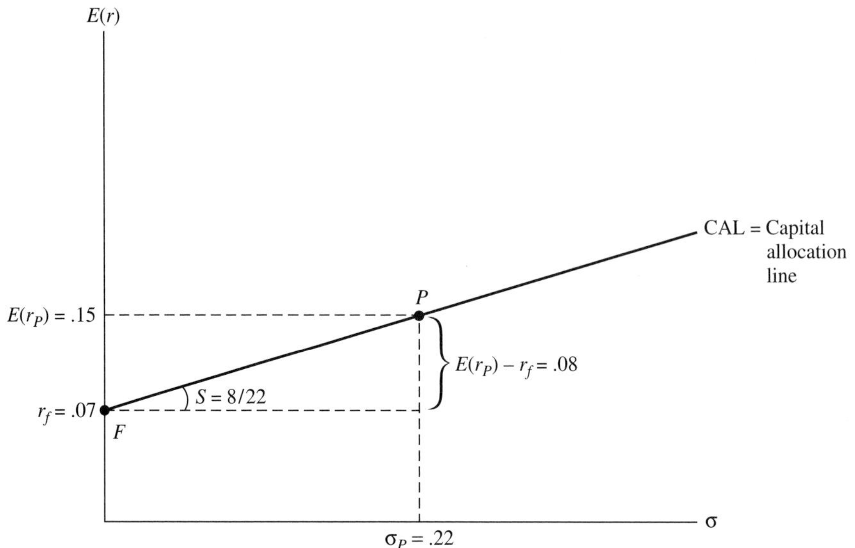


standard deviation—in other words, the measure of extra return per extra risk. For this reason, the slope also is called the **reward-to-variability ratio.**

A portfolio equally divided between the risky asset and the risk-free asset, that is, where $y = .5$, will have an expected rate of return of $E(r_C) = .07 + .5 \times .08 = .11$, implying a risk premium of 4 percent, and a standard deviation of $\sigma_C = .5 \times .22 = .11$, or 11 percent. It will plot on the line *FP* midway between *F* and *P*. The reward-to-variability ratio will be $S = .08/.22 = .36$.

---

**CONCEPT CHECK** Question 2. Can the reward-to-variability ratio, $S = [E(r_C) - r_f]/\sigma$, of any combination of the risky asset and the risk-free asset be different from the ratio for the risky asset taken alone, $[E(r_P) - r_f]/\sigma$, which in this case is .36?

---

What about points on the line to the right of portfolio *P* in the investment opportunity set? If investors can borrow at the (risk-free) rate of $r_f = 7$ percent, they can construct portfolios that may be plotted on the CAL to the right of *P*.

Suppose the investment budget is \$300,000, and our investor borrows an additional \$120,000, investing the total available funds in the risky asset. This is a *leveraged* position in the risky asset; it is financed in part by borrowing. In that case

$$y = \frac{420{,}000}{300{,}000} = 1.4$$

**Figure 6.4**
The opportunity set with differential borrowing and lending rates.

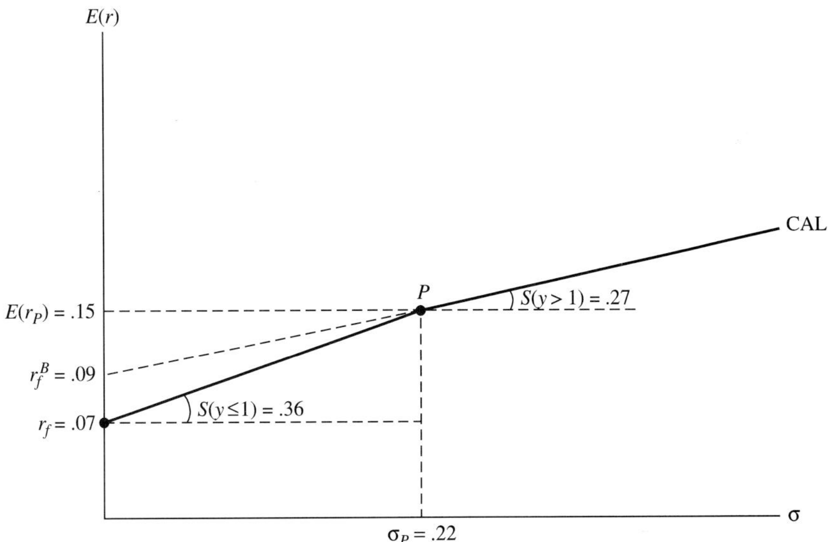


and $1 - y = 1 - 1.4 = -.4$, reflecting a short position in the risk-free asset, which is a borrowing position. Rather than lending at a 7 percent interest rate, the investor borrows at 7 percent. The distribution of the portfolio rate of return still exhibits the same reward-to-variability ratio:

$$E(r_C) = .07 + (1.4 \times .08) = .182$$
$$\sigma_C = 1.4 \times .22 = .308$$
$$S = \frac{E(r_C) - r_f}{\sigma_C}$$
$$= \frac{.182 - .07}{.308} = .36$$

As one might expect, the leveraged portfolio has a higher standard deviation than does an unleveraged position in the risky asset.

Of course, nongovernment investors cannot borrow at the risk-free rate. The risk of a borrower's default causes lenders to demand higher interest rates on loans. Therefore, the nongovernment investor's borrowing cost will exceed the lending rate of $r_f = 7$ percent. Suppose that the borrowing rate is $r_f^B = 9$ percent. Then, in the borrowing range the reward-to-variability ratio, the slope of the CAL, will be $[E(r_P) - r_f^B]/\sigma_P = .06/.22 = .27$. The CAL therefore will be "kinked" at point $P$ as shown in Figure 6.4. To the left of $P$ the investor is lending at 7 percent, and the slope of the CAL is .36. To the right of $P$, where $y > 1$, the investor is borrowing to finance extra investments in the risky asset, and the slope is .27.

In practice, borrowing to invest in the risky portfolio is easy and straightforward if you have a margin account with a broker. All you have to do is tell your broker that you want to buy "on margin." Margin purchases may not exceed 50 percent of the purchase value. Therefore, if your net worth in the account is \$300,000, the broker is allowed to lend you up to \$300,000 to purchase additional stock.[1] You would then have \$600,000 on the asset side of your account and \$300,000 on the liability side, resulting in $y = 2.0$.

**CONCEPT CHECK** Question 3. Suppose that there is a shift upward in the expected rate of return on the risky asset, from 15 percent to 17 percent. If all other parameters remain unchanged, what will be the slope of the CAL for $y \leq 1$ and $y > 1$?

## 6.4 RISK TOLERANCE AND ASSET ALLOCATION

We have shown how to develop the CAL, the graph of all feasible risk-return combinations available from different asset-allocation choices. The investor confronting the CAL now must choose one optimal combination from the set of feasible choices. This choice entails a trade-off between risk and return. Individual investor differences in risk aversion imply that, given an identical opportunity set (as described by a risk-free rate and a reward-to-variability ratio), different investors will choose different positions in the risky asset. In particular, the more risk-averse investors will choose to hold less of the risky asset and more of the risk-free asset.

In Chapter 5, we showed that the utility an investor derives from a portfolio with a given probability distribution of rates of return can be described by the expected return and variance of the portfolio rate of return. Specifically, we developed the following representation:

$$U = E(r) - \tfrac{1}{2}A\sigma^2$$

where $A$ is the coefficient of risk aversion. We interpret this expression to say that the utility from a portfolio increases as the expected rate of return increases, and it decreases when the variance increases. The relative magnitude of these changes is governed by the coefficient of risk aversion $A$. For risk-neutral investors, $A = 0$. Higher levels of risk aversion are reflected in larger values for $A$.

An investor who faces a risk-free rate, $r_f$, and a risky portfolio with expected return $E(r_P)$ and standard deviation $\sigma_P$ will find that, for any choice of $y$, the

[1] Margin purchases require the investor to maintain the securities in a margin account with the broker. If the value of the securities declines below a maintenance margin, a *margin call* is sent out, requiring a deposit to bring the net worth of the account up to the appropriate level. If the margin call is not met, regulations mandate that some or all of the securities be sold by the broker and the proceeds used to reestablish the required margin. See Chapter 3, Section 3.5, for a further discussion.

expected return of the complete portfolio is given by equation 6.1, part of which we repeat here:

$$E(r_C) = r_f + y[E(r_P) - r_f]$$

From equation 6.2, the variance of the overall portfolio is

$$\sigma_C^2 = y^2\sigma_P^2$$

The investor attempts to maximize his or her utility level, *U*, by choosing the best allocation to the risky asset, *y*. Typically, we write this problem as follows:

$$\underset{y}{\text{Max}}\ U = E(r_C) - \tfrac{1}{2}A\sigma_C^2 = r_f + y[E(r_P) - r_f] - \tfrac{1}{2}y^2A\sigma_P^2$$

where *A* is the coefficient of risk aversion.

Students of calculus will remember that the maximization problem is solved by setting the derivative of this expression to zero. Doing so and solving for *y* yields the optimal position for risk-averse investors in the risky asset, $y^*$, as follows.[2]

$$y^* = \frac{E(r_P) - r_f}{A\sigma_P^2} \qquad \textbf{(6.3)}$$

This solution shows that the optimal position in the risky asset is, as one would expect, *inversely* proportional to the level of risk aversion and the level of risk, as measured by the variance, and directly proportional to the risk premium offered by the risky asset.

Going back to our numerical example [$r_f$ = 7 percent, $E(r_P)$ = 15 percent, and $\sigma_P$ = 22 percent], the optimal solution for an investor with a coefficient of risk aversion, $A = 4$, is

$$y^* = \frac{.15 - .07}{4 \times .22^2} = .41$$

In other words, this particular investor will invest 41 percent of the investment budget in the risky asset and 59 percent in the risk-free asset. (Note that $r_f$, $E(r_P)$, and $\sigma_P$ must be expressed as decimals, or else it is necessary to change the scale of *A*.)

With 41 percent invested in the risky portfolio, the rate of return of the complete portfolio will have an expected return and standard deviation as follows:

$$\begin{aligned} E(r_C) &= .07 + .41 \times (.15 - .07) \\ &= .1028 \\ \sigma_C &= .41 \times .22 \\ &= .0902 \end{aligned}$$

[2] The derivative with respect to *y* equals $E(r_P) - r_f - yA\sigma_P^2$. Setting this expression equal to zero and solving for *y* yields equation 6.3.

**Figure 6.5**
Two indifference curves through a risky asset.

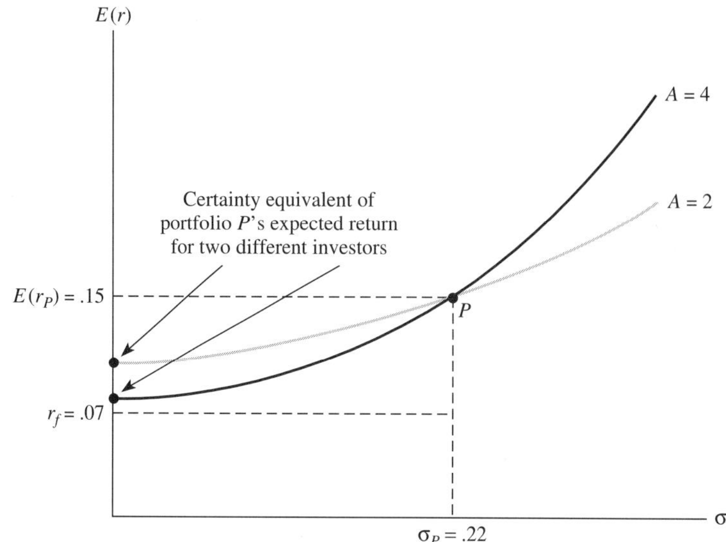


The risk premium of the complete portfolio is $E(r_C) - r_f = 3.28$ percent, which is obtained by taking on a portfolio with a standard deviation of 9.02 percent. Notice that 3.28/9.02 = .36, which is the reward-to-variability ratio assumed for this problem.

A less mathematical way of presenting this decision problem is to use indifference curve analysis. Recall from Chapter 5 that the indifference curve is a graph in the expected return–standard deviation plane of all points that result in a given level of utility. The curve then displays the investor's required trade-off between expected return and standard deviation.

For example, suppose that the initial portfolio under consideration is the risky asset itself, $y = 1$. The dark curve in Figure 6.5 represents the indifference curve for an investor with a degree of risk aversion, $A = 4$, that passes through the risky asset with $E(r_P) = 15$ percent and $\sigma_P = 22$ percent. The light curve, by contrast, shows an indifference curve going through $P$ with a smaller degree of risk aversion, $A = 2$. The light indifference curve is flatter, that is, the more risk-tolerant (less risk-averse) investor requires a smaller increase in expected return to compensate for a given increase in standard deviation. The intercept of the indifference curve with the vertical axis is the *certainty equivalent* of the risky portfolio's expected rate of return because it gives a risk-free return with the same utility as the risky portfolio. Notice in Figure 6.5 that the less risk-averse investor (with $A = 2$) has a higher certainty equivalent for a risky portfolio such as $P$ than the more risk-averse investor ($A = 4$).

Indifference curves can be drawn for many benchmark portfolios, representing various levels of utility. Figure 6.6 shows this set of indifference curves.

To show how to use indifference curve analysis to determine the choice of the optimal portfolio for a specific CAL, Figure 6.7 superimposes the graphs

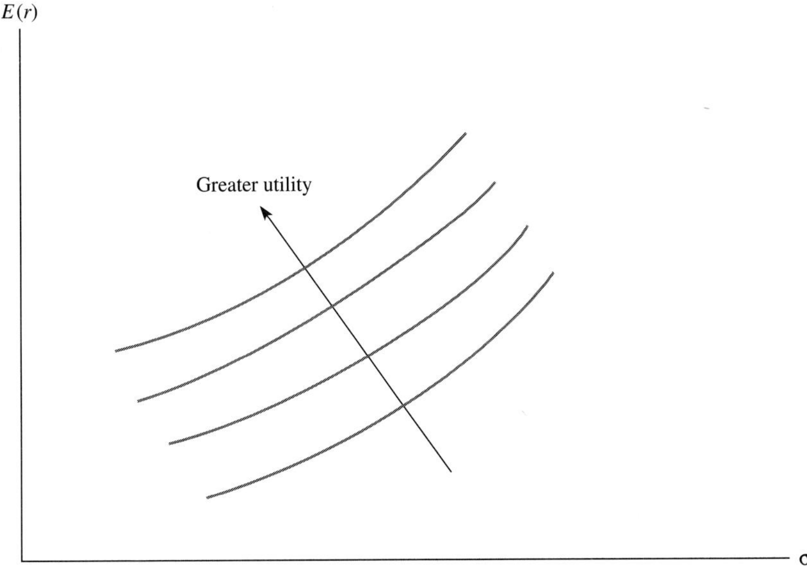


**Figure 6.6**
A set of indifference curves.

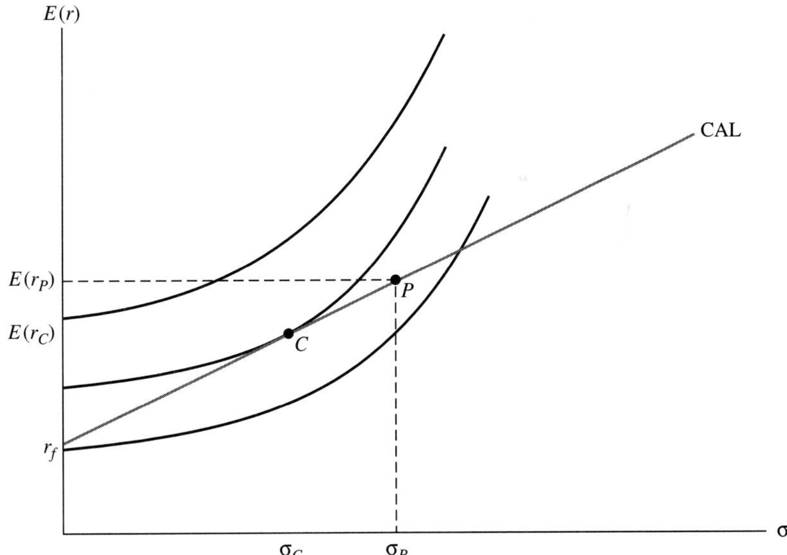


**Figure 6.7**
The graphical solution to the portfolio decision.

of the indifference curves on the graph of the investment opportunity set, the CAL.

The investor seeks the position with the highest feasible level of utility, represented by the highest possible indifference curve that touches the investment opportunity set. This is the indifference curve tangent to the CAL.

This optimal overall portfolio is represented by point $C$ on the investment opportunity set. Such a graphical approach yields the same solution as the algebraic approach

$$E(r_C) = .1028$$

and

$$\sigma_C = .0902$$

which yields $y^* = .41$.

In summary, the asset allocation process can be broken down into two steps: (1) determine the CAL; and (2) find the point of highest utility along that line.

---

**CONCEPT CHECK** Question 4.

*a*. If an investor's coefficient of risk aversion is $A = 3$, how does the optimal asset mix change? What are the new $E(r_C)$ and $\sigma_C$?

*b*. Suppose that the borrowing rate, $r_f^B = 9$ percent, is greater than the lending rate, $r_f = 7$ percent. Show, graphically, how the optimal portfolio choice of some investors will be affected by the higher borrowing rate. Which investors will *not* be affected by the borrowing rate?

---

## 6.5 PASSIVE STRATEGIES: THE CAPITAL MARKET LINE

The CAL is derived with the risk-free asset and "the" risky portfolio $P$. Determination of the assets to include in risky portfolio $P$ may result from a passive or an active strategy. A **passive strategy** describes a portfolio decision that avoids *any* direct or indirect security analysis.[3] At first blush, a passive strategy would appear to be naive. As will become apparent, however, forces of supply and demand in large capital markets may make such a strategy a reasonable choice for many investors.

A natural candidate for a passively held risky asset would be a well-diversified portfolio of common stocks. We already have said that a passive strategy requires that we devote no resources to acquiring information on any individual stock or group of stocks, so we must follow a "neutral" diversification strategy. One way is to select a diversified portfolio of stocks that mirrors the value of the corporate sector of the Canadian economy. This results in a value-weighted portfolio in which, for example, the proportion invested in Seagram's stock will be the ratio of Seagram's total market value to the market value of all listed stocks.

The most frequently used value-weighted stock portfolio in Canada is the Toronto Stock Exchange's composite index of the 300 large capitalization Cana-

---

[3] By "indirect security analysis" we mean the delegation of that responsibility to an intermediary, such as a professional money manager.

**Table 6.1** Annual Rates of Return for Common Stocks and 3-Month Bills, and the Risk Premium Over Bills on Common Stock

| | Common Stocks | | 3-Month Bills | | Risk Premium over Bills on Common Stocks | |
|---|---|---|---|---|---|---|
| | Mean | Standard Deviation | Mean | Standard Deviation | Mean | Standard Deviation |
| 1957–1968 | 10.32 | 16.74 | 4.07 | 1.04 | 6.26 | 17.00 |
| 1969–1980 | 12.52 | 19.05 | 7.76 | 3.16 | 4.75 | 18.04 |
| 1981–1994 | 9.21 | 15.09 | 10.41 | 3.63 | −1.20 | 16.92 |
| 1957–1994 | 10.60 | 16.53 | 7.57 | 3.87 | 3.03 | 17.16 |

Data from *ScotiaMcLeod's Handbook of Canadian Debt Market Indices, 1947–1994*. Reprinted by permission of Scotia Capital Markets Fixed Income Research.

dian corporations[4] (TSE 300). Table 6.1 shows the historical record of this portfolio. The last pair of columns shows the average risk premium over T-bills and its standard deviation. The risk premium of 3.03 percent and standard deviation of 17.16 percent over the entire period correspond to the figures of 8 percent and 22 percent we assumed for the risky portfolio example in Section 6.4.

We call the capital allocation line provided by one-month T-bills and a broad index of common stocks the **capital market line** (CML). A passive strategy generates an investment opportunity set that is represented by the CML.

How reasonable is it for an investor to pursue a passive strategy? Of course, we cannot answer such a question without comparing the strategy to the costs and benefits accruing to an active portfolio strategy. Some thoughts are relevant at this point, however.

First, the alternative active strategy is not free. Whether you choose to invest the time and cost to acquire the information needed to generate an optimal active portfolio of risky assets, or whether you delegate the task to a professional who will charge a fee, construction of an active portfolio is more expensive than construction of a passive one. The passive portfolio requires only small commissions on purchases of T-bills (or zero commissions if you purchase bills directly from the government) and management fees to a mutual fund company that offers a market index fund to the public. First Canadian's Equity Index Fund, for example, mimics the TSE 300 index. It purchases shares of the firms constituting the TSE 300 in proportion to the market values of the outstanding equity of each firm, and therefore essentially replicates the TSE 300 index. The fund thus duplicates the performance of this market index. It has low operating expenses (as a percentage of assets) when compared to other mutual stock funds precisely because it requires minimal managerial effort.

[4] For a discussion of value-weighted Canadian stock portfolios in asset allocation, see Paul Potvin, "Passive Management, the TSE 300 and the Toronto 35 Stock Indexes," *Canadian Investment Review* 5, no. 1 (Spring 1992).

A second reason supporting a passive strategy is the free-rider benefit. If we assume there are many active, knowledgeable investors who quickly bid up prices of undervalued assets and bid down overvalued assets (by selling), we have to conclude that at any time most assets will be fairly priced. Therefore, a well-diversified portfolio of common stock will be a reasonably fair buy, and the passive strategy may not be inferior to that of the average active investor. (We will explain this assumption and provide a more comprehensive analysis of the relative success of passive strategies in later chapters.)

To summarize, however, a passive strategy involves investment in two passive portfolios: virtually risk-free, short-term T-bills (or, alternatively, a money market fund), and a fund of common stocks that mimics a broad market index. The capital allocation line representing such a strategy is called the *capital market line.* Historically, based on data from 1957 to 1994, the passive risky portfolio offered an average risk premium of 3.03 percent and a standard deviation of 17.16 percent, resulting in a reward-to-variability ratio of .18. Passive investors allocate their investment budgets among instruments according to their degree of risk aversion.

We can use our analysis to deduce a typical investor's risk-aversion parameter. In October 1991, the total market value of the TSE 300 stocks was about 1.7 times the market value of all outstanding T-bills of less than a year's maturity. If we ignore all other assets (e.g., long-term bonds, foreign securities, and real estate) and pretend that all investors followed a passive strategy, then the average investor's position in the risky asset (the TSE 300) was

$$y = \frac{1.7}{1 + 1.7} = .63$$

What degree of risk aversion must investors have for this portfolio to be optimal? Assuming that the average investor uses the historical average risk premium (3.03 percent) and standard deviation (17.16 percent) to forecast future return and standard deviation, and noting that the weight in the risky portfolio was .63, we can work out the average investor's risk tolerance as follows:

$$y^* = \frac{E(r_M) - r_f}{A\sigma_M^2} = .63 = \frac{.0303}{A \times .1716^2}$$

which implies a coefficient of risk aversion of

$$A = \frac{.0294}{.63 \times .1716^2} = 1.63$$

This is, of course, mere speculation. We have assumed without basis that the average 1991 investor held the naive view that historical average rates of return and standard deviations are the best estimates of expected rates of return and risk, looking to the future. To the extent that in 1991 the average investor took advantage of contemporary information in addition to simple historical data, our estimate of $A = 1.63$ would be an unjustified inference.[5]

The equivalent figures for the United States, if Standard & Poor's composite index of the 500 largest corporations (S&P 500) is used as the value-weighted portfolio, yield a significantly different picture. Over the period 1926–1993, the risk premium of that portfolio over one-month T-bills averaged 8.6 percent, with a standard deviation of 20.9 percent. In 1990, the total market value of the S&P 500 stocks was about four times as large as the market value of all outstanding T-bills of less than six months' maturity. These numbers correspond to an average investor position of .8 in the risky asset (the S&P 500), yielding a coefficient of risk aversion of 2.46. It should be noted that the broad range of studies that take into account the full range of available assets places the degree of risk aversion for the representative U.S. investor in the range of 2.0–4.0.[6]

**CONCEPT CHECK** Question 5. Suppose that expectations about the TSE 300 index and the T-bill rate are the same as they were in 1991, but you find that a greater proportion is invested in T-bills today than in 1991. What can you conclude about the change in risk tolerance over the years since 1991?

## SUMMARY

**1.** Shifting funds from the risky portfolio to the risk-free asset is the simplest way to reduce risk. Other methods involve diversification of the risky portfolio (we take up these methods in later chapters).

**2.** T-bills provide a perfectly risk-free asset in nominal terms only. Nevertheless, the standard deviation of real rates on short-term T-bills is small compared to that of other assets such as long-term bonds and common stocks, so for the purpose of our analysis we consider T-bills as the risk-free asset. Money market funds hold, in addition to T-bills, short-term and relatively safe obligations such as CP and CDs. These entail some default risk, but again the additional risk is small relative to most other risky assets. For convenience, we often refer to money market funds as risk-free assets.

---

[5] A study by Kryzanowski and To estimated the risk-aversion coefficient for a variety of Canadian households. Their analysis is cross-sectional, and takes into account the effects of differential tax rates and inflation. Hence, the estimates are not directly comparable to the value of $A$ that we found. See Lawrence Kryzanowski and Minh Chau To, "Revealed Preferences for Risky Assets in Imperfect Markets," *Canadian Journal of Administrative Sciences* 3, no. 2 (December 1986).

[6] See, for example, I. Friend and M. Blume, "The Demand for Risky Assets," *American Economic Review* 64 (1974); or S. J. Grossman and R. J. Shiller, "The Determinants of the Variability of Stock Market Prices," *American Economic Review* 71 (1981).

**3.** An investor's risky portfolio (the risky asset) can be characterized by its reward-to-variability ratio, $S = [E(r_P) - r_f]/\sigma_P$. This ratio also is the slope of the CAL, the line that, when graphed, goes from the risk-free asset through the risky asset. All combinations of the risky asset and the risk-free asset lie on this line. All things considered, an investor would prefer a steeper-sloping CAL, because that means higher expected return for any level of risk. If the borrowing rate is greater than the lending rate, the CAL will be "kinked" at the point of the risky asset.

**4.** The investor's degree of risk aversion is characterized by the slope of his or her indifference curve. Indifference curves show, at any level of expected return and risk, the required risk premium for taking on one additional percentage of standard deviation. More risk-averse investors have steeper indifference curves; that is, they require a greater risk premium for taking on more risk.

**5.** The exact optimal position, $y^*$, in the risky asset is proportional to the risk premium and inversely proportional to the variance and degree of risk aversion:

$$y^* = \frac{E(r_P) - r_f}{A\sigma_P^2}$$

Graphically, this portfolio represents the point at which the indifference curve is tangent to the CAL.

**6.** A passive investment strategy disregards security analysis, targeting instead the risk-free asset and a broad portfolio of risky assets, such as the TSE 300 stock portfolio. If in 1991 investors took the mean historical return and standard deviation of the TSE 300 as proxies for its expected return and standard deviation, then the market values of outstanding T-bills and the TSE 300 stocks would imply a degree of risk aversion of about $A = 1.6$ for the average investor. The equivalent figure for U.S. investors in 1987 was 2.5, which is in line with other studies that estimate typical risk aversion for U.S. investors in the range of 2.0 through 4.0.

## Key Terms

Capital allocation decision
Asset allocation decision
Security selection decision
Risky asset
Complete portfolio
Risk-free asset
Capital allocation line (CAL)
Reward-to-variability ratio
Passive strategy
Capital market line (CML)

## Selected Readings

*The classic article describing the asset allocation choice, whereby investors choose the optimal fraction of their wealth to place in risk-free assets, is:*

Tobin, James. "Liquidity Preference as Behavior towards Risk." *Review of Economic Studies* 25 (February 1958).

*Practitioner-oriented approaches to asset allocation may be found in:*

Maginn, John L.; and Donald L. Tuttle. *Managing Investment Portfolios: A Dynamic Process,* 2nd edition. New York: Warren, Gorham, & Lamont, Inc., 1990.

*Similar practitioner-oriented Canadian contributions include:*

Auger, Robert; and Denis Parisien. "Understanding Asset Allocation." *Canadian Investment Review* 4, no. 1 (Spring 1991).

Potvin, Paul. "Passive Management, the TSE 300, and the Toronto 35 Stock Indexes." *Canadian Investment Review* 5, no. 1 (Spring 1992).

## Problems

You manage a risky portfolio with an expected rate of return of 17 percent and a standard deviation of 27 percent. The T-bill rate is 7 percent.

1. Your client chooses to invest 70 percent of a portfolio in your fund and 30 percent in a T-bill money market fund. What is the expected value and standard deviation of the rate of return on your client's portfolio?
2. Suppose that your risky portfolio includes the following investments in the given proportions:
   Stock *A:* 27 percent
   Stock *B:* 33 percent
   Stock *C:* 40 percent
   What are the investment proportions of your client's overall portfolio, including the position in T-bills?
3. What is the reward-to-variability ratio ($S$) of your risky portfolio?
4. Draw the CAL of your portfolio on an expected return–standard deviation diagram. What is the slope of the CAL? Show the position of your client on your fund's CAL.
5. Suppose that your client decides to invest in your portfolio a proportion $y$ of the total investment budget so that the overall portfolio will have an expected rate of return of 15 percent.
   *a.* What is the proportion $y$?
   *b.* What are your client's investment proportions in your three stocks and the T-bill fund?
   *c.* What is the standard deviation of the rate of return on your client's portfolio?
6. Suppose that your client prefers to invest in your fund a proportion $y$ that maximizes the expected return on the overall portfolio subject to the constraint that the overall portfolio's standard deviation will not exceed 20 percent.
   *a.* What is the investment proportion ($y$)?
   *b.* What is the expected rate of return on the overall portfolio?
7. Your client's degree of risk aversion is $A = 3.5$.
   *a.* What proportion ($y$) of the total investment should be invested in your fund?

*b.* What is the expected value and standard deviation of the rate of return on your client's optimized portfolio?

You estimate that a passive portfolio (i.e., one invested in a risky portfolio that mimics the TSE 300 stock index) yields an expected rate of return of 13 percent with a standard deviation of 25 percent.

**8.** Draw the CML and your fund's CAL on an expected return–standard deviation diagram.

*a.* What is the slope of the CML?

*b.* Characterize in one short paragraph the advantage(s) of your fund over the passive fund.

**9.** Your client ponders whether to switch the 70 percent that is invested in your fund to the passive portfolio.

*a.* Explain to your client the disadvantage(s) of the switch.

*b.* Show your client the maximum fee you could charge (as a percentage of the investment in your fund deducted at the end of the year) that would still leave him or her at least as well off investing in your fund as in the passive one. (Hint: The fee will lower the slope of your client's CAL by reducing the expected return net of the fee.)

**10.** Consider the client in problem 7 with $A = 3.5$.

*a.* If the client chose to invest in the passive portfolio, what proportion ($y$) would be selected?

*b.* What fee (percentage of the investment in your fund, deducted at the end of the year) can you charge to make the client indifferent between your fund and the passive strategy?

Problems 11–14 are more advanced and are based on the following assumptions. Suppose that the borrowing rate that your client faces is 9 percent. Continue to assume that the TSE 300 index has an expected return of 13 percent and a standard deviation of 25 percent.

**11.** Draw a diagram of the CML your client faces with the borrowing constraints. Superimpose on it two sets of indifference curves, one for a client who will choose to borrow, and one for a client who will invest in both the index fund and a money market fund.

**12.** What is the range of risk aversion for which the client will neither borrow nor lend, that is, for which $y = 1$?

**13.** Solve problems 11 and 12 for a client who uses your fund rather than an index fund.

**14.** Amend your solution to problem 10(*b*) for clients in the risk-aversion range that you found in problem 12.

**15.** Look at the data in Table 6.1 regarding the average risk premium of the TSE 300 over T-bills and the standard deviation of that risk premium. Suppose that the TSE 300 is your risky portfolio.

*a.* If your risk-aversion coefficient is 2 and you believe that the entire 1957–1994 period is representative of future expected performance, what fraction of your portfolio should be allocated to T-bills and what fraction to equity?

*b.* What if you believe that the 1981–1994 period is representative?

*c.* What do you conclude upon comparing your answers to (a) and (b)?

**16.** What do you think would happen to the expected return on stocks if investors perceived higher volatility in the equity market? Relate your answer to equation 6.3.

**17.** You manage an equity fund with an expected risk premium of 10 percent and an expected standard deviation of 14 percent. The rate on Treasury bills is 6 percent. Your client chooses to invest $60,000 of her portfolio in your equity fund and $40,000 in a T-bill money market fund. What is the expected return and standard deviation of return on your client's portfolio?

| | Expected Return | Standard Deviation of Return |
|---|---|---|
| a. | 8.4% | 8.4% |
| b. | 8.4% | 14.0% |
| c. | 12.0% | 8.4% |
| d. | 12.0% | 14.0% |

**18.** What is the reward-to-variability ratio for the *equity fund* in problem 17?

*a.* 0.71

*b.* 1.00

*c.* 1.19

*d.* 1.91

*Chapter* 7

# Optimal Risky Portfolios

**IN CHAPTER 6 WE DISCUSSED THE CAPITAL ALLOCATION DECISION.** That decision governs how an investor chooses between risk-free assets and "the" optimal portfolio or risky assets. This chapter explains how to construct that optimal risky portfolio.

We begin at the simplest level, with a discussion of how diversification can reduce the variability of portfolio returns. After establishing this basic point, we examine efficient diversification strategies at the asset allocation and security selection levels. We start with a simple, restricted example of asset allocation that excludes the risk-free asset. To that effect we use two risky mutual funds: a long-term bond fund and a stock fund. With this example we investigate the relationship between investment proportions and the resulting portfolio expected return and standard deviation. We then add a risk-free asset (e.g., T-bills) to the menu of assets and determine the optimal asset allocation. We do so by combining the principles of optimal allocation between risky assets and risk-free assets (from Chapter 6) with the risky portfolio construction methodology.

Moving from asset allocation to security selection, we first generalize our discussion of restricted asset allocation (with only two risky assets) to a universe of many risky securities. This generalization relies on the celebrated Markowitz portfolio selection model[1] that identifies the set of efficient stock portfolios from the available universe of securities. Proceeding to capital allocation, we show

[1] Harry Markowitz, *Portfolio Selection: Efficient Diversification of Investments* (New York: John Wiley, 1959).

how the best attainable capital allocation line emerges from the Markowitz algorithm. We pause to explain why portfolio optimization often is conducted in two stages, asset allocation and security selection, and discuss the potential inefficiency that may result from separating the asset allocation decision from security selection.

Finally, in the appendices to this chapter, we examine common fallacies regarding the power of diversification in the context of the insurance principle and the notion of time diversification.

## 7.1 Diversification and Portfolio Risk

Suppose that your risky portfolio is composed of only one stock. Dominion Computing Corporation (DCC). What would be the sources of risk to this "portfolio"? You might think of two broad sources of uncertainty. First, there is the risk that comes from conditions in the general economy, such as the business cycle, the inflation rate, interest rates, and exchange rates. None of these macroeconomic factors can be predicted with certainty, and all affect the rate of return that DCC stock eventually will provide. In addition to these macroeconomic factors there are firm-specific influences, such as DCC's success in research and development, and personnel changes. These factors affect DCC without noticeably affecting other firms in the economy.

Now consider a naive **diversification** strategy, in which you include additional securities in your risky portfolio. For example, suppose that you place half of your risky portfolio in an oil and minerals firm, Energy Resources Ltd (ERL), leaving the other half in DCC. What should happen to portfolio risk? To the extent that the firm-specific influences on the two stocks differ, we should reduce portfolio risk. For example, when oil prices fall, hurting ERL, computer prices might rise, helping DCC. The two effects are offsetting and stabilize portfolio return.

But why end diversification at only two stocks? If we diversify into many more securities, we continue to spread out our exposure to firm-specific factors, and portfolio volatility should continue to fall. Ultimately, however, even if we include a large number of risky securities in our portfolio, we cannot avoid risk altogether. To the extent that virtually all securities are affected by the common macroeconomic factors, we cannot eliminate our exposure to these risk sources. For example, if all stocks are affected by the business cycle, we cannot avoid exposure to business cycle risk no matter how many stocks we hold.

When all risk is firm-specific, as in Figure 7.1A, diversification can reduce risk to arbitrarily low levels. The reason is that with all risk sources independent, and with the portfolio spread across many securities, the exposure to any particular

**Figure 7.1**
Portfolio risk as a function of the number of stocks in the portfolio.

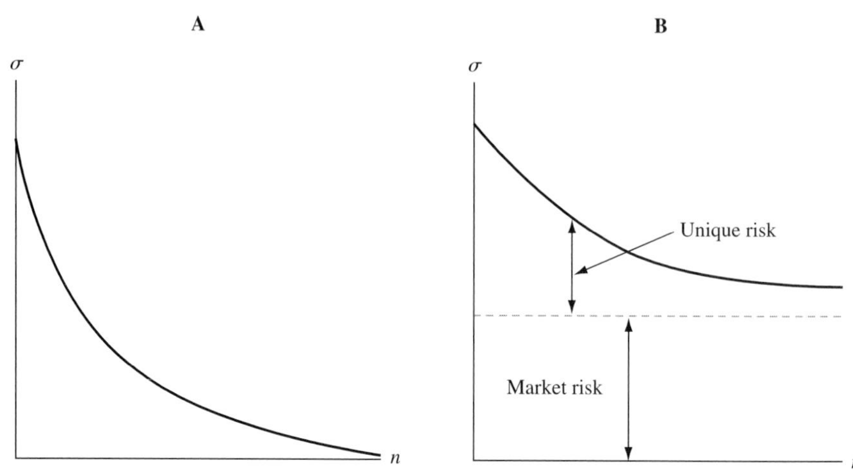


source of risk is reduced to a negligible level. This is just an application of the well-known law of averages. The reduction of risk to very low levels in the case of independent risk sources sometimes is called the **insurance principle,** because of the conventional belief that an insurance company depends on the risk reduction achieved through diversification when it writes many policies insuring against many independent sources of risk, with each policy being a small part of the company's overall portfolio. (See Appendix B of this chapter for a discussion of the insurance principle.)

When common sources of risk affect all firms, however, even extensive diversification cannot eliminate risk. In Figure 7.1B, portfolio risk measured by variance or standard deviation, falls as the number of securities increases, but it cannot be reduced to zero.[2] The risk that remains even after extensive diversification is called **market risk,** risk that is attributable to marketwide risk sources. Such risk also is called **systematic risk,** or **nondiversifiable risk.** In contrast, the risk that *can* be eliminated by diversification is called **unique risk, firm-specific risk, nonsystematic risk,** or **diversifiable risk.**

This analysis is borne out by empirical studies. Figure 7.2 shows the effect of portfolio diversification, using data on NYSE stocks.[3] The figure shows the average standard deviation of equally weighted portfolios constructed by selecting stocks at random as a function of the number of stocks in the portfolio. On average, portfolio risk does fall with diversification, but the power of diversification to reduce risk is limited by systematic or common sources of risk.

---

[2] The interested reader can find a more rigorous demonstration of these points in Appendix A. That discussion, however, relies on tools developed later in this chapter.

[3] L. Fisher and J. H. Lorie, "Some Studies of the Variability of Returns on Investments in Common Stocks," *Journal of Business*, 43 (April 1970).

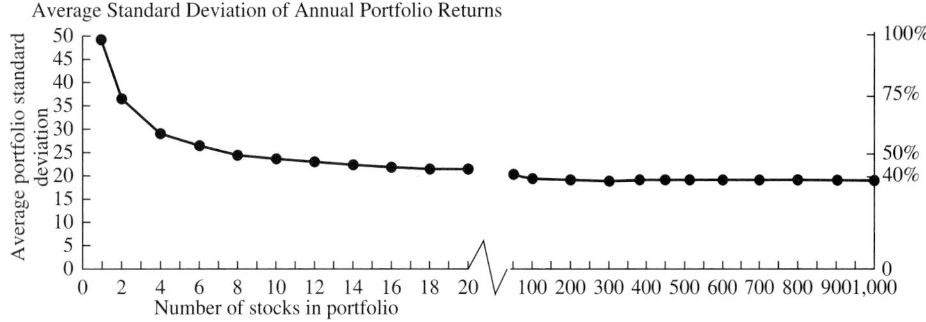


**Figure 7.2** Portfolio diversification. The average standard deviation of returns of portfolios composed of only one stock was 49.2 percent. The average portfolio risk fell rapidly as the number of stocks included in the portfolio increased. In the limit, portfolio risk could be reduced to only 19.2 percent.

Source: Edwin J. Elton and Martin J. Gruber, *Modern Portfolio Theory and Investment Analysis*, 2nd Edition (New York: John Wiley and Sons, 1989), p. 35, adapted by Meir Stotman, "How Many Stocks Make a Diversified Portfolio," *Journal of Financial and Quantitative Analysis* 22 (September 1987). Reprinted by permission.

## 7.2 Portfolios of Two Risky Assets

In the last section, we analyzed naive diversification, examining the risk of equally weighted portfolios composed of several securities. It is time now to study efficient diversification, whereby we construct risky portfolios to provide the lowest possible risk for any given level of expected return.

Constructing the optimal risky portfolio is a complicated statistical task. The *principles* we follow, however, are the same as those used to construct a portfolio from two risky assets only. We will analyze this easier process first and then backtrack a bit to see how we can generalize the technique to apply to more realistic cases.

Assume for this purpose that an investor is limited to two assets. To benefit from diversification, our investor chooses for the first asset shares in a mutual fund that maintains a broad portfolio of long-term debt securities ($D$) and for the second asset shares in a mutual fund that specializes in equities ($E$). The parameters of the joint probability distribution of returns are shown in Table 7.1.

**Table 7.1** Descriptive Statistics for Two Assets

| | Bonds (%) | | Stocks (%) |
|---|---|---|---|
| Expected return, $E(r)$ | 8 | | 13 |
| Standard deviation, $\sigma$ | 12 | | 20 |
| Covariance, $\text{Cov}(r_D, r_E)$ | | 72 | |
| Correlation coefficient, $\rho_{DE}$ | | .30 | |

A proportion denoted by $w_D$ is invested in the bond fund, and the remainder, $1 - w_D$, denoted $w_E$, is invested in the stock fund. The rate of return on this portfolio will be

$$r_p = w_D r_D + w_E r_E$$

where $r_p$ stands for the rate of return on the portfolio, $r_D$ the return on investment in the debt fund, and $r_E$ the return on investment in the equity fund.

As we noted in Chapter 5, the expected rate of return on the portfolio is a weighted average of expected return on the component securities with portfolio proportions as weights:

$$E(r_p) = w_D E(r_D) + w_E E(r_E) \tag{7.1}$$

The variance of the two-asset portfolio (rule 5 of Chapter 5) is

$$\sigma_p^2 = w_D^2 \sigma_D^2 + w_E^2 \sigma_E^2 + 2 w_D w_E \text{Cov}(r_D, r_E) \tag{7.2}$$

The first observation is that the variance of the portfolio, unlike the expected return, is *not* a weighted average of the individual asset variances. To understand the formula for the portfolio variance more clearly, recall that the covariance of a variable with itself (in this case the variable is the uncertain rate of return) is the variance of that variable; that is

$$\begin{aligned}
\text{Cov}(r_D, r_D) &= \sum_{\text{scenarios}} \Pr(\text{scenario})[r_D - E(r_D)][r_D - E(r_D)] \\
&= \sum_{\text{scenarios}} \Pr(\text{scenario})[r_D - E(r_D)]^2 \\
&= \sigma_D^2
\end{aligned}$$

Therefore, another way to write the variance of the portfolio is as follows:

$$\sigma_p^2 = w_D w_D \text{Cov}(r_D, r_D) + w_E w_E \text{Cov}(r_E, r_E) + 2 w_D w_E \text{Cov}(r_D, r_E)$$

In words, the variance of the portfolio is a weighted sum of covariances, where each weight is the product of the portfolio proportions of the pair of assets in the covariance term.

Why do we double the covariance between the two *different* assets in the last term of equation 7.2? This should become clear in the covariance matrix, Table 7.2, which is bordered by the portfolio weights.

**Table 7.2** Bordered Covariance Matrix

| | Covariances | |
|---|---|---|
| **Portfolio Weights** | $w_D$ | $w_E$ |
| $w_D$ | $\sigma_D^2$ | $\text{Cov}(r_D, r_E)$ |
| $w_E$ | $\text{Cov}(r_E, r_D)$ | $\sigma_E^2$ |

The diagonal (from top left to bottom right) of the covariance matrix is made up of the asset variances. The off-diagonal elements are the covariances. Note that

$$\text{Cov}(r_D, r_E) = \text{Cov}(r_E, r_D)$$

so that the matrix is symmetric. To compute the portfolio variance, we sum over each term in the matrix, first multiplying it by the product of the portfolio proportions from the corresponding row and column. Thus we have *one* term for each asset variance, but twice the term for each covariance pair because each covariance appears twice.

**CONCEPT CHECK**

Question 1.

*a.* Confirm that this simple rule for computing portfolio variance from the covariance matrix is consistent with equation 7.2.

*b.* Consider a portfolio of three funds, *X, Y,* and *Z,* with weights $w_X$, $w_Y$, and $w_Z$. Show that the portfolio variance is

$$w_X^2\sigma_X^2 + w_Y^2\sigma_Y^2 + w_Z^2\sigma_Z^2 + 2w_Xw_Y\text{Cov}(r_X, r_Y) + 2w_Xw_Z\text{Cov}(r_X, r_Z) + 2w_Yw_Z\text{Cov}(r_Y, r_Z)$$

As we discussed in Chapter 5, the portfolio variance is reduced if the covariance term is negative. This is the case in the use of hedge assets. It is important to recognize that, even if the covariance term is positive, thereby increasing portfolio volatility, the *portfolio* standard deviation still is less than the weighted average of the individual security standard deviations, unless the two securities are perfectly positively correlated.

To see this, recall from Chapter 5, equation 5.8 that the covariance can be written as

$$\text{Cov}(r_D, r_E) = \rho_{DE}\sigma_D\sigma_E$$

Substituting into equation 7.2, we can rewrite the variance and standard deviation of the portfolio as

$$\sigma_p^2 = w_D^2\sigma_D^2 + w_E^2\sigma_E^2 + 2w_Dw_E\sigma_D\sigma_E\rho_{DE} \qquad \textbf{(7.3)}$$

$$\sigma_p = \sqrt{\sigma_p^2} \qquad \textbf{(7.4)}$$

You can see from this information that the covariance term adds the most to the portfolio variance when the correlation coefficient, $\rho_{DE}$, is highest, that is, when it equals 1—as it would in the case of perfect positive correlation. In this case, the right-hand side of equation 7.3 is a perfect square, so it may be rewritten as follows:

$$\sigma_p^2 = (w_D\sigma_D + w_E\sigma_E)^2$$

or

$$\sigma_p = w_D\sigma_D + w_E\sigma_E$$

In other words, the standard deviation of the portfolio in the case of perfect positive correlation is just the weighted average of the component standard deviations. In all other cases, the correlation coefficient is less than 1, making the portfolio standard deviation *less* than the weighted average of the component standard deviations.

We know already from Chapter 5 that a hedge asset reduces the portfolio variance. This algebraic exercise adds the additional insight that the standard deviation of a portfolio of assets is less than the weighted average of the component security standard deviations, even when the assets are positively correlated. Because the portfolio expected return always is the weighted average of its component expected returns, while its standard deviation is less than the weighted average of the component standard deviations, *portfolio of less than perfectly correlated assets always offer better risk-return opportunities than the individual component securities on their own.* The less correlation between assets, the greater the gain in efficiency.

How low can portfolio standard deviation be? The lowest possible value of the correlation coefficient is $-1$, representing perfect negative correlation, in which case the portfolio variance is as follows:[4]

$$\sigma_p^2 = (w_D\sigma_D - w_E\sigma_E)^2$$

and the portfolio standard deviation is

$$\sigma_p = \text{Absolute value } (w_D\sigma_D - w_E\sigma_E)$$

Where $\rho = -1$, the investor has the opportunity of creating a perfectly hedged position. If the portfolio proportions are chosen as

[4] This expression also can be derived from equation 7.3. When $\rho_{DE} = -1$, equation 7.3 is a perfect square that can be factored as shown.

$$w_D = \frac{\sigma_E}{\sigma_D + \sigma_E}$$

$$w_E = \frac{\sigma_D}{\sigma_D + \sigma_E} = 1 - w_D$$

the standard deviation of the portfolio will equal zero.[5]

Let us apply this analysis to the data of the bond and stock funds as presented in Table 7.1. Using these data, the formulas for the expected return, variance, and standard deviation of the portfolio are

$$E(r_p) = 8w_D + 13w_E \quad \textbf{(7.5)}$$

$$\sigma_p^2 = 12^2 w_D^2 + 20^2 w_E^2 + 2 \times 72\, w_D w_E \quad \textbf{(7.6)}$$

$$\sigma_p = \sqrt{\sigma_p^2}$$

Now we are ready to experiment with different portfolio proportions to observe the effect on portfolio expected return and variance. Suppose we change the proportion invested in bonds. The effect on the portfolio's expected return is plotted in Figure 7.3. When the proportion invested in bonds varies from zero to one (so that the proportion in stock varies from one to zero), the portfolio expected return goes from 13 percent (the stock fund's expected return) to 8 percent (the expected return on bonds).

What happens to the right of this region, when $w_D > 1$ and $w_E < 0$? In this case, portfolio strategy would be to sell the stock fund short and invest the proceeds of the short sale in bonds. This will decrease the expected return of the portfolio. For example, when $w_D = 2$ and $w_E = -1$, expected portfolio return falls to 3 percent $[2 \times 8 + (-1) \times 13]$. At this point, the value of the bond fund in the portfolio is twice the net worth of the account. This extreme position is financed in part by short selling stocks equal in value to the portfolio's net worth.

The reverse happens when $w_D < 0$ and $w_E > 1$. This strategy calls for selling the bond fund short and using the proceeds to finance additional purchases of the equity fund.

Of course, varying investment proportions also has an effect on portfolio standard deviation. Table 7.3 presents portfolio standard deviations for different portfolio weights calculated from equations 7.3 and 7.4 for the assumed value of the correlation coefficient, .30, as well as for other values of $\rho$. Figure 7.4 shows the relationship between standard deviation and portfolio weights. Look first at the curve for $\rho = .30$. The graph shows that as the portfolio weight in the equity fund increases from zero to one, portfolio standard deviation first falls with the initial diversification from bonds into stocks but then rises again as the portfolio becomes heavily concentrated in stocks and again is undiversified.

[5] It is possible to drive portfolio variance to zero with perfectly positively correlated assets as well, but this would require short sales.

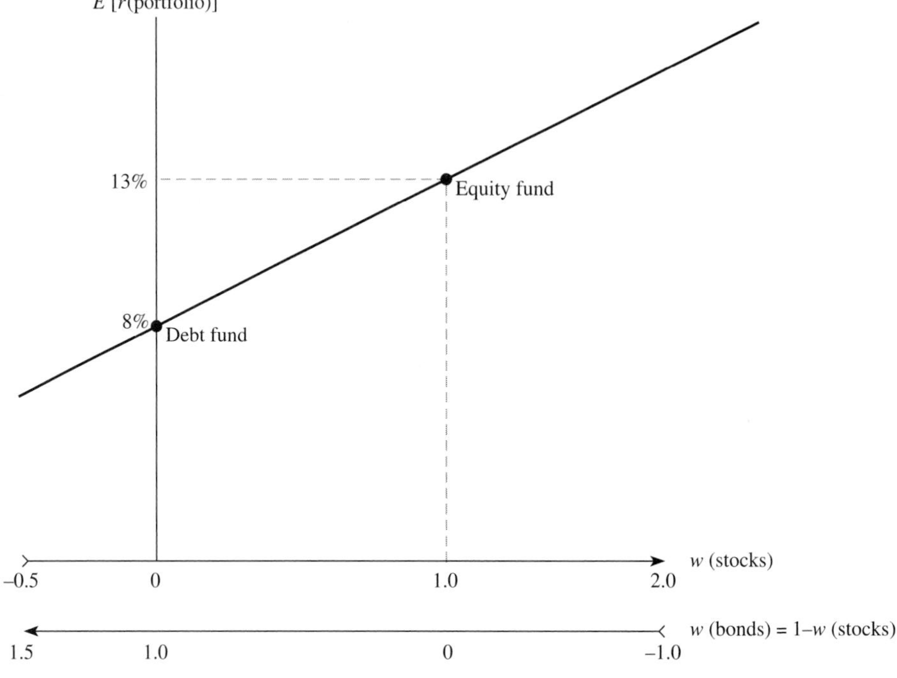


**Figure 7.3** Portfolio expected return as a function of investment proportions.

**Table 7.3** Portfolio Standard Deviation as a Function of Investment Proportions

| | | Standard Deviation (%) | | | |
|---|---|---|---|---|---|
| $w_D$ | $w_E$ | $\rho = -1$ | $\rho = 0$ | $\rho = 0.3$ | $\rho = 1$ |
| 0 | 1.00 | 20.00 | 20.00 | 20.00 | 20.00 |
| 0.25 | 0.75 | 12.00 | 15.30 | 16.16 | 18.00 |
| 0.50 | 0.50 | 4.00 | 11.66 | 13.11 | 16.00 |
| 0.75 | 0.25 | 4.00 | 10.30 | 11.53 | 14.00 |
| 1.00 | 0 | 12.00 | 12.00 | 12.00 | 12.00 |
| | minimum $\sigma_p$ | 0.00 | 10.20 | 11.45 | — |
| | $w_D$ at min $\sigma_p$ | 0.63 | 0.74 | 0.82 | — |

This pattern generally will hold as long as the correlation coefficient between the funds is not too high. For a pair of assets with a large positive correlation of returns, the portfolio standard deviation will increase monotonically from the low-risk asset to the high-risk asset. Even in this case, however, there is a positive (if small) value of diversification.

**Figure 7.4**
Portfolio standard deviation as a function of investment proportions.

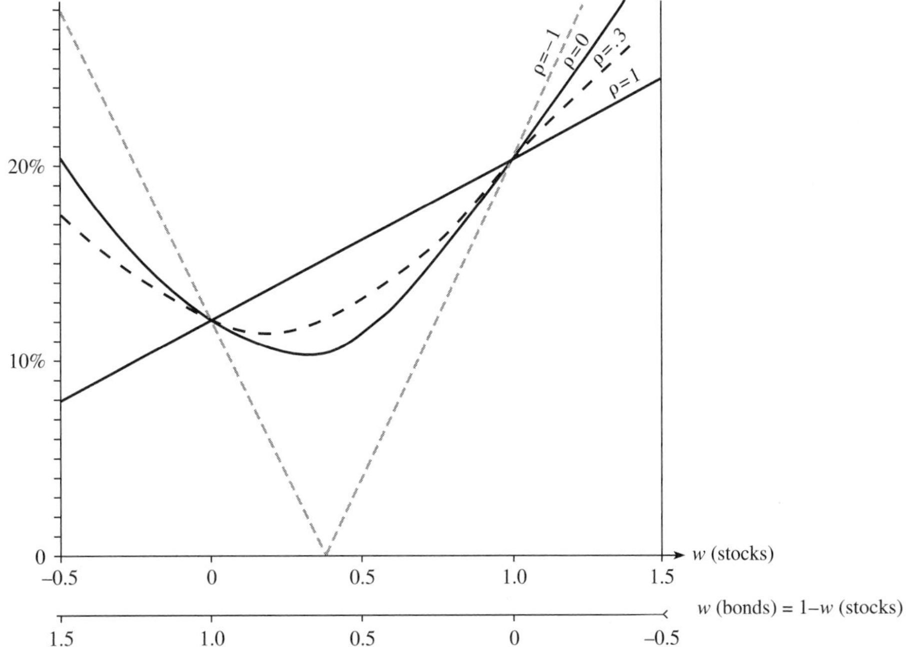


What is the minimum level to which portfolio standard deviation can be held? For the parameter values stipulated in Table 7.1, the portfolio weights that solve this minimization problem turn out to be:[6]

$$\begin{aligned} w_{\text{Min}}(D) &= \frac{\sigma_E^2 - \text{Cov}(r_D, r_E)}{\sigma_D^2 + \sigma_E^2 - 2\text{Cov}(r_D, r_E)} \\ &= \frac{20^2 - 72}{12^2 + 20^2 - 2 \times 72} \\ &= .82 \\ w_{\text{Min}}(E) &= 1 - .82 \\ &= .18 \end{aligned} \tag{7.7}$$

This minimum variance portfolio has a standard deviation of

$$\begin{aligned} \sigma_{\text{Min}}(P) &= [.82^2 \times 12^2 + .18^2 \times 20^2 + 2 \times .82 \times .18 \times 72]^{1/2} \\ &= 11.45\% \end{aligned}$$

as indicated in the next-to-last line of Table 7.3 for the column $\rho = .30$.

[6] This solution uses the minimization techniques of elementary calculus. Write out the expression for portfolio variance from equation 7.2, substitute $1 - w_D$ for $w_E$, differentiate the result with respect to $w_D$, set the derivative equal to zero, and solve for $w_D$. With a computer spreadsheet, however, you can obtain an accurate solution by generating a fine grid for Table 7.3 and observing the minimum.

The dark broken line in Figure 7.4 represents the portfolio standard deviation when $\rho = .30$ as a function of the investment proportions. It passes through the two undiversified portfolios of $w_D = 1$ and $w_E = 1$. Note that the **minimum-variance portfolio** has a standard deviation smaller than that of either of the individual component assets. This highlights the effect of diversification.

The other three lines in Figure 7.4 show how portfolio risk varies for other values of the correlation coefficient, holding the variances of each asset constant. These lines plot the values in the other three columns of Table 7.3.

The straight line connecting the undiversified portfolios of all-bonds or all-stocks, $w_D = 1$ or $w_E = 1$, demonstrates portfolio standard deviation with perfect positive correlation, $\rho = 1$. In this case, there is no advantage from diversification, and the portfolio standard deviation is the simple weighted average of the component asset standard deviations.

The solid curve below the $\rho = .30$ curve depicts portfolio risk for the case of uncorrelated assets, $\rho = 0$. With lower correlation between the two assets, diversification is more effective and portfolio risk is lower (at least when both assets are held in positive amounts). The minimum portfolio standard deviation when $\rho = 0$ is 10.29 percent (see Table 7.3), which again is lower than the standard deviation of either assets.

Finally, the upside-down triangular broken line illustrates the perfect hedge potential when the two assets are perfectly negatively correlated ($\rho = -1$). In this case, the solution for the minimum-variance portfolio is

$$\begin{aligned} w_{\text{Min}}(D;\rho = -1) &= \frac{\sigma_E}{\sigma_D + \sigma_E} \\ &= \frac{20}{12 + 20} \\ &= .625 \\ w_{\text{Min}}(E;\rho = -1) &= 1 - .625 \\ &= .375 \end{aligned}$$

and the portfolio variance (and standard deviation) is zero.

We can combine Figures 7.3 and 7.4 to demonstrate the relationship between the portfolio's level of risk (standard deviation) and the expected rate of return on that portfolio—given the parameters of the available assets. This is done in Figure 7.5. For any pair of investment proportions, $w_D$, $w_E$, we read the expected return from Figure 7.3 and the standard deviation from Figure 7.4. The resulting pairs of portfolio expected return and standard deviation are tabulated in Table 7.4 and plotted in Figure 7.5.

The dark cross-hatched curve in Figure 7.5 shows the **portfolio opportunity set** for $\rho = .30$. We call it the *portfolio opportunity set* because it shows the combination of expected return and standard deviation of all the portfolios that can be constructed from the two available assets. The broken and dotted lines show the portfolio opportunity set for other values of the correlation coefficient. The line farthest to the right, which is the straight line connecting the undiversi-

**Table 7.4** Portfolio Expected Returns and Standard Deviations with Various Correlation Coefficients

| | | | Portfolio Standard Deviation for Given Correlation | | | |
|---|---|---|---|---|---|---|
| $w_D$ | $w_E$ | $E(r_p)$ | $\rho = 1$ | $\rho = 0$ | $\rho = 0.3$ | $\rho = 1$ |
| 0 | 1.0 | 13.00 | 20.00 | 20.00 | 20.00 | 20.00 |
| 0.25 | 0.75 | 11.75 | 12.00 | 15.30 | 16.16 | 18.00 |
| 0.50 | 0.50 | 10.50 | 4.00 | 11.66 | 13.11 | 16.00 |
| 0.75 | 0.25 | 9.25 | 4.00 | 10.30 | 11.53 | 14.00 |
| 1.0 | 0 | 8.00 | 12.00 | 12.00 | 12.00 | 12.00 |
| | | | Minimum Variance Portfolio | | | |
| $w_D$(min) | | | 0.63 | 0.74 | 0.82 | — |
| $E(r_p)$ | | | 9.875 | 9.32 | 8.90 | — |
| $\sigma_p$ | | | 0.00 | 10.29 | 11.45 | — |

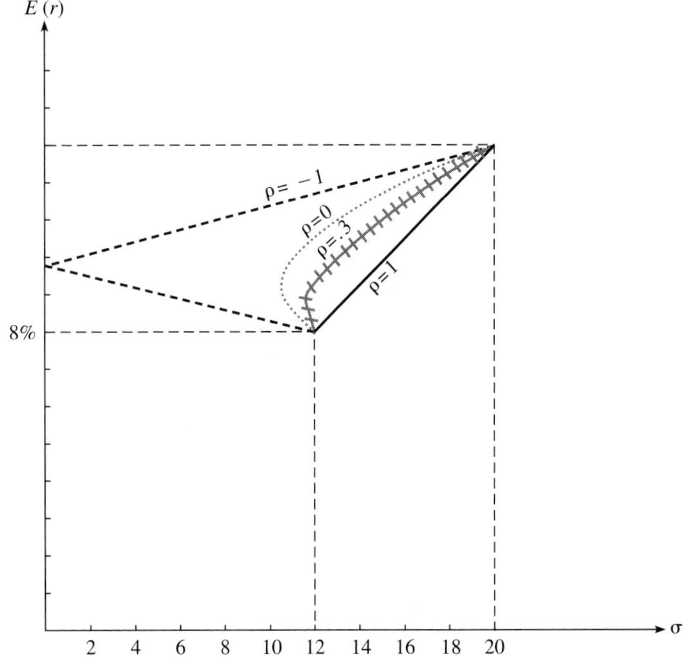


**Figure 7.5**
Portfolio expected return as a function of standard deviation.

fied portfolios, shows that there is no benefit from diversification when the correlation between the two assets is perfectly positive ($\rho = 1$). The opportunity set is not "pushed" to the northwest. The dotted line to the left of the dark curve shows that there is greater benefit from diversification when the correlation coefficient is zero than when it is positive.

Finally, the broken $\rho = -1$ lines show the effect of perfect negative correlation. The portfolio opportunity set is linear, but now it offers a perfect hedging opportunity and the maximum advantage from diversification.

To summarize, although the expected rate of return of any portfolio is simply the weighted average of the asset expected return, this is not true of the portfolio standard deviation. Potential benefits from diversification arise when correlation is less than perfectly positive. The lower the correlation coefficient, the greater the potential benefit of diversification. In the extreme case of perfect negative correlation, we have a perfect hedging opportunity and can construct a zero-variance portfolio.

Suppose now that an investor wishes to select the optimal portfolio from the opportunity set. The best portfolio will depend on risk aversion. Portfolios to the northeast in Figure 7.5 provide higher rates of return, but they impose greater risk. The best trade-off among these choices is a matter of personal preference. Investors with greater risk aversion will prefer portfolios to the southwest, with lower expected return, but lower risk.[7]

---

**CONCEPT CHECK** Question 2. Compute and draw the portfolio opportunity set for the debt and equity funds when the correlation coefficient between them is $\rho = .25$.

---

## 7.3 ASSET ALLOCATION WITH STOCKS, BONDS, AND BILLS

### The Optimal Risky Portfolio with Two Risky Assets and a Risk-Free Asset

What if we were still confined to the bond and stock funds, but now could also invest in risk-free T-bills yielding 5 percent? We start with a graphical solution. Figure 7.6 shows the opportunity set generated from the joint probability distribution of the bond and stock funds, using the data from Table 7.1.

Two possible capital allocation lines (CALs) are drawn from the risk-free rate ($r_f$ = 5 percent) to two feasible portfolios. The first possible CAL is drawn through the minimum-variance portfolio *A*, which is invested 82 percent in bonds and 18 percent in stocks (equation 7.7). Portfolio *A*'s expected return is

---

[7] Given a level of risk aversion, one can determine the portfolio that provides the highest level of utility. Recall from chapter 6 that we were able to describe the utility provided by a portfolio as a function of its expected return, $E(r_p)$, and its variance, $\sigma_p^2$, according to the relationship $U = E(r_p) - .005A\sigma_p^2$. The portfolio mean and variance are determined by the portfolio weights in the two funds, $w_E$ and $w_D$, according to equations 7.1 and 7.2. Using those equations, one can show, using elementary calculus, that the optimal investment proportions in the two funds are:

$$w_D = \frac{E(r_D) - E(r_E) + .01A(\sigma_E^2 - \sigma_D\sigma_E\rho_{DE})}{.01A(\sigma_D^2 + \sigma_E^2 - 2\sigma_D\sigma_E\rho_{DE})}$$

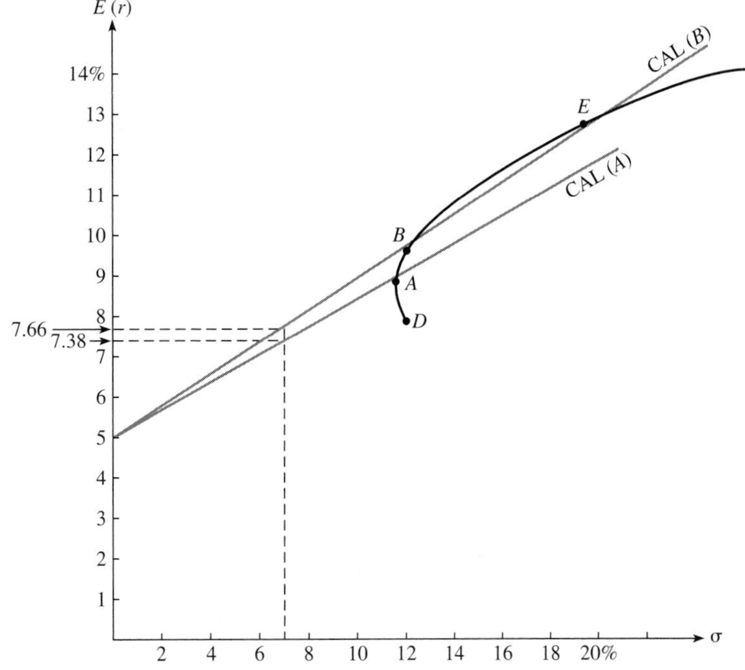


**Figure 7.6**
The opportunity set of the debt and equity funds and two feasible CALs.

$E(r_A) = 8.90$ percent, and its standard deviation is $\sigma_A = 11.45$ percent. With a T-bill rate of $r_f = 5$ percent, the **reward-to-variability ratio,** which is the slope of the CAL combining T-bills and the minimum-variance portfolio, is

$$S_A = \frac{E(r_A) - r_f}{\sigma_A}$$

$$= \frac{8.9 - 5}{11.45}$$

$$= .34$$

Now consider the CAL that uses portfolio *B* instead of *A*. Portfolio *B* invests 70 percent in bonds and 30 percent in stocks. Its expected return is 9.5 percent (giving it a risk premium of 4.5 percent), and its standard deviation is 11.70 percent. Thus, the reward-to-variability ratio on the CAL that is generated using portfolio *B* is

$$S_B = \frac{9.5 - 5}{11.7}$$

$$= .38$$

higher than the reward-to-variability ratio of the CAL that we obtained using the minimum-variance portfolio and T-bills.

If the CAL that uses portfolio *B* has a better reward-to-variability ratio than the CAL that uses portfolio *A*, then for any level of risk (standard deviation) that an investor is willing to bear, the expected return is higher with portfolio *B*. Figure 7.6 reflects this in showing that the CAL for portfolio *B* is above the CAL for portfolio *A*. In this sense, portfolio *B* dominates portfolio *A*.

In fact, the difference between the reward-to-variability ratios is

$$S_B - S_A = .04$$

This means we get four extra basis points expected return with $\text{CAL}_B$ for each percentage point increase in standard deviation.

Look at Figure 7.6 again. If we are willing to bear a standard deviation of $\sigma_p = 7$ percent, we can achieve a 7.38 percent expected return with the CAL of portfolio *A*:

$$\begin{aligned} E(r_p)(\text{CAL}_A;\ \sigma_p = 7\%) &= r_f + 7S_A \\ &= 5 + 7 \times .34 \\ &= 7.38\% \end{aligned}$$

With the CAL of portfolio *B*, we get an expected return of 7.66 percent:

$$\begin{aligned} E(r_p)(\text{CAL}_B;\ \sigma_p = 7\%) &= r_f + 7S_B \\ &= 5 + 7 \times .38 \\ &= 7.66\% \end{aligned}$$

This is a difference of $.04 \times 7 = .28$ percent, or 28 basis points.

But why stop at portfolio *B*? We can continue to ratchet the CAL upward until it ultimately reaches the point of tangency with the investment opportunity set. This must yield the CAL with the highest feasible reward-to-variability ratio. Therefore, the tangency portfolio, *P*, drawn in Figure 7.7, is the optimal risky portfolio to mix with T-bills. We can read the expected return and standard deviation of portfolio *P* from the graph in Figure 7.7:

$$E(r_p) = 11\%$$

$$\sigma_p = 14.2\%$$

In practice, we obtain an algebraic solution to this problem with a computer program. We can describe the process briefly, however.

The objective is to find the weights $w_D$, $w_E$ that result in the highest slope of the CAL (that is, the yield of the risky portfolio with the highest reward-to-variability ratio). Therefore, the objective is to maximize the slope of the CAL

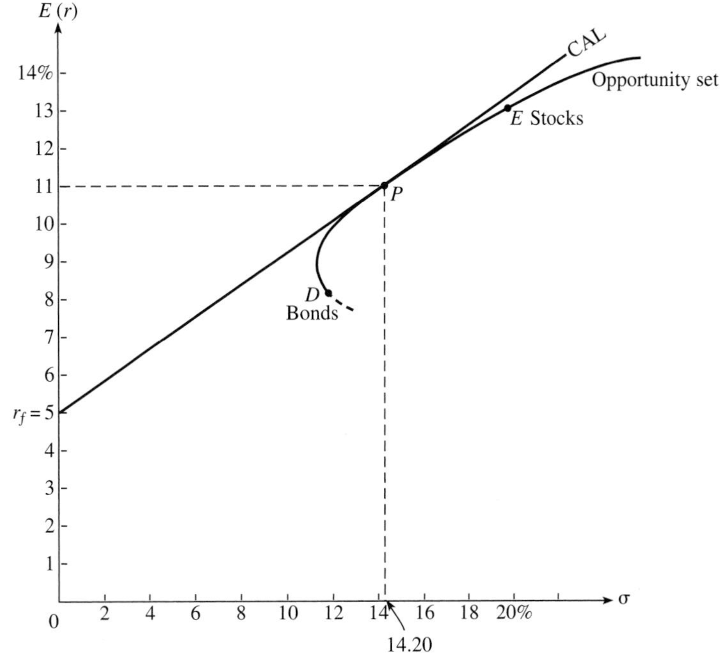


**Figure 7.7**
The opportunity set of the stock and bond funds with the optimal CAL and the optimal risky portfolio.

for any possible portfolio, $p$. Thus our *objective function* is the slope that we have called $S_p$:

$$S_p = \frac{E(r_p) - r_f}{\sigma_p}$$

For the portfolio with two risky assets, the expected return and standard deviation of portfolio $p$ are

$$E(r_p) = w_D E(r_D) + w_E E(r_E)$$
$$= 8w_D + 13w_E$$
$$\sigma_p = [w_D^2\sigma_D^2 + w_E^2\sigma_E^2 + 2w_D w_E \text{Cov}(r_D, r_E)]^{1/2}$$
$$= [144w_D^2 + 400w_E^2 + 2 \times 72w_D w_E]^{1/2}$$

When we maximize the objective function, $S_p$, we have to satisfy the constraint that the portfolio weights sum to one (100 percent), that is $w_D + w_E = 1$. Therefore, we solve a mathematical problem formally written as

$$\underset{w_i}{\text{Max}}\ S_p = \frac{E(r_p) - r_f}{\sigma_p}$$

subject to $\sum w_i = 1$. This is a standard problem in calculus.

In the case of two risky assets, the solution for the weights of the **optimal risky portfolio,** $P$, can be shown to be as follows:[8]

$$w_D = \frac{[E(r_D) - r_f]\sigma_E^2 - [E(r_E) - r_f]\text{Cov}(r_D,r_E)}{[E(r_D) - r_f]\sigma_E^2 + [E(r_E) - r_f]\sigma_D^2 - [E(r_D) - r_f + E(r_E) - r_f]\text{Cov}(r_D,r_E)} \quad \textbf{(7.8)}$$

$$w_E = 1 - w_D$$

Substituting our data, the solution is

$$\begin{aligned} w_D &= \frac{(8 - 5)400 - (13 - 5)72}{(8 - 5)400 + (13 - 5)144 - (8 - 5 + 13 - 5)72} \\ &= .40 \\ w_E &= 1 - .4 \\ &= .6 \end{aligned}$$

The expected return of this optimal risky portfolio is 11 percent [$E(r_p) = .4 \times 8 + .6 \times 13$]. The standard deviation is 14.2 percent:

$$\begin{aligned} \sigma_p &= (.4^2 \times 144 + .6^2 \times 400 + 2 \times .4 \times .6 \times 72)^{1/2} \\ &= 14.2\% \end{aligned}$$

The CAL using this optimal portfolio has a slope of

$$S_p = \frac{11 - 5}{14.2} = .42$$

which is the reward-to-variability ratio of portfolio $P$. Notice that this slope exceeds the slope of any of the other feasible portfolios that we have considered, as it must if it is to be the slope of the best feasible CAL.

In Chapter 6 we found the optimal *complete* portfolio given an optimal risky portfolio and the CAL generated by a combination of this portfolio and T-bills. Now that we have constructed the optimal risky portfolio, $P$, we can use the individual investor's degree of risk aversion, $A$, to calculate the optimal proportion of the complete portfolio to invest in the risky component.

An investor with a coefficient of risk aversion $A = 4$, would take a position in portfolio $P$ of

$$y = \frac{E(r_P) - r_f}{.01\, A\sigma_P^2} \quad \textbf{(7.9)}$$

$$= \frac{11 - 5}{.01 \times 4 \times 14.2^2}$$

$$= .7439$$

[8] The solution procedure is as follows. Substitute for $E(r_p)$ from equation 7.1 and for $\sigma_p$ from equation 7.2. Substitute $1 - w_D$ for $w_E$. Differentiate the resulting expression for $S_p$ with respect to $w_D$, set the derivative equal to zero, and solve for $w_D$.

Thus, the investor will invest 74.39 percent of his or her wealth in portfolio $P$ and 25.61 percent in T-bills. Portfolio $P$ consists of 40 percent in bonds, so the percentage of wealth in bonds will be $yw_D = .4 \times .7439 = .2976$, or 29.76 percent. Similarly, the investment in stocks will be $yw_E = .6 \times .7439 = .4463$, or 44.63 percent. The graphical solution of this problem is presented in Figures 7.8 and 7.9.

Once we have reached this point, generalizing to the case of many risky assets is straightforward. Before we move on, let us briefly summarize the steps we followed to arrive at the complete portfolio.

1. Specify the return characteristics of all securities (expected returns, variances, covariances).
2. Establish the risky portfolio:
   *a.* Calculate the optimal risky portfolio, $P$ (equation 7.8).
   *b.* Calculate the properties of portfolio $P$ using the weights determined in step (a) and equations 7.1 and 7.2.
3. Allocate funds between the risky portfolio and the risk-free asset:
   *a.* Calculate the fraction of the complete portfolio allocated to portfolio $P$ (the risky portfolio) and to T-bills (the risk-free asset) (equation 7.9).
   *b.* Calculate the share of the complete portfolio invested in each asset and in T-bills.

**Figure 7.8**
Determination of the optimal overall portfolio.

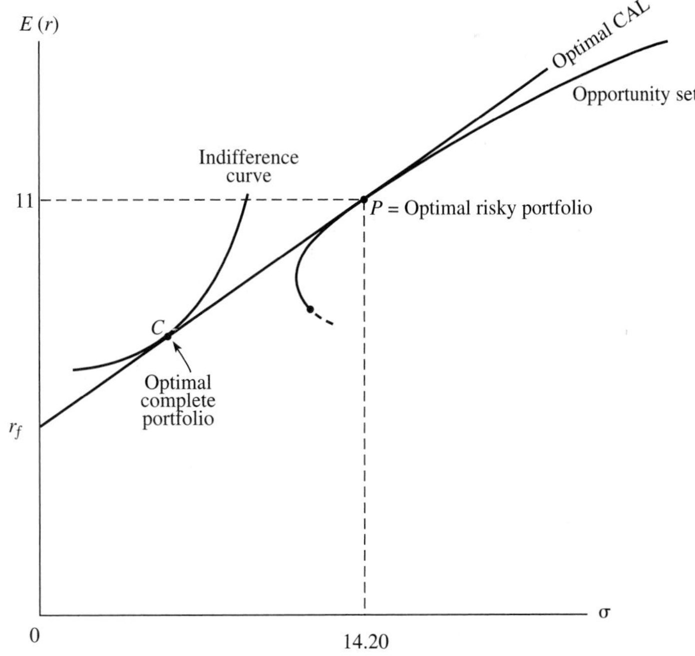

**Figure 7.9**
The proportions of the optimal overall portfolio.

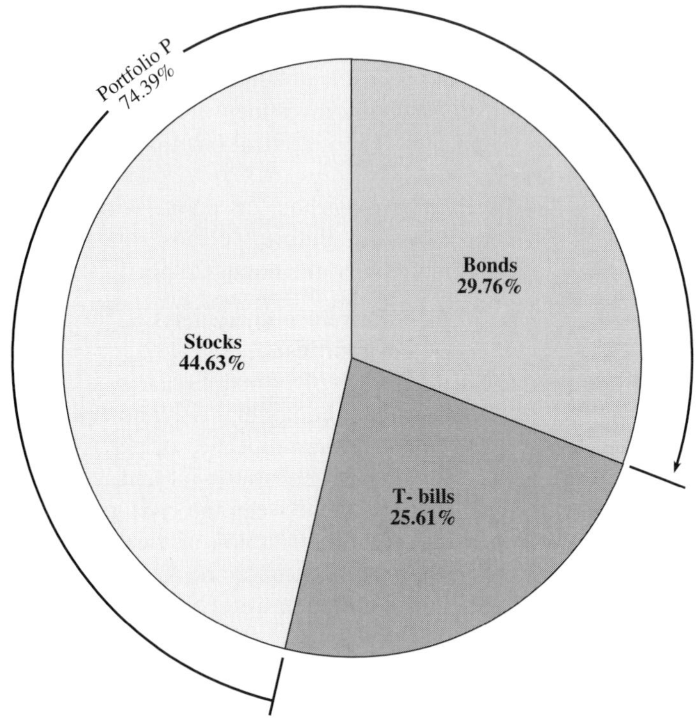


Before moving on, recall that the two assets in the asset allocation problem are already diversified portfolios. The diversification *within* each of these portfolios must be credited for most of the risk reduction, compared to undiversified single securities. For example, the standard deviation of the rate of return on an average stock is about 50 percent. In contrast, the standard deviation of our hypothetical stock index fund is only 20 percent, about equal to the historical standard deviation of the S&P 500 portfolio. This is evidence of the importance of diversification within the asset class. Asset allocation between bonds and stocks contributed incrementally to the improvement in the reward-to-volatility ratio of the complete portfolio. The CAL with stocks, bonds, and bills (Figure 7.7) shows that the standard deviation of the complete portfolio can be further reduced to 18 percent, while maintaining the same expected return of 13 percent as the stock portfolio.

---

**CONCEPT CHECK** Question 3. The universe of available securities includes two risky stock funds, *A* and *B,* and T-bills. The data for the universe are as follows:

| | Expected Return | Standard Deviation |
|---|---|---|
| *A* | .10 | .20 |
| *B* | .30 | .60 |
| T-bills | .05 | 0 |

The correlation coefficient between funds *A* and *B* is −.2.

*a.* Draw the opportunity set of funds *A* and *B*.

*b.* Find the optimal risky portfolio *P* and its expected return and standard deviation.

*c.* Find the slope of the CAL supported by T-bills and portfolio *P*.

*d.* How much will an investor with $A = 5$ invest in funds *A* and *B* and in T-bills?

## 7.4 THE MARKOWITZ PORTFOLIO SELECTION MODEL

### Security Selection

Now we can generalize the portfolio construction problem to the case of many risky securities and a risk-free asset. As in the two risky assets example, the problem has three parts. First, we identify the risk-return combinations available from the set of risky assets. Next, we identify the optimal portfolio of risky assets by finding the portfolio that results in the steepest CAL. Finally, we choose an appropriate complete portfolio by mixing the risk-free asset, T-bills, with the optimal risky portfolio. Before describing the process in detail, let us first present an overview.

The first step is to determine the risk-return opportunities available to the investor. These are summarized by the **minimum-variance frontier** of risky assets. This frontier is a graph of the lowest possible portfolio variance that can be attained for a given portfolio expected return. Given the set of data for expected returns, variances, and covariances, we can calculate the minimum-variance portfolio (or equivalently, minimum-standard deviation portfolio) for any targeted expected return. Performing such a calculation for many such expected return targets results in a pairing between expected returns and minimum-risk portfolios that offer those expected returns. The plot of these expected return–standard deviation pairs is presented in Figure 7.10.

Notice that all the individual assets lie to the right inside of the frontier, at least when we allow short sales in the construction of risky portfolios.[9] This tells us that risky portfolios composed of only a single asset are inefficient. Diversifying

[9] When short sales are prohibited, single securities may lie on the frontier. For example, the security with the highest expected return must lie on the frontier, as that security represents the *only* way that one can obtain a return that high, and so it also must be the minimum-variance way to obtain that return. When short sales are feasible, however, portfolios can be constructed that offer the same expected return and lower variance. These portfolios typically will have short positions in low expected-return securities.

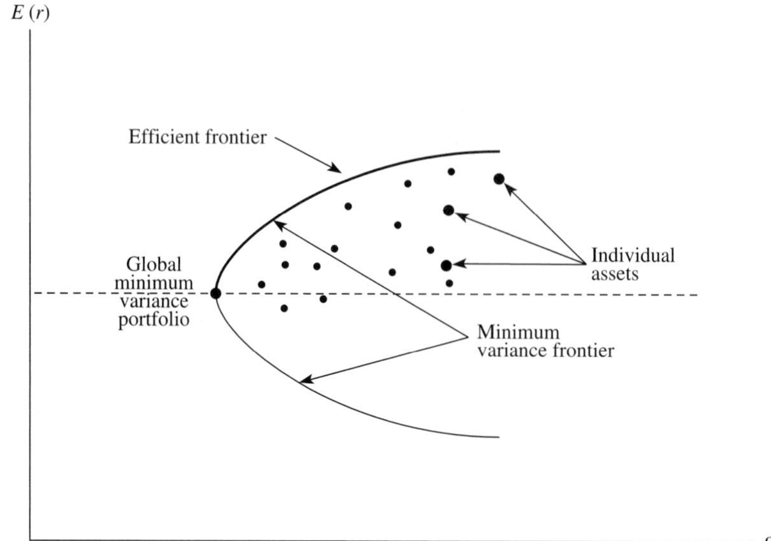


**Figure 7.10**
The minimum-variance frontier of risky assets.

investments leads to portfolios with higher expected returns and lower standard deviations.

All the portfolios that lie on the minimum-variance frontier, from the global minimum-variance portfolio and upward, provide the best risk-return combinations and thus are candidates for the optimal portfolio. The part of the frontier that lies above the global minimum-variance portfolio, therefore, is called the **efficient frontier.** For any portfolio on the lower portion of the minimum-variance frontier, there is a portfolio with the same standard deviation and a greater expected return positioned directly above it. Hence, the bottom part of the minimum-variance frontier is inefficient.

The second part of the optimization plan involves the risk-free asset. As before, we search for the capital allocation line with the highest reward-to-variability ratio (that is, the steepest slope) as shown in Figure 7.11.

The CAL that is supported by the optimal portfolio, *P,* is, as before, the one that is tangent to the efficient frontier. This CAL dominates all alternative feasible lines that may be drawn through the frontier. Portfolio *P,* therefore, is the optimal risky portfolio.

Finally, in the last part of the problem, the individual investor chooses the appropriate mix between the optimal risky portfolio *P* and T-bills, exactly as in Figure 7.8.

Now let us consider each part of the portfolio construction problem in more detail. In the first part of the problem, risk-return analysis, the portfolio manager needs, as inputs, a set of estimates for the expected returns of each security and a set of estimates for the covariance matrix. (In Part VI, Equities, we will examine the security valuation techniques and methods of financial analysis that analysts

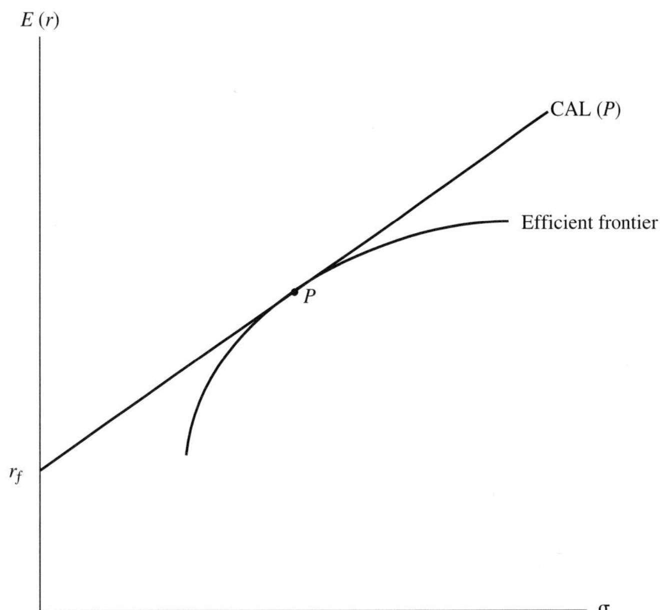


**Figure 7.11**
The efficient frontier of risky assets with the optimal CAL.

use. For now, we will assume that analysts already have spent the time and resources to prepare the inputs.)

Suppose that the horizon of the portfolio plan is one year. Therefore all estimates pertain to a one-year holding period return. Our security analysts cover $n$ securities. As of now, time zero, we observed these security prices: $P_1^0, \ldots, P_n^0$. The analysts derive estimates for each security's expected rate of return by forecasting end-of-year (time 1) prices: $E(P_1^1), \ldots, E(P_n^1)$, and the expected dividends for the period: $E(D_1), \ldots, E(D_n)$. The set of expected rates of return is then computed from

$$E(r_i) = \frac{E(P_i^1) + E(D_i) - P_i^0}{P_i^0}$$

The covariances among the rates of return on the analyzed securities (the covariance matrix) usually are estimated from historical data. Another method is to use a scenario analysis of possible returns from all securities instead of, or as a supplement to, historical analysis.

The portfolio manager now is armed with the $n$ estimates of $E(r_i)$ and the $n \times n$ estimates in the covariance matrix in which the $n$ diagonal elements are estimates of the variances, $\sigma_i^2$, and the $n^2 - n = n(n - 1)$ off-diagonal elements are the estimates of the covariances between each pair of asset returns. (You can verify this from Table 7.2 for the case $n = 2$.) We know that each covariance appears twice in this table, so actually we have $n(n - 1)/2$ different covariance estimates. If our portfolio management unit covers 50 securities, our security analysts need to deliver 50 estimates of expected returns, 50 estimates of variances, and 50 × 49/2 = 1,225 different estimates of covariances. This is a daunting task! (We show later how the number of required estimates can be reduced substantially.)

Once these estimates are compiled, the expected return and variance of any risky portfolio with weights in each security, $w_i$, can be calculated from the following formulas:[10]

$$E(r_p) = \sum_{i=1}^{n} w_i E(r_i) \tag{7.10}$$

$$\sigma_p^2 = \sum_{i=1}^{n} w_i^2 \sigma_i^2 + \sum_{\substack{i=1 \\ i \neq j}}^{n} \sum_{j=1}^{n} w_i w_j \text{Cov}(r_i, r_j) \tag{7.11}$$

We mentioned earlier that the idea of diversification is age-old. The phrase "don't put all your eggs in one basket" existed long before modern finance theory. It was not until 1952, however, that Harry Markowitz published a formal model of portfolio selection embodying diversification principles, ultimately earning himself the 1991 Nobel prize for economics. His model is precisely step one of portfolio management: the identification of the efficient set of portfolios, or, as it is often called, the efficient frontier of risky assets.

The principal idea behind the frontier set of risky portfolios is that, for any risk level, we are interested only in that portfolio with the highest expected return. Alternatively, the frontier is the set of portfolios that minimizes the variance for any target expected return.

Indeed, the two methods of computing the efficient set of risky portfolios are equivalent. To see this, consider the graphical representation of these procedures. Figure 7.12 shows the minimum-variance frontier.

The points marked by squares are the result of a variance-minimization program. We first draw the constraint, that is, a horizontal line at the level of required expected return. We then look for the portfolio with the lowest standard deviation that plots on this horizontal line—we look for the portfolio that will plot farthest to the left (smallest standard deviation) on that line. When we repeat this for various levels of required expected returns, the shape of the minimum-variance frontier emerges. We then discard the bottom (dotted) half of the frontier, because it is inefficient.

In the alternative approach, we draw a vertical line that represents the standard deviation constraint. We then consider all portfolios that plot on this line (have the same standard deviation) and choose the one with the highest expected return, that is, that portfolio falling highest on this vertical line. Repeating this procedure for various vertical lines (levels of standard deviation) gives us the points marked by circles that trace the upper portion of the minimum-variance frontier, the efficient frontier.

[10] Equation 7.11 follows from our discussion in Section 7.2 on using the bordered covariance matrix to obtain each term in the formula for the variance of a portfolio.

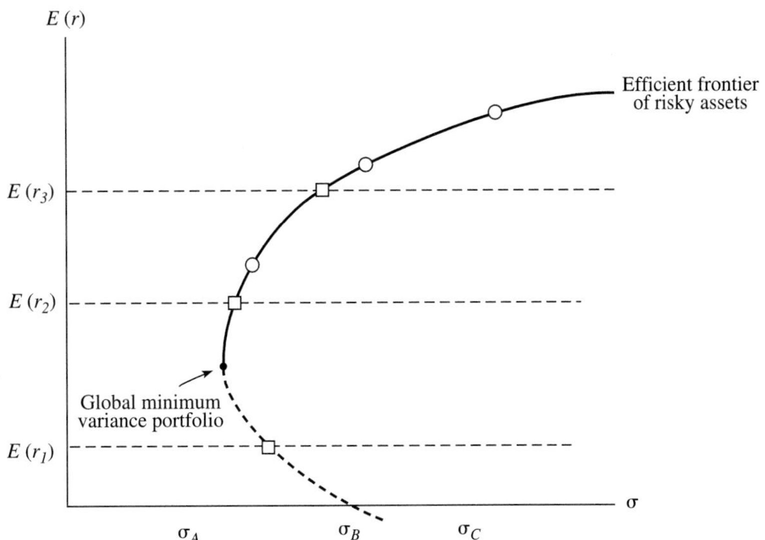


**Figure 7.12**
The efficient portfolio set.

When this step is completed, we have a list of efficient portfolios, because the solution to the optimization program includes the portfolio proportions, $w_i$, the expected return, $E(r_p)$, and standard deviation, $\sigma_p$.

Let us restate what our portfolio manager has done so far. The estimates generated by the analysts were transformed into a set of expected rates of return and a covariance matrix. This group of estimates we shall call the **input list.** This input list was then fed into the optimization program.

Before we proceed to the second step of choosing the optimal risky portfolio from the frontier set, let us consider a practical point. Some clients may be subject to additional constraints. For example, many institutions are prohibited from taking short positions in any asset. For these clients, the portfolio manager will add to the program constraints that rule out negative (short) positions in the search for efficient portfolios. In this special case it is possible that single assets may be, in and of themselves, efficient risky portfolios. For example, the asset with the highest expected return will be a frontier portfolio because, without the opportunity of short sales, the only way to obtain that rate of return is to hold the asset as one's entire risky portfolio.

Short-sale restrictions are by no means the only such constraints. For example, some clients may want to assure a minimal level of expected dividend yield on the optimal portfolio. In this case, the input list will be expanded to include a set of expected dividend yields $d_1, \ldots, d_n$ and the optimization program will include an additional constraint that ensures that the expected dividend yield of the portfolio will equal or exceed the desired level, $d$.

Portfolio managers can tailor the efficient set to conform to any desire of the client. Of course, any constraint carries a price tag in the sense that an efficient

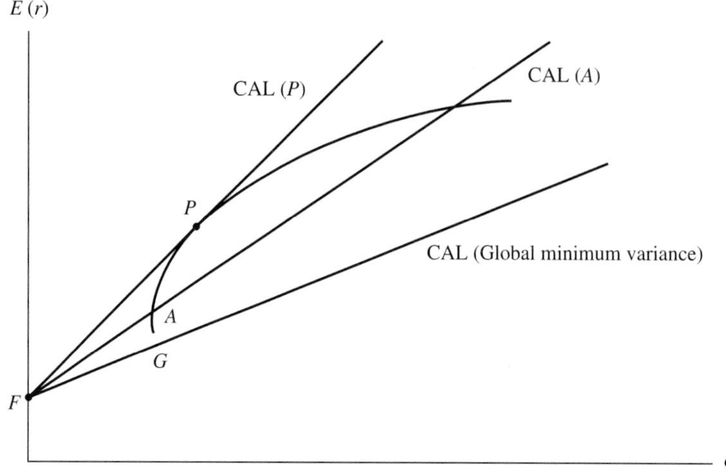


**Figure 7.13** Capital allocation lines with various portfolios from the efficient set.

frontier constructed subject to extra constraints will offer a reward-to-variability ratio inferior to that of a less constrained one. The client should be made aware of this cost and should reconsider constraints that are not mandated by law.

Another type of constraint that has become increasingly popular is aimed at ruling out investments in industries or countries considered ethically or politically undesirable. This is referred to as *socially responsible investing*. The nearby box contains an article from *The Globe and Mail* concerning socially responsible funds that constrain portfolio choice along several criteria. The article points out that one cost of such a policy is a potential reduction in return.

## Capital Allocation and Separation Property

We are now ready to proceed to step two. This step introduces the risk-free rate. Figure 7.13 shows the efficient frontier plus three CALs representing various portfolios from the efficient set. As before, we ratchet up the CAL by selecting different portfolios until we reach portfolio *P*, which is the tangency point of a line from *F* to the efficient frontier. Portfolio *P* maximizes the reward-to-variability ratio, the slope of the line from *F* to portfolios on the efficient frontier. At this point, our portfolio manager is done. Portfolio *P* is the optimal risky portfolio for the manager's clients. This is a good time to ponder our results and their implementation.

The most striking conclusion is that a portfolio manager will offer the same risky portfolio, *P*, to all clients regardless of their degree of risk aversion.[11] The

[11] Clients who impose special restrictions (constraints) on the manager, such as dividend yield, will obtain another optimal portfolio. Any constraint that is added to an optimization problem leads, in general, to a different and less desirable optimum compared to an unconstrained program.

## Ethical Investing Often Its Own Reward: Mixed Record Achieved by Funds That Shun Unsavoury Companies

"Can Canadian investors reap financial rewards while remaining true to their moral beliefs?"

This question is posed in the annual report of Investors Group Inc.'s *Summa Fund.* With assets of more than $60 million, this is the biggest of the so-called ethical funds in Canada.

The Summa Fund has a screening process that excludes certain companies as eligible investments. Excluded are companies primarily engaged in manufacturing or distributing alcohol and tobacco products; gambling; manufacturing weapons systems; and producing, importing, or distributing pornography. Also excluded are companies not practicing effective pollution control and companies supporting repressive regimes.

Other ethical funds have different exclusions. And, of course, there are problems of defining what is ethical. For example, what are repressive regimes and what constitutes supporting a repressive regime?

Common sense indicates that firms that limit their investment opportunities will earn lower returns in the long run. Defenders of ethical investment argue to the contrary—that environmentally and socially responsible companies have lower operating costs, since they have loyal clientele and don't face fines and lawsuits.

Further, defenders of ethical companies say that management may have implemented state-of-the-art operating techniques that are not only environmentally friendly but also cost-effective.

But a nonrestricted fund can replicate the portfolio of an ethical fund if appropriate, while still investing in profitable and other promising companies. Thus, its performance should surpass that of the ethical fund.

The recent performance of ethical funds has been a mixed bag. Most of the smaller funds have substantially underperformed market indexes over the past few years on both a nominal and risk-adjusted return basis.

However, *Ethical Growth Fund* and Investors' Summa Fund, the two largest ethical funds in Canada, have outperformed the average for Canadian equity funds for five and three years, respectively—the periods spanning the inception of each fund.

So there are at least two ethical fund managers that have overcome the barriers and done remarkably well over the past few years. Possibly these managers are particularly adroit at being first in finding and selecting innovative firms—at least for now.

The results suggest that this "first in" approach may reflect the ethical fund managers' superior effort or ability to pick stocks. It's almost as if increased skill is needed to combat the obvious operating constraints.

The bottom line: If you want to put your ethics in practice, you may pay a bit by earning a smaller return. At least that's what I expect to happen over the long term.

In practice, however, the opposite has occurred. The large ethical funds have performed well above average, which may well be a short-term fluke. But then again, maybe there is an interesting selection process taking place here. Do ethical funds attract the best managers?

In either case, the return cannot be measured strictly in dollars. Ethical investors argue that the implied social benefits are part of the return process.

degree of risk aversion of the client comes into play only in the selection of the desired point on the CAL. Thus, the only difference between clients' choices is that the more risk-averse client will invest more in the risk-free asset and less in the optimal risky portfolio, *P*, than will a less risk-averse client. However, both will use portfolio *P* as their optimal risky investment vehicle.

This result is called a **separation property;** it tells us that the portfolio choice problem may be separated into two independent tasks. The first task, determination of the optimal risky portfolio, *P*, is purely technical. Given the manager's input list, the best risky portfolio is the same for all clients, regardless of risk aversion. The second task, however, allocation of the complete portfolio to T-bills versus the risky portfolio, depends on personal preference. Here the client is the decision maker.

The crucial point is that the optimal portfolio *P* that the manager offers is the same for all clients. This result makes professional management more efficient and hence less costly. One management firm can serve any number of clients with relatively small incremental administrative costs.

In practice, however, different managers will estimate different input lists, thus deriving different efficient frontiers, and offer different "optimal" portfolios to their clients. The source of the disparity lies in the security analysis. It is worth mentioning here that the rule of GIGO (garbage in-garbage out) applies to security analysis, too. If the quality of the security analysis is poor, a passive portfolio such as a market index fund will result in a better CAL than an active portfolio that uses low-quality security analysis to tilt the portfolio weights toward seemingly favourable (seemingly mispriced) securities.

As we have seen, the optimal risky portfolios for different clients also may vary because of portfolio constraints such as dividend-yield requirements, tax considerations, or other client preferences. Nevertheless, this analysis suggests that only a very limited number of portfolios may be sufficient to serve the demands of a wide range of investors. This is the theoretical basis of the mutual fund industry.

The (computerized) optimization technique is the easiest part of the portfolio construction problem. The real arena of competition among portfolio managers is in sophisticated security analysis.

---

**CONCEPT CHECK** Question 4. Suppose that two portfolio managers who work for competing investment management houses each employ a group of security analysts to prepare the input list for the Markowitz algorithm. When all is completed, it turns out that the efficient frontier obtained by portfolio manager *A* dominates that of manager *B*. By domination we mean that *A*'s optimal risky portfolio lies northwest of *B*'s. Hence, given a choice, investors will always prefer the risky portfolio that lies on the CAL of *A*.

*a*. What should be made of this outcome?

*b.* Should it be attributed to better security analysis by *A*'s analysts?
*c.* Could it be that *A*'s computer program is superior?
*d.* If you were advising clients (and had an advance glimpse at the efficient frontiers of various managers), would you tell them to periodically switch their money around to the manager with the most northwesterly portfolio?

---

## Asset Allocation and Security Selection

As we have seen, the theories of security selection and asset allocation are identical. Both activities call for the construction of an efficient frontier and the choice of a particular portfolio from along that frontier. The determination of the optimal combination of securities proceeds in the same manner as the analysis of the optimal combination of asset classes. Why, then, do we (and the investment community) distinguish between asset allocation and security selection?

Three factors are at work. First, as a result of greater need and ability to save (for college education, recreation, longer life in retirement and health care needs, etc.), the demand for sophisticated investment management has increased enormously. Second, the growing spectrum of financial markets and financial instruments have put sophisticated investment beyond the capacity of most amateur investors. Finally, there are strong economic returns to scale in investment management. The end result is that the size of a competitive investment company has grown with the industry, and efficiency in organization has become an important issue.

A large investment company is likely to invest both in domestic and international markets and in a broad set of asset classes, each of which requires specialized expertise. Hence, the management of each asset-class portfolio needs to be decentralized, and it becomes impossible to simultaneously optimize the entire organization's risky portfolio in one stage (although this would be prescribed as optimal on *theoretical* grounds).

The practice is therefore to optimize the security selection of each asset-class portfolio independently. At the same time, top management continually updates the asset allocation of the organization, adjusting the investment budget of each asset-class portfolio. When changed frequently in response to intensive forecasting activity, the reallocations are called *market timing*. The shortcoming of this two-step approach to portfolio construction versus the theory-based one-step optimization approach is the failure to exploit the covariance of the individual securities in one asset-class portfolio with the individual securities in the other asset classes. Only the covariance matrix of the securities within each asset-class portfolio can be used. However, this loss might be small, due to the depth of diversification of each portfolio and the extra layer of diversification at the asset allocation level.

## 7.5 Optimal Portfolios with Restrictions on the Risk-Free Investment

The availability of a risk-free asset greatly simplifies the portfolio decision. When all investors can borrow and lend at that risk-free rate, we are led to a *unique* optimal risky portfolio that is appropriate for all investors, given a common input list. This portfolio maximizes the reward-to-variability ratio. All investors use the same risky portfolio and differ only in the proportion they invest in it and in the risk-free asset.

What if a risk-free asset is not available? Although T-bills are risk-free assets in nominal terms, their real returns are uncertain. Without a risk-free asset, there is no tangency portfolio that is best for all investors. In this case, investors have to choose a portfolio from the efficient frontier of risky assets redrawn in Figure 7.14.

Each investor will now choose the optimal risky portfolio by superimposing a particular set of indifference curves on the efficient frontier, as Figure 7.14 shows. The optimal portfolio, *P*, for the investor whose risk aversion is represented by the set of indifference curves in Figure 7.14 is tangent to the highest attainable indifference curve.

Investors who are more risk averse than the one represented in Figure 7.14 would have steeper indifference curves, meaning that the tangency portfolio would be of smaller standard deviation and expected return than portfolio *P*, such as portfolio *Q*. Conversely, investors who are more risk tolerant than the one represented in Figure 7.14 would be characterized by flatter indifference curves, resulting in a tangency portfolio of higher expected return and standard deviation than portfolio *P*, such as portfolio *S*. The common feature of all these rational

**Figure 7.14**
Individual portfolio selection without a risk-free asset.

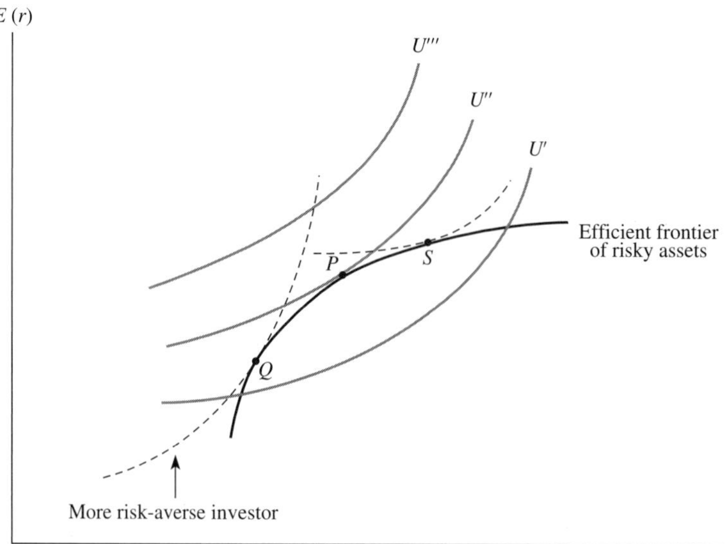

investors is that they choose portfolios on the efficient frontier; that is, they choose mean-variance efficient portfolios.

Even if virtually risk-free lending opportunities are available, many investors do face borrowing restrictions. They may be unable to borrow altogether, or, more realistically, they may face a borrowing rate that is significantly greater than the lending rate. Let us first consider investors who can lend without risk but are prohibited from borrowing.

When a risk-free investment is available but an investor can take only positive positions in it (he or she can lend at $r_f$, but cannot borrow), a CAL exists but is limited to the line *FP,* as in Figure 7.15.

Any investors whose preferences are represented by indifference curves with tangency portfolios on the portion *FP* of the CAL, such as portfolio *A,* are unaffected by the borrowing restriction. For such investors, the borrowing restriction is a nonbinding constraint, because they are net *lenders,* lending some of their money at rate $r_f$.

Aggressive or more risk-tolerant investors, who *would* choose portfolio *B* in the absence of the borrowing restriction, are affected, however. For them, the borrowing restriction is a binding constraint. Such investors will be driven to portfolios on the efficient frontier, such as portfolio *Q,* which have higher expected return and standard deviation than does portfolio *P* (but less than the unavailable portfolio *B*). Portfolios such as *Q,* which are on the efficient frontier of risky assets, represent a zero investment in the risk-free asset.

**Figure 7.15**
Individual portfolio selection with risk-free lending only.

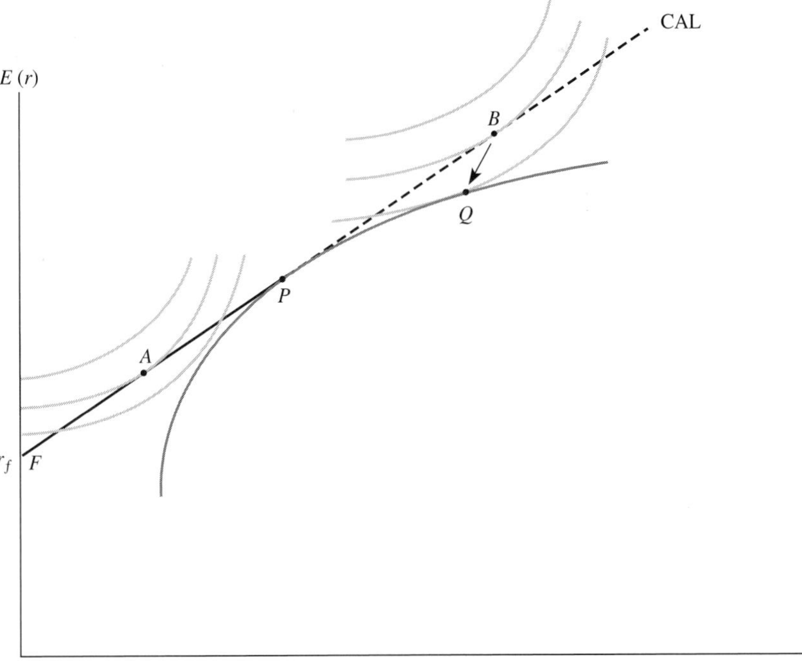

Finally, we consider a more realistic case, that of feasible borrowing, but at a higher rate than $r_f$. An individual who borrows to invest in a risky portfolio will have to pay an interest rate higher than the T-bill rate. The lender will require a premium commensurate with the probability of default. For example, the call money rate charged by brokers on margin accounts is higher than the T-bill rate.

Investors who face a borrowing rate greater than the lending rate confront a three-part CAL such as in Figure 7.16. $CAL_1$, which is relevant in the range $FP_1$, represents the efficient portfolio set for defensive (risk-averse) investors. These investors invest part of their funds in T-bills at rate $r_f$. They find that the tangency portfolio is $P_1$, and they choose a complete portfolio such as portfolio $A$ in Figure 7.17.

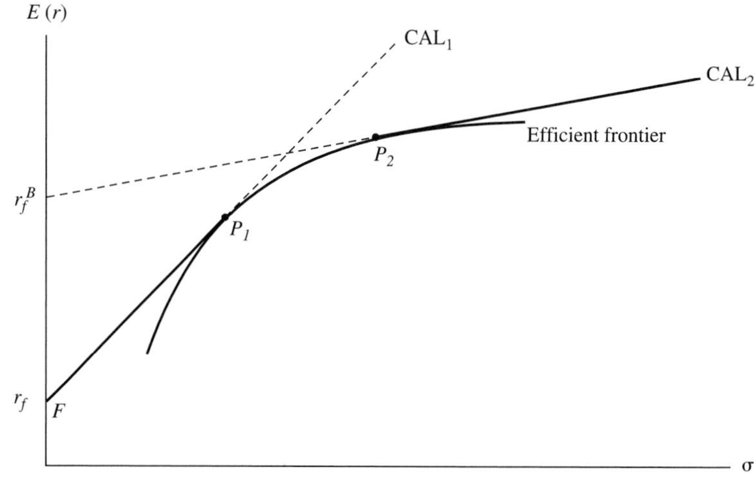


**Figure 7.16**
The investment opportunity set with differential rates for borrowing and lending.

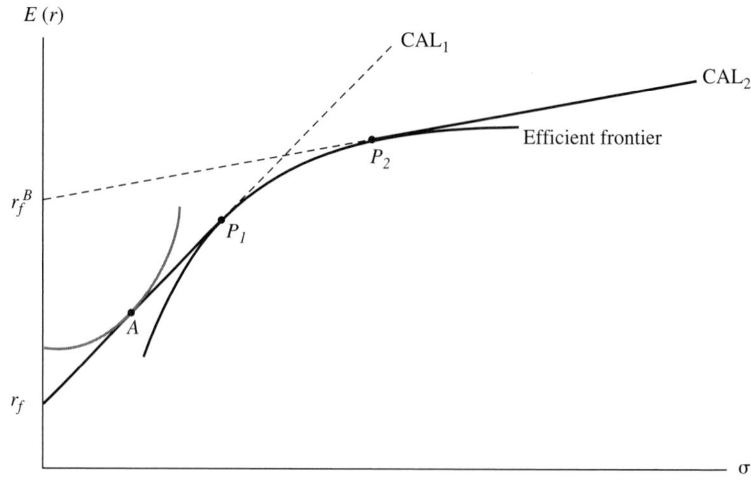


**Figure 7.17**
The optimal portfolio of defensive investors with differential borrowing and lending rates.

$CAL_2$, which is relevant in a range to the right of portfolio $P_2$, represents the efficient portfolio set for more aggressive, or risk-tolerant, investors. This line starts at the borrowing rate, $r_f^B$, but it is unavailable in the range $r_f^B P_2$, because *lending* (investing in T-bills) is available only at the risk-free rate $r_f$, less than $r_f^B$.

Investors who are willing to *borrow* at the higher rate, $r_f^B$, to invest in an optimal risky portfolio will choose portfolio $P_2$ as their risky investment vehicle. Such a case is described in Figure 7.18, which superimposes a relatively risk tolerant investor's indifference curve on $CAL_2$ of Figure 7.16. The investor with the indifference curve in Figure 7.18 chooses portfolio $P_2$ as the optimal risky portfolio and borrows to invest in it, arriving at overall portfolio *B*.

Investors in the middle range, neither defensive enough to invest in T-bills nor aggressive enough to borrow, choose a risky portfolio from the efficient frontier in the range $P_1P_2$. This case is described in Figure 7.19. The indifference curve representing the investor in Figure 7.19 leads to a tangency portfolio on the efficient frontier, portfolio *C*.

---

**CONCEPT CHECK**

Question 5. With differential lending and borrowing rates, only investors with approximately average degrees of risk aversion will choose a portfolio in the range $P_1P_2$ in Figure 7.17. Other investors will choose a portfolio on $CAL_1$, if they are more risk averse, or on $CAL_2$, if they are more risk tolerant.

*a.* Does this mean that investors with average risk aversion are more dependent on the quality of the forecasts that generate the efficient frontier?

*b.* Describe the trade-off between expected return and standard deviation for portfolios between $P_1$ and $P_2$ in Figure 7.17, compared with portfolios on $CAL_2$ beyond $P_2$.

---

**Figure 7.18**
The optimal portfolio of aggressive investors with differential borrowing and lending rates.

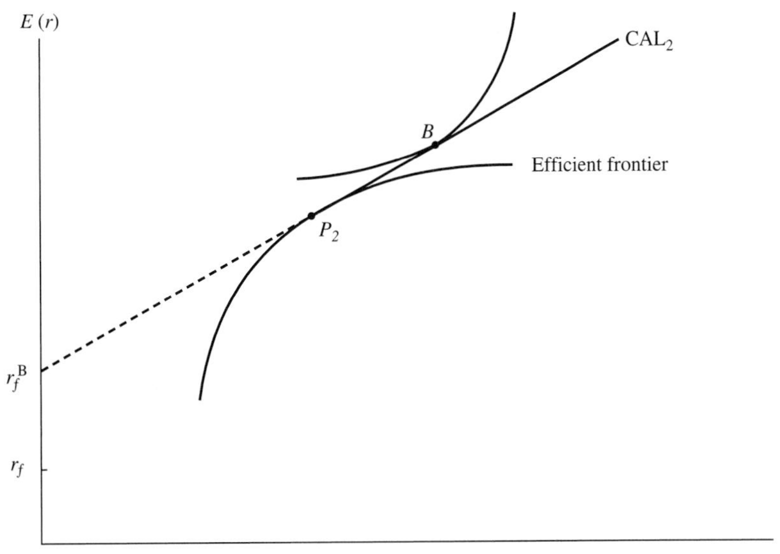

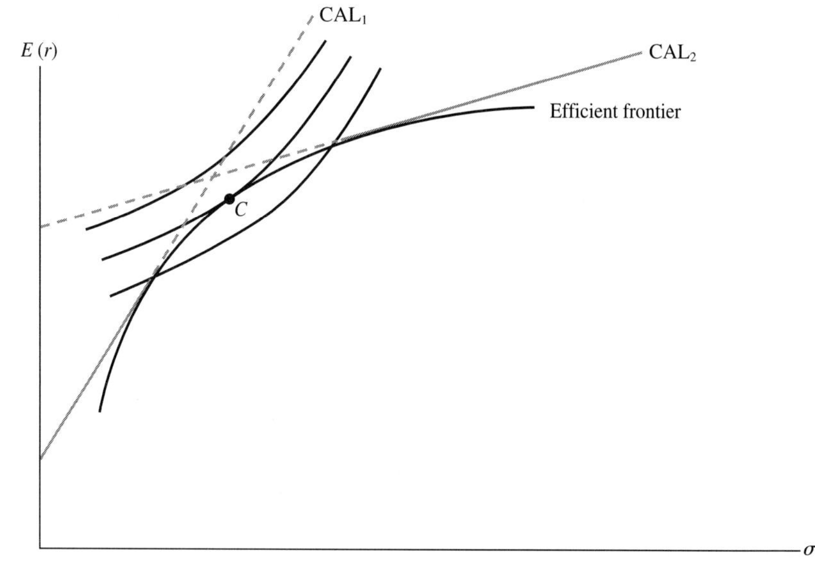


**Figure 7.19** The optimal portfolio of moderately risk-tolerant investors with differential borrowing and lending rates.

## 7.6 An Illustration of the Process of Asset Allocation

Now that we have seen the factors that enter into the formation of investment portfolios, we can relate these to the problems faced by an investor in choosing a personal portfolio. We can view the process of asset allocation as consisting of the following steps:

1. *Specify asset classes to be included in the portfolio.* The major classes usually considered are the following:
   *a.* Money market instruments (usually called cash).
   *b.* Fixed-income securities (usually called bonds).
   *c.* Stocks.
   *d.* Real estate.
   *e.* Precious metals.
   *f.* Other.
2. *Specify capital market expectations.* This step consists of using both historical data and economic analysis to determine the investor's expectations of future rates of return over the relevant holding period on the assets to be considered for inclusion in the portfolio.
3. *Derive the efficient portfolio frontier.* This step consists of finding portfolios that achieve the maximum expected return for any given degree of risk.
4. *Find the optimal asset mix.* This step consists of selecting the efficient portfolio that best meets the investor's risk and return objectives while satisfying any imposed constraints.

Let us illustrate how the process works by considering a simple example. We start the process by initially restricting our portfolio to cash, bonds, and stocks.

**Table 7.5** Probability Distribution of HPR on Stocks, Bonds, and Cash

| | | Holding Period Return | | |
|---|---|---|---|---|
| **State of Economy** | **Probability** | **Stocks (%)** | **Bonds (%)** | **Cash (%)** |
| Boom with low inflation | .1 | 74 | 4 | 6 |
| Boom with high inflation | .2 | 20 | −10 | 6 |
| Normal growth | .4 | 14 | 9 | 6 |
| Recession with low inflation | .2 | 0 | 35 | 6 |
| Recession with high inflation | .1 | −30 | 0 | 6 |
| Expected return | $E(r)$ | 14.0 | 9.0 | 6 |
| Standard deviation | $\sigma$ | 24.5 | 14.8 | 0 |

Correlation coefficient between stocks and bonds is −.2372.

Later we will consider how much of an improvement we can achieve by adding real estate and other asset classes.

## Specifying Capital Market Expectations

Having decided to restrict ourselves to cash, bonds, and stocks, we must specify our expectations of the holding period returns on these asset classes over the period until our next planned revision in the asset mix. Although professional investors revise their asset mix every three months, when they receive new information about the state of the economy, market developments may cause us to revise more frequently.[12] In our example, we will express all rates of return in annualized terms, but the holding period should be thought of as three months.

The set of capital market expectations must be in a form that allows assessment of both expected rates of return and risk. Sometimes investors will make only point forecasts of holding period returns on assets. These may serve as measures of expected rates of return, but they do not allow assessment of risks.

There are two sources of information relevant to forming capital market expectations: historical data on capital market rates and economic forecasts. The investment professional must exercise considerable judgment when deciding how much to rely on each of these two sources.

For example, suppose that, based entirely on economic forecasts derived from careful analysis of all the information we can assemble, we have determined the probability distribution of holding period returns exhibited in Table 7.5. Our assessment of the HPR on bonds comes from a consideration of a 30-year Canada bond with a 9 percent coupon. If there is normal growth, then we expect interest rates to remain at their current level and we will experience neither capital gains nor losses on the bond. Our HPR simply will equal the coupon rate of 9 percent.

[12] Many statistics, such as the CPI for inflation, are released monthly.

If there is a boom, then we think interest rates will rise and the price of the bond will fall. The amount by which interest rates will rise depends on whether there is a low or a high rate of inflation. With low inflation, interest rates will rise a little bit, causing a capital loss of only 5 percent on bonds, for a net HPR of 4 percent. However, if inflation is high, interest rates will rise a lot, causing a capital loss of 19 percent, for a net HPR of −10 percent on bonds.

If there is a recession, then we think that the direction of interest rates will depend on inflation. If there is low inflation, interest rates will fall, but if there is high inflation, they will rise despite the recession. In the low-inflation recessionary scenario, bonds will do very well, with an HPR of 35 percent. But in the high-inflation recessionary scenario, the bond price will fall by 9 percent, leaving an HPR of 0.

The assessment of the rates of return on stocks for each scenario is evident from Table 7.5. Stocks are expected to do best in a noninflationary boom and worst in an inflationary recession.

To the extent that these parameter estimates—either the means, the standard deviations, or the correlation coefficient—differ from what they have been in the past, we may want to adjust their values so that they conform more to historical experience. In the rest of our example, however, we will use the unadjusted numbers calculated in Table 7.5.

**CONCEPT CHECK**

Question 6. Suppose that you revised your assessment of the probabilities of each of the five economic scenarios in Table 7.5 as follows:

| | | Holding Period Return | | |
|---|---|---|---|---|
| **State of Economy** | **Probability** | **Stocks (%)** | **Bonds (%)** | **Cash (%)** |
| Boom with low inflation | .05 | 74 | 4 | 6 |
| Boom with high inflation | .2 | 20 | −10 | 6 |
| Normal growth | .5 | 14 | 9 | 6 |
| Recession with low inflation | .2 | 0 | 35 | 6 |
| Recession with high inflation | .05 | −30 | 0 | 6 |

What are your new estimates of expected returns, standard deviations, and correlations?

## Deriving the Efficient Portfolio Frontier

Given the probability distribution of holding period returns in Table 7.5, what is the efficient portfolio frontier? Since we are considering only two risky assets for inclusion in the portfolio, we can use the formula presented in Section 7.3 to find the optimal combination of stocks and bonds to be combined with risk-free assets.

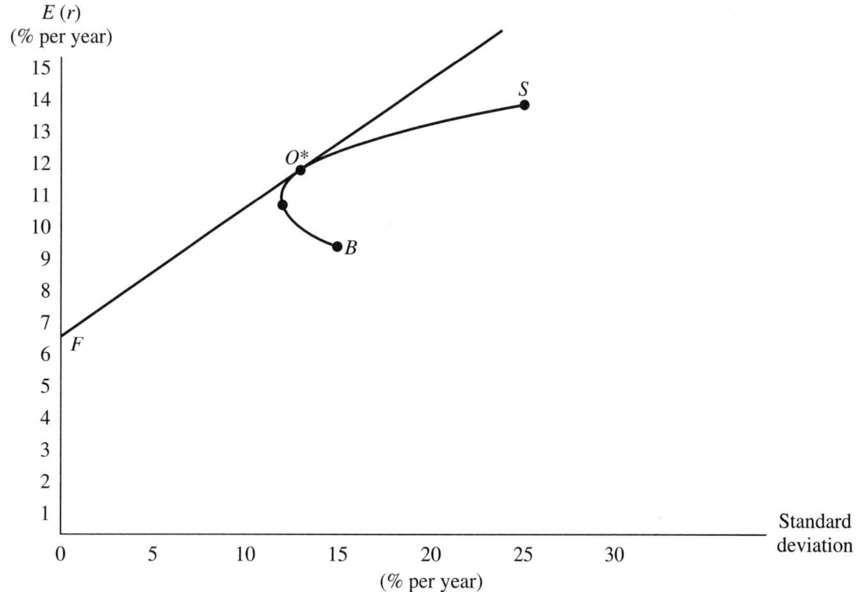


**Figure 7.20**
The risk-reward trade-off for portfolios of stocks, bonds, and cash.

Substituting in equation 7.8 we find that $w_D = .55$:

$$w_D = \frac{(9 - 6) \times 600 - (14 - 6) \times (-86)}{3 \times 600 + 8 \times 218 - (3 + 8)(-86)} = .55$$

Thus, the optimal stock-bond portfolio to be combined with cash is 45 percent stocks and 55 percent bonds.

Its expected HPR, $E(r^*)$, and standard deviation, $\sigma^*$, are

$$\begin{aligned} E(r^*) &= (1 - w_D)\, E(r_E) + w_D\, E(r_D) \\ &= .45 \times 14\% + .55 \times 9\% \\ &= 11.25\% \\ \sigma^{*2} &= (1 - w_D)^2\sigma_E^2 + w_D^2\sigma_D^2 + 2(1 - w_D)\, w_D \text{cov}(r_E, r_1) \\ &= .45^2 \times 600 + .55^2 \times 218 + 2 \times .45 \times .55 \times (-86) \\ &= 144.875 \\ \sigma^* &= 12.0\% \end{aligned}$$

Figure 7.20 displays the efficient portfolio frontier.

Point $F$ represents 100 percent invested in cash, point $B$ 100 percent in bonds, and point $S$ 100 percent in stocks. Point $O^*$ is the optimal combination of stocks and bonds (45 percent stocks and 55 percent bonds) to be combined with cash to form the investor's final portfolio. All efficient portfolios rest along the straight line connecting points $F$ and $O^*$. The slope of this efficient frontier, the reward-to-variability ratio, is:

$$S^* = \frac{E(r^*) - r_f}{\sigma^*}$$
$$= \frac{11.25\% - 6\%}{12.0}$$
$$= .4375$$

The fact that we have drawn the segment of the efficient frontier to the right of $O^*$ with the same slope as to the left reflects the assumption that we can borrow at a risk-free rate of 6 percent per year to buy the $O^*$ portfolio on margin. If the borrowing rate is higher than 6 percent per year, then the slope to the right of point $O^*$ will be lower than to the left.

If we rule out buying the $O^*$ portfolio on margin altogether, then the segment of the efficient frontier to the right of $O^*$ will be the curve linking points $O^*$ and $S$. This indicates that, to achieve an expected HPR higher than $E(r^*)$ in the absence of borrowing, we would have to increase the proportion of our portfolio invested in stocks and reduce the proportion in bonds relative to their proportions in $O^*$. The maximum expected HPR under these circumstances would be the expected HPR on stocks, achieved by investing 100 percent in stocks.

---

**CONCEPT CHECK** Question 7. What is the $O^*$ portfolio for the set of revised capital market parameters you derived in question 6?

---

## The Optimal Mix

Our choice of where to be on the efficient frontier will depend on our degree of risk aversion, as expressed by equation 7.9. For example, we might wonder how risk-averse we need to be to want to hold the portfolio $O^*$ itself, with nothing invested in cash. To find the answer, we set $y$ equal to 1 and solve for $A$. The answer is $A = 3.65$.

## Diversifying into Different Asset Classes

Diversification is a good thing in asset allocation. But can there be too much of a good thing? After all, there are many different asset categories. Should you have some of each in your portfolio: stocks, bonds, real estate, precious metals, art, collectibles, and so on? And if so, how much?

The basic principle of efficient diversification suggests that you never can be made worse off by broadening the set of assets included in your portfolio. However, when we quantify the improvement in portfolio efficiency resulting from including additional assets, we often find that it is not large enough to justify the additional time, trouble, and other transaction costs associated with implementing such a strategy.

For example, let us consider whether we should add real estate to our portfolio in the example above. The first thing we need is the mean, standard deviation,

**Table 7.6** Capital Market Expectations: Stocks, Bonds, and Real Estate

| | Stocks | Bonds | Real Estate | Cash |
|---|---|---|---|---|
| Expected HPR $E(r)$ | 14.0% | 9.0% | 10.0% | 6% |
| Standard deviation $\sigma$ | 24.5% | 14.8% | 20.0% | 0 |
| **CORRELATION COEFFICIENTS** | | | | |
| Stocks | 1.0 | −.24 | 0 | |
| Bonds | | 1.0 | 0 | |
| Real estate | | | 1.0 | |

and the correlations of the HPR on real estate with the returns on stocks and bonds. One way to derive them is from an expansion of the scenario analysis presented earlier in this chapter. Another way is by looking at past data.

Data on real estate holding period returns is not as readily available as data on stock and bond returns. One feasible approach, however, is to gather data on a few publicly traded real estate investment companies[13] and treat them as representative of real estate as a whole. The advantage of doing so is that we then can invest in the shares of those same REITs when it comes time to implement our investment policy.

Let us assume that we have used one or more of these methods to derive the following set of capital market parameters for real estate:

$$E(r_{\text{RE}}) = 10\% \text{ per year}$$

$$\sigma_{\text{RE}} = 20\%$$

$$\rho_{\text{RE},s} = 0 \text{ (correlation between real estate and stock returns)}$$

$$\rho_{\text{RE},b} = 0 \text{ (correlation between real estate and bond returns)}$$

In addition, let us use the parameters for stocks, bonds, and cash as we did in Table 7.5:

$$r_f = 6\%$$

$$E(r_E) = 14\% \quad \sigma_E = 24.5\%$$

$$E(r_D) = 9\% \quad \sigma_D = 14.8\%$$

$$\rho_{sb} = -.24 \text{ (correlation between stock and bond returns)}$$

Table 7.6 presents a convenient summary of these capital market assumptions.

We use a computer-based optimization program to find the optimal combination of risky assets to combine with cash.[14] Table 7.7 shows the new $O^*$ portfolio composition and characteristics, as well as the old.

Thus the reward-to-variability ratio that we face is .480, compared with .438 in the case without real estate. The optimal portfolio for an investor whose

---

[13] Opportunities for real estate investment were discussed in Chapter 3.

[14] The software diskette provided with the U.S. version of this text contains such a program.

**Table 7.7** The Optimal Combination of Risky Assets ($O^*$) with and without Real Estate

| | New | Old |
|---|---|---|
| **PORTFOLIO PROPORTIONS** | | |
| Stocks | 35% | 45% |
| Bonds | 43% | 55% |
| Real estate | 22% | |
| **PARAMETERS OF $O^*$ PORTFOLIO** | | |
| Expected HPR $E(r^*)$ | 11.0% | 11.25% |
| Standard deviation $\sigma^*$ | 10.4% | 12.0% |
| Reward-to-variability ratio $S^*$ | .480 | .438 |

coefficient of risk aversion is 3.65 and who previously would have chosen to hold the old $O^*$ portfolio with no cash would be

$$\begin{aligned} y &= \frac{E(r^*) - r_r}{A\sigma^2} \\ &= \frac{.11 - .06}{3.65 \times .0108} \\ &= 1.27 \end{aligned}$$

Thus, if this were you and if you had \$100,000 of your own money to invest, you should invest \$127,000 in the $O^*$ mutual fund, borrowing the other \$27,000 at an interest rate of 6 percent per year.

The mean and standard deviation of your optimal portfolio would be

$$\begin{aligned} E(r) &= r_f + 1.27[E(r^*) - r_f] \\ &= 6\% + 1.27(11\% - 6\%) \\ &= 12.35\% \\ \sigma &= 1.27\sigma^* \\ &= 1.27 \times 10.4\% \\ &= 13.21\% \end{aligned}$$

And your certainty-equivalent HPR would be

$$\begin{aligned} U &= E(r) - \tfrac{1}{2}A\sigma^2 \\ &= .1235 - .5 \times 3.65 \times .0175 \\ &= .092 \\ &= .92\% \text{ per year} \end{aligned}$$

This is .6 percent per year higher than the comparable certainty-equivalent HPR of 8.6 percent per year that you would have if you excluded real estate from your portfolio.

What can we conclude from all of this about the value of adding real estate to stocks, bonds, and cash in creating your investment portfolio? Is it worth the effort?

The first thing to point out is that the specific results we got are very sensitive to the specific assumptions that we made about the parameters of the probability distribution of the HPR on real estate. In our example, the reward-to-variability ratio goes up from .438 to .480, but had we assumed different numbers for the means, standard deviations, and correlation coefficients, the results could have been very different.

For example, had we assumed a higher value for the expected HPR on real estate, the optimization program would have indicated that we should invest much more heavily in it. The resultant increase in the reward-to-variability ratio would have been higher, too. By experimenting with the optimization program that accompanies the U.S. text, you can gain a feel for the contribution that real estate would make to improving the efficiency of your portfolio under a variety of assumptions about the relevant parameter values.

Whenever we add an asset class, the process is identical to the one described for real estate. We first must specify the mean and standard deviation of the HPR and its correlation with the other asset classes. Our optimization program then tells us what the optimal proportions of all risky assets are in the $O^*$ portfolio. We then can compute $E(r^*)$, $\sigma^*$, and $S^*$, and decide which combination of the risk-free asset and the new, expanded $O^*$ mutual fund is optimal for us.

For example, suppose we are thinking of adding gold to our portfolio. Suppose that we think that its $E(r)$ is 7 percent, its $\sigma$ is 20 percent, and its correlation with the other three risky assets is zero. Table 7.8 summarizes our capital market assumptions. What is the composition of the new $O^*$ portfolio, and how much do we gain by diversifying into gold?

Our portfolio optimization program tells us that the new $O^*$ has the following portfolio proportions:

| | |
|---|---|
| Stocks | 33% |
| Bonds | 41% |
| Real estate | 21% |
| Gold | 5% |

The expected return and risk of this new $O^*$ portfolio are

$$E(r^*) = 10.76\%$$
$$\sigma^* = 9.87\%$$

and the new reward-to-variability ratio is

$$S^* = .482$$

This compares with a reward-to-variability ratio of .480 for the previous case without gold. It would appear that the gain from adding gold to the portfolio is slight.

**Table 7.8** Capital Market Expectations: Stocks, Bonds, Real Estate, and Gold

| | Stocks | Bonds | Real Estate | Gold | Cash |
|---|---|---|---|---|---|
| Expected HPR $E(r)$ | 14.0% | 9.0% | 10.0% | 7.0% | 6% |
| Standard deviation $\sigma$ | 24.5% | 14.8% | 20.0% | 20.0% | 0 |
| **CORRELATION COEFFICIENTS** | | | | | |
| Stocks | 1.0 | −.24 | 0 | 0 | |
| Bonds | | 1.0 | 0 | 0 | |
| Real estate | | | 1.0 | 0 | |
| Gold | | | | 1.0 | |

In general, it seems to be true that, unless you can identify an additional asset that has a high expected HPR, the gain from further diversification will be slight. You can explore the gains from additional diversification, using your own capital market assumptions, with the aid of the portfolio optimization program provided with the U.S. version of this book.

## SUMMARY

**1.** The expected return of a portfolio is the weighted average of the component assets' expected returns with the investment proportions as weights.

**2.** The variance of a portfolio is the weighted sum of the elements of the covariance matrix with the product of the investment proportions as the weight. Thus, the variance of each asset is weighted by the square of its investment proportion. Each covariance of any pair of assets appears twice in the covariance matrix, and thus the portfolio variance includes twice each covariance weighted by the product of the investment proportions in each of the two assets.

**3.** Even if the covariances are positive, the portfolio standard deviation is less than the weighted average of the component standard deviations, as long as the assets are not perfectly positively correlated. Thus, portfolio diversification is of value as long as assets are less than perfectly correlated.

**4.** The greater an asset's *covariance* with the other assets in the portfolio, the more it contributes to portfolio variance. An asset that is perfectly negatively correlated with a portfolio can serve as a perfect hedge. The perfect hedge asset can reduce the portfolio variance to zero.

**5.** The efficient frontier is the graphical representation of a set of portfolios that maximize expected return for each level of portfolio risk. Rational investors will choose a portfolio on the efficient frontier.

**6.** A portfolio manager identifies the efficient frontier by first establishing estimates for the asset expected returns and the covariance matrix. This input list then is fed into an optimization program that reports as outputs the investment proportions, expected returns, and standard deviations of the portfolios on the efficient frontier.

**7.** In general, portfolio managers will arrive at different efficient portfolios due to a difference in methods and quality of security analysis. Managers compete on the quality of their security analysis relative to their management fees.

**8.** If a risk-free asset is available and input lists are identical, all investors will choose the same portfolio on the efficient frontier of risky assets: the portfolio tangent to the CAL. All investors with identical input lists will hold an identical risky portfolio, differing only in how much each allocates to this optimal portfolio and to the risk-free asset. This result is characterized as the separation principle of portfolio construction.

**9.** When a risk-free asset is not available, each investor chooses a risky portfolio on the efficient frontier. If a risk-free asset is available but borrowing is restricted, only aggressive investors will be affected. They will choose portfolios on the efficient frontier according to their degree of risk tolerance.

## Key Terms

Diversification
Insurance principle
Market risk
Systematic risk
Nondiversifiable risk
Unique risk
Firm-specific risk
Nonsystematic risk
Diversifiable risk
Minimum-variance portfolio
Portfolio opportunity set
Reward-to-variability ratio
Optimal risky portfolio
Minimum-variance frontier
Efficient frontier
Input list
Separation property

## Selected Readings

*Two frequently cited papers on the impact of diversification on portfolio risk are:*

Evans, John L.; and Stephen H. Archer. "Diversification and the Reduction of Dispersion: An Empirical Analysis." *Journal of Finance,* December 1968.

Wagner, W. H.; and S. C. Lau. "The Effect of Diversification on Risk." *Financial Analysts Journal,* November–December 1971.

*The seminal works on portfolio selection are:*

Markowitz, Harry M. "Portfolio Selection." *Journal of Finance,* March 1952.

Markowitz, Harry M. *Portfolio Selection: Efficient Diversification of Investments.* New York: John Wiley & Sons, Inc., 1959.

*Also see:*

Samuelson, Paul A. "Risk & Uncertainty: A Fallacy of Large Numbers." *Scientia* 98 (1963).

## Problems

The following data apply to problems 1–8:

A pension fund manager is considering three mutual funds. The first is a stock fund, the second is a long-term government and corporate bond fund, and the third is a T-bill money market fund that yields a rate of 9 percent. The probability distribution of the risky funds is as follows:

| | Expected Return | Standard Deviation |
|---|---|---|
| Stock fund (*S*) | .22 | .32 |
| Bond fund (*B*) | .13 | .23 |

The correlation between the fund returns is .15.

1. What are the investment proportions of the minimum-variance portfolio of the two risky funds, and what is the expected value and standard deviation of its rate of return?
2. Tabulate and draw the investment opportunity set of the two risky funds. Use investment proportions for the stock fund of zero to 100 percent in increments of 20 percent.
3. Draw a tangent from the risk-free rate to the opportunity set. What does your graph show for the expected return and standard deviation of the optimal portfolio?
4. Solve numerically for the proportions of each asset and for the expected return and standard deviation of the optimal risky portfolio.
5. What is the reward-to-variability ratio of the best feasible CAL?
6. You require that your portfolio yield an expected return of 15 percent and be efficient on the best feasible CAL.
   *a.* What is the standard deviation of your portfolio?
   *b.* What is the proportion invested in the T-bill fund and each of the two risky funds?
7. If you were to use only the two risky funds and will require an expected return of 15 percent, what must be the investment proportions of your portfolio? Compare its standard deviation to that of the optimized portfolio in problem 6. What do you conclude?
8. Suppose that you face the same opportunity set, but you cannot borrow. You wish to construct a portfolio with an expected return of 29 percent. What are the appropriate portfolio proportions and the resulting standard deviation? What reduction in standard deviation could you attain if you were allowed to borrow at the risk-free rate?
9. Stocks offer an expected rate of return of 18 percent, with a standard deviation of 22 percent. Gold offers an expected return of 10 percent with a standard deviation of 30 percent.
   *a.* In light of the apparent inferiority of gold with respect to both mean return and volatility, would anyone hold gold? If so, demonstrate graphically why one would do so.
   *b.* Given the data above, reanswer problem (a) with the additional assumption that the correlation coefficient between gold and stocks equals 1. Draw a graph illustrating why one would or would not hold gold in one's portfolio. Could this set of assumptions for expected re-

turns, standard deviations, and correlation represent an equilibrium for the security market?

**10.** Suppose that there are many stocks in the market and that the characteristics of stocks *A* and *B* are as follows:

| Stock | Expected Return | Standard Deviation |
|---|---|---|
| *A* | .10 | .05 |
| *B* | .15 | .10 |
| | Correlation = −1 | |

Suppose that it is possible to borrow at the risk-free rate, $r_f$. What must be the value of the risk-free rate? *Hint:* Think about constructing a risk-free portfolio from stocks *A* and *B*.

**11.** Assume that expected returns and standard deviations for all securities (including the risk-free rate for borrowing and lending) are known. True or false: In this case all investors will have the same optimal risky portfolio.

**12.** True or false: The standard deviation of the portfolio always is equal to the weighted average of the standard deviations of the assets in the portfolio.

**13.** Suppose that you have a project that has a .7 chance of doubling your investment in a year and a .3 chance of halving your investment in a year. What is the standard deviation of the rate of return on this investment?

**14.** Suppose that you have $1 million and the following two opportunities from which to construct a portfolio:

*a.* Risk-free asset earning .12 per year.

*b.* Risky asset earning .30 per year with a standard deviation of .40.

If you construct a portfolio with a standard deviation of .30, what will be the rate of return?

The following data apply to problems 15–17:

Hennessy & Associates manages a $30 million equity portfolio for the multi-manager Wilstead Pension Fund. Jason Jones, financial vice president of Wilstead, noted that Hennessy had rather consistently achieved the best record among Wilstead's six equity managers. Performance of the Hennessy portfolio had been clearly superior to that of the S&P 500 in four of the past five years. In the one less favourable year, the shortfall was trivial.

Hennessy is a "bottom-up" manager. The firm largely avoids any attempt to "time the market." It also focuses on selection of individual stocks, rather than the weighting of favoured industries.

There is no apparent conformity of style among the six equity managers. The five managers, other than Hennessy, manage portfolios aggregating $250 million made up of more than 150 individual issues.

Jones is convinced that Hennessy is able to apply superior skill to stock selection, but the favourable results are limited by the high degree of diversification in the portfolio. Over the years, the portfolio generally has held 40–50 stocks, with about 2 percent to 3 percent of total funds committed to each issue. The reason Hennessy seemed to do well most years was because the firm was able to identify each year 10 or 12 issues that registered particularly large gains.

Based on this overview, Jones outlined the following plan to the Wilstead pension committee:

"Let's tell Hennessy to limit the portfolio to no more than 20 stocks. Hennessy will double the commitments to the stocks that it really favours and eliminate the remainder. Except for this one new restriction, Hennessy should be free to manage the portfolio exactly as before."

All the members of the pension committee generally supported Jones' proposal, because all agreed that Hennessy had seemed to demonstrate superior skill in selecting stocks. Yet, the proposal was a considerable departure from previous practice, and several committee members raised questions. Respond to each of these questions:

**15.** Answer the following:
   *a.* Will the limitation of 20 stocks likely increase or decrease the risk of the portfolio? Explain.
   *b.* Is there any way Hennessy could reduce the number of issues from 40 to 20 without significantly affecting risk? Explain.

**16.** One committee member was particularly enthusiastic concerning Jones' proposal. He suggested that Hennessy's performance might benefit further from reduction in the number of issues to 10. If the reduction to 20 could be expected to be advantageous, explain why reduction to 10 might be less likely to be advantageous. (Assume that Wilstead will evaluate the Hennessy portfolio independently of the other portfolios in the fund.)

**17.** Another committee member suggested that, rather than evaluating each managed portfolio independently of other portfolios, it might be better to consider the effects of a change in the Hennessy portfolio on the total fund. Explain how this broader point of view could affect the committee decision to limit the holdings in the Hennessy portfolio to either 10 or 20 issues.

The following data apply to problems 18–20:
The correlation coefficients between pairs of stocks is as follows:

$$\text{Corr}(A, B) = .85;\ \text{Corr}(A, C) = .60;\ \text{Corr}(A, D) = .45$$

Each stock has an expected return of 8 percent.

**18.** If your entire portfolio now is comprised of stock *A* and you can add only one more, which of the following would you choose, and why?
   *a.* *B*
   *b.* *C*
   *c.* *D*
   *d.* Need more data

**19.** Would your answer to problem 18 change for more risk-averse or risk-tolerant investors? Explain.

**20.** Suppose that in addition to investing in one more stock you can invest in T-bills as well. How would you change your answers to problems 18 and 19?

**21.** Which *one* of the following portfolios *cannot* lie on the efficient frontier as described by Markowitz?

| | Portfolio | Expected Return | Standard Deviation |
|---|---|---|---|
| *a.* | *W* | 15% | 36% |
| *b.* | *X* | 12% | 15% |
| *c.* | *Z* | 5% | 7% |
| *d.* | *Y* | 9% | 21% |

**22.** Which of the following statements about portfolio diversification is *correct*?

*a.* Proper diversification can reduce or eliminate systematic risk.

*b.* Diversification reduces the portfolio's expected return because diversification reduces a portfolio's total risk.

*c.* As more securities are added to a portfolio, total risk typically would be expected to fall at a decreasing rate.

*d.* The risk-reducing benefits of diversification do not occur meaningfully until at least 30 individual securities are included in the portfolio.

## APPENDIX 7A: THE POWER OF DIVERSIFICATION

Section 7.1 introduced the concept of diversification and the limits to the benefits of diversification caused by systematic risk. Given the tools we have developed, we can reconsider this intuition more rigorously and at the same time sharpen our insight regarding the power of diversification.

Recall from equation 7.11 that the general formula for the variance of a portfolio is

$$\sigma_p^2 = \sum_{i=1}^{n} w_i^2 \sigma_i^2 + \sum_{\substack{j=1 \\ j \neq i}}^{n} \sum_{i=1}^{n} w_i w_j \mathrm{Cov}(r_i, r_f) \tag{7A.1}$$

Consider now the naive diversification strategy in which an equally weighted portfolio is constructed, meaning that $w_i = 1/n$ for each security. In this case, equation 7A.1 may be rewritten as follows:

$$\sigma_p^2 = \frac{1}{n} \sum_{i=1}^{n} \frac{1}{n} \sigma_i^2 + \sum_{\substack{j=1 \\ j \neq i}}^{n} \sum_{i=1}^{n} \frac{1}{n^2} \mathrm{Cov}(r_i, r_f) \tag{7A.2}$$

Note that there are $n$ variance terms and $n(n - 1)$ covariance terms in equation 7A.2.

If we define the average variance and average covariance of the securities as

$$\overline{\sigma}^2 = \frac{1}{n}\sum_{i=1}^{n} \sigma_i^2$$

$$\overline{\text{Cov}} = \frac{1}{n(n-1)}\sum_{\substack{i=1 \\ j \neq i}}^{n}\sum_{j=1}^{n} \text{Cov}(r_i, r_j)$$

we can express portfolio variance as

$$\sigma_p^2 = \frac{1}{n}\,\overline{\sigma}^2 + \frac{n-1}{n}\,\overline{\text{Cov}} \qquad \textbf{(7A.3)}$$

Now examine the effect of diversification. When the average covariance among security returns is zero, as it is when all risk is firm-specific, portfolio variance can be driven to zero. We see this from equation 7A.3: the second term on the right-hand side will be zero in this scenario while the first term approaches zero as $n$ becomes larger. Hence, when security returns are uncorrelated, the power of diversification to limit portfolio risk is unlimited.

However, the more important case is the one in which economywide risk factors impart positive correlation among stock returns. In this case, as the portfolio becomes more highly diversified ($n$ increases), portfolio variance remains positive. While firm-specific risk, represented by the first term in equation 7A.3, still is diversified away, the second term simply approaches $\overline{\text{Cov}}$ as $n$ becomes greater. [Note that $(n - 1)/n = 1 - 1/n$, which approaches 1 for large $n$.] Thus the irreducible risk of a diversified portfolio depends on the covariance of the returns of the component securities, which in turn is a function of the importance of systematic factors in the economy.

To see further the fundamental relationship between systematic risk and security correlations, suppose for simplicity that all securities have a common standard deviation, $\sigma$, and all security pairs have a common correlation coefficient $\rho$. Then the covariance between all pairs of securities is $\rho\sigma^2$, and equation 7A.3 becomes

$$\sigma_p^2 = \frac{1}{n}\,\sigma^2 + \frac{n-1}{n}\,\rho\sigma^2 \qquad \textbf{(7A.4)}$$

The effect of correlation is now explicit. When $\rho = 0$, we again obtain the insurance principle, where portfolio variance approaches zero as $n$ becomes greater. For $\rho > 0$, however, portfolio variance remains positive. In fact, for $\rho = 1$, portfolio variance equals $\sigma^2$ regardless of $n$, demonstrating that diversification is of no benefit: In the case of perfect correlation, all risk is systematic. More generally, as $n$ becomes greater, equation 7A.4 shows that systematic risk becomes $\rho\sigma^2$.

**Table 7A.1** Risk Reduction of Equally Weighted Portfolios in Correlated and Uncorrelated Universes

| Universe Size $n$ | Optimal Portfolio Proportion $1/n$(%) | $\rho = 0$ Standard Deviation (%) | $\rho = 0$ Reduction in $\sigma$ | $\rho = .4$ Standard Deviation (%) | $\rho = .4$ Reduction in $\sigma$ |
|---|---|---|---|---|---|
| 1 | 100 | 50.00 | 14.64 | 50.00 | 8.17 |
| 2 | 50 | 35.36 | | 41.83 | |
| 5 | 20 | 22.36 | 1.95 | 36.06 | .70 |
| 6 | 16.67 | 20.41 | | 35.36 | |
| 10 | 10 | 15.81 | .73 | 33.91 | .20 |
| 11 | 9.09 | 15.08 | | 33.71 | |
| 20 | 5 | 11.18 | .27 | 32.79 | .06 |
| 21 | 4.76 | 10.91 | | 32.73 | |
| 100 | 1 | 5.00 | .02 | 31.86 | .00 |
| 101 | .99 | 4.98 | | 31.86 | |

Table 7A.1 presents portfolio standard deviation as we include even greater numbers of securities in the portfolio for two cases: $\rho = 0$ and $\rho = .40$. The table takes $\sigma$ to be 50 percent. As one would expect, portfolio risk is greater when $\rho = .40$. More surprising, perhaps, is that portfolio risk diminishes far less rapidly as $n$ increases in the positive correlation case. The correlation among security returns limits the power of diversification.

Note that, for a 100-security portfolio, the standard deviation is 5 percent in the uncorrelated case—still significant when we consider the potential of zero standard deviation. For $\rho = .40$, the standard deviation is high, 31.86%, yet it is very close to undiversifiable systematic risk in the infinite-sized universe, $\sqrt{\rho\sigma^2} = \sqrt{.4 \times .50^2} = .3162$, or 31.62 percent. At this point, further diversification is of little value.

We also gain an important insight from this exercise. When we hold diversified portfolios, the contribution to portfolio risk of a particular security will depend on the *covariance* of that security's return with those of other securities, and *not* on the security's variance. As we shall see in Chapter 8, this implies that fair risk premiums also should depend on covariances rather than the total variability of returns.

**CONCEPT CHECK** Question 7A.1. Suppose that the universe of available risky securities consists of a large number of stocks, identically distributed with $E(r) = 15$ percent, $\sigma = 60$ percent, and a common correlation coefficient of $\rho = .5$.

*a.* What is the expected return and standard deviation of an equally weighted risky portfolio of 25 stocks?

*b.* What is the smallest number of stocks necessary to generate an efficient portfolio with a standard deviation equal to or smaller than 43 percent?

*c.* What is the systematic risk in this universe?

*d.* If T-bills are available and yield 10 percent, what is the slope of the CAL?

## Appendix 7B: The Insurance Principle: Risk-Sharing versus Risk-Pooling

Mean-variance analysis has taken a strong hold among investment professionals, and insight into the mechanics of efficient diversification has become quite widespread. Common misconceptions or fallacies about diversification still persist, however, and we will try to put some to rest.

It is commonly believed that a large portfolio of independent insurance policies is a necessary and sufficient condition for an insurance company to shed its risk. The fact is that a multitude of independent insurance policies is neither necessary nor sufficient for a sound insurance portfolio. Actually, an individual insurer who would not insure a single policy also would be unwilling to insure a large portfolio of independent policies.

Consider Paul Samuelson's (1963) story. He once offered a colleague 2-to-1 odds on a $1,000 bet on the toss of a coin. His colleague refused, saying "I won't bet because I would feel the $1,000 loss more than the $2,000 gain. But I'll take you on if you promise to let me make a hundred such bets."

Samuelson's colleague, as many others, might have explained his position, not quite correctly, that "One toss is not enough to make it reasonably sure that the law of averages will turn out in my favour. But with a hundred tosses of a coin, the law of averages will make it a darn good bet."

Another way to rationalize this argument is to think in terms of rates of return. In each bet you put up $1,000 and then get back $3,000 with a probability of one half, or zero with a probability of one half. The probability distribution of the rate of return is 200 percent with $p = ½$ and $-100$ percent with $p = ½$.

The bets are all independent and identical and therefore the expected return is $E(r) = ½(200) + ½(-100) = 50$ percent, regardless of the number of bets. The standard deviation of the rate of return on the portfolio of independent bets is[15]

$$\sigma(n) = \frac{\sigma}{\sqrt{n}}$$

where $\sigma$ is the standard deviation of a single bet:

$$\begin{aligned} \sigma &= [½(200 - 50)^2 + ½(-100 - 50)^2]^{1/2} \\ &= 150\% \end{aligned}$$

The rate of return on a sequence of bets, in other words, has a smaller standard deviation than that of a single bet. By increasing the number of bets we can reduce the standard deviation of the rate of return to any desired level. It seems at first glance that Samuelson's colleague was correct. But he was not.

The fallacy of the argument lies in the use of a rate of return criterion to choose from portfolios *that are not equal in size.* Although the portfolio is equally

---

[15] This follows from equation 7.11, setting $w_i = 1/n$ and all covariances equal to zero because of the independence of the bets.

weighted across bets, each extra bet increases the scale of the investment by \$1,000. Recall from traditional corporate finance that when choosing among mutually exclusive projects you cannot use the internal rate of return (IRR) as your decision criterion when the projects are of different sizes. You have to use the net present value (NPV) rule.

Consider the dollar profit (as opposed to rate of return) distribution of a single bet:

$$\begin{aligned} E(R) &= \tfrac{1}{2} \times 2{,}000 + \tfrac{1}{2} \times (-1{,}000) \\ &= \$500 \\ \sigma_R &= [\tfrac{1}{2}(2{,}000 - 500)^2 + \tfrac{1}{2}(-1{,}000 - 500)^2]^{1/2} \\ &= \$1{,}500 \end{aligned}$$

These are independent bets where the total profit from $n$ bets is the sum of the profits from the single bets. Therefore, with $n$ bets

$$\begin{aligned} E[R(n)] &= \$500n \\ \text{Variance}\left(\sum_{i=1}^{n} R_i\right) &= n\sigma_R^2 \\ \sigma_R(n) &= \sqrt{n\sigma_R^2} \\ &= \sigma_R\sqrt{n} \end{aligned}$$

so that the standard deviation of the dollar return *increases* by a factor equal to the square root of the number of bets, $n$, in contrast to the standard deviation of the rate of return, which *decreases* by a factor of the square root of $n$.

As further evidence, consider the standard coin-tossing game. Whether one flips a fair coin 10 times or 1,000 times, the expected percentage of heads flipped is 50 percent. One expects the actual proportion of heads in a typical running of the 1,000-toss experiment to be closer to 50 percent than in the 10-toss experiment. This is the law of averages.

But the actual number of heads typically will depart from its expected value by a greater amount in the 1,000-toss experiment. For example, 504 heads is close to 50 percent and is 4 more than the expected number. To exceed the expected number of heads by 4 in the 10-toss game would require 9 out of 10 heads, which is a much more extreme departure from the mean. In the many-toss case, there is more volatility of the number of heads and less volatility of the percentage of heads. This is the same when an insurance company takes on more policies: the dollar variance of its portfolio increases while the rate of return variance falls.

The lesson is this: Rate-of-return analysis is appropriate when considering mutually exclusive portfolios of equal size, which is what we did in all the examples so far. We applied a fixed investment budget, and we investigated only the consequences of varying investment proportions in various assets. But if an insurance company takes on more and more insurance policies, it is increasing portfolio dollar investments. The analysis that is called for in that case must be cast in terms of dollar profits, in much the same way that NPV is called for instead of

IRR when we compare different-sized projects. This is why risk-pooling (that is, accumulating independent risky prospects) does not act to eliminate risk.

Samuelson's colleague should have counteroffered: "Let's make 1,000 bets, each with your \$2 against my \$1." Then he would be holding a portfolio of fixed size, equal to \$1,000, which is diversified into 1,000 identical independent prospects. This would make the insurance principle work.

Another way for Samuelson's colleague to get around the riskiness of this tempting bet is to share the large bets with friends. Consider a firm engaging in 1,000 of Paul Samuelson's bets. In each bet the firm puts up \$1,000 and receives \$3,000 or nothing as before. Each bet is too large for you. Yet if you hold a 1/1,000 share of the firm, your position is exactly the same as if you were to make 1,000 small bets of \$2 against \$1. A 1/1,000 share of a \$1,000 bet is equivalent to a \$1 bet. Holding a small share of many large bets essentially allows you to replace a stake in one large bet with a diversified portfolio of manageable bets.

How does this apply to insurance companies? Investors can purchase insurance company shares in the stock market, so they can choose to hold as small a position in the overall risk as they please. No matter how great the risk of the policies, a large group of individual small investors will agree to bear the risk if the expected rate of return exceeds the risk-free rate. Thus, it is the sharing of risk among many shareholders that makes the insurance industry tick.

## Appendix 7C: The Fallacy of Time Diversification

The insurance story just discussed illustrates a misuse of rate of return analysis, specifically the mistake of comparing portfolios of different sizes. A more insidious version of this error often appears under the guise of "time diversification."

Consider the case of Mr. Frier, who has \$100,000. He is trying to figure out the appropriate allocation of this fund between risk-free T-bills that yield 10 percent and a risky portfolio that yields an annual rate of return with $E(r_p) = 15$ percent and $\sigma_p = 30$ percent.

Mr. Frier took a course in finance in his youth. He likes quantitative models, and after careful introspection he determines that his degree of risk aversion, $A$, is 4. Consequently, he calculates that his optimal allocation to the risky portfolio is

$$y = \frac{E(r_p) - r_f}{A\sigma_p^2} = \frac{.15 - .10}{4 \times .3^2}$$
$$= .14$$

which is a 14 percent investment (\$14,000) in the risky portfolio.

With this strategy, Mr. Frier calculates his complete portfolio expected return and standard deviation by

$$E(r_C) = r_f + y[E(r_p) - r_f]$$
$$= 10.70\%$$
$$\sigma_C = y\sigma_p$$
$$= 4.20\%$$

At this point, Mr. Frier gets cold feet because this fund is intended to provide the mainstay of his retirement wealth. He plans to retire in five years, and any mistake will be burdensome.

Mr. Frier calls Ms. Mavin, a highly recommended financial advisor. Ms. Mavin explains that indeed the time factor is all important. She cites academic research showing that asset rates of return over successive holding periods are independent. Therefore, she argues, returns in good years and bad years will tend to cancel out over the five-year period. Consequently, the average portfolio rate of return over the investment period will be less risky than would appear from the standard deviation of a single-year portfolio return. Because returns in each year are independent, Ms. Mavin tells Mr. Frier that a five-year investment is equivalent to a portfolio of five equally weighted independent assets. With such a portfolio, the (five-year) holding period return has a mean of

$$E[r_p(5)] = 15\% \text{ per year}$$

and standard deviation of[16]

$$\sigma_p(5) = \frac{30}{\sqrt{5}}$$
$$= 13.42\% \text{ per year}$$

Mr. Frier is relieved. He believes that the effective standard deviation has fallen from 30 percent to 13.42 percent, and that the reward-to-variability ratio is much better than his first assessment.

Is Mr. Frier's newfound sense of security warranted? Specifically, is Ms. Mavin's time diversification really a risk-reducer? Is it true that the standard deviation of the annualized *rate* of return over five years really is only 13.42 percent, as Mavin claims, compared with the 30 percent one-year standard deviation? But what about the volatility of Mr. Frier's total retirement fund?

With a standard deviation of the five-year average return of 13.42 percent, a one-standard-deviation disappointment in Mr. Frier's average return over the five-year period will affect final wealth by a factor of $(1 - .1342)^5 = .487$, meaning that final wealth will be less than one-half its expected value. This is a larger impact than the 30 percent one-year swing.

Ms. Mavin is wrong: Time diversification does not reduce risk. Although it is true that the *per year* average rate of return has a smaller standard deviation for

[16] The calculation for standard deviation is only approximate, because it assumes that the five-year return is the sum of each of the five one-year returns, and this formulation ignores compounding. The error is small, however, and does not affect the point we want to make.

a longer time horizon, it also is true that the uncertainty compounds over a greater number of years. Unfortunately, this latter effect dominates in the sense that the *total return* becomes more uncertain the longer the investment horizon.

Figures 7C.1 and 7C.2 show the fallacy of time diversification. They represent simulated returns to a stock investment and show the range of possible outcomes. While the confidence band around the expected rate of return on the investment narrows with investment life, the dollar confidence band widens.

Again, the coin-toss analogy is helpful. Think of each year's investment return as one flip of the coin. After many years, the average number of heads approaches 50 percent, but the possible deviation of total heads from one-half the number of flips still will be growing.

The lesson is, once again, that one should not use rate of return analysis to compare portfolios of different size. Investing for more than one holding period means that the amount at risk is growing. This is analogous to an insurer taking on more insurance policies. The fact that these policies are independent does not offset the effect of placing more funds at risk. Focus on the standard deviation of the rate of return should never obscure the more proper emphasis on the possible dollar values of a portfolio strategy.

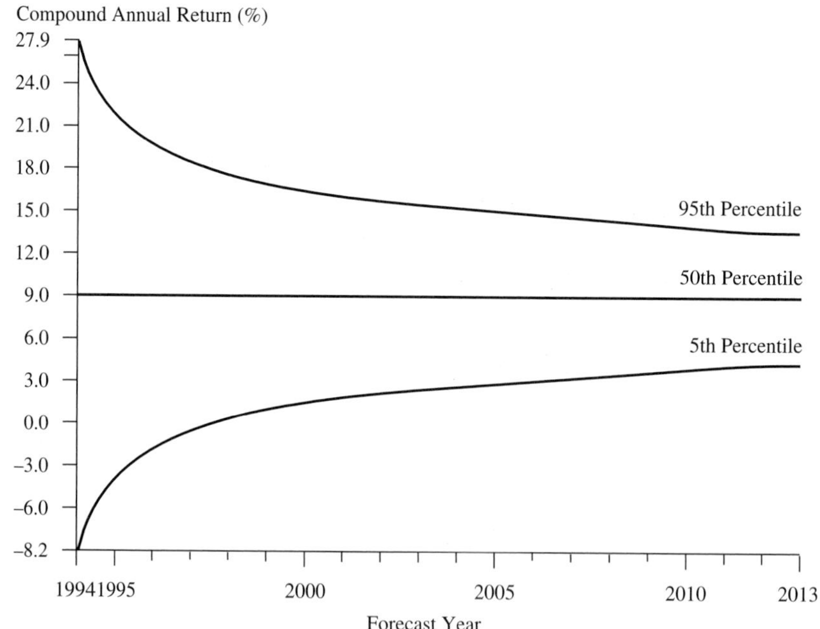


**Figure 7C.1**

Average rates of return on common stocks. Simulated total return distributions for the period 1994–2013. Geometric average annual rates.

Source: © Computed using data from *Stocks, Bonds, Bills, and Inflation: 1996 Yearbook,*™ Ibbotson Associates, Chicago (annually updates work by Roger G. Ibbotson and Rex A. Sinquefield). Used with permission. All rights reserved.

**Figure 7C.2**

Dollar returns on common stocks. Simulated distributions of nominal wealth index for the period 1994–2013 (year-end 1993 equals 1.00).

Source: © Computed using data from *Stocks, Bonds, Bills, and Inflation: 1996 Yearbook,*™ Ibbotson Associates, Chicago (annually updates work by Roger G. Ibbotson and Rex A. Sinquefield). Used with permission. 

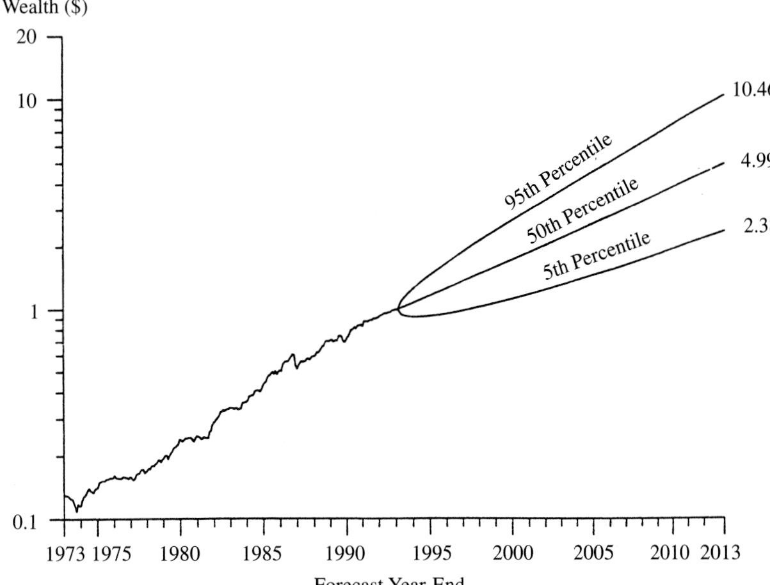

*Part III*

# Equilibrium in Capital Markets

*Chapter 8*

# The Capital Asset Pricing Model

**THE CAPITAL ASSET PRICING MODEL, ALMOST ALWAYS REFERRED TO AS THE CAPM, IS A CENTERPIECE OF MODERN FINANCIAL ECONOMICS.** The model gives us a precise prediction of the relationship that we should observe between the risk of an asset and its expected return. This relationship serves two vital functions. First, it provides a benchmark rate of return for evaluating possible investments. For example, if we are analyzing securities, we might be interested in whether the expected return we forecast for a stock is more or less than its "fair" return, given risk. Second, the model helps us to make an educated guess as to the expected return on assets that have not yet been traded in the marketplace. For example, how do we price an initial public offering of stock? How will a major new investment project affect the return investors require on a company's stock? Although the CAPM does not fully withstand empirical tests, it is widely used both because of the insight if offers and because its accuracy suffices for many important applications.

In this chapter we start with the basic version of the CAPM. We also show how the simple version may be extended without losing the insight and applicability of the model.

## 8.1 THE CAPITAL ASSET PRICING MODEL

The **capital asset pricing model** (CAPM) is a set of predictions concerning equilibrium expected returns on risky assets. We intend to explain it in one short chapter, but do not expect this to be easy going. Harry Markowitz laid down the foundation of modern portfolio management in 1952. The CAPM was developed 12 years later in articles by William Sharpe,[1] John Lintner,[2] and Jan Mossin.[3] The time for this gestation indicates that the leap from Markowitz's portfolio selection model to the CAPM is not trivial.

We will approach the CAPM by posing the question "what if," in which the "if" part refers to a simplified world. Posting an admittedly unrealistic world allows a relatively easy leap to the "then" part. Once we accomplish this, we can add complexity to the hypothesized environment one step at a time and see how the conclusions must be amended. This process allows us to derive a reasonably realistic and comprehensible model.

We can summarize the simplifying assumptions that lead to the basic version of the CAPM in the following list. The thrust of these assumptions is that we try to ensure that individuals are as alike as possible, with the notable exceptions of initial wealth and risk tolerance. We will see that conformity of investor behaviour vastly simplifies our analysis.

1. *There are many investors, each with an endowment (wealth) that is small compared to the total endowment of all investors.* Investors are price takers, in that they act as though security prices are unaffected by their own trades. This is the usual perfect competition assumption of microeconomics.
2. *All investors plan for one identical holding period.* This behaviour sometimes is said to be myopic (short-sighted) in that it ignores everything that might happen after the end of the single-period horizon. Myopic behaviour is, in general, suboptimal.
3. *Investments are limited to a universe of publicly traded financial assets, such as stocks and bonds, and to risk-free borrowing or lending arrangements.* This assumption rules out investment in nontraded assets such as in education (human capital), private enterprises, and governmentally funded assets such as town halls and nuclear submarines. It is assumed also that investors may borrow or lend any amount at a fixed, risk-free rate.
4. *Investors pay no taxes on returns and no transaction costs (commissions and service charges) on trades in securities.* In reality, of course, we know that investors are in different tax brackets and that this may govern the type of assets in which they invest. For example, tax implications may differ depending on whether the income is from interest, dividends, or capital gains. Furthermore, trading is costly, and commissions and fees depend on the size of the trade and the good standing of the individual investor.
5. *All investors are rational mean-variance optimizers, meaning that they all use the Markowitz portfolio selection model.*

---

[1] Sharpe, William, "Capital Asset Prices: A Theory of Market Equilibrium," *Journal of Finance*, September 1964.

[2] Lintner, John, "The Valuation of Risk Assets and the Selection of Risky Investments in Stock Portfolios and Capital Budgets," *Review of Economics and Statistics*, February 1965.

[3] Mossin, Jan, "Equilibrium in a Capital Asset Market," *Econometrica*, October 1966.

6. *All investors analyze securities in the same way and share the same economic view of the world.* The result is identical estimates of the probability distribution of future cash flows from investing in the available securities; that is, for any set of security prices, they all derive the same input list to feed into the Markowitz model. Given a set of security prices and the risk-free interest rate, all investors use the same expected returns and covariance matrix of security returns to generate the efficient frontier and the unique optimal risky portfolio. This assumption often is referred to as **homogeneous expectations** or beliefs.

These assumptions represent the "if" of our "what if" analysis. Obviously, they ignore many real-world complexities. With these assumptions, however, we can gain some powerful insights into the nature of equilibrium in security markets.

We can summarize the equilibrium that will prevail in this hypothetical world of securities and investors briefly. The rest of the chapter explains and elaborates on these implications.

1. All investors will choose to hold a portfolio of risky assets in proportions that duplicate representation of the assets in the **market portfolio** ($M$), which includes all traded assets. For simplicity, we shall often refer to all risky assets as stocks. The proportion of each stock in the market portfolio equals the market value of the stock (price per share multiplied by the number of shares outstanding) divided by the total market value of all stocks.
2. Not only will the market portfolio be on the efficient frontier, but it also will be the tangency portfolio to the optimal capital allocation line (CAL) derived by each and every investor. As a result, the capital market line (CML), the line from the risk-free rate through the market portfolio, $M$, is also the best attainable capital allocation line. All investors hold $M$ as their optimal risky portfolio, differing only in the amount invested in it versus in the risk-free asset.
3. The risk premium on the market portfolio will be proportional to the risk of the market portfolio and the market degree of risk aversion. Mathematically,

$$E(r_M) - r_f = \overline{A}\,\sigma_M^2$$

where $\sigma_M^2$ is the variance of the market portfolio and $A$ is the average degree of risk aversion across investors. Note that because $M$ is the optimal portfolio, which is efficiently diversified across all stocks, $\sigma_M^2$ is the systematic risk of this universe.
4. The risk premium on individual assets will be proportional to the risk premium on the market portfolio, $M$, and the *beta coefficient* of the security, relative to the market portfolio. We will see that beta measures the extent to which returns on the stock and the market move together. Formally, beta is defined as

$$\beta_i = \frac{\text{Cov}(r_i, r_M)}{\sigma_M^2}$$

and we can write

$$E(r_i) - r_f = \frac{\text{Cov}(r_i, r_M)}{\sigma_M^2}[E(r_M) - r_f]$$

$$= \beta_i[E(r_M) - r_f]$$

We will elaborate on these results and their implications shortly.

## Why Do All Investors Hold the Market Portfolio?

Given the assumptions of the previous section, it is easy to see that all investors will desire to hold identical risky portfolios. If all investors use identical Markowitz analysis (assumption 5) applied to the same universe of securities (assumption 3) for the same time horizon (assumption 2) and use the same input list (assumption 6), they all must arrive at the same determination of the optimal risky portfolio, the portfolio on the efficient frontier identified by the tangency line from T-bills to that frontier, as in Figure 8.1. This implies that if the weight of Seagram's (VO) stock, for example, in each common risky portfolio is 1 percent, then when we sum over all investors' portfolios to obtain the aggregate market portfolio, VO also will comprise 1 percent of the market portfolio. The same principle applies to the proportion of any stock in each investor's risky portfolio. As a result, the optimal risky portfolio of all investors is simply a share of the market portfolio, which we label *M* in Figure 8.1.

Now suppose that the optimal portfolio of our investors does not include the stock of some company such as Canadian Tire (CT). When all investors avoid

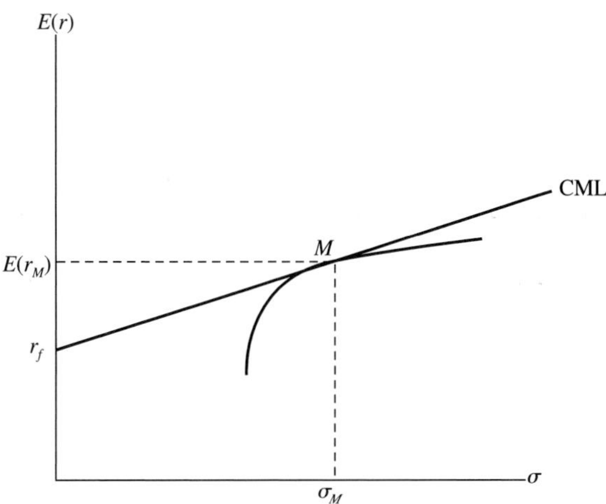


**Figure 8.1**
The efficient frontier and the capital market line.

CT stock, the demand is zero, and CT's price takes a free fall. As CT stock gets progressively cheaper, it becomes ever more attractive as an investment and all other stocks look (relatively) less attractive. Ultimately, CT reaches a price where it is profitable enough to include in the optimal stock portfolio.

Such a price adjustment process guarantees that all stocks will be included in the optimal portfolio. It shows that *all* assets have to be included in the market portfolio. The only issue is the price at which investors will be willing to include a stock in their optimal risky portfolio.

This may seem a roundabout way to derive a simple result: If all investors hold an identical risky portfolio, this portfolio has to be *M,* the market portfolio. Our intention, however, is to demonstrate a connection between this result and its underpinnings, the equilibrating process that is fundamental to security market operation.

## The Passive Strategy Is Efficient

In Chapter 6 we defined the CML (capital market line) as the CAL (capital allocation line) that is constructed from either a money market account or T-bills and the market portfolio. Perhaps now you can fully appreciate why the CML is an interesting CAL. In the simple world of the CAPM, *M* is the optimal tangency portfolio on the efficient frontier. This is shown in Figure 8.1.

In this scenario, the market portfolio, *M,* that all investors hold is based on the common input list, thereby incorporating all relevant information about the universe of securities. This means an investor can skip the trouble of doing specific analysis and obtain an efficient portfolio simply by holding the market portfolio. (Of course, if everyone were to follow this strategy, no one would perform security analysis, and this result would no longer hold. We discuss this issue in depth in Chapter 11 on market efficiency.)

Thus, the passive strategy of investing in a market index portfolio is efficient. For this reason, we sometimes call this result a **mutual fund theorem.** The mutual fund theorem is another incarnation of the separation property discussed in Chapter 7. Assuming that all investors choose to hold a market index mutual fund, we can separate portfolio selection into two components—a technological problem (creation of mutual funds by professional managers) and a personal problem that depends on an investor's risk aversion (allocation of the complete portfolio between the mutual fund and risk-free assets).

---

**CONCEPT CHECK** Question 1. If there are only a few investors who perform security analysis, and all others hold the market portfolio *M,* would the CML still be the efficient CAL for investors who do not engage in security analysis? Why or why not?

---

Of course, in reality different investment managers do create risky portfolios that differ from the market index. We attribute this in part to the use of different input lists in the formation of the optimal risky portfolio. Nevertheless, the significance of the mutual fund theorem is that a passive investor may view the market index as a reasonable first approximation of an efficient risky portfolio.

## The Risk Premium of the Market Portfolio

In Chapter 6 we discussed how individual investors go about deciding how much to invest in the risky portfolio. Returning now to the decision of how much to invest in portfolio $M$ versus in the risk-free asset, what can we deduce about the equilibrium risk premium of portfolio $M$?

We asserted earlier that the equilibrium risk premium on the market portfolio, $E(r_M) - r_f$, will be proportional to the average degree of risk aversion of the investor population and the risk of the market portfolio, $\sigma_M^2$. Now we can explain this result.

Recall that each individual investor chooses a proportion, $y$, allocated to the optimal portfolio $M$, such that

$$y = \frac{E(r_M) - r_f}{A\sigma_M^2} \tag{8.1}$$

In the simplified CAPM economy, risk-free investments involve borrowing and lending among investors. Any borrowing position must be offset by the lending position of the creditor. This means that net borrowing and lending across all investors must be zero and, in consequence, the average position in the risky portfolio is 100 percent, or $\bar{y} = 1$. Setting $y = 1$ in equation 8.1 and rearranging, we find that the risk premium on the market portfolio is related to its variance by the average degree of risk aversion:

$$E(r_M) - r_f = \bar{A}\sigma_M^2 \tag{8.2}$$

---

**CONCEPT CHECK**

Question 2. Data from the period 1957–1994 for the TSE 300 index yield the following statistics: Average excess return, 3.03 percent; standard deviation, 17.16 percent.

*a.* To the extent that these averages approximated investor expectations for the period, what must have been the average coefficient of risk aversion?

*b.* If the coefficient of risk aversion were actually 1.5, what risk premium would have been consistent with the market's historical standard deviation?

---

## Expected Returns on Individual Securities

The CAPM is built on the insight that the appropriate risk premium of an asset will be determined by its contribution to the risk of investors' overall portfolios. Portfolio risk is what matters to investors and governs the risk premiums they demand.

Suppose, for example, that we want to gauge the portfolio risk of Inco stock. We measure the contribution to the risk of the overall portfolio from holding Inco stock by its covariance with the market portfolio. To see why this is so, let us look again at the way the variance of the market portfolio is calculated. To calculate the variance of the market portfolio, we use the covariance matrix bordered by market portfolio weights, as discussed in Chapter 7. We highlight Inco in this depiction of the $n$ stocks in the market portfolio.

| **Portfolio Weights:** | $w_1$ | $w_2$ | ... | $w_I$ | ... | $w_n$ |
|---|---|---|---|---|---|---|
| $w_1$ | $\text{Cov}(r_1,r_1)$ | $\text{Cov}(r_1,r_2)$ | ... | $\text{Cov}(r_1,r_I)$ | ... | $\text{Cov}(r_1,r_n)$ |
| $w_2$ | $\text{Cov}(r_2,r_1)$ | $\text{Cov}(r_2,r_2)$ | ... | $\text{Cov}(r_2,r_I)$ | ... | $\text{Cov}(r_2,r_n)$ |
| · | · | · | | · | | · |
| · | · | · | | · | | · |
| · | · | · | | · | | · |
| $w_I$ | $\text{Cov}(r_I,r_1)$ | | ... | $\text{Cov}(r_I,r_I)$ | ... | $\text{Cov}(r_I,r_n)$ |
| · | · | · | | · | | · |
| · | · | · | | · | | · |
| · | · | · | | · | | · |
| $w_n$ | $\text{Cov}(r_n,r_1)$ | $\text{Cov}(r_n,r_2)$ | ... | $\text{Cov}(r_n,r_I)$ | ... | $\text{Cov}(r_n,r_n)$ |

Recall that we calculate the variance of the portfolio by summing over all the elements of the covariance matrix and multiplying each element by the portfolio weights from the row and the column. The contribution of one stock to portfolio variance therefore can be expressed as the sum of all the covariance terms in the row corresponding to the stock where each covariance is multiplied by both the portfolio weight from its row and the weight from its column.[4]

For example, the contribution of Inco's stock to the variance of the market portfolio is

$$w_I[w_1\text{Cov}(r_1,r_I) + w_2\text{Cov}(r_2,r_I) + \cdots + w_I\text{Cov}(r_I,r_I) + \cdots + w_n\text{Cov}(r_n,r_I)] \quad \textbf{(8.3)}$$

Equation 8.3 provides a clue about the respective roles of variance and covariance in determining asset risk. It shows us that, when there are many stocks in the economy, there will be many more covariance terms than variance terms. Consequently, the covariance of a particular stock with all other stocks might be expected to have more to do with that stock's contribution to total portfolio risk than does its variance. In fact, since each stock in equation 8.3 is weighted by its share in the market portfolio, we may summarize the term in brackets in the equation simply as the covariance of Inco with the market portfolio. In other

---

[4] An alternative and equally valid approach would be to measure Inco's contribution to market variance as the sum of the elements in the row *and* the column corresponding to Inco. In this case, Inco's contribution would be twice the sum in equation 8.3. The approach that we take in the text allocates contributions to portfolio risk among securities in a convenient manner in that the sum of the contributions of each stock equals the total portfolio variance, whereas the alternative measure of contribution would sum to twice the portfolio variance. This results from a type of double-counting, because adding both the rows and the columns for each stock would result in each entry in the matrix being added twice.

words, we can best measure the stock's contribution to the risk of the market portfolio by its covariance with that portfolio.

This should not surprise us. For example, if the covariance between Inco and the rest of the market is negative, then Inco makes a "negative contribution" to portfolio risk: By providing returns that move inversely with the rest of the market, Inco stabilizes the return on the overall portfolio. If the covariance is positive, Inco makes a positive contribution to overall portfolio risk because its returns amplify swings in the rest of the portfolio.

To prove this more rigorously, note that the rate of return on the market portfolio may be written as

$$r_M = \sum_{k=1}^{n} w_k r_k$$

Therefore the covariance of the return on Inco with the market portfolio is

$$\text{Cov}(r_I, r_M) = \text{Cov}\left(r_I, \sum_{k=1}^{n} w_k r_k\right) = \sum_{k=1}^{n} w_k \text{Cov}(r_I, r_k) \quad \textbf{(8.4)}$$

Comparing the last term of equation 8.4 to the term in brackets in equation 8.3, we can see that the covariance of Inco with the market portfolio is indeed proportional to the contribution of Inco to the variance of the market portfolio.

Having measured the contribution of Inco stock to market variance, we may determine the appropriate risk premium for Inco. We note first that the market portfolio has a risk premium of $E(r_M) - r_f$ and a variance of $\sigma_M^2$, for a reward-to-risk ratio of

$$\frac{E(r_M) - r_f}{\sigma_M^2} \quad \textbf{(8.5)}$$

This ratio often is called the **market price of risk**[5] because it quantifies the extra return that investors demand to bear portfolio risk. The ratio of risk premium to variance tells us how much extra return must be earned per unit of portfolio risk.

Suppose that investors wish to increase their position in the market portfolio by a tiny fraction, $\delta$, financed by borrowing at the risk-free rate. The increment to the portfolio expected excess return will be

$$\Delta E(r) = \delta[E(r_M) - r_f]$$

[5] We open ourselves to ambiguity in using this term, because the market portfolio's reward-to-variability ratio

$$\frac{E(r_M) - r_f}{\sigma_M}$$

is also sometimes referred to as the market price of risk.

The portfolio variance will increase by the variance of the incremental position in the market *plus* twice its covariance with the original position (100% in the market):

$$\Delta\sigma^2 = \delta^2\sigma_M^2 + 2\delta\text{Cov}(r_M,r_M)$$

If $\delta$ is infinitesimal, then its square will be negligible,[6] leaving the incremental variance as

$$\Delta\sigma^2 = 2\delta\text{Cov}(r_M,r_M) = 2\delta\sigma_M^2$$

The trade-off between the *incremental risk premium* and *incremental risk,* referred to as the *marginal price of risk,* is given by the ratio

$$\frac{\Delta E(r)}{\Delta\sigma^2} = \frac{E(r_M - r_f)}{2\sigma_M^2}$$

and equals one half the market price of risk in equation 8.5.

Now suppose that, instead, investors were to invest the increment $\delta$ in Inco stock, financed by borrowing at the risk-free rate. The increase in mean excess return is

$$\Delta E(r) = \delta[E(r_I) - r_f]$$

The increase in variance, here too, includes the variance of the incremental position in Inco *plus* twice its covariance with the market:

$$\Delta\sigma^2 = \delta^2\sigma_I^2 + 2\delta\text{Cov}(r_I,r_M)$$

Dropping the negligible term, the *marginal price* of risk of Inco is

$$\frac{\Delta E(r)}{\Delta\sigma^2} = \frac{E(r_I) - r_f}{2\text{Cov}(r_I,r_M)}$$

In equilibrium, the marginal price of risk of Inco stock has to equal that of the market portfolio. This is because, when the marginal price of risk of Inco is greater than the market's, investors can increase their portfolio *average* price of risk by increasing the weight of Inco in their portfolio. Moreover, as long as the price of Inco stock does not rise relative to the market, investors will keep buying Inco stock. The process will continue until stock prices adjust, so that the marginal price of risk of Inco equals that of the market. (The same process, in reverse, will equalize marginal prices of risk when Inco's initial marginal price of risk is less than that of the market portfolio.) Equating the marginal price of risk of Inco's stock to that of the market gets us the relationship between the risk premium of Inco and that of the market:

---

[6] For example, if $\delta$ is 1% (.01 of wealth), then its square is .0001 of wealth, one hundredth of the original value. The term $\delta\sigma_M^2$ will be smaller than $2\delta\text{Cov}(r_M,r_M)$ by an order of magnitude.

$$\frac{E(r_I) - r_f}{2\text{Cov}(r_I,r_M)} = \frac{E(r_M) - r_f}{2\sigma_M^2}$$

To determine the fair risk premium for Inco stock, we need only multiply the risk that Inco stock contributes to the variance of the market portfolio, which is $\text{Cov}(r_I,r_M)$, by the market price of risk. We thus find that $E(r_I) - r_f$, which is Inco's risk premium, should be

$$E(r_I) - r_f = \text{Cov}(r_I,r_M) \times \frac{E(r_M) - r_f}{\sigma_M^2}$$

Rearranging slightly, we obtain

$$E(r_I) - r_f = \frac{\text{Cov}(r_I,r_M)}{\sigma_M^2}[E(r_M) - r_f] \qquad \textbf{(8.6)}$$

The term $\text{Cov}(r_I,r_M)/\sigma_M^2$ measures the contribution of Inco stock to the variance of the market portfolio as a fraction of the total variance of the market portfolio and is referred to by the Greek letter **beta,** $\beta$. Using this measure, we can restate equation 8.6 as

$$E(r_I) = r_f + \beta_I[E(r_M) - r_f] \qquad \textbf{(8.7)}$$

This **expected return–beta relationship** is the most familiar expression of the CAPM to practitioners. We will have a lot more to say about the expected return–beta relationship shortly.

We see now why the assumptions that made individuals act similarly are so useful. If everyone holds an identical risky portfolio, then everyone will find that the beta of each asset with the market portfolio equals the asset's beta with his or her own risky portfolio. Hence, everyone will agree on the appropriate risk premium for each asset.

Does this mean that the fact that few real-life investors actually hold the market portfolio implies that the CAPM is of no practical importance? Not necessarily. Recall from Chapter 7 that reasonably well-diversified portfolios shed firm-specific risk and are left with only systematic or market risk. Even if one does not hold the precise market portfolio, a well-diversified portfolio will be so very highly correlated with the market that a stock's beta relative to the market still will be a useful risk measure.

In fact, several authors have shown that modified versions of the CAPM will hold true even if we consider differences among individuals leading them to hold different portfolios. For example, Brennan[7] examines the impact of differences in investors' personal tax rates on market equilibrium, and Mayers[8] looks at the

---

[7] Michael J. Brennan, "Taxes, Market Valuation, and Corporate Finance Policy," *National Tax Journal,* December 1973.

[8] David Mayers, "Nonmarketable Assets and Capital Market Equilibrium under Uncertainty," in M. C. Jensen (editor), *Studies in the Theory of Capital Markets* (New York: Praeger, 1972).

impact of nontraded assets, such as human capital (earning power). Both find that, although the market is no longer each investor's optimal risky portfolio, the expected return–beta relationship still should hold in a somewhat modified form.

If the expected return–beta relationship holds for any individual asset, it must hold for any combination of assets. Suppose that some portfolio $P$ has weight $w_k$ for stock $k$, where $k$ takes on values $1, \ldots, n$. Writing out the CAPM equation 8.7 for each stock and multiplying each equation by the weight of the stock in the portfolio, we obtain these equations, one for each stock:

$$\begin{aligned} w_1E(r_1) &= w_1r_f + w_1\beta_1[E(r_M) - r_f] \\ +\ w_2E(r_2) &= w_2r_f + w_2\beta_2[E(r_M) - r_f] \\ +\quad \ldots &= \ldots \\ +\ w_nE(r_n) &= w_nr_f + w_n\beta_n[E(r_M) - r_f] \\ \hline E(r_P) &= r_f + \beta_P[E(r_M) - r_f] \end{aligned}$$

Summing each column shows that the CAPM holds for the overall portfolio because $E(r_P) = \sum_k w_kE(r_k)$ is the expected return on the portfolio and $\beta_P = \sum_k w_k\beta_k$ is the portfolio beta. Incidentally, this result has to be true for the market portfolio itself.

$$E(r_M) = r_f + \beta_M[E(r_M) - r_f]$$

Indeed, this is a tautology because $\beta_M = 1$, as we can verify by demonstrating that

$$\beta_M = \frac{\text{Cov}(r_M,r_M)}{\sigma_M^2} = \frac{\sigma_M^2}{\sigma_M^2}$$

This also establishes 1 as the weighted average value of beta across all assets. If the market beta is 1, and the market is a portfolio of all assets in the economy, the weighted average beta of all assets must be 1. Hence betas greater than 1 are considered aggressive in that investment in high-beta stocks entails above-average sensitivity to market swings. Betas below 1 can be described as defensive.

---

**CONCEPT CHECK** Question 3. Suppose that the risk premium on the market portfolio is estimated at 8 percent with a standard deviation of 22 percent. What is the risk premium on a portfolio invested 25 percent in Inco and 75 percent in Noranda, if both have a beta of 1.15?

---

A word of caution: We all are accustomed to hearing that well-managed firms will provide high rates of return. We agree this is true if one measures the *firm's* return on investments in plant and equipment. The CAPM, however, predicts returns on investments in the *securities* of the firm.

Let us say that everyone knows a firm is well run. Its stock price will therefore be bid up and, consequently, returns to stockholders who buy at those high prices will not be excessive. Security prices, in other words, reflect public information about a firm's prospects, but only the risk of the company (as measured by beta in the context of the CAPM) should affect expected returns. In a rational market investors receive high expected returns only if they are willing to bear risk.

## The Security Market Line

We can view the expected return–beta relationship as a reward-risk equation. The beta of a security is the appropriate measure of its risk because beta is proportional to the risk that the security contributes to the optimal risky portfolio.

Risk-averse investors measure the risk of the optimal risky portfolio by its variance. In this world we would expect the reward, or the risk premium on individual assets, to depend on the risk that an individual asset contributes to the portfolio. The beta of a stock measures the stock's contribution to the variance of the market portfolio as a fraction of the total portfolio variance. Hence we expect, for any asset or portfolio, the required risk premium to be a function of beta. The CAPM confirms this intuition, stating further that the security's risk premium is directly proportional to both the beta and the risk premium of the market portfolio; that is, the risk premium equals

$$\beta[E(r_M) - r_f]$$

The expected return–beta relationship can be portrayed graphically as the **security market line** (SML) in Figure 8.2. Its slope is the risk premium of the market portfolio. At the point where $\beta = 1$ on the horizontal axis (which is the

**Figure 8.2**
The security market line.

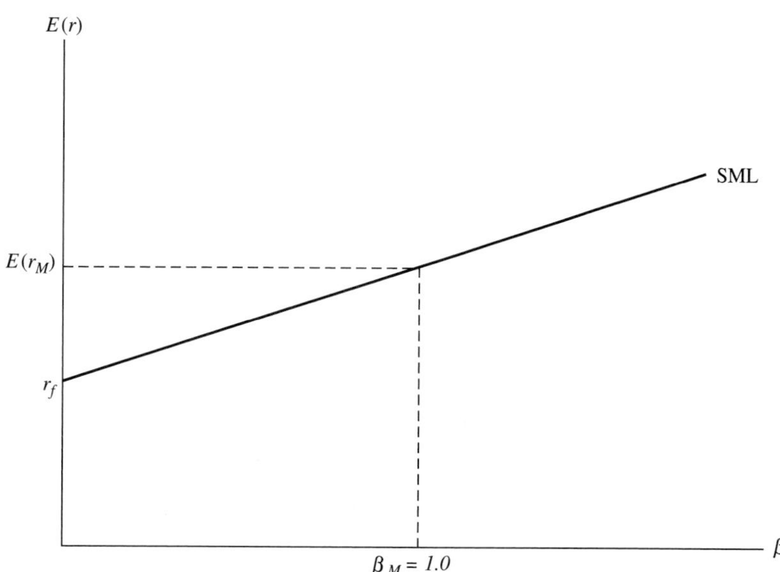

market portfolio's beta), we can read off the vertical axis the expected return on the market portfolio.

It is useful to compare the security market line to the capital market line. The CML graphs the risk premiums of efficient portfolios (that is, portfolios composed of the market and the risk-free asset) as a function of portfolio standard deviation. This is appropriate because standard deviation is a valid measure of risk for efficiently diversified portfolios that are candidates for an investor's overall portfolio. The SML, in contrast, graphs *individual asset* risk premiums as a function of asset risk. The relevant measure of risk for individual assets held as parts of well-diversified portfolios is not the asset's standard deviation or variance; it is, instead, the contribution of the asset to the portfolio variance, which we measure by the asset's beta. The SML is valid for both efficient portfolios and individual assets.

The security market line provides a benchmark for the evaluation of investment performance. Given the risk of an investment, as measured by its beta, the SML provides the required rate of return from that investment to compensate investors for risk, as well as the time value of money.

Because the security market line is the graphic representation of the expected return–beta relationship, "fairly priced" assets plot exactly on the SML; that is, their expected returns are commensurate with their risk. Given the assumptions we made in the beginning of this section, all securities must lie on the SML in market equilibrium. Nevertheless, we see here how the CAPM may be of use in the money-management industry. Suppose that the SML relation is used as a benchmark to assess the fair expected return on a risky asset. Then security analysis is performed to calculate the return actually expected. (Notice that we depart here from the simple CAPM world in that some investors now apply their own unique analysis to derive an "input list" that may differ from their competitors'.) If a stock is perceived to be a good buy, or underpriced, it will provide an expected return in excess of the fair return stipulated by the SML. Underpriced stocks, therefore, plot above the SML: given their betas, their expected returns are greater than dictated by the CAPM. Overpriced stocks plot below the SML.

The difference between the fair and actually expected rates of return on a stock is called the stock's **alpha,** denoted $\alpha$. For example, if the market is expected to be 14 percent, a stock has a beta of 1.2, and the T-bill rate is 10 percent, the SML would predict an expected return on the stock of $10 + 1.2\ (14 - 10) = 14.8$ percent. If one believed the stock would provide a return of 17 percent, the implied alpha would be 2.2 percent (see Figure 8.3).

---

**CONCEPT CHECK**

Question 4. Stock XYZ has an expected return of 12 percent and risk of $\beta = 1$. Stock ABC has expected return of 13 percent and $\beta = 1.5$. The market's expected return is 11 percent and $r_f = 5$ percent.

*a.* According to the CAPM, which stock is a better buy?

*b.* What is the alpha of each stock? Plot the SML and each stock's risk return point on one graph. Show the alphas graphically.

---

**Figure 8.3**
The SML and a positive-alpha stock.

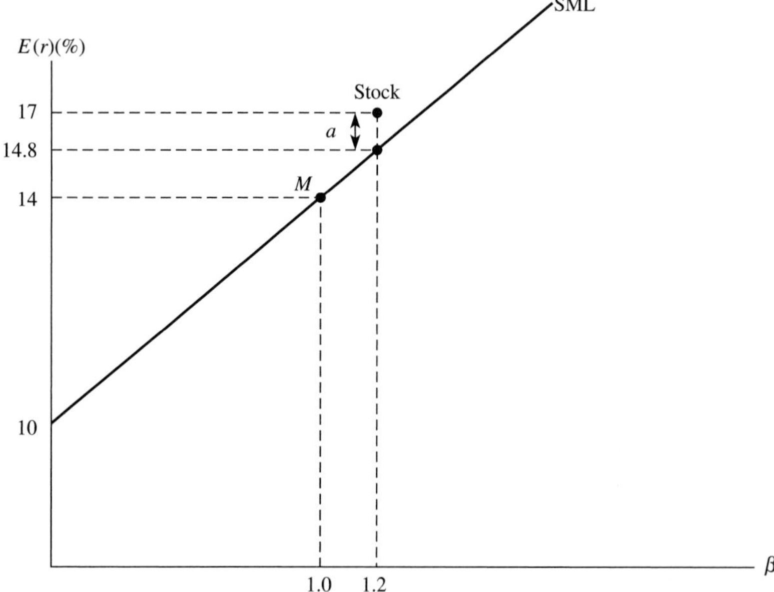


The CAPM also is useful in capital budgeting decisions. For a firm considering a new project, the CAPM can provide the return that the project needs to yield, based on its beta, to be acceptable to investors. Managers can use the CAPM to obtain this cutoff internal rate of return (IRR) or "hurdle rate" for the project.

---

**CONCEPT CHECK** Question 5. The risk-free rate is 8 percent and the expected return on the market portfolio is 12 percent. A firm considers a project that is expected to have a beta of 1.3.

*a.* What is the required rate of return on the project?
*b.* If the expected IRR of the project is 15 percent, should it be accepted?

---

Yet another use of the CAPM is in utility rate-making cases. In this case, the issue is the rate of return that a regulated utility should be allowed to earn on its investment in plant and equipment. Suppose that the equityholders have invested \$100 million in the firm and that the beta of the equity is .6. If the T-bill rate is 6 percent and the market risk premium is 4 percent, then the fair profits to the firm would be assessed as $6 + .6(4) = 8.4$ percent of the \$100 million investment, or \$8.4 million. The firm would be allowed to set prices at a level expected to generate these profits.

## 8.2 Extensions of the CAPM

The assumptions that allowed Sharpe to derive the simple version of the CAPM are admittedly unrealistic. Financial economists have been at work ever since the CAPM was devised to extend the model to more realistic scenarios.

There are two classes of extensions to the simple version of the CAPM. The first attempts to relax the assumptions that we outlined at the outset of the chapter. The second acknowledges the fact that investors worry about sources of risk other than the uncertain value of their securities, such as unexpected changes in the relative prices of consumer goods. This idea involves the introduction of additional risk factors besides security returns, and we will discuss it later in this chapter.

### The CAPM with Restricted Borrowing: The Zero-Beta Model

The CAPM is predicated on the assumption that all investors share an identical input list that they feed into the Markowitz algorithm. Thus all investors agree on the location of the efficient (minimum-variance) frontier, where each portfolio has the lowest variance among all feasible portfolios at a target expected rate of return. When all investors can borrow and lend at the safe rate, $r_f$, all agree on the optimal tangency portfolio and choose to hold a share of the market portfolio.

When there are constraints on risk-free lending and/or borrowing, we will see that the market portfolio is no longer the common optimal portfolio for all investors. One "restriction" on risk-free borrowing and lending is that, in a strict sense, once we account for inflation uncertainty there is no truly risk-free asset in the Canadian economy. Only treasury securities are entirely free of default risk, but these are nominal obligations, meaning that their real values are exposed to price level risk. In this sense, there is no risk-free asset in the economy. Other restrictions have to do with differences in the rates at which investors can borrow and lend.

When investors no longer can borrow or lend at a common risk-free rate, they may choose risky portfolios from the entire set of efficient frontier portfolios according to how much risk they choose to bear. The market is no longer the common optimal portfolio. In fact, with investors choosing different portfolios, it is no longer obvious whether the market portfolio, which is the aggregate of all investors' portfolios, will even be on the efficient frontier. If the market portfolio is no longer mean-variance efficient, then the expected return-beta relationship of the CAPM will no longer characterize market equilibrium.

An equilibrium expected return–beta relationship in the case of restricted risk-free investments has been developed by Fischer Black.[9] Black's model is fairly difficult and requires a good deal of facility with mathematics. Therefore, we will

[9] Fischer Black, "Capital Market Equilibrium with Restricted Borrowing," *Journal of Business,* July 1972.

satisfy ourselves with a sketch of Black's argument and spend more time with its implications.

Black's model of the CAPM in the absence of a risk-free asset rests on the three following properties of mean-variance efficient portfolios:

1. Any portfolio constructed by combining efficient portfolios is itself on the efficient frontier.
2. Every portfolio on the efficient frontier has a companion portfolio on the bottom half (the inefficient part) of the minimum-variance frontier with which it is uncorrelated. Because the portfolios are uncorrelated, the companion portfolio is referred to as the **zero-beta portfolio** of the efficient portfolio.

   The expected return of an efficient portfolio's zero-beta companion portfolio can be derived by the following graphical procedure. From any efficient portfolio such as *P* in Figure 8.4 draw a tangency line to the vertical axis. The intercept will be the expected return on portfolio *P*'s zero-beta companion portfolio, denoted *Z(P)*. The horizontal line from the intercept to the minimum-variance frontier identifies the standard deviation of the zero-beta portfolio. Notice in Figure 8.4 that different efficient portfolios such as *P* and *Q* have different zero-beta companions.

   These tangency lines are only helpful constructs—they do *not* signify that one can invest in portfolios with expected return-standard deviation pairs along the line. That would be possible only by mixing a risk-free asset

**Figure 8.4**
Efficient portfolios and their zero-beta companions.

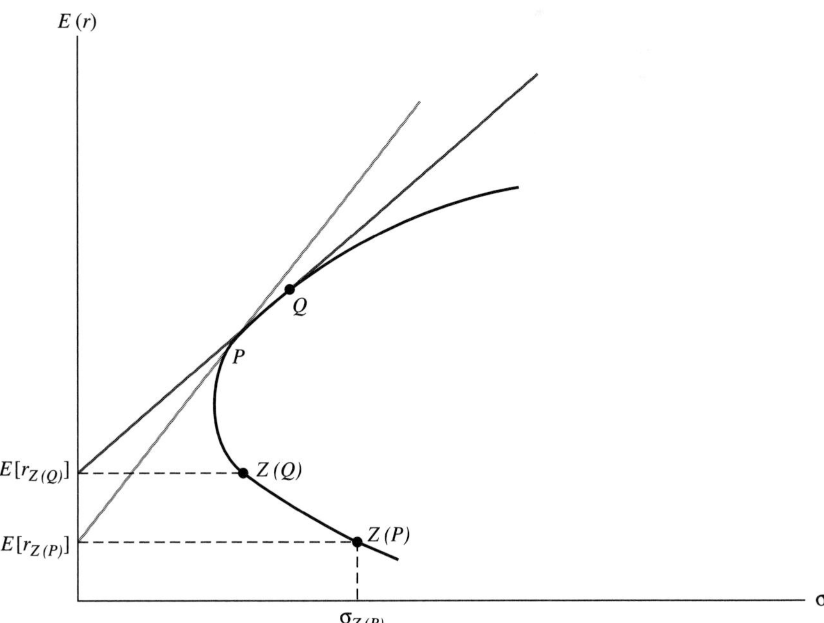

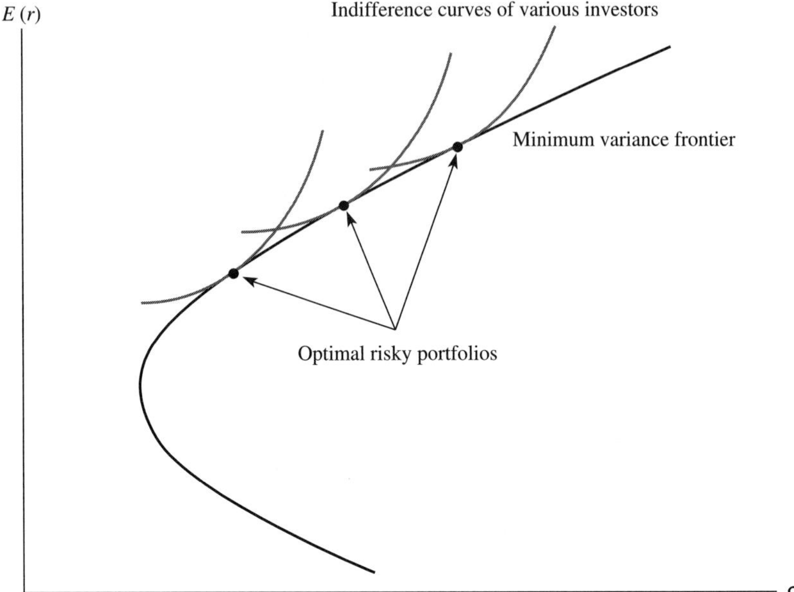


**Figure 8.5**
Portfolio selection with no risk-free assets.

with the tangency portfolio. In this case, however, we assume that risk-free assets are not available to investors.

3. The expected return of any asset can be expressed as an exact, linear function of the expected return on any two frontier portfolios. Consider, for example, the minimum-variance frontier portfolios *P* and *Q*. Black shows that the expected return on any asset *i* can be expressed as

$$E(r_i) = E(r_Q) + [E(r_P) - E(r_Q)]\frac{\text{Cov}(r_i,r_P) - \text{Cov}(r_P,r_Q)}{\sigma_P^2 - \text{Cov}(r_P,r_Q)} \quad \textbf{(8.8)}$$

Note that this last property has nothing to do with the market equilibrium. It is a purely mathematical property relating frontier portfolios and individual securities.

Given these three properties, it is easy to derive Black's model. The assumption of homogeneous expectations assures us that all investors use the same input list and compute the same minimum-variance frontier. Each investor will invest in an efficient portfolio according to his or her degree of risk aversion, as in Figure 8.5. The market portfolio, which is just the aggregate of all investors' portfolios, therefore is a combination of efficient portfolios and, by property 1, must itself be an efficient portfolio.

Next, recall equation 8.8 from property 3. Instead of using the arbitrarily chosen frontier portfolios *P* and *Q* in the equation, let us instead use as our two frontier portfolios the market portfolio, *M,* and its zero-beta companion, *Z(M).* This is a convenient pairing of portfolios because their mutual covariance is zero,

**Figure 8.6**
Capital market equilibrium with risk-free lending but no risk-free borrowing.

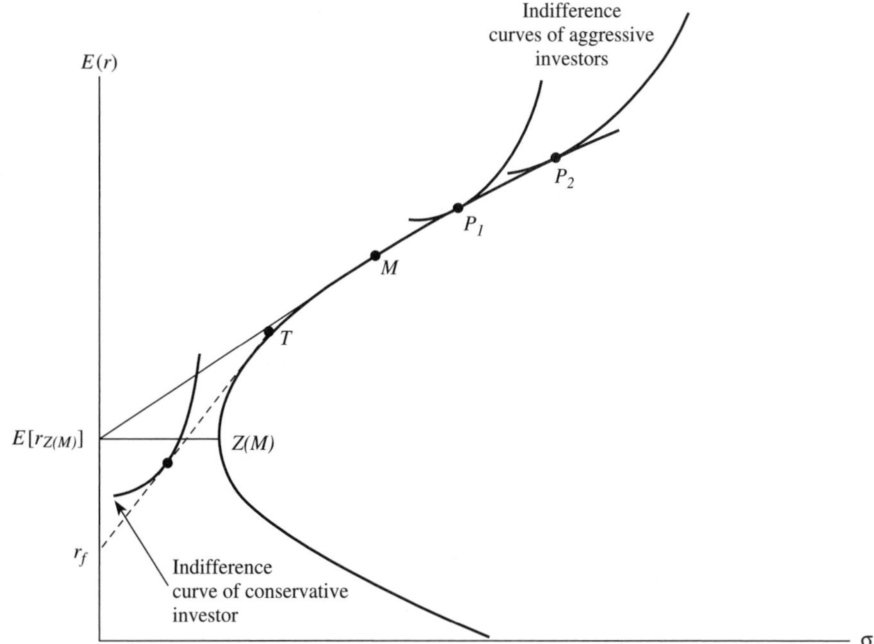


causing equation 8.8 to simplify. Specifically, because $\text{Cov}[r_M, r_{Z(M)}] = 0$, the expected return of any asset *i*, using *M* and *Z(M)* as the benchmark frontier portfolios, can be expressed as

$$E(r_i) = E[r_{Z(M)}] + E[r_M - r_{Z(M)}]\frac{\text{Cov}(r_i, r_M)}{\sigma_M^2} \tag{8.9}$$

where *P* from equation 8.8 has been replaced by *M* and *Q* has been replaced by *Z(M)*. Note that this is a variant of the simple CAPM, in which $r_f$ simply has been replaced with $E[r_{Z(M)}]$.

Although Black derived this variant of the CAPM for the case in which no risk-free asset exists, the approach we have taken can be applied to many related scenarios. For example, consider an economy in which investors can lend at the risk-free rate (can buy T-bills, for example) but cannot borrow funds to invest. We first explored portfolio selection for this situation in Section 7.5. Now we can explore market equilibrium.

Figure 8.6 shows that relatively conservative (risk-averse) investors will select the tangency portfolio, *T,* as their optimal risk portfolio and mix *T* with the safe asset. Relatively aggressive investors will choose efficient portfolios like $P_1$ or $P_2$. The market portfolio, *M,* will be a combination of these portfolios, all of which are efficient, meaning that the market also will be an efficient portfolio. Therefore, the zero-beta version of the CAPM will apply in this situation also.

A more realistic scenario is one in which the investor can lend at the risk-free rate, $r_f$, and borrow at a higher rate, $r_f^B$. This case also was considered in Chapter 7. The same arguments that we have just employed also can be used to establish the zero-beta CAPM in this situation. Problem 18 at the end of this chapter asks you to fill in the details of the argument for this situation.

---

**CONCEPT CHECK** Question 6. Suppose that the zero-beta portfolio exhibits returns that are, on average, greater than the rate on T-bills. Is this fact relevant to the question of the validity of the CAPM?

---

## Lifetime Consumption: The CAPM with Dynamic Programming

One of the restrictive assumptions of the simple version of the CAPM is that investors are myopic—they plan for one common holding period. Investors actually may be concerned with a lifetime consumption plan and a possible desire to leave a bequest to children. Consumption plans that are feasible for them depend on current wealth and future rates of return on the investment portfolio. These investors will want to rebalance their portfolios as often as required by changes in wealth.

However, Eugene Fama[10] shows that, even if we extend our analysis to a multiperiod setting, the single CAPM still may be appropriate. The key assumptions that Fama uses to replace myopic planning horizons are that investor preferences are unchanging over time and that the risk-free interest rate and probability distribution of security returns do not change unpredictably over time. Of course, this latter assumption is itself somewhat unrealistic. Extensions to the CAPM engendered by considering random changes to the so-called "investment opportunity set" are examined next.

## The Multifactor CAPM

The CAPM describes a fundamental expected return–beta relationship. Such a simple relationship implies that investors are concerned with, and hedge, only one source of risk: uncertainty about future security prices. In reality, investors must deal with many other sources of risk. Among these are:

1. Uncertain labour income.
2. Uncertain life expectancy.
3. Uncertain future investment opportunities.
4. Uncertain prices of consumption goods, such as oil or housing prices.

Investors will attempt to hedge these risks to the greatest extent possible. They will want to hold hedge portfolios that will reduce these additional uncertainties.

---

[10] Eugene F. Fama, "Multiperiod Consumption-Investment Decisions," *American Economic Review 60* (1970).

These extra hedging demands mean that our earlier treatment of portfolio demands must be modified.

Robert Merton[11] is responsible for the development of an expanded CAPM that accounts for the potential effects of these extra sources of uncertainty on security prices. The focal point of the model is not dollar returns per se but the consumption and investment made possible by an individual's wealth. Investors facing a broad list of risk factors must do more than hedge just the dollar value of their portfolios.

Suppose, for instance, that investors are concerned about oil price shocks, such as those that hit the North American economies during the 1970s and 1980s. In addition to the direct effect of the dramatic fluctuations in oil prices on stock market values, consumers and investors found that oil prices had substantial effects on unemployment and inflation, as well as on their own consumption. For most investors, oil price uncertainty had more impact in regard to their activities as consumers and employees than it did in regard to the value of energy stocks that they may have held in their portfolios.

It would not be surprising for individuals to search for investment vehicles to offset, or hedge, the risk they face from oil price uncertainty. A natural hedge security would be shares of energy sector stocks that should do well when the rest of the economy is harmed by an oil price shock. Investors would thus form hedge portfolios of such energy stocks to offset their oil price exposure. The optimal risky portfolio would then be one that adds to the market portfolio an additional position in the hedge portfolio of energy stocks.

This extra demand for energy stocks would change the prices and rates of return of these stocks. Because of their hedging value, investors would be willing to hold them even with an expected rate of return lower than that dictated by the simple CAPM. The simple expected return–beta relationship, therefore, needs to be generalized to account for the effects of extramarket hedging demands on equilibrium rates of return.

Merton has shown that these hedging demands will result in an expanded or "multifactor" version of the CAPM that recognizes the multidimensional nature of risk. For instance, in the case of oil price risk, Merton's model would imply that the expected return–beta relationship of the simple CAPM would be generalized to the following two-factor relationship:

$$E(r_1) - r_f = \beta_{iM}[E(r_M) - r_f] + \beta_{io}[E(r_o) - r_f]$$

where $\beta_{iM}$ is the beta of security $i$ with respect to the market portfolio, $\beta_{io}$ is the beta with respect to oil price risk, and $r_o$ is the rate of return on the portfolio that best hedges oil price uncertainty. The additional risk premium, $[E(r_o) - r_f]$, is associated with exposure to oil price uncertainty. More generally, we will have a beta and a risk premium for every significant source of risk that consumers try to hedge.

[11] Robert C. Merton, "An Intertemporal Capital Asset Pricing Model," *Econometrica* 41 (1973).

The multifactor CAPM provides us with a guide as to what kind of deviations from the single source of risk CAPM we can expect for various securities. The model does not resolve all issues, however. We must determine which sources of risk are indeed priced in capital markets and what portfolios most efficiently hedge those risks; this adds further complexity on top of the simple CAPM. We shall return to this topic at the end of the next chapter.

## 8.3 The CAPM and Liquidity: A Theory of Illiquidity Premiums

**Liquidity** refers to the cost and ease with which an asset can be converted into cash, that is, sold. Traders have long recognized the importance of liquidity, and some evidence suggests that illiquidity can reduce market prices substantially. For example, one study[12] finds that market discounts on closely held (and therefore nontraded) firms can exceed 30 percent. It also reports on an unusual class of stocks that was issued with a provision that prohibited public trading for two to three years, which traded at a discount of about 30 percent. Interestingly, such a discount is similar to the three-year risk premium on an average stock, which has been between 8 and 9 percent per year. This suggests that premiums for illiquidity can be roughly of the same magnitude as risk premiums and may deserve a comparable amount of attention.

A rigorous treatment of the value of liquidity has been developed by Amihud and Mendelson.[13] We believe that liquidity will become an important part of standard valuation and therefore present here a simplified version of their model.

Recall assumption 4 of the CAPM, that all trading is costless. In reality, no security is perfectly liquid, in that all trades involve some transaction cost. Investors prefer more liquid assets with lower transaction costs, so it should not surprise us to find that (all else being equal) relatively illiquid assets trade at lower prices, or equivalently, that the expected rate of return on illiquid assets must be higher. Therefore, an **illiquidity premium** must be impounded into the price of each asset. The impact of liquidity will depend on both the distribution of transaction costs across assets as well as the distribution of investors across investment horizons. We will use very simplified distributions to illustrate the effect of liquidity on equilibrium expected returns. However, you will see that these simplifications are expositional only and that the predicted effect of liquidity on equilibrium returns is quite general.

We will start with the simplest case, in which we can ignore systematic risk. Imagine, therefore, a world with a very large number of uncorrelated securities. Because the securities are uncorrelated, highly diversified portfolios of these se-

[12] Shannon P. Pratt, *Valuing a Business: The Analysis of Closely Held Companies,* 2nd ed. (Homewood, Ill.: Dow Jones–Irwin, 1989).

[13] Yakov Amihud and Haim Mendelson, "Asset Pricing and the Bid-Ask Spread," *Journal of Financial Economics* 17 (1986), pp. 223–49.

curities will have standard deviations nearly equal to zero. Therefore, the diversified market portfolio will be virtually as safe as the risk-free asset and yield an expected return equal to the risk-free rate. Moreover, the covariance between any pair of securities also is zero, implying that the beta of any security with the diversified market portfolio is zero. Therefore, according to the CAPM, all assets should have expected rates of return equal to that of the risk-free asset, which we will take to be T-bills.

Assume that investors know in advance for how long they intend to hold their portfolios, and suppose that there are $n$ types of investors, grouped by investment horizon. Type 1 investors intend to liquidate their portfolios in one period, type 2 investors in two periods, and so on, until the longest-horizon investors (type $n$) intend to hold their portfolios for $n$ periods.

Because we are now dealing with a multiperiod model, we should be careful in our comparison with the single-period CAPM. However, we've seen that Fama's work (see footnote 10) implies that even if investors have multiperiod investment horizons, the simple expected return–beta relationship of the CAPM still might describe equilibrium security returns. To stay as close as possible to Fama's assumptions, we will assume that as investors liquidate their portfolios, just enough investors of each type enter the market to take the place of those who depart. Thus, in each period, there is identical demand for securities, as Fama requires. However, even with these assumptions, the presence of trading costs *in conjunction with* differing investment horizons will require an adaptation of the CAPM.

We start with a simple structure of transactions costs as well, assuming that there are only two classes of securities: liquid and illiquid. These types of securities differ in their liquidation cost, the cost of selling the security at the end of the investment horizon. The liquidation cost of a class L (more liquid) stock to an investor with a horizon of $h$ years (a type $h$ investor) will reduce the per-period rate of return by $c_L/h$ percent. For example, if the combination of commissions and the bid-ask spread on a security resulted in a liquidation cost of 10 percent, then the per-period rate of return for an investor who holds the stock for 5 years would be reduced by approximately 2 percent per year, while the return on a 10-year investment would fall by only 1 percent per year.[14] Class I (illiquid) assets have higher liquidation costs that reduce the per-period return by $c_I/h$ percent, where $c_I$ is greater than $c_L$. Therefore, if you intend to hold a class L security for $h$ periods, your expected rate of return *net* of transaction costs is $E(r_L) - c_L/h$. There is no liquidation cost on T-bills.

The following table presents the expected rates of return investors would realize from the risk-free asset and class L and class I stock portfolios *assuming* that the simple CAPM is correct and all securities have an expected rate of return of $r$.

[14] This simple structure of liquidation costs allows us to derive a correspondingly simple solution for the effect of liquidity on expected returns. Amihud and Mendelson use a more general formulation but then need to rely on complex and more difficult-to-interpret mathematical programming. All that matters for the qualitative results below, however, is that illiquidity costs be less onerous to longer-term investors.

| **Asset:** | **Risk-Free** | **Class L** | **Class I** |
|---|---|---|---|
| Gross rate of return: | $r$ | $r$ | $r$ |
| One-period liquidation cost: | 0 | $c_L$ | $c_I$ |
| **Investor Type** | | **Net Rate of Return** | |
| 1 | $r$ | $r - c_L$ | $r - c_I$ |
| 2 | $r$ | $r - c_L/2$ | $r - c_I/2$ |
| . . . | . . . | . . . | . . . |
| $n$ | $r$ | $r - c_L/n$ | $r - c_I/n$ |

These net rates of return are inconsistent with a market in equilibrium, because with equal gross rates of return of $r$, all investors would prefer to invest in zero-transaction-cost T-bills. As a result, both class L and class I stock prices must fall, causing their expected rates of return to rise until investors are willing to hold these shares.

Suppose, therefore, that each gross return is higher by some fraction of liquidation cost. Specifically, assume that the gross expected rate of return on class L stocks is $r + xc_L$ and that of class I stocks is $r + yc_I$, where $x$ and $y$ are smaller than 1. (These fractions must be less than 1, or else diversified stock portfolios would dominate the risk-free asset in terms of net returns.) The *net* rate of return on class L stocks to an investor with a horizon of $h$ will be $(r + xc_L) - c_L/h = r + c_L(x - 1/h)$. In general, the rates of return to investors will be

| **Asset:** | **Risk-Free** | **Class L** | **Class I** |
|---|---|---|---|
| Gross rate of return: | $r$ | $r + xc_L$ | $r + yc_I$ |
| One-period liquidation cost: | 0 | $c_L$ | $c_I$ |
| **Investor Type** | | **Net Rate of Return** | |
| 1 | $r$ | $r + c_L(x - 1)$ | $r + c_I(y - 1)$ |
| 2 | $r$ | $r + c_L(x - 1/2)$ | $r + c_I(y - 1/2)$ |
| . . . | . . . | . . . | . . . |
| n | $r$ | $r + c_L(x - 1/n)$ | $r + c_I(y - 1/n)$ |

Notice that the liquidation cost has a greater impact on per-period returns for short-term investors. This is because the cost is amortized over fewer periods. As the horizon becomes very large, the per-period impact of the transaction cost approaches zero and the net rate of return approaches the gross rate.

Figure 8.7 graphs the net rate of return on the three asset classes for investors of differing horizons. The more illiquid stock has the lowest net rate of return for very short investment horizons because of its large liquidation costs. However, in equilibrium, the stock must be priced at a level that offers a rate of return high enough to induce some investors to hold it, implying that its gross rate of return must be higher than that of the more liquid stock. Therefore, for long enough

**Figure 8.7**
Net return as a function of investment horizon.

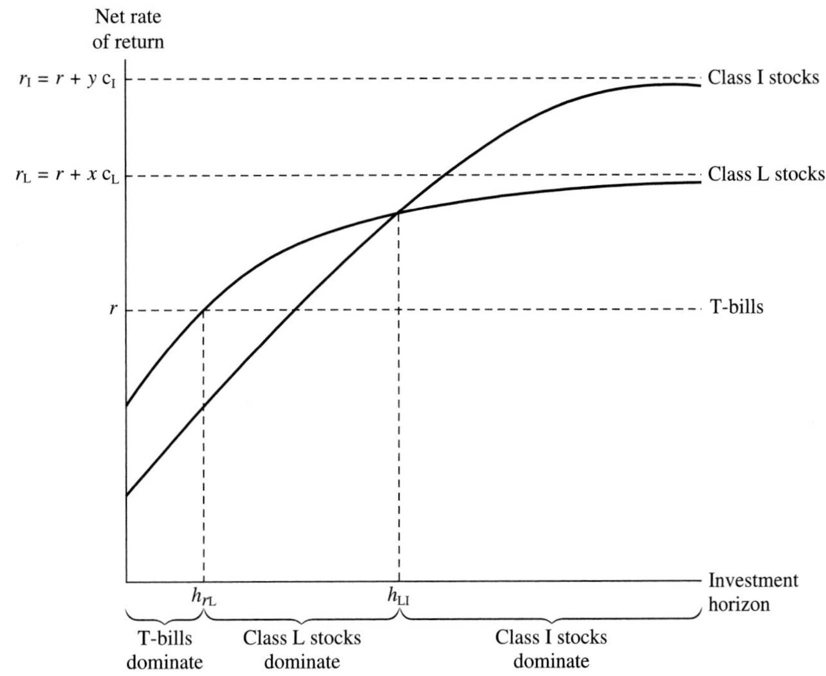


investment horizons, the net return on class I stocks will exceed that on class L stocks.

Both stock classes underperform T-bills for very short investment horizons, because the transactions costs then have the largest per-period impact. Ultimately, however, because the *gross* rate of return of stocks exceeds $r$ for a sufficiently long investment horizon, the more liquid stocks in class L will dominate bills. The threshold horizon can be read from Figure 8.7 as $h_{rL}$. Anyone with a horizon that exceeds $h_{rL}$ will prefer class L stocks to T-bills. Those with horizons below $h_{rL}$ will choose bills. For even longer horizons, because $c_I$ exceeds $c_L$, the net rate of return on relatively illiquid class I stocks will exceed that on class L stocks. Therefore, investors with horizons greater than $h_{LI}$ will specialize in the most illiquid stocks with the highest gross rate of return. These investors are harmed least by the effect of trading costs.

Now we can determine equilibrium illiquidity premiums. For the marginal investor with horizon $h_{LI}$, the *net* returns from class I and L stocks is the same. Therefore,

$$r + c_L(x - 1/h_{LI}) = r + c_I(y - 1/h_{LI})$$

We can use this equation to solve for the relationship between $x$ and $y$ as follows:

$$y = \frac{1}{h_{LI}} + \frac{c_L}{c_I}(x - \frac{1}{h_{LI}})$$

The expected gross return on illiquid stocks is then

$$r_{\mathrm{I}} = r + c_{\mathrm{L}}y = r + \frac{c_{\mathrm{I}}}{h_{\mathrm{LI}}} + c_{\mathrm{L}}\left(x - \frac{1}{h_{\mathrm{LI}}}\right) = r + c_{\mathrm{L}}x + \frac{1}{h_{\mathrm{LI}}}(c_{\mathrm{I}} - c_{\mathrm{L}}) \quad \textbf{(8.10)}$$

Recalling that the expected gross return on class L stocks is $r_{\mathrm{L}} = r - c_{\mathrm{L}}x$, we conclude that the illiquidity premium of class I versus class L stocks is

$$r_{\mathrm{I}} - r_{\mathrm{L}} = \frac{1}{h_{\mathrm{LI}}}(c_{\mathrm{I}} - c_{\mathrm{L}}) \quad \textbf{(8.11)}$$

Similarly, we can derive the liquidity premium of class L stocks over T-bills. Here, the marginal investor who is indifferent between bills and class L stocks will have investment horizon $h_{r\mathrm{L}}$ and a net rate of return just equal to $r$. Therefore, $r + c_{\mathrm{L}}(x - 1/h_{r\mathrm{L}}) = r$, implying that $x = 1/h_{r\mathrm{L}}$ and the liquidity premium of class L stocks must be $xc_{\mathrm{L}} = c_{\mathrm{L}}/h_{r\mathrm{L}}$. Therefore,

$$r_{\mathrm{L}} - r = \frac{1}{h_{r\mathrm{L}}}c_{\mathrm{L}} \quad \textbf{(8.12)}$$

There are two lessons to be learned from this analysis. First, as predicted, equilibrium expected rates of return are bid up to compensate for transaction costs, as demonstrated by equations 8.11 and 8.12. Second, the illiquidity premium is *not* a linear function of transaction costs. In fact, the incremental illiquidity premium steadily declines as transaction costs increase. To see that this is so, suppose that $c_{\mathrm{L}}$ is 1 percent and $c_{\mathrm{I}} - c_{\mathrm{L}}$ also is 1 percent. Therefore, the transaction cost increases by 1 percent as you move out of bills into the more liquid stock class and by another 1 percent as you move into the illiquid stock class. Equation 8.12 shows that the illiquidity premium of class L stocks over no-transaction-cost bills is then $1/h_{r\mathrm{L}}$, and equation 8.11 shows that the illiquidity premium of class I over class L stocks is $1/h_{\mathrm{LI}}$. But $h_{\mathrm{LI}}$ exceeds $h_{r\mathrm{L}}$ (see Figure 8.7), so we conclude that the incremental effect of illiquidity declines as we move into ever more illiquid assets.

The reason for this last result is simple. Recall that investors will self-select into different asset classes, with longer-term investors holding assets that have the highest gross return and the greatest illiquidity. For these investors, the effect of illiquidity is less costly because trading costs can be amortized over a longer horizon. Therefore, as these costs increase, the investment horizon associated with the holders of these assets also increases, which mitigates the impact on the required gross rate of return.

The distribution of investors also will affect the illiquidity premium. If many traders invest for a particular horizon, then the illiquidity premium will rise less rapidly around that horizon. Figure 8.8 illustrates this result. The curve labeled I corresponds to a relatively even distribution of investors across investment horizons. The curve labeled II, which flattens rapidly around the investment horizon $h^*$, would arise in the case that many investors have horizons of approximately $h^*$.

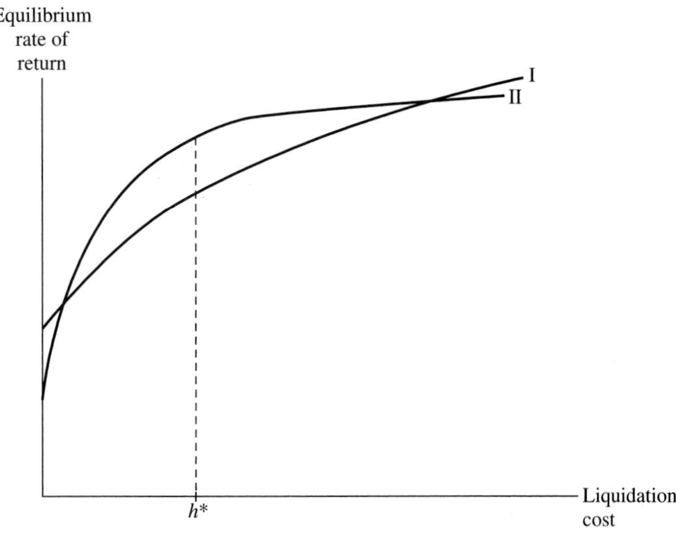


**Figure 8.8**

Rates of return as a function of liquidation cost for two populations with different distributions of investors across investment horizons.

**CONCEPT CHECK**

Question 7. Consider a very illiquid asset class of stocks, class V, with $c_V > c_I$. Use a graph like Figure 8.7 to convince yourself that there is an investment horizon, $h_{IV}$, for which an investor would be indifferent between stocks in illiquidity classes I and V. Analogously to equation 8.11, in equilibrium, the differential in gross returns must be

$$r_V - r_I = \frac{1}{h_{VI}}(c_V - c_I) < r_I - r_L < r_L - r$$

Our analysis so far has focused on the case of uncorrelated assets, allowing us to ignore issues of systematic risk. This special case turns out to be easy to generalize. If we were to allow for correlation among assets due to common systematic risk factors, we would find that the illiquidity premium is simply additive to the risk premium of the usual CAPM.[15] Therefore, we can generalize the CAPM expected return–beta relationship to include a liquidity effect as follows:

$$E(r_i) = r_f = \beta_i[E(r_M) - r_f] + f(c_i)$$

where $f(c_i)$ is a function of trading costs that measures the effect of the illiquidity premium given the trading costs of security $i$. We have seen that $f(c_i)$ is increasing

[15] The only assumption necessary to obtain this result is that for each level of beta, there are many securities within that risk class, with a variety of transaction costs. (This is essentially the same assumption used by Modigliani and Miller in their famous capital structure irrelevance proposition.) Thus, our earlier analysis could be applied within each risk class, resulting in an illiquidity premium that simply adds on to the systematic risk premium.

**Figure 8.9**

The relationship between illiquidity and average returns.

Derived from Yakov Amihud and Haim Mendelson, "Asset pricing and the Bid-Ask Spread," *Journal of Financial Economics* 17 (1986), pp. 223–49. Reprinted by permission.

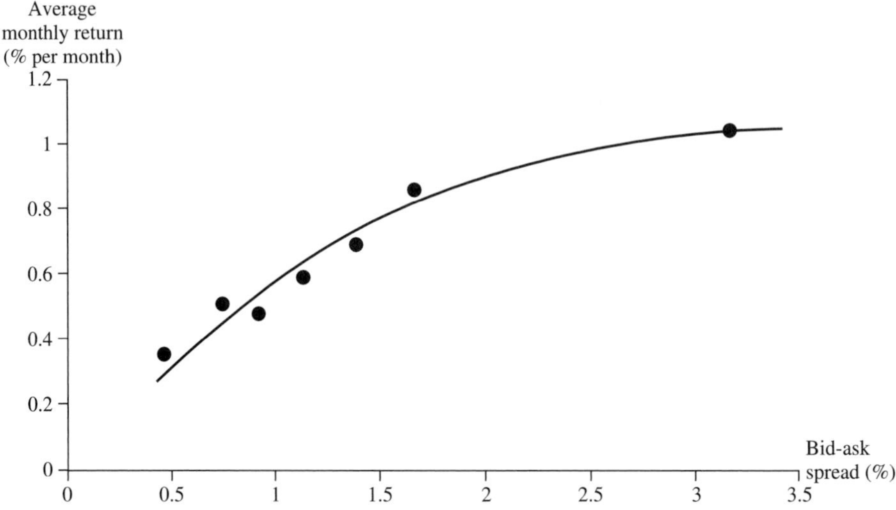


in $c_i$ but at a decreasing rate. The usual CAPM equation is modified because each investor's optimal portfolio is now affected by liquidation cost as well as risk-return considerations.

The model can be generalized in other ways as well. For example, even if investors do not know their investment horizon for certain, as long as investors do not perceive a connection between unexpected needs to liquidate investments and security returns, the implications of the model are essentially unchanged, with expected horizons replacing actual horizons in equations 8.11 and 8.12.

Amihud and Mendelson provide a considerable amount of empirical evidence that liquidity has a substantial impact on gross stock returns. We will defer our discussion of most of that evidence until Chapter 10. However, for a preview of the quantitative significance of the illiquidity effect, examine Figure 8.9 which is derived from their study. It shows that average monthly returns over the 1961–1980 period rise from 0.35 percent for the group of stocks with the lowest bid-ask spread (the most liquid stocks) to 1.024 percent for the highest-spread stocks. This is an annualized differential of about 8 percent, nearly equal to the historical average risk premium on the S&P 500 index! Moreover, as their model predicts, the effect of the spread on average monthly returns is nonlinear, with a curve that flattens out as spreads increase.

## SUMMARY

1. The CAPM assumes that investors are single-period planners who agree on a common input list from security analysis and seek mean-variance optimal portfolios.
2. The CAPM assumes that security markets are ideal in the sense that:
   *a.* They are large, and investors are price-takers.

*b.* There are no taxes or transaction costs.

*c.* All risky assets are publicly traded.

*d.* Investors can borrow and lend any amount at a fixed risk-free rate.

**3.** With these assumptions, all investors hold identical risky portfolios. The CAPM holds that in equilibrium the market portfolio is the unique mean-variance efficient tangency portfolio. Thus, a passive strategy is efficient.

**4.** The CAPM market portfolio is a value-weighted portfolio. Each security is held in a proportion equal to its market value divided by the total market value of all securities.

**5.** If the market portfolio is efficient and the average investor neither borrows nor lends, then the risk premium on the market portfolio is proportional to its variance, $\sigma_M^2$, and to the average coefficient of risk aversion across investors $\bar{A}$:

$$E(r_M) - r_f = .01 \times \bar{A}\sigma_M^2$$

**6.** The CAPM implies that the risk premium on any individual asset or portfolio is the product of the risk premium on the market portfolio and the beta coefficient:

$$E(r) - r_f = \beta[E(r_M) - r_f]$$

where the beta coefficient is the covariance of the asset with the market portfolio as a fraction of the variance of the market portfolio:

$$\beta = \frac{\text{Cov}(r, r_M)}{\sigma_M^2}$$

**7.** When risk-free investments are restricted but all other CAPM assumptions hold, then the simple version of the CAPM is replaced by its zero-beta version. Accordingly, the risk-free rate in the expected return–beta relationship is replaced by the zero-beta portfolio's expected return rate of return:

$$E(r_i) = E[r_{Z(M)}] + \beta_i E[r_M - r_{Z(M)}]$$

**8.** The simple version of the CAPM assumes that investors are myopic. When investors are assumed to be concerned with lifetime consumption and bequest plans but their tastes and security return distributions are stable over time, the market portfolio remains efficient and the simple version of the expected return–beta relationship holds.

**9.** The simple version of the CAPM must be modified when investors are concerned with extramarket sources of uncertainty pertaining to future consumption and investment opportunities. These concerns give rise to demands for securities that hedge these risks. With the extra hedging demands, equilibrium security returns will satisfy a multifactor version of the expected return–beta relationship.

**10.** Liquidity costs can be incorporated into the CAPM relationship. When there is a large number of assets with any combination of beta and liquidity cost $c_i$, the expected return is bid up to reflect this undesired property according to:

$$E(r_i) - r_f = \beta_i[E(r_M) - r_f] + f(c_i)$$

## Key Terms

Capital asset pricing model (CAPM)
Homogeneous expectations
Market portfolio
Mutual fund theorem
Market price of risk
Beta
Expected return–beta relationship
Security market line
Alpha
Zero-beta portfolio
Liquidity
Illiquidity premium

## Selected Readings

*A good introduction to the intuition of the CAPM is:*

Malkiel, Burton G. *A Random Walk Down Wall Street.* New York: W.W. Norton & Company, Inc., 1985.

*The four articles that established the CAPM are:*

Sharpe, William. "Capital Asset Prices: A Theory of Market Equilibrium." *Journal of Finance,* September 1964.

Lintner, John. "The Valuation of Risk Assets and the Selection of Risky Investments in Stock Portfolios and Capital Budgets." *Review of Economics and Statistics,* February 1965.

Mossin, Jan. "Equilibrium in a Capital Asset Market." *Econometrica,* October 1966.

Treynor, Jack. "Towards a Theory of Market Value of Risky Assets." Unpublished manuscript, 1961.

*A review of the simple CAPM and its variants is contained in:*

Jensen, Michael C. "The Foundation and Current State of Capital Market Theory." In Michael C. Jensen (editor), *Studies in the Theory of Capital Markets.* New York: Praeger Publishers, 1972.

*The zero-beta version of the CAPM appeared in:*

Black, Fischer. "Capital Market Equilibrium with Restricted Borrowing." *Journal of Business,* July 1972.

*Excellent practitioner-oriented discussions of the CAPM are:*

Mullins, David. "Does the Capital Asset Pricing Model Work?" *Harvard Business Review,* January/February 1982.

Rosenberg, Barr; and Andrew Rudd. "The Corporate Uses of Beta." In J. M. Stern and D. H. Chew, Jr. (editors), *The Revolution in Corporate Finance.* New York: Basil Blackwell, 1986.

## Problems

1. What is the beta of a portfolio with $E(r_p) = 20$ percent, if $r_f = 5$ percent and $E(r_M) = 15$ percent?
2. The market price of a security is $40. Its expected rate of return is 13 percent. The risk-free rate is 7 percent and the market risk premium is 8 percent. What will be the market price of the security if its covariance with the market portfolio doubles (and all other variables remain unchanged)?
3. You are a consultant to a large manufacturing corporation that is considering a project with the following net after-tax cash flows (in millions of dollars):

| Years from Now | After-Tax Cash Flow |
|---|---|
| 0 | −20 |
| 1–9 | 10 |
| 10 | 20 |

The project's beta is 1.7. Assuming that $r_f = 9$ percent and $E(r_M) = 19$ percent, what is the net present value of the project? What is the highest possible beta estimate for the project before its NPV becomes negative?

**4.** Are the following statements true or false?
   *a.* Stocks with a beta of zero offer an expected rate of return of zero.
   *b.* The CAPM implies that investors require a higher return to hold highly volatile securities.
   *c.* You can construct a portfolio with a beta of .75 by investing .75 of the budget in bills and the remainder in the market portfolio.

**5.** Consider the following table, which gives a security analyst's expected return on two stocks for two particular market returns:

| Market Return | Aggressive Stock | Defensive Stock |
|---|---|---|
| .05 | .02 | .035 |
| .20 | .32 | .14 |

   *a.* What are the betas of the two stocks?
   *b.* What is the expected rate of return on each stock if the market return is equally likely to be 5 percent or 20 percent?
   *c.* If the T-bill rate is 8 percent and the market return is equally likely to be 5 percent or 20 percent, draw the SML for this economy.
   *d.* Plot the two securities on the SML graph. What are the alphas of each?
   *e.* What hurdle rate should be used by the management of the aggressive firm for a project with the risk characteristics of the defensive firm's stock?

If the simple CAPM is valid, which of the following situations in problems 6–12 are possible? Explain. Consider each situation independently.

**6.**

| Portfolio | Expected Return | Beta |
|---|---|---|
| *A* | .20 | 1.4 |
| *B* | .25 | 1.2 |

**7.**

| Portfolio | Expected Return | Standard Deviation |
|---|---|---|
| *A* | .30 | .35 |
| *B* | .40 | .25 |

8.

| Portfolio | Expected Return | Standard Deviation |
|---|---|---|
| Risk-free | .10 | 0 |
| Market | .18 | .24 |
| *A* | .16 | .12 |

9.

| Portfolio | Expected Return | Standard Deviation |
|---|---|---|
| Risk-free | .10 | 0 |
| Market | .18 | .24 |
| *A* | .20 | .22 |

10.

| Portfolio | Expected Return | Beta |
|---|---|---|
| Risk-free | .10 | 0 |
| Market | .18 | 1.0 |
| *A* | .16 | 1.5 |

11.

| Portfolio | Expected Return | Beta |
|---|---|---|
| Risk-free | .10 | 0 |
| Market | .18 | 1.0 |
| *A* | .16 | .9 |

12.

| Portfolio | Expected Return | Standard Deviation |
|---|---|---|
| Risk-free | .10 | 0 |
| Market | .18 | .24 |
| *A* | .16 | .22 |

In problems 13–15, assume that the risk-free rate of interest is 8 percent and the expected rate of return on the market is 18 percent.

**13.** A share of stock sells for $100 today. It will pay a dividend of $9 per share at the end of the year. Its beta is 1. What do investors expect the stock to sell for at the end of the year?

**14.** I am buying a firm with an expected cash flow of $1,000 but am unsure of its risk. If I think the beta of the firm is zero, when in fact the beta is really 1, how much *more* will I offer for the firm than it is truly worth?

**15.** A stock has an expected rate of return of 6 percent. What is its beta?

**16.** Two investment advisors are comparing performance. One averaged a 19 percent rate of return and the other a 16 percent rate of return. However, the beta of the first investor was 1.5, whereas that of the second was 1.

*a.* Can you tell which investor was a better predictor of individual stocks (aside from the issue of general movements in the market)?

*b.* If the T-bill rate were 6 percent and the market return during the period were 14 percent, which investor would be the superior stock selector?

*c.* What if the T-bill rate were 3 percent and the market return were 15 percent?

**17.** In 1991, the rate of return on short-term government securities (perceived to be risk-free) was about 6 percent. Suppose the expected rate of return required by the market for a portfolio with a beta measure of 1 is 11 percent. According to the capital asset pricing model (security market line):

*a.* What is the expected rate of return on the market portfolio?

*b.* What would be the expected rate of return on a stock with $\beta = 0$?

*c.* Suppose you consider buying a share of stock at $40. The stock is expected to pay $3 in dividends next year and to sell then for $41. The stock risk has been evaluated by $\beta = -.5$. Is the stock overpriced or underpriced?

**18.** Suppose that you can invest risk free at rate $r_f$ but can borrow only at a higher rate, $r_f^B$. This case was first considered in Section 7.5.

*a.* Draw a minimum-variance frontier. Show on the graph the risky portfolio that will be selected by defensive investors. Show the portfolio that will be selected by aggressive investors.

*b.* What portfolios will be selected by investors who neither borrow nor lend?

*c.* Where will the market portfolio lie on the efficient frontier?

*d.* Will the zero-beta CAPM be valid in this scenario? Explain. Show graphically the expected return on the zero-beta portfolio.

**19.** Consider an economy with two classes of investors. Tax-exempt investors can borrow or lend at the safe rate, $r_f$. Taxed investors pay tax rate $t$ on all interest income, so their net-of-tax safe interest rate is $r_f(1 - t)$. Show that the zero-beta CAPM will apply to this economy and that $(1 - t)r_f < E[r_{Z(M)}] < r_f$.

**20.** Suppose that borrowing is restricted so that the zero-beta version of the CAPM holds. The expected return on the market portfolio is 17 percent, and on the zero-beta portfolio it is 8 percent. What is the expected return on a portfolio with a beta of 0.6?

**21.** The security market line depicts:

*a.* a security's expected return as a function of its systematic risk.

*b.* the market portfolio as the optimal portfolio of risky securities.

*c.* the relationship between a security's return and the return on an index.

*d.* the complete portfolio as a combination of the market portfolio and the risk-free asset.

**22.** Within the context of the capital asset pricing model (CAPM), assume:

- Expected return on the market = 15%
- Risk-free rate = 8%
- Expected rate of return on XYZ security = 17%
- Beta of XYZ security = 1.25

Which *one* of the following is *correct*?

*a.* XYZ is overpriced.

*b.* XYZ is fairly priced.

*c.* XYZ's alpha is −0.25%.

*d.* XYZ's alpha is 0.25%.

**23.** What is the expected return of a zero-beta security?

*a.* Market rate of return

*b.* Zero rate of return

*c.* Negative rate of return

*d.* Risk-free rate of return

**24.** Briefly explain whether investors should expect a higher return from holding Portfolio A versus Portfolio B under the Capital Asset Pricing Model (CAPM). Assume that both portfolios are fully diversified.

| | **Portfolio A** | **Portfolio B** |
|---|---|---|
| Systematic risk (beta) | 1.0 | 1.0 |
| Specific risk for each individual security | High | Low |

*Chapter 9*

# Index Models and the Arbitrage Pricing Theory

**THE EXPLOITATION OF SECURITY MISPRICING IN SUCH A WAY THAT RISK-FREE ECONOMIC PROFITS MAY BE EARNED IS CALLED ARBITRAGE.** It typically involves the simultaneous purchase and sale of equivalent securities (usually in different markets) in order to profit from discrepancies in their price relationship. The concept of arbitrage is central to the theory of capital markets. This chapter discusses the nature, and illustrates the use, of arbitrage. We show how to identify arbitrage opportunities and why investors will take as large a position as they can in arbitrage portfolios.

Perhaps the most basic principle of capital market theory is that equilibrium market prices are rational in that they rule out risk-free arbitrage opportunities. Pricing relationships that guarantee the absence of risk-free arbitrage possibilities are extremely powerful. If actual security prices allow for risk-free arbitrage, the result will be strong pressure on security prices to restore equilibrium. Only a few investors need be aware of arbitrage opportunities to bring about a large volume of trades, and these trades will bring prices back into balance.

The CAPM of the previous chapter gave us the security market line, a relationship between expected return and risk as measured by beta. The model discussed in this chapter, called the arbitrage pricing theory, or APT, also stipulates a relationship between expected return and risk, but it uses different assumptions and techniques. We explore this relationship using well-diversified portfolios, showing that these portfolios are priced to satisfy the CAPM expected return–beta relationship. Because all well-diversified portfolios have to satisfy that relationship, we show that all individual securities almost certainly satisfy this same relationship. This reasoning allows the derivation of an SML relationship that avoids reliance on the unobservable, theoretical market portfolio that is central to the CAPM. We also show how the simple single-factor APT easily can be generalized to a richer multifactor version.

The single-factor APT is based on the assumption that only one systematic common factor affects the returns of all securities. This assumption, however, was also at the origin of another class of models, known as *index* or *market models,* that predate the APT by several years. These models are initially introduced in order to simplify the computations of the Markowitz portfolio selection model. Since they also offer significant new insights into the nature of systematic risk versus firm-specific risk and constitute a good introduction to the concept of factor models of security returns, they will be examined in the first sections of this chapter.

## 9.1 A Single-Index Security Market

### Systematic Risk versus Firm-Specific Risk

The success of a portfolio selection rule depends on the quality of the input list, that is, the estimates of expected security returns and the covariance matrix. In the long run, efficient portfolios will beat portfolios with less reliable input lists and consequently inferior reward-to-risk trade-offs.

Suppose your security analysts can thoroughly analyze 50 stocks. This means that your input list will include the following:

$$\begin{aligned} n &= \quad 50 \text{ estimates of expected returns} \\ n &= \quad 50 \text{ estimates of variances} \\ (n^2 - n)/2 &= \underline{1{,}225} \text{ estimates of covariances} \\ & \quad\ 1{,}325 \text{ estimates} \end{aligned}$$

This is a formidable task, particularly in light of the fact that a 50-security portfolio is relatively small. Doubling $n$ to 100 will nearly quadruple the number of estimates to 5,150. If $n = 1{,}600$, roughly the number of TSE-listed stocks in 1990, we need nearly 1.3 *million* estimates.

Covariances between security returns occur because the same economic forces affect the fortunes of many firms. Some examples of common economic factors are business cycles, inflation, money-supply changes, technological changes, and prices of raw materials. All these (interrelated) factors affect almost all firms. Thus unexpected changes in these variables cause, simultaneously, unexpected changes in the rates of return on the entire stock market.

Suppose that we group all these economic factors and any other relevant common factors into one macroeconomic indicator and assume that it moves the security market as a whole. We further assume that, beyond this common effect, all remaining uncertainty in stock returns is firm-specific; that is, there is no other source of correlation between securities. Firm-specific events would include new inventions, deaths of key employees, and other factors that affect the fortune of the individual firm without affecting the broad economy in a measurable way.

We can summarize the distinction between macroeconomic and firm-specific factors by writing the return, $r_i$, realized on any security during some holding period as

$$r_i = E(r_i) + m_i + e_i \tag{9.1}$$

where $E(R_i)$ is the expected return on the security as of the beginning of the holding period, $m_i$ is the impact of unanticipated macroevents on the security's return during the period, and $e_i$ is the impact of unanticipated firm-specific events. Both $m_i$ and $e_i$ have zero expected values because each represents the impact of unanticipated events, which by definition must average out to zero.

We can gain further insight by recognizing that different firms have different sensitivities to macroeconomic events. Thus, if we denote the unanticipated component of the macro factor by $F$, and denote the responsiveness of security $i$ to macroevents by the Greek letter beta, $\beta_i$, then equation 9.1 becomes[1]

$$r_i = E(r_i) + \beta_i F + e_i \tag{9.2}$$

Equation 9.2 is known as a **factor model** for stock returns. It is easy to imagine that a more realistic decomposition of security returns would require more than one factor in equation 9.2. We treat this issue in subsequent sections. For now, let us examine the easy case with only one macro factor.

Of course, a factor model is of little use without specifying a way to measure the factor that is posited to affect security returns. One reasonable approach is to assert that the rate of return on a broad index of securities such as the TSE 300 is a valid proxy for the common macro factor. This approach leads to an equation similar to the factor model, which is called a **single-index model** because it uses the market index to proxy for the common or systematic factor.

According to the index model, we can separate the actual or realized rate of return on a security into macro (systematic) and micro (firm-specific) components

---

[1] You may wonder why we choose the notation $\beta$ for the responsiveness coefficient, since $\beta$ already has been defined in Chapter 8 in the context of the CAPM. The choice is deliberate, however. Our reason will be obvious shortly.

in a manner similar to that in equation 9.2. We write the rate of return on each security as a sum of three components:

| | Symbol |
|---|---|
| 1. The stock's expected return if the market is neutral, that is, if the market's excess return, $r_M - r_f$, is zero. | $\alpha_i$ |
| 2. The component of return due to movements in the overall market; $\beta_i$ is the security's responsiveness to market movements. | $\beta_i(r_M - r_f)$ |
| 3. The unexpected component due to unexpected events that are relevant only to this security (firm-specific). | $e_i$ |

The holding period excess rate of return on the stock, which measures the stock's relative performance, then can be stated as

$$r_i - r_f = \alpha_i + \beta_i(r_M - r_f) + e_i$$

Let us denote security excess returns over the risk-free rate using capital *R* and so rewrite this equation as

$$R_i = \alpha_i + \beta_i R_M + e_i \tag{9.3}$$

We write the index model in terms of excess returns over $r_f$ rather than in terms of total returns, because the level of the stock market return represents the state of the macroeconomy only to the extent that it exceeds or falls short of the rate of return on risk-free T-bills. For example, in the 1950s, when T-bills were yielding only a 3 percent or 4 percent rate of return, a return of 8 percent or 9 percent on the stock market would be considered good news. In contrast, in the early 1980s, when bills were yielding over 10 percent, that same 8 percent or 9 percent stock market return would signal disappointing macroeconomic news.[2]

Equation 9.3 says that each security therefore has two sources of risk: *market or "systematic" risk,* attributable to its sensitivity to macroeconomic factors as reflected in $R_M$, and *firm-specific risk* as reflected in *e*. If we denote the variance of the excess return on the market, $R_M$, as $\sigma_M^2$, then we can break the variance of the rate of return on each stock into two components:

| | Symbol |
|---|---|
| 1. The variance attributable to the uncertainty of the common macroeconomic factors. | $\beta_i^2\sigma_M^2$ |
| 2. The variance attributable to firm-specific uncertainty. | $\sigma^2(e_i)$ |

The covariance between $R_M$ and $e_i$ is zero because $e_i$ is defined as firm-specific, that is, independent of movements in the market. Hence, calling $\sigma_i^2$ the variance

[2] In practice, however, a "modified" index model is often used that is similar to equation 9.3 except that it uses total rather than excess returns. This practice is most common when daily data are used. In this case, the rate of return on bills is on the order of only about .02 percent per day, so total and excess returns are almost indistinguishable.

of the rate of return on security *i,* we find that

$$\sigma_i^2 = \beta_i^2\sigma_M^2 + \sigma^2(e_i)$$

The covariance between the excess rates of return on two stocks, for example, $R_i$ and $R_j$, derives only from the common factor, $R_M$, because $e_i$ and $e_j$ are each firm-specific and therefore presumed to be uncorrelated. Hence, the covariance between two stocks is

$$\text{Cov}(R_i,R_j) = \text{Cov}(\beta_i R_M, \beta_j R_M) = \beta_i\beta_j\sigma_M^2 \tag{9.4}$$

These calculations show that if we have

$n$ estimates of the expected returns, $E(R_i)$
$n$ estimates of the sensitivity coefficients, $\beta_i$
$n$ estimates of the firm-specific variances, $\sigma^2(e_i)$
1 estimate for the variance of the (common) macroeconomic factor, $\sigma_M^2$

then these $(3n + 1)$ estimates will enable us to prepare the input list for this single-index security universe. Thus for a 50-security portfolio we will need 151 estimates, rather than 1,325, and for a 100-security portfolio we will need only 301 estimates, rather than 5,150.

It is easy to see why the index model is such a useful abstraction. For large universes of securities, the data estimates required for this model are only a small fraction of what otherwise would be needed.

Another advantage is less obvious but equally important. The index model abstraction is crucial for specialization of effort in security analysis. If a covariance term had to be calculated directly for each security pair, then security analysts could not specialize by industry. For example, if one group were to specialize in the retail industry and another in the banking industry, who would have the common background necessary to estimate the covariance *between* Canadian Tire and CIBC? Neither group would have the deep understanding of other industries necessary to make an informed judgment of co-movements among industries. In contrast, the index model suggests a simple way to compute covariances. Covariances among securities are due to the influence of the single common factor, represented by the market index return, and can be easily estimated using equation 9.4.

The simplification derived from the index model assumption is, however, not without cost. The "cost" of the model lies in the restrictions it places on the structure of asset return uncertainty. The classification of uncertainty into a simple dichotomy—macro versus micro risk—oversimplifies sources of real-world uncertainty and misses some important sources of dependence in stock returns. For example, this dichotomy rules out industry events, events that may affect many firms within an industry without substantially affecting the broad macroeconomy.

Statistical analysis shows that the firm-specific components of some firms are correlated. Examples are the nonmarket components of stocks in a single industry, such as retail stocks or banking stocks. At the same time, statistical significance does not always correspond to economic significance. Economically speaking, the question that is more relevant to the assumption of a single-index model is whether portfolios constructed using covariances that are estimated on the basis of the single-factor or single-index assumption are significantly different from, and less efficient than, portfolios constructed using covariances that are estimated directly for each pair of stocks. In Part IV on active portfolio management, we explore this issue further.

---

**CONCEPT CHECK** Question 1. Suppose that the index model for stocks $A$ and $B$ is estimated with the following results:

$$R_A = .01 + .9R_M + e_A$$

$$R_B = -.02 + 1.1R_M + e_B$$

$$\sigma_M = .20$$

$$\sigma(e_A) = .3$$

$$\sigma(e_B) = .1$$

Find the standard deviation of each stock and the covariance between them.

---

## Estimating the Index Model

Equation 9.3 also suggests how we might go about actually measuring market and firm-specific risk. Suppose that we observe the excess return on the market index and a specific asset over a number of holding periods. We use as an example hypothetical monthly excess returns on the TSE 300 index and XYZ stock. We can summarize the results for a sample period in a **scatter diagram,** as illustrated in Figure 9.1.

The horizontal axis in Figure 9.1 measures the excess return (over the risk-free rate) on the market index, whereas the vertical axis measures the excess return on the asset in question (XYZ stock in our example). A pair of excess returns (one for the market index, one for XYZ stock) over a holding period constitutes one point on this scatter diagram. The points are numbered 1–12, representing excess returns for the TSE 300 and XYZ for each month from January–December. The single-index model states that the relationship between the excess returns on XYZ and the TSE 300 is given by

$$R_{XYZt} = \alpha_{XYZ} + \beta_{XYZ}R_{Mt} + e_{XYZt}$$

Note the resemblance of this relationship to a **regression equation.**

In a single-variable linear regression equation, the dependent variable plots around a straight line with an intercept $\alpha$ and a slope $\beta$. The deviations from the line, $e_t$, are assumed to be mutually independent and independent of the right-hand variable. Because these assumptions are identical to those of the index model, we can look at the index model as a regression model. The sensitivity of

**Figure 9.1** Characteristic line for XYZ.

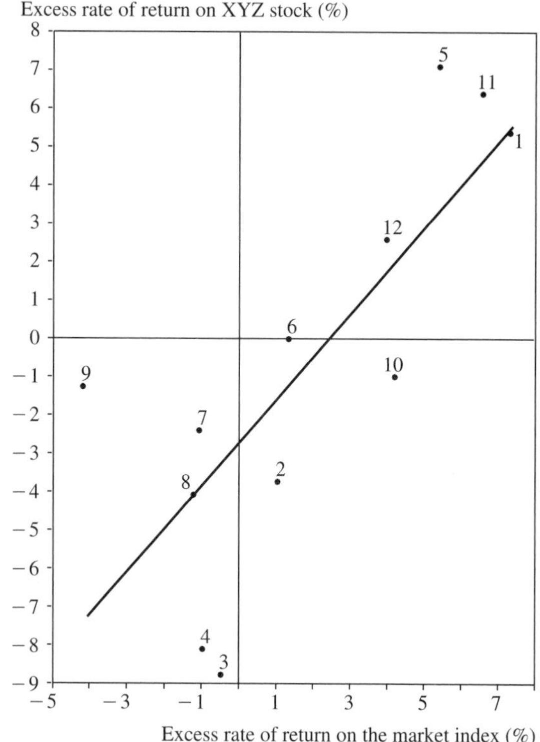


XYZ to the market, measured by $\beta_{XYZ}$, is the slope of the regression line. The intercept of the regression line is $\alpha$, and deviations of particular observations from the regression line are denoted $e$. These **residuals** are the parts of stock returns not explained by the independent variable (the market-index return); therefore they measure the impact of firm-specific events during the particular month. The parameters of interest, $\alpha$, $\beta$, and Var($e$), can be estimated using standard regression techniques.

Estimating the regression equation of the single-index model gives us the **security characteristic line** (SCL), which is plotted in Figure 9.1. (The regression results and raw data appear in Table 9.1.) The SCL is a plot of the typical excess return on a security over the risk-free rate as a function of the excess return on the market.

This sample of holding period returns is, of course, too small to yield reliable statistics. We use it only for demonstration. For this sample period we find that the beta coefficient of XYZ stock, as estimated by the slope of the regression line, is 1.1357, and that the intercept for this SCL is −2.59 percent per month.

For each month, our estimate of the residual, $e$, which is the deviation of XYZ's excess return from the prediction of the SCL, equals

**Table 9.1** Characteristic Line for XYZ Stock

| Month | XYZ Return | Market Return | Monthly T-Bill Rate | Excess XYZ Return | Excess Market Return |
|---|---|---|---|---|---|
| January | 6.06 | 7.89 | 0.65 | 5.41 | 7.24 |
| February | −2.86 | 1.51 | 0.58 | 3.44 | 0.93 |
| March | −8.18 | 0.23 | 0.62 | −8.79 | −0.38 |
| April | −7.36 | −0.29 | 0.72 | −8.08 | −1.01 |
| May | 7.76 | 5.58 | 0.66 | 7.10 | 4.92 |
| June | 0.52 | 1.73 | 0.55 | −0.03 | 1.18 |
| July | −1.74 | −0.21 | 0.62 | −2.36 | −0.83 |
| August | −3.00 | −0.36 | 0.55 | −3.55 | −0.91 |
| September | −0.56 | −3.58 | 0.60 | −1.16 | −4.18 |
| October | −0.37 | 4.62 | 0.65 | −1.02 | 3.97 |
| November | 6.93 | 6.85 | 0.61 | 6.32 | 6.25 |
| December | 3.08 | 4.55 | 0.65 | 2.43 | 3.90 |
| Mean | 0.02 | 2.38 | 0.62 | −0.60 | 1.75 |
| Standard deviation | 4.97 | 3.33 | 0.05 | 4.97 | 3.32 |

Regression results $r_{XYZ} = r_f = \alpha + \beta(r_M - r_f)$

| | $\alpha$ | $\beta$ |
|---|---|---|
| Estimated coefficient | −2.590 | 1.1357 |
| Standard error of estimate | (1.547) | (0.309) |

Variance of residuals = 12.601
Standard deviation of residuals = 3.550
R-SQR = 0.575

$$\text{Deviation} = \text{Actual} - \text{Predicted return}$$

$$e_{\text{XYZ}t} = R_{\text{XYZ}t} - (\beta_{\text{XYZ}} R_{Mt} + \alpha_{\text{XYZ}})$$

These residuals are estimates of the monthly unexpected *firm-specific* component of the rate of return on XYZ stock. Hence we can estimate the firm-specific variance by[3]

$$\sigma^2(e_{\text{XYZ}t}) = \frac{1}{10} \sum_{t=1}^{12} e_t^2 = 12.60$$

Therefore, the standard deviation of the firm-specific component of XYZ's return, $\sigma(e_{\text{XYZ}t})$, equals 3.55 percent per month.

[3] Because the mean of $e_t$ is zero, $e_t^2$ is the squared deviation from its mean. The average value of $e_t^2$ is therefore the estimate of the variance of the firm-specific component. We divide the sum of squared residuals by the degrees of freedom of the regression, $n - 2 = 12 - 2 = 10$, to obtain an unbiased estimate of $\sigma^2(e)$.

## The Index Model and Diversification

The index model, which was first suggested by Sharpe,[4] also offers insight into portfolio diversification. Suppose that we choose an equally weighted portfolio of $n$ securities. The excess rate of return on each security is given by

$$R_i = \alpha_i + \beta_i R_M + e_i$$

Similarly, we can write the excess return on the portfolio of stocks as

$$R_P = \alpha_P + \beta_P R_M + e_P \tag{9.5}$$

We now show that, as the number of stocks included in this portfolio increases, the part of the portfolio risk attributable to nonmarket factors becomes ever smaller. This part of the risk is diversified away. In contrast, the market risk remains, regardless of the number of firms combined into the portfolio.

To understand these results, note that the excess rate of return on this equally weighted portfolio, for which $w_i = 1/n$, is

$$R_P = \sum_{i=1}^{n} w_i R_i = \frac{1}{n}\sum_{i=1}^{n} R_i = \frac{1}{n}\sum_{i=1}^{n} (\alpha_i + \beta_i R_M + e_i)$$

$$= \frac{1}{n}\sum_{i=1}^{n} \alpha_i + \left(\frac{1}{n}\sum_{i=1}^{n} \beta_i\right) R_M + \frac{1}{n}\sum_{i=1}^{n} e_i \tag{9.6}$$

Comparing equations 9.5 and 9.6, we see that the portfolio has a sensitivity to the market given by

$$\beta_P = \frac{1}{n}\sum_{i=1}^{n} \beta_i$$

(which is the average of the individual $\beta_i$s), and it has a nonmarket return component of a constant (intercept)

$$\frac{1}{n}\sum_{i=1}^{n} \alpha_i$$

(which is the average of the individual alphas), plus the zero mean variable

$$e_P = \frac{1}{n}\sum_{i=1}^{n} e_i$$

which is the average of the firm-specific components. Hence the portfolio's variance is

$$\sigma_P^2 = \beta_P^2 \sigma_M^2 + \sigma^2(e_P) \tag{9.7}$$

The systematic risk component of the portfolio variance, which we defined as the part that depends on marketwide movements, is $\beta_P^2 \sigma_M^2$ and depends on the

[4] William F. Sharpe, "A Simplified Model of Portfolio Analysis," *Management Science,* January 1963.

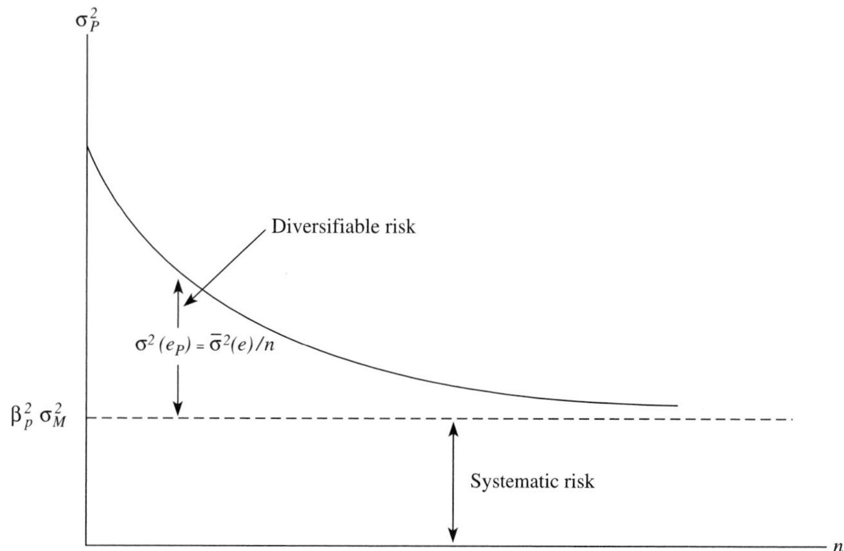


**Figure 9.2**
The variance of a portfolio with $\beta$ in the single-factor economy.

average of the sensitivity coefficients of the individual securities. This part of the risk depends on portfolio beta and $\sigma_M^2$ and will persist regardless of the extent of portfolio diversification. No matter how many stocks are held, their common exposure to the market will be reflected in portfolio systematic risk.[5]

In contrast, the nonsystematic component of the portfolio variance is $\sigma^2(e_P)$ and is attributable to firm-specific components, $e_i$. Because these $e_i$s are independent, and all have zero expected value, the law of averages can be applied to conclude that as more and more stocks are added to the portfolio, the firm-specific components tend to cancel out, resulting in ever-smaller nonmarket risk. Such risk is thus termed *diversifiable.* To see this more rigorously, examine the formula for the variance of the equally weighted "portfolio" of firm-specific components. Because the $e_i$s are all uncorrelated,

$$\sigma^2(e_P) = \sum_{i=1}^{n}\left(\frac{1}{n}\right)^2 \sigma^2(e_i) = \frac{1}{n}\,\overline{\sigma}^2(e)$$

where $\overline{\sigma}^2(e)$ is the average of the firm-specific variances. Since this average is independent of $n$, when $n$ gets large, $\overline{\sigma}^2(e_P)$ becomes negligible.

To summarize, as diversification increases, the total variance of a portfolio approaches the systematic variance, defined as the variance of the market factor multiplied by the square of the portfolio sensitivity coefficient, $\beta_P$. This is shown in Figure 9.2.

[5] Of course, one can always construct a portfolio with zero systematic risk by mixing negative $\beta$ and positive $\beta$ assets. The point of our discussion is that the vast majority of securities have a positive $\beta$, implying that well-diversified portfolios with small holdings in large numbers of assets will indeed have positive systematic risk.

Figure 9.2 shows that, as more and more securities are combined into a portfolio, the portfolio variance decreases because of the diversification of firm-specific risk. However, the power of diversification is limited. Even for very large *n,* risk remains because of the exposure of virtually all assets to the common, or market, factor. Therefore this systematic risk is said to be nondiversifiable.

This analysis is borne out by empirical analysis. We saw the effect of portfolio diversification on portfolio standard deviations in Figure 7.2. These empirical results are similar to the theoretical graph presented here in Figure 9.2.

The assumption that all security returns can be represented by equation 9.1 is the main assumption of the index model. It can be combined with other assumptions in order to lead to the CAPM. Alternatively, it can be used as the basis of the single-factor APT, examined in later sections.

**CONCEPT CHECK** Question 2. Reconsider the two stocks in Concept Check question (1). Suppose we form an equally weighted portfolio of *A* and *B*. What will be the nonsystematic standard deviation of that portfolio?

## 9.2 THE INDUSTRY VERSION OF THE INDEX MODEL

Not surprisingly, the index model has attracted the attention of practitioners. To the extent that it is approximately valid, it provides a convenient benchmark for security analysis. Also, as the accompanying box shows, it can generate instruments that allow investors to invest in the entire market.

A modern practitioner using the CAPM who has no special information about a security or insight that is unavailable to the general public will conclude that the security is "properly" priced. By "properly" priced, the analyst means that the expected return on the security is fair, given its risk, and therefore plots on the security market line. For instance, if one has no private information about Alcan's (AL) stock, then one should expect

$$E(r_{\text{AL}}) = r_f + \beta_{\text{AL}}[E(r_M) - r_f]$$

A portfolio manager who has a forecast for the market index, $E(r_M)$, and observes the risk-free T-bill rate, $r_f$, can use the model to determine the benchmark expected return for any stock. The beta coefficient, the market risk, $\sigma_M^2$, and the firm-specific risk, $\sigma^2(e)$, can be estimated from historical SCLs, that is, from regressions of security excess returns on market index excess returns.

There are many sources for such regression results. For instance, the Quantitative Analysis division of Nesbitt Burns Inc. publishes periodic estimates of stock

## Investing in the "Entire Market"—U.S. Index Funds

**by Leonard Goodall**

In the last 15 to 20 years a new type of investment instrument has emerged as a major factor in U.S. financial circles—the index fund. An index fund is a mutual fund which attempts to exactly reflect the investment performance of some general market. It does not try to outperform the market but rather to achieve the same level of success as the broader market.

Index funds began to emerge after the generally unsuccessful performance of professional money managers during the difficult financial years of the 1970s. Investors began to note that their mutual funds often performed worse than market averages, and journalists and other observers discovered that it was common for over half of all mutual funds to actually underperform the market in some years. It has been interesting in recent weeks to read articles pointing out that most U.S. mutual funds managers actually outperformed the general market in 1993. Why is this news? Precisely because it doesn't happen all that often!

This does not mean that mutual fund managers are stupid (though some may be). There are some practical reasons why it is difficult for them to outperform the market. First, there are always operating costs involved in fund management. There are no such costs figured into averages such as the Dow Jones Industrial Average or the Standard and Poor 500. Second, fund managers must always maintain some cash reserves. They may do this because they think that they can buy stocks later at lower levels, but at the very least they must always maintain some cash on hand to take care of the investor who wants to cash in shares.

The bottom line is that if managers are to outperform the general market, they must take their net investment funds after allowing for cash reserves and then outperform the market by enough to cover their operating costs, before they are even equal with the market averages. Only if they accomplish this, plus additional profits, can they be said to outperform the market.

There is another, more theoretical reason for the use of index funds. There are many students of the stock market who argue that the markets are "efficient," i.e., that all the information about the market is available to investors and that no one can outperform the market consistently over the long term. The person who looks like this year's "guru" will be next year's bum.

Indeed, this is the predominant theory among economic analysts. In 1990, three U.S. economists won the Nobel Prize for economics for their explanation of the efficient market theory.

There are, of course, investors who seem to outperform the market consistently enough to call the efficient market theory into question. Names like John Templeton, Peter Lynch, and Martin Zweig come to mind. Nevertheless, there is enough support for this theory that many investors will want to do at least some of their investing through index funds.

U.S. pension funds make heavy use of indexing. Two of the largest pension funds, College Retirement Equities Fund, which serves university faculty, and the California Public Employees Retirement System, both invest about two-thirds of their holdings on the basis of indexing and attempt to actively manage only the remaining portion of their investments.

The most common benchmark for index funds is the Standard and Poor 500, and there are several funds which attempt to reflect this average. Dreyfus Peoples Index (718) 895-1206, Fidelity Market Index (801) 534-1910, United Services All American Equity (210) 308-1222, and Vanguard Index Trust 500 (215) 648-6000 are funds which are based on the S&P 500. U.S. All American has the lowest minimum investment, requiring just $1,000.

Some index funds are more aggressive because

*(Continued)*

they track other indexes. Rushmore OTC Index Plus (301) 657-1510 is based on the NASDAQ 100; Vanguard Index Trust—Extended Market follows the Wilshire 4500; and Vanguard Small Capitalization tracks the Russell 2000 index.

There are also international index funds. The U.S. European Equity and the Vanguard International Equity Index—Europe both try to parallel the Morgan Stanley Capital International—Europe index. Vanguard International Equity Index—Pacific is based on the Morgan Stanley Capital International—Asia index.

The funds mentioned here are all no-load funds, and they have low operating expenses. As noted above, operating costs can reduce a fund's return, and it would not be wise to pay high management fees for a fund that is not being actively managed but is just designed to reflect the performance of an index.

It would be possible to build a balanced, diversified portfolio using just index funds. For example, a moderate risk investor might place 50 percent of his or her money in a fund based on the S&P 500, 30 percent in a fund which tracks one of the smaller stock indexes, and 20 percent in an international index fund. Such an investor may well find, in a few years, that the portfolio's performance compares very well with those which have been actively managed by a so-called stock market "guru."

Source: *Canadian Moneysaver,* May 1994. Reprinted by permission.

betas. It uses the TSE 300 index as the proxy for the market portfolio.[6] It relies on the 54 most recent monthly observations to calculate the regression parameters. Nesbitt Burns and most services[7] use total returns, rather than excess returns (deviations from T-bill rates), in their regressions. In this way they estimate a variant of our index model, which is

$$r = a + br_M + e \tag{9.8}$$

instead of

$$r - r_f = \alpha + \beta(r_M = r_f) + e \tag{9.9}$$

To see the effect of this departure, we can rewrite equation 9.8 as

$$r + r_f + \alpha + \beta r_M = \beta r_f + e = \alpha + r_f(1 - \beta) + \beta r_M + e \tag{9.10}$$

Comparing equations 9.8 and 9.10, you can see that if $r_f$ is constant over the sample period both equations have the same independent variable, $r_M$, and residual, $e$. Therefore the slope coefficient will be the same in the two regressions.[8]

However, the intercept that Nesbitt Burns calls alpha is really, using the parameters of the CAPM, an estimate of $\alpha + r_f(1 - \beta)$. The apparent justification for this procedure is that, on a monthly basis, $r_f(1 - \beta)$ is small and is apt to be

[6] Although the TSE 300 is the most easily available and most often used proxy for the market portfolio, it clearly does not include all stocks available for investment to Canadian investors. In addition to many Canadian stocks, it also ignores Canadians' opportunity to invest in foreign stocks. This should be taken into account when interpreting the results.

[7] Merrill Lynch and Value Line are two well-known sources of U.S. betas; Merrill Lynch uses monthly returns and the S&P 500 for the market proxy, while Value Line uses weekly returns and the NYSE index.

[8] Actually, $r_f$ does vary over time and so should not be grouped casually with the constant term in the regression. However, variations in $r_f$ are tiny compared with swings in the market return. The actual volatility in the T-bill rate has only a small impact on the estimated value of beta.

**Table 9.2** Estimates of Stock Total Return Betas

| | October 1984–March 1989 | | | April 1991–September 1995 | | |
|---|---|---|---|---|---|---|
| **Company** | **Beta** | **Alpha** | **% Expl. by Market** | **Beta** | **Alpha** | **% Expl. by Market** |
| Alcan Aluminum | 1.20 | 0.18 | 44.8 | 1.14 | 0.45 | 35.7 |
| Noranda Inc. | 1.76 | −1.02 | 62.0 | 1.56 | 0.23 | 53.5 |
| Imperial Oil A | 0.92 | −0.15 | 35.2 | 0.62 | −0.05 | 11.8 |
| Abitibi Price | 1.04 | 0.83 | 18.2 | 1.31 | 0.20 | 32.6 |
| Macmillan Bloedel | 1.49 | 0.64 | 47.0 | 1.29 | −0.90 | 43.4 |
| BC Sugar Refinery | 0.78 | 1.08 | 28.3 | 0.99 | −1.30 | 19.7 |
| Imasco Ltd. | 0.97 | 0.17 | 41.0 | 0.83 | 0.82 | 19.5 |
| Seagram's | 0.85 | 0.36 | 37.0 | 1.00 | 0.67 | 22.2 |
| Magna A | 1.80 | −1.47 | 45.5 | 0.70 | 3.90 | 5.6 |
| Dofasco Inc. | 1.16 | −0.44 | 55.1 | 1.85 | −1.03 | 33.4 |
| Northern Telecom | 1.07 | −1.38 | 36.8 | 1.08 | 0.13 | 14.9 |
| NOVA Corp. | 1.40 | 0.17 | 38.6 | 0.98 | 0.03 | 24.5 |
| Laidlaw Transportation B | 1.32 | 1.93 | 39.4 | 0.96 | −0.57 | 10.5 |
| BCE Inc. | 0.36 | 0.43 | 24.0 | 0.48 | 0.31 | 20.7 |
| Rogers Communications B | 1.64 | 3.93 | 33.8 | 1.41 | −0.06 | 25.9 |
| George Weston | 0.89 | 0.64 | 47.9 | 0.86 | −0.24 | 31.8 |
| Royal Bank of Canada | 0.72 | 0.46 | 38.0 | 0.91 | 0.01 | 32.3 |
| Canadian Pacific | 1.20 | −0.06 | 51.7 | 1.37 | −0.66 | 46.8 |

Data from the Quantitative Analysis division of Nesbitt Burns Inc. Reprinted by permission.

swamped by the volatility of actual stock returns. However, it is worth noting that for $\beta \neq 1$, the regression intercept in equation 9.8 will not equal the CAPM alpha as it does when excess returns are used as in equation 9.9.

## Company Beta Estimates

Table 9.2 illustrates some Nesbitt Burns estimates of equation 9.8 for a number of important Canadian firms, for two different periods of 54 months. For each period, after the company name, the next two columns show the beta and alpha coefficients. Remember that Nesbitt Burns' alpha is actually $\alpha + r_f(1 - \beta)$.

The next column, % Explained by Market, shows the square of the correlation coefficient, also known as $R$-square, between $r_i$ and $r_M$. The $R$-square statistic, which is sometimes called the *coefficient of determination,* gives the fraction of the variance of the dependent variable (the return on the stock) that is explained by movements in the independent variable (the return on the TSE 300 index). Recall from Section 9.1 that the part of the total variance of the rate of return on an asset, $\sigma^2$, that is explained by market returns is the systematic variance $\beta^2\sigma_M^2$. Hence the $R$-square is systematic variance over total variance, which tells us what fraction of a firm's volatility is attributable to market movements:

$$R\text{-square} = \frac{\beta^2\sigma_M^2}{\sigma^2}$$

The firm-specific variance, $\sigma^2(e)$, is the part of the asset variance that is unexplained by the market index. Therefore, because

$$\sigma^2 = \beta^2\sigma_M^2 + \sigma^2(e)$$

the coefficient of determination also may be expressed as

$$R^2 = 1 - \frac{\sigma^2(e)}{\sigma^2} \qquad \textbf{(9.11)}$$

The American brokerage firm Merrill Lynch provides another estimate of beta, called *adjusted beta*. The motivation for adjusting beta estimates is the observation that, on average, the beta coefficients of stocks seem to move toward 1 over time. One explanation for this phenomenon is intuitive. A business enterprise usually is established to produce a specific product or service, and a new firm may be more unconventional than an older one in many ways, from technology to management style. As it grows, however, a firm diversifies, first expanding to similar products and later to more diverse operations. As the firm becomes more conventional, it starts to resemble the rest of the economy even more. Thus, its beta coefficient will tend to change in the direction of 1.

Another explanation for this phenomenon is statistical. We know that the average beta over all securities is 1. Thus, before estimating the beta of a security our guess would be that it is 1. When we estimate this beta coefficient over a particular sample period, we sustain some unknown sampling error of the estimated beta. The greater the difference between our beta estimate and 1, the greater is the chance that we incurred a large estimation error and that, when we estimate this same beta in a subsequent sample period, the new estimate will be closer to 1.

The sample estimate of the beta coefficient is the best guess for the sample period. Given that beta has a tendency to evolve toward 1, however, a forecast of the future beta coefficient should adjust the sample estimate in that direction.

Merrill Lynch adjusts beta estimates in a simple way. It takes the sample estimate of beta and averages it with 1, using the weights of two-thirds and one-third:

$$\text{Adjusted beta} = \tfrac{2}{3}\ \text{sample beta} + \tfrac{1}{3}(1)$$

For instance, since Seagram's (VO) is actively traded on the NYSE, Merrill Lynch will be interested in providing an adjusted beta for it. Assuming it had the same estimate for beta of .85 for the 54 months ending in March 1989, the adjusted beta for Seagram's would be .90, taking it one-third of the way toward 1.

A comparison of the beta estimates between the two different periods shows that several of them were remarkably stable, even though they were estimated almost seven years apart. For instance, Alcan's beta went from 1.20 to 1.14; Macmillan Bloedel from 1.49 to 1.29; and Northern Telecom from 1.07 to 1.08. Others showed more variability: Seagram's went from 0.85 to 1.00, and Imperial Oil A from 0.92 to 0.62.

The sample period regression alpha for Seagram's for 1989 is .36. Since Seagram's beta is less than 1, we know that this means that the index model alpha estimate is somewhat smaller. As we did in equation 9.9, we have to subtract $(1 - \beta)r_f$ from the regression alpha to obtain the index model alpha.

---

**CONCEPT CHECK** Question 3. What was Seagram's CAPM alpha per month during the period covered by Nesbitt Burns 1989 regression if during this period the average monthly rate of return of T-bills was 0.8 percent?

---

By contrast, for 1995, where beta is exactly 1, the two alphas are the same. More importantly, these alpha estimates are ex-post (after the fact) measures. They do not mean that anyone could have forecast these alpha values ex ante (before the fact). In fact, the name of the game in security analysis is to forecast alpha values ahead of time. A well-constructed portfolio that includes long positions in future positive alpha stocks and short positions in future negative alpha stocks will outperform the market index. The key term here is *well constructed,* meaning that the portfolio has to balance concentration on high alpha stocks with the need for risk-reducing diversification. The beta and residual variance estimates from the index model regression make it possible to achieve this goal. (We examine this technique in more detail in part IV on active portfolio management.)

In the absence of special information concerning Seagram's, if our forecast for the market index is 14 percent and T-bills pay 6 percent, we learn from the Nesbitt Burns' estimates that the CAPM forecast for the rate of return on Seagram's stock is

$$\begin{aligned} E(\mathrm{r}_{\mathrm{VO}}) &= r_f + \beta \times [E(r_M) - r_f] \\ &= .06 + 1.00(.14 - .06) \\ &= .140 = 14\% \end{aligned}$$

## Industrial Sector Beta Estimates

In analyzing securities, it is often interesting to obtain statistical aggregates by industrial sector. Table 9.2 presented an extract from Nesbitt Burns' calculations for the TSE 300; in compiling that, the firm also estimates the sectoral statistics. The results for the two time periods are shown in Table 9.3; the 14 sectors also are broken down into subsectors in Nesbitt Burns' complete analysis. Note that even by aggregation, while some betas are extremely stable, other sectors show large variations for the two periods.

**Table 9.3** Estimates of Sector Total Return Betas

| | October 1984–March 1989 | | | April 1991–September 1995 | | |
|---|---|---|---|---|---|---|
| **Sector** | **Beta** | **Alpha** | **% Expl. by Market** | **Beta** | **Alpha** | **% Expl. by Market** |
| Metals and minerals | 1.40 | −0.04 | 63.6 | 1.19 | 0.21 | 55.4 |
| Gold and silver | 1.22 | 0.07 | 31.8 | 1.73 | 0.36 | 47.7 |
| Oil and gas | 1.03 | −0.51 | 49.3 | 0.90 | −0.18 | 27.8 |
| Paper/wood products | 1.38 | 0.41 | 70.9 | 1.17 | −0.14 | 50.0 |
| Consumer products | 0.91 | 0.12 | 72.8 | 0.76 | 0.57 | 35.4 |
| Industrial products | 1.07 | −0.54 | 77.2 | 1.19 | 0.15 | 61.5 |
| Real estate | 0.94 | 0.80 | 52.9 | 0.84 | −3.17 | 13.8 |
| Transportation | 1.22 | 0.69 | 48.6 | 1.01 | −1.07 | 21.6 |
| Pipelines | 0.96 | 0.24 | 56.8 | 0.55 | 0.11 | 31.6 |
| Utilities | 0.37 | 0.48 | 32.0 | 0.54 | 0.34 | 42.2 |
| Communications | 0.97 | 0.80 | 62.8 | 0.77 | 0.10 | 41.8 |
| Merchandising | 0.81 | 0.58 | 58.9 | 0.71 | −0.43 | 42.6 |
| Financial services | 0.84 | 0.41 | 69.2 | 0.92 | 0.17 | 51.6 |
| Management companies | 1.19 | 0.25 | 74.7 | 1.29 | −0.53 | 65.2 |

Data from the Quantitative Analysis division of Nesbitt Burns Inc. Reprinted by permission.

## 9.3 Arbitrage: Profits and Opportunities

A risk-free arbitrage opportunity arises when an investor can construct a **zero investment portfolio** that will yield a sure profit. A zero investment portfolio means that the investor need not use any of his or her own money. Obviously, to be able to construct a zero investment portfolio one has to be able to sell short at least one asset and use the proceeds to purchase (go long on) one or more assets. Even a small investor using short positions in this fashion can take a large position in such a portfolio.

An obvious case of an arbitrage opportunity arises when the law of one price is violated, as discussed in the Prologue. When an asset is trading at different prices in two markets (and the price differential exceeds transaction costs), a simultaneous trade in the two markets can produce a sure profit (the net price differential) without any investment. One simply sells short the asset in the high-priced market and buys it in the low-priced market. The net proceeds are positive, and there is no risk because the long and short positions offset each other.

In modern markets with electronic communications and instantaneous execution, arbitrage opportunities have become rare, but not extinct. The same technology that enables the market to absorb new information quickly also enables fast operators to make large profits by trading huge volumes at the instant that an arbitrage opportunity appears. This is the essence of program trading, to be discussed in Chapter 22.

**Table 9.4** Rate of Return Projections

| | High Real Interest Rates | | Low Real Interest Rates | |
|---|---|---|---|---|
| | **High Inflation** | **Low Inflation** | **High Inflation** | **Low Inflation** |
| Probability | .25 | .25 | .25 | .25 |
| **Stock** | | | | |
| Apex (*A*) | −20 | 20 | 40 | 60 |
| Bull (*B*) | 0 | 70 | 30 | −20 |
| Crush (*C*) | 90 | −20 | −10 | 70 |
| Dreck (*D*) | 15 | 3 | 15 | 36 |

**Table 9.5** Rate of Return Statistics

| | | | | Correlation Matrix | | | |
|---|---|---|---|---|---|---|---|
| **Stock** | **Current Price** | **Expected Return** | **Standard Deviation (%)** | ***A*** | ***B*** | ***C*** | ***D*** |
| *A* | $10 | 25 | 29.58% | 1.00 | −.15 | −.29 | .68 |
| *B* | 10 | 20 | 33.91 | −.15 | 1.00 | −.87 | −.38 |
| *C* | 10 | 32.5 | 48.15 | −.29 | −.87 | 1.00 | .22 |
| *D* | 10 | 22.25 | 8.58 | .68 | −.38 | .22 | 1.00 |

From the simple case of a violation of the law of one price, let us proceed to a less obvious (yet just as profitable) arbitrage opportunity. Imagine that four stocks are traded in an economy with only four distinct, possible scenarios. The rates of return on the four stocks for each inflation-interest rate scenario appear in Table 9.4. The current prices of the stocks and rate of return statistics are shown in Table 9.5.

Eyeballing the rate of return data, there seems no clue to any arbitrage opportunity lurking in this set of investments. The expected returns, standard deviations, and correlations do not reveal any particular abnormality.

Consider, however, an equally weighted portfolio of the first three stocks (Apex, Bull, and Crush) and contrast its possible future rates of return with those of the fourth stock, Dreck, as derived from Table 9.4.

| | High Real Interest Rates | | Low Real Interest Rates | |
|---|---|---|---|---|
| | **High Inflation Rate** | **Low Inflation Rate** | **High Inflation Rate** | **Low Inflation Rate** |
| Equally weighted portfolio (*A*, *B*, and *C*) | 23.33 | 23.33 | 20.00 | 36.67 |
| Dreck | 15.00 | 23.00 | 15.00 | 36.00 |

This analysis reveals that in all scenarios the equally weighted portfolio will outperform Dreck. The rate of return statistics of the two alternatives are

| | Mean | Standard Deviation | Correlation |
|---|---|---|---|
| Three-stock portfolio | 25.83 | 6.40 | .94 |
| Dreck | 22.25 | 8.58 | |

The two investments are not perfectly correlated; that is, they are not perfect substitutes, meaning there is no violation of the law of one price here. Nevertheless, the equally weighted portfolio will fare better under *any* circumstances; thus any investor, no matter how risk averse, can take advantage of this dominance. All that is required is for the investor to take a short position in Dreck and use the proceeds to purchase the equally weighted portfolio.[9] Let us see how it would work.

Suppose that we sell short 300,000 shares of Dreck and use the $3 million proceeds to buy 100,000 shares each of Apex, Bull, and Crush. The dollar profits in each of the four scenarios will be as follows:

| | | High Real Interest Rates | | Low Real Interest Rates | |
|---|---|---|---|---|---|
| Stock | Dollar Investment | High Inflation Rate | Low Inflation Rate | High Inflation Rate | Low Inflation Rate |
| Apex | $1,000,000 | $−200,000 | $200,000 | $400,000 | $ 600,000 |
| Bull | 1,000,000 | 0 | 700,000 | 300,000 | −200,000 |
| Crush | 1,000,000 | 900,000 | −200,000 | −100,000 | 700,000 |
| Dreck | −3,000,000 | −450,000 | −690,000 | −450,000 | −1,080,000 |
| Portfolio | 0 | $ 250,000 | $ 10,000 | $150,000 | $ 20,000 |

The first column verifies that the net investment in our portfolio is zero. Yet this portfolio yields a positive profit according to any scenario. This is a money machine. Investors will want to take an infinite position in such a portfolio because larger positions entail no risk of losses, yet yield ever-growing profits. Theoretically, even a single investor would take such large positions that the market would react to the buying and selling pressure: the price of Dreck has to come down and/or the prices of Apex, Bull, and Crush have to go up. The arbitrage opportunity will be eliminated.

**CONCEPT CHECK**

Question 4. Suppose that Dreck's price starts falling without any change in its per-share dollar payoffs. How far must the price fall before arbitrage between Dreck and the equally weighted portfolio is no longer possible? (Hint: what happens to the amount of the equally weighted portfolio that can be purchased with the proceeds of the short sale as Dreck's price falls?)

[9] Short selling is discussed in Chapter 3.

The idea that equilibrium market prices ought to be rational in the sense that prices will move to rule out arbitrage opportunities is perhaps the most fundamental concept in capital market theory. Violation of this restriction would indicate the grossest form of market irrationality.

The critical property of a risk-free arbitrage portfolio is that any investor, regardless of risk aversion or wealth, will want to take an infinite position in it so that profits will be driven to an infinite level. Because those large positions will force prices up or down until the opportunity vanishes, we can derive restrictions on security prices that satisfy the condition that no arbitrage opportunities are left in the marketplace.

There is an important difference between (risk-free) arbitrage and risk versus return dominance arguments in support of equilibrium price relationships. A dominance argument holds that when an equilibrium price relationship is violated, many investors will make portfolio changes. Each individual investor will make a limited change, though, depending on his or her degree of risk aversion. Aggregation of these limited portfolio changes over many investors is required to create a large volume of buying and selling, which in turn restores equilibrium prices. When arbitrage opportunities exist, by contrast, each investor wants to take as large a position as possible; hence it will not take many investors to bring about the price pressures necessary to restore equilibrium. For this reason, implications for prices derived from no-arbitrage arguments are stronger than implications derived from a risk versus return dominance argument.

The CAPM is an example of a dominance argument. The CAPM argues that all investors hold mean-variance efficient portfolios. If a security (or a bundle of securities) is mispriced, then investors will tilt their portfolios toward the underpriced and away from the overpriced securities. The resulting pressure on equilibrium prices results from many investors shifting their portfolios, each by a relatively small dollar amount. The assumption that a sufficiently large number of investors are mean-variance sensitive is critical, whereas the essence of the no-arbitrage condition is that even relatively few investors are enough to identify an arbitrage opportunity and then mobilize large dollar amounts to take advantage of it. Pressure on prices can result from only a few arbitrageurs.

Practitioners often use the terms *arbitrage* and *arbitrageurs* in ways other than our strict definition. *Arbitrageur* often is used to refer to a professional searching for mispriced securities in specific areas such as merger-target stocks, rather than to one who seeks strict (risk-free) arbitrage opportunities in the sense that no loss is possible. The search for mispriced securities rather than the more restrictive search for sure bets sometimes is called **risk arbitrage** to distinguish it from pure arbitrage.

To leap ahead, in Part VII we discuss "derivative" securities such as futures and options, where market values are completely determined by the prices of other securities or portfolios. For example, a call option on a stock has a value at maturity that is fully determined by the price of the stock. For such securities, strict arbitrage is a practical possibility, and the condition of no-arbitrage leads to exact pricing. In the case of stocks and other "primitive" securities (whose values are not determined strictly by a single asset or bundle of assets), no-arbitrage conditions must be obtained by appealing to diversification arguments.

## 9.4 Well-Diversified Portfolios and the APT

Stephen Ross developed the **Arbitrage Pricing Theory** (APT) in 1976.[10] As with our analysis of the CAPM, we begin with the simple version of his model, which assumes that only one systematic factor affects security returns. However, the usual discussion of the APT is concerned with the multifactor case, and we treat this richer model in Section 9.7.

Ross starts by examining a single-factor model similar in spirit to the index model introduced in section 9.1. As in that model, uncertainty in asset returns has two sources: a common or macroeconomic factor and a firm-specific or microeconomic cause. In the factor model, the common factor is assumed to have zero expected value, and it is meant to measure new information concerning the macroeconomy. New information has, by definition, zero expected value. There is no need, however, to assume that the factor can be proxied by the return on a market index portfolio.

If we call $F$ the deviation of the common factor from its expected value, $\beta_i$ the sensitivity of firm $i$ to that factor, and $e_i$ the firm-specific disturbance, the factor model states that the actual return on firm $i$ will equal its expected return plus a (zero expected value) random amount attributable to unanticipated economywide events, plus another (zero expected value) random amount attributable to firm-specific events.

Formally,

$$r_i = E(r_i) + \beta_i F + e_i$$

where $E(r_i)$ is the expected return on stick $i$. All the nonsystematic returns, the $e_i$s, are uncorrelated among themselves and uncorrelated with the factor, $F$.

To make the factor model more concrete, consider an example. Suppose that the macro factor, $F$, is taken to be the unexpected percentage change in GNP, and that the consensus is that GNP will increase by 4 percent this year. Suppose also that a stock's $\beta$ value is 1.2. If GNP increases by only 3 percent, then the value of $F$ would be $-1$ percent, representing a 1 percent disappointment in actual growth versus expected growth. Given the stock's beta value, this disappointment would translate into a return on the stock that is 1.2 percent lower than previously expected. This macro surprise, together with the firm-specific disturbance, $e_i$, determines the total departure of the stock's return from its originally expected value.

[10] Stephen A. Ross, "Return, Risk and Arbitrage," in I. Friend and J. Bicksler (editors), *Risk and Return in Finance* (Cambridge, Mass.: Ballinger, 1976).

## Well-Diversified Portfolios

Now we look at the risk of a portfolio of stocks. We first show that if a portfolio is well diversified, its firm-specific or nonfactor risk can be diversified away. Only factor (or systematic) risk remains. If we construct an $n$-stock portfolio with weights, $w_i$, $\Sigma\, w_i = 1$, then the rate of return on this portfolio is as follows:

$$r_P = E(r_P) + \beta_P F + e_P \tag{9.12}$$

where

$$\beta_P = \Sigma w_i \beta_i$$

is the weighted average of the $\beta_i$ of the $n$ securities. The portfolio nonsystematic component (which is uncorrelated with $F$) is

$$e_P = \Sigma w_i e_i$$

which also is a weighted average, in this case of the $e_i$ of each of the $n$ securities.

We can divide the variance of this portfolio into systematic and nonsystematic sources, as we saw in Section 9.1 (equation 9.7). The portfolio variance is

$$\sigma_P^2 = \beta_P^2 \sigma_F^2 + \sigma^2(e_P)$$

where $\sigma_F^2$ is the variance of the factor $F$, and $\sigma^2(e_P)$ is the nonsystematic risk of the portfolio, which is given by

$$\sigma^2(e_P) = \text{Variance}(\Sigma w_i e_i) = \Sigma w_i^2 \sigma^2(e_i)$$

Note that, in deriving the nonsystematic variance of the portfolio, we depend on the fact that the firm-specific $e_i$s are uncorrelated and hence that the variance of the "portfolio" of nonsystematic $e_i$s is the weighted sum of the individual nonsystematic variances (with the square of the investment proportions as weights).

If the portfolio were equally weighted, $w_i = 1/n$, then the nonsystematic variance would be

$$\sigma^2\left(e_P;\, w_i = \frac{1}{n}\right) = \Sigma\left(\frac{1}{n}\right)^2 \sigma^2(e_i) = \frac{1}{n}\Sigma\,\frac{\sigma^2(e_i)}{n} = \frac{1}{n}\,\overline{\sigma}^2(e_i)$$

In this case, we divide the average nonsystematic variance, $\overline{\sigma}^2(e_i)$, by $n$, so that when the portfolio gets large (in the sense that $n$ is large and the portfolio remains equally weighted across all $n$ stocks), the nonsystematic variance approaches zero.

---

**CONCEPT CHECK** Question 5. What will be the nonsystematic standard deviation of the equally weighted portfolio if the average value of $\sigma^2(e_i)$ equals .30, and (a) $n = 10$, (b) $n = 100$, (c) $n = 1{,}000$, and (d) $n = 10{,}000$? What do you conclude about the nonsystematic risk of large, diversified portfolios?

---

The set of portfolios for which the nonsystematic variance approaches zero as $n$ gets large consists of more portfolios than just the equally weighted portfolio.

Any portfolio for which each $w_i$ becomes consistently smaller as $n$ gets large (specifically where each $w_i^2$ approaches zero as $n$ gets large) will satisfy the condition that the portfolio nonsystematic risk will approach zero as $n$ gets large.

In fact, this property motivates us to define a **well-diversified portfolio** as one that is diversified over a large enough number of securities with proportions, $w_i$, each small enough that for practical purposes the nonsystematic variance, $\sigma^2(e_P)$, is negligible. Because the expected return of $e_P$ is zero, if its variance also is zero, we can conclude that any realized value of $e_P$ will be virtually zero. Rewriting equation 9.12, we conclude that for a well-diversified portfolio for all practical purposes

$$r_P = E(r_p) + \beta_P F$$

and

$$\sigma_P^2 = \beta_P^2 \sigma_F^2;\ \sigma_P = \beta_P \sigma_F$$

Large (mostly institutional) investors hold portfolios of hundreds and even thousands of securities; thus the concept of well-diversified portfolios clearly is operational in contemporary financial markets. Well-diversified portfolios, however, are not necessarily equally weighted.

As an illustration, consider a portfolio of 1,000 stocks. Let our position in the first stock be $w$ percent. Let the position in the second stock be $2w$ percent, the position in the third $3w$ percent, and so on. In this way our largest position (in the thousandth stock) is $1{,}000w$ percent. Can this portfolio possibly be well diversified, considering the fact that the largest position is 1,000 times the smallest position? Surprisingly, the answer is yes.

To see this, let us determine the largest weight in any one stock, in this case, the thousandth stock. The sum of the positions in all stocks must be 100 percent; therefore

$$w + 2w + \ldots + 1{,}000w = 100$$

Solving for $w$, we find that

$$w = .0002\%$$

$$1000w = .2\%$$

Our *largest* position amounts to only .2 of 1 percent. And this is very far from an equally weighted portfolio. Yet, for practical purposes, this still is a well-diversified portfolio.

## Betas and Expected Returns

Because nonfactor risk can be diversified away, only factor risk commands a risk premium in market equilibrium. Nonsystematic risk across firms cancels out in well-diversified portfolios, so that only the systematic risk of a security can be related to its expected returns.

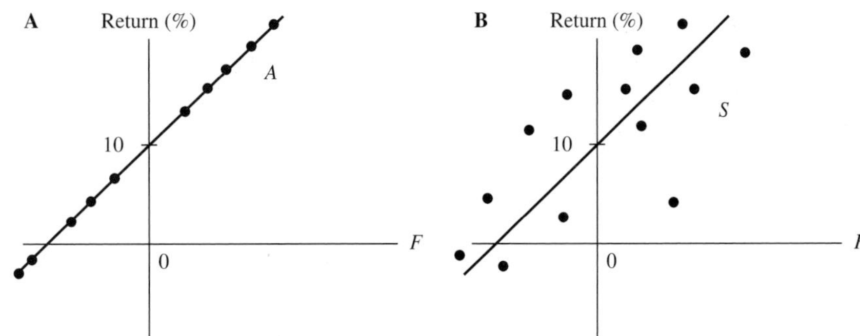


**Figure 9.3**
Returns as a function of the systematic factor. **A** = well-diversified portfolio ($A$); **B** = single stock ($S$).

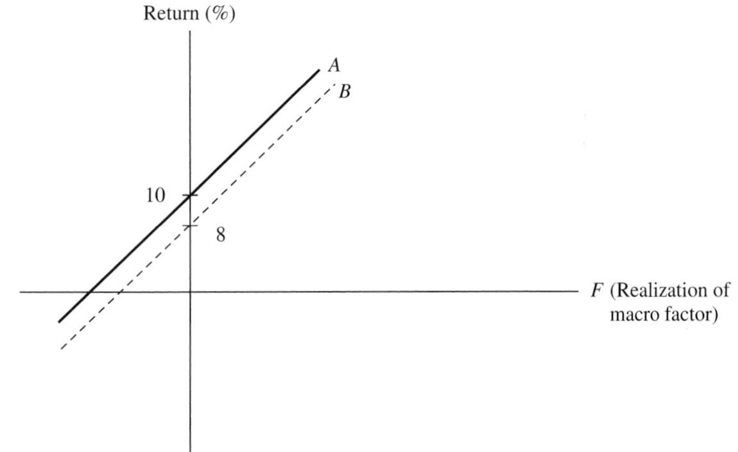


**Figure 9.4**
Returns as a function of the systematic factor: an arbitrage opportunity.

The solid line in Figure 9.3**A** plots the return of a well-diversified portfolio ($A$) with $\beta_A = 1$ for various realizations of the systematic factor. The expected return of portfolio $A$ is 10 percent: this is where the solid line crosses the vertical axis. At this point, the systematic factor is zero, implying no macro surprises. If the macro factor is positive, the portfolio's return exceeds its expected value; if it is negative, the portfolio's return falls short of its mean. The return on the portfolio is therefore

$$E(r_A) + \beta_A F = .10 + 1.0 \times F$$

Compare Figure 9.3**A** with Figure 9.3**B,** which is a similar graph for a single stock ($S$) with $\beta_S = 1$. The undiversified stock is subject to nonsystematic risk, which is seen in a scatter of points around the line. The well-diversified portfolio's return, in contrast, is determined completely by the systematic factor.

Now consider Figure 9.4, where the dashed line plots the return on another well-diversified portfolio, portfolio $B$, with an expected return of 8 percent and $\beta_B$ also equal to 1.0. Could portfolios $A$ and $B$ coexist with the return pattern

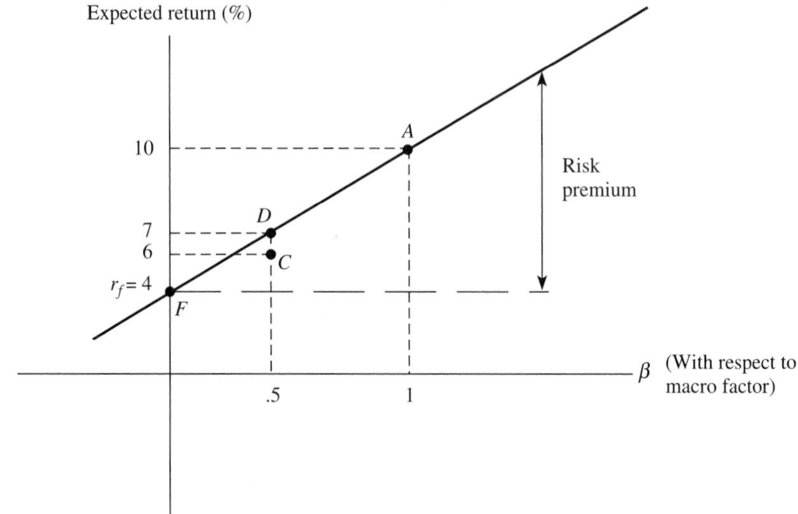


**Figure 9.5**
An arbitrage opportunity.

depicted? Clearly not: No matter what the systematic factor turns out to be, portfolio *A* outperforms portfolio *B*, leading to an arbitrage opportunity.

If you sell short \$1 million of *B* and buy \$1 million of *A*, a zero net investment strategy, your return would be \$20,000, as follows:

| | |
|---|---|
| $(.10 + 1.0 \times F) \times \$1$ million | (From long position in *A*) |
| $-(.08 + 1.0 \times F) \times \$1$ million | (From short position in *B*) |
| $.02 \times \$1$ million $= \$20{,}000$ | (Net proceeds) |

You make a risk-free profit because the factor risk cancels out across the long and short positions. Moreover, the strategy requires zero net investment. You should pursue it on an infinitely large scale until the return discrepancy between the two portfolios disappears. Portfolios with equal betas must have equal expected returns in market equilibrium, or arbitrage opportunities exist.

What about portfolios with different betas? We show now that their risk premiums must be proportional to beta. To see why, consider Figure 9.5. Suppose that the risk-free rate is 4 percent and that well-diversified portfolio *C*, with a beta of .5, has an expected return of 6 percent. Portfolio *C* plots below the line from the risk-free asset to portfolio *A*. Consider therefore a new portfolio, *D*, composed of half of portfolio *A* and half of the risk-free asset. Portfolio *D*'s beta will be $(\frac{1}{2} \times 0 + \frac{1}{2} \times 1.0) = .5$, and its expected return will be $(\frac{1}{2} \times 4 + \frac{1}{2} \times 10) =$ 7 percent. Now portfolio *D* has an equal beta but a greater expected return than does portfolio *C*. From our analysis in the previous paragraph we know that this constitutes an arbitrage opportunity.

We conclude that, to preclude arbitrage opportunities, the expected return on all well-diversified portfolios must lie on the straight line from the risk-free asset in Figure 9.5. The equation of this line will dictate the expected return on all well-diversified portfolios.

---

**CONCEPT CHECK** Question 6. Suppose that portfolio $E$ is well diversified with a beta of ⅔ and expected return of 9 percent. Would an arbitrage opportunity exist? If so, what would be the arbitrage opportunity?

---

Notice in Figure 9.5 that risk premiums are indeed proportional to portfolio betas. The risk premium is depicted by the vertical arrow, which measures the distance between the risk-free rate and the expected return on the portfolio. The risk premium is zero for $\beta = 0$, and rises in direct proportion to $\beta$.

## The Security Market Line

Now consider the market portfolio as a well-diversified portfolio, and let us measure the systematic factor as the unexpected return on the market portfolio. The beta of the market portfolio is 1, since that is the beta of the market portfolio with itself. Hence, the market portfolio is at point $A$ on the line in Figure 9.5, and we can use it to determine the equation describing that line. The intercept is $r_f$, and the slope is $E(r_M) - r_f$[rise $= E(r_M) - r_f$; run $= 1$], implying that the equation of the line is

$$E(r_P) = r_f + [E(r_M) - r_f]\beta_P \tag{9.13}$$

Hence, Figure 9.5 is identical to the SML relationship of the CAPM.

We have used the no-arbitrage condition to obtain an expected return-beta relationship identical to that of the CAPM, without the restrictive assumptions of the CAPM. This suggests that despite its restrictive assumptions, the main conclusion of the CAPM—namely, the SML expected return–relationship—is likely to be at least approximately valid.

It is worth noting that, in contrast to the CAPM, the APT does not require that the benchmark portfolio in the SML relationship be the true market portfolio. Any well-diversified portfolio lying on the SML of Figure 9.5 may serve as the benchmark portfolio. For example, one might define the benchmark portfolio as the well-diversified portfolio most highly correlated with whatever systematic factor is thought to affect stock returns. Accordingly, the APT has more flexibility than does the CAPM because problems associated with an unobservable market portfolio are not a concern.

In addition, the APT provides further justification for use of the index model in the practical implementation of the SML relationship. Even if the index portfolio is not a precise proxy for the true market portfolio, which is a cause of considerable concern in the context of the CAPM, we now know that if the index portfolio is sufficiently well diversified, the SML relationship should still hold true according to the APT.

So far we have demonstrated the APT relationship for well-diversified portfolios only. The CAPM expected return–beta relationship applies to single assets, as well as to portfolio. In the next section, we generalize the APT result one step further.

## 9.5 Individual Assets and the APT

We have demonstrated that, if arbitrage opportunities using well-diversified portfolios are to be ruled out, each portfolio's expected excess return must be proportional to is beta. For any two well-diversified portfolios $P$ and $Q$, this can be written as

$$\frac{E(r_P) - r_f}{\beta_P} = \frac{E(r_Q) - r_f}{\beta_Q} \tag{9.14}$$

The question is whether this relationship tells us anything about the expected rates of return on the component stocks. The answer is that if this relationship is to be satisfied by all well-diversified portfolios, it almost surely must be satisfied by all individual securities, although the proof of this proposition is somewhat difficult. We note at the outset that, intuitively, we must prove simply that nonsystematic risk does not matter for security returns. The expected return–beta relationship that holds for well-diversified portfolios also must hold for individual securities.

First, we show that if individual securities satisfy equation 9.14, so will all portfolios. If for any two stocks, $i$ and $j$, the same relationship holds exactly, that is,

$$\frac{E(r_i) - r_f}{\beta_i} = \frac{E(r_j) - r_f}{\beta_j} = K$$

where $K$ is a constant for all securities, then by cross-multiplying, we can write, for any security, $i$,

$$E(r_i) = r_f + \beta_i K$$

Therefore, for any portfolio $P$ with security weights $w_i$, we have

$$E(r_P) = \sum w_i E(r_i) = r_f \sum w_i + K \sum w_i \beta_i$$

Because $\Sigma w_i = 1$ and $\beta_P = \Sigma w_i \beta_i$, we have

$$E(r_P) = r_f + \beta_P K$$

Thus for all portfolios,

$$\frac{E(r_P) - r_f}{\beta_P} = K$$

and since all portfolios have the same $K$,

$$\frac{E(r_P) - r_f}{\beta_P} = \frac{E(r_Q) - r_f}{\beta_Q}$$

In other words, if the expected return–beta relationship holds for all single assets, then it will hold for all portfolios.

---

**CONCEPT CHECK** Question 7. Confirm the property expressed in equation 9.14 with a simple numerical example. Support that portfolio $P$ has an expected return of 10 percent, and $\beta$ of .5, whereas portfolio $Q$ has an expected return of 15 percent and $\beta$ of 1. The risk-free rate, $r_f$, is 5 percent.

*a.* Find $K$ for these portfolios, and confirm that they are equal.

*b.* Find $K$ for an equally weighted portfolio of $P$ and $Q$, and show that it equals $K$ for each individual security.

---

Now we show that it also is necessary that all securities satisfy the condition. To avoid extensive mathematics, we will satisfy ourselves with a less rigorous argument. Suppose that this relationship is violated for all single assets. Now create a pair of well-diversified portfolios from these assets. What are the chances that, in spite of the fact that for any two single assets this relationship

$$\frac{E(r_i) - r_f}{\beta_i} = \frac{E(r_j) - r_f}{\beta_j}$$

does not hold, the relationship *will* hold for the well-diversified portfolios as follows:

$$\frac{E(r_P) - r_f}{\beta_P} = \frac{E(r_Q) - r_f}{\beta_Q}$$

The chances are small, but it is possible that the relationships among the single securities are violated in offsetting ways so that somehow it holds for the pair of well-diversified portfolios.

Now construct yet another well-diversified portfolio. What are the chances that the violation of the relationships for single securities are such that the third portfolio also will fulfill the no-arbitrage expected return–beta relationship? Obviously, the chances are smaller still. But the relationship is possible. Continue with a fourth well-diversified portfolio, and so on. If the no-arbitrage expected return–beta relationship has to hold for infinitely many different, well-diversified portfolios, it must be virtually certain that the relationship holds for all individual securities.

We use the term *virtually certain* advisedly because we must distinguish this conclusion from the statement that all securities surely fulfill this relationship. The reason we cannot make the latter statement has to do with a property of well-diversified portfolios.

Recall that for a portfolio to qualify as well diversified it has to have very small positions in all securities. If, for example, only one security violates the expected return–beta relationship, then the effect of this violation for a well-diversified portfolio will be too small to be of importance for any practical purpose, and meaningful arbitrage opportunities will not arise. But if many securities violate the expected return–beta relationship, the relationship will no longer hold for well-diversified portfolios, and arbitrage opportunities will be available.

Consequently, we conclude that imposing the no-arbitrage condition on a single-factor security market implies maintenance of the expected return–beta relationship for all well-diversified portfolios and for all but possible, a *small* number of individual securities.

## 9.6 The CAPM, the Index Model, and the APT

The CAPM, the index model, and the APT all serve many of the same functions. They give us a benchmark for fair rates of return that can be used for capital budgeting, security evaluation, or investment performance evaluation. Moreover, they highlight the crucial distinction between nondiversifiable risk (factor risk), which requires a reward in the form of a risk premium, and diversifiable risk, which does not. The existence of all three models raises the question of what distinctions can be made between the assumptions and conclusions associated with each of them. In other words, what advantage is there in using any one of the models in preference to the others?

### Actual Returns versus Expected Returns

The CAPM is an elegant model. The question is whether it has real-world value—whether its implications are borne out by experience. Chapter 10 provides a range of empirical evidence on this point, but for now we will focus briefly on a more basic issue: is the CAPM testable even in principle?

For starters, one central prediction of the CAPM is that the market portfolio is a mean-variance efficient portfolio. Consider that the CAPM treats all traded risky assets. To test the efficiency of the CAPM market portfolio, we would need to construct a value-weighted portfolio of a huge size and test its efficiency. So far, this task has not been feasible. An even more difficult problem, however, is that the CAPM implies relationships among *expected* returns, whereas all we can observe are actual or realized holding period returns, and these need not equal prior expectations. Even supposing we could construct a portfolio to represent the CAPM market portfolio satisfactorily, how would we test its mean-variance efficiency? We would have to show that the reward-to-variability ratio of the market portfolio is higher than that of any other portfolio. However, this reward-to-variability ratio is set in terms of expectations, and we have no way to observe these expectations directly.

The problem of measuring expectations haunts us as well when we try to establish the validity of the second central set of CAPM predictions, the expected return–beta relationship. This relationship also is defined in terms of expected returns $E(r_i)$ and $E(r_M)$:

$$E(r_i) = r_f + \beta_i[E(r_M) - r_f] \tag{9.15}$$

The upshot is that, as elegant and insightful as the CAPM is, we must make additional assumptions to make it implementable and testable.

## The Index Model and Realized Returns

We have said that the CAPM is a statement about ex ante or expected returns, whereas in practice all anyone can observe directly are ex post or realized returns. To make the leap from expected to realized returns, we can employ the index model, which we will use in excess return form as

$$R_i = \alpha_i + \beta_i R_M + e_i \tag{9.16}$$

We saw in Section 9.1 how to apply standard regression analysis to estimate equation 9.16 using observable realized returns over some sample period. Let us now see how this framework for statistically decomposing actual stock returns meshes with the CAPM.

We start by deriving the covariance between the returns on stock $i$ and the market index. By definition, the firm-specific or nonsystematic component is independent of the marketwide or systematic component, that is, $\text{Cov}(R_M, e_i) = 0$. From this relationship, it follows that the covariance of the excess rate of return on security $i$ with that of the market index is

$$\begin{aligned}\text{Cov}(R_i, R_M) &= \text{Cov}(\beta_i R_M + e_i, R_M)\\ &= \beta_i \text{Cov}(R_M, R_M) + \text{Cov}(e_i, R_M)\\ &= \beta_i \sigma_M^2\end{aligned}$$

Note that we can drop $\alpha_i$ from the covariance terms because $\alpha_i$ is a constant and thus has zero covariance with all variables.

Because $\text{Cov}(R_i, R_M) = \beta_i \sigma_M^2$, the sensitivity coefficient, $\beta_i$, in equation 9.16, which is the slope of the regression line representing the index model, equals

$$\beta_i = \frac{\text{Cov}(R_i, R_M)}{\sigma_M^2}$$

The index model beta coefficient turns out to be the same beta as that of the CAPM expected return–beta relationship, except that we replace the (theoretical) market portfolio of the CAPM with the well-specified and observable market index.

**CONCEPT CHECK**

Question 8. The data below are drawn from a three-stock financial market that satisfies the single index model.

| Stock | Capitalization ($) | Beta | Mean Excess Return | Standard Deviation |
|---|---|---|---|---|
| *A* | 3,000 | 1.0 | .10 | .40 |
| *B* | 1,940 | .2 | .02 | .30 |
| *C* | 1,360 | 1.7 | .17 | .50 |

The single factor in this economy is perfectly correlated with the value-weighted index of the stock market. The standard deviation of the market index portfolio is 25 percent.

*a.* What is the mean excess return of the index portfolio?

*b.* What is the covariance between stock *A* and the index?

*c.* Break down the variance of stock *B* into its systematic and firm-specific components.

## The Index Model and the Expected Return–Beta Relationship

Recall that the CAPM expected return–beta relationship is, for any asset *i* and the (theoretical) market portfolio,

$$E(r_i) - r_f = \beta_i[E(r_M) - r_f]$$

where $\beta_i = \text{Cov}(r_i, r_M)/\sigma_M^2$. This is a statement about the mean or expected excess return of assets relative to the mean excess return of the (theoretical) market portfolio.

Assuming that the index *M* in equation 9.16 represents the true market portfolio, and taking the expectation of each side of equation 9.16 shows that the index model specification is

$$E(r_i) - r_f = \alpha_i + \beta_i[E(r_M) - r_f]$$

A comparison of the index model relationship to the CAPM expected return–beta relationship shows that the CAPM predicts that $\alpha_i$ must be zero for all assets. The alpha of a stock is its expected return in excess of (or below) the fair expected return as predicted by the CAPM. If the stock is fairly priced, its alpha must be zero.

We emphasize again that this is a statement about expected returns on a security. After the fact, of course, some securities will do better or worse than expected and will have returns higher or lower than predicted by the CAPM relationship; that is, they will exhibit positive or negative alphas over a sample period. But this superior or inferior performance could not have been forecast in advance.

Therefore, if we estimate the index model for several firms, using equation 9.16 as a regression equation, we should find that the ex post or realized alphas (the

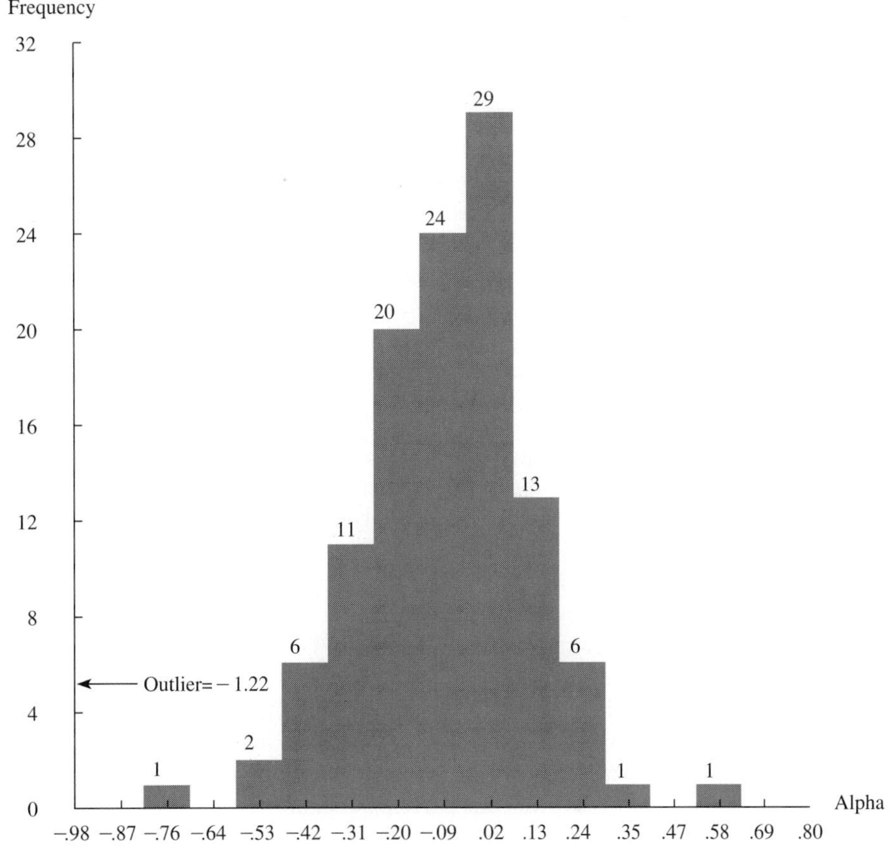


**Figure 9.6**
Frequency distribution of alphas.
From Michael C. Jensen, "The Performance of Mutual Funds in the Period 1945–1964," *Journal of Finance* 23 (May 1968). Reprinted by permission.

regression intercepts) for the firms in our sample center around zero. If the initial expectation for alpha were zero, as many firms would be expected to have a positive as a negative alpha for some sample period. The CAPM states that the *expected* value of alpha is zero for all securities, whereas the index model representation of the CAPM holds that the *realized* value of alpha should average out to zero for a sample of historical observed returns.

Some interesting evidence on this property was compiled by Michael Jensen,[11] who examined the alphas realized by mutual funds over the 10-year period 1955–1964. Figure 9.6 shows the frequency distribution of these alphas, which do indeed seem to be distributed around zero.

There is yet another applicable variation on the intuition of the index model, the **market model.** Formally, the market model states that the return "surprise"

[11] Michael C. Jensen, "The Performance of Mutual Funds in the Period 1945–1964," *Journal of Finance* 23 (May 1968).

of any security is proportional to the return surprise of the market, plus a firm-specific surprise:

$$r_i - E(r_i) = \beta_i[r_M - E(r_M)] + e_i$$

This equation divides returns into firm-specific and systematic components somewhat differently from the index model. If the CAPM is valid, however, you can see that, substituting for $E(r_i)$ from equation 9.15, the market model equation becomes identical to the index model we have just presented. For this reason the terms *index model* and *market model* sometimes are used interchangeably.

## Comparison with the APT

The APT is an extremely appealing model. It depends on the assumption that a rational equilibrium in capital markets precludes arbitrage opportunities. A violation of the APT's pricing relationships will cause extremely strong pressure to restore them, even if only a limited number of investors become aware of the disequilibrium.

Furthermore, the APT yields an expected return–beta relationship using a well-diversified portfolio that can be constructed practically from a large number of securities. In contrast, the CAPM is derived assuming an inherently unobservable "market" portfolio.

In spite of these appealing differences, the APT does not fully dominate the CAPM. The CAPM provides an unequivocal statement on the expected return–beta relationship for all assets, whereas the APT implies that this relationship holds for all but perhaps a small number of securities. This is an important difference, yet it is fruitless to pursue because the CAPM is not a readily testable model in the first place. A more productive comparison is between the APT and the index model.

As noted in the beginning of this chapter, the index model and the single-factor APT use virtually identical assumptions about the structure of security returns. Further, the index model relies on the assumptions of the CAPM with additional assumptions that: (1) a specified market index is virtually perfectly correlated with the (unobservable) theoretical market portfolio, and (2) the probability distribution of stock returns is stationary so that sample period returns can provide valid estimates of expected returns and variances.

The implication of the index model is that the market index portfolio is efficient and that the expected return–beta relationship holds for all assets. The assumption that the probability distribution of the security returns is stationary and the observability of the index make it possible to test the efficiency of the index and the expected return–beta relationship. The arguments leading from the assumptions to these implications rely on mean-variance efficiency; that is, if any security violates the expected return–beta relationship, then all investors (each relatively small) will tilt their portfolios so that their combined overall pressure on prices will restore an equilibrium that satisfies the relationship.

In contrast, the APT uses arbitrage arguments to obtain the expected return–beta relationship for well-diversified portfolios. Because it focuses on the no-arbitrage condition, without the further assumptions of the market or index model, the APT cannot rule out a violation of the expected return–beta relationship for any particular asset. For this, we need the CAPM assumptions and its dominance arguments.

**CONCEPT CHECK** Question 9. Can you sort out the nuances of the following maze of models?

*a.* CAPM
*b.* Single-factor APT model
*c.* Single index model
*d.* Market model

## 9.7 A MULTIFACTOR APT

We have assumed all along that there is only one systematic factor affecting stock returns. This simplifying assumption is in fact too simplistic. It is easy to think of several factors that might affect stock returns: business cycles, interest rate fluctuations, inflation rates, oil prices, and so on. Presumably, exposure to any of these factors will affect a stock's perceived riskiness and appropriate expected rate of return. We can use a multifactor version of the APT to accommodate these multiple sources of risk.

Suppose that we generalize the factor model expressed in equation 9.12 to a two-factor model:

$$r_i = E(r_i) + \beta_{i1}F_1 + \beta_{i2}F_2 + e_i \quad \textbf{(9.17)}$$

Factor 1 might be, for example, departures of GNP growth from expectations, and factor 2 might be unanticipated inflation. Each factor has a zero expected value because each measures the surprise in the systematic variable rather than the level of the variable. Similarly, the firm-specific component of unexpected return, $e_i$, also has zero expected value. Extending such a two-factor model to any number of factors is straightforward.

Establishing a multifactor APT proceeds along lines very similar to those we followed in the simple one-factor case. First, we introduce the concept of a **factor portfolio,** which is a well-diversified portfolio constructed to have a beta of 1 on one of the factors and a beta of 0 on any other factor. This is an easy restriction to satisfy because we have a large number of securities to choose from and a relatively small number of factors. Factor portfolios will serve as the benchmark portfolios for a multifactor generalization of the security market line relationship.

Suppose that the two factor portfolios, called portfolios 1 and 2, have expected returns $E(r_1) = 10$ percent and $E(r_2) = 12$ percent. Suppose further that the risk-free rate is 4 percent. The risk premium on the first factor portfolio becomes 10 percent − 4 percent = 6 percent, whereas that on the second factor portfolio is 12 percent − 4 percent = 8 percent.

Now consider an arbitrary, well-diversified portfolio, portfolio $A$, where beta on the first factor, $\beta_{A1} = .5$, and beta on the second factor, $\beta_{A2} = .75$. The multifactor APT states that the overall risk premium on this portfolio must equal the sum of the risk premiums required as compensation to investors for each source of systematic risk. The risk premium attributable to risk factor 1 should be the portfolio's exposure to factor 1, $\beta_{A1}$, multiplied by the risk premium earned on the first factor portfolio, $E(r_1) - r_f$. Therefore, the portion of portfolio $A$'s risk premium that is compensation for its exposure to the first risk factor is $\beta_{A1}[E(r_1) - r_f] = .5\ (.10 - .04) = .03$, whereas the risk premium attributable to risk factor 2 is $\beta_{A2}[E(r_2) - r_f] = .75\ (.12 - .04) = .06$. The total risk premium on the portfolio should be $.03 + .06 = .09$. Therefore, the total return on the portfolio should be .13, or 13 percent:

| | |
|---|---|
| .04 | Risk-free rate |
| +.03 | Risk premium for exposure to factor 1 |
| +.06 | Risk premium for exposure to factor 2 |
| .13 | Total expected return |

To see why the expected return on the portfolio must be 13 percent, consider the following argument. Suppose that the expected return on portfolio $A$ were 12 percent rather than 13 percent. This return would give rise to an arbitrage opportunity. Form a portfolio from the factor portfolios with the same betas as portfolio $A$. This requires weights of .5 on the first factor portfolio, .75 on the second factor portfolio, and −.25 on the risk-free asset. This portfolio has exactly the same factor betas as portfolio $A$: it has a beta of .5 on the first factor because of its .5 weight on the first factor portfolio, and it has a beta of .75 on the second factor.

However, in contrast to portfolio $A$, which as a 12 percent expected return, this portfolio's expected return is $(.5 \times 10) + (.75 \times 12) - (.25 \times 4) = 13$ percent. A long position in this portfolio and a short position in portfolio $A$ would yield an arbitrage profit. The total return per dollar long or short in each position would be

| | |
|---|---|
| $.13 + .5F_1 + .75\ F_2$ | (Long position in factor portfolios) |
| $-(.12 + .5\ F_1 + .75\ F_2)$ | (Short position in portfolio $A$) |
| $.01$ | |

for a positive and risk-free return on a zero net investment position.

To generalize this argument, note that the factor exposure of any portfolio, $P$, is given by its betas, $\beta_{P1}$ and $\beta_{P2}$. A competing portfolio formed from factor portfolios with weights $\beta_{P1}$ in the first factor portfolio, $\beta_{P2}$ in the second factor portfolio, and $1 - \beta_{P1} - \beta_{P2}$ in T-bills will have betas equal to those of portfolio $P$, and expected return of

$$E(r_P) = \beta_{P1}\,E(r_1) + \beta_{P2}\,E(r_2) + (1 - \beta_{P1} - \beta_{P2})\,r_f \qquad \textbf{(9.18)}$$

$$= r_f + \beta_{P1}\,[E(r_1) - r_f] + \beta_{P2}\,[E(r_2) - r_f]$$

Hence, many well-diversified portfolios with betas $\beta_{P1}$ and $\beta_{P2}$ must have the return given in equation 9.18 if arbitrage opportunities are to be precluded. If you compare equations 9.13 and 9.18, you will see that equation 9.18 is simply a generalization of the one-factor SML.

Finally, the extension of the multifactor SML of equation 9.18 to individual assets is precisely the same as for the one-factor APT. Equation 9.18 cannot be satisfied by every well-diversified portfolio unless it is satisfied by virtually every security taken individually. This establishes a multifactor version of the APT. Hence, the fair rate of return on any stock with $\beta_1 = .5$ and $\beta_2 = .75$ is 13 percent. Equation 9.18 thus represents the multifactor SML for an economy with multiple sources of risk.

**CONCEPT CHECK** Question 10. Find the fair rate of return on a security with $\beta_1 = .2$ and $\beta_2 = 1.4$.

One shortcoming of the multifactor APT is that it gives no guidance concerning the determination of the risk premiums on the factor portfolios. In contrast, the single-factor CAPM implies that the risk premium on the market is determined by the market's variance and the average degree of risk aversion across investors. On the other hand, the multifactor CAPM that we saw briefly in the previous chapter is very similar to the multifactor APT, and it also gives some guidance concerning the risk premiums on the factor portfolios.

As it turns out, it is not necessary to identify the true factor portfolios in order to estimate the expected return–beta relationship. Reisman and Shanken show (see the reading list) that the requirements from reference portfolios in the estimation procedure are not that stringent. The APT also gives little guidance about the nature of the common factors that influence security returns. For this reason, empirical applications of the APT rely either on statistical techniques to identify the factor portfolios or on a priori specifications of the factors on the basis of economic reasoning. The Chen, Roll, and Ross study (see the reading list), reviewed in detail in the next chapter, is an example of this latter approach.

## SUMMARY

**1.** A single-factor model of the economy classifies sources of uncertainty as systematic (macroeconomic) factors or firm-specific (microeconomic) factors. The index model assumes that the macro factor can be represented by a broad index of stock returns.

**2.** The single-index model drastically reduces the necessary inputs into the Markowitz portfolio selection procedure. It also aids in specialization of labour in security analysis.

**3.** If the index model specification is valid, then the systematic risk of a portfolio or asset equals $\beta^2\sigma_M^2$, and the covariance between two assets equals $\beta_i\beta_j\sigma_M^2$.

**4.** The index model is estimated by applying regression analysis to excess rates of return. The slope of the regression curve is the beta of an asset, whereas the intercept is the asset's alpha during the sample period. The regression line also is called the security characteristic line. The regression beta is equivalent to the CAPM beta, except that the regression uses actual returns and the CAPM is specified in terms of expected returns. The CAPM predicts that the average value of alphas measured by the index model regression will be zero.

**5.** A risk-free arbitrage opportunity arises when two or more security prices enable investors to construct a zero net investment portfolio that will yield a sure profit.

**6.** Rational investors will want to take infinitely large positions in arbitrage portfolios regardless of their degree of risk aversion.

**7.** The presence of arbitrage opportunities and the resulting large volume of trades will create pressure on security prices. This pressure will continue until prices reach levels that preclude arbitrage. Only a few investors need to become aware of arbitrage opportunities to trigger this process because of the large volume of trades in which they will engage.

**8.** When securities are priced so that there are no risk-free arbitrage opportunities, we say that they satisfy the no-arbitrage condition. Price relationships that satisfy the no-arbitrage condition are important because we expect them to hold in real-world markets.

**9.** Portfolios are called *well diversified* if they include a large number of securities and the investment proportion in each is sufficiently small. The proportion of a security in a well-diversified portfolio is small enough so that, for all practical purposes, a reasonable change in that security's rate of return will have a negligible effect on the portfolio rate of return.

**10.** In a single-factor security market, all well-diversified portfolios have to satisfy the expected return–beta relationship of the security market line in order to satisfy the no-arbitrage condition.

**11.** If all well-diversified portfolios satisfy the expected return–beta relationship, then all but a small number of securities almost satisfy this relationship.

**12.** The assumption of a single-factor security market made possible by the simple version of the APT, together with the no-arbitrage condition, implies the same expected return–beta relationship as does the CAPM, yet it does not require the restrictive assumptions of the CAPM and its (unobservable) market portfolio. The price of this generality is that the APT does not guarantee this relationship for all securities at all times.

**13.** A multifactor APT generalizes the single-factor model to accommodate several sources of systematic risk.

**14.** A multifactor CAPM's predictions differ from those of the multifactor APT insofar as the former predicts that common factors affecting security returns that are unrelated to future consumption uncertainty will not be priced. The multifactor APT, on the other hand, predicts that all such common factors will be priced. This distinction, however, is not likely to be meaningful empirically.

## Key Terms

Arbitrage
Factor model
Single-index model
Scatter diagram
Regression equation
Residuals
Security characteristic line
Zero investment portfolio
Risk arbitrage
Arbitrage pricing theory
Well-diversified portfolio
Market model
Factor portfolio

## Selected Readings

*The seminal paper relating the index model to the portfolio selection problem is:*

Sharpe, William F. "A Simplified Model of Portfolio Analysis." *Management Science,* January 1963.

*Stephen Ross developed the arbitrage pricing theory in two articles:*

Ross, S. A. "Return, Risk and Arbitrage." In I. Friend and J. Bicksler (editors), *Risk and Return in Finance.* Cambridge, Mass.: Ballinger, 1976.

Ross, S. A. "Arbitrage Theory of Capital Asset Pricing." *Journal of Economic Theory,* December 1976.

*Articles exploring the factors that influence common stock returns are:*

Bower, D. A.; R. S. Bower; and D. E. Logue. "Arbitrage Pricing and Utility Stock Returns." *Journal of Finance,* September 1984.

Chen, N. F.; R. Roll; and S. Ross. "Economic Forces and the Stock Market: Testing the APT and Alternative Asset Pricing Theories." *Journal of Business,* July 1986.

Sharpe, W. "Factors in New York Stock Exchange Security Returns, 1931–1979." *Journal of Portfolio Management,* Summer 1982.

*Articles exploring the requirement from reference portfolios for testing the expected return–beta relationship are:*

Reisman, H. "Reference Variables, Factor Structure, and the Approximate Multibeta Representation." *Journal of Finance,* September 1992.

Shanken, J. "Multivariate Proxies and Asset Pricing Relations: Living with the Roll Critique." *Journal of Financial Economics,* March 1987.

## Problems

**1.** A portfolio management organization analyzes 75 stocks and constructs a mean-variance efficient portfolio that is constrained to these 75 stocks.

*a.* How many estimates of expected returns, variances, and covariances are needed to optimize this portfolio?

*b.* If one could safely assume that stock market returns closely resemble a single-index structure, how many estimates would be needed?

**2.** The following are estimates for two of the stocks in problem (1).

| Stock | Expected Return | Beta | Firm-Specific Standard Deviation |
|---|---|---|---|
| *A* | .14 | .6 | .32 |
| *B* | .25 | 1.3 | .37 |

The market index has a standard deviation of .26.

*a.* What is the standard deviation of stocks *A* and *B*?

*b.* Suppose that we were to construct a portfolio with the following proportions:

| | | |
|---|---|---|
| Stock *A* | .33 | |
| Stock *B* | .38 | |
| T-bills | .29 | ($r_f$ = 9%) |

Compute the expected return, standard deviation, beta, and nonsystematic standard deviation of the portfolio.

**3.** Consider the following two regression curves for stocks *A* and *B*.

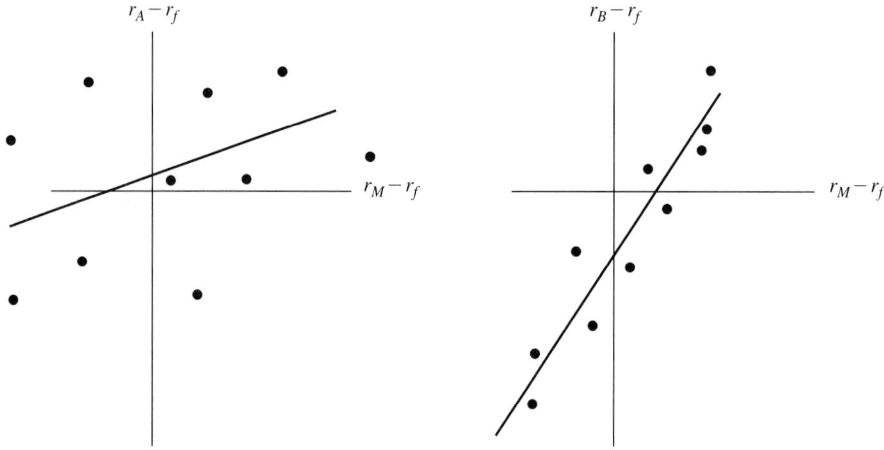


*a.* What stock has higher firm specific risk?

*b.* Which stock has greater systematic (market) risk?

*c.* Which stock has higher *R*-square?

*d.* Which stock has higher alpha?

*e.* Which stock has higher correlation with the market?

**4.** Consider the two (excess return) index model regression results for stocks *A* and *B*:

$$R_A = .01 + 1.2R_M$$
$$R^2 = .576$$
$$\sigma(e) = 10.3\%$$

$$R_B = -.02 + .8R_M$$
$$R^2 = .436$$
$$\sigma(e) = 9.1\%$$

*a.* Which stock has more firm-specific risk?
*b.* Which has greater market risk?
*c.* For which stock does market movement explain a greater fraction of return variability?
*d.* Which stock had an average return in excess of that predicted by the CAPM?
*e.* If $r_f$ were constant at 6 percent and the regression had been run using total rather than excess returns, what would have been the regression intercept for stock *A*?

Use the following data for problems 5–11. Suppose that the index model for stocks *A* and *B* is estimated with the following results:

$$R_A = .02 + .65R_M + e_A$$
$$R_B = .04 + 1.10R_M + e_B$$
$$\sigma_M = .25; R_A^2 = .15; R_B^2 = .30$$

**5.** What is the standard deviation of each stock?
**6.** Break down the variance of each stock to the systematic and firm-specific components.
**7.** What is the covariance and correlation coefficient between the two stocks?
**8.** What is the covariance between each stock and the market index?
**9.** Are the intercepts of the two regressions consistent with the CAPM? Interpret their values.
**10.** For portfolio *P* with investment proportions of .60 in *A* and .40 in *B*, rework problems (5), (6), and (8).
**11.** Rework problem 10 for portfolio *Q* with investment proportions of .50 in *P*, .30 in the market index, and .20 in T-bills.
**12.** Suppose that the following factors have been identified for the Canadian economy: the growth rate of industrial production, IP, and the inflation rate, IR. IP is expected to be 4 percent, and IR 6 percent. A stock with a beta of 1 on IP and .4 on IR currently is expected to provide a rate of return of 14 percent. If industrial production actually grows by 5 percent while the inflation rate turns out to be 7 percent, what is your revised estimate of the expected rate of return on the stock?

**13.** Suppose that there are two independent economic factors, $F_1$ and $F_2$. The risk-free rate is 7 percent, and all stocks have independent firm-specific components with a standard deviation of 50 percent. The following are well-diversified portfolios:

| Portfolio | Beta on $F_1$ | Beta on $F_2$ | Expected Return |
|---|---|---|---|
| *A* | 1.8 | 2.1 | 40 |
| *B* | 2.0 | −0.5 | 10 |

What is the expected return–beta relationship in this economy?

**14.** Consider the following data for a one-factor economy. All portfolios are well diversified.

| Portfolio | $E(r)$ | Beta |
|---|---|---|
| *A* | 10% | 1 |
| *F* | 4% | 0 |

Suppose that portfolio *B* is well diversified with a beta of ⅔ and expected return of 9 percent. Would an arbitrage opportunity exist? If so, what would be the arbitrage strategy?

**15.** The following is a scenario for three stocks constructed by the security analysts of Pf Inc.

| | | Scenario Rate of Return (%) | | |
|---|---|---|---|---|
| Stock | Price ($) | Recession | Average | Boom |
| *A* | 10 | −15 | 20 | 30 |
| *B* | 15 | 25 | 10 | −10 |
| *C* | 50 | 12 | 15 | 12 |

*a.* Construct an arbitrage portfolio using these stocks.

*b.* How might these prices change when equilibrium is restored? Give an example where a change in stock *C*'s price is sufficient to restore equilibrium, assuming that the dollar payoffs to stock *C* remain the same.

**16.** Assume that both portfolios *A* and *B* are well diversified, that $E(r_A) = .14$, and $E(r_B) = .148$. If the economy has only one factor, and $\beta_A = 1$ whereas $\beta_B = 1.1$, what must be the risk-free rate.

**17.** Assume that stock market returns have the market index as a common factor, and that all stocks in the economy have a beta of 1 on the market index. Firm-specific returns all have a standard deviation of .30.

Suppose that an analyst studies 20 stocks and finds that one half have an alpha of 3 percent, and the other half an alpha of −3 percent. Suppose the analyst buys $1 million of an equally weighted portfolio of the positive alpha stocks and shorts $1 million of an equally weighted portfolio of the negative alpha stocks.

*a.* What is the expected profit (in dollars) and standard deviation of the analyst's profit?

*b.* How does your answer change if the analyst examines 50 stocks instead of 20 stocks? 100 stocks?

**18.** Assume that security returns are generated by the single index model

$$R_i = \alpha_i + \beta_i R_M + e_i$$

where $R_i$ is the excess return for security *i*, and $R_M$ is the market's excess return. Suppose also that there are three securities, *A*, *B*, and *C*, characterized by the following data:

| Security | $\beta_i$ | $E(R_i)$ | $\sigma^2(e_i)$ |
|---|---|---|---|
| *A* | .8 | .10 | .05 |
| *B* | 1.0 | .12 | .01 |
| *C* | 1.2 | .14 | .10 |

*a.* If $\sigma_M^2 = .04$, calculate the variance of returns of securities *A*, *B*, and *C*.

*b.* Now assume that there are an infinite number of assets with return characteristics identical to those of *A*, *B*, and *C*, respectively. If one forms a well-diversified portfolio of type *A* securities, what will be the mean and variance of the portfolio's excess returns? What about portfolios composed only of type *B* or *C* stocks?

*c.* Is there an arbitrage opportunity in this market? What is it? Analyze the opportunity graphically.

**19.** The SML relationship states that the expected risk premium on a security in a one-factor model must be directly proportional to the security's beta. Suppose that this were not the case. For example, suppose that expected return rises more than proportionately with beta as in the figure below.

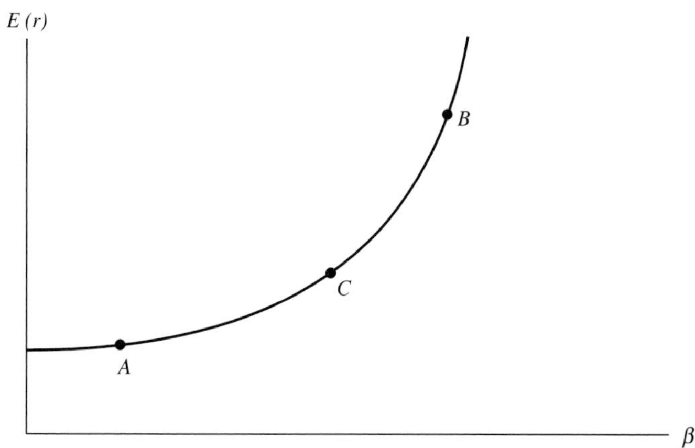


*a.* How could you construct an arbitrage portfolio? (Hint: Consider combinations of portfolios *A* and *B*, and compare the resultant portfolio to *C*.)

*b.* We will see in Chapter 10 that some researchers have examined the relationship between average return on diversified portfolios and the $\beta$ and $\beta^2$ of those portfolios. What should they have discovered about the effect of $\beta^2$ on portfolio return.

**20.** If the APT is to be a useful theory, the number of systematic factors in the economy must be small. Why?

**21.** The APT itself does not provide guidance concerning the factors that one might expect to determine risk premiums. How should researchers decide which factors to investigate? Why, for example, is industrial production a reasonable factor to test for a risk premium?

**22.** Consider the following multifactor (APT) model of security returns for a particular stock:

| Factor | Factor Beta | Factor Risk-Premium (%) |
|---|---|---|
| Inflation | 1.2 | 6 |
| Industrial production | 0.5 | 8 |
| Oil prices | 0.3 | 3 |

*a.* If T-bills currently offer a 6 percent yield, find the expected rate of return on this stock if the market views the stock as fairly priced.

*b.* Suppose that the market expected the values for the three macro factors given in the middle column below, but that the actual values turn out as given in the last column. Calculate the revised expectations for the rate of return on the stock once the "surprises" become known.

| Factor | Expected Rate of Change (%) | Actual Rate of Change (%) |
|---|---|---|
| Inflation | 5 | 4 |
| Industrial production | 3 | 6 |
| Oil prices | 2 | 0 |

**23.** Suppose that the market can be described by the following three sources of systematic risk with associated risk premiums:

| Factor | Risk Premium (%) |
|---|---|
| Industrial production ($I$) | 6 |
| Interest rates ($R$) | 2 |
| Consumer confidence ($C$) | 4 |

The return on a particular stock is generated according to the following equation:

$$r = 15\% + 1.0I + .5R + .75C + e$$

Find the equilibrium rate of return on this stock using the APT. The T-bill rate is 6 percent. Is the stock over- or underpriced? Explain.

**24.** Assume that both $X$ and $Y$ are well-diversified portfolios and the risk-free rate is 8 percent.

| Portfolio | Expected Return | Beta |
|---|---|---|
| *X* | 16% | 1.00 |
| *Y* | 12% | 0.25 |

In this situation you would conclude that Portfolios $X$ and $Y$:

*a.* Are in equilibrium?
*b.* Offer an arbitrage opportunity?
*c.* Are both underpriced?
*d.* Are both fairly priced?

**25.** According to the theory of arbitrage:

*a.* High-beta stocks are consistently overpriced.
*b.* Low-beta stocks are consistently overpriced.
*c.* Positive alpha stocks will quickly disappear.
*d.* Rational investors will arbitrage consistent with their risk tolerance.

**26.** A zero investment portfolio with a positive alpha could arise if:

*a.* The expected return of the portfolio equals zero.
*b.* The capital market line is tangent to the opportunity set.
*c.* The law of one price remains unviolated.
*d.* A risk-free arbitrage opportunity exists.

**27.** The arbitrage pricing theory (APT) differs from the capital asset pricing model (CAPM) because the APT:

*a.* Places more emphasis on market risk.
*b.* Minimizes the importance of diversification.
*c.* Recognizes multiple unsystematic risk factors.
*d.* Recognizes multiple systematic risk factors.

**28.** An investor will take as large a position as possible when an equilibrium price relationship is violated. This is an example of:

*a.* A dominance argument.
*b.* The mean-variance efficient frontier.
*c.* A risk-free arbitrage.
*d.* The capital asset pricing model.

**29.** A zero investment portfolio arises when:

*a.* An investor has only downside risk.
*b.* The law of prices remains unviolated.
*c.* The opportunity set is not tangent to the capital allocation line.
*d.* A risk-free arbitrage opportunity exists.

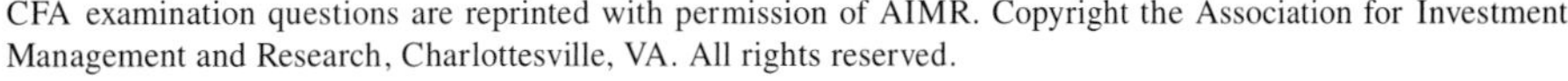

*Chapter* **10**

# Empirical Evidence on Security Returns

**BEFORE WE DISCUSS WHAT SORT OF EVIDENCE SUPPORTS THE IMPLICATIONS OF THE CAPM AND APT, WE MUST NOTE THAT THESE IMPLICATIONS ALREADY HAVE BEEN ACCEPTED IN WIDELY VARYING APPLICATIONS.** Consider the following:

1. Many professional portfolio managers use the expected return–beta relationship of security returns. Furthermore, many firms rate the performance of portfolio managers according to the reward-to-variability ratios they maintain and the average rates of return they realize relative to the SML.
2. Regulatory commissions use the expected return–beta relationship along with forecasts of the market index return as one factor in determining the cost of capital for regulated firms.
3. Court rulings on torts cases sometimes use the expected return–beta relationship to determine discount rates to evaluate claims of lost future income.
4. Many firms use the SML to obtain a benchmark hurdle rate for capital budgeting decisions.

These practices show that the financial community has passed a favourable judgment on the CAPM and the APT, if only implicitly.

In this chapter we consider the evidence along more explicit and rigorous lines. The first part of the chapter presents the methodology that has been deployed in testing the single-factor CAPM and APT and assesses the results.

The second part of the chapter provides an overview of current efforts to establish the validity of the multifactor versions of the CAPM and APT. Finally, we briefly report on current efforts to model the volatility of stock returns and their contribution to tests of the validity of the CAPM/APT.

Why lump together empirical works on the CAPM and APT? The CAPM is a theoretical construct that predicts *expected* rates of return on assets, relative to a market portfolio of all risky assets. It is difficult to test these predictions empirically because both expected returns and the exact market portfolio are unobservable (see Chapter 8). To overcome this difficulty, a single-factor or multifactor capital market usually is postulated, where a broad-based market index portfolio (such as the TSE 300) is assumed to represent the factor, or one of the factors. Furthermore, to obtain more reliable statistics, most tests have been conducted with the rates of return on well-diversified portfolios rather than on individual securities. For both of these reasons, tests that have been directed at the CAPM actually have been more suitable to establish the validity of the APT. We will see that it is more important to distinguish the empirical work on the basis of the factor structure that is assumed or estimated, than to distinguish between tests of the CAPM and the APT.

## 10.1 The Index Model and the Single-Factor APT

### The Expected Return–Beta Relationship

Recall that if the expected return–beta relationship holds with respect to an observable ex ante efficient index, $M$, the expected rate of return on any security $i$ is

$$E(r_i) = r_f + \beta_i[E(r_M) - r_f] \qquad \textbf{(10.1)}$$

where $\beta_i$ is defined as $\text{Cov}(r_i,r_M)/\sigma_M^2$.

This is the most commonly tested implication of the CAPM. Early simple tests followed three basic steps: establishing sample data, estimating the SCL (security characteristic line), and estimating the SML (security market line).

**Setting Up the Sample Data.** Determine a sample period of, for example, 60 monthly holding periods (five years). For each of the 60 holding periods, collect the rates of return on 100 stocks, a market portfolio proxy (the TSE 300 or the S&P 500 for U.S. studies), and the one-month (risk-free) T-bills. Your data thus consist of

$r_{it}$ $i = 1, \ldots, 100$, and $t = 1, \ldots, 60$.
Returns on the 100 stocks over the 60-month sample period.
$r_{Mt}$ Returns on the S&P 500 index over the sample period.
$r_{ft}$ Risk-free rate each month.
This constitutes a table of $102 \times 60 = 6{,}120$ rates of return.

**Estimating the SCL.** View equation 10.1 as a security characteristic line (SCL), as in Chapter 8. For each stock, $i$, you estimate the beta coefficient as the slope of a **first-pass regression** equation. (The terminology *first-pass* regression is due to the fact that the estimated coefficients will be used as input into a **second-pass regression.**)

$$r_{it} - r_{ft} = a_i + b_i(r_{Mt} - r_{ft}) + e_{it}$$

You will use the following statistics in later analysis:

$\overline{r_i - r_f}$ = Sample averages (over the 60 observations) of the excess return on each of the 100 stocks.
$b_i$ = Sample estimates of the beta coefficients of each of the 100 stocks.
$\overline{r_M - r_f}$ = Sample average of the excess return of the market index.
$\sigma^2(e_i)$ = Estimates of the variance of the residuals for each of the 100 stocks.

The sample average excess returns on each stock and the market portfolio are taken as estimates of expected excess returns, and the values of $b_i$ are estimates of the true beta coefficients for the 100 stocks during the sample period. The $\sigma^2(e_i)$ estimates the nonsystematic risk of each of the 100 stocks.

---

**CONCEPT CHECK** Question 1.

*a.* How many regressions estimates of the SCL do we have from the sample?
*b.* How many observations are there in each of the regressions?
*c.* To satisfy the CAPM, what should be the intercept in each of these regressions?

---

**Estimating the SML.** Now view equation 10.1 as a security market line (SML) with 100 observations for the stocks in your sample. You can estimate $\gamma_0$ and $\gamma_1$ in the following second-pass regression equation with $b_i$ from the first pass as the independent variable:

$$\overline{r_i - r_f} = \gamma_0 + \gamma_1 b_i \qquad i = 1, \ldots, 100 \qquad \textbf{(10.2)}$$

Compare equations 10.1 and 10.2; you should conclude that if the CAPM is valid, then $\gamma_0$ and $\gamma_1$ must satisfy

$$\gamma_0 = 0 \qquad \gamma_1 = \overline{r_M - r_f}$$

In fact, however, you can go a step further and argue that the key property of the expected return–beta relationship described by the SML is that the expected excess return on securities is determined *only* by the systematic risk (as measured by beta) and should be independent of the nonsystematic risk, as measured by the variance of the residuals, $\sigma^2(e_i)$, which also were estimated from the first-pass regression. These estimates can be added as a variable in equation 10.2 of an expanded SML that now looks like this:

$$\overline{r_i - r_f} = \gamma_0 + \gamma_1 b_i + \gamma_2 \sigma^2(e_i) \quad \textbf{(10.3)}$$

This *second-pass* regression is estimated with the hypotheses:

$$\gamma_0 = 0 \qquad \gamma_1 = \overline{r_M - r_f} \qquad \gamma_2 = 0$$

To the disappointment of early researchers, tests following this pattern consistently failed to support the index model. The results from such a test (first conducted by John Lintner[1] and later replicated by Merton Miller and Myron Scholes[2]) using annual data on 631 NYSE stocks for 10 years, 1954 to 1963, are (with returns expressed as decimals rather than percentages):

| | | | |
|---|---|---|---|
| Coefficient: | $\gamma_0 = .127$ | $\gamma_1 = .042$ | $\gamma_2 = .310$ |
| Standard error: | .006 | .006 | .026 |
| Sample average: | | $\overline{r_M - r_t} = .165$ | |

Such results are totally inconsistent with the CAPM. First, the estimated SML is "too flat"; that is, the $\gamma_1$ coefficient is too small. The slope should be $\overline{r_M - r_f}$ = .165 (16.5% per year), but it is estimated at only 0.42. The difference, .122, is about 20 times the standard error of the estimate, .006, which means that the measured slope of the SML is lower than it should be by a statistically significant margin. At the same time, the intercept of the estimated SML, $\gamma_0$, which is hypothesized to be zero, in fact equals .127, which is more than 20 times its standard error of .006.

**CONCEPT CHECK**

Question 2.
*a*. What is the implication of the empirical SML being "too flat"?
*b*. Do high- or low-beta stocks tend to outperform the predictions of the CAPM?

Second, and more damaging to the CAPM, is that nonsystematic risk seems to predict expected excess returns. The coefficient of the variable that measures nonsystematic risk, $\sigma^2(e_i)$, is .310, more than 10 times its standard error of .026.

There are, however, two principal flaws in these tests. The first is that statistical variation in stock returns introduces **measurement error** into the beta estimates, the *b* coefficients from the first-pass regressions. Using these estimates in place

[1] John Lintner, "Security Prices, Risk and Maximal Gains from Diversification," *Journal of Finance* 20 (December 1965).

[2] Merton H. Miller and Myron Scholes, "Rate of Return in Relation to Risk: A Reexamination of Some Recent Findings," in *Studies in the Theory of Capital Markets,* Michael C. Jensen ed. (New York: Praeger Publishers, 1972).

of the true beta coefficients in the estimation of the second-pass regression for the SML biases the estimates in the direction that we have observed: The measurement errors in the beta coefficients will lead to an estimate of the SML that is too flat and has a positive (rather than zero) intercept.

The second problem results from the fact that the variance of the residuals is correlated with the beta coefficients of stocks. Stocks that have high betas also tend to have high nonsystematic risk. Add this effect to the measurement problem, and the coefficient of nonsystematic risk, $\gamma_2$, in the second-pass regression will be upward biased.

Indeed, a well-controlled simulation test by Miller and Scholes confirms these arguments. In this test a random number generator simulated rates of return with covariances similar to observed ones. The average returns were made to agree exactly with the CAPM expected return–beta relationship. Miller and Scholes then used these randomly generated rates of return in the tests we have described as if they were observed from a sample of stock returns. The results of this "simulated" test were virtually identical to those reached using real data, despite the fact that the simulated returns were *constructed* to obey the SML, that is, the true $\gamma$ coefficients were $\gamma_0 = 0$, $\gamma_1 = .165 = \overline{r_M - r_f}$, and $\gamma_2 = 0$.

This postmortem of the early test gets us back to square one. We can explain away the disappointing test results, but we have no positive results to support the CAPM-APT implications.

The next wave of tests was designed to overcome the measurement error problem that led to biased estimates of the SML. The innovation in these tests was to use portfolios rather than individual securities. Combining securities into portfolios diversifies away most of the firm-specific part of returns, thereby enhancing the precision of the estimates of beta and the expected rate of return of the portfolio of securities. This mitigates the statistical problems that arise from measurement error in the beta estimates.

Obviously, however, combining stocks into portfolios reduces the number of observations left for the second-pass regression. For example, suppose that we wish to group 100 stocks into portfolios of 20 stocks each. If the assumption of a single-factor market is reasonably accurate, then the residuals of the 20 stocks in each portfolio will be practically uncorrelated and, hence, the variance of the portfolio residual will be about 1/20th the residual variance of the average stock. Thus, the portfolio beta in the first-pass regression will be estimated with far better accuracy. However, now consider the second-pass regression. With individual securities, we had 100 observations to estimate the second-pass coefficients. With portfolios of 20 stocks each we are left with only five observations for the second-pass regression.

To get the best of this trade-off, we need to construct portfolios with the largest possible dispersion of beta coefficients. Other things being equal, a sample yields more accurate regression estimates the more widely spaced are the observations of the independent variables. Consider the first-pass regressions where we estimate the SCL, that is, the relationship between the excess return on each stock and the market's excess return. If we have a sample with a great dispersion of market returns, we have a better shot at accurately estimating the effect of a change in the market return on the return of the stock. In our case, however, we have no control over the range of the market returns. But we can control the range of the independent variable of the second-pass regression, the portfolio betas. Rather than allocate 20 stocks to each portfolio randomly, we can rank portfolios by betas. Portfolio 1 will include the 20 highest-beta stocks and Portfolio 5 the 20 lowest-beta stocks. In that case, a set of portfolios with small nonsystematic components, $e_P$, and widely spaced betas will yield reasonably powerful tests of the SML.

A study by Black, Jensen, and Scholes[3] (BJS) pioneered this method. The researchers used an elaborate method to design the sample portfolios and estimate their betas. To illustrate, let us assume that the data set consists of 500 stocks over a long sample period. We would split the sample period into three subperiods:

Overall Sample Period of 500 Stock Returns

| Subperiod I: Preparing the Sample Portfolios | Subperiod II: First-Pass Regression | Subperiod III: Second-Pass Regression |
|---|---|---|
| Estimate *individual* stock betas and order them from highest to lowest beta. Form equally weighted portfolios of 50 stocks each, resulting in 10 portfolios from highest to lowest beta. This is a preparatory step for the first-pass regression. | Reestimate the betas of the 10 portfolios. These estimates will be used as the true betas for the SML estimates. The errors in measuring these betas are independent of the errors in the betas used to form the portfolios. This is the first-pass regression. | Use the average excess returns on the 10 portfolios from this period as estimates of the expected excess returns to regress on the betas from the previous subperiod. This is the second-pass regression. |

The BJS study uses all available NYSE stock returns over the period 1931 to 1965. The number of available stocks increased from 582 in 1931 to 1,094 in 1965. The available stocks are allocated to 10 portfolios; thus, portfolio size varies over the period from 58 to 110 stocks. The size and diversification of these portfolios reduces measurement error considerably.

Summary statistics for the 10 portfolios appear in Table 10.1. The betas of the 10 portfolios for the entire period (420 months) are shown in the first line of the table. They range from .4992 to 1.5614 and are fairly evenly spaced. The next two lines show the intercepts (denoted by $\alpha$) of the SCL for each portfolio. These values are small, and the ratios of these values to their standard errors [the $t$-statistics, $t(\alpha)$] are less than 2.0 for 9 out of the 10 portfolios. The pattern of these alpha values, however, begins to tell the story of the test results. The alphas are negative for high-beta portfolios ($\beta > 1$) and positive for low-beta portfolios ($\beta < 1$). This is a clue that, contrary to what the SML would imply,

[3] Fischer Black, Michael C. Jensen, and Myron Scholes, "The Capital Asset Pricing Model: Some Empirical Tests," in *Studies in the Theory of Capital Markets,* Michael C. Jensen, ed. (New York: Praeger Publishers, 1972).

**Table 10.1** Summary of Statistics for Time Series Tests (January 1931–December 1965)

| | Portfolio Number | | | | | | | | | | |
|---|---|---|---|---|---|---|---|---|---|---|---|
| **Item*** | **1** | **2** | **3** | **4** | **5** | **6** | **7** | **8** | **9** | **10** | $R_M$ |
| $\beta$ | 1.5614 | 1.3838 | 1.2483 | 1.1625 | 1.0572 | 0.9229 | 0.8531 | 0.7534 | 0.6291 | 0.4992 | 1.0000 |
| $\hat{\alpha} \cdot 10^2$ | −0.0829 | −0.1938 | −0.0649 | −0.0167 | −0.0543 | 0.0593 | 0.0462 | 0.0812 | 0.1968 | 0.2012 | |
| $t(\alpha)$ | −0.4274 | −1.9935 | −0.7597 | −0.2468 | −0.8869 | 0.7878 | 0.7050 | 1.1837 | 2.3126 | 1.8684 | |
| $\rho(\bar{R}, \bar{R}_M)$ | 0.9625 | 0.9875 | 0.9882 | 0.9914 | 0.9915 | 0.9833 | 0.9851 | 0.9793 | 0.9560 | 0.8981 | |
| $\rho(\bar{e}_t, \bar{e}_{t-1})$ | 0.0549 | −0.0638 | 0.0366 | 0.0073 | −0.0708 | −0.1248 | 0.1294 | 0.1041 | 0.0444 | 0.0992 | |
| $\sigma(\bar{e})$ | 0.0393 | 0.0197 | 0.0173 | 0.0137 | 0.0124 | 0.0152 | 0.0133 | 0.0139 | 0.0172 | 0.0218 | |
| $\bar{R}$ | 0.0213 | 0.0177 | 0.0171 | 0.0163 | 0.0145 | 0.0137 | 0.0126 | 0.0115 | 0.0109 | 0.0091 | 0.0142 |
| $\sigma$ | 0.1445 | 0.1248 | 0.1126 | 0.1045 | 0.0950 | 0.0836 | 0.0772 | 0.0685 | 0.0586 | 0.0495 | 0.0891 |

*$\bar{R}$ = Average monthly excess returns; $\sigma$ = Standard deviation of the monthly excess returns; $\rho$ = Correlation coefficient.
Sample size for each regression, 420.
Note: Returns are expressed as decimals rather than percentages.

Source: Modified from Fischer Black, Michael C. Jensen, and Myron Scholes, "The Capital Asset Pricing Model: Some Empirical Tests," in *Studies in the Theory of Capital Markets,* Michael C. Jensen, ed. (New York: Praeger Publishers, 1972). Copyright © 1972 by Praeger Publishers, Inc. Reprinted with permission of Greenwood Publishing Group, Inc., Westport, CT.

lower-beta portfolios earn consistently better risk-adjusted returns than higher-beta portfolios.

The next two lines in Table 10.1 show the correlation coefficients of the portfolio returns with the market index, $\rho(R_P,R_M)$, and the serial correlation of the nonsystematic component, *e,* of the portfolios between successive periods, $\rho(e_t,e_{t-1})$. The large size and corresponding diversification of the portfolios is such that we expect returns to be highly correlated with the market index. Indeed, the correlation coefficients range from .8981 to .9915. The nonsystematic components are not highly (auto) correlated from period to period: $\rho(e_t,e_{t-1})$ ranges from −.1248 to .1294.

From the last three lines of the table we know first that most of the risk of the 10 portfolios is systematic. The first of these lines shows the standard deviation of the residuals, our estimate of nonsystematic risk, $\sigma(e)$. The bottom line shows the standard deviation of the excess rate of return, $\sigma$. For the highest-beta portfolio, the monthly standard deviation was 14.45% per month, of which 3.93% is nonsystematic. For the lowest-beta portfolio, the standard deviation of the excess return was 4.95% per month, of which 2.18% is nonsystematic.

The next-to-last line in the table shows the average monthly excess returns for the 10 portfolios and the market (NYSE) index. The market index excess return averages 1.42% per month, and the average excess returns for the 10 portfolios range from .91% to 2.13% per month. As we should expect from the CAPM, the portfolios with betas lower than 1 earned less than the market index, and the portfolios with betas higher than 1 earned more.

Figure 10.1 shows the second-pass regression estimate of the SML for the entire period. The upper left-hand corner of Figure 10.1 reveals the disappointing

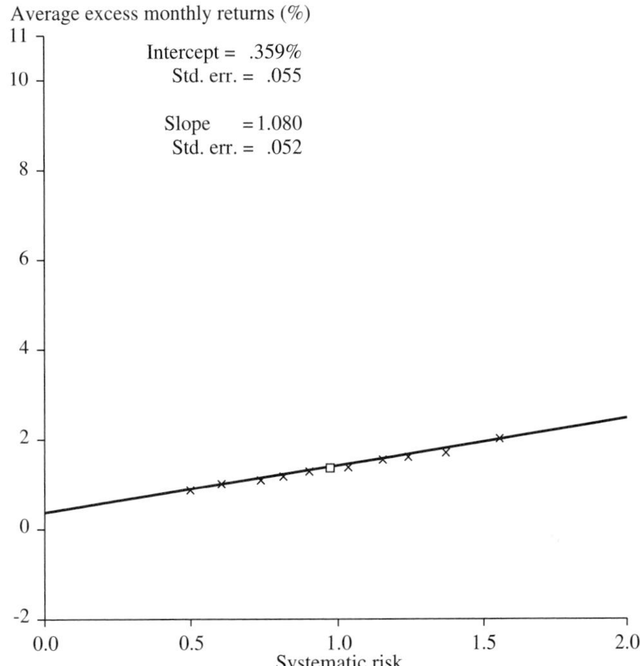


**Figure 10.1**

The second-pass regression estimate of the security market line.

Source: Fischer Black, Michael C. Jensen, and Myron Scholes, "The Capital Asset Pricing Model: Some Empirical Tests," in *Studies in the Theory of Capital Markets,* Michael C. Jensen, ed. (New York: Praeger Publishers, 1972). Copyright © 1972 by Praeger Publishers, Inc. Reprinted with permission of Greenwood Publishing Group, Inc., Westport, CT.

result for the CAPM hypothesis. The intercept of the estimated SML, the $\gamma_0$ coefficient, is 0.359 percent per month with a standard error of only 0.055 percent (its *t*-statistic is 6.53), so that the intercept, which is hypothesized by the CAPM to be zero, is positive and statistically significant.

The slope of the SML is 1.08. The CAPM hypothesis is that this slope, $\gamma_1$, should equal the expected excess return on the market index. For the sample period the market index averaged 1.42% per month. The difference, $\gamma_1 - (r_M - r_f)$, for this sample is thus −0.34% per month. The estimate SML is too flat again. The standard error of the estimate of $\gamma_1$ is 0.052%, so the difference (0.34%) is 6.54 times the standard error. Thus, the results are inconsistent with the CAPM hypothesis for $\gamma_1$.

Breaking the analysis into subperiods, BJS found no better results. Figure 10.2 shows the estimated SMLs for four subperiods. The intercepts are positive and statistically significant in three out of the four subperiods. Even worse, in the 1957 to 1965 subperiod, the slope of the SML has the wrong sign.

At this point, BJS bring up the possibility that perhaps the sample results may verify the zero-beta version of the CAPM. Recall from Chapter 8 that when borrowing is restricted, the CAPM expected return–beta relationship must be amended. As it turns out, all that is called for in moving to the zero-beta version of the CAPM is replacing the risk-free rate with the expected rate of return on the zero-beta portfolio (i.e., the minimum-variance portfolio uncorrelated with the market portfolio).

**Figure 10.2**

The estimated security market lines for four subperiods.

Source: Fischer Black, Michael C. Jensen, and Myron Scholes, "The Capital Asset Pricing Model: Some Empirical Tests," in *Studies in the Theory of Capital Markets,* Michael C. Jensen, ed. (New York: Praeger Publishers, 1972). Copyright © 1972 by Praeger Publishers, Inc. Reprinted with permission of Greenwood Publishing Group, Inc., Westport, CT.

**June 1931–September 1939**

Average excess monthly returns (%)

Intercept = .801%
Std. err. = .180

Slope = 3.041
Std. err. = .171

Systematic risk

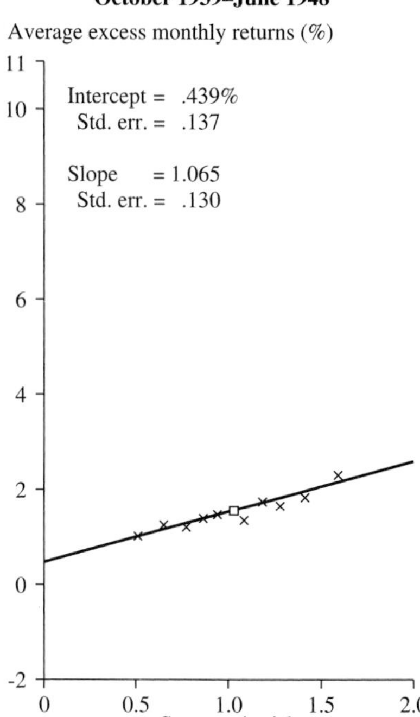


**July 1948–March 1957**

Average excess monthly returns (%)

Intercept = .777%
Std. err. = .105

Slope = .333
Std. err. = .099

Systematic risk

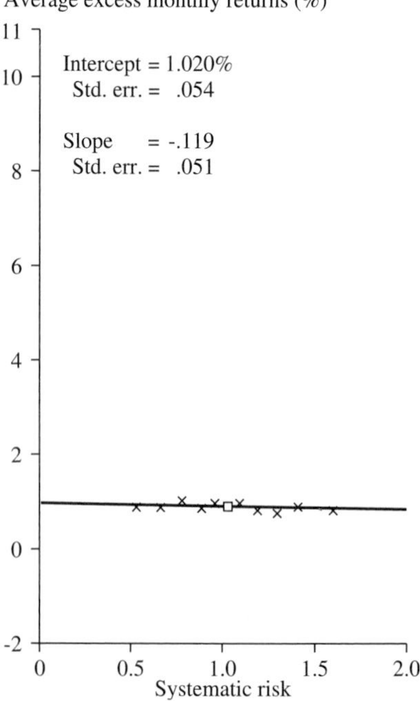

The representation of the CAPM expected return–beta relationship with a restriction on the risk-free investment (the zero-beta CAPM) is:

$$E(r_i) - E(r_{Z(M)}) = \beta_i[E(r_M) - E(r_{Z(M)})] \quad \textbf{(10.4)}$$

where $r_{Z(M)}$ is the rate of return on the zero-beta portfolio.

If we shift $E(r_{Z(M)})$ to the right-hand side and subtract the risk-free rate from both sides, equation 10.4 takes this form:

$$E(r_i) - r_f = E(r_{Z(M)}) - r_f + \beta_i[E(r_M) - E(r_{Z(M)})] \quad \textbf{(10.5)}$$

If we were to test this version of the CAPM, we would hypothesize that

$$\gamma_0 = E(r_{Z(M)}) - r_f$$

$$\gamma_1 = E(r_M) - E(r_{Z(M)})$$

To conduct their test, BJS needed to estimate returns on the zero-beta portfolio from the available data. To obtain these rates, they rearranged equation 10.5 and concluded that the actual rate of return on any stock in period $t$ (as opposed to the expected return) would be described by

$$r_{it} = r_{Zt}(1 - \beta_i) + r_{Mt}\beta_i + e_{it} \quad \textbf{(10.6)}$$

Using the previously estimated beta coefficient, the zero-beta rate is *estimated* from the return of each stock by

$$r_Z = (r_{it} - \beta_i)/(1 - \beta_i) \quad \textbf{(10.7)}$$

Note that the rate of return on each stock provides one estimate of the zero-beta rate. BJS use a statistically efficient technique to average these estimates across stocks and thus obtain, for each period, an efficient estimate of the zero-beta rate.

Using the time series of the estimated zero-beta rates for each subperiod, in conjunction with the market and individual stock returns, BJS examined the validity of the zero-beta version of the CAPM. Their major conclusions were:

**1.** The average return of the zero-beta portfolio is significantly greater than the risk-free rate.

**2.** The excess rate of return on the zero-beta portfolio explains some of the deviation of the results from the simple version of the CAPM, yet the regression estimates are not fully consistent with the zero-beta version of the CAPM either.

The fact that the average return on the zero-beta portfolio exceeds the risk-free rate is consistent with the restricted borrowing models of the CAPM presented in Chapter 8. It also is consistent with BJS's finding that the empirical SML is flatter than predicted by the simple CAPM.

**CONCEPT CHECK** Question 3. What should be the average return on the zero-beta portfolio in the BJS test according to the zero-beta version of the CAPM?

BJS tested the SML equation directly with negative results, with and without restrictions on risk-free lending and borrowing. They did not concern themselves with other specific implications of the CAPM, such as that expected returns are independent of nonsystematic risk or that the relationship between expected returns and beta is linear.

Fama and MacBeth[4] used the BJS methodology to verify that the observed relationship between average excess returns and beta is indeed linear and that nonsystematic risk does not explain average excess returns. Using 20 portfolios constructed according to the BJS methodology, Fama and MacBeth expanded the estimation of the SML equation to include the square of the beta coefficient (to test for linearity of the relationship between returns and betas) and the estimated standard deviation of the residual (to test for the explanatory power of nonsystematic risk). For a sequence of many subperiods, they estimated for each subperiod, the equation

$$r_i = \gamma_0 + \gamma_1\beta_i + \gamma_2\beta_i^2 + \gamma_3\sigma(e_i)$$

The term $\gamma_2$ measures potential nonlinearity of return, and $\gamma_3$ measures the explanatory power of nonsystematic risk, $\sigma(e_i)$. The Fama–MacBeth results show that the beta relationship is in fact linear ($\gamma_2$ is not significantly different from zero) and that nonsystematic risk does not explain average returns ($\gamma_3$ also is insignificant). At the same time, however, the authors reported that SMLs, in general, remain too flat and have a positive significant intercept.

We can summarize these conclusions:

1. The insights that are supported by the single-factor CAPM and APT are as follows:
   *a.* Expected rates of return are linear and increase with beta, the measure of systematic risk.
   *b.* Expected rates of return are not affected by nonsystematic risk.
2. The single-variable expected return–beta relationship predicted by either the risk-free rate or the zero-beta version of the CAPM is not fully consistent with empirical observation.

Thus, although the CAPM seems *qualitatively* correct, in that $\beta$ matters and $\sigma(e_i)$ does not, empirical tests do not validate its *quantitative* predictions.

**CONCEPT CHECK** Question 4. What would you conclude if you performed the Fama and MacBeth tests and found that the coefficients on $\beta^2$ and $\sigma(e)$ were positive?

[4] Eugene Fama and James MacBeth, "Risk, Return, and Equilibrium: Empirical Tests," *Journal of Political Economy* 81 (March 1973).

## Estimating Index Models for Canadian Stocks

Relatively few studies on the SML along the lines of the previous section have been done using Canadian data. The availability of data in computerized form was scarce until recent years. Furthermore, the Canadian financial markets present certain problems not encountered in the United States.

One of the earlier estimations of the SML in Canada was by Morin,[5] who used monthly return data on 620 securities trading continuously for at least five years on the TSE during the period 1957–1971. The basic methodology was the one developed by BJS, with its extensions by Fama and MacBeth. The market index was an equally weighted average of the returns of all securities in the databank.

The general flavour of the results can be obtained by quoting from the study's conclusions: "Overall, the empirical results of this study indicate that the capital asset pricing theory, in all its forms, fares poorly in attempting to explain differential returns on Canadian equities." The return–beta relationship turned out to be weak, erratic, and nonlinear, and implied unreasonably high estimates of the returns on low-risk assets.

Several other SML studies using Canadian data[6] reached conclusions that seem to confirm the basic outcome observed in the United States, namely that the single-variable expected return–beta relationship is, at best, only weakly supported by empirical work. For instance, Calvet and Lefoll[7] use monthly TSE security return data and a value-weighted index of all stocks in their databank as a market index. Although a significant linear relationship between systematic risk and portfolio returns was found almost always, the introduction of unsystematic risk and of the squared beta coefficient in the regression, as in the Fama–MacBeth study, showed both to be significant and more important than the beta.

Empirical research in Canadian financial markets is hindered by two effects that are not present to the same extent in the United States. The first is the existence of seasonal abnormal returns that are at variance with market efficiency; these will be examined in detail in the next chapter. The second is the persistent problem of **thin trading** in a majority of Canadian securities.

## Thin Trading

If transactions for many securities listed on the TSE are irregular and infrequent, then the prices quoted as closing by the exchange are unreliable and may also reflect situations that are no longer current. For instance, if a stock did not trade at all during a given month, then its recorded rate of return is zero during that

---

[5] Roger A. Morin, "Market Line Theory and the Canadian Equity Market," *Journal of Business Administration* 12, no. 1 (Fall 1980).

[6] For instance, J. D. Jobson and R. M. Korkie, "Some Tests of Linear Asset Pricing with Multivariate Normality," *Canadian Journal of Administrative Sciences* 2, no. 1 (June 1985).

[7] A. L. Calvet and J. Lefoll, "Risk and Return on Canadian Capital Markets," *Canadian Journal of Administrative Sciences* 5, no. 1 (March 1988).

**Table 10.2** Thin Trading Breakdown on TSE Listings between January 1970–December 1979

| | All Securities | | Securities Listed at Least 12 Months* | | Securities Listed for Whole 10-Year Period | | Broader "Fat" Category for 10-Year Group† | |
|---|---|---|---|---|---|---|---|---|
| | Number | % | Number | % | Number | % | Number | % |
| Fat | 112 | 5.3 | 78 | 4.3 | 38 | 6.0 | 156 | 24.6 |
| Moderate | 744 | 35.3 | 679 | 37.7 | 328 | 51.7 | 210 | 33.1 |
| Infrequent | 1251 | 59.4 | 1043 | 58.0 | 268 | 42.3 | 268 | 42.3 |
| **Total** | **2107** | **100.0** | **1800** | **100.0** | **634** | **100.0** | **634** | **100.0** |

*The prime difference between the all-securities and the 12-month groups is that warrants and rights are largely eliminated from the latter.

†This category includes any security for which a trade could always be found in the last five days of the month.
From D. J. Fowler, C. H. Rorke, and V. M. Jog, "Thin Trading and Beta Estimation Problems on the Toronto Stock Exchange," *Journal of Business Administration* 12, no. 1 (Fall 1980). Reprinted by permission.

month (in the absence of dividends). If many such securities and months occur in our database, then the statistical estimations of the SML will yield biased results.

Table 10.2 reproduces data from a study by Fowler, Rorke, and Jog[8] on the frequency of trading on the TSE during the period 1970–1979. The database contained 120 monthly returns for each security listed on the TSE during that period. The three categories of trading frequency distinguished by the authors were defined as follows: a "fat" security showed a trade during the closing day of each month; a "moderate" security was one that traded each month, but not necessarily on the last day; and an "infrequent" security was one that showed entire months without any trade. As the data show, this last category was by far the largest, accounting for 42–59 percent of the total, depending on the type of securities considered.

In addition to biases in the estimated coefficients, thinness of trading also causes heteroscedasticity,[9] that is, different variances of the residuals in the regressions. There are a number of procedures for correcting the biases arising out of thinness of trading, of which the one developed by Dimson[10] is perhaps the most popular. The Dimson method augments the single simultaneous market index term in the regression by two other terms, one with a lagged and one with a leading value of the index, each one with its own beta; an unbiased estimate of the "true" beta is equal to the sum of three estimated betas. Another bias-

[8] David J. Fowler, C. Harvey Rorke, and V. M. Jog, "Thin Trading and Beta Estimation Problems on the Toronto Stock Exchange," *Journal of Business Administration* 12, no. 1 (Fall 1980).

[9] David J. Fowler, C. Harvey Rorke, and V. M. Jog, "Heteroscedasticity, $R^2$ and Thin Trading on the Toronto Stock Exchange," *Journal of Finance* 34, no. 5 (December 1979).

[10] E. Dimson, "Risk Measurement When Shares Are Subject to Infrequent Trading," *Journal of Financial Economics* 7 (1979).

correcting method also was developed by Scholes and Williams,[11] but the small-sample properties of both methods are somewhat questionable.[12]

## The Efficiency of the Market Index—Roll's Critique

In 1977, while researchers were improving test methodology in an effort to conclusively endorse or reject the validity of the CAPM, Richard Roll[13] threw a monkey wrench into their machinery. In the now-classic "Roll's Critique" he argued not only that the tests of the expected return–beta relationship are invalid, but also that it is doubtful that the CAPM can ever be tested.

Roll's critique included the following observations:

1. There is a single testable hypothesis associated with the CAPM: The market portfolio is mean-variance efficient.
2. All the other implications of the model, the best-known being the linear relation between expected return and beta, follow from the market portfolio's efficiency and therefore are not independently testable. There is an "if and only if" relation between the expected return–beta relationship and the efficiency of the market portfolio.
3. In any sample of observations of individual returns, there will be an infinite number of ex post mean-variance efficient portfolios using the sample period returns and covariances (as opposed to the ex ante expected returns and covariances). Sample betas calculated between each such portfolio and individual assets will be exactly linearly related to sample mean returns. In other words, if betas are calculated against such portfolios, they will satisfy the SML relation exactly whether or not the true market portfolio is mean-variance efficient in an ex ante sense.
4. The CAPM is not testable unless we know the exact composition of the true market portfolio and use it in the tests. This implies that the theory is not testable unless *all* individual assets are included in the sample.
5. Using a proxy such as the S&P 500 for the market portfolio is subject to two difficulties. First, the proxy itself might be mean-variance efficient even when the true market portfolio is not. Conversely, the proxy may turn out to be inefficient, but obviously this alone implies nothing about the true market portfolio's efficiency. Furthermore, most reasonable market proxies will be very highly correlated with each other and with the true market whether or not they are mean-variance efficient. Such a high degree of correlation will make it seem that the exact composition of the market portfolio is unimportant, whereas the use of different proxies can lead to quite

[11] M. Scholes and J. Williams, "Estimating Betas from Nonsynchronous Data," *Journal of Financial Economics* 5 (1977).

[12] See Fowler, Rorke, and Jog, 1980.

[13] Richard Roll, "A Critique of the Asset Pricing Theory's Tests: Part I: On Past and Potential Testability of the Theory," *Journal of Financial Economics* 4 (1977).

different conclusions. This problem is referred to as **benchmark error,** because it refers to the use of an incorrect benchmark (market proxy) portfolio in the tests of the theory.

Roll's criticism requires us to think in terms of two contexts and three portfolios. The contexts are as follows:

1. Ex ante expectations of rates of return and covariances.
2. Ex post (sample) averages of rates of return and estimates of covariances.

Clearly, the ex post (realized) rates of return are random, and their measured averages and covariances are not necessarily equal to those that were expected ex ante.

Next, Roll argued that we have to worry about three types of portfolios:

1. The true (unobservable) market portfolio.
2. The portfolio that happens to be ex post efficient for a given sample of realized returns.
3. The portfolio that is chosen as the proxy for the market portfolio and is used to conduct the test.

Roll argued that the third portfolio, the market proxy, will be highly correlated with the first two portfolio. Because we do not know the exact composition of the true market portfolio, even if the data seem to support the expected return–beta relationship, we cannot tell whether this is (a) because we have tested the tautology that the ex post efficient portfolio (2) is indeed efficient, and therefore the expected return–beta relationship appears valid, or (b) that our index portfolio is in fact close enough to the unobservable market portfolio (1), and that *this* is the reason for the empirical finding of an expected return–beta relationship. Conversely, if we find that the results indicate that the expected return–beta relationship does not hold, we cannot tell whether the tests do not confirm the theory, or, instead, that the choice of the proxy for the market portfolio is inadequate.

Roll's critique was a serious blow to the CAPM. Indeed, it led to a now famous article in *Institutional Investor* called "Is Beta Dead?" However, the problems in testing the CAPM should not obscure the value of the model. The nearby box presents what we believe is a reasonably balanced view of the controversy.

With Roll's critique of the BJS and Fama–MacBeth methodology in mind, let us reassess the test results so far and consider what alternative tests might make sense. BJS used an equally weighted portfolio of all NYSE stocks as their proxy for the market portfolio. Because this portfolio included between 582 and 1,094 stocks throughout the sample period, there is no question that their market proxy was a well-diversified portfolio. The 10 test portfolios were equally weighted portfolios of between 58 and 110 stocks, also fairly well diversified. Perhaps we can view the BJS test really as a test of the APT, which applies only to well-diversified portfolios. As tests of the CAPM, however, Roll showed that the procedures are objectionable. Roll's critique tells us that all we can say about the BJS

# BETA IS DEAD! LONG LIVE BETA!

## Introduction

The philosophy of natural science as expounded by Karl Popper prescribes a logicoempiricist methodology for invalidating new theoretical models of the observed world, such as those hypothesized in the applied investment field by Harry Markowitz and Bill Sharpe. Their particular paradigm-shift has resulted in a plethora of theoretical investment models, including the capital asset pricing model (CAPM). Recent papers by Richard Roll, however, have suggested that the CAPM may not be susceptible to invalidation by such methodological tests.

The above paragraph shows quite clearly that it is, in fact, possible to do several things at once. Several imposing names are dropped, lots of long words are used, and a relatively simple statement is made utterly confusing—all in the same paragraph. The next Guinness Book of Records will surely have a new entry in this category, awarded to the author of the 1980 *Institutional Investor (II)* article entitled "Is Beta Dead?," who managed to keep up this kind of thing for seven pages, thereby utterly confusing hundreds of investment managers.

### About Theories

Modern portfolio theory (MPT) developed from the work done by Harry Markowitz in 1952 on portfolio selection. In essence, it is based on the single observation that the proper task of the investment manager is not simply to maximize expected return, but to do so at an acceptable level of risk. If this were not so, portfolios would consist solely of managers' favorite stocks, instead of combining different stocks which, although all not equally attractive when considered individually, together offer the maximum expected return for a given level of risk.

This observation itself was not new. The originality of Markowtiz's contribution lay in showing how investment risk could be measured and, hence, how mathematics could be used to select the best possible portfolio from all the different combinations of a chosen list of stocks.

There have been many refinements of the theory since. What is now commonly referred to as MPT is no longer a single theory, but several different theories or models, together with their applications. These models may be grouped into three main categories: versions of the market model, versions of the capital asset pricing model (CAPM), and versions of the efficient market hypothesis (EMH).

The most common misconception about MPT is that these three theoretical constructs are all part of the same one and that, therefore, they stand or fall together. While some of the applications depend on two or more of the models, the individual models themselves do not depend heavily on each other. It is thus quite possible that one could be "wrong" while the others were "right."

It is, in any case, a mistake to think in terms of theories being "right" or "wrong" absolutely. All theories are "wrong" in that sense, including, for example, Einstein's theory of relativity.

Karl Popper (see first sentence) is a philosopher of science who has pointed out that, even if a particular theory were "right," you could never actually prove it. All you can ever hope to do is prove that it is wrong. If you have a new theory, you keep testing it in as many different ways as possible to see if it doesn't work. As long as it works fairly well, you can assume that it might be right, but you will never know for sure. A good theory is generally reckoned to be one that works quite well most of the time.

Newton's theory about the way planets and stars move was considered to be a good theory for several hundred years. Then some smart engineer invented an extra-powerful telescope with a very accurate scale, and a bored astronomer who had nothing else to do one evening noticed that the orbit of Mercury, the smallest planet around these parts, wasn't quite

*(Continued)*

where it should be. Suddenly, Newton's theory wasn't so hot any more, and we all had to wait a few more years for Einstein to come along and say, "Well it's nearly right, but if you put in this extra wrinkle here . . . ," and so invent relativity.

Unfortunately for Einstein, smart engineers and bored astronomers are two a penny these days, even allowing for inflation, and they've already noticed one or two places where this theory is a tiny bit out.

Newton's theory is still taught in schools and is widely used in many different applications. To give a somewhat gruesome example, it is used for ranging artillery fire. The theory may not be exactly right, but it is certainly right enough to kill people. On the other hand, Einstein's theory was used to plot the flight of the Apollo spacecraft because Newton's theory wasn't good enough to prove the rigorous degree of accuracy required.

This point about a theory being useful without needing to be right was also made abut the CAPM in the *II* article mentioned earlier. In that article, Barr Rosenberg was quoted as saying, "While the model is false, it's not very false." All models are false in this sense; what matters is how false they are, and to what extent this affects their application.

## Much Ado about Nothing Very Much

Presumably, you may say, the *Institutional Investor* article on the demise of beta was supposed to be about something—but what exactly? The story the article was based on is actually more than five years old, and is quite simple.

In 1977 Richard Roll, the noted professor at UCLA, published the first of a series of academic papers showing that there is a bit of a problem with the CAPM. The problem has to do with something else Karl Popper said about theories: namely, that any new theory that someone thinks up should not be given the time of day unless it can be tested.

In the Middle Ages any young priest who wanted to get ahead would think up a new theory about how many angels could balance on the head of a pin. Karl Popper would have said that they were all wasting their time, since there was no way of testing their theories.

What Richard Roll did was to point out that the CAPM can't be tested either. His reason was that to test it you first need to get hold of "the market," and that can't be done. A lot of so-called testing had already been done using "market proxies" such as the S&P 500. Roll pointed out, quite correctly, that using different proxies gave you different answers; and that, in any case, a proxy was merely a proxy and not what we were supposed to be testing.

The problem with using a proxy is that it is not the efficient market portfolio one would like it to be, but is an inefficient portfolio (i.e., one containing diversifiable risk), representing a subset of the market. Roll showed that one of the mathematical consequences of this was likely to be consistent errors in the betas.

It is worth pointing out that nearly everyone now agrees with this just as everyone agrees that the CAPM is clearly not true. These errors are fundamentally different from the random errors that arise from the fact that betas are estimated statistically, rather than measured directly. We might also note, en passant, that the gentlemen with calculators continue to work out discounted present values, and that stocks still tend to go up and down together. The validity of EMH and the market model, meanwhile, remain unaffected by this controversy over CAPM.

The crucial point is this: Beta is supposed to measure the market-related risk of a stock or portfolio. By using the S&P 500 index as a market proxy, we are going to get betas that actually measure S&P 500-related risk. What we were hoping to do is to separate the total risk of a stock into its diversifiable and nondiversifiable components. By using a proxy that is itself an inefficient portfolio, we run the risk of not separating the total risk into the correct proportions. The S&P 500-related beta could be bigger or smaller than the "real" beta.

The "furious controversy" that the *II* article described is about how important these consistent errors in the betas are. If they are small (and there are good, though complex, reasons why this is likely to be the case), then we do not have much of a problem. If they are large, then we will have to be rather

*(Continued)*

careful in those applications in which it is likely to matter.

No doubt the "furious controversy" will continue to rage in academic circles for some time yet, and when the dust settles it may well turn out that the current version of the CAPM belongs in the same basket as theories about angels and pins. More than likely, though, academics will have thought up a different version of the CAPM that can be tested. And when some subtle variant of the present CAPM is finally vindicated, it is a fairly safe bet that beta will remain (though possibly in a different manifestation) the reigning measure of investment risk.

Is beta dead? One way to answer the question is to calculate (or buy) a few, and then watch what happens as the market goes up and down. The question then becomes fairly simple: Do portfolios of high (or medium, or low) beta stocks exaggerate (or match, or dampen) market swings? Answer: yes.

The fact of the matter is that betas do work, more or less well depending mostly on how sensible we've been in calculating them. All betas are relative to one or another market proxy. According to Einstein, everything else is relative too, so this should not be too much of a problem. Naturally something's beta will change if it is measured against different market indices. It will also change if it is measured against hemlines, which many experienced market men believe to be a very reliable market proxy. The point is that it has to be measured against something, and it is therefore up to the user to decide which market proxy is most appropriate.

We know that these theories are not perfectly "right," but we also know that they are not too "wrong." Using MPT can provide valuable information on the risks incurred in different investment strategies. In short, while the model is false, it's not very false, and even a model that is a bit false is a great deal better than no model at all.

Source: Jason MacQueen in Joel M. Stern and Donald H. Chew, eds., *The Revolution in Corporate Finance* (Oxford, England: Basil Blackwell, 1986). Originally published in *Chase Financial Quarterly*, Chase Manhattan Bank, New York. Reprinted with permission.

and Fama–MacBeth tests is that they, at best, constitute an attempt to verify a zero-beta version of the APT but provide no evidence about the CAPM.

Another inference we can draw from Roll's critique is that one way to test the CAPM is to test the efficiency of a market proxy. If we were to verify empirically that a legitimate market proxy is *the* efficient portfolio, we could endorse the CAPM's validity.

This is an important, albeit confusing, point. To relate it to first principles, we need first to distinguish portfolio mean-variance efficiency from information efficiency. The concept of informational efficiency relates to the question of whether an asset or portfolio is "fairly priced." By "fairly" we mean that the price reflects all available information. For example, does the price of Canadian Pacific stock reflect all available information about the earning potential of the corporation that arises from its current and expected future business plans? Chapter 11 is devoted to this concept and to the empirical issue of whether capital markets are informationally efficient.

The question of the informational efficiency of capital markets cannot be divorced from the question of mean-variance efficiency of asset portfolios, however. A central assumption of the simple CAPM is that all investors deduce the same input list from security analysis and hence construct identical efficient frontiers. Under these circumstances trade leads to the mean-variance efficiency of the market portfolio. However, this means that all investors use the same information when analyzing each asset. Therefore, according to CAPM hypothesis, all assets are informationally efficiently priced.

It is possible that capital markets are *informationally* efficient, but at the same time the CAPM is not valid and the market is not a *mean-variance* efficient portfolio. Roll, in addition to providing us with his now classic critique, realized this point and came up with a positive conclusion: Studies of the performance of professionally managed portfolios that were intended to test informational efficiency also may serve as indirect tests of the CAPM. If these tests lead to the conclusion that a market proxy portfolio consistently beats all professionally managed portfolios (on a risk-adjusted basis), then we may conclude that the market proxy is mean-variance efficient and the CAPM is valid. Conversely, if a professionally managed portfolio consistently outperforms the market proxy, then either the proxy is inadequate or the CAPM is invalid.

The motivation for comparing the performance of professional portfolio managers against the market proxy portfolio is simple. Professional managers are the best qualified to choose efficient portfolios, because they spend considerable resources on selecting and revising portfolios. Yet the CAPM predicts that all their efforts will fail, that one portfolio (the market portfolio) will outperform them all. If we find that, indeed, professional managers fail to beat the market proxy, the CAPM prediction is upheld. On the other hand, if professional managers can beat the proxy, we would have to conclude that the market proxy is inadequate and/or that the CAPM must be rejected.

The evidence on the performance of professional managers relative to a market proxy is strong. Sharpe[14] pioneered this line of investigation by studying the reward-to-variability ratio of 34 mutual funds. He concluded:

> We have shown that performance can be evaluated with a simple yet theoretically meaningful measure that considers both average return and risk. This measure precludes the 'discovery' of differences in performance due solely to differences in objectives (e.g., the high average returns typically obtained by funds that consciously hold risky portfolios). However, even when performance is measured in this manner there are differences among funds; and such differences do not appear to be entirely transitory. To a major extent they can be explained by differences in expense ratios, lending support to the view that the capital market is highly efficient and that good managers concentrate on evaluating risk and providing diversification, spending little effort (and money) on the search for incorrectly priced securities. However, past performance per se also explains some of the differences. Further work is required before the significance of this result can be properly evaluated. But the burden of the proof may reasonably be placed on those who argue the traditional view—that the search for securities whose prices diverge from their intrinsic value is worth the expense required.

[14] William Sharpe, "Mutual Fund Performance," *Journal of Business, Supplement on Security Prices* 39 (January 1966).

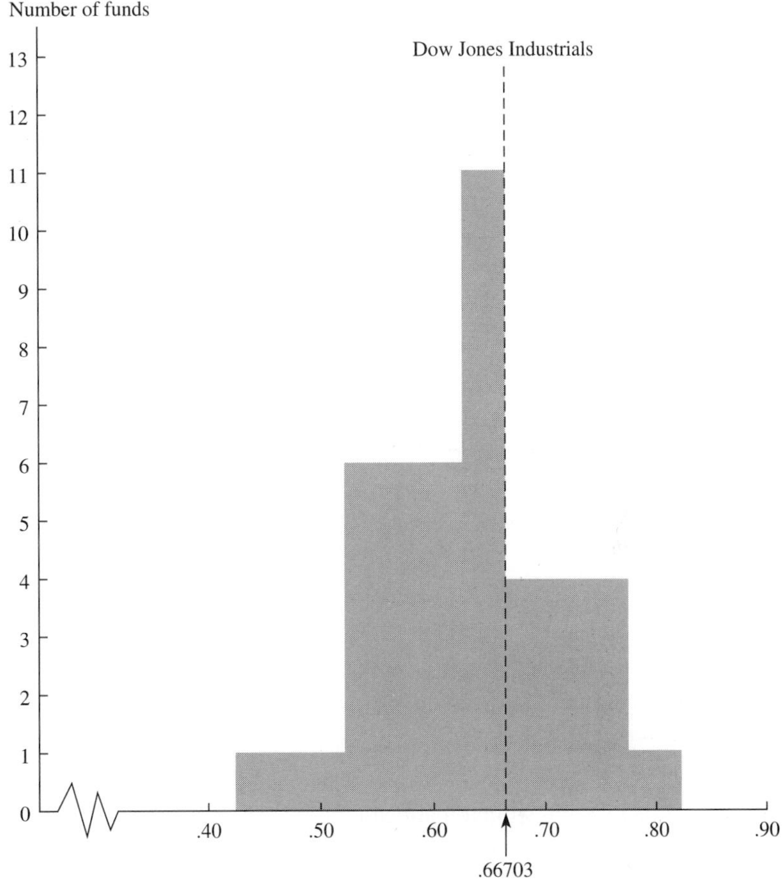


**Figure 10.3**
Mutual fund performance compared with the Dow Jones Industrials, 1954 to 1963.

Source: William Sharpe, "Mutual Fund Performance," *Journal of Business, Supplement on Security Prices* 39 (January 1966); published by the University of Chicago. Reprinted by permission.

Sharpe recorded the annual rate of return that investors realized from 34 mutual funds over the 10-year period 1954 to 1963. He then measured the reward-to-variability ratio for each fund, dividing the average rate of return by the standard deviation of returns, and compared these reward-to-variability ratios to that of the Dow Jones Industrial portfolio. The results are graphed in Figure 10.3. The figure shows that only 11 out of the 34 funds outperformed the Dow Jones Industrial portfolio, which is itself far from a satisfactory proxy for the theoretically efficient market portfolio.

Today, the picture is similar. Following Sharpe, several U.S. studies investigated more funds, used shorter intervals (months instead of years) to estimate variables, and, most important, included a more reasonable proxy for the market portfolio, such as the S&P 500 or the NYSE index. Their results were, overall, supportive of Sharpe's conclusions.

**Table 10.3** Real Performances and Systematic Risks

| Fund Number | $\alpha$ | $t$ Value | $\beta$ | $t$ Value | $R^2$ |
|---|---|---|---|---|---|
| 1 | 0.0086 | 1.1985 | 0.7406 | 8.182 | 0.6379 |
| 2 | −0.0049 | −0.5702 | 0.6852 | 6.330 | 0.5133 |
| 3 | −0.0030 | −0.6439 | 0.7785 | 13.202 | 0.8210 |
| 4 | −0.0051 | −1.2271 | 0.9084 | 17.250 | 0.8867 |
| 5 | −0.0048 | −1.2894 | 0.8189 | 17.477 | 0.8893 |
| 6 | −0.0055 | −1.2109 | 0.8681 | 14.992 | 0.8553 |
| 7 | −0.0084 | −1.1641 | 0.8773 | 9.664 | 0.7107 |
| 8 | −0.0016 | −0.1800 | 1.2356 | 10.680 | 0.7500 |
| 9 | 0.0069 | 0.9520 | 0.9916 | 10.795 | 0.7541 |
| 10 | 0.0015 | 0.4479 | 0.2973 | 6.995 | 0.5628 |
| 11 | 0.0150 | 2.0603 | 0.5849 | 6.365 | 0.5160 |
| 12 | −0.0102 | −1.6300 | 0.9232 | 11.690 | 0.7825 |
| 13 | −0.0012 | −0.2904 | 0.9190 | 17.657 | 0.8913 |
| 14 | 0.0053 | 0.8500 | 0.8398 | 10.720 | 0.7515 |
| 15 | −0.0015 | −0.1502 | 1.0495 | 7.976 | 0.6260 |
| 16 | −0.0016 | −0.1339 | 1.0809 | 6.953 | 0.5598 |
| 17 | 0.0061 | 0.8401 | 0.9468 | 10.276 | 0.7353 |

$t > 2.0245$ is the value of a 5 percent two-tail test with 38 degrees of freedom.

From A. L. Calvet and J. Lefoll, "The CAPM under Inflation and the Performance of Canadian Mutual Funds," *Journal of Business Administration,* 12, no. 1 (Fall 1980). Reprinted with permission.

A similar pattern emerges from Canadian studies. One example is a study by Calvet and Lefoll[15] that uses 17 mutual fund quarterly returns over the period 1966–1975. The funds included in the study were selected because they had less than 10 percent of their capital invested in foreign securities. The market portfolio was proxied by the TSE 300 index. The study also developed its own methodology in order to evaluate performance under inflationary conditions.

Results of the Calvet–Lefoll study appear in Table 10.3, which shows the Jensen alpha performance measure, the estimated constant term from the least-squares regression of fund excess returns on market excess returns, for all 17 funds. Only one fund (number 11) had a significantly positive alpha, indicating a slightly better performance than the market index of management fees are ignored. All other funds' performance measures were not significantly different from zero. These results remained virtually unchanged when performance was estimated with the "traditional" method that ignores inflation.

[15] A. L. Calvet and J. Lefoll, "The CAPM under Inflation and the Performance of Canadian Mutual Funds," *Journal of Business Administration* 12, no. 1 (Fall 1980).

These results are typical of all Canadian studies.[16] The conclusion from one,[17] which examined 40 Canadian mutual funds over the period 1967–1984, can be applied to all of them: ". . . Canadian mutual funds as a group were unable to perform significantly different from the market portfolio."

In the end, however, the question "How many managers beat the market portfolio over a given period?" is not very informative. First, we must be convinced that each of these managers shows a *statistically significant* superior performance (after adjusting for risk). Second, we must recognize that if a large number of managers are sampled, some are expected to succeed simply by the law of large numbers.

One way to account for the sampling problem is to subject managers' records to a test of persistence. Suppose you observe a sample of 100 managers over a period and split them in two groups of superior and inferior performers. Then you observe the same managers over the next period and split them again. The hypothesis is that, on average, success or failure of managers does not persist across time periods. Usually, however, a researcher obtains data on managers for a certain period. The sample is first divided into two subperiods, and then managers are ranked in each period. For example, one study[18] reported the following results:

| | **1979–1981 Winners** | **1979–1981 Losers** | **Total** |
|---|---|---|---|
| 1976–1978 winners | 44 | 19 | 63 |
| 1976–1978 losers | 19 | 44 | 63 |
| Total | 63 | 63 | 126 |

These results (which are repeated for more subperiods with similar statistics) indicate statistically significant persistence, suggesting that some managers may be consistently outperforming the market portfolio. As it turns out, however, this method, too, contains severe pitfalls.

Brown, Goetzmann, Ibbotson, and Ross[19] reported that the problems with studies of this type are twofold. First, they include only managers whose records are available for both subperiods and exclude managers that dropped out after the

[16] Dwight Grant, "Investment Performance of Canadian Mutual Funds, 1960–1974," *Journal of Business Administration* 8 (1976); and H. L. Dhingra, "Portfolio Volatility Adjustment by Canadian Mutual Funds," *Journal of Business Finance and Accounting* 5 (1978).

[17] H. Bishara, "Evaluation of the Performance of Canadian Mutual Funds (1967–1984)," *Proceedings of the Administrative Sciences Association of Canada* 1, part 1 (1987), p. 18.

[18] D. Hendricks, J. Patel, and R. Zeckhouser, "Hot Hands in Mutual Funds: The Persistence of Performance, 1974–1988," working paper, John F. Kennedy School of Government, Harvard University, 1991.

[19] Stephen J. Brown, William Goetzmann, Roger B. Ibbotson, and Stephen A. Ross, "Survivorship Bias in Performance Studies," *The Review of Financial Studies* 5 (1992), pp. 553–580. See also Burton G. Malkiel, "Returns from Investing in Equity Mutual Funds 1971 to 1991," *The Journal of Finance* 50, no. 2 (June 1995), pp. 549–572.

first subperiod. Some of these managers may have been replaced because their performance was poor. Using simulation, the study showed that if only 5% of the lowest-ranking managers get cut off after the first subperiod, results of the remaining sample may show strong persistence even if managers' success is uncorrelated from one period to the next.

A further complication arises from the possibility that managers may be using similar styles, and hence their portfolios' rates of return are correlated, period by period, although each of the returns may be uncorrelated from one period to the next. Such correlation may induce seeming persistence even when no manager is cut off after the first subperiod. When the lowest-ranking managers are cut off, such correlation exacerbates the survivorship bias.

## 10.2 Multiple Factors in Security Returns

Research into the multifactor nature of security returns is yet inconclusive. Identifying the factors and investigating the risk premiums of securities as a function of their factor loadings (betas) present greater statistical difficulties.

Two lines of inquiry have been pursued. In the first, researchers analyze security returns statistically to discern the significant factors and to construct portfolios that are highly correlated with those factors. They then estimate the average returns on these portfolios to determine whether these factors command risk premiums.

The second approach is to prespecify likely economic factors and identify portfolios that are highly correlated with these factors. The risk premiums on these portfolios are then estimated from sample average returns.

### Identifying Factors from Security Returns

In exploratory factor analysis, the exact number of factors is not known. Typically, a model with no factors is first fit to the data. This model assumes that asset returns are mutually uncorrelated. The goodness-of-fit measure from the model serves as a base value to express the total variability in returns. The researcher then fits a succession of factor models with increasing numbers of factors, comparing the goodness-of-fit measures of the various models. As each additional factor is added, a large improvement in the goodness-of-fit measures suggests that this is an important underlying factor that should be included. A small improvement in the fit suggests that the additional factor may have no real significance.

Factor analysis involving a large number of securities is a difficult task. In one of the most comprehensive studies to date, Lehman and Modest[20] used 750 NYSE and AMEX stocks to identify the factors. They concluded that, although the test results "may be interpreted as very weak evidence in favor of a ten factor model,"

[20] Bruce Lehman and David Modest, "The Empirical Foundation of the Arbitrage Pricing Theory," *Journal of Financial Economics* 21 (1988), pp. 213–54.

the tests actually "provide very little information regarding the number of factors which underlie the APT. As the analysis suggests, the tests have little power to discriminate among models with different numbers of factors."

Studies using Canadian data yield similar and even less satisfactory results. For instance, Kryzanowski and To,[21] who analyzed both U.S. and Canadian data, found that there was a much larger number of relevant factors (18 to 20) for the Canadian data, rather than the 10 or so found for the U.S. stocks. Further, the first factor was less important and associated with fewer securities for the Canadian than for the U.S. data. Hughes[22] found that only three or four factors were priced in the market in both samples that she used in her tests, but only the first factor turned out to be the same in both samples.

Paralleling the difficulty in identifying the factor structure from security returns, it has been difficult to demonstrate significant risk premiums on the **factor portfolios** that are constructed from this analysis. Although results may not be strong enough to disprove the hypothesis that the factor portfolios have insignificant risk premiums, the tests have little power to reject the hypothesis even when it is false. Reinganum and Conway[23] developed evidence that the large number of factors identified by factor analysis techniques may be a statistical fluke. Their work used a cross-validation technique to confirm the explanatory power of factor portfolios that are generated by factor analysis.

The cross-validation method splits the simple period rates of return into two subsamples of odd- and even-date rates of return. Factor analysis is used to identify factor portfolios from the odd-date subsample security returns. The rates of return from the even-date subsample are then used to test the explanatory power for these factor portfolios.

Suppose that the odd-date subsample produces 10 factor portfolios. We now compute the rates of return on the 10 portfolios for all the even dates. Let us assume that the first of the portfolios is the market index portfolio, $r_M$. Denote the other nine factor portfolio returns by $r_{P2}, \ldots, r_{P10}$. Next, we estimate 10 regression equations for all the stocks ($i = 1, \ldots$, n) using all the even-date returns ($t = 2, 4, \ldots, 10$) in the sample.

$$(1) \qquad r_{it} = r_{ft} + \beta_{iM}(r_{Mt} - r_{ft}) + e_{i1t}$$

$$(2) \qquad r_{it} = r_{ft} + \beta_{iM}(r_{Mt} - r_{ft}) + \beta_{iP2}(r_{P2t} - r_{ft}) + e_{i2t}$$

$$\vdots$$

$$(10) \qquad r_{it} = r_{ft} + \beta_{iM}(r_{Mt} - r_{ft}) + \beta_{iP2}(r_{P2t} - r_{ft}) + \beta_{iP3}(r_{P3} - r_{ft}) + \ldots \beta_{iP10}(r_{P10t} - r_{ft}) + e_{i10t}$$

[21] Lawrence Kryzanowski and Minh Chau To, "General Factor Models and the Structure of Security Returns," *Journal of Financial and Quantitative Analysis* 18, no. 1 (1983).

[22] Patricia J. Hughes, "A Test of the Arbitrage Pricing Theory Using Canadian Security Returns," *Canadian Journal of Administrative Sciences* 1, no. 2 (1984).

[23] Marc Reinganum and Dolores Conway, "Cross Validation Tests of the APT," *Journal of Business and Economic Statistics* 6 (January 1988).

For each of the 10 regressions, we estimate the variance of the residual $\sigma^2(e_{ikt})$, $k = 1, \ldots, 10$. The cross-validation test requires each additional factor portfolio to reduce the residual variance significantly.

The 10 first-pass factor portfolios appear in an order determined by their significance in the factor analysis of the odd-date subsample. In the second-pass (even-date) cross-validation test, Reinganum and Conway found in their U.S. data that, of the 10, only one factor portfolio (the market index) remained significant, whereas just one other was borderline significant in explaining the variability of the residuals. In a similar spirit, a Canadian study by Abeysekera and Mahajan[24] found that the return premiums of the three to eight factors identified from their first-pass tests were not significantly different from zero. The results demonstrate the statistical difficulties in identifying the factors that drive stock returns.

By design, these factor analysis tests are in the spirit of the APT rather than the multifactor CAPM. The portfolios that researchers identify statistically as factor portfolios are not constructed with regard to any economic meaning, and the chance that any of them can be identified as an obvious hedge for some prespecified risk to future consumption is small.

## Tests of Multifactor Equilibrium Models with Prespecified Factor Portfolios

The other avenue to test the multifactor equilibrium CAPM or APT is to choose portfolios that are designed to account for macroeconomic factors or hedge specific risks and to test the multifactor model with these portfolios.

A full-blown test of the multifactor equilibrium model, with prespecified factors and hedge portfolios, is as yet unavailable. A test of this hypothesis requires three stages:

1. Specification of risk factors.
2. Identification of hedge portfolios.
3. Test of the explanatory power and risk premiums of the hedge portfolios.

A step in this direction was made by Chen, Roll, and Ross,[25] who hypothesized several possible variables that might proxy for systematic factors:

1. MP = Monthly growth rate in industrial production.
2. DEI = Changes in expected inflation measured by changes in short-term (T-bill) interest rates.
3. UI = Unexpected inflation defined as the difference between actual and expected inflation.

---

[24] Sarath Abeysekera and Arvind Mahajan, "A Test of the APT in Pricing Canadian Stocks," *Canadian Journal of Administrative Sciences* 4, no. 2 (1987).

[25] Nai-Fu Chen, Richard Roll, and Stephen Ross, "Economic Forces and the Stock Market," *Journal of Business* 59 (1986).

**4.** UPR = Unexpected changes in borne risk premiums measured by the difference between the returns on corporate Baa bonds and long-term government bonds.

**5.** UTS = Unexpected changes in the term premium measured by the difference between the returns on long- and short-term government bonds.

With the identification of these potential economic factors, Chen, Roll, and Ross skipped the procedure of identifying factor portfolios (the portfolios that have the highest correlation with the factors). Instead, by using the factors themselves, they implicitly assumed that factor portfolios exist that are perfectly correlated with the factors. The factors now are used in a test similar to that of Fama–MacBeth.

A critical part of the methodology is the grouping of stocks into portfolios. Recall that in the single-factor tests portfolios were constructed to span a wide range of betas to enhance the power of the test. In a multifactor framework, the efficient criterion for grouping is less obvious. Chen, Roll, and Ross chose to group the sample stocks into 20 portfolios by size (market value of outstanding equity), a variable that is known to be associated with stock returns.

They first used five years of monthly data to estimate the factor betas of the 20 portfolios in a first-pass regression. This was accomplished by estimating the following regressions for each portfolio:

$$r = a + \beta_M r_M + \beta_{Mp} MP + \beta_{DEI} DEI + \beta_{UI} UI + \beta_{URS} URS + \beta_{UTS} UTS + e$$

where $M$ stands for the stock market index. Chen, Roll, and Ross used as the market index both the value-weighted NYSE index (VWNY) and the equally weighted NYSE index (EWNY).

Using the 20 sets of first-pass estimates of factor betas as the independent variables, they now estimated the second-pass regression (with 20 observations, one for each portfolio):

$$r = \gamma_0 + \gamma_M \beta_M + \gamma_{MP} \beta_{MP} + \gamma_{DEI} \beta_{DEI} + \gamma_{UI} \beta_{UI} + \gamma_{URS} \beta_{URS} + \gamma_{UTS} \beta_{UTS} + e$$

where the gammas become estimates of the risk premiums on the factors.

Chen, Roll, and Ross ran this second-pass regression for every month of their sample period, reestimating the first-pass factor betas once every 12 months. They ran the second-pass tests in four variations. First (Table 10.4, parts A and B), they excluded the market index altogether and used two alternative measures of industrial production ($YP$ based on annual growth of industrial production and $MP$ based on monthly growth). Finding that $MP$ is a more effective measure, they next included the two versions of the market index, *EWNY* and *VWNY*, one at a time (Table 10.4, parts C and D). The estimated risk premiums (the values for the parameters, $\gamma$) were averaged over all the second-pass regressions corresponding to each subperiod listed in Table 10.4.

Note in Table 10.4, parts C and D, that the two market indexes *EWNY* (equally weighted index of NYSE) and *VWNY* (the value-weighted NYSE index) are not

**Table 10.4** Economic Variables and Pricing (percent per month × 10), Multivariate Approach

| A | Years | *YP* | *MP* | *DEI* | *UI* | *UPR* | *UTS* | Constant |
|---|---|---|---|---|---|---|---|---|
| | 1958–84 | 4.341 | 13.984 | −.111 | −.672 | 7.941 | −5.8 | 4.112 |
| | | (.538) | (3.727) | (−1.499) | (−2.052) | (2.807) | (−1.844) | (1.334) |
| | 1958–67 | .417 | 15.760 | .014 | −.133 | 5.584 | .535 | 4.868 |
| | | (.032) | (2.270) | (.191) | (−.259) | (1.923) | (.240) | (1.156) |
| | 1968–77 | 1.819 | 15.645 | −.264 | −1.420 | 14.352 | −14.329 | −2.544 |
| | | (.145) | (2.504) | (−3.397) | (−3.470) | (3.161) | (−2.672) | (−.464) |
| | 1978–84 | 13.549 | 8.937 | −.070 | −.373 | 2.150 | −2.941 | 12.541 |
| | | (.774) | (1.602) | (−.289) | (−.442) | (.279) | (−.327) | (1.911) |

| B | Years | *MP* | *DEI* | *UI* | *UPR* | *UTS* | Constant |
|---|---|---|---|---|---|---|---|
| | 1958–84 | 13.589 | −.125 | −6.29 | 7.205 | −5.211 | 4.124 |
| | | (3.561) | (−1.640) | (−1.979) | (2.590) | (−1.690) | (1.361) |
| | 1958–67 | 13.155 | .006 | −.191 | 5.560 | −.008 | 4.989 |
| | | (1.897) | (.092) | (−.382) | (1.935) | (−.004) | (1.271) |
| | 1968–77 | 16.966 | −.245 | −1.353 | 12.717 | −13.142 | −1.889 |
| | | (2.638) | (−3.215) | (−3.320) | (2.852) | (−2.554) | (−.334) |
| | 1978–84 | 9.383 | −.140 | −.221 | 1.679 | −1.312 | 11.477 |
| | | (1.588) | (−.552) | (−.274) | (.221) | (−.149) | (1.747) |

| C | Years | *EWNY* | *MP* | *DEI* | *UI* | *UPR* | *UTS* | Constant |
|---|---|---|---|---|---|---|---|---|
| | 1958–84 | 5.021 | 14.009 | −.128 | .848 | .130 | −5.017 | 6.409 |
| | | (1.218) | (3.774) | (−1.666) | (−2.541) | (2.855) | (−1.576) | (1.848) |
| | 1958–67 | 6.575 | 14.936 | −.005 | −.279 | 5.747 | −.146 | 7.349 |
| | | (1.199) | (2.336) | (−.060) | (−.558) | (2.070) | (−.067) | (1.591) |
| | 1968–77 | 2.334 | 17.593 | −.248 | −1.501 | 12.512 | −9.904 | 3.542 |
| | | (.283) | (2.715) | (−3.039) | (−3.366) | (2.758) | (−2.015) | (.558) |
| | 1978–84 | 6.638 | 7.563 | −.132 | −.729 | 5.273 | −4.993 | 9.164 |
| | | (.906) | (1.253) | (−.529) | (−.847) | (.663) | (−.520) | (1.245) |

| D | Years | *YWNY* | *MP* | *DEI* | *UI* | *UPR* | *UTS* | Constant |
|---|---|---|---|---|---|---|---|---|
| | 1958–84 | −2.403 | 11.756 | −.123 | .795 | 8.274 | −5.905 | 10.713 |
| | | (−.633) | (3.054) | (−1.600) | (−2.376) | (2.972) | (−1.879) | (2.755) |
| | 1958–67 | 1.359 | 12.394 | .005 | −.209 | 5.204 | −.086 | 9.527 |
| | | (.277) | (1.789) | (.064) | (−.415) | (1.815) | (−.040) | (1.984) |
| | 1968–77 | −5.269 | 13.466 | −.255 | −1.421 | 12.897 | −11.708 | 8.582 |
| | | (−.717) | (2.038) | (−3.237) | (−3.106) | (2.955) | (−2.299) | (1.167) |
| | 1978–84 | −3.683 | 8.402 | −.116 | .739 | 6.056 | −5.928 | 15.452 |
| | | (−.491) | (1.432) | (−.458) | (−.869) | (.782) | (−.644) | (1.867) |

*VWNY* = Return on the value-weighted NYSE index; *EWNY* = Return on the equally weighted NYSE index; *MP* = Monthly growth rate in industrial production; *DEI* = Change in expected inflation; *UI* = Unanticipated inflation; *UPR* = Unanticipated change in the risk premium (Baa and under return—long-term government bond return); *UTS* = Unanticipated change in the term structure (long-term government bond return—Treasury-bill rate); and *YP* = Yearly growth rate in industrial production. Note that *t*-statistics are in parentheses.

Source: Modified from Nai-Fu Chen, Richard Roll, and Stephen Ross, "Economic Forces and the Stock Market," *Journal of Business* 59 (1986); published by the University of Chicago. Reprinted by permission.

significant (their $t$-statistics of 1.218 and $-0.633$ are less than 2 for the overall sample period and for each subperiod). Note also that the *VWNY* factor has the wrong sign in that it seems to imply a negative market-risk premium. Industrial production (*MP*), the risk premium on bonds (*UPR*), and unanticipated inflation (*UI*) are the factors that appear to have significant explanatory power.

A variant of the Chen, Roll, and Ross study was replicated with Canadian data by Otuteye,[26] but the results were not as satisfactory. While the exogenous variables were more or less similar to the ones used by Chen, Roll, and Ross, the market index (the return on a value-weighted portfolio of Canadian stocks) turned out to be highly significant, in contrast to the U.S. results.

The Chen, Roll, and Ross results must be treated as only preliminary in this line of inquiry, but they indicate that it may be possible to hedge some economic factors that affect future consumption risk with appropriate portfolios. A CAPM or APT multifactor equilibrium expected return–beta relationship may one day supersede the now widely used single-factor model.

It is very difficult to identify the portfolios that serve to hedge common sources of risk to future consumption opportunities. The two lines of research explore the data in search of such portfolios. Factor analysis techniques indicate the portfolios that may be providing hedge services. Researchers can then try to figure out what the source of risk is and how important it is. The second line of research attempts to guess the identity of economic variables that are correlated with consumption risk and determine whether they indeed explain rates of return.

**CONCEPT CHECK** Question 5. Compare the strategy of prespecifying the risk factor (as in Chen, Roll, and Ross's work) with that of explanatory factor analysis.

## 10.3 TIME-VARYING VOLATILITY AND THE STATE OF TESTS OF CAPITAL ASSET PRICES

In 1976, Fischer Black proposed to model the time-varying nature of asset-return volatility.[27] He suggested that such a model should include three effects. One is that the volatility depends on the stock price. (Generally, an increase in the stock price means a decrease in volatility.) A second is that the volatility tends to return to a long-term average. Finally, there are random changes in volatility. Although the idea was well received and widely cited, little was accomplished for quite a while.

[26] E. Otuteye, "How Economic Forces Explain Canadian Stock Returns," *Canadian Investment Review* 41 (Spring 1991), pp. 93–99.

[27] Fischer Black, "Studies in Stock Price Volatility Changes," *Proceedings of the 1976 Business Meeting of the Business and Economic Statistics Sections, American Statistical Association,* pp. 177–81.

In 1982, Robert F. Engle published a study[28] of U.K. inflation rates that measured their time-varying volatility. His model, named ARCH (autoregressive conditional heteroskedasticity), is based on the idea that a natural way to a variance forecast is to average it with the most recent squared "surprise" (i.e., the deviation of the rate of return from its mean). ARCH introduced a statistically efficient algorithm to do just that.

This methodology caught fire in empirical research. A survey conducted[29] in May 1990 listed over 250 papers that employ ARCH in financial models. Moreover, an algorithm has been developed[30] to perform a joint estimation of the time series variances and the relationship between the mean and variance of returns (ARCH-M). By applying this technique to an array of assets, tests that relate mean asset returns to covariances can be devised.

Examination of the state of the empirical evidence on security returns reveals four facts. First, direct tests of either a single or multifactor CAPM have rejected the expected return–beta relationship. At the same time, there is no solid evidence that professional managers can persistently outperform well-diversified portfolios by exploiting the failure of security returns to price some factors or, conversely, by exploiting diversifiable risk factors.

Second, there is ample evidence that past security returns exhibit statistical "anomalies" or apparent profitable trading rules that could have been exploited by portfolio managers to produce abnormal rates of return. (More on this in Chapter 11 on market efficiency). Such evidence is a reflection of the noted failure of the CAPM, which predicts that security alphas must average zero. Those who take this view must expect a more general theory to better explain asset returns.

Third, tests of extensions of the CAPM (that relax one or more of the simplifying assumptions) usually show that asset returns do indeed conform to the prediction of the modified model. One such example is the case of dividends and taxes.[31] A careful study of the joint effect of dividend yield and taxes shows that there is a positive but nonlinear association between common stock returns and dividend yields. Taxes drive investors in high tax brackets to tilt their portfolios toward lower-dividend-yield stocks, creating a dividend-clientele effect. The resultant relationship between dividend yield and expected returns violates the simple CAPM.

---

[28] Robert F. Engle, "Autoregressive Conditional Heteroskedasticity with Estimates of the Variance of U.K. Inflation," *Econometrica* 50 (1982), pp. 987–1008.

[29] Tim Bollerslev, Ray Y. Chou, Narayanan Jayaraman, and Kenneth F. Kroner, "ARCH Modeling in Finance: A Selective Review of the Theory and Empirical Evidence, with Suggestions for Future Research," *Journal of Econometrics* 48 (July/August 1992).

[30] Tim Bollerslev, Robert F. Engle, and Jeffrey M. Woolridge, "A Capital Asset Pricing Model with Time-Varying Covariances," *Journal of Political Economy* 96 (1989), pp. 116–31.

[31] Robert H. Litzenberger and Krishna Ramaswamy, "The Effects of Dividends on Common Stock Prices, Tax Effects or Information Effects," *Journal of Finance* 37 (1982).

A more interesting example is the issue of liquidity. A study of the effect of liquidity on asset returns[32] shows that liquidity accounts for much of the puzzling effect of firm size on asset returns (see Chapter 11). Thus, one view of the state of empirical research is that the anomalies we now observe are associated with some extensions of the CAPM. Observers of this school pin their hopes on improved specifications of tests of the CAPM.

Finally, there is still a long way to go in the accurate estimation of time-varying volatility (and the covariance structure) of asset returns and in the incorporation of these estimates in the prediction of security returns.

## Summary

**1.** Although the single-factor expected return–beta relationship has not yet been confirmed by scientific standards, its use is already commonplace in economic life.

**2.** Early tests of the single-factor CAPM rejected the SML, finding that nonsystematic risk did explain average security returns.

**3.** Later tests controlling for the measurement error in beta found not only that nonsystematic risk does not explain portfolio returns, but also that the estimated SML is too flat compared with what the CAPM would predict.

**4.** Tests using Canadian data found generally erratic results, with significant nonsystematic risk and nonlinear systematic risk as determinants of portfolio returns. Thin trading in the Canadian stock market can bias the tests.

**5.** Roll's critique implies that the usual CAPM test is a test only of the mean-variance efficiency of a prespecified market proxy and, therefore, that tests of the linearity of the expected return–beta relationship do not bear on the validity of the model.

**6.** Tests of the mean-variance efficiency of professionally managed portfolios against the benchmark of a prespecified market index conform with Roll's critique in that they provide evidence of the efficiency of the prespecific market index.

**7.** Empirical evidence suggests that most professionally managed portfolios in both Canada and the United States are outperformed by market indices, which lends weight to acceptance of the efficiency of those indices and, hence, the CAPM.

**8.** Factor analysis of security returns suggests that more than one factor may be necessary for a valid expected return–beta relationship. This technique, however, does not identify the economic factors behind the factor portfolios.

**9.** Work on prespecified economic factors is ongoing. Preliminary results suggest that factors such as unanticipated inflation do play a role in the expected return–beta relationship of security returns.

[32] Y. Amihud and H. Mendelson, "Asset Pricing and the Bid-Ask Spread," *Journal of Financial Economics* 17 (1986), pp. 223–49.

**10.** Volatility of stock returns is constantly changing. Empirical evidence on stock returns must account for this phenomenon. Contemporary researchers use the variations of the ARCH-M algorithm to estimate the level of volatility and its effect on mean returns.

## Key Terms

| | |
|---|---|
| First-pass regression | Thin trading |
| Second-pass regression | Benchmark error |
| Measurement error | Factor portfolios |

## Selected Readings


*The key readings concerning tests of the CAPM are still:*

Black, Fischer; Michael C. Jensen; and Myron Scholes. "The Capital Asset Pricing Model: Some Empirical Tests." In Michael C. Jensen (editor), *Studies in the Theory of Capital Markets.* New York: Praeger Publishers, 1972.

Fama, Eugene; and James MacBeth. "Risk, Return and Equilibrium: Empirical Tests." *Journal of Political Economy* 81 (1973), 607–36.

Roll, Richard. "A Critique of the Asset Pricing Theory's Tests." *Journal of Financial Economics* 4 (1977).

*Tests of the model using more recent econometric tools are:*

Gibbons, Michael. "Multivariate Tests of Financial Models." *Journal of Financial Economics* 10 (1982).

Jobson, J. D.; and R. M. Korkie. "Potential Performance and Tests of Portfolio Efficiency." *Journal of Financial Economics* 10 (1982).

*The factor analysis approach to testing multivariate models is treated in:*

Roll, Richard; and Stephen Ross. "An Empirical Investigation of the Arbitrage Pricing Theory." *Journal of Finance* 20 (1980).

Kryzanowski, L.; and M. C. To. "General Factor Models and the Structure of Security Returns." *Journal of Financial and Quantitative Analysis* 18, no. 1 (March 1982).

Lehman, Bruce; and David Modest. "The Empirical Foundation of the Arbitrage Pricing Theory." *Journal of Financial Economics* 21 (1988).

*A good paper that tests the APT with prespecified factors is:*

Chen, Nai-Fu; Richard Roll; and Stephen A. Ross. "Economic Forces and the Stock Market." *Journal of Business* 59 (1986).


## Problems

The following annual excess rates of return were obtained for six portfolios and a market index portfolio:

| | | Portfolios | | | | | |
|---|---|---|---|---|---|---|---|
| **Year** | **Market Index** | **A** | **B** | **C** | **D** | **E** | **F** |
| 1 | 26.4 | 38.1 | 32.6 | 23.6 | 15.2 | 11.9 | 38.0 |
| 2 | 17.9 | 21.9 | 20.2 | 17.6 | 14.6 | 11.8 | 19.8 |
| 3 | 13.4 | 13.4 | 15.1 | 13.0 | 13.2 | 9.0 | 14.4 |
| 4 | 10.6 | 9.8 | 10.4 | 11.4 | 12.1 | 11.0 | 9.7 |

1. Perform the first-pass regressions as did Black, Jensen, and Scholes, and tabulate the summary statistics as in Table 10.1.
2. Specify the hypotheses for a test of second-pass regression for the SML.
3. Perform the second-pass SML regression by regressing the average excess return on each portfolio on its beta.
4. Summarize your test results and compare them to the reported results in the text.
5. Group the six portfolios into three, maximizing the dispersion of the betas of the three resultant portfolios. Repeat the test and explain any changes in the results.
6. Explain Roll's critique as it applies to the tests performed in problems (1) to (5).
7. Compare the mean-variance efficiency of the six portfolios and the market index. Does the comparison support the CAPM?

Suppose that, in addition to the market factor that has been considered in problems (1) to (7), a second factor is considered. The values of this factor for years 1 to 4 were as follows:

| Year | Factor Value (%) |
|---|---|
| 1 | 13 |
| 2 | 17 |
| 3 | −21 |
| 4 | 27 |

8. Perform the first-pass regressions as did Chen, Roll, and Ross and tabulate the relevant summary statistics. (Hint: use a multivariable regression as in the Lotus spreadsheet package. Estimate the betas of the six portfolios on the two factors.)
9. Specify the hypothesis for a test of a second-pass regression for the multidimensional SML.
10. Do the data suggest a two-factor economy?
11. Can you identify a factor portfolio for the second factor?

**12.** Richard Roll, in an article on using the capital asset pricing model (CAPM) to evaluate portfolio performance, indicated that it may not be possible to evaluate portfolio management ability if there is an error in the benchmark used.

*a.* In evaluating portfolio performance, describe the general procedure, with emphasis on the benchmark employed.

*b.* Explain what Roll meant by the benchmark error and identify the specific problem with this benchmark.

*c.* Draw a graph that shows how a portfolio that has been judged as superior relative to a "measured" security market line (SML) can be inferior relative to the "true" SML.

*d.* Assume that you are informed that a given portfolio manager has been evaluated as superior when compared to the Dow Jones Industrial Average, the S&P 500, and the NYSE Composite index. Explain whether this consensus would make you feel more comfortable regarding the portfolio manager's true ability.

*e.* Although conceding the possible problem with benchmark errors as set forth by Roll, some contend this does not mean the CAPM is incorrect, but only that there is a measurement problem when implementing the theory. Others contend that because of benchmark errors the whole technique should be scrapped. Take and defend one of these positions.

---

*Part IV*

# Active Portfolio Management

# Chapter 11

# Market Efficiency

**IN THE 1950S, AN EARLY APPLICATION OF COMPUTERS IN ECONOMICS WAS FOR ANALYSIS OF ECONOMIC TIME SERIES.** Business cycle theorists felt that tracing the evolution of several economic variables over time would clarify and predict the progress of the economy through boom and bust periods. A natural candidate for analysis was the behaviour of stock market prices over time. Assuming that stock prices reflect the prospects of the firm, recurrent patterns of peaks and troughs in economic performance ought to show up in those prices.

Maurice Kendall examined this proposition in 1953.[1] He found to his great surprise that he could identify *no* predictable patterns in stock prices. Prices seemed to evolve randomly. They were as likely to go up as they were to go down on any particular day, regardless of past performance. The data provided no way to predict price movements.

At first blush, Kendall's results were disturbing to some financial economists. They seemed to imply that the stock market is dominated by erratic market psychology, or "animal spirits"—that it follows no logical rules. In short, the results appeared to confirm the irrationality of the market. On further reflection, however, economists came to reverse their interpretation of Kendall's study.

It soon became apparent that random price movements indicated a well-functioning or efficient market, not an irrational one. In this chapter we will

[1] Maurice Kendall, "The analysis of Economic Time Series, Part I: Prices," *Journal of the Royal Statistical Society* 96 (1953).

explore the reasoning behind what may seem a surprising conclusion. We show how competition among analysts leads naturally to market efficiency, and we examine the implications of the efficient market hypothesis for investment policy. We also consider empirical evidence that supports and contradicts the notion of market efficiency.

## 11.1 RANDOM WALKS AND THE EFFICIENT MARKET HYPOTHESIS

Suppose Kendall had discovered that stock prices are predictable. What a gold mine this would have been for investors! If they could use Kendall's equations to predict stock prices, investors would reap unending profits simply by purchasing stocks that the computer model implied were about to increase in price and by selling those stocks about to fall in price.

A moment's reflection should be enough to convince yourself that this situation could not persist for long. For example, suppose that the model predicts with great confidence that XYZ's stock price, currently at $100 per share, will rise dramatically in three days to $110. What would all investors with access to the model's prediction do today? Obviously, they would place a great wave of immediate buy orders to cash in on the prospective increase in stock price. No one holding XYZ, however, would be willing to sell. The net effect would be an *immediate* jump in the stock price to $110. The forecast of a future price increase will lead instead to an immediate price increase. In other words, the stock price will immediately reflect the "good news" implicit in the model's forecast.

This simple example illustrates why Kendall's attempt to find recurrent patterns in stock price movements was doomed to failure. A forecast about favourable *future* performance leads instead to favourable *current* performance, as market participants all try to get in on the action before the price jump.

More generally, one might say that any information that could be used to predict stock performance must already be reflected in stock prices. As soon as there is any information indicating that a stock is underpriced and therefore offers a profit opportunity, investors flock to buy the stock and immediately bid up its price to a fair level, where only ordinary rates of return can be expected. These "ordinary rates" are simply rates of return commensurate with the risk of the stock.

However, if prices are bid immediately to fair levels, given all available information, it must be that they increase or decrease only in response to new information. New information, by definition, must be unpredictable; if it could be predicted, then the prediction would be part of today's information. Thus stock prices that change in response to new (unpredictable) information also must move unpredictably.

This is the essence of the argument that stock prices should follow a **random walk,** that is, that price changes should be random and unpredictable.[2] Far from a proof of market irrationality, randomly evolving stock prices are the necessary consequence of intelligent investors competing to discover relevant information on which stocks to buy or sell before the rest of the market becomes aware of that information. Indeed, if stock price movements were predictable, that would be damning evidence of stock market inefficiency, because the ability to predict prices would indicate that all available information was not already reflected in stock prices. Therefore, the notion that stocks already reflect all available information is referred to as the **efficient market hypothesis** (EMH).[3]

## Competition as the Source of Efficiency

Why should we expect stock prices to reflect "all available information"? After all, if you are willing to spend time and money gathering information, it might seem reasonable that you could turn up something that has been overlooked by the rest of the investment community. When information is costly to uncover and analyze, one would expect investment analysis calling for such expenditures to result in an increased expected return. This point has been stressed by Grossman and Stiglitz.[4] They argue that investors will have an incentive to spend time and resources to analyze and uncover new information only if such activity is likely to generate higher investment returns. Therefore, in market equilibrium it makes sense that efficient information-gathering activity should be fruitful. Although we would not, therefore, go so far as to say that you absolutely cannot come up with new information, it still makes sense to consider the competition.

Consider an investment management fund currently managing a $5 billion portfolio. Suppose that the fund manager can devise a research program that could increase the portfolio rate of return by one tenth of one percent per year, a seemingly modest amount. This program would increase the dollar return to the portfolio by $5 billion × .001, or $5 million. Therefore, the fund would be willing to spend up to $5 million per year on research to increase stock returns by a mere one tenth of one percent per year. With such large rewards for such small increases in investment performance, it should not be surprising that professional portfolio managers are willing to spend large sums on industry analysts, computer

---

[2] Actually, we are being a little loose with terminology here. Strictly speaking, we should characterize stock prices as following a submartingale, meaning that the expected change in the price can be positive, presumably as compensation for the time value of money and systematic risk. Moreover, the expected return may change over time as risk factors change. A random walk is more restrictive in that it constrains successive stock returns to be independent *and* identically distributed. Nevertheless, the term *random walk* is commonly used in the looser sense that price changes are essentially unpredictable. We will follow this convention.

[3] Market efficiency should not be confused with the idea of efficient portfolios introduced in Chapter 7. An informationally efficient *market* is one in which information is rapidly disseminated and reflected in prices. An efficient *portfolio* is one with the highest expected return for a given level of risk.

[4] Sanford J. Grossman and Joseph E. Stiglitz, "On the Impossibility of Informationally Efficient Markets," *American Economic Review* 70 (June 1980).

support, and research effort and therefore that price changes are, generally speaking, difficult to predict.

With so many well-backed analysts willing to spend considerable resources on research, there will not be many easy pickings in the market. Moreover, the incremental rates of return on research activity are likely to be so small that only managers of the largest portfolios will find them worth pursuing.

Although it may not literally be true that "all" relevant information will be uncovered, it is virtually certain that there are many investigators hot on the trail of any leads that may improve investment performance. Competition among these many well-backed, highly paid, aggressive analysts ensures that, as a general rule, stock prices ought to reflect available information regarding their proper levels.

## Versions of the Efficient Market Hypothesis

It is common to distinguish among three versions of the EMH: the weak, semistrong, and strong forms of the hypothesis. These versions differ by their notions of what is meant by the term "all available information."

The **weak-form** hypothesis asserts that stock prices already reflect all information that can be derived by examining market trading data, such as the history of past prices, trading volume, or short interest. This version of the hypothesis implies that trend analysis is fruitless. Past stock price data are publicly available and virtually costless to obtain. The weak-form hypothesis holds that if such data ever conveyed reliable signals about future performance, all investors would have learned already to exploit the signals. Ultimately, the signals lose their value as they become widely known because a buy signal, for instance, would result in an immediate price increase.

The **semistrong-form** hypothesis states that all publicly available information regarding the prospects of a firm must be reflected already in the stock price. Such information includes, in addition to past prices, fundamental data on the firm's product line, quality of management, balance sheet composition, patents held, earning forecasts, and accounting practices. Again, if any investor has access to such information from publicly available sources, one would expect it to be reflected in stock prices.

Finally, the **strong-form** version of the efficient market hypothesis states that stock prices reflect all information relevant to the firm, even including information available only to company insiders. This version of the hypothesis is quite extreme. Few would argue with the notion that corporate officers have access to pertinent information long enough before public release to enable them to profit from trading on that information. Indeed, much of the activities of the provincial securities commissions is directed toward preventing insiders from profiting by exploiting their privileged situation. In Ontario, corporate officers, directors, and substantial owners are required to report trades in their firms' shares within 10 days of the end of the month in which the trade took place. These insiders, their relatives, and any associates who trade on information supplied by insiders are considered in violation of the law.

Defining insider trading is not always easy, however. After all, stock analysts are in the business of uncovering information not already widely known to market participants. As we saw in Chapter 3, the distinction between private and inside information is sometimes murky.

---

**CONCEPT CHECK** Question 1. If the weak form of the efficient market hypothesis is valid, must the strong form also hold? Conversely, does strong-form efficiency imply weak-form efficiency?

---

## 11.2 IMPLICATIONS OF THE EMH FOR INVESTMENT POLICY

### Technical Analysis

**Technical analysis** is essentially the search for recurring and predictable patterns in stock prices. Although technicians recognize the value of information that has to do with future economic prospects of the firm, they believe such information is not necessary for a successful trading strategy. Whatever the fundamental reason for a change in stock price, if the stock price responds slowly enough, the analyst will be able to identify a trend that can be exploited during the adjustment period. Technical analysis assumes a sluggish response of stock prices to fundamental supply and demand factors. This assumption is diametrically opposed to the notion of an efficient market.

Technical analysts sometimes are called *chartists* because they study records or charts of past stock prices, hoping to find patterns they can exploit to make a profit. As an example of technical analysis, consider the *relative strength* approach. The chartist compares stock performance over a recent period to performance of the market or other stocks in the same industry. A simple version of relative strength takes the ratio of the stock price to a market indicator, such as the TSE 300 index. If the ratio increases over time, the stock is said to exhibit relative strength, because its price performance is better than that of the broad market. Such strength presumably may continue for a long enough period to offer profit opportunities. We will explore this technique as well as several other tools of technical analysis further in Chapter 19.

The efficient market hypothesis predicts that technical analysis is without merit. The past history of prices and trading volume is publicly available at minimal cost. Therefore, any information that was ever available from analyzing past prices has already been reflected in stock prices. As investors compete to exploit their common knowledge of a stock's price history, they necessarily drive stock prices to levels where expected rates of return are commensurate with risk. At those levels, stocks are neither bad nor good buys. They are just fairly priced, meaning one should not expect abnormal returns.

Despite these theoretical considerations, some technically oriented trading strategies would have generated abnormal profits in the past. We will consider these strategies, and technical analysis more generally, in Chapter 19.

## Fundamental Analysis

**Fundamental analysis** uses earnings and dividend prospects of the firm, expectations of future interest rates, and risk evaluation of the firm to determine proper stock prices. Ultimately, it represents an attempt to determine the present discounted value of all the payments a stockholder will receive from each share of stock. If that value exceeds the stock price, the fundamental analyst will recommend purchasing the stock.

Fundamental analysts usually start with a study of past earnings and an examination of company balance sheets. They supplement this analysis with further detailed economic analysis, ordinarily including an evaluation of the quality of the firm's management, the firm's standing within its industry, and the prospects for the industry as a whole. The hope is to attain some insight into the future performance of the firm that is not yet recognized by the rest of the market. Chapters 17–18 provide a detailed discussion of the types of analyses that underlie fundamental analysis.

Once again, the efficient market hypothesis predicts that *most* fundamental analysis adds little value. If analysts rely on publicly available earnings and industry information, one analyst's evaluation of the firm's prospects is not likely to be significantly more accurate than another's. There are many well-informed, well-financed firms conducting such market research, and in the face of such competition, it will be difficult to uncover data not also available to other analysts. Only analysts with a unique insight will be rewarded.

Fundamental analysis is much more difficult than merely identifying well-run firms with good prospects. Discovery of good firms does an investor no good in and of itself if the rest of the market also knows those firms are good: if the knowledge is already public, the investor will be forced to pay a high price for those firms and will not realize a superior rate of return. The trick is not to identify firms that are good, but to find firms that are *better* than everyone else's estimate. Similarly, poorly run firms can be great bargains if they are not quite as bad as their stock prices suggest. This is why fundamental analysis is difficult. It is not enough to do a good analysis of a firm; you can make money only if your analysis is better than that of your competitors, because the market price is expected already to reflect all commonly available information.

## Active versus Passive Portfolio Management

By now it is apparent that casual efforts to pick stocks are not likely to pay off. Competition among investors ensures that any easily implemented stock evaluation technique will be used widely enough so that any insights derived will be reflected in stock prices. Only serious, time-consuming, and expensive techniques are likely to generate the *differential* insight necessary to generate trading profits.

Moreover, these techniques are economically feasible only for managers of large portfolios. If you have only $100,000 to invest, even a 1 percent per year improvement in performance generates only $1,000 per year, hardly enough to justify herculean efforts. The billion-dollar manager, however, reaps extra income of $10 million annually from the same 1 percent increment.

If small investors are not in a favoured position to conduct active portfolio management, what are their choices? The small investor probably is better off placing funds in a mutual fund. By pooling resources in this way, small investors can gain from economies of size.

More difficult decisions remain, though. Can investors be sure that even large mutual funds have the ability or resources to uncover mispriced stocks? Further, will any mispricing be sufficiently large to repay the costs entailed in active portfolio management?

Proponents of the efficient market hypothesis believe that active management is largely wasted effort and unlikely to justify the expenses incurred. Therefore, they advocate a **passive investment strategy** that makes no attempt to outsmart the market. A passive strategy aims only at establishing a well-diversified portfolio of securities without attempting to fund under- or overvalued stocks. Passive management usually is characterized by a buy-and-hold strategy. Because the efficient market theory indicates that stock prices are at fair levels, given all available information, it makes no sense to buy and sell securities frequently, which generates large brokerage fees without increasing expected performance.

One common strategy for passive management is to create an **index fund.** Such a fund aims to mirror the performance of a broad-based index of stocks. For example, the Toronto Dominion Bank sponsors a mutual fund called the Green Line Canadian Index Fund, which holds stocks in direct proportion to their weight in the TSE 300 stock price index. The performance of the Green Line Canadian Index Fund therefore replicates the performance of the TSE 300. Investors in this fund obtain broad diversification with relatively low management fees. The fees can be kept to a minimum because there is no need to pay analysts for assessing stock prospects or to incur transaction costs from high portfolio turnover.

As the nearby box shows, indexing has grown considerably in appeal in recent years, especially in the U.S. Many institutional investors now hold indexed bond portfolios in addition to indexed stock portfolios. Such bond portfolios aim to replicate the features of well-known bond indices. Managers of large portfolios, such as those of pension funds, often create their own indexed funds rather than paying a mutual fund manager to do so for them. A hybrid strategy also is fairly common, where the fund maintains a *passive core,* which is an indexed position, and augments that position with one or more actively managed portfolios.

---

**CONCEPT CHECK** Question 2. What would happen to market efficiency if *all* investors attempted to follow a passive strategy?

---

## Index Funds Work Hard for Your Money

Mutual funds are supposed to take some of the risk out of stock market investing, but there is a large gap between the top and bottom performers. If even this roll of the dice is too much for you, perhaps you should consider buying an index fund.

Index funds don't do any active stock picking. They strive to replicate the stock market's overall performance as measured by the Toronto Stock Exchange index or the Standard & Poor's Corp. 500 stock index in the United States.

On the surface, indexing makes sense. Given the stock market's natural efficiency, the odds are less than 50-50 that any given fund will beat the market over time. Factor in administrative expenses and a sales charge, in some cases, and you reduce your odds even further.

Since an indexed portfolio is largely predetermined, transaction fees are generally lower.

Also, the money in an index fund works harder. The funds, usually fully invested in stocks, need relatively little cash on hand for transactions. An actively managed fund sometimes has up to 25 percent of its assets in cash at any one time. While moving to cash can add significant value in the hands of an astute manager, cash generally doesn't earn much.

There is also a tax benefit in index funds, now that the $100,000 capital gains exemption has been eliminated. Less trading means fewer capital gains to be distributed to investors and taxed each year. An actively run fund will turn over its portfolio quite regularly.

Americans have fallen in love with index funds. The Vanguard 500 Portfolio, which tracks the S&P 500 index, has more than $9 billion (U.S.) in assets. It is among the largest domestic funds in the United States.

And why not? The S&P has produced an average annual return of more than 16 percent over the past decade.

More to the point, according to pension fund analysts SEI Corp., only one in three professional money managers was able to do any better.

"It's this lack of consistency that makes indexing so attractive to certain investors," says Gordon Garmaise of Garmaise Investment Technologies, a Toronto financial services consulting firm. "Many managers will outperform the benchmarks, but too many have failed to do so in recent years."

Although the case for indexing seems strong, it has its detractors—not all of whom manage money for a living.

Louis Lowenstein, professor of finance at Columbia University in New York, feels this passive approach only works for a while and is not sustainable.

"Indexing is like all one-decision strategies that substitute something mechanical for thinking."

Look at the Nifty Fifty of the early 1970s, Prof. Lowenstein says. Then, the popular wisdom said buy only the biggest companies in the market. But when the market turned in 1973 to 1974, these stocks led the decline. In fact, for several years after that, the Vanguard 500 index portfolio was an also-ran performer.

For Canadian investors who like the idea of a passive indexed portfolio, there are only a few funds to choose from.

"Canadians have not embraced this concept with the zeal we see in the United States," Mr. Garmaise says. "Fund marketers here have always concentrated on performance numbers and indexing is all about maintaining a steady hand."

Also, he added, it's more expensive to run an index fund in Canada. This means investors find less of a difference in management expense ratios compared with actively managed funds.

Right now, banks and insurance company funds dominate the index fund sector.

The Great-West Life Equity Index Fund, the largest of its type, has $321 million in assets. Others include Bank of Montreal's $183 million First

*(Continued)*

Canadian Equity Index, and Toronto-Dominion Bank's $87 million Green Line Canadian Index Fund.

There is nothing fancy here. Each fund is a plain vanilla bet on the TSE 300. Green Line also offers an S&P 500 index fund.

One caveat: All these funds will likely underperform the index by a larger margin than their expense ratios would suggest.

Expense ratios typically don't take into account taxes and the costs of rebalancing the portfolio to match the index. Nonetheless, these are investor costs and come out of the fund's returns. This tracking error is common to all index funds, although the economies of scale of large U.S.-based funds help keep it to a minimum.

One way to use an index fund is as a hedge against other more actively managed funds you might own. This is a common practice with large pension funds, which are usually more interested in risk management than in making a killing.

But Wendy Brodkin, a principal with the Toronto pension consulting firm Towers Perrin, thinks retail investors don't have the same level of patience as pension funds.

"In a strong market, it probably doesn't matter," she says, "but I can't see most people being willing to wait out a protracted drought in an index fund. They'll jump at the wrong time."

Unlike an index fund, an actively managed fund can take some steps to protect capital in a market decline, she said, such as selling stocks and raising cash levels.

Source: Gordon Powers, *The Globe and Mail,* November 3, 1994. Reprinted by permission.

## The Role of Portfolio Management in an Efficient Market

If the market is efficient, why not throw darts at *The Globe and Mail*'s stock quotations page instead of trying rationally to choose a stock portfolio? This is a tempting conclusion to draw from the notion that security prices are fairly set, but it is far too facile. There is a role for rational portfolio management, even in perfectly efficient markets.

You have learned that a basic principle in portfolio selection is diversification. Even if all stocks are priced fairly, each still poses firm-specific risks that can be eliminated through diversification. Therefore, rational security selection, even in an efficient market, calls for the selection of a well-diversified portfolio providing the systematic risk level that the investor wants.

Rational investment policy also requires that tax considerations be reflected in security choice. High tax-bracket investors generally will not want the same securities that low-bracket investors find favourable. For instance, high-bracket investors might want to tilt their portfolios in the direction of capital gains as opposed to dividend or interest income, because the option to defer the realization of capital gain income is more valuable the higher the current tax bracket. Hence these investors may prefer stocks that yield lower dividends yet offer greater expected capital gain income. They also will be more attracted to investment opportunities for which returns are sensitive to tax benefits, such as real estate ventures.

A third argument for rational portfolio management relates to the particular risk profile of the investor. For example, an executive for an auto parts firm whose annual bonus depends on his firm's profits generally should not invest additional amounts in auto stocks. To the extent that his or her compensation already depends on the auto industry's well-being, the executive already is overinvested in that industry and should not exacerbate the lack of diversification.

Investors of varying ages also might warrant different portfolio policies with regard to risk bearing. For example, older investors who are essentially living off savings might choose to avoid long-term bonds whose market values fluctuate dramatically with changes in interest rates (discussed in Part V). Because these investors are living off accumulated savings, they require conservation of principal. In contrast, younger investors might be more inclined toward long-term bonds. The steady flow of income over long periods of time that is locked in with long-term bonds can be more important than preservation of principal to those with long life expectancies.

In conclusion, there is a role for portfolio management even in an efficient market. Investors' optimal positions will vary according to factors such as age, tax bracket, risk aversion, and employment. The role of the portfolio manager in an efficient market is to tailor the portfolio to these needs, rather than to beat the market.

### Book Values versus Market Values

A somewhat common belief is the notion that book values are intrinsically more trustworthy than market values. Many firms, for example, are reluctant to issue additional stock when the market price of outstanding equity is lower than the book value of those shares. Issue under these circumstances is said to cause dilution of the original stockholder's ownership claim.

Perhaps this faith in book values derives from their stability. Although market values fluctuate daily, book values remain the same day in and day out. The stability of book values actually is a misleading virtue. Market prices fluctuate for a good reason: They move in response to new information about the economic prospects of the firm. The stability of book values in the face of new information is testament to their essential unreliability.

As an example of how book values can go wrong, imagine what would happen to the price of Imperial Oil stock if the price of oil were to double overnight. The stock price would increase for the very good reason that Imperial Oil's assets are now far more valuable. Yet the book value of Imperial Oil's assets would remain unchanged. Its stability in the face of changing conditions clearly shows it is not a guide to true value.

## 11.3 Event Studies

The notion of informationally efficient markets leads to a powerful research methodology. If security prices reflect all currently available information, then price changes must reflect new information. Therefore it seems that one should be able to measure the importance of an event of interest by examining price changes during the period in which the event occurs.

An **event study** describes a technique of empirical financial research that enables an observer to assess the impact of a particular event on a firm's stock price. A stock market analyst might want to study the impact of dividend changes on stock prices, for example. An event study would quantify the relationship between dividend changes and stock returns. Using the results of such a study together with a superior means of predicting dividend changes, the analyst could, in principle, earn superior trading profits.

Analyzing the impact of an announced change in dividends is more difficult than it might first appear. On any particular day stock prices respond to a wide range of economic news, such as updated forecasts for GNP, inflation rates, interest rates, or corporate profitability. Isolating the part of a stock price movement that is attributable to a dividend announcement is not a trivial exercise.

The statistical approach that researchers commonly use to measure the impact of a particular information release, such as the announcement of a dividend change, is a marriage of efficient market theory with the index model discussed in Chapter 9. We want to measure the unexpected return that results from an event. This is the difference between the actual stock return and the return that might have been expected given the performance of the market. This expected return can be calculated using the index model.

Recall that the index model holds that stock returns are determined by a market factor and a firm-specific factor. The stock return, $r_t$, during a given period, $t$, would be expressed mathematically as

$$r_t = a + br_{Mt} + e_t \tag{11.1}$$

where $r_{Mt}$ is the market's excess rate of return during the period and $e_t$ is the part of a security's return resulting from firm-specific events. The parameter $b$ measures sensitivity to the market return, and $a$ is the average rate of return the stock would realize in a period with a zero market return. Equation 11.1 therefore provides a decomposition of $r_t$ into market and firm-specific factors. The firm-specific return may be interpreted as the unexpected return that results from the event.

Determination of the firm-specific return in a given period requires that we obtain an estimate of the term $e_t$. Therefore, we rewrite equation 11.1:

$$e_t = r_t - (a + br_{Mt}) \tag{11.2}$$

Equation 11.2 has a simple interpretation: To determine the firm-specific component of a stock's return, subtract the return that the stock ordinarily would earn for a given level of market performance from the actual rate of return on the stock. The residual, $e_t$, is the stock's return over and above what one would predict based on broad market movements in that period, given the stock's sensitivity to the market.

For example, suppose that the analyst has estimated that $a = .5\%$ and $b = .8$. On a day that the market goes up by 1%, you would predict from equation 11.1

that the stock should rise by an expected value of .5% + .8 × 1% = 1.3%.[5] If the stock actually rises by 2%, the analyst would infer that firm-specific news that day caused an additional stock return of 2% − 1.3% = .7 percent. We sometimes refer to the term $e_t$ in equation 11.2 as the **abnormal return**—the return beyond what would be predicted from market movements alone.

The general strategy in event studies is to estimate the abnormal return around the date that new information about a stock is released to the market and attribute the abnormal stock performance to the new information. The first step in the study is to estimate parameters $a$ and $b$ for each security in the study. These typically are calculated using index model regressions, as described in Chapter 9, in a period before that in which the event occurs. The prior period is used for estimation so that the impact of the event will not affect the estimates of the parameters. Next, the information release dates for each firm are recorded. For example, in a study of the impact of merger attempts on the stock prices of target firms, the **announcement date** is the date on which the public is informed that a merger is to be attempted. Finally, the abnormal returns of each firm surrounding the announcement date are computed, and the statistical significance and magnitude of the typical abnormal return is assessed to determine the impact of the newly released information.

One concern that complicates event studies arises from *leakage* of information. Leakage occurs when information regarding a relevant event is released to a small group of investors before official public release. In this case, the stock price might start to increase (in the case of a "good news" announcement) days or weeks before the official announcement date. Any abnormal return on the announcement date is then a poor indicator of the total impact of the information release. A better indicator would be the **cumulative abnormal return,** which is simply the sum of all abnormal returns over the time period of interest. The cumulative abnormal return thus captures the total firm-specific stock movement for an entire period when the market might be responding to new information.

Figure 11.1 presents the results from a fairly typical event study. The authors of this study were interested in leakage of information before merger announcements and constructed a sample of 194 firms that were targets of a takeover attempt. In most takeovers, stockholders of the acquired firms sell their shares to the acquirer at substantial premiums over market value. Announcement of a takeover attempt is good news for shareholders of the target firm and therefore should cause stock prices to jump.

Figure 11.1 confirms the good-news nature of the announcements. On the announcement day, called day 0, the average cumulative abnormal return (CAR) for the sample of takeover candidates increases substantially, indicating a large and

[5] We know from Chapter 9, Section 9.3, that the CAPM implies that the intercept $a$ in equation 11.1 should equal $r_f(1 - \beta)$. Nevertheless, it is customary to estimate the intercept in this equation empirically rather than imposing the CAPM value. One justification for this practice is the empirically fitted security market lines seem flatter than predicted by the CAPM (see Chapter 10), which would make the intercept implied by the CAPM too small.

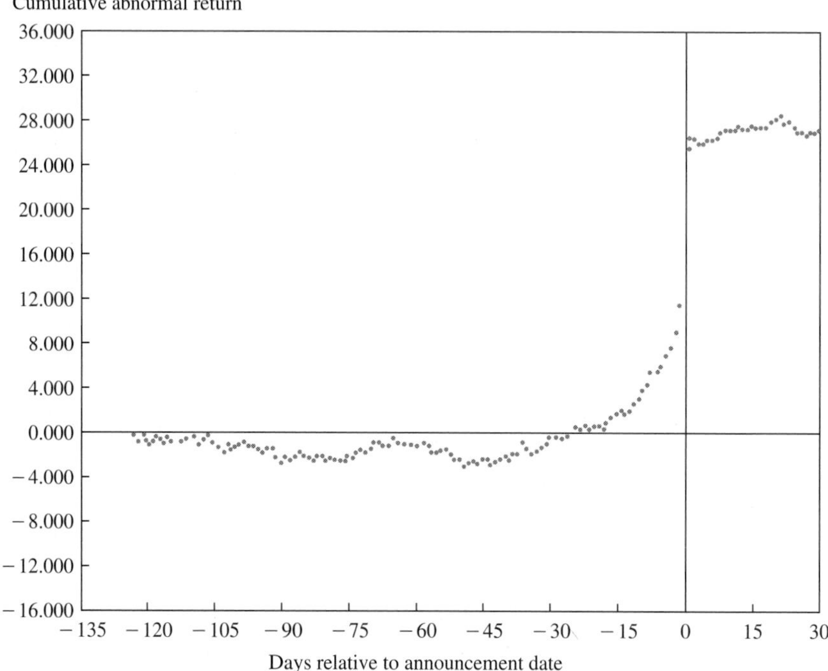


**Figure 11.1** Cumulative abnormal returns before takeover attempts: target companies.

From Arthur Keown and John Pinkerton, "Merger Announcements and Insider Trading Activity," *Journal of Finance* 36 (September 1981). Reprinted by permission.

positive abnormal return on the announcement date. Notice that immediately after the announcement date the CAR no longer increases or decreases significantly. This is in accord with the efficient market hypothesis. Once the new information became public, the stock prices jumped almost immediately in response to the good news. With prices once again fairly set, reflecting the effect of the new information, further abnormal returns on any particular day are equally likely to be positive or negative. In fact, for a sample of many firms, the average abnormal return will be extremely close to zero, and thus the CAR will show neither upward nor downward drift. This is precisely the pattern shown in Figure 11.1

The pattern of returns for the days preceding the public announcement date yields some interesting evidence about efficient markets and information leakage. If insider trading rules were perfectly obeyed and perfectly enforced, stock prices should show no abnormal returns on days before the public release of relevant news, because no special firm-specific information would be available to the market before public announcement. Instead, we should observe a clean jump in the stock price only on the announcement day. In fact, the prices of these takeover targets clearly start an upward drift 30 days before the public announcement. There are two possible interpretations of this pattern. One is that information is leaking to some market participants who then purchase the stocks before the public announcement. At least some abuse of insider trading rules is occurring.

Another interpretation is that in the days before a takeover attempt the public becomes suspicious of the attempt as it observes someone buying large blocks of stock. As acquisition intentions become more evident, the probability of an attempted merger is gradually revised upward so that we see a gradual increase in CARs. Although this interpretation is certainly a valid possibility, evidence of leakage appears almost universally in event studies, even in cases where the public's access to information is not gradual. It appears as if insider trading violations do occur.

Actually, securities commissions can take some comfort from patterns such as that in Figure 11.1. If insider trading rules were widely and flagrantly violated, we would expect to see abnormal returns earlier than they appear in these results. The CAR would turn positive as soon as acquiring firms decided on their takeover targets, because insiders would start trading immediately. By the time of the public announcement, the insiders would have bid up the stock prices of target firms to levels reflecting the merger attempt, and the abnormal returns on the actual public announcement date would be close to zero. The dramatic increase in the CAR that we see on the announcement date indicates that a good deal of these announcements were indeed news to the market and that stock prices did not already reflect complete knowledge about the takeovers. It would appear, therefore, that securities commission enforcement does have a substantial effect on restricting insider trading, even if some amount of it still persists.

Other studies, though, paint a less optimistic picture of securities trading regulation. For instance, the event studies methodology was applied by Kryzanowski[6] to investigate the effectiveness of trading suspensions in the three major Canadian stock exchanges (TSE, ME, and VSE) in arresting manipulative activities (mostly through dissemination of misleading information) on stock returns. The study identified stocks suspended from floor trading in these three exchanges over the period 1967–1973 because of alleged manipulation. It then examined the CARs in the weeks before and after the suspension event. These were significantly positive before, and significantly negative after, for up to 10 weeks around the suspension date. Hence, it appears that disseminating and exploiting misleading information about stocks is profitable. It also seems that investors were slow to react to the unfavourable information conveyed by the trading suspension.

---

**CONCEPT CHECK** Question 3. Suppose that we see negative abnormal returns (declining CARs) after an announcement date. Is this a violation of efficient markets?

---

[6] Lawrence Kyzanowski, "Misinformation and Regulatory Actions in the Canadian Capital Markets: Some Empirical Evidence," *The Bell Journal of Economics* 9, no. 2 (Fall 1978); and "The Efficacy of Trading Suspensions: A Regulatory Action Designed to Prevent the Exploitation of Monopoly Information," *Journal of Finance* 34 (December 1979).

## 11.4 Are Markets Efficient?

### The Issues

Not surprisingly, the efficient market hypothesis does not exactly arouse enthusiasm in the community of professional portfolio managers. It implies that a great deal of the activity of portfolio managers—the search for undervalued securities—is at best wasted effort and quite probably harmful to clients because it costs money and leads to imperfectly diversified portfolios. Consequently, the EMH has never been widely accepted among professionals, and debate continues today on the degree to which security analysis can improve investment performance. Before discussing empirical tests of the hypothesis, we want to note three factors that together imply that the debate probably never will be settled: the *magnitude issue,* the *selection bias issue,* and the *lucky event issue.*

**The Magnitude Issue.** Consider an investment manager overseeing a \$2 billion portfolio. If she can improve performance by only one tenth of one percent per year, that effort will be worth .001 × \$2 billion = \$2 million annually. This manager clearly would be worth her salary! Yet can we, as observers, statistically measure her contribution? Probably not: a one tenth of one percent contribution would be swamped by the yearly volatility of the market. Remember, the annual standard deviation of the well-diversified TSE 300 index has been more than 16 percent per year. Against these fluctuations, a small increase in performance would be hard to detect. Nevertheless, \$2 million remains an extremely valuable improvement in performance.

All might agree that stock prices are very close to fair values, and that only managers of large portfolios can earn enough trading profits to make the exploitation of minor mispricing worth the effort. According to this view, the actions of intelligent investment managers are the driving force behind the constant evolution of market prices to fair levels. Rather than ask the qualitative question, "Are markets efficient?" we ought to instead ask a more quantitative question: "How efficient are markets?"

**The Selection Bias Issue.** Suppose that you discover an investment scheme that could really make money. You have two choices: either publish your technique in *The Wall Street Journal* or *The Globe and Mail* to win fleeting fame, or keep your technique secret and use it to earn millions of dollars. Most investors would choose the latter option, which presents us with a conundrum. Only investors who find that an investment scheme cannot generate abnormal returns will be willing to report their findings to the whole world. Hence, opponents of the efficient-market view of the world always can use evidence that various techniques do not provide investment rewards as proof that the techniques that do work simply are not being reported to the public. This is a problem in *selection bias:* The outcomes we are able to observe have been preselected in favour of failed attempts.

## How To Guarantee a Successful Market Newsletter

Suppose you want to make your fortune publishing a market newsletter. You need first to convince potential subscribers that you have talent worth paying for. Ah, but what if you have no talent? The solution is simple: start eight newsletters.

In year one, let four of your newsletters predict an up-market and four a down-market. In year two, let half of the originally optimistic group of newsletters continue to predict an up-market and the other half a down-market. Do the same for the originally pessimistic group. Continue in this manner to obtain the above pattern of predictions ($U$ = prediction of an up-market, $D$ = prediction of a down-market).

After three years, no matter what has happened to the market, one of the newsletters would have had a perfect prediction record. This is because after three years there are $2^3 = 8$ outcomes for the market, and we have covered all eight possibilities with the eight newsletters. Now, we simply slough off the seven unsuccessful newsletters, and market the eighth newsletter based on its perfect track record. If we want to establish a newsletter with a perfect track record over a four-year period, we need $2^4 =$ 16 newsletters. A five-year period requires 32 newsletters, and so on.

After the fact, the one newsletter that was always right will attract attention for your uncanny foresight and investors will rush to pay large fees for its advice. Your fortune is made, and you never even researched the market!

*WARNING:* This scheme is illegal! The point, however, is that with hundreds of market newsletters, you can find one that has stumbled onto an apparently remarkable string of successful predictions without any real degree of skill. After the fact, *someone's* prediction history can seem to imply great forecasting skill. This person is the one we will read about in *The Wall Street Journal* and *The Globe and Mail;* the others will be forgotten.

**Newsletter Predictions**

| Year | 1 | 2 | 3 | 4 | 5 | 6 | 7 | 8 |
|---|---|---|---|---|---|---|---|---|
| 1 | *U* | *U* | *U* | *U* | *D* | *D* | *D* | *D* |
| 2 | *U* | *U* | *D* | *D* | *U* | *U* | *D* | *D* |
| 3 | *U* | *D* | *U* | *D* | *U* | *D* | *U* | *D* |

Therefore, we cannot fairly evaluate the true ability of portfolio managers to generate winning stock market strategies.

**The Lucky Event Issue.** In virtually any month it seems we read an article about some investor or investment company with a fantastic investment performance over the recent past. Surely the superior records of such investors disprove the efficient market hypothesis.

Yet this conclusion is far from obvious. As an analogy to the investment game, consider a contest to flip the most number of heads out of 50 trials using a fair coin. The expected outcome for any person is, of course, 50 percent heads and 50 percent tails. If 10,000 people, however, compete in this contest, it would not be surprising if at least one or two contestants flipped more than 75 percent heads. In fact, elementary statistics tells us that the expected number of contestants flipping 75 percent or more heads would be two. It would be silly, though, to crown these people the "head-flipping champions of the world." Obviously, they are simply the contestants who happened to get lucky on the day of the event. (See the accompanying box.)

The analogy to efficient markets is clear. Under the hypothesis that any stock is fairly priced given all available information, any bet on a stock is simply a coin toss. There is equal likelihood of winning or losing the bet. However, if many investors using a variety of schemes make fair bets, statistically speaking, *some* of those investors will be lucky and win a great majority of the bets. For every big winner, there may be many big losers, but we never hear of these managers. The winners, though, turn up in the financial press as the latest stock market gurus; then they can make a fortune publishing market newsletters.

Our point is that after the fact there will have been at least one successful investment scheme. A doubter will call the results luck, the successful investor will call it skill. The proper test would be to see whether the successful investors can repeat their performance in another period, yet this approach is rarely taken.

With these caveats in mind, we now turn to some of the empirical tests of the efficient markets hypothesis.

**CONCEPT CHECK** Question 4. The Fidelity Magellen Fund managed by Peter Lynch outperformed the S&P 500 in 11 of the 13 years that Lynch managed the fund, resulting in an average annual return more than 10 percent better than that of the index. Is this performance sufficient to dissuade you from a belief in efficient markets? If not, would *any* performance record be sufficient to dissuade you?

## 11.5 TESTS OF PREDICTABILITY IN STOCK MARKET RETURNS

### Returns over Short Horizons

Early tests of efficient markets were tests of the weak form. Could speculators find trends in past prices that would enable them to earn abnormal profits? This is essentially a test of the efficacy of technical analysis.

The already-cited work of Kendall and of Roberts,[7] both of whom analyzed the possible existence of patterns in stock prices, suggest that such patterns are not to be found. Fama[8] later analyzed "runs" of stock prices to see whether the stock market exhibits "momentum" that can be exploited. (A run is a sequence of consecutive price increases or decreases.) For example, if the last three changes in daily stock prices were positive, could we be more confident that the next move also would be up?

Fama classified daily stock price movements of each of the 30 Dow Jones industrial stocks as positive, zero, or negative in order to test persistence of runs.

[7] Harry Roberts, "Stock Market 'Patterns' and Financial Analysis: Methodological Suggestions," *Journal of Finance* 14 (March 1959).

[8] Eugene Fama, "The Behavior of Stock Market Prices," *Journal of Business* 38 (January 1965).

He found that neither positive nor negative returns persisted to an extent that could contradict the efficient market hypothesis. Although there was some evidence of runs over very short time intervals (less than one day), the tendency for runs to persist was so slight that any attempt to exploit them would generate trading costs in excess of the expected abnormal returns.

Fama's results indicate weak serial correlation in stock market returns. *Serial correlation* refers to the tendency for stock returns to be related to past returns. Positive serial correlation means that positive returns tend to follow positive returns (a momentum type of property). Negative serial correlation means that positive returns tend to be followed by negative returns (a reversal or "correction" property).

Using more powerful statistical tools, recent tests have confirmed Fama's results. Both Conrad and Kaul[9] and Lo and MacKinlay[10] have examined weekly returns of NYSE stocks and found positive serial correlation over short horizons. However, as in Fama's study, the correlation coefficients of weekly returns tend to be fairly small, at least for large stocks for which price data are the most reliably up to date. Thus, while these studies demonstrate price trends over short periods, the evidence does not clearly suggest the existence of trading opportunities.

A more sophisticated version of trend analysis is a **filter rule.** A filter technique gives a rule for buying or selling a stock depending on past price movements. One rule, for example, might be: "Buy if the last two trades each resulted in a stock price increase." A more conventional one might be: "Buy a security if its price increased by 1 percent and hold it until its price falls by more than 1 percent from the subsequent high." Alexander[11] and Fama and Blume[12] found that such filter rules generally could not generate trading profits.

The conclusion of the majority of weak-form tests using short-horizon returns is that the efficient market hypothesis is validated by stock market data. To be fair, however, one should note the criticism of efficient market skeptics, who argue that any filter rule or trend analysis that can be tested statistically is overly mechanical and cannot capture the finesse with which human investors can detect subtle but exploitable patterns in past prices.

## Returns over Long Horizons

While studies of short-horizon returns have detected minor positive serial correlation in stock market prices, more recent tests[13,14] of long-horizon returns (i.e.,

---

[9] Jennifer Conrad and Gautam Kaul, "Time-Variation in Expected Returns," *Journal of Business* 61 (October 1988), pp. 409–425.

[10] Andrew W. Lo and A. Craig MacKinlay, "Stock Market Prices Do Not Follow Random Walks: Evidence from a Simple Specification Test," *Review of Financial Studies* 1 (1988), pp. 41–66.

[11] Sidney Alexander, "Price Movements in Speculative Markets: Trends or Random Walks, No. 2," in Paul Cootner (editor), *The Random Character of Stock Market Prices* (Cambridge, Mass.: MIT Press, 1964).

[12] Eugene Fama and Marshall Blume, "Filter Rules and Stock Market Trading Profits," *Journal of Business* 39 (Supplement) (January 1966).

[13] Eugene F. Fama and Kenneth R. French, "Permanent and Temporary

returns over multiyear periods) have found suggestions of pronounced negative long-term serial correlation. The latter result has given rise to a "fads hypothesis," which asserts that stock prices might overreact to relevant news. Such overreaction leads to positive serial correlation (momentum) over short time horizons. Subsequent correction of the overreaction leads to poor performance following good performance and vice versa. The corrections mean that a run of positive returns eventually will tend to be followed by negative returns, leading to negative serial correlation over longer horizons. These episodes of apparent overshooting followed by correction give stock prices the appearance of fluctuating around their fair values and suggest that market prices exhibit excessive volatility compared to intrinsic value.[15]

These long-horizon results are dramatic, but the studies offer far from conclusive evidence regarding efficient markets. First, the study results need not be interpreted as evidence for stock market fads. An alternative interpretation of these results holds that they indicate only that market risk premiums vary over time. The response of market prices to variation in the risk premium can lead one to incorrectly infer the presence of mean reversion and excess volatility in prices. For example, when the risk premium and the required return on the market rises, stock prices will fall. When the market then rises (on average) at this higher rate of return, the data convey the impression of a stock price recovery. The impression of overshooting and correction is in fact no more than a rational response of market prices to changes in discount rates.

Second, these studies suffer from statistical problems. Because they rely on returns measured over long time periods, these tests of necessity are based on few observations of long-horizon returns. Moreover, it appears that much of the statistical support for mean reversion in stock market prices derives from returns during the Great Depression. Other periods do not provide strong support for the fads hypothesis.[16]

## Predictors of Broad Market Returns

Several studies have documented the ability of easily observed variables to predict market returns. For example, Fama and French[17] show that the return on the aggregate stock market tends to be higher when the dividend/price ratio, the divi-

---

Components of Stock Prices," *Journal of Political Economy* 96 (April 1988), pp. 246–273.

[14] James Poterba and Lawrence Summers, "Mean Reversion in Stock Prices: Evidence and Implications," *Journal of Financial Economics* 22 (October 1988), pp. 27–59.

[15] The fads debate started as a controversy over excess volatility. See Robert J. Shiller, "Do Stock Prices Move Too Much to Be Justified by Subsequent Changes in Dividends?" *American Economic Review* 71 (June 1971), pp. 421–436. However, it is now apparent that excess volatility and fads are essentially different ways of describing the same phenomenon. For a discussion of this issue, see John H. Cochrane, "Volatility Tests and Efficient Markets: A Review Essay," National Bureau of Economic Research Working Paper No. 3591, January 1991.

[16] Myung J. Kim, Charles R. Nelson, and Richard Startz, "Mean Reversion in Stock Prices? A Reappraisal of the Empirical Evidence," National Bureau of Economic Research Working Paper No. 2795, December 1988.

[17] Eugene F. Fama and Kenneth R. French, "Dividend Yields and Expected Stock Returns," *Journal of Financial Economics* 22 (October 1988), pp. 3–25.

dend yield, is high. Campbell and Shiller[18] find that the earnings yield can predict market returns. Keim and Stambaugh[19] show that bond market data, such as the spread between yields on high- and low-grade corporate bonds, also help predict broad market returns.

Again, the interpretation of these results is difficult. On the one hand, they may imply that stock returns can be predicted, in violation of the efficient market hypothesis. More probably, however, these variables are proxying for variation in the market risk premium. For example, given a level of dividends or earnings, stock prices will be lower and dividend and earnings yields will be higher when the risk premium (and therefore the expected market return) is larger. Thus, a high dividend or earnings yield will be associated with higher market returns. This does not indicate a violation of market efficiency—the predictability of market returns is due to predictability in the risk premium, not in risk-adjusted abnormal returns.

Fama and French[20] show that the yield spread between high- and low-grade bonds has greater predictive power for returns on low-grade bonds than for returns on high-grade bonds and greater predictive power for stock returns than for bond returns, suggesting that the predictability in returns is in fact a risk premium rather than evidence of market inefficiency. Similarly, the fact that the dividend yield on stocks helps to predict bond market returns suggests that the yield captures a risk premium common to both markets rather than mispricing in the equity market.

## 11.6 Portfolio Strategies and Market Anomalies

Fundamental analysis calls on a much wider range of information to create portfolios than does technical analysis, and tests of the value of fundamental analysis are thus correspondingly more difficult to evaluate. They have, however, revealed a number of so-called anomalies, that is, evidence that seems inconsistent with the efficient market hypothesis. We will review several such anomalies in the following pages.

We must note before starting that one major problem with these tests is that most require risk adjustments to portfolio performance and most use the CAPM to make the risk adjustments. We know that, although beta seems to be a relevant descriptor of stock risk, the empirically measured quantitative trade-off between risk as measured by beta and expected return differs from the predictions of the CAPM. If we use the CAPM to adjust portfolio returns for risk, we run the risk

[18] John Y. Campbell and Robert Shiller, "Stock Prices, Earnings and Expected Dividends," *Journal of Finance* 43 (July 1988), pp. 661–676.

[19] Donald B. Keim and Robert F. Stambaugh, "Predicting Returns in the Stock and Bond Markets," *Journal of Financial Economics* 17 (1986), pp. 357–390.

[20] Eugene F. Fama and Kenneth R. French, "Business Conditions and Expected Returns on Stocks and Bonds," *Journal of Financial Economics* 25 (November 1989), pp. 3–22.

that inappropriate adjustments will lead to the conclusion that various portfolio strategies can generate superior returns, when in fact it simply is the risk-adjustment procedure that has failed.

Another way to put this is to note that tests of risk-adjusted returns are *joint tests* of the efficient market hypothesis *and* the risk-adjustment procedure. If it appears that a portfolio strategy can generate superior returns, we must then decide whether this is due to a failure of the EMH or to an inappropriate risk-adjustment technique. Usually, the risk-adjustment technique is based on more questionable assumptions than is the EMH; by opting to reject the procedure, we are left with no conclusion about market efficiency.

An example of this issue is the discovery by Basu[21] that portfolios of low price-earnings ratio stocks have higher average returns than do high P/E portfolios. The **P/E effect** holds up even if returns are adjusted for portfolio beta. Is this a confirmation that the market systematically misprices stocks according to P/E ratios? This would be an extremely surprising and, to us, disturbing conclusion, because analysis of P/E ratios is such a simple procedure. Although it may be possible to earn superior returns using hard work and much insight, it hardly seems possible that such a simplistic technique is enough to generate abnormal returns. One possible interpretation of these results is that the model of capital market equilibrium is at fault in that the returns are not properly adjusted for risk.

This makes sense, because if two firms have the same expected earnings, then the riskier stock will sell at a lower price and lower P/E ratio. Because of its higher risk, the low P/E stock also will have higher expected returns. Therefore, unless the CAPM beta fully adjusts for risk, P/E will act as a useful additional descriptor of risk, and will be associated with abnormal returns if the CAPM is used to establish benchmark performance.

## The Small-Firm Effect

One of the most important anomalies with respect to the efficient market hypothesis is the so-called size, or **small-firm effect,** originally documented by Banz.[22] Banz found that both total and risk-adjusted rates of return tend to fall with increases in the relative size of the firm, as measured by the market value of the firm's outstanding equity. Dividing all NYSE stocks into five quintiles according to firm size, Banz found that the average annual return of firms in the smallest-size quintile was 19.8 percent greater than the average return of firms in the largest-size quintile.

---

[21] Sanjoy Basu, "The Investment Performance of Common Stocks in Relation to Their Price-Earnings Ratios: A Test of the Efficient Market Hypothesis," *Journal of Finance* 32 (June 1977), pp. 663–682; and "The Relationship between Earnings Yield, Market Value, and Return for NYSE Common Stocks: Further Evidence," *Journal of Financial Economics* 12 (June 1983).

[22] Rolf Banz, "The Relationship between Return and Market Value of Common Stocks," *Journal of Financial Economics* 9 (March 1981).

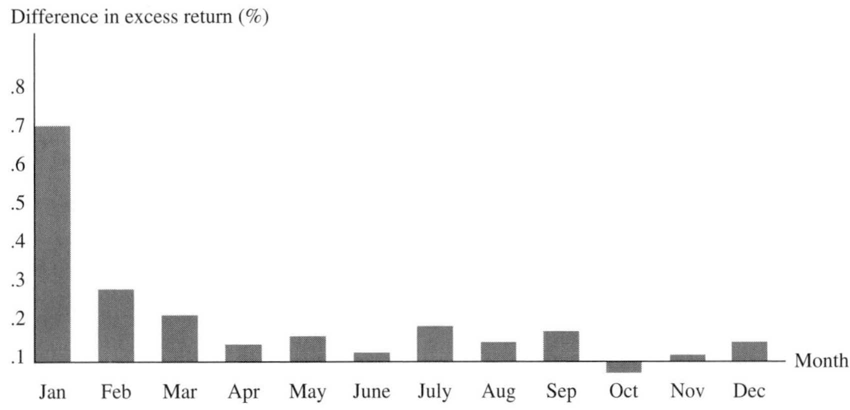


**Figure 11.2**
Average difference between daily excess returns (in percentages) of lowest-firm size and highest-firm size deciles for each month, 1963–1979.

Data from Donald B. Keim, "Size Related Anomalies and Stock Return Seasonality: Further Empirical Evidence," *Journal of Financial Economics* 12 (June 1983). Reprinted by permission.

This is a huge premium; imagine earning a premium of this size on a billion-dollar portfolio. Yet it is remarkable that following a simple (even simplistic) rule such as "invest in low capitalization stocks" should enable an investor to earn excess returns. After all, any investor can measure firm size at little cost. One would not expect such minimal effort to yield such large rewards.

Later studies (Keim,[23] Reinganum,[24] and Blume and Stambaugh,[25]) showed that the small-firm effect occurs virtually entirely in January, in fact, in the first two weeks of January. The size effect is in fact a "small-firm-in-January" effect.

Figure 11.2 illustrates the *January effect.* Keim ranked firms in order of increasing size as measured by market value of equity and then divided them into 10 portfolios grouped by the size of each firm. In each month of the year, he calculated the difference in the average excess return of firms in the smallest-firm portfolio and largest-firm portfolio. The average monthly differences over the years 1963–1979 appear in Figure 11.2. January clearly stands out as an exceptional month for small firms, with an average small-firm premium of .714 percent per day.

The results for the first five trading days in January are even more compelling. The difference in excess returns between the smallest-firm and largest-firm portfolios for the first five trading days of the year are as follows:

---

[23] Donald B. Keim, "Size Related Anomalies and Stock Return Seasonality: Further Empirical Evidence," *Journal of Financial Economics* 12 (June 1983).

[24] Marc R. Reinganum, "The Anomalous Stock Market Behavior of Small Firms in January: Empirical Tests for Tax-Loss Effects," *Journal of Financial Economics* 12 (June 1983).

[25] Marshall E. Blume and Robert F. Stambaugh, "Biases in Computed Returns: An Application to the Size Effect," *Journal of Financial Economics,* 1983.

| Trading Day | Differential Excess Return (Average for 1963–1979) |
|---|---|
| 1 | 3.20 |
| 2 | 1.68 |
| 3 | 1.25 |
| 4 | 1.14 |
| 5 | 0.89 |
| **Total** | **8.16** |

The total differential return is an amazing 8.16 percent over only five trading days.

Some researchers believe that the January effect is tied to tax-loss selling at the end of the year. The hypothesis is that many people sell stocks that have declined in price during the previous months to realize their capital losses before the end of the tax year. Such investors do not put the proceeds from these sales back into the stock market until after the turn of the year. At that point the rush of demand for stock places an upward pressure on prices that results in the January effect. Indeed, Ritter[26] shows that the ratio of stock purchases to sales of individual investors reaches an annual low at the end of December and an annual high at the beginning of January. The January effect is said to show up most dramatically for the smallest firms because the small-firm group includes, as an empirical matter, stocks with the greatest variability of prices during the year. The group therefore includes a relatively large number of firms that have declined sufficiently to induce tax-loss selling.

From a theoretical standpoint, this theory has substantial flaws. First, if the positive January effect is a manifestation of buying pressure, it should be matched by a symmetric negative December effect when the tax-loss incentives induce selling pressure. Second, the predictable January effect flies in the face of efficient market theory. If investors who do not already hold these firms know that January will bring abnormal returns to the small-firm group, they should rush to purchase stock in December to capture those returns. This would push buying pressure from January to December. Rational investors should not "allow" such predictable abnormal January returns to persist. However, small firms outperform large ones in January in every year of Keim's study, 1963–1979.

Despite these theoretical objections, some empirical evidence supports the belief that the January effect is connected to tax-loss selling. For example, Reinganum found that, within size class, firms that had declined more severely in price had larger January returns. This pattern is illustrated in Figure 11.3. Reinganum divided firms into quartiles based on the extent to which stock prices had declined during the year. Big price declines would be expected to generate big January returns if these firms tend to be unloaded in December and enjoy

[26] Jay R. Ritter, "The Buying and Selling Behavior of Individual Investors at the Turn of the Year," *Journal of Finance* 43 (July 1988), pp. 701–717.

**Figure 11.3**

Average daily returns in January for securities in the upper quartile and bottom quartile of the tax-loss selling distribution by market-value portfolio.

From Marc R. Reinganum, "The Anomalous Stock Market Behavior of Small Firms in January: Empirical Tests for Tax-Loss Effects," *Journal of Financial Economics* 12 (June 1983). Reprinted by permission.

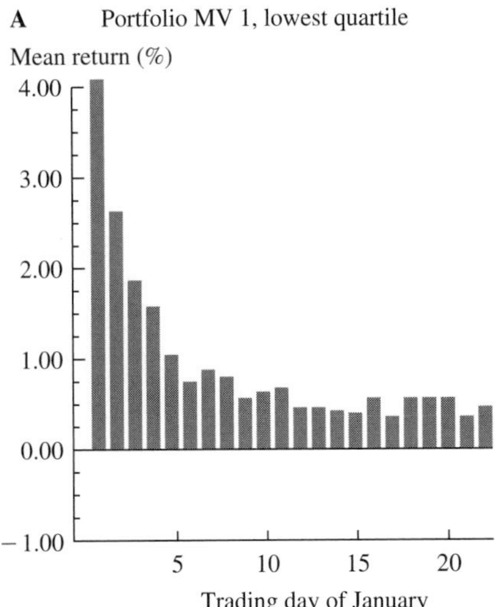


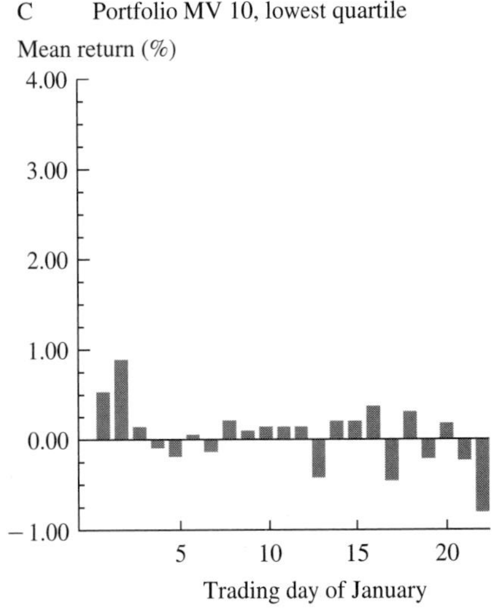


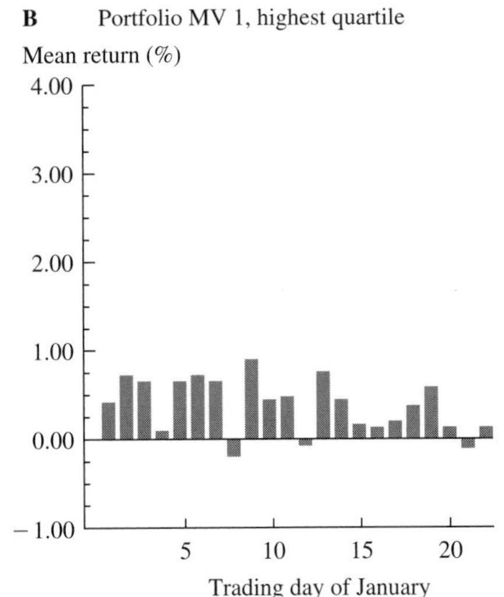


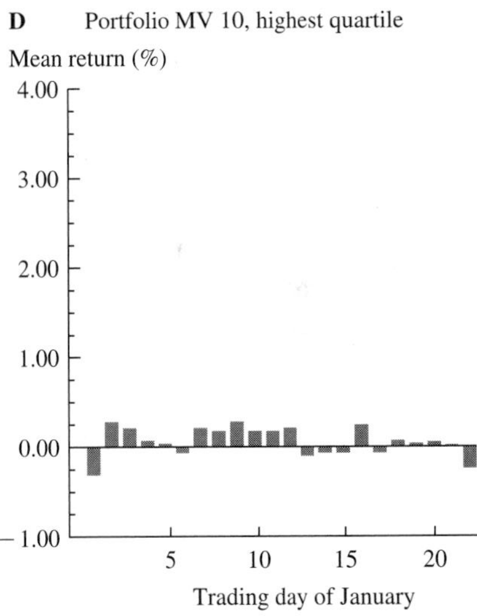


demand pressure in January. The figure shows that the lowest quartile (biggest tax loss) portfolios within each size group show the greatest January effect.

A size effect continues to persist, however, even after adjusting for taxes. Small firms that rose in price continue to show abnormal January returns (Figure 11.3**B**), while large firms that declined in price show no special January effect. Hence, although taxes appear to be associated with the abnormal January returns (Figure 11.3**A** compared with **B, C** compared with **D**), size per se remains a factor in January (Figure 11.3**A** compared with **C, B** compared with **D**).

Several Canadian studies confirm the ambiguous nature of the conclusions drawn from the U.S. results. Berges, McConnell, and Schlarbaum[27] found a significant January effect in Canadian stock returns, and this effect was more pronounced for firms with smaller values. The abnormally high January returns, however, were present during the entire period covered by the study (1951–1980), even though Canada did not introduce a capital gains tax until 1973. Thus, there is little evidence that tax-loss selling caused the January effect. A subsequent study by Tinic, Barone-Adesi, and West[28] confirmed the fact that tax-loss selling could not be the sole cause for the high January returns. This last study, however, did find some influence of the tax laws on the seasonality of returns, since the introduction of capital gains taxation in 1972 was shown to have some influence for stocks listed solely in Canada.

More recent Canadian work[29] attributes the January effect to portfolio rebalancing by professional portfolio managers in the securities industry. According to its arguments, such portfolio managers are rewarded at the end of the year with bonuses that are determined by the rate of return that they earned during the year. The managers invest the funds allocated to them in risky securities at the beginning of the year. If the securities produce a satisfactory return at some time during the year, the managers tend to lock in their returns (and their bonuses) by moving investments out of the equity market and into low-risk securities. The following January they move back into the equity market, thus producing the abnormal returns.

The fundamental question is why market participants do not exploit the January effect and thereby ultimately eliminate it by bidding stock prices to appropriate levels. One possible explanation lies in segmentation of the market into two groups: institutional investors who invest primarily in large firms, and individual investors who invest disproportionately in smaller-sized firms. According to this view, managers of large institutional portfolios are the moving force behind efficient markets. It is professionals who seek out profit opportunities and bid prices to their appropriate levels. Institutional investors do not seem to buy at the small-size end of the market, perhaps because of limits on allowed portfolio positions, so the small-firm anomaly persists without the force of their participation.

---

**CONCEPT CHECK**

Question 5. Does this market segmentation theory get the efficient market hypothesis off the hook, or are there still market mechanisms that, in theory, ought to act to eliminate the small firm anomaly?

---

[27] Angel Berges, John J. McConnell, and Gary G. Schlarbaum, "The Turn-of-the-Year in Canada," *Journal of Finance* 39, no. 1 (March 1984).

[28] Seha M. Tinic, Giovanni Barone-Adesi, and Richard R. West, "Seasonality in Canadian Stock Prices: A Test of the 'Tax-Loss-Selling' Hypothesis," *Journal of Financial and Quantitative Analysis* 21, no. 1 (March 1986).

[29] G. Athanassakos, "Portfolio Rebalancing and the January Effect in Canada," *Financial Analysts Journal,* November/December 1992; and "The January Effect: Solving the Mystery," *Canadian Investment Review,* Spring 1995.

**Table 11.1** January Effect by Degree of Neglect (1971–1980)

| | Average January Return (%) | Average January Return Minus Average Return During Rest of Year (%) | Average January Return after Adjusting for Systematic Risk (%) |
|---|---|---|---|
| **S&P 500 Companies** | | | |
| Highly researched | 2.48 | 1.63 | −1.44 |
| Moderately researched | 4.95 | 4.19 | 1.69 |
| Neglected | 7.62 | 6.87 | 5.03 |
| **Non-S&P 500 Companies** | | | |
| Neglected | 11.32 | 10.72 | 7.71 |

From Avner Arbel, "Generic Stocks: An Old Product in a New Package," *Journal of Portfolio Management*, Summer 1985. Reprinted by permission.

## The Neglected-Firm Effect

Arbel and Strebel[30] give another interpretation of the small-firm-in-January effect. Because small firms tend to be neglected by large institutional traders, information about such firms is less available. This information deficiency makes smaller firms riskier investments that command higher returns. "Brand-name" firms, after all, are subject to considerable monitoring from institutional investors that assures high-quality information, and presumably investors do not purchase "generic" stocks without the prospect of greater returns.

As evidence for the **neglected-firm effect,** Arbel[31] measures the information deficiency of firms using the coefficient of variation of analysts' forecasts of earnings. (The coefficient of variation is the ratio of standard deviation to mean and measures the dispersion of forecasts. It is a "noise-to-signal" ratio.) The correlation coefficient between the coefficient of variation and total return was .676, quite high, and statistically significant. In a related test, Arbel divided firms into highly researched, moderately researched, and neglected groups based on the number of institutions holding the stock. Table 11.1 shows that the January effect was largest for the neglected firms.

Work by Amihud and Mendelson[32] on the effect of liquidity on stock returns might be related to both the small-firm and neglected-firm effects. They argue that investors will demand a rate of return premium to invest in less liquid stocks, which entail higher trading costs (see Chapter 8 for more details). Indeed, spreads

---

[30] Avner Arbel and Paul J. Strebel, "Pay Attention to Neglected Firms," *Journal of Portfolio Management*, Winter 1983.

[31] Avner Arbel, "Generic Stocks: An Old Product in a New Package," *Journal of Portfolio Management*, Summer 1985.

[32] Yakov Amihud and Haim Mendelson, "Asset Pricing and the Bid-Ask Spread," *Journal of Financial Economics* 17 (December 1987), pp. 223–250; and "Liquidity, Asset Prices, and Financial Policy," *Financial Analysts Journal* 47 (November/December 1991), pp. 56–66.

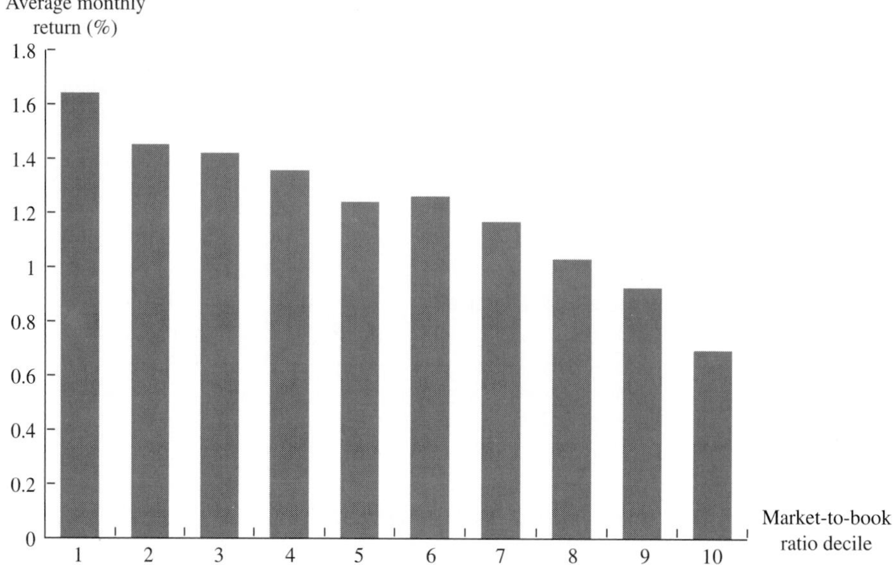


**Figure 11.4**
Average rate of return as a function of the ratio of market value to book value.

for the least liquid stocks easily can be more than 5 percent of stock value. In accord with their hypothesis, Amihud and Mendelson show that these stocks show a strong tendency to exhibit abnormally high risk-adjusted rates of return. Because small and less-analyzed stocks as a rule are less liquid, the liquidity effect might be a partial explanation of their abnormal returns. However, this theory does not explain why the abnormal returns of small firms should be concentrated in January. In any case, exploiting these effects can be more difficult than it would appear. The trading costs on small stocks can easily wipe out any apparent abnormal profit opportunity.

## Market-to-Book Ratios

Fama, French, and Reinganum[33] show that a very powerful predictor of returns across securities is the ratio of the market value of the firm's equity to the book value of equity. They stratify firms into 10 groups according to market-to-book ratios and examine the average monthly rate of return of each of the 10 groups during the period July 1963–December 1990. The decile with the lowest market-to-book ratio had an average monthly return of 1.65 percent, while the highest-ratio decile averaged only 0.72 percent per month. Figure 11.4 shows the pattern of returns across deciles. The dramatic dependence of returns on market-to-book ratio is independent of beta, suggesting either that low market-to-book ratio firms

[33] Eugene F. Fama and Kenneth R. French, "The Cross Section of Expected Stock Returns," *Journal of Finance* 47 (1992), pp. 427–65; Marc R. Reinganum, "The Anatomy of a Stock Market Winner," *Financial Analysts Journal,* March–April 1988, pp. 272–84.

are relatively underpriced, or that the market-to-book ratio is serving as a proxy for a risk factor that affects equilibrium-expected returns.

In fact, Fama and French found that after controlling for the size and market-to-book effects, beta seemed to have no power to explain average security returns. This was a severe blow to modern portfolio theory and its implication that a security's systematic risk should determine its risk premium and led many to ask, "Is beta dead again?" (See the box in Chapter 10 for a discussion of beta's "first death.")

Beta seems to have many lives, however. In a recent study, Kothari, Shanken, and Sloan[34] found that securities with high beta values do in fact have higher average returns when betas are estimated using annual rather than monthly returns. Moreover, their study revealed a market-to-book effect that is attenuated compared to the results in Fama and French, and is furthermore inconsistent across different samples of securities. Although these results do not disprove a market-to-book effect, Kothari, Shanken, and Sloan concluded that the empirical case for the importance of this ratio may be weaker than the Fama–French study would suggest.

**Reversals.** We considered above the possibility that the aggregate stock market overreacts to economic news. Several studies have examined the overreaction hypothesis using returns on individual stocks. DeBondt and Thaler,[35] Jegadeesh,[36] Lehman,[37] and Chopra, Lakonishok, and Ritter[38] all found strong tendencies for poorly performing stocks in one time period to experience sizable reversals over the subsequent period, while the best-performing stocks in a given period tend to follow with poor performance in the following period.

For example, the DeBondt and Thaler study found that if one were to rank in order the performance of stocks over a five-year period and then group stocks into portfolios based on investment performance, the base-period "loser" portfolio (defined as the 35 stocks with the worst investment performance) would outperform the "winner" portfolio (the top 35 stocks) by an average of 25% (cumulative return) in the following three-year period. This **reversal effect,** in which losers rebound and winners fade back, suggests that the stock market overreacts to relevant news. After the overreaction is recognized, extreme investment performance is reversed. This phenomenon would imply that a *contrarian* investment strategy—investing in recent losers and avoiding recent winners—should be profitable.

---

[34] S. P. Kothari, Jay Shanken, and Richard G. Sloan, "Another Look at the Cross-Section of Expected Stock Returns," *Journal of Finance* 50 (March 1995), pp. 185–224.

[35] Werner F. M. DeBondt and Richard Thaler, "Does the Stock Market Overreact?" *Journal of Finance* 40 (1985), pp. 793–805.

[36] Narasimhan Jegadeesh, "Evidence of Predictable Behavior of Security Returns," *Journal of Finance* 45 (September 1990), pp. 881–98.

[37] Bruce Lehman, "Fads, Martingales and Market Efficiency," *Quarterly Journal of Economics* 105 (February 1990), pp. 1–28.

[38] Navin Chopra, Josef Lakonishok, and Jay R. Ritter, "Measuring Abnormal Performance: Do Stocks Overreact?" *Journal of Financial Economics* 31 (1992), pp. 235–68.

It would be hard to explain apparent overreaction in the cross-section of stocks by appealing to time-varying risk premiums. Moreover, these returns seem pronounced enough to be exploited profitably.

However, a recent study by Ball, Kothari, and Shanken[39] suggests that the reversal effect may be an illusion. They showed that if portfolios are formed by grouping based on past performance periods ending in mid-year rather than in December (a variation in grouping strategy that ought to be unimportant), the reversal effect is substantially diminished. Moreover, the reversal effect seems to be concentrated in very low-priced stocks (e.g., prices of less than $1 per share), for which a bid-ask spread of even 1/8 can have a profound impact on measured return, and for which a liquidity effect may explain high average returns.[40] Finally, the *risk-adjusted* return of the contrarian strategy actually turns out to be statistically indistinguishable from zero, suggesting that the reversal effect is not an unexploited profit opportunity

The reversal effect also seems to be dependent on the time horizon of the investment. DeBondt and Thaler found reversals over long (multi-year) horizons, and the Jegadeesh and Lehman studies documented reversals over short horizons of a month or less. However, in an investigation of intermediate horizon stock price behavior (using 3-to-12-month holding periods), Jegadeesh and Titman[41] found that stocks exhibit a momentum property in which good or bad recent performance continues. This of course is the opposite of a reversal phenomenon.

## Risk Premiums or Anomalies?

The small firm, market-to-book, and reversal effects are currently among the most puzzling phenomena in empirical finance. there are several interpretations of these effects. First note that to some extent, these three phenomena may be related. The feature that small firms, low market-to-book firms, and recent "losers" seem to have in common is a stock price that has fallen considerably in recent months or years. Indeed, a firm can become a small firm, or a low market-to-book firm by suffering a sharp drop in price. These groups therefore may contain a relatively high proportion of distressed firms that have suffered recent difficulties.

Fama and French[42] argue that these effects can be explained as manifestations of risk premiums. Using an arbitrage pricing type of model, they show that stocks

[39] Ray Ball, S. P. Kothari, and Jay Shanken, "Problems in Measuring Portfolio Performance: An Application to Contrarian Investment Strategies," *Journal of Financial Economics* 37 (1995).

[40] This may explain why the choice of year-end versus mid-year grouping has such a significant impact on the results. Other studies have shown that close-of-year prices on the loser stocks are more likely to be quoted at the bid price. As a result, their initial prices are on average understated, and performance in the follow-up period is correspondingly overstated.

[41] Narasimhan Jegadeesh and Sheridan Titman, "Returns to Buying Winners and Selling Losers: Implications for Stock Market Efficiency," *Journal of Finance* 48 (March 1993), pp. 65–91.

[42] Eugene F. Fama and Kenneth R. French, "Common Risk Factors in the Returns on Stocks and Bonds," *Journal of Financial Economics* 33 (1993) pp. 3–56.

with higher "betas" (also known as factor loadings) on size or market-to-book factors have higher average returns; they interpret these returns as evidence of a risk premium associated with the factor. While size or market-to-book ratios per se are obviously not risk factors, they perhaps might act as proxies for more fundamental determinants of risk. Fama and French argue that these phenomena may therefore be consistent with a rational market in which expected returns are consistent with risk.

The opposite interpretation is offered by Lakonishok, Shleifer, and Vishney[43] who argue that these phenomena are evidence of inefficient markets, more specifically, of systematic errors in the forecasts of stock analysts. They believe that analysts extrapolate past performance too far into the future and therefore overprice firms with recent good performance and underprice firms with recent poor performance. Ultimately, when market participants recognize their errors, prices reverse. This explanation is obviously consistent with the reversal effect and also, to a degree, consistent with the small firm and market-to-book effects because firms with sharp price drops may tend to be small or have low market-to-book ratios.

Daniel and Titman[44] attempt to test whether these effects can in fact be explained as risk premia. They first classify firms according to size and market-to-book ratio and then further stratify portfolios based on the betas of each stock on size and market-to-book factors. They find that once size and market-to-book ratio are held fixed, the betas on these factors do not add any additional information about expected returns. They conclude that the characteristics per se, and not the betas on the size or market-to-book factors, influence returns. This result is inconsistent with the Fama-French interpretation that the high returns on these portfolios may reflect risk premia.

The Daniel and Titman results do not *necessarily* imply irrational markets. As noted, it might be that these characteristics per se measure a distressed condition that itself commands a return premium. Moreover, as we have noted, a good part of these apparently abnormal returns may be reflective of an illiquidity premium since small and low-priced firms tend to have bigger bid-ask spreads. Nevertheless, a compelling explanation of these results has yet to be devised.

## The Day-of-the Week Effect

The small-firm-in-January effect is one example of seasonality in stock market returns, a recurrent pattern of turn-of-the-year abnormal returns. Another recurrent pattern, and in several ways an even odder one, is the **weekend effect,**

---

[43] Josef Lakonishok, Andrei Shleifer, and Robert W. Vishney, "Contrarian Investment, Extrapolation, and Risk," *Journal of Finance* 49 (1994), pp. 1541–1578.

[44] Kent Daniel and Sheridan Titman, "Evidence of the Characteristics of Cross Sectional Variation in Stock Returns," working paper, Boston College, 1995.

documented in the United States by French[45] and Gibbons and Hess,[46] and in Canada by Hindmarch et al.,[47] Jaffe and Westerfield,[48] Condoyanni et al.,[49] and Chamberlain et al.[50] These researchers studied the pattern of stock returns from close of trading on Friday afternoon to close on Monday, to determine whether the three-day return spanning the weekend would be three times the typical return on a weekday. This was to be a test of whether the market operates on calendar time or trading time.

Much to their surprise, the typical Friday-to-Monday return was not larger than that of other weekdays—in fact, it was negative! Following is the mean return of the TSE 300 portfolio for each day of the week over the period March 1978–December 1985. The Monday return is based on closing price Friday to closing price Monday, the Tuesday return is based on Monday closing to Tuesday closing, and so on:

| | Monday | Tuesday | Wednesday | Thursday | Friday |
|---|---|---|---|---|---|
| Mean return | −.1512% | .0745% | .1251% | .1121% | .1378% |

The negative Monday effect is extremely large. On an annualized basis, assuming 250 trading days a year, the return is −37.8 percent (−.1512 percent × 250). Chamberlain, Cheung, and Kwan report that this effect was not confined to Monday's opening trading period but tended to persist throughout the entire day. It also tended to spill over onto Tuesday, especially whenever Monday was a stock market holiday, suggesting that the Monday effect was really a "first trading day" effect, at least in Canada. By contrast, the U.S. weekend effect does not extend beyond Monday's opening trading period.

The weekend effect poses a problem for efficient market theorists. In frictionless markets, one would expect this recurrent pattern to be "arbitraged away." Specifically, investors would sell stocks short late Friday afternoon and repurchase them on Monday afternoon at an expected lower price, thereby capturing an abnormal return. The selling on Friday would drive prices down on Friday to a fair level in the sense that the Friday–Monday return would be expected to be positive and commensurate with the risk of the stock market.

In practice, of course, such arbitrage activity would not pay. The magnitude of the weekend effect is not nearly large enough to offset the transaction costs in-

[45] Kenneth French, "Stock Returns and the Weekend Effect," *Journal of Financial Economics* 8 (March 1980).

[46] Michael Gibbons and Patrick Hess, "Day-of-the-Week Effects and Asset Returns," *Journal of Business* 54 (October 1981).

[47] S. Hindmarch, D. Jentsch, and D. Drew, "A Note on Canadian Stock Returns and the Weekend Effect," *Journal of Business Administration* 14 (1984).

[48] J. Jaffe and R. Westerfield, "The Weekend Effect in Common Stock Returns: The International Evidence," *Journal of Finance* 40 (June 1985).

[49] L. Condoyanni, J. O'Hanlon, and C. W. R. Ward, "Day-of-the-Week Effects on Stock Returns: International Evidence," *Journal of Business Finance and Accounting,* Summer 1987.

[50] T. W. Chamberlain, C. S. Cheung, and C. C. Y. Kwan, "Day-of-the-Week Patterns in Stock Returns: The Canadian Evidence," *Canadian Journal of Administrative Sciences* 5, no. 4 (December 1988).

volved in short selling and repurchasing the stocks. Hence, market frictions prevent the direct elimination of the weekend effect. Nevertheless, the effect should not be observed in efficient markets, even in the absence of direct arbitrage. If there is a predictable weekend effect, one would expect investors to shy away from purchases on Fridays, delaying them until Monday instead. Conversely, sales of stock originally scheduled for Monday optimally would be pushed up to the preceding Friday. This reshuffling of buying and selling would be enough to increase buy pressure relative to sell pressure on Mondays to the point where the weekend effect would be dissipated. The persistence of the effect seems to indicate that investors have not paid attention to the predictable price pattern.

## Inside Information

It would not be surprising if insiders were able to make superior profits trading in their firm's stock. The ability of insiders to trade profitably in their own stock has been documented in U.S. studies by Jaffe,[51] Seyhun,[52] Givoly and Palmon,[53] and others. Jaffe's was one of the earlier studies that documented the tendency for stock prices to rise after insiders intensively bought shares and to fall after intensive insider sales.

Similar results also were found in Canadian studies by Masse, Hanrahan, and Kushner[54] and Eckbo,[55] who examined the daily returns to companies targeted for mergers or acquisitions prior to the date of public announcement. They found evidence of significant abnormally high returns, which is consistent with the use of inside information to trade profitably in the market.

To enhance fairness, securities commissions require all insiders to register the changes in their holdings of company stock within 10 days of the end of the month in which the changes take place. Once the insiders file the required statements, the knowledge of their trades becomes public information. At that point, if markets are efficient, fully and immediately processing the released information, an investor should no longer be able to profit from following the pattern of those trades.

Surprisingly, early studies like Jaffe's seemed to indicate that following **insider transactions**—buying after insider purchases were reported and selling after insider sales—could offer substantial abnormal returns to an outside investor. This would be a clear violation of market efficiency, as the insider trading data are publicly available. However, a more recent and extensive U.S. study by Seyhun,

[51] Jeffrey F. Jaffe, "Special Information and Insider Trading," *Journal of Business* 47 (July 1974).

[52] H. Nejat Seyhun, " Insiders' Profits, Costs of Trading and Market Efficiency," *Journal of Financial Economics* 16 (1986).

[53] Dan Givoly and Dan Palmon, "Insider Trading and Exploitation of Inside Information: Some Empirical Evidence," *Journal of Business* 58 (1985).

[54] Isidore Masse, Robert Hanrahan, and Joseph Kushner, "Returns to Insider Trading: The Canadian Evidence," *Canadian Journal of Administrative Sciences* 5, no. 3 (September 1988).

[55] B. Espen Eckbo, "Mergers and the Market for Corporate Control: The Canadian Evidence," *Canadian Journal of Economics* 19, no. 2 (May 1986).

which carefully tracked the public release dates of the insider trading information, found that following insider transactions would be to no avail. Although there is some tendency for stock prices to increase even after public reports of insider buying, the abnormal returns are not of sufficient magnitude to overcome transaction costs.

The Canadian evidence yields similarly mixed conclusions. Baesel and Stein[56] investigated the performance of two insider groups on the TSE, ordinary insiders and insiders who were bank directors. Although both groups earned significant positive abnormal returns, the second group's such returns were higher. Fowler and Rorke[57] used monthly returns of firms listed on the TSE during the period 1967–1977 to investigate whether an outsider could realize abnormal returns by following insider transactions after they were publicly reported. They found that abnormal returns following "intense" buying or selling activity by insiders persisted for at least 12 months after the official release of the insider trading information. Moreover, the size of the returns indicated that trading profits could have been realized even after paying reasonable transactions costs. Similar results also were found in subsequent studies by Lee and Bishara,[58] for the period 1975–1983, and Suret and Cormier,[59] for the period May 1986–July 1988. These findings seem to indicate a clear violation of market efficiency for the TSE, at least for the periods covered by these studies.

On the other hand, a study by Heinkel and Kraus[60] on the Vancouver Stock Exchange (VSE) found rather weak evidence of the ability of insider trading to generate abnormal returns for insiders. The sample of firms that Heinkel and Kraus examined over the period June 1979–June 1, 1981 was rather atypical. It consisted of small resource companies listed on the VSE, for which insiders are by far the largest shareholders. Thus, although the results could be interpreted as evidence of market efficiency of the strong form, they cannot be extrapolated to other situations.

## The Value Line Enigma

The Value Line Investor Survey is an investment advisory service that ranks securities on a timeliness scale of one (best buy) to five (sell). Ranks are based on relative earnings and price performance across securities, price momentum, quar-

---

[56] Jerome Baesel and Garry Stein, "The Value of Information Inferences from the Profitability of Insider Trading," *Journal of Financial and Quantitative Analysis* 14 (September 1979).

[57] David J. Fowler and C. Harvey Rorke, "Insider Trading Profits on the Toronto Stock Exchange, 1967–1977," *Canadian Journal of Administrative Sciences* 5, no. 1 (March 1988).

[58] M. H. Lee and H. Bishara, "Recent Canadian Experience on the Profitability of Insider Trades," *The Financial Review* 24, no. 2 (May 1989).

[59] Jean-Marc Suret and Elise Cormier, "Insiders and the Stock Market," *Canadian Investment Review* 3, no. 2 (Fall 1990).

[60] Robert Heinkel and Alan Kraus, "The Effect of Insider Trading on Average Rates of Return," *Canadian Journal of Economics* 20, no. 3 (August 1987).

terly earnings momentum, and a measure of unexpected earnings in the most recent quarter.

Several studies have examined the predictive value of the Value Line recommendations. Black[61] found that portfolio 1 (the "buy" portfolio) had a risk-adjusted excess rate of return of 10 percent, while portfolio 5 (the "sell" portfolio) had an abnormal return of −10 percent. These results imply a fantastic potential value to the Value Line forecasts. Copeland and Mayers[62] performed a similar study, using a more sophisticated risk-adjustment technique, and found that the difference in the risk-adjusted performance of portfolios 1 and 5 was much smaller; portfolio 1 earned an abnormal six-month rate of return of 1.52 percent, while portfolio 5 earned an abnormal return of −2.97 percent. Even this smaller difference, however, seems to be a substantial deviation from the prediction of the efficient market hypothesis.

Given Value Line's apparent success in predicting stock performance, we would expect that changes in Value Line's timeliness rankings would result in abnormal returns for affected stocks. This seems to be the case. Stickel[63] shows that Value Line rankings generally are followed by abnormal stock returns in the expected direction. Interestingly enough, smaller firms tend to respond with greater sensitivity to rankings. This pattern is consistent with the neglected-firm effect in that the information contained in a ranking carries greater weight for firms that are less intensively monitored.

## The Market Crash of October 1987

The market crash of October 1987 seems to be a glaring counterexample to the efficient market hypothesis. If prices reflect market fundamentals, then defenders of the EMH must look for news on the nineteenth of October consistent with the 23 percent one-day decline in stock prices. Yet no events of such importance seem to have transpired on that date. The fantastic price swing is hard to reconcile with market fundamentals.

**CONCEPT CHECK** Question 6. Some say that continued worry concerning the U.S. trade deficit brought down the market on October 19. Is this explanation consistent with the EMH?

[61] Fischer Black, "Yes, Virginia, There Is Hope: Tests of the Value Line Ranking System," Graduate School of Business, University of Chicago, 1971.

[62] Thomas E. Copeland and David Mayers, "The Value Line Enigma (1965–1978): A Case Study of Performance Evaluation Issues," *Journal of Financial Economics* 11 (November 1982).

[63] Scott E. Stickel, "The Effect of Value Line Investment Survey Rank Changes on Common Stock Prices," *Journal of Financial Economics* 14 (1985).

## Mutual Fund Performance

We have documented some of the apparent chinks in the armour of efficient market proponents. Ultimately, however, the issue of market efficiency boils down to whether skilled investors can make consistent abnormal trading profits. The best test is simply to look at the performance of market professionals to see if that performance is superior to that of a passive index fund that buys and holds the market.

Such a test was carried out in Canada by Lawson,[64] who examined filter rules for buying or selling a stock depending on the trading activity of stock market professionals. He constructed a database of all transactions on the TSE over a 30-month period, which identified trades carried out by professional traders. The filter rules prescribed buying or selling a stock when professionals showed a corresponding "unusually high" buying or selling activity. Lawson found that his filters could not generate any trading profits and were in fact inferior to a strategy of buying and holding the stock.

Casual evidence also does not support claims that professionally managed portfolios can beat the market. In most of the past 15 years, the S&P 500 has outperformed the median professionally managed U.S. fund. In the decade ended in 1979, about 47 percent of equity fund managers outperformed the S&P 500. In the 1980s, only 37 percent beat the market.[65] Similar results were reported in the survey of the Canadian mutual funds studies in the previous chapter.

Of course, one might argue that there are good managers and bad managers, and that the good managers can, in fact, consistently outperform the index. The real test of this notion is to see whether managers with good performance in a given year can repeat that performance in a following year. In other words, is the abnormal performance due to luck or skill? Jensen[66] performed such a test using 10 years of data on 115 mutual funds, a total of 1,150 annual observations.

Jensen first risk-adjusted all returns using the CAPM to obtain portfolio alphas, or returns in excess of required return given risk. Then he tested to see whether managers with positive alphas tended to repeat their performance in later years. If markets are efficient, and abnormal performance is due solely to the luck of the draw, the probability of following superior performance in a given year with superior performance the next year should be 50 percent: Each year's abnormal return is essentially like the toss of a fair coin. This is precisely the pattern that Jensen found. Table 11.2 is reproduced from Jensen's study.

In row 1, we see that 574 positive alphas were observed out of the 1,150 observations, virtually 50 percent on the nose. Of these 574 positive alphas, 50.4

---

[64] William M. Lawson, "Market Efficiency: The Trading of Professionals on the Toronto Stock Exchange," *Journal of Business Administration* 12, no. 1 (Fall 1980).

[65] John C. Bogle, "Investing in the 1990s: Remembrance of Things Past, and Things Yet to Come," *Journal of Portfolio Management,* Spring 1991.

[66] Michael C. Jensen, "Risk, the Pricing of Capital Assets, and the Evaluation of Investment Portfolios," *Journal of Business* 42 (April 1969).

**Table 11.2** Mutual Fund Performance

| Number of Consecutive Positive Alphas So Far | Number of Observations | Cases in Which the Next Alpha is Positive (%) |
|---|---|---|
| 1 | 574 | 50.4 |
| 2 | 312 | 52.0 |
| 3 | 161 | 53.4 |
| 4 | 79 | 55.8 |
| 5 | 41 | 46.4 |
| 6 | 17 | 35.3 |

From Michael C. Jensen, "Risk, the Pricing of Capital Assets, and the Evaluation of Investment Portfolios," *Journal of Business* 42 (April 1969), published by The University of Chicago. Reprinted by permission.

percent were followed by positive alphas. So far, it appears that obtaining a positive alpha is pure luck, like a coin toss. Row 2 shows that 312 cases of two consecutive positive alphas were observed. Of these observations, 52 percent were followed by yet another positive alpha. Continuing, we see that 53.4 percent of three-in-a-row were followed by a fourth, and 55.8 percent of four-in-a-row were followed by a fifth.

The results so far are intriguing. They seem to suggest that most positive alphas are indeed obtained through luck. However, as more and more stringent filters are applied, the remaining managers show greater tendency to follow good performance with more good performance. This might suggest that there are a few, rare, superior managers who can consistently beat the market. However, at this point, the pattern collapses. Only 46.4 percent of the five-in-a-row group repeats the superior performance. Yet the sample size is too small to make statistically precise inferences about the population of managers.

The ultimate interpretation of these results is thus to some extent a matter of faith. However, it seems clear that it is not wise to invest with an actively managed fund chosen at random. The average alpha of all funds was slightly negative even *before* subtracting all the costs of management.

A more recent study performed by Frank Russell Company, reported in *The Wall Street Journal,* examined the consistency of performance of more than 100 equity managers. The question posed is whether managers that performed well in one period tend to perform well in subsequent periods. In other words, is performance consistent across time? To answer this question, the sample of managers was ranked according to total return in the 1983–1986 period. The managers were assigned to one of four groups based on their base-period performance. Then the performance of each group was computed in the 1987–1990 period. Figure 11.5 shows that the best performers in the 1983–1986 base period performed no better in 1987–1990 than the worst performers in the base period. The implication is that past performance has little predictive power concerning future

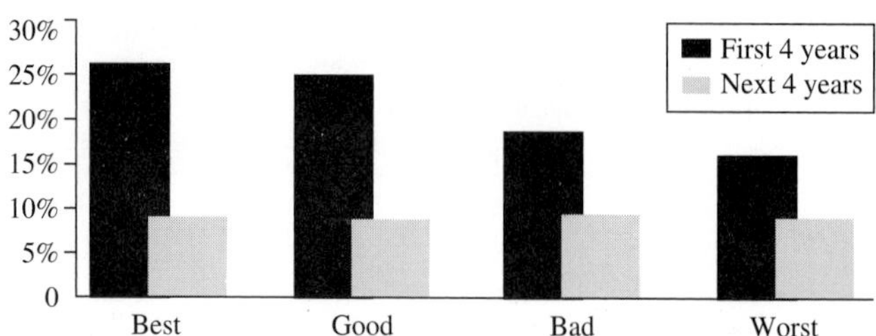


**Figure 11.5** Good, bad, and unpredictable.

performance. A similar conclusion was reached in an earlier study by Dunn and Theisen.[67]

More recent studies of the performance of mutual funds have reached mixed conclusions. Ippolito[68] examined returns of 143 mutual funds over the 1965–1984 period and found that returns net of expenses and fees (but not net of loads) provided an average alpha across funds of 0.83%. On the other hand, the performance of most funds was not statistically significantly different from that of a purely passive strategy. The alphas of 127 funds were statistically indistinguishable from zero. Four funds had alphas significantly negative and 12 had significantly positive alphas.

In contrast, Brinson, Hood, and Beebower[69] found that portfolio returns of 91 pension plans were harmed by attempts at active management. They compared actual returns to a benchmark computed by assuming plan managers had held indexed portfolios for the bond and stock sectors of their portfolios and had maintained constant weights across market sectors. They concluded that deviations from indexed positions within each market reduced average returns by 0.36% and that attempts to time the relative performance of fixed income versus equity markets reduced average returns by 0.66%.

Grinblatt and Titman[70] found evidence of abnormal returns and persistence of performance using five-year investment returns, but such persistence does not seem strong enough to be useful in forming investment strategies. Hendricks, Patel, and Zeckhauser[71] also documented some evidence of persistence. They found that investment performance in a base period tends to be predictive of per-

[67] Patricia Dunn and Rolf D. Theisen, "How Consistently Do Active Managers Win?" *Journal of Portfolio Management* 9 (Summer 1983).

[68] Richard A. Ippolito, "Efficiency with Costly Information: A Study of Mutual Fund Performance, 1965–1984," *Quarterly Journal of Economics* 104 (February 1989), pp. 1–24.

[69] Gary P. Brinson, L. Randolph Hood, and Gilbert L. Beebower, "Determinants of Portfolio Performance," *Financial Analysts Journal* 42 (July/August 1986), pp. 39–44.

[70] Mark Grinblatt and Sheridan Titman, "Mutual Fund Performance: An Analysis of Quarterly Portfolio Holdings, *Journal of Business* 62 (1989), pp. 393–416.

[71] Darryll Hendricks, Jayendu Patel, and Richard Zeckhauser, "Hot Hands in Mutual Funds: Short-Run Persistence of Relative Performance, 1974–1988," *Journal of Finance* 43 (March 1993), pp. 93–130.

formance over the next year, but no longer. Interestingly, poor performers in their study continued to underperform significantly while top performers continued to outperform but less dramatically.

Carhart[72] reported that much of the persistence in mutual fund performance is due to expenses rather than gross investment returns. This last point is important; although there can be no consistently superior performers in a fully efficient market, there *can* be consistently inferior performers. Repeated weak performance would not be due to an ability to pick bad stocks consistently (that would be impossible in an efficient market!) but could result from a consistently high expense ratio and consistently high portfolio turnover with the resulting trading costs. In this regard, it is interesting that Hendricks, Patel, and Zeckhauser also found that the strongest consistency was found among the weakest performers. Nevertheless, even allowing for expenses, some amount of performance persistence seems to be due to differences in investment strategy. Carhart found, however, that the evidence of persistence is concentrated at the two extremes. This suggests that there may be a small group of exceptional managers who can with some consistency outperform a passive strategy, but that for the majority of managers, over- or underperformance in any period is largely a matter of chance.

In contrast to the extensive studies of equity fund managers, there have been very few studies on the performance of bond fund managers. In a recent paper, however, Blake, Elton, and Gruber[73] examined the performance of fixed-income mutual funds. They found that, on average, bond funds underperform passive fixed-income indices by an amount roughly equal to expenses, and that there is no evidence that past performance can predict future performance. Their evidence is consistent with the hypothesis that bond managers operate in an efficient market in which performance before expenses is only as good as that of a passive index.

A Canadian study by Jog[74] confirms these findings for a sample of Canadian pension fund managers. The study used several different performance measures, which included the alphas, and four different benchmark portfolios, one of which was the TSE 300 index. The results, however, were virtually identical for all measures and benchmark portfolios: Managers of pension funds included in the sample failed to exhibit any significant or consistent ability to achieve superior risk-adjusted performance of the portfolios that they managed. Pension funds would have achieved a better risk-return combination by using combinations of suitable index funds.

---

[72] Mark M. Carhart, "Persistence in Mutual Fund Performance Re-examined," University of Chicago, mimeo, 1992; and "On Persistence in Mutual Fund Performance," University of Chicago, mimeo, 1994.

[73] Christopher R. Blake, Edwin J. Elton, and Martin J. Gruber, "The Performance of Bond Mutual Funds," *Journal of Business* 66 (July 1993), pp. 371–404.

[74] Vijay M. Jog, "Investment Performance of Pension Funds—A Canadian Study," *Canadian Journal of Administrative Sciences* 3, no. 1 (June 1986).

Thus, the evidence on the risk-adjusted performance of professional managers is mixed at best. We conclude that the performance of professional managers is broadly consistent with market efficiency. The amounts by which professional managers as a group beat or are beaten by the market fall within the margin of statistical uncertainty. In any event, it is quite clear that performance superior to passive strategies is far from routine. Studies show either that most managers cannot outperform passive strategies or that if there is a margin of superiority, it is small.

On the other hand, a small number of investment superstars—Peter Lynch (formerly of Fidelity's Magellan Fund), Warren Buffet (of Berkshire Hathaway), John Templeton (of Templeton Funds), and John Neff (of Vanguard's Windsor Fund) among them—have compiled career records that show a consistency of superior performance hard to reconcile with absolutely efficient markets. Nobel prize winner Paul Samuelson[75] reviews this investment hall of fame but points out that the records of the vast majority of professional money managers offer convincing evidence that there are no easy strategies to guarantee success in the securities markets.

## So, Are Markets Efficient?

There is a telling joke about two economists walking down the street. They spot a $20 bill on the sidewalk. One starts to pick it up, but the other one says, "Don't bother; if the bill were real someone would have picked it up already."

The lesson is clear. An overly doctrinaire belief in efficient markets can paralyze the investor and make it appear that no research effort can be justified. This extreme view is probably unwarranted. There are enough anomalies in the empirical evidence to justify the search for underpriced securities that clearly goes on.

The bulk of the evidence, however, suggests that any supposedly superior investment strategy should be taken with many grains of salt. The market is competitive *enough* that only differentially superior information or insight will earn money; the easy pickings have been picked. In the end it is likely that the margin of superiority that any professional manager can add is so slight that the statistician will not be able to detect it.

For the United States, we can safely conclude that markets are very efficient, but that rewards to the especially diligent, intelligent, or creative may in fact be waiting. In Canada, the anomalies are stronger and last longer, and the puzzle of the persistence of abnormal returns for several months following the reporting of unusual insider trading activity has not been satisfactorily explained. However,

---

[75] Paul Samuelson, "The Judgment of Economic Science on Rational Portfolio Management," *Journal of Portfolio Management* 16 (Fall 1989), pp. 4–12.

Canadian professional investment managers as a whole have shown no evidence of having exploited such inefficiencies.

## SUMMARY

**1.** Statistical research has shown that stock prices seem to follow a random walk with no discernible predictable patterns that investors can exploit. Such findings are now taken to be evidence of market efficiency, that is, of evidence that market prices reflect all currently available information. Only new information will move stock prices, and this information is equally likely to be good news or bad news.

**2.** Market participants distinguish among three forms of the efficient market hypothesis. The weak form asserts that all information to be derived from past stock prices already is reflected in stock prices. The semistrong form claims that all publicly available information is already reflected. The strong form, usually taken only as a straw man, asserts that all information, including insider information, is reflected in prices.

**3.** Technical analysis focuses on stock price patterns and on proxies for buy or sell pressure in the market. Fundamental analysis focuses on the determinants of the underlying value of the firm, such as current profitability and growth prospects. Since both types of analysis are based on public information, neither should generate excess profits if markets are operating efficiently.

**4.** Proponents of the efficient market hypothesis often advocate passive as opposed to active investment strategies. The policy of passive investors is to buy and hold a broad-based market index. They expend resources neither on market research nor on the frequent purchase and sale of stocks. Passive strategies may be tailored to meet individual investor requirements.

**5.** Event studies are used to evaluate the economic impact of events of interest, using abnormal stock returns. Such studies usually show that there is some leakage of inside information to some market participants before the public announcement date. Therefore insiders do seem to be able to exploit their access to information to at least a limited extent.

**6.** Empirical studies of technical analysis do not support the hypothesis that such analysis can generate superior trading profits. Only very short-term filters seem to offer any hope for profits, yet these are extremely expensive in terms of trading costs.

**7.** Several anomalies regarding fundamental analysis have been uncovered. These include the P/E effect, the small-firm effect, the neglected-firm effect, the weekend effect, the reversal effect, the market-to-book effect, the insider trading effect in Canada, and the Value Line Ranking System.

**8.** By and large, the performance record of professionally managed funds lends little credence to claims that professionals can consistently beat the market.

## Key Terms

| | |
|---|---|
| Random walk | Abnormal return |
| Efficient market hypothesis (EMH) | Announcement date |
| Weak-form EMH | Cumulative abnormal return |
| Semistrong-form EMH | Filter rule |
| Strong-form EMH | P/E effect |
| Technical analysis | Small-firm effect |
| Fundamental analysis | Neglected-firm effect |
| Passive investment strategy | Reversal effect |
| Index fund | Weekend effect |
| Event study | Insider transactions |

## Selected Readings

*One of the best treatments of the efficient market hypothesis is:*

Malkiel, Burton G. *A Random Walk Down Wall Street.* New York: W. W. Norton & Co., Inc., 1990. This paperback book provides an entertaining and insightful treatment of the ideas presented in this chapter as well as fascinating historical examples of securities markets in action.

*A more rigorous introduction to the theoretical underpinnings of the EMH, as well as a review of early empirical work, may be found in:*

Fama, Eugene F. "Efficient Capital Markets: A Review of Theory and Empirical Work." *Journal of Finance* 25 (May 1970).

*A more recent survey is:*

Fama, Eugene F. "Efficient Capital Markets: II." *Journal of Finance* 46 (December 1991).

## Problems

1. If markets are efficient, what should be the correlation coefficient between stock returns for two nonoverlapping time periods?
2. Which of the following most appears to contradict the proposition that the stock market is *weakly* efficient? Explain.
   *a.* Over 25 percent of mutual funds outperform the market on average.
   *b.* Insiders earn abnormal trading profits.
   *c.* Every January, the stock market earns above-normal returns.
3. Suppose that, after conducting an analysis of past stock prices, you come up with the following observations. Which would appear to *contradict* the *weak* form of the efficient market hypothesis? Explain.
   *a.* The average rate of return is significantly greater than zero.
   *b.* The correlation between the return during a given week and the return during the following week is zero.
   *c.* One could have made superior returns by buying stock after a 10 percent rise in price and selling after a 10 percent fall.
   *d.* One could have made higher than average capital gains by holding stock with low dividend yields.

**4.** Which of the following statements are true if the efficient market hypothesis holds?
   *a.* Future events can be forecast with perfect accuracy.
   *b.* Prices reflect all available information.
   *c.* Security prices change for no discernible reason.
   *d.* Prices do not fluctuate.

**5.** Which of the following observations would provide evidence *against* the *semistrong-form* version of the efficient market theory? Explain.
   *a.* Mutual fund managers do not on average make superior returns.
   *b.* You cannot make superior profits by buying (or selling) stocks after the announcement of an abnormal rise in dividends.
   *c.* Low P/E stocks tend to have positive abnormal returns.
   *d.* In any year, approximately 50 percent of pension funds outperform the market.

**6.** A successful firm like Seagram's has consistently generated large profits for years. Is this a violation of the EMH?

**7.** Suppose you find that prices of stocks before large dividend increases show on average consistently positive abnormal returns. Is this a violation of the EMH?

**8.** "If the business cycle is predictable, and a stock has a positive beta, the stock's returns also must be predictable," Respond.

**9.** Which of the following phenomena would be either consistent with or a violation of the efficient market hypothesis? Explain briefly.
   *a.* Nearly half of all professionally managed mutual funds are able to outperform the TSE 300 in a typical year.
   *b.* Money managers that outperform the market (on a risk-adjusted basis) in one year are likely to outperform it in the following year.
   *c.* Stock prices tend to be predictably more volatile in January than in other months.
   *d.* Stock prices of companies that announce increased earnings in January tend to outperform the market in February.
   *e.* Stocks that perform well in one week perform poorly in the following week.

**10.** "If all securities are fairly priced, all must offer equal market rates of return." Comment.

**11.** An index model regression applied to past monthly excess returns in ABC Corporation's stock price produces the following estimates, which are believed to be stable over time:

$$R_{ABC} = .10\% + 1.1\ R_M$$

If the market index subsequently rises by 8 percent and ABC's stock price rises by 7 percent, what is the abnormal change in ABC's stock price? The T-bill return during the month is 1 percent.

**12.** The monthly rate of return on T-bills is 1 percent. The market went up this month by 1.5 percent. In addition, AmbChaser, Inc., which has an equity beta of 2, surprisingly just won a lawsuit that awards it \$1 million immediately.

*a.* If the original value of AmbChaser equity were \$100 million, what would you guess was the rate of return of its stock this month?

*b.* What is your answer to (a) if the market had expected AmbChaser to win \$2 million?

**13.** In a recent, closely contested lawsuit, Apex sued Bpex for patent infringement. The jury came back today with its decision. The rate of return on Apex was $r_A = 3.1$ percent. The rate of return on Bpex was only $r_B = 2.5$ percent. The market today responded to very encouraging news about the unemployment rate, and $r_M = 3$ percent. The historical relationship between returns on these stocks and the market portfolio has been estimated from index model regressions as:

$$\text{Apex: } r_A = .2\% + 1.4\, r_M$$

$$\text{Bpex: } r_B = -.1\% + .6\, r_M$$

Based on these data, which company do you think won the lawsuit? (Note: On a daily basis, the rate of return on risk-free Treasury bills is close to zero.)

**14.** Dollar cost averaging means that you buy equal dollar amounts of a stock every period, for example, \$500 per month. The strategy is based on the idea that when the stock price is low, your fixed monthly purchase will buy more shares, and when the price is high, it will buy fewer shares. Averaging over time, you will end up buying more shares when the stock is cheaper and fewer when it is relatively expensive. Therefore, by design, you will exhibit good market timing. Evaluate this strategy.

**15.** Steady Growth Industries has never missed a dividend payment in its 94-year history. Does this make it more attractive to you as a possible purchase for your stock portfolio?

**16.** We know that the market should respond positively to good news and that good-news events, such as a coming end of a recession, can be predicted with at least some accuracy. Why, then, can we not predict the market will go up as the economy recovers?

**17.** If prices are as likely to increase as decrease, why do investors earn positive returns from the market on average?

**18.** You know that firm XYZ is very poorly run. On a scale of 1 (worst) to 10 (best), you would give it a score of 3. The market consensus evaluation is that the management score is only 2. Should you buy or sell the stock?

**19.** Good News Inc. just announced an increase in its annual earnings, yet its stock price fell. Is there a rational explanation for this phenomenon?

**20.** Some authors contend that professional managers are incapable of outperforming the market. Others come to an opposite conclusion. Compare and contrast the assumptions about the stock market that support (a) passive portfolio management, and (b) active portfolio management.

The following information should be used in solving problems 21 and 22

As director of research for a medium-sized investment firm, Jeff Cheney was concerned about the mediocre investment results experienced by the firm in recent years. He met with his two senior analysts to consider alternatives to the stock selection techniques employed in the past.

One of the analysts suggested that the current literature has examined the relationship between price earnings ratios (P/E) and securities returns. A number of studies had concluded that high P/E stocks tended to have higher betas and lower risk-adjusted returns than stocks with low P/E ratios.

The analysts also referred to recent studies analyzing the relationship between security returns and company size as measured by equity capitalization. The studies concluded that when compared to the TSE 300 index, small capitalization stocks tended to provide above-average risk-adjusted returns while large capitalization stocks tended to provide below-average risk-adjusted returns. It was further noted that little correlation was found to exist between a company's P/E ratio and the size of its equity capitalization.

Jeff's firm has employed a strategy of complete diversification and the use of beta as a measure of portfolio risk. He and his analysts were intrigued as to how these recent studies might be applied to their stock selection techniques and thereby improve their performance. Given the results of the studies indicated above:

**21.** Explain how the results of these studies might be used in the stock selection and portfolio management process. Briefly discuss the effects on the objectives of diversification and on the measurement of portfolio risk.

**22.** List the reasons and briefly discuss why this firm might *not* want to adopt a new strategy based on these studies in place of its current strategy of complete diversification and the use of beta as a measure of portfolio risk.

**23.** You are a portfolio manager meeting a client. During the conversation that followed your formal review of her account, your client asked the following question:

> "My grandson, who is studying investments, tells me that one of the best ways to make money in the stock market is to buy the stocks of small-capitalization firms on a Monday morning late in December and to sell the stocks one month later. What is he talking about?"

*a.* Identify the apparent market anomalies that would justify the proposed strategy.

*b.* Explain why you believe such a strategy might or might not work in the future.

*Chapter* 12

# Active Portfolio Management and Performance Measurement

SO FAR WE HAVE ALLUDED TO ACTIVE PORTFOLIO MANAGEMENT AS AN ALTERNATIVE TO PASSIVE MANAGEMENT BY INVESTMENT IN THE MARKET PORTFOLIO AND AS AN INPUT TO THE MARKOWITZ METHODOLOGY OF GENERATING THE OPTIMAL RISKY PORTFOLIO (CHAPTER 7). We have emphasized the theoretical result that efficient markets indicate a passive strategy. In Parts V and VI, we shall examine the approaches used professionally to obtain superior information about the bond and stock markets. You may well have wondered about the seeming contradiction between our equilibrium analysis in Part III—tempered by some of the evidence about efficient markets in Chapter 11—and the real-world environment, where profit-seeking investment managers use active management to exploit perceived market inefficiencies.

Despite the efficient market hypothesis, there are reasons to believe that active management can have effective results, but these need to be verified after the fact. It is possible to evaluate the performance of a portfolio manager, but it is not a simple matter; what the manager is trying to do as an investment strategy, and how this relates to individual investors, will cause different measures of performance to apply. Although the subject may seem technical, a close and accurate appraisal of performance is needed to cut through the arbitrary or nonspecific claims of success made by many professional managers.

We begin with a discussion of what one might expect from active management but illustrate how active management causes problems in evaluation. We then review the conventional approaches to risk adjustment for performance evaluation. We show the problems inherent in these approaches, even though they involve the use of specific theoretical measures, when they are applied in a complex world. Next we examine two forms of active portfolio management: market timing, which is based solely on macroeconomic factors, and security selection, which includes microeconomic forecasting. We then discuss some promising developments in the theory of performance evaluation and examine evaluation procedures used in the field. We conclude with some results and a discussion regarding the evaluation of actual performance.

The appendices present some technical details of measuring investment returns and two advanced analyses for assessing timing ability as an option and portfolio performance using a multifactor model.

## 12.1 The Objective of Active Management

How can a theory of active portfolio management be reconciled with the notion that markets are in equilibrium? Market efficiency prevails when many investors are willing to depart from maximum diversification, or a passive strategy, by adding mispriced securities to their portfolios in the hope of realizing abnormal returns. The competition for such returns ensures that prices will be near their "true" values. Most managers will not beat the passive strategy on a risk-adjusted basis. However, in the competition for rewards to investing, exceptional managers might beat the average forecasts built into market prices.

There is both economic logic and some empirical evidence to indicate that exceptional portfolio managers can beat the average forecast. Let us discuss economic logic first. We must assume that, if no analyst can beat the passive strategy, investors will be smart enough to divert their funds from strategies entailing expensive analysis to less expensive passive strategies. With less capital under active management and less research being produced, prices will no longer reflect sophisticated forecasts. The potential profit resulting from research will then increase and active managers using this research will again have superior performance.[1]

As for empirical evidence, consider the following: (1) some portfolio managers have produced streaks of abnormal returns that are hard to label as lucky outcomes; (2) the "noise" in realized rates is enough to prevent us from rejecting outright the hypothesis that some money managers have beaten the passive strategy by a statistically small, yet economically significant, margin; and (3) some anomalies in realized returns have been sufficiently persistent to suggest that portfolio managers who identified them in a timely fashion could have beaten the passive strategy over prolonged periods.

[1] This point is worked out fully in Sanford J. Grossman and Joseph E. Stiglitz, "On the Impossibility of Informationally Efficient Markets," *American Economic Review* 70 (June 1980).

These conclusions persuade us that there is a role for a theory of active portfolio management. Active management has an inevitable lure even if investors agree that security markets are nearly efficient.

Suppose that capital markets are perfectly efficient, an easily accessible market index portfolio is available, and this portfolio is, for all practical purposes, the efficient risky portfolio. Clearly, in this case security selection would be a futile endeavour. You would be better off with a passive strategy of allocating funds to a money market fund (the safe asset) and the market index portfolio.

At this point, the investment strategy ought to be straightforward, but there is still a need for some economic forecasting; $E(r_M)$ and $\sigma_M$ must be estimated to determine the investment proportion in the risky market portfolio, as we saw in Part II. Then, investment in fixed proportions in a risky portfolio, long-term bonds, and money market instruments requires some kind of index fund for each of these three assets. Faced with these hurdles, investors are likely to turn to professional managers who will attempt to distinguish themselves by claims and promises.

What does an investor expect from a professional portfolio, and how does this expectation affect the decisions of the manager? By now, we know the answer: The client wants high returns at an acceptable level of risk, provided by the right portfolio and the right proportion of that portfolio and safe assets. Fortunately, the theory of mean-variance efficiency allows us to separate the "product decision" (the right portfolio) and the "consumption decision" (the right allocation between the two assets). The technical question of finding a mean-variance efficient portfolio is for the manager to solve, while the allocation is determined between the manager and the client with respect to the latter's risk aversion. Clients will therefore rate managers based on their realized rates of return and corresponding reward-to-variability ratios.

William Sharpe's assessment of mutual fund performance[2] is the seminal work in the area of portfolio performance evaluation. Sharpe's measure, the reward-to-variability ratio or excess return over standard deviation, is now a common criterion for tracking performance of professionally managed portfolios. We will define it formally in the next section, but for now, we assume that it is a suitable basis for comparison.

Briefly, mean-variance portfolio theory implies that the objective of professional portfolio managers is to maximize the (ex ante) Sharpe measure, which entails maximizing the slope of the CAL (capital allocation line). A "good" manager is one whose CAL is steeper than the CAL representing the passive strategy of holding a market index portfolio. Clients can observe rates of return and compute the realized Sharpe measure (the ex post CAL) to evaluate the relative performance of their manager.

Ideally, clients would like to invest their funds with the most able manager, one who consistently obtains the highest Sharpe measure and presumably has real

---

[2] William F. Sharpe, "Mutual Fund Performance," *Journal of Business, Supplement on Security Prices* 39 (January 1966).

## Passive, Active Investors Square Off—Money Managers Debate Strategies and the Value of Fun in Life

TORONTO—Blindly matching stock indexes may be a valid part of investment strategy—but it's not much fun, says mutual fund manager Frank Mersch.

At a seminar at the Investment Funds Institute of Canada conference yesterday, he was pitted against Kathleen Taylor, an investment manager at Wells Fargo Nikko Investment Advisors Canada Ltd., who sang the praises of passive investing.

Passive investors buy all the stocks or bonds in a given market index, instead of trying to pick individual issues, citing evidence that fund managers often underperform the market.

They aim to capture moves in the broad market, often as part of asset allocation strategies.

Studies indicate that the choices and weightings of various types of financial assets that a portfolio holds—stocks, bonds or cash—have far more influence on investment returns than the particular shares or bonds bought. Passive managers also save on trading and research costs.

Wells Fargo Nikko is the world's largest marketer to institutional investors of index funds, managing about $170 billion (U.S.) of passive funds.

There's nothing passive about Mr. Mersch. Famed as an active trader, he has steered the $1.9 billion (Canadian) Altamira Equity Fund to a 22 percent annual rate of return over the past five years. That trounced the 9 percent annual return for an investor who bought all of the stocks in the Toronto Stock Exchange 300 index.

"There are managers out there who consistently outperform their benchmark and that alone refutes any passive-management thesis," Mr. Mersch said.

He cited Fidelity Investments' Peter Lynch and Altamira bond manager Will Sutherland.

Not that Mr. Mersch has any complaints about the index buyers—he says he's happy to make money off them. "Every six months or every year, the TSE will take 15 to 18 stocks out of the index and put 15 to 18 stocks into the index.

"We at Altamira are always trying to figure which are the new 15 stocks that are going in the TSE, so when the [passive investor] comes in to buy these stocks and drive them higher, it provides an opportunity for us to sell and derive an extraordinary rate of return."

He said later: "In this day of self-realization, in this day of the Internet, in this day of staying at home and not interacting with people, you've got to have some fun in your life."

"We're losing a lot of the fun of stock selection, money selection."

One Altamira client had 1,800 mutual fund transactions over a year, earning a return of about 32 percent, less than the 44 percent he would have received that same year by staying only in the Altamira Equity Fund, Mr. Mersch said.

But he said the client told Altamira: "If I'd stayed [invested in the fund all year], I wouldn't have had as much fun."

(Altamira has since introduced restrictions on short-term trading of its funds.)

Ms. Taylor wasn't taking that lying down: "I want to be able to retire with money in my bank account, money in my RRSP.

"I'd rather be able to have fun in my retirement and have the money to do it with, rather than lose it all through active management."

By Andrew Bell, *The Globe and Mail*, September 20, 1995, p. B10. Reprinted by permission.

forecasting ability. This is true for all clients, regardless of their degree of risk aversion. At the same time, each client must decide what fraction of investment funds to allocate to this manager, placing the remainder in a safe fund. If the manager's Sharpe measure is constant over time (and can be estimated by clients), the investor can compute the optimal fraction to be invested with the manager from equation 6.3, based on the portfolio long-term average return and variance. The remainder will be invested in a money market fund.

The manager's ex ante Sharpe measure from updated forecasts will be constantly varying. Clients may wish to increase their allocation to the risky portfolio when the forecasts are optimistic, and vice versa. However, it would be impractical to constantly communicate updated forecasts to clients and for them to constantly revise their allocation between the risky portfolios and risk-free asset.

Allowing managers to shift funds between their optimal risky portfolio and a safe asset according to their forecasts alleviates the problem. Indeed, many stock funds allow the managers reasonable flexibility to do just that. Managers can be assessed on their decisions of timing, when to invest in risky or safe portfolios, and selectivity (i.e., which risky assets to choose). For opinions on active management, see the nearby box.

## Performance Measurement under Active Management

We have seen already that the high variance of stock returns requires a very long observation period to determine performance levels with any statistical significance, even if portfolio returns are distributed with constant mean and variance. Imagine how this problem is compounded when portfolio return distributions are constantly changing. Before exploring formal measures, we want to give a preview of the problems faced in evaluation when managers change their portfolio composition as part of their active strategy.

It is acceptable to assume that the return distributions of passive strategies have constant mean and variance when the measurement interval is not too long. However, under an active strategy return distributions change by design, as the portfolio manager updates the portfolio in accordance with the dictates of financial analysis. In such a case, estimating various statistics from a sample period assuming a constant mean and variance may lead to substantial errors. Let us look at an example.

Suppose that the Sharpe measure of the passive strategy is 0.4. A portfolio manager is in search of a better, active strategy. Over the next two years, she executes first a low-risk strategy for the first year, then decides a high-risk strategy is best for the second year; as it turns out, she is successful in both years, delivering a Sharpe ratio of 0.5 each year and beating the passive strategy each time.

**Figure 12.1**
Portfolio returns.

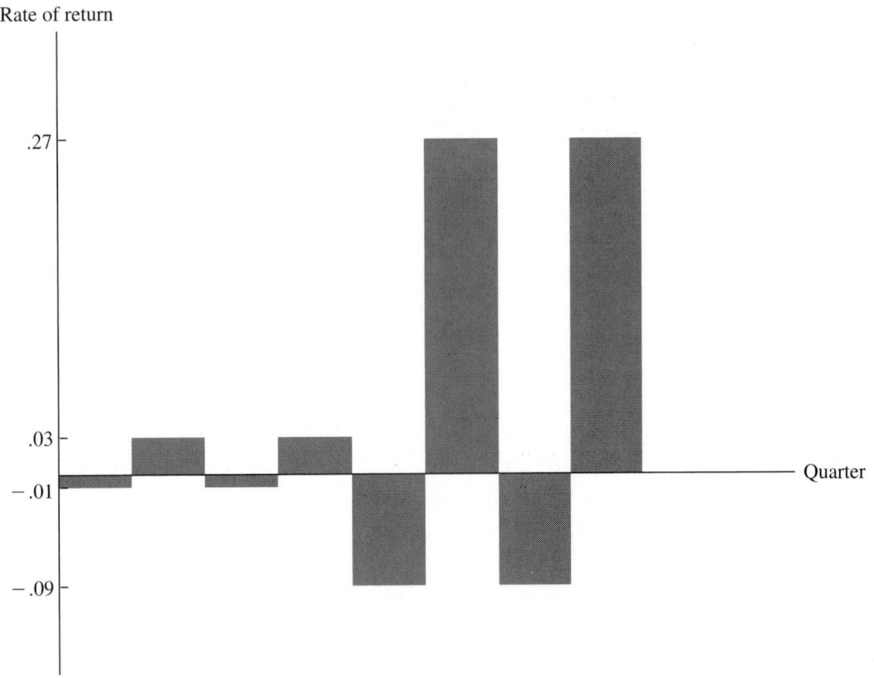


Figure 12.1 shows a pattern of (annualized) quarterly returns that are consistent with our description of the manager's strategy over two years. In the first four quarters the excess returns are −1 percent, 3 percent, −1 percent, and 3 percent, making for an average of 1 percent and standard deviation of 2 percent. In the next four quarters the returns are: −9 percent, 27 percent, −9 percent, and 27 percent, making for an average of 9 percent and a standard deviation of 18 percent. Since Sharpe's measure is average excess return divided by standard deviation, both years yield a ratio of 0.5. However, if we take the eight-quarter sequence as a single measurement period and measure the portfolio's mean and standard deviation over that full period, we will obtain an average excess return of 5 percent and standard deviation of 13.42 percent, making for a Sharpe measure of only .37. Since a higher Sharpe ratio is considered better, the active strategy is apparently inferior to the passive strategy!

What happened? The shift in the mean from the first four quarters to the next was not recognized as a shift in strategy. Instead, the difference in mean returns in the two years added to the *appearance* of volatility in portfolio returns. The active strategy with shifting means appears riskier than it really is and biases the estimate of the Sharpe measure downward. We conclude that for actively managed portfolios it is crucial to keep track of portfolio composition and changes in portfolio mean and risk.

## 12.2 The Conventional Theory of Performance Evaluation

Calculating average portfolio returns does not mean the task is done—returns must be adjusted for risk before they can be compared meaningfully. The simplest and most popular way to adjust returns for portfolio risk is to compare rates of return with those of other investment funds with similar risk characteristics. For example, high-yield bond portfolios are grouped into one "universe," growth stock, equity funds are grouped into another universe, and so on. Then the (usually time-weighted) average returns of each fund within the universe are ordered, and each portfolio manager receives a percentile ranking depending on relative performance within the **comparison universe.** For example, the manager with the ninth-best performance in a universe of 100 funds would be the 90th percentile manager: His performance was better than 90 percent of all competing funds over the evaluation period.

These relative rankings usually are displayed in a chart such as that in Figure 12.2. The chart summarizes performance rankings over four periods: one quarter, one year, three years, and five years. The top and bottom lines of each box are drawn at the rate of return of the 95th and 5th percentile managers. The three dotted lines correspond to the rates of return of the 75th, 50th (median), and 25th percentile managers. The diamond is drawn at the average return of a particular fund and the rectangle is drawn at the return of a benchmark index such as the TSE 300. The placement of the diamond within the box is an easy-to-read representation of the performance of the fund relative to the comparison universe.

This comparison of performance with other managers of similar investment style is a useful first step in evaluating performance. However, such rankings can be misleading. For example, within a particular universe, some managers may concentrate on particular subgroups, so that portfolio characteristics are not truly comparable. For example, within the equity universe, one manager may concentrate on high-beta stocks. Also, refinements are occurring. More sophisticated measures are being created, for example, indices based on fairly precise characterizations, such as small-capitalization firms or biotechnology firms. These measures help to establish standards for comparison, but they are generally not presented to the average investor in mass-circulation tabulations. Within fixed-income universes, durations can vary across managers. These considerations suggest that a more precise means for risk adjustment is desirable.

Methods of risk-adjusted performance evaluation using mean-variance criteria came on stage simultaneously with the capital asset pricing model. Jack Treynor,[3] William Sharpe,[4] and Michael Jensen[5] recognized immediately the implications

[3] Jack L. Treynor, "How to Rate Management Investment Funds," *Harvard Business Review* 43 (January–February 1966).

[4] William F. Sharpe, "Mutual Fund Performance," *Journal of Business* 39 (January 1966).

[5] Michael C. Jensen, "The Performance of Mutual Funds in the Period 1945–1964," *Journal of Finance,* May 1968; and "Risk, the Pricing of Capital Assets, and the Evaluation of Investment Portfolios," *Journal of Business,* April 1969.

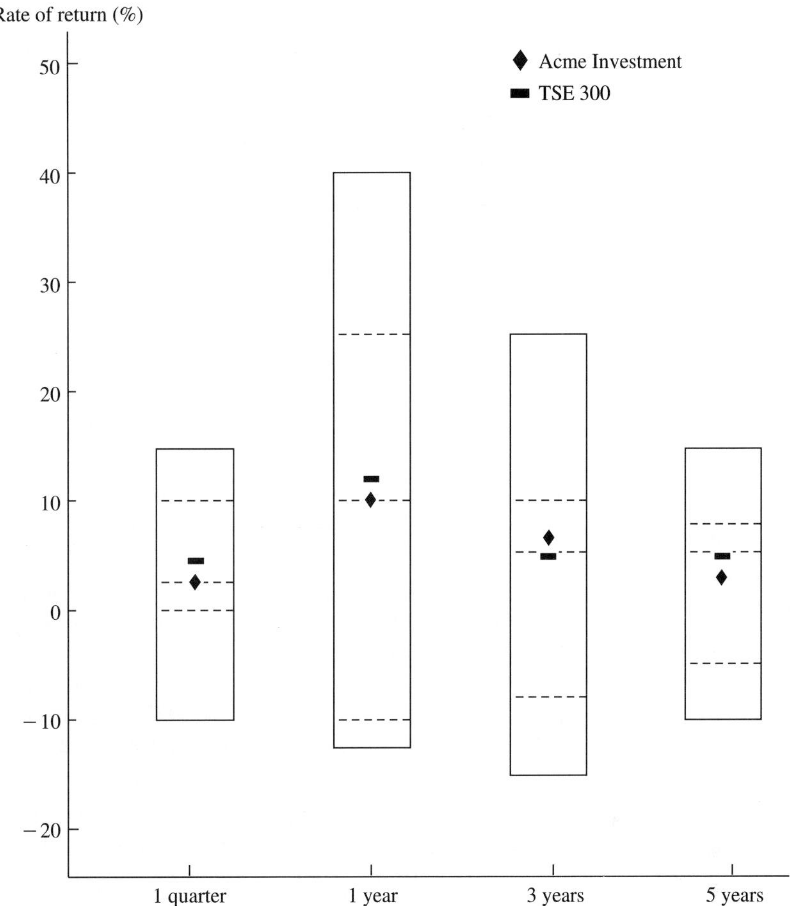


**Figure 12.2**
Universe comparison (periods ending December 31, 1991).

of the CAPM for rating the performance of managers. Within a short time, academicians were in command of a battery of performance measures, and a bounty of scholarly investigation of mutual fund performance was pouring from ivory towers. Shortly thereafter, agents emerged who were willing to supply rating services to portfolio managers eager for regular feedback. This trend has since lost some of its steam.

One explanation for the lagging popularity of risk-adjusted performance measures is the generally negative cast to the performance statistics. In nearly efficient markets it is extremely difficult for analysts to perform well enough to overcome costs of research and transaction costs. Indeed, we have seen that the most professionally managed equity funds generally underperform the TSE 300 index on both risk-adjusted and raw return measures. Another reason mean-variance criteria may have suffered relates to intrinsic problems in these measures, such as the one illustrated in the previous section.[6]

Let us begin by cataloguing some possible risk-adjusted performance measures and examining the circumstances in which each measure might be most relevant.

1. *Sharpe's measure:* $(\bar{r}_P - \bar{r}_f)/\sigma_P$
   **Sharpe's measure** divides average portfolio excess return over the sample period by the standard deviation of returns over that period. It measures the reward to (total) volatility trade-off.[7]
2. *Treynor's measure:* $(\bar{r}_P - \bar{r}_f)/\beta_P$
   Like Sharpe's, **Treynor's measure** gives excess return per unit of risk, but uses systematic risk instead of total risk.
3. *Jensen's measure:* $\alpha_P = \bar{r}_P - [\bar{r}_f + \beta_P(\bar{r}_M - \bar{r}_f)]$
   **Jensen's measure** is the average return on the portfolio over and above that predicted by the CAPM, given the portfolio's beta and the average market return. Jensen's measure is the portfolio's alpha value.
4. *Appraisal ratio:* $\alpha_P/\sigma(e_P)$
   The **appraisal ratio** divides the alpha of the portfolio by the nonsystematic risk of the portfolio. It measures abnormal return per unit of risk that in principle could be diversified away by holding a market index portfolio.

Each measure has some appeal. But each does not necessarily provide consistent assessments of performance, since the risk measures used to adjust returns differ substantially.

[6] A statistical analysis of the subject is presented in J. D. Jobson and R. M. Korkie, "Performance Hypothesis Testing with the Sharpe and Treynor Measures," *Journal of Finance* 36, no. 4 (September 1981).

[7] We place bars over $r_f$ as well as $r_P$ to denote the fact that since the risk-free rate may not be constant over the measurement period, we are taking a sample average, just as we do for $r_P$.

**CONCEPT CHECK** Question 1. Consider the following data for a particular sample period:

| | Portfolio $P$ | Market $M$ |
|---|---|---|
| Average return | .35 | .28 |
| Beta | 1.20 | 1.00 |
| Standard deviation | .42 | .30 |
| Nonsystematic risk, $\sigma(e)$ | .18 | 0.00 |

Calculate the following performance measures for portfolio $P$ and the market: Sharpe, Jensen (alpha), Treynor, and appraisal ratio. The T-bill rate during the period was .06. By which measures did portfolio $P$ outperform the market?

It is interesting to see how these measures are related to one another. Beginning with Treynor's measure, note that as the market index beta is 1.0, Treynor's measure for the market index is

$$T_M = \bar{r}_M - \bar{r}_f$$

The mean excess return of portfolio $P$ is

$$\bar{r}_P - \bar{r}_f = \alpha_P + \beta_P(\bar{r}_M - \bar{r}_f)$$

and thus its Treynor measure is

$$\begin{aligned} T_P &= \frac{\alpha_P + \beta_P(\bar{r}_M - \bar{r}_f)}{\beta_P} \\ &= \frac{\alpha_P}{\beta_P} + \bar{r}_M - \bar{r}_f \\ &= \frac{\alpha_P}{\beta_P} + T_M \end{aligned}$$

Treynor's measure compares portfolios on the basis of the alpha-to-beta ratio.[8] Note that this is very different in numerical value *and spirit* from the appraisal ratio, which is the ratio of alpha to residual risk.

The Sharpe measure for the market index portfolio is

$$S_M = \frac{\bar{r}_M - \bar{r}_f}{\sigma_M}$$

[8] Interestingly, although our definition of the Treynor measure is conventional, Treynor himself initially worked with the alpha-to-beta ratio. In this form, the measure is independent of the market. Both measures will rank-order portfolio performance identically, because they differ by a constant (the market's Treynor value). Some call the ratio of alpha-to-beta "modified alpha" or "modified Jensen's measure," not realizing that this is really Treynor's measure.

For portfolio $P$ we have

$$S_P = \frac{\bar{r}_P - \bar{r}_f}{\sigma_P} = \frac{\alpha_P + \beta_P(\bar{r}_M - \bar{r}_f)}{\sigma_P}$$

With some algebra that relies on the fact that $\rho^2$ between $P$ and $M$ is

$$\rho^2 = \frac{\beta^2\sigma_M^2}{\beta^2\sigma_M^2 + \sigma^2(e)} = \frac{\beta^2\sigma_M^2}{\sigma_P^2}$$

we find that

$$\begin{aligned} S_P &= \frac{\alpha_P}{\sigma_P} + \frac{\beta_P(\bar{r}_M - \bar{r}_f)}{\sigma_P} \\ &= \frac{\alpha_P}{\sigma_P} + \rho S_M \end{aligned}$$

This expression yields some insight into the process of generating valuable performance with active management. It is obvious that one needs to find significant-alpha stocks to establish potential value. A higher portfolio alpha, however, has to be tempered by the increase in standard deviation that arises when one departs from full diversification. The more we tilt toward high alpha stocks, the lower the correlation with the market index, $\rho$, and the greater the potential loss of performance value.

We conclude that it is important to use the performance measure that fits the relevant scenario. Evaluating portfolios by different performance measures may yield quite different results.

## Sharpe's Measure as the Criterion for Overall Portfolios

Suppose that Jane d'Arque constructs a portfolio and holds it for a considerable period of time. She makes no changes in portfolio composition during the period. In addition, suppose that the daily rates of return on all securities have constant means, variances, and covariances. This assures that the portfolio rate of return also has a constant mean and variance. These assumptions are unrealistic, but they will help us to focus on the key issue. They also are crucial to understanding the shortcoming of conventional applications of performance measurement.

Now we want to evaluate the performance of Jane's portfolio. Has she made a good choice of securities? This is really a three-pronged question. First, good choice compared with what alternatives? Second, in choosing between two distinct alternatives, what are the appropriate criteria to use to evaluate performance? Finally, having identified the alternatives and the performance criteria, is there a rule that will separate basic ability from the random luck of the draw?

Fortunately, our earlier chapters of this text help to determine portfolio choice criteria. If investor preferences can be summarized by a mean-variance utility function such as that introduced in Chapter 5, we can arrive at a relatively simple criterion. The particular utility function that we have used in this text is

$$U = E(r_P) - \tfrac{1}{2}A\sigma_P^2$$

where $A$ is the coefficient of risk aversion. With mean-variance preferences, we have seen that Jane will want to maximize her Sharpe measure (that is, the ratio $[E(r_P) - r_f]/\sigma_P$) of her *complete* portfolio of assets. Recall that this is the criterion that led to the selection of the tangency portfolio in Chapter 7. Jane's problem reduces to that of whether her overall portfolio is the one with the highest possible Sharpe ratio.

## Appropriate Performance Measures in Three Scenarios

To evaluate Jane's portfolio choice, we first ask whether she intends this portfolio to be her exclusive investment vehicle. If the answer is no, we need to know what her "complementary" portfolio is—the portfolio to which she is adding the one in question. The appropriate measure of portfolio performance depends critically on whether the portfolio is the entire investment fund or only a portion of the investor's overall wealth.

**Jane's Choice Portfolio Represents Her Entire Risky Investment Fund.** In this simplest case, we need to ascertain only whether Jane's portfolio has the highest possible (ex ante) Sharpe measure. But how can this be done? In principle we can follow these four steps:

1. Assume that her past security performance is representative of expected future performance, meaning that security returns over Jane's holding period exhibit averages and sample covariances that Jane might have anticipated.
2. Estimate the entire efficient frontier of risky assets from return data over Jane's holding period.
3. Using the risk-free rate at the time of decision, find the portfolio with the highest Sharpe measure.
4. Compare Jane's Sharpe measure to that of the best alternative.

This comprehensive approach, however, is problematic. It requires not only an extensive database and optimization techniques, but it also exacerbates the problem of inference from sample data. We have to rely on a limited sample to estimate the means and covariances of a very large set of securities. The verdict on Jane's choice will be subject to estimation errors. The very complexity of the procedure makes it hard to assess the reliability and significance of the verdict. Is there a second-best alternative?

In fact, it makes sense to compare Jane's choice to a restricted set of alternative portfolios that were easy for her to assess and invest in at the time of her decision. An obvious first candidate for this restricted set is the passive strategy, the market index portfolio. Other candidates are professionally managed active funds. The method to use to compare Jane's portfolio to any specific alternative is the same: compare their Sharpe measures.

In essence, when Jane's portfolio represents her entire investment fund for the holding period in question, the benchmark alternative is the market index or another specific portfolio. The performance criterion is the Sharpe measure of the actual portfolio versus the benchmark portfolios.

**Jane's Portfolio Is an Active Portfolio and Is Mixed with the Passive Market Index Portfolio.** How do we evaluate the optimal mix in this case? Call Jane's portfolio *P*, and denote the market portfolio by *M*. When the two portfolios are mixed optimally, it turns out (as we shall examine more closely in Section 12.4 that the square of the Sharpe measure of the composite portfolio, C, is given by

$$S_C^2 = S_M^2 + \left[\frac{\alpha_P}{\sigma(e_P)}\right]^2$$

where $\alpha_P$ is the abnormal return of the active portfolio, relative to the passive market portfolio, and $\sigma(e_P)$ is the diversifiable risk. The ratio $\alpha_P/\sigma(e_P)$ is thus the correct performance measure for *P* for this case, since it gives the improvement in the Sharpe measure of the overall portfolio attributable to the inclusion of *P*.

To see the intuition of this result, recall the single-index model:

$$r_P - r_f = \alpha_P + \beta_P(r_M - r_f) + e_P$$

If *P* is fairly priced, the $\alpha_P = 0$, and $e_P$ is just diversifiable risk that can be avoided. If *P* is mispriced, however, $\alpha_P$ no longer equals zero. Instead, it represents the expected abnormal return. Holding *P* in addition to the market portfolio thus brings a reward of $\alpha_P$ against the nonsystematic risk voluntarily incurred, $\sigma(e_P)$. Therefore, the ratio of $\alpha_P/\sigma(e_P)$ is the natural benefit-to-cost ratio for portfolio *P*. This performance measurement is sometimes called the appraisal ratio:

$$AR_P = \frac{\alpha_P}{\sigma(e_P)}$$

**Jane's Choice Portfolio Is One of Many Portfolios Combined into a Large Investment Fund.** This third case might describe the situation where Jane, as a corporate financial officer, manages the corporate pension fund. She parcels out the entire fund to a number of portfolio managers. Then she evaluates the performance of individual managers to reallocate parts of the fund to improve future performance. What is the correct performance measure?

We could continue to use the appraisal ratio if it were reasonable to assume that the complementary portfolio to *P* is approximately equal to the market index portfolio by virtue of its being spread among many managers and thus well diversified. The appraisal ratio is adequate in these circumstances. But you can imagine that the portfolio managers would take offense at this assumption. Jane, too,

**Table 12.1** Portfolio Performance

| | Portfolio $P$ | Portfolio $Q$ | Market |
|---|---|---|---|
| Beta | .90 | 1.60 | 1.0 |
| Excess return ($\bar{r} - \bar{r}_f$) | .11 | .19 | .10 |
| Alpha* | .02 | .03 | 0 |

*Alpha = Excess return − (Beta × Market excess return)
$= (\bar{r} - \bar{r}_f) - \beta(\bar{r}_M - \bar{r}_f)$
$= \bar{r} - [\bar{r}_f + \beta(\bar{r}_m - \bar{r}_f)]$

is likely to respond, "Do you think I am exerting all this effort just to end up with a passive portfolio?"

If we cannot treat this form of management as the same as investing in the index portfolio, we could make the following approximation. The benefit of portfolio $P$ to the entire diversified fund is measured by $P$'s alpha value. Although $\alpha_P$ is not a full measure of portfolio $P$'s performance value, it will give Jane some indication of $P$'s potential contribution to the overall portfolio. An even better solution, however, is to use Treynor's measure.

Suppose you determine that portfolio $P$ exhibits an alpha value of 2 percent. "Not bad," you tell Jane. But she pulls out of her desk a report and informs you that another portfolio, $Q$, has an alpha of 3 percent. "One hundred basis points is significant," says Jane. "Should I transfer some of my funds from $P$'s manager to $Q$'s?"

You tabulate the relevant data, as in Table 12.1 and graph the results as in Figure 12.3. Note that we plot $P$ and $Q$ in the mean return–beta (rather than the mean–standard deviation) plane, because we assume that $P$ and $Q$ are two of many subportfolios in the fund, and thus that nonsystematic risk will be largely diversified away, leaving beta as the appropriate risk measure. The security market line (SML) shows the value of $\alpha_P$ and $\alpha_Q$ as the distance of $P$ and $Q$ above this line.

Suppose that portfolio $Q$ can be mixed with T-bills. Specifically, if we invest $w_Q$ in $Q$ and $w_F = 1 - w_Q$ in T-bills, the resulting portfolio, $Q^*$, will have alpha and beta values proportional to $Q$'s alpha and beta and to $w_Q$:

$$\alpha_Q{}^* = w_Q \alpha_Q$$
$$\beta_Q{}^* = w_Q \beta_Q$$

Thus, all portfolios $Q^*$ generated from mixes of $Q$ and T-bills plot on a straight line from the origin through $Q$. We call it the T-line for the Treynor measure, which is the slope of this line.

Figure 12.3 shows the T-line for portfolio $P$ as well. You can see immediately that $P$ has a steeper T-line; despite its lower alpha, $P$ is a better portfolio in this case after all. For any *given* beta, a mixture of $P$ with T-bills will give a better alpha than a mixture of $Q$ with T-bills.

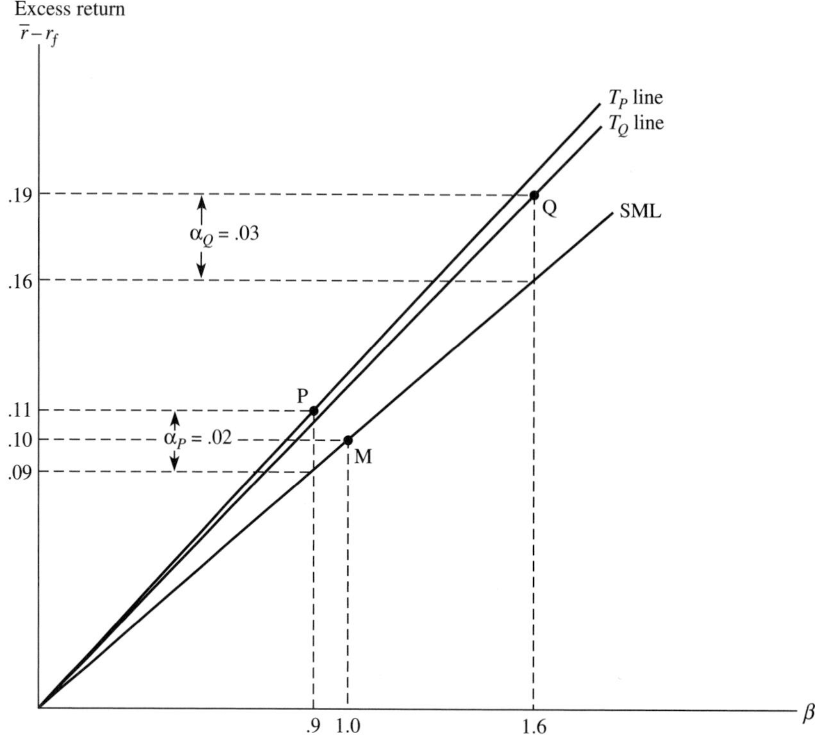


**Figure 12.3**
Treynor measure.

To see this, suppose that we choose to mix $Q$ with T-bills to create a portfolio $Q^*$ with a beta equal to that of $P$. We find the necessary proportion by solving for $w_Q$:

$$w_Q \beta_Q = 1.6 w_Q = \beta_P = .9$$
$$w_Q = 9/16$$

Portfolio $Q^*$ therefore has an alpha of

$$\alpha_Q{}^* = 9/16 \times 3$$
$$= 1.69\%$$

which, in fact, is less than that of $P$.

In other words, the slope of the T-line is the appropriate performance criterion for the third case. The slope of the T-line for $P$, denoted by $T_P$, is given by

$$T_P = \frac{\bar{r}_P - \bar{r}_f}{\beta_P}$$

Treynor's performance measure is appealing in the sense that it shows that when an asset is part of a large investment portfolio, you should weigh its mean

**Table 12.2** Excess Returns for Portfolios *P* and *Q* and the Benchmark *M* over 12 Months

| Month | Jane's Portfolio *P* | Alternative *Q* | Benchmark *M* |
|---|---|---|---|
| 1 | 3.58 | 2.81 | 2.20 |
| 2 | −4.91 | −1.15 | −8.41 |
| 3 | 6.51 | 2.53 | 3.27 |
| 4 | 11.13 | 37.09 | 14.41 |
| 5 | 8.78 | 12.88 | 7.71 |
| 6 | 9.38 | 39.08 | 14.36 |
| 7 | −3.66 | −8.84 | −6.15 |
| 8 | 5.56 | .83 | 2.74 |
| 9 | −7.72 | .85 | −15.27 |
| 10 | 7.76 | 12.09 | 6.49 |
| 11 | −4.01 | −5.68 | −3.13 |
| 12 | .78 | −1.77 | 1.41 |
| Year's average | 2.76 | 7.56 | 1.63 |
| Standard deviation | 6.17 | 14.89 | 8.48 |

excess return, $\bar{r}_P - \bar{r}_f$, against its *systematic* risk (as measured by beta), rather than against total or diversifiable risk (as measured by its standard deviation) to evaluate its contribution to performance.

## Actual Performance Measurement: An Example

Now that we have examined possible criteria for performance evaluation, we need to deal with a statistical issue: How can we derive an appropriate performance measure for ex ante decisions using ex post data? Before we plunge into a discussion of this problem, let us look at the rate of return on Jane's portfolio over the last 12 months. Table 12.2 shows the excess return recorded each month for Jane's portfolio *P*, one of her alternative portfolios, *Q*, and the benchmark market index portfolio *M*. The last rows in Table 12.2 give sample averages and standard deviations. From these, and regressions of *P* and *Q* on *M*, we obtain the necessary performance statistics.

The performance statistics in Table 12.3 show that portfolio *Q* is more aggressive than *P*, in the sense that its beta is significantly higher (1.40 versus .69). On the other hand, *P* appears better diversified from its residual standard deviation (1.95 percent versus 8.98 percent). Both portfolios have outperformed the benchmark market index portfolio, as is evident from their larger Sharpe measures and positive alphas.

Which portfolio is more attractive, based on reported performance? If *P* or *Q* represents the entire investment fund, *Q* would be preferable on the basis of its higher Sharpe measure (.51 versus .45). On the other hand, as an active portfolio

**Table 12.3** Performance Statistics

| | Portfolio *P* | Portfolio *Q* | Portfolio *M* |
|---|---|---|---|
| Sharpe's measure | .45 | .51 | .19 |
| SCL regression statistics | | | |
| Alpha | 1.63 | 5.28 | .00 |
| Beta | .69 | 1.40 | 1.00 |
| Treynor | 4.00 | 3.77 | 1.63 |
| $\sigma(e)$ | 1.95 | 8.98 | .00 |
| Appraisal ratio | .84 | .59 | .00 |
| *R*-SQR | .91 | .64 | 1.00 |

to be mixed with the market index, *P* is preferable to *Q*, as is evident from its appraisal ratio (.84 versus .59). For the third scenario, where *P* and *Q* are competing for a role as one of a number of subportfolios, the inadequacy of alpha as a performance measure is evident. Whereas *Q*'s alpha is larger (5.28 percent versus 1.63 percent), *P*'s beta is low enough to give it a better Treynor measure (4.00 versus 3.77), suggesting that it is superior to *Q* as one portfolio to be mixed with many others.

This analysis is based on 12 months of data only, a period too short to lend statistical significance to the conclusions. Even longer observation intervals may not be enough to make the decision clear-cut, which represents a further problem.

## 12.3 Market Timing

Professor Robert Merton began a seminar with finance professors several years ago by asking them to consider the following two different investment opportunities for available U.S. securities:

1. An investor who put $1,000 in 30-day commercial paper on January 1, 1927, and rolled over all proceeds into 30-day paper (or into 30-day T-bills after they were introduced) would have ended on December 31, 1978, 52 years later, with $3,600.
2. An investor who put $1,000 in the NYSE index on January 1, 1927, and reinvested all dividends in that portfolio would have ended on December 31, 1978, with $67,500.

Suppose we define **market timing** as the ability to tell (with certainty) at the beginning of each month whether the NYSE portfolio will outperform the 30-day paper portfolio. Accordingly, at the beginning of each month, the market timer shifts all funds into either cash equivalents (30-day paper) or equities (the NYSE portfolio), whichever is predicted to do better.

Merton asked the seminar participants to estimate what, beginning with $1,000 on the same date, the perfect timer would have amassed 52 years later? Out of the collected responses, the boldest guess was a few million dollars. The correct answer: $5.36 *billion*.

**CONCEPT CHECK** Question 2. What was the monthly and annual compounded rate of return for the three strategies over the period 1926–1978?

These numbers have some lessons for us. The first has to do with the power of compounding. Its effect is particularly important because more and more of the funds under management represent pension savings. The horizons of such investments may not be as long as 52 years, but by and large they are measured in decades, making compounding a significant factor.

Another result that may seem surprising at first is the huge difference between the end-of-period value of the all-safe asset strategy ($3,600) and that of the all-equity strategy ($67,500). Why would anyone invest in safe assets given this historical record? If you have internalized the lessons of previous chapters, you know the reason: risk. The average rates of return and the standard deviations on the all-bills and all-equity strategies presented by Merton are:

| | Arithmetic Mean | Standard Deviation |
|---|---|---|
| Bills | 2.55 | 2.10 |
| Equities | 10.70 | 22.14 |

The significantly higher standard deviation of the rate of return on the equity portfolio is commensurate with its significantly higher average return.

Can we also view the rate of return premium on the perfect-timing fund as a risk premium? The answer must be no, because the perfect timer never does worse than either bills or the market. The extra return is not compensation for the possibility of poor returns but is attributable to superior analysis. It is the value of superior information that is reflected in the tremendous end-of-period value of the portfolio.

Merton[9] pursued the issue of value information by simulating the returns, using the actual monthly return data, given perfect timing and also incorporating a charge for this timing ability. The monthly rate-of-return statistics for the all-equity portfolio and the timing portfolio are:

[9] Robert C. Merton, "On Market Timing and Investment Performance: An Equilibrium Theory of Value for Market Forecasts," *Journal of Business,* July 1981.

| Per Month | All Equities (%) | Perfect Timer No Charge (%) | Perfect Timer Fair Charge (%) |
|---|---|---|---|
| Average rate of return | .85 | 2.58 | .55 |
| Average excess return over return on safe asset | .64 | 2.37 | .34 |
| Standard deviation | 5.89 | 3.82 | 3.55 |
| Highest return | 38.55 | 38.55 | 30.14 |
| Lowest return | −29.12 | .06 | −7.06 |
| Coefficient of skewness | .42 | 4.28 | 2.84 |

Ignore for the moment the last column (Perfect Timer—Fair Charge). The first two rows of results are self-explanatory. The third item, standard deviation, requires some discussion. The standard deviation of the rate of return earned by the perfect market timer was 3.82 percent, far greater than the volatility of T-bill returns over the same period. Does this imply that (perfect) timing is a riskier strategy than investing in bills? No. For this analysis, standard deviation is a misleading measure of risk.

To see why, consider how you might choose between two hypothetical strategies: the first offers a sure rate of return of 5 percent; the second strategy offers an uncertain return that is given by 5 percent *plus* a random number that is zero with probability .5 and 5 percent with probability .5. The characteristics of each strategy are

| | Strategy 1 (%) | Strategy 2 (%) |
|---|---|---|
| Expected return | 5 | 7.5 |
| Standard deviation | 0 | 2.5 |
| Highest return | 5 | 10.0 |
| Lowest return | 5 | 5.0 |

Clearly, strategy 2 dominates strategy 1 since its rate of return is *at least* equal to that of strategy 1 and sometimes greater. No matter how risk averse you are, you will always prefer strategy 2 to strategy 1, despite the significant standard deviation of strategy 2. Compared to strategy 1, strategy 2 provides only "good surprises," so the standard deviation in this case cannot be a measure of risk.

These results are analogous to the case of the perfect timer compared with an all-equity or all-bills strategy. In every period, the perfect timer obtains at least as good a return and, in some cases, a better one. Therefore, the timer's standard deviation is a misleading measure of risk compared to an all-equity or all-bills strategy.

Returning to the empirical results, you can see that the highest rate of return is identical for the all-equity and the timing strategies, whereas the lowest rate of return is positive for the perfect timer and disastrous for the all-equity portfolio. Another reflection of this is seen in the coefficient of skewness, which measures the asymmetry of the distribution of returns. Because the equity portfolio is almost (but not exactly) normally distributed, its coefficient of skewness is very low at .42. In contrast, the perfect timing strategy effectively eliminates the negative tail of the distribution of portfolio returns (the part below the risk-free rate). Its returns are "skewed to the right," and its coefficient of skewness is therefore quite large, 4.28.

Now for the last column, Perfect Timer—Fair Charge, which is perhaps the most interesting. Most assuredly, the perfect timer will charge clients for such a valuable service. (The perfect timer may have other-worldly predictive powers, but saintly benevolence is unlikely.)

Subtracting a fair fee from the monthly rate of return of the timer's portfolio gives us an average rate of return lower than that of the passive, all-equity strategy. However, because the fee is *assumed* to be fair, the two portfolios (the all-equity strategy and the market timing with fee strategy) must be equally attractive after risk adjustment. In this case, again, the standard deviation of the market timing strategy (with fee) is of no help in adjusting for risk, because the coefficient of skewness remains high, 2.84. In other words, standard mean-variance analysis is quite complicated for valuing market timing. An alternative, option-based approach is given in Appendix B.

## The Value of Imperfect Forecasting

Unfortunately, managers are not perfect forecasters, as you and Merton know. It seems pretty obvious that if managers are right most of the time they are doing very well. However, when we say right "most of the time," we cannot refer merely to the percentage of time a manager is right. The weather forecaster in Tucson, Arizona, who *always* predicts no rain, may be right 90 percent of the time, but a high success rate for a "stopped-clock" strategy clearly is not evidence of forecasting ability.

Similarly, the appropriate measure of market forecasting ability is not the overall proportion of correct forecasts. If the market is up two days out of three and a forecaster always predicts a market advance, the two-thirds success rate is not a measure of forecasting ability. We need to examine both the proportion of bull markets ($r_M > r_f$) correctly forecast *and* the proportion of bear markets ($r_M < r_f$) correctly forecast.

If we call $P_1$ the proportion of the correct forecasts of bull markets and $P_2$ the proportion for bear markets, then $P_1 + P_2 - 1$ is the correct measure of timing ability. For example, a forecaster who always guesses correctly will have $P_1 = P_2 = 1$ and will show ability of 1 (100 percent). An analyst who always bets on a bear market will mispredict all bull markets ($P_1 = 0$), correctly "predict" all bear markets ($P_2 = 1$), and end up with timing ability of $P_1 + P_2 - 1 = 0$. If $C$ denotes the (call option) value of a perfect market timer, then $(P_1 + P_2 - 1)C$ measures the value of imperfect forecasting ability.

**CONCEPT CHECK** Question 3. What is the market timing score of someone who flips a fair coin to predict the market?

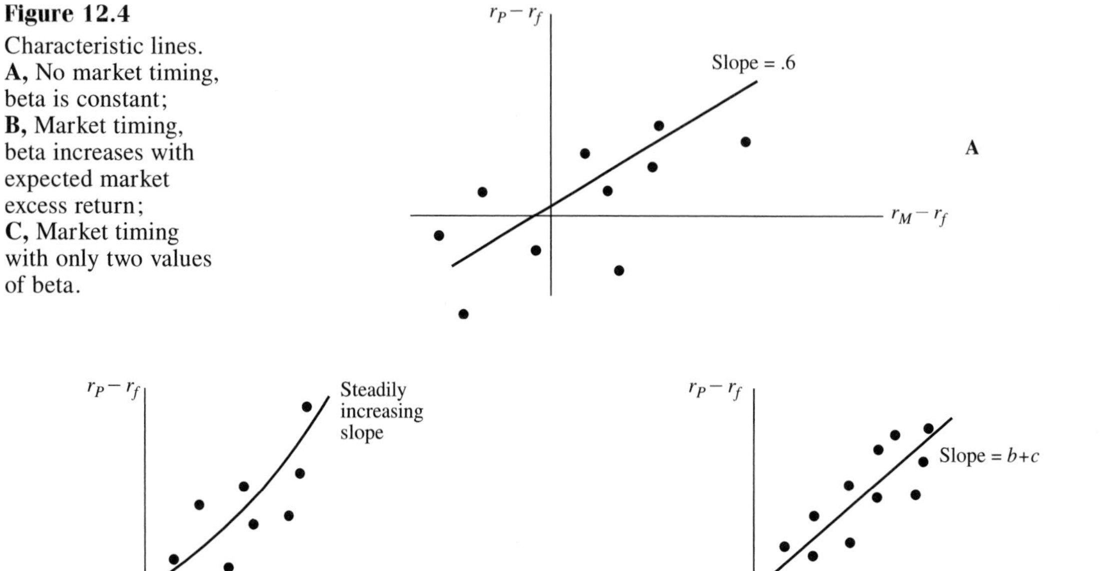


**Figure 12.4**
Characteristic lines.
**A,** No market timing, beta is constant;
**B,** Market timing, beta increases with expected market excess return;
**C,** Market timing with only two values of beta.

## Identifying Timing Ability

In its pure form, market timing involves shifting funds between a market index portfolio and a safe asset, such as T-bills or a money market fund, depending on whether the market as a whole is expected to outperform the safe asset. In practice, of course, most managers do not shift fully between T-bills and the market. How might we measure partial shifts into the market when it is expected to perform well?

To simplify, suppose that the investor holds only the market index portfolio and T-bills. If the weight on the market were constant, for example, 0.6, then the portfolio beta also would be constant, and the portfolio characteristic line would plot as a straight line with slope 0.6, as in Figure 12.4 A. If, however, the investor could correctly time the market, and shift funds into it in periods when the market does well, the characteristic line would plot as in Figure 12.4 B. The idea is that if the timer can predict bull and bear markets, the investor will shift more into the market when the market is about to go up. The portfolio beta and the slope of the characteristic line will be higher when $r_M$ is higher, resulting in the curved line that appears in Figure 12.4 B.

Treynor and Mazuy[10] propose that such a line can be estimated by adding a squared term to the usual linear index model:

$$r_P - r_f = a + b(r_M - r_f) + c(r_M - r_f)^2 + e_P$$

where $r_P$ is the portfolio return, and *a, b,* and *c* are estimated by regression analysis. If *c* turns out to be positive, we have evidence of timing ability, because this last term will make the characteristic line steeper as $r_M - r_f$ is larger. Treynor and Mazuy estimated this equation for a number of mutual funds but found little evidence of timing ability.

A similar and simpler methodology is proposed by Henriksson and Merton.[11] These authors suggest that the beta of the portfolio can take only two values: a large value if the market is expected to do well and a small value otherwise. Under this scheme, the portfolio characteristic line appears as Figure 12.4C. Such a line appears in regression form as

$$r_P - r_f = a + b(r_M - r_f) + c(r_M - r_f)D + e_P$$

where *D* is a dummy variable that equals 1 for $r_M > r_f$ and zero otherwise. Hence the beta of the portfolio is *b* in bear markets and $b + c$ in bull markets. Again, a positive value of *c* implies market timing ability.

Henriksson[12] estimated this equation for 116 mutual funds over the period 1968–1980. He found that the average value of *c* for the funds was *negative,* and equal to $-.07$, although the value was not statistically significant at the conventional 5 percent level. Eleven funds and significantly positive values of *c,* while eight had significantly negative values. Overall, 62 percent of the funds had negative point estimates of timing ability. In sum, the results showed little evidence of market timing ability. Perhaps this should be expected; given the tremendous values to be reaped by a successful market time, it would be surprising in nearly efficient markets to uncover clear-cut evidence of such skills. Other evidence may support the case for timing ability, as discussed in the accompanying box.

To illustrate a test for market timing, let's return to Table 12.2. Regressing the excess returns of portfolios *P* and *Q* on the excess returns on *M* and the square of these returns,

$$r_P - r_f = a_P + b_P(r_M - r_f) + c_P(r_M - r_f)^2 + e_P$$
$$r_Q - r_f = q_Q + b_Q(r_M - r_f) + c_Q(r_M - r_f)^2 + e_Q$$

---

[10] Jack L. Treynor and Kay Mazuy, "Can Mutual Funds Outguess the Market?" *Harvard Business Review* 43 (July–August 1966).

[11] Roy D. Henriksson and R. C. Merton, "On Market Timing and Investment Performance. II. Statistical Procedures for Evaulating Forecasting Skills," *Journal of Business* 54 (October 1981).

[12] Roy D. Henriksson, "Market Timing and Mutual Fund Performance: An Empirical Investigation," *Journal of Business* 57 (January 1984).

## THERE'S A CASE TO BE MADE FOR MARKET TIMING

To many mutual fund investors, the stock market's recent gyrations look a bit like a bungee jump. A sudden fall, a gut-wrenching jolt and several smaller rebounds—all of which eventually leave you hanging in midair.

Should you hang in through the ups and downs, or try to time things so that you move out near the predicted top and come back in near the bottom?

Sit still, most mutual fund sellers say; time, not timing, is what matters, and short-term volatility is part of the process of achieving long-term gains. But this attitude is largely driven by their not wanting huge amounts of money forever wandering in and out of their portfolios.

A buy-and-hold strategy seems to be the prevailing trend among brokers and fund dealers. With the advent of trailer fees (payments by mutual fund companies to salespeople from the annual management fee as long as the client remains in the fund), fund sellers are now better off by promoting accumulation than by generating commission dollars through continual fund trading.

And then there's Harland Hendrickson, a biochemistry PhD who left the halls of science several years ago to set up his own mutual fund dealership. An unabashed market timer, he thinks mutual fund investors can put extra money in their pockets by becoming a lot more active.

Each month, subscribers to his $199-a-year Edmonton-based Market Trend Follower newsletter receive specific recommendations on which mutual funds to buy and sell. (You can get a free copy by calling 403-466-2629.)

In hypothetical back tests, Mr. Hendrickson and partner Darcy Mountjoy claim an investor using their system would have outperformed a buy-and-hold strategy by a healthy margin. But what about real life?

So far, their aggressive RRSP model portfolio results are, theoretically, pretty impressive—although risky by anyone's standards, because they focus heavily on resource funds. From $50,000 invested on Jan. 1, 1993, the portfolio would now be worth $101,106, a rate of return roughly double what you'd have by just buying the TSE 300, excluding fees and commissions, he says.

More recently, they have been producing models for more conservative investors, but their track record is too short to be significant.

While readers are clearly believers, critics argue that market timing strategies like this are simply not sustainable over the long haul. The argument you hear most often is that an investor could easily miss out on the market's best days and months.

Missing the U.S. market's top 20 days over the five-year bull period leading up to the 1987 crash would have cut your overall return in half. That's the conclusion of a widely distributed University of Michigan study.

But a more recent 1993 University of Michigan study supported the flip side. After looking at a longer period (1963 to 1993), it discovered that missing the worst 90 days would have increased the annual return for someone mimicking the S&P 500 stock market index to 21.7 percent, compared with 11.8 percent for a buy-and-hold strategy.

More important, if a market timer missed both the worst and best 90 days, the return was still improved. There was more benefit in missing the worst days than in participating in the best.

The trouble with retroactive studies like these is that they have little to do with how real people actually behave. Few investors really stay in for the long haul and no one can call the market on a daily basis. But, according to Mr. Hendrickson, shifting in and out of mutual funds based on their price momentum can pay off.

Look at it this way. Most healthy bull markets show certain characteristics: declining or stable interest rates, broad investor participation, strong leadership among stocks and an identifiable uptrend

*(Continued)*

in market indices. The fewer of these features you see, the more cautiously you should tread.

Mr. Hendrickson's model hinges on two such indicators: the 39-week moving average of the S&P 500; and the 26-week moving average of the U.S. Federal Reserve Board discount rate. Viewed in tandem with other variables, he feels they provide a sound clue to the market's underlying trends.

What are they telling him now? Calling for a soft landing eventually, Mr. Hendrickson's model is still supporting stocks. But the recent sharp jump in interest rates has him feeling a bit more cautious.

Is he on to something? Well, buy-and-hold certainly makes sense for the new investor. But the closer you are to needing your money, the more dangerous it may be to hang on.

Remember the objective is to reduce the risk of being caught in a downdraft, not to always try to make a killing. In that sense, his strategy might be worth a look.

Source: Gordan Powers, *The Globe and Mail,* July 29, 1995. Reprinted by permission.

we derive the following statistics:

| | Portfolio | |
|---|---|---|
| **Estimate** | ***P*** | ***Q*** |
| Alpha (*a*) | 1.77 (1.77) | −2.29 (5.28) |
| Beta (*b*) | .70 ( .70) | 1.10 (1.40) |
| Timing (*c*) | .00 | .10 |
| *R*-SQR | .91 ( .91) | .98 ( .64) |

The numbers in parentheses are the regression estimates from the single variable regression reported in Table 12.3. The results reveal that portfolio *P* shows no timing. It is not clear whether this is a result of Jane's making no attempt at timing or that the effort to time was in vain and served only to increase portfolio variance unnecessarily.

The results for portfolio *Q,* however, reveal that timing has, in all likelihood, successfully been attempted. The timing coefficient, *c,* is estimated at .10. This describes a successful timing effort that was offset by unsuccessful stock selection. Note that the alpha estimate, *a,* is now −2.29 percent, as opposed to the 5.28 percent estimate derived from the regression equation that did not allow for the possibility of timing activity.

Indeed, this is an example of the inadequacy of conventional performance evaluation techniques that assume constant mean returns and constant risk. The market timer constantly shifts beta and mean return, moving into and out of the market. Whereas the expanded regression captures this phenomenon, the simple SCL does not. The relative desirability of portfolios *P* and *Q* remains unclear in the sense that the value of the timing success and selectivity failure of *Q* compared with *P* has yet to be evaluated. The important point for performance evaluation, however, is that expanded regressions can capture many of the effects of portfolio composition change that would confound the more conventional mean-variance measures.

## 12.4 Security Selection: The Treynor–Black Model

### Overview of the Treynor–Black Model

Security analysis is the other form of active portfolio management besides timing the overall market. Suppose that you are an analyst studying individual securities. It is quite likely that you will turn up several securities that appear to be mispriced. They offer positive anticipated alphas to the investor. But how do you exploit your analysis? Concentrating a portfolio on these securities entails a cost, namely, the firm-specific risk that you could shed by more fully diversifying. As an active manager you must strike a balance between aggressive exploitation of perceived security mispricing and diversification motives that dictate that a few stocks should not dominate the portfolio.

Treynor and Black[13] developed an optimizing model for portfolio managers who use security analysis. It represents a portfolio management theory that assumes security markets are *nearly* efficient. The essence of the model is this:

1. Security analysts in an active investment management organization can analyze in depth only a relatively small number of stocks out of the entire universe of securities. The securities not analyzed are assumed to be fairly priced.
2. For the purpose of efficient diversification, the market index portfolio is the baseline portfolio, which the model treats as the passive portfolio.
3. The macro forecasting unit of the investment management firm provides forecasts of the expected rate of return and variance of the passive (market index) portfolio.
4. The objective of security analysis is to form an active portfolio of a necessarily limited number of securities. Perceived mispricing of the analyzed securities is what guides the composition of this active portfolio.
5. Analysts follow several steps to make up the active portfolio and evaluate its expected performance:
   *a.* Estimate the beta of each analyzed security and its residual risk. From the beta and the macro forecast, $E(r_M) - r_f$, determine the *required* rate of return of the security.
   *b.* Given the degree of mispricing of each security, determine its expected return and expected *abnormal* return (alpha).
   *c.* Calculate the cost of less than full diversification. The nonsystematic risk of the mispriced stock, the variance of the stock's residual, offsets the benefit (alpha) of specializing in an underpriced security.
   *d.* Use the estimates for the values of alpha, beta, and residual risk to determine the optimal weight of each security in the active portfolio.

[13] Jack Treynor and Fischer Black, "How to Use Security Analysis to Improve Portfolio Selection," *Journal of Business,* January 1973.

*e.* Estimate the alpha, beta, and residual risk for the active portfolio according to the weights of the securities in the portfolio.

**6.** The macroeconomic forecasts for the passive index portfolio and the composite forecasts for the active portfolio are used to determine the optimal risky portfolio, which will be a combination of the passive and active portfolios.

Treynor and Black's model did not take the industry by storm. This is unfortunate for several reasons:

1. Just as even imperfect market timing ability has enormous value, security analysis of the sort Treynor and Black propose has similar potential value. Even with far from perfect security analysis, proper active management can add value.
2. The Treynor–Black model is conceptually easy to implement. Moreover, it is useful even when some of its simplifying assumptions are relaxed.
3. The model lends itself to use in decentralized organizations. This property is essential to efficiency in complex organizations.

## Portfolio Construction

Assuming that all securities are fairly priced, and using the index model as a guideline for the rate of return on fairly priced securities, the rate of return on the *i*th security is given by

$$r_i = r_f + \beta_i(r_M - r_f) + e_i \qquad \textbf{(12.1)}$$

where $e_i$ is the zero mean, firm-specific disturbance.

Absent security analysis, Treynor and Black (TB) take equation 12.1 to represent the rate of return on all securities and assume that the market portfolio, *M,* is the efficient portfolio. For simplicity, they also assume that the nonsystematic components of returns, $e_i$, are independent across securities. As for market timing, TB assume that the forecast for the **passive portfolio** already has been made, so that the expected return on the market index, $r_M$, as well as its variance, $\sigma_M^2$, has been assessed.

Now a portfolio manager unleashes a team of security analysts to investigate a subset of the universe of available securities. The objective is to form an active portfolio of positions in the analyzed securities to be mixed with the index portfolio. For each security, *k,* that is researched, we write the rate of return as

$$r_k = r_f + \beta_k(r_M - r_f) + e_k + \alpha_k \qquad \textbf{(12.2)}$$

where $\alpha_k$ represents the extra expected return (called the *abnormal return*) attributable to any perceived mispricing of the security. Thus for each security analyzed the research team estimates the parameters

$$\alpha_k,\ \beta_k,\ \sigma^2(e_k)$$

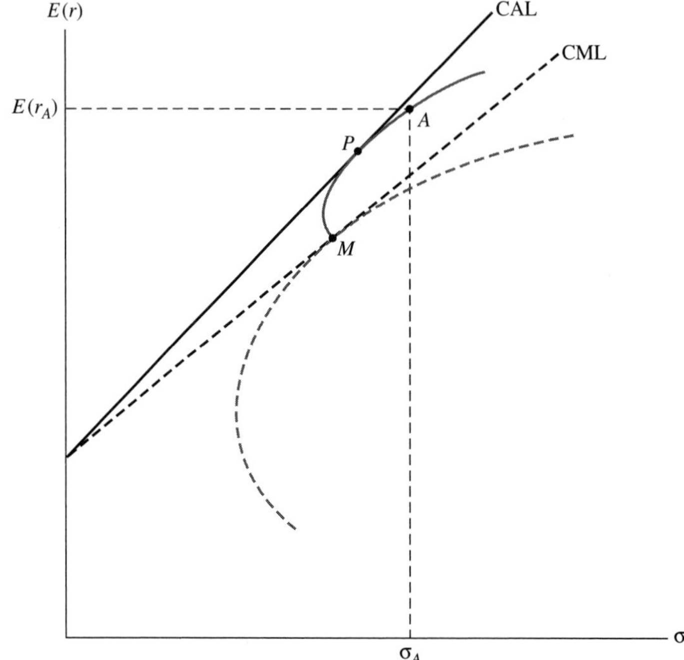


**Figure 12.5**
The optimization process with active and passive portfolios.

If all the $\alpha_k$ turn out to be zero, there would be no reason to depart from the passive strategy and the index portfolio $M$ would remain the manager's choice. However, this is a remote possibility. In general, there will be a significant number of non-zero alpha values, some positive and some negative.

One way to get an overview of the TB methodology is to examine what we should do with the active portfolio once we get it. Suppose that the **active portfolio** ($A$) has been constructed somehow and has the parameters

$$\alpha_A, \beta_A, \sigma^2(e_A)$$

Its total variance is the sum of its systematic variance, $\beta_A^2\sigma_M^2$, plus the nonsystematic variance $\sigma^2(e_A)$. Its covariance with the market index portfolio, $M$, is

$$\text{Cov}(r_A, r_M) = \beta_A\sigma_M^2$$

Figure 12.5 shows the optimization process with the active and passive portfolios. The dashed efficient frontier represents the universe of all securities assuming that they are all fairly priced, that is, that all alphas are zero. By definition, the market index, $M$, is on this efficient frontier and is tangent to the (broken) capital market line (CML). In practice the analysts do not need to know this frontier. They need only to observe the market index portfolio and construct a portfolio resulting in a capital allocation line that lies above CML. Given their perceived superior analysis, they will view the market index portfolio as inefficient: The active portfolio, *A*, constructed from mispriced securities must lie, by design, above the CML.

To locate the active portfolio *A* in Figure 12.5, we need its expected return and standard deviation. The standard deviation is

$$\sigma_A = [\beta_A^2\sigma_M^2 + \sigma^2(e_A)]^{1/2}$$

Because of the positive alpha value that is forecast for *A*, it plots above the (broken) CML with expected return

$$E(r_A) = \alpha_A + r_f + \beta_A[E(r_M) - r_f]$$

The optimal combination of the active portfolio, *A*, with the passive portfolio, *M*, is a simple application of the construction of optimal risky portfolios from two component assets that we first encountered in Chapter 7. Because the active portfolio is not perfectly correlated with the market index portfolio, we need to account for their mutual correlation in the determination of the optimal allocation between the two portfolios. This is evident from the solid efficient frontier that passes through *M* and *A*. It supports the optimal capital allocation line (CAL) and identifies the optimal risky portfolio, *P,* which combines portfolios *A* and *M,* and is the tangency point of the CAL to the efficient frontier. The active portfolio *A* in this example is not the ultimately efficient portfolio, because we need to mix *A* with the passive market portfolio to achieve greater diversification.

Let us now outline the algebraic approach to this optimization problem. If we invest a proportion, $w$, in the active portfolio and $1 - w$ in the market index, the portfolio return will be

$$r_p(w) = wr_A + (1 - w)r_M$$

We can use this equation to calculate Sharpe's measure (dividing the mean excess return by the standard deviation of the return) as a function of the weight, $w$, then find the optimal weight, $w^*$, that maximizes the measure. This is the value of $w$ that makes *P* the optimal tangency portfolio in Figure 12.5.

This maximization ultimately leads to the solution

$$w^* = \frac{w_0}{1 + (1 - \beta_A)w_0} \qquad \textbf{(12.3)}$$

where

$$w_0 = \frac{\alpha_A/\sigma^2(e_A)}{[E(r_M) - r_f]/\sigma_M^2}$$

Equation 12.3 actually is a restatement of the formula for determining the optimal weights to invest in two risky assets that you first encountered in Chapter 7. Here, we state the equation in terms of portfolio alphas relative to the CAPM, but the approach is identical.

First look at $w_0$. This would be the optimal weight in the active portfolio *if* its beta ($\beta_A$) were 1.0. This weight is a ratio of two measures. In the numerator is the reward from the active portfolio, $\alpha_A$, reflecting its mispricing, against the nonsystematic risk, $\sigma^2(e_A)$, incurred in holding it. This ratio is divided by an analogous measure for the index portfolio

$$\frac{E(r_M) - r_f}{\sigma_M^2}$$

which is the ratio of the reward from holding the index $E(r_M) - r_f$ to its risk, $\sigma_M^2$.

The intuition here is straightforward. We mix the active portfolio with the index for the benefit of diversification. The position to take in the active portfolio relative to the market portfolio depends on the ratio of the active portfolio's abnormal return, $\alpha_A$, to its potentially diversifiable risk, $\sigma^2(e_A)$. The optimal weights also will depend on the opportunities for diversification, which in turn depend on the correlation between the two portfolios and can be measured by $\beta_A$. To adjust the optimal weight for the fact that the beta of the active portfolio may not be 1.0, we compute $w^*$ in equation 12.3.

What is the reward-to-variability ratio of the optimal risky portfolio once we find the best mix, $w^*$, of the active and passive index portfolio? It turns out that if we compute the square of Sharpe's measure of the risky portfolio, we can separate the contributions of the index and active portfolios as follows:

$$\begin{aligned} S_P^2 &= S_M^2 + \frac{\alpha_A^2}{\sigma^2(e_A)} \\ &= \left[\frac{E(r_M) - r_f}{\sigma_M}\right]^2 + \left[\frac{\alpha_A}{\sigma(e_A)}\right]^2 \end{aligned} \quad \textbf{(12.4)}$$

This decomposition of the Sharpe measure of the optimal risky portfolio, which by the way is valid *only* for the optimal portfolio, tells us how to construct the active portfolio. Look at the last equality in equation 12.4. It shows that the highest Sharpe measure for the risky portfolio will be attained when we construct an active portfolio that maximizes the value of $\alpha_A/\sigma(e_A)$. The ratio of alpha to residual standard deviation of the active portfolio will be maximized when we choose a weight for the $k$th analyzed security as follows:

$$w_k = \frac{\alpha_k/\sigma^2(e_k)}{\sum_{i=1}^{n} \alpha_i/\sigma^2(e_i)} \quad \textbf{(12.5)}$$

This makes sense: The weight of a security in the active portfolio depends on the ratio of the degree of mispricing, $\alpha_k$, to the nonsystematic risk, $\sigma^2(e_k)$, of the security. The denominator, the sum of the ratio across securities, is a scale factor to guarantee that the weights sum to one.

Note from equation 12.4 that the square of Sharpe's measure of the optimal risky portfolio is increased over the square of the Sharpe measure of the passive (market-index) portfolio by the amount

$$\left[\frac{\alpha_A}{\sigma(e_A)}\right]^2$$

The ratio of the degree of mispricing, $\alpha_A$, to the nonsystematic standard deviation, $\sigma(e_A)$, becomes a natural performance measure of the active component of the risky portfolio. In Section 12.2, we identified this as the appraisal ratio.

We can also calculate the contribution of a single security in the active portfolio to the portfolio's overall performance. When the active portfolio contains $n$ analyzed securities, the total improvement in the squared Sharpe measure equals the sum of the squared appraisal ratios of the analyzed securities,

$$\left[\frac{\alpha_A}{\sigma(e_A)}\right]^2 = \sum_{i=1}^{n}\left[\frac{\alpha_i}{\sigma(e_i)}\right]^2$$

The appraisal ratio for each security, $\sigma_i/\sigma(e_i)$, is a measure of the contribution of that security to the performance of the active portfolio.

The best way to illustrate the Treynor-Black process is through an example. Suppose that the macroforecasting unit of Drex Portfolio Inc. (DPF) issues a forecast for a 15 percent market return. The forecast's standard error is 20 percent. The risk-free rate is 7 percent. The macro data can be summarized as follows:

$$E(r_M) - r_f = .08;\ \sigma_M = .20$$

At the same time, the security analysis division submits to the portfolio manager the following forecast of annual returns for the three securities that it covers:

| Stock | $\alpha$ | $\beta$ | $\sigma(e)$ |
|---|---|---|---|
| 1 | .07 | 1.6 | .45 |
| 2 | −.05 | 1.0 | .32 |
| 3 | .03 | .5 | .26 |

Note that the alpha estimates appear reasonably moderate. The estimates of the residual standard deviations are correlated with the betas, just as they are in reality. The magnitudes also reflect typical values for TSE stocks.

First, let us construct the optimal active portfolio implied by the security analyst input list. To do so we compute the appraisal ratios as follows:

| Stock | $\alpha/\sigma^2(e)$ | $\frac{\alpha_i}{\sigma^2(e_i)} \Big/ \sum_{i=1}^{3} \frac{\alpha_i}{\sigma^2(e_i)}$ |
|---|---|---|
| 1 | $.07/.45^2 = .3457$ | $.3457/.3012 = 1.1477$ |
| 2 | $-.05/.32^2 = -.4883$ | $-.4883/.3012 = -1.6212$ |
| 3 | $.03/.26^2 = .4438$ | $.4438/.3012 = 1.4735$ |
| Total | .3012 | 1.0000 |

The last column presents the optimal positions of each of the three securities in the active portfolio. Obviously, stock 2 has a negative weight. The magnitudes of the individual positions in the active portfolio (114.77 percent in stock 1, for example) seem quite extreme. However, this should not concern us because the active portfolio will later be mixed with the well-diversified market index portfolio, resulting in much more moderate positions, as we shall see shortly.

The forecasts for the stocks, together with the proposed composition of the active portfolio, lead to the following parameter estimates for the active portfolio:

$$\alpha_A = 1.1477 \times .07 + (-1.6212) \times (-.05) + 1.4735 \times .03 = .2056$$
$$\beta_A = 1.1477 \times 1.6 + (-1.6212) \times 1.0 + 1.4735 \times .5 = .9519$$
$$\sigma(e_A) = [1.477^2 \times .45^2 + (-1.6212)^2 \times .32^2 + 1.4735^2 \times .26^2]^{1/2} = .8262$$

Note that the negative weight (short position) on the negative alpha stock results in a positive contribution to the alpha of the active portfolio. Note also that because of the assumption that the stock residuals are uncorrelated, the active portfolio's residual variance is simply the weighted sum of the individual stock residual variances, with the squared portfolio proportions as weights.

The parameters of the active portfolio are now used to determine its proportion in the overall risky portfolio:

$$\begin{aligned} w_0 &= \frac{\alpha_A/\sigma^2(e_A)}{[E(r_M) - r_f]/\sigma_M^2} \\ &= \frac{.2056/.6826}{.08/.04} \\ &= .1506 \\ w^* &= \frac{w_0}{1 + (1 - \beta_A)w_0} \\ &= \frac{.1506}{1 + (1 - .9519) \times .1506} \\ &= .1495 \end{aligned}$$

Although the active portfolio's alpha is impressive (20.56 percent), its proportion in the overall risky portfolio, before adjustment for beta, is only 15.06 percent, because of its large nonsystematic risk (82.62 percent). Such is the importance of diversification. As it happens, the beta of the active portfolio is almost 1.0, and hence the correction for beta (from $w_0$ to $w^*$) is small, from 15.06 percent to 14.95 percent. The direction of the change makes sense. If the beta of the active portfolio is low (less than 1.0), there are more potential gains from diversification. Hence a smaller position in the active portfolio is called for. If the beta of the active portfolio were significantly greater than 1.0, a larger correction in the opposite direction would be called for.

The proportions of the individual stocks in the active portfolio, together with the proportion of the active portfolio in the overall risky portfolio, determine the proportions of each individual stock in the overall risky portfolio.

| Stock | Final Position |
|---|---|
| 1 | .1495 × 1.1477 = .1716 |
| 2 | .1495 × (−1.6212) = −.2424 |
| 3 | .1495 × 1.4735 = .2202 |
| Active portfolio | .1495 |
| Market portfolio | .8505 |
| | 1.0000 |

The parameters of the active portfolio and market-index portfolio are now used to forecast the performance of the optimal, overall risky portfolio. When optimized, a property of the risky portfolio is that its squared Sharpe measure increases by the square of the active portfolio's appraisal ratio:

$$S_P^2 = \left[\frac{E(r_M) - r_f}{\sigma_M}\right]^2 + \left[\frac{\alpha_A}{\sigma(e_A)}\right]^2$$
$$= .16 + .0619 = .2219$$

and hence the Sharpe measure of the active portfolio is $\sqrt{.2219} = .47$, compared with .40 for the passive portfolio.

**CONCEPT CHECK** Question 4.

*a.* When short positions are prohibited, the manager simply discards stocks with negative alphas. Using the preceding example, what would be the composition of the active portfolio if short sales were disallowed? Find the cost of the short-sale restriction in terms of the decline in performance of the new overall risky portfolio.

*b.* How would your answer change if the macro forecast is adjusted upward, for example, to $E(r_M) - r_f = 12$ percent, and short sales are again allowed?

## 12.5 PERFORMANCE ATTRIBUTION PROCEDURES

Traditionally, portfolio managers have distinguished themselves as either market-timers or stock-pickers. In this way, some have claimed an aptitude for timing the broad market swings by macroeconomic analysis; others, doubting the feasibility of this, have relied on **selectivity**—identifying equities that would perform well in particular economic climates. More recently, we have seen the emergence of managers who despair of either ability and operate index funds.

Rather than focus on risk-adjusted returns, practitioners often want simply to ascertain which decisions resulted in superior or inferior performance. Superior investment performance depends on an ability to be in the "right" securities at the right time. Such timing and selection ability may be considered broadly, for instance, being in equities as opposed to fixed-income securities when the stock market is performing well. Or it may be defined at a more detailed level, such as choosing the relatively better-performing stocks within a particular industry. Portfolio managers constantly make both broad-brush asset-market allocation decisions, as well as more detailed sector and security allocation decisions within markets. Performance attribution studies attempt to break down overall performance into discrete components that may be identified with a particular level of the portfolio selection process.

Recent characterizations of performance ability have extended the simpler timing–selectivity dichotomy by adding a policy variable representing asset allocation. As we have noted, market-timers do not actually switch from T-bills to index funds; rather, they have a standard or base allocation of portfolio weights to T-bills, government bonds, corporate bonds, domestic equities, foreign equities, and perhaps other assets. From this base allocation they shift weights as they see the various assets responding more favourably to changing market conditions.

Attribution studies start from the broadest asset allocation choices and progressively focus on ever-finer details of portfolio choice. The difference between a managed portfolio's performance and that of a benchmark portfolio then may be expressed as the sum of the contributions to performance of a series of decisions made at the various levels of the portfolio construction process. For example, one common attribution system breaks performance down into three components: (1) broad-asset market allocation choices across equity, fixed-income, and money markets, (2) industry (sector) choice within each market, and (3) security choice within each sector.

To illustrate the allocation of investment results to various decisions at different levels of portfolio construction, consider the attribution results for a hypothetical portfolio. The portfolio invests in stocks, bonds, and money market securities. The attribution analysis is presented in Tables 12.4–12.7. In Table 12.4, we see that the portfolio return over the month was 5.34 percent, which is compared to a benchmark return. The benchmark is the return gained on a **bogey portfolio.** The bogey portfolio represents what the portfolio manager would have earned by a passive strategy. "Passive" has two attributes. First, the asset allocation is set to neutral as determined by some market consensus, or more probably, according to what the client believes is appropriate to personal risk preferences and objectives. Second, within each asset class the funds are invested in an indexed portfolio such as the TSE 300, the ScotiaMcLeod index, and a money market index. Any departure from the benchmark's return by the manager's return must be due to either asset allocation or security selection, or both.

In Table 12.4, the neutral weights are 60 percent equity, 30 percent fixed-income, and 10 percent cash (money market securities). The bogey portfolio, composed of "investments" in each index with the 60/30/10 weights, returned 3.97 percent. The managed portfolio's measure of extra-market performance is positive and equal to its actual return less the return of the bogey: 5.34 − 3.97 = 1.37 percent. The next step is to allocate the 1.37 percent excess return to the separate decisions that contributed to it.

**Table 12.4** Performance of the Managed Portfolio

| Component | Benchmark Weight | Return of Index during Month (%) |
|---|---|---|
| **Bogey Performance and Excess Return** | | |
| Equity (TSE 300) | .60 | 5.81 |
| Bonds (ScotiaMcLeod) | .30 | 1.45 |
| Cash (money market) | .10 | 0.48 |
| Bogey = (.60 × 5.81) + (.30 × 1.45) + (.10 × 0.48) = 3.97% | | |
| Return of managed portfolio | | 5.34% |
| Return of bogey portfolio | | 3.97 |
| Excess return of managed portfolio | | 1.37% |

## Asset Allocation Decisions

As shown in Table 12.5, our hypothetical managed portfolio was invested in the equity, fixed-income, and money markets with weights 70 percent, 7 percent, and 23 percent, respectively. The portfolio's performance can derive from the departure of this weighting scheme from the benchmark 60/30/10 weights, as well as from superior or inferior results *within* each of the three broad markets. To iden-

**Table 12.5** Performance Attribution

| Market | (1) Actual Weight in Market | (2) Benchmark Weight in Market | (3) Excess Weight | (4) Market Return (%) | (5) = (3) × (4) Contribution to Performance (%) |
|---|---|---|---|---|---|
| **A. Contribution of Asset Allocation to Performance** | | | | | |
| Equity | .70 | .60 | .10 | 5.81 | .5810 |
| Fixed income | .07 | .30 | −.23 | 1.45 | −.3335 |
| Cash | .23 | .10 | .13 | 0.48 | .0624 |
| | Contribution of asset allocation | | | | .3099 |

| Market | (1) Portfolio Performance (%) | (2) Index Performance (%) | (3) Excess Performance (%) | (4) Portfolio Weight | (5) = (3) × (4) Contribution (%) |
|---|---|---|---|---|---|
| **B. Contribution of Selection to Total Performance** | | | | | |
| Equity | 7.28 | 5.81 | 1.47 | .70 | 1.03 |
| Fixed income | 1.89 | 1.45 | 0.44 | .07 | .03 |
| | Contribution of selection within markets | | | | 1.06 |

**Table 12.6** Sector Selection within the Equity Market

| Sector | (1) Beginning of Month Weights (%) Portfolio | (2) Beginning of Month Weights (%) TSE 300 | (3) Difference in Weights | (4) Sector Return | (5) Sector Over/Under Performance* | (6) = (3) × (5) Sector Allocation Contribution |
|---|---|---|---|---|---|---|
| Interest-sensitive | 29.72 | 31.99 | −2.27 | 6.4 | 0.9 | −2.04 |
| Consumer | 9.54 | 17.46 | −7.92 | 5.4 | −.1 | 0.79 |
| Resource | 10.31 | 21.52 | −11.21 | 3.7 | −1.8 | 20.18 |
| Energy | 24.29 | 9.31 | 14.98 | 8.4 | 2.9 | 43.44 |
| Industrial products | 19.03 | 9.83 | 9.2 | 8.3 | 2.8 | 25.76 |
| Transportation | 2.32 | 3.70 | −1.38 | −0.2 | −5.7 | 7.87 |
| Management companies | 4.79 | 6.19 | −1.4 | 2.1 | −3.4 | 4.76 |
| **Total** | | | | | | **100.76 basis points** |

*TSE 300 performance, excluding dividends, was 5.5 percent. Returns compared net of dividends.

tify the effect of the manager's asset allocation choice, we measure the performance of a hypothetical portfolio that would have invested in the *indices* for each market with weights 70/7/23. This return measures the individual effect of the shift away from the benchmark 60/30/10 weights, without allowing for any effects attributable to active management of the securities selected within each market. Superior performance relative to the bogey is achieved by overweighting investments in markets that turn out to perform relatively well and by underweighting poorly performing markets. The contribution of asset allocation to superior performance equals the sum over all markets of the excess weight in each market multiplied by the return of the market index.

Part **A** of Table 12.5 demonstrates that asset allocation contributed almost 31 basis points to the portfolio's overall excess return of 137 basis points. The major factor contributing to superior performance in this month was the heavy

**Table 12.7** Portfolio Attribution: Summary

| | | Contribution (Basis Points) |
|---|---|---|
| 1. Asset allocation | | 31.0 |
| 2. Selection | | |
| a. Equity excess return | | |
| i. Sector allocation | 101 | |
| ii. Security allocation | 46 | |
| | 147 × .70 (portfolio weight) = | 102.9 |
| b. Fixed-income excess return | 44 × .07 (portfolio weight) = | 3.1 |
| **Total excess return of portfolio** | | **137.0 basis points** |

weighting of the equity market in a month when the equity market had an excellent return of 5.81 percent.

## Sector and Security Allocation Decisions

If .31 percent of the excess performance can be attributed to advantageous asset allocation across markets, the remaining 1.06 percent must be attributable to sector and security selection within each market. Part **B** of Table 12.5 details the contribution of the managed portfolio's sector and security selection to total performance.

Part **B** shows that the equity component of the managed portfolio had a return of 7.28 percent versus a return of 5.81 percent for the TSE 300. The fixed-income return was 1.89 percent versus 1.45 percent for the ScotiaMcLeod index. The superior performance in equity and fixed-income markets weighted by the portfolio proportions invested in each market sums to the 1.06 percent contribution to performance attributable to sector and security selection.

Table 12.6 documents the sources of the equity component performance by each sector within the market. The first three columns detail the allocation of funds to the sectors in the equity market compared with their (hypothetical) representation in the TSE 300. Column 4 shows the rate of return of each sector, and column 5 documents the performance of each sector relative to the return of the TSE 300. The contribution of each sector's allocation presented in column 6 equals the product of the difference in the sector weight and the sector's relative performance.

Note that good performance (a positive contribution) derives from overweighting well-performing sectors, such as energy, or underweighting poorly performing sectors, such as transportation. The excess return of the equity component of the portfolio attributable to sector allocation alone is 1.01 percent. Since the equity component of the portfolio outperformed the TSE 300 by 1.47 percent (Table 12.5**B,** column (3)), we conclude that the effect of security selection within sectors must have contributed an additional 1.47 − 1.01 = .46 percent to the performance of the equity component of the portfolio.

A similar sector analysis can be applied to the fixed-income portion of the portfolio, but we do not show those results here.

## Summing Up Component Contributions

In this particular month, all facets of the portfolio selection process were successful. Table 12.7 details the contribution of each aspect of performance. Asset allocation across the major security markets contributes 31 basis points. Sector and security allocation within those markets contributes 106 basis points, for total excess portfolio performance of 137 basis points. The sector and security allocation of 106 basis points can be partitioned further. Sector allocation within the equity market results in excess performance of 100.76 basis points, and security selection within sectors contributes 46 basis points. (The total equity excess performance of 147 basis points is multiplied by the 70 percent weight in equity to obtain contribution to portfolio performance.) Similar partitioning could be done for the fixed-income sector.

## 12.6 Performance Evaluation

Performance evaluation has two very basic problems:

1. Many observations are needed for significant results even when portfolio mean and variance are constant.
2. Shifting parameters when portfolios are actively managed make accurate performance evaluation all the more elusive.

Although these objective difficulties cannot be overcome completely, it is clear that to obtain reasonably reliable performance measures we need to do the following:

1. Maximize the number of observations by taking more frequent return readings.
2. Specify the exact make-up of the portfolio to obtain better estimates of the risk parameters at each observation period.

Suppose an evaluator knows the exact portfolio composition at the opening of each day. Because the daily return on each security is available, the total daily return on the portfolio can be calculated. Furthermore, the exact portfolio composition allows the evaluator to estimate the risk characteristics (variance, beta, residual variance) for each day. Thus, daily risk-adjusted rates of return can be obtained. Although a performance measure for one day is statistically unreliable, the number of days with such rich data accumulates quickly. Performance evaluation that accounts for frequent revision in portfolio composition is superior by far to evaluation that assumes constant risk characteristics over the entire measurement period.

What sort of evaluation takes place in practice? Performance reports for portfolio managers traditionally have been based on quarterly data over 5–10 years. Currently, managers of mutual funds are required to disclose the exact composition of their portfolios only semiannually. Trading activity that immediately precedes the reporting date is known as "window dressing." Rumor has it that window dressing involves changes in portfolio composition to make it look as if the manager chose successful stocks. If Seagram's performed well over the quarter, for example, a portfolio manager will make sure that his or her portfolio includes a lot of Seagram's on the reporting date, whether or not it did during the quarter and whether or not Seagram's is expected to perform as well over the next quarter. Of course, portfolio managers deny such activity, and we know of no published evidence to substantiate the allegation. However, if window dressing is quantitatively significant, even the reported quarterly composition data can be misleading. Mutual funds publish portfolio values on a daily basis, which means the rate of return for each day is publicly available, but portfolio composition is not.

Moreover, mutual fund managers have had considerable leeway in the presentation of both past investment performance and fees charged for management services. The resultant noncomparability of net-of-expense performance numbers has made meaningful comparison of funds difficult. This may be changing, however; the OSC has moved toward greater disclosure in the reporting of fees. Awareness of the fees may help to evaluate performance based on the actual invested capital.

Traditional academic research uses monthly, weekly, and, more recently, even daily data. But such research makes no use of changes in portfolio composition because the data usually are unavailable. Therefore, performance evaluation is unsatisfactory in both the academic and practitioner communities.

Portfolio managers reveal their portfolio composition only when they have to, which so far is quarterly. This is not nearly sufficient for adequate evaluation. However, current computer and communication technology makes it easy to use daily composition data for evaluation purposes. If the technology required for meaningful evaluation is in place, implementation of more accurate performance measurement techniques could improve welfare by enabling the public to identify the truly talented investment managers. In the United States, the Association of Investment Management and Research has published an extensive set of performance presentation standards encouraging the presentation of regular reporting periods and intervals, comparative indices, and expense effects.

## Professional Performance Reporting

The most widely available report on mutual funds is published regularly by the major financial newspapers in Canada. For example, *The Globe and Mail*'s Report on Business survey of mutual funds appears monthly and provides a summary of the realized performance of Canadian funds. In an attempt to provide meaningful comparisons, the funds are grouped by type, including: balanced, dividend (income), Canadian equity, U.S. equity, international equity, as well as money market, bond, mortgage and real estate funds; the Canadian, U.S. and international equity funds ought to be growth-oriented by contrast with the balanced and dividend funds. The report also provides a measure of volatility on a one-to-five scale. The tables within the report list returns for periods ranging from three months to ten years, where these are net of management fees and include reinvestment of dividends. An average for the group is given in addition to other individual information of interest to investors, including details of sales commissions or "loads."

A far more informative appraisal is provided by firms whose primary purpose is to track performance of managers for funds who are their clients. Individual components of performance are measured to examine the success or failure of the manager in beating the index or the average of similar-objective funds. There are four major services that specialize in providing these analyses in Canada: SEI

Financial Services, Comstat Capital Sciences, CTUCS, and Intersec Research Corp. Between them they track performance for over 2,000 investment portfolios.

Software providing similar information also is available to individuals to aid in the assessment of funds. For instance, Portfolio Analytics Limited provides statistical information about mutual funds on disk through a service called "FundTrak." Also, a number of on-line data services provide information on fund performance in addition to stock data.

An additional problem in performance evaluation has received considerable attention from researchers in recent years. The issue is known as **survivorship bias,** which refers to the measurement of results from a population whose membership varies over time; put more simply, badly performing funds disappear, and their poor results are not counted in determining average performance. In consequence, the reported average for mutual fund performance exceeds the ex ante results that an investor can expect from a randomly selected fund. Brown et al[14] exposed the problem in a 1992 article. A number of articles have examined the question of performance persistence by mutual fund managers, with Brown and Goetzmann[15] reporting on the effect of survival bias in such studies. A 1995 study of this phenomenon for Canadian funds is summarized by Curwood et al.[16]

## Empirical Studies of Canadian Performance

A number of studies of the general performance of Canadian mutual funds have been conducted, using a variety of techniques and investigating different phenomena. Researchers have investigated the stability of the funds' betas, the effects of inflation and fund size, performance in good and bad markets, and the general question of the value of managerial expertise.

An early study by Grant[17] used Jensen's measure to compare performance over the period 1960–1974. By examining the stability of the risk measure beta and performance, Grant found that funds were unable to satisfy the objectives that they set for themselves; that is, the revealed instability meant that an investor could not guarantee either high or low growth and risk by investing in funds with defined objectives. Similarly, Dhingra found that both average returns and volatility were unstable over time, as we previously noted.

Calvet and Lefoll[18] investigated the inflationary effect on returns and concluded that the real returns of funds were not superior to those of the TSE 300;

---

[14] S. J. Brown, W. N. Goetzmann, R. G. Ibottson, and S. A. Ross, "Survivorship Bias in Performance Studies," *Review of Financial Studies* 5 (1992), pp. 553–80.

[15] S. J. Brown and W. N. Goetzmann, "Performance Persistence," *The Journal of Finance* 50 (June 1995), pp. 679–98.

[16] B. Curwood, S. Hadjiyannakis, P. Halpern, and K. Taylor, "How Survivorship Bias Skews Results of Comparative Measurement Universes," *Canadian Investment Review* 8 (Winter 1995/1996), pp. 9–12.

[17] D. Grant, "Investment Performance of Canadian Mutual Funds: 1960–1974," *Journal of Business Administration* 8 (Fall 1976).

[18] A. L. Calvet and J. Lefoll, "The CAPM under Inflation and the Performance of Canadian Mutual Funds," *Journal of Business Administration* 12, no. 1 (Fall 1980).

real and nominal returns revealed that inflation did not explain the return-generating mechanism of the market or fund returns. Martel, Khoury, and M'zali[19] used a multicriterion evaluation and the Sharpe and Treynor indices in a study to determine the effect of fund size. The data were drawn from a sample of 34 funds from 1981–1986, and they identified a combined index incorporating the TSE 300, S&P 500, and the EAFE (for international effects). Their conclusion was that fund size was associated with superior performance for this sample.

Fund performance for the period 1967–1984 was analyzed by Bishara,[20] who concluded that Canadian funds could not outperform the market. He subdivided his fund universe into balanced, income, and growth funds and considered their returns over boom and recession periods. His findings concluded that while growth funds managed to match the index return, the balanced and income funds were inferior to the index over the whole period and during one boom.[21]

The more specific issue of identifying timing and selectivity ability has received less attention. There is difficulty in defining the two skills where these tend to be related to the regression characteristics rather than to their intuitive, economic characteristics. Admati et al[22] have presented two alternative structures for testing these abilities, based on the alternative definitions. The normal regression-based approach is identified as a portfolio approach; this stresses the use of obvious portfolios to be used for timing decisions, such as the T-bill and index fund portfolios, and examines the regression residuals for different managers. A newer approach is to use a factor model that will relate to the economic factors giving rise to timing and selecting decisions. In both cases, the issue is the quality of information possessed by the manager; the information will affect the performance of individual assets and the portfolios either directly, by analysis of the assets, or through the factors that generate returns on the assets and portfolios.

Few Canadian studies have focused on the timing issue, although Dhingra did find that the volatilities of fund portfolios were not stationary.[23] A recent study, however, by Weigel and Ilkiw[24] investigated market timing effected by two methods: **tactical asset allocation** (TAA) models and **swing fund management.** They

---

[19] Jean-Marc Martel, Nabil Khoury, and Bouchra M'zali, "Relationship between Mutual Funds' Size and Their 'Performance,' " *Finance Proceedings,* Administrative Sciences Association of Canada 8 (1987). See also J.-M. Martel, N. T. Khoury, and M. Bergeron, "An Application of a Multicriteria Approach to Portfolio Comparisons," *Journal of the Operations Research Society* 39, no. 7 (1988); and N. T. Khoury and J.-M Martel, "The Relationship between Risk-Return Characteristics of Mutual Funds and Their Size," *Finance* 11, no. 2 (1990).

[20] Halim Bishara, "Evaluation of the Performance of Canadian Mutual Funds (1967–1984)," *Finance Proceedings,* Administrative Sciences Association of Canada 9 (1988).

[21] These statements must be appreciated in the light of the diminishing statistical significance that accompanies sample size reduction; each of the stated results is significant.

[22] A. R. Admati, S. Bhattacharya, P. Pfleiderer, and S. A. Ross, "On Timing and Selectivity," *Journal of Finance* 41, no. 3 (July 1986).

[23] H. L. Dhingra, "Portfolio Volatility Adjustment by Canadian Mutual Funds," *Journal of Business Finance and Accounting* 5, no. 4 (1978).

[24] Eric J. Weigel and John H. Ilkiw, "Market Timing Skill in Canada: An Assessment," *Canadian Investment Review* 4, no. 1 (Spring 1991).

have a very specific interpretation of the two terms, where TAA is generally used for both. Swing fund management describes the more traditional practice of switching weights in response to intuitive appraisal of the economy and asset class response. TAA is the result of computerized decision rules and relies on the use of options and other derivative instruments to effect rapid and cost-effective adjustments to the portfolio mix. The study found TAA to be a superior approach, but the authors qualified the reliability of their results due to data limitations.

In further research of the subject, Carlton and Osborn investigated the choice of the base portfolio from which tactical switches were made as a result of timing decisions.[25] They found this factor to be unimportant in assessing managerial ability.

A thorough study of performance attribution by Kryzanowski, Lalancette and To used an intertemporal asset pricing model to investigate returns, risk, and performance in Canadian mutual fund portfolios.[26] They concluded that Canadian managers had significant performance in both stock-picking and timing; unfortunately, in both abilities their results were negative.

## SUMMARY

**1.** A truly passive portfolio strategy entails holding the market index portfolio and a money market fund. Determining the optimal allocation to the market portfolio requires an estimate of its expected return and variance, which in turn suggests delegating some analysis to professionals.

**2.** Active portfolio managers attempt to construct a risky portfolio that maximizes the reward-to-variability (Sharpe) radio.

**3.** The shifting mean and variance of actively managed portfolios make it even harder to assess performance. A typical example is the attempt of portfolio managers to time the market, resulting in ever-changing portfolio betas.

**4.** The appropriate performance measure depends on the role of the portfolio to be evaluated. Appropriate performance measures are as follows:

*a. Sharpe:* when the portfolio represents the entire investment fund.

*b. Appraisal ratio:* when the portfolio represents the active portfolio to be optimally mixed with the passive portfolio.

*c. Treynor:* when the portfolio represents one subportfolio of many.

**5.** Many observations are required to eliminate the effect of the "luck of the draw" from the evaluation process, because portfolio returns commonly are very "noisy."

---

[25] Colin G. Carlton and John C. Osborn, "The Determinants of Balanced Fund Performance," *Canadian Investment Review* 4, no. 1 (Spring 1991).

[26] Lawrence Kryzanowski, Simon Lalancette, and Minh Chau To, "Performance Attribution Using a Multivariate Intertemporal Asset Pricing Model with One State Variable," *Canadian Journal of Administrative Sciences* II, no. 1 (March 1994).

**6.** The value of perfect market timing ability is considerable. The rate of return to a perfect market timer will be uncertain. However, its risk characteristics are not measurable by standard measures of portfolio risk, because perfect timing dominates a passive strategy, providing "good surprises" only.

**7.** With imperfect timing, the value of a timer who attempts to forecast whether stocks will outperform bills is given by the conditional probabilities of the true outcome given the forecasts: $P_1 + P_2 - 1$. Thus, if the value of perfect timing is given by the option value, $C$, then imperfect timing has the value $(P_1 + P_2 - 1)C$.

**8.** A simple way to measure timing and selection success simultaneously is to estimate an expanded SCL, with a quadratic term added to the usual index model.

**9.** The Treynor-Black security selection model envisions that a macroeconomic forecast for market performance is available and that security analysts estimate abnormal expected rates of return, $\alpha$, for various securities. Alpha is the expected rate of return on a security beyond that explained by its beta and the security market line. In the Treynor-Black model, the weight of each analyzed security is proportional to the ratio of its alpha to its nonsystematic risk, $\sigma^2(e)$.

**10.** Once the active portfolio is constructed, its alpha value, nonsystematic risk, and beta can be determined from the properties of the component securities. The optimal risky portfolio, $P$, is then constructed by holding a position in the active portfolio according to the ratio of $\alpha_P$ to $\sigma^2(e_P)$, divided by the analogous ratio for the market index portfolio. Finally, this position is adjusted by the beta of the active portfolio.

**11.** When the overall risky portfolio is constructed using the optimal proportions of the active portfolio and passive portfolio, its performance, as measured by the square of Sharpe's measure, is improved (over that of the passive, market index portfolio) by the amount$[\alpha_A/\sigma(e_A)]^2$.

**12.** The contribution of each security to the overall improvement in the performance of the active portfolio is determined by its degree of mispricing and nonsystematic risk. The contribution of each security to portfolio performance equals $[\alpha_i/\sigma(e_i)]^2$, so that for the optimal risky portfolio,

$$S_P^2 = \left[\frac{E(r_M) - r_f}{\sigma_M^2}\right]^2 + \sum_{i=1}^{n}\left[\frac{\alpha_i}{\sigma(e_i)}\right]^2$$

**13.** Common attribution procedures partition performance improvements to asset allocation, sector selection, and security selection. Performance is assessed by calculating departures of portfolio composition from a benchmark or neutral portfolio.

**14.** Empirical studies of mutual fund performance have not revealed any ability to outperform the market index or time market swings.

## Key Terms

Comparison universe
Sharpe's measure
Treynor's measure
Jensen's measure
Appraisal ratio
Market timing
Passive portfolio
Active portfolio
Selectivity
Bogey portfolio
Survivorship bias
Tactical asset allocation
Swing fund management

## Selected Readings


*The mean-variance based performance evaluation literature is based on early papers by:*

Sharpe, William F. "Mutual Fund Performance." *Journal of Business* 39 (January 1966).

Treynor, Jack L. "How to Rate Management Investment Funds." *Harvard Business Review* 43 (January–February 1966).

Jensen, Michael C. "The Performance of Mutual Funds in the Period 1945–1964." *Journal of Finance,* May 1968.

Jensen, Michael C. "Risk, the Pricing of Capital Assets, and the Evaluation of Investment Portfolios." *Journal of Business,* April 1969.

*A recent review of investment performance is given by a number of notable researchers in the twentieth anniversary edition of the Journal of Portfolio Management including:*

Sharpe, William F. "The Sharpe Ratio." *Journal of Portfolio Management* 21, (Fall 1994).

*The problems that arise when conventional mean-variance measures are calculated in the presence of a shifting-return distribution are treated in:*

Dybvig, Philip H.; and Stephen A. Ross. "Differential Information and Performance Measurement Using a Security Market Line." *Journal of Finance* 40 (June 1985).

*The separation of investment ability into timing versus selection activity derives from:*

Fama, Eugene F. "Components of Investment Performance." *Journal of Finance* 25 (June 1970).

*Key empirical papers on timing versus selection are:*

Admati, A. R.; S. Bhattacharya; P. Pfleiderer; and S. A. Ross. "On Timing and Selectivity." *Journal of Finance* 41, no. 3 (July 1986).

Henriksson, Roy D. "Market Timing and Mutual Fund Performance: An Empirical Investigation." *Journal of Business* 57 (January 1984).

Henriksson, Roy D.; and R. C. Merton. "On Market Timing and Investment Performance. II. Statistical Procedures for Evaluating Forecasting Skills." *Journal of Business* 54 (October 1981).

Kon, S. J.; and F. D. Jen. "The Investment Performance of Mutual Funds: An Empirical Investigation of Timing, Selectivity, and Market Efficiency." *Journal of Business* 52 (April 1979).

Lee, Cheng-Few; and Shafiqur Rahman. "Market Timing, Selectivity, and Mutual Fund Performance: An Empirical Investigation." *Journal of Business* 63, no. 2 (April 1990).

Treynor, Jack, L.; and Kay Mazuy. "Can Mutual Funds Outguess the Market?" *Harvard Business Review* 43 (July–August 1966).

*The valuation of market timing ability using the option pricing framework was developed in:*

Merton, Robert C. "On Market Timing and Investment Performance: An Equilibrium Theory of Value for Market Forecasts." *Journal of Business,* July 1981.

*The Treynor-Black model was laid out in:*

Treynor, Jack and Fischer Black. "How to Use Security Analysis to Improve Portfolio Selection." *Journal of Business,* January 1973.

## Problems

1. The five-year history of annual rates of return in excess of the T-bill rate for two competing stock funds is

| The Bull Fund | The Unicorn Fund |
|---|---|
| −21.7 | −1.3 |
| 28.7 | 15.5 |
| 17.0 | 14.4 |
| 2.9 | −11.9 |
| 28.9 | 25.4 |

   *a.* How would these funds compare in the eye of the risk-neutral potential client?

   *b.* How would these finds compare by Sharpe's measure?

   *c.* If a risk-averse investor (with a coefficient of risk aversion $A = 3$) had to choose one of these funds to mix with T-bills, which fund would be better to choose, and how much should be invested in that fund on the basis of the available data?

2. Based on current dividend yields and expected capital gains, the expected rates of return on portfolios *A* and *B* are .11 percent and .14 percent, respectively. The beta of *A* is 0.8, while that of *B* is 1.5. The T-bill rate is currently .06, while the expected rate of return of the TSE 300 index is .12. The standard deviation of portfolio *A* is .10 annually, that of *B* is .31, and that of the TSE 300 index is .20.

   *a.* If you currently hold a market-index portfolio, would you choose to add either of these portfolios to your holdings? Explain.

   *b.* If instead you could invest *only* in T-bills and *one* of these portfolios, which would you choose?

3. Consider the two (excess return) index-model regression results for stocks *A* and *B*. The risk-free rate over the period was .06, and the market's average return was .14.

   (i) $r_A - r_f = .01 + 1.2(r_M - r_f)$

   $R$-SQR $= .576$

   Residual standard deviation, $\sigma(e_A) = 10.3\%$

   Standard deviation of $r_A - r_f = .261$

(ii) $r_B - r_f = .02 + .8(r_M - r_f)$
$R$-SQR $= .436$
Residual standard deviation, $\sigma(e_B) = 19.1\%$
Standard deviation of $r_B - r_f = .249$

*a.* Calculate the following statistics for each stock:
   i. Alpha
   ii. Appraisal ratio
   iii. Sharpe measure
   iv. Treynor measure

*b.* Which stock is the best choice under the following circumstances?
   i. This is the only risky asset to be held by the investor.
   ii. This stock will be mixed with the rest of the investor's portfolio, currently composed solely of holdings in the market index fund.
   iii. This is one of many stocks that the investor is analyzing to form an actively managed stock portfolio.

**4.** A portfolio manager summarizes the input from the macro and micro forecasters in the following table:

**Micro Forecasts**

| Asset | Expected Return (%) | Beta | Residual Standard Deviation |
|---|---|---|---|
| Stock *A* | 20 | 1.3 | 58 |
| Stock *B* | 18 | 1.8 | 71 |
| Stock *C* | 17 | .7 | 60 |
| Stock *D* | 12 | 1.0 | 55 |

**Macro Forecasts**

| Asset | Expected Return (%) | Standard Deviation |
|---|---|---|
| T-bills | 8 | 0 |
| Passive equity portfolio | 16 | 23 |

*a.* Calculate expected excess returns, alpha values, and residual variances for these stocks.

*b.* Construct the optimal risky portfolio.

*c.* What is Sharpe's measure for the optimal portfolio, and how much of it is contributed by the active portfolio?

*d.* What should be the exact make-up of the complete portfolio for an investor with a coefficient of risk aversion of 2.8?

**5.** Recalculate problem 4 for a portfolio manager who is not allowed to short-sell securities.

*a.* What is the cost of the restriction in terms of Sharpe's measure?

*b.* What is the utility loss to the investor ($A = 2.8$) given his new complete portfolio?

**6.** Evaluate the timing and selection abilities of four managers whose performances are plotted in the following four scatter diagrams:

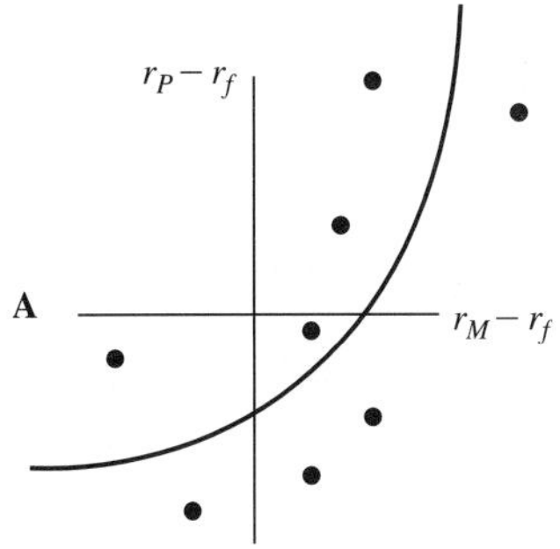


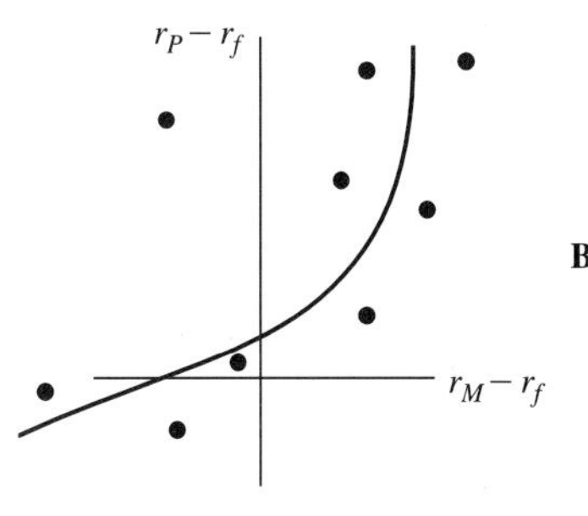


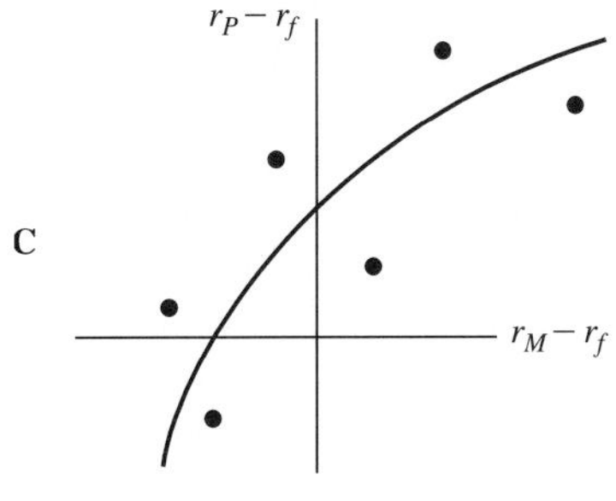


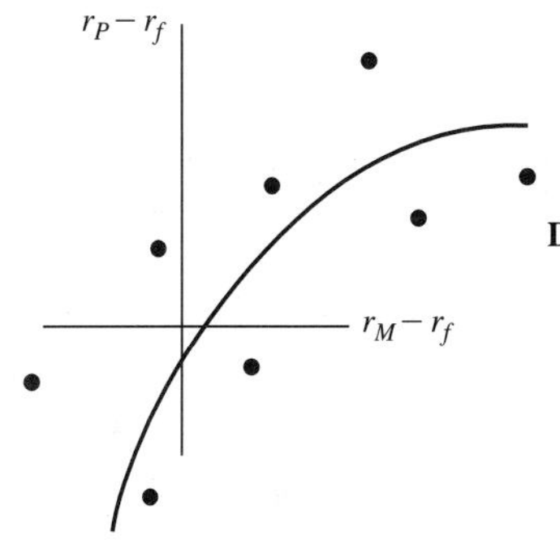


**7.** In scrutinizing the record of two market timers, a fund manager comes up with the following table:

| | | |
|---|---|---|
| Number of months that $r_M > r_f$ | 135 | |
| Correctly predicted by timer *A* | | 78 |
| Correctly predicted by timer *B* | | 86 |
| Number of months that $r_M < r_f$ | 92 | |
| Correctly predicted by timer *A* | | 57 |
| Correctly predicted by timer *B* | | 50 |

What are the conditional probabilities, $P_1$ and $P_2$, and the total ability parameters for timers *A* and *B*?

**8.** A portfolio management house approximates the return-generating process by a two-factor model and uses two-factor portfolios to construct its passive portfolio. The input table that is constructed by the house analysts looks as follows:

**Micro Forecasts**

| Asset | Expected Return (%) | Beta on *M* | Beta on *H* | Residual Standard Deviation (%) |
|---|---|---|---|---|
| Stock *A* | 20 | 1.2 | 1.8 | 58 |
| Stock *B* | 18 | 1.4 | 1.1 | 71 |
| Stock *C* | 17 | .5 | 1.5 | 60 |
| Stock *D* | 12 | 1.0 | .2 | 55 |

**Macro Forecasts**

| Asset | Expected Return (%) | Standard Deviation (%) |
|---|---|---|
| T-bills | 8 | 0 |
| Factor *M* portfolio | 16 | 23 |
| Factor *H* portfolio | 10 | 18 |

The correlation coefficient between the two-factor portfolios is .6.

*a.* What is the optimal passive portfolio?

*b.* By how much is the optimal passive portfolio superior to the single-factor passive portfolio, *M*, in terms of Sharpe's measure?

*c.* Analyze the utility improvement to the $A = 2.8$ investor relative to holding portfolio *M* as the sole risky asset that arises from the expanded macro model of the portfolio manager.

**9.** Construct the optimal active and overall risky portfolio with the data from problem (8) with no restrictions on short sales.

*a.* What is the Sharpe measure of the optimal risky portfolio and what is the contribution of the active portfolio to that measure?

*b.* Compare the risky portfolio to that from problem (4).

*c.* Analyze the utility value of the optimal risky portfolio for the $A = 2.8$ investor. Compare to problem (4).

**10.** Recalculate problem (9) with a short-sale restriction. Compare the results to those from problems (5) and (9).

**11.** Consider the following information regarding the performance of a money manager in a recent month. The table presents the actual return of each sector of the manager's portfolio in column 1, the fraction of the portfolio allocated to each sector in column 2, the benchmark or neutral sector allocations in column 3, and returns of sector indices in column 4.

| | Actual Return | Actual Weight | Benchmark Weight | Index Return |
|---|---|---|---|---|
| Equity | .02 | .70 | .60 | .025 (TSE 300) |
| Bonds | .01 | .20 | .30 | .012 (ScotiaMcLeod) |
| Cash | .005 | .10 | .10 | .005 |

*a.* What was the manager's return for the month? What was her overperformance or underperformance?

*b.* What was the contribution of security selection to relative performance?

*c.* What was the contribution of asset allocation to relative performance? Confirm that the sum of selection and allocation contributions equals her total "excess" return relative to the bogey.

**12.** Conventional wisdom says that one should measure a manager's investment performance over an entire market cycle. What arguments support this contention? What arguments contradict it?

**13.** Does the use of universes of managers with similar investment styles to evaluate relative investment performance overcome the statistical problems associated with instability of beta or total variability?

**14.** During a particular year, the T-bill rate was 6 percent, the market return was 14 percent, and a portfolio manager with beta of .5 realized a return of 10 percent.

*a.* Evaluate the manager based on the portfolio alpha.

*b.* Reconsider your answer to part (a) in view of the Black–Jensen–Scholes finding that the security market line is too flat. Now how do you assess the manager's performance?

**15.** The chairman provides you with the following data, covering one year, concerning the portfolios of two of the fund's equity managers (Firm *A* and Firm *B*). Although the portfolios consist primarily of common stocks, cash reserves are included in the calculation of both portfolio betas and performance. By way of perspective, selected data for the financial markets are included in the following table:

| | Total Return (%) | Beta |
|---|---|---|
| Firm *A* | 24.0 | 1.0 |
| Firm *B* | 30.0 | 1.5 |
| TSE 300 | 21.0 | |
| ScotiaMcLeod Total Bond Index | 31.0 | |
| 91-day Treasury bills | 12.0 | |

*a.* Calculate and compare the risk-adjusted performance of the two firms relative to each other and to the TSE 300.

*b.* Explain *two* reasons the conclusions drawn from this calculation may be misleading.

CFA

**16.** Carl Karl, a portfolio manager for the Alpine Trust Company, has been responsible since 1975 for the City of Alpine's Employee Retirement Plan, a municipal pension fund. Alpine is a growing community, and city services and employee payrolls have expanded in each of the past 10 years. Contributions to the plan in fiscal 1980 exceeded benefit payments by a three-to-one ratio.

The plan's Board of Trustees directed Karl five years ago to invest for total return over the long term. However, as trustees of this highly visible public fund, they cautioned him that volatile or erratic results could cause them embarrassment. They also noted a state statute that mandates that not more than 25 percent of the plan's assets (at cost) be invested in common stocks.

At the annual meeting of the trustees in November 1980, Karl presented the following portfolio and performance report to the board:

Alpine Employee Retirement Plan

| Asset Mix as of 9/30/80 | At Cost (Millions) | | At Market (Millions) | |
|---|---|---|---|---|
| Fixed income assets: | | | | |
| Short-term securities | $ 4.5 | 11.0% | $ 4.5 | 11.4% |
| Long-term bonds and mortgages | 26.5 | 64.7 | 23.5 | 59.5 |
| Common stocks | 10.0 | 24.3 | 11.5 | 29.1 |
| | $41.0 | 100.0% | $39.5 | 100.0% |

Investment Performance

| | Annual Rates of Return For Period Ending 9/30/80 | |
|---|---|---|
| | 5 Years | 1 Year |
| Total Alpine Fund: | | |
| Time-weighted* | 8.2% | 5.2% |
| Dollar-weighted (internal)* | 7.7% | 4.8% |
| Assumed actuarial return | 6.0% | 6.0% |
| U.S. Treasury bills | 7.5% | 11.3% |
| Large sample of pension funds (average 60% equities, 40% fixed income) | 10.1% | 14.3% |
| Common stocks—Alpine Fund | 13.3% | 14.3% |
| Average portfolio beta coefficient | 0.90 | 0.89 |
| Standard & Poor's 500 stock index | 13.8% | 21.1% |
| Fixed income securities—Alpine Fund | 6.7% | 1.0% |
| Salomon Brothers' bond index | 4.0% | −11.4% |

*See Appendix A for an explanation of these terms.

Karl was proud of his performance, and thus he was chagrined when a trustee made the following critical observations:

*a.* "Our one-year results were terrible, and it's what you've done for us lately that counts most."

*b.* "Our total fund performance was clearly inferior compared to the large sample of other pension funds for the last five years. What else could this reflect except poor management judgment?"

*c.* "Our common stock performance was especially poor for the five-year period."

*d.* "Why bother to compare your returns to the return from Treasury bills and the actuarial assumption rate? What your competition could have earned for us or how we would have fared if invested in a passive index (which doesn't charge a fee) are the only relevant measures of performance."

*e.* "Who cares about time-weighted return? If it can't pay pensions, what good is it?"

Appraise the merits of each of these statements and give counterarguments that Mr. Karl can use.

**17.** The Retired Fund is an open-ended mutual fund composed of $500 million in U.S. bonds and U.S. Treasury bills. This fund has had a portfolio duration (including T-bills) of between three and nine years. Retired has shown first-quartile performance over the past five years, as measured by an independent fixed-income measurement service. However, the directors of the fund would like to measure the market timing skill of the fund's sole bond investment manager. An external consulting firm has suggested the following three methods:

*I.* Method I examines the value of the bond portfolio at the beginning of every year and then calculates the return that would have been achieved had that same portfolio been held throughout the year. This return would then be compared with the return actually obtained by the fund.

*II.* Method II calculates the average weighting of the portfolio in bonds and T-bills for each year. Instead of using the actual bond portfolio, the return on a long-bond market index and T-bill index would be used. For example, if the portfolio on average was 65 percent in bonds and 35 percent in T-bills, the annual return on a portfolio invested 65 percent in a long-bond index and 35 percent in T-bills would be calculated. This return is compared with the annual return that would have been generated using the indices and the manager's actual bond/T-bill weighting for each quarter of the year.

*III.* Method III examines the net bond purchase activity (market value of purchases less sales) for each quarter of the year. If net purchases were positive (negative) in any quarter, the performance of the bonds would be evaluated until the net purchase activity became negative (positive). Positive (negative) net purchases would be viewed as a bullish (bearish) view taken by the manager. The correctness of this view would be measured.

Critique *each* method with regard to market timing measurement problems.

**18.** A plan sponsor with a portfolio manager who invests in small-capitalization, high-growth stocks should have the plan sponsor's performance measured against which *one* of the following?

*a.* S&P 500 index.

*b.* Wilshire 5000 index

*c.* Dow Jones Industrial Average.

*d.* S&P 400 index.

---

## Appendix 12A: Measuring Investment Returns

We already have defined the holding period return as the difference between the end of period and initial values plus interim cash flows (dividends or interest), divided by the initial value. This concept is clear for a single period, as we see from the simple example that follows. Suppose you purchase today for \$50 a stock paying a \$2 dividend; if in one year you sell it for \$53, your rate of return is simply the gain (\$53 − \$50), plus a dividend of \$2 divided by cost (\$50). Then (3 + 2)/50 gives a return of 10 percent. The financial mathematics technique of internal rate of return yields the same result. Equating the initial investment to the end-of-year proceeds of (\$53 + \$2) discounted by $1 + r$ (the unknown rate) gives the solution $r = .10$ again.

### Dollar-Weighted Returns versus Time-Weighted Returns

When we consider investments over a period during which cash has been added to or withdrawn from the portfolio, measuring the rate of return becomes more difficult. To continue our example, suppose that you were to purchase a second share of the same stock at the end of the first year and hold both shares until the end of year 2, at which point you sell each share for \$54.

Total cash outlays are

| Time | Outlay |
|---|---|
| 0 | \$50 to purchase first share |
| 1 | \$53 to purchase second share a year later |

Proceeds are

| Time | Proceeds |
|---|---|
| 1 | \$2 dividend from initially purchased share |
| 2 | \$4 dividend from the 2 shares held in the second year, plus \$108 received from selling both shares at \$54 each |

Using the discounted cash flow (DCF) approach, we can solve the average return over the two years by equating the present values of the cash inflows and outflows:

$$50 + \frac{53}{1 + r} = \frac{2}{1 + r} + \frac{112}{(1 + r)^2}$$

resulting in $r = 7.117$ percent.

This value is called the **dollar-weighted rate of return** on the investment. It is "dollar weighted" because the stock's performance in the second year, when two shares of stock are held, has a greater influence on the average overall return than the first-year return, when only one share is held.

This investment approach, buying an equal amount of shares each period with new cash, is not unrealistic. A popular variant, in fact, is called **dollar-cost averaging.** Instead of buying a second share, you invest another $50 after one year. Notice the effect of this is to buy fewer shares at a higher price, or more shares at a lower price if the price should fall. In the example above, you only purchase 1/1.06 shares and receive that portion of the dividend. Skipping the arithmetic details, we find that $r$ rises to 7.145 percent with the revised cash flows. This strategy for investing ignores inflation and increased ability to invest, but it can be practised on a monthly basis, with periodic increases in the averaging quantity.

An alternative to the internal or dollar-weighted return is the **time-weighted return.** This method ignores the number of shares of stock held in each period. The stock return in the first year was 10 percent. (A $50 purchase provided $2 in dividends and $3 in capital gains.) In the second year, the stock had a starting value of $53 and sold at year-end for $54, for a total one-period rate of return of $3 ($2 dividend plus $1 capital gain) divided by $53 (the stock price at the start of the second year), or 5.66 percent. The time-weighted rate of return is the average of 10 percent and 5.66 percent, which is 7.83 percent. This average return considers only the period-by-period returns without regard to the amounts invested in the stock in each period.

Note that the dollar-weighted return is less than the time-weighted return in this example. The reason is that the stock fared relatively poorly in the second year, when the investor was holding more shares. The greater weight that the dollar-weighted average places on the second-year return results in a lower measure of investment performance. In general, dollar- and time-weighted returns will differ, and the difference can be positive or negative depending on the configuration of period returns and portfolio composition.

Which measure of performance is superior? They both have their place, depending on what the investment pattern is, and that depends upon who is doing the investing. In the money management industry, portfolio managers are subject to the withdrawal and contribution wishes of their clients. Specifically in open-ended funds, the total asset value is based both on investor net contributions and past performance; calculation of net asset value (NAV) per unit is the basis for redemptions or purchases, which is a result of the portfolio performance since the last calculation. Total portfolio value is adjusted by net contributions and net increases in component asset prices; for closed-end funds, only the latter is relevant. The same two effects occur in the case of pension fund management, as contributions are made and benefits paid. Consequently, the money management industry uses time-weighted returns for performance evaluation.

**CONCEPT CHECK** Question 12A.1. Shares of XYZ Corp. pay a \$2 dividend at the end of every year on December 31. An investor buys two shares of the stock on January 1 at a price of \$20 each, sells one of those shares for \$22 a year later on the next January 1, and sells the second share an additional year later for \$19. Find the time- and dollar-weighted rates of return on the two-year investment.

## Arithmetic Averaging versus Geometric Averaging

Our example took the arithmetic average of the two annual returns for the time-weighted average of 7.83 percent. The principle of compounding lends itself to the computation of a geometric average instead. If stock had been purchased to yield the combined returns of growth with dividend reinvestment, the factors of 1.10 and 1.0566 lead to a compound growth rate of

$$(1 + r_G)^2 = (1.10)(1.0566)$$

Taking the square root of each side gives the result. In general terms, for an $n$-period investment, the geometric average rate of return is given by

$$1 + r_G = [(1 + r_1)(1 + r_2) \ldots (1 + r_n)]^{1/n} \qquad \textbf{(12A.1)}$$

where $r_t$ is the return in each time period. By contrast, the arithmetic average rate of return is given by

$$r_G = (r_1 + r_2 + \ldots + r_n) \times 1/n \qquad \textbf{(12A.2)}$$

The geometric average return in this example, 7.81 percent, is slightly less than the arithmetic average return, 7.83 percent. This is a general property: Geometric averages never exceed arithmetic averages, and the difference between the two becomes greater as the variability of period-by-period returns becomes greater. The general rule when returns are expressed as decimals, is

$$r_G \approx r_A - \sigma^2/2 \qquad \textbf{(12A.3)}$$

where $\sigma^2$ is the variance of returns. Equation 12A.3 is exact when the returns are normally distributed.

For example, consider Table 12A.1, which presents arithmetic and geometric returns over the period 1949–1987 for a variety of investments. The arithmetic averages all exceed the geometric averages, and the difference is greatest for stocks of small firms, where annual returns exhibit the greatest standard deviation. Indeed, the difference between the two averages falls to zero only when there is no variation in yearly returns, although the table indicates that, by the time the standard deviation falls to a level characteristic of T-bills, the difference is quite small.

Here is another return question. In the case of time-weighted averages, which is the superior measure of investment performance, the arithmetic average or the geometric average? The geometric average has considerable appeal because it rep-

**Table 12A.1** Selected Canadian Annual Returns by Investment Class, 1949–1987

| | | | Arithmetic Returns | | |
|---|---|---|---|---|---|
| | **Geometric Average** | **Arithmetic Average** | **Maximum** | **Minimum** | **Standard Deviation** |
| **Equities (Value Weighted)** | | | | | |
| Small firms | 15.08 | 18.93 | 46.41 | −27.85 | 19.61 |
| Large firms | 11.07 | 12.45 | 51.40 | −26.78 | 17.59 |
| All firms | 11.15 | 12.50 | 51.30 | −28.29 | 17.82 |
| **Equities (Equal Weighted)** | | | | | |
| Small firms | 20.23 | 23.83 | 80.72 | −32.72 | 29.70 |
| Large firms | 12.22 | 13.93 | 46.41 | −27.85 | 19.60 |
| All firms | 15.51 | 18.62 | 59.30 | −27.35 | 23.83 |
| Long-term industrial bonds | 6.22 | 6.62 | 43.36 | −7.60 | 9.69 |
| Long-term Canada bonds | 5.22 | 5.64 | 45.81 | −5.82 | 10.17 |
| Treasury bills | 5.90 | 5.98 | 19.09 | 0.51 | 4.16 |
| Inflation | 4.69 | 4.76 | 12.32 | −1.73 | 3.76 |

Adapted from James E. Hatch and Robert W. White, *Canadian Stocks, Bonds, Bills, and Inflation: 1950–1987* (Charlottesville, Va.: The Financial Analysts Research Foundation, 1988). Reprinted by permission.

resents exactly the constant rate of return we would have needed to earn in each year to match actual performance over some past investment period. It is an excellent measure of *past* performance. However, if our focus is on future performance, then the arithmetic average is the statistic of interest because it is an unbiased estimate of the portfolio's expected future return (assuming, of course, that the expected return does not change over time). In contrast, because the geometric return over a sample period is always less than the arithmetic mean, it constitutes a downward-biased estimator of the stock's expected return in any future year.

To illustrate this concept, suppose that in any period a stock will either double in value ($r = 100$ percent) with probability of .5, or halve in value ($r = -50$ percent) with probability .5. The table following illustrates these outcomes:

| Investment Outcome | Final Value of Each Dollar Invested | One-Year Rate of Return |
|---|---|---|
| Double | $2 | 100% |
| Halve | $0.50 | −50% |

Suppose that the stock's performance over a two-year period is characteristic of the probability distribution, doubling in one year, and halving in the other. The stock's price ends up exactly where it started, and the geometric average annual return is zero:

$$1 + r_G = [(1 + r_1)(1 + r_2)]^{1/2}$$
$$= [(1 + 1)(1 - .50)]^{1/2}$$
$$= 1$$

so that

$$r_G = 0$$

which confirms that a zero year-by-year return would have replicated the total return earned on the stock.

The expected annual future rate of return on the stock, however, is *not* zero: it is the arithmetic average of 100 percent and −50 percent: (100 − 50)/2 = 25 percent. To confirm this, note that there are two equally likely outcomes for each dollar invested: either a gain of \$1 (when $r$ = 100 percent) or a loss of \$.50 (when $r$ = −50 percent). The expected profit is (\$1 − \$.50)/2 = \$.25, for a 25 percent expected rate of return. The profit in the good year more than offsets the loss in the bad year, despite the fact that the geometric return is zero. The arithmetic average return thus provides the best guide to expected future returns from an investment.

You might question the assumption of a pattern of doubling or halving with equal probability. Why not plus or minus 50 percent, symmetrically? The answer is that plus 100 and minus 50 percent *is* symmetric, in a multiplicative or geometric sense. In fact, the prospects of plus or minus the same percent should not be considered equal; one hundred percent is double or nothing, and nothing means you are out. Bringing utilities into the picture, you might be indifferent between plus 100 and minus 50 percent. The arithmetic average, your expected gain, is the wealth you will have and it will have a certain utility; but that is different from your expected utility for the gamble.

This argument carries forward into multiperiod investments. Consider, for example, all the possible outcomes over a two-year period:

| Investment Outcome | Final Value of Each Dollar Invested | Total Return over Two Years |
|---|---|---|
| Double, double | \$4 | 300% |
| Double, halve | \$1 | 0 |
| Halve, double | \$1 | 0 |
| Halve, halve | \$.25 | −75% |

The expected final value of each dollar invested is (4 + 1 + 1 + .25)/4 = \$1.5625 for two years, again indicating an average rate of return of 25 percent per year, equal to the arithmetic average. Note that an investment yielding 25 percent per year with certainty will yield the same final compounded value as the expected final value of this investment, as $1.25^2 = 1.5625$. The arithmetic average return on the stock is [300 + 0 + 0 + (−75)]/4 = 56.25 percent per two years, for an effective annual return of 25 percent, that is, $1.5625^{1/2} - 1$. In contrast, the geometric mean return is zero:

$$[(1 + 3)(1 + 0)(1 + 0)(1 - .75)]^{1/4} = 1.0$$

Again, the arithmetic average is the better guide to *future* performance.

---

**CONCEPT CHECK** Question 12A.2. Suppose that a stock now selling for $100 will either increase in value by 15 percent by year-end with probability .5 or fall in value by 5 percent with probability .5. The stock pays no dividends.

*a.* What are the geometric and arithmetic mean returns on the stock?
*b.* What is the expected end-of-year value of the share?
*c.* Which measure of expected return is superior?

---

### Appendix 12A: Key Terms

Dollar-weighted rate of return
Dollar-cost averaging
Time-weighted return

### Appendix 12A: Problems

**1.** Consider the rate of return of stocks ABC and XYZ.

| Year | $r_{ABC}$ | $r_{XYZ}$ |
|---|---|---|
| 1 | .20 | .30 |
| 2 | .10 | .10 |
| 3 | .14 | .18 |
| 4 | .05 | .00 |
| 5 | .01 | −.08 |

*a.* Calculate the arithmetic average return on these stocks over the sample period.
*b.* Which stock has greater dispersion around the mean?
*c.* Calculate the geometric average returns of each stock. What do you conclude?
*d.* If you were equally likely to earn a return of 20 percent, 10 percent, 14 percent, 5 percent, or 1 percent in each of the five annual returns for stock ABC, what would be your expected rate of return? What if the five outcomes were those of stock XYZ?

**2.** XYZ stock price and dividend history are as follows:

| Year | Beginning of Year Price | Dividend Paid at Year-End |
|---|---|---|
| 1991 | $100 | $4 |
| 1992 | $110 | $4 |
| 1993 | $ 90 | $4 |
| 1994 | $ 95 | $4 |

An investor buys three shares of XYZ at the beginning of 1991, buys another two shares at the beginning of 1992, sells one share at the beginning of 1993, and sells all four remaining shares at the beginning of 1994.

*a.* What are the arithmetic and geometric average time-weighted rates of return for the investor?

*b.* What is the dollar-weighted rate of return? Hint: Carefully prepare a chart of cash flows for the *four* dates corresponding to the turn of the year for January 1, 1991, to December 31, 1994. If your calculator cannot calculate internal rate of return, you will have to use trial and error.

CFA

**3.** In measuring the comparative performance of different fund managers, the preferred method of calculating rate of return is:

*a.* Internal
*b.* Time-weighted
*c.* Dollar-weighted
*d.* Income

**4.** Which *one* of the following is a valid benchmark against which a portfolio's performance can be measured over a given time period?

*a.* The portfolio's dollar-weighted rate of return.
*b.* The portfolio's time-weighted rate of return.
*c.* The portfolio manager's "normal" portfolio.
*d.* The average beta of the portfolio.

**5.** Assume you invested in an asset for two years. The first year you earned a 15 percent return, and the second year you earned a *negative* 10 percent return. What was your annual geometric return?

*a.* 1.7 percent
*b.* 2.5 percent
*c.* 3.5 percent
*d.* 5.0 percent

CFA

**6.** Assume you purchased a rental property for $50,000 and sold it one year later for $55,000 (there was no mortgage on the property). At the time of the sale, you paid $2,000 in commissions and $600 in taxes. If you received $6,000 in rental income (all of it received at the end of the year), what annual rate of return did you earn?

*a.* 15.3 percent
*b.* 15.9 percent
*c.* 16.8 percent
*d.* 17.1 percent

**7.** A portfolio of stocks generates a $-9$ percent return in 1990, a 23 percent return in 1991, and a 17 percent return in 1992. The annualized return (geometric mean) for the entire period is:

*a.* 7.2 percent.
*b.* 9.4 percent.
*c.* 10.3 percent.
*d.* None of the above.

**8.** A two-year investment of $2,000 results in a return of $150 at the end of the first year and a return of $150 at the end of the second year, in addition to the return of the original investment. The internal rate of return on the investment is:

*a.* 6.4 percent.
*b.* 7.5 percent.
*c.* 15.0 percent.
*d.* None of the above.

**9.** In measuring the performance of a portfolio, the time-weighted rate of return is superior to the dollar-weighted rate of return because:

*a.* When the rate of return varies, the time-weighted return is higher.
*b.* The dollar-weighted return assumes all portfolio deposits are made on day 1.
*c.* The dollar-weighted return can only be estimated.
*d.* The time-weighted return is unaffected by the timing of portfolio contributions and withdrawals.

## APPENDIX 12B: OPTION PRICING OF TIMING ABILITY

Merton's approach to analyzing the pattern of returns to the perfect market timer was to recognize that perfect foresight is equivalent to holding a call option on the equity portfolio. We shall explore options in depth in Part VII, but for now we can identify a call option as a right, but not an obligation, to acquire an asset at a predetermined "exercise" price. The perfect timer has the option here to invest 100 percent in either the safe asset or the equity portfolio, whichever will yield the higher return. This is shown in Figure 12B.1. The rate of return is bounded from below by $r_f$.

To see the value of information as an option, suppose that the market index currently is at $S_0$, and that a call option on the index has an exercise price of $X = S_0(1 + r_f)$. If the market outperforms bills over the coming period, $S_T$ will exceed $X$, whereas it will be less than $X$ otherwise. Now look at the payoff to a portfolio consisting of this option and $S_0$ dollars invested in bills:

| | **Payoff to Portfolio** | |
|---|---|---|
| | $S_T < X$ | $S_T \geq X$ |
| Bills: | $S_0(1 + r_f)$ | $S_0(1 + r_f)$ |
| Option: | 0 | $S_T - X$ |
| Total | $S_0(1 + r_f)$ | $S_T$ |

The portfolio pays the risk-free return when the market is bearish (that is, the market return is less than the risk-free rate) and pays the market return when the market is bullish and beats bills. Such a portfolio is a perfect market timer. Consequently, we can measure the value of perfect ability as the value of the call

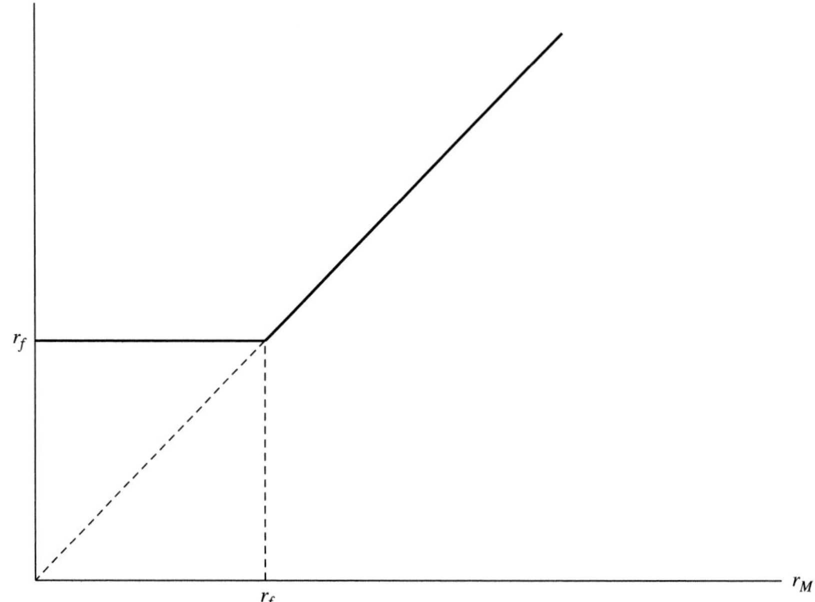


**Figure 12B.1**
Rate of return of a perfect market timer.

option, because a call enables the investor to earn the market return only when it exceeds $r_f$.

This insight lets Merton value timing ability using the theory of option valuation, and from this we calculate our fair charge for timing. Each month, we calculate the option value based on the current $s_0$ and $r_f$, this value is then subtracted from the portfolio payoff, which is converted to a rate of return to determine the monthly statistics.

## Appendix 12C: Multifactor Models and Active Portfolio Management

Perhaps in the foreseeable future a multifactor structure of security returns will be developed and accepted as conventional wisdom. So far, our analytical framework for active portfolio management seems to rest on the validity of the index model, that is, on a single-factor security model. Despite this appearance, a multifactor structure will not affect the construction of the active portfolio because the entire Treynor–Black analysis focuses on the residuals of the index model. If we were to replace the one-factor model with a multifactor model, we would continue to form the active portfolio by calculating each security's alpha relative to its fair return (give its betas on *all* factors) and again would combine the active portfolio with the portfolio that would be formed in the absence of security analysis. The multifactor framework, however, does raise several new issues in portfolio management.

You saw in Chapter 9 how the index model simplifies the construction of the input list necessary for portfolio optimization programs. If

$$r_i - r_f = \alpha_i + \beta_i(r_M - r_f) + e_i$$

adequately describes the security market, then the variance of any asset is the sum of systematic and nonsystematic risk: $\sigma^2(r_i) = \beta_i^2\sigma_M^2 + \sigma^2(e_i)$, and the covariance between any two assets is $\beta_i\beta_j\sigma_M^2$.

How do we generalize this rule to use in a multifactor model? To simplify, let us consider a two-factor world, and let us call the two-factor portfolios *M* and *H*. Then we generalize the index model to

$$\begin{aligned} r_i - r_f &= \beta_{iM}(r_M - r_f) + \beta_{iH}(r_H - r_f) + \alpha_i + e_i \\ &= r_\beta + e_i \end{aligned} \tag{12C.1}$$

$\beta_M$ and $\beta_H$ are the betas of the security relative to portfolios *M* and *H*. Given the rates of return on the factor portfolios, $r_M$ and $r_H$, the fair excess rate of return over $r_f$ on a security is denoted $r_\beta$ and its expected abnormal return is $\alpha_i$.

How can we use equation 12C.1 to form optimal portfolios? Suppose that investors simply wish to maximize the Sharpe measures of their portfolios. The factor structure of equation 12C.1 can be used to generate the inputs for the Markowitz portfolio selection algorithm. The variance and covariance estimates are now more complex, however:

$$\begin{aligned} \sigma^2(r_i) &= \beta_{iM}^2\sigma_M^2 + \beta_{iH}^2\sigma_H^2 + 2\beta_{iM}\beta_{iH}\text{Cov}(r_M,r_H) + \sigma^2(e_i) \\ \text{Cov}(r_i,r_j) &= \beta_{iM}\beta_{jM}\sigma_M^2 + \beta_{iH}\beta_{jH}\sigma_H^2 + (\beta_{iM}\beta_{jH} + \beta_{jM}\beta_{iH})\text{Cov}(r_M,r_H) \end{aligned}$$

Nevertheless, the informational economy of the factor model still is valuable, because we can estimate a covariance matrix for an *n*-security portfolio from:

*n* estimates of $\beta_{iM}$
*n* estimates of $\beta_{iH}$
*n* estimates of $\sigma^2(e_i)$
1 estimate of $\sigma_M^2$
1 estimate of $\sigma_H^2$

rather than $n(n + 1)/2$ separate variance and covariance estimates. Thus, the factor structure continues to simplify portfolio construction issues.

The factor structure also suggests an efficient method to allocate research effort. Analysts can specialize in forecasting means and variances of different factor portfolios. Having established factor betas, they can form a covariance matrix to be used together with expected security returns generated by the CAPM or APT to construct an optimal passive risky portfolio. If active analysis of individual stocks also is attempted, the procedure of constructing the optimal active portfolio and its optimal combination with the passive portfolio is identical to that followed in the single-factor case.

It is likely, however, that the factor structure of the market has hedging implications. This means that clients will be willing to accept an inferior Sharpe measure (in terms of dollar returns) to maintain a risky portfolio that has the desired hedge qualities. Portfolio optimization for these investors obviously is more complicated, requiring specific information on client preferences. The portfolio manager will not be able to satisfy diverse clients with one portfolio.

In the case of the multifactor market, even passive investors (meaning those who accept market prices as "fair") need to do a considerable amount of work. They need forecasts of the expected return and volatility of each factor return, and they need to determine the appropriate weights on each factor portfolio to maximize their expected utility. Such a process is straightforward in principle, but quickly becomes analytically demanding.

*Chapter 13*

# International Investing

**ALTHOUGH IT IS COMMON IN CANADA TO USE THE TSE 300 AS THE MARKET INDEX PORTFOLIO, SUCH PRACTICE IS IN SOME WAYS INAPPROPRIATE.** Equities actually comprise barely 10 percent of total Canadian wealth and a far smaller percentage of world wealth. In one sense, international investing may be viewed as no more than a straightforward generalization of our earlier treatment of portfolio selection with a larger menu of assets from which to construct a portfolio. One faces similar issues of diversification, security analysis, security selection, and asset allocation. On the other hand, international investments pose some problems not encountered in domestic markets. Among these are the presence of exchange rate risk, restrictions on capital flows across national boundaries, an added dimension of political risk and country-specific regulations, and different accounting practices in different countries.

In this chapter we will see the importance of world markets and the benefits of diversification for risk-return trade-offs; we also introduce the possibilities for making international investments. We then examine the effect of currency fluctuations on returns. Following this, we review the processes of appraising international investing, including the identification of factors underlying those returns and the determination of success in selecting areas and assets for portfolios in the context of active, rather than passive, international investment. Finally, we examine the issue of segmentation of markets, which underlies the expected benefits of diversification across national or regional borders.

## 13.1 International Investments

### The World Market Portfolio

Canadian investors have shown themselves to be far less prone than their American neighbours to limit their investment horizons to the national boundaries. The presence and influence of foreign investors and markets serve to focus Canadian attention on alternatives to domestic investment; while the proximity of the United States makes it the dominant figure in our international perspective, European and Far Eastern nations already and increasingly are receiving substantial attention from investors. The internationalization of trade, beyond the traditional markets for major corporations such as Alcan, Inco, and the banks, implies that Canadians can and must diversify their portfolio holdings into foreign assets in order to hedge foreign currency and economic fluctuations.

The portfolio holdings of an investor in any country should serve to protect his or her future consumption opportunities, given the prices faced domestically; but these prices are affected by foreign economic conditions and pricing relative to the proportion that foreign trade represents in the domestic economy. Thus in the United States, where domestic production and consumption represent the vast majority of economic activity, foreign economic events have had less and later effect on domestic conditions; in contrast, Canadian conditions react swiftly and directly to external events, particularly in the United States. Canadians, therefore, have far more need to link themselves to foreign financial markets in order to hedge their portfolios and their consumption opportunities from adverse international events.

While Canadians, by nature, may be more inclined to underestimate the size of their securities markets rather than the opposite, these markets in fact represent only a small fraction of the world markets. Tables 13.1 and 13.2 present, respectively, the comparative sizes of world equity and bond markets.[1] The Canadian market values in 1993 and 1994 represented about 2.4 percent in both cases; that left about $28 trillion (U.S.) of foreign securities for investment opportunities. As we noted in Chapter 1, Canadians can easily invest in U.S. securities; but these represented only some 37 percent of the equity markets and 46 percent of the bond markets. (Note that Table 13.2 refers to bonds denominated in U.S. dollars rather than issued by U.S. debtors.) Furthermore, we shall see that for Canadian portfolios, U.S. securities offer little in the way of diversification, which is the key opportunity to be exploited in considering foreign securities.

[1] Another $1.6 trillion can be added by emerging markets including Taiwan, Korea, Mexico, Malaysia, Thailand, and South Africa.

**Table 13.1** Comparative Sizes of World Equity Markets, 1994*

| Area or Country | $ Billion | % of Total |
|---|---|---|
| **Europe** | 3,275 | 25.9 |
| United Kingdom | 1,145 | 9.1 |
| West Germany | 477 | 3.8 |
| France | 444 | 3.5 |
| Switzerland | 284 | 2.2 |
| Netherlands | 224 | 1.8 |
| Italy | 177 | 1.4 |
| Spain | 151 | 1.2 |
| Sweden | 118 | 0.9 |
| Belgium | 84 | 0.7 |
| Other countries | 171 | 1.4 |
| **Pacific Area** | 4,435 | 35.1 |
| Japan | 3,624 | 28.7 |
| Australia | 212 | 1.7 |
| Singapore | 139 | 1.1 |
| Hong Kong | 241 | 1.9 |
| **North America** | 4,914 | 38.9 |
| United States | 4,626 | 36.6 |
| Canada | 288 | 2.3 |
| **Developed Markets** | **12,640** | **100.0** |

*Because of rounding error, column sums may not equal totals.

From Bruno Solnik, *International Investments,* 3rd edition, Exhibit 6.1 © 1996 Addison-Wesley Publishing Company, Inc. Reprinted by permission of Addison-Wesley Longman Publishing Company, Inc.

## International Diversification

From our discussion of the power of diversification in Chapter 7, we know that adding to a portfolio assets that are not perfectly correlated will improve the best attainable reward-to-volatility ratio. Given increasing globalization, might not foreign securities provide a feasible way to extend diversification?

Figure 7.2 revealed the results of a classic study on U.S. equities that showed the benefits of diversification. The results of a subsequent study are summarized in Figure 13.1 which demonstrates the marked reduction in risk that can be achieved by including foreign, as well as U.S., stocks in a portfolio. The graph presents the standard deviation of equally weighted portfolios of various sizes as a percentage of the average standard deviation of a one-stock portfolio. For example, a value of 20 means that the diversified portfolio has only 20 percent of the standard deviation of a typical stock. The graphs in Figure 13.1 are presented in terms of the standard deviation of the dollar-denominated returns to make them relevant to U.S. investors. Clearly, given the high correlation between U.S. and

**Table 13.2** Size of Major Bond Markets at Year End, 1993*

| Bond Market | Total Publicly Issued | Public Issues in All Markets (%) |
|---|---|---|
| U.S. dollar | $ 7,547.2 | 46.3 |
| Japanese yen | 3,044.0 | 18.7 |
| Deutsche mark | 1,590.8 | 9.8 |
| Italian lira | 780.7 | 4.8 |
| French franc | 748.6 | 4.6 |
| U.K. pound sterling | 436.6 | 2.7 |
| Canadian dollar | 393.0 | 2.4 |
| Belgian franc | 301.3 | 1.8 |
| Dutch guilder | 227.5 | 1.4 |
| Danish krone | 227.4 | 1.4 |
| Swiss franc | 200.7 | 1.2 |
| Swedish krona | 186.4 | 1.1 |
| ECU | 144.6 | 0.9 |
| Spanish peseta | 144.4 | 0.9 |
| Australian dollar | 106.1 | 0.7 |
| Others | 227.3 | 1.4 |
| **Total** | **$16,306.5** | **100.0** |

*Nominal value outstanding, billions of U.S. dollars equivalent.

Modified from Bruno Solnik, *International Investments* 3rd edition, Exhibit 9.1 © 1996 Addison-Wesley Publishing Company, Inc. Reprinted by permission of Addison-Wesley Longman Publishing Company, Inc.

Canadian stocks, similar improvement can be achieved by adding foreign stocks to a Canadian portfolio.

Figure 13.1 demonstrates that rational investors should invest across borders. Adding international investments to national investments enhances the power of portfolio diversification. Table 13.3 presents results from a study of equity returns showing that, although the correlation coefficients between the Canadian stock index and stock index portfolios of other large industrialized economies are positive, they are much smaller than 1. While the correlation between the Canadian and U.S. indexes is 0.72, for European markets, it is typically around 0.45 and for other markets, below 0.30 (earlier, more extensive data show this pattern more clearly). In contrast, correlation coefficients between diversified U.S. portfolios—with 40 to 50 securities, for example—typically exceed 0.9. The imperfect correlation across national boundaries allows for the improvement in diversification potential that shows up in Figure 13.1.

**CONCEPT CHECK** Question 1. What would Figure 13.1 look like if we next introduced the possibility of diversifying into bond investments in addition to foreign equity?

A different perspective on opportunities for international diversification appears in Figure 13.2. Here we examine risk-return opportunities offered by

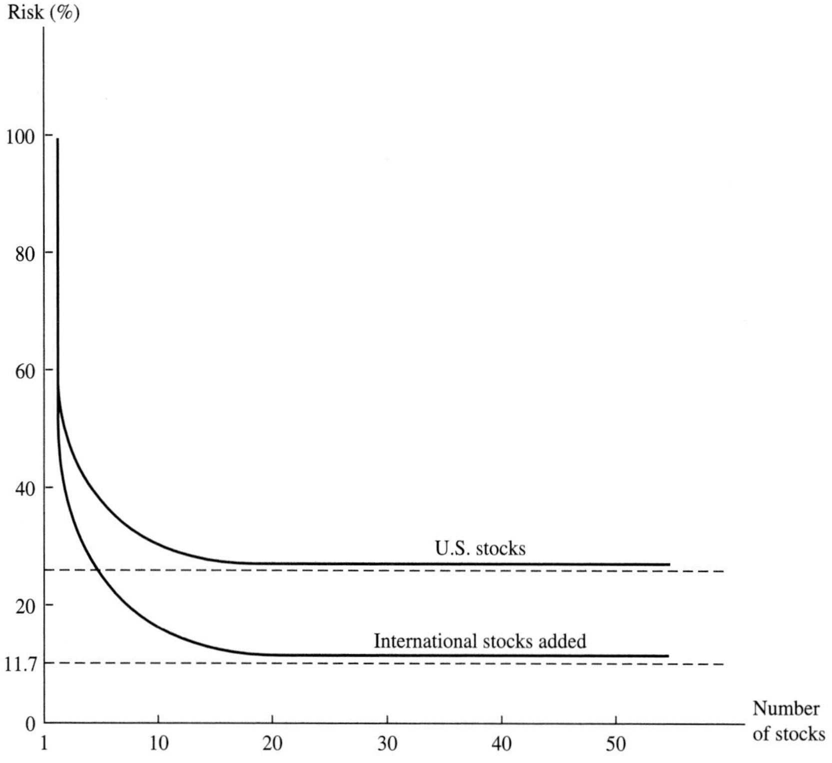


**Figure 13.1** International diversification.

Modified from B. Solnik, "Lessons for International Asset Allocation" *Financial Analysts Journal,* July 1994. Reprinted by permission.

national equity indices, alone and combined into portfolios. For example, we see that world stocks plotted to the northwest of U.S. stocks for this 10-year period, offering higher average return and lower risk than U.S. stocks alone. (All returns are calculated in terms of U.S. dollars.) Of course, the efficient frontier generated from these assets offers the best possible risk-return pairs; these are vastly superior to the risk-return profile of U.S. or Canadian stocks alone. A more recent study (1979–1989) by Marmer is summarized in Figure 13.3, which shows the improvement in the efficient frontier for portfolios of bills, bonds, and stocks when international assets are added to Canadian assets.

Investing in foreign markets is difficult for individual investors, due to institutional restrictions, inhibited access to the markets, and lack of information. Consequently, there has been a recent increase in the creation of both regional and single-country mutual funds; these include the Far East, Germany, Spain, Mexico, and Thailand as examples of markets in different stages of development. While these funds tend to be listed on the TSE or NYSE as closed-end funds, ordinary open-ended funds are another possibility. A study by Chua and Woodward[2] has examined the opportunities for diversification by Canadian investors

[2] J. H. Chua and R. S. Woodward, "International Diversification for Small Canadian Investors through Mutual Funds," *Canadian Journal of Administrative Sciences,* September 1987.

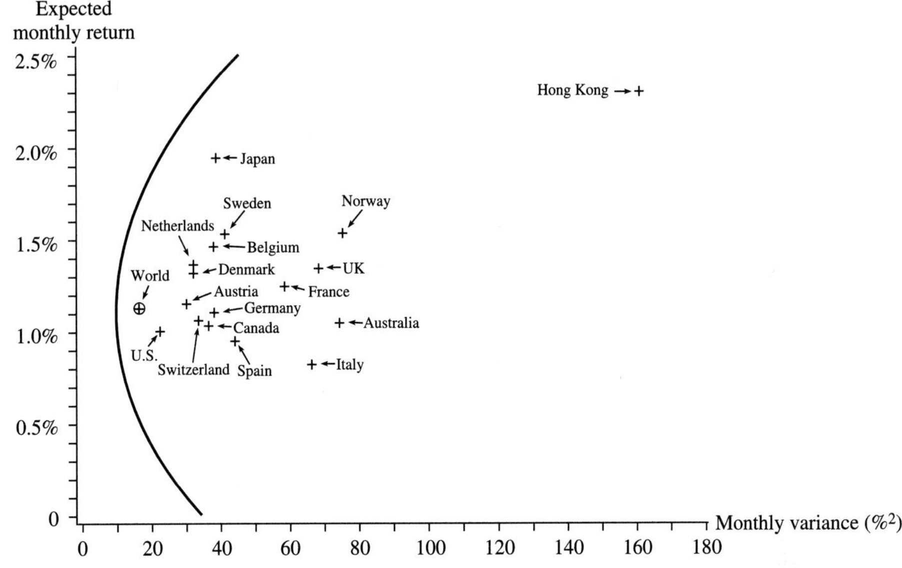


**Figure 13.2**
The minimum variance frontier. The minimum variance frontier is calculated from the unconditional means, variances, and convariances of 17 country returns. The returns are in U.S. dollars and are from Morgan Stanley Capital International. The data are from 1970:2–1989:5 (232 observations).

From Campbell R. Harvey, "The World Price of Covariance Risk," *Journal of Finance* 46 (March 1991) pp. 111–58. Reprinted by permission.

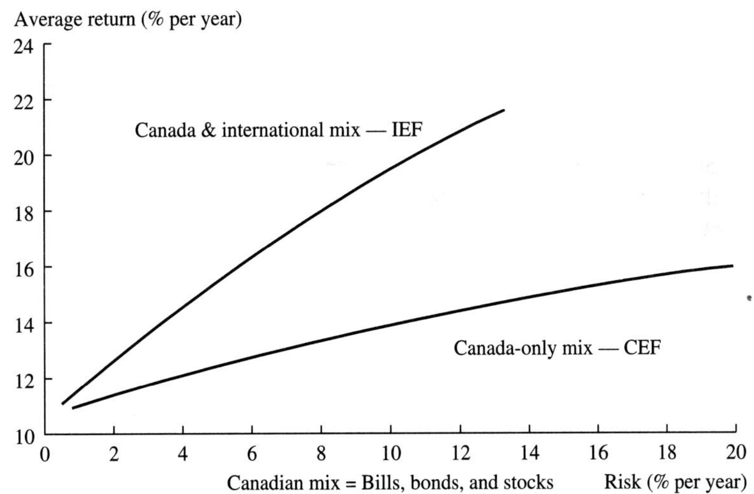


**Figure 13.3**
Canada-only efficient frontier versus Canada and international efficient frontier, 1979–1989.

From H. S. Marmer, "International Investing: A New Canadian Perspective," *Canadian Investment Review* 4, no. 1 (Spring 1991). Reprinted by permission.

through investment in foreign-domiciled mutual funds, readily available from Canadian brokers. The authors examined the risk-return characteristics of portfolios of funds from Canada, the United States, and the United Kingdom, individually and in combination, and compared the results with the market indexes and efficient frontiers for those separate markets, and again in combination. They found that significant diversification benefits existed for Canadian investors who augmented their portfolios with foreign mutual funds, especially for more risk-averse

**Table 13.3** Correlation Coefficients of Monthly Percentage Changes in Major Stock Market Indices (Local Currencies, June 1981–September 1987)

| Portfolio | Australia | Austria | Belgium | Canada | Denmark | France | Germany |
|---|---|---|---|---|---|---|---|
| World | .57 | .29 | .62 | .75 | .47 | .61 | .54 |
| Australia | — | .16 | .32 | .59 | .28 | .37 | .28 |
| Austria | | — | .46 | .18 | .30 | .43 | .55 |
| Belgium | | | — | .38 | .45 | .64 | .63 |
| Canada | | | | — | .30 | .44 | .30 |
| Denmark | | | | | — | .35 | .39 |
| France | | | | | | — | .57 |
| Germany | | | | | | | — |
| Hong Kong | | | | | | | |
| Italy | | | | | | | |
| Japan | | | | | | | |
| Netherlands | | | | | | | |
| Norway | | | | | | | |
| Spain | | | | | | | |
| Sweden | | | | | | | |
| Switzerland | | | | | | | |
| United Kingdom | | | | | | | |

Note: The correlations are based on monthly data from 1970:2–1989:5 (232 observations). The country returns are calculated in U.S. dollars in excess of the holding-period return on the Treasury bill that is closest to 30 days maturity.

Source: Campbell R. Harvey, "The World Price of Covariance Risk," *Journal of Finance* 46 (March 1991), pp. 111–58. Reprinted by permission.

investors. For the time period under consideration, 1973–1983, mutual fund performance exceeded that of the market indices; this finding runs counter to the usual results for mutual fund performance (examined in Chapter 10). Hence, the study illustrates both the advantages of international diversification and the question of active versus passive portfolio management.

Canadian interest in the international sector is evidenced by the increase in the allowable foreign assets in pension and retirement fund portfolios from 10 percent to 20 percent in 1994. Pension funds have for many years invested up to the limit; increasingly, the allowable foreign component is being filled with overseas stocks, rather than the original U.S. companies. (See the accompanying box.)

## Techniques for Investing Internationally

Investors have a number of alternatives for achieving international exposure in their portfolios, the most direct being difficult for individuals. Large, or institutional, investors can invest directly in shares of companies trading on foreign exchanges, except in certain developing markets where foreign investment is

**Table 13.3** (Continued)

| Hong Kong | Italy | Japan | Netherlands | Norway | Spain | Sweden | Switzerland | United Kingdom | United States |
|---|---|---|---|---|---|---|---|---|---|
| .41 | .42 | .63 | .74 | .50 | .41 | .50 | .68 | .67 | .86 |
| .36 | .24 | .28 | .40 | .41 | .32 | .36 | .42 | .46 | .47 |
| .21 | .24 | .25 | .43 | .28 | .29 | .27 | .49 | .23 | .12 |
| .32 | .42 | .46 | .65 | .53 | .40 | .44 | .67 | .50 | .41 |
| .29 | .27 | .28 | .55 | .45 | .28 | .35 | .48 | .52 | .72 |
| .31 | .26 | .39 | .45 | .33 | .30 | .30 | .44 | .35 | .33 |
| .24 | .44 | .41 | .58 | .47 | .36 | .33 | .62 | .52 | .42 |
| .28 | .34 | .42 | .66 | .37 | .34 | .39 | .74 | .38 | .33 |
| — | .22 | .32 | .42 | .29 | .24 | .27 | .34 | .35 | .29 |
| | — | .38 | .36 | .25 | .35 | .30 | .38 | .34 | .22 |
| | | — | .45 | .17 | .35 | .33 | .43 | .35 | .27 |
| | | | — | .52 | .38 | .43 | .73 | .62 | .56 |
| | | | | — | .25 | .38 | .48 | .40 | .44 |
| | | | | | — | .31 | .33 | .30 | .25 |
| | | | | | | — | .47 | .39 | .38 |
| | | | | | | | — | .55 | .49 |
| | | | | | | | | — | .49 |

restricted. Small investors still have satisfactory opportunities that include the purchase of:

1. Foreign shares on U.S. markets.
2. International closed-end mutual funds.
3. International open-end mutual funds.

Before describing these options, we should recall that among the stocks available for investment, there are both domestic and foreign companies, which are commonly known as *multinational firms.* Almost all large banks would qualify for this label, but there are also numerous nonfinancial enterprises, such as Alcan, Nestlé, IBM and Unilever. Such firms can be characterized as conducting many, if not all, of their primary activities, including obtaining raw materials, production, sales, and financing, in a large number of countries. Typically, these firms derive a majority of their profits from foreign sales. Hence, we can conclude that their financial results will depend on the economic conditions all around the world, and thus are themselves internationally diversified. Analysis

## Eluding Foreign Limits on RRSPs: Some Mutual Funds Have Found Loopholes to Gain the Higher Returns of International Exposure

Restrictions on foreign content have long been a source of frustration for RRSP investors. If you want your savings sheltered, you've got to buy almost exclusively Canadian, though other investment pastures may seem greener. Even in this era of global investing, the federal government has made few concessions on RRSPs. The tax rules governing foreign property holdings are being eased, but only gradually. Under provisions in 1990's federal budget that have yet to be enacted, the 10 percent foreign limit was to rise to 12 percent in 1990 and 14 percent in 1991, eventually reaching 20 percent by 1994. Consequently, most international mutual funds can form only part of an RRSP investor's portfolio up to the prescribed foreign property limit.

For every rule, though, there's a loophole. At least two mutual fund companies, Global Strategy Financial Inc. and the Guardian Group of Funds Ltd., offer funds that have high levels of foreign exposure but are fully RRSP-eligible. They're able to do so thanks largely to Canadian bonds denominated in foreign currencies, and foreign interest-bearing notes of Canadian issuers. And in the Global Strategy Canadian Fund, which despite its name invests mostly overseas, index options serve as a proxy for foreign equity markets.

THE VALUE OF GLOBAL DIVERSIFICATION—OVER THE PAST DECADE, EQUITY PORTFOLIOS WITH A FOREIGN FLAVOR EARNED HIGHER RETURNS AND WERE LESS RISKY.

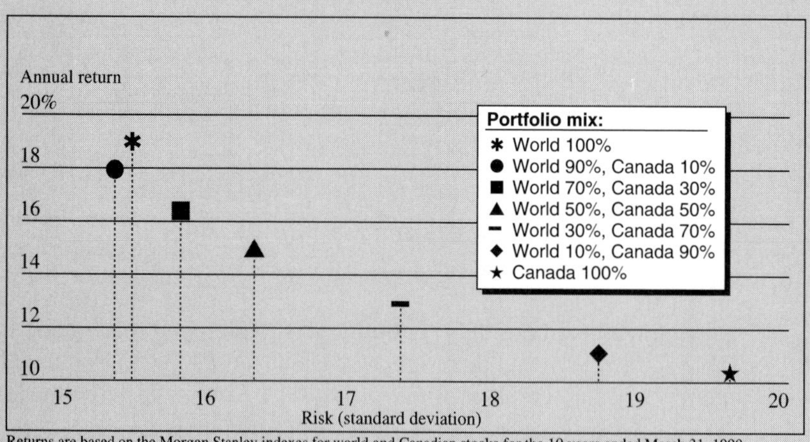


Returns are based on the Morgan Stanley indexes for world and Canadian stocks for the 10 years ended March 31, 1990.

Source: Templeton International. Ivy Wong/*Financial Times.*

*(Continued)*

"Investors ought to have the opportunity in the context of their RRSPs to get more diversification," says Richard Wernham, Global's president. He argues that for the same reason you shouldn't load your portfolio with a single stock, you shouldn't invest solely in a single national market. The RRSP rules force investors to give up potentially higher returns as well. To illustrate that point, Global Strategy uses the example of $3,500 invested in equities each year for 10 years during the 1980s. A representative portfolio of global stocks would have been worth $112,800 at the end of the period, compared with $71,000 for a portfolio based on the Toronto Stock Exchange 300 total-return index.

Global uses hedging strategies—combining stock index options and cash instruments—to mimic the performance of foreign equity markets. Specifically, it invests 8 percent of its Canadian Fund in options and 64 percent in cash, for a total of 72 percent in foreign equity exposure. If the equity markets stumble, the options expire worthless, but the cash component continues to generate interest and remains a currency play in relation to the Canadian dollar. Hence, the potential loss is limited.

"This is actually a less risky strategy than buying equities," says Wernham. He acknowledges that the gains are limited too; index options can only match the performance of the underlying market.

Launched in December 1987 as the Global Strategy RRSP Fund, the renamed Canadian Fund adopted its current investment mandate last January. Over the year ended November 30, it was the second-best performer among Canadian equity funds, with a return of minus 0.1 percent; its two-year compound return is still well above average at 5 percent. Global retains a London adviser to the fund, N.M. Rothschild Asset Management Ltd. An arm of the venerable British merchant bank, Rothschild is in charge of day-to-day management of the Global Strategy Income Fund and World Money Fund.

The Guardian Group, too, has a London money-management firm, Kleinwort Benson-Investment Management Ltd., to run its International Income Fund. The three-year-old fund had an above-average 8.9 percent return for the 12 months ended in November, though its three-year compound return is a lacklustre 1.9 percent. "You do lose some flexibility," says adviser Richard Conyers of Kleinwort Benson. The RRSP rules restrict the choice of issuers and maturities, and also the opportunity to trade bonds of similar quality for those at more attractive prices.

But these constraints have only a slight impact on fund returns. Conyers estimates the tax rules reduce the rate of return he's able to earn by only 0.1 percent. That reflects the growing efficiency of world financial markets. With the world bond market having become so integrated, he says, there are fewer opportunities to take advantage of price anomalies.

Ultimately, the performance of an internationally oriented bond fund depends on skills other than being able to get around Canadian-content rules. A new fund launched last year by the Templeton group, the fully RRSP-eligible Templeton Heritage Bond Fund, is capable of having a high degree of foreign exposure. But so far the managers have chosen to use up only half of the current limit. "We've used only 5 percent of our foreign content right now and that's a reflection of our investment views," says Don Reed, president and CEO of Templeton Management Ltd. He says that the current high levels and firmness of the Canadian dollar make it less attractive to have foreign exposure in the fund.

For some investors, buying Canadian may well be a smart RRSP strategy. To reduce currency risk, it makes sense for Canadians to have domestic assets well represented in their RRSPs. But it's a sounder strategy if executed on its own merits, rather than because it is imposed by restrictive tax laws.

Source: Rudy Luukko *The Financial Times of Canada,* January 14, 1991. Reprinted by permission of the author and *The Financial Times of Canada*.

of multinationals requires a more widely based approach than does analysis of purely domestic firms.[3]

These firms may be bought on Canadian or U.S. exchanges in most cases, with the largest Canadian multinationals trading on both. In addition to the U.S. multinationals, one can, of course, purchase other U.S. firms for specific U.S. exposure. There are also a number of the largest European, Japanese, and Mexican companies that trade on the NYSE in the form of **American Depository Receipts,** or ADRs. ADRs are issued by U.S. financial institutions, or by the firms themselves, and represent claims to a number of shares in the foreign firm, issued abroad but held on deposit in the United States.

Over the last decade, there has been a major expansion in the number of closed-end mutual funds whose purpose is to invest in specific countries (**single-country funds**), regions, or internationally in developing markets. Table 13.4 lists most of the funds available in 1995; *The Wall Street Journal* publishes a weekly report on these, including comparisons of price and asset value as well as weekly and annual performance. Most of the major mutual fund groups include developing markets and regional equity funds as well as both equity and bond international funds.

Although closed-end funds typically trade at a discount to asset value, foreign funds tend to trade at a premium as they offer a service, diversification, that investors cannot provide themselves in foreign markets.[4] In this case, it would seem better to invest in open-end funds, which sell at asset value. As an interesting note on the investment policies of closed- and open-end funds, Templeton and Morgan Stanley offer both types of funds managed by the same advisors. On one recent occasion, it was observed that, for both these firms, the performance of the closed-end versions exceeded the open-end fund results by almost exactly the amount of the premium, suggesting excellent market efficiency in pricing. How could this happen? Closed-end funds are able to be fully invested if desired, since the investors' funds have been collected and need not be refunded. The open-end funds, on the other hand, must always maintain a cash reserve for investors who wish to cash in, so their returns must be lower due to the short-term rates; given the higher volatility of foreign markets, and the investor reactions, cash reserves for international funds are quite high.

## Exchange Rate Risk

International investing poses unique challenges for Canadian investors. Information in foreign markets may be less timely and more difficult to come by. In

---

[3] A study on the effectiveness of diversification through multinationals reveals, however, that the price of this diversification may be lower risk-adjusted performance; see S. Foerster, R. Reinders, and M. Thorfinnson, "Are Investors Rewarded for the Foreign Exposure of Canadian Corporations?" *Canadian Investment Review* 5, no. 1 (Spring 1992).

[4] On the other hand, the premium on foreign funds appears to be related to investment restrictions in the particular countries involved. See C. Bonser–Neal, G. Brauer, R. Neal, and S. Wheatley, "International Investment Restrictions and Closed-End Country Fund Prices," *Journal of Finance* 45 (June 1990).

**Table 13.4** Closed-End International Funds Listed on the NYSE

| Ticker Symbol | Name |
|---|---|
| **Australia & Asia** | |
| APB | Asia Pacific Fund |
| APF | Morgan Stanley Asia Pacific |
| GRR | Asia Tigers Fund |
| TGF | Emerging Tigers Fund |
| FAE | Fidelity Advisors Emerging Asia |
| SHF | Schroder Asian Growth |
| SAF | Scudder New Asia Fund |
| CHN | China Fund |
| GCH | Greater China Fund |
| JFC | Jardine Fleming China |
| TCH | Templeton China World |
| TDF | Templeton Dragon Fund |
| TVF | Templeton Vietnam Fund |
| IAF | 1st Australia Fund |
| FPF | 1st Philippine |
| IFN | India Fund |
| IGF | India Growth Fund |
| JFI | Jardine Fleming India Fund |
| IIF | Morgan Stanley India Fund |
| IF | Indonesia Fund |
| JGF | Jakarta Growth Fund |
| JOF | Japan OTC Equity Fund |
| JEQ | Japan Equity Fund |
| KF | Korea Fund |
| KEF | Korea Equity Fund |
| KIF | Korean Investment Fund |
| FAK | Fidelity Advisors Korea Fund |
| MF | Malaysia Fund |
| PKF | Pakistan Investment Fund |
| ROC | R.O.C. Taiwan Fund |
| SGF | Singapore Fund |
| TWN | Taiwan Fund |
| TYW | Taiwan Equity Fund |
| TTF | Thai Fund |
| TC | Thai Capital Fund |
| **Europe & Middle East** | |
| OST | Austria Fund |
| FRG | Emerging Germany Fund |
| EF | Europe Fund |
| IBF | 1st Iberian Fund |
| FRF | France Growth Fund |
| FGF | Future Germany Fund |
| GER | Germany Fund |
| GSP | Growth Fund of Spain |
| IRL | Irish Investment Fund |
| ITA | Italy Fund |

**Table 13.4** (*Concluded*)

| Ticker Symbol | Name |
|---|---|
| **Europe & Middle East** (*Concluded*) | |
| GF | New Germany Fund |
| PGF | Portugal Fund |
| SNF | Spain Fund |
| SWZ | Swiss Helvetia Fund |
| TKF | Turkish Investment Fund |
| UKM | U.K. Fund |
| ISL | 1st Israel Fund |
| EME | For. & Col. Em. Middle East |
| **Latin America** | |
| AF | Argentina Fund |
| BZF | Brazil Fund |
| BZL | Brazilian Equity Fund |
| CH | Chile Fund |
| MEF | Emerging Mexico Fund |
| LDF | Latin America Discovery Fund |
| LAM | Latin America Investment |
| LAQ | Latin America Equity Fund |
| MXF | Mexico Fund |
| MXE | Mexico Equity & Income |
| **South Africa** | |
| ASA | ASA Ltd. |
| AFF | Morgan Stanley Africa Fund |
| NSA | New South Africa Fund |
| SOA | Southern Africa Fund |
| **Global Funds** | |
| CLM | Clemente Global Growth |
| ETF | Emerging Markets Telecom |
| EMG | Emerging Markets Infrastructure |
| GPF | Global Privatization Fund |
| GTD | GT Global Developing Markets |
| MSF | Morgan Stanley Emerging Markets |
| EMF | Templeton Emerging Markets |
| VLU | Worldwide Value Fund |

smaller economies with correspondingly smaller securities markets, one can encounter higher transaction costs and liquidity problems. There also is a need for special expertise concerning political risk. **Political risk** arises from the possibility of the expropriation of assets, changes in tax policy, the possibility of restrictions on the exchange of foreign currency for domestic currency, or other changes in the business climate of a country.

In addition to these risks, international investing entails exchange rate risk. The dollar return from a foreign investment depends not only on the returns in the foreign currency, but also on the dollar–foreign currency exchange rate.

For example, consider an investment in England in risk-free British government bills paying 10 percent annual interest in British pounds. These U.K. bills would be the risk-free asset to a British investor—but not for a Canadian investor. Suppose, for example, that the initial **exchange rate** is \$2 per pound, and that the Canadian investor starts with \$20,000. Those funds can be exchanged for £10,000 and invested at a risk-free 10 percent rate providing £11,000 in one year. However, what if the dollar–pound exchange rate varies over the course of the year? Suppose that the pound depreciates during the year, so that by year end only \$1.80 is required to purchase £1. Despite the positive 10 percent pound-denominated return, the dollar-denominated return will be negative. The £11,000 can be exchanged at the year-end exchange rate for only \$19,800 (11,000 × 1.80), resulting in a loss of \$200 relative to the initial \$20,000 investment, for a dollar-denominated return of −1 percent.

Let us generalize. The \$20,000 is exchanged for \$20,000/$E_0$ pounds, where $E_0$ denotes the original exchange rate (\$2/£). The U.K. investment grows to $(20{,}000/E_0)[1 + r_f(\text{UK})]$ British pounds, where $r_f(\text{UK})$ is the risk-free rate in the United Kingdom. The pound proceeds ultimately are converted back to dollars at the subsequent exchange rate $E_1$, for total dollar proceeds of $20{,}000(E_1/E_0)[1 + r_f(\text{UK})]$. Therefore the dollar-denominated return on the investment in British bills is

$$1 + r(\text{C}) = [1 + r_f(\text{UK})]E_1/E_0 \qquad \textbf{(13.1)}$$

We see in equation 13.1 that the dollar-denominated return for a Canadian investor equals the pound-denominated return multiplied by the exchange rate "return." For a Canadian investor, the investment in the British bill in fact is a combination of a safe investment in the United Kingdom and a risky investment in the performance of the pound relative to the dollar. In this case the pound fared poorly, falling from a value of \$2 to only \$1.80. The loss on the pound more than offset the earnings on the British bill.

---

**CONCEPT CHECK** Question 2. Calculate the rate of return in dollars to a Canadian investor holding the British bill, using the same data as above, if the year-end exchange rate is:

*a.* $E_1$ = \$2.00/£
*b.* $E_1$ = \$2.20/£

---

In this example, the exchange rate risk could have been hedged using a forward contract in foreign exchange. Foreign currency forward contracts (to be examined in Chapter 22) establish future rates of exchange at specified dates that can be guaranteed in the present. If the forward exchange rate had been $F$ = \$1.93/£ when the investment was made, the Canadian investor could have locked in a risk-free dollar-denominated return by locking in the year-end exchange rate at \$1.93/£. In this case, the risk-free Canadian return would have been 6.15 percent:

$$
\begin{aligned}
[1 + r_f(\text{UK})](F/E_0) &= (1.10)(1.93/2.00) \\
&= 1.0615
\end{aligned}
$$

Let us investigate the steps that would be taken to lock in the dollar-denominated returns.

| Initial Transaction | End-of-Year-Proceeds in Dollars |
|---|---|
| 1. Exchange \$20,000 for £10,000 and invest at 10% in U.K. | £11,000 × $E_1$ |
| 2. Enter a contract to deliver £11,000 for dollars at the (forward) exchange rate, \$1.93/£ | £11,000(1.93 − $E_1$) |
| Total | £11,000 × \$1.93/£ = \$21,230 |

The forward contract entered in step 2 exactly offsets the exchange rate risk incurred in step 1.

The Canadian investor can lock in a risk-free dollar-denominated return either by investing in the United Kingdom and hedging exchange rate risk or by investing in risk-free Canadian assets. Because the returns on two risk-free strategies must be equal, we conclude that

$$
[1 + r_f(\text{UK})]\frac{F}{E_0} = 1 + r_f(\text{C})
$$

$$
\frac{F}{E_0} = \frac{1 + r_f(\text{C})}{1 + r_f(\text{UK})}
$$

which is the interest rate parity relationship for a single period. (This interest rate parity relationship will be explored at length in Chapter 22.)

Unfortunately, such perfect exchange rate hedging is usually not so easy. In our example, we knew exactly how many pounds to sell in the forward market because the pound-denominated proceeds in the United Kingdom were risk-free. If the U.K. investment had not been in bills but instead were in risky U.K. equity, we would not know the ultimate value in pounds of our U.K. investment or therefore how many pounds to sell forward. Thus, the hedging opportunity offered by foreign exchange forward contracts would be imperfect. To summarize, the generalization of equation 13.1 is that

$$
1 + r(\text{C}) = [1 + r(\text{foreign})](E_1/E_0) \tag{13.2}
$$

where $r$(foreign) is the possibly risky return earned in the currency of the foreign investment. The only opportunity for perfect hedging is in the special case that $r$ (foreign) is itself a known number.

**Table 13.5** Domestic and Foreign Investments: Annualized Average Returns and Return Standard Deviations for 1973–1987

| Period | TSE 300 | Unhedged EAFE | Local EAFE | Hedged EAFE | Unhedged S&P 500 | Local S&P 500 | Hedged S&P 500 | Canadian Paper | Canadian Bonds |
|---|---|---|---|---|---|---|---|---|---|
| **1973–1987** | | | | | | | | | |
| Return | 11.0 | 17.7 | 12.0 | 16.0 | 11.8 | 9.8 | 10.7 | 10.8 | 9.7 |
| Standard deviation | 22.2 | 27.2 | 17.3 | 19.3 | 17.8 | 18.0 | 18.5 | 1.2 | 14.5 |
| **1973–1977** | | | | | | | | | |
| Return | 1.6 | 4.6 | −0.2 | 0.2 | 1.7 | −0.2 | 0.8 | 8.6 | 7.2 |
| Standard deviation | 12.4 | 21.6 | 18.0 | 19.5 | 18.8 | 18.2 | 19.2 | 1.7 | 8.5 |
| **1978–1982** | | | | | | | | | |
| Return | 18.3 | 14.5 | 13.8 | 20.8 | 16.8 | 14.0 | 14.5 | 14.0 | 8.1 |
| Standard deviation | 26.1 | 18.6 | 7.9 | 7.6 | 12.4 | 12.8 | 12.3 | 4.1 | 13.9 |
| **1983–1987** | | | | | | | | | |
| Return | 13.8 | 36.2 | 23.7 | 29.0 | 17.5 | 16.4 | 17.7 | 9.9 | 13.9 |
| Standard deviation | 20.4 | 27.1 | 11.6 | 12.4 | 14.4 | 15.5 | 16.0 | 1.5 | 14.9 |

From Robert Auger and Denis Parisien, "The Risks and Rewards of Global Investing," *Canadian Investment Review* 2, no. 1 (Spring 1989). Reprinted by permission.

**CONCEPT CHECK** Question 3. How many pounds would need to be sold forward to hedge exchange rate risk in the above example if

*a.* $r(\text{UK}) = 20\%$
*b.* $r(\text{UK}) = 30\%$

Although one may wish to hedge the exchange rate risk, another opinion maintains that domestic consumption is dependent upon the prices of foreign goods and thus, currency fluctuations in one's portfolio actually help to hedge this risk to consumption. As such, once a foreign component has been determined for a portfolio, it is best to leave it unhedged. In fact, a study by Auger and Parisien[5] for 1973–1987 data including Canadian assets, U.S. equities (S&P 500), and international equities (Morgan Stanley's EAFE index, described in the following section) analyzes the effect of foreign currency hedging on internationally diversified portfolios for Canadian investors. While the unhedged EAFE portfolio had a slightly higher rate of return of 17.7 percent for volatility of 27.2 percent, the hedged equivalent return of 16.0 percent was obtained for a volatility of only 19.3 percent. Table 13.5, reproduced from their study, shows the returns and volatilities for various portfolios and periods; the results show the local currency returns and the Canadian dollar equivalents, with and without hedging. Note that the TSE 300 is clearly dominated by the hedged EAFE portfolio.

[5] Robert Auger and Denis Parisien, "The Risks and Rewards of Global Investing," *Canadian Investment Review* 2, no. 1 (Spring 1989).

**Table 13.6** Relative Importance of World, Industrial, Currency, and Domestic Factors in Explaining Return of a Stock

| | Average $R^2$ of Regression on Factors | | | | |
|---|---|---|---|---|---|
| | Single-Factor Tests | | | | |
| Locality | World | Industrial | Currency | Domestic | Joint Test—All Four Factors |
| Switzerland | 0.18 | 0.17 | 0.00 | 0.38 | 0.39 |
| West Germany | 0.08 | 0.10 | 0.00 | 0.41 | 0.42 |
| Australia | 0.24 | 0.26 | 0.01 | 0.72 | 0.72 |
| Belgium | 0.07 | 0.08 | 0.00 | 0.42 | 0.43 |
| Canada | 0.27 | 0.24 | 0.07 | 0.45 | 0.48 |
| Spain | 0.22 | 0.03 | 0.00 | 0.45 | 0.45 |
| United States | 0.26 | 0.47 | 0.01 | 0.35 | 0.55 |
| France | 0.13 | 0.08 | 0.01 | 0.45 | 0.60 |
| United Kingdom | 0.20 | 0.17 | 0.01 | 0.53 | 0.55 |
| Hong Kong | 0.06 | 0.25 | 0.17 | 0.79 | 0.81 |
| Italy | 0.05 | 0.03 | 0.00 | 0.35 | 0.35 |
| Japan | 0.09 | 0.16 | 0.01 | 0.26 | 0.33 |
| Norway | 0.17 | 0.28 | 0.00 | 0.84 | 0.85 |
| Netherlands | 0.12 | 0.07 | 0.01 | 0.34 | 0.31 |
| Singapore | 0.16 | 0.15 | 0.02 | 0.32 | 0.33 |
| Sweden | 0.19 | 0.06 | 0.01 | 0.42 | 0.43 |
| All Countries | 0.18 | 0.23 | 0.01 | 0.42 | 0.46 |

Modified from Bruno Solnik, *International Investments,* 3rd Edition, Exhibit 7.6 © 1996 Addison-Wesley Publishing Company, Inc. Reprinted by permission of Addison-Wesley Longman Publishing Company, Inc.

## 13.2 Analysis of International Investing

### Factor Models and International Investing

Analysis of stocks from an international perspective, especially of multinationals, presents a good opportunity for an application of multifactor models of security returns. Natural factors might include the following:

1. A world stock index
2. A national (domestic) stock index
3. Industrial sector indices
4. Currency movements

Solnik and de Freitas[6] use such a framework. Table 13.6 presents some of their results for several countries. The first four columns of numbers present the $R^2$ of

[6] Bruno Solnik and A. de Freitas, "International Factors of Stock Price Behavior," CESA working paper, February 1986, cited in Bruno Solnik, *International Investments,* 3rd Ed., (Reading, Mass.: Addison-Wesley Publishing Co., 1996).

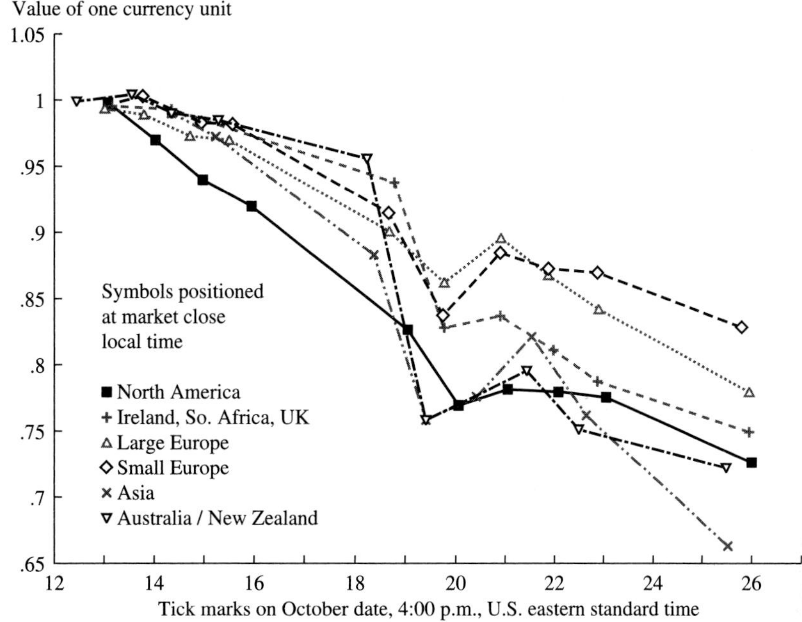


**Figure 13.4**
Regional indices around the crash, October 14–October 26, 1987.

From Richard Roll, "The International Crash of October 1987," *Financial Analysts Journal,* September–October 1988. Reprinted by permission.

various one-factor regressions. Recall that the $R^2$ measures the percentage of return volatility of a company's stock that can be explained by the factor treated as the independent or explanatory variable. Solnik and de Freitas estimate the factor regressions for many firms in a given country and report the average $R^2$ across the firms in that country. The table reveals that the domestic factor seems to be the dominant influence on stock returns. Whereas the domestic index alone generates an average $R^2$ of .42 across all countries, adding the three additional factors (in the last column of the table) increases average $R^2$ to only .46.

On the other hand, evidence of a world market factor clearly emerges from the market crash of October 1987. Despite the fact that equity returns across borders show only moderate correlation (Table 13.3), equity index returns in October in all 23 countries considered in a study by Richard Roll[7] were negative. Figure 13.4 reproduced from Roll's study, shows the value of regional equity indices (starting from a value of 1.0) during October. The correlation among returns is obvious and suggests some underlying world factor common to all economies. Roll also found that the beta of a country's equity index on a world index (estimated through September 1987) was the best predictor of that index's response to the crash, lending further support to the importance of a world factor.

[7] Richard Roll, "The International Crash of October 1987," *Financial Analyst's Journal,* September–October 1988.

**Table 13.7** Equity Returns, 1960–1980

| | Average Return | Standard Deviation of Return | Beta | Alpha |
|---|---|---|---|---|
| Australia | 12.20 | 22.80 | 1.02 | 1.52 |
| Austria | 10.30 | 16.90 | .01 | 4.86 |
| Belgium | 10.10 | 13.80 | .45 | 2.44 |
| Canada | 12.10 | 17.50 | .77 | 2.75 |
| Denmark | 11.40 | 24.20 | .60 | 2.91 |
| France | 8.10 | 21.40 | .50 | .17 |
| Germany | 10.10 | 19.90 | .45 | 2.41 |
| Italy | 5.60 | 27.20 | .41 | −1.92 |
| Japan | 19.00 | 31.40 | .81 | 9.49 |
| Netherlands | 10.70 | 17.80 | .90 | .65 |
| Norway | 17.40 | 49.00 | −.27 | 13.39 |
| Spain | 10.40 | 19.80 | .04 | 4.73 |
| Sweden | 9.70 | 16.70 | .51 | 1.69 |
| Switzerland | 12.50 | 22.90 | .87 | 2.66 |
| United Kingdom | 14.70 | 33.60 | 1.47 | 1.76 |
| United States | 10.20 | 17.70 | 1.08 | −.69 |

From Roger G. Ibbotson, Richard C. Carr, and Anthony W. Robinson, "International Equity and Bond Returns," *Financial Analysts Journal,* July/August 1982. Reprinted by permission.

## Equilibrium in International Capital Markets

As for domestic assets, we can look to the CAPM or APT to predict expected rates of return in an international capital market equilibrium. However, these models must be adapted somewhat for the international context.

For example, one might expect that a world CAPM would result simply by replacing a narrow domestic market portfolio with a broad world market portfolio, and measuring betas relative to the world portfolio. Indeed, this approach was pursued in part of a paper by Ibbotson, Carr, and Robinson,[8] who calculated betas of equity indices of several countries against a world equity index, with all returns denominated in U.S. dollars. Their results appear in Table 13.7. The betas for different countries show surprising variability.

Whereas such a straightforward generalization of the simple CAPM is a reasonable first step, it is subject to some problems:

1. Taxes, transaction costs, and capital barriers across countries make it difficult and less attractive for investors to hold a world index portfolio. Some assets are simply unavailable to foreign investors.
2. Investors in different countries view exchange rate risk from the perspective of different domestic currencies. Thus, they will not agree on the risk char-

[8] Roger G. Ibbotson, Richard C. Carr, and Anthony W. Robinson, "International Equity and Bond Returns," *Financial Analysts Journal,* July/August 1982.

acteristics of various securities and, therefore, will not derive identical efficient frontiers.

3. Investors in different countries tend to consume different baskets of goods, either because of differing tastes, or because of tariffs, transportation costs, or taxes. Therefore, if relative prices of goods vary over time, the inflation risk perceived by investors in different countries also will differ.

These problems suggest that the simple CAPM will not work as well in an international context as it would if all markets were fully integrated. Indeed, some evidence suggests that assets that are less accessible to foreign investors carry higher risk premiums.[9]

The APT seems better designed for the international context, since the special risk factors that arise in this setting can be treated like any other risk factor. For example, similar to the four-factor model of Chen, Roll, and Ross for U.S. equities, returns could be described by a like number of factors, including world economic activity and currency movements for international effects, an industry-specific measure, and some measure of domestic market performance relative to world performance.

## Passive and Active International Investing

When we discuss investment strategies in the purely domestic context, we use a market index portfolio such as the TSE 300 as a benchmark passive equity investment. This suggests that a world market index might be a useful starting point for a passive international strategy.

Several major U.S. investment houses have composed indices of non-U.S. (actually non-North American) stocks. The most widely used index of these is the Europe, Australia, Far East, or **EAFE index** computed by Morgan Stanley. Morgan Stanley also has an alternative EAFE index using GDP rather than market value for country weighting. However, there are now several additional indices of world equity performance. Capital International Indices has published several indicators of international equity performance since 1968. Now Salomon Brothers, First Boston, and Goldman Sachs also publish world equity indices. Portfolios designed to mirror or even replicate the country, currency, and company representation of these indices would be the obvious generalization of the purely domestic passive equity strategy.

An issue that sometimes arises in the international context is the appropriateness of market-capitalization weighting schemes in the construction of international indices. Capitalization weighting is far and away the most common approach. However, some argue that it might not be the best weighting scheme in an international context. This is in part because different countries have differing

[9] Vihang Errunza and Etienne Losq, "International Asset Pricing under Mild Segmentation: Theory and Test," *Journal of Finance* 40 (March 1985).

proportions of their corporate sector organized as publicly traded firms. For example, in 1993, U.K. firms received a total weighting of 16.7 percent of the EAFE index in terms of market value of equity, but accounted for only 8 percent of the gross domestic product (GDP) of the EAFE countries. In contrast, French firms represented 5.8 percent of the market-value weighted index, despite the fact that France accounted for fully 11.4 percent of EAFE GDP.

Some argue that it is more appropriate to weight international indexes by GDP rather than market capitalization because an internationally diversified portfolio should purchase shares in proportion to the broad asset base of each country, and GDP might be a better measure of the importance of a country in the international economy than the value of its outstanding stocks. Others have even suggested weights proportional to the import share of various countries. The argument is that investors who wish to hedge the price of imported goods might choose to hold securities in foreign firms in proportion to the goods imported from those countries.

Another problem with market capitalization weights arises from the practice of **cross-holdings** that tend to overstate the aggregate value of outstanding equity. Cross-holdings refer to equity investments that firms make in other firms. These purchases can increase the sum of the market values of outstanding equity. For instance, a $10 million holding by firm *A* in firm *B* will increase *A*'s equity by $10 million but will not decrease firm *B*'s equity. The aggregate equity in the market will be increased by this $10 million, even though the individual shareholder's equity holdings will not increase by $10 million. Clearly there will be no increase in real assets due to this financial asset held by firm *A*.

French and Poterba[10] have calculated the effect of cross-holdings on the U.S. and Japanese equity markets. The Japanese system of business alliances (known as *keiretsus*) leads to extensive cross-holdings. They find that in mid-1990, the value of the Japanese equity market falls from $3,266 billion to $1,623 billion when cross-holdings are netted out. In contrast, in the United States, where cross-holdings are minimal, the value of equity falls only slightly, from $3,044 billion to $3,006 billion.

Table 13.8 uses data from 1993 to illustrate the different weightings that would emerge for the EAFE countries using market capitalization and GDP. The differing methodologies result in substantially different weights for some countries. In particular, Japan had a market-value weight of 48.3 percent despite that fact that its GDP was only 33.4 percent of the EAFE total. This disproportionate weight was due primarily to much higher price earnings ratios in Japan in 1993 and the more common practice of cross-holdings in Japan.

Active portfolio management in an international context may be viewed similarly as an extension of active domestic management. In principle, one would form an efficient frontier from the full menu of world securities and determine

[10] Kenneth R. French and James M. Poterba, "Were Japanese Stock Prices Too High?" *Journal of Financial Economics* 29 (October 1991), pp. 337–63.

**Table 13.8** Weighting Schemes for EAFE Countries

| Country | Market Capitalization | Gross Domestic Product (GDP) |
|---|---|---|
| Australia | 2.4% | 2.4% |
| Austria | 0.4 | 1.6 |
| Belgium | 1.1 | 1.9 |
| Denmark | 0.6 | 1.2 |
| Finland | 0.3 | 0.8 |
| France | 5.8 | 11.4 |
| Germany | 6.7 | 15.4 |
| Hong Kong | 3.3 | 0.9 |
| Italy | 1.9 | 9.2 |
| Ireland | 0.2 | 0.4 |
| Japan | 48.3 | 33.4 |
| Malaysia | 1.6 | 0.5 |
| New Zealand | 0.3 | 0.3 |
| Netherlands | 2.9 | 2.8 |
| Norway | 0.3 | 0.9 |
| Singapore | 0.9 | 1.4 |
| Spain | 1.8 | 4.6 |
| Sweden | 1.3 | 1.8 |
| Switzerland | 4.2 | 2.1 |
| U.K. | 16.7 | 8.0 |

Source: Bruce Clarke and Anthony W. Ryan, "Proper Overseas Benchmark a Critical Choice," *Pensions and Investments,* May 30, 1994, p. 28. Reprinted by permission.

the optimal risky portfolio. Even in the domestic context, the need for specialization in various asset classes usually calls for a two-step procedure in which asset allocation is fixed initially, and then security selection within each asset class is determined. The complexities of the international market argue even more strongly for the primacy of asset allocation, and this is the perspective often taken in the evaluation of active portfolio management. Performance attribution of international managers focuses on these potential sources of abnormal returns: currency selection, country selection, stock selection within countries, and cash-bond selection within countries.

We can measure the contribution of each of these factors following a manner similar to the performance attribution techniques introduced in Chapter 12.

1. **Currency selection** measures the contribution to total portfolio performance attributable to exchange rate fluctuations relative to the investor's benchmark currency, the Canadian dollar. We can measure currency selection as the weighted average of the appreciation, $E_1/E_0$, of each currency represented in the portfolio, using as weights the fraction of the portfolio invested in each currency. We might use a benchmark such as the EAFE index to compare a portfolio's currency selection for a particular period to

**Table 13.9** Example of Performance Attribution: International

| | EAFE* Weight | Return on Equity Index | $E_1/E_0$ | Manager's Weight | Manager's Return |
|---|---|---|---|---|---|
| Europe | .30 | .10 | 1.10 | .35 | .08 |
| Australia | .10 | .05 | .90 | .10 | .07 |
| Far East | .60 | .15 | 1.30 | .55 | .18 |

With the above data we can make the following calculations:

**Currency selection:** EAFE: .30 × 1.10 + .10 × .90 + .60 × 1.30 = 1.20 (20% appreciation)
Manager: .35 × 1.10 + .10 × .90 + .55 × 1.30 = 1.19
Loss of 1% relative to EAFE.

**Country selection:** EAFE: .30 × .10 + .10 × .05 + .60 × .15 = .125
Manager: .35 × .10 + .10 × .05 + .55 × .15 = .1225
Loss of .25% relative to EAFE.

**Stock selection:** (.08 − .10).35 + (.07 − .05).10 + (.18 − .15).55 = .0115
Contribution of 1.15% relative to EAFE.

*E, Europe; A, Australia; FE, Far East.

a passive benchmark. EAFE currency selection would thus be computed as the weighted average of $E_1/E_0$ of the currencies represented in the EAFE portfolio, using as weights the fraction of the EAFE portfolio invested in each currency.

2. **Country selection** measures the contribution to performance attributable to investing in the better-performing stock markets of the world. It can be measured as the weighted average of the *equity-index* returns of each country, using as weights the share of the manager's portfolio in each country. To measure a manager's contribution relative to a passive strategy, we might compare country selection to the weighted average across countries of equity index returns, using as weights the share of the EAFE portfolio in each country.
3. **Stock selection** ability may be measured as the weighted average of equity returns *in excess of the equity index* in each country. In this instance, we would use local currency returns and use as weights the investments in each country.
4. **Cash/bond selection** may be measured as the excess return derived from weighting bonds and bills differently from some benchmark weights.

An example of international performance attribution is presented in Table 13.9.

**CONCEPT CHECK** Question 4. What would the manager's country and currency selection have been if her portfolio weights were 40 percent in Europe, 20 percent in Australia, and 40 percent in the Far East?

**Table 13.10** Stock Market Valuation

| Index | P/BV | P/CE | P/E | Yield |
|---|---|---|---|---|
| **International indexes** | | | | |
| World | 2.26 | 9.9 | 26.7 | 2.2 |
| North America | 2.51 | 10.0 | 20.1 | 2.8 |
| EAFE | 2.13 | 9.9 | 33.8 | 1.9 |
| Europe | 1.94 | 8.3 | 22.6 | 3.1 |
| Pacific | 2.30 | 12.2 | 53.1 | 1.0 |
| **National indexes** | | | | |
| Australia | 1.72 | 10.6 | 17.2 | 3.4 |
| Austria | 1.67 | 7.5 | loss | 1.1 |
| Belgium | 1.59 | 6.9 | 20.1 | 4.2 |
| Canada | 1.77 | 11.4 | 44.7 | 2.5 |
| Denmark | 2.40 | 8.7 | 19.2 | 1.7 |
| Finland | 1.50 | 10.2 | loss | 0.9 |
| France | 1.55 | 7.7 | 27.2 | 3.1 |
| Germany | 2.10 | 6.2 | 60.3 | 2.4 |
| Hong Kong | 2.16 | 14.2 | 16.6 | 2.9 |
| Ireland | 1.97 | 11.6 | 15.3 | 2.4 |
| Italy | 1.77 | 7.9 | n.s. | 1.4 |
| Japan | 2.33 | 11.9 | 88.0 | 0.7 |
| Malaysia | 3.61 | 19.5 | 28.4 | 1.0 |
| Netherlands | 1.71 | 7.8 | 17.6 | 3.5 |
| New Zealand | 1.89 | 10.1 | 13.7 | 4.3 |
| Norway | 1.95 | 6.6 | 16.3 | 1.7 |
| Singapore | 1.96 | 12.6 | 20.4 | 1.3 |
| Spain | 1.50 | 6.7 | n.s. | 3.4 |
| Sweden | 2.31 | 12.0 | 30.1 | 1.3 |
| Switzerland | 2.10 | 9.6 | 17.5 | 1.8 |
| United Kingdom | 2.22 | 9.7 | 15.5 | 4.2 |
| U.S.A. | 2.58 | 9.9 | 19.5 | 2.8 |

Valuation: P/BV: price to book-value ratio;
P/CE: price to cash earnings (earnings + depreciation) ratio;
P/E: price earnings ratio;
Yield: gross dividend yield;
n.s.: not significant.

Source: Morgan Stanley Capital International, May 31, 1994. Reprinted from Bruno Solnik, *International Investments,* 3rd Edition, Exhibit 7.4 © 1996 Addison-Wesley Publishing Company, Inc. Reprinted by permission of Addison-Wesley Longman Publishing Company, Inc.

Under active portfolio management, the problem of stock analysis and selection is much more complicated than for the domestic case. Many of the standard ratios (such as price-earnings) in foreign countries will be significantly different from the accepted norms in Canada or the United States, which are comparable. This difference may often be due to different accounting practices or institutional requirements in the foreign country, but also different levels for ratios may reflect alternative attitudes regarding risk as seen in leverage and reserves for losses. Table 13.10 shows a wide range for four ratios in the more developed markets (without considering the situation for developing nations); the most widely recognized of these is the Japanese P/E, here seen as almost five times the Canadian P/E.

## 13.3 Integration of Canadian and International Markets

### Integration versus Segmentation in Markets

Investigation of the benefits of international investment leads immediately to the question of whether assets listed in different capital markets offer the same risk-return characteristics. Interlisting of stocks on various world exchanges makes them accessible to investors in those markets and places them in direct competition as financial assets with the domestic securities of those markets. One might suspect that the inevitable result of this would be that all assets in all markets would display the same risk-return characteristics, at least relative to some world index or common factors. Were this the case, we would describe the markets as being fully **integrated.** In contrast to this, if assets in different markets retained different risk-return characteristics or were priced according to different and country-specific factors, we would describe these markets as **segmented.**

The existence of market segmentation is ascribed to both indirect and legal barriers to investment by all potential investors in all potential assets. Indirect barriers are defined as those previously mentioned problems besetting the foreign investor, such as lack of access to financial information or ability to trade efficiently in the securities. Legal barriers include restrictions on foreign ownership or of foreign investment by individuals or institutions, such as the limitation placed on Canadian pension funds. Interlisting of securities tends to alleviate the indirect barriers but usually cannot solve legal barriers.

We have seen in Table 13.10 that various important financial ratios have been found to vary widely across the different markets shown. This might be taken as evidence of clear segmentation of the many markets, possibly excepting the Canadian and U.S. markets with their similar ratios, given the relevance of these ratios to market valuation. Yet these statistics must be recognized as dependent upon the market conditions under which they were compiled; prices are high relative to earnings during recessions. Furthermore, the different markets are not homogeneous in terms of the firms that comprise the indices; the Canadian market is disproportionately high in natural resource companies. Financial ratios vary appropriately across different industries, and the different comparisons of specific national markets leads to a variety of aggregates of ratios.

Consideration of financial ratios is a dated approach to valuation, however, and cannot provide reliable evidence as to market segmentation. Modern financial theory prescribes the comparison of ex post risk-return measures and the sensitivity to market factors as evidence. Recent interest in the subject of market integration and segmentation has led to a number of theoretical and empirical studies to test which of the two descriptions is accurate. Generally, these tests involve attempts to price international assets by appeal to multifactor models, as described in the previous section; both multifactor CAPM and APT models have been used. Modeling the effects of barriers causing segmentation is difficult, however, given the problem of defining and quantifying imperfections in the markets. Hence, the risk premiums for the various factors cannot be reliably established. Alternatively, theory suggests that the integration of a smaller market with larger markets will result in a lowering of expected returns in the smaller market, due to increased liquidity and demand, but more importantly, due to a lowering of the risk premium. Interlisting of securities should produce a lowering of risk premiums for these securities at least; thus the event of interlisting can be studied to test for an observed reduction as of the occurrence of the event.[11]

## Integration of Canadian and U.S. Markets

Canadian markets offer a unique opportunity to researchers to study the question of segmentation versus integration since they are close to U.S. markets both institutionally and geographically; the economies are closely linked, corporations are governed by essentially similar rules and practices, and both debt and equity instruments of both countries are sold to and traded by investors of both countries, with interlisting of many stocks. Yet the different tax treatment of dividends in the two countries implies that ex-dividend day returns should differ for stocks in the two markets; interlisted stocks were shown by Booth and Johnston[12] to behave differently from domestically traded stocks. Comparison of interlisted and domestic stocks can provide statistically significant results to demonstrate segmentation. Furthermore, a case for integration between the two markets can be made more strongly than for integration of a third market with either of the two. Statistical methods can be used to test for the different characteristics of integration as would be expected under the closely linked versus distant markets.

Most empirical studies of Canadian and U.S. returns differ in their conclusions as to whether the two markets are truly integrated. Hatch and White[13] examined the comparative returns of U.S. and Canadian stock markets, and noted that U.S. stocks had a higher return than did Canadian but had a slightly lower risk; they rationalized this as resulting from a lower beta for Canadian stocks, relative to a world index. Brennan and Schwartz[14] rejected integration of the two markets over the period 1968–1980 based on a combined index, but their analysis does not correct for the substantial double-counting of interlisted stocks. Extending the

[11] Gordon J. Alexander, Cheol S. Eun, and S. Janakiramanan, "Asset Pricing and Dual Listing on Foreign Capital Markets: A Note," *Journal of Finance* 42 (March 1987).

[12] L. D. Booth and D. J. Johnston, "The Ex-Dividend Day Behavior of Canadian Stock Prices: Tax Changes and Clinetele Effects," *Journal of Finance* 39 (June 1984).

[13] J. E. Hatch and R. W. White, "A Canadian Perspective on Canadian and United States Capital Market Returns: 1950–1983," *Financial Analysts Journal* 42 (May–June 1986).

[14] M. J. Brennan and E. Schwartz, "Asset Pricing in a Small Economy: A Test of the Omitted Assets Model," in Spremann (ed.), *Survey of Developments in Modern Finance* (New York: Springer-Verlag, 1986).

period to 1982, Jorion and Schwartz[15] found the same result by using a two-factor CAPM approach; the model was designed to eliminate the commonality between the domestic and international components. They found that the international index did not account for all the returns in Canadian stocks, leaving a priceable national component; hence, they concluded there was evidence of segmentation. A recent study by Mittoo[16] finds evidence that both time and interlisting are significant in explaining the segmentation issue. Using both CAPM and APT approaches, it is revealed that data prior to 1982 support segmentation, while integration is indicated afterward; furthermore, interlisted stocks after 1982 show integration, but domestically listed stocks suggest segregation. The data were restricted to TSE 35 companies to avoid thin-trading problems and natural resource factor loading, and to a time period where regulatory impediments to integration were absent. Alexander, Eun, and Janakiramanan[17] tested the reduction in expected required returns following interlisting for the period 1969–1982. They investigated both Canadian and non-North American stocks that were listed on the NYSE, AMEX, or NASDAQ, and found a significant distinction between the Canadian and non-Canadian groups; as hypothesized, the Canadian stocks experienced a much smaller return reduction than did the others. In fact, the Canadian results were found to be insignificant, leading them to the conclusion that the foreign markets are definitely segmented from the U.S., but that the Canadian market may not have been.

In conclusion, we can say that there are institutional and sectoral explanations for an apparent segmentation of Canadian and U.S. markets; at the same time, similarities and accessibility of the two markets suggest little if any differential pricing is likely and that virtual integration is possible.

## SUMMARY

**1.** Canadian assets comprise only a small fraction of the world wealth portfolio. International capital markets offer important opportunities for portfolio diversification with enhanced risk-return characteristics.

**2.** Investors can diversify internationally by buying multinational firms on Canadian or U.S. markets or by buying closed- or open-ended mutual funds that invest in specific countries, regions, or internationally in general.

**3.** Exchange rate risk imparts an extra source of uncertainty to investments denominated in foreign currencies. Much of that risk can be hedged in foreign exchange futures or forward markets, but unless the foreign currency rate of return is known, a perfect hedge is not feasible.

---

[15] P. Jorion and E. Schwartz, "Integration vs. Segmentation in the Canadian Stock Market," *Journal of Finance* 41 (July 1986).

[16] Usha R. Mittoo, "Additional Evidence on Integration in the Canadian Stock Market," *Journal of Finance* 47 (December 1992).

[17] Gordon J. Alexander, Cheol S. Eun, and S. Janakiramanan, "International Listings and Stock Returns: Some Empirical Evidence," *Journal of Financial and Quantitative Analysis* 23 (1988). This is a typical example of the event study methodology, described in Chapter 11.

**4.** A factor model applied to international investing would include a world factor, as well as the usual domestic factors. Although some evidence suggests that domestic factors dominate stock returns, the October 1987 crash provides evidence of an important international factor.

**5.** Several world market indices can form a basis for passive international investing. Active international management can be partitioned into currency selection, country selection, stock selection, and cash/bond selection.

**6.** Financial markets in different countries may be integrated or segmented, depending or whether factors that influence security prices are universal or specific to the countries.

**7.** The benefits of international diversification are increased if market segmentation exists. Studies indicate that Canadian markets are at most mildly segmented from U.S. markets. For Canadian investors, overseas investment offers the greatest diversification opportunities.

## Key Terms

American Depository Receipt (ADR)
Single-country fund
Political risk
Exchange rate
EAFE index
Cross-holdings
Currency selection
Country selection
Stock selection
Cash/bond selection
Integrated
Segmented

## Selected Readings

*Comprehensive textbooks on international facets of investing are:*

Solnik, Bruno. *International Investments* (3rd edition). Reading, Mass.: Addison-Wesley Publishing, Co., Inc., 1996.

Grabbe, J. Orlin. *International Financial Markets.* New York: Elsevier Science Publishers, 2nd Edn, 1991.

*A text with a greater emphasis on corporate applications and foreign exchange risk management is:*

Shapiro, Alan C. *Multinational Financial Management.* Boston: Allyn & Bacon, Inc., 1986.

*A good book of readings is:*

Lessard, Donald R. (editor). *International Financial Management: Theory and Application.* New York: John Wiley & Sons, 1985.

*Some recent Canadian empirical studies on international diversification include the works mentioned in the footnotes and:*

Marmer, Harry S. "International Investing: A New Canadian Perspective." *Canadian Investment Review* 4, no. 1 (Spring 1991).

## Problems

1. Suppose that a Canadian investor wishes to invest in a British firm currently selling for £40 per share. The investor has $10,000 to invest, and the current exchange rate is $2/£.

*a*. How many shares can the investor purchase?

*b*. Fill in the table below for rates of return after one year in each of the nine scenarios.

| Price per Share (£) | Pound-Denominated Return (%) | Dollar-Dominated Return for Year-End Exchange Rate | | |
|---|---|---|---|---|
| | | $1.80/£ | $2/£ | $2.20/£ |
| £35 | | | | |
| £40 | | | | |
| £45 | | | | |

*c*. When is the dollar-denominated return equal to the pound-denominated return?

**2.** If each of the nine outcomes in problem (1) is equally likely, find the standard deviation of both the pound- and dollar-denominated rates of return.

**3.** Now suppose that the investor in problem (1) also sells forward £5,000 at a forward exchange rate of $2.10/£.

*a*. Recalculate the dollar-denominated returns for each scenario.

*b*. What happens to the standard deviation of the dollar-denominated return?

**4.** Calculate the contribution of total performance from currency, country, and stock selection for the following manager:

| | EAFE Weight | Return on Equity Index | $E_1/E_0$ | Manager's Weight | Manager's Return |
|---|---|---|---|---|---|
| Europe | .30 | .20 | .9 | .35 | .18 |
| Australia | .10 | .15 | 1.0 | .15 | .20 |
| Far East | .60 | .25 | 1.1 | .50 | .20 |

**5.** If the current exchange rate is $1.75/£, the one-year forward exchange rate is $1.85/£, and the interest rate on British government bills is 8 percent per year, what risk-free dollar-denominated return can be locked in by investing in the British bills?

**6.** If you were to invest $10,000 in the British bills of problem (5), how would you lock in the dollar-denominated return?

**7.** A U.S. pension plan hired two offshore firms to manage the non-U.S. equity portion of its total portfolio. Each firm was free to own stocks in any country market included in Capital International's Europe, Australia, and Far East index (EAFE) and free to use any form of dollar and/or nondollar cash or bonds as an equity substitute or reserve. After three years had elapsed, the records of the managers and the EAFE index were as shown below:

Summary: Contributions to Return

| | Currency Selection (%) | Country Selection (%) | Stock Selection (%) | Cash/Bond Allocation (%) | Total Return Recorded (%) |
|---|---|---|---|---|---|
| Manager *A* | 9.0 | 19.7 | 3.1 | 0.6 | 14.4 |
| Manager *B* | 7.4 | 14.2 | 6.0 | 2.8 | 15.6 |
| Composite of *A* & *B* | 8.2 | 16.9 | 4.5 | 1.7 | 15.0 |
| EAFE index | 12.9 | 19.9 | — | — | 7.0 |

You are a member of the plan sponsor's Pension Committee, which will soon meet with the plan's consultant to review manager performance. In preparation for this meeting, you go through the following analysis:

*a.* Briefly describe the strengths and weaknesses of each manager, relative to the EAFE index data.

*b.* Briefly explain the meaning of the data in the "Currency" column.

**8.** John Irish, CFA, is an independent investment advisor who is assisting Alfred Darwin, the head of the Investment Committee of General Technology Corporation, to establish a new pension fund. Darwin asks Irish about international equities and whether the Investment Committee should consider them as an additional asset for the pension fund.

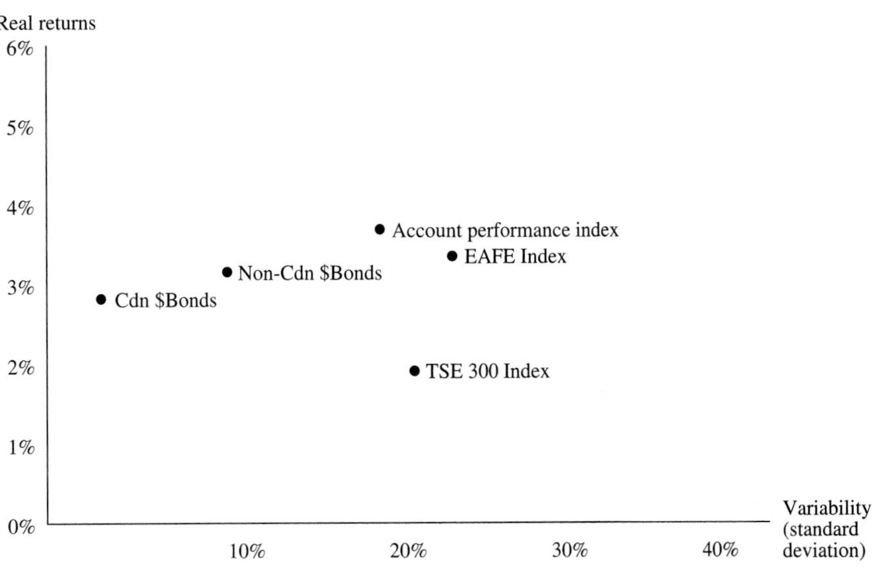


**Annualized historical performance data: 14 years ended Dec. 31, 1983**

*a*. Explain the rationale for including international equities in General's equity portfolio. Identify and describe *three* relevant considerations in formulating your answer.
*b*. List *three* possible arguments against international equity investment and briefly discuss the significance of each.
*c*. To illustrate several aspects of the performance of international securities over time, Irish shows Darwin the accompanying graph of investment results experienced by a Canadian pension fund in the 1970–1983 period. Compare the performance of the Canadian dollar and non-Canadian dollar equity and fixed-income asset categories, and explain the significance of the result of the account performance index relative to the results of the four individual asset class indices.

**9.** A global equity manager is assigned to select stocks from a universe of large stocks throughout the world. The manager will be evaluated by comparing his returns to the return on the MSCI World Market Portfolio, but she is free to hold stocks from various countries in whatever proportions she finds desirable. Results for a given month are contained in the following table.

| Country | Weight in MSCI Index | Manager's Weight | Manager's Return in Country | Return of Stock Index for That Country |
|---|---|---|---|---|
| U.K. | .15 | .30 | 20% | 12% |
| Japan | .30 | .10 | 15 | 15 |
| U.S. | .45 | .40 | 10 | 14 |
| Germany | .10 | .20 | 5 | 12 |

*a*. Calculate the total value added by all the manager's decisions for this period.
*b*. Calculate the value added (or subtracted) by her *country* allocation decisions.
*c*. Calculate the value added from her stock selection ability within countries. Confirm that the sum of the contributions to value added from her country allocation plus security selection decisions equals total over- or underperformance.

**10.** Renée Michaels, CFA, plans to invest $1 million in U.S. government cash equivalents for the next 90 days. Michaels' client has authorized her to use non-U.S. government cash equivalents, but only if the currency risk is hedged to U.S. dollars by using forward currency contracts.
*a*. Calculate the U.S. dollar value of the hedged investment at the end of 90 days for *each* of the two cash equivalents in the table below. Show all calculations.
*b*. Briefly explain the theory that best accounts for your results.
*c*. Based upon this theory, estimate the implied interest rate for a 90-day U.S. government cash equivalent.

| Interest Rates 90-Day Cash Equivalents | |
|---|---|
| Japanese government | 7.6% |
| German government | 8.6% |

Exchange Rates: Currency Units per U.S. Dollar

| | Spot | 90-Day Forward |
|---|---|---|
| Japanese yen | 133.05 | 133.47 |
| German deutsche mark | 1.5260 | 1.5348 |

**11.** After much research on the developing economy and capital markets of the country of Otunia, your firm, GAC, has decided to include an investment in the Otunia stock market in its Emerging Markets Commingled Fund. However, GAC has not yet decided whether to invest actively or by indexing. Your opinion on the active versus indicing decision has been solicited. A summary of the research findings follows.

Otunia's economy is fairly well diversified across agricultural and natural resources, manufacturing (both consumer and durable goods), and a growing finance sector. Transaction costs in securities markets are relatively large in Otunia because of high commissions and government "stamp taxes" on securities trades. Accounting standards and disclosure regulations are quite detailed, resulting in wide public availability of reliable information about companies' financial performance.

Capital flows into and out of Otunia, and foreign ownership of Otunia securities are strictly regulated by an agency of the national government. The settlement procedures under these ownership rules often cause long delays in settling trades made by nonresidents. Senior finance officials in the government are working to deregulate capital flows and foreign ownership, but GAC's political consultant believes that isolationist sentiment may prevent much real progress in the short run.

*a.* Briefly discuss *four* aspects of the Otunia environment that favor investing actively *and four* aspects that favor indexing.

*b.* Recommend whether GAC should invest in Otunia actively or by indexing and justify your recommendation based on the factors identified in part (a).

*Part V*

# Fixed-Income Securities

# Chapter 14

# Bond Prices and Yields

**IN THE PREVIOUS CHAPTERS ON RISK AND RETURN RELATIONSHIPS, WE HAVE TREATED SECURITIES AT A HIGH LEVEL OF ABSTRACTION.** We have assumed implicitly that a prior, detailed analysis of each security already has been performed, and that its risk and return features have been assessed.

We turn now to specific analyses of particular security markets. We examine valuation principles, determinants of risk and return, and portfolio strategies commonly used within and across the various markets.

We begin by analyzing **fixed-income securities**. A fixed-income security is a claim on a specified periodic stream of income. Fixed-income securities have the advantage of being relatively easy to understand because the level of payments is fixed in advance. Risk considerations are minimal as long as the issuer of the security is sufficiently creditworthy. That makes these securities a convenient starting point for our analysis of the universe of potential investment vehicles.

The bond is the basic fixed-income security, and this chapter reviews the principles of bond pricing. We show how bond prices are set in accordance with market interest rates, and why bond prices change with those rates. After examining the Canada bond market, where default risk may be ignored, we move to the corporate bond sector. Here, we look at the determinants of credit risk and the default premium built into bond yields. We examine the impact of call and convertibility provisions on prices and yields. Finally, we discuss certain tax rules that apply to fixed income investments and show how to calculate after-tax returns.

## 14.1 BOND CHARACTERISTICS

A **bond** is a borrowing arrangement in which the borrower issues (sells) an IOU to the investor. The arrangement obligates the issuer to make specified payments to the bondholder on specified dates. A typical *coupon bond* obligates the issuer to make semiannual payments of interest, called coupon payments, to the bondholder for the life of the bond, and then to pay in addition the bond's **par value** (equivalently, **face value**) at the bond's maturity date. The **coupon rate** of the bond is the coupon payment divided by the bond's par value.

To illustrate, a bond with a par value of $1,000 and a coupon rate of 8 percent might be sold to a buyer for $1,000. The bondholder is then entitled to a payment of 8 percent of $1,000, or $80 per year, for the stated life of the bond, say 30 years. The $80 payment typically comes in two semiannual installments of $40 each. At the end of the 30-year life of the bond, the issuer also pays the $1,000 par value to the bondholder.

Bonds usually are issued with coupon rates set high enough to induce investors to pay par value to buy the bond. Sometimes, however, **zero-coupon bonds** are issued that make no coupon payments. In this case, investors receive par value at the maturity date, but they receive no interest payments until then: The bond has a coupon rate of zero. These bonds are issued at prices considerably below par value, and the investor's return comes solely from the difference between the issue price and the payment of par value at maturity. We will return to these bonds below.

### Canada Bonds

Figure 14.1 is an excerpt from the listing of bond issues in *The Globe and Mail.* Canada bond maturities range up to 30 years. The bonds are issued in denominations of $1,000 or more and make semiannual coupon payments.

Some bonds are callable. They are easily identified in a listing such as Figure 14.1 because of a range of years appears in the maturity date column. The first date is the time at which the bond is first callable. The second date is the maturity date of the bond. The bond may be called by the issuer at any coupon date in the call period, but it must be retired by the maturity date. No such bonds appear in Figure 14.1.

The highlighted bond in Figure 14.1 matures in December 2001. Its coupon rate is 9.75 percent. Par value is $1,000; thus, the bond pays interest of $97.50 per year in two semiannual payments of $48.75. Payments are made in June and December of each year. The quoted price is the average of the bid and ask prices.[1]

[1] Recall that the bid price is the price at which you can sell the bond to a dealer. The ask price, which is slightly higher, is the price at which you can buy the bond from a dealer.

**Figure 14.1**
Listings of Canadian bonds.

From the *Globe and Mail,* June 30, 1995. Reprinted by permission.

# Canadian Bonds

## Provided by RBC Dominion Securities

**Selected quotations, with changes since the previous day, on actively traded bond issues. Yields are calculated to full maturity, unless marked C to indicate callable date. Price is the midpoint between final bid and ask quotations June 29, 1995.**

| Issuer | Coupon | Maturity | Price | Yield | $ Chg |
|---|---|---|---|---|---|
| **GOVERNMENT OF CANADA** | | | | | |
| CANADA | 7.75 | 15 SEP 96 | 100.885 | 6.954 | -0.320 |
| CANADA | 8.00 | 15 MAR 97 | 101.585 | 6.984 | -0.460 |
| CANADA | 7.50 | 1 JUL 97 | 100.755 | 7.086 | -0.520 |
| CANADA | 6.25 | 1 FEB 98 | 97.715 | 7.235 | -0.630 |
| CANADA | 6.50 | 1 SEP 98 | 97.685 | 7.330 | -0.740 |
| CANADA | 5.75 | 1 MAR 99 | 94.775 | 7.403 | -0.690 |
| CANADA | 7.75 | 1 SEP 99 | 100.975 | 7.469 | -0.770 |
| CANADA | 9.25 | 1 DEC 99 | 106.443 | 7.503 | -0.838 |
| CANADA | 8.50 | 1 MAR 00 | 103.805 | 7.512 | -0.870 |
| CANADA | 9.75 | 1 JUN 01 | 109.826 | 7.649 | -0.993 |
| CANADA | 9.50 | 1 OCT 01 | 108.875 | 7.679 | -1.050 |
| CANADA | 9.75 | 1 DEC 01 | 110.313 | 7.679 | -1.034 |
| CANADA | 8.50 | 1 APR 02 | 103.800 | 7.761 | -1.125 |
| CANADA | 7.25 | 1 JUN 03 | 96.462 | 7.857 | -1.041 |
| CANADA | 7.50 | 1 DEC 03 | 97.528 | 7.906 | -1.088 |
| CANADA | 10.25 | 1 FEB 04 | 114.293 | 7.920 | -1.213 |
| CANADA | 6.50 | 1 JUN 04 | 90.850 | 7.952 | -1.050 |
| CANADA | 9.00 | 1 DEC 04 | 106.802 | 7.957 | -1.218 |
| CANADA | 8.75 | 1 DEC 05 | 105.340 | 7.983 | -1.305 |
| CANADA | 10.00 | 1 JUN 08 | 114.939 | 8.110 | -1.205 |
| CANADA | 9.50 | 1 JUN 10 | 111.362 | 8.167 | -1.274 |
| CANADA | 9.00 | 1 MAR 11 | 107.049 | 8.191 | -1.268 |
| CANADA | 10.25 | 15 MAR 14 | 119.066 | 8.232 | -1.370 |
| CANADA | 9.75 | 1 JUN 21 | 115.233 | 8.308 | -1.473 |
| CANADA | 8.00 | 1 JUN 23 | 96.600 | 8.314 | -1.300 |
| CANADA | 9.00 | 1 JUN 25 | 107.458 | 8.319 | -1.447 |
| CMHC | 8.80 | 1 MAR 00 | 104.473 | 7.636 | -0.871 |
| REAL RETURNS | 4.25 | 1 DEC 21 | 95.825 | 4.522 | -1.500 |
| **PROVINCIAL** | | | | | |
| ALBERTA | 7.00 | 20 AUG 97 | 99.739 | 7.128 | -0.542 |
| ALBERTA | 8.50 | 1 SEP 99 | 103.364 | 7.538 | -0.817 |
| ALBERTA | 6.38 | 1 JUN 04 | 89.435 | 8.059 | -1.034 |
| B C | 7.00 | 9 JUN 99 | 98.549 | 7.430 | -0.687 |
| B C | 9.00 | 9 JAN 02 | 105.532 | 7.897 | -1.101 |
| B C | 9.00 | 21 JUN 04 | 105.515 | 8.121 | -1.154 |
| B C | 8.50 | 23 AUG 13 | 100.240 | 8.472 | -1.130 |
| B C | 8.00 | 8 SEP 23 | 94.045 | 8.561 | -1.250 |
| HYDRO QUEBEC | 9.25 | 2 DEC 96 | 102.775 | 7.137 | -0.400 |
| HYDRO QUEBEC | 10.88 | 25 JUL 01 | 112.585 | 8.195 | -0.970 |
| HYDRO QUEBEC | 11.00 | 15 AUG 20 | 118.825 | 9.082 | -1.350 |
| HYDRO QUEBEC | 9.63 | 15 JUL 22 | 105.225 | 9.102 | -1.250 |
| MANITOBA | 6.75 | 24 AUG 95 | 100.065 | 6.126 | +0.020 |
| MANITOBA | 7.00 | 19 APR 99 | 98.154 | 7.564 | -0.727 |
| MANITOBA | 7.88 | 7 APR 03 | 98.590 | 8.120 | -1.023 |
| MANITOBA | 10.50 | 5 MAR 31 | 120.790 | 8.614 | -1.600 |
| NEW BRUNSWIC | 7.00 | 17 MAR 98 | 99.075 | 7.378 | -0.700 |
| NEW BRUNSWIC | 8.38 | 26 AUG 02 | 101.950 | 8.008 | -1.100 |
| NEW BRUNSWIC | 8.50 | 28 JUN 13 | 98.825 | 8.629 | -1.100 |
| NEWFOUNDLAND | 10.13 | 22 NOV 14 | 108.925 | 9.132 | -1.200 |

| Issuer | Coupon | Maturity | Price | Yield | $ Chg |
|---|---|---|---|---|---|
| NOVA SCOTIA | 9.60 | 30 JAN 22 | 107.325 | 8.877 | -1.350 |
| ONTARIO HYD | 10.88 | 8 JAN 96 | 101.900 | 7.002 | -0.150 |
| ONTARIO HYD | 7.25 | 31 MAR 98 | 99.509 | 7.445 | -0.691 |
| ONTARIO HYD | 9.63 | 3 AUG 99 | 106.628 | 7.698 | -0.818 |
| ONTARIO HYD | 8.63 | 6 FEB 02 | 102.774 | 8.071 | -1.086 |
| ONTARIO HYD | 9.00 | 24 JUN 02 | 104.776 | 8.089 | -1.148 |
| ONTARIO | 8.75 | 16 APR 97 | 102.472 | 7.235 | -0.482 |
| ONTARIO | 9.00 | 15 SEP 04 | 104.454 | 8.295 | -1.159 |
| ONTARIO | 7.50 | 7 FEB 24 | 86.935 | 8.750 | -1.150 |
| P E I | 9.75 | 30 APR 02 | 107.775 | 8.233 | -1.100 |
| P E I | 11.00 | 19 SEP 11 | 118.950 | 8.783 | -1.200 |
| QUEBEC | 8.00 | 30 MAR 98 | 101.015 | 7.575 | -0.690 |
| QUEBEC | 10.25 | 7 APR 98 | 106.475 | 7.593 | -0.700 |
| QUEBEC | 10.25 | 15 OCT 01 | 109.750 | 8.225 | -0.950 |
| QUEBEC | 9.38 | 16 JAN 23 | 102.635 | 9.112 | -1.220 |
| SASKATCHEWAN | 9.88 | 6 JUL 99 | 107.335 | 7.710 | -0.808 |
| SASKATCHEWAN | 9.50 | 16 AUG 04 | 107.313 | 8.336 | -1.171 |
| SASKATCHEWAN | 9.60 | 4 FEB 22 | 108.500 | 8.768 | -1.310 |
| TORONTO -MET | 10.38 | 4 SEP 01 | 110.925 | 8.085 | -1.050 |
| **CORPORATE** | | | | | |
| AGT LIMITED | 9.50 | 24 AUG 04 | 107.250 | 8.347 | -1.125 |
| AVCO FIN | 8.75 | 15 MAR 00 | 103.125 | 7.935 | -0.875 |
| BELL CANADA | 9.20 | 1 JUN 99 | 104.875 | 7.727 | -0.875 |
| BELL CANADA | 9.50 | 15 JUN 02 | 106.875 | 8.181 | -1.250 |
| BELL CANADA | 9.70 | 15 DEC 32 | 108.625 | 8.901 | -1.500 |
| BC TELEPHONE | 9.65 | 8 APR 22 | 108.125 | 8.850 | -1.375 |
| CDN IMP BANK | 7.10 | 10 MAR 04 | 92.750 | 8.285 | -1.125 |
| CDN IMP BANK | 9.65 | 31 OCT 14 | 107.625 | 8.819 | -1.125 |
| CDN UTIL | 8.43 | 1 JUN 05 | 101.000 | 8.278 | -1.250 |
| CDN UTIL | 9.40 | 1 MAY 23 | 106.250 | 8.793 | -1.375 |
| IMASCO LTD | 8.38 | 23 JUN 03 | 100.000 | 8.374 | -1.000 |
| INTERPRV PIP | 8.20 | 15 FEB 24 | 92.875 | 8.889 | -1.125 |
| MOLSON BREW | 8.20 | 11 MAR 03 | 98.875 | 8.398 | -1.000 |
| NVA SCOT PWR | 9.75 | 2 AUG 19 | 107.625 | 8.971 | -1.375 |
| NOVA GAS | 8.30 | 15 JUL 03 | 99.625 | 8.364 | -1.000 |
| NOVA GAS | 9.90 | 16 DEC 24 | 109.625 | 8.966 | -1.375 |
| PANCDN PETE | 8.75 | 9 NOV 05 | 102.750 | 8.345 | -1.250 |
| ROYAL BANK | 10.50 | 1 MAR 02 | 111.750 | 8.172 | -1.250 |
| TALISMAN | 9.45 | 22 DEC 99 | 105.375 | 7.993 | -0.875 |
| TALISMAN | 9.80 | 22 DEC 04 | 107.375 | 8.642 | -1.125 |
| THOMSON CORP | 9.15 | 6 JUL 04 | 104.250 | 8.466 | -1.125 |
| TRANSCDA PIP | 9.45 | 20 MAR 18 | 104.625 | 8.967 | -1.250 |
| UNION GAS | 9.75 | 13 DEC 04 | 108.125 | 8.480 | -1.125 |
| WSTCOAST ENE | 9.50 | 10 JAN 00 | 105.875 | 7.926 | -0.875 |
| WSTCOAST ENE | 9.70 | 15 NOV 04 | 107.750 | 8.481 | -1.125 |
| WSTCOAST ENE | 9.90 | 10 JAN 20 | 109.250 | 8.961 | -1.250 |

**MAPLE LEAF WARRANTS**

| Underlying Issue | Type | Expiry | Strike | Price | $ Chg |
|---|---|---|---|---|---|
| CAN 9.00 DEC 04 | C | 14 FEB 96 | 101.800 | 5.355 | -0.980 |

## ScotiaMcLeod Indexes

| Index | Close | % chg | Yield | Chg | 52 wk High | 52 wk Low |
|---|---|---|---|---|---|---|
| Short | 245.15 | -0.52 | 7.357 | 0.22 | 246.85 | 217.36 |
| Mid | 266.92 | -0.79 | 7.926 | 0.17 | 270.07 | 226.59 |
| Long | 285.89 | -0.92 | 8.452 | 0.11 | 289.91 | 235.76 |
| Universe | 267.16 | -0.72 | 7.840 | 0.17 | 269.98 | 228.76 |

## Benchmarks

| Issuer | Coupon | Maturity | Price | Yield | $ chg |
|---|---|---|---|---|---|
| U.S. Treasury | 7 5/8 | Feb/25 | 112 21/32 | 6.64 | -1 28/32 |
| British gilt | 8.5 | Oct/05 | 100 2/32 | 8.48 | -10/32 |
| German | 6.875 | May/05 | 99.81 | 6.90 | -0.67 |
| Japan #174 | 4.5 | Jun/05 | 114.86 | 2.595 | +0.61 |

Although bonds are sold in denominations of $1,000 par value, the prices are quoted as a percentage of par value. Therefore, the price of the bond is 110.313 percent of par value or $1103.13.

The column labeled "Yield" is the yield to maturity on the bond. The yield to maturity is a measure of the average rate of return to an investor who purchases the bond for the quoted price and holds it until its maturity date. We will have much to say about yield to maturity below.

Bonds generally are traded over the counter, meaning that the market for the bonds is a loosely organized network of bond dealers linked together by a computer quotation system. (See Chapter 3 for a comparison of exchange and OTC trading.) In practice, the bond market can be quite "thin," in that there are few investors interested in trading a particular bond at any particular time. On any day it might be difficult to find a buyer or seller for a particular issue, which introduces some "liquidity risk" into the bond market. It may be difficult to sell one's holdings quickly if the need arises.

This lack of liquidity may be a partial explanation for the inefficiencies that some studies claim to have uncovered in the Canadian bond market. These inefficiencies imply that some Canada bonds are traded below or above their "correct" values, where the latter are estimated from the entire universe of Canada bonds and T-bills. This, in turn, may give rise to arbitrage profits. Such mispricings were quite frequent in earlier years, but they have been much less so more recently.[2]

**Accrued Interest and Quoted Bond Prices.** The bond prices that you see quoted in the financial pages are not actually the prices that investors pay for the bond. This is because the quoted price does not include the interest that accrues between coupon payment dates.

If a bond is purchased between coupon payments, the buyer must pay the seller for accrued interest, the prorated share of the upcoming semiannual coupon. For example, if 40 days have passed since the last coupon payment, and there are 182 days in the semiannual coupon period, the seller is entitled to a payment of accrued interest of 40/182 of the semiannual coupon. The sale, or *invoice price,* of the bond would equal the stated price plus the accrued interest.

To illustrate, suppose that the coupon rate is 8 percent. Then the semiannual coupon payment is \$40. Because 40 days have passed since the last coupon payment, the accrued interest on the bond is \$40 × (40/182) = \$8.79. If the quoted price of the bond is \$990, then the invoice price will be \$990 + \$8.79 = \$998.79.

The practice of quoting bond prices net of accrued interest explains why the price of a maturing bond is listed at \$1,000 rather than \$1,000 plus one coupon payment. A purchaser of an 8 percent coupon bond one day before the bond's maturity would receive \$1,040 on the following day and so should be willing to pay a total price of \$1,040 for the bond. In fact, \$40 of that total payment constitutes the accrued interest for the preceding half-year period. The bond price is quoted net of accrued interest in the financial pages and thus appears as \$1,000.

---

[2] See Tim Appelt and Ramaswamy Krishnan, "Valuation, Mispricing and Change in the Canadian Bond Market", and John Rumsey, "Same Maturity, Different Yields?", both in *Canadian Investment Review*, Spring 1994.

## Corporate Bonds

Like the government, corporations borrow money by issuing Bonds. Figure 14.1 also shows corporate bond listings from *The Globe and Mail.* The data presented follow the same format as Government of Canada and provincial bond listings. For example, the BC Telephone 9.65 bond pays a coupon rate of 9.65 percent and matures in 2022. Like government bonds, corporate bond listings quote the average of the bid and asked prices, as well as the APR or bond equivalent yield. By contrast, U.S. corporate bond listings quote the *current yield,* which is simply the annual coupon payment divided by the bond price. Unlike yield to maturity, the current yield ignores any prospective capital gains or losses based on the bond's price relative to par value. The last column shows the change in closing price from the previous day. Like government bonds, corporate bonds sell in units of $1,000 par value but are quoted as a percentage of par value.

Bonds issued in Canada today can be either *registered bonds* or *bearer bonds.* For registered bonds, the issuing firm keeps records of the owner of the bond and can mail interest checks to him or her. Registration of bonds is clearly helpful to tax authorities in the enforcement of tax collection. In contrast, bearer bonds are traded without any record of ownership. The investor's physical possession of the bond certificate is the only evidence of ownership.

**Call Provisions on Corporate Bonds.** Many corporate bonds are issued with call provisions. The call provision allows the issuer to repurchase the bond at a specified *call price* before the maturity date. For example, if a company issues a bond with a high coupon rate when market interest rates are high. and interest rates later fall, the firm might like to retire the high-coupon debt and issue new bonds at a lower coupon rate to reduce interest payments. This is called *refunding.*

The call price of a bond is commonly set at an initial level near par value plus one annual coupon payment. The call price falls as time passes, gradually approaching par value.

Callable bonds typically come with a period of call protection, an initial time during which the bonds are not callable. Such bonds are referred to as *deferred* callable bonds.

The option to call the bond is valuable to the firm, allowing it to buy back the bonds and refinance at a lower interest rate when market rates fall. Of course, the firm's benefit is the bondholder's burden. Holders of called bonds forfeit their bonds for the call price, thereby giving up the prospect of an attractive rate of interest on their original investment. To compensate investors for this risk, callable bonds are issued with higher coupons and promised yields to maturity than noncallable bonds.

Figure 14.2 shows the terms of a callable bond issued by The Bank of Nova Scotia as described in *Moody's Bank and Finance Manual.* The bond was issued in 1977 but was not callable until 1993. After 1993, the call price falls until it eventually reaches par value after September 14, 1995. Therefore, bondholders have complete call protection until 1993. However, *limited* amounts of the

**Figure 14.2**
Callable bond issued by The Bank of Nova Scotia.

From Moody's Bank and Finance Manual 1991. Reprinted by permission.

**17. The Bank of Nova Scotia sinking fund debenture 9 1/2s, due 1997:**

OUTSG.—Oct. 31, 1990, C$36,375,000.

DATED—Sept. 15, 1977. DUE—Sept. 15, 1997.

INTEREST—M&S 15. Principal and interest will be payable at any branch of the Bank in Canada.

TRUSTEE—Montreal Trust Company Canada.

DENOMINATION—Coupon, $1,000, $5,000 and $25,000 registrable as to principal only and fully registered, $1,000 and full multiples thereof.

CALLABLE—As a whole or in part at any time on at least 30 days' notice to each Sept. 14 as follows:

1933. . . . . 101.50 1994. . . . 101.00 1995. . . . . 100.50

And thereafter at 100. Also callable for mandatory and optional sinking fund purposes at 100 plus accrued interest.

SINKING FUND—Annually, on Sept. 15, 1983–96, cash (or debs.), to retire $1,500,000 principal amount of debs.; plus similar optional payments.

SECURITY—Subordinate to all senior debt.

INDENTURE MODIFICATION—Indenture may be modified, except as provided, with consent of 66 2/3% of debs. outstg.

PURPOSE—Proceeds will be used to augment the Bank's general fund.

OFFERED—($50,000,000) at $100 plus accrued interest on Aug. 16, 1977, through Wood Gundy Ltd., Burns Fry Ltd., Dominion Securities Ltd., and associates.

bonds may be called at par value starting in 1983 as part of the provisions of the sinking fund.

---

**CONCEPT CHECK** Question 1. Suppose that a corporation issues two bonds with identical coupon rates and maturity dates. One bond is callable, however, whereas the other is not. Which bond will sell at a higher price?

---

**Convertible Bonds.** **Convertible bonds** give bondholders an option to exchange each bond for a specified number of shares of common stock of the firm. The *conversion ratio* gives the number of shares for which each bond may be exchanged. To see the value of this right, suppose a convertible bond that is issued at par value of $1,000 is convertible into 40 shares of a firm's stock. The current stock price is $20 per share, so the option to convert is not profitable now. Should the stock price later rise to $30, however, each bond may be converted profitably into $1,200 worth of stock. The *market conversion value* is the current value of the shares for which the bonds may be exchanged. At the $20 stock price, for example, the bond's conversion value is $800. The *conversion premium* is the excess of the bond value over its conversion value. If the bond were selling currently for $950, its premium would be $150.

Convertible bonds give their holders the ability to share in the price appreciation of the company's stock. Again, this benefit comes at a price; convertible bonds offer lower coupon rates and stated or promised yields to maturity than do nonconvertible bonds. At the same time, the actual return on the convertible bond may exceed the stated yield to maturity if the option to convert becomes profitable.

We discuss convertible and callable bonds further in Chapter 20.

**Retractable and Extendible Bonds.** A relatively new development is the **retractable bond**. Whereas the callable bond gives the issuer the option to retire the bond at the call date or to continue to the maturity date, the retractable bond gives the option to the bondholder. Thus, if the bond's coupon rate is below current market yields, the bondholder will choose to redeem the bond early, through retraction. An **extendible bond**, on the other hand, allows the bondholder to retain the bond for an additional period beyond maturity, which he or she will do if the coupon exceeds current rates; such a bond is known as a *put bond* in the United States. These additional privileges granted to the bondholders are paid for by a slightly lower coupon.

**Floating-Rate Bonds. Floating-rate bonds** make interest payments that are tied to some measure of current market rates. For example, the rate might be adjusted annually to the current T-bill rate plus 2 percent. If the one-year T-bill rate at the adjustment date is 4 percent, the bond's coupon rate over the next year would then be 6 percent. This arrangement means that the bond always pays approximately current market rates.

The major risk involved in floaters has to do with changing credit conditions. The yield spread is fixed over the life of the security, which may be many years. If the financial health of the firm deteriorates, then a greater yield premium would be required than is offered by the security. In this case, the price of the bond would fall. Although the coupon rate on floaters adjusts to changes in the general level of market interest rates, it does not adjust to changes in the financial condition of the firm.

## Preferred Stock

Although preferred stock strictly speaking is considered to be equity, it often is included in the fixed-income universe. This is because, like bonds, preferred stock promises to pay a specified stream of dividends. However, unlike bonds, the failure to pay the promised dividend does not result in corporate bankruptcy. Instead, the dividends owed simply cumulate, and the common stockholders may not receive any dividends until the preferred stockholders have been paid in full. In the event of bankruptcy, the claims of preferred stockholders to the firm's assets have lower priority than those of bondholders, but higher priority than those of common stockholders.

Most preferred stock pays a fixed dividend. Therefore, it is in effect a perpetuity, providing a level cash flow indefinitely. In the last few years, however, adjustable or floating rate preferred stock has become popular. Floating rate preferred stock is much like floating rate bonds. The dividend rate is linked to a measure of current market interest rates and is adjusted at regular intervals.

### Other Issuers

There are, of course, several issuers of bonds in addition to the federal government and private corporations. For example, provinces, crown corporations, and local governments issue bonds. They also appear in the listings of Figure 14.1.

## 14.2 Default Risk

Although bonds generally *promise* a fixed flow of income, that income stream is not riskless unless the investor can be sure the issuer will not default on the obligation. While government bonds may be treated as free of default risk, this is not true of corporate bonds. If the company goes bankrupt, the bondholders will not receive all the payments they have been promised. Therefore, the actual payments on these bonds are uncertain, for they depend to some degree on the ultimate financial status of the firm.

Bond default risk is measured by both Moody's and Standard & Poor's in the United States and by Canadian Bond Rating Service (CBRS) and Dominion Bond Rating Service (DBRS) in Canada; the two U.S. rating services also rate several Canadian issues. All rating agencies assign letter grades to the bonds of corporations and municipalities to reflect their assessment of the safety of the bond issue. The top rating is AAA (Standard & Poor's and DBRS), Aaa (Moody's), and A++ (CBRS). Moody's modifies each rating class with a 1, 2, or 3 suffix (e.g., Aaa1, Aaa2, Aaa3) to provide a finer gradation of ratings. S&P uses a + or − modification, and the two Canadian services use the terms (*high*) and (*low*) as modifiers.

Bonds rated BBB or above (S&P and DBRS), Baa or above (Moody's), and B++ or above (CBRS) are considered **investment grade bonds**, whereas lower-rated bonds are classified as **speculative grade** or **junk bonds**. Certain regulated institutional investors such as insurance companies have not always been allowed to invest in speculative grade bonds.

Figure 14.3 provides the definitions of each bond rating classification.

### Junk Bonds

Junk bonds, also known as *high-yield bonds,* are nothing more than speculative grade (low-rated or unrated) bonds. Before 1977, almost all junk bonds were "fallen angels," that is, firm-issued bonds that originally had investment grade ratings but that had since been downgraded. In 1977, however, firms began to issue "original-issue junk."

Much of the credit for this innovation is given to Drexel Burnham Lambert and especially its trader, Michael Milken. Drexel had long enjoyed a niche as a junk bond trader and had established a network of potential investors in junk bonds. Its reasoning for marketing original-issue junk, so-called emerging credits, lay in the belief that default rates on these bonds did not justify the large yield spreads commonly exhibited in the marketplace. Firms not able to muster an investment

**Figure 14.3** Definitions of each bond rating class.

### *Bond Ratings*

| | **Very high quality** | **High quality** | **Speculative** | **Very poor** |
|---|---|---|---|---|
| CBRS | A++ A+ | A B++ | B+ B | C D |
| DBRS | AAA AA | A BBB | BB B | C D |
| Standard & Poor's | AAA AA | A BBB | BB B | CCC D |
| Moody's | Aaa Aa | A Baa | Ba B | Caa C |

At times all services have used adjustments to these ratings. S&P uses plus and minus signs: A+ is the strongest A rating and A− the weakest. Moody's uses a 1, 2 or 3 designation—with 1 indicating the strongest. CBRS and DBRS use a (high) for the strongest and a (low) for the weakest designations.

| **CBRS** | **DBRS** | **Moody's** | **S&P** | |
|---|---|---|---|---|
| A++ | AAA | Aaa | AAA | Debt rated Aaa and AAA has the highest rating. Capacity to pay interest and principal is extremely strong. |
| A+ | AA | Aa | A | Debt rated Aa and AA has a very strong capacity to pay interest and repay principal. Together with the highest rating, this group comprises the high-grade bond class. |
| A | A | A | A | Debt rated A has a strong capacity to pay interest and repay principal, although it is somewhat more susceptible to the adverse effects of changes in circumstances and economic conditions than debt in higher-rated categories. |
| B++ | BBB | Baa | BBB | Debt rated Baa and BBB is regarded as having an adequate capacity to pay interest and repay principal. Whereas it normally exhibits adequate protection parameters, adverse economic conditions or changing circumstances are more likely to lead to a weakened capacity to pay interest and repay principal for debt in this category than in higher-rated categories. These bonds are medium-grade obligations. |
| B+<br>B<br>C<br>C | BB<br>B<br>CCC<br>CC | Ba<br>B<br>Caa<br>Ca | BB<br>B<br>CCC<br>CC | Debt rated in these categories is regarded, on balance, as predominantly speculative with respect to capacity to pay interest and repay principal in accordance with the terms of the obligation. BB and Ba indicate the lowest degree of speculation, and CC and Ca the highest degree of speculation. Although such debt will likely have some quality and protective characteristics, these are outweighed by large uncertainties or major risk exposures to adverse conditions. Some issues may be in default. |
| C | C | C | C | This rating is reserved for income bonds on which no interest is being paid. |
| D | D | D | D | Debt rated D is in default, and payment of interest and/or repayment of principal is in arrears. |

Data from various editions of *Standard & Poor's Bond Guide, Moody's Bond Guide, CBRS Canadian Credit Review,* and *DBRS Bond Rating.*

Modified from Stephen A. Ross and Randolph W. Westerfield, *Corporate Finance* (St. Louis: Times Mirror/Mosby College Publishing, 1988). Reprinted by permission.

## There's Gold in Canadian Junk Bonds

New York bond traders have locked in huge profits recently from cheap Canadian corporate bonds purchased over the past year when companies sank into difficulty.

Canadian investors have largely missed the boat on the distressed bonds, blaming the small size of our market for a lack of investment vehicles.

But some analysts and traders say high-risk mutual funds investing in Canadian junk bonds are an inevitable future development because of the potential profits.

Distressed bonds of companies such as Trizec Corp., Ltd., Gentra, Inc. (formerly Royal Trustco Ltd.), Brainalea Ltd., Stelco Inc., Algoma Steel Inc., and Olympia & York Developments Ltd. have rallied recently after sinking to steep bargain rates.

Stelco's 10.4% 2009 bond, for example, has climbed to $99 recently from $30 at the beginning of last year. Gentra's 11¼% 1998 bond has climbed to $74 from $50 in January 1993.

Corporate bond prices rise when investors believe they have a better chance of being repaid, usually as a company's financial health improves or as the likelihood increases that its assets will be successfully liquidated to repay debt.

Canadian and U.S. bond traders and analysts say the improved market only drives home the loss to Canadians who have sent their distressed bonds across the border to U.S. buyers in a virtually one-way market.

They estimate more than $1 billion par value of Canadian distressed bonds were sold in 1993, and almost 100% of the sales went to the U.S. or other foreign buyers.

One distressed-bond salesman for a U.S. investment company said Canadian institutions are forced by their conservative mandates to sell bonds that sink below investment-grade, often at huge losses. They are similarly not allowed to purchase junk bonds for their investment portfolios.

"Canadians are incompetent and stupid," he said bluntly. "They're so risk-averse they sell out at 20¢ on the dollar when they're worth 80¢ on the dollar."

Many U.S. institutional investors have the same type of investment limitations as Canadian institutions, but the difference in the U.S. is the presence of large investment funds that specialize in junk bonds. Their rapid growth during the past five years has created a huge market for distressed bonds, and they do not hesitate to search the Canadian market to find them.

They are known as junk bond funds, or, more formally, as high-yield bond funds because the junk bonds pay a higher yield because of their lower prices. The U.S. junk bond market was estimated at US $70 billion last year.

"If there were junk bond funds in Canada, you could make terrific returns," says Brian Berner of Berner & Co. Inc., a Toronto-based distressed-securities house. "They've made a fortune out of the Canadian market in the last year."

Berner says he did a theoretical portfolio of Canadian distressed bonds, and it showed a 63% return for 1993.

But setting up a Canadian high-yield mutual fund is not an easy solution, says one Canadian bond trader at a Toronto-based securities firm.

He says Canada's market for distressed securities is too small to make it possible to have full-time analysts examining the opportunities in the market, which is a crucial requirement for the very high-risk investments.

"It's highly profitable, but it requires a degree of knowledge and focus and our market here I don't think is big enough for anyone to do it."

Canada not only lacks sufficient amounts of capital, he says, but it especially lacks enough capital slated for high-risk investing. Canada's supply of distressed bonds, although growing, is also very small compared to U.S. supplies, he says.

"It's not because Canadians are risk-averse, but when you don't have large, deep pockets you can't

*(Continued)*

afford to take $5 million and go and roll with it," he says.

One Toronto-based trader says it is only a matter of time until Canadians start to take advantage of the investment opportunity. He believes high-yield funds are inevitable in Canada, likely within the next three years.

"We're 10 years behind the U.S.," he says. "By 1997 it will be a nice little business."

A key development, he argues, is the introduction of U.S. debt-rating agencies into the Canadian market. He argues that with both Moody's Investors Service Inc. and Standard & Poor's Corp. opening offices in Canada, there will be more interest in Canadian bonds.

"Things are going to get more and more professional," he says. "Somebody's going to open shop and sell a higher-yield mutual fund."

Julian Schroeder, a specialist in Canadian bonds at New York's BDS Securities Corp., says investors in the U.S. have especially been attracted to Canadian bonds during the past year. He says, for example, that he bought a Bramalea bond at $15 that was recently selling for $45, and bought a Trizec bond for $58 that recently hit $83.

"The investors are pretty much value-oriented investors here," Schroeder said. "They'll play wherever there's value, and I would say Canada continues to be under-followed in this country. People who take the time to look into it will be rewarded."

Perhaps the biggest problem this month is thinning markets and declining opportunities as prices rise. The flood of U.S. interest is drying up supply and making hidden bargains harder to find.

"Everybody and his brother is looking for opportunities," says a trader in the Toronto office of a U.S.-based investment company. "A 10-year U.S. Treasury yields 5¼% and a decent junk bond yields 8%."

It will not be a long-term phenomenon, however, as long as Canadian companies continue to fall into trouble and see their bonds sink in price.

"There will be another one tomorrow," one trader predicts confidently. "They're like buses, but in Canada they're not as frequent."

**Examples of Junk Bond Price Increases in the Past Year:**

| | Jan. 31/94 Price | Jan. 4/93 Price |
|---|---|---|
| Stelco 13½% Oct. 2000 | $98 | $30 |
| Stelco 10⅞% Sept. 1994 | $99 | $30 |
| Stelco 10.40% Nov. 2009 | $99 | $30 |
| Olympia & York 10.7% Nov. 93* | $68 | $60 |
| Olympia & York 11% Nov. 98 | $68 | $60 |
| Trizec 11⅛% June 1996 | $78 | $70 |
| Trizec 10¼% June 1999 | $79 | $65 |
| Royal Trustco (now Gentra Inc.) | | |
| 11¼ May 1998 | $74 | $50 |
| 11.3% May 1998 | $86 | $55 |
| 11.8% May 1998 | $88 | $55 |

*Bond is still outstanding although past maturity date.

Source: Wood Gundy Inc.

Source: Janet McFarland, *Financial Post*, February 5, 1994, p. 19. Reprinted by permission.

grade rating were happy to have Drexel (and other investment bankers) market their bonds directly to the public, as this opened up a new source of financing. Junk issues were a lower-cost financing alternative than borrowing from banks.

High-yield bonds gained considerable notoriety in the 1980s when they were used as financing vehicles in leveraged buyouts and hostile takeover attempts. High-yield bonds also were extremely popular with investors. Although such bonds constituted only 3.7 percent of the corporate bond market in 1977, they accounted for 23 percent of the market by 1987.

Shortly thereafter, however, the junk bond market suffered. The legal difficulties of Drexel and Michael Milken in connection with Wall Street's insider trading scandals of the late 1980s tainted the junk bond market. Drexel agreed to pay $650 million in fines and plead guilty to six felony charges to avoid racketeering charges. Milken was indicted on racketeering and security fraud charges, resigned from Drexel, and eventually agreed in a plea bargain to plead guilty to six felony charges and to pay $600 million in fines. Moreover, as the high-yield bond market tumbled in late 1989, Drexel suffered large losses in its own billion-dollar portfolio of junk bonds. In February 1990, Drexel filed for bankruptcy.

At the height of Drexel's difficulties, the high-yield bond market nearly dried up. New issues of high-yield bonds fell from $24 billion in 1989 to less than $1 billion in 1990, and prices on these issues fell so severely that their yields exceeded U.S. Treasury yields by about 7.5 percentage points, the largest margin in history. Since then, the market has rebounded. New issues in 1993 were a record-breaking $55 billion in the U.S. Further, the nearby box indicates this investor interest in junk bonds has also had an impact in Canada. It is, however, worth noting that the average credit quality of high-yield debt issues in 1993 was higher than the average quality in the boom years of the 1980s.

## Determinants of Bond Safety

Bond rating agencies base their quality ratings largely on an analysis of the level and trend of some of the issuer's financial ratios. The key ratios used to evaluate safety are:

1. *Coverage ratios*—Ratios of company earnings to fixed costs. For example, the *times-interest-earned ratio* is the ratio of earnings before interest payments and taxes to interest obligations. The *fixed-charge coverage ratio* adds lease payments and sinking fund payments to interest obligations to arrive at the ratio of earnings to all fixed cash obligations. Low or falling coverage ratios signal possible cash flow difficulties.
2. *Leverage ratio*—Debt to equity ratio. A too-high leverage ratio indicates excessive indebtedness, signaling the possibility the firm will be unable to earn enough to satisfy the obligations on its bonds.
3. *Liquidity ratios*—The two common liquidity ratios are the *current ratio* (current assets/current liabilities) and the *quick ratio* (current assets excluding inventories/current liabilities). These ratios measure the firm's ability to pay bills coming due with cash currently being collected.
4. *Profitability ratio*—Measures of rates of return on assets or equity. Profitability ratios are indicators of a firm's overall financial health. The *return on assets* (earnings before interest and taxes divided by total assets) is the most popular of these measures. Firms with higher return on assets should be better able to raise money in security markets because they offer prospects for better returns on the firm's investments.
5. *Cash flow to debt ratio*—This is the ratio of total cash flow to outstanding debt.

Standard & Poor's several years ago computed three-year median values of

**Table 14.1** Rating Classes and Median Financial Ratios, 1983–1985

| Rating Category | Fixed-Charge Coverage Ratio | Cash Flow to Long-Term Debt | Return on Capital (%) | Long-Term Debt to Capital(%) |
|---|---|---|---|---|
| AAA | 7.48 | 3.09 | 25.60 | 8.85 |
| AA | 4.43 | 1.18 | 22.05 | 18.88 |
| A | 2.93 | .75 | 18.03 | 24.46 |
| BBB | 2.30 | .46 | 12.10 | 31.54 |
| BB | 2.04 | .27 | 13.80 | 42.52 |
| B | 1.51 | .19 | 12.01 | 52.04 |
| CCC | 0.75 | .15 | 2.70 | 69.28 |

Source: Standard & Poor's *Debt Rating Guide,* 1986. Reprinted by permission of Standard & Poor's Ratings Group.

selected ratios for firms in each of the four investment grade classes, which we present in Table 14.1. Of course, ratios must be evaluated in the context of industry standards, and analysts differ in the weights they place on particular ratios. Nevertheless, Table 14.1 demonstrates the tendency of ratios to improve along with the firm's rating class.

Direct statistical tests of the ability of financial ratios to predict bond ratings in the five top rating classes of the Canadian Bond Rating Service (CBRS) were conducted in a study by Barnes and Byng.[3] The study examined 27 financial variables that included ratios similar to those in Table 14.1, as well as variables representing the size and earnings stability of the firm. The results showed that the observed ratings assigned by CBRS in the years 1972, 1978, and 1983 could be predicted fairly accurately by an appropriate set of weights applied to the 27 variables for each year. These weights, though, tended to change from year to year, and the accuracy of one year's predictors tended to deteriorate with time.

In fact, the heavy dependence of bond ratings on publicly available financial data is evidence of an interesting phenomenon. You might think that an increase or a decrease in a bond rating would cause substantial bond price gains or losses, but this is not the case. Weinstein[4] found that bond prices move in *anticipation* of rating changes, which is evidence that investors themselves track the financial status of bond issuers. This is consistent with an efficient market. Rating changes actually largely confirm a change in status that has been reflected in security prices already. Holthausen and Leftwich[5] however, found that bond rating downgrades (but not upgrades) are associated with abnormal returns in the stock of the affected company.

[3] Tom Barnes and Tom Byng, "The Prediction of Corporate Bond Ratings: The Canadian Case," *Canadian Journal of Administrative Sciences* 5, no. 3 (September 1988).

[4] Mark I. Weinstein, "The Effect of a Rating Change Announcement on Bond Price," *Journal of Financial Economics,* December 1977.

[5] Robert W. Holthausen and Richard W. Leftwich, "The Effect of Bond Rating Changes on Common Stock Prices," *Journal of Financial Economics* 17 (September 1986).

**Figure 14.4**
Discriminant analysis.

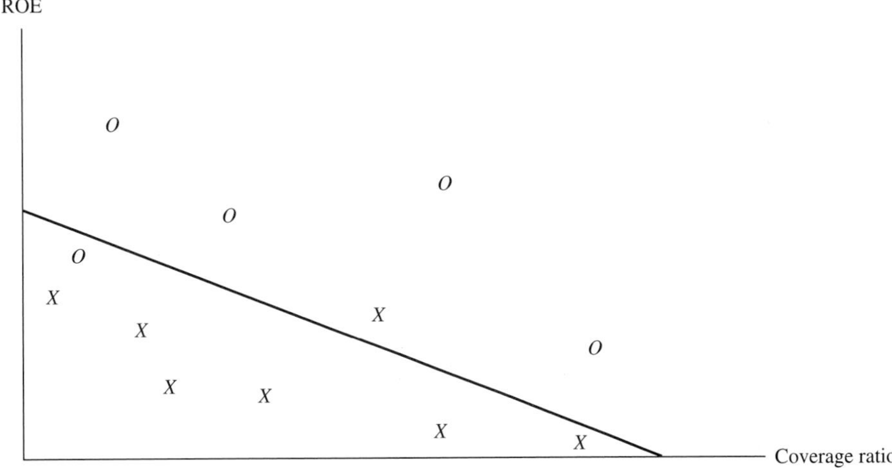


Many studies have tested whether financial ratios can in fact be used to predict default risk. One of the best-known series of tests has been conducted by Edward Altman, who has used discriminant analysis to predict bankruptcy. With this technique, a firm is assigned a score based on its financial characteristics. If its score exceeds a cutoff value, the firm is deemed creditworthy. A score below the cutoff value indicates significant bankruptcy risk in the near future.

To illustrate the technique, suppose that we were to collect data on the return on equity (ROE) and coverage ratios of a sample of firms and then keep records of any corporate bankruptcies. In Figure 14.4 we plot the ROE and coverage ratios for each firm using *X* for firms that eventually went bankrupt and *O* for those who remained solvent. Clearly, the *X* and *O* firms show different patterns of data, with the solvent firms typically showing higher values for the two ratios.

The discriminant analysis determines the equation of the line that best separates the *X* and *O* observations. Suppose that the equation of the line is $.75 = .9 \times \text{ROE} + .4 \times \text{Coverage}$. Each firm is assigned a "Z-score" equal to $.9 \times \text{ROE} + .4 \times \text{Coverage}$ using the firm's ROE and coverage ratios. If the Z-score exceeds .75, the firm plots above the line and is considered a safe bet; Z-scores below .75 foretell financial difficulty.

The discriminant analysis method was applied to a sample of Canadian firms in a study by Altman and Lavallee,[6] who found the following equation to best separate failing and nonfailing firms:

[6] Edward I. Altman and Marion Y. Lavalee, "Business Failure Classification in Canada," *Journal of Business Administration* 12, no. 1 (Fall 1980).

$$Z = 0.234 \frac{\text{Sales}}{\text{Total assets}} + 0.972 \frac{\text{Net after-tax profits}}{\text{Total debt}} + 1.002 \frac{\text{Current assets}}{\text{Current liabilities}} - 0.531 \frac{\text{Total debt}}{\text{Total assets}} + 0.612\,(\text{Rate of equity growth} - \text{Rate of asset growth})$$

Firms with Z-scores above 1.626 were deemed safe; 81.5 percent of these were still in business in the next year. In contrast, 85.2 percent of bankrupt firms had Z-scores below 1.626 the year before they failed.

A rather more sceptical view of the ability of financial ratios to predict default risk emerges from a Canadian study of *small-business* debt (mainly bank loans) by Kryzanowski and To.[7] They found that default risk depended on variables such as the firm's size and age, the type of loan, and the project performance assessment made by the lending institution. Several important financial ratios were examined, and none of them were found to be a significant determinant of default risk. It seems, therefore, that financial ratios are not good indicators of such risk for small businesses.

---

**CONCEPT CHECK** Question 2. Suppose we add to the Altman–Lavallee equation a new variable equal to market value of equity/book value of debt. Would you expect this variable to receive a positive or negative coefficient?

---

## Bond Indentures

A bond is issued with an **indenture**, which is the contract between the issuer and the bondholder. Part of the indenture is a set of restrictions on the firm issuing the bond to protect the rights of the bondholders. Such restrictions include provisions relating to collateral, sinking funds, dividend policy, and further borrowing. The issuing firm agrees to these so-called *protective covenants* in order to market its bonds to investors concerned about the safety of the bond issue.

**Sinking Funds.** Bonds call for the payment of par value at the end of the bond's life. This payment constitutes a large cash commitment for the issuer. To help ensure the commitment does not create a cash flow crisis, the firm agrees to establish a **sinking fund** to spread the payment burden over several years. The fund may operate in one of two ways:

1. The firm may repurchase a fraction of the outstanding bonds in the open market each year.

---

[7] Lawrence Kryzanowski and Minh Chau To, "Small-Business Debt Financing: An Empirical Investigation of Default Risk," *Canadian Journal of Administrative Sciences* 2, no. 1 (June 1985).

2. The firm may purchase a fraction of outstanding bonds at a special call price associated with the sinking fund provision. The firm has an option to purchase the bonds at either the market price or the sinking fund price, whichever is lower. To allocate the burden of the sinking fund call fairly among bondholders, the bonds chosen for the call are selected at random based on serial numbers.[8]

The sinking fund call differs from a conventional bond call in two important ways. First, the firm can repurchase only a limited fraction of the bond issue at the sinking fund call price. At best, some indentures allow firms to use a *doubling option,* which allows repurchase of double the required number of bonds at the sinking fund call price. Second, the sinking fund call price generally is lower than the call price established by other call provisions in the indenture. The sinking fund call price usually is set at the bond's par value.

Although sinking funds ostensibly protect bondholders by making principal repayment more likely, they can hurt the investor. If interest rates fall and bond prices rise, firms will benefit from the sinking fund provision that enables them to repurchase their bonds at below-market prices. In these circumstances, the firm's gain is the bondholder's loss.

One bond issue that does not require a sinking fund is a *serial bond issue.* In a serial bond issue, the firm sells bonds with staggered maturity dates. As bonds mature sequentially, the principal repayment burden for the firm is spread over time just as it is with a sinking fund. Serial bonds do not include call provisions.

**Subordination of Further Debt.** One of the factors determining bond safety is total outstanding debt of the issuer. If you bought a bond today, you would be understandably distressed to see the firm tripling its outstanding debt tomorrow. Your bond would be of lower quality than it appeared when you bought it. To prevent firms from harming bondholders in this manner, **subordination clauses** restrict the amount of additional borrowing. Additional debt might be required to be subordinated in priority to existing debt; that is, in the event of bankruptcy, *subordinated* or *junior* debtholders will not be paid unless and until the prior senior debt is fully paid off. For this reason, subordination is sometimes called a "me-first rule," meaning the senior (earlier) bondholders are to be paid first in the event of bankruptcy.

**Dividend Restrictions.** Covenants also limit firms in the amount of dividends they are allowed to pay. These limitations protect the bondholders because they force the firm to retain assets rather than paying them out to stockholders. A typical restriction disallows payments of dividends if cumulative dividends paid since the firm's inception exceed cumulative net income plus proceeds from sales of stock.

---

[8] Although it is uncommon, the sinking fund provision also may call for periodic payments to a trustee, with the payments invested so that the accumulated sum can be used for retirement of the entire issue at maturity.

**Collateral.** Some bonds are issued with specific collateral behind them. **Collateral** can take several forms, but it represents a particular asset of the firm that the bondholders receive if the firm defaults on the bond. If the collateral is property, the bond is called a *mortgage bond.* If the collateral takes the form of other securities held by the firm, the bond is a *collateral trust bond.* In the case of equipment, the bond is known as an *equipment obligation bond.* This last form of collateral is used most commonly by firms such as railroads, where the equipment is fairly standard and can be easily sold to another firm should the firm default and the bondholders acquire the collateral.

Because of the specific collateral that backs them, collaterized bonds generally are considered the safest variety of corporate bonds. General **debenture** bonds by contrast do not provide for specific collateral; they are *unsecured* bonds. The bondholder relies solely on the general earning power of the firm for the bond's safety. If the firm defaults, debenture owners become general creditors of the firm. Because they are safer, collateralized bonds generally offer lower yields than general debentures.

## 14.3 BOND PRICING

### Review of the Present Value Relationship

Because a bond's coupon payments and principal repayment all occur months or years in the future, the price an investor would be willing to pay for a claim to those payments depends on the value of dollars to be received in the future compared to dollars in hand today. The *present value* of a claim to a dollar to be paid in the future is the market price at which that claim would sell if it were traded in the securities market.

We know that the present value of a dollar to be received in the future is less than one dollar.The time spent waiting to receive the dollar imposes an opportunity cost on the investor—if the money is not in hand today, it cannot be invested to start generating income immediately. Denoting the current market interest rate by $r$, the present value of a dollar to be received $n$ years from now is $1/(1 + r)^n$.

To see why this is so, consider an example in which the interest rate is 5 percent, ($r = .05$). According to the present value rule, the value of \$1 to be received in 10 years would be $1/(1.05)^{10} = \$.614$. A little over 61 cents is the amount that would be paid in the marketplace for a claim to a payment of \$1 in 10 years. This is because a person investing today at the going 5 percent rate of interest realizes that only \$.614 needs to be set aside now in order to provide a final value of \$1 in 10 years as $\$.614 \times 1.05^{10} = \$1.00$. The present value formula tells us exactly how much an investor should be willing to pay for a claim to a future cash flow. This value will be the current price of the claim.

We simplify for now by assuming there is one interest rate that is appropriate for discounting cash flows of any maturity, but we can relax this assumption easily. In practice, there may be different discount rates for cash flows accruing in different periods. For the time being, however, we ignore this refinement.

## Bond Pricing

To value a security, we discount its expected cash flows by the appropriate discount rate. The cash flows from a bond consist of coupon payments until the maturity date plus the final payment of par value. Therefore

$$\text{Bond value} = \text{Present value of coupons} + \text{Present value of par value}$$

If we call the maturity date $T$ and the interest rate $r$, the bond value can be written as

$$\text{Bond value} = \sum_{t=1}^{T} \frac{\text{Coupon}}{(1+r)^t} + \frac{\text{Par value}}{(1+r)^T} \qquad \textbf{(14.1)}$$

The summation sign in equation 14.1 directs us to add the present value of each coupon payment; each coupon is discounted based on the time until it will be paid. The first term on the right-hand side of equation 14.1 is the present value of an annuity. The second term is the present value of a single amount, the final payment of the bond's par value.

**An Example: Bond Pricing.** We discussed earlier an 8 percent coupon, 30-year maturity bond with par value of $1,000 paying 60 semiannual coupon payments of $40 each. Suppose that the interest rate is 8 percent annually, or 4 percent per six-month period. Then the value of the bond can be written as

$$\text{Price} = \sum_{t=1}^{60} \frac{\$40}{(1.04)^t} + \frac{\$1{,}000}{(1.04)^{60}} \qquad \textbf{(14.2)}$$

For notational simplicity, we can write equation 14.2 as

$$\text{Price} = \$40 \times \text{PA}(4\%, 60) + \$1{,}000 \times \text{PF}(4\%, 60)$$

where PA(4%, 60) represents the present value of an annuity of $1 when the interest rate is 4 percent and the annuity lasts for 60 six-month periods, and PF(4%, 60) is the present value of a single payment of $1 to be received in 60 periods.

It is easy to confirm that the present value of the bond's 60 semiannual coupon payments of $40 each is $904.94, whereas the $1,000 final payment of par value has a present value of $95.06, for a total bond value of $1,000. You can perform these calculations on any financial calculator or use a set of present value tables.

In this example, the coupon rate equals yield to maturity, and the bond price equals par value. If the interest rate were not equal to the bond's coupon rate, the bond would not sell at par value. For example, if the interest rate were to rise to 10 percent (5 percent per six months), the bond's price would fall by $189.29, to $810.71, as follows

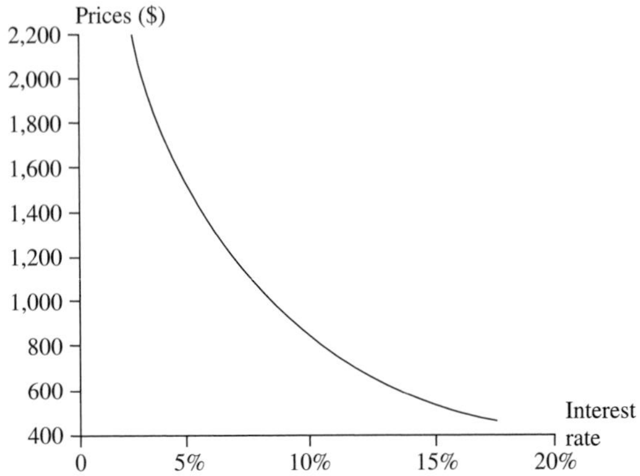


**Figure 14.5** The inverse relationship between bond prices and yields.

**Table 14.2** Bond Prices at Different Interest Rates (8% coupon bond, coupons paid semiannually)

| | Bond Price at Given Market Interest Rate | | | | |
|---|---|---|---|---|---|
| **Time to Maturity** | **4%** | **6%** | **8%** | **10%** | **12%** |
| 1 year | 1,038.83 | 1,029.13 | 1,000.00 | 981.41 | 963.33 |
| 10 years | 1,327.03 | 1,148.77 | 1,000.00 | 875.35 | 770.60 |
| 20 years | 1,547.11 | 1,231.15 | 1,000.00 | 828.41 | 699.07 |
| 30 years | 1,695.22 | 1,276.76 | 1,000.00 | 810.71 | 676.77 |

$$\begin{aligned}&\$40 \times \text{PA}(5\%, 60) + \$1{,}000 \times \text{PF}(5\%, 60)\\ &= \$757.17 + \$53.54\\ &= \$810.71\end{aligned}$$

At a higher interest rate, the present value of the payments to be received by the bondholder is lower. Therefore, the bond price will fall as market interest rates rise. This illustrates a crucial general rule in bond valuation. When interest rates rise, bond prices must fall because the present values of the bond's payments are obtained by discounting at a higher interest rate.

Figure 14.5 shows the price of the 30-year, 8 percent coupon bond for a range of interest rates. The negative slope illustrates the inverse relationship between prices and yields. Note also from the figure (and from Table 14.2) that the shape of the curve implies that an increase in the interest rate results in a price decline that is smaller than the price gain resulting from a decrease of equal magnitude in the interest rate. This property of bond prices is called *convexity* because of the convex shape of the bond price curve. This curvature reflects the fact that progressive increases in the interest rate result in progressively smaller reductions in the bond price.[9] Therefore, the price curve becomes flatter at higher interest rates.

---

**CONCEPT CHECK** Question 3. Calculate the price of the bond for a market interest rate of 3% per half year. Compare the capital gains for the interest rate decline to the losses incurred when the rate increases to 5%.

---

Corporate bonds typically are issued at par value. This means that the underwriters of the bond issue (the firms that market the bonds to the public for the issuing corporation) must choose a coupon rate that very closely approximates market yields. In a primary issue of bonds, the underwriters attempt to sell the newly issued bonds directly to their customers. If the coupon rate is inadequate, investors will not pay par value for the bonds.

After the bonds are issued, bondholders may buy or sell bonds in secondary markets, such as the over-the-counter market, where many U.S. and all Canadian bonds trade. In these secondary markets, bond prices move in accordance with market forces. The bond prices fluctuate inversely with the market interest rate.

The inverse relationship between price and yield is a central feature of fixed-income securities. Interest rate fluctuations represent the main source of risk in the fixed-income market, and we devote considerable attention in Chapter 16 to assessing the sensitivity of bond prices to market yields. For now, however, it is sufficient to highlight one key factor that determines that sensitivity, namely, the maturity of the bond.

A general rule in evaluating bond price risk is that, keeping all other factors the same, the longer the maturity of the bond, the greater the sensitivity of price to fluctuations in the interest rate. For example, consider Table 14.2, which presents the price of an 8 percent coupon bond at different market yields and times to maturity. For any departure of the interest rate from 8 percent (the rate at which the bond sells at par value), the change in the bond price is smaller for shorter times to maturity.

This makes sense. If you buy the bond at par with an 8 percent coupon rate, and market rates subsequently rise, then you suffer a loss: You have tied up your money earning 8 percent when alternative investments offer higher returns. This is reflected in a capital loss on the bond—a fall in its market price. The longer the period for which your money is tied up, the greater the loss, and, correspondingly, the greater the drop in the bond price. In Table 14.2, the row for one-year maturity bonds shows little price sensitivity—that is, with only one year's earnings at stake, changes in interest rates are not too threatening. But for 30-year maturity bonds, interest rate swings have a large impact on bond prices.

---

[9] The progressively smaller impact of interest rate increases results from the fact that at higher rates the bond is worth less. Therefore, an additional increase in rates operates on a smaller initial base, resulting in a smaller price reduction.

This is why short-term government securities such as T-bills are considered to be the safest. They are free not only of default risk, but also largely of price risk attributable to interest rate volatility.

## 14.4 Bond Yields

We have noted that the current yield of a bond measures only the cash income provided by the bond as a percentage of bond price and ignores any prospective capital gains or losses. We would like a measure of rate of return that accounts for both current income as well as the price increase or decrease over the bond's life. The yield to maturity is the standard measure of the total rate of return of the bond over its life. However, it is far from a perfect measure, and we will explore several variations of this statistic.

### Yield to Maturity

In practice, an investor considering the purchase of a bond is not quoted a promised rate of return. Instead, the investor must use the bond price, maturity date, and coupon payments to infer the return offered by the bond over its life. The **yield to maturity** (YTM) is a measure of the average rate of return that will be earned on a bond if it is bought now and held until maturity. To calculate the yield to maturity, we solve the bond price equation for the interest rate given the bond's price.

For example, suppose an 8 percent coupon, 30-year bond is selling at \$1,276.76. What average rate of return would be earned by an investor purchasing the bond at this price? To answer this question, we find the interest rate at which the present value of the remaining bond payments equals the bond price. This is the rate that is consistent with the observed price of the bond. Therefore, we solve for $r$ in the following equation.

$$\$1{,}276.76 = \sum_{t=1}^{60} \frac{\$40}{(1+r)^t} + \frac{\$1{,}000}{(1+r)^{60}}$$

or, equivalently

$$1{,}276.76 = 40 \times \text{PA}(r, 60) + 1{,}000 \times \text{PF}(r, 60)$$

These equations have only one unknown variable, the interest rate, $r$. You can use a financial calculator to confirm that the solution to the equation is $r = .03$, or 3 percent per half year.[10] This is considered the bond's yield to maturity, as the bond would be fairly priced at \$1,276.76 if the fair market rate of return on the bond over its entire life were 3 percent per half year.

[10] Without a financial calculator, you still could solve the equation, but you would need to use a trial-and-error approach.

The financial press reports yields on an annualized basis, however, and annualizes the bond's semiannual yield using simple interest techniques, resulting in an annual percentage rate, or APR. Yields annualized using simple interest are also called "bond equivalent yields." Therefore, the semiannual yield would be doubled and reported in the newspaper as a bond equivalent yield of 6 percent. The *effective* annual yield of the bond, however, accounts for compound interest. If one earns 3 percent interest every six months, then after one year, each dollar invested grows with interest to $\$1 \times (1.03)^2 = 1.0609$, and the effective annual interest rate on the bond is 6.09 percent.

The bond's yield to maturity is the internal rate of return on an investment in the bond. The yield to maturity can be interpreted as the compound rate of return over the life of the bond under the assumption that all bond coupons can be reinvested at an interest rate equal to the bond's yield to maturity. Yield to maturity is widely accepted as a proxy for average return.

Yield to maturity is different from the *current yield* of a bond, which is the bond's annual coupon payment divided by the bond price. For example, for the 8 percent, 30-year bond currently selling at \$1,276.76, the current yield would be \$80/\$1,276.76 = .0627, or 6.27 percent per year. In contrast, recall that the effective annual yield to maturity is 6.09 percent. For this bond, which is selling at a premium over par value (\$1,276 rather than \$1,000), the coupon rate (8 percent) exceeds the current yield (6.27 percent), which exceeds the yield to maturity (6.09 percent). The coupon rate exceeds current yield because the coupon rate divides the coupon payments by par value (\$1,000) rather than by the bond price (\$1,276). In turn, the current yield exceeds yield to maturity because the yield to maturity accounts for the built-in capital loss on the bond; the bond bought today for \$1,176 will eventually fall in value to \$1,000 at maturity.

**CONCEPT CHECK** Question 4. What will be the relationship among coupon rate, current yield, and yield to maturity for bonds selling at discounts from par?

## Yield to Call

Yield to maturity is calculated on the assumption that the bond will be held until maturity. What if the bond is callable, however, and may be retired prior to the maturity date? How should we measure average rate of return for bonds subject to a call provision?

Figure 14.6 illustrates the risk of call to the bondholder. The upper line is the value at various market interest rates of a "straight" (i.e., noncallable) bond with par value \$1,000, an 8 percent coupon rate, and a 30-year time to maturity. If interest rates fall, the bond price, which equals the present value of the promised payments, can rise substantially.

Now consider a bond that has the same coupon rate and maturity date but is callable at 110 percent of par value, or \$1,100. When interest rates fall, the present value of the bond's *scheduled* payments rises, but the call provision allows

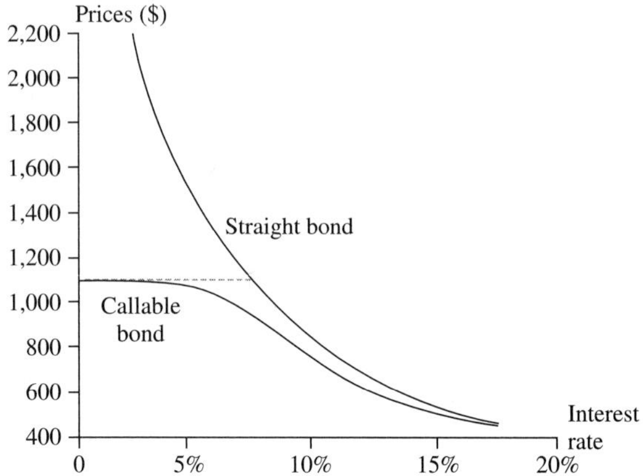


**Figure 14.6**
Bond prices: Callable and straight debt

the issuer to repurchase the bond at the call price. If the call price is less than the present value of the scheduled payments, the issuer can call the bond at the expense of the bondholder.

The lower line in Figure 14.6 is the value of the callable bond. At high interest rates, the risk of call is negligible, and the values of the straight and callable bonds converge. At lower rates, however, the values of the bonds begin to converge, with the difference reflecting the value of the firm's opinion to reclaim the callable bond at the call price. At very low rates, the bond is called, and its value is simply the call price, $1,100.

This analysis suggests that bond market analysts might be more interested in a bond's yield to call rather than yield to maturity if the bond is especially vulnerable to being called. The yield to call is calculated just like the yield to maturity except that the time until call replaces the time until maturity, and the call price replaces the par value.

For example, suppose the 8 percent coupon, 30-year maturity bonds sells for $1,150 and is callable in 10 years at a call price of $1,100. Its yield to maturity and yield to call would be calculated using the following inputs:

| | **Yield to Call** | **Yield to Maturity** |
|---|---|---|
| Coupon payment | $40 | $40 |
| Number of semiannual periods | 20 periods | 60 periods |
| Final payment | $1,100 | $1,000 |
| Price | $1,150 | $1,150 |

The yield to call is then 6.64 percent, whereas yield to maturity is 6.82 percent.

We have noted that most callable bonds are issued with an initial period of call protection. In addition, an implicit form of call protection operates for bonds selling at deep discounts from their call prices. Even if interest rates fall a bit, deep-discount bonds still will sell below the call price and thus will not be subject to a call.

Premium bonds that might be selling near their call prices, however, are especially apt to be called if rates fall further. If interest rates fall, a callable premium bond is likely to provide a lower return than could be earned on a discount bond whose potential price appreciation is not limited by the likelihood of a call. As a consequence, investors in premium bonds often are more interested in the bond's yield to call than its yield to maturity, because it may appear to them that the bond will be retired at the call date.

---

**CONCEPT CHECK**

Question 5. The yield to maturity on two 10-year maturity bonds currently is 7 percent. Each bond has a call price of $1,100. One bond has a coupon rate of 6 percent, the other 8 percent. Assume for simplicity that bonds are called as soon as the present value of their remaining payments exceeds their call price. What will be the capital gain on each bond if the market interest rate suddenly falls to 6 percent?

Question 6. A 20-year maturity 9 percent coupon bond paying coupons semiannually is callable in 5 years at a call price of $1,050. The bond currently sells at a yield to maturity of 8 percent. What is the yield to call?

---

## Yield to Maturity and Default Risk

Because corporate bonds are subject to default risk, we must distinguish between the bond's promised yield to maturity and its expected yield. The promised or stated yield will be realized only if the firm meets the obligations of the bond issue. Therefore, the stated yield is the *maximum possible* yield to maturity of the bond. The expected yield to maturity must take into account the possibility of a default.

For example, in August 1993, Wang Laboratories, Inc., was in bankruptcy proceedings, and its bonds due in 2009 were selling at about 35 percent of par value, resulting in a yield to maturity of over 26 percent. Investors did not really expect these bonds to provide a 26 percent rate of return. They recognized that bondholders were very unlikely to receive all the payments promised in the bond contract and that the yield based on *expected* cash flows was far less than the yield based on *promised* cash flows.

To illustrate the difference between expected and promised yield to maturity, suppose a firm issued a 9 percent coupon bond 20 years ago. The bond now has 10 years left until its maturity date but the firm is having financial difficulties. Investors believe that the firm will be able to make good on the remaining interest payments, but that at the maturity date, the firm will be forced into bankruptcy, and bondholders will receive only 70 percent of par value. The bond is selling at $750.

Yield to maturity (YTM) would then be calculated using the following inputs:

| | Expected YTM | Stated YTM |
|---|---|---|
| Coupon payment | $45 | $45 |
| Number of semiannual periods | 20 periods | 20 periods |
| Final payment | $700 | $1,000 |
| Price | $750 | $750 |

The yield to maturity based on promised payments is 13.7 percent. Based on the expected payment of $700 at maturity, however, the yield to maturity would be only 11.6 percent. The stated yield to maturity is greater than the yield investors actually expect to receive.

**CONCEPT CHECK** Question 7. What is the expected yield to maturity if the firm is in even worse condition and investors expect a final payment of only $600?

To compensate for the possibility of default, corporate bonds must offer a **default premium.** The default premium is the difference between the promised yield on a corporate bond and the yield of an otherwise-identical government bond that is riskless in terms of default. If the firm remains solvent and actually pays the investor all of the promised cash flows, the investor will realize a higher yield to maturity than would be realized from the government bond. If, however, the firm goes bankrupt, the corporate bond is likely to provide a lower return than the government bond. The corporate bond has the potential for both better and worse performance than the default-free Treasury bond. In other words, it is riskier.

The pattern of default premiums offered on risky bonds is sometimes called the *risk structure of interest rates.* The greater the default risk, the higher the default premium. Figure 14.7 shows the yield to maturity of bonds of different risk classes since 1977. You can see here clear evidence of default-risk premiums on promised yields.

One particular manner in which yield spreads seem to vary over time is related to the business cycle. Yield spreads tend to be wider when the economy is in a recession. Apparently, investors perceive a higher probability of bankruptcy when the economy is faltering, even holding bond ratings constant. They require a commensurately higher default premium. This is sometimes termed a *flight to quality,* meaning that investors move their funds into safer bonds unless they can obtain larger premiums on lower-rated securities.

## Realized Compound Yield versus Yield to Maturity

We have noted that yield to maturity will equal the rate of return realized over the life of the bond if all coupons are reinvested at an interest rate equal to the bond's yield to maturity. Consider, for example, a two-year bond selling at par value

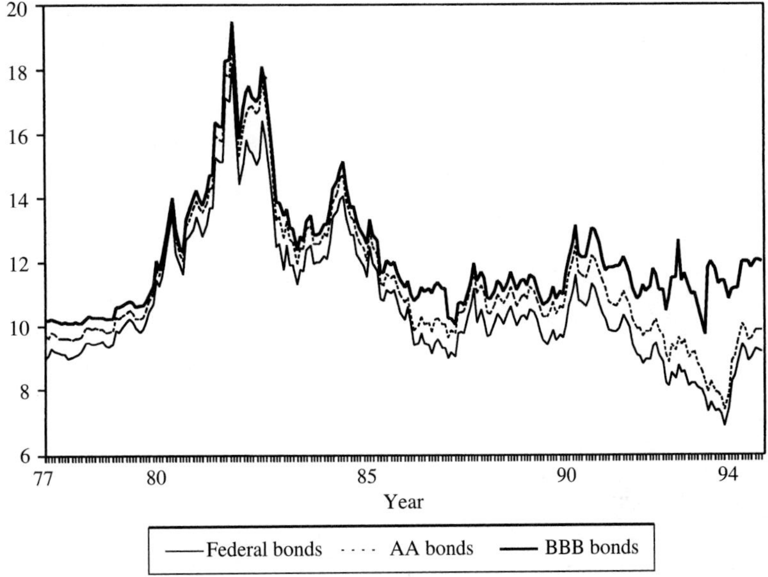


**Figure 14.7**
Yields on long-term bonds.

paying a 10 percent coupon once a year. The yield to maturity is 10 percent. If the \$100 coupon payment is reinvested at an interest rate of 10 percent, the \$1,000 investment in the bond will grow after two years to \$1,210, as illustrated in Figure 14.8, Panel A. The coupon paid in the first year is reinvested and grows with interest to a second-year value of \$110, which, together with the second coupon payment and payment of par value in the second year, results in a total value of \$1,210. The compound growth rate of invested funds, therefore, is calculated from

$$\$1{,}000\,(1 + y_{\text{realized}})^2 = \$1{,}210$$
$$y_{\text{realized}} = .10 = 10\%$$

With a reinvestment rate equal to the 10 percent yield to maturity, the *realized* compound yield equals yield to maturity.

But what if the reinvestment rate is not 10 percent? If the coupon can be invested at more than 10 percent, funds will grow to more than \$1,210, and the realized compound return will exceed 10 percent. If the reinvestment rate is less than 10 percent, so will be the realized compound return.

Suppose, for example, that the interest rate at which the coupon can be invested equals 8 percent. The following calculations are illustrated in Panel **B** of Figure 14.8:

| | |
|---|---|
| Future value of first coupon payment with interest earnings | \$100 × 1.08 = \$ 108 |
| Cash payment in second year (final coupon plus par value) | \$1,100 |
| Total value of investment with reinvested coupons | \$1,208 |

**Figure 14.8**
Growth of invested funds.

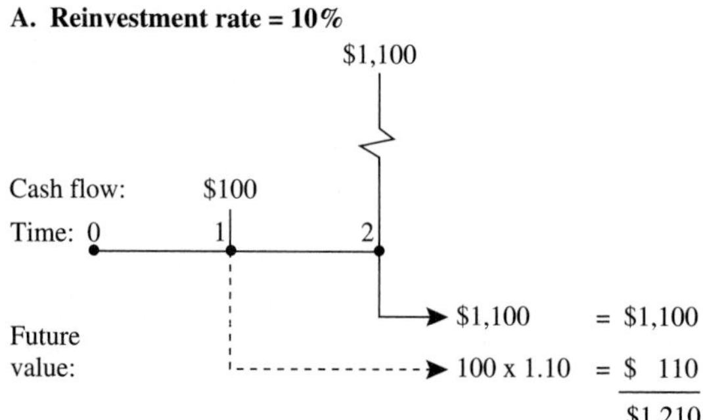


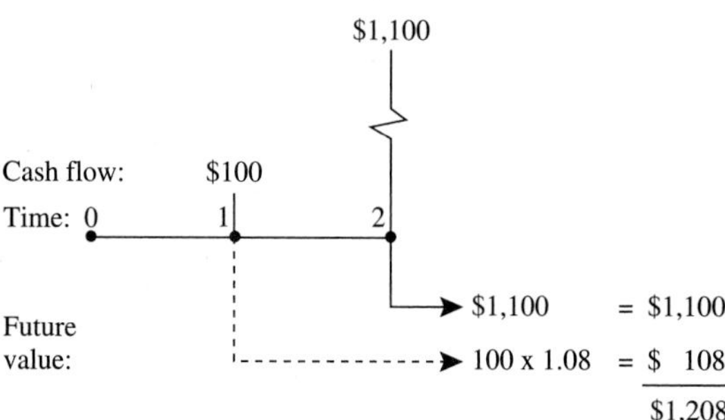


The realized compound yield is computed by calculating the compound rate of growth of invested funds, assuming that all coupon payments are reinvested. The investor purchased the bond for par at $1,000, and this investment grew to $1,208.

$$\$1{,}000\ (1 + y_{\text{realized}})^2 = \$1{,}208$$
$$y_{\text{realized}} = .0991 = 9.91\%$$

This example highlights the problem with conventional yield to maturity when reinvestment rates can change over time. Conventional yield to maturity will not equal realized compound return. However, in an economy with future interest rate uncertainty, the rates at which interim coupons will be reinvested are not yet known. Therefore, although realized compound yield can be computed *after* the investment period ends, it cannot be computed in advance without a forecast of future reinvestment rates. This reduces much of the attraction of the realized yield measure.

## Yield to Maturity versus Holding Period Return

You should not confuse the rate of return on a bond over any particular holding period with the bond's yield to maturity. The yield to maturity is defined as the single discount rate at which the present value of the payments provided by the bond equals its price. The yield to maturity is a measure of the average rate of return over the bond's life if it is held until maturity. In contrast, the holding period return equals income earned over a period (including capital gains or losses) as a percentage of the bond price at the start of the period. The holding period return can be calculated for any holding period based on the income generated over that period.

For example, if a 30-year bond paying an annual coupon of \$80 is purchased for \$1,000, its yield to maturity is 8 percent. If the bond price increases to \$1,050 by year end, its yield to maturity will fall below 8 percent (the bond is now selling above par value, so yield to maturity must be less than the 8 percent coupon rate), but the holding period return for the year is greater than 8 percent:

$$\text{Holding period return} = \frac{\$80 + (\$1{,}050 - \$1{,}000)}{\$1{,}000} = .13, \text{ or } 13\%$$

## 14.5 Bond Prices Over Time

As we noted earlier, a bond will sell at par value when its coupon rate equals the market interest rate. In these circumstances, the investor receives fair compensation for the time value of money in the form of the recurring interest payments. No further capital gain is necessary to provide fair compensation.

When the coupon rate is lower than the market interest rate, the coupon payments alone will not provide investors as high a return as they could earn elsewhere in the market. To receive a fair return on such an investment, investors also need to earn price appreciation on their bonds. The bonds, therefore, would have to sell below par value to provide a "built-in" capital gain on the investment.

To illustrate this point, suppose a bond was issued several years ago when the interest rate was 7 percent. The bond's annual coupon rate was thus set at 7 percent. (We will suppose for simplicity that the bond pays its coupon annually.) Now, with three years left in the bond's life, the interest rate is 8 percent per year. The bond's fair market price is the present value of the remaining annual coupons plus payment of par value. That present value is

$$\$70 \times \text{PA}(8\%, 3) + \$1{,}000 \times \text{PF}(8\%, 3) = \$974.23$$

which is less than par value.

In another year, after the next coupon is paid, the bond would sell at

$$\$70 \times \text{PA}(8\%, 2) + \$1{,}000 \times \text{PF}(8\%, 2) = \$982.17$$

thereby yielding a capital gain over the year of \$7.94. If an investor had purchased the bond at \$974.23, the total return over the year would equal the coupon payment plus capital gain, or \$70 + \$7.94 = \$77.94. This represents a rate of return of \$77.94/\$974.23, or 8 percent, exactly the current rate of return available elsewhere in the market.

**CONCEPT CHECK** Question 8. What will the bond price be in yet another year, when only one year remains until maturity? What is the rate of return to an investor who purchases the bond at $982.17 and sells it one year hence?

When bond prices are set according to the present value formula, any discount from par value provides an anticipated capital gain that will augment a below-market coupon rate just sufficiently to provide a fair total rate of return. Conversely, if the coupon rate exceeds the market interest rate, the interest income by itself is greater than that available elsewhere in the market. Investors will bid up the price of these bonds above their par values. As the bonds approach maturity, they will fall in value because fewer of these above-market coupon payments remain. The resulting capital losses offset the large coupon payments so that the bondholder again receives only a fair rate of return.

Problem 7 at the end of the chapter asks you to work through the case of the high coupon bond. Figure 14.9 traces out the price paths of high and low coupon bonds (net of accrued interest) as time to maturity approaches. The low coupon bond enjoys capital gains, whereas the high coupon bond suffers capital losses.

We use these examples to show that each bond offers investors the same total rate of return. Although the capital gain versus income components differ, the price of each bond is set to provide competitive rates, as we should expect in well-functioning capital markets. Security returns all should be comparable on an after-tax risk-adjusted basis. If they are not, investors will try to sell low-return securities, thereby driving down the prices until the total return at the now-lower price is competitive with other securities. Prices should continue to adjust until all securities are fairly priced, in that expected returns are appropriate (given necessary risk and tax adjustments).

## Zero-Coupon Bonds

*Original issue discount* bonds are less common than coupon bonds issued at par. These are bonds that are issued intentionally with low coupon rates that cause the bond to sell at a discount from par value. An extreme example of this type of bond is the *zero-coupon bond,* which carries no coupons and must provide all its return in the form of price appreciation. Zeroes provide only one cash flow to their owners, and that is on the maturity date of the bond.

Government of Canada Treasury bills are examples of short-term zero-coupon instruments. The Bank of Canada issues or sells a bill for some amount ranging from $1,000 to $1 million, agreeing to repay that amount at the bill's maturity. All of the investor's return comes in the form of price appreciation over time.

Longer-term zero-coupon bonds are commonly created synthetically. Several investment banking firms buy coupon-paying Government of Canada or provincial bonds and sell rights to single payments backed by the bonds. These bonds are said to be *stripped* of coupons, and often are called *strips.* They often have colorful names such as TIGRs, Cougars, or Sentinels. The single payments are,

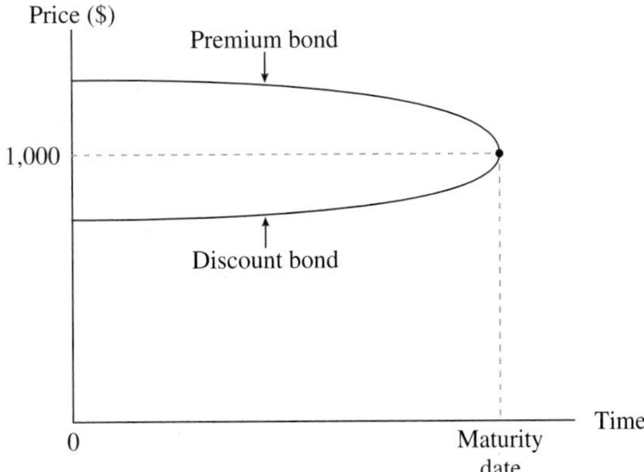


**Figure 14.9**
Price paths of coupon bonds.

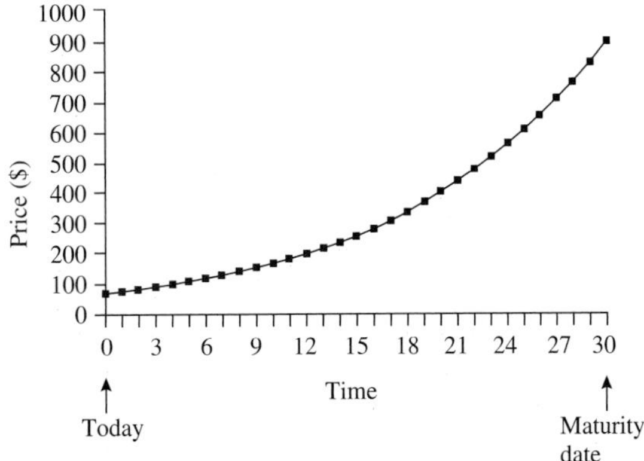


**Figure 14.10**
The price of a 30-year zero-coupon bond over time. Price equals 1,000/$(1.10)^T$ where $T$ is time until maturity.

in essence, zero-coupon bonds collateralized by the original securities and so are virtually free of default risk (see the nearby box).

What should happen to prices of zeroes as time passes? On their maturity date, zeroes must sell for par value. Before maturity, however, they should sell at discounts from par, because of the time value of money. As time passes, price should approach par value. In fact, if the interest rate is constant, a zero's price will increase at exactly the rate of interest.

To illustrate this property, consider a zero with 30 years until maturity, and suppose the market interest rate is 10 percent per year. The price of the bond today will be $\$1,000/(1.10)^{30} = \$57.31$. Next year, with only 29 years until maturity, the price will be $\$1,000/(1.10)^{29} = \$63.04$, a 10 percent increase over its previous-year value. Because the par value of the bond is now discounted for one fewer year, its price has increased by the one-year discount factor.

Figure 14.10 presents the price path of a 10-year zero-coupon bond until its maturity date for an annual market interest rate of 10 percent. The bond's price rises exponentially, not linearly, until its maturity.

## Strip Bonds Hedge Against Low Inflation

With inflation and interest rates low, investors are advised to buy short-term strip bonds instead of the traditional long-term bonds.

Strips are created by dealers who buy regular government, or corporate, bonds and notionally remove the coupons. They then sell the coupon portion and the principal upon maturity, separately, as strip bonds.

Strips carry the same date and credit rating as the original bond. The big difference is interest payments and price. Regular bonds pay semiannual interest and investors must usually put up almost the entire face value.

Strip bonds pay no interest and only the face value is redeemed at maturity. However, strips are sold at a big discount to the face value. The price reflects market expectations of inflation and interest rates.

The commission to the dealer is built into the price. Yields are based on the difference between the price and the face value.

For example, a $1,000 Government of Canada strip that matures on April 1, 1996, currently costs about $874, including the commission to the broker. That means for $874, the strip holder is entitled to $1,000 from the issuer, the Government of Canada, on that date. The annual yield is 5.68 percent.

The market for strips is generally more volatile relative to the market for interest-bearing bonds. That means prices of stripped bonds tend to fluctuate more.

Like all bonds, when interest rates rise, strip prices generally fall because the yield is no longer attractive, compared to other investment options. Conversely, when interest rates drop, strip prices usually rise.

In recent years, some strip holders have made big profits selling strips they bought during the high-interest days of the late 1980s.

"From about May 1990 to the present, anyone who bought a strip stood to make a substantial gain," says Pauline Cronin, vice president and director of fixed-income investor services at Burns Fry Ltd. in Toronto.

Cronin adds that some investors made up to a 25 percent return on the sale of their strip.

But now, with interest rates low, Cronin and others suggest investors buy strips that expire within 10 years.

"I believe that we will see U.S. interest rates heading back up and a little higher inflation," says Hugh Hamill, a broker with ScotiaMcLeod Inc. in Calgary.

"So, for RRSP accounts, I'm recommending investors stay short-term with strips between five and seven years."

Hamill and others say investors planning for retirement should plan to keep the strip to its maturity.

"You should look at the strip coupons as an anchor in your RRSP account," says Hank Cunningham, fixed income manager at First Marathon Securities Ltd. in Toronto. He suggests buying several strips with different maturity dates. If interest rates rise, the investor will have money maturing at different times which can be reinvested.

Cunningham notes that many strips offer a better return than guaranteed investment certificates. For example, a $1,000 British Columbia strip that expires on Aug. 21, 1998, has an annual yield of 6.7 percent. That compares to about 6 percent for a five-year GIC.

"You can usually do about one percentage point better with a strip than GICs,"says another dealer who asked not to be named.

Falling interest rates have put a glut of strips on the market. As a result, Cronin says, some dealers have developed a new strip product called strip bond packages.

These are created when dealers buy up blocks of strips with different maturity dates and sell them as a single package. The advantage of these packages

*(Continued)*

for investors is that they provide a series of future payments over several years.

Some brokers are also offering strips that provide some inflation-proofing. For example, Richardson Greenshields of Canada Ltd. has marketed a 28½-year strip that guarantees a 4 percent yield above inflation.

However they are packaged, strip bonds have grown in to a booming business.

"The market has evolved into a $70-billion market since strips started in 1981," says Hank Cunningham of First Marathon. "They are ideal for retirement planning."

Source: Paul Waldie, *Financial Post,* November 1, 1993. Reprinted by permission.

## After-Tax Returns

The tax authorities recognize that the "built-in" price appreciation on original issue discount (OID) bonds such as zero-coupon bonds represents an implicit interest payment to the holder of the security. Revenue Canada, therefore, calculates a price appreciation schedule to impute taxable interest income for the built-in appreciation during a tax year, even if the asset is not sold or does not mature until a future year. Any additional gains or losses that arise from changes in market interest rates are treated as capital gains or losses if the OID bond is sold during the tax year.

Let's consider an example. If the interest rate originally is 10 percent, the 30-year zero would be issued at a price of $\$1{,}000/(1.10)^{30} = \$57.31$. The following year, Revenue Canada calculates what the bond price would be if the yield remains at 10 percent. This is $\$1{,}000/(1.10)^{29} = \$63.04$. Therefore, the tax authorities impute interest income of $\$63.04 - \$57.31 = \$5.73$. This amount is subject to tax. Notice that the imputed interest income is based on a "constant yield method" that ignores any changes in market interest rates.

If interest rates actually fall, let's say to 9.9 percent, the bond price actually will be $\$1{,}000/(1.099)^{29} = \$64.72$. If the bond is sold, then the difference between \$64.72 and \$63.04 will be treated as capital gains income and taxed at the capital gains tax rate. If the bond is not sold, then the price difference is an unrealized capital gain and does not result in taxes in that year. In either case, the investor must pay taxes on the \$5.73 of imputed interest at the rate of ordinary income.

The same reasoning is applied to the taxation of other original issue discount bonds, even if they are not zero-coupon bonds. Consider, as an example, a 30-year maturity bond that is issued with a coupon rate of 4 percent and a yield to maturity of 8 percent. For simplicity, we will assume that the bond pays coupons once annually. Because of the low coupon rate, the bond will be issued at a price far below par value, specifically at a price of \$549.69. If the bond's yield to maturity remains at 8 percent, then its price in one year will rise to \$553.66. (Confirm this for yourself.) This provides a pretax holding period return of exactly 8 percent.

$$\text{HPR} = \frac{\$40 + (\$553.66 - \$549.69)}{\$549.69} = .08$$

The increase in the bond price based on a constant yield, however, is treated as interest income, so the investor is required to pay taxes on imputed interest income of $553.66 − $549.69 = $3.97. If the bond's yield actually changes during the year, the difference between the bond's price and the "constant-yield value" of $553.66 will be treated as capital gains income if the bond is sold.

---

**CONCEPT CHECK** Question 9. Suppose that the yield to maturity of the 4 percent coupon, 30-year maturity bond actually falls to 7 percent by the end of the first year, and that the investor sells the bond after the first year. If the investor's tax rate on interest income is 36 percent and the tax rate on capital gains is 28 percent, what is the investor's after-tax rate of return?

---

## SUMMARY

**1.** Fixed-income securities are distinguished by their promise to pay a fixed or specified stream of income to their holders. The coupon bond is a typical fixed-income security.

**2.** Government bonds have original maturities greater than one year. They are issued at or near par value, with their prices quoted net of accrued interest.

**3.** When bonds are subject to potential default, the stated yield to maturity is the maximum possible yield to maturity that can be realized by the bondholder. In the event of default, however, that promised yield will not be realized. To compensate bond investors for default risk, bonds must offer default premiums, that is, promised yields in excess of those offered by default-free government securities. If the firm remains healthy, its bonds will provide higher returns than government bonds. Otherwise, the returns may be lower.

**4.** Bond safety is often measured using financial ratio analysis. Bond indentures are another safeguard to protect the claims of bondholders. Common indentures specify sinking fund requirements, collateralization of the loan, dividend restrictions, and subordination of future debt.

**5.** Callable bonds should offer higher promised yields to maturity to compensate investors for the fact that they will not realize full capital gains should the interest rate fall and the bonds be called away from them at the stipulated call price. Bonds often are issued with a period of call protection. In addition, discount bonds selling significantly below their call price offer implicit call protection.

**6.** Retractable and extendible bonds give the bondholder rather than the issuer the option to terminate or extend the life of the bond.

**7.** Convertible bonds may be exchanged, at the bondholder's discretion, for a specified number of shares of stock. Convertible bondholders "pay" for this option by accepting a lower coupon rate on the security.

**8.** Floating-rate bonds pay a fixed premium over a reference short-term interest rate. Risk is limited because the rate paid is tied to current market conditions.

**9.** The yield to maturity is the single interest rate that equates the present value of a security's cash flows to its price. Bond prices and yields are inversely related. For premium bonds, the coupon rate is greater than the current yield, which is greater than the yield to maturity. The order of these inequalities is reversed for discount bonds.

**10.** The yield to maturity often is interpreted as an estimate of the average rate of return to an investor who purchases a bond and holds it until maturity. This interpretation is subject to error, however. Related measures are yield to call, realized compound yield, and expected (versus promised) yield to maturity.

**11.** Prices of zero-coupon bonds rise exponentially over time, providing a rate of appreciation equal to the interest rate. Revenue Canada treats this price appreciation as imputed taxable interest income to the investor.

## Key Terms

Fixed income securities
Bond
Par value
Face value
Coupon rate
Zero-coupon bonds
Convertible bonds
Retractable bond
Extendible bond
Floating-rate bonds
Investment grade bonds
Speculative grade
Junk bonds
Indenture
Sinking fund
Subordination clauses
Collateral
Debenture
Yield to maturity
Default premium

## Selected Readings

*A comprehensive treatment of price issues related to fixed-income securities is given in:*

Fabozzi, Frank J. *Bond Markets, Analysis, and Strategies,* 2nd edition. Englewood Cliffs, N.J.: Prentice Hall, 1993.

*Surveys of fixed-income instruments and investment characteristics are contained in:*

Fabozzi, Frank J.; T. Dessa Fabozzi; and Irvin M. Pollack. *The Handbook of Fixed Income Securities,* Homewood, Ill.: Business One Irwin, 1991.

Stigum, Marcia; and Frank J. Fabozzi. *The Dow-Jones Guide to Bond and Money Market Investments.* Homewood, Ill.: Dow Jones–Irwin, 1987.

*Surveys of Canadian fixed-income instruments can be found in:*

Hunter, W. T. *Canadian Financial Markets.* Peterborough, Ont.: Broadview, 1988.

Canadian Securities Institute. *The Canadian Securities Course* (annual).

*Canadian references on retractable and extendible bonds include:*

Ananthanarayanan, A.L.; and Eduardo Schwartz. "Retractable and Extendible Bonds: The Canadian Experience." *Journal of Finance* 35, no. 1 (March 1980).

Dipchand, Cecil R.; and Robert J. Hanrahan. "Exit and Exchange Option Values on Government of Canada Retractable Bonds." *Financial Management* 8, no. 3 (Autumn 1979).

## Problems

1. Which security has a higher *effective* annual interest rate?
   *a.* A three-month T-bill selling at $97,645.
   *b.* A coupon bond selling at par and paying a 10 percent coupon semiannually.
2. Treasury bonds paying an 8 percent coupon rate with *semiannual* payments currently sell at par value. What coupon rate would they have to pay in order to sell at par if they paid their coupons *annually*?
3. Two bonds have identical times to maturity and coupon rates. One is callable at 105, the other at 110. Which should have the higher yield to maturity? Why?
4. Consider a bond with a 10 percent coupon and with yield to maturity = 8 percent. If the bond's yield to maturity remains constant, then in one year, will the bond price be higher, lower, or unchanged? Why?
5. Consider an 8 percent coupon bond selling for $953.10 with three years until maturity making *annual* coupon payments. The interest rates in the next three years will be, with certainty, $r_1 = 8\%$, $r_2 = 10\%$, and $r_3 = 12\%$. Calculate the yield to maturity and realized compound yield of the bond.
6. Assume you have a one-year investment horizon and are trying to choose among three bonds. All have the same degree of default risk and mature in 10 years. The first is a zero-coupon bond that pays $1,000 at maturity. The second has an 8 percent coupon rate and pays the $80 coupon once per year. The third has a 10 percent coupon rate and pays the $100 coupon once per year.
   *a.* If all three bonds are now priced to yield 8 percent to maturity, what are their prices?
   *b.* If you expect their yields to maturity to be 8 percent at the beginning of next year, what will their prices be then? What is your before-tax holding period return on each bond? If your tax bracket is 30 percent on ordinary income and 20 percent on capital gains income, what will your after-tax rate of return be on each?
   *c.* Recalculate your answer to (*b*) under the assumption that you expect the yields to maturity on each bond to be 7 percent at the beginning of next year.
7. Consider a bond paying a coupon rate of 10 percent per year semiannually when the market interest rate is only 4 percent per half year. The bond has three years until maturity.
   *a.* Find the bond's price today and six months from now after the next coupon is paid.
   *b.* What is the total rate of return on the bond?
8. A newly issued bond pays its coupons once annually. Its coupon rate is 5 percent, its maturity is 20 years, and its yield to maturity is 8 percent.
   *a.* Find the holding period return for a one-year investment period if the bond is selling at a yield to maturity of 7 percent by the end of the year.

*b.* If you sell the bond after one year, what taxes will you owe if the tax rate on interest income is 40 percent and the tax rate on capital gains income is 30 percent?

*c.* What is the after-tax holding period return on the bond?

*d.* Find the realized compound yield *before taxes* for a two-year holding period, assuming that (1) you sell the bond after two years; (2) the bond yield is 7 percent at the end of the second year; and (3) the coupon can be reinvested for one year at a 3 percent interest rate.

*e.* Use the tax rates in part (*b*) to compute the *after-tax* two-year realized compound yield. Remember to take account of OID tax rules.

**9.** A bond with a coupon rate of 7 percent makes semiannual coupon payments on January 15 and July 15 of each year. *The Globe and Mail* reports the price for the bond on January 30 at 100.02. What is the invoice price of the bond? The coupon period has 182 days.

**10.** A bond has a current yield of 9 percent and a yield to maturity of 10 percent. Is the bond selling above or below par value? Explain.

**11.** Is the coupon rate of the bond in problem (10) more or less than 9 percent?

**12.** A newly issued 20-year maturity, zero-coupon bond is issued with a yield to maturity of 8 percent and a face value of $1,000. Find the imputed interest income in the first, second, and last year of the bond's life.

**13.** A newly issued 10-year maturity, 4 percent coupon bond making *annual* coupon payments is sold to the public at a price of $800. What will be an investor's taxable income from the bond over the coming year? The bond will not be sold at the end of the year. The bond is treated as an original issue discount bond.

**14.** A 30-year maturity, 8 percent coupon bond paying coupons semiannually is callable in five years at a call price of $1,100. The bond currently sells at a yield to maturity of 7 percent (3.5 percent per half-year).

*a.* What is the yield to call?

*b.* What is the yield to call if the call price is only $1,050?

*c.* What is the yield to call if the call price is $1,100, but the bond can be called in two years instead of five years?

**15.** A 10-year bond of a firm in severe financial distress has a coupon rate of 14 percent and sells for $900. The firm is currently renegotiating the debt, and it appears that the lenders will allow the firm to reduce coupon payments on the bond to one-half the originally contracted amount. The firm can handle these lower payments. What is the stated and expected yield to maturity of the bonds? The bond makes its coupon payments annually.

**16.** A two-year bond with a par value of $1,000 making annual coupon payments of $100 is priced at $1,000. What is the yield to maturity of the bond? What will be the realized compound yield to maturity if the one-year interest rate next year turns out to be (a) 8 percent, (b) 10 percent, (c) 12 percent?

**17.** The stated yield to maturity and realized compound yield to maturity of a (default-free) zero-coupon bond always will be equal. Why?

**18.** Suppose that today's date is April 15. A bond with a 10 percent coupon paid semiannually every January 15 and July 15 is listed as selling at an ask price of 101.04. If you buy the bond from a dealer today, what price will you pay for it?

**19.** In June 1982, when the yield to maturity (YTM) on long-term bonds was about 14 percent, many observers were projecting an eventual decline in these rates. It was not unusual to hear of customers urging portfolio managers to "lock in" these high rates by buying some new issues with these high coupons. You recognize that it is not possible to really lock in such returns for coupon bonds because of the potential reinvestment rate problem if rates decline. Assuming the following expectations for a five-year bond bought at par, compute the total realized compound yield (without taxes) for the bond below.

Coupon: 14% (assume annual interest payments at end of each year).
Maturity: Five years.
One-year reinvestment rates during:
Year 2, 3: 10%.
Year 4, 5: 8%.

**20.** Assume that in 1988 two firms, PG and CLX, were concurrently to undertake private debt placements with the following contractual details:

| | PG | CLX |
|---|---|---|
| Issue size | $1 billion | $100 million |
| Issue price | 100 | 100 |
| Maturity | 1993* | 2003 |
| Coupon | 10% | 11% |
| Collateral | First mortgage | Unsecured |
| First call date | 1998 | 1995 |
| Call price | 111 | 106 |
| Sinking fund — beginning | nil | 1993 |
| — amount | nil | $5 million/year |

*Extendable at the option of the holder for an additional 10 years (to 2003) with no change in coupon rate.

Ignoring credit quality, identify four features of these issues that might account for the lower coupon on the PG debt. Explain.

**21.** A large forest product manufacturer has outstanding two Baa-rated, $150 million par amount, intermediate-term debt issues:

| | 10.10% notes | Floating-Rate Notes |
|---|---|---|
| Maturity | 1995 | 1992 |
| Issue date | 6-12-85 | 9-27-84 |
| Callable (beginning on) | 6-15-91 | 10-01-89 |
| Callable at | 100 | 100 |
| Sinking fund | None | None |
| Current coupon | 10.10% | 9.9% |
| Coupon changes | Fixed | Every 6 months |
| Rate adjusts to | — | 1% above 6-month T-bill rate |
| Range since issued | — | 12.9%–8.3% |
| Current price | 73 3/8 | 97 |
| Current yield | 13.77% | 10.3% |
| Yield to maturity | 15.87% | — |
| Price range since issue | 100–72 | 102–93 |

Given these data:

*a.* State the minimum coupon rate of interest at which the firm could sell a fixed-rate issue at par due in 1995. Assume the same indenture provisions as the 10.10 percent notes and disregard any tax considerations.

*b.* Give two reasons why the floating-rate notes are not selling at par.

*c.* State and justify whether the risk of call is high, moderate, or low for the fixed-rate issue.

*d.* Assuming a decline in interest rates is anticipated, identify and justify which issue would be most appropriate for an actively managed bond portfolio where total return is the primary objective.

*e.* Explain why yield to maturity is not valid for the floating-rate note.

**22.** You have the following information about a convertible bond issue:

Burroughs Corp.
7¼% Due 8/1/2010

| | |
|---|---|
| Agency rating (Moody's/S&P) | A3/A– |
| Conversion ratio | 12.882 |
| Market price of convertible | $102.00 |
| Market price of common stock | $ 66.00 |
| Dividend per share — common | $ 2.60 |
| Call price (first call — 8/1/1990) | $106.00 |
| Estimated floor price | $ 66.50 |

Using this information, calculate the following values and show calculations.

*a.* Market conversion value.

*b.* Conversion premium per common share.

*c.* Current yield—convertible.

*d.* Dividend yield—common.

**23.** As the portfolio manager for a large pension fund, you are offered the following bonds:

| | Coupon | Maturity | Price | Call Price | Yield to Maturity |
|---|---|---|---|---|---|
| Edgar Corp. (new issue) | 14.00% | 2002 | $101 3/4 | $114 | 13.75% |
| Edgar Corp. (new issue) | 6.00 | 2002 | 48 1/8 | 103 | 13.60 |

Assuming you expect a decline in interest rates over the next three years, identify which of the bonds you would select. Justify your answer.

**24.** *a.* In terms of option theory, explain the impact on the offering yield of adding a call feature to a proposed bond issue.

*b.* Explain the impact on the bond's expected life of adding a call feature to a proposed bond issue.

*c.* Describe *one* advantage and *one* disadvantage of including callable bonds in a portfolio.

**25.** Philip Morris may issue a 10-year maturity fixed-income security, which might include a sinking-fund provision and either refunding or call protection.

*a.* Describe a sinking-fund provision.

*b.* Explain the impact of a sinking-fund provision on:

i. The expected average life of the proposed security.

ii. Total principal and interest payments over the life of the proposed security.

*c.* From the investor's point of view, explain the rationale for demanding a sinking-fund provision.

**26.** The multiple-choice problems following are based on questions that appeared in past CFA examinations.

*a.* The spread between Treasury and BAA corporate bond yields widens when:

i. Interest rates are low.

ii. There is economic uncertainty.

iii. There is a "flight from quality."

iv. All of the above.

*b.* The market risk of an AAA-rated preferred stock relative to an AAA-rated bond is:

i. Lower

ii. Higher

iii. Equal

iv. Unknown

*c.* A bond with a call feature:

i. Is attractive because the immediate receipt of principal plus premium produces a high return.

ii. Is more apt to be called when interest rates are high because the interest saving will be greater.
iii. Will usually have a higher yield than a similar noncallable bond.
iv. None of the above.

*d.* The yield to maturity on a bond is:
i. Below the coupon rate when the bond sells at a discount, and above the coupon rate when the bond sells at a premium.
ii. The discount rate that will set the present value of the payments equal to the bond price.
iii. The current yield plus the average annual capital gains rate.
iv. Based on the assumption that any payments received are reinvested at the coupon rate.

*e.* A particular bond has a yield to maturity on an APR basis of 12.00 percent but makes equal quarterly payments. What is the effective annual yield to maturity?
i. 11.45 percent
ii. 12.00 percent
iii. 12.55 percent
iv. 37.35 percent

*f.* In which *one* of the following cases is the bond selling at a discount?
i. Coupon rate is greater than current yield, which is greater than yield to maturity.
ii. Coupon rate, current yield, and yield to maturity are all the same.
iii. Coupon rate is less than current yield, which is less than yield to maturity.
iv. Coupon rate is less than current yield, which is greater than yield to maturity.

*g.* Consider a five-year bond with a 10 percent coupon that has a present yield to maturity of 8 percent. If interest rates remain constant, one year from now the price of this bond will be:
i. Higher
ii. Lower
iii. The same
iv. Par

*h.* Serial obligation bonds differ from *most* other bonds because:
i. They are secured by the assets and taxing power of the issuer.
ii. Their par value is usually well below $1,000.
iii. Their term to maturity is usually very long (30 years or more).
iv. They possess multiple maturity dates.

*i.* Which *one* of the following is *not* an advantage of convertible bonds for the investor?
i. The yield on the convertible will typically be higher than the yield on the underlying common stock.
ii. The convertible bond will likely participate in a major upward move in the price of the underlying common stock.

iii. Convertible bonds typically are secured by specific assets of the issuing company.
iv. Investors normally may convert to the underlying common stock.

*j.* The call feature of a bond means the:
i. Investor can call for payment on demand.
ii. Investor can only call if the firm defaults on an interest payment.
iii. Issuer can call the bond issue before the maturity date.
iv. Issuer can call the issue during the first three years.

*k.* The annual interest paid on a bond relative to its prevailing market price is called its:
i. Promised yield
ii. Yield to maturity
iii. Coupon rate
iv. Current yield

*l.* Which *one* of the following statements about convertible bonds is *false*?
i. The yield on the convertible typically will be higher than the yield on the underlying common stock.
ii. The convertible bond will likely participate in a major upward movement in the price of the underlying common stock.
iii. Convertible bonds typically are secured by specific assets of the issuing company.
iv. A convertible bond can be valued as a straight bond with an attached option.

*m.* All else being equal, which *one* of the following bonds would be *most likely* to sell at the highest yield?
i. Callable debenture
ii. Puttable mortgage bond
iii. Callable mortgage bond
iv. Puttable debentures

*n.* Yields on nonconvertible preferred stock usually are lower than yields on bonds of the same company because of differences in:
i. Marketability
ii. Risk
iii. Taxation
iv. Call protection

*o.* The yield to maturity on a bond is:
i. Below the coupon rate when the bond sells at a discount and above the coupon rate when the bond sells at a premium.
ii. The interest rate that makes the present value of the payments equal to the bond price.
iii. Based on the assumption that all future payments received are reinvested at the coupon rate.
iv. Based on the assumption that all future payments received are reinvested at future market rates.

*Chapter* 15

# The Term Structure of Interest Rates

**IN CHAPTER 14, WE ASSUMED FOR THE SAKE OF SIMPLICITY THAT THE SAME CONSTANT INTEREST RATE IS USED TO DISCOUNT CASH FLOWS OF ANY MATURITY.** In the real world this is rarely the case. We have seen, for example, that in late 1994 short-term bonds and notes carried yields to maturity only slightly higher than 5 percent while the longest-term bonds offered yields above 8 percent. At the time these bond prices were quoted, however, the longer-term securities had higher yields anyway. This, in fact, is a common empirical pattern.

In this chapter we explore the pattern of interest rates for different-term assets. We attempt to identify the factors that account for that pattern and determine what information may be derived from an analysis of the so-called **term structure of interest rates,** the structure of interest rates for discounting cash flows of different maturities.

## 15.1 THE TERM STRUCTURE UNDER CERTAINTY

What do you conclude from the observation that longer-term bonds offer higher yields to maturity? One possibility is that longer-term bonds are riskier and that the higher yields are evidence of a risk premium that compensates for interest rate risk. Another possibility is that investors expect interest rates to rise and that the higher average yields on long-term bonds reflect the anticipation of high interest rates in the latter years of the bond's life. We will start our analysis of these possibilities with the easiest case: a world with no uncertainty where investors already know the path of future interest rates.

**Table 15.1** Interest Rates on One-Year Bonds in Coming Years

| Year | Interest Rate |
|---|---|
| 0 (Today) | 8% |
| 1 | 10 |
| 2 | 11 |
| 3 | 11 |

## Bond Pricing

The interest rate for a given time interval is called the **short interest rate** for that period. Suppose that all participants in the bond market are convinced that the short rates for the next four years will follow the pattern in Table 15.1.

Of course, market participants cannot look up such a sequence of short rates in the financial press. All they observe there are prices and yields of bonds of various maturities. Nevertheless, we can think of the short-rate sequence of Table 15.1 as the series of interest rates that investors keep in the back of their minds when they evaluate the prices of different bonds. Given this pattern of rates, what prices might we observe on various maturity bonds? To keep the algebra simple, for now we will treat only a zero-coupon bond.

A bond paying $1,000 in one year would sell today for $1,000/1.08 = $925.93. Similarly, a two-year maturity bond would sell today at price

$$P = \frac{\$1{,}000}{(1.08)(1.10)} = \$841.75 \qquad \textbf{(15.1)}$$

This is the present value of the future $1,000 cash flow, because $841.75 would need to be set aside now to provide a $1,000 payment in two years. After one year, the $841.75 set aside would grow to $841.75(1.08) = $909.09 and after the second year to $909.09(1.10) = $1,000.

In general, we may write the present value of $1 to be received after $n$ periods as

$$\text{PV of \$1 in } n \text{ periods} = \frac{1}{(1 + r_1)(1 + r_2) \ldots (1 + r_n)}$$

where $r_i$ is the one-year interest rate that will prevail in year $i$. Continuing in this manner, we find the values of the three- and four-year bonds as shown in the middle column of Table 15.2.

From the bond prices we can calculate the yield to maturity on each bond. Recall that the yield is the *single* interest rate that equates the present value of the bond's payments to the bond's price. Although interest rates may vary over time,

**Table 15.2** Prices and Yields of Zero-Coupon Bonds

| Time to Maturity | Price | Yield to Maturity |
|---|---|---|
| 1 | $925.93 | 8.000% |
| 2 | 841.75 | 8.995 |
| 3 | 758.33 | 9.660 |
| 4 | 683.18 | 9.993 |

**Figure 15.1**
Yield curve.

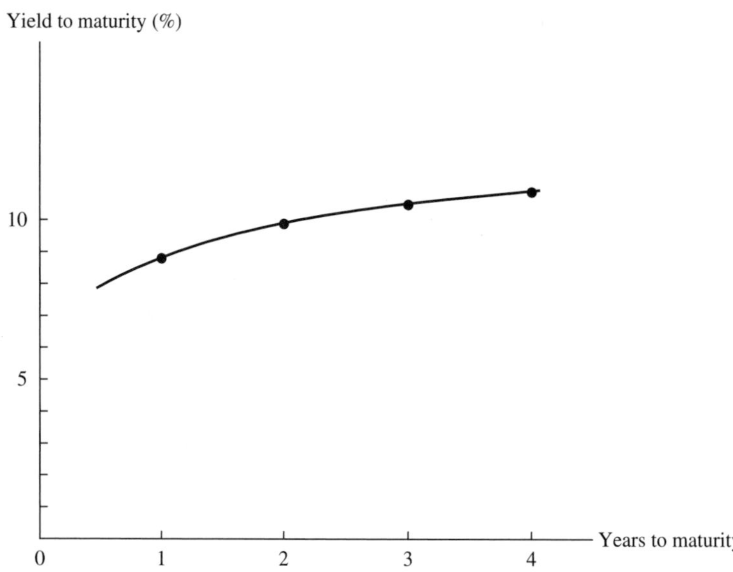


the yield to maturity is calculated as one "average" rate that is applied to discount all of the bond's payments. For example, the yield on the two-year zero-coupon bond, which we will call $y_2$, is the interest rate that satisfies

$$841.75 = 1{,}000/(1 + y_2)^2 \tag{15.2}$$

which we solve for $y_2 = .08995$. We repeat the process for the two other bonds, with results as reported in the table. For example, we find $y_3$ by solving

$$758.33 = 1{,}000/(1 + y_3)^3$$

Now we can make a graph of the yield to maturity on the four bonds as a function of time to maturity. This graph, which is called the **yield curve,** appears in Figure 15.1.

While the yield curve in Figure 15.1 rises smoothly, a wide range of curves may be observed in practice. Figure 15.2 presents three such curves. Panel **A** is the yield curve from October 1995, which is upward sloping. Panel **B** is a hump-

**Figure 15.2**
Treasury yield curves.

Source: Various editions of *The Globe and Mail.* Reprinted by permission.

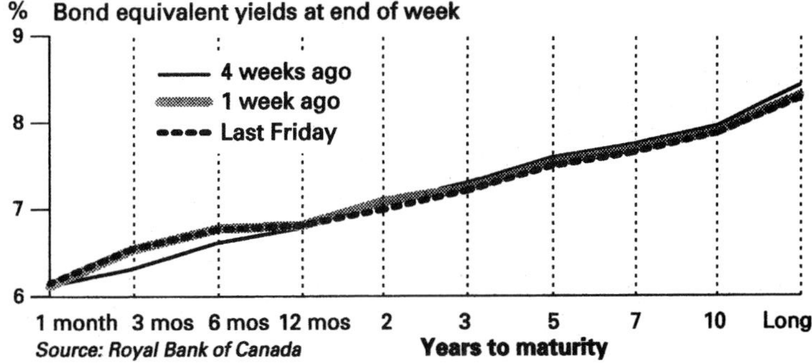


**A.** (October 20, 1995)
Rising yield curve

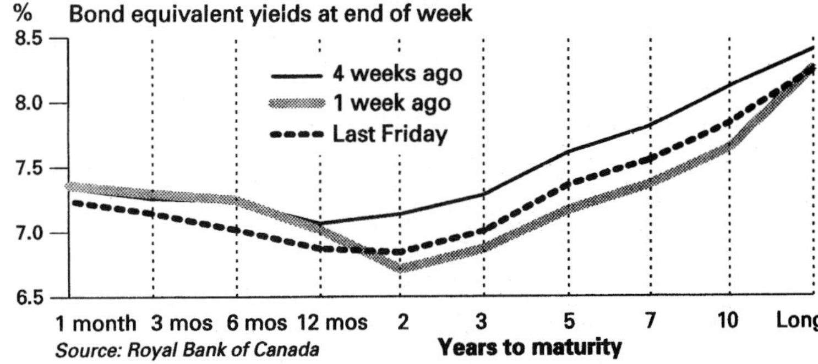


**B.** (June 12, 1995)
Hump-shaped yield curve

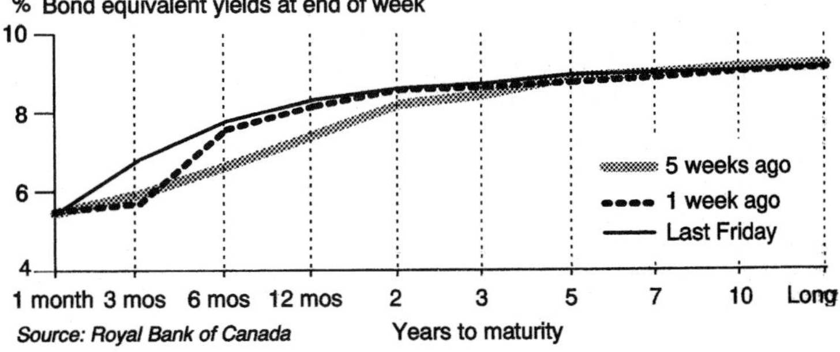


**C.** (January 2, 1995)
Flat yield curve

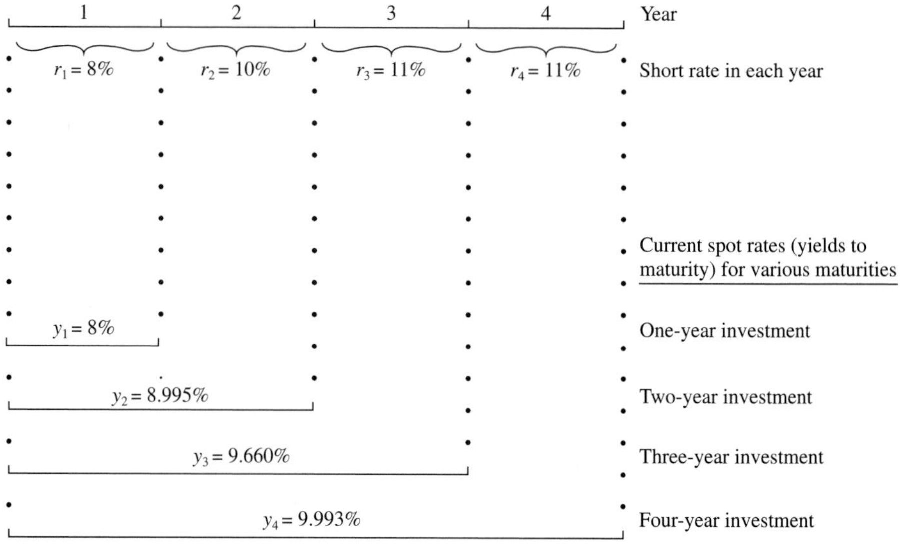


**Figure 15.3** Short rates versus spot rates.

shaped curve, first falling and then rising. The yield curve in Panel **C** is essentially flat after a while.

The yield to maturity on zero-coupon bonds is sometimes called the **spot rate** that prevails today for a period corresponding to the maturity of the zero. The yield curve, or equivalently, the last column of Table 15.2, thus presents the spot rates for four maturities. Note that the spot rates or yields do *not* equal the one-year interest rates for each year.

To emphasize the differences between the sequence of *short* rates for each future year, and *spot* rates for different maturity dates, examine Figure 15.3. The first line of data presents the short rate for each annual period. The lower lines present the spot rates or equivalently, the yields to maturity, for different holding periods that extend from the present to each relevant maturity date.

The yield on the two-year bond is close to the average of the short rates for years one and two. This makes sense because if interest rates of 8 percent and 10 percent will prevail in the next two years, then (ignoring compound interest) a sequence of two one-year investments will provide a cumulative return of 18 percent. Therefore, we would expect a two-year bond to provide a competitive total return of about 18 percent, which translates into an annualized yield to maturity of 9 percent, just about equal to the 8.995 percent yield we derived in Table 15.2. Because the yield is a measure of the average return over the life of the bond, it should be determined by the market interest rates available in both years one and two.

In fact, we can be more precise. Notice that equations 15.1 and 15.2 each relate the two-year bond's price to appropriate interest rates. Combining equations 15.1 and 15.2, we find

$$841.75 = \frac{1{,}000}{(1.08)(1.10)} = \frac{1{,}000}{(1 + y_2)^2}$$

so that

$$(1 + y_2)^2 = (1.08)(1.10)$$

and

$$1 + y_2 = [(1.08)(1.10)]^{1/2} = 1.08995$$

Similarly,

$$1 + y_3 = [(1 + r_1)(1 + r_2)(1 + r_3)]^{1/3}$$

and

$$1 + y_4 = [(1 + r_1)(1 + r_2)(1 + r_3)(1 + r_4)]^{1/4} \qquad \textbf{(15.3)}$$

and so on. Thus, the yields are in fact averages of the interest rates in each period. However, because of compound interest, the relationship is not an arithmetic average but a geometric one.

## Holding-Period Returns

What is the rate of return on each of the four bonds in Table 15.2 over a one-year holding period? You might think at first that higher-yielding bonds would provide higher one-year rates of return, but this is not the case. In our simple world with no uncertainty all bonds must offer identical rates of return over any holding period. Otherwise, at least one bond would be dominated by the others in the sense that it would offer a lower rate of return than would combinations of other bonds; no one would be willing to hold the bond, and its price would fall. In fact, despite their different yields to maturity, each bond will provide a rate of return over the coming year equal to this year's short interest rate.

To confirm this point, we can compute the rates of return on each bond. The one-year bond is bought today for $925.93 and matures in one year to its par value of $1,000. Because the bond pays no coupon, total income is $1,000 − $925.93 = $74.07, and the rate of return is $74.07/$925.93 = .08, or 8 percent. The two-year bond is bought today for $841.75. Next year the interest rate will be 10 percent, and the bond will have one year left until maturity. It will sell for $1,000/1.10 = $909.09. Thus, the *holding-period return* is ($909.09 − $841.75)/ $841.75 = .08, again implying an 8 percent rate of return. Similarly, the three-year bond will be purchased for $758.33 and will be sold at year-end for $1,000/(1.10)(1.11) = $819.00, for a rate of return of ($819.00 − $758.33)/ $758.33 = .08, again, an 8 percent return.

---

**CONCEPT CHECK** Question 1. Confirm that the return on the four-year bond also will be 8 percent.

---

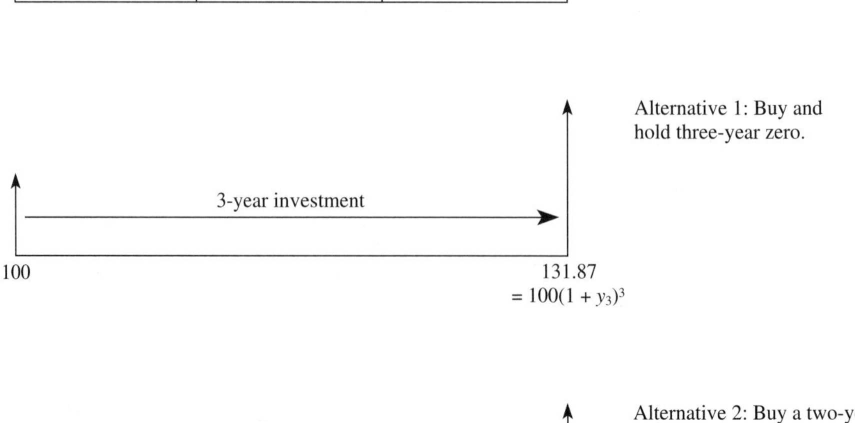


**Figure 15.4**
Two three-year investment programs.

Therefore we conclude that, when interest rate movements are known with certainty, if all bonds are fairly priced, all will provide equal one-year rates of return. The higher yields on the longer-term bonds merely reflect the fact that future interest rates are higher than current rates, and that the longer bonds are still alive during the higher-rate period. Owners of the short-term bonds receive lower yields to maturity, but they can reinvest or "roll over" their proceeds for higher yields in later years when rates are higher. In the end, both long-term bonds and short-term rollover strategies provide equal returns over the holding period, at least in a world of interest rate certainty.

## Forward Rates

Unfortunately, investors do not have access to short-term interest rate quotations for coming years. What they do have are newspaper quotations of bond prices and yields to maturity. Can they infer future short rates from the available data?

Suppose we are interested in the interest rate that will prevail during year three, and we have access only to the data reported in Table 15.2. We start by comparing two alternatives, illustrated in Figure 15.4.

1. Invest in a three-year zero-coupon bond.
2. Invest in a two-year zero-coupon bond. After two years, reinvest the proceeds in a one-year bond.

Assuming an investment of \$100, under strategy (1), with a yield to maturity of 9.660 percent on three-year zero-coupon bonds, our investment would grow to $\$100(1.0966)^3 = \$131.87$. Under strategy (2), the \$100 investment in the two-year bond would grow after two years to $\$100(1.08995)^2 = \$118.80$. Then in the third year it would grow by an additional factor of $1 + r_3$.

In a world of certainty both of these strategies must yield exactly the same final payoff. If strategy (1) were to dominate strategy (2), no one would hold two-year bonds; their prices would fall and their yields would rise. Likewise if strategy (2) dominated strategy (1), no one would hold three-year bonds. Therefore, we can conclude that $\$131.87 = \$118.80(1 + r_3)$, which implies that $(1 + r_3) = 1.11$, or $r_3 = 11$ percent. This is in fact the rate that will prevail in year three, as Table 15.1 indicates. Thus, our method of obtaining the third-period interest rate does provide the correct solution in the certainty case.

More generally, the comparison of the two strategies establishes that the return on a three-year bond equals that on a two-year bond and rollover strategy:

$$100(1 + y_3)^3 = 100(1 + y_2)^2(1 + r_3)$$

so that $1 + r_3 = (1 + y_3)^3/(1 + y_2)^2$. Generalizing for the certainty case, a simple rule for inferring a future short interest rate from the yield curve of zero-coupon bonds is to use the following formula:

$$(1 + r_n) = (1 + y_n)^n/(1 + y_{n-1})^{n-1} \qquad \textbf{(15.4)}$$

where $n$ denotes the period in question and $y_n$ is the yield to maturity of a zero-coupon bond with an $n$-period maturity.

Equation 15.4 has a simple interpretation. The numerator on the right-hand side is the total growth factor of an investment in an $n$-year zero held until maturity. Similarly, the denominator is the growth factor of an investment in an $(n - 1)$-year zero. Because the former investment lasts for one more year than the latter, the difference in these growth factors must be the rate of return available in year $n$ when the $(n - 1)$-year zero can be rolled over into a one-year investment.

Of course, when future interest rates are uncertain, as they are in reality, there is no meaning to inferring "the" future short rate. No one knows today what the future interest rate will be. At best, we can speculate as to its expected value and associated uncertainty. Nevertheless, it still is common to use equation 15.4 to investigate the implications of the yield curve for future interest rates. In recognition of the fact that future interest rates are uncertain, we call the interest rate that we infer in this matter the **forward interest rate** rather than the *future short rate,* because it need not be the interest rate that actually will prevail at the future date.

If the forward rate for period $n$ is $f_n$, we define $f_n$ by the equation

$$1 + f_n = (1 + y_n)^n/(1 + y_{n-1})^{n-1}$$

Equivalently, we may rewrite the equation as

$$(1 + y_n)^n = (1 + y_{n-1})^{n-1}(1 + f_n) \qquad \textbf{(15.5)}$$

In this formulation, the forward rate is *defined* as the "break-even" interest rate that equates the return on an $n$-period zero-coupon bond to that of a $(n-1)$-period zero-coupon bond rolled over into a one-year bond in year $n$. The actual total returns on the two $n$-year strategies will be equal if the spot interest rate in year $n$ turns out to equal $f_n$.

We emphasize that the interest rate that actually will prevail in the future need not equal the forward rate, which is calculated from today's data. Indeed, it is not even necessarily the case that the forward rate equals the expected value of the future short interest rate. This is an issue that we address in much detail shortly. For now, however, we note that forward rates do equal future short rates in the special case of interest rate certainty.

## 15.2 Measuring the Term Structure

Thus far we have focused on default-free zero-coupon bonds. These bonds are easiest to analyze because their maturity is given by their single payment. In practice, however, the great majority of bonds pay coupons, and most available data pertain to coupon bonds, so we must develop a general approach to calculate spot and forward rates from prices of coupon bonds.

Equations 15.4 and 15.5 for the determination of the forward rate from available yields apply only to zero-coupon bonds. They were derived by equating the returns to competing investment strategies that both used zeros. If coupon bonds had been used in those strategies, we would have had to deal with the issue of coupons paid and reinvested during the investment period, which complicates the analysis.

A further complication arises from the fact that bonds with different coupon rates can have different yields even if their maturities are equal. For example, consider two bonds, each with a two-year time to maturity and annual coupon payments. Bond $A$ has a 3 percent coupon; bond $B$ a 12 percent coupon. Using the interest rates of Table 15.1, we see that bond $A$ will sell for

$$\frac{\$30}{1.08} + \frac{\$1{,}030}{(1.08)(1.10)} = \$894.78$$

At this price its yield to maturity is 8.98 percent. Bond $B$ will sell for

$$\frac{\$120}{1.08} + \frac{\$1{,}120}{(1.08)(1.10)} = \$1{,}053.87$$

at which price its yield to maturity is 8.94 percent. Because bond $B$ makes a greater share of its payments in the first year when the interest rate is lower, its yield to maturity is slightly lower. Because bonds with the same maturity can have different yields, we conclude that a single yield curve relating yields and times to maturity cannot be appropriate for all bonds.

The solution to this ambiguity is to perform all of our analysis using the yield curve for zero-coupon bonds, sometimes called the *pure yield curve.* Our goal, therefore, is to calculate the pure yield curve even if we have to use data on more common coupon-paying bonds.

The trick we use to infer the yield curve from data on coupon bonds is to treat each coupon payment as a separate "mini" zero-coupon bond. A coupon bond then becomes just a "portfolio" of many zeros. Indeed, we saw in the previous chapter that most zero-coupon bonds are created by stripping coupon payments from coupon bonds and repackaging the separate payments from many bonds into portfolios with common maturity dates. By determining the price of each of these "zeroes," we can calculate the yield to that maturity date for a single-payment security and thereby construct the pure yield curve.

The simplest way to apply this technique is by successive estimations of the implied spot rates from the observed prices of coupon bonds of increasing maturities. This method is known as *bootstrapping.* As a specific example, consider the Canada bond prices observed on June 29, 1995, as presented in Figure 14.1 of the previous chapter. The Treasury bill yields observed on that same day were 6.90 percent, 6.86 percent, and 6.87 percent, respectively for three months, six months, and one year. We shall use the bootstrapping technique to estimate the implied spot rates for the maturity dates of the first two Canada bonds of Figure 14.1.

The first bond has a coupon rate of 7.75 percent, a market price of $1,008.85, and a maturity date of September 15, 1996. The corresponding values for the second bond are 8 percent, $1,015.85, and March 15, 1997. Since there are approximately 2.5 months between June 29 and September 15, the purchase of the first bond entitles the buyer to three payments of $38.75 × (2.5/6), $38.75, and $1,038.75, in 2.5, 8.5, and 14.5 months, respectively. Similarly, the second bond corresponds to cash flows of $40 × (2.5/6), $40, $40, and $1,040 in 2.5, 8.5, 14.5, and 20.5 months. Hence, if $y_3$ and $y_4$ are the spot rates corresponding to the maturity dates of the two bonds, then their purchase prices must satisfy the equations

$$1{,}008.85 = \frac{38.75 \times \dfrac{2.5}{6}}{(1.069)^{2.5/12}} + \frac{38.75}{(1.0686)^{8.5/12}} + \frac{1{,}038.75}{(1 + y_3)^{14.5/12}}$$

$$1{,}015.85 = \frac{40 \times 2.5/6}{(1.069)^{2.5/12}} + \frac{40}{(1.0686)^{8.5/12}} + \frac{40}{(1 + y_3)^{14.5/12}} + \frac{1{,}040}{(1 + y_4)^{20.5/12}}$$

In these two equations we assume that the spot rates in 2.5 months and 8.5 months are equal to the three-month and six-month T-bill rates, respectively. Solving the first equation gives us an implied spot rate of $y_3 = 7.12\%$. Substituting this value into the second one and solving for $y_4$, we get $y_4 = 7.14\%$. These two values are the spot rates corresponding to September 16, 1996, and March 15, 1997. We now can use them, together with the T-bill rates, to find the implied spot rate for the next highest-maturity bond for which we have a price observation.

**CONCEPT CHECK** Question 2. A T-bill with six-month maturity and $10,000 face value sells for $9,700. A one-year maturity T-bond paying semiannual coupons of $40 sells for $1,000. Find the current six-month short rate and the forward rate for the following six-month period.

When we analyze many bonds, such an inference procedure is more difficult, in part because of the greater number of bonds and time periods, but also because not all bonds give rise to identical estimates for the discounted value of a future $1 payment. In other words, there seem to be apparent error terms in the pricing relationship.[1] Nevertheless, treating these errors as random aberrations, we can use a statistical approach to infer the pattern of forward rates embedded in the yield curve.

To see how the statistical procedure would operate, suppose that we observe many coupon bonds, indexed by *i,* selling at prices $P_i$. The coupon and/or principal payment (the cash flow) of bond *i* at time *t* is denoted $\text{CF}_{it}$, and the present value of a $1 payment at time *t,* which is the implied price of a zero-coupon bond that we are trying to determine, is denoted $d_t$. Then for each bond we may write the following:

$$\begin{aligned} P_1 &= d_1\text{CF}_{11} + d_2\text{CF}_{12} + d_3\text{CF}_{13} + \ldots + e_1 \\ P_2 &= d_1\text{CF}_{21} + d_2\text{CF}_{22} + d_3\text{CF}_{23} + \ldots + e_2 \\ P_3 &= d_1\text{CF}_{31} + d_2\text{CF}_{32} + d_3\text{CF}_{33} + \ldots + e_3 \\ &\vdots \\ P_n &= d_1\text{CF}_{n1} + d_2\text{CF}_{n2} + d_3\text{CF}_{n3} + \ldots + e_n \end{aligned} \tag{15.6}$$

Each line of equation system 15.6 equates the price of the bond to the sum of its cash flows, discounted according to time until payment. The last term in each equation, $e_i$, represents the error term that accounts for the deviations of a bond's price from the prediction of the equation.

Students of statistics will recognize that equation 15.6 is a simple system of equations that can be estimated by regression analysis. The dependent variables are the bond prices, the independent variables are the cash flows, and the coefficients $d_t$ are to be estimated from the observed data.[2] The estimates of $d_t$ are our inferences of the present value of $1 to be paid at time *t.* The pattern of $d_t$ for various times to payment is called the *discount function,* because it gives the discounted value of $1 as a function of time until payment. From the discount

[1] We will consider later some of the reasons for the appearance of these error terms.

[2] In practice, variations of regression analysis called "splining techniques" usually are used to estimate the coefficients. This method was first suggested by McCulloch in the following two articles: J. Huston McCulloch, "Measuring the Term Structure of Interest Rates," *Journal of Business* 44 (January 1971); and "The Tax Adjusted Yield Curve," *Journal of Finance* 30 (June 1975).

function, which is equivalent to a list of zero-coupon bond prices for various maturity dates, we can calculate the yields on pure zero-coupon bonds. We would use government securities in this procedure to avoid complications arising from default risk.

Before leaving the issue of the measurement of the yield curve, it is worth pausing briefly to discuss the error terms. Why is it that all bond prices do not conform exactly to a common discount function that sets price equal to present value? Two reasons relate to factors not accounted for in the regression analysis of equation 15.6: taxes and options associated with the bond.

Taxes affect bond prices because investors care about their after-tax return on investment. Therefore, the coupon payments should be treated as net of taxes. Similarly, if a bond is not selling at par value, Revenue Canada requires that a "built-in" interest payment be imputed by amortizing the difference between the price and the par value of the bond. These considerations are difficult to capture in a mathematical formulation because different individuals are in different tax brackets, meaning that the net-of-tax cash flows from a given bond depend on the identity of the owner. Moreover, the specification of equation 15.6 implicitly assumes that the bond is held until maturity: It discounts *all* the bond's coupon and principal payments. This, of course, ignores the investor's option to sell the bond before maturity and so to realize a different stream of income from that described by equation 15.6. Moreover, it ignores the investor's ability to engage in *tax-timing options.* For example, an investor whose tax bracket is expected to change over time may benefit by realizing capital gains during the period when the tax rate is the lowest.

Another feature affecting bond pricing is the call provision. First, if the bond is callable, how do we know whether to include in equation 15.6 coupon payments in years following the first call date? Similarly, the date of the principal repayment becomes uncertain. More important, one must realize that the issuer of the callable bond will exercise the option to call only when it is profitable to do so. Conversely, the call provision is a transfer of value away from the bondholder who has "sold" the option to call to the bond issuer. The call feature therefore will affect the bond's price and introduce further error terms in the simple specification of equation 15.6.

Finally, we must recognize that the yield curve is based on price quotes that often are somewhat inaccurate. Price quotes used in the financial press may be stale (i.e., out of date), even if only by a few hours. Moreover, they may not represent prices at which dealers actually are willing to trade.

## 15.3 Interest Rate Uncertainty and Forward Rates

Let us turn now to the more difficult analysis of the term structure when future interest rates are uncertain. We have argued so far that, in a certain world, different investment strategies with common terminal dates must provide equal rates of return. For example, two consecutive one-year investments in zeroes would need to offer the same total return as an equal-sized investment in a two-year zero. Therefore, under certainty,

$$(1 + r_1)(1 + r_2) = (1 + y_2)^2$$

What can we say when $r_2$ is not known today?

For example, referring once again to Table 15.1, suppose that today's rate, $r_1 = 8\%$, and that the expected rate next year is $E(r_2) = 10\%$. If bonds were priced based only on the expected value of the interest rate, then a one-year zero would sell for \$1,000/1.08 = \$925.93, and a two-year zero would sell for \$1,000/[(1.08)(1.10)] = \$841.75, just as in Table 15.2.

But now consider a short-term investor who wishes to invest only for one year. She can purchase the one-year zero and lock in a riskless 8 percent return because she knows that at the end of the year, the bond will be worth its maturity value of \$1,000. She also can purchase the two-year zero. Its *expected* rate of return also is 8 percent: Next year, the bond will have one year to maturity, and we expect that the one-year interest rate will be 10 percent, implying a price of \$909.09 and a holding-period return of 8 percent. But the rate of return on the two-year bond is risky. If next year's interest rate turns out to be above expectations, that is, greater than 10 percent, the bond price will be below \$909.09, and conversely, if $r_2$ turns out to be less than 10 percent, the bond price will exceed \$909.09. Why should this short-term investor buy the risky two-year bond when its expected return is 8 percent, no better than that of the risk-free one-year bond? Clearly, she would not hold the two-year bond unless it offered an expected rate of return greater than the riskless 8 percent return available on the competing one-year bond. This requires that the two-year bond sell at a price lower than the \$841.75 value we derived when we ignored risk.

Suppose, for example, that most investors have short-term horizons and are willing to hold the two-year bond only if its price falls to \$819. At this price, the expected holding-period return on the two-year bond is 11 percent (because 909.09/819 = 1.11). The risk premium of the two-year bond, therefore, is 3 percent; it offers an expected rate of return of 11 percent versus the 8 percent risk-free return on the one-year bond. At this risk premium, investors are willing to bear the price risk associated with interest rate uncertainty.

In this environment, the forward rate, $f_2$, no longer equals the expected short rate, $E(r_2)$. Although we have assumed that $E(r_2) = 10\%$, it is easy to confirm that $f_2 = 13\%$. The yield to maturity on the two-year zero selling at \$819 is 10.5 percent, and

$$1 + f_2 = \frac{(1 + y_2)^2}{1 + y_1} = \frac{1.105^2}{1.08} = 1.13$$

This result—that the forward rate exceeds the expected short rate—should not surprise us. We defined the forward rate as the interest rate that would need to prevail in the second year to make the long- and short-term investments equally attractive, ignoring risk. When we account for risk, it is clear that short-term investors will shy away from the long-term bond unless it offers an expected return greater than that offered by the one-year bond. Another way of putting this is to say that investors will require a risk premium to hold the longer-term bond. The risk-averse investor would be willing to hold the long-term bond only if $E(r_2)$ is less than the break-even value, $f_2$, because the lower the expectation of $r_2$, the greater the anticipated return on the long-term bond.

Therefore, if most individuals are short-term investors, bonds must have prices that make $f_2$ greater than $E(r_2)$. The forward rate will embody a premium compared with the expected future short-interest rate. This **liquidity premium** compensates short-term investors for the uncertainty about the price at which they will be able to sell their long-term bonds at the end of the year.[3]

---

**CONCEPT CHECK** Question 3. Suppose that the required liquidity premium for the short-term investor is 1 percent. What must $E(r_2)$ be if $f_2$ is 10 percent?

---

Perhaps surprisingly, we also can imagine scenarios in which long-term bonds can be perceived by investors to be *safer* than short-term bonds. To see how, we now consider a "long-term" investor, who wishes to invest for a full two-year period. Suppose that the investor can purchase a two-year \$1,000 par value zero-coupon bond for \$841.75 and lock in a guaranteed yield to maturity of $y_2 = 9\%$. Alternatively, the investor can roll over two one-year investments. In this case an investment of 841.75 would grow in two years to $841.75 \times (1.08)(1 + r_2)$, which is an uncertain amount today because $r_2$ is not yet known. The break-even year-two interest rate is, once again, the forward rate, 10 percent, because the forward rate is defined as the rate that equates the terminal value of the two investment strategies.

The expected value of the payoff of the rollover strategy is $841.75(1.08)[1 + E(r_2)]$. If $E(r_2)$ equals the forward rate, $f_2$, then the expected value of the payoff from the rollover strategy will equal the *known* payoff from the two-year maturity bond strategy.

If this a reasonable presumption? Once again, it is only if the investor does not care about the uncertainty surrounding the final value of the rollover strategy. Whenever that risk is important, the long-term investor will not be willing to engage in the rollover strategy unless its expected return exceeds that of the two-year bond. In this case, the investor would require that

$$(1.08)[1 + E(r_2)] > (1.09)^2 = (1.08)(1 + f_2)$$

which implies that $E(r_2)$ exceeds $f_2$. The investor would require that the expected period two interest rate exceed the break-even value of 10 percent, which is the forward rate.

---

[3] *Liquidity* refers to the ability to sell an asset easily at a predictable price. Because long-term bonds have greater price risk, they are considered less liquid in this context and thus must offer a premium.

Therefore, if all investors were long-term investors, no one would be willing to hold short-term bonds unless those bonds offered a reward for bearing interest rate risk. In this situation, bond prices would be set at levels such that rolling over short bonds would result in greater expected returns than holding long bonds. This would cause the forward rate to be less than the expected future spot rate.

For example, suppose that in fact $E(r_2) = 11\%$. The liquidity premium therefore is negative: $f_2 - E(r_2) = 10\% - 11\% = -1\%$. This is exactly opposite from the conclusion that we drew in the first case of the short-term investor. Clearly, whether forward rates will equal expected future short rates depends on investors' readiness to bear interest rate risk, as well as their willingness to hold bonds that do not correspond to their investment horizons.

## 15.4 Theories of the Term Structure

### The Expectations Hypothesis

The simplest theory of the term structure is the **expectations hypothesis.** A common version of this hypothesis states that the forward rate equals the market consensus expectation of the future short interest rate; in other words, that $f_2 = E(r_2)$, and that liquidity premiums are zero. Because $f_2 = E(r_2)$, we may relate yields on long-term bonds to expectations of future interest rates. In addition, we can use the forward rates derived from the yield curve to infer market expectations of future short rates. For example, with $(1 + y_2)^2 = (1 + r_1)(1 + f_2)$ from equation 15.5, we may also write that $(1 + y_2)^2 = (1 + r_1)[1 + E(r_2)]$ if the expectations hypothesis is correct. The yield to maturity would thus be determined solely by current and expected future one-period interest rates. An upward-sloping yield curve would be clear evidence that investors anticipate increases in interest rates.

**Concept Check**

Question 4. If the expectations hypothesis is valid, what can we conclude about the premiums necessary to induce investors to hold bonds of different maturities from their investment horizons?

### Liquidity Preference

We noted in our discussion of long- and short-term investors that short-term investors will be unwilling to hold long-term bonds unless the forward rate exceeds the expected short interest rate, $f_2 > E(r_2)$, whereas long-term investors will be unwilling to hold short bonds unless $E(r_2)$ exceeds $f_2$. In other words, both groups of investors require a premium to induce them to hold bonds with maturities different from their investment horizons. Advocates of the **liquidity preference theory** of the term structure believe that short-term investors dominate the market so that, generally speaking, the forward rate exceeds the expected short rate. The excess of $f_2$ over $E(r_2)$, the liquidity premium, is predicted to be positive.

**CONCEPT CHECK** Question 5. The liquidity premium hypothesis also holds that *issuers* of bonds prefer to issue long-term bonds. How would this preference contribute to a positive liquidity premium?

To illustrate the differing implications of these theories for the term structure of interest rates, consider a situation in which the short interest rate is expected to be constant indefinitely. Suppose that $r_1 = 10\%$ and that $E(r_2) = 10\%$, $E(r_3) = 10\%$, and so on. Under the expectations hypothesis, the two-year yield to maturity could be derived from the following:

$$(1 + y_2)^2 = (1 + r_1)[1 + E(r_2)]$$
$$= (1.10)(1.10)$$

so that $y_2$ equals 10 percent. Similarly, yields on all-maturity bonds would equal 10 percent.

In contrast, under the liquidity preference theory, $f_2$ would exceed $E(r_2)$. For the sake of illustration, suppose that $f_2$ is 11 percent, implying a 1 percent liquidity premium. Then, for two-year bonds:

$$(1 + y_2)^2 = (1 + r_1)(1 + f_2)$$
$$= (1.10)(1.11) = 1.221$$

implying that $1 + y_2 = 1.105$. Similarly, if $f_3$ also equals 11 percent, then the yield on three-year bonds would be determined by

$$(1 + y_3)^3 = (1 + r_1)(1 + f_2)(1 + f_3)$$
$$= (1.10)(1.11)(1.11) = 1.35531$$

implying that $1 + y_3 = 1.1067$. The plot of the yield curve in this situation would be given as in Figure 15.5**A**. Such an upward-sloping yield curve is commonly observed in practice.

If interest rates are expected to change over time, then the liquidity premium may be overlaid on the path of expected spot rates to determine the forward interest rate. Then the yield to maturity for each date will be an average of the single-period forward rates. Several such possibilities for increasing and declining interest rates appear in Figure 15.5 **B** to **D.**

## Market Segmentation and Preferred Habitat Theories

Both the liquidity premium and the expectations hypothesis of the term structure implicitly view bonds of different maturities as potential substitutes for each other. An investor considering holding bonds of one maturity possibly can be lured instead into holding bonds of another maturity by the prospect of earning a risk premium. In this sense markets for bonds of all maturities are inextricably linked, and yields on short and long bonds are determined jointly in market equilibrium. Forward rates cannot differ from expected short rates by more than a fair

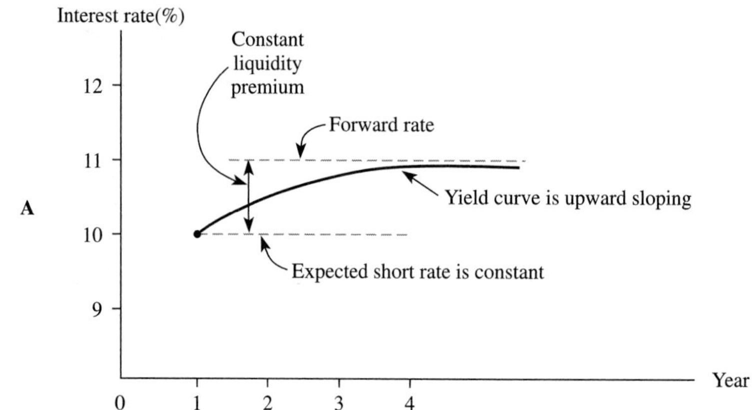


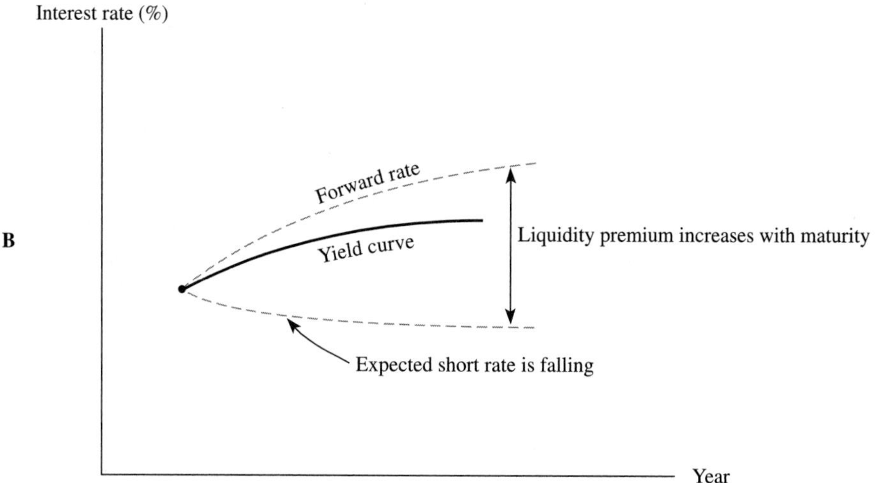


**Figure 15.5**
Yield curves. **A,** Constant expected short rate. Liquidity premium of 1 percent. Result is a rising yield curve. **B,** Declining expected short rates. Increasing liquidity premiums. Result is a rising yield curve despite falling expected interest rates.

liquidity premium, or else investors will reallocate their fixed-income portfolios to exploit what they perceive as abnormal profit opportunities elsewhere.

In contrast, the **market segmentation theory** holds that long- and short-maturity bonds are traded in essentially distinct or segmented markets, each of which finds its own equilibrium independently. The activities of long-term borrowers and lenders determine rates on long-term bonds. Similarly, short-term traders set short rates independently of long-term expectations. The term structure of interest rates, in this view, is determined by the equilibrium rates set in the various maturity markets.

This view of the market is not common today. Both borrowers and lenders seem to compare long and short rates, as well as expectations of future rates,

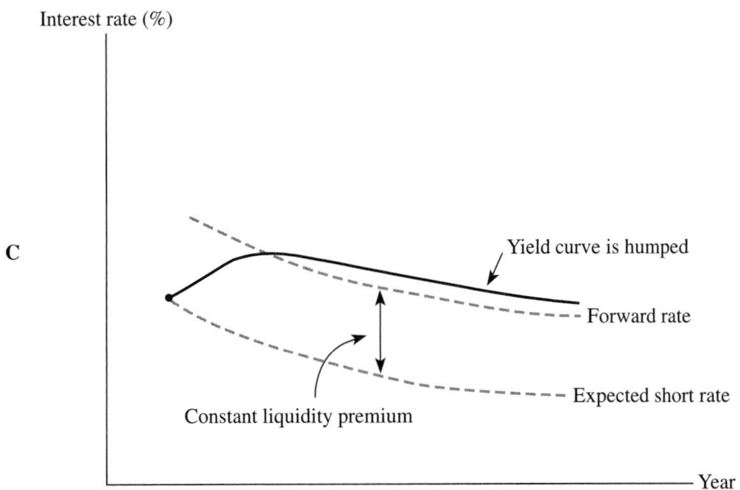


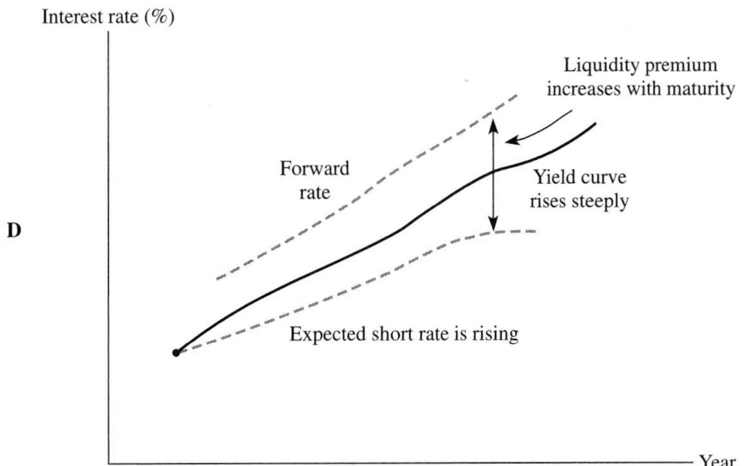


**Figure 15.5**
*(Concluded)*
**C,** Declining expected short rates. Constant liquidity premiums. Result is a hump-shaped yield curve. **D,** Increasing expected short rates. Increasing liquidity premiums. Result is a sharply increasing yield curve.

before deciding whether to borrow or lend long- or short-term. That they make these comparisons, and are willing to move into a particular maturity if it seems sufficiently profitable to do so, means that all-maturity bonds compete with each other for investors' attention, which implies that the rate on a bond of any given maturity is determined with an eye toward rates on competing bonds. This view of the market is called the **preferred habitat theory:** Investors prefer specific maturity ranges but can be induced to switch if premiums are sufficient. Markets are not so segmented that an appropriate premium cannot attract an investor who prefers one bond maturity to consider a different one.

## 15.5 Interpreting the Term Structure

We have seen that under certainty, one plus the yield to maturity on a zero-coupon bond is simply the geometric average of one plus the future short rates that will prevail over the life of the bond. This is the meaning of equation 15.3, which we repeat here:

$$1 + y_n = [(1 + r_1)(1 + r_2) \ldots (1 + r_n)]^{1/n}$$

When future rates are uncertain, we modify equation 15.3 by replacing future short rates with forward rates:

$$1 + y_n = [(1 + r_1)(1 + f_2)(1 + f_3) \ldots (1 + f_n)]^{1/n} \quad \textbf{(15.7)}$$

Thus, there is a direct relationship between yields on various maturity bonds and forward interest rates. This relationship is the source of the information that can be gleaned from an analysis of the yield curve.

First, we ask what factors can account for a rising yield curve. Mathematically, if the yield curve is rising, $f_{n+1}$ must exceed $y_n$. In words, the yield curve is upward sloping at any maturity date, *n,* for which the forward rate for the coming period is greater than the yield at that maturity. This rule follows from the notion of the yield to maturity as an average (albeit a geometric average) of forward rates.

If the yield curve is to rise as one moves to longer maturities, it must be the case that extension to a longer maturity results in the inclusion of a "new" forward rate that is higher than the average of the previously observed rates. This is analogous to the observation that if a new student's test score is to increase the class average, that student's score must exceed the class's average without her score. To raise the yield to maturity, an above-average forward rate must be added to the other rates in the averaging computation.

For example, if the yield to maturity on three-year bonds is 9 percent, then the yield on four-year bonds will satisfy the following equation:

$$(1 + y_4)^4 = (1.09)^3(1 + f_4)$$

If $f_4 = .09$, then $y_4$ also will equal .09. (Confirm this!) If $f_4$ is greater than 9 percent, $y_4$ will exceed 9 percent, and the yield curve will slope upward.

**Concept Check** Question 6. Look back at Tables 15.1 and 15.2. Show that $y_4$ would exceed $y_3$ if and only if the interest rate for period four had been greater than 9.66 percent, which was the yield to maturity on the three-year bond, $y_3$.

Given that an upward-sloping yield curve is always associated with a forward rate higher than the spot, or current, yield, we need to ask next what can account for that higher forward rate. Unfortunately, there always are two possible answers to this question. Recall that the forward rate can be related to the expected future short rate according to this equation:

$$f_n = E(r_n) + \text{Liquidity premium}$$

where the liquidity premium might be necessary to induce investors to hold bonds of maturities that do not correspond to their preferred investment horizons.

By the way, the liquidity premium need not be positive, although that is the position generally taken by advocates of the liquidity premium hypothesis. We showed previously that if most investors have long-term horizons, the liquidity premium could be negative.

In any case, the equation shows that there are two reasons that the forward rate could be high. Either investors expect rising interest rates, meaning that $E(r_n)$ is high, or they require a large premium for holding longer-term bonds. Although it is tempting to infer from a rising yield curve that investors believe that interest rates will eventually increase, this is not a valid inference. Indeed, Figure 15.5**A** provides a simple counterexample to this line of reasoning. There, the spot rate is expected to stay at 10 percent forever. Yet there is a constant 1 percent liquidity premium so that all forward rates are 11 percent. the result is that the yield curve continually rises, starting at a level of 10 percent for one-year bonds, but eventually approaching 11 percent for long-term bonds as more and more forward rates at 11 percent are averaged into the yields to maturity.

Therefore, although it is true that expectations of increases in future interest rates can result in a rising yield curve, the converse is not true: A rising yield curve does not in and of itself imply expectations of higher future interest rates. This is the heart of the difficulty in drawing conclusions from the yield curve. The effects of possible liquidity premiums confound any simple attempt to extract expectations from the term structure. But estimating the market's expectations is a crucial task, because only by comparing your own expectations to those reflected in market prices can you determine whether you are relatively bullish or bearish on interest rates.

One very rough approach to deriving expected future spot rates is to assume that liquidity premiums are constant. An estimate of that premium can be subtracted from the forward rate to obtain the market's expected interest rate. For example, again making use of the example plotted in Figure 15.5**A,** the researcher would estimate from historical data that a typical liquidity premium in this economy is 1 percent. After calculating the forward rate from the yield curve to be 11 percent, the expectation of the future spot rate would be determined to be 10 percent.

This approach has little to recommend it for two reasons. First, it is next to impossible to obtain precise estimates of a liquidity premium. The general approach to doing so would be to compare forward rates and eventually realized future short rates and to calculate the average difference between the two. However, the deviations between the two values can be quite large and unpredictable because of unanticipated economic events that affect the realized short rate. The data do not contain enough information to calculate a reliable estimate of the expected premium. Second, there is no reason to believe that the liquidity premium should be constant. Figure 15.6 shows the rate of return variability of Canada

**Figure 15.6**
Price volatility of long-term bonds, 1977–1994.

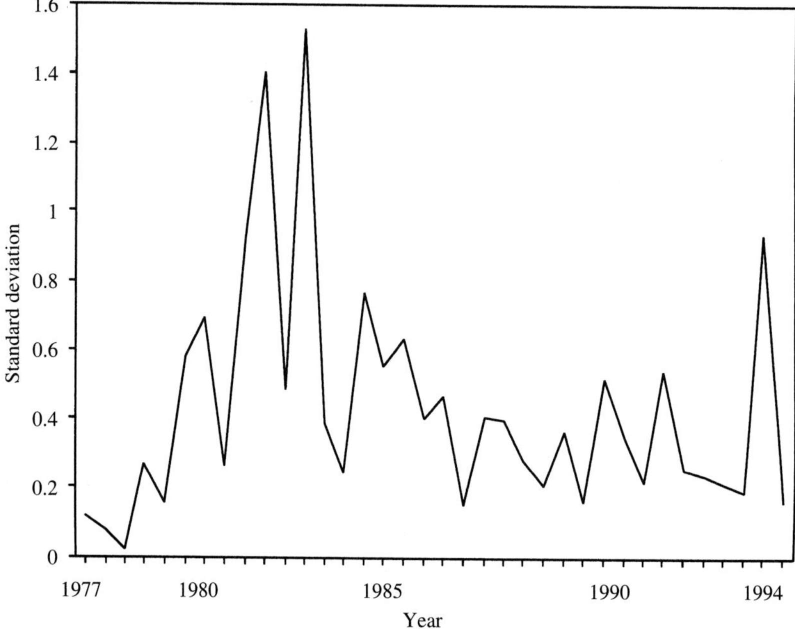


long-term bonds since 1977. Interest rate risk fluctuated dramatically during the period. So might we expect risk premiums on various maturity bonds to fluctuate, and empirical evidence suggests that term premiums do in fact fluctuate over time.[4] Still, as the accompanying box indicates, very steep yield curves are interpreted by many market professionals as warning signs of impending rate increases.

The usually observed upward slope of the yield curve, especially for short maturities, is the empirical basis for the liquidity premium doctrine that long-term bonds offer a positive liquidity premium. In the face of this empirical regularity, perhaps it is valid to interpret a downward-sloping yield curve as evidence that interest rates are expected to decline. If **term premiums,** the spread between yields on long- and short-term bonds, generally are positive, then anticipated declines in rates could account for a downward-sloping yield curve.

Figure 15.7 presents a history of yields on short-term and long-term Canada bonds. Yields on the longer-term bonds *generally* exceed those on the short-term bonds, meaning that the yield curve generally slopes upward. Moreover, the exceptions to this rule seem to precede episodes of falling short rates, which, if anticipated, would induce a downward-sloping yield curve. For example,

[4] See, for example, Richard Startz, "Do Forecast Errors or Term Premia Really Make the Difference between Long and Short Rates?" *Journal of Financial Economics* 10 (1982).

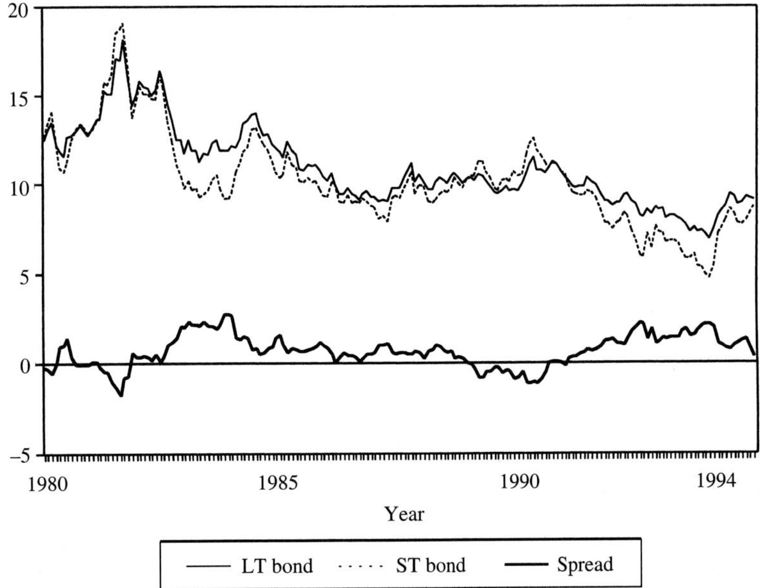


**Figure 15.7**
Yields on long-term versus short-term government securities: term spread, 1980–1994.

1989–90 were years in which short-term yields exceeded long-term yields. These years preceded a drastic drop in the general level of rates.

Why might interest rates fall? There are two factors to consider: the real rate and the inflation premium. Recall that the nominal interest rate is composed of the real rate plus a factor to compensate for the effect of inflation:

$$1 + \text{Nominal rate} = (1 + \text{Real rate})(1 + \text{Inflation rate})$$

or approximately,

$$\text{Nominal rate} = \text{Real rate} + \text{Inflation rate}$$

Therefore, an expected change in interest rates can be due to changes either in expected real rates or expected inflation rates. Usually, it is important to distinguish between these two possibilities because the economic environments associated with them may vary substantially. High real rates may indicate a rapidly expanding economy, high budget deficits, and tight monetary policy. Although high inflation rates also can arise out of a rapidly expanding economy, inflation also may be caused by rapid expansion of the money supply or supply-side shocks to the economy, such as interruptions in oil supplies. These factors have very different implications for investments. Even if we conclude from an analysis of the yield curve that rates will fall, we need to analyze the macroeconomic factors that might cause such a decline.

## Shapely Curves

For the seventh time in 12 months, America's Federal Reserve increased interest rates on February 1st. The half-point rise. which lifted the federal funds rate to 6 percent and the discount rate to 5.25 percent, had been widely expected. the question now, however, is whether it will prove to be the last.

Most economists are predicting a slowdown in growth this year. The question is whether it will come early enough to prevent overheating, and so relieve the Fed of the need to raise interest rates more aggressively. Although most economists are still forecasting a "soft landing" (in which annual growth conveniently slows to 2.5 percent, and stays there), a small but growing number now expect the economy to remain robust in early 1995; the eventual slowdown will therefore be much sharper.

The latter group of economists has become mesmerised by the shape of the yield curve—the graph that plots yields on securities of different maturities. In the past, the shape of this curve (more precisely, the gap in yields between long- and short-term bonds) has proved to be a good leading indicator of economic activity.

Why should this be? In normal times, investors demand higher yields on longer-dated bonds to compensate them for the greater risk, but the required premium varies according to their expectations of growth, inflation, and thus the future path of interest rates. For example, the yield curve sloped steeply upwards in 1992–93, reflecting the market's expectation that future growth—and hence inflation and short-term interest rates—would increase. Investors therefore demanded a bigger premium on securities with a long maturity.

By contrast, when the Fed lifts short-term interest rates in order to dampen growth, the gap between long- and short-term bond yields usually narrows in a pincer movement. While yields on shorter-term bonds are pulled up by rising short-term interest rates, those on long-term bonds fall as inflationary expectations ease. If the Fed continues to tighten policy, short-term rates eventually rise above long-term rates and the yield curve becomes "inverted". Because investors expect weaker growth in the future, and hence lower interest rates, they will accept lower rates on long-term bonds.

### A Fatal Inversion

As a forecasting tool, the yield curve has impressive credentials: It has become inverted 12–18 months before every recession during the past 40 years, and only once over that period has there been a false alarm, when an inversion of the curve was not followed by a recession. That was in 1965–66, when heavy government spending during the Vietnam war helped to avert a full recession, and growth merely slowed.

So what is the curve signaling now? Since late 1992, the gap between ten-year and three-year Treasury bonds has narrowed from 200 basis points (one-hundredths of one percent) to only 25 points (see chart), the smallest gap since the 1990 recession. On past experience, this signals a sharp slowdown in 1995–96 but not, as yet, a recession.

The Fed is playing a tough game: It must weigh up future inflationary risks against the danger of pushing the economy into recession. The snag is that monetary policy is not a science: There are long lags of around 18 months before changes in interest rates affect economic activity, and the extent of their impact is unclear. Alan Greenspan, the Fed's chairman, cannot, except by luck, bring the rate of growth exactly in line with the economy's productive potential. The best he can do to avoid a recession is to prevent serious overheating.

*(Continued)*

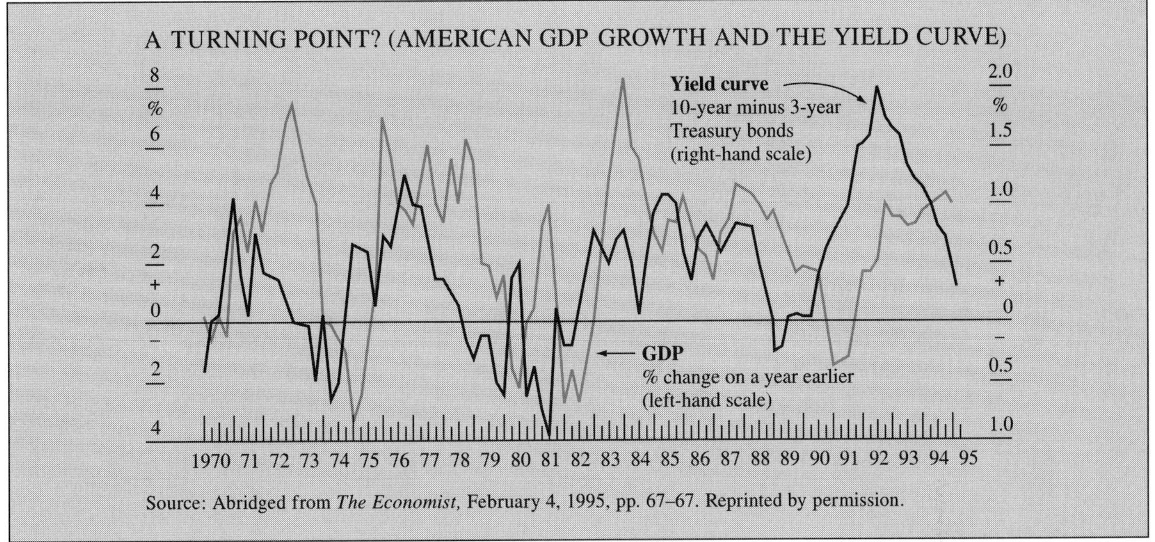


Source: Abridged from *The Economist,* February 4, 1995, pp. 67–67. Reprinted by permission.

## Summary

**1.** The term structure of interest rates refers to the interest rates for various terms to maturity embodied in the prices of default-free zero-coupon bonds.

**2.** In a world of certainty all investments must provide equal total returns for any investment period. Short-term holding-period returns on all bonds would be equal in a risk-free economy, and all would be equal to the rate available on short-term bonds. Similarly, total returns from rolling over short-term bonds over longer periods would equal the total returns available from long-maturity bonds.

**3.** A pure yield curve could be plotted easily from a complete set of zero-coupon bonds. In practice, however, most bonds carry coupons, payable at different future times, so that yield-curve estimates usually must be inferred from prices of coupon bonds. Measurement of the term structure is completed by tax issues such as tax timing options and the different tax brackets of different investors.

**4.** The forward rate of interest is the break-even future interest rate that would equate the total return from a rollover strategy to that of a longer-term zero-coupon bond. It is defined by the equation

$$(1 + y_n)^n(1 + f_{n+1}) = (1 + y_{n+1})^{n+1}$$

where $n$ is a given number of periods from today. This equation can be used to show that yields to maturity and forward rates are related by the equation

$$(1 + y_n)^n = (1 + r_1)(1 + f_2)(1 + f_3) \ldots (1 + f_n)$$

**5.** A common version of the expectations hypothesis holds that forward interest rates are unbiased estimates of expected future interest rates. However, there are good reasons to believe that forward rates differ from expected short rates by a risk premium known as a *liquidity premium*. A liquidity premium can cause the yield curve to slope upward even if no increase in short rates is anticipated.

**6.** The existence of liquidity premiums makes it extremely difficult to infer expected future interest rates from the yield curve. Such an inference would be made easier if we could assume the liquidity premium remained reasonably stable over time. However, both empirical and theoretical insights cast doubt on the constancy of that premium.

## Key Terms

Term structure of interest rates
Short interest rate
Yield curve
Spot rate
Forward interest rate
Liquidity premium
Expectations hypothesis
Liquidity preference theory
Market segmentation theory
Preferred habitat theory
Term premiums

## Selected Readings

*A detailed presentation of yield-curve analytics and relationships among spot rates, yields to maturity, and realized compound yields is contained in:*

Homer, Sidney; and Martin Liebowitz. *Inside the Yield Book: New Tools for Bond Market Strategy.* Englewood Cliffs, N.J.: Prentice Hall, 1972.

*A discussion of the various versions of the expectations hypothesis is:*

Cox, John; Jonathan Ingersoll; and Stephen Ross. "A Reexamination of Traditional Hypotheses about the Term Structure of Interest Rates." *Journal of Finance* 36 (September 1981).

*Evidence on liquidity premiums may be found in:*

Fama, Eugene. "The Information in the Term Structure." *Journal of Financial Economics* 13 (1984).

Mankiw, N. Gregory. "The Term Structure of Interest Rates Revisited." *Brookings Papers on Economic Activity* 61 (1986).

*Problems in the measurement of the yield curve are treated in:*

McCulloch, J. Houston. "The Tax-Adjusted Yield Curve." *Journal of Finance* 30 (June 1975).

## Problems

**1.** *a.* Briefly explain why bonds of different maturities have different yields in terms of the (*i*) expectations, (*ii*) liquidity, and (*iii*) segmentation hypotheses.

*b.* Briefly describe the implications of each of the three hypotheses when the yield curve is (*i*) upward sloping, and (*ii*) downward sloping.

2. Which one of the following is false?
   *a.* The liquidity preference hypothesis indicates that, all things being equal, longer maturities will have a higher yield.
   *b.* The basic conclusion of the expectations hypothesis is that the long-term rate is equal to the anticipated short-term rate.
   *c.* The expectations hypothesis indicates a flat yield curve if anticipated future short-term rates are equal to current short-term rates.
   *d.* The segmentation hypothesis contends that borrowers and lenders are constrained to particular segments of the yield curve.
3. Under the expectations hypothesis, if the yield curve is upward sloping, the market must expect an increase in short-term interest rates. Is this statement true, false, or uncertain? Why?
4. Under the liquidity preference theory, if inflation is expected to be falling over the next few years, long-term interest rates will be higher than short-term rates. Is this statement true, false, or uncertain? Why?
5. The following is a list of prices for zero-coupon bonds of various maturities. Calculate the yields to maturity of each bond and the implied sequence of forward rates.

| Maturity (Years) | Price of Bond($) |
|---|---|
| 1 | 943.40 |
| 2 | 898.47 |
| 3 | 847.62 |
| 4 | 792.16 |

6. Assuming that the expectations hypothesis is valid, compute the expected price path of the four-year bond in problem (3) as time passes. What is the rate of return of the bond in each year? Show that the expected return equals the forward rate for each year.

7. The following table shows yields to maturity of U.S. Treasury securities as of January 1, 1993:

| Term to Maturity (in years) | Yield to Maturity |
|---|---|
| 1 | 3.50% |
| 2 | 4.50 |
| 3 | 5.00 |
| 4 | 5.50 |
| 5 | 6.00 |
| 10 | 6.60 |

   *a.* Based on the data in the table, calculate the implied forward one-year rate of interest at January 1, 1996.

*b.* Describe the conditions under which the calculated forward rate would be an unbiased estimate of the one-year spot rate of interest at January 1, 1996.

Assume that one year earlier, on January 1, 1992, the prevailing term structure for U.S. Treasury securities was such that the implied forward one-year rate of interest on January 1, 1996, was significantly higher than the corresponding rate implied by the term structure on January 1, 1993.

*c.* On the basis of the pure expectations theory of the term structure, briefly discuss *two* factors that could account for such a decline in the implied forward rate.

**8.** Would you expect the yield on a callable bond to lie above or below a yield curve fitted from noncallable bonds?

**9.** The current yield curve for default-free zero-coupon bonds is as follows:

| Maturity (Years) | YTM |
|---|---|
| 1 | 10% |
| 2 | 11 |
| 3 | 12 |

*a.* What are the implied one-year forward rates?

*b.* Assume that the pure expectations hypothesis of the term structure is correct. If market expectations are accurate, what will the pure yield curve, that is, the yields to maturity on one- and two-year zero-coupon bonds, be next year?

*c.* If you purchase a two-year zero-coupon bond now, what is the expected total rate of return over the next year? What if it were a three-year zero-coupon bond? (Hint: Compute the current and expected future prices.) Ignore taxes.

*d.* What should be the current price of a three-year maturity bond with a 12 percent coupon rate paid annually? If you purchased it at that price, what would your total expected rate of return be over the next year (coupon plus price change)? Ignore taxes.

**10.** The term structure for zero-coupon bonds is currently:

| Maturity (Years) | YTM |
|---|---|
| 1 | 4% |
| 2 | 5 |
| 3 | 6 |

Next year at this time, *you* expect it to be:

| Maturity (Years) | YTM |
|---|---|
| 1 | 5% |
| 2 | 6 |
| 3 | 7 |

*a.* What do *you* expect the rate of return to be over the coming year on a three-year zero-coupon bond?

*b.* Under the expectations theory, what yield to maturity does the market expect to observe on one- and two-year zeroes next year? Is the market's expectation of the return on the three-year bond more or less than yours?

**11.** The yield to maturity on one-year zero-coupon bonds is currently 7 percent; the YTM on two-year zeroes is 8 percent. The federal government plans to issue a two-year maturity *coupon* bond, paying coupons once per year with a coupon rate of 9 percent. The face value of the bond is $100.

*a.* At what price will the bond sell?

*b.* What will be the yield to maturity on the bond?

*c.* If the expectations theory of the yield curve is correct, what is the market expectation of the price that the bond will sell for next year?

*d.* Recalculate your answer to (*c*) if you believe in the liquidity preference theory and you believe that the liquidity premium is 1 percent.

**12.** Below is a list of prices for zero-coupon bonds of various maturities.

| Maturity (Years) | Price of $1,000 Par Bond (Zero Coupon) |
|---|---|
| 1 | 943.40 |
| 2 | 873.52 |
| 3 | 816.37 |

*a.* An 8.5 percent coupon $1,000 par bond pays an annual coupon and will mature in three years. What should be the yield to maturity on the bond?

*b.* If at the end of the first year the yield curve flattens out at 8 percent, what will be the one-year holding-period return on the coupon bond?

**13.** Prices of zero-coupon bonds reveal the following pattern of forward rates:

| Year | Forward Rate |
|---|---|
| 1 | 5% |
| 2 | 7 |
| 3 | 8 |

In addition to the zero-coupon bond, investors also may purchase a three-year bond making annual payments of $60 with a par value of $1,000.

*a.* What is the price of the coupon bond?

*b.* What is the yield to maturity of the coupon bond?

*c.* Under the expectations hypothesis, what is the expected realized compound yield of the coupon bond?

*d.* If you forecast that the yield curve in one year will be flat at 7 percent, what is your forecast for the expected rate of return on the coupon bond for the one-year holding period?

**14.** You observe the following term structure:

| | Effective Annual YTM |
|---|---|
| 1-year zero-coupon bond | 6.1% |
| 2-year zero-coupon bond | 6.2 |
| 3-year zero-coupon bond | 6.3 |
| 4-year zero-coupon bond | 6.4 |

*a.* If you believe that the term structure next year will be the same as today's, will the one-year or the four-year zeroes provide a greater expected one-year return?

*b.* What if you believe in the expectations hypothesis?

**15.** Canada bonds represent a significant holding in many pension portfolios. You decide to analyze the yield curve for Canada bonds.

*a.* Using the data in the table below, calculate the five-year spot and forward rates assuming annual compounding. Show your calculations.

**Canada Bond Yield Curve Data**

| Years to Maturity | Par Coupon Yield-to-Maturity | Calculated Spot Rates | Calculated Forward Rates |
|---|---|---|---|
| 1 | 5.00 | 5.00 | 5.00 |
| 2 | 5.20 | 5.21 | 5.42 |
| 3 | 6.00 | 6.05 | 7.75 |
| 4 | 7.00 | 7.16 | 10.56 |
| 5 | 7.00 | — | — |

*b.* Define and describe each of the following three concepts:

- Yield to maturity
- Spot rate
- Forward rate

Explain how these *three* concepts are related.

You are considering the purchase of a zero-coupon Canada bond with four years to maturity.

*c.* Based on the above yield curve analysis, calculate both the expected yield to maturity and the price for the security. Show your calculations.

**16.** The yield to maturity (YTM) on one-year maturity zero-coupon bonds is 5 percent and the YTM on two-year maturity zero-coupon bonds is 6 percent. The yield to maturity on two-year maturity coupon bonds with coupon rates of 12 percent (paid annually) is 5.8 percent. What arbitrage opportunity is available for an investment banking firm? What is the profit on the activity?

**17.** Suppose that a one-year zero-coupon bond with a face value of $100 currently sells at $94.34, while a two-year zero sells at $84.99. You are considering the purchase of a two-year maturity bond making *annual* coupon payments. The face value of the bond is $100, and the coupon rate is 12 percent per year.

*a.* What is the yield to maturity of the two-year zero? The two-year coupon bond?

*b.* What is the forward rate for the second year?

*c.* If the expectations hypothesis is accepted, what are (*i*) the expected price of the coupon bond at the end of the first year, and (*ii*) the expected holding period return on the coupon bond over the first year?

*d.* Will the expected rate of return be higher or lower if you accept the liquidity preference hypothesis?

Chapter 16

# Fixed-Income Portfolio Management

**IN THIS CHAPTER, WE TURN TO VARIOUS STRATEGIES THAT FIXED-INCOME PORTFOLIO MANAGERS CAN PURSUE, MAKING A DISTINCTION BETWEEN PASSIVE AND ACTIVE STRATEGIES.** A *passive investment strategy* takes market prices of securities as fairly set. Rather than attempting to beat the market by exploiting superior information or insight, passive managers act to maintain an appropriate risk/return balance given market opportunities. One special case of passive management is an immunization strategy that attempts to insulate or immunize the portfolio from interest rate risk.

An *active investment strategy* attempts to achieve returns more than commensurate with the risk borne. In the context of fixed-income management, this style of management can take two forms: Active managers either use interest rate forecasts to predict movements in the entire fixed-income market, or they employ some form of intramarket analysis to identify particular sectors of the fixed-income market or particular bonds that are relatively mispriced.

We start our discussion with an analysis of the sensitivity of bond prices to interest rate fluctuations. The concept of duration, which measures interest rate sensitivity, is basic to formulating both active and passive fixed-income strategies. We turn next to passive strategies and show how duration-matching strategies can be used to immunize the holding period return of a fixed-income portfolio from interest rate risk. Finally, we explore a variety of active strategies, including intramarket analysis, interest rate forecasting, and interest rate swaps.

## 16.1 Management of Interest Rate Risk

In the previous chapters we have seen that there is an inverse relationship between bond prices and yields, that this effect is stronger as maturity lengthens, and that it is even more so for zero-coupon bonds. A portfolio of bonds will therefore be affected in different ways by changing interest rates in relation to the yields and maturities of its holdings. Since interest rates can be quite volatile (during the 1980s, bond volatility often exceeded stock volatility), the value of a supposedly safe government bond portfolio can be quite risky. (See the nearby box.)

A bond portfolio manager will react to interest rate risk according to the motivation for forming that portfolio and the need for payout from it. As a simple example, suppose you wanted to have $10,000 in five years, having some capital already. You could simply buy a five-year Canada bond and collect interest as time passed, concluding with redemption for your objective. Alternatively, you could buy one-year T-bills and roll them over, or you could buy a 10-year Treasury and sell it after five years.

If you faced a normal rising yield curve, the last strategy would promise the greatest yield, but the sale price in five years would probably not be exactly $10,000; you would be exposed to *price risk.* The T-bill possibility offers you the lowest yield, but it guarantees you the going rate; here you face *reinvestment rate risk,* as each year you must reinvest at the going rate. You also face this in the five-year bond, however, because you must do something with the semiannual coupon payments. (We saw this in Section 14.4 of Chapter 14.) If you examine the cash flows, you can see that if rates rise, interim prices of bonds will fall but the opportunities for reinvesting coupon income improve; if you sell the bond at a loss and reinvest at a higher rate, you will be compensated in terms of higher cash flows to maturity. Ultimately, the higher interim rates will leave you with higher accumulated cash flows than if rates had stayed constant. Of course, with perfect foresight, you could have delayed the bond purchase until rates peaked, avoiding the price drop and locking in the higher return. If instead rates fall during the investment, you will actually accumulate less cash.

The idea of matching maturities for your needs sounds reasonable, but it doesn't eliminate all the interest rate risk. In fact, it is what we shall define as *duration* that needs to be matched. Indeed, the best alternative is to buy a five-year zero-coupon bond, with a duration of five years, at a price of the discounted present value of $10,000.

Management of interest rate risk has used duration-based strategies for some time now. Increasing sophistication and the design of new instruments have opened up other strategies using derivatives like swaps and futures. We shall explore how managers attempt to control the risk of their portfolios, keeping in mind that a passive or active strategy must be followed so as to be consistent with the requirements for payouts from the portfolio and the acceptability of taking risks to increase gains. First we need to clarify the nature of the risk and the characteristics of duration, which is the fundamental tool in measuring that risk.

# LUNGE FOR LIQUIDITY FUELLED BOND PLUNGE

**The Wall Street Journal**
**New York**

After two days of mayhem in the financial markets, U.S. President Bill Clinton interrupted his California vacation in late March and phoned economic adviser Robert Rubin back at the White House to ask a simple question: Why? For about half an hour, the subdued Wall Street veteran struggled to explain why long-term interest rates were soaring and bond prices plunging. Economic fundamentals didn't provide the answer, he said.

The market was functioning differently than it had in the past.

After only two small Federal Reserve Board moves to tighten credit, here was the fastest fall in U.S. bond prices in more than a decade.

And nearly everyone, from the resident White House expert on the markets to the seasoned chairman of the Federal Reserve to the managers of the biggest portfolios in the world, seemed confounded.

Today, with the bond market finally taking a respite, the causes of the global chain reaction are beginning to emerge. A confluence of factors triggered the exaggerated price decline: not only the Fed's first boost in short-term rates in five years, but also the signs of strength in the U.S. economy, heavy use of leverage by traders, and the unexpected collapse of trade talks with Japan.

But once it got going, the decline was accelerated by a global lunge for liquidity by money managers—wielding huge international portfolios and securities that didn't exist a decade ago—who had bet wrong and saw no choice but to sell whatever they could.

"I just remember losing money and staying up nights trying to peddle things, and being unable to sell anything at the market price," recalls money manager Michael Steinhardt. He was so leveraged he was losing a stunning $7 million (U.S.) with every 100th of a percentage point move in European interest rates.

The three-month bond plunge lifted the yield on 30-year U.S. Treasury bonds from about 6.2 percent in early February to above 7.6 percent in early May.

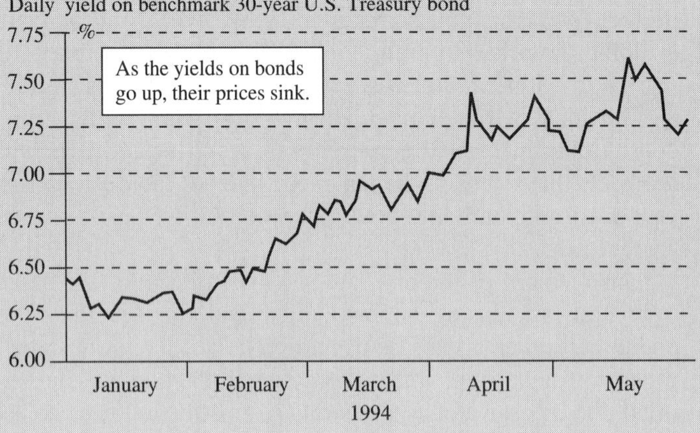


(Continued)

William Gross, bond manager at Pacific Investment Management Co. in Newport Beach, Calif., listened to the market collapse over a speaker that broadcast the bond futures pit at the Chicago Board of Trade. "You don't have to look at a screen to know whether the market is moving—you can hear the panic," he says. "When the market would sink, it sounded something akin to childbirth." The ramifications were broad. Mortgage rates shot up more than 1.5 percentage points and Corporate debt offerings dried up.

How did it happen? A look behind the scenes at the market's spring meltdown provides some clues. The proliferation of mortgage-backed securities played a little-appreciated role. As homeowners slowed their refinancing—thereby lengthening the maturities of securities based on home loans—the securities lost value faster than they would have before. In response, holders of these securities sold longer-term U.S. Treasury bonds to reduce the maturity of the rest of their holdings, pushing long-term rates up further, a phenomenon Federal Reserve Bank of New York economists are now studying.

The world didn't look so complicated when Fed officials met in Washington February 4 to raise rates, reasoning that an expanding economy no longer needed the prod of exceptionally low short-term borrowing costs. Only alarmists were talking about inflation.

Long-term rates, although up from unsustainable, low levels of last fall, were still low. Markets were calm.

Fed chairman Alan Greenspan argued that the markets would respond well to a quarter-percentage-point increase in short-term interest rates.

Others argued that markets would respond even better to a half-point increase. But the most persuasive advocate of the larger increase, vice chairman David Mullins, wasn't there because he had just announced his resignation. Surprisingly, top White House economist Alan Blinder (later nominated to succeed Mr. Mullins) told colleagues at the time that he, too, favoured the bigger move.

As he usually does, Mr. Greenspan prevailed. A few yards away, Mr. Mullins winced as he saw the news move across his computer screen that Friday.

Fed officials expected long-term rates to rise—indeed, some talked about pricking a speculative bubble in the bond market—but none was prepared for what was to follow.

For the past couple of years, the president of the New York Federal Reserve Bank, William McDonough, has pondered a nightmare scenario in which the financial system might be paralyzed by mere rumours that a big bank had lost so much money—not from lending but from trading—that others refused to trade with it.

On the morning of March 2, the nightmare threatened to come true.

Rumours were rampant about Bankers Trust New York Corp., which had derived 56 percent of its billion-dollar 1993 profit from trading.

According to the rumours, Bankers Trust had lost $1 billion trading with its own capital; other scuttlebutt held that the bank had told its traders to stop taking positions.

Because Bankers Trust had devoted so much of its resources to hedge-fund-like trading with its own capital, there was some plausibility to the notion that it had suffered hedge-fund-size losses. Indeed, Bankers' own proprietary traders, led by Kelly Doherty and his fixed-income lieutenant Barney Tumey, had made a series of losing bets on bond markets in Germany, France, Britain, Italy, Japan, and Latin America.

As Mr. Doherty would later explain to colleagues, such a diversified portfolio would be expected to do well—unless all the markets went down at the same time. But partly because of the heavy selling by hedge funds and other traders, the markets all did fall at once. The result was the first quarterly trading loss for Bankers Trust in 10 years and, subsequently, the resignations—which some traders believe were forced—of several traders.

The setback was nowhere near the crippling blow rumoured. But it was serious enough to prompt the bank to order its traders to curtail their trading for the rest of the quarter. And that decision

*(Continued)*

apparently caused the rumours to snowball. "Rumours take on a life of their own in periods of increased volatility" in the markets, says bank analyst Carole Berger of Salomon Brothers Inc. Because of them, Bankers Trust stock initially didn't open March 2, contributing to a panicky atmosphere that sent the Dow Jones industrial average plunging 50 points in the first half-hour.

Mr. McDonough, in constant touch with Washington, increased the frequency of his calls to top bankers, trying both to gather intelligence for the Fed and to offer calming reassurance about Bankers Trust. "The thing that makes it unusual," he says, "is that this happened to one of the most highly regarded banks in the country, with a return on equity of 26 percent in 1993." Says Mr. Gross, the California bond manager: "The fact that Bankers as well as other firms were involved in this gigantic game . . . was certainly wreaking havoc on the financial markets and probably producing higher interest rates than would normally have existed."

Just before 11 a.m. on March 2, after consulting with the Fed, Bankers Trust issued what in ordinary circumstances would have been a ho-hum statement: "Operations thus far for 1994 have been profitable." The message: Losses weren't severe enough to endanger the bank.

Because of Bankers Trust's reputation and the quiet assurances from top Fed officials, the statement worked, and the bullet was dodged. Stock and bond prices quickly rebounded, although Bankers Trust shares closed down $2.25 or 2.9 percent. At the end of the day, the yield on 30-year U.S. Treasury bonds was 6.77 percent.

On March 22, Fed policymakers sat down to contemplate the damage they had done. Although they had raised rates only a quarter point, the yield on 30-year bonds was up nearly half a point from early February. Instead of convincing the markets that they were heading off inflation, they inadvertently fueled fears that an inflation virus was already afoot.

Mr. Greenspan had said the Fed was moving rates from a level that was spurring the economy to a "neutral" level. But no one knew where that level was. (Last Tuesday, in raising rates another half point, the Fed implied that it thinks rates now are close to neutral.) The Fed staff came to the March 22 meeting laden with charts showing the unusual correlation between U.S. and foreign bond markets and showing how much the bond market had reacted to past turning points in Fed policy. The Fed quickly decided to raise rates another quarter point. But the meeting dragged on over a disagreement about a contingency plan to aid Mexico in case of a run on the peso.

Bonds soared after the Fed announcement—but the good news was short-lived. The next day Mexican presidential candidates Luis Donaldo Colosio was slain. Another set of chain reactions was under way.

At Chase Manhattan Bank, Joseph Boyle, who manages trading in emerging market securities, told traders in New York to come in at 2:30 a.m. on March 24 to handle an expected flood of orders from London. What he didn't anticipate was that investors would respond to the slaying by unloading not just Mexican securities but also those from other emerging markets, from Argentina to the Philippines.

J. P. Morgan, which had already sold off the bulk of its own holdings in emerging markets, began to avoid trading emerging-market debt for its clients by reducing the size of trades it would make to $2 million from $5 million and making its bid and asked prices unattractive.

With new financial instruments such as derivatives—which can be crafted to rise and fall in value depending on the relationships between, say, a Mexican bond and a U.S. bond—fluctuations in one market can be transmitted rapidly to others. Sensing that the world was even riskier than it had seemed before, big investors pulled back further, selling whatever they could, which in many cases meant U.S. Treasury bonds. "You don't sell what you should. You sell what you can," says Neil Soss, chief economist of CS First Boston, in what could be the T-shirt slogan for the veterans of the bond market crash of 1994.

*(Continued)*

At the end of March, the 30-year bond had crossed the 7 percent threshold—and there was just about to be another explosion in the chain reaction.

In late March, David Askin of Askin Capital Management was telling investors of the turmoil in the mortgage-backed-securities market. Earlier, he had boasted that he had developed a "market-neutral" strategy for buying certain variants of mortgage-backed securities that supposedly would make money whichever way interest rates moved. He managed about $600 million, much of which he had raised in 1993 in a 10-month marketing blitz.

He also had borrowed heavily, boosting his portfolio of mortgage-backed securities to $2.5 billion in value.

With markets plummeting, anxious Wall Street creditors, including Kidder Peabody & Co., Lehman Brothers, and Bear Stearns & Co., began to crowd Askin Capital. By mid-March, prices of mortgage securities had fallen so far that Mr. Askin received two margin calls. To meet them, he sold bonds, but he was unable to raise enough cash.

Word of his troubles spread fast. In addition to worries about Askin Capital's ability to repay, Wall Street has its own inventory to hedge—as much as $30 billion of mortgage-backed securities.

Like any bonds, mortgage-backed securities decline in market value when interest rates rise. But they also are affected by the speed with which people refinance their houses, a process that involves prepaying the original mortgage. The spring surge in interest rates slowed prepayments so much that the average life of mortgage-backed securities was stretching out like Silly Putty. They suddenly became longer-term bonds—which, by nature, are riskier because they are more sensitive to changes in interest rates. To compensate for this, the universal response on Wall Street was to lighten up on other long-term securities, primarily by selling 10-year Treasury notes.

"I remember certain days when our mortgage desk would sell $1 billion of 10-years," says Peter Hirsch, manager of government securities trading at Salomon Brothers. A senior trader at Lehman Brothers says the firm had to sell "many hundreds of millions" of 10-year notes to offset its $220 million exposure to Mr. Askin's mortgage-backed bonds. Traders estimate that all told, Wall Street sold as much as $20 billion of 10-year notes during March and April to offset its mortgage-security risk.

On March 30 and 31, Mr. Askin's bonds were seized by his creditors, contributing to the urge to sell 10-year notes. Then other mortgage portfolios began selling the notes as well—a hedge fund started by Cargill Inc. and several Askin-style mutual funds managed by Piper Capital Management of Minneapolis. The selling reached a peak in the first week in April. And as the yield on 10-year Treasury notes rose, so did the yield on the 30-year bond.

On April 4, it reached 7.4 percent.

Mr. Clinton finished his telephone conversation with Mr. Rubin and walked out to face the ubiquitous pack of reporters, then outside the Zamorano Fine Arts Academy Elementary School in San Diego. Distilling Mr. Rubin's message, he told them on March 31: "There is no underlying economic justification . . . for any increase in long-term interest rates. . . . Some of these corrective things will happen from time to time, but there's no reason for people to overreact." During the bond meltdown, Mr. Rubin has mainly tried to infuse a sense of calm, even on the most unruly days.

On Friday, April 1, the Labor Department jarred the market with the word that employers had hired twice as many workers in March as Wall Street had anticipated. The chaos continued. The bond market was whipsawed: The Fed raised interest rates, and in Germany, the Bundesbank cut them. The U.S. dollar plunged and recovered. By early May, the yield on 30-year bonds was above 7.6 percent.

Then the Fed sought to draw the spring trauma to a close last Tuesday, hoisting short-term rates by a bold half percentage point and making clear that it intends to sit tight for a while. The bond market enthusiastically pushed bond prices up, bring the yield on 30-year bonds back to 7.26 percent. That's still a full percentage point higher than it was in early

*(Continued)*

February. But the White House, the Fed and the bond traders breathed a collective sigh of relief, hoping that the worst was over.

The bond market plunge of 1994 may be remembered as the episode that provided investors big and small, corporate treasurers, bankers, and regulators a jolt they sorely needed. Some sophisticated-sounding strategies were shown to be little more than bets that bonds wouldn't reverse course. If traders were once spellbound by leverage, which fuelled their huge profits in 1993, they were reminded that it can also multiply losses. Naive investors who diverted savings from low-rate accounts to bond funds now realize they were taking on risks.

In shaking out the excesses, the long bond's steep fall taught banks and their regulators to prepare for big swings in prices, particularly in the value of derivatives. Finance officers who turned corporate treasuries into profit centres have seen the danger of strategies some didn't fully understand. The Fed has been reminded of its awesome ability to trigger market turbulence, perhaps even more now because of the links between various markets and the speed with which information moves.

Source: *The Globe and Mail,* May 23, 1994, pp. B1, B8. Reprinted by permission.

Note: This story was written by David Wessel in Washington and Laura Jereski and Randall Smith in New York.

## 16.2 Bond Duration

### Interest Rate Sensitivity

We begin with a quick review of the price reaction of equal maturity coupon and zero-coupon bonds to the same change in market yields. In Table 16.1, the first part gives the current prices of an 8 percent coupon bond for three different maturities ($T$) at market yields of 8 and 9 percent; because they are semiannual paying bonds, the stated annual yield is twice the true six-month yield. The second part of the table shows the discount prices paid for zero-coupon bonds of the same maturities. Clearly, the percentage change in price is greater for the zero-coupon bond, increasingly so as maturity lengthens.

The lower sensitivity of the coupon bond is due to the fact that it is not simply a 10- or 20-year maturity instrument. The 10-year bond is a contract for a series of 20 payments of different "maturity," most of which occur well before the maturity of the bond. The effective maturity of the bond is a sort of average of these maturities. The zero-coupon bond, by contrast, has a single payment with an unquestioned maturity.

**Table 16.1** Prices of 8 Percent Coupon Bond and Zero-Coupon Bonds

| Yield to Maturity (APR) | $T$ = 1 Year | $T$ = 10 Years | $T$ = 20 Years |
|---|---|---|---|
| **8% Coupon Bond** | | | |
| 8% | 1,000 | 1,000 | 1,000 |
| 9% | 990.64 | 934.96 | 907.99 |
| Change in price (%)* | 0.94% | 6.50% | 9.20% |
| **Zero-Coupon Bond** | | | |
| 8% | 924.56 | 456.39 | 208.29 |
| 9% | 915.73 | 414.64 | 171.93 |
| Change in price (%)* | 0.96% | 9.15% | 17.46% |

*Equals value of bond at a 9 percent yield to maturity divided by value of bond at (the original) 8 percent yield, minus 1.

## Calculating Duration

To deal with the ambiguity of the "maturity" of a bond making many payments, we need a measure of the average maturity of the bond's promised cash flows to serve as a useful summary statistic of the effective maturity of the bond. We also would like to use the measure as a guide to the sensitivity of a bond to interest rate changes, because we have noted that price sensitivity tends to increase with time to maturity.

Frederick Macaulay[1] termed the effective maturity concept the **duration** of the bond and suggested that duration be computed as the weighted average of the times to each coupon or principal payment made by the bond. He recommended that the weight of each payment be measured by the "importance" of that payment to the value of the bond—specifically, that the weight for each payment be the proportion of the total value of the bond accounted for by that payment. This proportion is just the present value of the payment divided by the bond price.

Therefore the weight, denoted $w_t$, associated with the cash flow at time $t$ ($CF_t$) would be

$$w_t = \frac{CF_t/(1 + y)^t}{\text{Bond price}}$$

where $y$ is the bond's yield to maturity. The numerator on the right-hand side of this equation is the present value of all payments forthcoming from the bond.

[1] Frederick Macaulay, *Some Theoretical Problems Suggested by the Movements of Interest Rates, Bond Yields, and Stock Prices in the United States since 1856* (New York: National Bureau of Economic Research, 1938).

**Table 16.2** Calculating the Duration of Two Bonds

| | (1) Time until Payment (in Years) | (2) Payment | (3) Payment Discounted at 5% Semiannually | (4) Weight* | (5) Column 1 Multiplied by Column 4 |
|---|---|---|---|---|---|
| **Bond A** | | | | | |
| 8% bond | .5 | $ 40 | $ 38.095 | .0395 | .0198 |
| | 1.0 | 40 | 36.281 | .0376 | .0376 |
| | 1.5 | 40 | 34.553 | .0358 | .0537 |
| | 2.0 | 1,040 | 855.611 | .8871 | 1.7742 |
| Sum: | | | $964.540 | 1.0000 | 1.8853 |
| **Bond B** | | | | | |
| Zero-coupon bond | .5–1.5 | $ 0 | $ 0 | 0 | 0 |
| | 2.0 | 1,000 | 822.70 | 1.0 | 2 |
| Sum: | | | $822.70 | 1.0 | 2 |

*Weight = Present value of each payment (column 3) divided by the bond price, $964.54 for bond A and $822.70 for bond B.

These weights sum to 1, because the sum of the cash flows discounted at the yield to maturity equals the bond price.

Using these values to calculate the weighted average of the times until the receipt of each of the bond's payments, we obtain Macauley's duration formula:

$$D = \sum_{t=1}^{T} t w_t \tag{16.1}$$

As an example of the application of equation 16.1, we derive in Table 16.2 the durations of 8 percent coupon and zero-coupon bonds, each with two years to maturity. We assume that the yield to maturity on each bond is 10 percent, or 5 percent per half-year.

The numbers in column 5 are the products of time to payment and payment weight. Each of these products corresponds to one of the terms in equation 16.1, which indicates that we calculate the duration of the bonds by adding the numbers in column 5. The duration of the zero-coupon bond is exactly equal to its time to maturity, two years. This makes sense, because with only one payment, the average time until payment must be the bond's maturity. In contrast, the two-year coupon bond has a shorter duration of 1.8853 years.

Duration is a key concept in fixed-income portfolio management for at least three reasons. First, it is a simple summary statistic of the effective average maturity of the portfolio. Second, it turns out to be an essential tool in immunizing portfolios from interest rate risk. (We will explore this application in Section 16.3.) Third, duration is a measure of the interest rate sensitivity of a portfolio, which we will explore here.

We already have noted that long-term bonds are more sensitive to interest rate movements than are short-term bonds. The duration measures enables us to quantify this relationship. Specifically, it can be shown that when interest rates change, the proportional change in a bond's price can be related to the change in its yield to maturity, $y$, according to the rule:

$$\frac{\Delta P}{P} = -D \times \left[\frac{\Delta(1 + y)}{1 + y}\right] \qquad \textbf{(16.2)}$$

The proportional price change equals the proportional change in 1 plus the bond's yield times the bond's duration. Therefore, bond price volatility is proportional to the bond's duration, and duration becomes a natural measure of interest rate exposure.[2]

Practitioners commonly use equation 16.2 in a slightly different form. They define "modified duration" as $D^* = D/(1 + y)$, note that $\Delta(1 + y) = \Delta y$, and rewrite 16.2 as

$$\Delta P/P = -D^*\Delta y \qquad \textbf{(16.2A)}$$

The percentage change in bond price is just the product of modified duration and the change in the bond's yield to maturity.

To confirm the relationship between duration and the sensitivity of bond price to interest rate changes, let's compare the interest rate sensitivity of the price of the two-year coupon bond in Table 16.2, which has a duration of 1.8853 years, to the sensitivity of a zero-coupon bond with maturity and duration of 1.8853 years. Both should have equal interest rate exposure if duration is a useful measure of price sensitivity.

The coupon bond sells for \$964.5404 at the initial semiannual interest rate of 5 percent. If the bond's semiannual yield increases by one basis point (1/100 of a percent) to 5.01 percent, its price will fall to \$964.1942, a percentage decline of .0359 percent. The zero-coupon bond has a maturity of $1.8853 \times 2 = 3.7706$ half-year periods. (Because we use a half-year interest rate of 5 percent, we also need to define duration in terms of a number of half-year periods to maintain consistency of units.) At the initial half-year interest rate of 5 percent, it sells at a price of \$831.9623 ($\$1{,}000/1.05^{3.7706}$). Its price falls to \$831.6636 ($\$1{,}000/1.0501^{3.7706}$) when the interest rate increases, for an identical .0359 percent capital loss. We conclude that equal-duration assets are in fact equally sensitive to interest rate movements. Incidentally, this example confirms the validity of equation 16.2. Note that the equation predicts that the proportional price change of the two bonds should have been $3.7706 \times .0001/1.05 = .000359$, or .0359 percent, exactly as we found from direct computation.

---

[2] Actually, equation 16.2 is only approximately valid for large changes in the bond's yield. The approximation becomes exact as one considers smaller, or localized, changes in yields. Students of calculus will recognize that duration is proportional to the derivative of the bond's price with respect to changes in the bond's yield:

$$D^* = -(1/P)(dP/dy)$$

As such, it gives a measure of the slope of the bond price curve only in the neighbourhood of the current price.

**Table 16.3** Bond Durations (in Years) (Initial Bond Yield = 8 percent APR)

| | Coupon Rates (per Year) | | | |
|---|---|---|---|---|
| **Years to Maturity** | **6%** | **8%** | **10%** | **12%** |
| 1 | .985 | .980 | .976 | .972 |
| 5 | 4.361 | 4.218 | 4.095 | 3.990 |
| 10 | 7.454 | 7.067 | 6.772 | 6.541 |
| 20 | 10.922 | 10.292 | 9.870 | 9.568 |
| Infinite (perpetuity) | 13.000 | 13.000 | 13.000 | 13.000 |

**CONCEPT CHECK** Question 1.

*a*. Calculate, as in Table 16.3, the price and duration of a two-year maturity, 9 percent coupon bond making annual coupon payments when the market interest rate is 10 percent.

*b*. Now suppose the interest rate increases to 10.05 percent. Calculate the new value of the bond and the percentage change in the bond's price.

*c*. Calculate the percentage change in the bond's price predicted by the duration formula in Equation 16.2 or 16.2A. Compare this value to your answer for (*b*).

## Duration Properties

The sensitivity of a bond's price to changes in market interest rates is influenced by three key factors: time to maturity, coupon rate, and yield to maturity. These determinants of price sensitivity are important to fixed-income portfolio management. Therefore, we summarize some of the important relationships in the following eight rules. These rules also are illustrated in Figure 16.1, which contains plots of durations of bonds of various coupon rates, yields to maturity, and times to maturity.

We already have established:

### Rule 1 for duration

The duration of a zero-coupon bond equals its time to maturity.

We also have seen that the two-year coupon bond has a lower duration than the two-year zero because coupons early in the bond's life lower the bond's weighted average time until payments. This illustrates another general property:

### Rule 2 for duration

Holding maturity constant, a bond's duration is higher when the coupon rate is lower.

This rule is attributable to the impact of early coupon payments on the average maturity of a bond's payments. The higher these coupons, the more they reduce the weighted average maturity of the payments. Compare the plots in Figure 16.1 of the durations of the 3 percent coupon and 15 percent coupon bonds, each with identical yields of 15 percent. The plot of the duration of the 15 percent coupon bond lies below the corresponding plot for the 3 percent coupon bond.

**Rule 3 for duration**

Holding the coupon rate constant, a bond's duration generally increases with its time to maturity. Duration always increases with maturity for bonds selling at par or at a premium to par.

This property of duration is fairly intuitive. What is surprising is that duration need not always increase with time to maturity. It turns out that for some deep discount bonds, duration may fall with increases in maturity. However, for virtually all traded bonds, it is safe to assume that duration increases with maturity.

Notice in Figure 16.1 that for the zero-coupon bond, maturity and duration are equal. However, for coupon bonds duration increases by less than a year with a year's increase in maturity. The slope of the duration graph is less than one.

Although long-maturity bonds generally will be high-duration bonds, duration is a better measure of the long-term nature of the bond because it also accounts for coupon payments. Time to maturity is an adequate statistic only when the bond pays no coupons; then, maturity and duration are equal.

Notice also in Figure 16.1 that the two 15 percent coupon bonds have different durations when they sell at different yields to maturity. The lower-yield bond has greater duration. This makes sense, because at lower yields the more distant payments made by the bond have relatively greater present values and account for a greater share of the bond's total value. Thus, in the weighted-average calculation of duration, the distant payments receive greater weights, which results in a higher duration measure. This establishes rule 4:

**Rule 4 for duration**

Holding other factors constant, the duration of a coupon bond is higher when the bond's yield to maturity is lower.

Rule 4 applies to coupon bonds. For zeroes, of course, duration equals time to maturity, regardless of the yield to maturity.

Finally, we develop some algebraic rules for the duration of securities of special interest. These rules are derived from and consistent with the formula for duration given in equation 16.1 but may be easier to use for long-term bonds.

**Rule 5 for duration**

The duration of a level perpetuity is $(1 + y)/y$. For example, at a 10 percent yield, the duration of a perpetuity that pays \$100 once a year forever will equal $1.10/.10 = 11$ years, but at an 8 percent yield it will equal $1.08/.08 = 13.5$ years.

**Figure 16.1** Bond duration versus bond maturity.

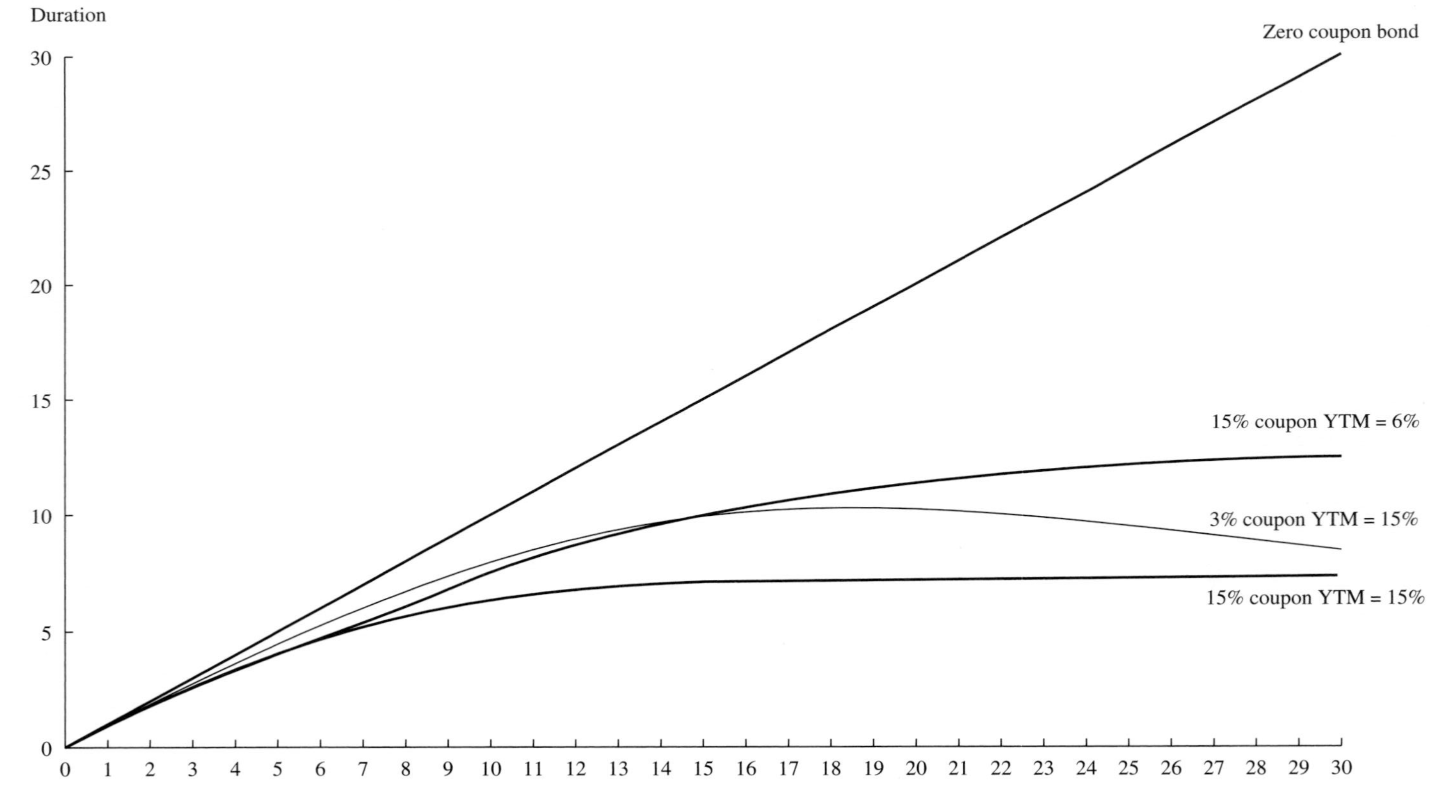

Rule 5 makes it obvious that maturity and duration can differ substantially. The maturity of the perpetuity is infinite, whereas the duration of the instrument at a 10 percent yield is only 11 years. The present-value-weighted cash flows early on in the life of the perpetuity dominate the computation of duration.

Notice from Figure 16.1 that as their maturities become ever longer, the durations of the two coupon bonds with yields of 15 percent both converge to the duration of the perpetuity with the same yield, 7.67 years.

---

**CONCEPT CHECK** Question 2. Show that the duration of the perpetuity increases as the interest rate decreases in accordance with rule 4.

---

### Rule 6 for duration

The duration of a level annuity is equal to the following:

$$\frac{1+y}{y} - \frac{T}{(1+y)^T - 1}$$

where $T$ is the number of payments and $y$ is the annuity's yield per payment period. For example, a 10-year annual annuity with a yield of 8 percent will have a duration of

$$\frac{1.08}{.08} - \frac{10}{1.08^{10} - 1} = 4.87 \text{ years}$$

### Rule 7 for duration

The duration of a coupon bond equals the following:

$$\frac{1+y}{y} - \frac{(1+y) + T(c-y)}{c[(1+y)^T - 1] + y}$$

where $c$ is the coupon rate per payment period, $T$ is the number of payment periods, and $y$ is the bond's yield per payment period. For example, a 10 percent coupon bond with 20 years until maturity and paying coupons semiannually would have a 5 percent semiannual coupon and 40 payment periods. If the yield to maturity were 4 percent per half-year period, the bond's duration would be

$$\frac{1.04}{.04} - \frac{1.04 + 40(.05 - .04)}{.05[1.04^{40} - 1] + .04} = 19.74 \text{ half-years}$$

$$= 9.87 \text{ years}$$

This calculation reminds us again of the importance of maintaining consistency between the time units of the payment period and interest rate. When the bond pays a coupon semiannually, we must use the effective semiannual interest rate and semiannual coupon rate in all calculations. This unit of time (one half-year) is then carried into the duration measure, when we calculate duration to be 19.74 half-year periods.

**Rule 8 for duration**

For coupon bonds selling at par value, rule 7 simplifies to the following formula for duration:

$$\frac{1+y}{y}\left[1-\frac{1}{(1+y)^T}\right]$$

Durations can vary widely among traded bonds. Table 16.3 presents durations computed from rule 7 for several bonds all assumed to pay semiannual coupons and to yield 4 percent per half-year. Notice that duration decreases as coupon rates increase and generally increases with time to maturity. According to Table 16.3 and equation 16.2, if the interest rate were to increase from 8 percent to 8.1 percent, the 6 percent coupon 20-year bond would fall in value by about 1.01 percent (10.922 × .1%/1.08), while the 10 percent coupon 1-year bond would fall by only 0.090 percent. Notice also from Table 16.3 that duration is independent of coupon rate only for the perpetual bond.

## 16.3 Passive Bond Management

Passive managers take bond prices as fairly set and seek to control only the risk of their fixed-income portfolio. Two broad classes of passive management are pursued in the fixed-income market. The first is an indexing strategy that attempts to replicate the performance of a given bond index. The second broad class of passive strategies are known as **immunization** techniques and are used widely by financial institutions such as insurance companies and pension funds. These are designed to shield the overall financial status of the institution from exposure to interest rate fluctuations. While both indexing and immunization strategies are alike in that they accept market prices as correctly set, they are very different in terms of risk exposure. A **bond index portfolio** will have the same risk-reward profile as the bond market index to which it is tied. In contrast, immunization strategies seek to establish a virtually zero-risk profile, in which interest rate movements have no impact on the value of the firm.

### Bond Index Funds

In principle, bond market indexing is similar to stock market indexing. The idea is to create a portfolio that mirrors the composition of an index that measures the broad market. Thus, stock index funds will purchase shares of each firm in the TSE 300 or S&P 500 in proportion to the market value of outstanding equity, to create index portfolios. A similar strategy is used for bond index funds, but as we shall see shortly, several modifications are required because of difficulties unique to the bond market and its indices.

The major indices of the Canadian bond market are compiled by Scotia-McLeod, its Universe Index being the relevant one. In the United States, there are three: the Salomon Brothers Broad Investment Grade (BIG) Index, the Lehman Brothers Aggregate Index, and the Merrill Lynch Domestic Master Index. These bond indices are market value-weighted indices of total returns on (U.S.) government, corporate, mortgage-backed, and Yankee (foreign issuer, U.S. dollar-denominated) bonds with maturities greater than one year; as time passes and the maturity of a bond falls below one year, the bond is dropped from the indices.

The first problem that arises in the formation of a bond index portfolio is that the index includes a vast number of securities (the U.S. indices include more than 5,000); hence, it is quite difficult to purchase each security in the index in proportion to its market value. Moreover, many bonds are very thinly traded, especially in Canada.

Bond index funds also present more difficult rebalancing problems than do stock index funds. Bonds are continually dropped from the index as their maturities fall below one year. Moreover, as new bonds are issued, they are added to the index. Therefore, in contrast to equity indices, the securities used to compute bond indices constantly change. As they do, the manager must update or rebalance the portfolio to ensure a close match between the composition of the portfolio and the bonds included in the index. The fact that bonds generate considerable interest income that must be reinvested further complicates the job of the index fund manager.

In practice, it is deemed infeasible to replicate precisely the broad bond indices. Instead, a stratified sampling or *cellular* approach is often pursued. The market is stratified by various characteristics such as maturity, credit risk of issuer, and coupon. Then, based on the percentage representation of the bond universe in the cells thus created, a portfolio is formed with representative bonds from each cell; the performance of the portfolio is supposed to match that of the index. Evidence from measurement of the *tracking error* between the performance of the portfolio and the index is supportive of the validity of this practice.[3]

The ScotiaMcLeod bond indices actually are based only on those bonds that are considered to be available for public investment. Those bonds that are held by the Bank of Canada in particular and other institutions that buy on issue to hold to maturity are not included in calculating the value weighting. This realization points to the well-known illiquidity of the Canadian bond market, which has a bearing on the subject of index funds. In the late 1980s, ScotiaMcLeod created a Canadian bond index fund but was disappointed with the results. The same problems that make an index portfolio difficult to maintain in the U.S. market were exaggerated in Canada, such that the fund became infeasible. There also proved to be very little interest for the fund from Canadian institutional and professional investors.

As we noted, the purpose of a bond index portfolio is to limit the interest rate exposure to that of the whole market, as captured by the index. This end may be

---

[3] Salomon Brothers found that a $100 million index fund could track the BIG index with an average absolute tracking error of only 4 basis points per month, as reported in Sharmin Mossavar-Rahmani, *Bond Index Funds* (Chicago: Probus Publishing Co., 1991).

insufficient for many financial institutions, which wish to protect either the current or future values of their portfolios. For instance, banks need to maintain current net worth for regulatory reasons; pension funds need to guarantee a certain future value when liabilities will mature. Let us therefore turn to a discussion of how interest rate risk can be controlled using immunization strategies.

## Net Worth Immunization

Many banks have a natural mismatch between asset and liability maturity structures. Bank liabilities are primarily the deposits owed to customers, most of which are very short term in nature and consequently of low duration. Bank assets, by contrast, are composed largely of outstanding commercial and consumer loans or mortgages. These assets are of longer duration than are deposits, and their values are correspondingly more sensitive to interest rate fluctuations. In periods when interest rates increase unexpectedly, banks can suffer serious decreases in net worth—their assets can fall in value by more than their liabilities.

Flannery and James[4] have shown that prices of bank stock do in fact tend to fall when interest rates rise. In another study, Kopcke and Woglom[5] found that, when measured by market values, total liabilities exceeded total assets for some savings banks in Connecticut in several years during the 1970s, a period following significant increases in interest rates. Had these banks been required to carry their assets at market value on their balance sheets, they would have been declared insolvent. Clearly, banks are subject to interest rate risk.

The watchword in bank portfolio strategy has become asset and liability management. Techniques called *gap management* were developed to limit the "gap" between asset and liability durations. Adjustable rate mortgages are one way to reduce the duration of bank asset portfolios. Unlike conventional mortgages, adjustable rate mortgages do not fall in value when market interest rates rise, because the rates they pay are tied to an index of the current market rate. Even if it is imperfect or entails lags, indexing greatly diminishes sensitivity to interest rate fluctuations. On the other side of the balance sheet, the introduction of bank certificates of deposit with fixed terms to maturity serves to lengthen the duration of bank liabilities, also reducing the duration gap.

One way to view gap management is to consider that the bank is attempting to equate the durations of assets and liabilities to effectively immunize its overall position from interest rate movements. Because bank assets and liabilities are roughly equal in size, if their durations also are equal, any change in interest rates will affect the values of assets and liabilities equally. Interest rates would have no effect on net worth, in other words. Therefore, net worth immunization requires

---

[4] Mark J. Flannery and Christopher M. James, "The Effect of Interest Rate Changes on the Common Stock Returns of Financial Institutions," *Journal of Finance* 39 (September 1984).

[5] Richard W. Kopcke and Geoffrey R. H. Woglom, "Regulation Q and Savings Bank Solvency—The Connecticut Experience," *The Regulation of Financial Institutions,* Federal Reserve Bank of Boston Conference Series, no. 21, 1979.

a portfolio duration of zero. This will result if assets and liabilities are equal in both magnitude and duration.

---

**CONCEPT CHECK** Question 3. If assets and liabilities are not equal, then immunization requires that $D_A A = D_L L$, where $D$ denotes duration and $A$ and $L$ denote assets and liabilities, respectively. Explain why the simpler condition $D_A = D_L$ is no longer valid in this case.

---

## Target Date Immunization

Pension funds are different from banks. They think more in terms of future commitments than current net worth. Pension funds have an obligation to provide workers with a flow of income upon their retirement, and they must have sufficient funds available to meet those commitments. As interest rates fluctuate, both the value of the assets held by the fund and the rate at which those assets generate income fluctuate. The pension fund manager therefore may want to protect or "immunize" the future accumulated value of the fund at some target date against interest rate movements.

Pension funds are not alone in this concern. Any institution with a future fixed obligation might consider immunization a reasonable risk management policy. Insurance companies, for example, also pursue immunization strategies. Indeed, the notion of immunization was introduced by F. M. Redington,[6] an actuary for a life insurance company.

The idea behind immunization is that with duration-matched assets and liabilities, the ability of the asset portfolio to meet the firm's obligations should be unaffected by interest rate movements. As an example of immunization, suppose that a pension fund is obligated to pay out $14,693.28 in five years. If the current market interest rate is 8 percent, the present value of that obligation is $10,000. The plan chooses to fund the obligation with $10,000 of 8 percent *annual* coupon bonds, selling at par value, with six years to maturity. As the duration of the bond is (from rule 8) five years, the single-payment obligation should be immunized by the bond.

Table 16.4 shows that if interest rates remain at 8 percent, then the accumulated funds from the bond will grow to exactly the $14,693.28 obligation. Over the five-year period, the year-end coupon income of $800 is reinvested at the prevailing 8 percent market interest rate. At the end of the period, the bonds can be sold for $10,000; they will still sell at par value because the coupon rate still equals the market interest rate. Total income after five years from reinvested coupons and the sale of the bond is precisely $14,693.28.

---

[6] F. M. Redington, "Review of the Principle of Life-Office Valuations," *Journal of the Institute of Actuaries* 78 (1952).

**Table 16.4** Terminal Value of a Bond Portfolio after Five Years (All Proceeds Reinvested)

| Payment Number | Time Remaining until Obligation | Accumulated Value of Invested Payment | | |
|---|---|---|---|---|
| **Rates Remain at 8%** | | | | |
| 1 | 4 | $800 \times (1.08)^4$ | = | $ 1,088.39 |
| 2 | 3 | $800 \times (1.08)^3$ | = | 1,007.77 |
| 3 | 2 | $800 \times (1.08)^2$ | = | 933.12 |
| 4 | 1 | $800 \times (1.08)^1$ | = | 864.00 |
| 5 | 0 | $800 \times (1.08)^0$ | = | 800.00 |
| Sale of bond | 0 | 10,800/1.08 | = | 10,000.00 |
| | | | | $14,693.28 |
| **Rates Fall to 7%** | | | | |
| 1 | 4 | $800 \times (1.07)^4$ | = | $ 1,048.64 |
| 2 | 3 | $800 \times (1.07)^3$ | = | 980.03 |
| 3 | 2 | $800 \times (1.07)^2$ | = | 915.92 |
| 4 | 1 | $800 \times (1.07)^1$ | = | 856.00 |
| 5 | 0 | $800 \times (1.07)^0$ | = | 800.00 |
| Sale of bond | 0 | 10,800/1.07 | = | 10,093.46 |
| | | | | $14,694.05 |
| **Rates Increase to 9%** | | | | |
| 1 | 4 | $800 \times (1.09)^4$ | = | $ 1,129.27 |
| 2 | 3 | $800 \times (1.09)^3$ | = | 1,036.02 |
| 3 | 2 | $800 \times (1.09)^2$ | = | 950.48 |
| 4 | 1 | $800 \times (1.09)^1$ | = | 872.00 |
| 5 | 0 | $800 \times (1.09)^0$ | = | 800.00 |
| Sale of bond | 0 | 10,800/1.09 | = | 9,908.26 |
| | | | | $14,696.02 |

Note: The sale price of the bond portfolio equals the portfolio's final payment ($10,800) divided by $1 + r$, because the time to maturity of the bonds will be one year at the time of sale.

However, Table 16.4 shows that if interest rates fall to 7 percent, the total funds will accumulate to $14,694.05, providing a small surplus of 77 cents. If rates increase to 9 percent, as at the bottom of Table 16.4, the fund accumulates to $14,696.02, providing a small surplus of $2.74.

Several points are worth highlighting. First, notice that duration-matching balances the trade-off between the accumulated value of the coupon payments (reinvestment rate risk) and the sale value of the bond (price risk). Thus, when interest rates fall, the coupons grow less than in the base case, but the gain on the sale of the bond offsets the coupon shortfall. When interest rates rise, the resale value of the bond falls, but the coupons make up for this loss with their higher accumulated interest. The net surplus in the fund is trivial, especially compared to the change in the value of the accumulated coupons or resale value taken alone. Because the bonds were chosen with a duration equal to the payout horizon (ver-

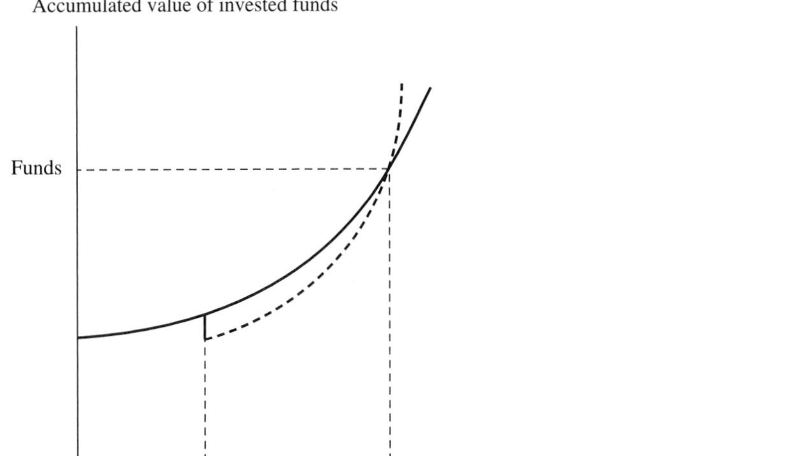


**Figure 16.2**
Growth of invested funds. The solid line curve represents the growth of portfolio value at the original interest rate. If interest rates increase at time $t^*$, the portfolio value falls but increases thereafter at the faster rate represented by the broken curve. At time $D$ (duration), the curves cross.

ify this using rule 8), price risk offsets reinvestment rate risk perfectly, and the accumulated value of the bonds at the horizon is unaffected by interest rate fluctuations. Figure 16.2, showing the capital loss occurring at the time of the rate increase, illustrates the duration effect.

As we noted, immunization also can be analyzed in terms of present values as opposed to future values. Figure 16.3 presents a graph of the present values of the bond and the single-payment obligation as a function of the interest rate. Notice that at the current rate of 8 percent the values are equal and the obligation is fully funded by the bond. Moreover, the two present value curves are tangent at $y = 8$ percent. As market yields change, the change in value of both the asset and the obligation is equal, so the obligation remains fully funded. For greater changes in the interest rate, however, the present value curves diverge. This is related to the fact that the fund actually shows some surplus in year 5 at market interest rates other than 8 percent.

Why is there any surplus in the fund? After all, we claimed that a duration-matched asset and liability mix would result in indifference to interest rate shifts. Actually, such a claim is valid only for *small* changes in the interest rate, because as bond yields change, so too does duration. (Recall rule 4 for duration and footnote 2.) In our example, although the duration of the bond is indeed equal to 5.0 years at a yield to maturity of 8 percent, it rises to 5.02 years when its yield falls to 7 percent and drops to 4.97 years at $y = 9$ percent; that is, the bond and the obligation were not duration matched *across* the interest rate shift, so that the position was not fully immunized. (This explains the slight surpluses in Table 16.4 which were not round-off errors.)

The increased curvature in Figure 16.3 is referred to as **convexity,** as the coupon bond has more convexity than the single payment obligation (and the

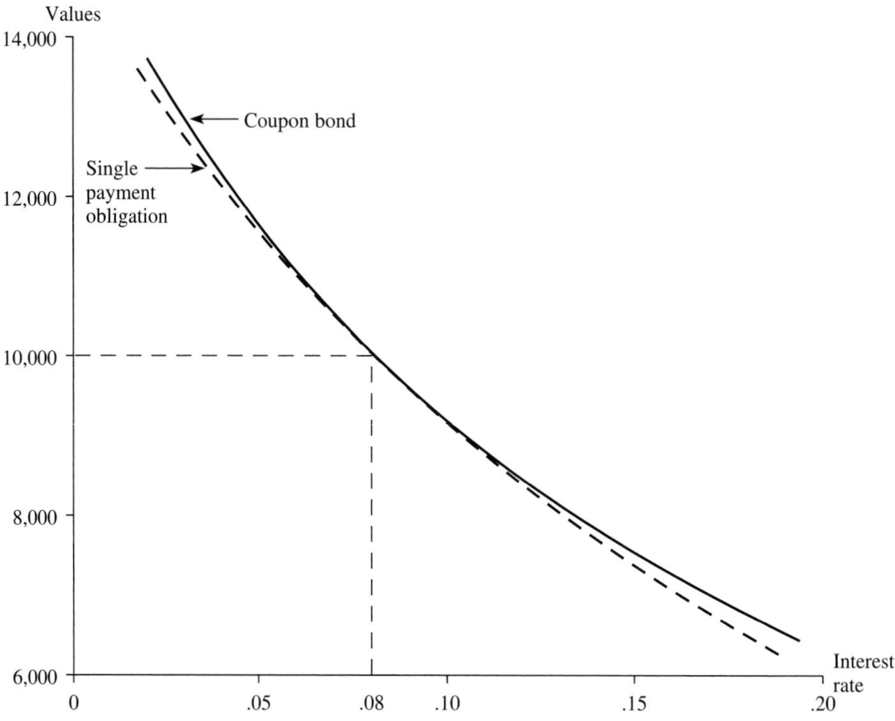


**Figure 16.3**
Immunization.

equivalent single payment asset).[7] Under this property, the value of a coupon bond rises more, and falls less, than that of an equal duration zero-coupon bond as interest rates fall and rise. This implies that instruments with earlier cash flows are actually more valuable than those with later cash flows, but of the same duration, in the immunization of portfolios.

This example highlights the importance of **rebalancing** immunized portfolios. As interest rates and asset durations change, a manager must rebalance the portfolio of fixed-income assets continually to realign its duration with the duration of the obligation. Moreover, even if interest rates do not change, asset durations *will* change solely because of the passage of time. Recall from Figure 16.2 that duration generally decreases less rapidly than does maturity. Thus, even if an obligation is immunized at the outset, as time passes the durations of the asset and liability will fall at different rates. Without portfolio rebalancing, durations will become unmatched and the goals of immunization will not be realized. Obviously, immunization is a passive strategy only in the sense that it does not involve attempts to identify undervalued securities. Immunization managers still actively update and monitor their positions.

[7] As in footnote 2, which refers to the price $P$ as a continuous function of the yield $y$, this curve is depicted in Figure 16.3; the slope $dP/dy$ is negative and the curvature is given by $d^2P/dy^2$. Formally, convexity is defined by the second derivative of the price with respect to the yield.

As an example of the need for rebalancing, consider a portfolio manager facing an obligation of \$19,487 in seven years, which, at a current market interest rate of 10 percent, has a present value of \$10,000. Right now, suppose that the manager wishes to immunize the obligation by holding only three-year zero-coupon bonds and perpetuities paying annual coupons. (Our focus on zeroes and perpetuities will serve to keep the algebra simple.) At current interest rates, the perpetuities have a duration of 1.10/.10 = 11 years; the duration of the zero is simply three years.

For assets with equal yields, the duration of a portfolio is the weighted average of the durations of the assets comprising the portfolio. To achieve the desired portfolio duration of seven years, the manager would have to choose appropriate values for the weights of the zero and the perpetuity in the overall portfolio. Call $w$ the zero's weight and $(1 - w)$ the perpetuity's weight. Then $w$ must be chosen to satisfy the equation

$$w \times 3 \text{ years} + (1 - w) \times 11 \text{ years} = 7 \text{ years}$$

which implies that $w = 1/2$. The manager invests \$5,000 in the zero-coupon bond and \$5,000 in the perpetuity, providing annual coupon payments of \$500 per year indefinitely. The portfolio duration is then seven years, and the position is immunized.

Next year, even if interest rates do not change, rebalancing will be necessary. The present value of the obligation has grown to \$11,000, because it is one year closer to maturity. The manager's funds also have grown to \$11,000: The zero-coupon bonds have increased in value from \$5,000 to \$5,500 with the passage of time, while the perpetuity has paid its annual \$500 coupon and is still worth \$5,000. However, the portfolio weights must be changed. The zero-coupon bond now will have a duration of 2 years, while the perpetuity remains at 11 years. The obligation is now due in six years. The weights must now satisfy the equation

$$w \times 2 + (1 - w) \times 11 = 6$$

which implies that $w = 5/9$. Now, the manager must invest a total of \$11,000 × 5/9 = \$6,111.11 in the zero. This requires that the entire \$500 coupon payment be invested in the zero and that an additional \$111.11 of the perpetuity be sold and invested in the zero in order to maintain an immunized position.

Of course, rebalancing of the portfolio entails transaction costs as assets are bought or sold, so one cannot rebalance continuously. In practice, an appropriate compromise must be established between the desire for perfect immunization, which requires continual rebalancing, and the need to control trading costs, which dictates less-frequent rebalancing.[8]

[8] For a comparison of duration and maturity matching with tax effects, see E. Z. Prisman and Y. Tiam, "Immunization in Markets with Tax-Clientele Effects: Evidence from the Canadian Market," *Journal of Financial and Quantitative Analysis* 29, no. 2, June 1994.

**CONCEPT CHECK** Question 4. What would be the immunization weights in the second year if the interest rate had fallen to 8 percent?

## Cash Flow Matching and Dedication

The problems associated with immunization seem to have an easy solution. Why not simply buy a zero-coupon bond that provides a payment in an amount exactly sufficient to cover the projected cash outlay? If we follow the principle of **cash flow matching,** we automatically immunize the portfolio from interest rate movements because the cash flow from the bond and the obligation exactly offset each other.

Cash flow matching on a multiperiod basis is referred to as a **dedication strategy.** In this case, the manager selects either zero-coupon or coupon bonds that provide cash flows in each period that match a series of obligations. Since the dedicated portfolio provides the cash necessary to pay the firm's liabilities regardless of the eventual path of interest rates, there is no need for rebalancing.

Cash flow matching is not widely pursued probably because of the constraints that it imposes on bond selection. Immunization-dedication strategies are appealing to firms that do not wish to bet on general movements in interest rates, but these firms may want to immunize using bonds that they perceive are undervalued. Cash flow matching, however, places so many more constraints on the bond selection process that it can be impossible to pursue a dedication strategy using only "underpriced" bonds. Firms looking for underpriced bonds give up exact and easy dedication for the possibility of achieving superior returns from the bond portfolio.

Sometimes, cash flow matching is not possible. To match cash flow for a pension fund that is obligated to pay out a perpetual flow of income to current and future retirees, the pension fund would need to purchase fixed-income securities with maturities ranging up to hundreds of years. Such securities do not exist, making exact dedication infeasible. Immunization is easy, however. If the interest rate is 8 percent, for example, the duration for the pension fund obligation is $1.08/.08 = 13.5$ years (see rule 5 above). Therefore, the fund can immunize its obligation by purchasing zero-coupon bonds with a maturity of 13.5 years and a market value equal to that of the pension liabilities.

**CONCEPT CHECK** Question 5. How would an increase in trading costs affect the attractiveness of dedication immunization?

## Other Problems with Conventional Immunization

If you look back at the definition of duration in equation 16.1, you note that it uses the bond's yield to maturity to calculate the weight applied to each coupon payment. Given this definition and limitations on the proper use of yield to maturity, it is perhaps not surprising that this notion of duration is strictly valid only for a flat yield curve for which all payments are discounted at a common interest rate.

If the yield curve is not flat, then the definition of duration must be modified and $CF_t/(1 + y)^t$ replaced with the present value of $CF_t$, where the present value of each cash flow is calculated by discounting with the appropriate interest rate from the yield curve corresponding to the date of the *particular* cash flow, instead of by discounting with the *bond's* yield to maturity. Moreover, even with this modification, duration matching will immunize portfolios only for parallel shifts in the yield curve. Clearly, this sort of restriction is unrealistic. As a result, much work has been devoted to generalizing the notion of duration. Multifactor duration models have been developed to allow for tilts and other distortions in the shape of the yield curve, in addition to shifts in its level. (We refer to some of this work in the suggested readings at the end of this chapter.) However, it does not appear that the added complexity of such models pays off in terms of substantially greater effectiveness.[9]

There is an extensive literature on the design and testing of immunization strategies. Gagnon and Johnson[10] investigated the success of duration- versus convexity-based strategies for asset-liability matching to solve the problem of fluctuating interest rates, finding the duration-based approach to be more effective. Bierwag, Fooladi, and Roberts[11] analyzed a sophisticated strategy known as M-squared minimization and found it to perform less well than anticipated, while Fooladi and Roberts[12] also conducted an empirical study of Canadian bond portfolio management. These analyses point to the complexity of bond trading and the difficulties in attaining the objectives stated for various types of portfolios.

Finally, immunization can be an inappropriate goal in an inflationary environment. Immunization is essentially a nominal notion and makes sense only for nominal liabilities. It makes no sense to immunize a projected obligation that will grow with the price level using nominal assets, such as bonds. For example, if your child will attend college in 15 years and if the annual cost of tuition is expected to be $15,000 at that time, immunizing your portfolio at a locked-in terminal value of $15,000 is not necessarily a risk-reducing strategy. The tuition obligation will vary with the realized inflation rate, whereas the asset portfolio's final value will not. In the end, the tuition obligation will not necessarily be matched by the value of the portfolio.

---

[9] G. O. Bierwag, G. C. Kaufman, and A. Toevs (editors), *Innovations in Bond Portfolio Management: Duration Analysis and Immunization* (Greenwich, Conn.: JAI Press, 1983). See also, G. O. Bierwag and G. S. Roberts, "Single-Factor Duration Models," *The Journal of Financial Research* 13, no. 1 (Spring 1990), pp. 23–38.

[10] Louis Gagnon and Lewis D. Johnson, "Dynamic Immunization under Stochastic Interest Rates," *Journal of Portfolio Management* 20, no. 3 (Spring 1994), pp. 48–54. Johnson also has written a series of articles on extending the notion of duration to equity portfolios, which appeared in *Financial Analysts Journal* in 1989, 1990, and 1992 and in *Canadian Journal of Administrative Sciences* in March 1991.

[11] G. O. Bierwag, I. Fooladi, and G. S. Roberts, "Designing an Immunized Portfolio—Is M-Squared the Key," *Journal of Banking and Finance* 17 (December 1993), pp. 1147–70.

[12] I. Fooladi and G. S. Roberts, "Bond Portfolio Immunization: Canadian Tests," *Journal of Economics and Business* 44 (February 1992), pp. 3–17.

On this note, it is worth pointing out that immunization is a goal that may well be inappropriate for many investors who would find a zero-risk portfolio strategy unduly conservative. Full immunization is a fairly extreme position for a portfolio manager to pursue.

## 16.4 Active Bond Management

### Sources of Potential Profit

Broadly speaking, there are two sources of potential value in active bond management. The first is interest rate forecasting, which tries to anticipate movements across the entire spectrum of the fixed-income market. If interest rate declines are anticipated, managers will increase portfolio duration (and vice versa). The second source of potential profit is identification of relative mispricing within the fixed-income market. An analyst, for example, might believe that the default premium on one particular bond is unnecessarily large and, therefore, that the bond is underpriced.

These techniques will generate abnormal returns only if the analyst's information or insight is superior to that of the market. One cannot profit from knowledge that rates are about to fall if everyone else in the market is aware of this. In that case, the anticipated rates already are built into bond prices in the sense that long-duration bonds are already selling at higher prices that reflect the anticipated fall in future short rates. If the analyst does not have information before the market does, it will be too late to act on that information—prices will have responded already to the news. This follows from the discussion of market efficiency.

For now, we simply repeat that valuable information is differential information. In this context it is worth noting that interest rate forecasters have a notoriously poor track record. If you consider this record, you will approach attempts to time the bond market with caution.

Homer and Liebowitz[13] have coined a popular taxonomy of active bond portfolio strategies. They characterize portfolio rebalancing activities as one of four types of *bond swaps.*

In the first swaps, the investor typically believes that the yield relationship between bonds or sectors is only temporarily out of alignment. When the aberration is eliminated, gains can be realized on the underpriced bond. The period of realignment is called the *workout period.*

1. The **substitution swap** is an exchange of one bond for a nearly identical substitute. The substituted bonds should be of essentially equal coupon, maturity, quality, call features, sinking fund provisions, and so on. This swap

[13] Sidney Homer and Martin L. Liebowitz, *Inside the Yield Book: New Tools for Bond Market Strategy* (Englewood Cliffs, N. J.: Prentice-Hall, 1972).

would be motivated by a belief that the market has temporarily mispriced the two bonds, and that the discrepancy between the prices of the bonds represents a profit opportunity.

2. The **intermarket spread swap** is pursued when an investor believes that the yield spread between two sectors of the bond market is temporarily out of line. For example, if the current spread between corporate and government bonds is considered too wide and is expected to narrow, the investor will shift from government bonds to corporate bonds. If the yield spread does in fact narrow, corporates will outperform governments.
3. The **rate anticipation swap** is pegged to interest rate forecasting. In this case, if investors believe that rates will fall, they will swap to bonds of greater duration. Conversely, when rates are expected to rise, they will swap low-duration bonds.
4. The **pure yield pickup swap** is pursued not in response to perceived mispricing, but as a means of increasing return by holding higher-yield bonds. This must be viewed as an attempt to earn an expected term premium in higher-yield bonds. The investor is willing to bear the interest rate risk that this strategy entails.

We can add a fifth swap, called a **tax swap,** to this list. This simply refers to a swap to exploit some tax advantage. For example, an investor may swap from one bond that has decreased in price to another if realization of capital losses is advantageous for tax purposes.

Investors and analysts commonly use this classification of strategies, at least implicitly. Twenty years after Homer and Liebowitz characterized these swaps, however, the financial world's perspective requires broadening the opportunities to include derivative and foreign fixed-income assets as a sector of the bond market, and consideration of foreign interest rates in determining a bond strategy. Where Canadian analysts might earlier have examined only the U.S. prognosis, they now also compare overseas opportunities.

We can see some of these strategies reflected in the March 1992 analysis by Burns Fry (now Nesbitt Burns), for example, revealed by the following quotations from the fixed-income sections of their recommendations:

Over the next 12 months, however, long Canada yields are expected to fall roughly 50 bps [basic points] to 8.70 percent. A drop of 40 basis points in long Treasury yields will narrow long spreads to 110 basis points. C$ weakness and political uncertainty pose risks to the near term outlook, but longer-term fundamentals continue to look constructive. A fixed-income portfolio overweighted in long Canadas and higher-quality provincials is recommended. The BFGFA [Burns Fry Gifford Fong Associates] Canada Long Bond Index has a total return potential of 12 percent compared to the BFGFA Bond Universe return of 10 percent.[14]

[14] Reprinted from *Asset Selection* by permission of Burns Fry Limited. © Copyright 1992.

This analysis accompanies a recommendation that due to higher expected returns in the equity market, a slight overweighting of equities relative to bonds and a major emphasis on both relative to cash are indicated. We recognize the advice as rate anticipation, which follows from Burns Fry's overall macroeconomic analysis. Given the firm's belief in falling rates, it recommends long asset durations.

At the end of the general analysis comes the specific intermarket spread analysis that expresses Burns Fry's view that yield relationships across the government and corporate (as included in the Bond Universe) offer better potential returns in the Canada and general government sectors.

In its *Advantage* recommendation, Burns Fry reveals other examples of intermarket spread awareness and of pure yield pickup as it discusses foreign and domestic instruments and its portfolio adjustments. The accompanying box reproduces the firm's fixed-income report. We note its preoccupation with the upward pressure on Canadian rates and downward pressure on the exchange rate value of the dollar brought on by fiscal and political problems. Domestically, the firm takes advantage of the superior yield offered by MBSs, while other alternatives to government bonds are becoming relatively overpriced. On the other hand, in *Fixed Income Facts,*[15] Burns Fry expresses some optimism by noting that the same domestic problems have pushed the risk premium on Canadas, which it refers to as an "incentive rate," to a level that will reward longer-horizon investors and recommends purchase on the basis of picking up a bonus in the yield.

## Horizon Analysis

One form of interest rate forecasting is called **horizon analysis.** The analyst using this approach selects a particular holding period and predicts the yield curve at the end of that period. Given a bond's time to maturity at the end of the holding period, its yield can be read from the predicted yield curve and its end-of-period price calculated. Then the analyst adds the coupon income and prospective capital gain of the bond to obtain the total return on the bond over the holding period.

For example, suppose that a 20-year maturity 10 percent coupon bond currently yields 9 percent and sells at \$1,092.01. An analyst with a five-year time horizon would be concerned about the bond's price and the value of reinvested coupons five years hence. At that time, the bond will have a 15-year maturity, so the analyst will predict the yield on 15-year maturity bonds at the end of the five-year period to determine the bond's expected price. Suppose that the yield is expected to be 8 percent. Then the bond's end-of-period price will be (assuming 30 semiannual coupon payments):

$$50 \times \text{PA}(4\%,30) + 1{,}000 \times \text{PF}(4\%,30) = \$1{,}172.92$$

The capital gain on the bond therefore will be \$80.91.

---

[15] *Fixed Instrument Facts,* Burns Fry Limited. © Copyright 1992.

# Burns Fry Fixed-Income Report

### From "Canadas" to "Bunds"

We sold nearly half our Government of Canada 9.25 percent bonds of 01 Oct. 96 at $104.25.

We bought $50,000 face value of a German Bund, the Deutsche Republic 6⅜ percent of 20 Oct. 97 at 93.20 DM with an annual yield of 7.77 percent.

This is the first time we have bought a German Bund and we are proceeding cautiously.

The Deutsche Republic bonds are German government bonds rated triple A.

We chose a German government bond over a DM-pay Canadian or an ECU-denominated bond because we wanted maximum liquidity. The Deutsche Republic bonds trade like our Canadas.

### Foreigns

- Faced with increased need by both federal and provincial governments to fund increasing deficits, there will be a good deal of supply in our domestic bond market putting downward pressure on bond prices.
- We may see a lower Canadian dollar as international investors become increasingly concerned with our domestic financing problems and constitutional debates.
- We may see more foreign selling of our bonds for the same reasons.
- Investors have realized strong profits in our bonds. The last year has been stellar for investors holding Canadian bonds.
- We could see Ontario bond ratings decline and many international investors, particularly European, see Ontario as representative of our entire domestic market.

In summary, we have taken profits in the Canadian market and positioned ourselves to benefit from:

1. A pending bull market in Germany; rates are expected to decline through 1992, and
2. An appreciating German mark versus the Canadian dollar, with our dollar being expected to weaken somewhat through 1992 in response to economic and political woes.

### Domestics

*We sold* our Ontario Hydro 9.75 percent of 15 Jan. 93 at $101¾ and the remaining Government of Canada 9.25 percent of 01 Oct. 96 at $104.15, a 10 basis point difference from the first sale.

It is expected that the yield curve will flatten, that short rates are at or near their lows, that inflation is under control for the time being, and that long rates will drift downward but continue to be volatile.

*We bought* $50,000 face value of First Line Trust 8½ percent 01 Oct. 94 at $100.90 with a semiannual yield of 7.96 percent and an annual yield of 8.12 percent. This is a three-year prepayable mortgage backed security.

The MBS market for short-term maturities is trading at a substantial discount relative to other fixed income investments. Yield is currently about 1 percent over Canadas while in other fixed income areas, corporates, Euros, and coupons, we're seeing spreads narrowing.

Meanwhile, the coupons paid by the bond will be reinvested over the five-year period. The analyst must predict a reinvestment rate at which the invested coupons can earn interest. Suppose that the assumed rate is 4 percent per six-month period. If all coupon payments are reinvested at this rate, the value of the 10 semiannual coupon payments with accumulated interest at the end of the five years will be $600.31. (This amount can be solved for as the future value of a $50 annuity after 10 periods with per period interest of 4 percent.) The total return provided by the bond over the five-year period will be $80.91 + $600.31 = $681.22, for a total five-year holding period return of $681.22/$1,092.01 = .624, or 62.4 percent.

The analyst repeats this procedure for many bonds and selects the ones promising superior holding period returns for the portfolio.

---

**CONCEPT CHECK** Question 6. Consider a 30-year 8 percent coupon bond currently selling at $896.81. The analyst believes that in five years the yield on 25-year bonds will be 8.5 percent. Should she purchase the 20-year bond just discussed or the 30-year bond today?

---

A particular version of the horizon analysis, popular among money managers, is called **riding the yield curve.** If the yield curve is upward sloping *and* if it is projected that the curve will not shift during the investment horizon, then as bond maturities fall with the passage of time, their yields also will fall as they "ride" the yield curve toward the lower yields of shorter-term bonds. The decrease in yields will contribute to capital gains on the bonds.

To illustrate, suppose that the yield to maturity on 10-year bonds currently is 9 percent, while that on 9-year bonds is 8.8 percent. A $1,000 par value 10-year zero-coupon bond can be bought today for $\$1,000/1.09^{10} = \$422.41$. In one year, if yields on 9-year bonds are still 8.8 percent, the bond will sell for $\$1,000/1.088^{9} = \$468.10$, for a one-year return of 10.82 percent. In contrast, if the bond's yield remained at 9 percent, it would sell after one year for $\$1,000/1.09^{9} = \$460.43$, offering a 9 percent rate of return.

The danger of riding the yield curve is that the yield curve will, in fact, rise over time. Indeed, according to the expectations hypothesis, an upward-sloping curve is evidence that market participants expect interest rates to be rising over time.

## Contingent Immunization

**Contingent immunization** is a mixed passive-active strategy suggested by Liebowitz and Weinberger.[16] To illustrate, suppose that interest rates currently are

[16] Martin L. Liebowitz and Alfred Weinberger, "Contingent Immunization—Part I: Risk Control Procedures," *Financial Analysts Journal* 38 (November–December 1982).

10 percent and that a manager's portfolio is worth \$10 million right now. At current rates the manager could lock in, via conventional immunization techniques, a future portfolio value of \$12.1 million after two years. Now suppose that the manager wishes to pursue active management but is willing to risk losses only to the extent that the terminal value of the portfolio would not drop lower than \$11 million. Since only \$9.09 million (\$11 million/$1.1^2$) is required to achieve this minimum acceptable terminal value and the portfolio currently is worth \$10 million, the manager can afford to risk some losses at the outset and might start off with an active strategy rather than immediately immunizing.

The key is to calculate the funds required to lock in via immunization a future value of \$11 million at current rates. If $T$ denotes the time left until the horizon date, and $r$ is the market interest rate at any particular time, then the value of the fund necessary to guarantee an ability to reach the minimum acceptable terminal value is \$11 million/$(1 + r)^T$, because this size of portfolio, if immunized, will grow risk-free to \$11 million by the horizon date. This value becomes the trigger point: If and when actual portfolio value dips to the trigger point, active management will cease. *Contingent* upon reaching the trigger point, an immunization strategy is initiated instead, guaranteeing that the minimal acceptable performance can be realized.

Figure 16.4 illustrates two possible outcomes in a contingent immunization strategy. In Figure 16.4**A,** the portfolio falls in value and hits the trigger point at time $t^*$. At that point, immunization is pursued and the portfolio rises smoothly to the \$11 million terminal value. In Figure 16.4**B,** the portfolio does well, never reaches the trigger point, and is worth more than \$11 million at the horizon date.

**CONCEPT CHECK**

Question 7. What would be the trigger point with a three-year horizon, an interest rate of 12 percent, and a minimum acceptable terminal value of \$10 million?

## An Example of a Fixed-Income Investment Strategy

As an example of an analytical fixed-income portfolio strategy, we might consider the approach of RBC Dominion Securities presented in its New Year 1990 *Strategy* book. The initial discussion concerned the macroeconomic analysis for Canada, as influenced by the U.S. economy. On this basis, it predicted easier Bank of Canada monetary policy due to slow economic growth, but only after evidence of reduced inflationary pressure. An inverted yield curve was expected to return to normal. Risks to this prediction were then advanced, including the escape of the U.S. economy from recession (which of course did not materialize), the danger of reduced rate spreads with respect to the United States and of dollar devaluation, and the resultant threat of foreign partial withdrawal from the Canadian bond market.

Given the uncertainties, RBC outlined three scenarios (optimistic, pessimistic, and most likely) for interest rates at the end of the year and assigned them probabilities. This projection then allowed them to calculate the expected one-year

**Figure 16.4**
Contingent immunization.

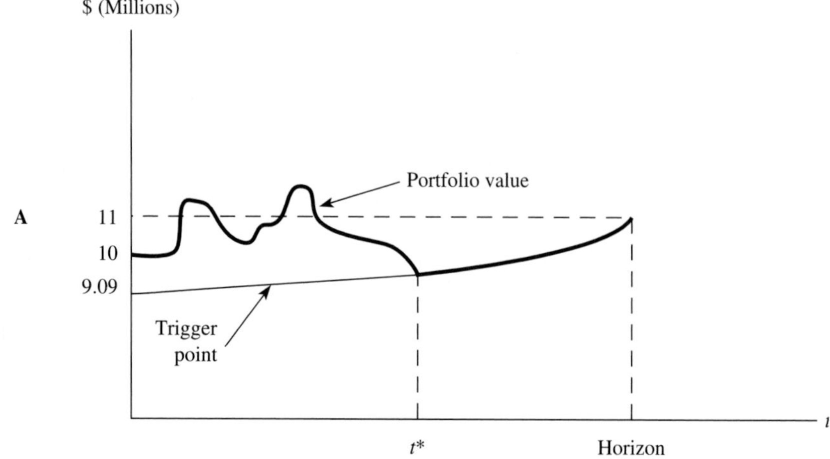


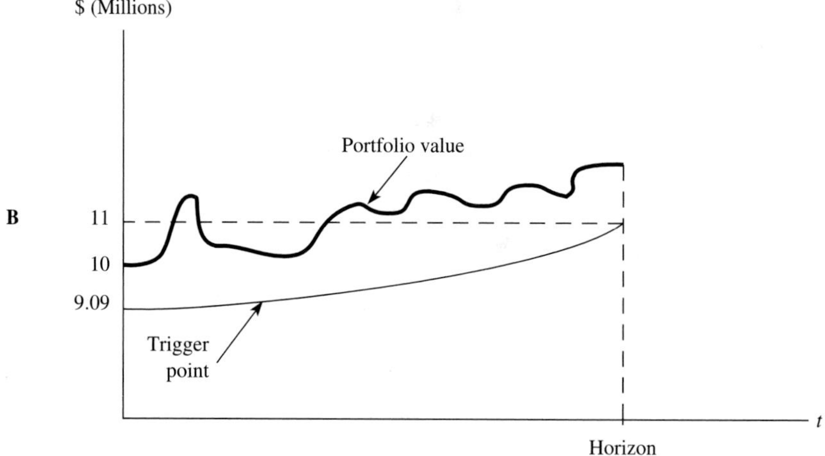


HPR from following alternative portfolio strategies. From this analysis, they concluded:

Under these sets of conditions, Canada 9.50 percent September 1, 1993, offers the best potential for maximizing year-over-year rate of return with an indicated holding period yield of 12.95 percent, marginally ahead of the 12.52 percent weighted return projected for Canada 9.75 percent October 1, 1997, and well ahead of the weighted 11.03 percent return forecast for Canada 9.50 percent June 1, 2010. Given our outlook for 1990, it is difficult to justify term commitments beyond the three- to four-year period unless current yields move back up to higher levels. [They mean *before* investing.] At this juncture we would advocate commitments be limited to the 1993 area and, consequently, recommend new investments be focused on Canada 9.50 percent September 1, 1993. Containment of weighted duration to 2.92 years is consistent with this approach, as additional return, only attainable under the "optimistic" scenario, would require a doubling or more in term and duration.[17]

To summarize the key features of RBC's strategy, we can make the following observations:

1. The firm recognizes the difficulty in attempting to forecast interest rate moves given the uncertain conditions and also appreciates the dependence on U.S. factors. It expressly observes the necessity for the Canadian yield premium in order to attract foreign capital.
2. The firm believes in the use of expected value analysis and the simulation of portfolio payoffs to determine the effects of choosing a strategy.
3. Consistent with this unpredictable future and cautious approach, it recommends a portfolio that minimizes potential loss and gain associated with a longer duration.

## 16.5 Interest Rate Swaps

**Interest rate swaps** have emerged recently as a major fixed-income tool. An interest rate swap is a contract between two parties to exchange a series of cash flows similar to those that would result if the parties instead were to exchange equal dollar values of different types of bonds. Swaps arose originally as a means of managing interest rate risk. The volume of swaps has increased from virtually zero in 1980 to over $3 trillion by 1993. (Interest rate swaps do not have anything to do with the Homer–Leibowitz bond swap taxonomy set out earlier.)

To illustrate how swaps work, consider the manager of a large portfolio that currently includes $100 million par value of long-term bonds paying an average coupon rate of 7 percent. The manager believes that interest rates are about to rise. As a result, he would like to sell the bonds and replace them with either short-term or floating-rate issues. However, it would be exceedingly expensive in terms of transaction costs to replace the portfolio every time the forecast for interest rates is updated. A cheaper and more flexible way to modify the portfolio is for the managers to "swap" the $7 million per year in interest income the portfolio currently generates for an amount of money that is tied to the short-term interest rate. That way, if rates do rise, so will the portfolio's interest income.

A swap dealer might advertise its willingness to exchange or "swap" a cash flow based on the six-month LIBOR rate for one based on a fixed rate of 7 percent. (The LIBOR, or London Interbank Offer Rate, is the interest rate at which banks borrow from each other in the Eurodollar market. It is the most commonly used short-term interest rate in the swap market.) The portfolio manager would then enter into a swap agreement with the dealer to *pay* 7 percent on "notional principal" of $100 million and *receive* payment of the LIBOR rate on that amount

[17] Reprinted from *Strategy* 10, no. 1, by permission of RBC Dominion Securities. © Copyright 1990.

of notional principal.[18] In other words, the manager swaps a payment of .07 × \$100 million for a payment of LIBOR × \$100 million. The manager's *net* cash flow from the swap agreement is therefore (LIBOR − .07) × \$100 million.

Now consider the net cash flow to the manager's portfolio in three interest rate scenarios:

| | LIBOR Rate | | |
|---|---|---|---|
| | 6.5% | 7.0% | 7.5% |
| Interest income from bond portfolio (= 7% of \$100 million bond portfolio) | \$7,000,000 | \$7,000,000 | \$7,000,000 |
| Cash flow from swap [= (LIBOR − 7%) × Notional principal of \$100 million] | (500,000) | 0 | 500,000 |
| Total (= LIBOR × \$100 million) | \$6,500,000 | \$7,000,000 | \$7,500,000 |

Notice that the total income on the overall position—bonds plus swap agreement—is now equal to the LIBOR rate in each scenario times \$100 million. The manager has in effect converted a fixed-rate bond portfolio into a synthetic floating-rate portfolio.

You can see now that swaps can be immensely useful for firms in a variety of applications. For example, a corporation that has issued fixed-rate debt can convert it into synthetic floating-rate debt by entering a swap to receive a fixed interest rate (offsetting its fixed-rate coupon obligation) and pay a floating rate. Or, a bank that pays current market interest rates to its depositors might enter a swap to receive a floating rate and pay a fixed rate on some amount of notional principal. This swap position, added to its floating rate deposit liability, would result in a net liability of a fixed stream of cash. The bank might then be able to invest in long-term fixed-rate loans without encountering interest rate risk.

What about the swap dealer? Why is the dealer, which is typically a financial intermediary such as a bank, willing to take on the opposite side of the swaps desired by these participants?

Consider a dealer who takes on one side of a swap, let's say paying LIBOR and receiving a fixed rate. The dealer will search for another trader in the swap market who wishes to receive a fixed rate and pay LIBOR. When the two swaps are combined, the dealer's position is effectively neutral on interest rates, paying LIBOR on one swap and receiving it on another. Similarly, the dealer pays a fixed rate on one swap and receives it on another. The dealer becomes little more than

[18] The participants to the swap do not loan each other money. They agree only to exchange a fixed cash flow for a variable cash flow that depends on the short-term interest rate. This is why the principal is described as *notional*. The notional principal is simply a way to describe the size of the swap agreement. In this example, the parties to the swap exchange a 7 percent fixed rate for the LIBOR rate; the difference between LIBOR and 7 percent is multiplied by notional principal to determine the cash flow exchanged by the parties.

**Figure 16.5**
Interest rate swap.

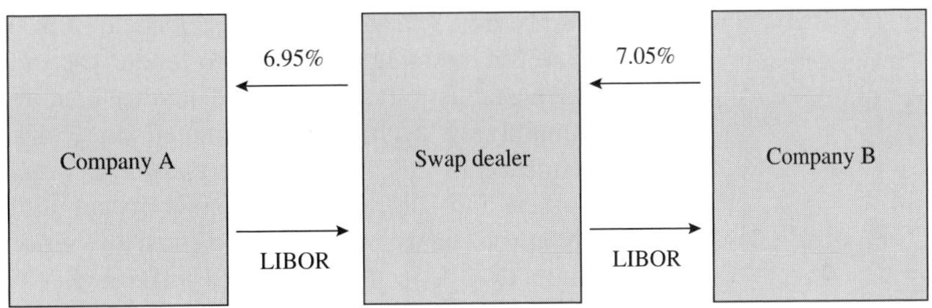


Company B pays a fixed rate of 7.05% to the swap dealer in return for LIBOR. Company A receives 6.95% from the dealer in return for LIBOR. The swap dealer realized a cash flow each period equal to .1% of notional principal.

an intermediary, funneling payments from one party to the other.[19] The dealer finds this activity profitable because he or she will charge a bid-ask spread on the transaction. This is illustrated in Figure 16.5. The bid-ask spread in the example illustrated in Figure 16.5 is 0.1% of notional principal each year.

---

**CONCEPT CHECK**

Question 8. A pension fund holds a portfolio of money market securities which the manager believes are paying excellent yields compared to other comparable-risk short-term securities. However, the manager believes that interest rates are about to fall. What type of swap will allow the fund to continue to hold its portfolio of short-term securities while at the same time benefiting from a decline in rates?

---

## SUMMARY

**1.** Even default-free bonds such as Canada issues are subject to interest rate risk. Longer-term bonds generally are more sensitive to interest rate shifts than are short-term bonds. A measure of the average life of a bond is Macaulay's duration, defined as the weighted average of the times until each payment made by the security, with weights proportional to the present value of the payment.

**2.** Duration is a direct measure of the sensitivity of a bond's price to a change in its yield. The proportional change in bond's price equals the negative of duration multiplied by the proportional change in $1 + y$.

[19] Actually, things are a bit more complicated. The dealer is more than just an intermediary because he or she bears the credit risk that one or the other of the parties to the swap might default on the obligation. Referring to Figure 16.5, if firm A defaults on its obligation, for example, the swap dealer still must maintain its commitment to firm B. In this sense, the dealer does more than simply pass through cash flows to other swap participants.

**3.** Immunization strategies are characteristic of passive fixed-income portfolio management. Such strategies attempt to render the individual or firm immune to movements in interest rates. This may take the form of immunizing net worth, or, instead, immunizing the future accumulated value of a fixed-income portfolio.

**4.** Immunizations of a fully funded plan is accomplished by matching the durations of assets and liabilities. To maintain an immunized position as time passes and interest rates change, the portfolio must be periodically rebalanced. Classic immunization also depends on parallel shifts in flat yield curve. Given that this assumption is unrealistic, immunization generally will be less than complete. To mitigate this problem, multifactor duration models can be used to allow for variation in the shape of the yield curve.

**5.** A more direct form of immunization is dedication, or cash flow matching. If a portfolio is perfectly matched in cash flow with projected liabilities, rebalancing will be unnecessary.

**6.** Active bond management consists of interest rate forecasting techniques and intermarket spread analysis. One popular taxonomy classifies active strategies as substitution swaps, intermarket spread swaps, rate anticipation swaps, or pure yield pickup swaps.

**7.** Horizon analysis is a type of interest rate forecasting. In this procedure, the analyst forecasts the position of the yield curve at the end of some holding period and, from that yield curve, predicts corresponding bond prices. Bonds then can be ranked according to expected total returns (coupon plus capital gain) over the holding period.

**8.** Interest rate swaps are major recent developments in the fixed-income market. In these arrangements, parties trade the cash flows of different securities without actually exchanging any securities directly. This is a useful tool to manage the duration of a portfolio. It also has been used by corporations to borrow at advantageous interest rates in foreign credit markets that are viewed as more hospitable than domestic credit markets.

## Key Terms

Duration
Immunization
Bond index portfolio
Convexity
Rebalancing
Cash flow matching
Dedication strategy
Substitution swap
Intermarket spread swap
Rate anticipation swap
Pure yield pickup swap
Tax swap
Horizon analysis
Riding the yield curve
Contingent immunization
Interest rate swaps

## Selected Readings

*Duration and immunization are analyzed extensively in the literature. Good treatments are:*

Bierwag, G. O. *Duration Analysis.* Cambridge, Mass.: Ballinger Publishing Company, 1987.

Weil, Roman. "Macaulay's Duration: An Appreciation." *Journal of Business* 46 (October 1973).

*Useful general references to techniques of fixed-income portfolio management may be found in a book of readings used by the Institute of Chartered Financial Analysts:*

Fong, H. Gifford. "Portfolio Construction—Fixed Income." In John L. Maginn and Donald L. Tuttle (editors), *Managing Investment Portfolios: A Dynamic Process,* 2d edition. Boston: Warren, Gorham & Lamont, 1990.

*Active bond management strategies are discussed in:*

Fabozzi, Frank J. *Bond Markets, Analysis, and Strategies,* 2d edition. Englewood Cliffs, N.J.: Prentice-Hall, 1993.

*Bond indexing is treated in:*

Mossavar-Rahmani, Sharmin. *Bond Index Funds.* Chicago: Probus Publishing Co., 1991.

*For a detailed analysis of swaps, see:*

Brown, Keith C., and Donald J. Smith. *Interest Rate and Currency Swaps: A Tutorial.* Charlottesville, Institute of Chartered Financial Analysts, 1995.

## Problems

1. A nine-year bond has a yield of 10 percent and a duration of 7.194 years. If the market yield changes by 50 basis points, what is the percentage change in the bond's price?
2. Find the duration of a 6 percent coupon bond making *annual* coupon payments if it has three years until maturity and has a yield to maturity of 6 percent. What is the duration if the yield to maturity is 10 percent?
3. Find the duration of the bond in problem (2) if the coupons are paid semiannually.
4. Rank the durations of the following pairs of bonds:
   *a.* Bond *A* is an 8 percent coupon bond, with a 20-year time to maturity selling at par value. Bond *B* is an 8 percent coupon bond, with a 20-year maturity time selling below par value.
   *b.* Bond *A* is a 20-year noncallable coupon bond with a coupon rate of 8 percent, selling at par. Bond *B* is a 20-year callable bond with a coupon rate of 9 percent, also selling at par.

5. Rank the following bonds in order of descending duration:

| Bond | Coupon (%) | Time to Maturity (Years) | Yield to Maturity (%) |
|---|---|---|---|
| *A* | 15 | 20 | 10 |
| *B* | 15 | 15 | 10 |
| *C* | 0 | 20 | 10 |
| *D* | 8 | 20 | 10 |
| *E* | 15 | 15 | 15 |

6. An insurance company must make payments to a customer of $10 million in one year and $4 million in five years. The yield curve is flat at 10 percent.
   *a.* If it wants to fully fund and immunize its obligation to this customer with a *single* issue of a zero-coupon bond, what maturity bond must it purchase?
   *b.* What must be the face value and market value of that zero-coupon bond?
7. Currently, the term structure is as follows: one-year bonds yield 7 percent, two-year bonds yield 8 percent, three-year bonds and greater maturity bonds all yield 9 percent. An investor is choosing between one-, two-, and three-year maturity bonds all paying *annual* coupons of 8 percent, once a year. Which bonds should she buy if she strongly believes that at year-end the yield curve will be flat at 9 percent?
8. You will be paying $10,000 a year in tuition expenses at the end of the next two years. Bonds currently yield 8 percent.
   *a.* What is the present value and duration of your obligation?
   *b.* What maturity zero-coupon bond would immunize your obligation?
   *c.* Suppose you buy a zero-coupon bond with value and duration equal to your obligation. Now suppose the rates immediately increase to 9 percent. What happens to your net position, that is, to the difference between the value of the bond and that of your tuition obligation? What if rates fall to 7 percent?
9. What types of interest rate swaps would be appropriate for a corporation holding long-term assets that it funded with floating-rate bonds?
10. A corporation has issued a $10 million issue of floating-rate bonds on which it pays an interest rate 1 percent over the LIBOR rate. The bonds are selling at par value. The firm is worried that rates are about to rise, and it would like to lock in a fixed interest rate on its borrowings. The firm sees that dealers in the swap market are offering swaps of LIBOR for 7 percent. What interest rate swap will convert the firm's interest obligation into one resembling a synthetic fixed-rate loan? What interest rate will it pay on that synthetic fixed-rate loan?
11. Pension funds pay lifetime annuities to recipients. If a firm will remain in business indefinitely, the pension obligation will resemble a perpetuity. Suppose, therefore, that you are managing a pension fund with obligations to make perpetual payments of $2 million per year to beneficiaries. The yield to maturity on all bonds is 16 percent.
    *a.* If the duration of 5-year maturity bonds with coupon rates of 12 percent (paid annually) is 4 years and the duration of 20-year maturity bonds with coupon rates of 6 percent (paid annually) is 11 years, how much of each of these coupon bonds (in market value) will you want to hold to both fully fund and immunize your obligation?
    *b.* What will be the *par value* of your holdings in the 20-year coupon bond?

**12.** You are managing a portfolio of $1 million. Your target duration is 10 years, and you can choose from two bonds: a zero-coupon bond with maturity of five years and a perpetuity, each currently yielding 5 percent.

*a.* How much of each bond will you hold in your portfolio?

*b.* How will these fractions change *next year* if target duration is now nine years?

**13.** My pension plan will pay me $10,000 once a year for a 10-year period. The first payment will come in exactly five years. The pension fund wants to immunize its position.

*a.* What is the duration of its obligation to me? The current interest rate is 10 percent per year.

*b.* If the plan uses 5-year and 20-year zero-coupon bonds to construct the immunized position, how much money ought to be placed in each bond? What will be the *face value* of the holdings in each zero?

**14.** The ability to *immunize* a bond portfolio is very desirable for bond portfolio managers in some instances.

*a.* Discuss the components of interest rate risk—that is, assuming a change in interest rates over time, explain the two risks faced by the holder of a bond.

*b.* Define immunization and discuss why a bond manager would immunize his portfolio.

*c.* Explain why a duration-matching strategy is a superior technique to a maturity-matching strategy for the minimization of interest rate risk.

*d.* Explain in specific terms how you would use a zero-coupon bond to immunize a bond portfolio. Discuss why a zero-coupon bond is an ideal instrument in this regard.

*e.* Explain how contingent immunization, another bond portfolio management technique, differs from normal *immunization*. Discuss why a bond portfolio manager would engage in *contingent immunization*.

**15.** You are the manager for the bond portfolio of a pension fund. The policies of the fund allow for the use of active strategies in managing the bond portfolio. It appears that the economic cycle is beginning to mature, inflation is expected to accelerate, and in an effort to contain the economic expansion, central bank policy is moving toward constraint. For each of the situations below, *state* which one of the two bonds you would prefer. *Briefly justify* your answer in each case.

*a.* Government of Canada (Canadian pay), 10 percent due in 1984 and priced at 98.75 to yield 10.50 percent to maturity; or Government of Canada (Canadian pay), 10 percent due in 1995 and priced at 91.75 to yield 11.19 percent to maturity.

*b.* Texas Power and Light Co., 7½ due in 2002, rated AAA, and priced at 62 to yield 12.78 percent to maturity; or Arizona Public Service Co., 7.45 due to 2002, rated A−, and priced at 56 to yield 14.05 percent to maturity.

*c.* Commonwealth Edison, 2¾ due in 1999, rated Baa, and priced at 25 to yield 14.9 percent to maturity; or Commonwealth Edison, 15⅜ due in 2000, rated Baa, and priced at 102.75 to yield 14.9 percent to maturity.

*d.* Shell Oil Co., 8½ sinking fund debentures due in 2000, rated AAA (sinking fund begins 9/80 at par), and priced at 69 to yield 12.91 percent to maturity; or Warner-Lambert, 8⅞ sinking fund debentures due in 2000, rated AAA (sinking fund begins 4/86 at par), and priced at 75 to yield 12.31 percent to maturity.

*e.* Bank of Montreal (Canadian pay), 12 percent certificates of deposit due in 1985, rated AAA, and priced at 100 to yield 12 percent to maturity; or Bank of Montreal (Canadian pay), floating rate notes due in 1991, rated AAA. Coupon currently set at 10.65 percent and priced at 100 (coupon adjusted semiannually to 0.5 percent above the three-month Government of Canada Treasury bill rate).

**16.** Active bond management, as contrasted with a passive buy-and-hold strategy, has gained increased acceptance as investors have attempted to maximize the total return on bond portfolios under their management. The following bond swaps could have been made in recent years as investors attempted to increase the total returns on their portfolios. From the information presented below, identify the reason(s) investors may have made each swap.

| Action | | Call | Price | YTM (%) |
|---|---|---|---|---|
| a. Sell | Baa1 Georgia Pwr. 1st mtg. 11⅝% due 2000 | 108.24 | 75⅝ | 15.71 |
| Buy | Baa1 Georgia Pwr. 1st mtg. 7⅜ due 2001 | 105.20 | 51⅛ | 15.39 |
| b. Sell | Aaa Amer. Tel & Tel notes 13¼% due 1991 | 101.50 | 96⅛ | 14.02 |
| Buy | U.S. Treasury notes 14¼% due 1991 | NC | 102.15 | 13.83 |
| c. Sell | Aa1 Chase Manhattan zero-coupon due 1992 | NC | 25¼ | 14.37 |
| Buy | Aa1 Chase Manhattan float rate notes due 2009 | 103.90 | 90¼ | — |
| d. Sell | A1 Texas Oil & Gas 1st mtg. 8¼% due 1997 | 105.75 | 60 | 15.09 |
| Buy | U.S. Treasury bond 8¼% due 2005 | NC | 65.60 | 12.98 |
| e. Sell | A1 K mart convertible deb. 6% due 1999 | 103.90 | 62¾ | 10.83 |
| Buy | A2 Lucky Stores S.F. deb. 11¾% due 2005 | 109.86 | 73 | 16.26 |

**17.** Your client is concerned about the apparent inconsistency between the following two statements.

- Short-term interest rates are more volatile than long-term rates.
- The rates of return of long-term bonds are more volatile than returns on short-term securities.

Discuss why these two statements are not necessarily inconsistent.

**18.** A fixed-income portfolio manager is unwilling to realize a rate of return of less than 3 percent annually over a five-year investment period on a portfolio currently valued at $1 million. Three years later, the interest rate is 8 percent. What is the trigger point of the portfolio at this time, that is, how low can the value of the portfolio fall before the manager will be forced to immunize to be assured of achieving the minimum acceptable return?

**19.** A 30-year maturity bond has a 7 percent coupon rate, paid annually. It sells today for $867.42. A 20-year maturity bond has 6.5 percent coupon rate, also paid annually. It sells today for $879.50. A bond market analyst forecasts that in five years, 25-year maturity bonds will sell at yields to maturity of 8 percent and that 15-year maturity bonds will sell at yields of 7.5 percent. Because the yield curve is upward sloping, the analyst believes that coupons will be invested in short-term securities at a rate of 6 percent. Which bond offers the higher expected rate of return over the five-year period?

---

*Part VI*

# Equities

*Chapter* 17

# Security Analysis

**THE DILEMMA FOR THE PORTFOLIO MANAGER AND THE INVESTOR IS WHETHER TO FOLLOW THE IMPLICATION OF THE EMPIRICAL EVIDENCE AND THE THEORY OF MARKET EFFICIENCY OR TO IGNORE IT; SHOULD ONE ACCEPT A PASSIVE INVESTMENT STRATEGY OF AN INDEX FUND OR WILL THE EFFORT AND EXPENSE OF ACTIVE MANAGEMENT PROVIDE A SUPERIOR PORTFOLIO?** You saw in our discussion of market efficiency that finding undervalued securities is hardly easy. At the same time, there are enough doubts about the accuracy of the efficient market hypothesis that the search for such securities should not be dismissed out of hand. Moreover, it is the continuing search for mispriced securities that maintains a nearly efficient market. Even infrequent discoveries of minor mispricing justify the salary of a stock market analyst.

The area of security analysis can be divided into fundamental analysis and technical analysis. **Fundamental analysis** refers to the search for information concerning the current and prospective profitability of a company in order to discover its fair market value. **Technical analysis** embraces the use of information contained in stock market data to identify trends that will uncover trading opportunities. Empirical evidence suggests that neither of these approaches, especially the latter, is fruitful on the whole, but both are widely practiced and must be understood.

Fundamental analysis has various aspects to it, including an economic analysis of how the firm will react to potential future conditions that will affect earnings; alternatively, the analyst can examine the recent financial results of the firm in the hope of finding unrecognized value. In this chapter, we see how valuation based on cash flow can be estimated from earnings; earnings themselves are predicted by examining economic conditions. In the following two chapters, we examine financial statement analysis and technical analysis.

We start with a discussion of alternative measures of the value of a company. From there, we review *dividend discount models,* from the simple growth model to compound variants; this leads to an examination of how earnings and dividend payouts are related to growth. Next, we turn to price/earnings (or P/E) ratios, which are employed widely by analysts but must be used carefully. We explain how P/E ratios are indicative of growth potential for the firm, and thus of dividends. At this point, we discuss two alternative strategies, growth investing and value investing. Finally, we examine the broader issue of how economic conditions affect the prospects of the firm. First, we analyze the effect of inflation, and then we identify key macroeconomic variables and discuss business cycles; from there we consider industry analysis and the sensitivity of the firm to the general environment.

## 17.1 The Balance Sheet Approach to Valuation

Underlying all valuation approaches, there must be an appeal to the fundamental accounting relationship between total assets and liabilities. The elementary result is known as **book value,** which determines the equity and other liability claims against the assets of the firm. Adjusted for interest rate considerations, the values of liabilities are generally fairly accurate in terms of market value; assets, on the other hand, depend upon accounting conventions dealing with acquisition cost and age. This historical basis may be quite irrelevant if the firm is likely to be wound up; in this case assets are sold at their **liquidation value,** which may be quite low if a quick liquidation is needed.

Even liquidation can lead to increased values for assets, such as land, that do not depreciate; the historical cost basis may be quite unrealistic. Instead, we have the notion of **replacement value,** under which assets can be acquired at current values. These values would reflect supply and demand, incorporating to some extent the cash flows that these assets might generate in similar or competing uses. It is argued that the market value of a firm having no unique ability cannot rise much above replacement value, as competitors would replicate the firm to gain the same cash flows. This idea is popular among economists, who refer to the ratio of market price to replacement cost of the firm's common stock as

**Tobin's *q*.**[1] Theoretically, this value should tend to one in the long run; however, evidence shows wide and lengthy departures from the norm.[2]

A market valuation model accepts the accounting relationship as implicitly recognized by investors. They can proceed from the balance sheet and calculate the market value of equity as the present value of net operating revenues (after tax), less the market value of any debt claims; the latter value is itself a discounted valuation of the cash flows to the liabilities. Or, they can find equity value by discounting net cash flows available to equityholders, after subtracting debt payments from operating revenues. (We have ignored noncash items such as depreciation in talking about revenues and cash flows.) The value that is calculated in this way is known as **intrinsic value.** When we see the price of equity in the market, it defines total equity value; this plus the value of liabilities must equal the present value of the cash flows derived from the firm's operation of its assets, or the value of total assets.

To be more precise about the preceding discussion, let's assume that there are one million shares of ABC stock trading at \$10 per share and \$5 million of 10 percent coupon perpetual debt, with no income tax and no depreciation. ABC is a no-growth firm and investors want a 15 percent rate of return on investment. The dividend per share of $D$ each year must be $k = 15\%$ times the share price ($P = \$10$). Total dividend payments ($n \times D$) are the residual of operating income (OI) less interest payments ($\text{I} = 10\% \times \$5$ million); hence, reversing the process, we can conclude that operating income in millions is:

$$\text{OI} = \text{I} + n \times D = \$.5 + 1 \times .15 \times \$10 = \$2 \text{ (million)}$$

Therefore, \$2 million of earnings are generated by the assets of the firm, which must be worth \$15 million; we recognize this by observing the share price and using the balance sheet equation:

$$V = B + S = B + n \times P = \$5 + 1 \times \$10 = \$15 \text{ (million)}$$

In arriving at the price $P = \$10$, the market must have predicted operating earnings of \$2 million and subtracted interest payments to get net income of \$1.5 million, or \$1.50 per share. Alternatively, we can capitalize operating income, estimated as \$2 million, at an overall cost of 13⅓ percent (the weighted average cost of capital) to find asset value of \$15 million. Subtracting the debt of \$5 million, we derive the share price of \$10.

The process of identifying superior values always seems circular in practice; we have a chicken and egg problem of needing the capitalization rate for the share price, and the price for the rate. There are ways to break into the circle, however; if we use the CAPM or comparable companies, we can infer the cost of equity

[1] The ratio is named after the Novel prize-winning economist James Tobin. For a discussion of Tobin's $q$ and its role in monetary theory, see James Tobin, "A General Equilibrium Approach to Monetary Theory," *Journal of Money, Credit, and Banking*, February 1969.

[2] See, for example, Lawrence H. Summers, "Taxation and Corporate Investment: A $q$-Theory Approach," *Brookings Papers on Economic Activity*, 1981.

**Table 17.1** Northern Telecom Balance Sheet, December 31, 1990 ($ million)

| Assets | Liabilities and Owners' Equity | |
|---|---|---|
| 4,435 | Liabilities | 1,236 |
| | Common Equity | 3,253 |
| | (243,516,231 shares outstanding) | |

capital. Then if we predict, for example, that earnings will be higher, at $2.5 million, we quickly calculate:

$$P = D/k = (\text{OI} - \text{I})/(n \times k)$$
$$= (\$2.5 - .5)/(1 \times .15) = \$13.33$$

Since the market price of $10 is below this, ABC is a buy. The earnings estimate must be higher or the capitalization rate lower than market estimates in order for there to be an opportunity. In a simplified way, this is what analysts must do: estimate earnings, determine cash flows to equity, and capitalize them. As we shall see, a more realistic case would also require an estimate of *growth* in earnings.

In a perfect and simple economic setting, we might expect all of these accounting-based and market values to be about the same. Realistic depreciation rules applied to assets bought at competitive prices should yield values that equate to replacement values; and in a competitive environment, this also would equal capitalized values of earnings from those assets. Reality, however, is far different. Consider, for example, the figures for Northern Telecom given in Table 17.1. In 1990, Northern Telecom had a 1990 book value of $4.435 billion in assets and $1.236 billion of debt; with 243.5 million shares outstanding, its equity book value was $3.253 billion, or $13.36 per share. Yet the market price was $32.50 at year end. At the same time, Canadian Pacific (CP) traded at $19.75, while its book value was $24.55 per share. Not only are the two discrepancies large and in opposite directions, the CP assets apparently can be bought at a bargain price, contrary to a popular belief that book value should be a floor price. Understanding why these differences occur is part of the analyst's job.

**CONCEPT CHECK**

Question 1. You expect the price of IBX stock to be $59.77 per share a year from now. Its current market price is $50, and you expect it to pay a dividend one year from now of $2.15 a share.

*a.* What is the stock's expected dividend yield, rate of price appreciation, and holding period return?

*b.* If the stock has a beta of 1.15, the risk-free rate is 6 percent per year, and the expected rate of return on the market portfolio is 14 percent per year, what is the required rate of return on IBX stock?

*c.* What is the intrinsic value of IBX stock, and how does it compare to the current market price?
*d.* If there are one million shares and debt is \$20 million paying 8 percent, what are the operating earnings and the value of assets?

## 17.2 Dividend Discount Models

Elementary financial mathematics provides us with some simple formulas for the value of the share price based on cash flows.[3] Under the **dividend discount model (DDM),** we can consider the infinite flow of dividends or the payment of a dividend and sale of the share at the end of a single period; these can be shown to be consistent. Thus, for a stream of dividends $D_t$, a discount rate $k$, and ending price $P_1$, we see that

$$V_0 = \frac{D_1}{1+k} + \frac{D_2}{(1+k)^2} + \frac{D_3}{(1+k)^3} + \ldots = \frac{D_1 + P_1}{1+k} \quad \textbf{(17.1)}$$

This model appears to give problems in the case of a company paying no dividends; but either the company will eventually decide to pay dividends—even a single liquidating dividend—or it never will and its value will be zero. Predicting an infinite stream of dividends could be challenging, and that is still needed in order to calculate $P_1$ recursively from future dividends; consequently, we usually move to a model for some growth pattern in dividends.

The basic model is known as the **constant growth DDM** or the *Gordon model,* after its formulator, Myron J. Gordon. A constant growth rate in dividends, $g$, leads to the simple formula

$$V_0 = \frac{D_1}{k-g} \quad \textbf{(17.2)}$$

When the market price, $P_0$, is presumed to be the value, this can be inverted to yield the intuitive result

$$k = \frac{D_1}{P_0} + g \quad \textbf{(17.3)}$$

which states that the required return equals the current dividend yield plus the capital gain (the growth in the price).

The analyst or investor using this formula again must escape the circularity trap if an investment opportunity is to be found. Given the market price and a consensus on $k$, we infer the presumed growth rate. Analysis of financial results and market conditions may lead to the conclusion of a higher growth rate than

[3] These elementary results are derived in standard corporation finance texts; for those not familiar with them or those needing a review, the appendix gives the details.

implied by price. If the assumed $k$ is accepted, then 17.2 will lead to a higher price estimate and a buy recommendation. By contrast, acceptance of the growth rate, combined with a feeling that the risk assessment implied by the discount rate $k$ is too low, would imply that the price is too high, with sale recommended.

Estimation of a higher value is not the end of the process. If the market persists in its view of growth and risk, yet you feel the price should be higher, you may never see the fruits of your analysis, even if you're right. How quickly the market recognizes what you see determines how quickly the price will converge to true value. If in one year the stock is correctly priced, there will be a substantial holding period return (HPR). For example, if $g = 10\%$ and $k = 15\%$ for an anticipated dividend of \$1, Equation 17.2 gives a price of $\$1/(.15 - .10) = \$20$. If the market currently sees only \$18 of value but corrects in one year, then at that time, $P_1$ will be based on $D_2$ of \$1.10, or \$22. Your HPR will be

$$r = (D_1 + P_1 - P_0)/P_0 = (1.10 + 22 - 18)/18 = .2833$$

The 28⅓ percent return for one year is well above the required return of 15 percent. If the market never catches on, the return from Equation 17.3 is calculated as (1/18) + .10, or 15.5 percent; this is higher than the supposed requirement for a return of 15 percent.

---

**CONCEPT CHECK** Question 2.

*a.* IBX's stock dividend at the end of this year is expected to be \$2.15, and it is expected to grow at 11.2 percent per year forever. If the required rate of return on IBX stock is 15.2 percent per year, what is its intrinsic value?

*b.* If IBX's current market price is equal to this intrinsic value, what is next year's expected price?

*c.* If an investor were to buy IBX stock now and sell it after receiving the \$2.15 dividend a year from now, what is the expected capital gain (i.e., price appreciation) in percentage terms? What is the dividend yield, and what would be the holding period return?

---

## Stock Prices and Investment Opportunities

The major practical issue in evaluating socks is forecasting the cash flows. Generally firms expand, leading to growth in sales, earnings, and dividends. As we develop this issue, let us start with a simple case that illustrates the growth issue.

Consider two companies, No-Opps and Good-Opps, each with expected earnings in the coming year of \$5 per share. Both companies could in principle pay out all of these earnings as dividends, maintaining a perpetual dividend flow of \$5 per share. If the market capitalization rate were $k = 12.5$ percent, both companies would then be valued at $D_1/k = \$5/.125 = \$40$ per share. Neither firm would grow in value, because with all earnings paid out as dividends, and no earnings reinvested in the firm, both companies' capital stock and earnings capacity would remain unchanged over time; earnings and dividends would not grow.

Actually, we are referring here to earnings net of the funds necessary to maintain the productivity of the firm's capital, that is, earnings net of "economic depreciation." In other words, the earnings figure should be interpreted as the maximum amount of money the firm could pay out each year in perpetuity without depleting its productive capacity. For this reason, the net earnings number may be quite different from the accounting earnings figure that the firm reports in its financial statements. (We explore this further in the next chapter.)

Now suppose one of the firms, Good-Opps, engages in projects that generate a return on investment of 15 percent, which is greater than the required rate of return, $k = 12.5$ percent. It would be foolish for such a company to pay out all of its earnings as dividends. If Good-Opps retains or plows back some of its earnings into its highly profitable projects, it can earn a 15 percent rate of return for its shareholders, while if it pays out all earnings as dividends, it forgoes the projects, leaving shareholders to invest the dividends in other opportunities at a fair market rate of only 12.5 percent. Suppose, therefore, Good-Opps lowers its **dividend payout ratio** (the fraction of earnings paid out as dividends) from 100 percent to 40 percent, maintaining a **plowback ratio** (the fraction of earnings reinvested in the firm) of 60 percent. The plowback ratio is also referred to as the **earnings retention ratio.**

The dividend of the company, therefore, will be $2 (40 percent of $5 earnings) instead of $5. Will share price fall? No—it will rise! Although dividends initially fall under the earnings reinvestment policy, subsequent growth in the assets of the firm because of reinvested profits will generate growth in future dividends, which will be reflected in today's share price.

How much growth will be generated? Suppose Good-Opps starts with plant and equipment of $100 million and is all equity financed. With a return on investment or equity (ROE) of 15 percent, total earnings are ROE × $100 million = .15 × $100 million = $15 million. There are 3 million shares of stock outstanding, so earnings per share are $5, as posited above. If 60 percent of the $15 million in this year's earnings is reinvested, then the value of the firm's capital stock will increase by 0.60 × $15 million = $9 million, or by 9 percent. The percentage increase in the capital stock is the rate at which income was generated (ROE) times the plowback ratio (the fraction of earnings reinvested in more capital), which we will denote as $b$.

Now endowed with 9 percent more capital, the company earns 9 percent more income and pays out 9 percent higher dividends. The growth rate of the dividends, therefore, is

$$\begin{aligned} g &= \text{ROE} \times b \\ &= .15 \times .60 \\ &= .09 \end{aligned}$$

If the stock price equals its intrinsic value, it should sell at

$$P_0 = \frac{D_1}{k - g} = \frac{\$2}{.125 - .09} = \$57.14$$

When Good-Opps pursued a no-growth policy and paid out all earnings as dividends, the stock price was only \$40. When it reduced current dividends and plowed funds back into the company, the growth rate increased enough to cause the stock price to increase.

The difference between the no-growth price of \$40 and the actual price of \$57.14 can be ascribed to the present value of the company's excellent investment opportunities. One way to think of the company's value is to describe its stock price as the sum of the no-growth value (the value of current earnings per share, $E_1$, in perpetuity) plus the present value of these growth opportunities, which we will denote as PVGO. In terms of the example we have been following, PVGO = 17.14:

$$P_0 = \frac{E_1}{k} + \text{PVGO}$$

$$57.14 = 40 + 17.14 \quad \textbf{(17.4)}$$

It is important to recognize that growth per se is not what investors desire. Growth enhances company value only if it is achieved by investments in projects with attractive profit opportunities (i.e., with ROE $> k$). To see why, let's now consider Good-Opps' unfortunate sister company, No-Opps. No-Opps' ROE is only 12.5 percent, just equal to the required rate of return, $k$. The NPV of its investment opportunities is zero. We've seen that following a zero-growth strategy with $b = 0$ and $g = 0$. The value of No-Opps will be $E_1/k = \$5/.125 = \$40$ per share. Now suppose that No-Opps chooses a plowback ratio of $b = .60$, the same as Good-Opps' plowback. Then $g$ would be

$$\begin{aligned} g &= \text{ROE} \times b \\ &= 0.125 \times 0.60 \\ &= 0.075 \end{aligned}$$

and the stock price becomes

$$P_0 = \frac{D_1}{k - g} = \frac{\$2}{.125 - .075} = \$40$$

no different from the no-growth strategy.

In the case of No-Opps, the dividend reduction used to free funds for reinvestment in the firm generates only enough growth to maintain the stock price at the current level. This is as it should be: If the firm's projects yield only what investors can earn on their own, shareholders cannot be made better off by a high reinvestment rate policy. This demonstrates that "growth" is not the same as growth opportunities. To justify reinvestment, the firm must engage in projects with better prospective returns than those shareholders can find elsewhere. Notice also that the PVGO of No-Opps is zero: PVGO $= P_0 - E_1/k = 40 - 40 = 0$. With ROE $= k$, there is no advantage to plowing funds back into the firm; this shows up as PVGO of zero.

**CONCEPT CHECK** Question 3.

*a.* Calculate the price of a firm with a plowback ratio of .60 if its ROE is 20 percent. Earnings are expected to be $E_1 = \$5$ per share, and $k = 12.5$ percent; find the PVGO for this firm.

*b.* Suppose the ROE is only 10 percent and $k = 15$ percent; what will be the stock price? What is the PVGO and why would you expect this firm to be a takeover target?

## Life Cycles and Multistage Growth Models

As useful as the constant growth DDM formula is, you need to remember that it is based on a simplifying assumption, namely, that the dividend growth rate will be constant forever. In fact, firms typically pass through life cycles with very different dividend profiles in different phases. In early years, there are ample opportunities for profitable reinvestment in the company. Payout ratios are low, and growth is correspondingly rapid. In later years, the firm matures, production capacity is sufficient to meet market demand, competitors enter the market, and attractive opportunities for reinvestment may become harder to find. In this mature phase, the firm may choose to increase the dividend payout ratio, rather than retain earnings. The dividend level increases, but thereafter grows at a slower rate because of fewer company growth opportunities.

Table 17.2 demonstrates this profile. It gives Value Line's forecasts of return on assets, dividend payout ratio, and three-year growth rate in earnings per share for a sample of the firms included in the semiconductor industry versus those in the northeast region electric utility group. (We compare return on assets rather than return on equity because the latter is affected by leverage, which tends to be far greater in the electric utility industry than in the semiconductor industry. Return on assets measures operating income per dollar of total assets, regardless of whether the source of the capital supplied is debt or equity. We will return to this issue in the next chapter.)

The semiconductor firms as a group have had attractive investment opportunities. The average return on assets of these firms is forecast to be 13.3 percent, and the firms have responded with quite high plowback ratios. Many of these firms pay no dividends at all. The high return on assets and high plowback result in rapid growth. The average growth rate of earnings per share in this group is projected at 9.8 percent. In contrast, the electric utilities are more representative of mature firms. Their return on assets is lower, at 7.6 percent; their dividend payout is higher, at 76.4 percent; and their average growth is lower, at 2.8 percent.

To value companies with temporarily high growth, analysts use a multistage version of the dividend discount model. Dividends in the early high-growth period are forecasted and their combined present value is calculated. Then, once the firm is projected to settle down to a steady growth phase, the constant growth DDM is applied to value the remaining stream of dividends.

**Table 17.2** Financial Ratios in Two Industries

| | Return on Assets (%) | Payout Ratio (%) | Growth Rate 1994–97 (%) |
|---|---|---|---|
| **Semiconductors** | | | |
| Analog Devices | 13.0 | 0.0 | 22.1 |
| Cirrus Logic | 14.5 | 0.0 | 15.5 |
| Intel | 19.0 | 11.0 | 2.4 |
| Micron Technologies | 13.5 | 5.0 | 10.7 |
| Motorola | 11.5 | 19.0 | 9.5 |
| National Semiconductor | 13.0 | 16.5 | 6.3 |
| Novellus | 14.0 | 0.0 | 13.4 |
| Teradyne | 9.5 | 0.0 | 4.0 |
| Texas Instruments | 12.0 | 27.0 | 4.6 |
| *Average* | 13.3 | 8.7 | 9.8 |
| **Electric Utilities** | | | |
| Boston Edison | 8.0 | 75.0 | 3.3 |
| Central Maine Power | 7.5 | 77.0 | 1.3 |
| Central Vermont | 9.0 | 79.0 | 4.6 |
| Commonwealth Energy | 7.5 | 77.0 | 2.0 |
| Consolidated Edison | 8.0 | 76.0 | 2.0 |
| Eastern Utilities | 8.0 | 65.0 | 5.1 |
| Long Island Lighting | 6.0 | 78.0 | 4.2 |
| New England Electric | 7.5 | 79.0 | 2.6 |
| Northeastern Utilities | 7.0 | 82.0 | 0.0 |
| *Average* | 7.6 | 76.4 | 2.8 |

Source: The *Value Line Investment Survey,* 1993. Reprinted by permission.

As an example from the list of semiconductors, we analyze Motorola, a major electronic designer and manufacturer. Figure 17.1 is a *Value Line Investment Survey* report on Motorola, with some of the relevant information highlighted.

Motorola's beta appears at the circled A, the recent stock price at the B, the per share dividend payments at the C, the ROE (referred to as percent earned on net worth) at the D, and the dividend payout ratio (referred to as percent of all dividends to net profits) at the E. The rows ending at C, D, and E are historical time series. The boldfaced italicized entries under 1994 are estimates for that year. Similarly, the entries in the far right column (labeled 96–98) are forecasts for some time between 1996 and 1998, which we will take to be 1997.

Note that while dividends were \$.54 per share in 1994, dividends forecast for 1997 are \$.90; hence, Value Line forecasts rapid short-term growth in dividends, nearly 20 percent per year. If we use linear interpolation between 1994 and 1997, we obtain dividend forecasts as follows:

| | |
|---|---|
| 1994 | \$.54 |
| 1995 | \$.66 |
| 1996 | \$.78 |
| 1997 | \$.90 |

**Figure 17.1** *Value Line Investment Survey* report on Motorola.

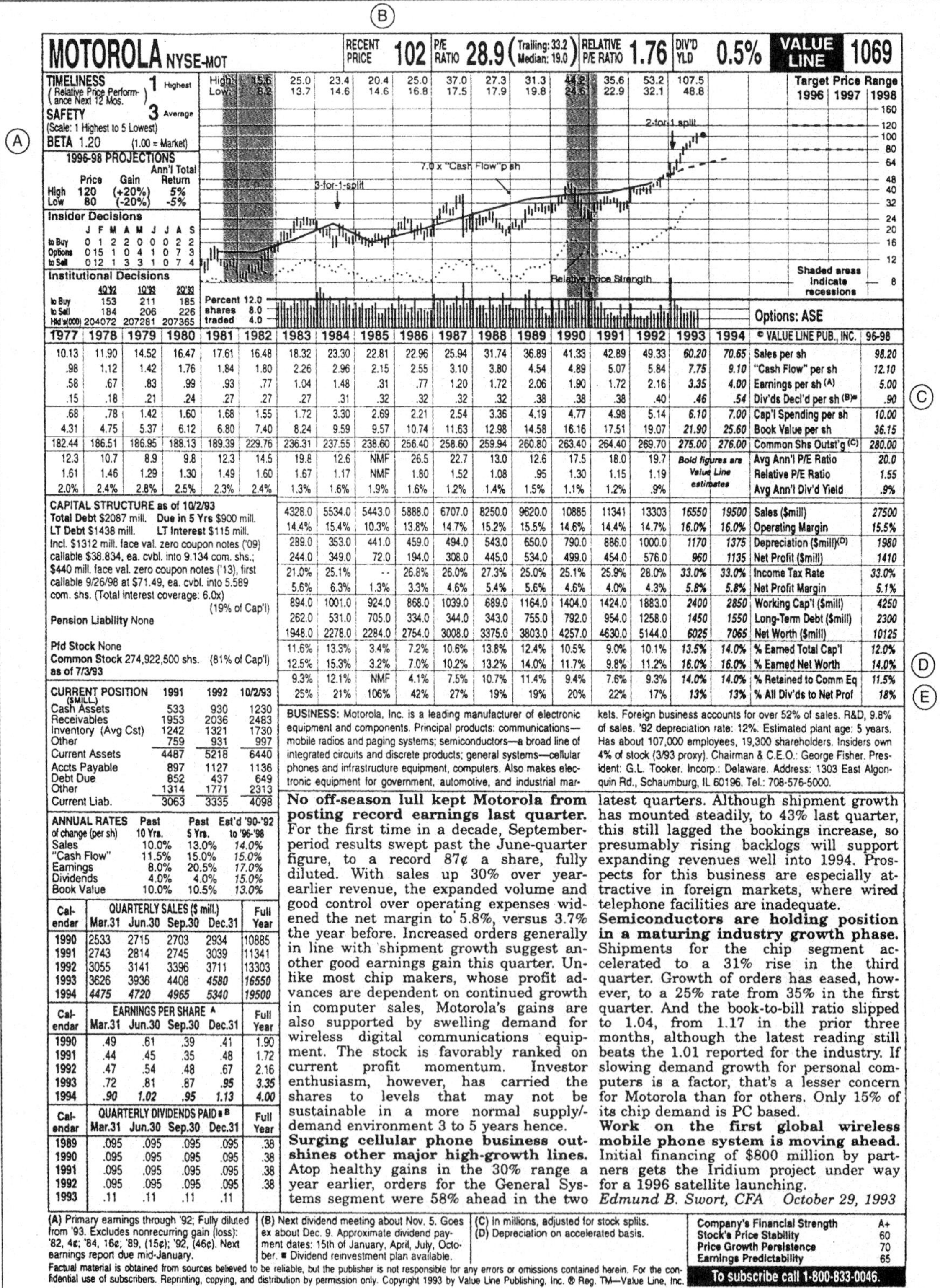

(B)

**MOTOROLA** NYSE-MOT | RECENT PRICE **102** | P/E RATIO **28.9** (Trailing: 33.2 Median: 19.0) | RELATIVE P/E RATIO **1.76** | DIV'D YLD **0.5%** | **VALUE LINE** **1069**

(A)

TIMELINESS (Relative Price Performance Next 12 Mos.) **1** Highest

SAFETY **3** Average

(Scale: 1 Highest to 5 Lowest)

BETA 1.20 (1.00 = Market)

**1996-98 PROJECTIONS**

| | Price | Gain | Ann'l Total Return |
|---|---|---|---|
| High | 120 | (+20%) | 5% |
| Low | 80 | (-20%) | -5% |

**Insider Decisions**

| | J | F | M | A | M | J | J | A | S |
|---|---|---|---|---|---|---|---|---|---|
| to Buy | 0 | 1 | 2 | 2 | 0 | 0 | 0 | 2 | 2 |
| Options | 0 | 15 | 1 | 0 | 4 | 1 | 0 | 7 | 3 |
| to Sell | 0 | 12 | 1 | 3 | 3 | 1 | 0 | 7 | 4 |

**Institutional Decisions**

| | 4Q'92 | 1Q'93 | 2Q'93 |
|---|---|---|---|
| to Buy | 153 | 211 | 185 |
| to Sell | 184 | 206 | 226 |
| Hld's(000) | 204072 | 207281 | 207365 |

| | 1982 | 1983 | 1984 | 1985 | 1986 | 1987 | 1988 | 1989 | 1990 | 1991 | 1992 | 1993 |
|---|---|---|---|---|---|---|---|---|---|---|---|---|
| High | 15.6 | 25.0 | 23.4 | 20.4 | 25.0 | 37.0 | 27.3 | 31.3 | 44.2 | 35.6 | 53.2 | 107.5 |
| Low | 8.2 | 13.7 | 14.6 | 14.6 | 16.8 | 17.5 | 17.9 | 19.8 | 24.6 | 22.9 | 32.1 | 48.8 |



Target Price Range 1996 | 1997 | 1998

Options: ASE

| | 1977 | 1978 | 1979 | 1980 | 1981 | 1982 | 1983 | 1984 | 1985 | 1986 | 1987 | 1988 | 1989 | 1990 | 1991 | 1992 | 1993 | 1994 | 96-98 |
|---|---|---|---|---|---|---|---|---|---|---|---|---|---|---|---|---|---|---|---|
| Sales per sh | 10.13 | 11.90 | 14.52 | 16.47 | 17.61 | 16.48 | 18.32 | 23.30 | 22.81 | 22.96 | 25.94 | 31.74 | 36.89 | 41.33 | 42.89 | 49.33 | *60.20* | *70.65* | *98.20* |
| "Cash Flow" per sh | .98 | 1.12 | 1.42 | 1.76 | 1.84 | 1.80 | 2.26 | 2.96 | 2.15 | 2.55 | 3.10 | 3.80 | 4.54 | 4.89 | 5.07 | 5.84 | *7.75* | *9.10* | *12.10* |
| Earnings per sh (A) | .58 | .67 | .83 | .99 | .93 | .77 | 1.04 | 1.48 | .31 | .77 | 1.20 | 1.72 | 2.06 | 1.90 | 1.72 | 2.16 | *3.35* | *4.00* | *5.00* |
| Div'ds Decl'd per sh (B)■ | .15 | .18 | .21 | .24 | .27 | .27 | .27 | .31 | .32 | .32 | .32 | .32 | .38 | .38 | .38 | .40 | *.46* | *.54* | *.90* |
| Cap'l Spending per sh | .68 | .78 | 1.42 | 1.60 | 1.68 | 1.55 | 1.72 | 3.30 | 2.69 | 2.21 | 2.54 | 3.36 | 4.19 | 4.77 | 4.98 | 5.14 | *6.10* | *7.00* | *10.00* |
| Book Value per sh | 4.31 | 4.75 | 5.37 | 6.12 | 6.80 | 7.40 | 8.24 | 9.59 | 9.57 | 10.74 | 11.63 | 12.98 | 14.58 | 16.16 | 17.51 | 19.07 | *21.90* | *25.60* | *36.15* |
| Common Shs Outst'g (C) | 182.44 | 186.51 | 186.95 | 188.13 | 189.39 | 229.76 | 236.31 | 237.55 | 238.60 | 256.40 | 258.60 | 259.94 | 260.80 | 263.40 | 264.40 | 269.70 | *275.00* | *276.00* | *280.00* |
| Avg Ann'l P/E Ratio | 12.3 | 10.7 | 8.9 | 9.8 | 12.3 | 14.5 | 19.8 | 12.6 | NMF | 26.5 | 22.7 | 13.0 | 12.6 | 17.5 | 18.0 | 19.7 | *Bold figures are* | | *20.0* |
| Relative P/E Ratio | 1.61 | 1.46 | 1.29 | 1.30 | 1.49 | 1.60 | 1.67 | 1.17 | NMF | 1.80 | 1.52 | 1.08 | .95 | 1.30 | 1.15 | 1.19 | *Value Line* | | *1.55* |
| Avg Ann'l Div'd Yield | 2.0% | 2.4% | 2.8% | 2.5% | 2.3% | 2.4% | 1.3% | 1.6% | 1.9% | 1.6% | 1.2% | 1.4% | 1.5% | 1.1% | 1.2% | .9% | *estimates* | | *.9%* |
| Sales ($mill) | | | | | | | 4328.0 | 5534.0 | 5443.0 | 5888.0 | 6707.0 | 8250.0 | 9620.0 | 10885 | 11341 | 13303 | *16550* | *19500* | *27500* |
| Operating Margin | | | | | | | 14.4% | 15.4% | 10.3% | 13.8% | 14.7% | 15.2% | 15.5% | 14.6% | 14.4% | 14.7% | *16.0%* | *16.0%* | *15.5%* |
| Depreciation ($mill)(D) | | | | | | | 289.0 | 353.0 | 441.0 | 459.0 | 494.0 | 543.0 | 650.0 | 790.0 | 886.0 | 1000.0 | *1170* | *1375* | *1980* |
| Net Profit ($mill) | | | | | | | 244.0 | 349.0 | 72.0 | 194.0 | 308.0 | 445.0 | 534.0 | 499.0 | 454.0 | 576.0 | *960* | *1135* | *1410* |
| Income Tax Rate | | | | | | | 21.0% | 25.1% | -- | 26.8% | 26.0% | 27.3% | 25.0% | 25.1% | 25.9% | 28.0% | *33.0%* | *33.0%* | *33.0%* |
| Net Profit Margin | | | | | | | 5.6% | 6.3% | 1.3% | 3.3% | 4.6% | 5.4% | 5.6% | 4.6% | 4.0% | 4.3% | *5.8%* | *5.8%* | *5.1%* |
| Working Cap'l ($mill) | | | | | | | 894.0 | 1001.0 | 924.0 | 868.0 | 1039.0 | 689.0 | 1164.0 | 1404.0 | 1424.0 | 1883.0 | *2400* | *2850* | *4250* |
| Long-Term Debt ($mill) | | | | | | | 262.0 | 531.0 | 705.0 | 334.0 | 344.0 | 343.0 | 755.0 | 792.0 | 954.0 | 1258.0 | *1450* | *1550* | *2300* |
| Net Worth ($mill) | | | | | | | 1948.0 | 2278.0 | 2284.0 | 2754.0 | 3008.0 | 3375.0 | 3803.0 | 4257.0 | 4630.0 | 5144.0 | *6025* | *7065* | *10125* |
| % Earned Total Cap'l | | | | | | | 11.6% | 13.3% | 3.4% | 7.2% | 10.6% | 13.8% | 12.4% | 10.5% | 9.0% | 10.1% | *13.5%* | *14.0%* | *12.0%* |
| % Earned Net Worth | | | | | | | 12.5% | 15.3% | 3.2% | 7.0% | 10.2% | 13.2% | 14.0% | 11.7% | 9.8% | 11.2% | *16.0%* | *16.0%* | *14.0%* |
| % Retained to Comm Eq | | | | | | | 9.3% | 12.1% | NMF | 4.1% | 7.5% | 10.7% | 11.4% | 9.4% | 7.6% | 9.3% | *14.0%* | *14.0%* | *11.5%* |
| % All Div'ds to Net Prof | | | | | | | 25% | 21% | 106% | 42% | 27% | 19% | 19% | 20% | 22% | 17% | *13%* | *13%* | *18%* |

© VALUE LINE PUB., INC.

(C) (D) (E)

**CAPITAL STRUCTURE as of 10/2/93**
**Total Debt** $2087 mill. **Due in 5 Yrs** $900 mill.
**LT Debt** $1438 mill. **LT Interest** $115 mill.
Incl. $1312 mill. face val. zero coupon notes ('09) callable $38.834, ea. cvbl. into 9.134 com. shs.; $440 mill. face val. zero coupon notes ('13), first callable 9/26/98 at $71.49, ea. cvbl. into 5.589 com. shs. (Total interest coverage: 6.0x) (19% of Cap'l)

**Pension Liability** None

**Pfd Stock** None
**Common Stock** 274,922,500 shs. (81% of Cap'l) as of 7/3/93

| CURRENT POSITION ($MILL.) | 1991 | 1992 | 10/2/93 |
|---|---|---|---|
| Cash Assets | 533 | 930 | 1230 |
| Receivables | 1953 | 2036 | 2483 |
| Inventory (Avg Cst) | 1242 | 1321 | 1730 |
| Other | 759 | 931 | 997 |
| Current Assets | 4487 | 5218 | 6440 |
| Accts Payable | 897 | 1127 | 1136 |
| Debt Due | 852 | 437 | 649 |
| Other | 1314 | 1771 | 2313 |
| Current Liab. | 3063 | 3335 | 4098 |

| ANNUAL RATES of change (per sh) | Past 10 Yrs. | Past 5 Yrs. | Est'd '90-'92 to '96-'98 |
|---|---|---|---|
| Sales | 10.0% | 13.0% | *14.0%* |
| "Cash Flow" | 11.5% | 15.0% | *15.0%* |
| Earnings | 8.0% | 20.5% | *17.0%* |
| Dividends | 4.0% | 4.0% | *15.0%* |
| Book Value | 10.0% | 10.5% | *13.0%* |

| Calendar | QUARTERLY SALES ($ mill.) Mar.31 | Jun.30 | Sep.30 | Dec.31 | Full Year |
|---|---|---|---|---|---|
| 1990 | 2533 | 2715 | 2703 | 2934 | 10885 |
| 1991 | 2743 | 2814 | 2745 | 3039 | 11341 |
| 1992 | 3055 | 3141 | 3396 | 3711 | 13303 |
| 1993 | 3626 | 3936 | 4408 | *4580* | *16550* |
| 1994 | *4475* | *4720* | *4965* | *5340* | *19500* |

| Calendar | EARNINGS PER SHARE A Mar.31 | Jun.30 | Sep.30 | Dec.31 | Full Year |
|---|---|---|---|---|---|
| 1990 | .49 | .61 | .39 | .41 | 1.90 |
| 1991 | .44 | .45 | .35 | .48 | 1.72 |
| 1992 | .47 | .54 | .48 | .67 | 2.16 |
| 1993 | .72 | .81 | .87 | *.95* | *3.35* |
| 1994 | *.90* | *1.02* | *.95* | *1.13* | *4.00* |

| Calendar | QUARTERLY DIVIDENDS PAID ■ B Mar.31 | Jun.30 | Sep.30 | Dec.31 | Full Year |
|---|---|---|---|---|---|
| 1989 | .095 | .095 | .095 | .095 | .38 |
| 1990 | .095 | .095 | .095 | .095 | .38 |
| 1991 | .095 | .095 | .095 | .095 | .38 |
| 1992 | .095 | .095 | .095 | .095 | .38 |
| 1993 | .11 | .11 | .11 | .11 | |

**BUSINESS:** Motorola, Inc. is a leading manufacturer of electronic equipment and components. Principal products: communications—mobile radios and paging systems; semiconductors—a broad line of integrated circuits and discrete products; general systems—cellular phones and infrastructure equipment, computers. Also makes electronic equipment for government, automotive, and industrial markets. Foreign business accounts for over 52% of sales. R&D, 9.8% of sales. '92 depreciation rate: 12%. Estimated plant age: 5 years. Has about 107,000 employees, 19,300 shareholders. Insiders own 4% of stock (3/93 proxy). Chairman & C.E.O.: George Fisher. President: G.L. Tooker. Incorp.: Delaware. Address: 1303 East Algonquin Rd., Schaumburg, IL 60196. Tel.: 708-576-5000.

**No off-season lull kept Motorola from posting record earnings last quarter.** For the first time in a decade, September-period results swept past the June-quarter figure, to a record 87¢ a share, fully diluted. With sales up 30% over year-earlier revenue, the expanded volume and good control over operating expenses widened the net margin to 5.8%, versus 3.7% the year before. Increased orders generally in line with shipment growth suggest another good earnings gain this quarter. Unlike most chip makers, whose profit advances are dependent on continued growth in computer sales, Motorola's gains are also supported by swelling demand for wireless digital communications equipment. The stock is favorably ranked on current profit momentum. Investor enthusiasm, however, has carried the shares to levels that may not be sustainable in a more normal supply/-demand environment 3 to 5 years hence.

**Surging cellular phone business outshines other major high-growth lines.** Atop healthy gains in the 30% range a year earlier, orders for the General Systems segment were 58% ahead in the two latest quarters. Although shipment growth has mounted steadily, to 43% last quarter, this still lagged the bookings increase, so presumably rising backlogs will support expanding revenues well into 1994. Prospects for this business are especially attractive in foreign markets, where wired telephone facilities are inadequate.

**Semiconductors are holding position in a maturing industry growth phase.** Shipments for the chip segment accelerated to a 31% rise in the third quarter. Growth of orders has eased, however, to a 25% rate from 35% in the first quarter. And the book-to-bill ratio slipped to 1.04, from 1.17 in the prior three months, although the latest reading still beats the 1.01 reported for the industry. If slowing demand growth for personal computers is a factor, that's a lesser concern for Motorola than for others. Only 15% of its chip demand is PC based.

**Work on the first global wireless mobile phone system is moving ahead.** Initial financing of $800 million by partners gets the Iridium project under way for a 1996 satellite launching.

*Edmund B. Swort, CFA October 29, 1993*

(A) Primary earnings through '92; Fully diluted from '93. Excludes nonrecurring gain (loss): '82, 4¢; '84, 16¢; '89, (15¢); '92, (46¢). Next earnings report due mid-January.

(B) Next dividend meeting about Nov. 5. Goes ex about Dec. 9. Approximate dividend payment dates: 15th of January, April, July, October. ■ Dividend reinvestment plan available.

(C) In millions, adjusted for stock splits.
(D) Depreciation on accelerated basis.

| | |
|---|---|
| **Company's Financial Strength** | A+ |
| **Stock's Price Stability** | 60 |
| **Price Growth Persistence** | 70 |
| **Earnings Predictability** | 65 |



Source: Motorola, October 29, 1993. 

Now let us assume the dividend growth rate levels off in 1997. What is a good guess for that steady-state growth rate? Value Line forecasts a dividend payout ratio of 0.18 and an ROE of 14.0 percent, implying long-term growth will be

$$g = \text{ROE} \times b = 14\% \times (1 - .18) = 11.5\%$$

Our estimate of Motorola's intrinsic value using an investment horizon of 1997 is therefore obtained from a version of Equation 17.1, which we restate here:

$$V_{1993} = \frac{D_{1994}}{(1+k)} + \frac{D_{1995}}{(1+k)^2} + \frac{D_{1996}}{(1+k)^3} + \frac{D_{1997} + P_{1997}}{(1+k)^4}$$

$$= \frac{.54}{1+k} + \frac{.66}{(1+k)^2} + \frac{.78}{(1+k)^3} + \frac{.90 + P_{1997}}{(1+k)^4}$$

Here, $P_{1997}$ represents the forecasted price at which we can sell our shares of Motorola at the end of 1997, when dividends enter their constant growth phase. That price, according to the constant growth DDM, should be

$$P_{1997} = \frac{D_{1998}}{k - g} = \frac{D_{1997}(1+g)}{k - g} = \frac{.90(1.115)}{k - .115}$$

The only variable remaining to be determined in order to calculate intrinsic value is the market capitalization rate, $k$.

One way to obtain $k$ is from the CAPM. Observe from the Value Line data that Motorola's beta is 1.20. The risk-free rate in 1993 was about 3 percent. Suppose that the market risk premium were forecasted at 7.75 percent.[4] This would imply that the forecast for the market return was

$$\text{Risk-free rate} + \text{Market risk premium} = 3\% + 7.75\% = 10.75\%$$

Therefore, we can solve for the market capitalization rate for Motorola as

$$\begin{aligned} k &= r_f + \beta[E(r_M) - r_f] \\ &= 3\% + 1.2[10.75\% - 3\%] \\ &= 12.3\% \end{aligned}$$

Our guess for the stock price in 1997 is thus

$$P_{1997} = \frac{\$.90(1.115)}{.123 - .115} = \$125.44$$

and today's estimate of intrinsic value is

$$V_{1993} = \frac{.54}{(1.123)} + \frac{.66}{(1.123)^2} + \frac{.78}{(1.123)^3} + \frac{.90 + 125.44}{(1.123)^4} = \$80.99$$

[4] The historical risk premium on the market portfolio has been closer to 8.5 percent. However, stock analysts in 1993 were relatively pessimistic about market performance over the short term. While the historical risk premium is a guide as to the typical risk premium one might expect from the market, there is no reason that the risk premium cannot vary somewhat from period to period.

We know from the Value Line report that Motorola's actual price was \$102 (at the circled B). Our intrinsic value analysis indicates Motorola was overpriced. Should we sell our holdings of Motorola or even sell Motorola short?

Perhaps. But before betting the farm, stop to consider how firm our estimate is. We've had to guess at dividends in the near future, the ultimate growth rate of those dividends, and the appropriate discount rate. Moreover, we've assumed Motorola will follow a relatively simple two-stage growth process. In practice, the growth of dividends can follow more complicated patterns. Even small errors in these approximations could upset a conclusion.

For example, suppose that we have underestimated Motorola's growth prospects and that the actual growth rate in the post-1997 period will be 11.8 percent rather than 11.5 percent, a change of only 0.3 percentage points. Using the higher growth rate in the dividend discount model would result in an intrinsic value in 1993 of \$128.65, which actually is greater than the stock price. Our conclusion regarding intrinsic value versus price is reversed.

This exercise shows that finding bargains is not as easy as it seems. While the DDM is easy to apply, establishing its inputs is more of a challenge. This should not be surprising. In even a moderately efficient market, finding profit opportunities has to be more involved than sitting down with Value Line for a half hour.

The exercise also highlights the importance of performing sensitivity analysis when you attempt to value stocks. Your estimates of stock values are no better than your assumptions. Sensitivity analysis will highlight the inputs that need to be most carefully examined. For example, we just found that very small changes in the estimated growth rate for the post-1997 period would result in big changes in intrinsic value. Similarly, small changes in the assumed capitalization rate would change intrinsic value substantially. On the other hand, reasonable changes in the dividends forecast between 1993 and 1997 would have a small impact on intrinsic value.

**CONCEPT CHECK**

Question 4. Confirm that the intrinsic value of Motorola using $g = 11.8$ percent is \$128.65. Hint: First calculate the stock price in 1997. Then, calculate the present value of all interim dividends plus the present value of the 1997 sales price.

## 17.3 EARNINGS, GROWTH, AND P/E RATIOS

Financial analysts tend to focus on earnings rather than dividends, and for good reason. Dividend payments are to a great degree discretionary—management can declare and pay whatever dividends it chooses, provided that in the long run the firm has the required cash flow. In fact, as Miller and Modigliani[5] have demon-

[5] See M. Miller and F. Modigliani, "Dividend Policy, Growth and the Valuation of Shares," *Journal of Business,* October 1961.

strated, simply by issuing additional equity, cash can be raised to satisfy dividend requirements. In modern theory, dividends are used by management to signal the firm's cash flow prospects in the future; for this reason, analysts are more interested in the change in dividends than the actual amounts. What Miller and Modigliani have proved is that the investment opportunities leading to future earnings are what count, and this is what analysts work hard to estimate.

The relationship between earnings and dividends in any period $t$, assuming no external equity financing, is

$$\text{Dividends}_t = \text{Earnings}_t - \text{Reinvested earnings}_t$$

Using this expression in the discounted dividend expression given in equation 17.1 we have

$$V_0 = \sum_{t=1}^{\infty} \frac{D_t}{(1+k)^t} = \sum_{t=1}^{\infty} \frac{E_t}{(1+k)^t} - \sum_{t=1}^{\infty} \frac{I_t}{(1+k)^t} \tag{17.5}$$

There is a convenient result for this expression when the expected ROE on reinvested earnings is $k$; since the NPV of new investment is zero, the retention of earnings from dividends is pointless and the value remains the same as full payout with no growth. That means we can simply capitalize expected earnings for value, or $V_0 = E(E_1)/k$.

Much of the real-world discussion of stock market valuation concentrates on the firm's **price/earnings multiple,** the ratio of price per share to earnings per share. Our discussion of growth opportunities shows why stock market analysts focus on this multiple, commonly called the *P/E ratio.* Both companies considered in our earlier example, No-Opps and Good-Opps, had earnings per share, EPS, of $5, but Good-Opps reinvested 60 percent of earnings in prospects with an ROE of 15 percent, while No-Opps paid out all earnings as dividends. No-Opps had a price of $40, giving it a P/E multiple of 40/5 = 8.0. while Good-Opps sold for $57.14, giving it a multiple of 57.14/5 = 11.4. This observation suggests the P/E ratio might serve as a useful indicator of expectations of growth opportunities. We can see this explicitly by rearranging Equation 17.4 to

$$\frac{P_0}{E_1} = \frac{1}{k}\left[1 + \frac{\text{PVGO}}{E/k}\right] \tag{17.6}$$

When PVGO = 0, Equation 17.6 shows that $P_0 = E_1/k$. The stock is valued like a nongrowing perpetuity of $\text{EPS}_1$. The P/E ratio is just $1/k$. However, as PVGO becomes an increasingly dominant contributor to price, the P/E ratio can rise dramatically. The Ratio of PVGO to $E/k$ has a simple interpretation. It is the ratio of the component of firm value due to growth opportunities to the component of value due to assets already in place (i.e., the no-growth value of the firm, $E/k$). When future growth opportunities dominate the estimate of total value, the firm will command a high price relative to current earnings. Thus, a high P/E multiple appears to indicate a firm is endowed with ample growth opportunities. In 1994, Motorola's P/E ratio was 25; Boston Edison's P/E ratio at this time was 9. The difference can only be justified by the belief of investors that Motorola had higher growth prospects. In fact, Motorola's stream of earnings grew more than eightfold between 1977 and 1994, while Boston Edison's earnings only increased by a factor of 2.3. Apparently, investors expected the pattern to continue.

Clearly, it is differences in expected growth opportunities that justify particular differentials in P/E ratios across firms. The P/E ratio actually is a reflection of the market's optimism concerning a firm's growth prospects. In their use of a P/E ratio, analysts must decide whether they are more or less optimistic than the market. If they are more optimistic, they will recommend buying the stock.

There is a way to make these insights more precise. Look again at the constant growth DDM formula, $P_0 = D_1/(k - g)$. Now recall that dividends equal the earnings that are *not* reinvested in the firm: $D_1 = E_1(1 - b)$. Recall also that $g = \text{ROE} \times b$. Hence, substituting for $D_1$ and $g$, we find that

$$P_0 = \frac{E_1(1 - b)}{k - \text{ROE} \times b}$$

implying the P/E ratio is

$$\frac{P_0}{E_1} = \frac{1 - b}{k - \text{ROE} \times b} \qquad \textbf{(17.7)}$$

It is easy to verify that the P/E ratio increases with ROE. This makes sense, because high ROE projects give the firm good opportunities for growth.[6] We also can verify that the P/E ratio increases for higher $b$ as long as ROE exceeds $k$. This too makes sense. When a firm has good investment opportunities, the market will reward it with a higher P/E multiple if it exploits those opportunities more aggressively by plowing back more earnings into those opportunities.

Remember we noted, however, that growth is not desirable for its own sake. Examine Table 17.3 where we use Equation 17.7 to compute both growth rates and P/E ratios for different combinations of ROE and $b$. While growth always increases with the plowback rate (move across the rows in Table 17.3**A**), the P/E ratio does not (move across the rows in panel **B**). In the top row of Table 17.3**B,** the P/E falls as the plowback rate increases. In the middle row, it is unaffected by plowback. In the third row, it increases.

This pattern has a simple interpretation. When the expected ROE is less than the required return, $k$, investors prefer that the firm pay out earnings as dividends rather than reinvest earnings in the firm at an inadequate rate of return. That is, for ROE lower than $k$, the value of the firm falls as plowback increases. Conversely, when ROE exceeds $k$, the firm offers superior investment opportunities, so the value of the firm is enhanced as those opportunities are more fully exploited by increasing the plowback rate.

---

[6] Note that Equation 17.7 is a simple rearrangement of the DDM formula, with $\text{ROE} \times b = g$. Because that formula requires that $g < k$ Equation 17.7 is valid only when $\text{ROE} \times b < k$.

**Table 17.3** Effect of ROE and Plowback on Growth and the P/E Ratio

| | Plowback Rate ($b$) | | | |
|---|---|---|---|---|
| **ROE (%)** | **0** | **.25** | **.50** | **.75** |
| **A. Growth rate, $g$(%)** | | | | |
| 10 | 0 | 2.5 | 5.0 | 7.5 |
| 12 | 0 | 3.0 | 6.0 | 9.0 |
| 14 | 0 | 3.5 | 7.0 | 10.5 |
| **B. P/E Ratio** | | | | |
| 10 | 8.33 | 7.89 | 7.14 | 5.56 |
| 12 | 8.33 | 8.33 | 8.33 | 8.33 |
| 14 | 8.33 | 8.82 | 10.00 | 16.67 |

Assumption: $k = 12$ percent per year.

Finally, where ROE just equals $k$, the firm offers "break-even" investment opportunities with a fair rate of return. In this case, investors are indifferent between reinvestment of earnings in the firm or elsewhere at the market capitalization rate, because the rate of return in either case is 12 percent. Therefore, the stock price is unaffected by the plowback rate.

One way to summarize these relationships is to say the higher the plowback rate, the higher the growth rate, but a higher plowback rate does not necessarily mean a higher P/E ratio. A higher plowback rate increases P/E only if investments undertaken by the firm offer an expected rate of return higher than the market capitalization rate. Otherwise, higher plowback hurts investors because it means more money is sunk into prospects with inadequate rates of return.

**CONCEPT CHECK** Question 5. ABC stock has an expected ROE of 12 percent per year, expected earnings per share of \$2, and expected dividends of \$1.50 per share. Its market capitalization rate is 10 percent per year.

*a.* What are its expected growth rate, its price, and its P/E ratio?

*b.* If the plowback rate were 0.4, what would be the expected dividend per share, growth rate, price, and P/E ratio?

## Pitfalls in P/E Analysis

No description of P/E analysis is complete without issuing some caveats in its use. First, consider that the denominator in the ratio is accounting earnings, which are defined according to generally accepted accounting principles, including the use of historical cost in depreciation and inventory valuation. In particular, these earnings are not *economic earnings,* which are net of economic depreciation; this means that the earnings from which payout or plowback are calculated should be

## ARE P/E RATIOS MEANINGFUL?

Sorting Toronto Stock Exchange-listed stocks into those with the highest and lowest price-earnings ratios produces some startling results. Those results in turn lead to an almost inescapable conclusion: In many cases, price-earnings ratios are virtually meaningless.

In theory, stocks that trade at extremely high multiples of share earnings—more than 30 to 40 times—should be seen by the market as absurdly overvalued and drop in price to a more reasonable level. However, some technology stocks routinely trade at even higher multiples.

Similarly, stocks with low price-earnings valuations—lower than four to five times share earnings—should look abnormally cheap and be snapped up by investors. Yet whole groups of stocks—such as lumber and steel stocks—are trading at less than five times earnings.

The list of high P/E stocks contains names like **Tee-Comm Electronics Inc.,** at 321 times earnings for the most recent 12 months; **Maple Leaf Gardens Ltd.,** at 219 times; **Caledonia Mining Corp.,** 110 times; **BCE Mobile Telecommunications Inc.,** 79 times; and **Ford Motor Co. of Canada Ltd.** at 71 times.

Tee-Comm is a good example of one factor that often makes price-earnings multiples irrelevant. As with many technology stocks, investors are valuing the company not so much on what it earned in the past 12 months, but on what is *could* earn in the next year—or even the year after that.

The company makes satellite television equipment and is part of the Expressvu consortium, which has received a lot of publicity for its plan to offer programming to Canadian consumers this fall. Tee-Comm's stock rose to as high as $10.25 this month from less than $3 last year, based on expectations of revenue from the service.

BCE Mobile and **Clearnet Communications Inc.** also show up on the list for similar reasons. Neither company is valued on its earnings, because both are spending massive sums to expand telecommunications networks. In fact, it's surprising they have any earnings at all.

A similar company, **Rogers Cantel Mobile Communications Inc.,** consistently loses money—and yet investors are willing to pay $30 for the stock. Industry analysts say such companies are usually valued on the basis of their cash flow, using arcane measurements such as price-to-EBITDA (earnings before interest, taxes, depreciation and amortization).

Speculative resource stocks, such as Caledonia Mining, also are usually valued not on what they have earned, but on what they might earn. Caledonia, which has gold properties and is exploring for diamonds in the Northwest Territories, has been hyped in the past by a U.S.-based stock tip sheet called The Oxford Club. The stock has been as high as $10.

Although most are not as high as Caledonia, many gold companies trade at high P/Es. They do this because gold investors focus not on earnings but on what the company's reserves—the gold still in the ground—will be worth in the future. That, of course, depends on where the price of gold will be—one of the market's favourite guessing games.

Ford of Canada falls into a different category—in fact, into several categories. First it is a subsidiary of U.S. auto giant Ford Motor Co., and until recently the parent owned 94 percent of the stock, making it thinly traded—which exaggerates swings in the share price.

And second, the parent recently announced it was buying the stock it didn't already own at $150 a share—a hefty premium to the trading price—which pushed the stock up. Other thinly traded Canadian subsidiaries on the high P/E list include **Xerox Canada Inc.** and **Canadian Marconi Co.**

Maple Leaf Gardens also is on the list for a number of reasons, one of which is likely continuing takeover speculation—although an attempted buy-

*(Continued)*

out by investor Steve Stavro is tied up in court.

The stock also is thinly traded. Finally, it is likely trading on earnings expectations, because the hockey players' lockout crimped this past year's earnings badly, but future results aren't expected to be hit as hard.

When it comes to the low P/E list, an obvious pattern emerges: the majority of stocks with extremely low multiples are steel and forest products, particularly lumber, companies. These include **Algoma Steel Inc.** at 1.3 times; **Harris Steel Group Inc.** at 3.6 times; **Riverside Forest Products Ltd.** at 4.3 times; and **Slocan Forest Products Ltd.** at 4.8 times.

The reason is simple, say industry watchers, such as Steve Laciak of First Marathon Securities. In the same way that technology investors assume earnings will rise in the next year or two, investors looking at steel and forest industry stocks already are discounting what they see as future declining earnings.

"The steel sector has seen its top, and started its downturn," Mr. Laciak says. The peak in earnings also appears to have lasted for a relatively short time, he says. "It's peaked for a very thin period of time, and so P/Es haven't gotten as high as they have in previous cycles."

Mr. Laciak expects earnings to continue to erode as demand for steel drops, thanks in part to an economic slowdown in the United States and falling production of automobiles. However, the subject is open to debate.

"The question you have to ask is: Are we into a period where prices are eroding, and will keep eroding for the next couple of years—or do you think they will slow down and bounce back?"

If you feel, as some market analysts do, that the economic slowdown will be a slow and measured one—instead of a massive drop that plunges North America into recession—then you might feel that the discount some steel and forestry stocks are trading at is overly severe.

In fact, U.S. investors have been buying some Canadian forestry stocks despite the fact that earnings for that industry are widely considered to have peaked. These investors feel that Canadian stocks are trading at lower multiples than their U.S. counterparts.

There are a few stocks on the list that don't fall into this cyclical mold: perennially unloved takeover artist **Onex Corp.** trades at 4.3 times earnings, for example, but this has little to do with the fact that—among other things—it owns an auto parts company.

Onex-watchers say it is more likely a result of several factors: the company holds stakes in many companies, and is often given a discount because it is not what investors call a "pure play" on one industry. The market also is leery of Onex's specialty—leveraged buyouts.

Mathew Ingram, *Toronto Globe & Mail*, June 21, 1995, p. B.11. Reprinted by permission.

*after* provisions to maintain the productive capacity. Inflation causes historic depreciation and inventory costs to underrepresent true economic values, since replacement costs will rise. Historically, P/E ratios have tended to be lower when inflation has been higher. This reflects the market's assessment that earnings in these periods are of "lower quality," being distorted by inflation; at the same time, higher interest rates associated with inflation are consistent with lower multiples.

Another confounding factor in the use of P/E ratios is related to the business cycle. The concept of a normal P/E ratio, as used in this section, assumes implicitly that earnings rise at a constant rate. Actual reported earnings can fluctuate dramatically around a trend line over the business cycle. The "normal" P/E ratio predicted by Equation 17.7 is the ratio of today's price to the trend value of future earnings, but P/E ratios appearing in financial pages and on screens are based on

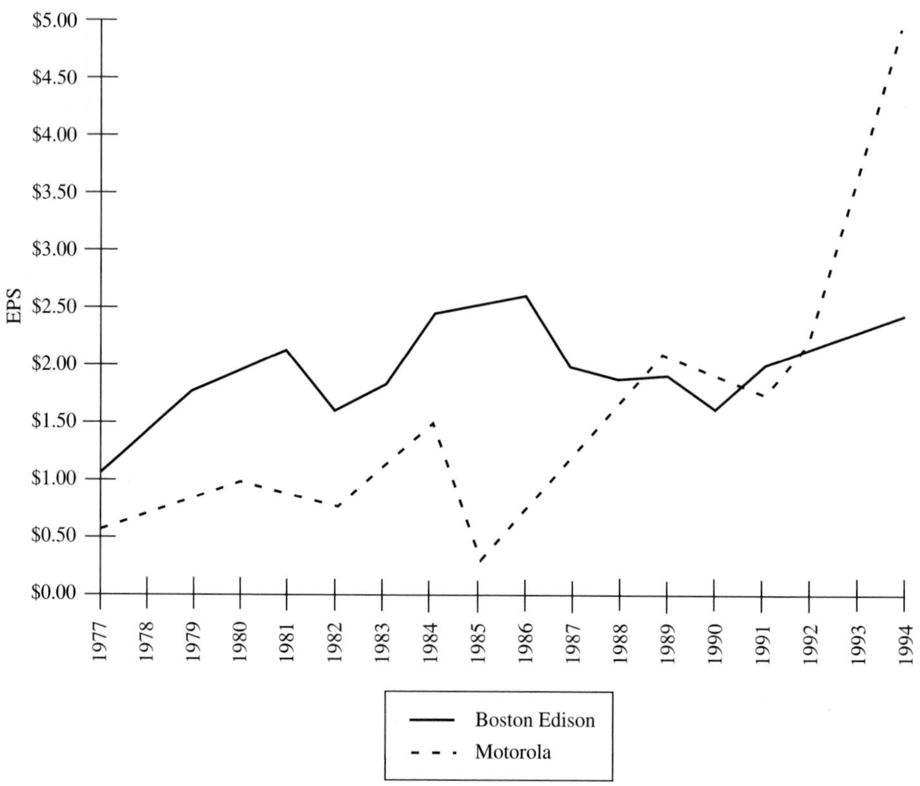


**Figure 17.2** Earnings per share, 1977–1994.

past reported earnings. Clearly, current accounting earnings can differ considerably from future economic earnings. For this reason, analysts often refer to "forward" or "trailing" earnings and P/E ratios. (See the accompanying box.)

Since P/E ratios are based on growth prospects, and different industries have very different potential, as the case of Motorola and Boston Edison typifies, we find different P/E ratios to be "normal" across industry lines. We also should recognize that different industries respond to the business cycle at different times; some pick up early in the cycle, while others lag in the cycle. What we expect to see in reported P/E ratios, therefore, can vary widely. A company that is still experiencing good earnings, but that can be expected to undergo a drastic decrease in profits, will show a low P/E as investors efficiently lower the price in anticipation of lower earnings. After, or in the middle of, a recession, many companies will have extremely high P/Es, given the current low earnings and anticipated recovery. P/E ratios can easily range from 3 to 100, suggesting a 33⅓ percent or 1 percent return on equity!

Figures 17.2 and 17.3 graph the earnings per share and P/E ratios of Motorola and Boston Edison respectively, since 1977. Motorola's fluctuating earnings reflect its sensitivity to the business cycle (beta is 1.4), while Boston Edison has a much

**Figure 17.3**
Price/earnings ratios, 1977–1994.

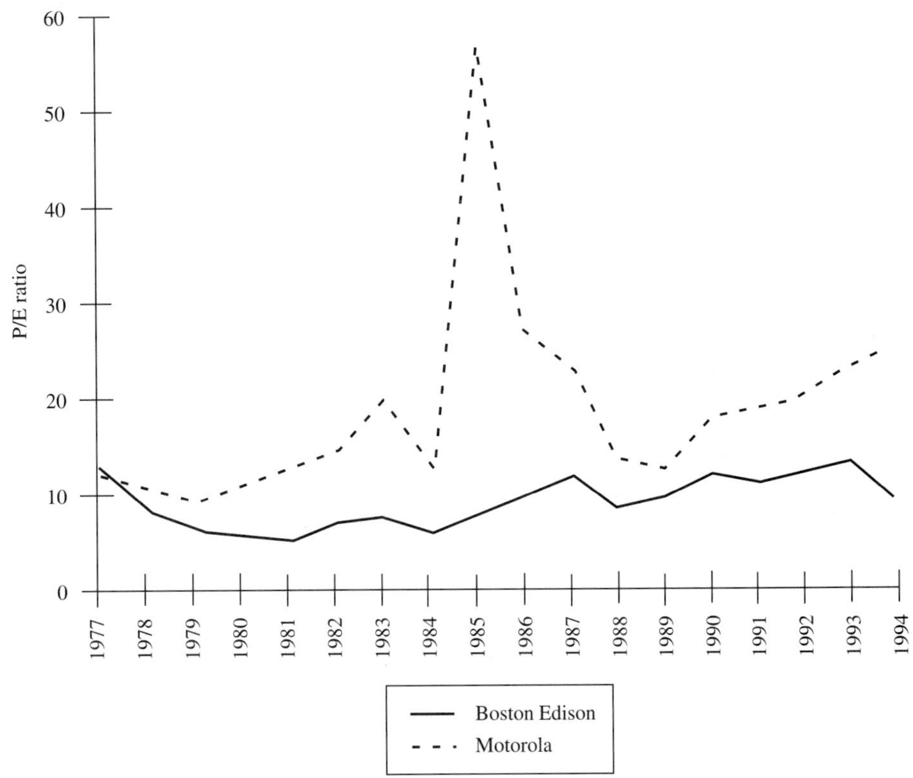


more stable trend (beta is .75). In 1985, when Motorola's earnings fell to $.61, its P/E ratio reached 56.3; if earnings had been a more normal 2.5 times this level, the P/E would have been only 22, more typical of other values.

## 17.4 Growth or Value Investing

Many investment advisers express their approach to portfolio building as either "value investing" or "growth investing." The former is considered to be more conservative and the latter more rewarding, as it entails more risk. Others insist that all investing must be value-based, and that when growth opportunities are undervalued they become value opportunities. The two terms are generally accepted as implying a choice between companies for which there are superior growth prospects and those where fundamental analysis reveals unrecognized value. A more formal definition states that a **growth company** is one for which the growth rate is greater than the market average due to the opportunity to reinvest earnings at a rate greater than the market's required rate of return. (Note that this definition fits with the three stages of company life cycles.) Value is found in companies that can invest only at the market capitalization rate; the value is there because investors overlook these firms as they bid up the price of growth companies.

In fact, value investors rely upon misperceptions as to the real growth prospects of so-called growth companies, leaving true value in stable companies. There is considerable evidence to justify this approach. Growth investing assumes that there is a degree of persistence in growth trends such that superior returns can be generated from investing in companies with a record of growth; this return must justify the risk that actively growing firms often experience financial setbacks during downturns in the economy. More established, stable firms have greater financial resources to weather these difficulties. A famous study by I. M. D. Little in 1962 showed that, for British firms, those identified as growth companies in the first period were no more likely than other firms to be so identified in the second period; that is, there was no persistence of the growth characteristic. Subsequent studies of American firms showed the same results; growth could be identified only ex post.

Investors pay a premium price for future earnings of growth companies, captured by the high P/E ratio; should that growth fail to materialize, they will have inferior returns. Therefore, value investing in companies whose future earnings are much easier to predict will have a higher payoff. On the other hand, surely companies in growing industries with unique products to sell—the Microsofts and Newbridge Networks of tomorrow—can be identified as growth companies. Ex post, they are easy to spot; the skill of being an analyst lies in finding them before their success occurs.

## The Graham Technique

No presentation of fundamental security analysis would be complete without a discussion of the ideas of Benjamin Graham, the greatest of the investment "gurus." Until the evolution of modern portfolio theory in the latter half of this century, Graham was the single most important thinker, writer, and teacher in the field of investment analysis. His influence on investment professionals remains very strong.

Graham's magnum opus is *Security Analysis,* written with Columbia Professor David Dodd in 1934. By analyzing a firm's financial statements carefully, Graham felt one could identify bargain stocks. Over the years, he developed many different rules for determining the most important financial ratios and the critical values for judging a stock to be undervalued. Through its many editions, his book has had a profound influence on investment professionals. It has been so influential and successful, in fact, that widespread adoption of Graham's techniques has led to the elimination of the very bargains they are designed to identify.

In a 1976 seminar, Graham said:

I am no longer an advocate of elaborate techniques of security analysis in order to find superior value opportunities. This was a rewarding activity, say 40 years ago, when our textbook "Graham and Dodd" was first published; but the situation has changed a good deal since then. In the old days any well-trained security analyst could do a good professional job of selecting undervalued issues through detailed studies; but in the light of the enormous amount of research now being carried on, I doubt whether in most cases such extensive efforts will generate sufficiently superior selections to justify their cost. To that very limited extent I'm on the side of the "efficient market" school of thought now generally accepted by the professors.[7]

Nonetheless, in that same seminar Graham suggested a simplified approach to identify bargain stocks:

My first, more limited, technique confines itself to the purchase of common stocks at less than their working-capital value, or net current-asset value, giving no weight to the plant and other fixed assets, and deducting all liabilities in full from the current assets. We used this approach extensively in managing investment funds, and over a 30-odd-year period we must have earned an average of some 20 percent per year from this source. For a while, however, after the mid-1950s, this brand of buying opportunity became very scarce because of the pervasive bull market. But it has returned in quantity since the 1973–1974 decline. In January 1976 we counted over 100 such issues in the Standard & Poor's *Stock Guide*—about 10 percent of the total. I consider it a foolproof method of systematic investment—once again, not on the basis of individual results but in terms of the expectable group outcome.

There are two convenient sources of information for those interested in trying out the Graham technique. Both Standard & Poor's *Outlook* and the *Value Line Investment Survey* carry lists of stocks selling below net working capital.

## 17.5 Corporate Finance and the Free Cash Flow Approach

In both the discounted dividend and capitalized earnings approaches to equity valuation we made the assumption that the only source of financing of new equity investment in the firm was retained earnings. How would our results be affected if we allowed external equity financing of new investments? How would they be affected if we assumed debt financing of new investments? In other words, how do dividend policy and capital structure affect the value of a firm's shares?

The classic answer to these questions was provided by Modigliani and Miller (MM) in a series of articles that have become the foundation for the modern

[7] As cited by John Train in *Money Masters* (New York: Harper & Row, Publishers, Inc., 1987). Graham is reported to have attributed his success in investing to the purchase of growth stocks rather than to reliance on fundamental analysis.

theory of corporate finance,[8] and we will briefly explain the main points of their theory.[9]

MM claim that if we take as given a firm's future investments, then the value of its existing common stock is not affected by how those investments are financed. Therefore, neither the firm's dividend policy nor its capital structure should affect the value of a share of its equity.

The basic reasoning underlying the MM theory is that the intrinsic value of the equity in a firm is the present value of the net cash flows to shareholders that can be produced by the firm's existing assets plus the net present value of any investments to be made in the future. Given those existing and expected future investments, the firm's dividend and financing decisions will affect only the form in which existing shareholders will receive their future returns, that is, as dividends or capital gains, but not their present value.

As a by-product of their proof of these propositions, MM show the equivalence of three seemingly different approaches to valuing the equity in a firm. The first two are the discounted dividend and capitalized earnings approaches presented in the earlier parts of this chapter. The third is the free cash flow approach.

This third approach starts with an estimate of the value of the firm as a whole and derives the value of the equity by subtracting the market value of all nonequity claims. The estimate of the value of the firm is found as the present value of cash flows, assuming all-equity financing, plus the net present value of tax shields created by using debt. This approach is similar to that used by the firm's own management in capital budgeting, or the valuation approach that another firm would use in assessing the firm as a possible acquisition target.

For example, consider the MiMo Corporation. Its cash flow from operations before interest and taxes was $1 million in the year just ended, and it expects that this will grow by 6 percent per year forever. To make this happen, the firm will have to invest an amount equal to 15 percent of pretax cash flow each year. The tax rate is 30 percent. Depreciation was $10,000 in the year just ended and is expected to grow at the same rate as the operating cash flow. The appropriate market capitalization rate for the unleveraged cash flow is 10 percent per year, and the firm currently has debt of $2 million outstanding.

MiMo's projected free cash flow for the coming year is

| | |
|---|---:|
| Before-tax cash flow from operations | $1,060,000 |
| Depreciation | 106,000 |
| Taxable income | 954,000 |
| Taxes (at 30%) | 286,200 |

[8] The original two papers are M. Miller and F. Modigliani, "Dividend Policy, Growth and the Valuation of Shares," *Journal of Business,* October 1961; and F. Modigliani and M. Miller, "The Cost of Capital, Corporation Finance, and the Theory of Investment," *American Economic Review,* June 1958. Miller has since revised his views in "Debt and Taxes," *Journal of Finance,* May 1976, and Modigliani his in "Debt, Dividend Policy, Taxes, Inflation and Market Valuation," *Journal of Finance,* May 1982.

[9] For a more complete treatment see Stephen A. Ross and Randolph W. Westerfield, and Jeffrey F. Jaffe, *Corporate Finance* (Homewood, Ill.: Richard D. Irwin, Inc., 1993) Chapters 15 and 16.

| | |
|---|---|
| After-tax unleveraged income | 667,800 |
| After-tax cash flow from operations (after-tax unleveraged income plus depreciation) | 773,800 |
| New investment (15% of cash flow from operations) | 159,000 |
| Free cash flow (after-tax cash flow from operations minus new investment) | 614,800 |

It is important to realize that this projected free cash flow is what the firm's cash flow would be under all-equity financing. It ignores the interest expense on the debt, as well as any tax savings resulting from the deductibility of the interest expense.

The present value of all future free cash flows is:

$$V_0 = \frac{C_1}{k - g}$$

$$= \frac{\$614{,}800}{.1 - .06} = \$15{,}370{,}000$$

Thus the value of the whole firm, debt plus equity, is \$15,370,000. Since the value of the debt is \$2 million, the value of the equity is \$13,370,000.

If we believe that the use of financial leverage enhances the total value of the firm, then we should add to the \$15,370,000 estimate of the firm's unleveraged value the gain from leverage. Thus, if in our example we believe that the tax shield provided by the deductibility of interest payments on the debt increases the firm's total value by \$.5 million, the value of the firm would be \$15,870,000 and the value of the equity \$13,870,000.

In reconciling this free cash flow approach with either the discounted dividend or the capitalized earnings approaches, it is important to realize that the capitalization rate to be used in the present value calculation is different. In the free cash flow approach it is the rate appropriate for unleveraged equity, whereas in the other two approaches it is the rate appropriate for leveraged equity. Since leverage affects the stock's beta, these two capitalization rates will be different. The usual application of this approach is in assessing potential acquisition targets or in considering a financial restructuring of a firm to increase value. The analyst who believes a firm is ripe for a takeover or might benefit greatly from restructuring would use this technique to identify the potential gains from making an investment before the change was announced. We have only sketched the analysis needed.[10]

## 17.6 Inflation and Equity Valuation

What about the effects of inflation on stock prices? We start with an "inflation-neutral" case in which all *real* variables, and therefore the stock price, are unaffected by inflation, and then we explore the ways in which reality might differ.

[10] For a deeper analysis of this, see Richard A. Brealey and Stewart C. Myers, *Principles of Corporate Finance*, 4th edition (New York: McGraw-Hill, Inc., 1991) Chapters 16 and 17.

Consider the case of Inflatotrend, a firm that in the absence of inflation pays out all earnings as dividends. Earnings and dividends per share are $1, and there is no growth. We will use asterisked (*) letters to denote variables in the no-inflation case, or what represents the real value of variables. We again consider an equilibrium capitalization rate, $k^*$, of 10 percent per year. The price per share of this stock should be $10:

$$P_0 = \frac{\$1}{.1} = \$10$$

Now imagine that inflation ($i$) is 6 percent per year, but that the values of the other economic variables adjust so as to leave their real values unchanged. Specifically, the *nominal* capitalization rate, $k$, becomes $(1 + k^*)(1 + i) - 1 = 1.10 \times 1.06 - 1 = .166$, or 16.6 percent, and the expected nominal growth rate of dividends, $g$, is now 6 percent, which is necessary to maintain a constant level of real dividends. The *nominal* dividend expected at the end of this year is therefore $1.06 per share.

If we apply the constant growth DDM to these nominal variables we get the same price as in the no-inflation case:

$$P_0 = \frac{E(D_1)}{k - g} = \frac{\$1.06}{.166 - .060} = \$10$$

Thus, as long as real values are unaffected, the stock's current price is unaffected by inflation.

Note that the expected nominal dividend yield, $E(D_1)/P_0$, is 10.6 percent and the expected nominal capital gains rate, $[E(P_1) - P_0]/P_0$ is 6 percent. Almost the entire 6.6 percent increase in nominal HPR comes in the form of expected capital gains. A capital gain is necessary if the real value of the stock is to remain unaffected by inflation.

Let us see how these assumptions affect the other variables: earnings and the plowback ratio. To illuminate what otherwise may be confusing implications, we can explore a simplified story behind the examples above.

Inflatotrend produces a product that requires purchase of inventory at the beginning of each year, processing, and sale of the finished product at the end of the year. Last year there was no inflation. The inventory cost $10 million. Labor, rent, and other processing costs (paid at year-end) were $1 million, and revenue was $12 million. Assuming no taxes, earnings were $1 million.

| | |
|---|---|
| Revenue | $12 million |
| − Labor and rent | 1 million |
| − Cost of goods sold | 10 million |
| Earnings | $ 1 million |

All earnings are distributed as dividends to the one million shareholders. Because the only invested capital is the $10 million in inventory, the ROE is 10 percent.

This year inflation of 6 percent is expected, and all prices are expected to rise at that rate. As inventory is paid for at the beginning of the year it will still cost \$10 million. However, revenue will be \$12.72 million instead of \$12 million, and other costs will be \$1.06 million.

Nominal Earnings

| | |
|---|---|
| Revenue | \$12.72 million |
| − Labor and rent | 1.06 million |
| − Cost of goods sold | 10.00 million |
| Earnings | \$ 1.66 million |
| ROE | 16.6% |

Note that the amount required to replace inventory at year's end is \$10.6 million, rather than the beginning cost of \$10 million, so the amount of cash available to distribute as dividends is \$1.06 million, not the reported earnings of \$1.66 million.

A dividend of \$1.06 million would be just enough to keep the real value of dividends unchanged and at the same time allow for maintenance of the same real value of inventory. The reported earnings of \$1.66 million overstate true economic earnings, in other words.

We thus have the following set of relationships:

| | No Inflation | 6% Inflation |
|---|---|---|
| Dividends | \$1 million | \$1.06 million |
| Reported earnings | \$1 million | \$1.66 million |
| ROE | 10% | 16.6% |
| Plowback ratio | 0 | .36145 |
| Price of a share | \$10 | \$10 |
| P/E ratio | 10 | 6.0241 |

There are some surprising findings in this case of "neutral" inflation, that is, inflation that leaves the real interest rate and real earnings unaffected. While nominal dividends rise at the rate of inflation, 6 percent, reported earnings increase initially by 66 percent. In subsequent years, as long as inflation remains at a constant rate of 6 percent, earnings will grow at 6 percent.

Note also that the plowback ratio rises from 0 to .36145. Although plowback in the no-inflation case was zero, positive plowback of reported earnings now becomes necessary to maintain the level of inventory at a constant real value. Inventory must rise from a nominal level of \$10 million to a level of \$10.6 million to maintain its real value. This inventory investment requires reinvested earnings of \$.6 million.

**CONCEPT CHECK** Question 6. Assume that Inflatotrend has a 4 percent annual expected constant growth rate of earnings if there is no inflation. $E(E_1^*)$ = \$1 per share; ROE* = 10 percent per year; $b^* = .4$; and $k^* = 10$ percent per year.

*a*. What is the current price of a share ex-dividend?
*b*. What are the expected real dividend yield and rate of capital appreciation?
*c*. If the firm's real revenues and dividends are unaffected by inflation, and expected inflation is 6 percent per year, what should be the nominal growth rate of dividends, the expected nominal dividend yield, the expected ROE, and the nominal plowback ratio?

---

Thus, the proportion of reported income that must be retained and reinvested to keep the real growth rate of earnings at zero is .36145 if inflation is 6 percent per year. Multiplying this plowback ratio by the nominal ROE of 16.6 percent produces a nominal growth rate of dividends of 6 percent, which is equal to the inflation rate:

$$\begin{aligned} g &= b \times \text{ROE} \\ &= .36145 \times 16.6\% \\ &= 6\% \text{ per year} \end{aligned}$$

More generally, the relationship between nominal and real variables is:

| Variable | Real | Nominal |
|---|---|---|
| Growth rate | $g^*$ | $g = (1 + g^*)(1 + i) - 1$ |
| Capitalization rate | $k^*$ | $k = (1 + k^*)(1 + i) - 1$ |
| Return on equity | ROE* | $\text{ROE} = (1 + \text{ROE}^*)(1 + i) - 1$ |
| Expected dividend | $E(D_1^*)$ | $E(D_1) = (1 + i)E(D_1^*)$ |
| Plowback ratio | $b^*$ | $b = \dfrac{(1 + b^* \times \text{ROE}^*)(1 + i) - 1}{(1 + \text{ROE}^*)(1 + i) - 1}$ |

Note that it is not true that $E(E_1) = (1 + i)E(E_1^*)$. That is, expected reported earnings do not, in general, equal expected real earnings times one plus the inflation rate. The reason, as you have seen, is that stated earnings do not accurately measure the cost of replenishing assets.

For example, cost of goods sold is treated as if it were $10 million, even though it now costs $10.6 million to replace the inventory. Original cost accounting in this case distorts the measured cost of goods sold, which in turn distorts the reported earnings figures. We will return to this point in Chapter 18.

Note also the effect of inflation on the P/E ratio. In our example, the P/E ratio drops from 10 in the no-inflation scenario to 6.0241 in the 6 percent inflation scenario. This is entirely a result of the fact that the reported earnings figure gets distorted by inflation and overstates true economic earnings.

This is true in the real world too, not just in our simplified example, Many companies show gains in reported earnings during inflationary periods, even though real earnings may be unaffected. This is one reason analysts must interpret data on the past behaviour of P/E ratios over time with greater care.

For many years, financial economists considered stocks to be an inflation-neutral investment in the sense that we have described. They believed, and many of them still believe, that changes in the rate of inflation, whether expected or unexpected, have no effect on the expected real rate of return on common stocks.

Recent empirical research, however, seems to indicate that real rates of return are negatively correlated with inflation. In terms of the simple constant growth rate DDM, this would mean that an increase in inflation is associated with (but is not necessarily caused by) either a decrease in $E(D_1)$, an increase in $k$, a decrease in $g$, or some combination of all three.

One school of thought[11] believes that economic "shocks" such as oil price hikes can cause a simultaneous increase in the inflation rate and a decline of expected real earnings (and dividends). This would result in a negative correlation between inflation and real stock returns.

A second view[12] is that the higher the rate of inflation, the riskier real stock returns are perceived to be. The reasoning here is that higher inflation is associated with greater uncertainty about the economy, which tends to induce a higher required rate of return on equity. In addition, a higher $k$ implies a lower level of stock prices.

A third perspective[13] is that higher inflation results in lower real dividends because our tax system causes lower after-tax real earnings as the inflation rate rises.

Finally, there is the view[14] that many investors in the stock market suffer from a form of "money illusion." Investors mistake the rise in the nominal rate of interest for a rise in the real rate. As a result, they undervalue stocks in a period of higher inflation.

## 17.7 Macroeconomic Analysis

In order to forecast a firm's earnings, an analyst must consider the business environment in which it operates. For many firms, macroeconomic and industry circumstances have a greater influence on profits than does the firm's relative performance within its industry. Many portfolio managers attempt to identify superior firms based on their specific advantages, looking at past performance and financial statements, as we shall consider in the next chapter; others prefer to do a "top-down" analysis, examining the state of the economy and its implications for the industry in which the firm operates.

We present here a brief review of macroeconomics, mentioning the kind of factors that economists, working with the analysts, would examine in order to

---

[11] See Eugene F. Fama, "Stock Returns, Real Activity, Inflation, and Money," *American Economic Review,* September 1981.

[12] See Burton Malkiel, *A Random Walk Down Wall Street,* 4th Edition (New York: W. W. Norton & Co., Inc., 1985).

[13] See Martin Feldstein, "Inflation and the Stock Market," *American Economic Review,* December 1980.

[14] See Franco Modigliani and Richard Cohn, "Inflation, Rational Valuation, and the Market," *Financial Analysts Journal,* March–April 1979.,

identify the current stage of the business cycle and predict the direction of economic variables. This information is then used by analysts to consider its effect on the industries that they cover in looking for particular companies that excel. This approach to investing is closely tied to the notion of timing the market. We illustrate a means of estimating the market response to the business cycle, especially using the level of interest rates in discounting predicted earnings, and we discuss some of the factors relevant to the sensitivity of the various industry classifications.

## The Macro Economy

Some of the key variables that analysts use to assess the state of the macro economy include the *gross domestic product* (GDP), the *unemployment rate, inflation, interest rates,* and the *budget deficit.* The GDP measures the total production of goods and services and allows the tracking of the rate of growth in the economy; this can be more narrowly focused on industrial production. Employment statistics and capacity utilization rates help analysts determine whether the economy may be overheating. This is closely related to the inflation rate, where various precise measures are used to identify the cause and probable course of inflationary pressures. The perceived trade-off between inflation and unemployment is at the heart of many macroeconomic policy disputes. Interest rates generally respond to inflation, but they are managed by the central bank policy as well. They also follow from the budget deficit, which is the difference between government spending and revenues. Government borrowing as a result of deficits puts upward pressure on interest rates; excessive borrowing will "crowd out" private borrowing by forcing up interest rates.

In an export-dependent economy, such as Canada's, the international variables of the *exchange rate* and the *current account* are crucial. Exchange rates, primarily against the U.S. dollar, determine the balance between exports and imports; they also affect inflation through the domestic cost of imported goods. The current account is determined by the difference between the value of imports and exports and by international transfers of investment funds; these transfers depend greatly on the investment decisions of foreigners holding Canadian assets and Canadians holding foreign assets. Persistent trade deficits (the major component of the current account) will cause the dollar to depreciate. Thus, we have a complex interplay of forces affecting interest rates, inflation, and exchange rates resulting from government policies and private investment and production decisions.

## Demand and Supply Shocks and Government Policy

A useful way to organize the analysis of the factors that might influence the macro economy is to classify any impact as a demand or supply shock. A **demand shock** is an event that affects the demand for goods and services. Examples of positive demand shocks are reductions in tax rates, increases in the money supply, increases in government spending, or increases in foreign export demand.

A **supply shock** is an event that influences production capacity and costs. Examples of supply shocks are droughts that might reduce quantities of crops, changes in the immigration policies that increase the number of skilled labourers, or changes in the labour code governing wage rates or union activity.

Demand shocks usually are characterized by aggregate output moving in the same direction as interest rates and inflation. Thus, an increase in government spending will stimulate the economy and increase GDP, with a likely increase in borrowing, interest rates, and even inflation. A supply shock has the opposite effect—aggregate output usually moves counter to interest rates and inflation. Increases in world prices of oil increase production costs and prices of finished goods; the inflationary pressure results in higher interest rates and lower production as individuals are less able to purchase more expensive goods.

The federal government has two broad classes of macroeconomic tools with which it attempts to regulate the economy—those that affect demand and those affecting supply. **Fiscal policy** includes taxation and government spending, and has a pronounced effect on demand. Increases in taxes directly restrict consumption and rapidly rein in the economy. An increase in government spending, on the other hand, fuels demand and can cause a prompt increase in production. An increase in one without a corresponding increase in the other changes the deficit; thus a stimulative or restrictive shock can be given to the economy.

The other tool of demand-side policy is **monetary policy,** which refers to the manipulation of the money supply and works mainly through its impact on interest rates. The money supply is increased or decreased by the purchase or sale of securities by the Bank of Canada; the money paid for a security by the bank is a direct increase to the money supply. The bank also can raise or lower the bank rate to make borrowing more or less costly, thereby affecting investment. These tools are easier to implement but less effective than fiscal policy. Many economists believe that an increased money supply leads only to inflation in the long run.

The failure of economic policy to manage the economy of most western nations in past decades, as evidenced by high inflation, high deficits, and high unemployment, as well as severe recessions induced by restrictive monetary policies, has been blamed on the inadequacies of demand-side policies. Consequently, the 1980s saw the emergence of supply-side economics. This approach focuses on the productive capacity of the economy. Its goal is to create an environment in which workers and owners of capital have the maximum incentive and ability to produce and develop goods. Hence, the emphasis is on tax policy and the incentives that it defines; lower tax rates lead to more incentives to provide capital and labour, thereby enhancing economic growth.

## Business Cycles

The economy recurrently experiences periods of expansion and contraction, although the length and depth of those cycles can be irregular. This pattern of

**Table 17.4** Components of Leading Economic Indicators' Composite Index

| Retail Sales | Manufacturing |
|---|---|
| Furniture and appliances | New orders—durables |
| Other durable sales | Ratio of shipments to stocks |
| | Average work week |
| **Financial** | Business and personnel services employment |
| Real money supply | |
| Toronto stock market (TSE 300) | **House Spending** |
| | U.S. Index |

recession and recovery is called the **business cycle.** Given this cyclical nature, it is not surprising that the cycle can be predicted. Statistics Canada has developed a set of cyclical indicators to help forecast and measure short-term fluctuations in economic activity. **Leading economic indicators** are those economic series that tend to rise or fall in advance of the rest of the economy.

Ten series are grouped into a widely followed composite index of leading economic indicators, as specified in Table 17.4. Figure 17.4 graphs percent changes in the composite leading indicator series against changes in the GDP and the coincident series of industrial production for the years 1985–1995. It is not at all apparent that the leading indicator series is earning its title over this period!

The stock market price index is a leading indicator.[15] Unfortunately, this makes the series of leading indicators much less useful for investment policy—by the time the series predicts an upturn, the market already has made its move. While the business cycle may be somewhat predictable, the stock market may not be. This is one more manifestation of the efficient market hypothesis. Various industries, however, respond early or late in the cycle, while others are more insensitive. Forest products encompass two subsectors: lumber, which responds to home construction as interest rates fall, and pulp and paper, which follows business activity as advertising and packaging increase. Since interest rates fall as a recession deepens, lumber company profits pick up earlier than do pulp and paper; the efficient market anticipates the increased profits by raising the equity prices. You might miss the gains in forest product companies specializing in lumber operations, but still have time to invest in the pulp and paper companies.

## 17.8 The Aggregate Stock Market and Industry Analysis

### Explaining Past Behaviour

Most scholars and serious analysts would agree that, although the stock market appears to have a substantial life of its own, responding perhaps to bouts of mass

[15] See, for example, Stanley Fischer and Robert C. Merton, "Macroeconomics and Finance: The Role of the Stock Market," *Carnegie–Rochester Conference Series on Public Policy* 21 (1984).

**Figure 17.4** Composite leading indicator, GDP, and industrial production in Canada.

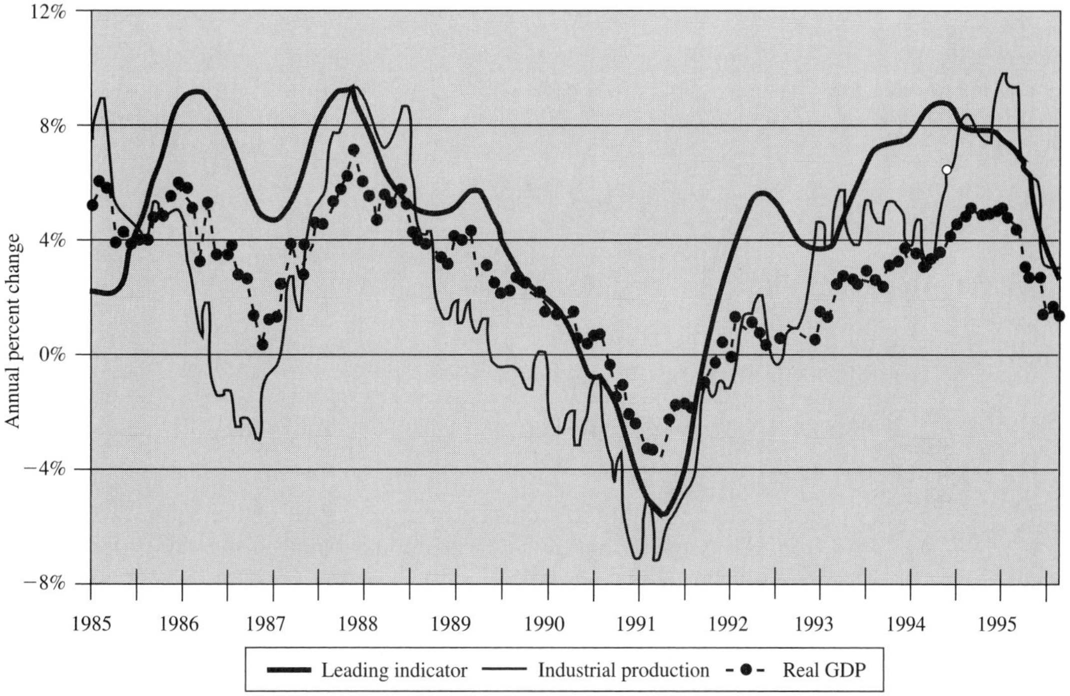

Source: Statistics Canada, Series D100031, I37035, I37026. Reprinted by permission.

euphoria and then panic, economic events and the anticipation of such events do have a substantial effect on stock prices.[16] Perhaps the two factors with the greatest impact are interest rates and corporate profits.

Figure 17.5 shows the behaviour of the difference between the yield to maturity on long-term Canada bonds and the earnings-to-price ratio (i.e., the earning yield) of the TSE 300 stock index over the 35-year period 1955–1990. Our discussion of valuation models earlier in this chapter gives us some insights into the relationship between these two yields. Let us assume that the expected ROE on future real investments in the corporate sector is equal to the equity capitalization rate and that current earnings per share equal expected future earnings per share; then, in the absence of inflation, the earnings yield on the TSE 300 represents the expected real rate of return on the stock market. This should be equal to the yield to maturity on Canada bonds plus a risk premium, which may change slowly over time.

Inflation will alter this relationship for several reasons. First, as shown earlier in this chapter, even in the case of neutral inflation, reported earnings tend to rise

[16] For a discussion of the current debate on the rationality of the stock market, see the suggested readings at the end of this chapter.

**Figure 17.5**
Long-term bond yield minus earnings yield of TSE 300.
From Burns Fry Limited Equity Investment Strategy Group (September 1990). Reprinted with permission.

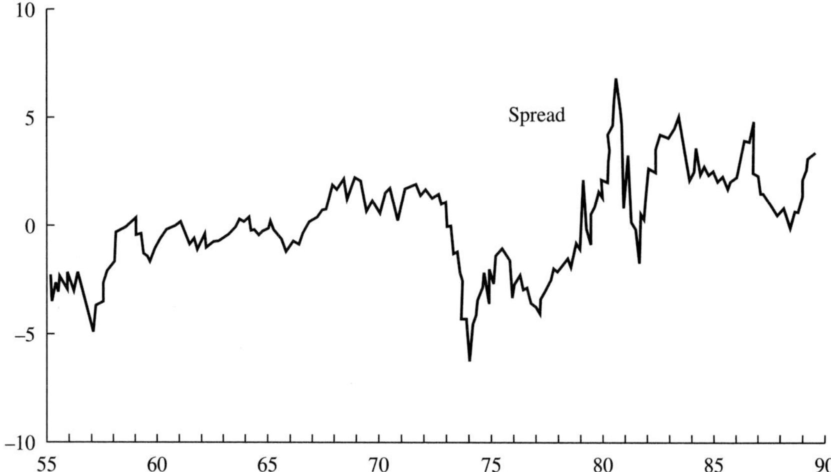


in a period of high inflation. Thus, at least part of the sharp drop in the 1970s from the graph in Figure 17.5 can be attributed to the sharp rise in the rate of inflation during that period.

However, a more important fact is that the yield to maturity on long-term bonds is a nominal rate that embodies the inflation expectations of market participants. The earnings yield on common stocks, on the other hand, is a real yield. Thus, if stocks are inflation neutral, the difference between the earnings yield on stocks and the yield to maturity on Canada bonds will reflect both the risk premium on stocks and the expected long-run inflation rate. This implies that when the expected rate of inflation is low, the earnings yield on stocks should exceed the yield to maturity on bonds, and when the expected rate of inflation is high, the reverse should be true.

For example, suppose that in the absence of inflation the earnings yield on stocks is 9 percent per year and the yield to maturity on bonds 3 percent per year, implying an equity risk premium of 6 percent per year. As you can see in Figure 17.5, the equity risk premium was near zero in the late 1960s and early 1970s, until (approximately) the first oil shock of 1973. Now suppose the expected rate of inflation is 8 percent per year. If stocks are inflation neutral, the earnings yield will still be 9 percent. But the yield to maturity on bonds, since it is a nominal rate, will jump to 11 percent per year. Thus, the yield to maturity on bonds will exceed the earnings yield on stocks by 2 percent per year, the difference between the expected rate of inflation (8 percent per year) and the equity risk premium (6 percent per year). These hypothetical relationships are summarized in Table 17.5.

Something like this appears to be what actually happened in the 1980s. Of course, other things that might have affected stock and bond yields were happening during this period as well. Perhaps the most important were changes in the relative risk of stocks and bonds. Long-term bonds, in particular, became much

**Table 17.5** Effect of Inflation on Stock and Bond Yields

| Rate of Inflation | Earnings Yield on Stocks (% per Year) | Yield to Maturity on Bonds (% per Year) |
|---|---|---|
| 0% | 9% | 3% |
| 8 | 9 | 11 |

riskier during this period as a result of changes in Bank of Canada monetary policy and the variability in the inflation rate.

## Forecasting the Stock Market

What can we learn from all of this future rate of return on stocks? First, a note of optimism. Although timing the stock market is a very difficult and risky game, it is not impossible.

In the early 1980s, several serious scholars of the stock market were predicting that as the rate of inflation came down the stock market would do extraordinarily well. For example, in the fourth edition of his classic book, *A Random Walk Down Wall Street,* Malkiel[17] predicted a compound rate of return of 17 percent per year during the decade of the 1980s. In fact, the average compound rate of return on the S&P 500 during the five-year period 1982–1987 was 17 percent per year. (The equivalent rate on the TSE 300 during the same period was 13.8 percent per year.)

In addition, by the summer of 1987 (on the eve of the October 1987 stock market crash), many market analysts were warning that the market was seriously overvalued. The ensuing debacle is now history. However, if market history teaches us anything at all, it is that the market has great variability. Thus, although we can use a variety of methods to derive a forecast of the expected holding period return on the market, uncertainty surrounding that forecast will always be high.

The most popular approach to forecasting the stock market is the earnings multiplier approach applied at the aggregate level. The first step is to forecast corporate profits for the coming period (either a quarter or a full year). Then an estimate of the earnings multiplier is derived, based on a forecast of long-term interest rates. The product of the two forecasts is the point forecast of the end-of-period level of the market. Table 17.6 illustrates an application of this method. The table reflects the use of sensitivity analysis in the projections, with alternative earnings and Treasury yields; we also can vary the spread between Treasury and earnings yields.

Other analysts use an aggregate version of the discounted dividend model rather than an earnings multiplier approach. All of these models rely heavily on

[17] Burton Malkiel, *A Random Walk Down Wall Street,* 4th edition (New York: W. W. Norton Co., 1985.)

**Table 17.6** TSE 300 Price Targets under Various Scenarios

| | 9–12 Month Target | Other Interest Rate Possibilities | | The Bull Scenario |
|---|---|---|---|---|
| Canada bond interest rate* | 7.50% | 7.25% | 7.00% | 6.50% |
| P/E ratio | 15.4x† | 16.0x | 16.7x | 18.2x |
| EPS (midpoint of 1994 and 1995 estimates) | $320 | $320 | $320 | $360 |
| TSE price target one year out | 4928 | 5120 | 5344 | 6552 |

*Forecast year-end Canada bond.

†Assumes a TSE 300 earnings yield 100 basis points below the bond yield. Our reasoning is that, even though the earnings yield exceeded the bond yield for most of the post-World War II era, the earnings yield has been below the bond yield for most of the recent period, beginning with the high-inflation era and extending into the current time. We believe one of the explanations for this current relationship is the abundant liquidity that is buoying the market. In recognition of the market's willingness to accept a lower earnings yield, we assume a 6.5 percent earnings yield, which implies a P/E of 15.4x. Other tests validate this type of number.

forecasts of such macroeconomic variables as GNP, interest rates, and the rate of inflation, which are themselves very difficult to predict accurately.

## Industry Analysis

Whatever the means an analyst uses to forecast the macro economy, it is necessary to determine the implication of that forecast for specific industries. Not all industries are equally sensitive to the business cycle. For example, consider Figure 17.6, which shows how various sectors of the economy responded to the recession in 1990 and 1991. While the traditional industries of transportation, construction, and manufacturing contracted, the emerging industry of communications and the evolving financial sector kept expanding through the recession.

Industries are classified in a variety of ways. Government statistics are based on one classification. Two U.S. stock rating services categorize companies and provide analysis by industry aggregation. Standard & Poor computes stock price indices for about 100 groups, while the *Value Line Investment Survey* forecasts performance for about 90 industry groups.

Three factors will determine the sensitivity of a firm's earnings to the business cycle. First is the sensitivity of sales. Necessities such as food, drugs, and medical services will show little sensitivity to business conditions. Other industries with low sensitivity with be those for which income is not a crucial determinant of demand, such as tobacco products. In contrast, firms in industries such as machine tools, steel, autos, and transportation are highly sensitive to the state of the economy.

The second factor determining business cycle sensitivity is operating leverage, which refers to the division between fixed and variable costs. (Fixed costs are those the firm incurs regardless of its production levels. Variable costs are those that rise or fall as the firm produces more or less product.) Firms with variable as opposed to fixed costs will be less sensitive to business conditions, because in

**Figure 17.6**
Sectoral response to the recession.

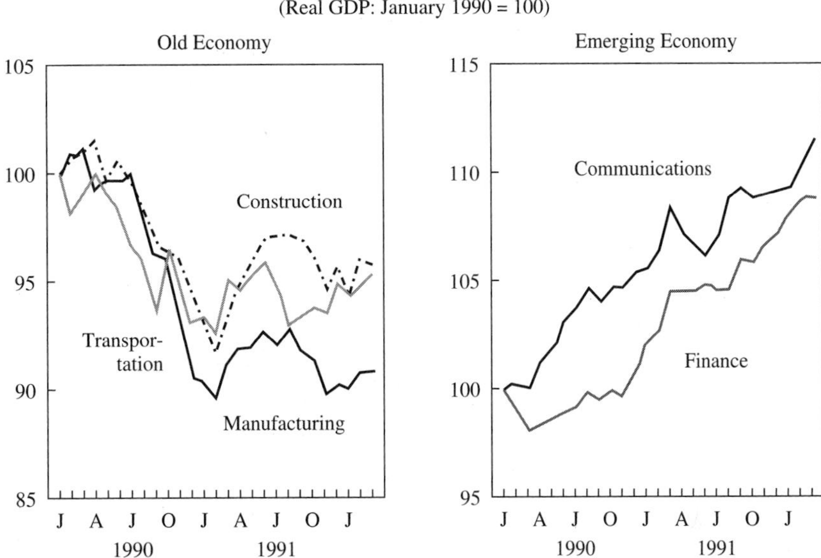


economic downturns these firms can reduce costs as output falls in response to falling sales. Profits for firms with high fixed costs will swing more widely with sales because costs do not move to offset revenue variability. Firms with high fixed costs are said to have high operating leverage, as small swings in business conditions can have large impacts on profitability.

An example might help illustrate this concept. Consider two firms operating in the same industry with identical revenues in all phases of the business cycle: recession, normal, and expansion. Firm A has short-term leases on most of its equipment and can reduce its lease expenditures when production slackens. It has fixed costs of $5 million and variable costs of $1 per unit of output. Firm B has long-term leases on most of its equipment and must make lease payments regardless of economic conditions. Its fixed costs are higher, $8 million, but its variable costs are only $.50 per unit. Table 17.7 shows that firm A will do better in recessions than firm B, but not as well in expansions. A's costs move in conjunction with its revenues to help performance in downturns and impede performance in upturns.

The third factor influencing business cycle sensitivity is financial leverage, which is the use of borrowing. Interest payments on debt must be paid regardless of sales. They are fixed costs that also increase the sensitivity of profits to business conditions. We will have more to say about financial leverage in Chapter 18.

Investors should not always prefer industries with lower sensitivity to the business cycle. Firms in sensitive industries will have high-beta stocks and are riskier. But while they swing lower in downturns, they also swing higher in upturns. As always, the issue you need to address is whether the expected return on the investment is fair compensation for the risks borne.

Just as there is a life cycle for firms, there is a corresponding **industry life cycle;** in fact, to a great extent the individual firm's life cycle depends upon the stages of its industry's cycle. When the industry is in its earlier stages, we expect to see high rates of return on high investment and low dividends; late in the cycle, during maturity, there will be predictable cash flows and corresponding dividends. Typically, there will be a start-up stage characterized by rapid growth, a consolidation stage with slower growth that still exceeds that of the general economy, a maturity stage that matches average growth, and a stage of relative decline encompassing relatively slow growth or shrinkage.

During the start-up stage, the novelty of the major products leads to extremely rapid sales and earnings growth, as we have seen in the high technology area; identification of the eventual industry leaders is difficult at first. During the consolidation phase, those leaders become apparent and their performance will parallel that of the industry. During maturity, the dominant firms will produce stable cash flows and may in fact have great appeal to value investors, as their P/E multiples will be much lower. In the stage of decline, competition from newer products or lower cost suppliers makes it difficult to generate profits.

Another factor is the relationship between industry structure and profitability. Returns are limited in a competitive structure, which can be characterized by the following:

- Threat of entry—Barriers to entry deter new entrants who put pressure on price and profits.
- Rivalry between existing competitors—Slow industry growth, high fixed costs, and homogeneous products all lead to price pressure (such as in the airline industry).
- Pressure from substitute products—Newer industries will generally be able to set higher prices.
- Bargaining power of buyers—Industries such as auto parts manufacturing have limited outlets for their products and little opportunity to demand higher profit margins.
- Bargaining power of suppliers—Profits also can be squeezed when there is little competition or substitutability among suppliers, as in the case of a unionized labour force.

A different approach to classification is taken by Peter Lynch, who had amazing success as a portfolio manager by avoiding many growth companies, especially if unknown. He characterized companies on the basis of their source of value, rather than the nature of their business, and labeled them as:

- Slow growers—Large mature companies with excess cash flows.
- Stalwarts—Large, noncyclical companies with well-recognized brand names (probably international), such as Coca-Cola.
- Fast growers—Small, aggressive new firms, growing at 20 to 25 percent annually, due to industry growth or increasing market share.
- Cyclicals—Firms with predictable sales and profit cycles.

**Table 17.7** Operating Leverage

| | Recession Scenario | | Normal Scenario | | Expansion Scenario | |
|---|---|---|---|---|---|---|
| | Firm A | Firm B | Firm A | Firm B | Firm A | Firm B |
| Sales (million units) | 5 | 5 | 6 | 6 | 7 | 7 |
| Price per unit | $ 2 | $ 2 | $ 2 | $ 2 | $ 2 | $ 2 |
| Revenue ($ million) | 10 | 10 | 12 | 12 | 14 | 14 |
| Fixed costs ($ million) | 5 | 8 | 5 | 8 | 5 | 8 |
| Variable costs ($ million) | 5 | 2.5 | 6 | 3 | 7 | 3.5 |
| Total costs ($ million) | $10 | $10.5 | $11 | $11 | $12 | $11.5 |
| Profits | $ 0 | $ (0.5) | $ 1 | $ 1 | $ 2 | $ 2.5 |

- Turnarounds—Distressed firms that have a good probability of recovery (Chrysler is well-known, but Repap is a recent Canadian example).
- Asset plays—Firms whose assets are not reflected in the stock price, being hidden in real estate, tax-loss carryforwards, or intangible assets not yielding immediate cash flows.

Analysts seeking unrecognized value must be familiar with the response of industries to the business cycle and with the relative strengths of firms within the different industries. Experience and intelligent appraisal of the economic factors and financial statements can be combined in the process of investing based on timing and security selection. The auto industry is notoriously cyclical as both industry and consumers postpone decisions to replace existing vehicles during recessions. A vehicle that is one year older is a little bit rustier and less reliable than before and more needful of replacement. Therefore the pressure to purchase increases, leading to relatively high auto sales following the low sales due to postponement. *When* the inevitable purchasing will start is a timing decision. Whether Japanese cars or the Big Three—and which of them—will get more of those sales is a question of selectivity; and whether perhaps the leading Canadian parts supplier, Magna International, will have more leverage to increased sales is a further question. The analyst is paid to resolve these questions.

**CONCEPT CHECK** Question 7. In Table 17.7, what will be profits in the three scenarios for a firm C with fixed costs of $2 million and variable costs of $1.50 per unit? What are your conclusions regarding operating leverage and business risk?

## SUMMARY

1. One approach to estimating intrinsic value is to focus on the firm's book value, either as it appears on the balance sheet or as adjusted to reflect current replacement cost of assets or liquidation value. Another approach is to focus on the present value of expected future dividends, earnings, or free cash flow.

**2.** The constant growth version of the DDM asserts that if dividends are expected to grow at a constant rate forever, then the intrinsic value of a share is determined by the formula

$$V_0 = D_1/(k - g)$$

The more realistic DDMs allow for several stages of earnings growth. Usually there is an initial stage of rapid growth, followed by a final stage of constant growth at a lower sustainable rate.

**3.** The expected growth rate of earnings is related both to the firm's ROE and to its dividend policy. The relationship can be expressed as

$$g = (\text{ROE on new investment}) \times (\text{Retention ratio})$$

**4.** Stock market analysts devote considerable attention to a company's price to earnings ratio. The P/E ratio is a useful measure of the market's assessment of the firm's growth opportunities. Firms with no growth opportunities should have a P/E ratio that is just the reciprocal of the capitalization rate, $k$. As growth opportunities become a progressively more important component of the value of the firm, the P/E ratio will increase.

**5.** You can relate any DDM to a simple capitalized earnings model by comparing the expected ROE on future investments to the market capitalization rate, $k$. If the two rates are equal, then the stock's intrinsic value reduces to expected earnings per share (EPS) divided by $k$.

**6.** Many analysts form their estimate of a stock's value by multiplying their forecast of next year's EPS by a P/E multiple derived from some empirical rule. This rule can be consistent with some version of the DDM, although often it is not.

**7.** Two approaches to portfolio building are value and growth investing. The first looks for value in slow growth firms that are overlooked; the second searches for firms growing faster than average, with earnings reinvested at greater than the required return on equity.

**8.** The free cash flow approach is the one used most often in corporate finance. The analyst first estimates the value of the entire firm as the present value of expected future free cash flows, assuming all-equity financing, then adds the value of tax shields arising from debt financing, and finally subtracts the value of all claims other than equity. This approach will be consistent with the DDM and capitalized earnings approaches as long as the capitalization rate is adjusted to reflect financial leverage.

**9.** We explored the effects of inflation on stock prices in the context of the constant growth DDM. Although traditional theory has held that inflation has a neutral effect on real stock returns, recent historical evidence shows a striking negative correlation between inflation and real stock market returns.

**10.** Macroeconomic analysis plays a major role in fundamental analysis; economists identify supply and demand shocks to the macro economy and the business cycle and use these in predicting future returns in the markets.

**11.** The models presented in this chapter can be used to explain and to forecast the behaviour of the aggregate stock market. The key macroeconomic variables that determine the level of stock prices in the aggregate are interest rates and corporate profits.

**12.** The business cycle is the economy's recurring pattern of expansions and recessions. Industries differ in their sensitivity to the business cycle, both in the degree and timing of their response.

**13.** Industry analysis examines aspects of performance, such as cyclical sensitivity, stages within an industry's life cycle, and competitive pressures.

## Key Terms

Fundamental analysis
Technical analysis
Book value
Liquidation value
Replacement cost
Tobin's *q*
Intrinsic value
Dividend discount model (DDM)
Constant growth DDM
Dividend payout ratio
Plowback ratio
Earnings retention ratio
Price/earnings multiple
Growth company
Demand shock
Supply shock
Fiscal policy
Monetary policy
Business cycle
Leading economic indicators
Industry life cycle

## Selected Readings

*For the key issues in the recent debate about the link between fundamentals and stock prices see:*

Merton, Robert C. "On the Current State of the Stock Market Rationality Hypothesis." In *Macroeconomics and Finance, Essays in Honor of Franco Modigliani,* ed. Rudiger Dornbusch, Stanley Fischer, and John Bossons. Cambridge, Mass.: MIT Press, 1986.

Cutler, David M.; James M. Poterba; and Lawrence H. Summers. "What Moves Stock Prices?" *Journal of Portfolio Management* 15 (Spring 1989), pp. 4–12.

West, Kenneth D. "Bubbles, Fads, and Stock Price Volatility Tests: A Partial Evaluation." *Journal of Finance* 43 (July 1988), pp. 639–55.

## Problems

**1.** *a.* Computer stocks currently provide an expected rate of return of 16 percent. MBI, a large computer company, will pay a year-end dividend of $2 per share. If the stock is selling at $50 per share, what must be the market's expectation of the growth rate of MBI dividends?

*b.* If dividend growth forecasts for MBI are revised downward to 5 percent per year, what will happen to the price of MBI stock? What will happen to the company's price-earnings ratio?

2. *a.* MF Corp. has an ROE of 16 percent and a plowback ratio of 50 percent. If the coming year's earnings are expected to be \$2 per share, at what price will the stock sell? The market capitalization rate is 12 percent.
   *b.* What price do you expect MF shares to sell for in three years?

3. The constant growth dividend discount model can be used both for the valuation of companies and for the estimation of the long-term total return of a stock.

   Assume: \$20 = the price of a stock today
   8% = the expected growth rate of dividends
   \$0.60 = the annual dividend one year forward

   *a.* Using *only* the above data, compute the expected long-term total return on the stock using the constant growth dividend discount model. Show calculations.
   *b.* Briefly discuss two disadvantages of the constant growth dividend discount model in its application to investment analysis.
   *c.* Identify two alternative methods to the dividend discount model for the valuation of companies.
4. The market consensus is that Analog Electronic Corporation has an ROE of 9 percent, a beta of 1.25, and it plans to maintain indefinitely its traditional plowback ratio of 2/3. This year's earnings were \$3 per share. The annual dividend was just paid. The consensus estimate of the coming year's market return is 14 percent, and T-bills currently offer a 6 percent return.
   *a.* Find the price at which Analog stock should sell.
   *b.* Calculate the P/E ratio.
   *c.* Calculate the present value of growth opportunities.
   *d.* Suppose your research convinces you Analog will announce momentarily that it will immediately reduce its plowback ratio to 1/3. Find the intrinsic value of the stock. The market is still unaware of this decision. Explain why $V_0$ no longer equals $P_0$ and why $V_0$ is greater or less than $P_0$.
5. If the expected rate of return of the market portfolio is 15 percent and a stock with a beta of 1.0 pays a dividend yield of 4 percent, what must the market believe is the expected rate of price appreciation on that stock?
6. The FI Corporation's dividends per share are expected to grow indefinitely by 5 percent per year.
   *a.* If this year's year-end dividend is \$8 and the market capitalization rate is 10 percent per year, what must the current stock price be according to the DDM?
   *b.* If the expected earnings per share are \$12, what is the implied value of the ROE on future investment opportunities?

*c.* How much is the market paying per share for growth opportunities (that is, for an ROE on future investments that exceeds the market capitalization rate)?

**7.** Using the data provided, discuss whether the common stock of Dominion Tobacco Company is attractively priced based on at least three different valuation approaches. (Hint: use the asset value, DDM, and earnings multiplier approaches.)

| | Dominion Tobacco | S&P 500 |
|---|---|---|
| Recent price | $27.00 | $290 |
| Book value per share | $ 6.42 | |
| Liquidation value per share | $ 4.90 | |
| Replacement costs of assets per share | $ 9.15 | |
| Anticipated next year's dividend | $ 1.20 | $ 8.75 |
| Estimated annual growth in dividends and earnings | 10.0% | 7.0% |
| Required return | 13.0% | |
| Estimated next year's EPS | $ 2.40 | $16.50 |
| P/E ratio based on next year's earnings | 11.3 | 17.6 |
| Dividend yield | 4.4% | 3.0% |

**8.** The risk-free rate of return is 10 percent, the required rate of return on the market is 15 percent, and High-Flyer stock has a beta coefficient of 1.5. If the dividend per share expected during the coming year, $D_1$, is $2.50 and $g = 5$ percent, at what price should a share sell?

**9.** Your preliminary analysis of two stocks has yielded the information set forth below. The market capitalization rate for both stock *A* and stock *B* is 10 percent per year.

| | Stock *A* | Stock *B* |
|---|---|---|
| Expected return on equity, ROE | 14% | 12% |
| Estimated earnings per share, $E_1$ | $ 2.00 | $ 1.65 |
| Estimated dividends per share, $D_1$ | $ 1.00 | $ 1.00 |
| Current market price per share, $P_0$ | $27.00 | $25.00 |

*a.* What are the expected dividend payout ratios for the two stocks?
*b.* What are the expected dividend growth rates of each?
*c.* What is the intrinsic value of each stock?
*d.* In which, if either, of the two stocks would you choose to invest?

**10.** The Tennant Company, founded in 1870, has evolved into the leading producer of large-sized floor sweepers and scrubbers, which are ridden by their operators. Some of its financial data are presented in the following table:

Tennant Company
Selected Historic Operating and Balance Sheet Data (000 Omitted)
As of December 31

| | 1980 | 1986 | 1992 |
|---|---|---|---|
| Net sales | $47,909 | $109,333 | $166,924 |
| Cost of goods sold | 27,395 | 62,373 | 95,015 |
| Gross profits | 20,514 | 46,960 | 71,909 |
| Selling, general, and administrative expenses | 11,895 | 29,649 | 54,151 |
| Earnings before interest and taxes | 8,619 | 17,311 | 17,758 |
| Interest on long-term debt | 0 | 53 | 248 |
| Pretax income | 8,619 | 17,258 | 17,510 |
| Income taxes | 4,190 | 7,655 | 7,692 |
| After-tax income | 4,429 | 9,603 | 9,818 |
| Total assets | $33,848 | $ 63,555 | $106,098 |
| Total common stockholders' equity | 25,722 | 46,593 | 69,516 |
| Long-term debt | 6 | 532 | 2,480 |
| Total common shares outstanding | 5,654 | 5,402 | 5,320 |
| Earnings per share | $ .78 | $ 1.78 | $ 1.85 |
| Dividends per share | .28 | .72 | .96 |
| Book value per share | 4.55 | 8.63 | 13.07 |

*a*. Based on these data, calculate a value for Tennant common stock by applying the constant growth dividend discount model. Assume an investor's required rate of return is a five percentage point premium over the current risk-free rate of return of 7 percent.

*b*. To your disappointment, the calculation you completed in part (*a*) results in a value below the stock's current market price. Consequently, you apply the constant growth DDM using the same required rate of return as in your calculation for part (*a*), but using the company's stated goal of earning 20 percent per year on stockholders' equity and maintaining a 35 percent dividend payout ratio. However, you find you are unable to calculate a meaningful answer. Explain why you cannot calculate a meaningful answer, and identify an alternative DDM that may provide a meaningful answer.

**11.** You are a portfolio manager considering the purchase of Nucor common stock. Nucor is the preeminent "mini-mill" steel producer in the United States. Mini-mills use scrap steel as their raw material and produce a limited number of products, primarily for the construction market. You are provided the following information:

Nucor Corporation

| | |
|---|---|
| Stock price (Dec. 30, 1990) | $53.00 |
| 1990 Estimated earnings | $ 4.25 |
| 1990 Estimated book value | $25.00 |
| Indicated dividend | $ 0.40 |
| Beta | 1.10 |
| Risk-free return | 7.0% |
| High grade corporate bond yield | 9.0% |
| Risk premium — stocks over bonds | 5.0% |

*a.* Calculate the expected stock market return. Show your calculations.
*b.* Calculate the implied total return of Nucor stock.
*c.* Calculate the required return of Nucor stock using the security market line model.
*d.* Briefly discuss the attractiveness of Nucor based on these data.

**12.** The stock of Nogro Corporation is currently selling for $10 per share. Earnings per share in the coming year are expected to be $2. The company has a policy of paying out 50 percent of its earnings each year in dividends. The rest is retained and invested in projects that earn a 20 percent rate of return per year. This situation is expected to continue indefinitely.
*a.* Assuming the current market price of the stock reflects its intrinsic value as computed using the constant growth rate DDM, what rate of return do Nogro's investors require?
*b.* By how much does its value exceed what it would be if all earnings were paid as dividends and nothing were reinvested?
*c.* If Nogro were to cut its dividend payout ratio to 25 percent, what would happen to its stock price? What if Nogro eliminated the dividend?

**13.** Chiptech, Inc., is an established computer chip firm with several profitable existing products as well as some promising new products in development. The company earned $1 a share last year and just paid out a dividend of $.50 per share. Investors believe the company plans to maintain its dividend payout ratio at 50 percent. ROE equals 20 percent. Everyone in the market expects this situation to persist indefinitely.
*a.* What is the market price of Chiptech stock? The required return for the computer chip industry is 15 percent, and the company has just gone ex-dividend (i.e., the next dividend will be paid a year from now, at $t = 1$).
*b.* Suppose you discover that Chiptech's competitor has developed a new chip that will eliminate Chiptech's current technological advantage in this market. This new product, which will be ready to come to the market in two years, will force Chiptech to reduce the prices of its chips to remain competitive. This will decrease ROE to 15 percent and, because of falling demand for its product, Chiptech will decrease the plowback ratio to .40. The plowback ratio will be decreased at the end of the

second year, at $t = 2$; the annual year-end dividend for the second year (paid at $t = 2$) will be 60 percent of that year's earnings. What is your estimate of Chiptech's intrinsic value per share? Hint: carefully prepare a table of Chiptech's earnings and dividends for each of the next three years. Pay close attention to the change in the payout ratio in $t = 2$.

*c.* No one else in the market perceives the threat to Chiptech's market. In fact, you are confident that no one else will become aware of the change in Chiptech's competitive status until the competitor firm publicly announces its discovery near the end of year two. What will be the rate of return on Chiptech stock in the coming year (that is, between $t = 0$ and $t = 1$)? In the second year (between $t = 1$ and $t = 2$)? In the third year (between $t = 2$ and $t = 3$)? Hint: pay attention to when the *market* catches on to the new situation. A table of dividends and market prices over time might help.

**14.** The risk-free rate of return is 8 percent, the expected rate of return on the market portfolio is 15 percent, and the stock of Xyrong Corporation has a beta coefficient of 1.2. Xyrong pays out 40 percent of its earnings in dividends, and the latest earnings announced were $10 per share. Dividends were just paid and are expected to be paid annually. You expect that Xyrong will earn an ROE of 20 percent per year on all reinvested earnings forever.

*a.* What is the intrinsic value of a share of Xyrong stock?

*b.* If the market price of a share is currently $100, and you expect the market price to be equal to the intrinsic value one year from now, what is your expected one-year holding-period return on Xyrong stock?

**15.** The Digital Electronic Quotation System (DEQS) Corporation pays no cash dividends currently and is not expected to for the next five years. Its latest EPS was $10, all of which was reinvested in the company. The firm's expected ROE for the next five years is 20 percent per year, and during this time it is expected to continue to reinvest all of its earnings. Starting six years from now, the firm's ROE on new investments is expected to fall to 15 percent, and the company is expected to start paying out 40 percent of its earnings in cash dividends, which it will continue to do forever after. DEQS's market capitalization rate is 15 percent per year.

*a.* What is your estimate of DEQS's intrinsic value per share?

*b.* Assuming its current market price is equal to its intrinsic value, what do you expect to happen to its price over the next year? The year after?

*c.* What effect would it have on your estimate of DEQS's intrinsic value if you expected DEQS to pay out only 20 percent of earnings starting in year six?

**16.** At year-end 1991, the Wall Street consensus was that Philip Morris' earnings and dividends would grow at 20 percent for five years, after which growth would fall to a market-like 7 percent. Analysts also projected a required rate of return of 10 percent for the U.S. equity market. You are provided with the following information:

Philip Morris Corporation
Selected Financial Data
Years Ending December 31
($ millions except per share data)

| | 1991 | 1981 |
|---|---|---|
| Earnings per share | $4.24 | $0.66 |
| Dividends per share | 1.19 | 0.25 |
| Stockholders' equity | 12,512 | 3,234 |
| Total liabilities and stockholders' equity | $47,384 | $9,180 |
| **Other Data** | | |
| **Philip Morris:** | | |
| Common shares outstanding (millions) | 920 | 1,003 |
| Closing price common stock | $80.250 | $6.125 |
| **S&P 500 Stock Index:** | | |
| Closing price | $417.09 | $122.55 |
| Earnings per share | 16.29 | 15.36 |
| Book value per share | 161.08 | 109.43 |

*a.* Using the data in the accompanying table and the multistage dividend discount model, calculate the intrinsic value of Philip Morris stock at year-end 1991. Assume a similar level of risk for Philip Morris stock as for the typical U.S. stock. Show all work.

*b.* Using the data in the table, calculate Philip Morris' price/earnings ratio and the price/earnings ratio relative to the S&P 500 stock index as of December 31, 1991.

*c.* Using the data in the table, calculate Philip Morris' price/book ratio and the price/book ratio relative to the S&P 500 stock index as of December 31, 1991.

**17.** *a.* State *one* major advantage and *one* major disadvantage of *each* of the *three* valuation methodologies you used to value Philip Morris stock in the previous problem.

*b.* State whether Philip Morris stock is undervalued or overvalued as of December 31, 1991. Support your conclusion using your answers to the previous problem and any data provided. (The past ten-year average S&P 500 stock index relative price/earnings and price/book ratios for Philip Morris were 0.80 and 1.61, respectively.)

**18.** The Duo Growth Company just paid a dividend of $1 per share. The dividend is expected to grow at a rate of 25 percent per year for the next three years and then to level off to 5 percent per year forever. You think the appropriate market capitalization rate is 20 percent per year.

*a.* What is your estimate of the intrinsic value of a share of the stock?

*b.* If the market price of a share is equal to this intrinsic value, what is the expected dividend yield?

*c.* What do you expect its price to be one year from now? Is the implied capital gain consistent with your estimate of the dividend yield and the market capitalization rate?

**19.** The Generic Genetic (GG) corporation pays no cash dividends currently and is not expected to for the next four years. Its latest EPS was $5, all of which was reinvested in the company. The firm's expected ROE for the next four years is 20 percent per year, during which time it is expected to continue to reinvest all of its earnings. Starting five years from now, the firm's ROE on new investments is expected to fall to 15 percent per year. GG's market capitalization rate is 15 percent per year.

*a.* What is your estimate of GG's intrinsic value per share?

*b.* Assuming its current market price is equal to its intrinsic value, what do you expect to happen to its price over the next year?

**20.** The MoMi Corporation's cash flow from operations before interest and taxes was $2 million in the year just ended, and its expects that this will grow by 5 percent per year forever. To make this happen, the firm will have to invest an amount equal to 20 percent of pretax cash flow each year. The tax rate is 34 percent. Depreciation was $200,000 in the year just ended and is expected to grow at the same rate as the operating cash flow. The appropriate market capitalization rate for the unleveraged cash flow is 12 percent per year, and the firm currently has debt of $4 million outstanding. Use the free cash flow approach to value the firm's equity.

**21.** You are trying to forecast the expected level of the aggregate Toronto stock market for the next year. Suppose the current three-month Treasury bill rate is 8 percent, the yield to maturity on 10+-year Canada bonds is 10 percent per year, the expected rate of inflation is 5 percent per year, and the expected EPS for the TSE 300 is $300. What is your forecast, and why?

**22.** Consider two firms producing videocassette recorders. One uses a highly automated robotics process, while the other uses human workers on an assembly line and pays overtime when there is heavy production demand.

*a.* Which firm will have higher profits in a recession? In a boom?

*b.* Which firm's stock will have a higher beta?

**23.** Here are four industries and four forecasts for the macroeconomy. Choose the industry that you would expect to perform best in each scenario.

*Industries:* Housing construction, health care, gold mining, steel production.

**Economic Forecasts**

*Deep recession:* Falling inflation, falling interest rates, falling GDP.

*Superheated economy:* Rapidly rising GDP, increasing inflation and interest rates.

*Healthy expansion:* Rising GDP, mild inflation, low unemployment.

*Stagflation:* Falling GDP, high inflation.

**24.** In which stage of the industry life cycle would you place the following industries? Warning: there often is considerable room for disagreement concerning the "correct" answers to this question.
*a.* Oil well equipment
*b.* Computer hardware
*c.* Computer software
*d.* Genetic engineering
*e.* Railroads

**25.** For each pair of firms, choose the one that you think would be more sensitive to the business cycle.
*a.* General Autos or General Pharmaceuticals.
*b.* Friendly Airlines or Happy Cinemas.

**26.** Choose an industry and identify the factors that will determine its performance in the next three years. What is your forecast for performance in that time period?

**27.** You have $5,000 to invest for the next year and are considering three alternatives:
*a.* A money market fund with an average maturity of 30 days offering a current yield of 6 percent per year.
*b.* A one-year savings deposit at a bank offering an interest rate of 7.5 percent.
*c.* A 20-year Canada bond offering a yield to maturity of 9 percent per year.

What role does your forecast of future interest rates play in your decisions?

**28.** General Weedkillers dominates the chemical weed control market with its patented product Weed-ex. The patent is about to expire, however. What are your forecasts for changes in the industry? Specifically, what will happen to industry prices, sales, and profit prospects of General Weedkillers, and the profit prospects of its competitors? What stage of the industry life cycle do you think is relevant for the analysis of this market?

CFA

**29.** Which one of the following statements *best* expresses the central idea of countercyclical fiscal policy?
*a.* Planned government deficits are appropriate during economic booms, and planned surpluses are appropriate during economic recessions.
*b.* The balanced budget approach is the proper criterion for determining annual budget policy.
*c.* Actual deficits should equal actual surpluses during a period of deflation.
*d.* Government deficits are planned during economic recessions, and surpluses are utilized to restrain inflationary booms.

CFA

**30.** The supply-side view stresses that:
*a.* Aggregate demand is the major determinant of real output and aggregate employment.

*b.* An increase in government expenditures and tax rates will cause real income to rise.

*c.* Tax rates are a major determinant of real output and aggregate employment.

*d.* Expansionary monetary policy will cause real output to expand without causing the rate of inflation to accelerate.

**31.** Which *one* of the following propositions would a strong proponent of supply-side economics be *most* likely to stress?

*a.* Higher marginal tax rates will lead to a reduction in the size of the budget deficit and lower interest rates because they expand government revenues.

*b.* Higher marginal tax rates promote economic inefficiency and thereby retard aggregate output because they encourage investors to undertake low productivity projects with substantial tax-shelter benefits.

*c.* Income redistribution payments will exert little impact on real aggregate supply because they do not consume resources directly.

*d.* A tax reduction will increase the disposable income of households. Thus, the primary impact of a tax reduction on aggregate supply will stem from the influence of the tax change on the size of the budget deficit or surplus.

**32.** How would an economist who believes in crowding out complete the following sentence? "The increase in the budget deficit causes real interest rates to rise, and therefore private spending and investment to

*a.* Increase."

*b.* Stay the same."

*c.* Decrease."

*d.* Initially increase but eventually decrease."

**33.** If the central monetary authorities want to reduce the supply of money to slow the rate of inflation, the central bank should:

*a.* Sell government bonds, which will reduce the money supply; this will cause interest rates to rise and aggregate demand to fall.

*b.* Buy government bonds, which will reduce the money supply; this will cause interest rates to rise and aggregate demand to fall.

*c.* Decrease the discount rate, which will lower the market rate of interest; this will cause both costs and prices to fall.

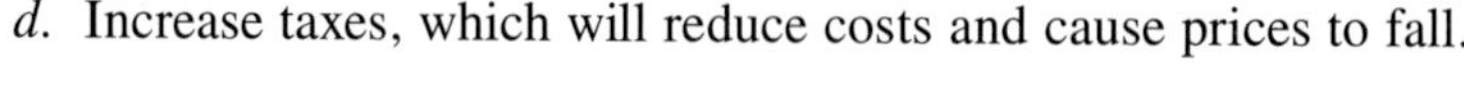

*d.* Increase taxes, which will reduce costs and cause prices to fall.

## APPENDIX 17A: DERIVATION OF THE DIVIDEND DISCOUNT MODEL

Consider an investor who buys a share of Steady State Electronics stock, planning to hold it for one year. The intrinsic value of the share is the present value of the dividend to be received at the end of the first year, $D_1$, and the expected sales price, $P_1$. We will henceforth use the simplest notation $P_1$ instead of $E(P_1)$ to avoid clutter. Keep in mind, though, future prices and dividends are unknown, and we are dealing with expected values, not certain values. Discounting at the cost of equity, $k$,

$$V_0 = \frac{D_1 + P_1}{1 + k} \tag{17A.1}$$

While dividends are fairly predictable given a company's history, you might ask how we can estimate $P_1$, the year-end price. According to Equation 17A.1, $V_1$ (the year-end value) will be

$$V_1 = \frac{D_2 + P_2}{1 + k}$$

If we assume the stock will be selling for its intrinsic value next year, then $V_1 = P_1$, and we can substitute this value for $P_1$ into Equation 17A.1 to find

$$V_0 = \frac{D_1}{1 + k} + \frac{D_2 + P_2}{(1 + k)^2}$$

This equation may be interpreted as the present value of dividends plus sales price for a two-year holding period. Of course, now we need to come up with a forecast of $P_2$. Continuing in the same way, we can replace $P_2$ by $(D_3 + P_3)/(1 + k)$, which relates $P_0$ to the value of dividends plus the expected sales price for a three-year holding period.

More generally, for a holding period of $H$ years, we can write the stock value as the present value of dividends over the $H$ years, plus the ultimate sale price, $P_H$

$$V_0 = \frac{D_1}{1 + k} + \frac{D_2}{(1 + k)^2} + \cdots + \frac{D_H + P_H}{(1 + k)^H} \tag{17A.2}$$

Note the similarity between this formula and the bond valuation formula developed in Chapter 14. Each relates price to the present value of a stream of payments (coupons in the case of bonds, dividends in the case of stocks) and a final payment (the face value of the bond, or the sales price of the stock). The key differences in the case of stocks are the uncertainty of dividends, the lack of a fixed maturity date, and the unknown sales price at the horizon date. Indeed, one can continue to substitute for price indefinitely to conclude

$$V_0 = \frac{D_1}{1+k} + \frac{D_2}{(1+k)^2} + \frac{D_3}{(1+k)^3} + \cdots \qquad \textbf{(17A.3)}$$

Equation 17A.3 states that the stock price should equal the present value of all expected future dividends into perpetuity. As discussed in Section 17.2, this formula is called the *dividend discount model (DDM)* of stock prices.

It is tempting, but incorrect, to conclude from Equation 17A.3 that the DDM focuses exclusively on dividends and ignores capital gains as a motive for investing in stock. Indeed, we assume explicitly in Equation 17A.1 that capital gains (as reflected in the expected sales price, $P_1$) are part of the stock's value. At the same time, the price at which you can sell a stock in the future depends on dividend forecasts at that time.

The reason only dividends appear in Equation 17A.3 is not that investors ignore capital gains. It is instead that those capital gains will be determined by dividend forecasts at the time the stock is sold. That is why in Equation 17A.2 we can write the stock price as the present value of dividends plus sales price for *any* horizon date. $P_H$ is the present value at time $H$ of all dividends expected to be paid after the horizon date. That value is then discounted back to today, time 0. The DDM asserts that stock prices are determined ultimately by the cash flows accruing to stockholders, and those are dividends.[18]

## The Constant Growth DDM

Equation 17A.3 as it stands is still not very useful in valuing a stock, because it requires dividend forecasts for every year into the indefinite future. For a more structured valuation approach, we need to introduce some simplifying assumptions. A useful first pass at the problem is to assume that Steady State Electronics dividends are trending upward at a stable growth rate, which we will call $g$. Then if $g = .05$, and the most recently paid dividend was $D_0 = 3.81$, expected future dividends would be

$$\begin{aligned} D_1 &= D_0(1+g) = 3.81 \times 1.05 = 4.00 \\ D_2 &= D_0(1+g)^2 = 3.81 \times (1.05)^2 = 4.20 \\ D_3 &= D_0(1+g)^3 = 3.81 \times (1.05)^3 = 4.41 \end{aligned}$$

and so on.

Using these dividend forecasts in Equation 17A.3, we solve for intrinsic value as

$$V_0 = \frac{D_0(1+g)}{1+k} + \frac{D_0(1+g)^2}{(1+k)^2} + \frac{D_0(1+g)^3}{(1+k)^3} + \cdots$$

[18] If investors never expected a dividend to be paid, then this model implies that the stock would have no value. To reconcile the fact that nondividend-paying stocks do have a market value with this model, one must assume that investors expect that some day it may pay out some cash, even if only a liquidating dividend.

This equation can be simplified to

$$V_0 = \frac{D_0(1 + g)}{k - g} = \frac{D_1}{k - g} \qquad \textbf{(17A.4)}$$

Note in Equation 17A.4 that we divide $D_1$ (not $D_0$) by $k - g$ to calculate intrinsic value. If the market capitalization rate for Steady State is 12 percent, now we can use Equation 17A.4 to show that the intrinsic value of a share of Steady State stock is

$$\frac{\$400}{.12 - .05} = \$57.14$$

Equation 17A.4 is called the *constant growth DDM* or the *Gordon model,* after Myron J. Gordon, who popularized the model. It should remind you of the formula for the present value of a perpetuity. If dividends were expected not to grow, then the dividend stream would be a simple perpetuity, and the valuation formula would be $P_0 = D_1/k$. Equation 17A.4 is a generalization of the perpetuity formula to cover the case of a *growing* perpetuity. As $g$ increases, the stock price also rises.[19]

The constant growth DDM is valid only when $g$ is less than $k$. If dividends were expected to grow forever at a rate faster than $k$, the value of the stock would be infinite. If an analyst derives an estimate of $g$ that is greater than $k$, that growth rate must be unsustainable in the long run. The appropriate valuation model to use in this case is a multistage DDM such as that discussed in Section 17.2.

---

19 Proof that the intrinsic value, $V_0$, of a stream of cash dividends growing at a constant rate, $g$, is equal to $\frac{D_1}{k - g}$.

By definition,

$$V_0 = \frac{D_1}{1 + k} + \frac{D_1(1 + g)}{(1 + k)^2} + \frac{D_1(1 + g)^2}{(1 + k)^3} + \cdots \qquad \textbf{(a)}$$

Multiplying through by $(1 + k)/(1 + g)$, we obtain

$$\frac{(1 + k)}{(1 + g)} V_0 = \frac{D_1}{(1 + g)} + \frac{D_1}{(1 + k)} + \frac{D_1(1 + g)}{(1 + k)^2} + \cdots \qquad \textbf{(b)}$$

Subtracting Equation (a) from Equation (b), we find that

$$\frac{(1 + k)}{(1 + g)} V_0 - V_0 = \frac{D_1}{(1 + g)}$$

which implies

$$\frac{(k - g)V_0}{(1 + g)} = \frac{D_1}{(1 + g)}$$

$$V_0 = \frac{D_1}{k - g}$$

The constant growth DDM is so widely used by stock market analysts that it is worth exploring some of its implications and limitations. The constant growth rate DDM implies that a stock's value will be greater:

1. The larger its expected dividend per share.
2. The lower the market capitalization rate, $k$.
3. The higher the expected growth rate of dividends.

Another implication of the constant growth model is that the stock price is expected to grow at the same rate as dividends. To see this, suppose Steady State stock is selling at its intrinsic value of \$57.14, so that $V_0 = P_0$. Then,

$$P_0 = \frac{D_1}{k - g}$$

Note that price is proportional to dividends. Therefore, next year, when the dividends paid to Steady State stockholders are expected to be higher by $g = 5$ percent, price also should increase by 5 percent. To confirm this, note

$$D_2 = \$4(1.05) = \$4.20$$
$$P_1 = D_2/(k - g) = \$4.20/(.12 - .05) = \$60.00$$

which is 5 percent higher than the current price of \$57.14. To generalize,

$$P_1 = \frac{D_2}{k - g} = \frac{D_1(1 + g)}{k - g} = \frac{D_1}{k - g}(1 + g)$$
$$= P_0(1 + g)$$

Therefore, the DDM implies that in the case of constant growth of dividends, the rate of price appreciation in any year will equal that constant growth rate, $g$.

## Appendix 17B: Contingent Claims Approach to Equity Valuation

In recent years, the theory of contingent claims pricing has been applied to common stocks.[20] This approach can be a useful adjunct to the valuation models presented earlier—especially the free cash flow model—if a firm has substantial debt in its capital structure. In this approach, common stock is viewed as a call option on the assets of the firm, with an exercise price equal to the face value of the debt.

For example, suppose the Hidett Corporation has assets worth \$100 million and debt with a face value of \$100 million. Although the book value of the equity may be zero, the common stock may still have a substantial market value. The equity is a call option in the sense that if the shareholders pay off the debt at its face

[20] See Scott Mason and Robert C. Merton, "The Role of Contingent Claims Analysis in Corporate Finance," in Altman and Subramanyam (editors), *Recent Advances in Corporate Finance* (Homewood, Ill.: Richard D. Irwin, Inc., 1985).

value at maturity, then they can keep the firm's assets; otherwise assets will belong to the creditors.

Viewing the equity of Hidett Corporation as a call option on the assets of the firm gives considerable insight into the determinants of its value, as well as a well-known methodology for estimating it. A detailed exposition of the techniques used is contained in Part VII, but one insight is worth mentioning now.

How will the value of Hidett's common stock be affected if the riskiness of the firm's assets (as measured by the standard deviation of their market value) increases? The answer is that the value of the common stock will increase, just as the price of an option increases when the standard deviation of the underlying security increases.

*Chapter* **18**

# Financial Statement Analysis

**IN THE PREVIOUS CHAPTER, WE EXPLORED EQUITY VALUATION TECHNIQUES.** These techniques take as inputs the firm's dividends and earnings prospects. While the valuation analyst is interested in economic earnings streams, only financial accounting data are readily available. What can we learn from a company's accounting data that can help us estimate the intrinsic value of its common stock?

In this chapter, we are not trying to develop the art of financial statement analysis, but rather to show how it relates to stock valuation analysis. We present much more complicated financial statements than are often seen in elementary corporate finance texts; this is to show the complexity and the potential variety of statements. In addition to discussing how to analyze the statements, we also show the importance of analysts' appraisals of sales and accounting information in forecasting economic earnings and the difficulties they have in formulating those appraisals. The market reaction to the combination of accounting releases and forecasts is important to understand.

We start by reviewing the basic sources of such data—the income statement, the balance sheet, and the statement of cash flows. We next discuss the difference between economic and accounting earnings. While economic earnings are more important for issues of valuation, we examine evidence suggesting that, whatever their shortcomings, accounting data still are useful in assessing the economic prospects of the firm. We show how analysts use financial ratios to explore the sources of a firm's profitability and evaluate the "quality" of its earnings in a systematic fashion. We also examine the impact of debt policy on various financial ratios. Finally, we conclude with a discussion of the limitations of financial statement analysis as a tool in uncovering mispriced securities. Some of these limitations are due to differences in firms' accounting procedures, while others arise from inflation-induced distortions in accounting numbers.

## 18.1 The Major Financial Statements

### The Income Statement

The **income statement** is a summary of the profitability of the firm over a period of time, such as a year. It presents revenues generated during the operating period, the expenses incurred during that same period, and the company's net income, which is simply the difference between revenues and expenses.

It is useful to distinguish four broad classes of expenses: cost of goods sold (COGS), which is the direct cost attributable to producing the product sold by the firm; salaries, advertising, and other costs of operating the firm that are not directly attributable to production; interest expense on the firm's debt; and taxes on earnings owed to federal and local governments. Typically, this simple breakdown of expenses is not immediately recognizable in the income statements of larger firms. Table 18.1 presents a 1995 income statement for Imperial Oil, which shows the consolidated amounts from its four business divisions. Revenues are derived from operational and investment sources; because of the interrelationship between the divisions, the unconsolidated statements also show interdivisional payments. Imperial Oil chooses to segregate its expenses by listing exploration, purchases of inputs, and operating expenses separately, all of which are part of COGS. Depreciation usually is mentioned as an additional production expense, but depletion also is a major item for a resource company as its reserves (of oil and gas, in this case) are used; as similar items governed by specified formulas, these two are merged in the expenses category. Federal excise taxes also are significant factors in determining the firm's operating costs.

Aggregating the total revenues less the sum of operating expenses (including overhead, which has been included without mention by Imperial in its category of operating expenses) gives total net revenues, often called *operating income.* At this point, peripheral sources of income or expense are included with other adjustments to obtain earnings before interest and taxes (EBIT). Imperial has noted unusual items in previous years due to workforce reductions and closing expenses; the resulting figure of $923 million for earnings before income taxes (*not* EBIT) can be used to reconstruct EBIT by adding back the financing cost already subtracted. Thus EBIT for Imperial is $923 plus $208, or $1,131 million. This is what the firm would have earned if not for its obligations to its creditors and the income tax authorities, and it is a measure of the profitability of the firm's operations ignoring the cost of debt financing. Finally, the effect of income taxes leads to net income, the "bottom line" of the income statement.

**Table 18.1** Consolidated Statement of Earnings for Imperial Oil (Millions of Dollars for the Years Ended December 31)

| | 1995 | 1994 | 1993 | 1992 | 1991 |
|---|---|---|---|---|---|
| **Revenues** | | | | | |
| Operating revenues | **9,285** | 8,805 | 8,757 | 8,939 | 9,412 |
| Interest and investment income | **159** | 100 | 108 | 175 | 62 |
| Total revenues | **9,444** | 8,905 | 8,865 | 9,114 | 9,474 |
| **Expenses** | | | | | |
| Exploration | **75** | 46 | 52 | 70 | 89 |
| Purchases of crude oil and products | **3,706** | 3,436 | 3,325 | 3,465 | 3,597 |
| Operating | **2,666** | 2,746 | 2,801 | 2,982 | 3,469 |
| Federal excise tax | **1,120** | 1,019 | 986 | 983 | 966 |
| Depreciation and depletion | **746** | 786 | 861 | 894 | 833 |
| Financing costs (11) | **208** | 172 | 177 | 166 | 216 |
| Total expenses | **8,521** | 8,205 | 8,202 | 8,560 | 9,170 |
| Unusual items (2) | **—** | (47) | (95) | (101) | (31) |
| Earnings before income taxes | **923** | 653 | 568 | 453 | 273 |
| Income taxes (7) | **409** | 294 | 289 | 258 | 111 |
| Net earnings | **514** | 359 | 279 | 195 | 162 |
| **Per-Share Information (Dollars)** | | | | | |
| Net earnings | **2.67** | 1.85 | 1.44 | 1.01 | 0.84 |
| Dividends | **1.90** | 4.80 | 1.80 | 1.80 | 1.80 |

(The notes are part of these consolidated financial statements.)

## The Balance Sheet

While the income statement provides a measure of the profitability over a period of time, the **balance sheet** provides a "snapshot" of the financial condition of the firm at a particular point in time. The balance sheet is a list of the firm's assets and liabilities at that moment. The difference in assets and liabilities is the net worth of the firm, also called *shareholders' equity*. Like income statements, balance sheets are reasonably standardized in presentation. Table 18.2 is the balance sheet of Imperial Oil for year-end 1995.

The first section of the balance sheet gives a listing of the assets of the firm. Current assets are presented first. These are cash and other items such as accounts receivable or inventories that will be converted into cash within one year. Imperial next lists the value of investments it has made and of related goodwill from past acquisitions in additon to the usual entry of the company's property, plant, and equipment. The sum of current and long-term assets, plus other adjustments, gives total assets, the last line of the assets side of the balance sheet.

**Table 18.2** Consolidated Balance Sheet for Imperial Oil (Millions of Dollars at December 31)

| | 1995 | 1994 | 1993 | 1992 | 1991 |
|---|---|---|---|---|---|
| **Assets** | | | | | |
| Current assets | **273** | 409 | 605 | 265 | 286 |
| Cash | | | | | |
| Marketable securities at amortized cost (3) | **378** | 859 | 874 | 757 | 7 |
| Promissory notes of an Exxon Corporation subsidiary (13) | **1,191** | — | — | — | — |
| Accounts receivable | **1,006** | 1,045 | 954 | 1,065 | 1,095 |
| Inventories of crude oil and products (14) | **385** | 384 | 402 | 468 | 604 |
| Materials, supplies, and prepaid expenses | **90** | 100 | 129 | 140 | 178 |
| Total current assets | **3,323** | 2,797 | 2,964 | 2,695 | 2,170 |
| Investments and other long-term assets | **254** | 264 | 152 | 159 | 204 |
| Property, plant, and equipment (1) | **8,170** | 8,538 | 9,389 | 9,965 | 10,760 |
| Goodwill | **305** | 329 | 356 | 373 | 400 |
| Total assets | **12,052** | 11,928 | 12,861 | 13,192 | 13,534 |
| **Liabilities** | | | | | |
| Current liabilities | **—** | — | — | — | 58 |
| Short-term debt | | | | | |
| Accounts payable and accrued liabilities (13) | **1,508** | 1,297 | 1,222 | 1,373 | 1,514 |
| Income taxes payable | **418** | 284 | 436 | 247 | 110 |
| Total current liabilities | **1,926** | 1,581 | 1,658 | 1,620 | 1,682 |
| Long-term debt (4) | **1,971** | 1,977 | 2,030 | 2,222 | 2,356 |
| Other long-term obligations (5) | **1,097** | 1,148 | 1,149 | 1,137 | 1,007 |
| Commitments and contingent liabilities (8) | | | | | |
| Total liabilities | **4,994** | 4,706 | 4,837 | 4,979 | 5,045 |
| Deferred income taxes | **1,150** | 1,227 | 1,458 | 1,577 | 1,699 |
| **Shareholders' Equity** | | | | | |
| Common shares at stated value (10) | **2,903** | 2,977 | 2,977 | 2,977 | 2,977 |
| Net earnings retained and used in the business | **3,018** | 3,589 | 3,659 | 3,813 | 3,999 |
| At beginning of year | | | | | |
| Net earnings for the year | **514** | 359 | 279 | 195 | 162 |
| Share purchases (10) | **(162)** | — | — | — | — |
| Dividends | **(365)** | (930) | (349) | (349) | (348) |
| At end of year | **3,005** | 3,018 | 3,589 | 3,659 | 3,813 |
| Total shareholders' equity | **5,908** | 5,995 | 6,566 | 6,636 | 6,790 |
| Total liabilities, deferred income taxes, and shareholders' equity | **12,052** | 11,928 | 12,861 | 13,192 | 13,534 |

The liability and shareholders' equity side is similarly arranged. First come short-term or current liabilities, such as accounts payable, accrued taxes, and debts due within one year. Following this is long-term debt and other liabilities due in more than a year, as well as other adjustments. The difference between total assets and total liabilities is shareholders' equity. This is the net worth or book value of the firm. Shareholders' equity is divided between preferred (none here) and common shareholders. The latter section usually is divided into value of common shares, contributed surplus (additional paid-in capital), and retained earnings; the first two of these represent the proceeds realized from the sale of shares to the public, while retained earnings derive from the buildup of equity from profits plowed back into the firm.

## The Statement of Changes in Financial Position

The **statement of changes in financial position** is also referred to as a *statement of cash flows* or *flow of funds statement.* It is a report of the cash flow generated by the firm's operations, investments, and financial activities. The income statement and balance sheet are based on accrual methods of accounting, which means revenues and expenses are recognized when incurred, even if no cash has yet been exchanged; this third statement, however, recognizes only the results of transactions in which cash changes hands. For example, if goods are sold now, with payment due in 60 days, the income statement will treat the revenue as generated when the sale occurs, and the balance sheet will be immediately augmented by accounts receivable less inventory; but the statement of changes in financial position will not recognize the transaction until the bill is paid and the cash is in hand.

Table 18.3 is the 1995 consolidated statement of changes in financial position for Imperial Oil. The first item under cash from operating activities is net income. The next entries modify that figure by components of income that have been recognized, but for which cash has not yet been exchanged. An increase in accounts receivable, for example, means income has been claimed on the income statement, but cash has not yet been collected. Hence, increases in accounts receivable reduce the cash flows realized from operations in this period. Similarly, increases in accounts payable mean expenses have been incurred, but cash has not yet left the firm. Any payment delay increases the company's net cash flows in this period.

Another major difference between the income statement and the statement of changes in financial position involves depreciation (and depletion for Imperial), which is a major addition to income in the adjustment section of cash provided in Table 18.3. The income statement attempts to "smooth" large capital expenditures over time to reflect a measure of profitability not distorted by large infrequent expenditures. The depreciation expense on the income statement is a way of doing this by recognizing capital expenditures over a period of many years rather than at the specific time of those expenditures.

The statement of cash flows, however, recognizes the cash implication of a capital expenditure when it occurs. It will ignore the depreciation "expense" over time, but will account for the full capital expenditure when it is paid in the second section, entitled cash flows from investing activities. Exploration expense is treated analogously.

Rather than smooth or allocate expenses over time, as in the income statement, the statement of cash flows reports cash flows separately for operations, investing, and financing activities. This way, any large cash flows (such as those for big

**Table 18.3** Consolidated Statement of Cash Flows for Imperial Oil (Millions of Dollars Inflow (Outflow) for the Years Ended December 31)

| | 1995 | 1994 | 1993 | 1992 | 1991 |
|---|---|---|---|---|---|
| **Operating Activities** | | | | | |
| Net earnings | **514** | 359 | 279 | 195 | 162 |
| Exploration expenses[(a)] | **75** | 46 | 52 | 70 | 89 |
| Depreciation and depletion | **746** | 786 | 861 | 894 | 833 |
| (Gain)/loss from asset sales and writedowns (2) | **—** | — | 55 | 101 | (94) |
| Deferred income taxes and other | **(39)** | (124) | (81) | (112) | 3 |
| Cash flow from earnings | **1,296** | 1,067 | 1,166 | 1,148 | 993 |
| Receivables | **55** | (120) | 126 | 57 | 400 |
| Inventories and prepaids | **11** | (45) | 77 | 174 | 208 |
| Liabilities | **280** | (119) | 69 | 57 | (421) |
| Change in operating assets and liabilities | **346** | (284) | 272 | 288 | 187 |
| Cash from operating activities | **1,642** | 783 | 1,438 | 1,436 | 1,180 |
| **Investing Activities** | | | | | |
| Capital and exploration expenditures[(a)] | **(570)** | (540) | (538) | (467) | (574) |
| Proceeds from asset sales | **135** | 559 | 122 | 245 | 410 |
| Marketable securities—net | **481** | 14 | (117) | (750) | (5) |
| Promissory notes of an Exxon Corporation subsidiary—net (13) | **(1,191)** | — | — | — | — |
| Cash from (used in) investing activities | **(1,145)** | 33 | (533) | (972) | (169) |
| Cash flow before financing activities | **497** | 816 | 905 | 464 | 1,011 |
| **Financing Activities** | | | | | |
| Long-term debt and capital lease | **1** | — | — | — | 228 |
| Repayment of long-term debt | **(40)** | (82) | (216) | (78) | (410) |
| Short-term debt—net | **—** | — | — | (58) | (241) |
| Common shares issued (purchased) (10) | **(236)** | — | — | — | 111 |
| Dividends paid | **(358)** | (930) | (349) | (349) | (347) |
| Cash used in financing activities | **(633)** | (1,012) | (565) | (485) | (659) |
| Increase (decrease) in cash | **(136)** | (196) | 340 | (21) | 352 |
| Cash at beginning of year | **409** | 605 | 265 | 286 | (66) |
| Cash at end of year | **273** | 409 | 605 | 265 | 286 |

[(a)]Exploration expenses, deducted in arriving at net earnings, are reclassified and included in investing activities in the consolidated statement of cash flows.

investments) can be recognized explicitly as nonrecurring, without affecting the measure of cash flow generated by operating activities.

The second section of the statement of cash flows is the accounting of cash flows from investing activities. These entries are investments in the capital stock necessary for the firm to maintain or enhance its productive capacity, and other financial investments; note that Imperial invested in $1,191 million of promissory notes of another subsidiary of its parent, Exxon.

Finally, the last section of the statement lists the cash flows resulting from financing activities. Issuance of securities will contribute positive cash flows, while repurchasing or redeeming securities will consume cash. For example, in 1995 Imperial repaid $40 million of debt versus the $1 million that it issued; additionally, its share repurchases and dividends used a significant amount ($594 million) of cash, leading to a final reduction in cash for the year of $136 million. Notice that while dividends paid are included in the cash flows from financing, interest payments on debt are included with operating activities, presumably because unlike dividends, interest payments are not discretionary.

The statement of cash flows provides evidence on the well-being of a firm. If a company cannot pay its dividends and maintain the productivity of its capital stock out of cash flow from operations, for example, and it must resort to borrowing to meet these demands, this is a serious warning that the firm cannot maintain dividend payout at its current level in the long run. The statement of cash flows will reveal this developing problem, when it shows that cash flow from operations is inadequate and that borrowing is being used to maintain dividend payments at unsustainable levels.

## 18.2 Accounting versus Economic Earnings

We've seen that stock valuation models require a measure of economic earnings or sustainable cash flow that can be paid out to stockholders without impairing the productive capacity of the firm. In contrast, **accounting earnings** are affected by several conventions regarding the valuation of assets, such as inventories (e.g., LIFO versus FIFO treatment), and by the way some expenditures, such as capital investments, are recognized over time (as depreciation expenses). We will discuss problems with some of these accounting conventions in greater detail later in the chapter. In addition to these accounting issues, as the firm makes its way through the business cycle, its earnings will rise above or fall below the trend line that might more accurately reflect sustainable economic earnings. This introduces an added complication in interpreting net income figures. One might wonder how closely accounting earnings approximate economic earnings and, correspondingly, how useful accounting data might be to investors attempting to value the firm.[1]

In fact, the net income figure on the firm's income statement does convey considerable information concerning a firm's prospects. We see this in the fact that stock prices tend to increase when firms announce earnings greater than market analysts or investors anticipate. There are several studies to this effect.

[1] In "The Trouble with Earnings," *Financial Analysts Journal,* September–October 1972, Jack Treynor points out some important difficulties with the accounting concept of earnings. In particular, he argues that the trouble stems from accountants' attempts to measure the value of assets.

In one well-known study, Foster, Olsen, and Shevlin[2] used time series of earnings for many firms to forecast the coming quarter's earnings announcement. They estimated an equation for more than 2,000 firms between 1974 and 1981:

$$E_{i,t} = E_{i,t-4} + a_i(E_{i,t-1} - E_{i,t-5}) + g_i$$

where

$E_{i,t}$ = Earnings of firm $i$ in quarter $t$

$a_i$ = Adjustment factor for firm $i$

$g_i$ = Growth factor for firm $i$

The rationale is that this quarter's earnings, $E_{i,t}$, will equal last year's earnings for the same quarter, $E_{i,t-4}$, plus a factor representing recent above-trend earnings performance as measured by the difference between last quarter's earnings and the corresponding quarter's earnings a year earlier, plus another factor that represents steady earnings growth over time. Regression techniques are used to estimate $a_i$ and $g_i$. Given these estimates, the equation is used together with past earnings to forecast future earnings.

Now it is easy to determine earnings surprises. Simply take the difference between actual earnings and forecasted or expected earnings, and see whether earnings surprises correlate with subsequent stock price movements.

Before doing so, however, these researchers introduced an extra refinement (first suggested by Latane and Jones[3]). Instead of using the earnings forecast error itself as the variable of interest, they first divided the forecast errors for each period by the standard deviation of forecast errors calculated from earlier periods; they effectively deflated the earnings surprise in a particular quarter by a measure of the typical surprise in an average quarter. This discounts forecast errors for firms with historically very unpredictable earnings. A large error for such firms might not be as significant as for a firm with typically very predictable earnings. The resulting "normalized" forecast error commonly is called the "standardized unexpected earnings" (SUE) measure. SUE is the variable that was correlated with stock price movements.

Each earnings announcement was placed in 1 of 10 deciles ranked by the magnitude of SUE, and the abnormal returns of the stock in each decile were calculated. The abnormal return in a period is the portfolio return after adjusting for both the market return in that period and the portfolio beta. It measures return over and above what would be expected given market conditions in that period. Figure 18.1 is a graph of the cumulative abnormal returns.

The results of this study are dramatic. The correlation between SUE ranking and abnormal returns across deciles is as predicted. There is a large abnormal

---

[2] George Foster, Chris Olsen, and Terry Shevlin, "Earnings Releases, Anomalies, and the Behavior of Security Returns," *The Accounting Review* 59, no. 4 (October 1984).

[3] H. A. Latane and C. P. Jones, "Standardized Unexpected Earnings—1971–1977," *Journal of Finance,* June 1979.

**Figure 18.1**
Cumulative abnormal returns in response to earnings announcements.

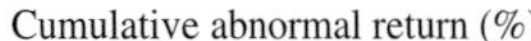


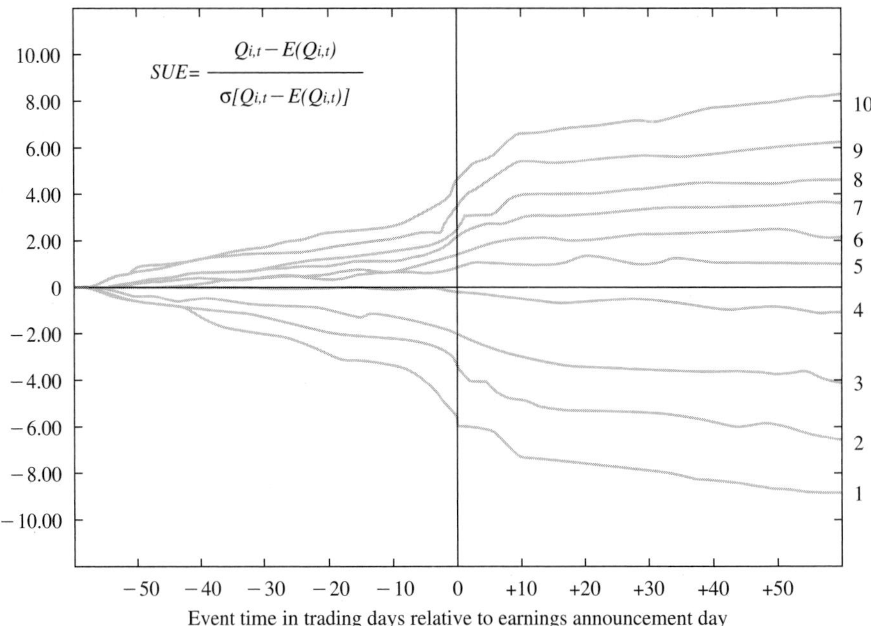


return (a large increase in cumulative abnormal return) on the earnings announcement day (time 0). The abnormal return is positive for high-SUE and negative for low-SUE (actually negative-SUE) firms.

The more remarkable, and disturbing, results of the study concerns stock price movements *after* the announcement date. The cumulative abnormal returns of high-SUE stocks continue to grow even after the earnings information becomes public, while the low-SUE firms continue to suffer negative abnormal returns. The market appears to adjust to the earnings information only gradually, resulting in a sustained period of abnormal returns.

Evidently, one can earn abnormal profits simply by waiting for earnings announcements and purchasing a stock portfolio of high-SUE companies. These are precisely the types of predictable continuing trends that ought to be impossible in an efficient market. This finding is not unique.

Some research suggests that the post-announcement drift in security prices might be related in part to trading costs. Bernard and Thomas[4] find that post-announcement abnormal returns increase with the magnitude of SUE until the earnings surprise becomes fairly large. Beyond this point, they speculate, the change in the perceived value of the firm due to the earnings announcement is so

[4] Victor L. Bernard and Jacob K. Thomas, "Post-Earnings-Announcement Drift: Delayed Price Response or Risk Premium?" *Journal of Accounting Research* 27 (1989), pp. 1–36.

large that transaction costs no longer impede trading. They also point out that post-announcement abnormal returns are larger for smaller firms, for which trading costs are higher. Still, these results do not satisfactorily explain the post-announcement drift anomaly. First, while trading costs may explain the existence of post-announcement drift, they do not explain why the total *post-announcement* abnormal return is higher for high-SUE firms. Second, Bernard and Thomas show that firms with positive earnings surprises in one quarter exhibit positive abnormal returns at the earnings announcement in the *following* quarter, suggesting that the market does not fully account for the implications of current earnings announcements when it revises its expectations for future earnings. This suggests informational inefficiency, leaving this phenomenon a topic for future research.

## Analysts' Forecasts and Stock Returns

You might wonder whether security analysts can predict earnings more accurately than can mechanical time series equations. After all, analysts have access to these statistical equations and to other qualitative and quantitative data. The evidence seems to be that analysts in fact do outperform such mechanical forecasts. Two recent Canadian studies analyzed the effect on stock prices of the release of estimated earnings by analysts and of revisions to forecasts announced by analysts. Their findings were consistent with earlier U.S. studies.[5] Both studies used the data contained in publicly available summary reports of analysts' forecasts.

In a test of market efficiency, Brown, Richardson, and Trzcinka[6] determined that there is a positive correlation between analysts' forecasts and abnormal returns in individual stocks. The forecasts of stock prices, presumably based on earnings estimates, are reported in the Research Evaluation Service of the *Financial Post Information Service.* The authors found that use of the service in a trading strategy led to significant excess returns, net of transactions costs. They also tested the significance of the benchmark for risk adjustment and concluded that the result was independent of the choice of a CAPM or APT approach; hence, they demonstrated that use of the simpler CAPM methodology was justified in this context.

L 'Her and Suret[7] examined the reaction to earnings revisions by measuring abnormal returns. Using the information in the *Institutional Brokers Estimate System* (IBES), they divided earnings revisions into quintiles by magnitude of the percentage change from greatest downward revision (quintile 1) to greatest upward revision (quintile 5). The findings were remarkably similar to those in the

[5] A good survey of American studies is given in D. Givoly and J. Lakonishok, "Properties of Analysts' Forecasts of Earnings: A Review and Analysis of the Research," *Journal of Accounting Literature,* 1984.

[6] Lawrence Brown, Gordon Richardson, and Charles Trzcinka, "Strong-Form Efficiency on the Toronto Stock Exchange: An Analysis of Analyst Price Forecasts," *Contemporary Accounting Research,* Spring 1991.

[7] Jean-Francois L 'Her and Jean-Marc Suret, "The Reaction of Canadian Securities to Revisions of Earnings," *Contemporary Accounting Research,* Spring 1991.

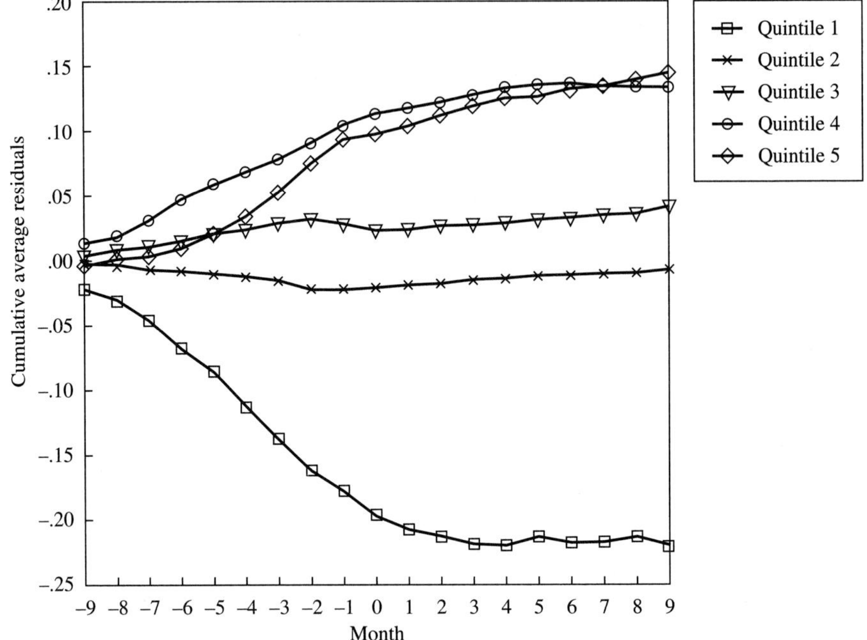


**Figure 18.2**
Cumulative average residuals in response to forecast revisions.

Latane and Jones study. Cumulative average residuals were recorded for the nine-month periods preceding and following the release by IBES of the revisions, as shown in Figure 18.2. Although most of the price reaction occurred in anticipation of the announcement, the extreme cases (quintiles 5 and 1) showed that abnormal returns persisted for nine months following release for upward revisions, but for only three months for downward revisions. (On the other hand, the reaction to unfavourable revisions was much more pronounced over the 18-month period.) Findings such as these may lead one to suspect the causality; it is possible that analysts revise their forecasts in response to price changes, which they interpret as inside information.

In an interesting observation, L 'Her and Suret note that segregating the data by industrial sector gave varied results. Using a three-sector classification, they found that the primary sector, with unpredictable commodity prices determining earnings, did not react to earnings revisions, while the other two sectors did; the secondary sector had a major reaction, such that purchase or sale of stock, including commissions, after an announced revision yielded significant gains. They also noted that if the revision occurs close to the end of the fiscal year, the signal is more reliable.

The *Value Line Investment Survey* is an influential service that provides reports of most of the recognized publicly traded stocks in the United States, including many large Canadian firms. Brown and Rozeff[8] compared earnings forecasts from Value Line with those made using a sophisticated statistical technique called a Box-Jenkins model. The Value Line forecasts generally were more accurate. Whereas 54 percent of the Box-Jenkins forecasts were within 25 percent of the realized values, and 26.5 percent were within 10 percent, 63.5 percent of the Value Line forecasts were within 25 percent and 23 percent were within 10 percent. Apparently, the qualitative data and firm-specific fundamental analysis that analysts bring to bear are of value.[9]

## 18.3 Return on Equity

### Past versus Future ROE

We noted in Chapter 17 that **return on equity (ROE)** is one of the two basic factors in determining a firm's growth rate of earnings. There are two sides to using ROE. Sometimes it is reasonable to assume that future ROE will approximate its past value, but a high ROE in the past does not necessarily imply a firm's future ROE will be high.

A declining ROE, on the other hand, is evidence that the firm's new investments have offered a lower ROE than its past investments. The best forecast of future ROE in this case may be lower than the most recent ROE. The vital point for an analyst is not to accept historical values as indicators of future values. Data from the recent past may provide information regarding future performance, but the analyst should always keep an eye on the future. It is expectations of future dividends and earnings that determine the intrinsic value of the company's stock.

### Financial Leverage and ROE

An analyst interpreting the past behaviour of a firm's ROE or forecasting its future value must pay careful attention to the firm's debt-equity mix and to the interest rate on its debt. An example will show why. Suppose Nodett is a firm that is all equity financed and has total assets of $100 million. Assume it pays corporate taxes at the rate of 40 percent of taxable earnings.

Table 18.4 shows the behaviour of sales, earnings before interest and taxes, and net profits under three scenarios representing phases of the business cycle. It also shows the behaviour of two of the most commonly used profitability measures: operating **return on assets (ROA),** which equals EBIT/assets, and ROE, which equals net profits/equity.

Somdett is an otherwise identical firm to Nodett, but $40 million of its $100 million of assets are financed with debt bearing an interest rate of 8 percent. It

[8] Lawrence D. Brown and Michael Rozeff, "The Superiority of Analysts' Forecasts as Measures of Expectations: Evidence from Earnings," *Journal of Finance,* March 1978.

[9] See Section 19.5 for more on Value Line.

**Table 18.4** Nodett's Profitability over the Business Cycle

| Scenario | Sales ($ millions) | EBIT ($ millions) | ROA (% per year) | Net Profit ($ millions) | ROE ($ per year) |
|---|---|---|---|---|---|
| Bad year | 80 | 5 | 5 | 3 | 3 |
| Normal year | 100 | 10 | 10 | 6 | 6 |
| Good year | 120 | 15 | 15 | 9 | 9 |

**Table 18.5** Impact of Financial Leverage on ROE

| | | Nodett | | Somdett | |
|---|---|---|---|---|---|
| Scenario | EBIT ($ millions) | Net Profits ($ millions) | ROE (%) | Net Profits* ($ millions) | ROE† (%) |
| Bad year | 5 | 3 | 3 | 1.08 | 1.8 |
| Normal year | 10 | 6 | 6 | 4.08 | 6.8 |
| Good year | 15 | 9 | 9 | 7.08 | 11.8 |

*Somdett's after-tax profits are given by .6(EBIT − $3.2 million).
†Somdett's equity is only $60 million.

pays annual interest expense of $3.2 million. Table 18.5 shows how Somdett's ROE differs from Nodett's.

Note that annual sales, EBIT, and therefore ROA for both firms are the same in each of the three scenarios, that is, business risk for the two companies is identical. It is their financial risk that differs. Although Nodett and Somdett have the same ROA in each scenario, Somdett's ROE exceeds that of Nodett in normal and good years and is lower in bad years.

We can summarize the exact relationship among ROE, ROA, and leverage in the following equation:[10]

[10] The derivation of equation 18.1 is as follows:

$$\begin{aligned}
\text{ROE} &= \frac{\text{Net profit}}{\text{Equity}} \\
&= \frac{\text{EBIT} - \text{Interest} - \text{Taxes}}{\text{Equity}} \\
&= \frac{(1 - \text{Tax rate})(\text{EBIT} - \text{Interest})}{\text{Equity}} \\
&= (1 - \text{Tax rate})\frac{(\text{ROA} \times \text{Assets} - \text{Interest rate} \times \text{Debt})}{\text{Equity}} \\
&= (1 - \text{Tax rate})\left[\text{ROA} \times \frac{(\text{Equity} + \text{Debt})}{\text{Equity}} - \text{Interest rate} \times \frac{\text{Debt}}{\text{Equity}}\right] \\
&= (1 - \text{Tax rate})\left[\text{ROA} + (\text{ROA} - \text{Interest rate})\frac{\text{Debt}}{\text{Equity}}\right]
\end{aligned}$$

$$\text{ROE} = (1 - \text{Tax rate})\left[\text{ROA} + (\text{ROA} - \text{Interest rate})\frac{\text{Debt}}{\text{Equity}}\right] \quad \textbf{(18.1)}$$

The relationship has the following implications. If there is no debt or if the firm's ROA equals the interest rate on its debt, its ROE will simply equal (1 − Tax rate) × ROA. If its ROA exceeds the interest rate, then its ROE will exceed (1 − Tax rate) × ROA by an amount that will be greater the higher the debt-to-equity ratio.

This result makes intuitive sense: If ROA exceeds the borrowing rate, the firm earns more on its money than it pays out to creditors. The surplus earnings are available to the firm's owners, the equityholders, which raises ROE. If, on the other hand, ROA is less than the interest rate, then ROE will decline by an amount that depends on the debt-to-equity ratio.

To illustrate the application of equation 18.1, we can use the numerical example in Table 18.5. In a normal year, Nodett has an ROE of 6 percent, which is .6(1 − Tax rate) × its ROA of 10 percent. However, Somdett, which borrows at an interest rate of 8 percent and maintains a debt/equity ratio of ⅔, has an ROE of 6.8 percent. The calculation using equation 18.1 is

$$\begin{aligned}\text{ROE} &= .6[10\% + (10\% - 8\%)\tfrac{2}{3}] \\ &= .6[10\% + \tfrac{4}{3}\%] \\ &= 6.8\%\end{aligned}$$

The important point to remember is that increased debt will make a positive contribution to a firm's ROE only if the firm's ROA exceeds the interest rate on the debt.

Note also that financial leverage increases the risk of the equityholder returns. Table 18.5 shows that ROE on Somdett is worse than that of Nodett in bad years. Conversely, in good years, Somdett outperforms Nodett because the excess of ROA over ROE provides additional funds for equityholders. The presence of debt makes Somdett more sensitive to the business cycle than Nodett. Even though the two companies have equal business risk (reflected in their identical EBITs in all three scenarios), Somdett carries greater financial risk than Nodett.

Even if financial leverage increases the expected ROE of Somdett relative to Nodett (as it seems to in Table 18.5), this does not imply the market value of Somdett's equity will be higher.[11] Financial leverage increases the risk of the firm's equity as surely as it raises the expected ROE.

Increased operating leverage has a similar effect in magnifying the results of increased sales into greater percentage increases in EBIT. Higher fixed costs work as do fixed financial charges; until sales reach a certain level, lower operating leverage will be superior in terms of EBIT. Given the principle of matching the financing of fixed assets with long-term capital, high operating leverage companies

[11] This is the essence of the debate on the Modigliani–Miller theorems regarding the effect of financial leverage on the value of the firm. For a discussion of the issues and evidence, see footnotes 9 and 10 in Chapter 17.

will probably have higher debt loads and interest charges. Thus total leverage, a product of financial and operating leverage, will be even higher, indicating a greater sensitivity to the sales cycle. Conceivably, lower operating leverage combined with higher financial leverage could make one firm equally sensitive to sales changes as another with the reversed leverage position; practically, it is unlikely to happen. Risk and cyclical response tend to be high or low by the nature of the particular industry, where optimal operating structures will suggest roughly equal degrees of operating leverage, financed with similar debt ratios.

**CONCEPT CHECK** Question 1. Mordett is a company with the same assets as Nodett and Somdett but a debt-to-equity ratio of 1.0 and an interest rate of 9 percent. What would its net profit and ROE be in a bad year, a normal year, and a good year?

## 18.4 RATIO ANALYSIS

### Decomposition of ROE

To understand the factors affecting a firm's ROE, including its trend over time and its performance relative to competitors, analysts often "decompose" ROE into the product of a series of ratios. Each component ratio is in itself meaningful, and the process serves to focus the analyst's attention on the separate factors influencing performance.[12]

One useful decomposition of ROE is

$$\text{ROE} = \frac{\text{Net profit}}{\text{Pretax profit}} \times \frac{\text{Pretax profit}}{\text{EBIT}} \times \frac{\text{EBIT}}{\text{Sales}} \times \frac{\text{Sales}}{\text{Assets}} \times \frac{\text{Assets}}{\text{Equity}}$$

$$(1) \times (2) \times (3) \times (4) \times (5)$$

These five ratios are given for Nodett and Somdett under three different economic scenarios in Table 18.6.

The product of factors 3 and 4 is EBIT/Assets or the ROA. Factor 3 is known as the firm's operating profit margin or **return on sales** (ROS). ROS shows operating profit per dollar of sales. In an average year, Nodett's ROS is 0.10, or 10 percent; in a bad year, it is 0.0625, or 6.25 percent; and in a good year, it is .125, or 12.5 percent. Factor 4, the ratio of sales to assets, is known as **asset turnover** (ATO). It indicates the efficiency of the firm's use of assets in the sense that it measures the annual sales generated by each dollar of assets. In a normal year, Nodett's ATO is 1.0 per year, meaning that sales of $1 per year were generated per dollar of assets. In a bad year, this ratio declines to 0.8 per year, and in a good year, it rises to 1.2 per year. Since the two factors are independent of finan-

[12] This kind of decomposition of ROE is often called the *Du Pont system*.

**Table 18.6** Ratio Decomposition Analysis for Nodett and Somdett

| | ROE | (1) Net Profit / Pretax Profit | (2) Pretax Profit / EBIT | (3) EBIT / Sales (ROS) | (4) Sales / Assets (ATO) | (5) Assets / Equity | (6) Compound Leverage Factor (2) × (5) |
|---|---|---|---|---|---|---|---|
| **Bad Year** | | | | | | | |
| Nodett | .030 | .6 | 1.000 | .0625 | .800 | 1.000 | 1.000 |
| Somdett | .018 | .6 | .360 | .0625 | .800 | 1.667 | .600 |
| **Normal Year** | | | | | | | |
| Nodett | .060 | .6 | 1.000 | .100 | 1.000 | 1.000 | 1.000 |
| Somdett | .068 | .6 | .680 | .100 | 1.000 | 1.667 | 1.134 |
| **Good Year** | | | | | | | |
| Nodett | .090 | .6 | 1.000 | .125 | 1.200 | 1.000 | 1.000 |
| Somdett | .118 | .6 | .787 | .125 | 1.200 | 1.667 | 1.311 |

cial leverage, they are identical for the two firms under all scenarios, as is factor 1, known as the *tax-burden ratio.* Ratio 1 is unaffected by the business cycle, provided the tax code and the policies of the firm to deal with the tax burden remain unchanged.

Factors 2 and 5, unlike the others, are affected by capital structure. Factor 2 is the ratio of pretax profits to EBIT. The firm's pretax profits will be greatest when there are no interest payments to be made to debt holders. In fact, another way to express this ratio is

$$\frac{\text{Pretax profits}}{\text{EBIT}} = \frac{\text{EBIT} - \text{Interest expense}}{\text{EBIT}}$$

We will call this factor the *interest-burden* (IB) ratio. The higher the degree of financial leverage, the lower the IB ratio, with a maximum value of 1, as for Nodett, reflecting the absence of interest payments; this is unchanging under economic conditions. For Somdett, however, because interest expense is fixed in dollar amounts while EBIT varies, the IB ratio varies from a low of 0.36 in a bad year to a high of 0.787 in a good year.

Factor 5, the ratio of assets to equity, is a measure of the firm's degree of financial leverage. It is called the **leverage ratio** and is equal to 1 + the debt-to-equity ratio.[13] In our numerical example in Table 18.6, Nodett has a leverage ratio of 1 while Somdett's is 1.667. From our discussion in Section 18.3, we know that

[13] $\frac{\text{Assets}}{\text{Equity}} = \frac{\text{Equity} + \text{Debt}}{\text{Equity}} = 1 + \frac{\text{Debt}}{\text{Equity}}$

**Table 18.7** Differences between ROS and ATO across Industries

| | ROS | × | ATO | = | ROA |
|---|---|---|---|---|---|
| Supermarket chain | .02 | | 5.0 | | .10 |
| Gas utility | .20 | | 0.5 | | .10 |

financial leverage helps boost ROE only if ROA is greater than the interest rate on the firm's debt. How is this fact reflected in the ratios of Table 18.6?

The answer is that to measure the full impact of leverage in this framework, the analyst must take the product of the IB and leverage ratios (that is, factors 2 and 5, shown in Table 18.6 as column 6). For Nodett, factor 6, which we call the *compound leverage factor,* remains a constant 1.0 under all three scenarios. But for Somdett, we see that the compound leverage factor is greater than 1 in normal years (1.134) and in good years (1.311), indicating the positive contribution of financial leverage to ROE. It is less than 1 in bad years, reflecting the fact that when ROA falls below the interest rate, ROE falls with increased use of debt.

We can summarize all of these relationships as follows:

$$\text{ROE} = \text{Tax burden} \times \text{Interest burden} \times \text{Margin} \times \text{Turnover} \times \text{Leverage}$$

Because

$$\text{ROA} = \text{Margin} \times \text{Turnover}$$

and

$$\text{Compound leverage factor} = \text{Interest burden} \times \text{Leverage}$$

we can decompose ROE equivalently as follows:

$$\text{ROE} = \text{Tax burden} \times \text{ROA} \times \text{Compound leverage factor}$$

Table 18.6 compares firms with the same ROS and ATO but different degrees of financial leverage. Comparison of ROS and ATO usually is meaningful only in evaluating firms in the same industry. Cross-industry comparisons of these two ratios often are meaningless and can even be misleading.

For example, let us take two firms with the same ROA of 10 percent per year. The first is a supermarket chain, the second is a gas utility. As Table 18.7 shows, the supermarket chain as a "low" ROS of 2 percent and achieves a 10 percent ROA by "turning over" its assets five times per year. The capital-intensive utility, on the other hand, has a "low" ATO of only 0.5 times per year and achieves its 10 percent ROA by having an ROS of 20 percent. The point here is that a "low" ROS or ATO ratio need not indicate a troubled firm. Each ratio must be interpreted in light of industry norms.

Even within an industry, ROS and ATO sometimes can differ markedly among firms pursuing different marketing strategies. In the retailing industry, for example, Holt-Renfrew pursues a high-margin, low-ATO policy compared to Zellers, which pursues a low-margin, high-ATO policy.

**CONCEPT CHECK** Question 2. Do a ratio decomposition analysis for Mordett of question 1, preparing a table similar to Table 18.6.

## Turnover and Other Asset Utilization Ratios

It is often helpful in understanding a firm's ratio of sales to assets to compute comparable efficiency-of-utilization, or turnover, ratios for subcategories of assets. For example, fixed-asset turnover would be

$$\frac{\text{Sales}}{\text{Fixed assets}}$$

This ratio measures sales per dollar of the firm's money tied up in fixed assets.

To illustrate how you can compute this and other ratios from a firm's financial statements, consider Growth Industries, Inc. (GI). GI's income statement and opening and closing balance sheets for the years 19X1, 19X2, and 19X3 appear in Table 18.8. GI's total asset turnover in 19X3 was 0.303, which was below the industry average of 0.4. To understand better why GI underperformed, we decide to compute asset utilization ratios separately for fixed assets, inventories, and accounts receivable.

GI's sales in 19X3 were $144 million. Its only fixed assets were plant and equipment, which were $216 million at the beginning of the year and $259.2 million at year's end. Average fixed assets for the year were, therefore, $237.6 million [($216 million + $259.2 million)/2]. GI's fixed asset turnover for 19X3 was $144 million per year/$237.6 million = .606 per year. In other words, for every dollar of fixed assets, there were $.606 in sales during the year 19X3.

Comparable figures for the fixed-asset turnover ratio for 19X1, 19X2, 19X3, and the 19X3 industry average are

| 19X1 | 19X2 | 19X3 | 19X3 Industry Average |
|---|---|---|---|
| .606 | .606 | .606 | .700 |

GI's fixed asset turnover has been stable over time and below the industry average.

Whenever a financial ratio includes one item from the income statement, which covers a period of time, and another from the balance sheet, which is a "snapshot" taken at a particular time, the practice is to take the average of the beginning and end-of-year balance sheet figures. Thus, in computing the fixed-asset turnover ratio you divide sales (from the income statement) by average fixed assets (from the balance sheet).

**Table 18.8** Growth Industries Financial Statements, 19X1–19X3 ($ thousands)

| | 19X0 | 19X1 | 19X2 | 19X3 |
|---|---|---|---|---|
| **Income Statements** | | | | |
| Sales revenue | | $100,000 | $120,000 | $144,000 |
| Cost of goods sold (including depreciation) | | 55,000 | 66,000 | 79,200 |
| Depreciation | | 15,000 | 18,000 | 21,600 |
| Selling and administrative expenses | | 15,000 | 18,000 | 21,600 |
| Operating income | | 30,000 | 36,000 | 43,200 |
| Interest expense | | 10,500 | 19,095 | 34,391 |
| Taxable income | | 19,500 | 16,905 | 8,809 |
| Income tax (40% rate) | | 7,800 | 6,762 | 3,524 |
| Net income | | 11,700 | 10,143 | 5,285 |
| **Balance Sheets (End of Year)** | | | | |
| Cash and marketable securities | $ 50,000 | $ 60,000 | $ 72,000 | $ 86,400 |
| Accounts receivable | 25,000 | 30,000 | 36,000 | 43,200 |
| Inventories | 75,000 | 90,000 | 108,000 | 129,600 |
| Net plant and equipment | 150,000 | 180,000 | 216,000 | 259,200 |
| **Total assets** | **$300,000** | **$360,000** | **$432,000** | **$518,400** |
| Accounts payable | $ 30,000 | $ 36,000 | $ 43,200 | $ 51,840 |
| Short-term debt | 45,000 | 87,300 | 141,957 | 214,432 |
| Long-term debt (8% bonds maturing in 19X7) | 75,000 | 75,000 | 75,000 | 75,000 |
| **Total liabilities** | **$150,000** | **$198,300** | **$260,157** | **$341,272** |
| Shareholders' equity (1 million shares outstanding) | $150,000 | $161,700 | $171,843 | $177,128 |
| **Other data** | | | | |
| Market price per common share at year-end | | $93.60 | $61.00 | $21.00 |

Another widely followed turnover ratio is the inventory turnover ratio, which is the ratio of cost of goods sold per dollar of inventory. It is usually expressed as cost of goods sold (instead of sales revenue) divided by average inventory. It measures the speed with which inventory is turned over.

In 19X1, GI's cost of goods sold (less depreciation) was $40 million, and its average inventory was $82.5 million [($75 million + $90 million)/2]. Its inventory turnover was 0.485 per year ($40 million/$82.5 million). In 19X2 and 19X3, inventory turnover remained the same and continued below the industry average of 0.5 per year.

The ratio of accounts receivable to sales also is a measure of efficiency. This ratio usually is computed as (Average accounts receivable/Sales) × 365. The result is a number called the **average collection period,** or **days receivables,** which equals the total credit extended to customers per dollar of daily sales. It is the number of days' worth of sales tied up in accounts receivable. You also can think of it as the average lag between the date of sale and the date payment is received. In 19X3, the industry average was 60 days, while for GI the ratio was

$$\frac{(\$36 \text{ million} + \$43.2 \text{ million})/2}{\$144 \text{ million}} \times 365 = 100.4 \text{ days}$$

In summary, use of these ratios lets us see that GI's poor total asset turnover relative to the industry is in part caused by lower-than-average fixed asset turnover and inventory turnover and higher than average days receivables. This suggests GI may be having problems with excess plant capacity along with poor inventory and receivables management procedures.

## Liquidity and Coverage Ratios

Liquidity and interest coverage ratios are of great importance in evaluating the riskiness of a firm's securities. They aid in assessing the financial strength of the firm.

Liquidity ratios include the current ratio, quick ratio, and interest coverage ratio.

1. **Current ratio:** Current assets/Current liabilities. This ratio measures the ability of the firm to pay off its current liabilities by liquidating its current assets (i.e., turning them into cash). It indicates the firm's ability to avoid insolvency in the short run. GI's current ratio in 19X1, for example, was (60 + 30 + 90)/(36 + 87.3) = 1.46. In other years, it was

| 19X1 | 19X2 | 19X3 | 19X3 Industry Average |
|---|---|---|---|
| 1.46 | 1.17 | .97 | 2.0 |

   This represents an unfavourable time trend and poor standing relative to the industry.
2. **Quick ratio:** (Cash + Receivables)/Current liabilities. This ratio also is called the **acid test ratio.** It has the same denominator as the current ratio, but its numerator includes only cash, cash equivalents, and receivables. The quick ratio is a better measure of liquidity than the current ratio for firms whose inventory is not readily convertible into cash. GI's quick ratio shows the same disturbing trends as its current ratio:

| 19X1 | 19X2 | 19X3 | 19X3 Industry Average |
|---|---|---|---|
| .73 | .58 | .49 | 1.0 |

3. **Interest coverage ratio:** EBIT/Interest expense. This ratio often is called **times interest earned.** It is closely related to the interest-burden ratio discussed in the previous section. A high coverage ratio tells the firm's shareholders and lenders that the likelihood of bankruptcy is low because annual earnings are significantly greater than annual interest obligations. It is widely used by both lenders and borrowers in determining the firm's debt

capacity and is a major determinant of the firm's bond rating. GI's interest coverage ratios are

| 19X1 | 19X2 | 19X3 | 19X3 Industry Average |
|---|---|---|---|
| 2.86 | 1.89 | 1.26 | 5 |

GI's interest coverage ratio has fallen dramatically over this three-year period, and by 19X3 it is far below the industry average. Probably its credit rating has been declining as well, and no doubt GI is considered a relatively poor credit risk in 19X3.

## Market Price Ratios

There are two market price ratios: the market-to-book-value ratio and the price/earnings ratio.

The **market-to-book-value ratio** (P/B) equals the market price of a share of the firm's common stock divided by its *book value,* that is, shareholders' equity per share. Analysts sometimes consider the stock of a firm with a low market-to-book value to be a "safer" investment, seeing the book value as a "floor" supporting the market price.

Analysts presumably view book value as the level below which market price will not fall because the firm always has the option to liquidate, or sell, its assets for their book values. However, this view is questionable. In fact, some firms, such as Digital Equipment, do sometimes sell for less than book value. Nevertheless, low market-to-book-value ratio is seen by some as providing a "margin of safety," and some analysts will screen out or reject high P/B firms in their stock selection process.

Proponents of the P/B screen would argue that, if all other relevant attributes are the same for two stocks, the one with the lower P/B ratio is safer. Although there may be firms for which this approach has some validity, book value does not necessarily represent liquidation value, which renders the margin of safety notion unreliable.

The theory of equity valuation offers some insight into the significance of the P/B ratio. A high P/B ratio is an indication that investors think a firm has opportunities of earning a rate of return on their investment in excess of the market capitalization rate, $k$.

To illustrate this point, we can return to the numerical example in Chapter 17, Section 17.3 and its accompanying table. That example assumes the market capitalization rate is 12 percent per year. Now add the assumptions that the book value per share is $8.33, and that the coming year's expected EPS is $1, so that in the case for which the expected ROE on future investment also is 12 percent, the stock will sell at $1/.12 = $8.33, and the P/B ratio will be 1.

Table 18.9 shows the P/B ratio for alternative assumptions about future ROE and plowback ratio. Reading down any column, you can see how the P/B ratio

**Table 18.9** P/B under Varying ROE and Plowback Ratios

| | Plowback Ratio (*b*) | | | |
|---|---|---|---|---|
| **ROE** | **0** | **25%** | **50%** | **75%** |
| 10% | 1.00 | .95 | .86 | .67 |
| 12% | 1.00 | 1.00 | 1.00 | 1.00 |
| 14% | 1.00 | 1.06 | 1.20 | 2.00 |

The assumptions and formulas underlying this table are: $E_1$ = \$1; book value per share = \$8.33; $k$ = 12% per year.

$$g = b \times \text{ROE}$$
$$P_0 = \frac{(1 - b)E}{k - g}$$
$$\text{P/B} = P_0/\$8.33$$

changes with ROE. The numbers reveal that, for a given plowback ratio, the higher the expected ROE, the higher is the P/B ratio. This makes sense, because the greater the expected profitability of the firm's future investment opportunities, the greater its market value as an ongoing enterprise compared with the cost of acquiring its assets.

We've noted that the **price/earnings ratio** that is based on the firm's financial statements and reported in newspaper stock listings is not the same as the price/earnings multiple that emerges from a discounted dividend model. The numerator is the same (the market price of the stock), but the denominator is different. The P/E ratio uses the most recent past accounting earnings, while the P/E multiple predicted by valuation models uses expected future economic earnings.

Many security analysts pay careful attention to the accounting P/E ratio in the belief that among low P/E stocks they are somehow more likely to find bargains than with high P/E stocks. The idea is that you can acquire a claim on a dollar of earnings more cheaply if the P/E ratio is low. For example, if the P/E ratio is 8, you pay \$8 per share per \$1 of *current* earnings, while if the P/E is 12, you must pay \$12 for a claim on \$1 of current earnings.

Note, however, that current earnings may differ substantially from future earnings. The higher P/E stock still may be a bargain relative to the low P/E stock if its earnings and dividends are expected to grow at a faster rate. Our point is that ownership of the stock conveys the right to future earnings, as well as to current earnings. An exclusive focus on the commonly reported accounting P/E ratio can be shortsighted, because by its nature it ignores future growth in earnings.

An efficient markets adherent will be skeptical of the notion that a strategy of investing in low P/E stocks would result in an expected rate of return greater than that of investing in high or medium P/E stocks having the same risk. The empirical evidence on this question is mixed, but if the strategy had worked in the past, it almost surely would not work in the future because too many investors would be following it.[14]

Before leaving the P/B and P/E ratios, it is worth pointing out the relationship among these ratios and ROE:

$$\begin{aligned} \text{ROE} &= \frac{\text{Earnings}}{\text{Book value}} \\ &= \frac{\text{Market price}}{\text{Book value}} \div \frac{\text{Market price}}{\text{Earnings}} \\ &= \text{P/B ratio} \div \text{P/E ratio} \end{aligned}$$

By rearranging the terms, we find that a firm's **earnings yield,** the ratio of earnings to price, is equal to its ROE divided by the market-to-book-value ratio:

$$\frac{E}{P} = \frac{\text{ROE}}{\text{P/B}}$$

Thus, a company with a high ROE can have a relatively low earnings yield because its P/B ratio is high. This indicates a high ROE does not in and of itself imply the stock is a good buy: The price of the stock already may be bid up to reflect an attractive ROE. If so, the P/B ratio will be above 1.0, and the earnings yield to stockholders will be below the ROE, as the equation demonstrates. The relationship shows that a strategy of investing in the stock of high ROE firms may produce a lower holding-period return than investing in those with a low ROE.

Clayman (1987)[15] found that investing in the stock of 29 "excellent" companies, with mean reported ROE of 19.05 percent during the period 1976 to 1980, produced results much inferior to investing in 39 "unexcellent" companies, those with a mean ROE of 7.09 percent during the period. An investor putting equal dollar amounts in the stocks of the unexcellent companies would have earned a portfolio rate of return over the 1981–1985 period that was 11.3 percent higher per year than the rate of return on a comparable portfolio of excellent company stocks.

---

**CONCEPT CHECK** Question 3. What were GI's ROE, P/E, and P/B ratios in the year 19X3? How do they compare to the industry average ratios, which were:

ROE = 8.64%

P/E = 8

P/B = .69

How does GI's earnings yield in 19X3 compare to the industry's average?

---

[14] See the discussion of this point in Chapter 11, on market efficiency.

[15] Michelle Clayman, "In Search of Excellence: The Investor's Viewpoint," *Financial Analysts Journal,* May/June 1987.

## 18.5 An Illustration of Financial Statement Analysis

In her 19X3 annual report to the shareholders of Growth Industries, Inc., the president wrote: "19X3 was another successful year for Growth Industries. As in 19X2, sales, assets, and operating income all continued to grow at a rate of 20 percent." Is she right?

We can evaluate her statement by conducting a full-scale ratio analysis of Growth Industries. Our purpose is to assess GI's performance in the recent past, to evaluate its future prospects, and to determine whether its market price reflects its intrinsic value.

Table 18.10 shows the key financial ratios we can compute from GI's financial statements. The president is certainly right about the growth in sales, assets, and operating income. Inspection of GI's key financial ratios, however, contradicts her first sentence: 19X3 was not another successful year for GI—it appears to have been another miserable one.

ROE has been declining steadily from 7.51 percent in 19X1 to 3.03 percent in 19X3. A comparison of GI's 19X3 ROE to the 19X3 industry average of 8.64 percent makes the deteriorating time trend appear especially alarming. The low and falling market-to-book-value ratio and the falling price/earnings ratio indicate investors are less and less optimistic about the firm's future profitability.

The fact that ROA has not been declining, however, tells us that the source of the declining time trend in GI's ROE must be inappropriate use of financial leverage. And we see that, while GI's leverage ratio (column 5) climbed from 2.117 in 19X1 to 2.723 in 19X3, its interest-burden ratio (column 2) fell from 0.650 to 0.204—with the net result that the compound leverage factor fell from 1.376 to 0.556.

The rapid increase in short-term debt from year to year and the concurrent increase in interest expense make it clear that, to finance its 20 percent growth rate in sales, GI has incurred sizable amounts of short-term debt at high interest

**Table 18.10** Key Financial Ratios of Growth Industries, Inc.

| Year | ROE | (1) Net Profit / Pretax Profit | (2) Pretax Profit / EBIT | (3) EBIT / Sales (ROS) | (4) Sales / Assets (ATO) | (5) Assets / Equity | (6) Compound Leverage Factor (2) × (5) | (7) ROA (3) × (4) | P/E | P/B |
|---|---|---|---|---|---|---|---|---|---|---|
| 19X1 | 7.51% | .6 | .650 | 30% | .303 | 2.117 | 1.376 | 9.09% | 8 | .58 |
| 19X2 | 6.08 | .6 | .470 | 30 | .303 | 2.375 | 1.116 | 9.09 | 6 | .35 |
| 19X3 | 3.03 | .6 | .204 | 30 | .303 | 2.723 | .556 | 9.09 | 4 | .12 |
| Industry average | 8.64% | .6 | .800 | 30% | .400 | 1.500 | 1.200 | 12.00% | 8 | .69 |

**Table 18.11** Growth Industries Statement of Cash Flows ($ Thousands)

| | 19X1 | 19X2 | 19X3 |
|---|---|---|---|
| **Cash Flow from Operating Activities** | | | |
| Net income | $ 11,700 | $ 10,143 | $ 5,285 |
| + Depreciation | 15,000 | 18,000 | 21,600 |
| + Decrease (increase) in accounts receivable | (5,000) | (6,000) | (7,200) |
| + Decrease (increase) in inventories | (15,000) | (18,000) | (21,600) |
| + Increase in accounts payable | 6,000 | 7,200 | 8,640 |
| | $ 12,700 | $ 11,343 | $ 6,725 |
| **Cash Flow from Investing Activities** | | | |
| Investment in plant and equipment* | $(45,000) | $(54,000) | $(64,800) |
| **Cash Flow from Financing Activities** | | | |
| Dividends paid† | $ 0 | $ 0 | $ 0 |
| Short-term debt issued | 42,300 | 54,657 | 72,475 |
| Change in cash and marketable securities‡ | $ 10,000 | $ 12,000 | $ 14,400 |

*Gross investment equals increase in net plant and equipment plus depreciation.

†We can conclude that no dividends are paid because stockholders' equity increases each year by the full amount of net income, implying a plowback ratio of 1.0.

‡Equals cash flow from operations plus cash flow from investment activities plus cash flow from financing activities. Note that this equals the yearly change in cash and marketable securities on the balance sheet.

rates. The firm is paying rates of interest greater than the ROA it is earning on the investment financed with the new borrowing. As the firm has expanded, its situation has become ever more precarious.

In 19X3, for example, the average interest rate on short-term debt was 20 percent versus an ROA of 9.09 percent. (We compute the average interest rate on short-term debt by taking the total interest expense of $34,391,000, subtracting the $6 million in interest on the long-term bonds, and dividing by the beginning-of-year short-term debt of $141,957,000.)

GI's problems become clear when we examine its statement of cash flows in Table 18.11. The statement is derived from the income statement and balance sheet in Table 18.8. GI's cash flow from operations is falling steadily, from $12,700,000 in 19X1 to $6,725,000 in 19X3. The firm's investment in plant and equipment, by contrast, has increased greatly. Net plant and equipment (i.e., net of depreciation) rose from $150,000,000 in 19X0 to $259,200,000 in 19X3. This near doubling of the capital assets makes the decrease in cash flow from operations all the more troubling.

The source of the difficulty is GI's enormous amount of short-term borrowing. In a sense, the company is being run as a pyramid scheme. It borrows more and more each year to maintain its 20 percent growth rate in assets and income. However, the new assets are not generating enough cash flow to support the extra interest burden of the debt, as the falling cash flow from operations indicates.

Eventually, when the firm loses its ability to borrow further, its growth will be at an end.

At this point, GI stock might be an attractive investment. Its market price is only 12 percent of its book value, and with a P/E ratio of 4, its earnings yield is 25 percent per year. GI is a likely candidate for a takeover by another firm that might replace GI's management and build shareholder value through a radical change in policy.

**CONCEPT CHECK** Question 4. You have the following information for IBX Corporation for the years 1991 and 1988 (all figures are in $ millions):

| | 1991 | 1988 |
|---|---|---|
| Net income | $ 253.7 | $ 239.0 |
| Pretax income | 411.9 | 375.6 |
| EBIT | 517.6 | 403.1 |
| Average assets | 4,857.9 | 3,459.7 |
| Sales | 6,679.3 | 4,537.0 |
| Shareholders' equity | 2,233.3 | 2,347.3 |

What is the trend in IBX's ROE, and how can you account for it in terms of tax burden, margin, turnover, and financial leverage?

## 18.6 Comparability and Limitations

### The Problem

Financial statement analysis gives us a good amount of ammunition for evaluating a company's performance and future prospects, but comparing financial results of different companies is not so simple. There is more than one acceptable way to represent various items of revenue and expense according to generally accepted accounting principles (GAAP). This means that two firms may have exactly the same economic income yet very different accounting incomes.

Furthermore, interpreting a single firm's performance over time is complicated when inflation distorts the dollar measuring rod. Comparability problems are especially acute in this case, because the impact of inflation on reported results often depends on the particular method the firm adopts to account for inventories and depreciation. The security analyst must adjust the earnings and the financial ratio figures to a uniform standard before attempting to compare financial results across firms and over time.

Comparability problems can arise out of the flexibility of GAAP guidelines in accounting for inventories and depreciation and in adjusting for the effects of inflation. Other important potential sources of noncomparability include the capitalization of leases and other expenses and the treatment of pension costs, but they are beyond the scope of this book. Analysts also may choose to include or exclude nonrecurring items such as write-offs, reserves, and gains or losses from discontinued operations in reporting earnings. Similarly, analysts may treat intangibles differently when estimating book value.

## Inventory Valuation

There are two commonly used ways to value inventories: **LIFO** (last-in, first-out), and **FIFO** (first-in, first-out). The difference is best explained using a numerical example. Suppose Generic Products Inc. (GPI) has a constant inventory of 1 million units of generic goods. The inventory turns over once per year, meaning that the ratio of cost of goods sold to inventory is 1.

The LIFO system calls for valuing the million units used up during the year at the current cost of production, so that the last goods produced are considered the first ones to be sold. The FIFO system assures that the units used up or sold are the ones that were added to inventory first, and therefore that goods sold should be valued at original cost. If the price of generic goods were constant, for example, at the level of $1, the book value of inventory and the cost of goods sold would be the same $1 million under both systems. But suppose the price of generic goods rises by 10 cents during the year as a result of general inflation. LIFO accounting would result in a cost of goods sold of $1.1 million, while the end-of-year balance sheet value of the one million units in inventory remains $1 million. The balance sheet value of inventories is measured as the cost of the goods still in inventory. Under LIFO, the last goods produced are assumed to be sold at the current cost of $1.10; the goods remaining are thus the previously produced goods, at a cost of only $1. You can see that although LIFO accounting accurately measures the cost of goods sold, it understates the current value of the remaining inventory in an inflationary environment.

In contrast, under FIFO accounting the cost of goods sold would be $1 million, and the end-of-year balance sheet value of the inventory would be $1.1 million. The result is that the LIFO firm has both a lower profit and a lower balance sheet of inventories than the FIFO firm.

LIFO is to be preferred to FIFO in computing economic earnings (i.e., real sustainable cash flow), because it uses up-to-date prices to evaluate the cost of goods sold. However, LIFO accounting induces balance sheet distortions when it values investment in inventories at original cost. This practice results in an upward bias in ROE, since the investment base on which return is earned is undervalued.

Canadian tax law requires that firms use FIFO accounting in determining their taxable income, but they are free to use LIFO in their internal or annual reporting. In the case of a discrepancy between accounting methods used, an adjustment must be made for the deferred tax credit or liability that is created with respect to the reported financial statements.

## Depreciation

Depreciation comparability problems include one more wrinkle. A firm can use different depreciation methods for tax purposes than for other reporting purposes. Canadian firms must use an accelerated depreciation method (declining balance for most depreciable assets) to calculate the capital cost allowance (CCA) for tax purposes; they are free, however, to use straight-line CCA in published financial statements. There are also differences across firms in their estimates of the depreciable life of plant, equipment, and other depreciable assets.

The major problem related to depreciation, however, is caused by inflation. Because conventional depreciation is based on historical costs rather than on the current replacement cost of assets, measured depreciation in periods of inflation is understated relative to replacement cost, and *real* economic income (sustainable cash flow) is correspondingly overstated.

The situation is similar to what happens in FIFO inventory accounting. Conventional depreciation and FIFO both result in an inflation-induced overstatement of real income, because both use original cost instead of current cost to calculate income. For example, suppose Generic Products Inc. has a machine with a three-year useful life that originally cost $3 million. Annual straight-line depreciation is $1 million, regardless of what happens to the replacement cost of the machine. Suppose inflation in the first year turns out to be 10 percent. Then the true annual depreciation expense is $1.1 million in current terms, while conventionally measured depreciation remains fixed at $1 million per year. Accounting income therefore overstates *real* economic income by the inflation factor, $100,000. Again, if firms use straight-line depreciation for reported statements while using declining balance for tax purposes, a discrepancy with respect to tax liability is created; consequently, the appropriate adjustment must be noted in the statements.

## Inflation and Interest Expense

If inflation can cause distortions in the measurement of a firm's inventory and depreciation costs, it has perhaps an even greater effect on the calculation of *real* interest expense. Nominal interest rates include an inflation premium that compensates the lender for inflation-induced erosion in the *real* value of principal. From the perspective of both lender and borrower, part of what is conventionally measured as interest expense should be treated more properly as repayment of principal.

For example, suppose Generic Products has debt outstanding with a face value of $10 million, paying 10 percent per year. Interest expense, as conventionally measured, is therefore $1 million per year. However, suppose inflation during the year is 6 percent, so that the real interest rate is 4 percent. Then $600,000 of what appears as interest expense on the income statement is really an inflation premium, or compensation for the anticipated reduction in the real value of the

$10 million principal; only $400,000 is *real* interest expense. The $600,000 reduction in the purchasing power of the outstanding principal may be thought of as repayment of principal, rather than as an interest expense. Real income of the firm is therefore understated by $600,000. Mismeasurement of real interest means that inflation deflates the statement of real income. The effects of inflation on the reported values of inventories and depreciation that we have discussed work in the opposite direction.

These distortions might by chance cancel each other out, so that the reported income figure is an unbiased estimate of real economic income. Although this seems extremely improbable for any individual firm, there is some evidence that these distortions have approximately offset one another for the aggregate corporate sector of the U.S. economy during the past 20 years.[16] In both Canada and the United States, the responsible accounting bodies (in Canada, the Canadian Institute of Chartered Accountants, or CICA) have tried to impose a requirement for inflation-adjusted accounting reports as supplements to regular statements. Reportedly, however, security analysts by and large ignore the inflation-adjusted data, particularly since this adds another element of noncomparability. Consequently, the requirement has been dropped in both jurisdictions.

**CONCEPT CHECK** Question 5. In a period of rapid inflation, companies ABC and XYZ have the same *reported* earnings. ABC uses LIFO inventory accounting, has relatively fewer depreciable assets, and has more debt than XYZ. XYZ uses FIFO inventory accounting. Which company has the higher *real* income, and why?

## Limitations

The efficient market hypothesis (EMH) refutes the possibility of gleaning additional information of value from the published financial statements of a company. Yet, as discussed in Chapter 12, analysis must be valuable in order to justify the efforts of well-paid analysts in looking for mispriced assets; active management depends upon the identification of opportunities for investment. Financial theory has been slow to accept the possibility that financial statement analysis may have more than the smallest and shortest-lived effect in making extraordinary gains; instead it suggests that the practice of analysis adds to market information, which leads to efficient pricing. Accounting theorists have been more inclined to look for the value in their products and their analyses.

Michael Brennan[17] discusses two aspects of accounting information and its relation to stock prices in a review article. He presents the results of research on

[16] F. Modigliani and R. Cohn, "Inflation, Rational Valuation and the Market," *Financial Analysts Journal*, March/April 1979.

[17] Michael J. Brennan, "A Perspective on Accounting and Stock Prices," *The Accounting Review* 66, no. 1 (January 1991), pp. 67–79.

market reactions to the release of new information and on the use of accounting information in the determination of value and of stock prices. He suggests that the definition and presentation of accounting data must be carefully controlled when academic studies of the significance of accounting information are conducted.

Ou and Penman[18], in two articles, demonstrate that accounting information presented in annual statements is not only retrospective but prospective in revealing future results. They claim that financial statements capture fundamentals that are not reflected in prices, contrary to the assertions of the semistrong form of efficiency; in fact, financial statements contain information that can predict future stock returns. Furthermore, they define an accounting measure from the released information that they assert is relevant to future earnings rather than the current earnings revealed in the income statement. The stock returns predicted by their measure are shown to be negatively correlated with the returns predicted by P/E ratios.

## SUMMARY

**1.** The primary focus of the security analyst should be the firm's real economic earnings rather than its reported earnings. Accounting earnings as reported in financial statements can be a biased estimate of real economic earnings, although empirical studies reveal that reported earnings convey considerable information concerning a firm's prospects.

**2.** A firm's ROE is a key determinant of the growth rate of its earnings. ROE is affected profoundly by the firm's degree of financial leverage. An increase in a firm's debt-to-equity ratio will raise its ROE and hence its growth rate only if the interest rate on the debt is less than the firm's return on assets.

**3.** It often is helpful to the analyst to decompose a firm's ROE ratio into the product of several accounting ratios and to analyze their separate behaviour over time and across companies within an industry. A useful breakdown is

$$\text{ROE} = \frac{\text{Net profits}}{\text{Pretax profits}} \times \frac{\text{Pretax profits}}{\text{EBIT}} \times \frac{\text{EBIT}}{\text{Sales}} \times \frac{\text{Sales}}{\text{Assets}} \times \frac{\text{Assets}}{\text{Equity}}$$

**4.** Other accounting ratios that have a bearing on a firm's profitability and/or risk are fixed asset turnover, inventory turnover, days receivables, and current, quick, and interest coverage ratios.

**5.** Two ratios that make use of the market price of the firm's common stock in addition to its financial statements are the market-to-book-value ratio and the price/earnings ratio. Analysts sometimes take low values for these ratios as a margin of safety or a sign that the stock is a bargain.

[18] Jane A. Ou and Stephen H. Penman, "Financial Statement Analysis and the Prediction of Stock Returns," *Journal of Accounting and Economics* 11 (1985), pp. 295–329; and "Accounting Measurement, Price-Earnings Ratio, and the Information Content of Security Prices," *Journal of Accounting Research* 27 (Spring 1989), pp. 111–44.

**6.** A strategy of investing in stocks with high reported ROE seems to produce a lower rate of return to the investor than investing in low ROE stocks. This implies that high reported ROE stocks are overpriced compared with low ROE stocks.

**7.** A major problem in the use of data obtained from a firm's financial statements is comparability. Firms have a great deal of latitude in how they choose to compute various items of revenue and expense. It is therefore necessary for the security analyst to adjust accounting earnings and financial ratios to a uniform standard before attempting to compare financial results across firms.

**8.** Comparability problems can be acute in a period of inflation. Inflation can create distortions in accounting for inventories, depreciation, and interest expense.

## Key Terms

Income statement
Balance sheet
Statement of changes in financial position
Accounting earnings
Economic earnings
Return on equity
Return on assets
Profit margin
Return on sales
Asset turnover
Leverage ratio
Average collection period (Days receivables)
Current ratio
Quick ratio (Acid test ratio)
Interest coverage ratio (Times interest earned)
Market-to-book-value ratio
Price/earnings ratio
Earnings yield
LIFO
FIFO

## Selected Readings

*The classic book on the use of financial statements in equity valuation, now in its fifth edition, is:*

Cottle, S.; R. Murray; and F. Block. *Graham and Dodd's Security Analysis.* New York: McGraw-Hill, Inc., 1988.

## Problems

1. The Crusty Pie Co., which specializes in the production of apple turnovers, has a return on sales higher than the industry average, yet its ROA is the same as the industry average. How can you explain this?
2. The ABC Corporation has a profit margin on sales below the industry average, yet its ROA is above the industry average. What does this imply about its asset turnover?
3. Firm A and firm B have the same ROA, yet firm A's ROE is higher. How can you explain this?

The following problems are based on questions that appeared in past CFA examinations:

**4.** Which of the following *best* explains a ratio of "net sales to average net fixed assets" that *exceeds* the industry average?
   *a.* The firm expanded its plant and equipment in the past few years.
   *b.* The firm makes less efficient use of its assets than other firms.
   *c.* The firm has a lot of old plant and equipment.
   *d.* The firm uses straight-line depreciation.

**5.** The rate of return on assets is equivalent to:
   *a.* Profit margin × Total asset turnover
   *b.* Profit margin × Total asset turnover × Leverage ratio/Interest expense
   *c.* $\dfrac{\text{Net income + Interest expense net of income tax + Minority interest in earnings}}{\text{Average total assets}}$
   *d.* $\dfrac{\text{Net income + Minority interest in earnings}}{\text{Average total assets}}$
      *i.* (*a*) only
      *ii.* (*a*) and (*c*)
      *iii.* (*b*) only
      *iv.* (*b*) and (*d*)

**6.** Which one of the following is *true*?
   *a.* During inflation, LIFO makes the income statement less representative than if FIFO were used.
   *b.* During inflation, FIFO makes the balance sheet less representative than if LIFO were used.
   *c.* After inflation ends, distortion due to LIFO will disappear as inventory is sold.
   *d.* None of the above.

**7.** The financial statements for Seattle Manufacturing Corporation are to be used to compute the following ratios for 1996 (Tables 18A and 18B).
   *a.* Return on total assets.
   *b.* Earnings per share of common stock.
   *c.* Acid test ratio.
   *d.* Interest coverage ratio.
   *e.* Receivables collection period.
   *f.* Leverage ratio.

**8.** The financial statements for Chicago Refrigerator Inc. are to be used to compute the following ratios for 1995 (Tables 18C and 18D).
   *a.* Quick ratio.
   *b.* Return on assets.
   *c.* Return on common shareholders' equity.
   *d.* Earnings per share of common stock.
   *e.* Profit margin.
   *f.* Times interest earned.

**Table 18A** Seattle Manufacturing Corp. Consolidated Balance Sheet, as of December 31 ($ Millions)

| | 1995 | 1996 |
|---|---|---|
| **Assets** | | |
| Current assets | | |
| Cash | $ 6.2 | $ 6.6 |
| Short-term investment in commercial paper | 20.8 | 15.0 |
| Accounts receivable | 77.0 | 93.2 |
| Inventory | 251.2 | 286.0 |
| Prepaid manufacturing expense | 1.4 | 1.8 |
| **Total current assets** | **$356.6** | **$402.6** |
| Leased property under capital leases net of accumulated amortization | 181.4 | 215.6 |
| Other | 6.2 | 9.8 |
| **Total assets** | **$544.2** | **$628.0** |

**Table 18B** Seattle Manufacturing Corp. Income Statement, Years Ending December 31 ($ Millions)

| | 1985 | 1986 |
|---|---|---|
| Sales | $1,166.6 | $1,207.6 |
| Other income, net | 12.8 | 15.6 |
| **Total revenues** | **$1,179.4** | **$1,223.2** |
| Cost of sales | $ 912.0 | $ 961.2 |
| Amortization of leased property | 43.6 | 48.6 |
| Selling and administrative expense | 118.4 | 128.8 |
| Interest expense | 16.2 | 19.8 |
| **Total costs and expenses** | **$1,090.2** | **$1,158.4** |
| Income before income tax | $ 89.2 | $ 64.8 |
| Income tax | 19.2 | 10.4 |
| **Net income** | **$ 70.0** | **$ 54.4** |

*g.* Inventory turnover.
*h.* Leverage ratio.

9. The financial statements for Atlas Corporation are to be used to compute the following ratios for 1994 (Tables 18E and 18F).
*a.* Acid test ratio.
*b.* Inventory turnover.
*c.* Earnings per share.
*d.* Interest coverage.
*e.* Leverage.

**Table 18C** Chicago Refrigerator Inc. Balance Sheet, as of December 31 ($ Thousands)

| | 1994 | 1995 |
|---|---|---|
| **Assets** | | |
| Current assets | | |
| Cash | $ 683 | $ 325 |
| Accounts receivable | 1,490 | 3,599 |
| Inventories | 1,415 | 2,423 |
| Prepaid expenses | 15 | 13 |
| **Total current assets** | **$3,603** | **$6,360** |
| Property, plant, equipment, net | 1,066 | 1,541 |
| Other | 123 | 157 |
| **Total assets** | **$4,792** | **$8,058** |
| **Liabilities** | | |
| Current liabilities | | |
| Notes payable to bank | $ — | $ 875 |
| Current portion of long-term debt | 38 | 116 |
| Accounts payable | 485 | 933 |
| Estimated income tax | 588 | 472 |
| Accrued expenses | 576 | 586 |
| Customer advance payment | 34 | 963 |
| **Total current liabilities** | **$1,721** | **$3,945** |
| Long-term debt | 122 | 179 |
| Other liabilities | 81 | 131 |
| **Total liabilities** | **$1,924** | **$4,255** |
| **Shareholders' Equity** | | |
| Common stock, $1 par value: 1,000,000 shares authorized; 550,000 and 829,000 outstanding, respectively | $ 550 | $ 829 |
| Preferred stock, Series A 10%; $25 par value; 25,000 authorized; 20,000 and 18,000 outstanding, respectively | 500 | 450 |
| Additional paid-in capital | 450 | 575 |
| Retained earnings | 1,368 | 1,949 |
| **Total shareholders' equity** | **$2,868** | **$3,803** |
| **Total liabilities and shareholders' equity** | **$4,792** | **$8,058** |

**10.** Philip Morris Corporation is a major consumer products company operating worldwide. The company's brand names have immediate recognition in most markets and include Marlboro, Benson & Hedges, Kraft, Kool-Aid, Jell-O, Miller, and Maxwell House. Some of these brands were the result of acquisitions, but many of them have been established through years of marketing effort and advertising expenditures.

Philip Morris is the world leader in tobacco products, and this line is its primary source of profits. Tobacco product sales are growing slowly, particularly in the U.S., for both health and economic reasons. However,

**Table 18D** Chicago Refrigerator Inc. Income Statement, Years Ending December 31 ($ Thousands)

| | 1994 | 1995 |
|---|---|---|
| Net sales | $7,570 | $12,065 |
| Other income, net | 261 | 345 |
| **Total revenues** | **$7,831** | **$12,410** |
| Cost of goods sold | $4,850 | $ 8,048 |
| General administrative and marketing expenses | 1,531 | 2,025 |
| Interest expense | 22 | 78 |
| **Total costs and expenses** | **$6,403** | **$10,151** |
| Net income before tax | $1,428 | $ 2,259 |
| Income tax | 628 | 994 |
| **Net income** | **$ 800** | **$ 1,265** |

cigarette prices have increased much faster than the rate of inflation in the U.S. due to a combination of excise tax pressure and aggressive pricing by Philip Morris and other tobacco companies. One justification for this trend put forth by the tobacco industry is that the price increases are necessary to cover the extensive legal fees arising from the large number of negligence and liability suits now pending against tobacco companies.

For many years, Philip Morris has been redeploying the growing excess cash flow from operations (defined as cash over and above that necessary to sustain the intrinsic growth of the basic business). The strategy has been to consistently increase dividends, repurchase common shares, and make acquisitions in consumer nondurable businesses. Dividends have been raised in every year over the past decade, and shares have been steadily repurchased at prices well above book value. Some repurchased stock is held as Treasury stock, and the remainder has been retired. Philip Morris also has made many sizable acquisitions (almost all on a purchase basis), which have added substantial goodwill to the balance sheet.

Philip Morris uses the LIFO method for costing all domestic inventories and the straight-line method for recording depreciation. Goodwill and other intangibles are amortized on a straight-line basis over 40 years. The company was an early adopter of FAS 106, "Employers' Accounting for Postretirement Benefits Other than Pensions," doing so on the immediate recognition basis on January 1, 1991, for all U.S. employee benefit plans. The 1991 year-end accrued postretirement health care cost liability amounted to $1,854 million.

Use the financial statement data in Table 18G to answer the following questions.

*a.* Using the Du Point method, *identify* and *calculate* Philip Morris' *five* primary components of return on equity for the years 1981 and 1991.

**Table 18E** Atlas Corporation Consolidated Balance Sheet, as of December 31 ($ Millions)

| | 1993 | 1994 |
|---|---|---|
| **Assets** | | |
| Current assets | | |
| Cash | $ 3.1 | $ 3.3 |
| Short-term investment in commercial paper | 2.9 | — |
| Accounts receivable | 38.5 | 46.6 |
| Inventory | 125.6 | 143.0 |
| Prepaid manufacturing expense | .7 | .9 |
| **Total current assets** | **$170.8** | **$193.8** |
| Leased property under capital leases net of accumulated amortization | $ 90.7 | $107.8 |
| Other | 3.1 | 4.9 |
| **Total assets** | **$264.6** | **$306.5** |
| **Liabilities** | | |
| Current liabilities | | |
| Accounts payable | $ 71.6 | $ 81.7 |
| Dividends payable | 6.5 | 6.0 |
| Current portion of long-term debt | 6.0 | 8.3 |
| Current portion of obligation under capital leases | 9.4 | 11.3 |
| Estimated taxes on income | 5.4 | 4.9 |
| **Total current liabilities** | **$ 98.9** | **$112.2** |
| Long-term debt | $ 43.2 | $ 53.5 |
| Obligations under capital leases | 70.4 | 82.9 |
| **Total liabilities** | **$212.5** | **$248.6** |
| **Shareholders' Equity** | | |
| Common stock $10 par value: 2,000,000 shares authorized; 1,340,000 and 1,500,000 outstanding, respectively | $ 13.4 | $ 15.0 |
| Additional paid-in capital | 13.2 | 13.5 |
| Retained earnings | 25.5 | 29.4 |
| **Total shareholders' equity** | **$ 52.1** | **$ 57.9** |
| **Total liabilities and shareholders' equity** | **$264.6** | **$306.5** |

Using these components, *calculate* the return on equity for *both* years. *Show* all work.

*b.* Using your answers to part (*a*), *identify* the *two* most significant components contributing to the observed difference in Philip Morris' ROE between 1981 and 1991. *Briefly discuss* the likely reasons for the changes in those components.

*c.* *Calculate* Philip Morris' sustainable growth rate (i.e., ROE × *b*) using the 1981 data. The company's actual compound annual growth rate in earnings per share over the 1981–91 period was 20.4 percent. *Discuss* why the sustainable growth rate was or was not a good predictor of actual growth over the 1981–91 period.

**Table 18F** Atlas Corporation Income Statement, Years Ending December 31 ($ Millions)

| | 1993 | 1994 |
|---|---|---|
| Sales | $583.3 | $603.8 |
| Other income, net | 6.4 | 2.8 |
| **Main revenues** | **$589.7** | **$606.6** |
| Cost of sales | $456.0 | $475.6 |
| Amortization of leased property | 21.8 | 24.3 |
| Selling and administrative expenses | 59.2 | 64.4 |
| Interest expense | 8.1 | 9.9 |
| **Total costs and expenses** | **$545.1** | **$574.2** |
| Income before tax | $ 44.6 | $ 32.4 |
| Income tax | 9.6 | 5.2 |
| **Net income** | **$ 35.0** | **$ 27.2** |

**11.** Just before the onset of inflation, a firm switched from FIFO to LIFO. If nothing else changed, the inventory turnover for the next year would be:
*a.* Higher.
*b.* Lower.
*c.* Unchanged.
*d.* Unpredictable from the information given.

**12.** In an inflationary period, the use of FIFO will make which *one* of the following more realistic than the use of LIFO?
*a.* Balance sheet.
*b.* Income statement.
*c.* Cash flow statement.
*d.* None of the above.

**13.** A company acquires a machine with an estimated 10-year service life. If the company uses the sum-of-the-years-digits depreciation method instead of the straight-line method:
*a.* Income will be higher in the 10th year.
*b.* Total depreciation expense for the 10 years will be lower.
*c.* Depreciation expense will be lower in the first year.
*d.* Scrapping the machine after eight years will result in a larger loss.

**14.** Why might a firm's ratio of long-term debt to long-term capital be lower than the industry average, but its ratio of income-before-interest-and-taxes to debt-interest charges be lower than the industry average?
*a.* The firm has higher profitability than average.
*b.* The firm has more short-term debt than average.
*c.* The firm has a high ratio of current assets to current liabilities.
*d.* The firm has a high ratio of total cash flow to total long-term debt.

**Table 18G** Philip Morris Corporation Selected Financial Statements and Other Data Years Ending December 31 ($ millions except per share data)

| | 1991 | 1981 |
|---|---|---|
| **Income Statement** | | |
| Operating revenue | $56,458 | $10,886 |
| Cost of sales | 25,612 | 5,253 |
| Excise taxes on products | 8,394 | 2,580 |
| Gross profit | $22,452 | $ 3,053 |
| Selling, general, and administrative expenses | 13,830 | 1,741 |
| Operating income | $ 8,622 | $ 1,312 |
| Interest expense | 1,651 | 232 |
| Pretax earnings | $ 6,971 | $ 1,080 |
| Provision for income taxes | 3,044 | 420 |
| Net earnings | $ 3,927 | $ 660 |
| Earnings per share | $4.24 | $0.66 |
| Dividends per share | $1.91 | $0.25 |
| **Balance Sheet** | | |
| Current assets | $12,594 | $ 3,733 |
| Property, plant, and equipment, net | 9,946 | 3,583 |
| Goodwill | 18,624 | 634 |
| Other assets | 6,220 | 1,230 |
| Total assets | $47,384 | $ 9,180 |
| Current liabilities | $11,824 | $ 1,936 |
| Long-term debt | 14,213 | 3,499 |
| Deferred taxes | 1,803 | 455 |
| Other liabilities | 7,032 | 56 |
| Stockholders' equity | 12,512 | 3,234 |
| Total liabilities and stockholders' equity | $47,384 | $ 9,180 |
| **Other Data** | | |
| Philip Morris: | | |
| Common shares outstanding (millions) | 920 | 1,003 |
| Closing price common stock | $80.250 | $6.125 |
| S&P 500 Stock Index: | | |
| Closing price | 417.09 | 122.55 |
| Earnings per share | 16.29 | 15.36 |
| Book value per share | 161.08 | 109.43 |

15. Assuming continued inflation, a firm that uses LIFO will tend to have a _______ current ratio than a firm using FIFO, and the difference will tend to _______ as time passes.
    *a.* Higher, increase.
    *b.* Higher, decrease.

**Table 18H** Income Statements and Balance Sheets

| | 1985 | 1989 |
|---|---|---|
| **Income Statement Data** | | |
| Revenues | $542 | $979 |
| Operating income | 38 | 76 |
| Depreciation and amortization | 3 | 9 |
| Interest expense | 3 | 0 |
| Pretax income | 32 | 67 |
| Income taxes | 13 | 37 |
| Net income after tax | 19 | 30 |
| **Balance Sheet Data** | | |
| Fixed assets | $ 41 | $ 70 |
| Total assets | 245 | 291 |
| Working capital | 123 | 157 |
| Total debt | 16 | 0 |
| Total shareholders' equity | 159 | 220 |

*c.* Lower, decrease.
*d.* Lower, increase.

**16.** In a cash flow statement prepared in accordance with FASB 95, cash flow from investing activities *excludes:*
*a.* Cash paid for acquisitions.
*b.* Cash received from sale of fixed assets.
*c.* Inventory increase due to new (internally developed) product line.
*d.* All of the above.

**17.** Cash flow from operating activities *includes:*
*a.* Inventory increases resulting from acquisitions.
*b.* Inventory changes due to changing exchange rates.
*c.* Interest paid to bondholders.
*d.* Dividends paid to stockholders.

**18.** Cash flow from investing activities *excludes:*
*a.* Cash paid for acquisitions.
*b.* Cash received from sale of fixed assets.
*c.* Inventory increase due to new (internally developed) product line.
*d.* All of the above.

**19.** The Du Pont formula defines the net return on shareholders' equity as a function of the following components:

- Operating margin
- Asset turnover
- Interest burden
- Financial leverage
- Income tax rate

Using *only* the data in Table 18H:

*a*. Calculate each of the five components listed above for 1985 and 1989, and calculate the return on equity (ROE) for 1985 and 1989, using all of the five components.

*b*. Briefly discuss the impact of the changes in asset turnover and financial leverage on the change in ROE from 1985 to 1989.

---

# Chapter 19

# Technical Analysis

**IN THE TWO PREVIOUS CHAPTERS, WE EXAMINED FUNDAMENTAL ANALYSIS OF EQUITY, CONSIDERING HOW THE GENERAL MACROECONOMIC ENVIRONMENT AND THE SPECIFIC PROSPECTS OF THE FIRM OR INDUSTRY MIGHT AFFECT THE PRESENT VALUE OF THE DIVIDEND STREAM THE FIRM CAN BE EXPECTED TO GENERATE.** In this chapter, we examine technical analysis. Technical analysis focuses more on past price movements of a company than on the underlying fundamental determinants of future profitability. Technicians believe that past price and volume data signal future price movements.

Such a view is diametrically opposed to that of the efficient market hypothesis, which holds that all historical data must be reflected in stock prices already. As we lay out the basics of technical analysis in this chapter, we will point out the contradiction between the assumptions on which these strategies are based and the notion of well-functioning capital markets with rational and informed traders.

## 19.1 TECHNICAL ANALYSIS

Technical analysis is, in most instances, an attempt to exploit recurring and predictable patterns in stock prices to generate abnormal trading profits. Technicians do not necessarily deny the value of fundamental information such as we have discussed in the past two chapters. Many technical analysts believe stock prices eventually "close in" on their fundamental values. Technicians believe, nevertheless, that shifts in market fundamentals can be discerned before the impact of those shifts is fully reflected in prices. As the market adjusts to a new equilibrium, astute traders can exploit these price trends.

Technicians also believe that market fundamentals can be perturbed by irrational factors. More or less random fluctuations in price will accompany any underlying trend. If these fluctuations dissipate slowly, they can be taken advantage of for abnormal profits.

These presumptions, of course, clash head-on with those of the efficient market hypothesis (EMH) and with the logic of well-functioning capital markets. According to the EMH, a shift in market fundamentals should be reflected in prices immediately. According to technicians, though, that shift will lead to a gradual price change that can be recognized as a trend. Such easily exploited trends in stock market prices would be damning evidence against the EMH, as they would indicate profit opportunities that market participants had left unexploited.

The line between some technical analysis and fundamental analysis is hard to draw. In Section 19.5, we discuss the Value Line methodology and its success. Much of its analysis is fundamental, referring to financial data; but ultimately, it produces an index as a function of observable, realized data, and recommends purchase or not on this basis. Similarly, new, rigorously tested filters have been devised to identify firms that should yield superior risk-adjusted returns. These might include the Fama–French identification of ratios that offer further explanatory power for returns than given by traditional beta, or patterns of return persistence or price reversal that lead to trading rules. Economic rationalization of the plausibility of these rules makes them appear acceptable strategies. Even if the pricing defies the CAPM, the EMH would argue that investors should react and reprice these securities so that the pattern no longer prevails. If not, then this is technical analysis that works.

A more subtle version of technical analysis holds that there are patterns in stock prices that can be exploited, but that once investors identify and attempt to profit from these patterns their trading activity affects prices, thereby altering price patterns. This means the patterns that characterize market prices will be constantly evolving, and only the best analysts who can identify new patterns earliest will be rewarded. We call this phenomenon *self-destructing* patterns and explore it further later in the chapter.

The notion of evolving patterns is consistent with almost but not quite efficient markets. It allows for the possibility of temporarily unexploited profit opportunities, but it also views market participants as aggressively exploiting those opportunities once they are uncovered. The market is continually groping toward full efficiency, but it is never quite there.

This is in some ways an appealing middle position in the ongoing debate between technicians and proponents of the EMH. Ultimately, however, it is an untestable hypothesis. Technicians will always be able to identify trading rules that would have worked in the past but need not work any longer. Is this evidence of a once viable trading rule that has not been eliminated by competition? Perhaps. But it is far more likely that the trading rule could have been identified only after the fact.

Until technicians can prove rigorous evidence that their trading rules provide *consistent* trading profits, we must doubt the viability of those rules. As you saw in the chapter on the efficient market hypothesis, the evidence on the performance of professionally managed funds does not support the efficacy of technical analysis.

## 19.2 CHARTING

Technical analysts are sometimes called *chartists* because they study records or charts of past stock prices and trading volume, hoping to find patterns they can exploit to make a profit. In this section, we examine several specific charting strategies.

### The Dow Theory

The **Dow theory,** named after its creator Charles Dow (who established *The Wall Street Journal*), is the most famous of technical analyses. The aim of the Dow theory is to identify long-term trends in stock market prices. The two indicators used are the Dow Jones Industrial Average (DJIA) and the Dow Jones Transportation Average (DJTA). The DJIA is the key indicator of underlying trends, while the DJTA usually serves as a check to confirm or reject that signal.

The Dow theory posits three forces simultaneously affecting stock prices:

1. The *primary trend* is the long-term movement of prices, lasting from several months to several years.
2. *Secondary* or *intermediate trends* are caused by short-term deviations of prices from the underlying trend line. These deviations are eliminated via *corrections* when prices revert back to trend values.
3. *Tertiary* or *minor trends* are daily fluctuations of little importance.

Figure 19.1 represents these three components of stock price movements. In this figure, the primary trend is upward, but intermediate trends result in short-lived market declines lasting a few weeks. The intraday minor trends have no long-run impact on price.

Figure 19.2 depicts the course of the DJIA during 1988. The primary trend is upward, as evidenced by the fact that each market peak is higher than the previous peak (point F versus D versus B). Similarly, each low is higher than the previous low (E versus C versus A). This pattern of upward-moving "tops" and "bottoms" is one of the key ways to identify the underlying primary trend. Notice in Figure 19.2 that, despite the upward primary trend, intermediate trends still can lead to short periods of declining prices (points B through C, or D through E).

The Dow theory incorporates notions of support and resistance levels in stock prices. A **support level** is a value below which the market is relatively unlikely to fall. A **resistance level** is a value above which it is difficult to rise. Support

**Figure 19.1**

Dow theory trends.

From Melanie F. Bowman and Thom Hartle, "Dow Theory," *Technical Analysis of Stocks and Commodities* (September 1990), p. 690. Reprinted by permission.

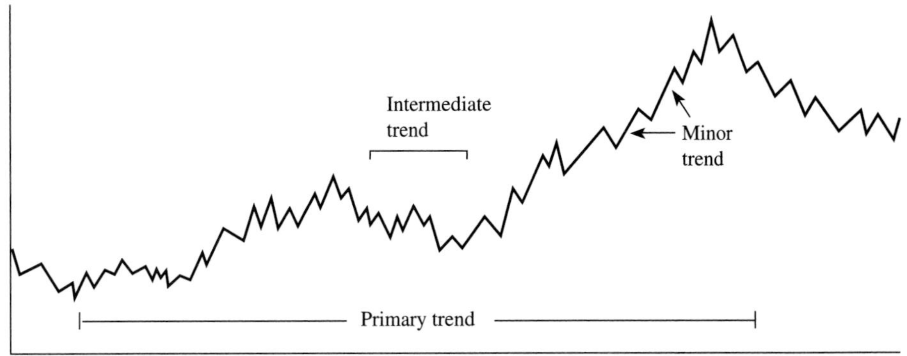


The primary trend is typically measured in years and the intermediate trend is measured in weeks to months, while the minor trend will last from days to weeks.

**Figure 19.2**

Dow Jones Industrial Average, January–November 1988.

From Melanie F. Bowman and Thom Hartle, "Dow Theory," *Technical Analysis of Stocks and Commodities* (September 1990), p. 690. Reprinted by permission.

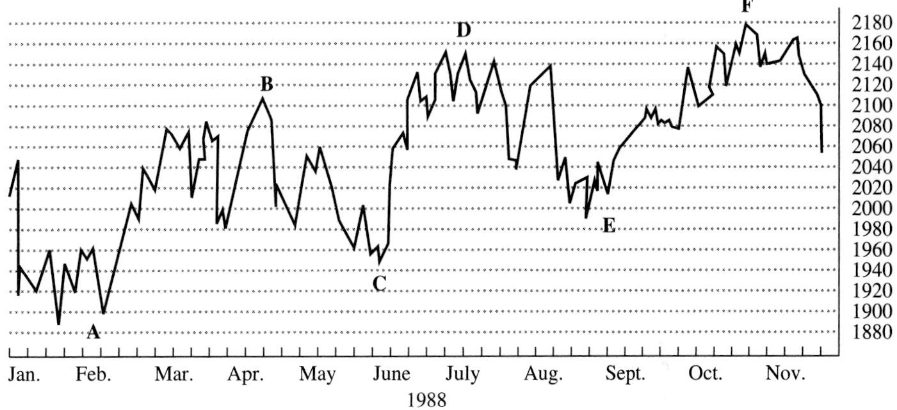


During 1988 the DJIA was bullish as points B, D, and F and points A, C, and E were a series of higher highs and higher lows, respectively.

and resistance levels are determined by the recent history of prices. In Figure 19.3, the price at point C would be viewed as a resistance level because the recent intermediate-trend high price was unable to rise above C. Hence, piercing the resistance point is a bullish signal. The fact that he transportation index also pierces its resistance level at point D confirms the bull market signal.

Technicians see resistance and support levels as resulting from common psychological investor traits. Consider, for example, stock XYZ, which traded for several months at a price of $72 and then declined to $65. If the stock eventually begins to increase in price, $72 is a natural resistance level because the many investors who bought originally at $72 will be eager to sell their shares as soon as they can break even on their investment. Whenever prices near $72, a wave of selling pressure will develop. Such activity imparts to the market a type of "memory" that allows past price history to influence current stock prospects.

**Figure 19.3**
Dow theory signals—confirmation simulation.

From Melanie F. Bowman and Thomas Hartle, "Dow Theory," *Technical Analysis of Stocks and Commodities* (September 1990), p. 690. Reprinted by permission.

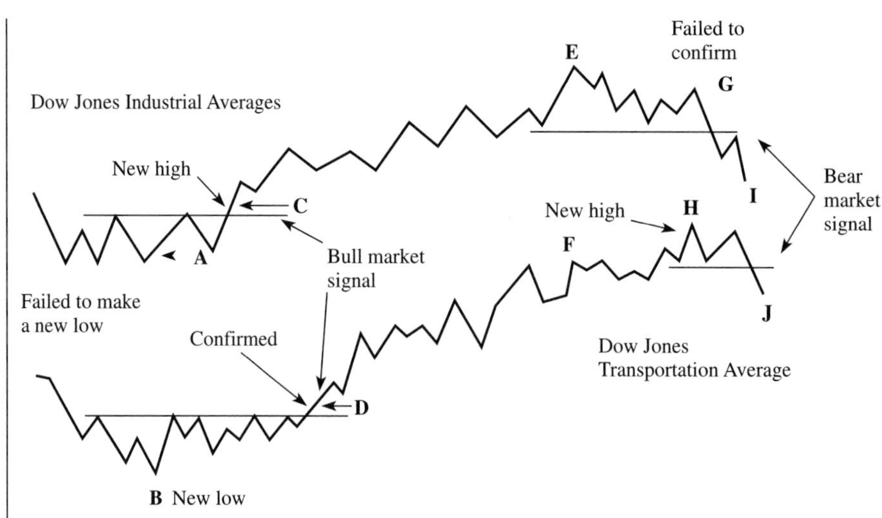


A simulated example of confirmation and nonconfirmation by the DJIA and the DJTA.

**CONCEPT CHECK** Question 1. Describe how technicians might explain support levels.

At point G, the DJIA fails to move to a higher high when the DJTA reaches a higher high at point H. This contradictory signal, called a *nonconfirmation,* is a warning sign. At points I and J, both indices fall below the low points of the previous trading range, which is taken as a signal of the end of the primary bull market.

In evaluating the Dow theory, don't forget the lessons of the efficient market hypothesis. The Dow theory is based on a notion of predictably recurring price patterns. Yet the EMH holds that if any pattern is exploitable, many investors would attempt to profit from such predictability, which would ultimately move stock prices and cause the trading strategy to self-destruct. While Figure 19.2 certainly appears to describe a classic upward primary trend, one always must wonder whether we can see that trend only *after* the fact. Recognizing patterns as they emerge is far more difficult.

A recent variation on the Dow theory is the Elliott wave theory. Like the Dow theory, the idea behind Elliott waves is that stock prices can be described by a set of wave patterns. Long-term and short-term wave cycles are superimposed and result in a complicated pattern of price movements, but by interpreting the cycles, one can, according to the theory, predict broad movements.

## Other Charting Techniques

The Dow theory posits a particular, and fairly simple, type of pattern in stock market prices: long-lasting trends with short-run deviations around those trends.

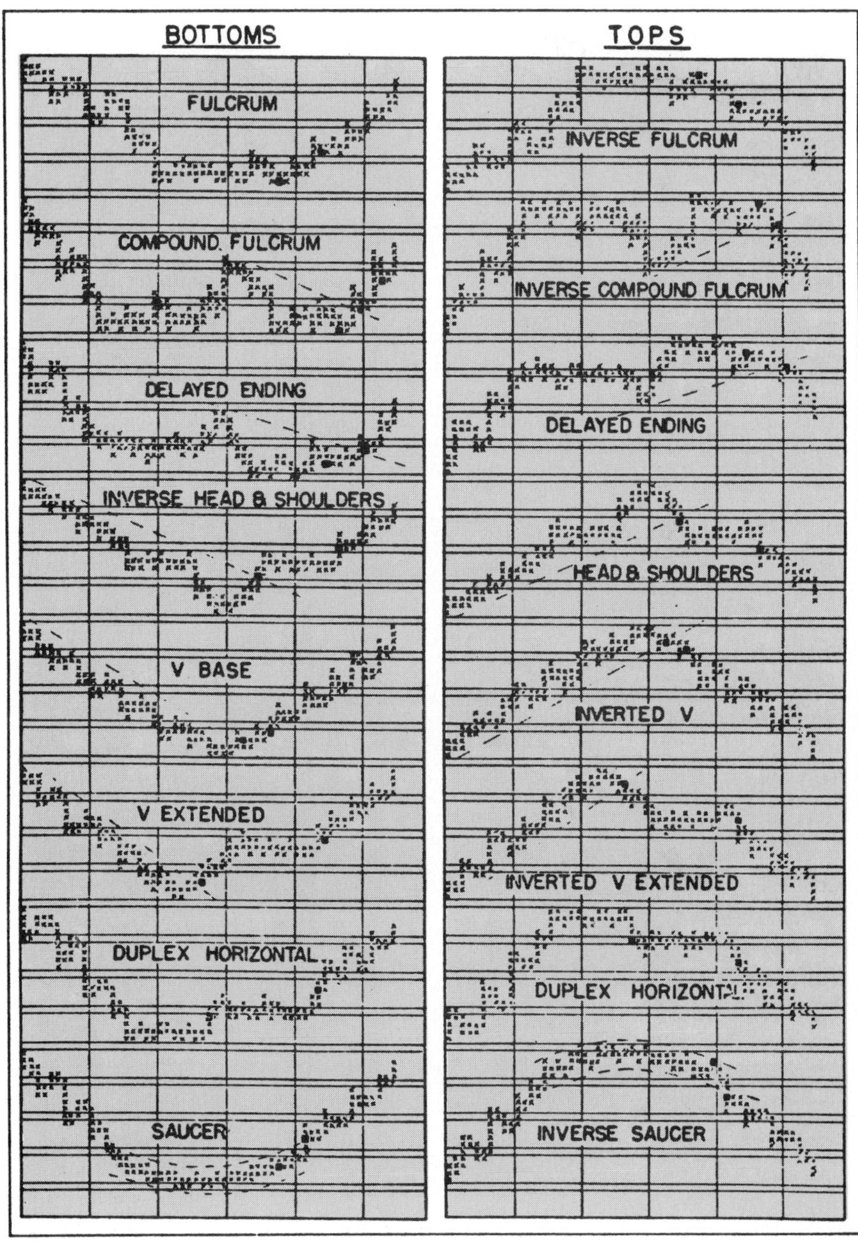


**Figure 19.4**
Chart representation of market bottoms and tops.
From Irwin Shishko, "Techniques of Forecasting Commodity Prices," *Commodity Yearbook* (New York: Commodity Research Bureau, 1965), p. 4. Reprinted by permission.

Not surprisingly, several more involved patterns have been identified in stock market prices. Figure 19.4 illustrates several of these patterns. If stock prices actually follow any of these patterns, profit opportunities result. The patterns are reasonably straightforward to discern, meaning future prices can be extrapolated from current prices.

**Figure 19.5**
Point and figure chart for Table 19.1.

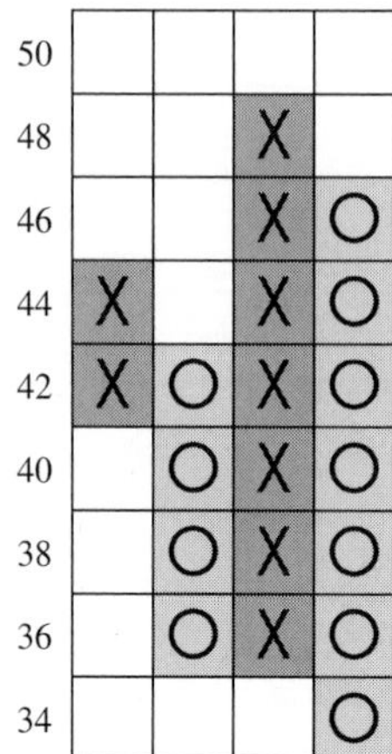


**Table 19.1** Stock Price History

| Date | Price | Date | Price |
|---|---|---|---|
| January 2 | 40 | February 1 | 40* |
| January 3 | 40-½ | February 2 | 41 |
| January 4 | 41 | February 5 | 40-½ |
| January 5 | 42* | February 6 | 42* |
| January 8 | 41-½ | February 7 | 45* |
| January 9 | 42-½ | February 8 | 44-½ |
| January 10 | 43 | February 9 | 46* |
| January 11 | 43-¾ | February 12 | 47 |
| January 12 | 44* | February 13 | 48* |
| January 15 | 45 | February 14 | 47-½ |
| January 16 | 44 | February 15 | 46† |
| January 17 | 41-½† | February 16 | 45 |
| January 18 | 41 | February 19 | 44* |
| January 19 | 40* | February 20 | 42* |
| January 22 | 39 | February 12 | 41 |
| January 23 | 39-½ | February 22 | 40* |
| January 24 | 39-¾ | February 23 | 41 |
| January 25 | 38* | February 26 | 40-½ |
| January 26 | 35* | February 27 | 38* |
| January 29 | 36† | February 28 | 39 |
| January 30 | 37 | March 1 | 36* |
| January 31 | 39* | March 2 | 34* |

A variant on pure trend analysis is the *point and figure chart* depicted in Figure 19.5. This figure has no time dimension. It simply traces significant upward or downward moves in stock prices without regard to their timing. The data for Figure 19.5 come from Table 19.1.

Suppose, as in Table 19.1, that a stock's price is currently $40. If the price rises by at least $2, you put an X in the first column at $42 in Figure 19.5. Another

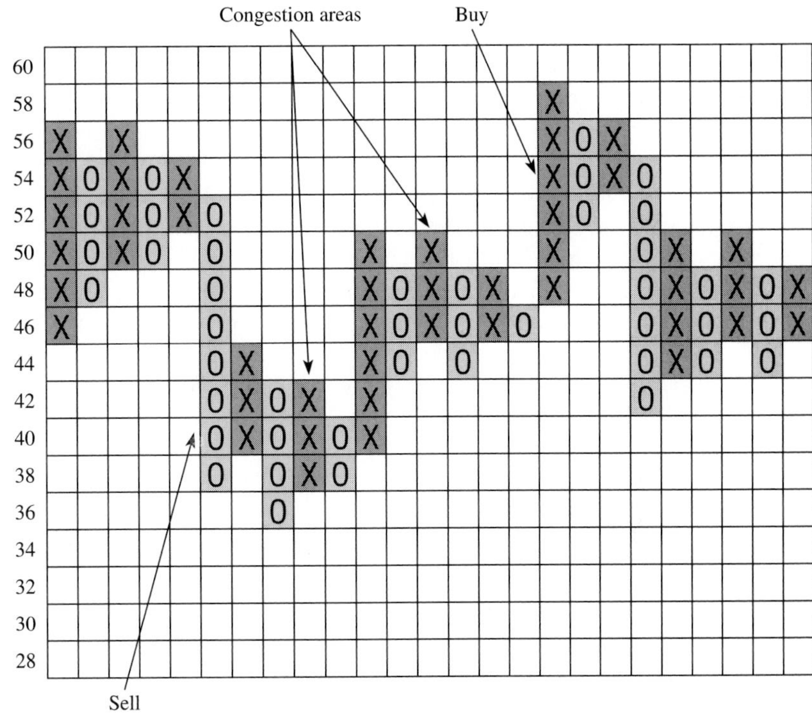


**Figure 19.6**
Point and figure chart with sell signal, buy signal, and congestion areas.

increase of at least $2 calls for placement of another X in the first column, this time at the $44 level. If the stock then falls by at least $2, you start a new column and put an O next to $42. Each subsequent $2 price fall results in another O in the second column. When prices reverse yet again and head upward, you begin the third column with an X denoting each consecutive $2 price increase.

The asterisks in Table 19.1 mark an event resulting in the placement of a new X or O in the chart. The daggers denote price movements that result in the start of a new column of Xs or Os.

Sell signals are generated when the stock price *penetrates* previous lows, and buy signals occur when previous high prices are penetrated. A *congestion area* is a horizontal band of Xs and Os created by several price reversals. These three regions are indicated in Figure 19.6.

One can devise point and figure charts using price increments other than $2, but it is customary in setting up a chart to require reasonably substantial price changes before marking pluses or minuses.

---

**Concept Check** Question 2. Draw a point and figure chart using the history in Table 19.1 with price increments of $3.

---

## A Warning

The search for patterns in stock market prices is nearly irresistible, and the ability of the human eye to discern apparent patterns is remarkable. Unfortunately, it is possible to perceive patterns that really don't exist. Consider Figure 19.7, which presents simulated and actual values of the Dow Jones Industrial Average during 1956 taken from a famous study by Harry Roberts.[1] In Figure 19.7**B,** it appears as though the market presents a classic head-and-shoulders pattern where the middle hump (the head) is flanked by two shoulders. When the price index "pierces the right shoulder"—a technical trigger point—it is believed to be heading lower, and it is time to sell your stocks. Figure 19.7**A** also looks like a "typical" stock market patterns. Can you tell which of the two graphs is constructed from the real value of the Dow and which from the simulated data? Figure 19.7**A** is based on the real data. The graph in **B** was generated using "returns" created by a random number generator. These returns *by construction* were patternless, but the simulated price path that is plotted appears to follow a pattern much like that of **A.**

Figure 19.8 shows the weekly price changes behind the two panels in Figure 19.7. Here the randomness in both series—the stock price as well as the simulated sequence—is obvious.

A problem related to the tendency to perceive patterns where they don't exist is data mining. After the fact, you can always find patterns and trading rules that would have generated enormous profits. If you test enough rules, some will have worked in the past. Unfortunately, picking a theory that would have worked after the fact carries no guarantee of future success.

In this regard, consider a curious investment rule that has worked with uncanny precision since 1967. In years that an original National Football League team wins the Superbowl (played in January), bet on the stock market rising for the rest of the year. In years that a team from the American Football Conference that was not originally an NFL team wins, bet on a market decline.

Between 1967 and 1990, the NYSE index rose in the year following the Superbowl 15 of the 17 times that an NFC or original NFL team won. The market fell in six out of seven years that an AFC team won. Despite the overwhelming past success of this rule, would you use it to invest your money? We suspect not.

In evaluating trading rules, you should always ask whether the rule would have seemed reasonable *before* you looked at the data. If not, you might be buying into the one arbitrary rule among many that happened to have worked in the recent past. The hard but crucial question is whether there is reason to believe that what worked in the past should continue to work in the future.

---

[1] Harry Roberts, "Stock Market 'Patterns' and Financial Analysis: Methodological Suggestions," *Journal of Finance* 14 (March 1959), pp. 701–717.

**Figure 19.7**

Actual and simulated levels for stock market prices of 52 weeks.

From Harry Roberts, "Stock Market 'Patterns' and Financial Analysis: Methodological Suggestions," *Journal of Finance* (March 1959), pp. 5–6. Reprinted by permission.

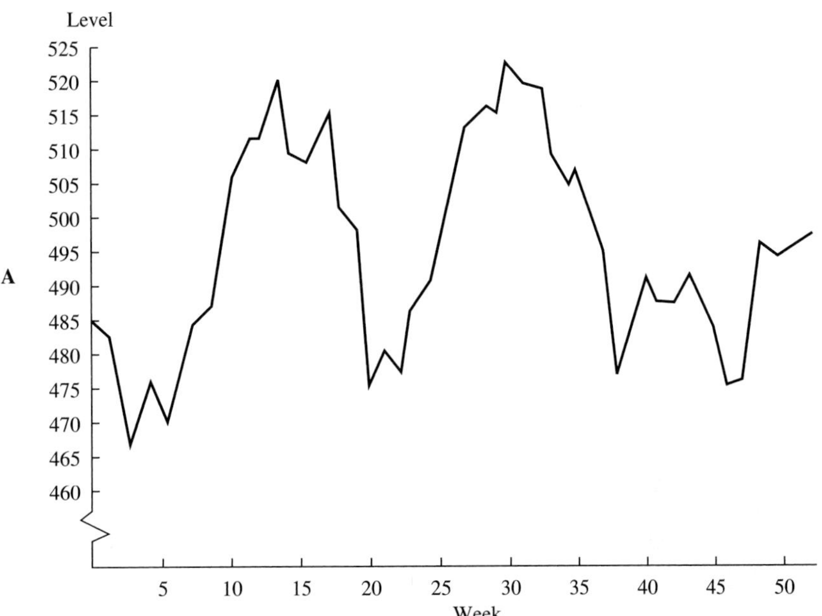


Friday closing levels, December 30, 1955—December 28, 1956, Dow Jones Industrial Average.

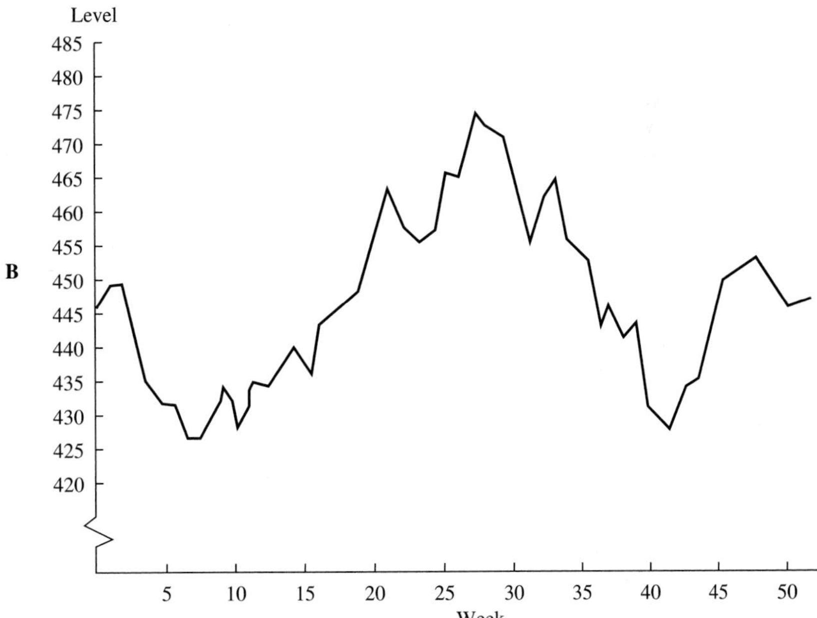

**Figure 19.8**
Actual and simulated changes in weekly stock prices for 52 weeks.

From Harry Roberts, "Stock Market 'Patterns' and Financial Analysis: Methodological Suggestions," *Journal of Finance* (March 1959), pp. 5–6. Reprinted by permission.

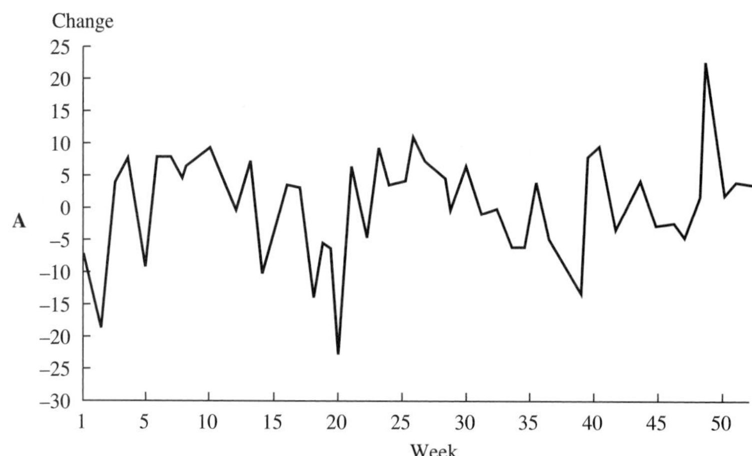


Changes from Friday to Friday (closing) January 6, 1956–December 28, 1956, Dow Jones Industrial Average.

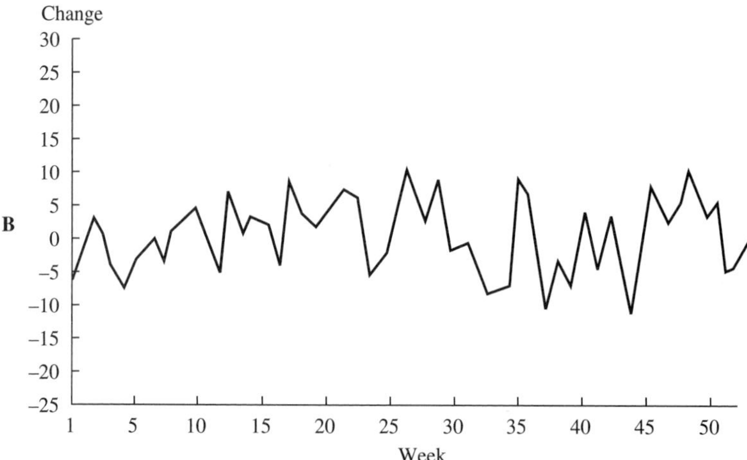


## 19.3 Technical Indicators

Technical analysts use technical indicators besides charts to assess prospects for market declines or advances. We will examine some popular indicators in this section.

Market volume sometimes is used to measure the strength of a market rise or fall. Increased investor participation in a market advance or retreat is viewed as a measure of the significance of the movement. Technicians consider market advances to be a more favourable omen of continued price increases when they are associated with increased trading volume. Similarly, market reversals are consid-

**Figure 19.9**
Market diary.

From *The Wall Street Journal*, October 18, 1990. Reprinted by permission of *The Wall Street Journal*, © 1990 Dow Jones & Company, Inc. All Rights Reserved Worldwide.

**DIARIES**

| NYSE | WED | TUES | WK AGO |
|---|---|---|---|
| Issues traded | 1,981 | 1,988 | 1,900 |
| Advances | 659 | 487 | 356 |
| Declines | 833 | 1,077 | 1,200 |
| Unchanged | 489 | 424 | 434 |
| New highs | 6 | 5 | 1 |
| New lows | 248 | 276 | 278 |
| z/Adv vol (000) | 68,074 | 29,694 | 25,874 |
| zDecl vol (000) | 74,617 | 105,139 | 129,075 |
| zTotal vol (000) | 161,260 | 149,570 | 167,890 |
| Closing tick[1] | −418 | −111 | −378 |
| Closing trin[1] | .87 | 1.60 | 1.48 |
| zBlock trades | 3,503 | 3,077 | 3,558 |

[1] The net difference of the number of stocks closing higher than their previous trade from those closing lower, NYSE trading only.
[2] A comparison of the number of advancing and declining issues with the volume of shares rising and falling. Generally, a trin of less than 1.00 indicates buying demand: above 1.00 indicates selling pressure.
z-NYSE or AMEX only.

ered more bearish when associated with higher volume. The **trin** statistic is the ratio of the number of advancing to declining issues divided by the ratio of volume in advancing versus declining issues:

$$\text{Trin} = \frac{\text{Number advancing/Number declining}}{\text{Volume advancing/Volume declining}}$$

This expression can be rearranged as:

$$\text{Trin} = \frac{\text{Volume declining/Number declining}}{\text{Volume advancing/Number advancing}}$$

Therefore, trin is the ratio of average volume in declining issues to average volume in advancing issues. Ratios above 1.0 are considered bearish because the falling stocks would then have higher average volume than the advancing stocks, indicating net selling pressure. *The Wall Street Journal* reports trin every day in the market diary section, as in Figure 19.9.

Note, however, for every buyer, there must a seller of stock. Rising volume in a rising market should not necessarily indicate a larger imbalance of buyers versus sellers. For example, a trin statistic above 1.0, which is considered bearish, could equally well be interpreted as indicating that there is more *buying* activity in declining issues.

The **breadth** of the market is a measure of the extent to which movements in a market index are reflected widely in the price movements of all the stocks in the market. The most common measure of breadth is the spread between the number of stocks that advance and decline in price. If advances outnumber declines by a wide margin, then the market is viewed as being stronger because the rally is widespread. A standard indicator of the current breadth is the **tick,** computed as

**Table 19.2** Breadth

| Day | Advances | Declines | Net Advances | Cumulative Breadth |
|---|---|---|---|---|
| 1 | 802 | 748 | 54 | 54 |
| 2 | 917 | 640 | 277 | 331 |
| 3 | 703 | 772 | −69 | 262 |
| 4 | 512 | 1122 | −610 | −348 |
| 5 | 633 | 1004 | −371 | −719 |

Note: The sum of advances and declines varies across days because some stock prices are unchanged.

the net difference between the number of stocks trading higher than their previous trade price and the number trading lower. These breadth numbers also are reported daily in *The Wall Street Journal* (see Figure 19.9).

Some analysts cumulate breadth data each day, as in Table 19.2. The cumulative breadth for each day is obtained by adding that day's net advances (or declines) to the previous day's total. The direction of the cumulated series is then used to discern broad market trends.

**Short interest** is the total number of shares of stock currently sold short in the market. Some technicians interpret short interest as bullish, some as bearish. The bullish perspective is that because all short sales must be covered (i.e., short-sellers eventually must purchase shares to return the ones they have borrowed), short interest represents latent future demand for the stocks. As short sales are covered, the demand created by the share purchase will force prices up.

The bearish interpretation of short interest is based on the fact that short-sellers tend to be larger, more sophisticated investors. Accordingly, increased short interest reflects bearish sentiment by those investors "in the know," which would be a negative signal of the market's prospects. Assogvabi, Khoury, and Yourougou have used the volume of outstanding short interest on the TSE to test asymmetry in the price-volume relationship. Their findings show that the ratio of short positions to total shares outstanding is significantly related to the sensitivity of the volume of transactions to price changes.[2]

Just as short-sellers tend to be larger institutional traders, odd-lot traders are almost always small individual traders. (An odd lot is a transaction of fewer than 100 shares; 100 shares is one round lot.) the **odd-lot theory** holds that these small investors tend to miss key market turning points, typically buying stocks after a bull market has already run its course and selling too late into a bear market. Therefore, the theory suggests that when odd-lot traders are widely buying, you should sell, and vice versa.

[2] See Tov Assogvabi, Nabil Khoury, and Pierre Yourougou, "Short Interest and the Asymmetry of the Price-Volume Relationship in the Canadian Stock Market," *Journal of Banking and Finance* 19, No. 8 (November 1995), pp. 1341-58.

*The Wall Street Journal* publishes odd-lot trading data every day. You can construct an index of odd-lot trading by computing the ratio of odd-lot purchases to sales. A ratio substantially above 1.0 is bearish because it implies small traders are net buyers.

*Barron's* computes a confidence index using data from the bond market. The presumption is that actions of bond traders reveal trends that will emerge soon in the stock market.

The **confidence index** is the ratio of the average yield on 10 top-rated corporate bonds divided by the average yield on 10 intermediate-grade corporate bonds. The ratio will always be below 100 percent because higher-rated bonds will offer lower promised yields to maturity. When bond traders are optimistic about the economy, however, they might require smaller default premiums on lower-rated debt. Hence, the yield spread will narrow, and the confidence index will approach 100 percent. Therefore, higher values of the confidence index are bullish signals.

---

**CONCEPT CHECK** Question 3. Yields on lower-rated debt will rise after fears of recession have spread through the economy. This will reduce the confidence index. Should the stock market now be expected to fall or will it already have fallen?

---

**Relative strength** measures the extent to which a security has outperformed or underperformed either the market as a whole or its particular industry. Relative strength is computed by calculating the ratio of the price of the security to a price index for the industry. For example, the relative strength of IBM versus the computer industry would be measured by movements in the ratio of Price (IBM)/Price (computer industry index). A rising ratio implies IBM has been outperforming the rest of the industry. If relative strength can be assumed to persist over time, then this would be a signal to buy IBM.

Similarly, the relative strength of an industry relative to the whole market can be computed by tracking the ratio of the industry price index to the market price index.

Some technical indicators are depicted in charts of individual stocks, industry groups, or the entire market. Thus charting services may include graphs of the relative strength and of the **advance-decline line,** which is the common indicator of market breadth. In addition to these, **moving averages** computed on 13-week, 26-week, or 200-day periods are watched closely by many technicians; failure of the current price to break through a moving average line is interpreted to indicate that the existing trend in the price graph will prevail, while a convincing breakthrough implies a reversal and thus the establishment of a new trend.

## 19.4 TECHNICAL ANALYSIS FOR CANADIAN INVESTORS

The subject of technical analysis followed in Canada can be dividend along macro and micro lines. Broadly, the market in Canada can be viewed as following that in the United States, as evidenced by the high degree of correlation between them.

**Figure 19.10**
Market breadth.
From *The Financial Post,* October 5, 1996. Reprinted by permission.

**Market Diaries**

| | Volume 00s | Previous day 00s | Advances | Adv. vol 00s | Declines | Dec. vol 00s | Unchanged | Issues traded | New highs | New lows |
|---|---|---|---|---|---|---|---|---|---|---|
| Toronto | 1002873 | 999822 | 511 | 555028 | 376 | 316952 | 300 | 1187 | 94 | 15 |
| Montreal | 214814 | 188580 | 214 | 119414 | 134 | 66158 | 122 | 470 | 37 | 5 |
| Vancouver | 347862 | 368585 | 340 | 179850 | 337 | 115223 | 181 | 858 | 22 | 10 |
| Alberta | 165016 | 176629 | 158 | 69179 | 155 | 63440 | 114 | 427 | 10 | 8 |
| New York | 4676300 | 3894818 | 1789 | 3020694 | 704 | 1069696 | 745 | 3238 | 294 | 26 |
| AMEX | 219006 | 187556 | 298 | 123152 | 220 | 60842 | 204 | 722 | 33 | 12 |
| NASDAQ | 5743767 | 5864577 | 2243 | 3462185 | 1845 | 1759598 | 1224 | 5312 | 260 | 66 |

In response to this, a brokerage house can predict the direction of the market by performing technical analysis on the S&P 500 or by following the Dow theory. If market timing is the objective, then either an in-house analysis can be pursued or predictions can be obtained from U.S. affiliates or other sources.

At the level of the individual company, there is an important dichotomy. For those companies that are actively traded on the NYSE, such as Northern Telecom or Alcan, information is likely to be available from U.S. sources; the relevant price behaviour to follow is that on the NYSE, at least as much as that on the TSE. For smaller companies, however, Canadian investment advisors must perform their own technical analysis. This will be done using the same measures as are used in the United States, such as relative strength and charts displaying patterns and trends.

The information on Canadian stocks available to investors is somewhat more limited. Brokers may have displayed on their screens the technical indicators such as the trin and tick for the NYSE; more recently, trin and tick have also been available for TSE stocks. This will enable traders (if they so believe) to speculate on short-run movements in the market, for either Canadian or U.S. securities. Other U.S. indicators like odd-lot trading and the confidence index are not computed, although short interest figures are available.

*The Financial Post* gives a daily report of market breadth for Canadian markets as well as the three major U.S. markets, as illustrated in Figure 19.10; in addition, there are daily price and volume charts for the TSE 300, as illustrated in Figure 19.11, and the block trade report (shown in Chapter 2). Investors can also consult the *Graphoscope,* available by subscription or at libraries. This document presents charts on Canadian stocks, commodities, indices, and foreign markets and currencies, giving the advance-decline line and the moving average. The *Independent Survey Co.* gives similar information, including relative strength.

One area where academics are less inclined to reject technical analysis is in commodity trading. For whatever reasons, chart patterns seem to offer information about future prices.[3] In Figure 19.12, the chart pattern for the relative performance of the TSE gold index versus gold illustrates how the analysis may be applied.

**Figure 19.11** TSE 300 index and market volume.

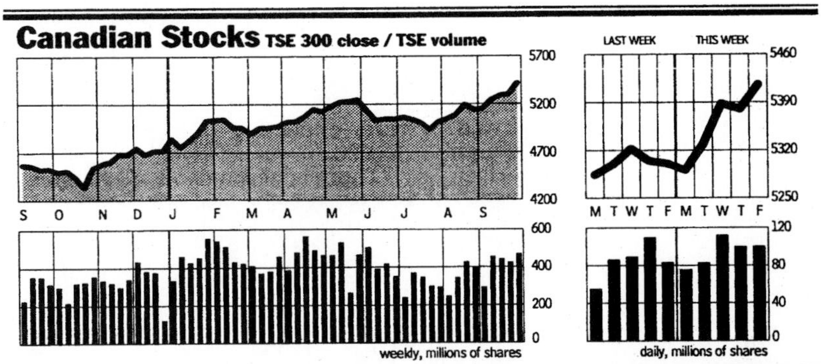

**Canadian Stocks** TSE 300 close / TSE volume

| Index | Close | Net chg | % chg | 52W high | 52W low | — Yr over yr — net chg | % chg | — Yr to date — net chg | % chg |
|---|---|---|---|---|---|---|---|---|---|
| TSE 300 | 5415.71 | +35.70 | +0.66 | 5415.71 | 4280.03 | +923.09 | +20.55 | +702.17 | +14.90 |
| TSE 200 | 329.47 | +1.89 | +0.58 | 329.53 | 252.03 | +59.59 | +22.08 | +46.54 | +16.45 |
| TSE 100 | 327.92 | +2.23 | +0.68 | 327.94 | 260.25 | +55.05 | +20.17 | +41.61 | +14.53 |
| Toronto 35 | 283.55 | +2.15 | +0.76 | 283.57 | 222.99 | +47.45 | +20.10 | +35.06 | +14.11 |
| ME Market Portfolio | 2677.43 | +30.37 | +1.15 | 2677.43 | 2094.00 | +486.54 | +22.21 | +360.04 | +15.54 |
| VSE Composite | 1209.63 | −0.50 | −0.04 | 1472.55 | 760.77 | +374.87 | +44.91 | +413.70 | +51.98 |
| ASE Combined | 2455.67 | +14.00 | +0.57 | 2591.36 | 1259.16 | +1138.09 | +86.38 | +990.06 | +67.55 |

From *The Financial Post,* October 5, 1996. Reprinted by permission.

## 19.5 The Value Line System

The Value Line ranking system may be the most celebrated and well-documented example of successful stock analysis. Value Line is the largest investment advisory service in the world. Besides publishing the *Value Line Investment Survey,* which provides information on investment fundamentals for approximately 1,700 publicly traded companies, Value Line also ranks each of these stocks according to their anticipated price appreciation over the next 12 months. Stocks ranked in group 1 are expected to perform the best, while those in group 5 are expected to perform the worst. Value Line calls this "ranking for timeliness."

Figure 19.13 shows the performance of the Value Line ranking system over the 25 years from 1965 to March 1990. Over the total period, the different groups performed just as the rankings would predict, and the differences were quite large. The total 25-year price appreciation for the group 1 stocks was 3,083 percent (or 14.8 percent per year) compared to 15 percent (or 0.5 percent per year) for group 5.

[3] See, for example, Stephen J. Taylor, "Trading Futures Using a Channel Rule," *Journal of Futures Markets* 14, no. 2 (April 1994), pp. 215–36.

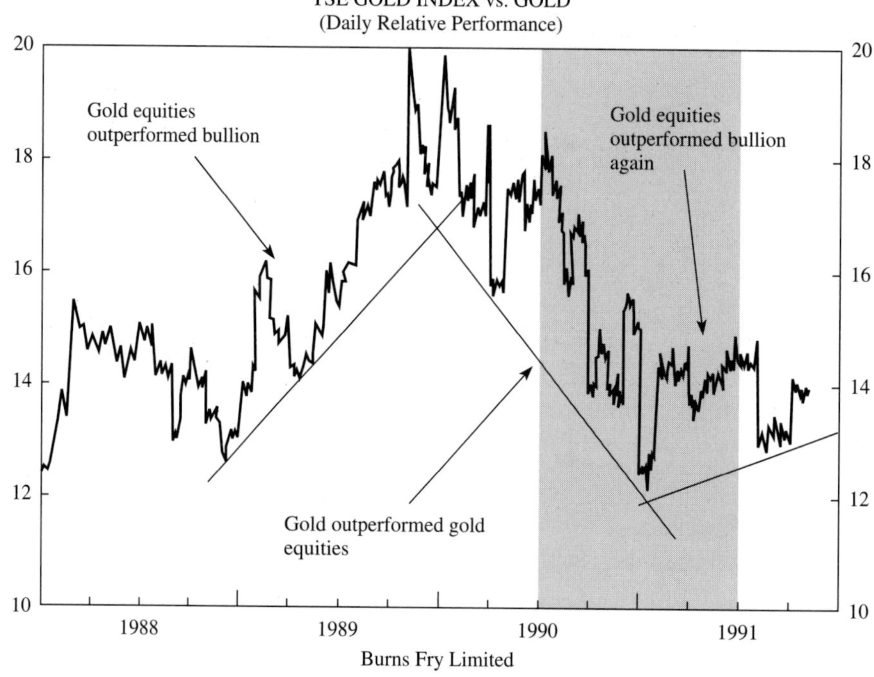


**Figure 19.12** TSE gold index versus gold (daily relative performance).

From Burns Fry Investment Research, *Gold Chart Book,* December 1991. Reprinted by permission of Burns Fry Ltd.

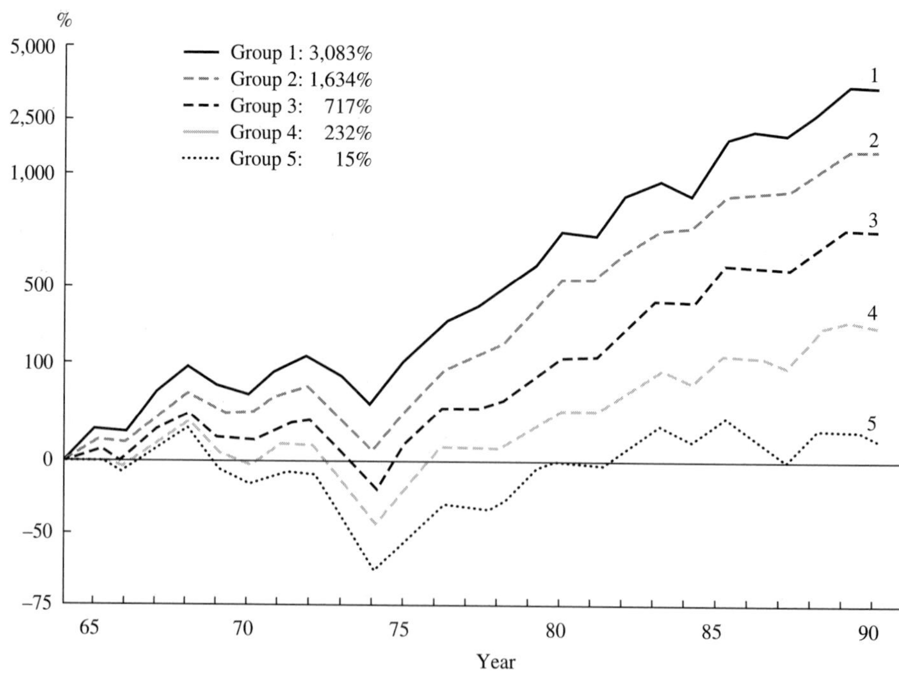


**Figure 19.13** Record of Value Line ranking for timeliness (without allowing for changes in rank, 1965–1990).

From *Value Line Selection & Opinion,* April 20, 1990. Reprinted by permission.

How does the Value Line ranking system work? As Bernhard[4] explains, the ranking procedure has three components: (1) relative earnings momentum, (2) earnings surprise, and (3) a value index. Most (though not all) of the Value Line criteria are technically oriented, relying on either price momentum or relative strength. Points assigned for each factor determine the stock's overall ranking.

The relative earnings momentum factor is calculated as each company's year-to-year change in quarterly earnings divided by the average change for all stocks.

The earnings surprise factor has to do with the difference between actual reported quarterly earnings and Value Line's estimate. The points assigned to each stock increase with the percentage difference between reported and estimated earnings.

The value index is calculated from the following regression equation:

$$V = a + b_1x_1 + b_2x_2 + b_3x_3$$

where

$x_1$ = A score from 1 to 10 depending on the relative earnings momentum ranking, compared with the company's rank for the last 10 years;

$x_2$ = A score from 1 to 10 based on the stock's relative price, with ratios calculated in a similar way to the earnings ratio;

$x_3$ = The ratio of the stock's latest 10-week average relative price (stock price divided by the average price for all stocks) to its 52-week average relative price.

and $a$, $b_1$, $b_2$, and $b_3$ are the coefficients from the regression estimated on 12 years of data.

Finally, the points for each of the three factors are added, and the stocks are classified into five groups according to the total score.

Investing according to this system does seem to produce superior results on paper, as Figure 19.13 shows. Yet as the accompanying box points out, in practice, things are not so simple—Value Line's own mutual funds have not kept up even with the broad market averages. The box illustrates that even apparently successful trading rules can be difficult to implement in the market.

## 19.6 Can Technical Analysis Work in Efficient Markets?

### Self-Destructing Patterns

It should be abundantly clear from our presentation that most of technical analysis is based on ideas totally at odds with the foundations of the efficient market hypothesis. The EMH follows from the idea that rational profit-seeking investors will act on new information so quickly that prices will nearly always reflect all

[4] See the suggested readings that conclude this chapter.

# PAYING THE PIPER: ON PAPER, VALUE LINE'S PERFORMANCE IN PICKING STOCKS IS NOTHING SHORT OF DAZZLING . . . FOR AN INVESTOR TO CAPITALIZE ON THAT PERFORMANCE IS A DIFFERENT MATTER

Value Line, Inc., publishes the *Value Line Investment Survey,* that handy review of 1,652 companies. Each week the survey rates stocks from I (best buys) to V (worst). Can you beat the market following these rankings? Value Line tracks the performance of group I from April 1965, when a new ranking formula went into effect. If you bought group I then and updated your list every week, you would have a gain of 15,391 percent by June 30. That means $10,000 would have grown to about $1.5 million, dividends excluded. The market is up only 245 percent since 1965, dividends excluded.

Quite an impressive record. There is only one flaw: It ignores transaction costs. Do transaction costs much matter against a performance like that? What does the investor lose in transaction costs? A percentage point a year? Two percent?

None other than Value Line provides an answer to this question, and the answer is almost as startling as the paper performance. Since late 1983, Value Line has run a mutual fund that attempts to track I precisely. Its return has averaged a dismal 11 percentage points a year worse than the hypothetical results in group I. The fund hasn't even kept up with the market (see chart).

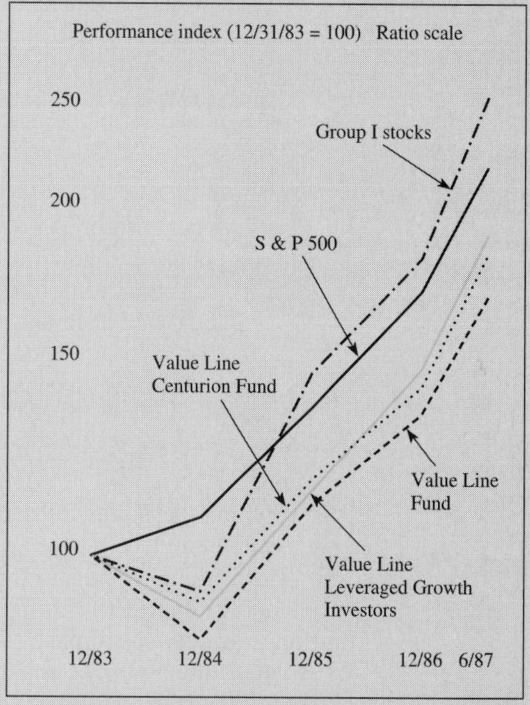


What went wrong? "Inefficiencies and costs of implementation," says Mark Tavel, manager of the fund, Value Line Centurion.

This is not to denigrate Value Line's undeniably impressive stock-picking record. Far from it: one of the funds run for Value Line by Tavel, Leveraged Growth Investors, shines on Forbes' mutual fund honor roll. (Leveraged Growth and the flagship Value Line Fund use the ranking system, but not as closely as Centurion.)

The point here is to illustrate the folly of constant trading. It's a familiar story, but one that investors are prone to forget in the middle of a bull market. It costs money to run the racetrack, and the fellow who steps up to the betting window pays. Wall Street's revenues top $50 billion a year. People who trade pay the bill, and people who try to beat the market with a lot of trading pay dearly.

The Value Line Centurion Fund's turnover is 200 percent a year. That's quite a bit of turnover—although by no means the highest in the business. The turnover is high because in a typical week, 4 of the

*(Continued)*

100 group I stocks drop down in rank and have to be replaced with new group I stocks. It's not impossible for traders like Centurion to beat the market, but they start out with a handicap.

All of which means that paper performance can be pretty fanciful. "Anytime hypothetical returns are offered as proof of a particular investing style, one should also swallow a large grain of salt," says Cam Schmidt of Potomac Investment Management, a money manager in Bethesda, Maryland, that brought the Value Line discrepancy to *Forbes'* attention.

What are these inefficiencies and costs? And what do they tell investors about the perils of in-and-out trading?

Fund overhead is not a big item? At the $244 million Centurion, which is available only through variable life and annuity policies sold by Guardian Life, the annual expense ratio averages 0.6 percent. Nor are brokerage commissions large. Funneled at about 5 cents a share mostly to a captive Value Line broker, commissions eat up to 0.4 percent of Centurion's assets per year.

So far we have 1 percent. Where's the other 10 percent of the shortfall? Bid-ask spreads, for one. A stock quoted at 39 to sellers might cost a buyer 39½—or even 41 or 42 if the buyer wants a lot of it. With about 95 of the 100 group I stocks at any given time in the Centurion portfolio, Tavel needs to amass an average $2.5 million position in each. Some of these companies have $150 million or less in outstanding shares. The very smallest Tavel doesn't even try to buy.

Timing explains some of the gulf between hypothetical and actual results. The hypothetical performance assumes a purchase at the Wednesday close before publication of the new rankings. Most subscribers get their surveys on Friday morning, however, and buy at the Friday opening—if they are lucky. An internal Value Line rule forbids the funds to act on rank changes before Friday morning.

Why, then, are Wednesday prices used in the performance claims? Because, says Samuel Eisenstadt, Value Line's chief of statistics, until recently that was all Value Line had in its database. Wednesday prices were gathered because it takes nine days to compute, print, and mail the results. The hypothetical buy, then, would come a week after the closing prices used to calculate the rankings, and a day and a half before a real buyer could act on the advice. Eisenstadt says a conversion to Friday night scoring is under way and will no doubt depress reported performance.

A day makes all the difference. A 1985 study by Scott Stickel, now an assistant professor at Wharton, showed that almost all of the excess return on a group I stock is concentrated on three days, almost evenly divided: the Friday when subscribers read about the stock's being promoted into group I, the Thursday before, and the Monday following. Wait until Tuesday to buy and you might as well not subscribe.

Why are prices moving up on Thursday, the day before publication? Eisenstadt suspects the Postal Service of acting with uncharacteristic efficiency in some parts of the country, giving a few subscribers an early start. Another reason for an uptick: Enough is known about the Value Line formula for smart investors to anticipate a rank change by a few days. The trick is to watch group II (near-top) stocks closely. If a quarterly earnings report comes in far better than the forecast published in *Value Line,* grab the stock. "What happens if you're wrong? You're stuck with a group II stock with terrific earnings," says Eisenstadt.

Come Friday at 9:30 A.M., the throng is at the starting gate. Tavel says he often gets only a small portion of his position established before the price starts to run away from him. How are the individual investors faring? Probably no better. True, a 200-share order is not by itself going to move the market the way Tavel's 20,000-share order will. But if both orders arrive at the opening bell, the small investor is in no position to get a good price. Individuals aren't paying the fund overhead, but then they pay higher commissions than Tavel.

What of the future? Value Line's magic was built on its computer-quick response to favourable earnings reports. Now computers are nothing special. Significantly, they're becoming a lot more common among individual investors, the people who buy the small-cap stocks where the ranking system has

*(Continued)*

shown its strength. Eisenstadt concedes: "Everyone's playing this earnings surprise game now." But he insists that there's no firm evidence yet that the ranking system is falling apart.

Even if the ranking system loses some of its effectiveness, however, it would be premature to write off Value Line, which trades over the counter near 27. Many of the survey's 120,000 subscribers pay $495 a year just to get the detailed financial histories of the companies in it. Indeed, considering that subscriptions are on the upswing and that it costs maybe $50 to print and mail one, favourable earnings surprises may be in store. If you don't like the horses, buy stock in the track.



publicly available information. Technical analysis, on the other hand, posits the existence of long-lived trends that play out slowly and predictably. Such patterns, if they exist, would violate the EMH notion of essentially unpredictable stock price changes.

An interesting question is whether a technical rule that seems to work will continue to work in the future once it becomes widely recognized. A clever analyst may occasionally uncover a profitable trading rule, but the real test of efficient markets is whether the rule itself becomes reflected in stock prices once its value is discovered.

Suppose, for example, the Dow theory predicts an upward primary trend. If the theory is widely accepted, it follows that many investors will attempt to buy stocks immediately in anticipation of the price increase; the effect would be to bid up prices sharply and immediately rather than at the gradual, long-lived pace initially expected. The Dow theory's predicted trend would be replaced by a sharp jump in prices. It is in this sense that price patterns ought to be *self-destructing.* Once a useful technical rule (or price pattern) is discovered, it ought to be invalidated once the mass of traders attempts to exploit it.

For the prediction of a technical indicator to work, enough believers must trade correspondingly to bring about the anticipated price behaviour. In this sense, the trading rule may become self-fulfilling. If everyone were to believe, however, the necessary anticipation of the price movement would eliminate any potential gain. Technicians are happy to admit that they rely on enough believers to produce the effect, but enough skeptics to allow it to continue; alternatively, smaller investors can follow the rules, but institutional investors moving large blocks of stock are unable to profit from technical strategies.

An instructive example of this phenomenon is the evidence by Jegadeesh[5] and Lehmann[6] that stock prices seem to obey a reversal effect; specifically, the best-

---

[5] Narasimhan Jegadeesh, "Evidence of Predictable Behavior of Security Prices," *Journal of Finance* 45 (September 1990), pp. 881–898.

[6] Bruce Lehmann, "Fads, Martingales and Market Efficiency," *Quarterly Journal of Economics* 105 (February 1990), pp. 1–28.

performing stocks in one week or month tend to fare poorly in the following period, while the worst performers follow up with good performance. Such a phenomenon can be used to form a straightforward technically based trading strategy: Buy shares that recently have done poorly and sell shares that recently have done well. Lehmann shows such a strategy would have been extremely profitable in the past. Lehmann notes that Rosenberg Institutional Equity Management and the College Retirement Equity Fund now use return reversal strategies in their actively managed portfolios. These activities presumably should eliminate existing profit opportunities by forcing prices to their "correct" levels.

On the other hand, Foerster, Prihar and Schmitz[7] report evidence of testing for return persistence in Canadian equities. Identifying superior returns in previous quarters, they show that the top performing decile of the data set continues to outperform the market on a risk-adjusted basis. Both before and after transaction costs, a policy of investing in a portfolio of that top decile (revised quarterly) yields extremely high returns—approximately three times those of the TSE. The results of quarterly persistence in Canada appear to contradict the abovementioned monthly reversals in the U.S.[8] They find, however, that the bottom decile has quite average returns, which might indicate reversal for poor performers.

Under the area of market microstructure studies, Blume, Easley and O'Hara[9] have investigated the importance of analyzing trading volume in determining the underlying pressure on price. Increased volume is likely to be an indication of superior information possessed by some investors. This information as to the true equilibrium value of the stock will cause an increase in buying or selling by insiders. Uninformed investors must take account of the volume information in order to restore strong-form efficiency. Recognition of the volume may allow technical traders to trade and profit before the equilibrium value is identified.

Yet another recent study[10] offers conclusive evidence that even the simplest of technical trading strategies can be profitable, especially before transaction costs. The charting practices discussed earlier in the chapter, such as determining moving averages and price breakouts, were subjected to more sophisticated statistical analyses (including the GARCH technique) and shown to offer significantly better returns than trading on the basis of no technical signals. These effects are at odds with market efficiency and at the same time, consistent with the viability of technical analysis. The real test of these trading rules will come now that the potential of the strategies has been uncovered.

---

[7] Steven Foerster, Anoop Prihar, and John Schmitz, "Price Momentum Models and How They Beat the Canadian Equity Markets," *Canadian Investment Review* VII, no. 4 (Winter, 1995), pp. 9–13.

[8] N. Jegadeesh and S. Titman, "Returns to Buying Winners and Selling Losers: Implications for Stock Market Efficiency," *The Journal of Finance* 48 (March 1993), pp. 65–91.

[9] Marshall Blume, David Easley, and Maureen O'Hara, "Market Statistics and Technical Analysis: The Role of Volume," *The Journal of Finance* 49 (March 1994), pp. 153–82.

[10] William Brock, Josef Lakonishok, and Blake LeBaron, *The Journal of Finance* 47 (December 1992), pp. 1661–99.

Thus, the market dynamic is one of a continual search for profitable trading rules, followed by destruction by overuse of those rules found to be successful, followed by more search for yet-undiscovered rules.

## A New View of Technical Analysis

Brown and Jennings[11] offer a rigorous foundation for the potential efficacy of technical analysis. They envision an economy where many investors have private information regarding the ultimate value of a stock. Moreover, as time passes, each investor acquires additional information. Each investor can infer something of the information possessed by other traders by observing the price at which securities trade. The entire sequence of past prices can turn out to be useful in the inference of the information held by other traders. In this sense, technical analysis can be useful to traders even if all traders rationally use all information available to them.

Most discussions of the EMH envision public information commonly available to all traders and ask only if prices reflect that information. In this sense, the Brown and Jennings framework is more complex. Here, different individuals receive different private signals regarding the value of a firm. As prices unfold, each trader infers the good-news or bad-news nature of the signals received by other traders and updates assessments of the firm accordingly. Prices *reveal* as well as *reflect* information and become useful data to traders. Without addressing specific technical trading rules, the Brown and Jennings model is an interesting and innovative attempt to reconcile technical analysis with the usual assumption of rational traders participating in efficient markets.

## SUMMARY

**1.** Technical analysis is the search for recurring patterns in stock market prices. It is based essentially on the notion that market prices adjust slowly to new information and, thus, is at odds with the efficient market hypothesis.

**2.** The Dow theory is the earliest chart-based version of technical analysis. The theory posits the existence of primary, intermediate, and minor trends that can be identified on a chart and acted on by an analyst before the trends fully dissipate. Other trend-based theories are based on relative strength and the point and figures chart.

**3.** Technicians believe high volume and market breadth accompanying market trends add weight to the significance of a trend.

**4.** Odd-lot traders are viewed as uninformed, which suggests informed traders should pursue trading strategies in opposition to their activity. In contrast, short-sellers are viewed as informed traders, lending credence to their activity.

---

[11] David Brown and Robert H. Jennings, "On Technical Analysis," *Review of Financial Studies* 2 (1989), pp. 527–552.

**5.** Value Line's ranking system uses technically based data and has shown great ability to discriminate between stocks with good and poor prospects, but the Value Line mutual fund that uses this system most closely has been only a mediocre performer, suggesting that implementation of the Value Line timing system is difficult.

**6.** New theories of information dissemination in the market suggest there may be a role for the examination of past prices in formulating investment strategies. They do not, however, support the specific charting patterns currently relied on by technical analysts.

## Key Terms

Dow theory
Support level
Resistance level
Trin
Breadth
Tick
Short interest
Odd-lot theory
Confidence index
Relative strength
Advance-decline line
Moving average

## Selected Readings

*A magazine devoted to technical analysis is Technical Analysis of Stocks and Commodities.*

*The Value Line method is described in:*

Bernhard, Arnold. *Value Line Methods of Evaluating Common Stocks.* New York: Arnold Bernhard and Co., 1979.

## Problems

1. Consider the graph of stock prices over a two-year period in Figure 19A. Identify likely support and resistance levels.
2. Use the data from *The Globe and Mail* in Figure 19.10 to construct the trin ratio for the market. Is the trin ratio bullish or bearish?
3. Calculate market breadth using the same data as in problem (2). Is the signal bullish or bearish?
4. Collect data on the TSE 300 for a period covering a few months. Try to identify primary trends. Can you tell whether the market currently is in an upward or downward trend?
5. The ratio of put to call options outstanding is viewed by some as a technical indicator. Do you think a high ratio is viewed as bullish or bearish? Should it be?

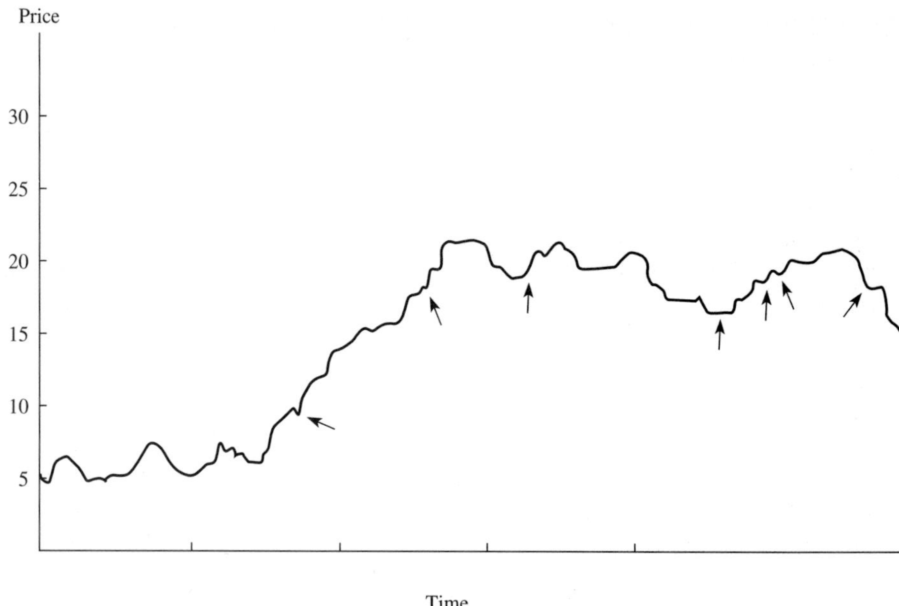


**Figure 19A**
Simulated stock prices over time.

6. Table 19A presents price data for Computers, Inc., and a computer industry index. Does Computers, Inc., show relative strength over this period?
7. Use the data in Table 19A to compute a five-day moving average for Computers, Inc. Can you identify any buy or sell signals?
8. Construct a point and figure chart for Computers, Inc., using the data in Table 19A. Use $2 increments for your chart. Do the buy or sell signals derived from your chart correspond to those derived from the moving average rule (see problem [7])?
9. Table 19B on page 774 contains data on market advances and declines. Calculate cumulative breadth and decide whether this technical signal is bullish or bearish.
10. Is the confidence index rising or falling, given the following information?

| | This Year | Last Year |
|---|---|---|
| Yield on top-rated corporate bonds | 8% | 9% |
| Yield on intermediate-grade corporate bonds | 9% | 10% |

**Table 19A** Computers, Inc., Stock Price History

| Trading Day | Computers, Inc. | Industry Index |
|---|---|---|
| 1 | 19⅝ | 50.0 |
| 2 | 20 | 50.1 |
| 3 | 20½ | 50.5 |
| 4 | 22 | 50.4 |
| 5 | 21⅛ | 51.0 |
| 6 | 22 | 50.7 |
| 7 | 21⅞ | 50.5 |
| 8 | 22½ | 51.1 |
| 9 | 23⅛ | 51.5 |
| 10 | 23⅞ | 51.7 |
| 11 | 24½ | 51.4 |
| 12 | 23¼ | 51.7 |
| 13 | 22⅛ | 52.2 |
| 14 | 22 | 52.0 |
| 15 | 20⅝ | 53.1 |
| 16 | 20¼ | 53.5 |
| 17 | 19¾ | 53.9 |
| 18 | 18¾ | 53.6 |
| 19 | 17½ | 52.9 |
| 20 | 19 | 53.4 |
| 21 | 19⅝ | 54.1 |
| 22 | 21½ | 54.0 |
| 23 | 22 | 53.9 |
| 24 | 23⅛ | 53.7 |
| 25 | 24 | 54.8 |
| 26 | 25¼ | 54.5 |
| 27 | 26¼ | 54.6 |
| 28 | 27 | 54.1 |
| 29 | 27½ | 54.2 |
| 30 | 28 | 54.8 |
| 31 | 28½ | 54.2 |
| 32 | 28 | 54.8 |
| 33 | 27½ | 54.9 |
| 34 | 29 | 55.2 |
| 35 | 29¼ | 55.7 |
| 36 | 29½ | 56.1 |
| 37 | 30 | 56.7 |
| 38 | 28½ | 56.7 |
| 39 | 27¾ | 56.5 |
| 40 | 28 | 56.1 |

**Table 19B** Market Advances and Decline

| Day | Advances | Declines |
|---|---|---|
| 1 | 906 | 704 |
| 2 | 653 | 986 |
| 3 | 721 | 789 |
| 4 | 503 | 968 |
| 5 | 497 | 1095 |
| 6 | 970 | 702 |
| 7 | 1002 | 609 |
| 8 | 903 | 722 |
| 9 | 850 | 748 |
| 10 | 766 | 766 |

*Part VII*

# Derivative Assets

*Chapter* 20

# Options and Other Derivatives: Introduction

A **RELATIVELY RECENT, BUT EXTREMELY IMPORTANT CLASS OF FINANCIAL ASSETS IS DERIVATIVE SECURITIES, OR SIMPLY DERIVATIVES.** These are securities whose prices are determined by, or "derive from," the prices of other securities. These assets also are called *contingent claims* because their payoffs are contingent on the prices of other securities.

Options and futures contracts are both derivative securities. We will see that their payoffs depend on the value of other securities. Swaps, which we discussed in Chapter 16, also are derivatives. Because the value of derivatives depends on the value of other securities, they can be powerful tools for both hedging and speculation. We will investigate these applications in the next three chapters, starting in this chapter with options.

Trading of standardized options contracts on a national exchange started in the United States in 1973 when the Chicago Board Options Exchange (CBOE) began listing call options. These contracts were almost immediately a great success, crowding out the previously existing over-the-counter trading in stock options.

Options contracts are traded now on several U.S. exchanges. They are written on common stock, stock indices, foreign exchange, agricultural commodities, precious metals, and interest rate futures. In addition, the over-the-counter market also has enjoyed a tremendous resurgence in recent years as trading in custom-tailored options has exploded. Popular and potent tools in modifying portfolio characteristics, options have become essential tools a portfolio manager must understand.

In Canada, organized exchange trading of standardized option contracts began in 1975–1976 in Montreal and Toronto. The following year the two exchanges merged their options-clearing corporations, forming TransCanada Options Inc. (TCO). The Vancouver Stock Exchange joined TCO in 1984. TCO was renamed Canadian Derivatives Clearing Corporation in 1996.

Derivatives have received some bad press in recent years, principally because they have been involved in several high profile financial scandals, like the 1995 failure of the Barings Investment Bank in the U.K. Most, if not all, such scandals have stemmed from fraudulent actions coupled with an insufficient understanding of the instruments. In fact, derivatives are simply tools to hedge or manage risk, and they don't deserve their bad name. While it is true that they are relatively difficult to master, it is also true, as we shall see, that the rewards from their use will largely repay the effort.

This chapter is an introduction to options markets. It explains how puts and calls work and examines their investment characteristics. Popular option strategies are considered next. Finally, the chapter provides a brief overview of securities with embedded options, such as callable or convertible bonds.

## 20.1 The Option Contract

A **call option** gives its holder the right to purchase an asset for a specified price, called the **exercise price** or **strike price,** on or before a specified expiration date. For example, a July call option on Seagram's stock with an exercise price of $40 entitles its owner to purchase Seagram's stock for a price of $40 at any time up to and including the expiration date in July. The holder of the call is not required to exercise the option. It will be profitable for the holder to exercise the call only if the market value of the asset to be purchased exceeds the exercise price. When the market price does exceed the exercise price, the option holder either may sell the option, or "call away" the asset for the exercise price and reap a profit. Otherwise, the option may be left unexercised. If it is not exercised before the expiration date of the contract, a call option simply expires and no longer has value.

The purchase price of the option is called the *premium*. It represents the compensation the purchaser of the call must pay for the ability to exercise the option if it becomes profitable. Sellers of call options, who are said to *write* calls, receive premium income now as payment against the possibility that they will be forced at some later date to deliver the asset in return for an exercise price lower than the market value of the asset. If the option is left to expire worthless because the exercise price remains above the market price of the asset, then—aside from transaction costs—the writer of the call clears a profit equal to the premium income derived from the initial sale of the option.

A **put option** gives its holder the right to *sell* an asset for a specified exercise or strike price on or before a given expiration date. A July put on Seagram's with exercise price $40 thus entitles its owner to sell Seagram's stock to the put writer at a price of $40 at any time before expiration in July, even if the market price of Seagram's is less than $40. Whereas profits on call options increase when the asset increases in value, profits on put options increase when the asset value falls. The put is exercised only if its holder can deliver an asset with market value less than the exercise price in return for the exercise price.

Options and futures contracts sometimes are called *derivative securities.* Their values derive from the values of the underlying primary security. For example, the value of a Seagram's option depends on the price of Seagram's stock. For this reason, options and futures contracts also are called *contingent claims:* payoff is contingent on the prices of other securities.

An option is said to be **in the money** when its exercise would produce profits for its holder; an option is **out of the money** when exercise would be unprofitable. A call option is in the money when the exercise price is below the asset's value, because purchase at the exercise price would be profitable. It is out of the money when the exercise price exceeds the asset value; no one would exercise the right to purchase for the exercise price an asset worth less than that price. Conversely, put options are in the money when the exercise price exceeds the asset's value because delivery of the lower-valued asset in exchange for the exercise price would be profitable. Options are at the money when the exercise price and asset price are equal.

## Options Trading

Some options trade on over-the-counter (OTC) markets. An OTC market offers the advantage that the terms of the option contract—the exercise price, maturity date, and number of shares committed—can be tailored to the needs of the traders. The costs of establishing an OTC option contract, however, are higher than for exchange-traded options. Today, most option trading takes place on organized exchanges. The OTC market in customized options also is thriving.

Options contracts traded on exchanges are standardized by allowable maturity dates and exercise prices for each listed option. Each stock option contract provides for the right to buy or sell 100 shares of stock. (If stock splits occur after the contract is listed, adjustments are required. We discuss adjustments in option contract terms later in this section.)

Standardization of the terms of listed option contracts means that all market participants trade in a limited and uniform set of securities. This increases the depth of trading in any particular option, which lowers trading costs and results in a more competitive market. Therefore, exchanges offer two important benefits: ease of trading, which flows from a central marketplace where buyers and sellers or their representatives congregate; and a liquid secondary market, where buyers and sellers of options can transact quickly and cheaply.

Figure 20.1 is a reproduction of listed stock option quotations from *The Globe and Mail;* only the options that traded that day are quoted. Note the option listed (arrow) for shares of Corel Corp. In the first line, following the company name and the letter C, it is indicated that the last recorded price on the Toronto Stock Exchange for Corel stock was $18½ per share. Options are traded on Corel at exercise prices varying in $2.5 increments. These values are also called *strike prices* and are given in the first column of numbers, next to the expiration month.

The exchanges offer options on stocks with exercise prices that bracket the stock price. Exercise prices generally are set at intervals of either $2.5 or $5, depending on whether the price of the stock is below or above $35; however, tighter intervals also can be set for low stock prices. If the stock price moves outside the range of exercise prices of the existing set of options, new options with appropriate exercise prices may be offered. Therefore, at any time both in-the-money and out-of-the-money options will be listed, as in the Corel example.

The next four groups or rows of numbers provide the bid, asked, and closing prices of call and put options on Corel shares that traded that day, with expiration dates of April, May, July, and October. The contracts expire on the Saturday following the third Friday of the month. Notice that the prices of Corel call options decrease as one moves down each column, toward progressively higher exercise prices. This makes sense, because the right to purchase a share at a given exercise price is worth less as that exercise price increases. At an exercise price of $20, the July Corel call had a closing price of $1.15, whereas the option to purchase for an exercise price of $22½ sold for only $.55.

Many options may go an entire day without trading. Because trading is infrequent (especially in Canada), it is not unusual to find option prices that appear out of line with other prices. You might find, for example, two calls with different exercise prices that seem to sell for equal prices. This discrepancy arises because the last trades for these options may have occurred at different times during the day. At any moment the call with the lower exercise price must be worth more than an otherwise-identical call with a higher exercise price.

Several rows, distinguished by a P, report prices of put options with various strike prices and times to maturity. Notice that, in contrast to call options, put prices increase with the exercise price. The right to sell a share of Corel at a price of $20 obviously is less valuable than the right to sell it at $22½.

Figure 20.1 illustrates that the maturities of most exchange-traded options tend to be fairly short, ranging up to only several months. For larger firms, however, longer-term options are traded with maturities ranging up to three years. These options are called LEAPS (for Long-term Equity Anticipation Securities).

**Figure 20.1** Listed Trans Canada Options quotations.

# Trans Cana

Trans Canada Options combine Montreal, Toronto and Vancouver option trading. P is a put.

**Five most active TCO option classes**

| | Volume | Op Int |
|---|---|---|
| TVX Gold Inc | 2347 | 8249 |
| Rogers Com Cl B | 1750 | 5671 |
| Seagram Co. | 1158 | 4998 |
| TSE 35 Index | 1080 | 11159 |
| Cott Corp. | 766 | 6135 |

| Series | | Bid | Ask | Last | Vol | Op Int |
|---|---|---|---|---|---|---|
| **Abitibi Price** | | | C $20⅛ | Opt Vol | | 20 |
| SP 20 | | 1.600 | 1.800 | 1.800 | 20 | 25 |
| **Agnico-Eagle** | | | C $17⅜ | Opt Vol | | 46 |
| MY 17 | | 1.050 | 1¼ | 1¼ | 10 | 114 |
| JN 15 | | 2⅝ | 3 | 2.950 | 6 | 216 |
| 16 | | 2 | 2¼ | 2.150 | 10 | 257 |
| 18 | | 0.850 | 1.050 | 0.900 | 10 | 10 |
| SP 17 | | 2.100 | 2.350 | 2.150 | 10 | 114 |
| **Air Canada** | | | C $6⅞ | Opt Vol | | 214 |
| JY 6 | P | 0.200 | 0.300 | 0.200 | 10 | 1010 |
| 7 | | 0.300 | 0.400 | 0.350 | 6 | 3779 |
| 8 | | 0.100 | 0.200 | 0.150 | 50 | 1969 |
| OC 7 | | 0.600 | 0.650 | 0.600 | 70 | 686 |
| 8 | | 0.300 | 0.350 | 0.300 | 78 | 180 |
| **Alcan Alumin.** | | | C $39 | Opt Vol | | 248 |
| AP 37½ | | 1.700 | 1.850 | 1.800 | 70 | 1508 |
| 40 | | 0.350 | 0½ | 0.400 | 20 | 1968 |
| MY 35 | P | 0.100 | 0¼ | 0.090 | 20 | 40 |
| 40 | | 0.850 | 1 | 0.900 | 20 | 1020 |
| 40 | P | 1¾ | 1.900 | 1.900 | 20 | 20 |
| JY 35 | P | 0½ | 0.650 | 0.600 | 40 | 225 |
| 37½ | | 3.050 | 3.300 | 3.050 | 10 | 372 |
| 40 | | 1.700 | 1.850 | 1.700 | 23 | 437 |
| 40 | P | 2.350 | 2.600 | 2.600 | 20 | 20 |
| OC 40 | | 2½ | 2.700 | 2½ | 5 | 210 |
| **Alcan Leaps 96** | | | C $39 | Opt Vol | | 52 |
| JA 20 | | 19⅝ | 20⅝ | | | 5 |
| 20 | P | 0.010 | 0½ | | | 20 |
| 25 | | 14⅞ | 15⅝ | 15 | 3 | 86 |
| 25 | P | 0.010 | 0½ | | | 20 |
| 30 | | 10½ | 11¼ | 10 | 1 | 102 |
| 30 | P | 0.150 | 0.600 | | | 146 |
| 35 | | 6¾ | 7¼ | 7 | 33 | 108 |
| 35 | P | 1.100 | 1.800 | | | 57 |
| 40 | | 3¾ | 4½ | 3.850 | 15 | 87 |
| 40 | P | 2.900 | 3.650 | | | 23 |
| **Alcan Leaps 97** | | | C $39 | Opt Vol | | 11 |
| JA 30 | | 12¾ | 13¾ | 13 | 2 | 68 |
| 30 | P | 0.650 | 1.150 | | | 51 |
| 35 | | 9⅝ | 10 | | | 98 |
| 35 | P | 1.800 | 2.800 | | | 50 |
| 40 | | 6⅛ | 6¼ | 6¼ | 9 | 77 |
| 40 | P | 4.050 | 5 | | | 60 |
| **Barrick Gold** | | | C $35⅝ | Opt Vol | | 480 |
| AP 30 | | 5¼ | 5½ | 5¼ | 30 | 3123 |
| 32½ | | 2.850 | 3.100 | 3.100 | 97 | 3657 |
| 35 | | 0.900 | 1.050 | 1 | 23 | 1440 |
| 35 | P | 0.650 | 0.800 | 0.700 | 15 | 149 |
| 37½ | | 0.100 | 0.300 | 0¼ | 10 | 634 |
| MY 35 | | 1.550 | 1¾ | 1.700 | 65 | 195 |
| 35 | P | 1.100 | 1.300 | 1.200 | 10 | 39 |
| 37½ | | 0½ | 0.700 | 0¾ | 70 | 70 |
| JY 32½ | | 4.050 | 4¼ | 4.200 | 10 | 4748 |
| 35 | | 2½ | 2.700 | 2.800 | 11 | 938 |
| 37½ | | 1.300 | 1½ | 1.400 | 15 | 15 |
| OC 30 | | 6⅞ | 7⅛ | 7⅛ | 5 | 159 |
| 32½ | | 5⅛ | 5⅜ | 5 | 100 | 2430 |
| 37½ | | 2.350 | 2½ | 2½ | 19 | 15 |
| **Barrick Lps96** | | | C $35⅝ | Opt Vol | | 128 |
| JA 25 | | 11⅝ | 12 | | | 166 |
| 25 | P | 0.200 | 0.400 | | | 270 |
| 30 | | 8 | 8⅜ | 8⅜ | 20 | 261 |
| 30 | P | 0.900 | 1.150 | | | 250 |
| 35 | | 4.650 | 4.900 | 4.700 | 3 | 515 |
| 35 | P | 2.600 | 2.950 | 2.850 | 5 | 219 |
| 40 | | 2.300 | 2½ | 2.400 | 50 | 881 |
| 40 | P | 5½ | 5⅞ | | | 27 |
| 45 | | 1.150 | 1¼ | 1.350 | 50 | 690 |
| 45 | P | 9⅝ | 10 | | | 32 |
| **Barrick Lps97** | | | C $35⅝ | Opt Vol | | 59 |
| JA 25 | | 14⅛ | 14⅝ | 14⅝ | 26 | 103 |
| 25 | P | 0.800 | 1 | | | 273 |
| 30 | | 10⅞ | 10⅞ | 10⅞ | 30 | 275 |
| 30 | P | 1.600 | 1.950 | | | 49 |
| 35 | | 8 | 8⅜ | | | 120 |
| 35 | P | 3.400 | 3¾ | 3.450 | 3 | 98 |
| 40 | | 5⅝ | 5¾ | | | 400 |
| 40 | P | 6⅛ | 6½ | | | 24 |
| **Biochem** | | | C $22½ | Opt Vol | | 244 |
| AP 22 | | 0.950 | 1.150 | 1 | 20 | 238 |
| MY 20 | | 3 | 3¼ | 3.200 | 8 | 77 |
| JN 24 | | 1.150 | 1.350 | 1¼ | 108 | 245 |
| 24 | P | 2.200 | 2.450 | 2.350 | 108 | 118 |
| **Biochem Lps 96** | | | C $22½ | Opt Vol | | 30 |
| JA 10 | | 13 | 13½ | | | 100 |
| 10 | P | 0.010 | 0.300 | | | |
| 12 | | 11⅛ | 11⅝ | | | 3 |
| 12 | P | 0.010 | 0.350 | | | 20 |
| 14 | | 9⅝ | 9⅞ | | | 1010 |
| 14 | P | 0.150 | 0.600 | | | 1020 |
| 16 | | 7⅝ | 8⅛ | | | 1805 |
| 16 | P | 0.200 | 0.650 | | | 60 |
| 18 | | 6⅛ | 6⅝ | | | 1757 |
| 18 | P | 0.550 | 1 | | | 55 |
| 20 | | 4.600 | 5⅛ | | | 2005 |
| 20 | P | 1.150 | 1.650 | | | 90 |
| 22 | | 3.600 | 4.100 | | | 2249 |
| 22 | P | 2.050 | 2.550 | | | 25 |
| 24 | | 2.800 | 3.300 | 3.450 | 30 | 537 |
| 24 | P | 2.950 | 3.450 | | | |
| **Biochem Lps 97** | | | C $22½ | Opt Vol | | 25 |
| JA 10 | | 13⅝ | 14⅛ | | | 1713 |
| 10 | P | 0.020 | 0½ | | | 37 |
| 12 | | 12⅛ | 12⅝ | | | 28 |
| 12 | P | 0.150 | 0.650 | | | 5 |
| 14 | | 10⅝ | 11⅛ | | | 50 |
| 14 | P | 0.450 | 0.950 | | | 22 |
| 16 | | 9⅛ | 9⅝ | | | 94 |
| 16 | P | 0.800 | 1.300 | | | 28 |
| 18 | | 7⅞ | 8⅜ | | | 41 |
| 18 | P | 1.350 | 1.850 | | | 2 |
| 20 | | 6¾ | 7¼ | | | 32 |
| 20 | P | 2.200 | 2.700 | | | 1 |
| 22 | | 5⅝ | 6⅛ | | | 39 |
| 22 | P | 3.200 | 3.700 | 3.450 | 25 | 147 |
| 24 | | 4.950 | 5½ | | | 2 |
| 24 | P | 4.150 | 4.650 | | | 70 |
| **Bk Mont** | | | C $26⅝ | Opt Vol | | 7 |
| AP 23 | | 3.700 | 3.950 | 4 | 3 | 43 |
| JY 27 | | 0.600 | 0¾ | 0¾ | 4 | 517 |
| **Bk Mont Leaps96** | | | C $26⅝ | Opt Vol | | |
| JA 22 | | 4.800 | 5¼ | | | 179 |
| 22 | P | 0.010 | 0½ | | | 56 |
| 24 | | 3.300 | 3.550 | | | 313 |
| 24 | P | 0¼ | 0.850 | | | 62 |
| 26 | | 1.550 | 1.950 | | | 333 |
| 26 | P | 0.600 | 1.200 | | | 194 |
| 28 | | 0.650 | 1 | | | 467 |
| 28 | P | 1.650 | 2¼ | | | 80 |
| 30 | | 0.200 | 0.600 | | | 271 |
| 30 | P | 3.150 | 3¾ | | | |
| 32 | | 0.040 | 0.350 | | | 130 |
| 32 | P | 5⅛ | 5⅝ | | | |
| **Bk Mont Leaps97** | | | C $26⅝ | Opt Vol | | |
| JA 24 | | 4.450 | 4.950 | | | 152 |
| 24 | P | 0.450 | 1.200 | | | 16 |
| 26 | | 2.900 | 3.400 | | | 113 |
| 26 | P | 0.950 | 1.700 | | | 50 |
| 28 | | 1.950 | 2.350 | | | 289 |
| 28 | P | 1.850 | 2.600 | | | 10 |
| **Bk Nova Scotia** | | | C $26¾ | Opt Vol | | 35 |
| AP 25 | | 1¾ | 2 | 2 | 30 | 60 |
| MY 27 | | 0½ | 0¾ | 0.650 | 5 | 55 |
| **Bk NS Leaps 96** | | | C $26¾ | Opt Vol | | |
| JA 20 | | 6⅝ | 7⅛ | | | 131 |
| 20 | P | 0.050 | 0.300 | | | 10 |
| 25 | | 2.450 | 2⅞ | | | 2809 |
| 25 | P | 0.450 | 0.950 | | | 50 |
| 30 | | 0½ | 0.700 | | | 424 |
| 30 | P | 3.400 | 3.900 | | | 67 |
| 35 | | 0.050 | 0¼ | | | 165 |
| 35 | P | 8¼ | 8⅞ | | | |
| **Bk NS Leaps 97** | | | C $26¾ | Opt Vol | | |
| JA 20 | | 7½ | 8 | | | 31 |
| 20 | P | 0.200 | 0.700 | | | 18 |
| 25 | | 3.850 | 4.350 | | | 88 |
| 25 | P | 1.350 | 1.850 | | | 116 |
| 30 | | 1.600 | 2.100 | | | 171 |
| 30 | P | 3.800 | 4.300 | | | 20 |
| **Bombardier Cl B** | | | C $27¼ | Opt Vol | | 66 |
| AP 23 | | 4.100 | 4.350 | 4.350 | 5 | 196 |
| 27 | | 0½ | 0.700 | 0.700 | 41 | 284 |
| JY 27 | | 1½ | 1¾ | 1.450 | 10 | 143 |
| OC 27 | | 2.150 | 2.400 | 2¼ | 10 | 386 |
| **Bombrd Leaps96** | | | C $27¼ | Opt Vol | | 10 |
| JA 10 | | 17¼ | 17⅝ | | | 166 |
| 10 | P | 0.010 | 0.100 | | | 57 |
| 12 | | 15⅛ | 15⅝ | | | 1500 |
| 12 | P | 0.010 | 0.200 | | | 27 |
| 14 | | 13⅛ | 13⅝ | | | 185 |
| 14 | P | 0.010 | 0.200 | | | 12 |
| 16 | | 11⅛ | 11⅝ | | | 137 |
| 16 | P | 0.010 | 0¼ | | | 22 |
| 18 | | 9⅛ | 9⅝ | | | 139 |
| 18 | P | 0.010 | 0¼ | | | 16 |
| 20 | | 7⅝ | 8⅛ | | | 582 |
| 20 | P | 0.100 | 0.350 | | | 56 |
| 22 | | 6 | 6½ | 6 | 10 | 162 |
| 22 | P | 0.040 | 0.450 | | | 70 |
| 24 | | 4¼ | 4¾ | | | 337 |
| 24 | P | 0.400 | 0.600 | | | 107 |
| 26 | | 2.950 | 3.450 | | | 114 |
| 26 | P | 0¾ | 1.150 | | | 30 |
| 28 | | 1.900 | 2.400 | | | 77 |
| 28 | P | 1.700 | 2.150 | | | 20 |
| **Bombrd Leaps97** | | | C $27¼ | Opt Vol | | |
| JA 18 | | 11 | 11½ | | | 106 |
| 18 | P | 0.020 | 0.450 | | | 20 |
| 20 | | 9½ | 9⅞ | | | 93 |
| 20 | P | 0.100 | 0.550 | | | 10 |
| 22 | | 7⅜ | 8⅛ | | | 41 |
| 22 | P | 0.200 | 0.650 | | | 3 |
| 24 | | 6⅝ | 7 | | | 131 |
| 24 | P | 0½ | 0.950 | | | 12 |
| 26 | | 5⅜ | 5¾ | | | 92 |
| 26 | P | 1.100 | 1.550 | | | 30 |
| 28 | | 4.200 | 4.600 | | | 90 |
| 28 | P | 1.950 | 2.400 | | | 10 |
| **BCE Inc** | | | C $43 | Opt Vol | | 322 |
| AP 45 | | 0.150 | 0.200 | 0.200 | 100 | 586 |
| 45 | P | 1.800 | 2.050 | 1.900 | 10 | 10 |
| MY 42½ | | 1.350 | 1.600 | 1.400 | 40 | 97 |
| AG 40 | | 3.850 | 4.100 | 4 | 40 | 54 |
| 42½ | | 2.200 | 2.350 | 2.350 | 80 | 324 |
| 45 | | 0.800 | 1.050 | 1 | 32 | 404 |
| 45 | P | 2.100 | 2.350 | 2.100 | 5 | 120 |
| NV 42½ | | 2.600 | 2.850 | 2.850 | 5 | 20 |
| 45 | | 1.350 | 1.600 | 1½ | 10 | 78 |
| **Cambior Inc** | | | C $16⅜ | Opt Vol | | 272 |
| AP 14 | | 2¼ | 2½ | 2.400 | 125 | 124 |
| MY 14 | | 2.400 | 2.650 | 2½ | 20 | 520 |
| 15 | | 1.550 | 1.800 | 1¾ | 25 | 133 |
| 15 | P | 0.060 | 0.300 | 0.100 | 20 | 118 |
| AG 15 | | 2.200 | 2.450 | 2.550 | 33 | 122 |
| 17 | | 1.050 | 1.300 | 1¼ | 22 | 175 |
| NV 16 | | 2.100 | 2.350 | 2.200 | 27 | 73 |
| **Cascades Inc** | | | C $7¾ | Opt Vol | | 40 |
| OC 7 | | 1.150 | 1.350 | 1.350 | 40 | 40 |
| **Cascades Lps96** | | | C $7¾ | Opt Vol | | |
| JA 5 | | 3 | 3.400 | | | 138 |
| 5 | P | 0.010 | 0.300 | | | |
| 6 | | 2.100 | 2.400 | | | 20 |
| 6 | P | 0.050 | 0.350 | | | |
| 7 | | 1.350 | 1.650 | | | 148 |
| 7 | P | 0.200 | 0½ | | | 26 |
| 8 | | 0¾ | 1.050 | | | 107 |
| 8 | P | 0½ | 0.800 | | | 35 |
| 9 | | 0.400 | 0.650 | | | 294 |
| 9 | P | 1.150 | 1½ | | | 87 |
| **Cascades Lps97** | | | C $7¾ | Opt Vol | | |
| JA 6 | | 2.900 | 3.300 | | | 135 |
| 6 | P | 0.150 | 0½ | | | 5 |
| 7 | | 2.150 | 2½ | | | 146 |
| 7 | P | 0.300 | 0.650 | | | 10 |
| 8 | | 1.650 | 1.850 | | | 156 |
| 8 | P | 0.650 | 1 | | | 20 |
| 9 | | 1 | 1.350 | | | 143 |
| 9 | P | 1.150 | 1.550 | | | 35 |
| **Cdn Impl Lps 96** | | | C $33⅝ | Opt Vol | | |
| JA 30 | | 4.850 | 5⅛ | | | 395 |
| 30 | P | 0.350 | 0.600 | | | 51 |
| 35 | | 1.800 | 2.050 | | | 213 |
| 35 | P | 2 | 2¼ | | | 115 |
| 40 | | 0.400 | 0.650 | | | 217 |
| 40 | P | 6¼ | 6½ | | | |
| **Cdn Impl Lps 97** | | | C $33⅝ | Opt Vol | | 10 |
| JA 30 | | 6¼ | 6⅝ | 6⅝ | 10 | 53 |
| 30 | P | 0.700 | 0.950 | | | 12 |
| 35 | | 3.350 | 3.600 | | | 66 |
| 35 | P | 2.200 | 2.450 | | | 135 |
| **Cdn Occidental Petroleum** | | | C $37½ | Opt Vol | | 15 |
| MY 38 | | 0.800 | 1.050 | 0.900 | 10 | 10 |
| SP 37 | | 2.700 | 2.950 | 2.800 | 5 | 5 |
| **Cdn Pacific** | | | C $21 | Opt Vol | | 10 |
| NV 22 | | 1 | 1¼ | 1.100 | 10 | 10 |
| **Cdn Tire Cl A** | | | C $13¾ | Opt Vol | | 40 |
| AP 12 | | 1¾ | 1.950 | 1.800 | 40 | 267 |
| **CdnPac Leaps 96** | | | C $21 | Opt Vol | | |
| JA 15 | | 5⅞ | 6⅜ | | | 106 |
| 15 | P | 0.100 | 0.200 | | | 20 |
| 20 | | 2.300 | 2¾ | | | 261 |
| 20 | P | 0.650 | 0.900 | | | 183 |
| 25 | | 0.450 | 0.700 | | | 318 |
| 25 | P | 3.850 | 4.350 | | | 6 |
| **CdnPac Leaps 97** | | | C $21 | Opt Vol | | |
| JA 15 | | 6⅞ | 7⅜ | | | 58 |
| 15 | P | 0.100 | 0.350 | | | 29 |
| 20 | | 3.400 | 3.800 | | | 93 |
| 20 | P | 1.050 | 1.300 | | | 95 |
| 25 | | 1.350 | 1.600 | | | 96 |
| 25 | P | 3.850 | 4.350 | | | 72 |
| **Corel Corp.** ← | | | C $18⅛ | Opt Vol | | 275 |
| AP 17½ | | 1 | 1.150 | 0.900 | 20 | 267 |
| 20 | | 0.200 | 0¼ | 0.150 | 10 | 930 |
| 20 | P | 1.700 | 1.950 | 1.700 | 30 | 265 |
| 22½ | P | 4 | 4½ | 4.100 | 10 | |
| MY 20 | | 0.350 | 0.400 | 0.350 | 50 | 90 |
| JY 17½ | | 2¼ | 2.350 | 2.350 | 120 | 253 |
| 20 | | 1.150 | 1.300 | 1.150 | 10 | 889 |
| 22½ | | 0½ | 0.700 | 0.550 | 20 | 780 |
| OC 20 | | 1¾ | 1.850 | 1¾ | 5 | 82 |
| **Cott Corp.** | | | C $11½ | Opt Vol | | 766 |
| AP 10 | | 1.650 | 1.850 | 1.700 | 10 | 10 |
| 10 | P | 0.150 | 0.300 | 0.300 | 94 | 94 |
| 12 | | 0¼ | 0.400 | 0¼ | 20 | 334 |
| 12 | P | 0¾ | 0.900 | 0.800 | 118 | 558 |
| 14 | P | 2½ | 2¾ | 2.650 | 20 | 115 |
| MY 10 | | 1.850 | 2.050 | 1.900 | 20 | 20 |
| 12 | | 0.650 | 0.700 | 0.650 | 22 | 137 |
| 12 | P | 1.050 | 1¼ | 1.050 | 45 | 230 |
| 14 | | 0.150 | 0.300 | 0.200 | 50 | 189 |
| JN 12 | | 0.850 | 1 | 0.850 | 35 | 270 |
| 12 | P | 1.200 | 1¼ | 1¼ | 30 | 682 |
| 14 | | 0.300 | 0.450 | 0.400 | 20 | 688 |
| 14 | P | 2.700 | 2.950 | 2.850 | 50 | 478 |
| 16 | P | 4½ | 4¾ | 4.650 | 26 | 170 |
| SP 10 | P | 0.700 | 0.850 | 0.700 | 10 | 10 |
| 12 | | 1.400 | 1.600 | 1.350 | 10 | 48 |
| 12 | P | 1.550 | 1¾ | 1.700 | 100 | 302 |
| 14 | | 0.700 | 0.850 | 0¾ | 30 | 256 |
| 14 | P | 2.950 | 3.200 | 2.900 | 30 | 60 |
| 16 | P | 4.650 | 4.900 | 4.550 | 26 | 26 |
| **CAE Inc.** | | | C $8¼ | Opt Vol | | 10 |
| JN 8 | | 0.550 | 0.700 | 0.550 | 10 | 1188 |
| **CDA Mar 2011 9** | | | C $103.35 | Opt Vol | | 49 |
| AP 102 | | 1.450 | 1.700 | 1.400 | 20 | 106 |
| 104 | | 0.300 | 0.550 | 0½ | 4 | 33 |
| MY 104 | | 0¾ | 1 | 0.650 | 4 | 50 |
| JN 104 | | 1.050 | 1.300 | 1.200 | 20 | 70 |
| SP 104 | | 1.650 | 1.900 | 1¾ | 1 | 5 |
| **CDA Oct 2001 9.5** | | | C $105.95 | Opt Vol | | 4 |
| AP 90 | | 15.650 | 16¼ | 15.950 | 4 | |
| **Delrina Corp** | | | C $19½ | Opt Vol | | 179 |
| AP 20 | | 0.700 | 0.950 | 0.700 | 45 | 125 |
| JN 17½ | | 3.100 | 3.600 | 3.100 | 5 | 34 |
| 17½ | P | 0.800 | 1.050 | 1 | 20 | 119 |
| 20 | | 1¾ | 2 | 1¾ | 10 | 76 |
| 22½ | | 0.900 | 1.150 | 1.050 | 10 | 169 |
| 22½ | P | 3.450 | 3.950 | 3.550 | 12 | 24 |
| SP 17½ | P | 1.600 | 1.850 | 1.850 | 33 | 85 |
| 20 | | 3 | 3½ | 3 | 32 | 52 |
| 22½ | | 2.050 | 2.550 | 2.050 | 10 | 172 |
| 25 | | 1.400 | 1.650 | 1½ | 2 | 42 |
| **Dofasco Inc** | | | C $17¾ | Opt Vol | | 75 |
| AP 17 | | 0.800 | 1.050 | 1.050 | 10 | 10 |
| JN 18 | | 0.800 | 1.050 | 0.800 | 20 | 220 |
| 18 | P | 0.900 | 1.150 | 0.950 | 40 | 244 |
| SP 17 | P | 0¾ | 1 | 0.850 | 5 | 55 |
| **Domtar Inc** | | | C $11¼ | Opt Vol | | 90 |
| MY 9 | | 2.300 | 2.550 | 2.550 | 10 | 281 |
| 11 | | 0¾ | 1 | 0.900 | 50 | 435 |
| NV 12 | | 1.200 | 1.350 | 1.350 | 30 | 130 |
| **Echo Bay Mines** | | | C $14¾ | Opt Vol | | 10 |
| JY 16 | | 0¾ | 0.950 | 1 | 10 | 127 |
| **Gulf Canada Resources** | | | C $6 | Opt Vol | | 135 |
| MY 5 | | 1.200 | 1.400 | 1 | 100 | 497 |
| JN 6 | | 0.600 | 0.850 | 0.450 | 35 | 106 |
| **Hemlo Gold Mines** | | | C $15⅝ | Opt Vol | | 17 |
| MY 14 | | 1.350 | 1.600 | 1.400 | 3 | |
| JY 15 | | 1 | 1¼ | 1 | 10 | 130 |
| OC 16 | | 1 | 1.200 | 1 | 4 | 4 |
| **Imperial Oil Ltd** | | | C $50¼ | Opt Vol | | 25 |
| MY 50 | | 1.400 | 1.650 | 1.400 | 10 | 321 |
| AG 47½ | P | 0.700 | 0.950 | 1.150 | 5 | 10 |
| 50 | P | 1.650 | 1.900 | 2 | 10 | 10 |
| **Inco Ltd** | | | C $39¾ | Opt Vol | | 152 |
| AP 37½ | | 2.300 | 2.450 | 2.400 | 17 | 365 |
| 40 | | 0.700 | 0.800 | 0.650 | 80 | 677 |
| MY 37½ | | 2.850 | 3 | 2.950 | 5 | 93 |
| 37½ | P | 0.450 | 0.550 | 0.600 | 50 | 1634 |
| **John Labatt Ltd** | | | C $21¼ | Opt Vol | | 708 |
| MY 20 | | 2 | 2.100 | 1.950 | 50 | 1272 |
| 21 | | 1¼ | 1½ | 1½ | 30 | 2844 |
| 21 | P | 0.550 | 0¾ | 0.650 | 5 | 35 |
| 22 | | 0.900 | 1 | 0.950 | 323 | 3552 |
| 23 | | 0.650 | 0¾ | 0¾ | 170 | 3017 |
| AG 21 | | 2.050 | 2.300 | 2 | 6 | 122 |
| NV 22 | | 2.150 | 2.400 | 2.400 | 124 | 291 |
| **Kinross Gold** | | | C $8⅛ | Opt Vol | | 89 |
| JN 7 | | 1¼ | 1.450 | 1¼ | 15 | 2210 |
| 8 | | 0½ | 0.700 | 0½ | 4 | 2061 |
| AG 8 | | 0¾ | 0.950 | 0.900 | 70 | 90 |
| **Laidlaw Inc B** | | | C $12⅛ | Opt Vol | | 15 |
| JN 13 | | 0¼ | 0.400 | 0.300 | 5 | 71 |
| SP 13 | P | 1.150 | 1.350 | 1.100 | 10 | 12 |
| **Laidlaw Leaps96** | | | C $12⅛ | Opt Vol | | 2 |
| JA 6 | | 6⅛ | 6⅝ | | | 767 |
| 6 | P | 0.010 | 0.350 | | | 56 |
| 8 | | 4.450 | 4.800 | | | 444 |
| 8 | P | 0.050 | 0.400 | | | 154 |
| 10 | | 2.650 | 3 | | | 1320 |
| 10 | P | 0.090 | 0.400 | | | 541 |
| 12 | | 1.300 | 1.550 | 1.300 | 2 | 599 |
| 12 | P | 0.550 | 0.700 | | | 151 |
| 14 | | 0¼ | 0.450 | | | 493 |
| 14 | P | 1.950 | 2.300 | | | 69 |
| **Laidlaw Leaps97** | | | C $12⅛ | Opt Vol | | |
| JA 6 | | 6¾ | 7⅛ | | | 2 |
| 6 | P | 0.010 | 0.350 | | | |
| 8 | | 5 | 5⅝ | | | 17 |
| 8 | P | 0.030 | 0.400 | | | |
| 10 | | 3.400 | 3¾ | | | 32 |
| 10 | P | 0¼ | 0.600 | | | 50 |
| 12 | | 2.200 | 2.550 | | | 160 |
| 12 | P | 0¾ | 1.100 | | | 30 |
| 14 | | 1¼ | 1.600 | | | 43 |
| 14 | P | 2.050 | 2.400 | | | 10 |
| **Mac Bloedel** | | | C $18¼ | Opt Vol | | 143 |
| AP 16 | | 2.300 | 2½ | 2¼ | 10 | |
| 17 | P | 0.010 | 0.100 | 0.050 | 20 | 1276 |
| 18 | | 0½ | 0.600 | 0½ | 8 | 1072 |
| 19 | | 0.100 | 0.150 | 0.150 | 30 | 220 |
| JY 16 | | 2.600 | 2.800 | 2.800 | 10 | 80 |
| 19 | | 0.650 | 0¾ | 0¾ | 60 | 186 |
| OC 17 | | 2.150 | 2.300 | 2¼ | 5 | 230 |

# da Options

| Series | | Bid | Ask | Last | Vol | Op Int |
|---|---|---|---|---|---|---|
| **Methanex Corp.** | | | C | $14¼ | Opt Vol | 80 |
| AP 15 | | 0.100 | 0¼ | 0.150 | 15 | 149 |
| JN 16 | | 0.450 | 0.600 | 0½ | 10 | 352 |
| SP 14 | P | 1.200 | 1.400 | 1.350 | 35 | 99 |
| 18 | | 0.450 | 0.550 | 0.450 | 20 | 121 |
| **Mitel Corp.** | | | C | $6½ | Opt Vol | 180 |
| JN 6 | | 0.800 | 0.950 | 0.800 | 40 | 1291 |
| SP 6 | | 1.050 | 1¼ | 1.050 | 40 | 404 |
| 8 | | 0.200 | 0.300 | 0¼ | 100 | 140 |
| **Moore Corp Ltd** | | | C | $26½ | Opt Vol | 13 |
| AG 27½ | | 1.150 | 1.400 | 1.150 | 5 | 324 |
| NV 25 | P | 1.350 | 1.600 | 1.350 | 8 | 8 |
| **Natl Bk Leaps 96** | | | C | $9⅞ | Opt Vol | |
| JA 7 | | 3.050 | 3.450 | | | 245 |
| 7 | P | 0.010 | 0.350 | | | 10 |
| 8 | | 2.100 | 2½ | | | 188 |
| 8 | P | 0.020 | 0.350 | | | 20 |
| 9 | | 1.300 | 1.650 | | | 286 |
| 9 | P | 0.200 | 0.550 | | | 155 |
| 10 | | 0½ | 0.850 | | | 725 |
| 10 | P | 0.550 | 0.900 | | | 389 |
| 12 | | 0.050 | 0.300 | | | 860 |
| 12 | P | 2.150 | 2½ | | | 41 |
| **Natl Bk Leaps 97** | | | C | $9⅞ | Opt Vol | |
| JA 8 | | 2.550 | 2.950 | | | 65 |
| 8 | P | 0¼ | 0.650 | | | 109 |
| 9 | | 1.700 | 2.100 | | | 109 |
| 9 | P | 0.450 | 0.850 | | | 82 |
| 10 | | 1.050 | 1.450 | | | 213 |
| 10 | P | 0¾ | 1.150 | | | 90 |
| 12 | | 0¼ | 0.650 | | | 167 |
| 12 | P | 2.150 | 2.550 | | | 94 |
| **Newbridge $CD** | | | C | $42⅞ | Opt Vol | 193 |
| AP 42½ | P | 1.050 | 1.300 | 1.200 | 60 | 70 |
| 45 | P | 2.650 | 2.800 | 2.550 | 5 | 155 |
| 50 | | 0.010 | 0.100 | 0.050 | 50 | 188 |
| MY 42½ | P | 1.900 | 2.150 | 1¾ | 13 | 38 |
| 47½ | | 0.800 | 0.950 | 0.900 | 7 | 16 |
| JN 42½ | P | 2.450 | 2.700 | 2.400 | 20 | 20 |
| 45 | | 2¼ | 2.400 | 2.550 | 4 | 33 |
| 47½ | | 1.350 | 1.600 | 1½ | 5 | 68 |
| 50 | | 0.850 | 1 | 0.900 | 7 | 61 |
| 55 | | 0¼ | 0.400 | 0.450 | 1 | 49 |
| 60 | | 0.030 | 0.150 | 0.150 | 1 | 173 |
| SP 42½ | P | 3.600 | 3.950 | 3.700 | 20 | 20 |
| **Noranda Inc.** | | | C | $24⅝ | Opt Vol | 38 |
| AP 21 | | 3.600 | 3.850 | 3.400 | 5 | |
| AG 23 | P | 0½ | 0¾ | 0¾ | 10 | 131 |
| 26 | | 0.800 | 0.850 | 0.800 | 13 | 291 |
| NV 25 | | 1.650 | 1.900 | 1.600 | 10 | 25 |
| **Northern Tel** | | | C | $52⅞ | Opt Vol | 284 |
| AP 50 | | 2.950 | 3.300 | 2.800 | 6 | 373 |
| 50 | P | 0.010 | 0.200 | 0.150 | 10 | 204 |
| 52½ | | 1.050 | 1.300 | 1 | 20 | 598 |
| 55 | | 0¼ | 0.350 | 0.300 | 175 | 328 |
| 55 | P | 2.100 | 2.350 | 2.150 | 10 | 200 |
| MY 52½ | P | 1.150 | 1.350 | 1.400 | 10 | 86 |
| JY 52½ | P | 1.800 | 2.050 | 2 | 10 | 65 |
| 55 | | 1.700 | 1.950 | 1.600 | 33 | 780 |
| 55 | P | 3.100 | 3.400 | 3 | 10 | 20 |
| **Nortl Leaps 96** | | | C | $52⅞ | Opt Vol | 15 |
| JA 25 | | 29 | 29½ | | | 53 |
| 25 | P | 0.010 | 0¼ | | | 60 |
| 30 | | 24¼ | 24¾ | | | 38 |
| 30 | P | 0.010 | 0¼ | | | 92 |
| 35 | | 19½ | 20 | | | 26 |
| 35 | P | 0.010 | 0¼ | | | 43 |
| 40 | | 14¾ | 15¼ | | | 119 |
| 40 | P | 0.050 | 0.300 | | | 74 |
| 45 | | 10⅝ | 10⅞ | | | 138 |
| 45 | P | 0.550 | 0.800 | | | 108 |
| 50 | | 6⅝ | 7⅛ | 6⅞ | 5 | 508 |
| 50 | P | 1.800 | 2.050 | | | 100 |
| 55 | | 3.850 | 4.350 | | | 243 |
| 55 | P | 4 | 4½ | | | 1 |
| 60 | | 2 | 2½ | | | 10 |
| 60 | P | 7½ | 8 | 7¾ | 10 | |
| **Nortl Leaps 97** | | | C | $52⅞ | Opt Vol | 12 |
| JA 35 | | 21¾ | 22¼ | | | 31 |
| 35 | P | 0.100 | 0.350 | | | 1 |
| 40 | | 17½ | 18 | | | 14 |
| 40 | P | 0.550 | 0.800 | | | 40 |
| 45 | | 13¾ | 14¼ | | | 174 |
| 45 | P | 1½ | 1¾ | | | 16 |
| 50 | | 10½ | 11 | 10¼ | 2 | 182 |
| 50 | P | 2.900 | 3.400 | | | 21 |
| 55 | | 7⅝ | 8⅛ | | | 187 |
| 55 | P | 5¼ | 5¾ | | | 10 |
| 60 | | 5½ | 6 | 5⅝ | 10 | 31 |
| 60 | P | 8½ | 9 | | | |
| **Nova Corp.** | | | C | $12 | Opt Vol | 58 |
| AP 12 | | 0.200 | 0.350 | 0.350 | 10 | 1100 |
| JY 12 | P | 0.450 | 0.550 | 0½ | 10 | 295 |
| 13 | | 0.350 | 0.450 | 0.400 | 15 | 344 |
| OC 12 | | 1.100 | 1.300 | 1.100 | 18 | 235 |
| 13 | P | 1 | 1¼ | 1.200 | 5 | 5 |
| **Nova Leaps 96** | | | C | $12 | Opt Vol | 20 |
| JA 7 | | 5 | 5½ | | | 209 |
| 7 | P | 0.010 | 0¼ | | | 140 |
| 9 | | 3.700 | 3¾ | | | 414 |
| 9 | P | 0.100 | 0¼ | | | 173 |
| 11 | | 2.200 | 2.400 | | | 937 |
| 11 | P | 0.300 | 0.400 | | | 272 |
| 13 | | 0.900 | 1.050 | 0.900 | 10 | 831 |
| 13 | P | 0.900 | 1.200 | 0.900 | 10 | 206 |
| 15 | | 0.400 | 0½ | | | 429 |
| 15 | P | 2.550 | 2.950 | | | 10 |
| **Nova Leaps 97** | | | C | $12 | Opt Vol | 2 |
| JA 9 | | 4 | 4½ | | | 100 |
| 9 | P | 0¼ | 0½ | | | |
| 11 | | 2.650 | 3.050 | | | 135 |
| 11 | P | 0.550 | 0¾ | | | 208 |
| 13 | | 1¾ | 2 | | | 683 |
| 13 | P | 1.200 | 1.550 | | | 50 |
| 15 | | 0.850 | 1.100 | 1 | 2 | 255 |
| 15 | P | 2½ | 3 | | | 25 |
| **Pegasus Gold** | | | C | $17⅝ | Opt Vol | 40 |
| AG 20 | | 0.950 | 1.150 | 1 | 8 | 124 |
| NV 15 | | 4.050 | 4.300 | 4.050 | 20 | 20 |
| 17 | | 2.700 | 2.950 | 2.700 | 2 | 16 |
| 17 | P | 1.600 | 1.800 | 1.700 | 10 | 10 |
| **Petro-Canada** | | | C | $12¼ | Opt Vol | 15 |
| JN 11 | | 1¼ | 1.350 | 1¼ | 15 | 73 |
| **Placer Dome** | | | C | $33⅛ | Opt Vol | 208 |
| AP 29 | | 4.200 | 4.450 | 4¾ | 50 | 185 |
| 32½ | | 1.200 | 1.450 | 1.350 | 100 | 552 |
| 35 | | 0¼ | 0.400 | 0.300 | 10 | 412 |
| MY 35 | | 0.650 | 0.850 | 0¾ | 20 | 215 |
| JY 30 | | 4.400 | 4.650 | 4.650 | 8 | 289 |
| 35 | | 1½ | 1¾ | 1.600 | 20 | 67 |
| **Placer Leaps 96** | | | C | $33⅛ | Opt Vol | 12 |
| JA 20 | | 13¾ | 14¼ | | | 138 |
| 20 | P | 0.010 | 0½ | | | 87 |
| 25 | | 9¼ | 10¼ | | | 302 |
| 25 | P | 0.150 | 0.650 | | | 123 |
| 30 | | 5⅝ | 6⅝ | | | 691 |
| 30 | P | 1.300 | 1.800 | 1.800 | 2 | 218 |
| 35 | | 2.850 | 3¼ | | | 321 |
| 35 | P | 3.400 | 4.400 | | | 13 |
| 40 | | 1½ | 2 | 1½ | 10 | 409 |
| 40 | P | 7 | 8 | | | 25 |
| **Placer Leaps 97** | | | C | $33⅛ | Opt Vol | 5 |
| JA 25 | | 11¼ | 12¼ | | | 93 |
| 25 | P | 0¾ | 1¼ | | | 99 |
| 30 | | 8 | 9 | 8⅛ | 5 | 175 |
| 30 | P | 2¼ | 3.050 | | | 28 |
| 35 | | 5⅝ | 6⅜ | | | 145 |
| 35 | P | 4.450 | 5½ | | | 50 |
| **Ranger Oil Cda** | | | C | $9 | Opt Vol | 6 |
| OC 10 | | 0.450 | 0.550 | 0½ | 6 | 76 |
| **Repap Enterprises** | | | C | $10¼ | Opt Vol | 10 |
| MY 9 | | 1½ | 1.650 | 1.650 | 10 | 10 |
| **Rogers Com Cl B** | | | C | $17⅜ | Opt Vol | 1750 |
| JY 21 | | 0.100 | 0.200 | 0.200 | 1750 | 1760 |
| **Royal Bk Cda** | | | C | $29 | Opt Vol | 36 |
| JY 30 | | 0.600 | 0¾ | 0.550 | 32 | 604 |
| OC 30 | | 0.950 | 1.100 | 0.900 | 4 | 94 |
| **Royal Bk Lps96** | | | C | $29 | Opt Vol | 50 |
| JA 25 | | 4.700 | 5 | | | 560 |
| 25 | P | 0.150 | 0.350 | | | 212 |
| 30 | | 1.300 | 1½ | 1½ | 50 | 2209 |
| 30 | P | 1.700 | 2 | | | 192 |
| 35 | | 0.200 | 0.450 | | | 399 |
| 35 | P | 5½ | 6½ | | | |
| **Royal Bk Lps97** | | | C | $29 | Opt Vol | |
| JA 25 | | 5⅞ | 6⅜ | | | 302 |
| 25 | P | 0½ | 0.800 | | | 57 |
| 30 | | 2.700 | 2.900 | | | 263 |
| 30 | P | 2 | 2½ | | | 20 |
| 35 | | 1.100 | 1½ | | | 167 |
| 35 | P | 5½ | 6½ | | | |
| **Royal Oak Mines** | | | C | 475 | Opt Vol | 105 |
| JN 6 | | 0.100 | 0.200 | 0.150 | 30 | 580 |
| SP 5 | | 0½ | 0.650 | 0½ | 30 | 544 |
| 6 | | 0.200 | 0.300 | 0.300 | 45 | 210 |
| **Seagram Co.** | | | C | $38¾ | Opt Vol | 1158 |
| AP 37½ | P | 0.300 | 0.550 | 0¼ | 40 | 53 |
| 40 | | 0.400 | 0½ | 0¾ | 210 | 414 |
| 40 | P | 1.400 | 1.650 | 1.050 | 55 | 82 |
| 42½ | | 0.050 | 0¼ | 0.300 | 50 | 176 |
| MY 37½ | | 2.050 | 2.550 | 3.300 | 50 | 50 |
| 40 | | 1.100 | 1.150 | 1¼ | 264 | 505 |
| 40 | P | 1.700 | 1.950 | 1.700 | 215 | 355 |
| 42½ | | 0¼ | 0½ | 0.650 | 80 | 50 |
| JY 37½ | | 2¾ | 3¼ | 4 | 50 | 50 |
| 40 | | 1.550 | 1.800 | 2.200 | 60 | 685 |
| 40 | P | 2.100 | 2.350 | 1.700 | 9 | 70 |
| 42½ | | 0¾ | 0.900 | 1.150 | 10 | 262 |
| OC 37½ | P | 1.300 | 1.550 | 1.150 | 65 | 70 |
| **Seagram Lps 96** | | | C | $38¾ | Opt Vol | 40 |
| JA 30 | | 9½ | 10 | | | 89 |
| 30 | P | 0.100 | 0.350 | | | 74 |
| 35 | | 5½ | 6 | 7 | 10 | 87 |
| 35 | P | 0¾ | 1¼ | | | 71 |
| 40 | | 3.300 | 3.400 | 4.400 | 25 | 100 |
| 40 | P | 2.800 | 3 | | | 503 |
| 45 | | 1.300 | 1.450 | 1¾ | 5 | 104 |
| 45 | P | 6¼ | 6¾ | | | 30 |
| 50 | | 0¼ | 0.450 | | | |
| 50 | P | 11⅛ | 11⅝ | | | |
| **Seagram Lps 97** | | | C | $38¾ | Opt Vol | 41 |
| JA 35 | | 8 | 8½ | 9⅛ | 10 | 32 |
| 35 | P | 1.400 | 1.550 | | | 51 |
| 40 | | 5 | 5½ | 6⅝ | 10 | 40 |
| 40 | P | 3½ | 4 | 3.400 | 10 | 60 |
| 45 | | 3.300 | 3.400 | 3¾ | 10 | 65 |
| 45 | P | 6¼ | 6⅝ | 5 | 1 | 25 |
| 50 | | 1¼ | 1¾ | | | |
| 50 | P | 11⅜ | 11⅞ | | | |
| **Stelco Inc A** | | | C | $7⅜ | Opt Vol | 93 |
| MY 8 | | 0.200 | 0¼ | 0.200 | 50 | 190 |
| SP 7 | | 0.900 | 1.050 | 0.900 | 13 | 36 |
| 8 | | 0.600 | 0.650 | 0.600 | 30 | 218 |
| **SHL Systemhouse Inc.** | | | C | $8⅛ | Opt Vol | 10 |
| JN 7 | | 1.300 | 1½ | 1.300 | 10 | 60 |
| **TransCan Lps96** | | | C | $17⅝ | Opt Vol | |
| JA 16 | | 2.300 | 2.550 | | | 46 |
| 16 | P | 0¼ | 0.450 | | | 10 |
| 18 | | 1.050 | 1.300 | | | 736 |
| 18 | P | 0.950 | 1.100 | | | 81 |
| 20 | | 0.400 | 0.650 | | | 227 |
| 20 | P | 2.350 | 2.600 | | | 26 |
| 22 | | 0.100 | 0¼ | | | 84 |
| 22 | P | 4.350 | 4.600 | | | 20 |
| **TransCan Lps97** | | | C | $17⅝ | Opt Vol | 25 |
| JA 16 | | 2.900 | 3.100 | | | 270 |
| 16 | P | 0.450 | 0.650 | | | 62 |
| 18 | | 1.900 | 2 | 1.900 | 25 | 235 |
| 18 | P | 1.150 | 1.400 | | | 150 |
| 20 | | 0.950 | 1.200 | | | 177 |
| 20 | P | 2.350 | 2.600 | | | 15 |
| **TransCanadaPipe** | | | C | $17⅝ | Opt Vol | 25 |
| AG 16 | | 1.950 | 2.150 | 2.050 | 10 | 10 |
| NV 18 | P | 0.800 | 0.950 | 0.800 | 15 | 15 |
| **TD Bank Leap96** | | | C | $20¼ | Opt Vol | |
| JA 15 | | 5⅜ | 6⅜ | | | 72 |
| 15 | P | 0.010 | 0½ | | | 6 |
| 20 | | 1.850 | 1.900 | | | 635 |
| 20 | P | 0.850 | 1¼ | | | 237 |
| 25 | | 0.150 | 0.350 | | | 706 |
| 25 | P | 4.450 | 5¼ | | | |
| **TD Bank Leap97** | | | C | $20¼ | Opt Vol | |
| JA 15 | | 6¼ | 6⅞ | | | 20 |
| 15 | P | 0.050 | 0.550 | | | |
| 20 | | 2.900 | 3.300 | | | 207 |
| 20 | P | 1.100 | 1.600 | | | 105 |
| 25 | | 0.700 | 1 | | | 56 |
| 25 | P | 4.550 | 5⅜ | | | |
| **TSE 100 Index** | | | C | $259.92 | Opt Vol | 15 |
| AP 255 | P | 0.550 | 0.700 | 0½ | 10 | 20 |
| 265 | | 0.700 | 0.850 | 0.950 | 5 | 40 |
| **TSE 35 Index** | | | C | $226.94 | Opt Vol | 1080 |
| AP 220 | | 7¾ | 8¼ | 8⅞ | 5 | 55 |
| 220 | P | 0.200 | 0.350 | 0¼ | 5 | 379 |
| 225 | P | 0.900 | 1.100 | 0.950 | 30 | 448 |
| 227 | | 2.100 | 2.300 | 2.450 | 165 | 200 |
| 227 | P | 1.800 | 2 | 1.900 | 175 | 336 |
| 230 | | 1.050 | 1¼ | 1.150 | 50 | 396 |
| 230 | P | 3.150 | 3½ | 3.350 | 71 | 222 |
| 232 | | 0.350 | 0.550 | 0.600 | 130 | 340 |
| 235 | | 0.050 | 0¼ | 0.200 | 25 | 288 |
| MY 225 | P | 2.150 | 2.450 | 2¼ | 14 | 154 |
| 227 | | 4.150 | 4.550 | 4.600 | 9 | 9 |
| 230 | | 2.650 | 2.950 | 2.700 | 52 | 60 |
| 232 | | 1.600 | 1.800 | 1.700 | 20 | 105 |
| 235 | P | 6⅝ | 7⅛ | 6⅜ | 5 | 40 |
| JN 205 | P | 0.400 | 0.600 | 0.450 | 300 | 331 |
| 215 | | 15¼ | 15¾ | 16 | 5 | 1005 |
| 215 | P | 1.100 | 1.300 | 1¼ | 1 | 59 |
| 225 | | 7⅜ | 7⅞ | 8⅛ | 13 | 354 |
| 230 | P | 4.900 | 5⅜ | 5⅛ | 5 | 45 |
| **TVX Gold Inc** | | | C | $9¾ | Opt Vol | 2347 |
| AP 8 | | 1¾ | 1.850 | 1.650 | 20 | 57 |
| 10 | | 0.200 | 0¼ | 0.200 | 2160 | 576 |
| MY 10 | | 0.400 | 0.450 | 0.300 | 30 | 30 |
| JY 9 | | 1.050 | 1.150 | 0.950 | 20 | 249 |
| 9 | P | 0.350 | 0.400 | 0.450 | 7 | 75 |
| 10 | | 0.600 | 0.700 | 0.650 | 90 | 553 |
| OC 8 | | 2.050 | 2.200 | 2.200 | 10 | 10 |
| 9 | | 1.400 | 1½ | 1.400 | 15 | 60 |
| 10 | | 0.900 | 1 | 0.800 | 5 | 116 |

**Total contract volume**
**13,094**
**Total open interest**
**363,997**

**CONCEPT CHECK** Question 1.

*a*. What will be the proceeds and net profits to an investor who purchases the April maturity Corel calls with exercise price \$20 if the stock price at maturity is \$15? What if the stock price at maturity is \$25?

*b*. Now answer part (*a*) for an investor who purchases an April maturity Corel put option with exercise price \$20.

## American and European Options

An **American option** allows its holder to exercise the right to purchase (call) or sell (put) the underlying asset on *or before* the expiration date. A **European option** allows for exercise of the option only on the expiration date. American options, because they allow more leeway than do their European counterparts, generally will be more valuable. Virtually all traded options in Canada and the United States are American. Foreign currency options and stock index options traded on the Chicago Board Options Exchange in the United States, and stock index options traded on the Toronto Stock Exchange in Canada, are notable exceptions to this rule, however.

## Adjustments in Option Contract Terms

Because options convey the right to buy or sell shares at a stated price, stock splits would radically alter their value if the terms of the option contract were not adjusted to account for the stock split. For example, reconsider the call options in Figure 20.1. If Corel were to announce a ten-for-one split, its share price would fall from \$18½ to about \$1.85. A call option with exercise price \$20 would be just about worthless, with virtually no possibility that the stock would sell at more than \$20 before the option expired.

To account for a stock split, the exercise price is reduced by the factor of the split, and the number of options held is increased by that factor. For example, the original Corel call option with exercise price of \$20 would be altered after a ten-for-one split to ten new options, with each option carrying an exercise price of \$2.0. A similar adjustment is made for stock dividends of more than 10 percent; the number of shares covered by each option is increased in proportion to the stock dividend, and the exercise price is reduced by that proportion.

In contrast to stock dividends, cash dividends do not affect the terms of an option contract. Because payment of a cash dividend reduces the selling price of the stock without inducing offsetting adjustments in the option contract, the value of the option is affected by dividend policy. Other things being equal, call option values are lower for high dividend-payout policies, because such policies slow the rate of increase of stock prices; conversely, put values are higher for high dividend payouts. (Of course, the option values do not rise or fall on the dividend payment or ex-dividend dates. Dividend payments are anticipated, so the effect of the payment already is built into the original option price.)

**CONCEPT CHECK** Question 2. Suppose that Corel's stock price at the exercise date is $25, and the exercise price of the call is $20. What is the profit on one option contract? After a ten-for-one split, the stock price is $2.5, the exercise price is $2.0, and the option holder now can purchase 1,000 shares. Show that the split leaves option profits unaffected.

## The Option Clearing Corporation

The Option Clearing Corporation (OCC) is jointly owned by the exchanges on which stock options are traded. It is the clearinghouse for options trading. In Canada, it is called Canadian Derivatives Clearing Corporation (CDCC)[1] and is owned by the Montreal, Toronto, and Vancouver Stock Exchanges.

Buyers and sellers of options who agree on a price will consummate the sale of the option. At this point the OCC steps in, by placing itself between the two traders and becoming the effective buyer of the option from the writer and the effective writer of the option to the buyer. All individuals, therefore, deal only with the OCC, which effectively guarantees contract performance.

When an option holder exercises an option, the OCC arranges for a member firm with clients who have written that option to make good on the option obligation. The member firm, in turn, selects from its clients who have written that option to fulfill the contract. The selected client must either deliver 100 shares of stock at a price equal to the exercise price for each call option contract written, or purchase 100 shares at the exercise price for each put option contract written.

Because the OCC guarantees contract performances, option writers are required to post margin amounts to guarantee that they can fulfill their obligations under the option contract. The margin required is determined, in part, by the amount by which the option is in the money, because that value is an indicator of the potential obligation of the option writer upon exercise of the option. When the required margin exceeds the posted margin, the writer will receive a margin call. The holder of the option need not post margin, because the holder will exercise the option only if it is profitable to do so. After purchasing the option, no further money is at risk.

Margin requirements are determined, in part, by the other securities held in the investor's portfolio. For example, a call option writer owning the stock against which the option is written can satisfy the margin requirement simply by allowing a broker to hold that stock in the brokerage account. The stock is then guaranteed to be available for delivery should the call option be exercised. If the underlying security is not owned, however, the margin requirement is determined by both the value of the underlying security and the amount by which the option is in or out of the money. Out-of-the-money options require less margin from the writer, because expected payouts are lower.

---

[1] CDCC used to be called TransCanada Options Inc. (TCO) until 1996.

## Other Listed Options

Options on assets other than stocks also are widely traded, especially in the United States. These include options on market and industry indices; foreign currency; and even the future prices of agricultural products, gold, silver, fixed-income securities, and stock indices. We will discuss these in turn.

**Index Options.** An index option is a call or put based on a stock market index such as the TSE 35, the TSE 100, or the New York Stock Exchange Index. Index options are traded on several broad-based indices, as well as on a few industry-specific indices. We discussed many of these indices in Chapter 2.

The construction of the indices can vary across contracts or exchanges. For example, the TSE 35 index is a value-weighted average of 35 major Canadian stocks in the TSE 300 stock group. The weights are proportional to the market value of outstanding equity for each stock. The Major Market Index, by contrast, is a price-weighted average of 20 U.S. stocks, most of which are in the Dow Jones Industrial Average group, whereas the Value Line Index is an equally weighted arithmetic average of roughly 1,700 U.S. stocks.

In contrast to stock options, index options do not require that the call writer actually "deliver the index" upon exercise, or that the put writer "purchase the index." Instead, a cash settlement procedure is used. The profits that would accrue upon exercise of the option are calculated, and the option writer simply pays that amount to the option holder. The profits are equal to the difference between the exercise price of the option and the value of the index. For example, if the TSE 35 index is at $230 when a call option on the index with exercise price $220 is exercised, the holder of the call receives a cash payment of $10 multiplied by the contract multiplier of 100, or $1,000 per contract. The TSE 100 and TSE 35 traded options are listed at the end of Figure 20.1. Figure 20.2 is a sample listing of various index options from *The Financial Post.* These include options on several foreign stock indices.

**Foreign Currency Options.** A currency option offers the right to buy or sell a quantity of foreign currency for a specified amount of domestic currency. Several foreign currency options were introduced by the Montreal Exchange in the 1980s, but they met with little success and were subsequently withdrawn. In the United States, foreign currency options have traded on the Philadelphia Stock Exchange since December 1982. Since then, the Chicago Board Options Exchange (CBOE) and Chicago Mercantile Exchange (CME) also have listed foreign currency options.

Currency option contracts on U.S. exchanges call for purchase or sale of the currency in exchange for a specified number of U.S. dollars. Contracts are quoted in cents or fractions of a cent per unit of foreign currency. The size of each option contract is specified for each listing. The call option on the British pound, for example, entitles its holder to purchase 31,250 pounds for a specified number of cents per pound on or before the expiration date. For instance, on December 31,

**Figure 20.2**
Index options.
Source: *The Financial Post,* May 31, 1996.
Reprinted by permission.

**Index Options** Thurs., May 30, 1996
Figures supplied by Star Data Systems Inc.

**S&P 500 Comp** Close 671.70

| Strike | Calls June | Calls July | Calls Aug | Puts June | Puts July | Puts Aug |
|---|---|---|---|---|---|---|
| 605 | r | r | s | r | 2 1/4 | s |
| 610 | 59 | r | r | 3/4 | 2 1/8 | r |
| 620 | 54 3/4 | r | r | 1 1/4 | 3 5/8 | 4 5/8 |
| 625 | r | r | s | 1 1/8 | 3 1/4 | s |
| 630 | r | r | r | 1 3/8 | 3 1/2 | 6 3/8 |
| 635 | 40 1/2 | r | s | 1 1/2 | 3 7/8 | s |
| 640 | 31 | 35 3/8 | r | 2 3/16 | 5 1/4 | 9 |
| 645 | 26 1/4 | 31 1/2 | s | 2 5/16 | 6 3/4 | s |
| 650 | 21 1/2 | r | r | 3 | 6 5/8 | 9 5/8 |
| 655 | 18 1/4 | r | s | 3 3/4 | 7 7/8 | s |
| 660 | 18 1/2 | r | r | 4 7/8 | 8 3/4 | 12 3/8 |
| 665 | 14 3/4 | r | s | 6 | 9 7/8 | s |
| 670 | 10 3/4 | 17 3/4 | 19 | 8 | 12 1/8 | 18 1/2 |
| 675 | 8 | 13 7/8 | r | 10 1/8 | 14 1/2 | 16 1/2 |
| 680 | 5 5/8 | 11 3/8 | 13 5/8 | 12 3/4 | 20 3/8 | r |
| 685 | 3 1/2 | 9 1/8 | s | 15 | 22 | s |
| 690 | 2 5/16 | 5 3/4 | 9 1/4 | 17 3/4 | r | 28 |
| 695 | 1 1/2 | 4 3/4 | s | 22 1/2 | 24 | s |
| 700 | 1 | 4 | 7 3/4 | 31 1/4 | r | r |
| 705 | 3/8 | s | 5 1/4 | r | s | r |
| 710 | 5/16 | s | 5 1/4 | r | s | r |
| 715 | 1/4 | s | r | r | s | r |
| 725 | 1/16 | 1/2 | 2 1/4 | r | r | r |

Total call vol. 36,064 Total put vol. 36,605
Prev. open int. 447,835 Prev. open int. 535,881

**S&P 100** Close 649.09

| Strike | Calls June | Calls July | Calls Aug | Puts June | Puts July | Puts Aug |
|---|---|---|---|---|---|---|
| 605 | r | 47 7/8 | r | 1 1/4 | 3 1/4 | r |
| 610 | r | 42 1/2 | r | 1 9/16 | 4 1/8 | 7 3/4 |
| 615 | 38 | r | r | 1 3/4 | 6 | 8 3/4 |
| 620 | 34 1/4 | r | r | 2 1/8 | 5 5/8 | 8 |
| 625 | 31 3/8 | 29 5/8 | r | 2 3/4 | 6 3/8 | 10 7/8 |
| 630 | 26 | 28 | r | 3 3/8 | 7 3/8 | 11 |
| 635 | 20 1/2 | 23 | r | 4 1/4 | 8 | 11 5/8 |
| 640 | 16 1/4 | 22 1/2 | 24 1/2 | 5 3/8 | 10 1/8 | 13 1/2 |
| 645 | 12 7/8 | 20 1/4 | r | 6 7/8 | 12 | 17 |
| 650 | 9 3/4 | 15 1/2 | 20 1/2 | 8 3/4 | 13 1/2 | r |
| 655 | 7 | 14 | 17 1/2 | 11 1/4 | 15 | 19 |
| 660 | 4 3/4 | 10 3/8 | 13 7/8 | 14 | 18 1/4 | r |
| 665 | 3 1/8 | 8 1/2 | r | 17 5/8 | 20 3/4 | r |
| 670 | 2 | 6 1/4 | 8 5/8 | 20 1/4 | 24 5/8 | 26 5/8 |
| 675 | 1 1/8 | 4 3/4 | r | 25 | r | r |
| 680 | 5/8 | 3 1/2 | r | r | r | r |
| 685 | 7/16 | 2 3/8 | 5 1/8 | r | r | r |

Total call vol. 109,452 Total put vol. 91,898
Prev. open int. 228,865 Prev. open int. 291,579

**S&P Mid-cap 400** Close 240.54

| Strike | Calls June | Calls July | Calls Aug | Puts June | Puts July | Puts Aug |
|---|---|---|---|---|---|---|
| 230 | r | r | r | r | r | 4 |
| 240 | 3 1/4 | r | r | 3 1/2 | 5 | r |
| 245 | r | r | r | 6 1/8 | r | r |

Total call vol. 20 Total put vol. 1,218
Prev. open int. 17,815 Prev. open int. 21,664

**Major Market** Close 595.64

| Strike | Calls June | Calls July | Calls Aug | Puts June | Puts July | Puts Aug |
|---|---|---|---|---|---|---|
| 525 | r | s | s | 1/2 | s | s |
| 530 | r | r | s | 1/2 | r | s |
| 535 | r | s | s | 9/16 | s | s |
| 540 | r | r | r | 11/16 | r | r |
| 550 | r | r | r | r | r | 5 3/4 |
| 560 | r | r | r | 1 3/8 | r | r |
| 565 | r | r | r | r | 6 1/4 | r |
| 570 | r | r | r | 2 | 5 3/8 | 9 1/2 |
| 575 | r | r | r | 4 | r | r |
| 580 | r | r | r | 3 5/8 | r | r |
| 585 | 17 1/8 | r | r | 4 3/8 | r | r |
| 590 | r | r | r | 6 1/4 | 13 | r |
| 595 | 9 5/8 | r | r | 7 3/4 | r | r |
| 600 | 7 5/8 | 11 1/8 | r | 9 1/4 | 17 | r |

Total call vol. 65 Total put vol. 564
Prev. open int. 3,780 Prev. open int. 8,959

**Japan Index** Close 222.22

| Strike | Calls June | Puts June |
|---|---|---|
| 175 | 46 1/8 | r |
| 215 | r | 1 1/2 |
| 220 | 5 1/4 | 3 1/4 |

Total call vol. 304 Total put vol. 140
Prev. open int. 16,684 Prev. open int. 13,299

**Toronto 35** Close 271.30

| Strike | Calls June | Calls July | Calls Sep | Puts June | Puts July | Puts Sep |
|---|---|---|---|---|---|---|
| 230 | r | s | r | r | s | 0.35 |
| 240 | r | s | r | r | s | 0.65 |
| 250 | 19.60 | s | r | r | s | r |
| 255 | 14.80 | r | r | r | r | r |
| 260 | 9.90 | r | r | 0.35 | r | r |
| 262.50 | r | s | s | 0.50 | s | s |
| 265 | r | r | r | 1.15 | r | r |
| 267.50 | 4.80 | 5.50 | s | 1.15 | r | s |
| 270 | 3.30 | r | r | 2.70 | r | 5.10 |
| 272.50 | 1.25 | r | s | 3.10 | r | s |
| 275 | 1.00 | 2.45 | r | 4.70 | r | r |
| 277.50 | 0.35 | r | s | r | r | s |

Total call vol. 395 Total put vol. 128
Open int. 4,305 Open int. 5,869

1994 the March call option with strike price of 155 cents was quoted at 3.34 cents on the Philadelphia Exchange, which means that each contract cost $\$.0334 \times 31{,}250 = \$1{,}043.75$. The current exchange rate was 156 cents per pound on that date. Therefore, the option was in the money by 1 cent, the difference between the current exchange (156 cents) and the exercise price of 155 cents per pound.

**Futures Options.** Futures options give their holders the right to buy or sell a specified futures contract, using as a future price the exercise price of the option. Although the delivery process is slightly complicated, the terms of futures options contracts are designed, in effect, to allow the option to be written on the futures price itself. The option holder receives upon exercise a profit equal to the difference between the current futures price on the specified asset and the exercise price of the option. Thus, if the futures price is, for example, \$37, and the call has an exercise price of \$35, the holder who exercises the call option on the futures gets a payoff of \$2.

**Interest Rate Options.** Options on Canada bonds are traded on the Montreal and Toronto exchanges via TCO. Figure 20.1 shows two such bonds (denoted by CDA in the listing) traded that particular day. There also are options on Canada Bond futures and bankers' acceptances futures.

Options on particular U.S. Treasury notes and bonds are listed on the American Exchange and the CBOE. Options also are traded on Treasury bills, certificates of deposit, GNMA pass-through certificates, and yields on Treasury securities. Options on several interest rate futures, such as Treasury bonds, Treasury notes, municipal bonds, and LIBOR also trade on various US exchanges.

## 20.2 Values of Options at Expiration

### Call Options

Recall that a call option gives the right to purchase a security at the exercise price. If you hold a call option on Seagram's stock with an exercise price of $30 and Seagram's currently sells at $40, you can exercise your option to purchase the stock at $30 and simultaneously sell the shares at the market price of $40, clearing $10 per share. On the other hand, if the shares sell below $30, you can sit on the option and do nothing, realizing no further gain or loss. The value of the call option at expiration equals:

$$\text{Payoff to call holder} = \begin{cases} S_T - X & \text{if } S_T > X \\ 0 & \text{if } S_T \le X \end{cases}$$

where $S_T$ is the value of the stock at expiration and $X$ is the exercise price. This formula emphasizes the option property, because the payoff cannot be negative. That is, the option is exercised only if $S_T$ exceeds $X$. If $S_T$ is less than $X$, exercise does not occur and the option expires with zero value. The loss to the option holder in this case equals the price originally paid for the right to buy at the exercise price.

The value at expiration of the call on Seagram's with exercise price $30 is given by the following schedule:

| Seagram's value: | $20 | $30 | $40 | $50 | $60 |
|---|---|---|---|---|---|
| Option value: | 0 | 0 | $10 | $20 | $30 |

For Seagram's prices at or below $30, the option is worthless. Above $30, the option is worth the excess of Seagram's price over $30. The option's value increases by $1 for each dollar increase in the Seagram's stock price. This relationship can be depicted graphically, as in the solid (top) line of Figure 20.3.

The solid line of Figure 20.3 depicts the value of the call at maturity. The net *profit* to the holder of the call equals the gross payoff less the initial investment in the call. Suppose the call cost $10. Then the profit to the call holder would be as given in the broken (bottom) line of Figure 20.3. At option expiration, the

**Figure 20.3**
Payoff and profit to call option at expiration.

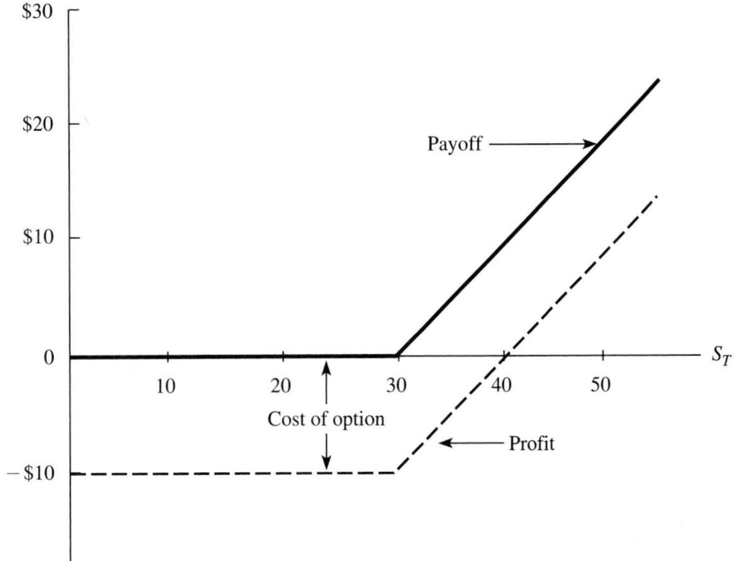


investor has suffered a loss of $10 if the stock price is less than $30. Profits do not become positive unless the stock price at expiration exceeds $40. The break-even point is $40, because at that point the payoff to the call, $S_T - X = \$40 - \$30 = \$10$, equals the cost paid to acquire the call. Hence, the call holder profits only if the stock price is higher.

Conversely, the writer of the call incurs losses if the stock price is high. In that scenario, the writer will receive a call and will be obligated to deliver a stock worth $S_T$ for only $X$ dollars:

$$\text{Payoff to call writer} = \begin{cases} -(S_T - X) & \text{if } S_T \geq X \\ 0 & \text{if } S_T < X \end{cases}$$

The call writer, who is exposed to losses if Seagram's stock increases in price, is willing to bear this risk in return for the option premium. Figure 20.4 depicts the payoff and profit diagrams for the call writer. Notice that these are just the mirror images of the corresponding diagrams for call holders. The break-even point for the option writer also is $40. The (negative) payoff at that point just offsets the premium originally received when the option was written.

## Put Options

A put option conveys the right to sell an asset at the exercise price. In this case, the holder will not exercise the option unless the asset sells for *less* than the exercise price. For example, if Seagram's shares were to fall to $30, a put option with exercise price $40 could be exercised to give a $10 profit to its holder. The

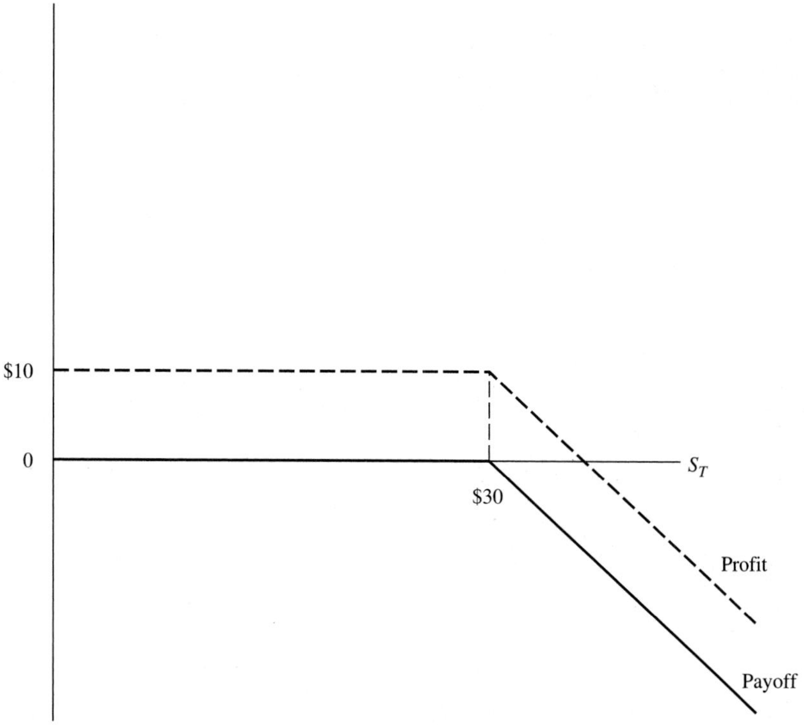


**Figure 20.4**
Payoff and profit to call writers at expiration.

holder would purchase a share of Seagram's for $30 and simultaneously deliver it to the put option writer for the exercise price of $40.

The value of a put option at expiration is

$$\text{Payoff to call holder} = \begin{cases} X - S_T & \text{if } S_T \leq X \\ 0 & \text{if } X_T > X \end{cases}$$

The solid (top) line in Figure 20.5 illustrates the payoff at maturity to the holder of a put option on Seagram's stock with an exercise price of $40. If the stock price at option maturity is above $40, the put has no value, because the right to sell the shares at $40 would not be exercised. Below a price of $40, the put value at expiration increases by $1 for each dollar that the stock price falls. The dashed (bottom) line in Figure 20.5 is a graph of the put option owner's profit at expiration, net of the initial cost of the put.

---

**CONCEPT CHECK** Question 3. Analyze the strategy of put writing.

*a.* What is the payoff to a put writer as a function of the stock price?
*b.* What is the profit?
*c.* Draw the payoff and profit graphs.
*d.* When do put writers do well? When do they do poorly?

---

**Figure 20.5**
Payoff and profit to put option at expiration.

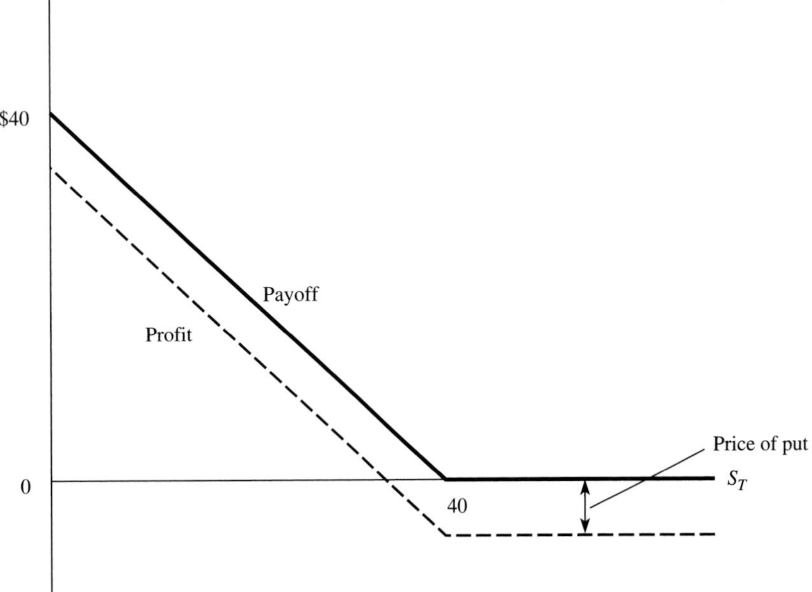


Writing puts *naked* (i.e., writing a put without an offsetting position in the stock for hedging purposes) exposes the writer to losses if the market falls. Writing naked out-of-the-money puts was once considered an attractive way to generate income, since it was believed that, as long as the market did not fall sharply before the option expiration, the option premium could be collected without the put holder ever exercising the option against the writer. Because only sharp drops in the market could result in losses to the writer of the put, the strategy was not viewed as overly risky. However, in the wake of the market crash of October 1987, such put writers suffered huge losses. Participants now perceive much greater risk to this strategy.

## Options versus Stock Investments

Call options are bullish investments; that is, they provide profits when stock prices increase. Puts, in contrast, are bearish investments. Symmetrically, writing calls is bearish and writing puts is bullish. Because option values depend on market movements, purchase of options may be viewed as a substitute for direct purchase or sale of a stock. Why might an option strategy be preferable to direct stock transactions?

For example, why would you purchase a call option rather than buy Seagram's stock directly? Maybe you have some information that leads you to believe that Seagram's stock will increase in value from its current level, which in our examples we will take to be $40. You know your analysis could be incorrect, and that Seagram's also could fall in price. Suppose that a six-month maturity call option with exercise price $35 currently sells for $8, and that the six-month interest rate is 5 percent. Consider these three strategies for investing a sum of money, for example, $4,000. For simplicity, suppose that Seagram's will not pay any dividends until after the six-month period.

Strategy *A:* Purchase 100 shares of Seagram stock.
Strategy *B:* Purchase 500 call options on Seagram's with exercise price $35. (This would require 5 contracts, each for 100 shares.)
Strategy *C:* Purchase 100 call options for $800. Invest the remaining $3,200 in six-month T-bills, to earn 5 percent interest.

Let us trace the possible values of these three portfolios when the options expire in six months as a function of Seagram's stock price at that time.

| Seagram's Price | $20 | $30 | $40 | $50 | $60 |
|---|---|---|---|---|---|
| Value of portfolio *A:* | $2,000 | $3,000 | $4,000 | $5,000 | $ 6,000 |
| Value of portfolio *B:* | 0 | 0 | 2,500 | 7,500 | 12,500 |
| Value of portfolio *C:* | 3,360 | 3,360 | 3,860 | 4,860 | 5,860 |

Portfolio *A* will be worth 100 times the share value of Seagram's. Portfolio *B* is worthless unless Seagram's sells for more than the exercise price of the call. Once that point is reached, the portfolio is worth 1,000 times the excess of the stock price over the exercise price. Finally, portfolio *C* is worth $3,360 from the investment in T-bills ($\$3,200 \times 1.05 = \$3,360$) plus any profits from the 100 call options. Remember that each of these portfolios involves the same $4,000 initial investment. The rates of return on these three portfolios are as follows:

| Seagram's Price | $20 | $30 | $40 | $50 | $60 |
|---|---|---|---|---|---|
| *A* (all stock) | −50% | −25% | 0.0% | 25% | 50% |
| *B* (all options) | −100.0% | −100.0% | −37.5% | 87.5% | 212.5% |
| *C* (options plus bills) | −16% | −16% | −3.5% | 21.5% | 46.5% |

These rates of return are illustrated in Figure 20.6.

Comparing the returns to portfolios *B* and *C* to those of the simple investment in Seagram's stock represented by portfolio *A,* we see that options offer two interesting features. First, an option offers leverage. Compare the returns of portfolio *B* and *A.* When Seagram's stock falls in price to $30, the value of portfolio *B* falls precipitously to zero, a rate of return of −100 percent. Conversely, if the stock price increases by 25 percent, from $40 to $50, the all-option portfolio jumps in value by a disproportionate 87.5 percent. In this sense, calls are a leveraged investment on the stock. Their values respond more than proportionately to changes in the stock value. Figure 20.6 vividly illustrates this point. The slope of the all-option portfolio is far steeper than the all-stock portfolio, reflecting its greater proportional sensitivity to the value of the underlying security. The leverage factor is the reason that investors (illegally) exploiting inside information commonly choose options as their investment vehicle.

The potential insurance value of options is the second interesting feature, as portfolio *C* shows. The T-bill plus option portfolio cannot be worth less than

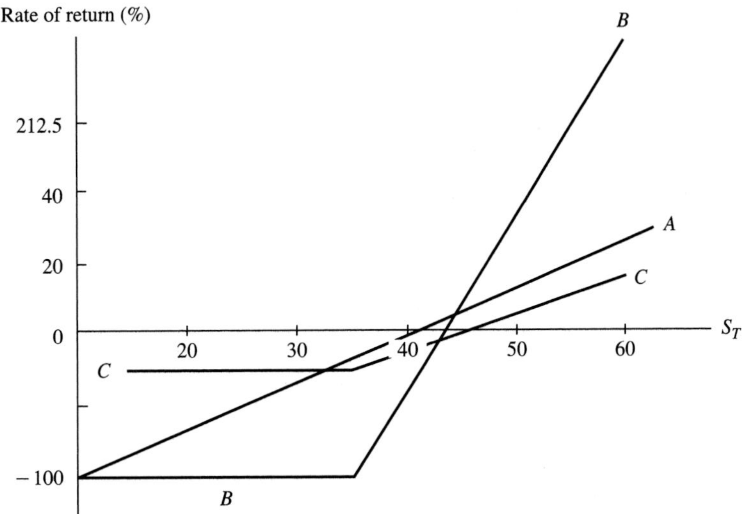


**Figure 20.6**
Rates of return to three strategies.

\$3,360 after six months, since the option can always be left to expire worthless. The worst possible rate of return on portfolio *C* is −16 percent, compared to a (theoretically) worst possible rate of return on Seagram's stock of −100 percent if the company were to go bankrupt. Of course, this insurance comes at a price: When Seagram's does well, portfolio *C* does not perform quite as well as portfolio *A*.

## 20.3 Option Strategies

An unlimited variety of payoff patterns can be achieved by combining puts and calls with various exercise prices. The following subsections explain the motivation and structure of some of the more popular methods.

### Protective Put

Imagine that you would like to invest in a stock, for example, Seagram's, but that you are unwilling to bear potential losses beyond some given level. Investing in the stock alone is quite risky, because in principle you could lose all the money you invest. Instead you might consider investing in stock together with a put option on the stock. Table 20.1 illustrates the total value of your portfolio at option expiration.

Whatever happens to the stock price, you are guaranteed a payoff equal to the put option's exercise price because the put gives you the right to sell Seagram's for the exercise price even if the stock price is below that value.

Figure 20.7 illustrates the payoff and profit to this **protective put** strategy. The solid line in Figure 20.7C is the total payoff; the dashed line is displaced

**Table 20.1** Payoff to Protective Put Strategy

| | $S_T \le X$ | $S_T > X$ |
|---|---|---|
| Stock | $S_T$ | $S_T$ |
| Put | $X - S_T$ | 0 |
| Total | $X$ | $S_T$ |

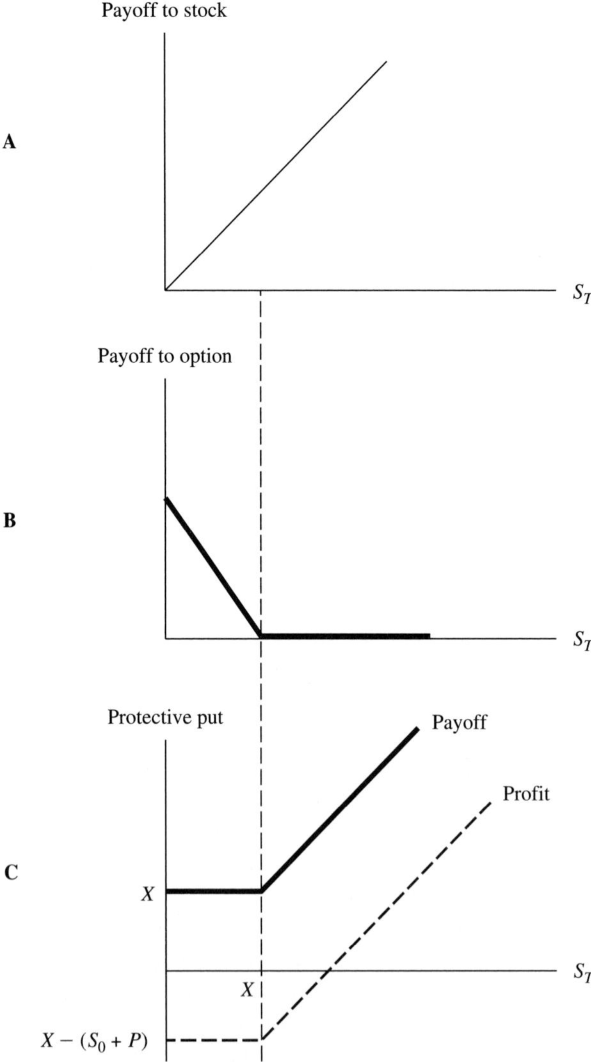


**Figure 20.7** Value of a protective put position at expiration.

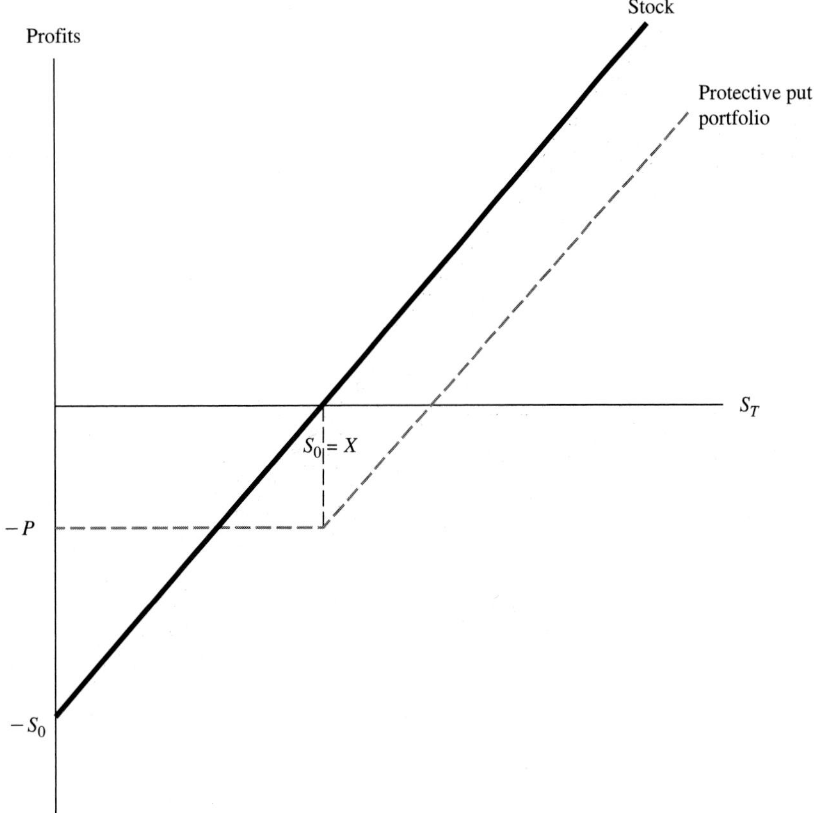


**Figure 20.8**
Protective put versus stock investment.

downward by the cost of establishing the position, $S_0 + P$. Notice that potential losses are indeed limited.

It is instructive to compare the profit to the protective put strategy with that of the stock investment. For simplicity, consider an at-the-money protective put, so that $X = S_0$. Figure 20.8 compares the profits for the two strategies. The profit on the stock is zero if the stock price remains unchanged, and $S_T = S_0$. It rises or falls by $1 for every $1 swing in the ultimate stock price. The profit on the stock plus put portfolio is negative and equal to the cost of the put if $S_T$ is below $S_0$. The profit on the overall protective put position increases one for one with increases in the stock price, once $S_T$ exceeds $S_0$.

Figure 20.8 makes it clear that the protective put offers some insurance against stock price declines in that it limits losses. Indeed, as we shall see in Chapter 21, protective put strategies provide a form of *portfolio insurance.* The cost of the protection is that, in the case of stock price increases, your profit is reduced by

## Protective Puts versus Stop-Loss Orders

We have seen that protective puts guarantee that the end-of-period value of a portfolio will equal or exceed the put's exercise price. As a specific example, consider a share of stock protected by a European put option with one-year maturity and an exercise price of $40. Even if the stock at year-end is selling below $40, the put can be exercised and the stock can be sold for the exercise price, locking in a minimum payoff of $40.

Another common tool to protect a portfolio position is the stop-loss order. This is an order to your broker to sell your stock when and if its price falls to some lower boundary, such as $40 per share. Thus, should the stock price fall substantially, your shares will be sold before losses mount, so that your proceeds will not fall below $40 per share.

It would seem that the stop-loss order provides the same stock price insurance offered by the protective put. However, the stop-loss order can be executed by your broker for no extra cost. Does this mean that the stop-loss order is effectively a free put option? What does the put offer that the stop-loss order does not?

To resolve this seeming paradox, look at Figure 20.9, which graphs one possible path for the stock price over the course of the year. Notice that, although the stock price falls below $40 at time *t*, it ultimately recovers and ends the year at $60. The protective put will end the year worth $60—the put will expire worthless, but the stock will be worth $60. The stop-loss order, however, required that the stock be sold at time *t* as soon as its price fell below $40. This strategy will yield by year-end only $40 plus any interest accumulated between time *t* and the end of the year, far less than the payoff on the protective put strategy.

The protective put strategy does offer an advantage over the stop-loss strategy. With a stop-loss order in force, the investor realizes the $40 lower bound if the stock price *ever* reaches that boundary because the stock is sold as soon as the boundary is reached. Even if the stock price rebounds from the $40 limit, the investor using the stop-loss order will not share in the gain. The holder of the put option, on the other hand, need not exercise when the stock hits $40. Instead, the option holder may wait until the end of the year to exercise the option, knowing that the $40 exercise price is guaranteed regardless of how far the stock falls, but should the stock price recover, the stock still will be held and any gain will be captured.*

*Another disadvantage of the stop-loss order, which is of a more practical nature, is that the selling price is not guaranteed. Problems in executing trades could lead to a transaction at a price lower than $40.

the cost of the put, which turned out to be unneeded. The accompanying box and Figure 20.9 illustrate the relative merits of protective puts versus stop-loss orders.

### Covered Call

A **covered call** position is the purchase of a share of stock with a simultaneous sale of a call on that stock. The position is "covered" because the obligation to deliver the stock is covered by the stock held in the portfolio. Writing an option without an offsetting stock position is called, by contrast, *naked option writing.* The payoff to a covered call, presented in Table 20.2, equals the stock value minus

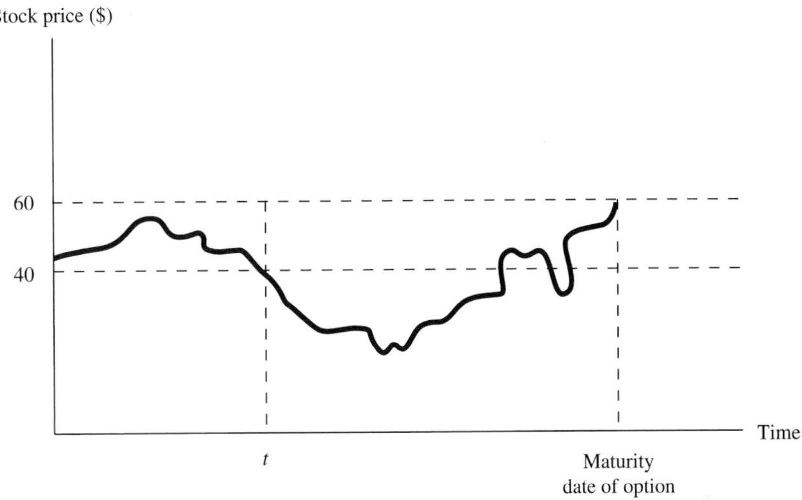


**Figure 20.9**
Stop-loss versus protective put.

**Table 20.2** Payoff to a Covered Call

| | $S_T \leq X$ | $S_T > X$ |
|---|---|---|
| Payoff of stock | $S_T$ | $S_T$ |
| −Payoff of call | $-0$ | $-(S_T - X)$ |
| Total | $S_T$ | $X$ |

the payoff of the call. The call payoff is subtracted because the covered call position involves issuing a call to another investor who can choose to exercise it to profit at your expense.

The solid line in Figure 20.10**C** illustrates the payoff pattern. We see that the total position is worth $S_T$ when the stock price at time $T$ is below $X$, and rises to a maximum of $X$ when $S_T$ exceeds $X$. In essence, the sale of the call option means that the call writer has sold the claim to any stock value above $X$ in return for the initial premium (the call price). Therefore, at expiration the position is worth, at most $X$. The dashed line of Figure 20.10**C** is the net profit to the covered call.

Writing covered call options has been a popular investment strategy among institutional investors. Consider the managers of a fund invested largely in stocks. They might find it appealing to write calls on some or all of the stock in order to boost income by the premiums collected. Although they thereby forfeit potential capital gains should the stock price rise above the exercise price, if they view $X$ as the price at which they plan to sell the stock anyway, then the call may be viewed as enforcing a king of "sell discipline." The written call guarantees that the stock sale will take place as planned.

**Figure 20.10**
Value of a covered call position at expiration.

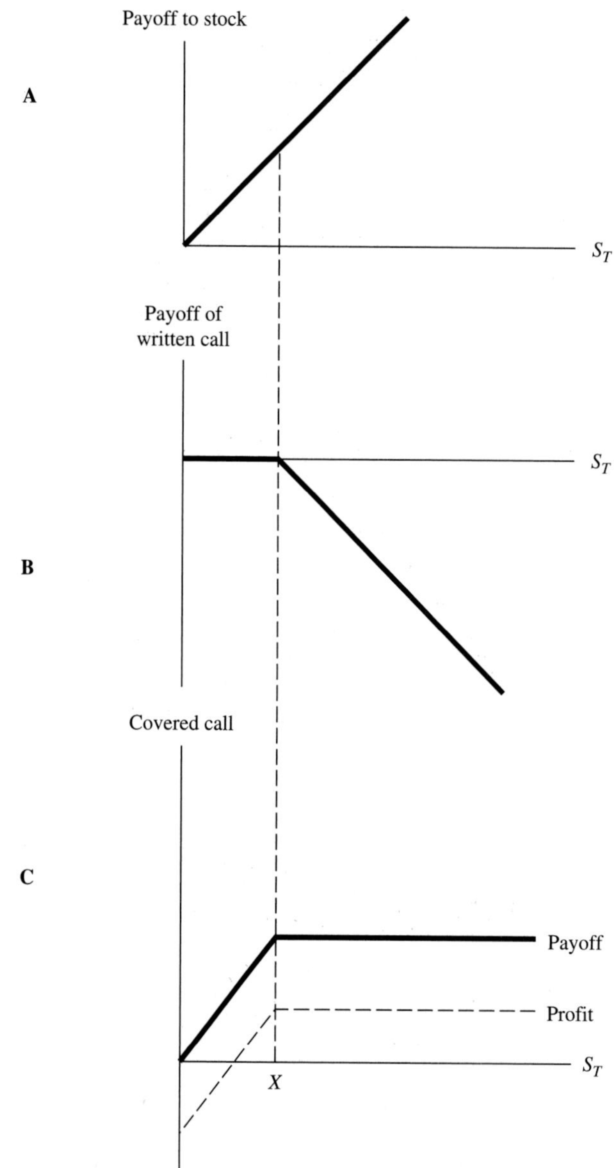


For example, assume a pension fund is holding 1,000 shares of Seagram's stock, with a current price of $40 per share. Suppose that management intends to sell all 1,000 shares if the share price hits $45 and that a call expiring in 90 days with an exercise price of $45 is currently selling for $2. By writing 10 Seagram's call contracts (100 shares each) the fund can pick up $2,000 in extra income. The fund would lose its share of profits from any movement of Seagram's stock above \$45 per share, but given that it would have sold its shares at \$45, it would not have realized those profits anyway.

## Straddle

A **straddle** is established by buying both a call and a put on a stock, each with the same exercise price, $X$, and the same expiration date, $T$. Straddles are useful strategies for investors who believe that a stock will move a lot in price, but who are uncertain about the direction of the move. For example, suppose you believe that an important court case that will make or break a company is about to be settled, and the market is not yet aware of the situation. The stock will either double in value if the case is settled favourably, or it will drop by half if the settlement goes against the company. The straddle position will do well regardless of the outcome, because its value is highest when the stock price makes extreme upward or downward moves from $X$.

The worst-case scenario for a straddle is no movement in the stock price. If $S_T$ equals $X$, both the call and the put expire worthless, and the investor's outlay for the purchase of the two positions is lost. Straddle positions, in other words, are bets on volatility. An investor who establishes a straddle must view the stock as more volatile than the market does. The payoff to straddle is presented in Table 20.3.

The solid line in Figure 20.11**C** illustrates this payoff. Notice that the portfolio payoff is always positive, except at the one point where the portfolio has zero value, $S_T = X$. You might wonder why all investors do not pursue such a no-lose strategy. Remember, however, that the straddle requires that both the put and call be purchased. The value of the portfolio at expiration, although never negative, still must exceed the initial cash outlay for the investor to clear a profit.

The broken line in Figure 20.11**C** is the profit to the straddle. The profit line lies below the payoff line by the cost of purchasing the straddle, $P + C$. It is clear from the diagram that the straddle position generates a loss unless the stock price deviates substantially from $X$. The stock price must depart from $X$ by the total amount expended to purchase the call and the put for the purchaser of the straddle to clear a profit.

**Table 20.3** Payoff to a Straddle

| | $S_T \leq X$ | $S_T > X$ |
|---|---|---|
| Payoff of call | 0 | $S_T - X$ |
| +Payoff of put | $+(X - S_T)$ | +0 |
| Total | $X - S_T$ | $S_T - X$ |

**Figure 20.11**
Payoff and profit to a straddle at expiration.

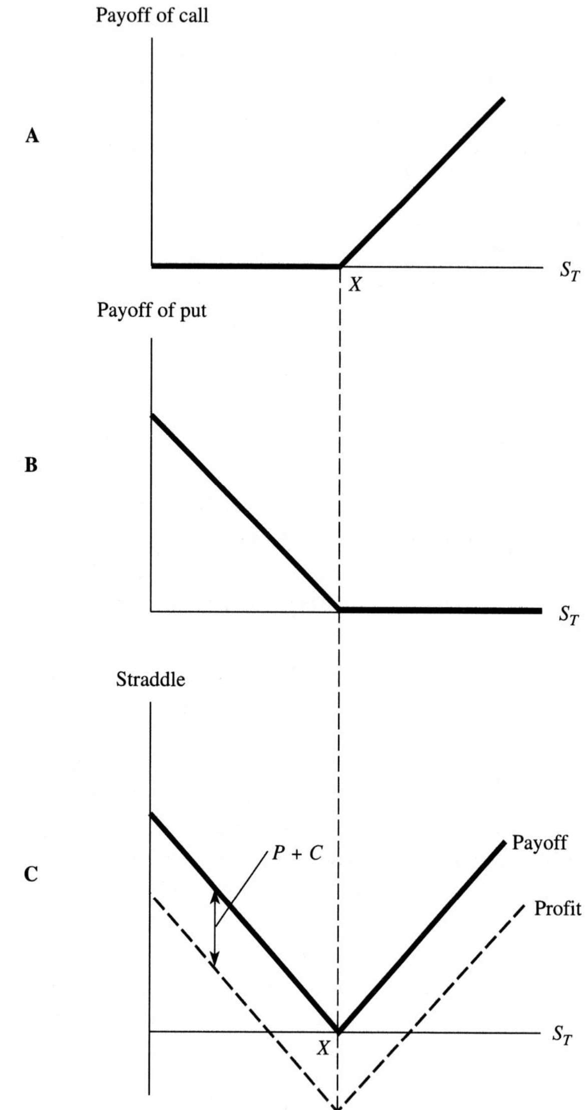


*Strips* and *straps* are variations of straddles. A strip is two puts and one call on a security with the same exercise price and maturity date. A strap is two calls and one put.

**CONCEPT CHECK** Question 4. Graph the profit and payoff diagrams for strips and straps.

## Spreads

A **spread** is a combination of two or more call options (or two or more puts) on the same stock with differing exercise prices or times to maturity. Some options will be held long, while others are written. A *money spread* involves the purchase of one option and the simultaneous sale of another with a different exercise price. A *time* spread refers to the sale and purchase of options with differing expiration dates.

Consider a money spread in which one call option is bought with an exercise price $X_1$, while another call with an identical expiration date but higher exercise price, $X_2$, is written. The payoff to this position will be the difference in the value of the call held and the value of the call written, as shown in Table 20.4.

Notice that we now have three instead of two outcomes to distinguish: the lowest-price region where $S_T$ is below both exercise prices, a middle region where $S_T$ is between the two exercise prices, and a high-price region where $S_T$ exceeds both exercise prices. Figure 20.12 illustrates the payoff and profit to this strategy, which is called a *bullish spread* because the payoff either increases or is unaffected by stock price increases. Holders of bullish spreads benefit from stock price increases.

One motivation for a bullish spread might be that the investor believes that one option is overpriced relative to another. For example, if the investor believes that an $X = \$135$ call is cheap compared to an $X = \$150$ call, he or she might establish the spread, even without a strong desire to take a bullish position in the stock.

A product called CAPS, which mimics European vertical spreads on the S&P 100 and S&P 500 indices and the Major Market index, began trading in the U.S. a few years ago. The spread position, which is long one option and short another, is in effect traded as a single security. For example, the exercise price of the long call position is accompanied by a higher exercise price called the cap price. The cap price is in effect the exercise price of the call that would be written in an explicit spread position. Similarly, put CAPS accompany the stated exercise price with a lower cap price. The spread between the exercise price and the cap price is 30 points on the S&P contracts, and 20 points on the MMI contract. CAPS differ from actual spread positions in that they are automatically exercised as soon as the index reaches the cap price.

**Table 20.4** Payoff to a Bullish Vertical Spread

| | $S_T \le X_1$ | $X_1 < S_T \le X_2$ | $S_T > X_2$ |
|---|---|---|---|
| Payoff of call, exercise price = $X_1$ | 0 | $S_T - X_1$ | $S_T - X_1$ |
| −Payoff of call, exercise price = $X_2$ | −0 | −0 | $-(X_T - X_2)$ |
| Total | 0 | $S_T - X_1$ | $X_2 - X_1$ |

**Figure 20.12**
Value of a bullish spread position at expiration.

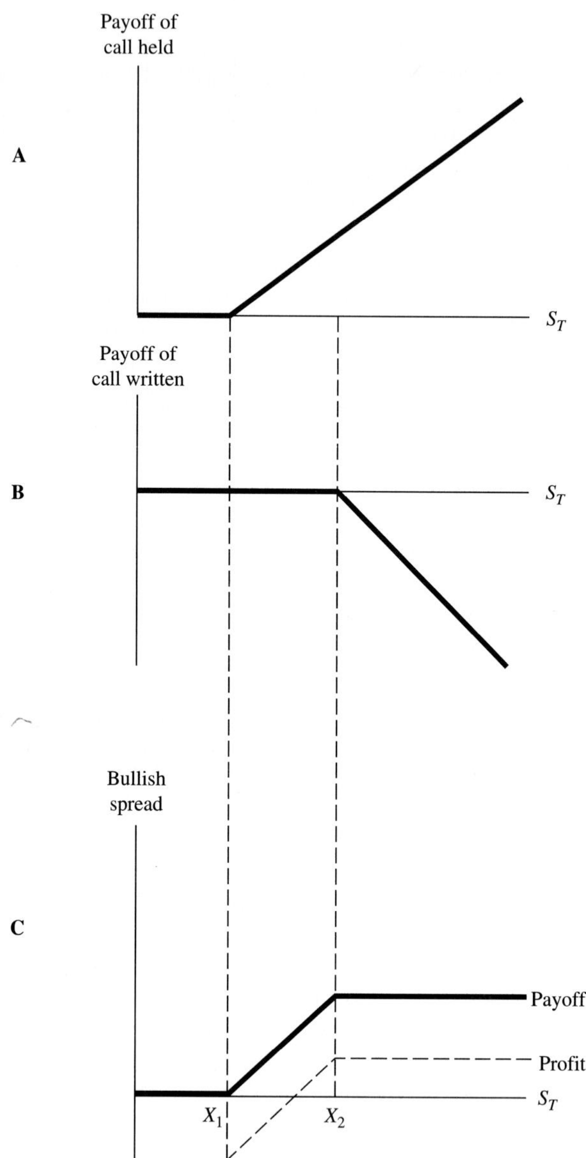


## 20.4 The Put-Call Parity Relationship

Suppose that you buy a call option and write a put option, each with the same exercise price, $X$, and the same expiration date, $T$. At expiration, the payoff on your investment will equal the payoff to the call, minus the payoff that must be made on the put. The payoff for each option will depend on whether the ultimate stock price, $S_T$, exceeds the exercise price at contract expiration.

**Figure 20.13**
The payoff pattern of a long call–short put position.

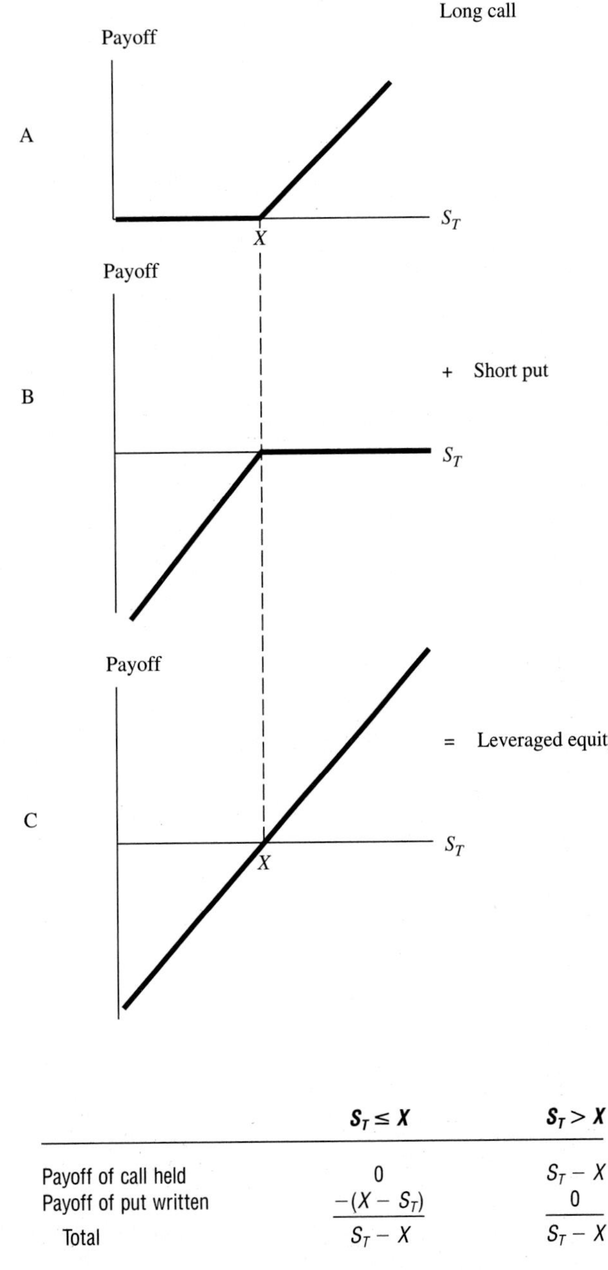


| | $S_T \le X$ | $S_T > X$ |
|---|---|---|
| Payoff of call held | 0 | $S_T - X$ |
| Payoff of put written | $-(X - S_T)$ | 0 |
| Total | $S_T - X$ | $S_T - X$ |

Figure 20.13 illustrates this payoff pattern. Compare the payoff to that of a portfolio made up of the stock plus a borrowing position, where the money to be paid back will grow, with interest, to $X$ dollars at the maturity of the loan. Such a position, in fact, is a *leveraged* equity position in which $X/(1 + r_f)^T$ dollars is borrowed today (so that $X$ will be repaid at maturity) and $S_0$ dollars are invested

in the stock. The total payoff of the leveraged equity position is $S_T - X$, the same as that of the option strategy. Thus the long call–short put position replicates the leveraged equity position. Again, we see that option trading allows us to construct artificial leverage.

Because the option portfolio has a payoff identical to that of the leveraged equity position, the costs of establishing the two positions must be equal. The net cost of establishing the option position is $C - P$; the call is purchased for $C$, while the written put generates premium income of $P$. Likewise, the leveraged equity position requires a net cash outlay of $S_0 - X/(1 + r_f)^T$, the cost of the stock less the proceeds from borrowing. Equating these costs, we conclude that

$$C - P = S_0 - X/(1 + r_f)^T \tag{20.1}$$

Equation 20.1 is called the **put-call parity theorem** because it represents the proper relationship between put and call prices. If the parity relationship is ever violated, an arbitrage opportunity arises. For example, suppose that you confront these data for a certain stock:

| | |
|---|---|
| Stock price | \$110 |
| Call price (6-month maturity, $X$ = \$105) | \$ 17 |
| Put price (6-month maturity, $X$ = \$105) | \$ 5 |
| Risk-free interest rate | 10.25 percent annual yield, or 5 percent per 6 months |

We use these data in the put-call parity theorem to see if parity is violated:

$$C - P \overset{?}{=} S_0 - X/(1 + r_f)^T$$
$$17 - 15 \overset{?}{=} 110 - 105/1.05$$
$$12 \overset{?}{=} 10$$

Parity is violated. To exploit the mispricing, you can buy the relatively cheap portfolio (the stock plus borrowing position represented on the right-hand side of equation 20.1 and sell the relatively expensive portfolio (the long call–short put position corresponding to the left-hand side—i.e., write a call and buy a put).

Let us examine the payoff to this strategy. In six months, the stock will be worth $S_T$. The \$100 borrowed will be paid back with interest, resulting in a cash outflow of \$105. The written call will result in a cash outflow of $S_T$ – \$105 if $S_T$ exceeds \$105.

Table 20.5 summarizes the outcome. The immediate cash inflow is \$2. In six months, the various positions provide exactly offsetting cash flows: the \$2 inflow is thus realized without any offsetting outflows. This is an arbitrage opportunity that will be pursued on a large scale until buying and selling pressures restore the parity condition expressed in Equation 20.1.

Equation 20.1 actually applies only to options on stocks that pay no dividends before the maturity date of the option. The extension of the parity condition for European call options on dividend-paying stocks is, however, straightforward. Problem (4) at the end of the chapter leads you through the extension of the parity relationship. The more general formulation of the put-call parity condition is:

**Table 20.5** Arbitrage Strategy

| | | Cash Flow in 6 Months | |
|---|---|---|---|
| **Position** | **Immediate Cash Flow** | $S_T \le 105$ | $S_T > 105$ |
| Buy stock | −110 | $S_T$ | $S_T$ |
| Borrow $X/(1 + r_f)^T = \$100$ | +100 | −105 | −105 |
| Sell call | + 17 | 0 | $-(S_T - 105)$ |
| Buy put | − 5 | $105 - S_T$ | 0 |
| Total | 2 | 0 | 0 |

$$P = C - S_0 + \text{PV}(X) + \text{PV(dividends)} \qquad \textbf{(20.2)}$$

where PV(dividends) is the present value of the dividends that will be paid by the stock during the life of the option. If the stock does not pay dividends, Equation 20.2 becomes identical to Equation 20.1.

Notice that this generalization would apply as well to European options on assets other than stocks. Instead of using dividend income per se in Equation 20.2, we would let any income paid only by the underlying asset play the role of the stock dividends. For example, European put and call options on bonds would satisfy the same parity relationship, except that the bond's coupon income would replace the stock's dividend payments in the parity formula.

Even this generalization, however, applies only to European options, as the cash flow stream from the two portfolios represented by the two sides of Equation 20.2 will match only if each position is held until maturity. If a call and a put may be optimally exercised at different times before their common expiration date, then the equality of payoffs cannot be assured, or even expected, and the portfolio will have different values.

Let's see how well parity works with real data from Figure 20.1, using Seagram's options. The May call on Seagram with exercise price \$40 and time to expiration of 43 days cost \$1.25, while the put cost \$1.70, Seagram was selling for \$38.75, and the annualized interest rate on this date for 90-day T-bills was 8.4 percent. According to parity, we should find that

$$\$1.25 - \$1.70 = \$38.75 - \$40/(1.084)^{43/365}$$
$$-\$.45 = -\$.87$$

In this case, parity is violated by 42 cents per share. Does this amount outweigh the brokerage fees involved in attempting to exploit the mispricing? Probably not. Moreover, given the infrequent trading of options that we have noted, this discrepancy from parity could be due to "stale prices." Indeed, we note from Figure 20.1 that the last recorded price for the call used in this example lies outside its corresponding bid and asked prices, implying that the last recorded trade in this option took place before the bid and asked prices took their closing values.

## 20.5 Option-Like Securities

Even if you never trade an option directly, you still need to appreciate the properties of options in formulating any investment plan. Why? Many other financial instruments and agreements have features that convey implicit or explicit options to one or more parties. If you are to value and use these securities correctly, you must understand these option attributes.

### Callable Bonds

You know from Chapter 14 that many corporate bonds are issued with call provisions entitling the issuer to buy bonds back from bondholders at some time in the future at a specified call price. This provision conveys a call option to the issuer, where the exercise price is equal to the price at which the bond can be repurchased. A callable bond arrangement is essentially a sale of a *straight bond* (a bond with no option features such as callability or convertibility) to the investor and the concurrent issuance of a call option by the investor to the bond-issuing firm.

There must be some compensation for offering this implicit call option to the firm. If the callable bond were issued with the same coupon rate as a straight bond, we would expect it to sell at a discount to the straight bond equal to the value of the call. To sell callable bonds at par, firms must issue them with coupon rates higher than the coupons on straight debt. The higher coupons are the investor's compensation for the call option retained by the issuer. Coupon rates usually are selected so that the newly issued bond will sell at par value.

Figure 20.14 illustrates the option-like property of a callable bond. The horizontal axis is the value of a straight bond with terms otherwise identical to the

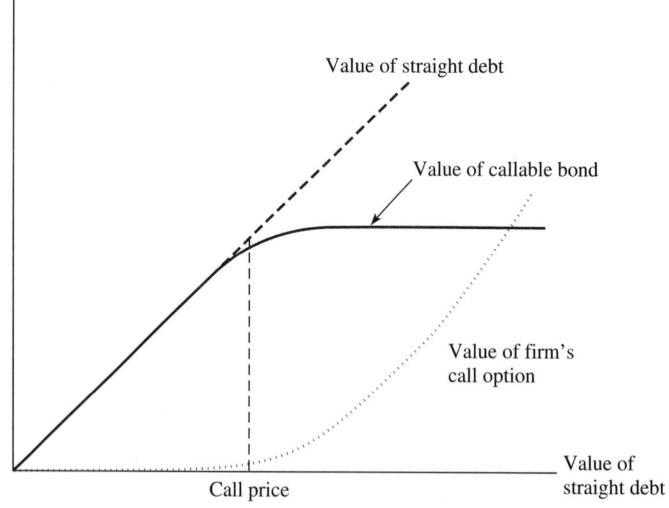


**Figure 20.14**
Values of callable bonds compared with straight bonds.

callable bond. The 45-degree dashed line represents the value of straight debt. The solid line is the value of the callable bond, and the dotted line is the value of the call option retained by the firm. A callable bond's potential for capital gains is limited by the firm's option to repurchase at the call price.

**CONCEPT CHECK** Question 5. How is a callable bond similar to a covered call strategy on a straight bond?

The option inherent in callable bonds is actually more complex than an ordinary call option, because usually it may be exercised only after some initial period of call protection. Also, the price at which the bond is callable may change over time. Unlike exchange-listed options, these features are defined in the initial bond offering and will depend on the needs of the issuing firm and its perception of the market's tastes.

**CONCEPT CHECK** Question 6. Suppose that the period of call protection is extended. How will the coupon rate that is required for the bond to sell at par value change?

### Convertible Securities

Convertible bonds and convertible preferred stock convey options to the holder of the security rather than to the issuing firm. The convertible security typically gives its holder the right to exchange each bond or share of preferred stock for a fixed number of shares of common stock, regardless of the market prices of the securities at the time.

**CONCEPT CHECK** Question 7. Should a convertible bond issued at par value have a higher or lower coupon rate than a nonconvertible bond issued at par?

For example, a bond with a conversion ratio of 10 allows its holder to convert one bond of par value $1,000 into 10 shares of common stock. Alternatively, the conversion price in this case is $100: To receive 10 shares of stock, the investor sacrifices bonds with face value $1,000, or $100 of face value per share. If the present value of the bond's scheduled payments is less than 10 times the value of one share of stock, it may pay to convert; that is, the conversion option is in the money. A bond worth $950 with a conversion ratio of 10 could be converted profitably if the stock were selling above $95, since the value of the 10 shares received for each bond surrendered would exceed $950. Most convertible bonds are issued "deep out of the money"; that is, the issuer sets the conversion ratio so that conversion will not be profitable unless there is a substantial increase in stock prices and/or decrease in bond prices from the time of issue.

A bond's conversion value equals the value it would have if you converted it into stock immediately. Clearly, a bond must sell for at least its conversion value. If it did not, you could purchase the bond, convert it immediately, and clear a risk-free profit. This condition could never persist, because all investors would pursue such a strategy, which ultimately would bid up the price of the bond.

The straight bond value or "bond floor" is the value the bond would have if it were not convertible into stock. The bond must sell for more than its straight bond value because a convertible bond is in fact a straight bond plus a valuable call option. Therefore the convertible bond has two lower bounds on its market price: the conversion value and the straight bond value.

Figure 20.15**A** illustrates the value of the straight debt as a function of the stock price of the issuing firm. For healthy firms the straight debt value is almost independent of the value of the stock because default risk is small. However, if the firm is close to bankruptcy (stock prices are low), default risk increases, and the straight bond value falls. Figure 20.15**B** shows the conversion value of the bond, and **C** compares the value of the convertible bond to these two lower bounds.

When stock prices are low, the straight bond value is the effective lower bound, and the conversion option is nearly irrelevant. The convertible will trade like straight debt. When stock prices are high, the bond's price is determined by its conversion value. With conversion all but guaranteed, the bond is essentially equity in disguise.

We can illustrate with two examples:

| | Bond A | Bond B |
|---|---|---|
| Annual coupon | $80 | $80 |
| Maturity date | 10 years | 10 years |
| Quality rating | Baa | Baa |
| Conversion ratio | 20 | 25 |
| Stock price | $30 | $50 |
| Conversion value | $600 | $1,250 |
| Market yield on 10-year Baa-rated bonds | 8.5% | 8.5% |
| Value as straight debt | $967 | $967 |
| Actual bond price | $972 | $1,255 |
| Reported yield to maturity | 8.42% | 4.76% |

Bond A has a conversion value of only $600. Its value as straight debt, in contrast, is $967. This is the present value of the coupon and principal payments at a market rate for straight debt of 8.5 percent. The bond's price is $972, so the premium over straight bond value is only $5, reflecting the low probability of conversion. Its reported yield to maturity based on scheduled coupon payments and the market price of $972 is 8.42 percent, close to that of straight debt.

The conversion option on Bond B is in the money. Conversion value is $1,250, and the bond's price, $1,255, reflects its value as equity (plus $5 for the protection the bond offers against stock price declines). The bond's reported yield is 4.76 percent, far below the comparable yield on straight debt. The big yield sacrifice

**Figure 20.15**
Value of a convertible bond as a function of stock price. **A**—Straight debt value, or bond floor. **B**—Conversion value of the bond. **C**—Total value of convertible bond.

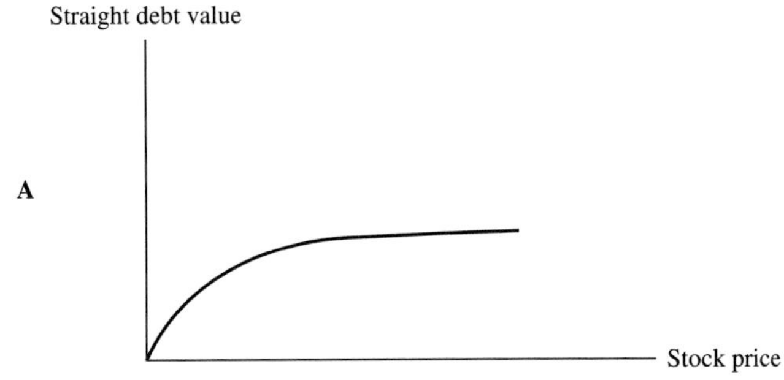


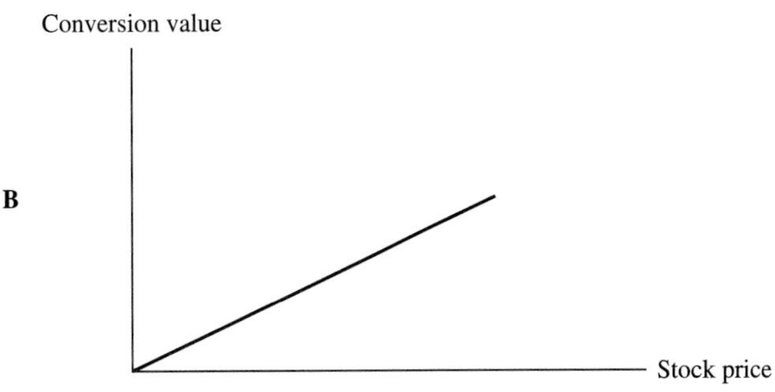


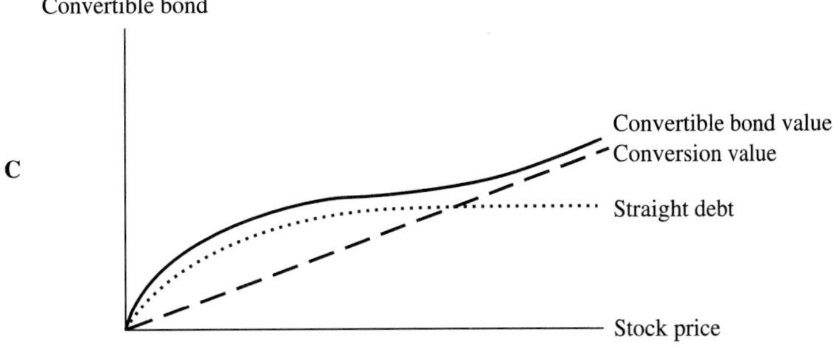


is attributable to the far greater value of the conversion option. In theory, we could value convertible bonds by treating them as straight debt plus call options. In practice, however, this approach is often impractical for several reasons:

1. The conversion price frequently increases over time, which means the exercise price for the option changes.
2. Stocks may pay several dividends over the life of the bond, further complicating the option valuation analysis.
3. Most convertibles also are callable at the discretion of the firm. In essence, the investor and the firm hold options on each other. If the firm exercises

its call option to repurchase the bond, the bondholders typically have a month during which they still can convert. When firms use a call option, while knowing that bondholders will choose to convert, the firm is said to have *forced a conversion*. These conditions together mean that the actual maturity of the bond is indeterminate.

## Warrants

**Warrants** are essentially call options issued by the firm. One important difference between calls and warrants is that exercise of a warrant requires the firm to issue a new share of stock—the total number of shares outstanding increases. Exercise of a call option requires only that the writer of the call deliver an already-issued share of stock to discharge the obligation. In that case, the number of shares outstanding remains fixed. Also unlike call options, warrants result in a cash flow to the firm when the exercise price is paid by the warrant holder. These differences mean that warrant values will differ somewhat from the values of call options with identical terms.

Like convertible debt, warrant terms may be tailored to meet the needs of the firm. Also like convertible debt, warrants generally are protected against stock splits and dividends in that the exercise price and the number of warrants held are adjusted to offset the effects of the split.

Warrants often are issued in conjunction with another security. Bonds, for example, may be packaged together with a warrant "sweetener," frequently a warrant that may be sold separately. This is called a *detachable warrant*.

The issue of warrants and convertible securities creates the potential for an increase in outstanding shares of stock if exercise occurs. Exercise obviously would affect financial statistics that are computed on a per-share basis, so annual reports must provide earnings-per-share (EPS) figures under the assumption that all convertible securities and warrants are exercised. These figures are called *fully diluted* earnings per share.[2]

## Collateralized Loans

Most loan arrangements require that the borrower put up collateral to guarantee that the loan will be paid back. In the event of default, the lender takes possession of the collateral. A non-recourse loan gives the lender no recourse beyond the right to the collateral; that is, the lender may not sue the borrower for further payment if the collateral turns out not to be valuable enough to repay the loan.

This arrangement, it turns out, gives an implicit call option to the borrower. The borrower, for example, is obligated to pay back $L$ dollars at the maturity of the loan. The collateral will be worth $S_T$ dollars at maturity. (Its value today is $S_0$.)

---

[2] We should note that the exercise of a convertible bond need not reduce EPS. Diluted EPS will be less than undiluted EPS only if interest saved (per share) on the converted bonds is less than the prior EPS.

The borrower has the option to wait until loan maturity and repay the loan only if the collateral is worth more than the $L$ dollars he or she borrowed. If the collateral is worth less than $L$, the borrower can default on the loan, discharging the obligation by forfeiting the collateral, which is worth only $S_T$.

Another way of describing such a loan is to view the borrower as, in effect, turning over the collateral to the lender but retaining the right to reclaim it by paying off the loan. The transfer of the collateral with the right to claim it is equivalent to a payment of $S_0$ dollars, less a future recovery of a sum that resembles a call option with exercise price $L$. Basically, the borrower turns over collateral and keeps an option to "repurchase" it for $L$ dollars at the maturity of the loan if $L$ turns out to be less than $S_T$. This is, of course, a call option.

A third way to look at a collateralized loan is to assume the borrower will repay the $L$ dollars with certainty but also retain the option to sell the collateral to the lender for $L$ dollars, even if $S_T$ is less than $L$. In this case, the sale of the collateral would generate the cash necessary to satisfy the loan. The ability to "sell" the collateral for a price of $L$ dollars represents a put option, which guarantees that the borrower can raise enough money to satisfy the loan by turning over the collateral.

It is strange to think that we can describe the same loan as involving either a put option or a call option, since the payoffs to calls and puts are so different. Yet the equivalence of the two approaches is nothing more than a reflection of the put-call parity relationship. In our call option description of the loan, the value of the borrower's liability is $S_0 - C$: The borrower turns over the asset, which is a transfer of $S_0$ dollars, but retains a call, which is worth $C$ dollars. In the put-option description the borrower is obligated to pay $L$ dollars but retains the put, which is worth $P$: The present value of this net obligation is $L/(1 + r_f)^T - P$. Because these alternative descriptions are equivalent ways of viewing the same loan, the value of the obligations must be equal:

$$S_0 - C = L/(1 + r_f)^T - P \qquad \textbf{(20.3)}$$

Treating $L$ as the exercise price of the option, Equation 20.3 is simply the put-call parity relationship.

Figure 20.16**A** illustrates the value of the payment to be received by the lender, which equals the minimum of $S_T$ or $L$. Figure 20.16**B** shows that this amount can be expressed as $S_T$ minus the payoff of the call implicitly written by the lender and held by the borrower. Figure 20.16**C** shows that it also can be viewed as a receipt of $L$ dollars minus the proceeds of the put option.

## Levered Equity and Risky Debt

Investors holding stock in incorporated firms are protected by limited liability, which means that if the firm cannot pay its debts, the firm's creditors may attach only the firm's assets and may not sue the corporation's equity holders for further payment. In effect, any time the corporation borrows money, the maximum possible collateral for the loan is the total of the firm's assets. If the firm declares

**Figure 20.16**
Collateralized loan.

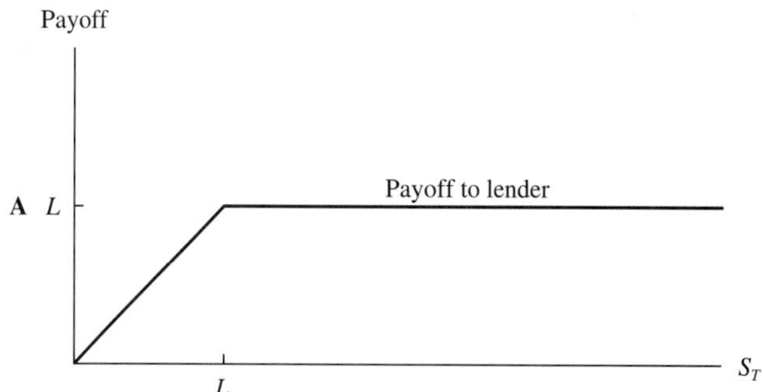


When $S_T$ exceeds $L$, the loan is repaid and the collateral is reclaimed. Otherwise, the collateral is forfeited and the total loan repayment is worth only $S_T$.

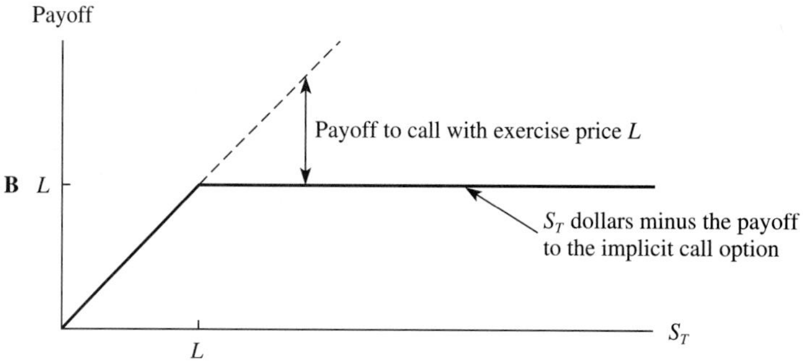


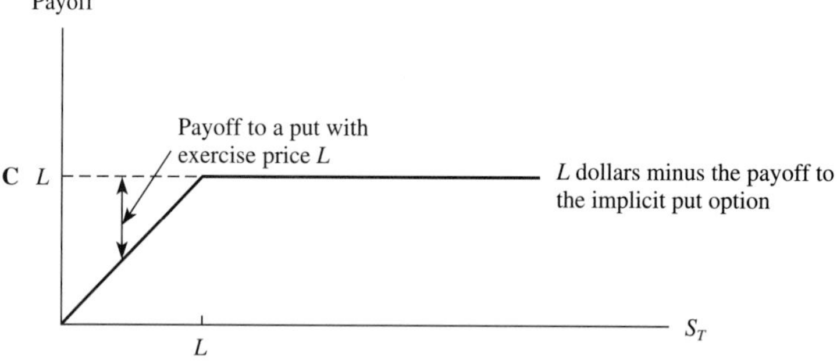


bankruptcy, we can interpret this as an admission that the assets of the firm are insufficient to satisfy the claims against it. The corporation may discharge its obligations by transferring ownership of the firm's assets to the creditors.

Just as with non-recourse collateralized loans, the required payment to the creditors represents the exercise price of the implicit option, while the value of the firm is the underlying asset. The equity holders have a put option to transfer their ownership claims on the firm to the creditors in return for the face value of the firm's debt.

Alternatively, we may view the equity holders as retaining a call option. They have, in effect, already transferred their ownership claim on the firm to the creditors but have retained the right to reacquire the ownership claims on the firm by paying off the loan. Hence, the equity holders have the option to "buy back" the firm for a specified price—they have a call option.

The significance of this observation is that the values of corporate bonds can be estimated using option pricing techniques. The default premium required of risky debt, in principle, can be estimated using option valuation models. These will be considered in the next chapter.

## 20.6 Financial Engineering

One of the attractions of options is the ability they provide to create investment positions with payoffs that depend in a variety of ways on the values of other securities. We have seen evidence of this capability in the various options strategies examined in Section 20.3. Options also can be used to custom design new securities or portfolios with desired patterns of exposure to the price of an underlying security. In this sense, options (and futures contracts, to be discussed in Chapter 23) provide the ability to engage in *financial engineering,* the creation of portfolios with specified payoff patterns. The nearby box discusses the rapid pace of this innovation.

Most financial engineering takes place for institutional investors. However, some applications have been designed for the retail market. A second box in this section, entitled "Derivatives Widely Used," provides some information on the use of options and futures applications in Canada.

A recent innovation is the bond, note, or certificate of deposit that allows its holder to participate in an equity index growth. Such certificates of deposit are sometimes known as *bull CDs.* Unlike conventional CDs, which pay a fixed rate of interest, bull CDs pay depositors a specified fraction of the increase in the rate of return on a market index such as the S&P 500, while guaranteeing a minimum rate of return should the market fall.

The *protected index notes* (PINs) are a Canadian variant of bull CDs. They are discount notes issued by the Export Development Corporation (EDC) and denominated in U.S. dollars. Unlike conventional notes, the PINs are redeemable at any time prior to maturity at the larger of the following prices: the original par price, or the par price multiplied by the ratio of the S&P 500 index at redemption time to 1.05 times the value of the index at the time of issuance.

This arrangement is clearly a type of call option. If the market rises, the investor profits according to the relative rise in the index; if the market falls, the investor is guaranteed to receive at least the par value. The return to the prospective investor is at least equal to the ratio of par value to purchase value, and it can increase in proportion to the rise of the S&P index. Just as clearly, the issuer offering these notes is in effect writing call options and can hedge its position by buying index calls in the U.S. options market. Figure 20.17 shows the nature of the issuer's obligation to its depositors.

## Mathematicians Race to Develop New Kinds of Trading Instruments

From the quiet cubicles at International Business Machines Corp.'s central research facility here to secretive research labs inside brokerage firms, mathematicians are working on Wall Street's computer revolution, part two.

Over the past five years, Wall Street has spent enormously to upgrade its computing horsepower. Now, researchers at IBM and major securities firms are trying to harness that computing muscle with a new generation of "analytics," or sophisticated mathematical computer models that identify hundreds of never-before-imagined trades in stocks, bonds, and currencies.

For example, computers at Algorithms Inc., a Toronto firm, recently created a synthetic option on the benchmark Nikkei Index of 225 Japanese stocks. Produced by the computer out of a combination of Nikkei stock-index futures and exchange-traded stock-index options, the synthetic Nikkei option cost less than the real thing; this allowed traders at a Canadian investment bank to make $500,000 on a single trade.

Myron Scholes, who developed the widely used Black-Scholes option pricing model in 1973 with Fischer Black, says high-powered computers have extended the application of his model greatly. "The people who don't have these [analytics] are going to be relatively obsolete," says Mr. Scholes, who recently joined Salomon Brothers Inc.'s high-tech bond trading department as a managing director. (He is also a professor of finance at Stanford University.)

For years, Wall Street's computers were used for little more than fast accounting programs, known as spreadsheets. Now, some Wall Street firms are using mathematical formulas that imitate how traders think about and look at markets—but several hundred times faster than humans can. The next generation of analytics, in development at IBM and other research labs, seeks to apply elaborate financial theories—such as the "Markowitz mean variance model," for instance—to markets for up-to-the-minute use.

The development of analytics is one of the most closely guarded secrets inside Wall Street firms. Competition for clients has never been more intense; the only monopoly available to Wall Street now may be the proprietary mathematics of analytical systems that ferret out profit opportunities in markets that are ruthlessly efficient.

So closely guarded are the mathematics at O'Connor & Associates, a Chicago futures and options trading firm, that clients and even family members are barred from the trading floor at O'Connor's headquarters. Visitors can observe the firm at work only from a catwalk 20 feet above the trading floor. An O'Connor executive says the firm has "about 40 people developing analytical software for trading purposes, and about 100 traders using these systems."

Elsewhere, IBM is working on a mathematical model that will allow investors to assemble hundreds of portfolios in seconds that have various shadings of investment risk and reward.

But no matter how refined the mathematical model Wall Street researchers build, the markets often prove elusive. Unlike physics, Mr. Winograd notes, finance has very few basic laws. "Economics hasn't had its Newton or its Einstein," he says. "Basic statistical behavior is still in question. Human beings are not molecules."

But that's precisely why Wall Street firms seek out mathematicians. Since markets are run by humans, there will always be imperfections that can be turned into profits. Or, in Mr. Winograd's words, "that's why you can make tons of money; or lose tons of money."

Source: Craig Torres, *The Wall Street Journal,* October 18, 1991. Reprinted by permission of *The Wall Street Journal,* 

## DERIVATIVES WIDELY USED

A survey of Canadian money managers responsible for more than $230-billion in assets shows that 76 percent use derivatives.

The most widely used derivatives are options on Canadian stocks, followed by forward rate agreements, Canadian stock index futures and options, and international stock index futures and options.

"Exchange-traded derivative products appear to be more widely used and accepted than over-the-counter instruments," said Ted Dixon of the Fraser Institute of Vancouver, which did the survey. (Letters were sent to 144 pension fund and investment managers, 50 of whom responded.)

Derivatives, which are tied to the value of an underlying security, have been in the news recently because of big losses sustained by some financial institutions.

When asked to explain the losses, money managers blamed inadequate supervision of derivative traders by their firms.

Six in ten managers said they did not actively hedge foreign-currency exposure.

"It appears that most fund managers want the currency exposure offered by international investments," Mr. Dixon said.



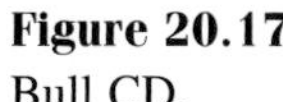
**Figure 20.17**
Bull CD.

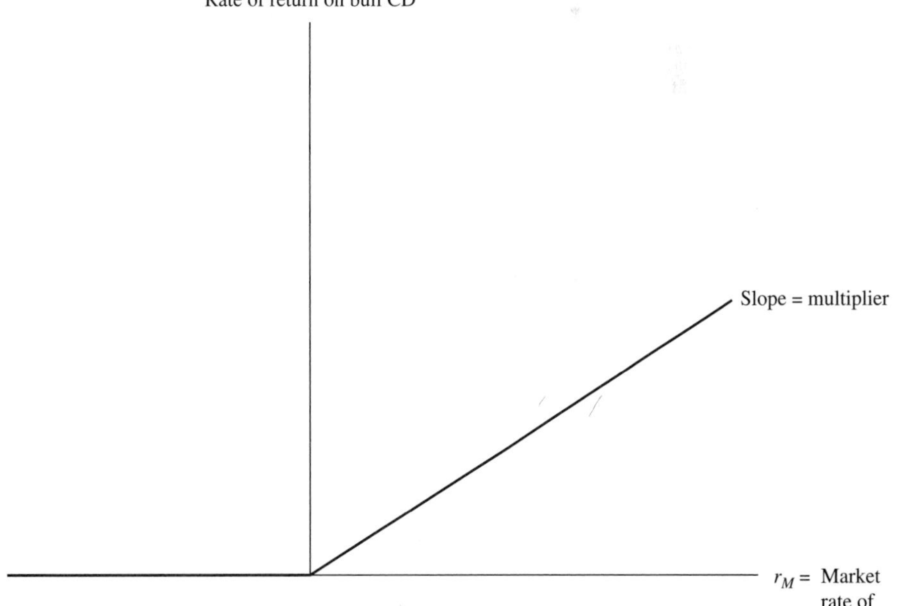

Bull CDs are similar to PINs, except that the holder may receive only a fraction (say 70 percent) of the growth in the index; this fraction is known as the *participation rate* or *multiplier,* and it is set by the issuer. The PIN is essentially a bull CD with a multiplier equal to 1/1.05. In valuing PINs we are especially interested in the *inverse multiplier,* equal in this example to 1.05.

How can one value a PIN or bull CD at any time prior to expiration? To answer this, note various features of the option:

1. At exercise the PIN holder receives the par value, or (1/1.05) times (par value) times the realized return on the S&P 500 index, whichever is greater. If the PIN sells at par at issuance, then the payoff at exercise time per dollar invested is equal to the larger of 1, and (1/1.05) times (1 plus the market rate of return $r_M$ as measured by the index).
2. Suppose that we want to replicate this pattern of payments, by using call options on the index and a riskless investment (say a T-bill or a conventional CD) with rate of return $r_f$. If $C$ is the value of a call option on one unit of the index, with exercise price equal to 1.05 times the value $S_0$ of the index at issuance, then the ratio $C/(1.05S_0)$ is the value of a contingent claim that pays at exercise time the larger of 0, and/or (1/1.05) times $(1 + r_M)$ minus 1. Hence, a portfolio of this contingent claim plus an amount $1/(r_f + 1)$ invested in the riskless investment pays the larger of 1, or (1/1.05) times $(1 + r_M)$, the same as the PIN. To avoid arbitrage, this portfolio must, therefore, have a value equal to that of the PIN at issuance, divided by the par value.
3. To determine whether the PIN should sell at par at issuance it suffices, therefore, to evaluate the quantity $C/(1.05S_0) + 1/(r_f + 1)$: If it is equal to 1, then the PIN should sell at par; it should sell above or below par if the above quantity is respectively greater or smaller than 1.

As an example, suppose that $r_f = 6$ percent per year (3 percent for six months), and that the index is currently at \$240, implying that $1.05S_0 = 252$. The six-month maturity calls on the market index with an exercise price of \$252 are currently valued at \$10. Then the test quantity is equal to \$10/\$252 + 1/1.03 = 1.011 per dollar of par value. Therefore, the PIN should sell at slightly above par.

This PIN is a bull CD with a multiplier equal to 1/1.05. This version of the bull CD has several variants. Investors can purchase bull CDs that guarantee a positive minimum return, perhaps in combination with a smaller multiplier. In this case, the bull CD per unit par value is replicated by an index call option (with value $C$) plus a riskless investment portfolio. The call option has an exercise price equal to the inverse multiplier times $(r_{min} + 1)$ times the value of the index at issuance, where $r_{min}$ is the guaranteed minimum return; the riskless investment is $(1 + r_{min})/(1 + r_f)$. The test quantity, the riskless investment plus $C$ divided by the inverse multiplier times the index at issuance, is again compared to 1 to determine whether the instrument should be sold at par. Another variant is the *bear CD,* which pays depositors a fraction of any *fall* in the market index. For example, a bear CD might offer a rate of return of .6 times any percentage decline in the S&P 500.

**CONCEPT CHECK** Question 8. Continue to assume that $r_f = 6$ percent, the appropriate calls sell for \$10, the multiplier is still 1/1.05, and the market index is at 240. What would be the value of bull CDs per unit at par value if they offer a guaranteed minimum return of 1 percent on a six-month deposit?

## 20.7 EXOTIC OPTIONS

Options markets have been tremendously successful. Investors clearly value the portfolio strategies made possible by trading options; this is reflected in the heavy trading volume in these markets. Success breeds imitation, and in recent years we have witnessed considerable innovation in the range of option instruments available to investors. Part of this innovation has occurred in the market for customized options, which now trade in active over-the-counter markets. Many of these options have terms that would have been highly unusual even a few years ago; they are therefore called "exotic options." In this section, we will survey some of the more interesting variants of these new instruments.

### Asian Options

You already have been introduced to American and European options. *Asian options* are options with payoffs that depend on the *average* price of the underlying asset during at least some portion of the life of the option. For example, an Asian call option may have a payoff equal to the average stock price over the last three months minus the strike price if that value is positive, and zero otherwise. These options may be of interest, for example to firms that wish to hedge a profit stream that depends on the average price of a commodity over some period of time.

### Barrier Options

*Barrier options* have payoffs that depend not only on some asset price at option expiration, but also on whether the underlying asset price has crossed through some "barrier." For example, a down-and-out option is one type of barrier option that automatically expires worthless if and when the stock price falls below some barrier price. Similarly, down-and-in options will not provide a payoff unless the stock price *does* fall below some barrier at least once during the life of the option. These options also are referred to as knock-out and knock-in options.

### Lookback Options

*Lookback options* have payoffs that depend in part on the minimum or maximum price of the underlying asset during the life of the option. For example, a lookback call option might provide a payoff equal to the *maximum* stock price minus the exercise price. Such an option provides (for a fee, of course) a form of perfect market timing, providing the call holder with a payoff equal to the one that would accrue if the asset were purchased for $X$ dollars and later sold at what turns out to be its high price.

## Currency-Translated Options

*Currency-translated options* have either asset or exercise prices denominated in a foreign currency. A good example of such an option is the *quanto,* which allows an investor fix in advance the exchange rate at which an investment in a foreign currency can be converted back into dollars. The right to translate a fixed amount of foreign currency into dollars at a given exchange rate is a simple foreign exchange option. Quantos are more interesting, however, because, the amount of currency that will be translated into dollars depends on the investment performance of the foreign security. Therefore, a quanto in effect provides a *random number* of options.

## Binary Options

Binary of "bet" options have fixed payoffs that depend on whether a condition is satisfied by the price of the underlying asset. For example, a binary call option might pay off a fixed amount of $100 if the stock price at maturity exceeds the exercise price.

There are many more exotic options that we do not have room to discuss, and new ones are continually being created. For a comprehensive review of these options and their valuation (which is far more complex than the valuation of the simple options emphasized in this chapter), we refer you to the collection of articles compiled by RISK Magazine listed in the Suggested Readings at the end of the chapter.

## Summary

**1.** A call option is the right to buy an asset at an agreed-upon exercise price. A put option is the right to sell an asset at a given exercise price.

**2.** American options allow exercise on or before the expiration date. European options allow exercise only on the expiration date. Most traded options are American in nature.

**3.** Options are traded on stocks, stock indices, foreign currencies, fixed-income securities, and several futures contracts.

**4.** Options can be used either to increase an investor's exposure to an asset price or to provide insurance against volatility of asset prices. Popular option strategies include covered calls, protective puts, straddles, and spreads.

**5.** The put-call parity theorem relates the prices of put and call options. If the relationship is violated, arbitrage opportunities result. Specifically, the relationship that must be satisfied is that

$$P = C - S_0 + \text{PV}(X) + \text{PV}(\text{dividends})$$

where $X$ is the exercise price of both the call and the put options; PV($X$) is the present value of a claim to $X$ dollars to be paid at the expiration date of the options; and PV(dividends) is the present value of dividends to be paid before option expiration.

**6.** Many commonly traded securities embody option characteristics. Examples include callable bonds, convertible bonds and warrants. Other arrangements, such as collateralized loans and limited-liability borrowing can be analyzed as conveying implicit options to one or more parties.

**7.** Bull and bear CDs are in fact options and may be valued by comparing them to the prices of market-traded options.

**8.** Trading in so-called exotic options now takes place in an active over-the-counter market.

## Key Terms

Call option
Exercise price (Strike price)
Put option
In the money
Out of the money
At the money
American option
European option
Protective put
Covered call
Straddle
Spread
Put-call parity theorem
Warrant

## Selected Readings

*Good treatments of the institutional organization of option markets in the United States and Canada can be found in the following:*

Chicago Board Options Exchange. *Reference Manual.* (The CBOE also publishes a *Margin Manual* that provides an overview of margin requirements on many option positions.)

Montreal Exchange. *The Profitable Option: Guide to the Stock Options Market,* August 1992; *LEAPS Options: An Investor's Guide,* May 1995; and *Interest Rate Options: An Investor's Guide,* June 1995.

*An excellent discussion of option trading strategies is:*

Black, Fischer. "Fact and Fantasy in the Use of Options." *Financial Analysts Journal,* July/August 1975.

*The Winter 1992 issue of the* Journal of Applied Corporate Finance *highlights financial innovation. The issue contains several articles on the use of futures and options in new security design and risk management.*

*RISK Magazine is an excellent source of material on current developments in option pricing, applications of derivative instruments, and new developments in the derivatives markets. It has assembled a collection of articles that have appeared in its previous issues on option pricing generally and exotic options in particular in:*

*From Black-Scholes to Black Holes: Frontiers in Options.* London: RISK Magazine, 1992.

*A description and empirical evaluation of several characteristics of Canadian option markets is in:*

Mandron, Alix. "Some Empirical Evidence about Canadian Stock Options, Part I: Valuation; Part II: Market Structure." *Canadian Journal of Administrative Sciences* 5, no. 2 (June 1988).

*An overview of derivative instruments traded in Canadian financial markets is in:*
Gagnon, Louis. "Exchange-Traded Financial Derivatives in Canada: Finally Off the Launching Pad." *Canadian Investment Review,* Fall 1990.
*For more on protected index notes (PINs), see:*
Perrakis, Stylianos; Sylvain Brisebois; Carl Pelland; and Carole Larson. "Decoding the PIN Numbers." *Canadian Investment Review,* Winter 1995/96.

## Problems

**1.** Suppose you think ABC stock is going to appreciate substantially in value in the next six months. Also suppose that the stock's current price, $S_0$, is \$100, and the call option expiring in six months has an exercise price, *X,* of \$100 and is selling at a price, *C,* of \$10. With \$10,000 to invest, you are considering three alternatives.

*a.* Invest all \$10,000 in the stock, buying 100 shares.
*b.* Invest all \$10,000 in 1,000 options (10 contracts).
*c.* Buy 100 options (one contract) for \$1,000, and invest the remaining \$9,000 in a money market fund paying 4 percent in interest over six months (8 percent per year).

What is your rate of return for each alternative for four stock prices six months from now? Summarize your results in the following table and diagram.

Rate of Return on Investment

| | Price of Stock 6 Months from Now | | | |
|---|---|---|---|---|
| **Stock Price:** | **80** | **100** | **110** | **120** |
| a. All stocks (100 shares) | | | | |
| b. All options (1,000 shares) | | | | |
| c. Bills + 100 options | | | | |

Rate of return

0

$S_T$

**2.** The common stock of the PUTT Corporation has been trading in a narrow price range for the past month, and you are convinced that it is going to break far out of that range in the next three months. You do not know whether it will go up or down, however. The current price of the stock is \$100 per share, and the price of a three-month call option at an exercise price of \$100 is \$10. The stock will pay no dividends for the next three months.

*a.* If the risk-free interest rate is 10 percent per year, what must be the price of a three-month put option on PUTT stock at an exercise price of \$100?

*b.* What would be a simple options strategy to exploit your conviction about the stock price's future movement? How far would it have to move in either direction for you to make a profit on your initial investment?

**3.** The common stock of the CALL Corporation has been trading in a narrow range around \$50 per share for months, and you are convinced that it is going to stay in that range for the next three months. The price of a three-month put option with an exercise price of \$50 is \$4. The stock will pay no dividends for the next three months.

*a.* If the risk-free interest rate is 10 percent per year, what must be the price of a three-month call option on CALL stock at an exercise price of \$50 if it is at the money?

*b.* What would be a simple options strategy using a put and a call to explain your conviction about the stock price's future movement? What is the most money you can make on this position? How far can the stock price move in either direction before you lose money?

*c.* How can you create a position involving a put, a call, and risk-free lending that would have the same payoff structure as the stock at expiration? What is the net cost of establishing that position now?

**4.** In this problem, we derive the put-call parity relationship for European options on stocks that pay dividends before option expiration. For simplicity, assume that the stock makes one dividend payment of \$D per share at the expiration date of the option.

*a.* What is the value of a stock-plus-put position on the expiration date of the option?

*b.* Now consider a portfolio comprising a call option and a zero-coupon bond with the same maturity date as the option and with face value ($X + D$). What is the value of this portfolio on the option expiration date? You should find that its value equals that of the stock-plus-put portfolio regardless of the stock price.

*c.* What is the cost of establishing the two portfolios in parts (*a*) and (*b*)? Equate the costs of these portfolio, and you will derive the put-call parity relationship, Equation 20.2.

**5.** *a.* A butterfly spread is the purchase of one call at exercise price $X_1$, the sale of two calls at exercise price $X_2$, and the purchase of one call at exercise price $X_3$. $X_1$ is less than $X_2$, and $X_2$ is less than $X_3$ by equal amounts, and all calls have the same expiration date. Graph the payoff diagram to this strategy.

*b.* A vertical combination is the purchase of a call with exercise price $X_2$ and a put with exercise price $X_1$, with $X_2$ greater than $X_1$. Graph the payoff to this strategy.

**6.** A bearish spread is the purchase of a call with exercise price $X_2$ and the sale of a call with exercise price $X_1$, with $X_2$ greater than $X_1$. Graph the payoff to this strategy and compare it to Figure 20.12.

**7.** You are attempting to formulate an investment strategy. On the one hand, you think there is great upward potential in the stock market and would like to participate in the upward move if it materializes. However, you are not able to afford substantial stock market losses and so cannot run the risk of a stock market collapse, which you also think is a possibility. Your investment advisor suggests a protective put position: Buy both shares in a market index stock fund and put options on those shares with three-month maturity and exercise price of $260. The stock index is currently selling for $300. However, your uncle suggests you instead buy a three-month call option on the index fund with exercise price $280 and buy three-month T-bills with face value $280.

*a.* On the same graph, draw the *payoffs* to each of these strategies as a function of the stock fund value in three months. (Hint: Think of the options as being on one "share" of the stock index fund, with the current price of each share of the index equal to $300.)

*b.* Which portfolio must require a greater initial outlay to establish? (Hint: Does either portfolio provide a final payoff that is always at least as great as the payoff of the other portfolio?)

*c.* Suppose the market prices of the securities are as follows:

| | |
|---|---|
| Stock fund | $300 |
| T-bill (face value $280) | $270 |
| Call (exercise price $280) | $ 40 |
| Put (exercise price $260) | $ 2 |

Make a table of the profits realized for each portfolio for the following values of the stock price in three months: $S_T$ = $0, $260, $280, $300, $320.

Graph the profits to each portfolio as a function of $S_T$ on a single graph.

*d.* Which strategy is riskier? Which should have a higher beta?

*e.* Explain why the data for the securities given in part (*c*) do *not* violate the put-call parity relationship.

**8.** The agricultural price support system guarantees farmers a minimum price for their output. Describe the program provisions as an option. What is the asset? The exercise price?

**9.** In what ways is owning a corporate bond similar to writing a put option? A call option?

**10.** An executive compensation scheme might provide a manager a bonus of $1,000 for every dollar by which the company's stock price exceeds some cutoff level. In what way is this arrangement equivalent to issuing the manager call options on the firm's stock?

**11.** Consider the following options portfolio. You write an April maturity call option on Seagram's with exercise price 42½. You write an April Seagram's put option with exercise price 40.
   *a.* Graph the payoff of this portfolio at option expiration as a function of Seagram's stock price at that time.
   *b.* What will be the profit/loss on this position if Seagram's is selling at 41 on the option maturity date? What if Seagram's is selling at 45? Use *The Globe and Mail* listing from Figure 20.1 to answer this question.
   *c.* At what two stock prices will you just break even on your investment?
   *d.* What kind of "bet" is this investor making; that is, what must this investor believe about Seagram's stock price in order to justify this position?

**12.** Consider the following portfolio. You write a put option with exercise price 90 and buy a put option on the same stock with the same maturity date with exercise price 95.
   *a.* Plot the value of the portfolio at the maturity date of the options.
   *b.* On the same graph, plot the profit of the portfolio. Which option must cost more?

**13.** A Ford put option with strike price 60 trading on the Acme options exchange sells for $2. To your amazement, Ford put with the same maturity selling on the Apex options exchange, but with strike price 62, also sells for $2. If you plan to hold the options positions to maturity, devise a zero-net-investment arbitrage strategy to exploit the pricing anomaly. Draw the profit diagram at maturity for your position.

**14.** Using the Seagram's option prices in Figure 20.1, calculate the market price of a riskless zero-coupon bond with face value $40 that matures in April on the same date as the listed options.

**15.** You buy a share of stock, write a one-year call option with $X = \$10$, and buy a one-year put option with $X = \$10$. Your net outlay to establish the entire portfolio is $9.50. What is the risk-free interest rate? The stock pays no dividends.

**16.** Demonstrate that an at-the-money call option on a given stock must cost more than an at-the-money put option with the same maturity. Hint: Use put-call parity.

**17.** You write a put option with $X = 100$ and buy a put with $X = 110$. The puts are on the same stock and have the same maturity date.
   *a.* Draw the payoff graph for this strategy.
   *b.* Draw the profit graph for this strategy.
   *c.* If the underlying stock has positive beta, does this portfolio have positive or negative beta?

**18.** Joe Finance has just purchased an indexed stock fund, currently selling at \$400 per share. To protect against losses, Joe also purchased an at-the-money European put option on the fund for \$20, with exercise price \$400, and three-month time to expiration. Sally Calm, Joe's financial advisor, points out that Joe is spending a lot of money on the put. She notes that three-month puts with strike prices of \$390 cost only \$15 and suggests that Joe use the cheaper put.

*a.* Analyze the strategies of Joe and Sally by drawing the *profit* diagrams for the stock-plus-put positions for various values of the stock fund in three months.

*b.* When does Sally's strategy do better? When does it do worse?

*c.* Which strategy entails greater systematic risk?

**19.** You write a call option with $X = 50$ and buy a call with $X = 60$. The options are on the same stock and have the same maturity date. One of the calls sells for \$3; the other sells for \$9.

*a.* Draw the payoff graph for this strategy at the option maturity date.

*b.* Draw the profit graph for this strategy.

*c.* What is the break-even point for this strategy? Is the investor bullish or bearish on the stock?

**20.** Devise a portfolio using only call options and shares of stock with the following value (payoff) at the option maturity date. If the stock price currently is 53, what kind of bet is the investor making?

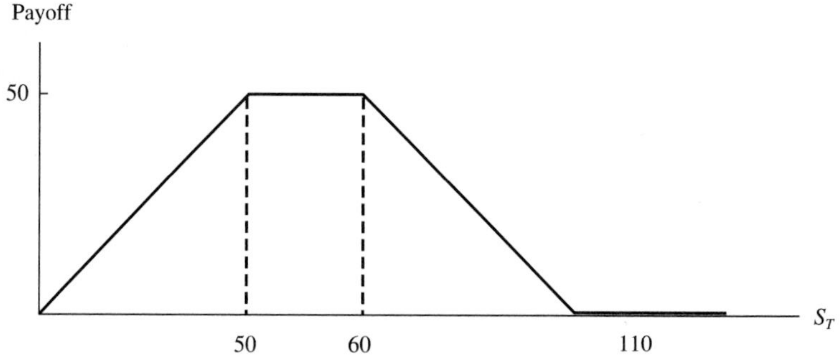


The following problem is based on a question that appeared in a past CFA examination:

**21.** On the death of his grandmother several years ago, Bill Melody received as a bequest from her estate 2,000 shares of General Motors common stock. The price of the stock at time of distribution from the estate was \$75 a share, and this became the cost basis of Melody's holding. Late in 1990, Melody agreed to purchase a new condominium for his parents at a total cost of \$160,000, payable in full upon its completion in March 1991. Melody planned to sell the General Motors stock in order to raise funds to purchase the condominium.

At year-end 1990, GM's market price was around $75 a share, but it looked to be weakening. This concerned Melody, for if the price of the stock were to drop by a significant amount before he sold, the proceeds would not be sufficient to cover the purchase of the condominium in March 1991.

Melody visited with three investment counseling firms to seek advice in developing a strategy that, at a minimum, would protect the value of his principal at or near $150,000 ($75 a share). Ideally, the strategy would enhance the value to $160,000 so Melody would have the total cost of the condominium. Four alternatives were discussed:

*a.* Melody's own opinion was to sell the General Motors stock at $75 a share and invest the proceeds in a 10 percent certificate of deposit maturing in three months.

*b.* Anderson Investment Advisors suggested Melody write a March 1991 call option on his General Motors stock holding at a strike price of $80. The March 1991 calls were quoted at $2.

*c.* Cole Capital Management suggested Melody purchase March 1991 at-the-money put contracts on General Motors, now quoted at $2.

*d.* MBA Associates suggested Melody keep the stock, purchase March 1991 at-the-money put contracts on GM, and finance the purchase by selling March calls with a strike price of $80.

Disregarding transaction costs, dividend income, and margin requirements, rank order the four alternatives in terms of their fulfilling the strategy of at least preserving the value of Melody's principal at $150,000 and preferably increasing the value to $160,000 by March 1991. Support your conclusions by showing the payoff structure of each alternative.

---

*Chapter 21*

# Option Valuation

**IN THE PREVIOUS CHAPTER, WE EXAMINED OPTION MARKETS AND STRATEGIES.** We noted that many securities contain embedded options that affect both their values and their risk-return characteristics. In this chapter, we turn our attention to option valuation issues. To understand most option-valuation models requires considerable mathematical and statistical background. Still, many of the ideas and insights of these models can be demonstrated in simple examples, and we will concentrate on these.

We start with a discussion of the factors that ought to affect option prices. After this discussion, we present several bounds within which option prices must lie. Next, we turn to quantitative models. First, we examine one particular valuation formula, the famous Black-Scholes model, one of the most significant breakthroughs in finance theory in the past three decades. Next, we look at some of the more important applications of option-pricing theory in portfolio management and control. Finally, we examine an alternative option valuation approach, called "two-state" or "binomial" option pricing, and its extensions.

## 21.1 Option Valuation: Introduction

### Intrinsic and Time Values

Consider a call option that is out of the money at the moment, with the stock price below the exercise price. This does not mean the option is valueless. Even though immediate exercise today would be unprofitable, the call retains a positive value because there is always a chance the stock price will increase sufficiently by the expiration date to allow for profitable exercise. If not, the worst that can happen is that the option will expire with zero value.

The value $S_0 - X$ sometimes is called the **intrinsic value** of in-the-money call options because it gives the payoff that could be obtained by immediate exercise. Intrinsic value is set equal to zero for out-of-the-money or at-the-money options. The difference between the actual call price and the intrinsic value commonly is called the *time value* of the option.

"Time value" is an unfortunate choice of terminology because it may confuse the option's time value with the time value of money. Time value in the options context refers simply to the difference between the option's price and the value the option would have if it were expiring immediately. It is the part of the option's value that may be attributed to the fact that it still has positive time to expiration.

Most of an option's time value typically is a type of "volatility value." As long as the option holder can choose not to exercise, the payoff cannot be worse than zero. Even if a call option is out of the money now, it still will sell for a positive price because it offers the potential for a profit if the stock price increases, while imposing no risk of additional loss should the stock price fall. The volatility value lies in the value of the right to not exercise the option if that action would be unprofitable. The option to exercise, as opposed to the obligation to exercise, provides insurance against poor stock price performance.

As the stock price increases substantially, it becomes more likely that the call option will be exercised by expiration. In this case, with exercise all but assured, the volatility value becomes minimal. As the stock price gets ever larger, the option value approaches the "adjusted" intrinsic value, the stock price minus the present value of the exercise price, $S_0 - PV(X)$.

Why should this be? If you are virtually certain the option will be exercised and the stock purchased for X dollars, it is as though you own the stock already. The stock certificate, with a value today of $S_0$, might as well be sitting in your safe-deposit box now, as it will be there in only a few months. You just haven't paid for it yet. The present value of your obligation is the present value of $X$, so the net value of the call option is $S_0 - PV(X)$.[1]

Figure 21.1 illustrates the call option valuation function. The option always increases in value with the stock price. The slope is greatest, however, when the option is deep in the money. In this case, exercise is all but assured, and the option increases in price one for one with the stock price. The value curve shows that when the stock price is low, the option is nearly worthless because there is almost no chance that it will be exercised. When the stock price is very high, the option value approaches adjusted intrinsic value. In the midrange case, where the option

---

[1] This discussion presumes the stock pays no dividends until after option expiration. If the stock does pay dividends before maturity, then there *is* a reason you would care about getting the stock now rather than at expiration—getting it now entitles you to the interim dividend payments. In this case, the adjusted intrinsic value of the option must subtract the value of the dividends the stock will pay out before the call is exercised. Adjusted intrinsic value would more generally be defined as $S_0 - PV(X) - PV(D)$, where $D$ is the dividend to be paid before option expiration.

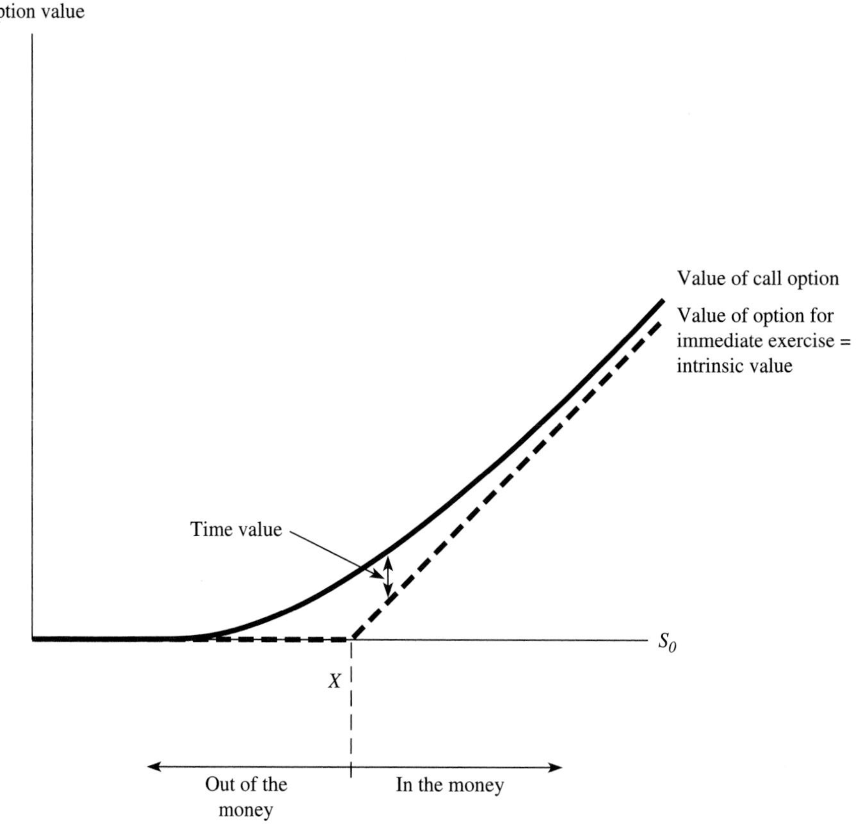


**Figure 21.1**
Call option value before expiration.

is approximately at the money, the option curve diverges from the straight lines corresponding to adjusted intrinsic value. This is because while exercise today would have a negligible (or negative) payoff, the volatility value of the option is quite high in this region.

## Determinants of the Value of a Call Option

We can identify at least six factors that should affect the value of a call option: the stock price, the exercise price, the volatility of the stock price, the time to expiration, the interest rate, and the dividend rate of the stock. The call option should increase in value with the stock price and decrease in value with the exercise price because the payoff to a call, if exercised, equals $S_T - X$. The magnitude of the expected payoff from the call increases with the difference of $S_0 - X$.

Call option value also increases with the volatility of the underlying stock price. To see why, consider circumstances where possible stock prices at expiration may range from \$10 to \$50 compared with a situation where stock prices may range only from \$20 to \$40. In both cases the expected stock price will be \$30. Suppose that the exercise price on a call option is also \$30. What are the option payoffs?

High-Volatility Scenario

| | | | | | |
|---|---|---|---|---|---|
| Stock price | \$10 | \$20 | \$30 | \$40 | \$50 |
| Option payoff | 0 | 0 | 0 | \$10 | \$20 |

If each outcome is equally likely, with probability .2, the expected payoff to the option under high-volatility conditions will be \$6.

Low-Volatility Scenario

| | | | | | |
|---|---|---|---|---|---|
| Stock price | \$20 | \$25 | \$30 | \$35 | \$40 |
| Option payoff | 0 | 0 | 0 | \$ 5 | \$10 |

Again, with equally likely outcomes, the expected payoff to the option is half as much, only \$3.

Despite the fact that the average stock price in each scenario is \$30, the average option payoff is greater in the high-volatility scenario. The source of this extra value is the limited loss that an option holder can suffer, or the volatility value of the call. No matter how far below \$30 the stock price drops, the option holder will get \$0. Obviously, extremely poor stock price performance is no worse for the call option holder than is moderately poor performance. In the case of good stock performance, however, the option will expire in the money, and it will be more profitable the higher the stock price. Thus, extremely good stock outcomes can improve the option payoff without limit, but extremely poor outcomes cannot worsen the payoff below zero. This asymmetry means that volatility in the underlying stock price increases the expected payoff to the option, thereby enhancing its value.

**CONCEPT CHECK** Question 1. Should a put option also increase in value with the volatility of the stock?

Similarly, longer time to expiration increases the value of a call option. For more distant expiration dates, the range of likely stock prices expands, which has an effect similar to that of increased volatility. Moreover, as time to expiration increases, the present value of the exercise price falls, thereby benefiting the call option holder and increasing the option value. As a corollary to this issue, call option values are higher when interest rates rise (holding the stock price constant), because higher interest rates also reduce the present value of the exercise price.

Finally, the dividend payout policy of the firm affects option values. A high-dividend payout policy puts a drag on the rate of growth of the stock price. For any expected total rate of return on the stock, a higher dividend yield must imply

**Table 21.1** Determinants of Call Option Values

| Variable Increases | Value of Call Option |
|---|---|
| Stock price, $S$ | Increases |
| Exercise price, $X$ | Decreases |
| Volatility, $\sigma$ | Increases |
| Time to expiration, $T$ | Increases |
| Interest rate, $r_f$ | Increases |
| Cash dividend payouts | Decreases |

a lower expected rate of capital gain. This drag on stock price appreciation decreases the potential payoff from the call option, thereby lowering the call value. Table 21.1 summarizes these relationships.

**CONCEPT CHECK** Question 2. Prepare a table like Table 21.1 for the determinants of put option values. How should put values respond to increases in $S$, $X$, $\sigma$, $T$, $r_f$, and dividend payouts?

## 21.2 RESTRICTIONS ON OPTION VALUES

Several quantitative models of option pricing have been devised, and we will examine some of these in this chapter. All models, however, rely on simplifying assumptions. You might wonder which properties of option values are truly general and which depend on the particular simplifications. To start with, we will consider some of the more important general properties of option prices. Some of these properties have important implications for the effect of stock dividends on option values and the possible profitability of early exercise of an American option.

### Restrictions on the Value of a Call Option

The most obvious restriction on the value of a call option is that its value must be zero or positive. Because the option need not be exercised, it cannot impose any liability on its holder; moreover, as long as there is any possibility that at some point the option can be exercised profitably, the option will command a positive price. Its payoff must be zero at worst, and possibly positive, so that investors are willing to pay a positive amount to purchase it.

We can place another lower bound on the value of a call option. Suppose that the stock will pay a dividend of $D$ dollars just before the expiration date of the option, denoted by $T$ (where today is time zero). Now compare two portfolios, one consisting of a call option on one share of stock and the other a leveraged equity position consisting of that share and borrowing of $(X + D)/(1 + r_f)^T$ dollars. The loan repayment is $X + D$ dollars, due on the expiration date of the option. For example, for a half-year maturity option with exercise price \$70, dividends to be paid of \$5, and effective annual interest of 10 percent, you would purchase one share of stock and borrow $\$75/(1.10)^{1/2} = \$71.51$. In six months, when the loan matures, the payment due is \$75.

At that time, the payoff to the leveraged equity position would be

| | In General | Our Numbers |
|---|---|---|
| Stock value | $S_T + D$ | $S_T + 5$ |
| −Payback of loan | $-(X + D)$ | $-75$ |
| Total | $S_T - X$ | $S_T - 70$ |

where $S_T$ denotes the stock price at the option expiration date. Notice that the payoff to the stock is the ex-dividend stock value plus dividends received. Whether the total payoff to the stock-plus-borrowing position is positive or negative depends on whether $S_T$ exceeds $X$. The net cash outlay required to establish this leveraged equity position is $S_0 - \$71.51$, or, more generally, $S_0 - (X + D)/(1 + r_f)^T$, that is, the current price of the purchased stock, $S_0$, less the initial cash inflow from the borrowing position.

The payoff to the call option will be $S_T - X$ if the option expires in the money and zero otherwise. Thus, the option payoff is equal to the leveraged equity payoff when that payoff is positive and is greater when the leveraged equity position has a negative payoff. Because the option payoff always is greater than or equal to that of the leveraged equity position, the option price must exceed the cost of establishing that position.

In our case the value of the call must be greater than $S_0 - (X + D)/(1 + r_f)^T$, or, more generally,

$$C \geq S_0 - \text{PV}(X) - \text{PV}(D)$$

where PV($X$) denotes the present value of the exercise price and PV($D$) is the present value of the dividends the stock will pay at the option's expiration. More generally, we can interpret PV($D$) as the present value of any and all dividends to be paid prior to the option expiration date. Because we know already that the value of a call option must be non-negative, we may conclude that $C$ is greater than the *maximum* of either 0 or $S_0 - \text{PV}(X) - \text{PV}(D)$.

We also can place an upper bound on the possible value of the call: simply the stock price. No one would pay more than $S_0$ dollars for the right to purchase a stock currently worth $S_0$ dollars. Thus, $C \leq S_0$.

Figure 21.2 demonstrates graphically the range of prices that is ruled out by these upper and lower bounds for the value of a call option. Any option value outside the shaded area is not possible according to the restrictions we have derived. Before expiration, the call option value normally will be *within* the allowable range, touching neither the upper nor lower bounds, as in Figure 21.3.

**Figure 21.2**
Range of possible call option values.

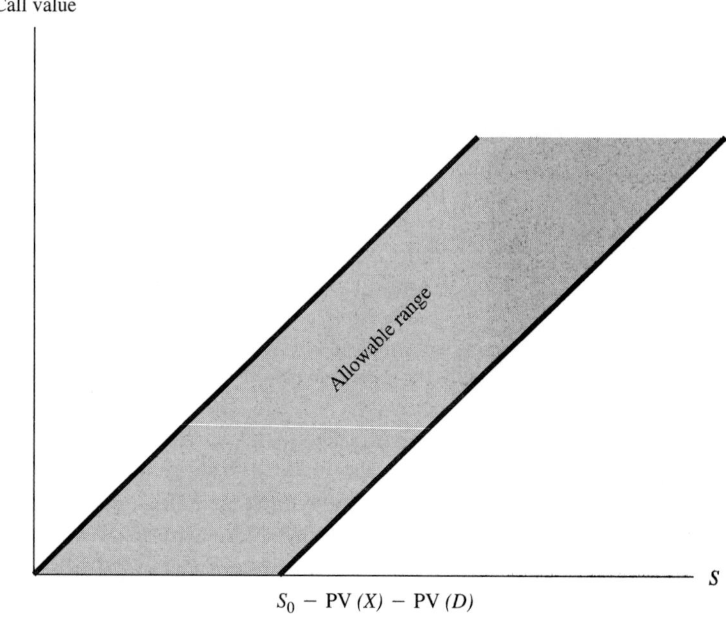


**Figure 21.3**
Call option value as a function of the stock price.

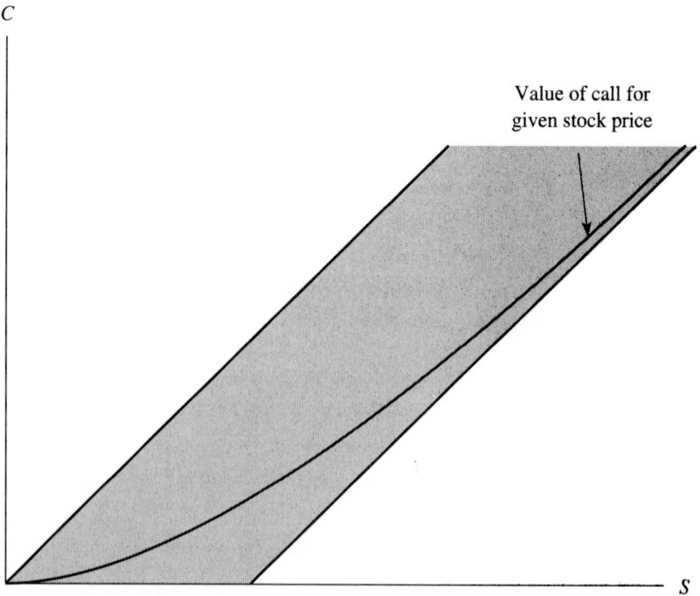

## Early Exercise and Dividends

A call option holder who wants to close out that position has two choices: exercise the call or sell it. If the holder exercises at time $t$, the call will provide a profit of $S_t - X$, assuming, of course, that the option is in the money. We have just seen that the option can be sold for at least $S_t - \text{PV}(X) - \text{PV}(D)$. Therefore, for an option on a nondividend-paying stock, $C$ is greater than $S_t - \text{PV}(X)$. Because the present value of $X$ is less than $X$ itself, it follows that

$$C \geq S_t - \text{PV}(X) \geq S_t - X$$

The implication here is that the proceeds from a sale of the option (at price $C$) must exceed the proceeds from an exercise ($S_t - X$). It is economically more effective to keep the call option "alive" rather than "killing" it through early exercise. In other words, calls on nondividend-paying stocks are worth more alive than dead.

If it never pays to exercise a call option before maturity, the right to exercise early actually must be valueless. The right of the American call holder to exercise early is irrelevant because it will never pay to exercise early. We have to conclude that the values of otherwise-identical American and European call options on stocks paying no dividends are equal. If we can find the value for the European call, we also will have found the value of the American call. Therefore, any valuation formula for European call options will apply as well to American calls on nondividend-paying stocks.

As most stocks do pay dividends, you may wonder whether this result is just a theoretical curiosity. It is not: Reconsider our argument and you will see that all that we really require is that the stock pay no dividends *until the option expires.* This condition will be true for many real-world options.

For American *put options,* however, the optimality of early exercise is most definitely a possibility. To see why, consider a simple example. Suppose that you purchase a put option on a stock. Soon the firm goes bankrupt, and the stock price falls to zero. Of course you want to exercise now, because the stock price can fall no lower. Immediate exercise gives you immediate receipt of the exercise price, which can be invested to start generating income. Delay in exercise means a time-value-of-money cost. The right to early exercise of a put option before maturity must have value.

Now suppose instead that the firm is only nearly bankrupt, with the stock selling at just a few cents. Immediate exercise may still be optimal. After all, the stock price can fall by only a very small amount, meaning that the proceeds from future exercise cannot be more than a few cents greater than the proceeds from immediate exercise. Against this possibility of a tiny increase in proceeds must be weighed the time-value-of-money cost of deferring exercise. Clearly, there is some stock price below which early exercise is optimal.

This argument also proves that the American put must be worth more than its European counterpart. The American put allows you to exercise anytime before maturity. Because the right to exercise early may be useful in some circumstances,

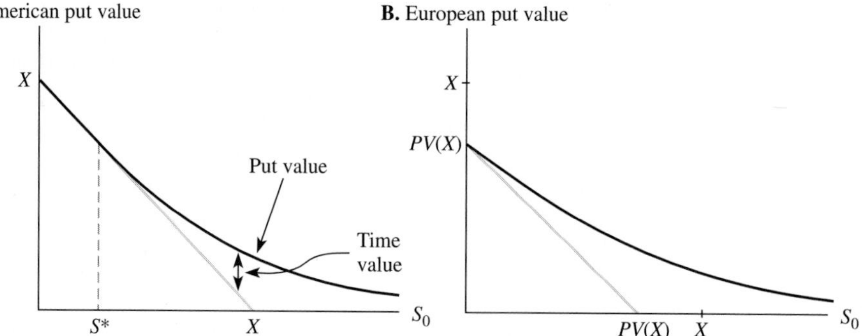


**Figure 21.4** Put option values as a function of the current stock price.

it will command a positive price in the capital market. The American put therefore will sell for a higher price than a European put with otherwise identical terms.

Figure 21.4**A** illustrates the value of an American put option as a function of the current stock price, $S_0$. Once the stock price drops below a critical value, denoted $S^*$ in the figure, exercise becomes optimal. At that point the option-pricing curve is tangent to the straight line depicting the intrinsic value of the option. If and when the stock price reaches $S^*$, the put option is exercised and its payoff equals its intrinsic value.

In contrast, the value of the European put, which is graphed in Figure 21.4**B,** does not asymptote to the intrinsic value line. Because early exercise is prohibited, the maximum value of the European put is PV($X$), which occurs at the point $S_0 = 0$. Obviously, for a long enough horizon, PV($X$) can be made arbitrarily small.

**CONCEPT CHECK** Question 3. In light of this discussion, explain why the put-call parity relationship is valid only for European options on nondividend-paying stocks. If the stock pays no dividends, what *inequality* for American options would correspond to the parity theorem?

## 21.3 THE BLACK-SCHOLES FORMULA

Financial economists searched for years for a workable option-pricing model before Black and Scholes[2] and Merton[3] derived a formula for the value of a call option. Now widely used by option-market participants, the **Black-Scholes**

[2] Fischer Black and Myron Scholes, "The Pricing of Options and Corporate Liabilities," *Journal of Political Economy* 81 (May/June 1973).

[3] Robert C. Merton, "Theory of Rational Option Pricing," *Bell Journal of Economics and Management Science* 4 (Spring 1973).

**pricing** formula is

$$C_0 = S_0N(d_1) - Xe^{-rT}N(d_2) \tag{21.1}$$

where

$$d_1 = \frac{\ln(S_0/X) + (r + \sigma^2/2)T}{\sigma\sqrt{T}}$$

$$d_2 = d_1 - \sigma\sqrt{T}$$

and where

$C_0$ = Current option value
$S_0$ = Current stock price
$X$ = Exercise price
$r$ = Risk-free interest rate (the annualized continuously compounded rate on a safe asset with the same maturity as the expiration of the option, which is to be distinguished from $r_f$, the discrete period interest rate)
$T$ = Time to maturity of options in years
$\sigma$ = Standard deviation of the annualized continuously compounded rate of return of the stock
ln = Natural logarithm function
$e$ = 2.71828, the base of the natural log function
$N(d)$ = The probability that a random draw from a standard normal distribution will be less than $d$ (this equals the percentage of the area under the normal curve up to $d$, as shown in Figure 21.5)

The option value does not depend on the expected rate of return on the stock. In a sense this information is already built into the formula with inclusion of the stock price, which itself depends on the stock's risk-and-return characteristics. This version of the Black-Scholes formula is predicated on the assumption that the stock pays no dividends.

Although you may find the Black-Scholes formula intimidating, we can explain it first at a somewhat intuitive level. The trick is to view the $N(d)$ terms (loosely!) as risk-adjusted probabilities that the call option will expire in the money. First, look at Equation 21.1 when both $N(d)$ terms are close to 1, indicating a very high probability that the option will be exercised. Then the call option value is equal to $S_0 - Xe^{-rT}$, which is what we called earlier the adjusted intrinsic value, $S_0 -$ PV($X$). This makes sense: If exercise is certain, we have a claim on a stock with current value $S_0$ and an obligation with present value PV($X$), or, with continuous compounding, $Xe^{-rT}$.

Now look at Equation 21.1 when the $N(d)$ terms are close to zero, meaning that the option almost certainly will not be exercised. Then the equation confirms that the call is worth nothing. For middle-range values of $N(d)$ between 0 and 1, Equation 21.1 tells us that the call value can be viewed as the present value of the call's potential payoff adjusting for the probability of in-the-money expiration.

How do the $N(d)$ terms serve as risk-adjusted probabilities? This question quickly leads us into advanced statistics. Notice, however, that $d_1$ and $d_2$ both

**Figure 21.5**
A standard normal curve.

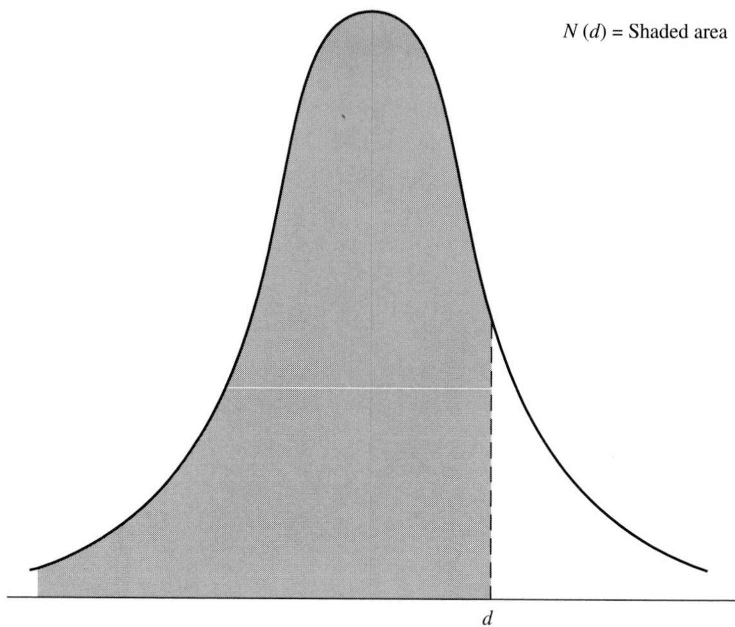


increase as the stock price increases. Therefore, $N(d_1)$ and $N(d_2)$ also increase with higher stock prices. This is the property we would desire of our "probabilities." For higher stock prices relative to exercise prices, future exercise is more likely.

In fact, you can use the Black-Scholes formula fairly easily. Suppose that you want to value a call option under the following circumstances:

| | |
|---|---|
| Stock price | $S_0 = 100$ |
| Exercise price | $X = 95$ |
| Interest rate | $r = .10$ |
| Time to expiration | $T = .25$ (one-fourth year) |
| Standard deviation | $\sigma = .5$ |

First calculate

$$d_1 = \frac{\ln(100/95) + (.10 + .5^2/2) \times .25}{.5\sqrt{.25}} = .43$$

$$d_2 = .43 - .5\sqrt{.25} = .18$$

Next find $N(d_1)$ and $N(d_2)$. The values of the normal distribution are tabulated and may be found in many statistics textbooks. A table of $N(d)$ is provided here as Table 21.2. The table reveals (using interpolation) that

**Table 21.2** Cumulative Normal Distribution

| *d* | *N*(*d*) | *d* | *N*(*d*) | *d* | *N*(*d*) |
|---|---|---|---|---|---|
| −3.00 | .0013 | −1.42 | .0778 | −0.44 | .3300 |
| −2.95 | .0016 | −1.40 | .0808 | −0.42 | .3373 |
| −2.90 | .0019 | −1.38 | .0838 | −0.40 | .3446 |
| −2.85 | .0022 | −1.36 | .0869 | −0.38 | .3520 |
| −2.80 | .0026 | −1.34 | .0901 | −0.36 | .3594 |
| −2.75 | .0030 | −1.32 | .0934 | −0.34 | .3669 |
| −2.70 | .0035 | −1.30 | .0968 | −0.32 | .3745 |
| −2.65 | .0040 | −1.28 | .1003 | −0.30 | .3821 |
| −2.60 | .0047 | −1.26 | .1038 | −0.28 | .3897 |
| −2.55 | .0054 | −1.24 | .1075 | −0.26 | .3974 |
| −2.50 | .0062 | −1.22 | .1112 | −0.24 | .4052 |
| −2.45 | .0071 | −1.20 | .1151 | −0.22 | .4129 |
| −2.40 | .0082 | −1.18 | .1190 | −0.20 | .4207 |
| −2.35 | .0094 | −1.16 | .1230 | −0.18 | .4286 |
| −2.30 | .0107 | −1.14 | .1271 | −0.16 | .4365 |
| −2.25 | .0122 | −1.12 | .1314 | −0.14 | .4443 |
| −2.20 | .0139 | −1.10 | .1357 | −0.12 | .4523 |
| −2.15 | .0158 | −1.08 | .1401 | −0.10 | .4602 |
| −2.10 | .0179 | −1.06 | .1446 | −0.08 | .4681 |
| −2.05 | .0202 | −1.04 | .1492 | −0.06 | .4761 |
| −2.00 | .0228 | −1.02 | .1539 | −0.04 | .4841 |
| −1.98 | .0239 | −1.00 | .1587 | −0.02 | .4920 |
| −1.96 | .0250 | −0.98 | .1635 | 0.00 | .5000 |
| −1.94 | .0262 | −0.96 | .1685 | 0.02 | .5080 |
| −1.92 | .0274 | −0.94 | .1736 | 0.04 | .5160 |
| −1.90 | .0287 | −0.92 | .1788 | 0.06 | .5239 |
| −1.88 | .0301 | −0.90 | .1841 | 0.08 | .5319 |
| −1.86 | .0314 | −0.88 | .1894 | 0.10 | .5398 |
| −1.84 | .0329 | −0.86 | .1949 | 0.12 | .5478 |
| −1.82 | .0344 | −0.84 | .2005 | 0.14 | .5557 |
| −1.80 | .0359 | −0.82 | .2061 | 0.16 | .5636 |
| −1.78 | .0375 | −0.80 | .2119 | 0.18 | .5714 |
| −1.76 | .0392 | −0.78 | .2177 | 0.20 | .5793 |
| −1.74 | .0409 | −0.76 | .2236 | 0.22 | .5871 |
| −1.72 | .0427 | −0.74 | .2297 | 0.24 | .5948 |
| −1.70 | .0446 | −0.72 | .2358 | 0.26 | .6026 |
| −1.68 | .0465 | −0.70 | .2420 | 0.28 | .6103 |
| −1.66 | .0485 | −0.68 | .2483 | 0.30 | .6179 |
| −1.64 | .0505 | −0.66 | .2546 | 0.32 | .6255 |
| −1.62 | .0526 | −0.64 | .2611 | 0.34 | .6331 |
| −1.60 | .0548 | −0.62 | .2676 | 0.36 | .6406 |
| −1.58 | .0571 | −0.60 | .2743 | 0.38 | .6480 |
| −1.56 | .0594 | −0.58 | .2810 | 0.40 | .6554 |
| −1.54 | .0618 | −0.56 | .2877 | 0.42 | .6628 |
| −1.52 | .0643 | −0.54 | .2946 | 0.44 | .6700 |
| −1.50 | .0668 | −0.52 | .3015 | 0.46 | .6773 |
| −1.48 | .0694 | −0.50 | .3085 | 0.48 | .6844 |
| −1.46 | .0721 | −0.48 | .3156 | 0.50 | .6915 |
| −1.44 | .0749 | −0.46 | .3228 | 0.52 | .6985 |

**Table 21.2** Continued

| d | N(d) | d | N(d) | d | N(d) |
|---|---|---|---|---|---|
| 0.54 | .7054 | 1.18 | .8810 | 1.82 | .9556 |
| 0.56 | .7123 | 1.20 | .8849 | 1.84 | .9671 |
| 0.58 | .7191 | 1.22 | .8888 | 1.86 | .9686 |
| 0.60 | .7258 | 1.24 | .8925 | 1.88 | .9699 |
| 0.62 | .7324 | 1.26 | .8962 | 1.90 | .9713 |
| 0.64 | .7389 | 1.28 | .8997 | 1.92 | .9726 |
| 0.66 | .7454 | 1.30 | .9032 | 1.94 | .9738 |
| 0.68 | .7518 | 1.32 | .9066 | 1.96 | .9750 |
| 0.70 | .7580 | 1.34 | .9099 | 1.98 | .9761 |
| 0.72 | .7642 | 1.36 | .9131 | 2.00 | .9772 |
| 0.74 | .7704 | 1.38 | .9162 | 2.05 | .9798 |
| 0.76 | .7764 | 1.40 | .9192 | 2.10 | .9821 |
| 0.78 | .7823 | 1.42 | .9222 | 2.15 | .9842 |
| 0.80 | .7882 | 1.44 | .9251 | 2.20 | .9861 |
| 0.82 | .7939 | 1.46 | .9279 | 2.25 | .9878 |
| 0.84 | .7996 | 1.48 | .9306 | 2.30 | .9893 |
| 0.86 | .8051 | 1.50 | .9332 | 2.35 | .9906 |
| 0.88 | .8106 | 1.52 | .9357 | 2.40 | .9918 |
| 0.90 | .8159 | 1.54 | .9382 | 2.45 | .9929 |
| 0.92 | .8212 | 1.56 | .9406 | 2.50 | .9938 |
| 0.94 | .8264 | 1.58 | .9429 | 2.55 | .9946 |
| 0.96 | .8315 | 1.60 | .9452 | 2.60 | .9953 |
| 0.98 | .8365 | 1.62 | .9474 | 2.65 | .9960 |
| 1.00 | .8414 | 1.64 | .9495 | 2.70 | .9965 |
| 1.02 | .8461 | 1.66 | .9515 | 2.75 | .9970 |
| 1.04 | .8508 | 1.68 | .9535 | 2.80 | .9974 |
| 1.06 | .8554 | 1.70 | .9554 | 2.85 | .9978 |
| 1.08 | .8599 | 1.72 | .9573 | 2.90 | .9981 |
| 1.10 | .8643 | 1.74 | .9591 | 2.95 | .9984 |
| 1.12 | .8686 | 1.76 | .9608 | 3.00 | .9986 |
| 1.14 | .8729 | 1.78 | .9625 | 3.05 | .9989 |
| 1.16 | .8770 | 1.80 | .9641 | | |

$$N(.43) = .6664$$
$$N(.18) = .5714$$

Thus, the value of the call option is

$$\begin{aligned} C &= 100 \times .6664 - (95e^{-.10\times.25}) \times .5714 \\ &= 66.64 - 52.94 = \$13.70 \end{aligned}$$

What if the option price were in fact \$15? Is the option mispriced? Maybe, but before betting your fortune on that, you may want to reconsider the valuation analysis. First, like all models, the Black-Scholes formula is based on some simplifying abstractions that make the formula only approximately valid: the stock will pay no dividends until after the option expiration date; interest rate $r$ and standard deviation $\sigma$ are constant; and stock prices are continuous, ruling out sudden jumps.

Second, even within the context of the model, you must be sure of the accuracy of the parameters used in the formula. Four of these—$S_0$, $X$, $T$, and $r$—are straightforward. The stock price, exercise price, and time to maturity may be read directly from the option pages. The interest rate used is the money market rate for a maturity equal to that of the option. The last input, however, the standard deviation of the stock return, is not directly observable. It must be estimated from historical data, from scenario analysis, or from the prices of other options, as we will describe momentarily. Because the standard deviation must be estimated, it is always possible that discrepancies between an option price and its Black-Scholes value are simply artifacts of error in the estimation of the stock's volatility.

In fact, market participants often give the option valuation problem a different twist. Rather than calculating a Black-Scholes option value for a given stock standard deviation, they ask instead, "What standard deviation would be necessary for the option price that I can see to be consistent with the Black-Scholes formula?" This is called the **implied volatility** of the option, the volatility level for the stock that the option price implies. From the implied standard deviation, investors judge whether they think the actual stock standard deviation exceeds the implied volatility. If it does, the option is considered a good buy; if actual volatility seems greater than the implied volatility, its fair price would exceed the observed price.

**CONCEPT CHECK** Question 4. Consider the option in the example selling for $15 with Black-Scholes value of $13.70. Is its implied volatility more or less than .5?

Another variation is to compare two options on the same stock with equal expiration dates but different exercise prices. The option with the higher implied volatility would be considered relatively expensive, because a higher standard deviation is required to justify its price. The analyst might consider buying the option with the lower implied volatility and writing the option with the higher implied volatility.

## Dividends and Call Option Valuation

We noted earlier that the Black-Scholes call option formula applies to stocks that do not pay dividends. When dividends are to be paid before the option expires, we need to adjust the formula. The payment of dividends raises the possibility of early exercise and, for most realistic dividend payout schemes, the valuation formula becomes significantly more complex than the Black-Scholes equation.

We can apply some simple rules of thumb to approximate the option value, however. One popular approach, originally suggested by Black,[4] calls for adjust-

[4] Fischer Black, "Fact and Fantasy in the Use of Options," *Financial Analysts Journal* 31 (July–August 1975).

ing the stock price downward by the present value of any dividends that are to be paid before option expiration. Such an adjustment will take dividends into account by reflecting their eventual impact on the stock price. The option value then may be computed as before, assuming that the option will be held to expiration.

This procedure would yield a very good approximation of option value for European call options that must be held until maturity, but it does not allow for the fact that the holder of an American call option might choose to exercise the option just before a dividend. The current value of a call option, assuming that the option will be exercised just before the ex-dividend date, might be greater than the value of the option—assuming it will be held until maturity. Although holding the option until maturity allows greater effective time to expiration, which increases the option value, it also entails more dividend payments, lowering the expected stock price at maturity and thereby lowering the current option value.

For example, suppose that a stock selling at $20 will pay a $1 dividend in four months, whereas the call option on the stock does not expire for six months. The effective annual interest rate is 10 percent, so that the present value of the dividend is $\$1/(1.10)^{1/3} = \$0.97$. Black suggests that we can compute the option value in one of two ways:

1. Apply the Black-Scholes formula assuming early exercise, thus using the actual stock price of $20 and a time to expiration of four months (the time until the dividend payment).
2. Apply the Black-Scholes formula assuming no early exercise, using the dividend-adjusted stock price of $\$20 - \$0.97 = \$19.03$ and a time to expiration of six months.

The greater of the two values is the estimate of the option value, recognizing that early exercise might be optimal. In other words, the so-called *pseudo-American* call option value is the maximum of the value derived by assuming that the option will be held until expiration and the value derived by assuming that the option will be exercised just before an ex-dividend date. Even this technique is not exact, however, for it assumes that the option holder makes an irrevocable decision now on when to exercise, when in fact the decision is not binding until exercise notice is given.[5]

## Put Option Valuation

We have concentrated so far on call option valuation. We can derive Black-Scholes European put option values from call option values using the put-call

[5] An exact formula for American call valuation on dividend-paying stocks has been developed in Richard Roll, "An Analytic Valuation Formula for Unprotected American Call Options on Stocks with Known Dividends," *Journal of Financial Economics* 5 (November 1977). The technique has been discussed and revised in Robert Geske, "A Note on an Analytical Formula for Unprotected American Call Options on Stocks with Known Dividends," *Journal of Financial Economics* 7 (December 1979); Robert E. Whaley, "On the Valuation of American Call Options on Stocks with Known Dividends," *Journal of Financial Economics* 9 (June 1981); and Giovanni Barone-Adesi and Robert E. Whaley, "Efficient Analytic Approximations of American Option Values," *Journal of Finance* 42, no. 2 (June 1987). Note that these are difficult papers, however.

parity theorem. To value the put option, we simply calculate the value of the corresponding call option in Equation 21.1 from the Black-Scholes formula, and solve for the put option value as

$$\begin{aligned} P &= C + \text{PV}(X) - S_0 \\ &= C + Xe^{-rT} - S_0 \end{aligned} \qquad \textbf{(21.2)}$$

We must calculate the present value of the exercise price using continuous compounding to be consistent with the Black-Scholes formula.

Using data from the Black-Scholes call option example ($C = \$13.70$; $X = \$95$; $S = \$100$; $r = .10$; and $T = .25$), we find that a European put option on that stock with identical exercise price and time to maturity is worth

$$P = \$13.70 + \$95e^{-.10\times.25} - \$100 = \$6.35$$

As we noted traders can do, we might then compare this formula value to the actual put price as one step in formulating a trading strategy.

Equation 21.2 is valid for European puts on nondividend-paying stocks. Listed put options are American options that offer the opportunity of early exercise, however, and we have seen that the right to exercise puts early can turn out to be valuable. This means that an American option must be worth more than the corresponding European option. Therefore, Equation 21.2 describes only the lower bound on the true value of the American put. However, in many applications the approximation is very accurate.[6]

## 21.4 Using the Black-Scholes Formula

### Hedge Ratios and the Black-Scholes Formula

In Chapter 20, Section 20.2, we considered two investments in Seagram's: 100 shares of Seagram's stock or 500 call options on Seagram's. We saw that the call option position was more sensitive to swings in Seagram's stock price than the all-stock position. To analyze the overall exposure to a stock price more precisely, however, it is necessary to quantify these relative sensitivities. A tool that enables us to summarize the overall exposure of portfolios of options with various exercise prices and times to maturity is the **hedge ratio.** An option's hedge ratio is the change in the price of an option for a $1 increase in the stock price. Therefore, a call option has a positive hedge ratio and a put option has a negative hedge ratio. The hedge ratio is commonly called the option's **delta.**

[6] For a more complete treatment of American put valuation, see R. Geske and H. E. Johnson, "The American Put Valued Analytically," *Journal of Finance* 39 (December 1984), pp. 1511–24.

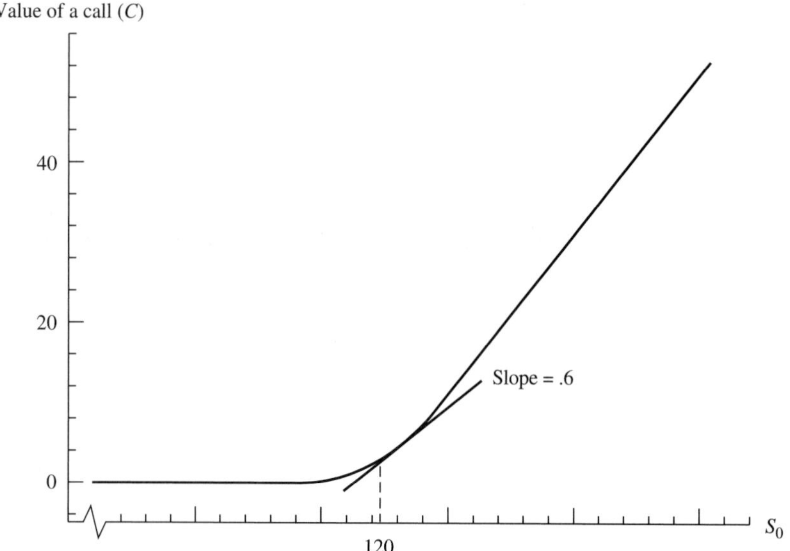


**Figure 21.6**
Call option value and hedge ratio.

If you were to graph the option value as a function of the stock value as we have done for a call option in Figure 21.6, the hedge ratio is simply the slope of the value function evaluated at the current stock price. For example, suppose that the slope of the curve at $S_0 = \$120$ equals .60. As the stock increases in value by \$1, the option increases by approximately \$.60, as the figure shows.

For every call option written, .60 shares of stock would be needed to hedge the investor's portfolio. For example, if one writes 10 options and holds six shares of stock, according to the hedge ratio of .6, a \$1 increase in stock price will result in a gain of \$6 on the stock holdings, whereas the loss on the 10 options written will be 10 × \$0.60, an equivalent \$6. The stock price movement leaves total wealth unaltered, which is what is required of a hedged position. The investor holding the stock and option in proportions dictated by their relative price movements hedges the portfolio.

Black-Scholes hedge ratios are particularly easy to compute. It turns out that the hedge ratio for a call is $N(d_1)$, and the hedge ratio for a put is $N(d_1) - 1$. We defined $N(d_1)$ as part of the Black-Scholes formula (Equation 21.1). Recall that $N(d)$ stands for the area under the standard normal curve up to $d$. Therefore, the call option hedge ratio must be positive and less than 1, whereas the put option hedge ratio is negative and of smaller absolute value than 1.

Figure 21.6 verifies the insight that the slope of the call option valuation function is indeed less than 1, approaching 1 only as the stock price becomes extremely large. This tells us that option values change less than one-for-one with changes in stock prices. Why should this be? Suppose that an option is so far in the money that you are absolutely certain it will be exercised. In that case, every dollar increase in the stock price would indeed increase the option value by $1. However, if there is a reasonable chance that the call option will expire out of the money even after a moderate stock price gain, a $1 increase in the stock price will not necessarily increase the ultimate payoff to the call; therefore, the call price will not respond by a full dollar.

The fact that hedge ratios are less than 1 does not conflict with our earlier observation that options offer leverage and are quite sensitive to stock price movements. Although *dollar* movements in option prices are slighter than dollar movements in the stock price, the *rate of return* volatility of options remains greater than stock return volatility because options sell at smaller prices. In our example, with the stock selling at $120 and a hedge ratio of 0.6, an option with exercise price $120 may sell for $5. If the stock price increases to $121, the call price would be expected to increase by only $.60, to $5.60. The percentage increase in the option value is $.60/$5.00 = 12 percent, however, whereas the stock price increase is only $1/$120 = .83 percent. In this case, we would say that the *elasticity* of the option is 12 percent/.83 percent = 14.4. For every 1 percent increase in the stock price, the option price increases by 14.4 percent. This ratio, the percent change in option price per percent change in stock price, is called the **option elasticity.**

**CONCEPT CHECK** Question 5. What is the elasticity of a put option currently selling for $4 with exercise price $120 and hedge ratio −.4, if the stock price is currently $122?

The hedge ratio is an essential tool in portfolio management and control. An example will illustrate.

Consider two portfolios, one holding 750 Seagram's calls and 200 shares of Seagram's, and the other holding 800 shares of Seagram's. Which portfolio has greater dollar exposure to Seagram's price movements? You can answer this question easily using the hedge ratio.

Each option changes in value by $H$ dollars for each dollar change in stock price, where $H$ stands for the hedge ratio. Thus, if $H$ equals 0.6, the 750 options are equivalent to 450 (.6 × 750) shares in terms of the response of their market value to Seagram's stock price movements. The first portfolio has less dollar sensitivity to Seagram's, because the 450 share-equivalents of the options plus the 200 shares actually held are less than the 800 shares held in the second portfolio.

This is not to say, however, that the first portfolio is less sensitive to Seagram's in terms of its rate of return. As we noted in discussing option elasticities, the first portfolio may be of lower total value than the second, so despite its lower sensitivity in terms of total market value, it might have greater rate of return sensitivity. Because a call option has a lower market value than the stock, its price changes more than proportionally with stock price changes, even though its hedge ratio is less than 1.

## Portfolio Insurance

In Chapter 20 we showed that protective put strategies offer a sort of insurance policy on an asset. The protective put has proved to be extremely popular with investors. Even if the asset price falls, the put conveys the right to sell the asset for the exercise price, which is a way to lock in a minimum portfolio value. With an at-the-money put ($X = S_0$), the maximum loss that can be realized is the cost of the put. The asset can be sold for $X$, which equals its original value, so even if the asset price falls, the investor's net loss over the period is just the cost of the put. If the asset value increases, however, upside potential is unlimited. Figure 21.7 graphs the profit or loss on a protective put position as a function of the change in the value of the underlying asset.

Although the protective put is a simple and convenient way to achieve **portfolio insurance,** there are practical difficulties in trying to insure a portfolio of stocks. First, unless the investor's portfolio corresponds to a standard market index for which puts are traded, a put option on the portfolio will not be available for purchase. In addition, if index puts are used to protect a nonindexed portfolio, tracking errors can result. For example, if the portfolio falls in value while the market index rises, the put will fail to provide the intended protection. Tracking error limits the investor's freedom to pursue active stock selection, because such error will be greater as the managed portfolio departs more substantially from the market index.

**Figure 21.7**
Return characteristics for a portfolio with a protective put.

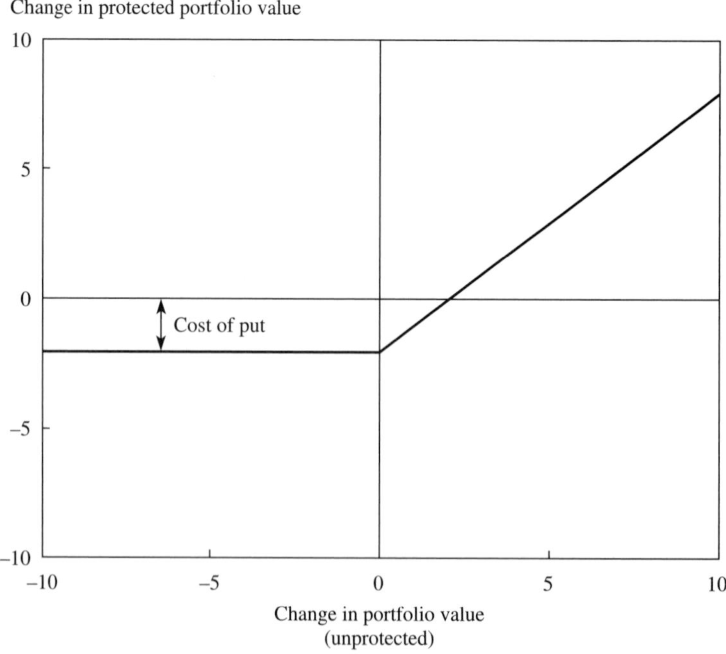

Moreover, the desired horizon of the insurance program must match the maturity of a traded put option in order to establish the appropriate protective put position. Whereas most insurance programs have horizons of several years, traded index options in Canada have been limited to maturities of less than one year. Rolling over a sequence of short-term puts, which might be viewed as a response to this problem, introduces new risks because the prices at which successive puts will be available in the future are not known today.

Providers of portfolio insurance with horizons of several years, therefore, cannot rely on the simple expedient of purchasing protective puts for their clients' portfolios. Instead, they follow trading strategies that replicate the payoffs to the protective put position.

Here is the general idea: Even if a put option on the desired portfolio with the desired expiration date does not exist, a theoretical option pricing model (such as the Black-Scholes model) can be used to determine how that option's price would respond to the portfolio's value if the option did in fact trade. For example, if stock prices were to fall, the put option would increase in value. The option model could quantify this relationship. The next exposure of the (hypothetical) protective put portfolio to swings in stock prices is the sum of the exposures of the two components of the portfolio, the stock and the put. The net exposure of the portfolio equals the equity exposure less the (offsetting) put option exposure. We can create "synthetic" protective put positions by holding a quantity of stocks with the same net exposure to market swings as the hypothetical protective put position. The key to this strategy is the option's delta or hedge ratio, that is, the change in the price of the protective put option per change in the value of the underlying stock portfolio.

An example will clarify the procedure. Suppose that a portfolio is currently valued at $100 million. An at-the-money put option on the portfolio might have a hedge ratio or delta of −.6, meaning that the option's value swings $.60 for every dollar change in portfolio value, but in an opposite direction. Suppose the stock portfolio falls in value by 2 percent. The profit on a hypothetical protective put position (if the put existed) would be as follows (in millions of dollars):

| | |
|---|---|
| Loss on stocks: 2% of $100 | = $2.00 |
| Gain on put: .6 × $2 | = $1.20 |
| Net loss: | = $ .80 |

We create the synthetic option position by selling a proportion of shares equal to the put option's delta (that is, selling 60 percent of the shares), and placing the proceeds in risk-free T-bills. The rationale is that the hypothetical put option would have offset 60 percent of any change in the stock portfolio's value, so one must reduce portfolio risk directly by selling off 60 percent of the equity and putting the proceeds into a risk-free asset. Total return on a synthetic protective put position with $60 million in risk-free investments, such as T-bills, and $40 million in equity is

**Figure 21.8**
Hedge ratios change as the stock price fluctuates.

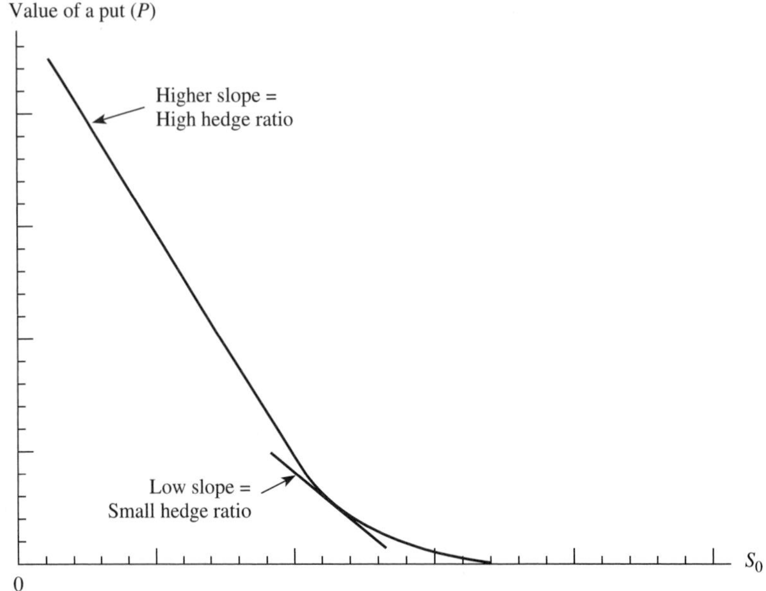


| | | |
|---|---|---|
| Loss on stocks: 2% of \$40 | = | \$.80 |
| Loss on bills: | = | 0 |
| Net loss: | = | \$.80 |

The synthetic and actual protective put positions have equal returns. We conclude that if you sell a proportion of shares equal to the put option's delta and place the proceeds in cash equivalents, your exposure to the stock market will equal that of the desired protective put position.

The difficulty with this procedure is that deltas constantly change. Figure 21.8 shows that, as the stock price falls, the magnitude of the appropriate hedge ratio increases. Therefore, market declines require extra hedging, that is, additional conversions of equity into cash. This constant updating of the hedge ratio is called **dynamic hedging.**

Dynamic hedging is one reason portfolio insurance has been said to contribute to market volatility. Market declines trigger additional sales of stock as portfolio insurers strive to increase their hedging. These additional sales are seen as reinforcing or exaggerating market downturns.

In practice, portfolio insurers do not actually buy or sell stocks directly when they update their hedge positions. Instead, they minimize trading costs by buying or selling stock index futures as a substitute for sale of the stocks themselves. As you will see in the following chapter, stock prices and index futures prices usually are very tightly linked by cross-market arbitrageurs so that futures transactions can be used as reliable proxies for stock transactions. Instead of selling equities based on the put option's delta, insurers will sell an equivalent number of futures contracts.[7]

Several U.S. portfolio insurers suffered great setbacks on October 19, 1987, when the Dow Jones Industrial Average fell by more than 500 points. We can describe what happened then so you can appreciate the complexities of applying a seemingly straightforward hedging concept:

1. Market volatility was much greater than ever encountered before. Put option deltas based on historical experience were too low, and insurers underhedged, held too much equity, and suffered excessive losses.
2. Prices moved so fast that insurers could not keep up with the necessary rebalancing. They were chasing deltas that kept getting away from them. In addition, the futures market saw a "gap" opening, where the opening price was nearly 10 percent below the previous day's close. The price dropped before insurers could update their hedge ratios.
3. Execution problems were severe. First, current market prices were unavailable, with the trade execution and price quotation system hours behind, which made computation of correct hedge ratios impossible. Moreover, trading in stocks and stock futures ceased altogether during some periods. The continuous rebalancing capability that is essential for a viable insurance program simply vanished during the precipitous market collapse.
4. Futures prices traded at steep discounts to their proper levels compared to reported stock prices, thereby making the sale of futures (as a proxy for equity sales) to increase hedging seem expensive. Although we will see in the next chapter that stock index futures prices normally exceed the value of the stock index, on October 19, 1987, futures sold far below the stock index level. The so-called cash-to-futures spread was negative most of the day. When some insurers gambled that the futures price would recover to its usual premium over the stock index and chose to defer sales, they remained underhedged. As the market fell further, their portfolios experienced substantial losses.

Although most observers believe that the portfolio insurance industry will never recover from the market crash, delta hedging is still alive and well in Wall Street in the mid-1990s. Dynamic hedges are widely used by large firms to hedge potential losses from the options they write. These traders are, however, increasingly aware of the practical difficulties in implementing dynamic hedges in very volatile markets. For instance, direct, rather than synthetic option strategies now appear more attractive. Today long-term index options called LEAPS (for long-term equity anticipation securities) trade on the CBOE with maturities of a few years. These long-term options also are traded in Canada, although only for some stocks, and not for indices.

---

[7] Notice, however, that the use of index futures reintroduces the problem of tracking error between the portfolio and the market index.

In Canada, portfolio insurance was until very recently virtually nonexistent. There are too few derivative instruments and too little liquidity in the markets to allow efficient dynamic hedging of Canadian stock portfolios. Nonetheless, the situation appears to be changing, and several derivative instruments suitable for hedging purposes are offered over-the-counter to portfolio managers. The accompanying box documents the increasing use of derivatives by Canadian pension fund managers and explores some of the reasons for the lags in their adoption relative to their U.S. counterparts.

## 21.5 BINOMIAL OPTION PRICING

### Two-State Option Pricing

A complete understanding of the Black-Scholes formula is difficult without a substantial mathematics background. Nevertheless, we can develop valuable insight into option valuation by considering a particularly simple special case. Assume that a stock price can take only two possible values at option expiration: The stock will either increase to a given higher price or decrease to a given lower price. Although this may seem an extreme simplification, it allows us to come closer to understanding more complicated and seemingly more realistic models. Moreover, we can extend this approach to accept far more reasonable specifications of stock price behaviour. In fact, several major financial firms employ variants of this simple model to value options and securities with option-like features.

Suppose that the stock currently sells at $100 and that by year-end the price either will double to $200 or be cut in half to $50. A call option on the stock might specify an exercise price of $125 and a time to expiration of one year. Suppose the interest rate is 8 percent. At year-end, the payoff to the holder of the call option either will be zero if the stock falls or $75 if the stock price goes to $200.

Compare this payoff to that of a portfolio consisting of one share of the stock and borrowing of $46.30 at the interest rate of 8 percent. The payoff to this portfolio also depends on the stock price at year-end:

| | | |
|---|---|---|
| Value of stock | $50 | $200 |
| −Repayment of loan with interest | −$50 | −$ 50 |
| Total | $ 0 | $150 |

The payoff of this portfolio is exactly twice the option value regardless of the stock price. In other words, two call options will exactly replicate the payoff to the portfolio; two call options, therefore, should have the same price as the cost of establishing the portfolio. We know the cost of establishing the portfolio is $100 for the stock, less the $46.30 proceeds from borrowing. Hence, the two calls should sell at

$$2C = \$100 - \$46.30$$

## From Suspicion to Optimism

Derivatives are viewed with either suspicion or optimism by Canadian pension plan sponsors. Suspicious sponsors view derivatives as speculative instruments and steer well clear of derivative-based strategies. Optimistic sponsors see derivatives as prudent risk management tools and increasingly embrace their use. While the majority of sponsors would probably list themselves under the former rubric, the number of Canadian pension plans using derivatives has increased significantly since 1990—albeit the absolute number is still small.

Hard data on derivative use by Canadian pension plans is limited and often only anecdotal, but it is clear that derivative use is growing rapidly: Using *Benefits Canada*'s annual pension fund survey, the number of plans reporting derivative use increased from 18 in 1990 to 48 in 1993, a 166 percent increase over four years (Table 1). The survey also indicated that derivatives are increasingly used to provide foreign exposure. In 1990, seven plans reported using derivatives for foreign exposure and in 1993 the number had risen to 17, an increase of 142 percent.

Because the *Benefits Canada* survey is voluntary and covers only Canada's largest pension plans, it may underestimate the true growth of derivative use. For example, additional data collected by Frank Russell Canada (FRC) reveal that the number of Canadian pension plans using derivatives for foreign exposure actually increased from seven in 1990 to at least 31 in 1993. This is a 400 percent increase over four years, or more than twice the growth rate suggested by the *Benefits Canada* survey. The larger estimate better represents the growth in derivative use by Canadian pension plans, with the caveats that high growth rate is a function of the small starting base and that the absolute number of plans using derivatives is still small.

**Figure 1** Daily Futures Volume

The value of futures contracts compared to the value of actual stocks and bonds traded for seven countries

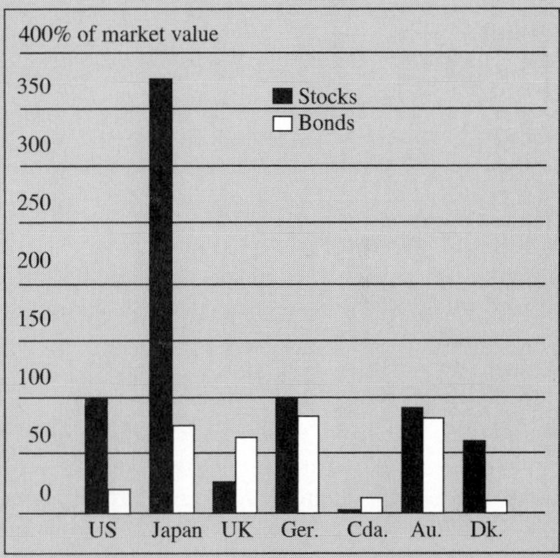


Source: First Quadrant, based on 4 months ending Dec. 31, 1993.

### Barriers To Derivatives Use

While derivatives are increasingly used by Canadian pension plans, they are underused relative to non-pension financial institutions such as banks, brokerage firms, and insurance companies. Canada's experience is not unique. Even the U.S. pension industry underuses derivatives, albeit to a lesser extent. This has led more than one derivative advocate to ask: "If derivatives are so great, why don't more pension plans use them?"

There is a threefold response to this rhetorical question. First, many of the derivatives that are useful to pension plans are still relatively new and it takes time for new products to be accepted. This is especially true of an industry that manages other people's retirement money under regulatory and plan member scrutiny.

(Continued)

**Table 1 Derivatives' Growth**

| | 1990 | 1991 | 1992 | 1993 | Growth 1990–93 |
|---|---|---|---|---|---|
| Number of plans using derivatives* | 18 | 40 | 36 | 48 | 166% |
| Percent using derivatives | 22 | 50 | 36 | 40 | |
| Number of plans using derivatives for foreign exposure | 7 | 11 | 13 | 17 | 142% |

*In 1990–91 there were 80 respondents to Benefits Canada's survey, in 1992, 100 respondents, and in 1993, there were 120 respondents. Source: Benefits Canada.

Second, derivative strategies can appear complicated to the uninitiated which produces a "space shuttle" syndrome in the minds of many sponsors. "It's an engineering marvel, but you're not going to get me to go for a ride." The syndrome is regularly reinforced by negative articles in the media. For example, the lead article in the March 7, 1994 issue of *Fortune* magazine was titled "The risk that won't go away" and had the attention grabbing subtitle "Like alligators in a swamp, derivatives lurk in the global economy; even CEOs of companies that use them don't understand them."

Finally, there is the cultural gap between traditional "Graham and Dodd" investors that tend to be well represented on pension investment committees and the quantitative "financial engineers" that design, advocate, and implement derivative-based strategies. The opinion of many traditional investors was colourfully expressed by Alan Abelson of *Barron's* in a recent article: "Stocks and bonds are instruments; derivatives are instruments of the devil (and even he doesn't always understand them)."

Canadian pension plans that are using derivatives tend to use non-Canadian derivatives which has hindered the development of Canada's derivative markets. The Toronto 35 futures contract trades at only 3 percent of the value of stock trading in Canada. This compares with 100 percent for the S&P 500 contract in the U.S., and a remarkable 380 percent for the Nikkei in Japan. Even in Australia, which is a resource-based economy like Canada, the All Ordinaries futures contract trades at 90 percent of the value of Australian stock trading. Canada's long bond contract trades at a higher 18 percent of the bond market value, but this percentage is still low relative to fixed-income futures contracts in other countries, other than Denmark.

Six reasons are often cited to explain why domestic derivatives are so little used by Canadian pension plans. First, established Canadian investment counseling firms have little incentive to commit the time and resources needed to learn and use derivatives. Second, in-house managers among most of Canada's largest pension plans have, until very recently, shown little interest in learning and using derivatives.

Third, the status of derivatives as permissible pension investments has been uncertain. However, the move to "prudent portfolio" from "legal list" regulation has removed this concern.

Fourth, the derivative strategies that have most appealed to Canadian plan sponsors are those strategies which increase exposure to non-Canadian investments. This means using non-Canadian derivatives.

Fifth, neither the current Toronto 35 futures contract nor its TSE 300 antecedent closely tracked the composition of the Canadian stock portfolios of most pension plans. The introduction of a TSE 100 futures contract should remove this limitation. Finally, the continued illiquidity of Canada's derivative markets makes pricing inefficient and, by implica-

**Table 2 The Choices** (Derivative Strategies Currently Marketed to Pension Funds in Canada)

| | |
|---|---|
| • Equitizing cash | • Collars |
| • Securitizing cash | • Alpha transfer |
| • Tactical asset allocation | • Passive currency hedging |
| • Portfolio insurance | • Active currency hedging |
| • Bond/Call | • Synthetic equity |
| • Interest rate swaps | • Synthetic bonds |
| • Equity swaps | • Market neutral |
| • Arbitrage | • Duration management |

*(Continued)*

tion, makes effective hedging, speculation, and arbitrage difficult. Canadian pension funds employing derivative strategies to manage the risk profile of portfolios of Canadian securities may use U.S. exchange-traded derivatives because of their high liquidity or the OTC market because of its flexibility.

Because pension money is nervous money, Canadian pension sponsors have been slow to embrace derivative strategies. But this is changing as the advantages of derivatives become more apparent. The rapid growth in derivative use since 1990 foreshadows even more rapid growth in the future, manifested not only in the number of plans using derivatives, but also the dollar value of underlying assets to which derivatives are applied. It will not be all smooth sailing. One can expect the advance to be stalled by a future horror story about some pension plan's derivative strategy that went wrong. But after the dust settles, the advantages of derivatives will still be obvious and the advance will continue.

John Ilkiw, *Canadian Investment Review*, Summer 1994, pp. 19–21. Reprinted by permission.

or each call should sell at $C$ = \$26.85. Thus, given the stock price, exercise price, interest rate, and volatility of the stock price (as represented by the magnitude of the up or down movements), we can derive the fair value for the call option.

This valuation approach relies heavily on the notion of replication. With only two possible end-of-year values of the stock, the returns to the leveraged stock portfolio replicate the returns to the call option and therefore command the same market price. This notion of replication is behind most option pricing formulas. For more complex price distributions for stocks, the replication technique is correspondingly more complex, but the principles remain the same.

One way to view the role of replication is to note that, using the numbers assumed for this example, a portfolio made up of one share of stock and two call options written is perfectly hedged. Its year-end value is independent of the ultimate stock price:

| | | |
|---|---|---|
| Stock value | \$50 | \$200 |
| −Obligations from two calls written | − 0 | −\$150 |
| Net payoff | \$50 | \$ 50 |

The investor has formed a risk-free portfolio, with a payout of \$50. Its value must be the present value of \$50, or \$50/1.08 = \$46.30. The value of the portfolio, which equals \$100 from the stock held long, minus 2$C$ from the two calls written, should equal \$46.30. Hence, \$100 − 2$C$ = \$46.30, or $C$ = \$26.85.

The ability to create a perfect hedge is the key to this argument. The hedge guarantees the end-of-year payout, which can be discounted using the risk-free interest rate. To find the value of the option in terms of the value of the stock, we do not need to know the option's or the stock's beta or expected rate of return. (Recall that this also was true of Black-Scholes option valuation.) The perfect hedging, or replication, approach enables us to express the value of the option in terms of the current value of the stock without this information. With a hedged position the final stock price does not affect the investor's payoff, so the stock's risk-and-return parameters have no bearing.

The hedge ratio of this example is one share of stock to two calls, or one half. For every option written, one-half share of stock must be held in the portfolio to hedge away risk. This ratio has an easy interpretation in this context: It is the ratio of the range of the values of the option to those of the stock across the two possible outcomes. The option is worth either zero or \$75, for a range of \$75. The stock is worth either \$50 or \$200, for a range of \$150. The ratio of ranges, 75/150, is one half, which is the hedge ratio we have established.

The hedge ratio equals the ratio of ranges because the option and stock are perfectly correlated in this two-state example. When the returns of the option and stock are perfectly correlated, a perfect hedge requires that option and stock be held in a fraction determined only by relative volatility.

The generalization of the hedge ratio for the other two-state option problems is

$$H = \frac{C^+ - C^-}{S^+ - S^-}$$

where $C^+$ and $C^-$ refer to the call option's value when the stock goes up or down, respectively, and $S^+$ and $S^-$ are the stock prices in the two states. The hedge ratio, $H$, is thus the ratio of the swings in the possible end-of-period values of the option and the stock. If the investor writes one option and holds $H$ shares of stock, the value of the portfolio will be unaffected by the stock price. In this case, option pricing is easy: Simply set the value of the hedged portfolio equal to the present value of the known payoff.

---

**CONCEPT CHECK** Question 6. Intuitively, would you expect the hedge ratio to be higher or lower when the call option is more in the money? (You can confirm your intuition in problem 3 at the end of the chapter.)

---

Using our example, the option pricing technique would proceed as follows:

1. Given the possible end-of-year stock prices, $S^+ = 200$ and $S^- = 50$, and the exercise price of \$125, calculate that $C^+ = 75$ and $C^- = 0$. The stock price range is thus \$150, while the option price range is \$75.
2. Find that the hedge ratio is $75/150 = .5$.
3. Find that a portfolio made up of .5 shares with one written option would have an end-of-year value of \$25 with certainty.
4. Show that the present value of \$25 with a one-year interest rate of 8 percent is \$23.15.
5. Set the value of the hedged position to the present value of the certain payoff:

$$.5S_0 - C_0 = 23.15$$
$$\$50 - C_0 = \$23.15$$

**6.** Solve for the call's value, $C_0 = \$26.85$.

What if the option were overpriced, perhaps selling for \$30? Then you can make arbitrage profits. Here is how:

| | Initial Cash Flow | CF in 1 Year for Each Possible Stock Price | |
|---|---|---|---|
| | | $S = 50$ | $S = 200$ |
| 1. Write two options | 60 | 0 | −150 |
| 2. Purchase one share | −100 | 50 | 200 |
| 3. Borrow \$40 at 8% interest, and repay in 1 year | 40 | −43.20 | −43.20 |
| Total | 0 | 6.80 | 6.80 |

Although the net initial investment is zero, the payoff in one year is positive and riskless. If the option were underpriced, one would simply reverse this arbitrage strategy: Buy the option, and shortsell the stock to eliminate price risk. Note, by the way, that the present value of the profit to the arbitrage strategy above exactly equals twice the amount by which the option is overpriced. The present value of the risk-free profit of \$6.80 at an 8 percent interest rate is \$6.30. With two options written in this strategy, this translates to a profit of \$3.15 per option, exactly the amount by which the option was overpriced: \$30 versus the "fair value" of \$26.85.

**CONCEPT CHECK** Question 7. Suppose the call option in the above example had been underpriced, selling at \$24. Formulate the arbitrage strategy to exploit the mispricing, and show that it provides a riskless cash flow in one year of \$3.08 per option purchased.

## Generalizing the Two-State Approach

Although the two-state stock price model seems simplistic, we can generalize it to incorporate more realistic assumptions. To start, suppose that we were to break up the year into two six-month segments, and then assert that over each half-year segment the stock price could take on two values. In this case we will say it can increase 10 percent or decrease 5 percent. A stock initially selling at 100 could follow these possible paths over the course of the year:

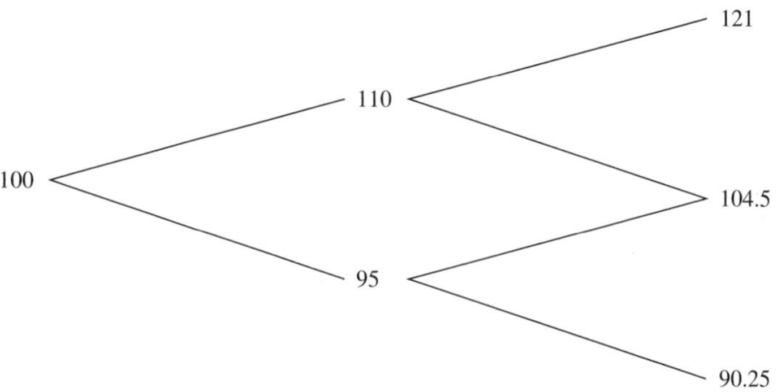


The midrange value of 104.5 can be attained by two paths: an increase of 10 percent followed by a decrease of 5 percent, or a decrease of 5 percent followed by a 10 percent increase.

There are now three possible end-of-year values for the stock and three for the option.

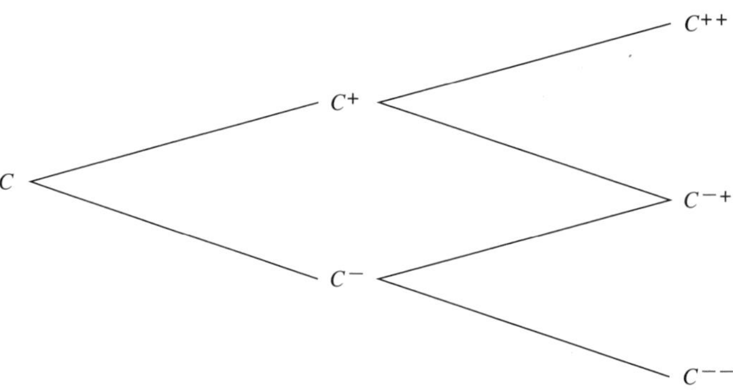


Using methods similar to those we followed above, we could value $C^+$ from knowledge of $C^{++}$ and $C^{+-}$, then value $C^-$ from knowledge of $C^{-+}$ and $C^{--}$, and finally value $C$ from knowledge of $C^+$ and $C^-$. There is no reason to stop at six-month intervals. We could next break up the year into 4 three-month units, or 12 one-month units, or 365 one-day units, each of which would be posited to have a two-state process. Although the calculations become quite numerous and correspondingly tedious, they are easy to program into a computer, and such computer programs are used widely by participants in the securities market.

As we break the year into progressively finer subintervals, the range of possible year-end stock prices expands and, in fact, will ultimately take on a lognormal distribution.[8] This can be seen from an analysis of the event tree for the stock for a period with three subintervals:

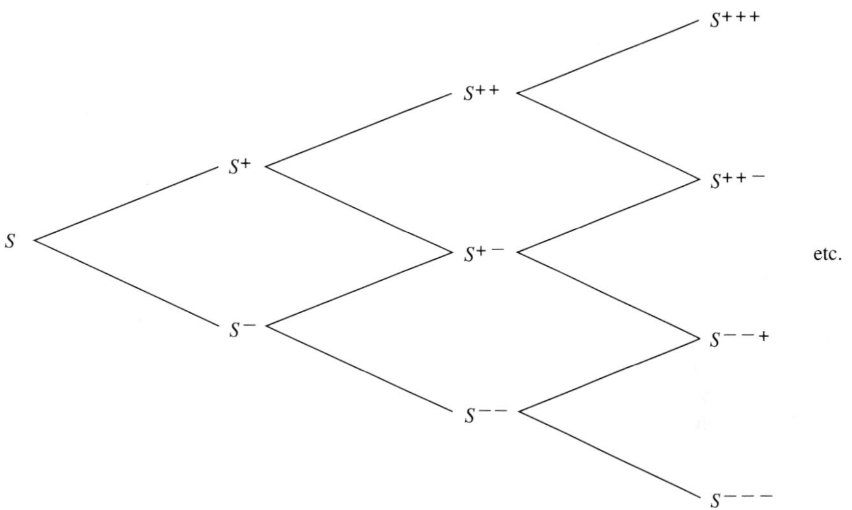


First, notice that as the number of subintervals increases, the number of possible stock prices also increases. Second, notice that extreme events such as $S^{+++}$ or $S^{---}$ are relatively rare, since they require either three consecutive increases or decreases in the three subintervals. More moderate, or midrange results such as $S^{++-}$ can be arrived at by more than one path—any combination of two price increases and one decrease will result in stock price $S^{++-}$. Thus the midrange values will be more likely, and the stock price distribution will acquire the familiar bell-shaped pattern discussed in Chapter 5. The probability of each outcome is described by the binomial distribution, and this multiperiod approach to option pricing is therefore called the binomial model.

For example, using our initial stock price of $100, equal probability of stock price increases or decreases, and three intervals for which the possible price increase is 5 percent and the possible price decrease is 3 percent, we would obtain the probability distribution of stock prices from the following calculations. There are eight possible combinations for the stock price movements in the three periods: $+++$, $++-$, $+-+$, $-++$, $+--$, $-+-$, $--+$, $---$. Each has

[8] Actually, more complex considerations enter here. The limit of this process is lognormal only if we assume also that stock prices move continuously, by which we mean that over small time intervals only small price movements can occur. This rules out rare events such as sudden, extreme price moves in response to dramatic information (like a takeover attempt). For a treatment of this type of "jump process," see John C. Cox and Stephen A. Ross, "The Valuation of Options for Alternative Stochastic Processes," *Journal of Financial Economics* 3 (January–March 1976); or Robert C. Merton, "Option Pricing When Underlying Stock Returns Are Discontinuous," *Journal of Financial Economics* 3 (January–March 1976).

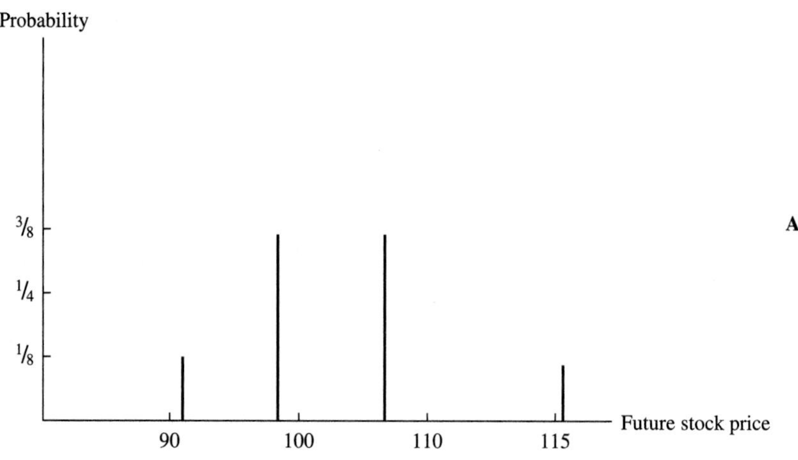


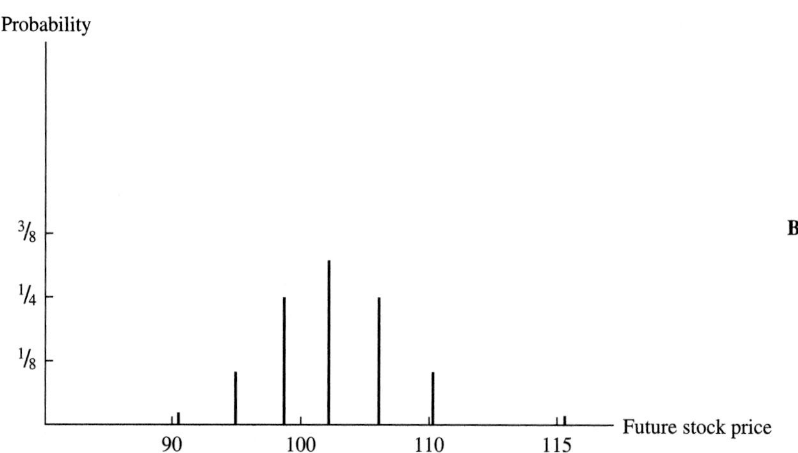


**Figure 21.9** Probability distributions. **A**—Possible outcomes and associated probabilities for stock prices after three periods. The stock price starts at \$100, and in each period it can increase by 5% or decrease by 3%. **B**—Each period is subdivided into two smaller subperiods. Now there are six periods, and in each of these the stock price can increase by 2.5% or fall by 1.5%. Notice that as the number of periods increases the stock price distribution approaches the familiar bell-shaped curve.

probability of ⅛. Therefore the probability distribution of stock prices at the end of the last interval would be as follows:

| Event | Probability | Stock Price |
|---|---|---|
| 3 up movements | ⅛ | $100 \times 1.05^3 = 115.76$ |
| 2 up and 1 down | ⅜ | $100 \times 1.05^2 \times .97 = 106.94$ |
| 1 up and 2 down | ⅜ | $100 \times 1.05 \times .97^2 = 98.79$ |
| 3 down movements | ⅛ | $100 \times .97^3 = 91.27$ |

The midrange values are three times as likely to occur as the extreme values. Figure 21.9**A** is a graph of the frequency distribution for this example. Notice that the graph is beginning to take on the familiar appearance of the bell-shaped curve. In fact, as the number of intervals increases, as in Figure 21.9**B** the frequency distribution progressively approaches the lognormal distribution rather than the normal distribution. (Recall our discussion in the appendix to Chapter 5 on why the lognormal distribution is superior to the normal as a means of modeling stock prices.)

Suppose that we were to continue subdividing the interval in which stock prices are posited to move up or down. Eventually, each node of the event tree would correspond to an infinitesimally small time interval. The possible stock price movement within that time interval would be correspondingly small. As those many intervals pass, the end-of-period stock price would more and more closely resemble a lognormal distribution. Thus the apparent oversimplification of the two-state model can be overcome by progressively subdividing any period into many subperiods.

At any node, one still could set up a portfolio that would be perfectly hedged over the next tiny time interval. Then, at the end of that interval, upon reaching the next node, a new hedge ratio could be computed and the portfolio composition could be revised to remain hedged over the coming small interval. By continuously revising the hedge position, the portfolio would remain hedged and would earn a risk-free rate of return over each interval. This is dynamic hedging, which calls for continued updating of the hedge ratio as time passes. In fact, Black and Scholes used a dynamic hedge approach to derive their option valuation formula, and you saw in our discussion of portfolio insurance that a dynamic hedge strategy is required for the stock plus bills portfolio to replicate the payoff to a protective put.

## 21.6 Multinomial Option Pricing

### Complete and Incomplete Markets

The binomial model described in the previous section assumes that in every subinterval the stock price can take exactly two possible values, up or down by given amounts. We saw that in such a model it is possible to replicate the option with a portfolio containing exactly two assets, the stock and a riskless loan at the prevailing rate of interest. This correspondence of available assets and possible stock values in every subinterval is crucial to the use of the model for option pricing.

Consider again the example of the previous section, where a stock that sells at \$100 can by year-end either double to \$200 or be cut in half to \$50. Now, however, suppose that there is also a third possibility, that the stock keeps the original price of \$100. If the interest rate is 8 percent, can we still use the replication method to value the option with exercise price of \$125 and one year time to expiration?

The answer to this question is no. At year-end, the option payoff is either zero if the stock falls or stays the same or \$75 if it rises. The portfolio that we examined in the previous section, with one share of the stock and borrowing of \$46.30 at 8 percent, now yields the following contingent payoffs:

| | | | |
|---|---|---|---|
| Value of stock | \$50 | \$100 | \$200 |
| Repayment of loan with interest | −50 | −50 | −50 |
| Total | \$ 0 | \$ 50 | \$150 |

The holder of this portfolio would get twice the option value when the stock goes up or down, *plus* \$50 whenever the stock stays the same. Hence, the value of the portfolio can no longer be equal to twice that of the option, since it is clearly greater.

In fact, it can be shown that there is no portfolio involving only the stock and borrowed funds capable of replicating this option. Suppose that a replicating portfolio contains $x$ shares and \$$y$ of borrowed funds. Its future value must be equal to that of the option for all possible values of the stock. This means that:

$$50x - 1.08y = 0,\ 100x - 1.08y = 0,\ 200x - 1.08y = 75$$

This system has no solution, since it has three equations and only two unknowns. This implies that there is no portfolio capable of replicating the option. The reason for this is that there are more possible future values of the stock than there are assets to form a replicating portfolio.

In the binomial model, there are only two future "states of the world" as far as the stock price is concerned. In our example, the stock can only go down to \$50 (state 1), or up to \$200 (state 2). Suppose also that we have two assets, also numbered 1 and 2, each one of them yielding a payoff equal to \$1 if the corresponding state occurs, and 0 otherwise; their respective values are $v_1$ and $v_2$. These assets are known as *elementary* or *primitive* securities, and they are a very convenient analytical tool in valuing options or other derivative assets.

With these elementary assets we now can replicate every other asset in our binomial model. Thus, the stock is equivalent to a portfolio of 50 units of asset 1 and 200 units of asset 2, and any riskless investment corresponds to portfolios having equal numbers of units of assets 1 and 2. This helps us determine the two elementary assets' values, $v_1$ and $v_2$:

$$50v_1 + 200v_2 = 100$$
$$v_1 + v_2 = 1/1.08$$

Solving this system, we find $v_1 = 0.5679$, and $v_2 = 0.358$. With these prices it is now very easy to price the option with exercise price \$125: It is simply equal to $75v_2 = 75 \times 0.358 = 26.85$, which is the value found in the previous section.

We now can see why the notion of replication can be applied to the binomial model but breaks down when there is a third "state of the world." In such a case we have three elementary assets, each one paying \$1 when the corresponding state of the world occurs, and zero otherwise. Let us number them 1, 2, and 3, corresponding to the ascending order of future stock price, and denote their corresponding values by $v_1$, $v_2$, and $v_3$; then one share would be equivalent to a portfolio of 50 units of asset 1, 100 units of asset 2, and 200 units of asset 3. However, we now have only *two* equations to determine the three unknown elementary asset values $v_1$, $v_2$, and $v_3$:

$$50v_1 + 100v_2 + 200v_3 = 100$$
$$v_1 + v_2 + v_3 = 1/1.08 \quad \textbf{(21.3)}$$

Here, the observable stock price and rate of interest are insufficient to give us unique values of the three elementary assets. There are more states of the world (and, hence, elementary assets) than there are observable assets. This indeterminacy is the mirror image of the impossibility to find a portfolio replicating a given option.

A market that has as many independent observable assets as there are future states of the world is said to be *complete.* By contrast, **incomplete markets** are those that have fewer such assets than there are states of the world; real-world markets generally are assumed to be incomplete.[9] The binomial model is the only complete market model if our states of the world are classified by a stock's future payoffs and if we observe only the optioned stock and the riskless rate of interest.

## Generalizing the Binomial Option Pricing Model

A unique set of elementary asset values consistent with the observed stock price and rate of interest does not exist in incomplete markets. Consequently, a unique option price cannot be derived by the replication method. For instance, there are infinitely many values of $v_3$, the elementary asset that pays $1 when the stock goes up and zero otherwise, that satisfy the two equations of Equation 21.3 corresponding to the stock price and rate of interest. Each one of these $v_3$ values would yield a different value of the option with exercise price equal to $125, since the option's payoff is zero in all other states of the world.

This indeterminacy is rather disturbing, given that a stock price model with three (or more) states is otherwise very similar to the two-state model. In both types of models we can subdivide the year into progressively finer subintervals, approaching at the limit *the same* lognormal distribution. For such a distribution, the appropriate option value is given by the Black-Scholes formula. Do all admissible option values, derived from the values of $v_3$ satisfying the two equations in Equation 21.3 similarly approach the Black-Scholes option price at the limit?

The answer is again no. While there are infinitely many option values consistent with the observed stock price and rate of interest, only a given subset of them, contained between an upper and a lower bound, converge at the limit to the Black-Scholes option value. This set of option values constitutes, therefore, the appropriate generalization of the binomial model when the number of possible future stock prices exceeds two.

The two bounds that define the appropriate option values depend not only on the size of the future stock prices, but also on their probabilities. Suppose, for instance, that in our previous example the stock price either could double or be

[9] See the remarks in W. Sharpe, *Investments,* 2d edition (Englewood Cliffs, N.J.: Prentice Hall, 1988), pp. 99–101.

cut in half, each with probability equal to ¼, and could stay the same with probability equal to ½. The expected value of the stock price would be equal to

$$.25 \times 50 + .5 \times 100 + .25 \times 200 = 112.5$$

This corresponds to a return of 12.5 percent, which is higher than the rate on interest of 8 percent. For stock price distributions with expected returns higher than the rate of interest, it can be shown that upper and lower bounds on the admissible option values are equal to the expected present values of the call payoff with the expectations taken over transformed[10] stock price distributions. In this example, the transformed probabilities for the upper bound are .304, .464, and .232 for stock prices of 50, 100, and 200, respectively; they give an upper bound equal to 75 × .232/1.08 = \$16.11. The corresponding transformed probabilities for the lower bound are .263, .526, and .211, yielding a lower bound equal to 75 × .211/1.08 = \$15.86.

Thus, option prices with an exercise price of \$125 must lie between \$15.86 and \$16.11 in this three-state option pricing model. As we subdivide the time period into increasingly finer partitions, the distance between the two bounds tends to decrease. At the limit, both bounds become equal to the Black-Scholes option value.

## 21.7 Empirical Evidence

There have been an enormous number of empirical tests of the option pricing model. For the most part, the results of the studies have been positive in that the Black-Scholes model generates option values fairly close to the actual prices at which options trade. At the same time, some regular empirical failures of the model have been noted. Geske and Roll[11] have argued that these empirical results can be attributed to the failure of the Black-Scholes model to account for the possible early exercise of American calls on stocks that pay dividends. Indeed, they show that the theoretical bias induced by this failure exactly corresponds to the actual "mispricing" observed empirically.

Whaley[12] examines the performance of the Black-Scholes formula relative to that of the pseudo-American and true American option formulas. His findings also indicate that formulas that allow for the possibility of early exercise do better at

[10] Let $p_1$, $p_2$, and $p_3$ denote the three probabilities corresponding to the down, stay-the-same, and up states, respectively. Then for the upper bound the probabilities are transformed into $p_1 = Q + (1 - Q)p_1$, $p_2 = (1 - Q)p_2$, $p_3 = (1 - Q)p_3$, where $Q$ is equal to (112.5 − 108)/(112.5 − 50) in our example, the ratio of the difference between the expected future stock price and the rate of interest, to the difference between the expected stock price and the lowest possible stock value. The transformation for the lower bound is slightly more complicated. See S. Perrakis, "Preference-Free Option Prices When the Stock Return Can Go Up, Go Down, or Stay the Same," *Advances in Futures and Options Research,* 1988.

[11] Robert Geske and Richard Roll, "On Valuing American Call Options with the Black-Scholes European Formula," *Journal of Finance* 39 (June 1984).

[12] Robert E. Whaley, "Valuation of American Call Options on Dividend-Paying Stocks: Empirical Tests," *Journal of Financial Economics* 10 (1982).

pricing than does the Black-Scholes formula. Whaley's results indicate that the Black-Scholes formula performs worst for options on stocks with high dividend payouts. The true American call option formula, on the other hand, seems to fare equally well in the prediction of option prices on stocks with high or low dividend payouts.

A more skeptical view of the Black-Scholes formula or, indeed, of any other option pricing formula presented in the literature, comes out of the tests performed by Rubinstein.[13] He has found that all formulas exhibit systematic biases in their predictions, in terms of both the exercise price and the time to expiration of the options. Fortunately these biases are not, in most cases, sufficiently large to have major economic consequences for option holders using the Black-Scholes formulas as if it were the true option value.

More recently, however, Rubinstein[14] has pointed out that the performance of the Black-Scholes model has deteriorated in recent years in the sense that options on the same stock with the same strike price which *should* have the same implied volatility actually exhibit progressively different implied volatilities. He attributes this to an increasing fear of another market crash like that experienced in 1987, and notes that, consistent with this hypothesis, out-of-the-money put options are priced higher (that is, with higher implied volatilities) than other puts. He suggests a method to extend the option valuation framework to allow for these issues.

A different type of empirical test on option pricing examines whether the observed call option prices satisfy the general restrictions stated in the first section of this chapter. These restrictions are independent of any particular option pricing model. The major difficulty in carrying out the tests is the simultaneous observation of corresponding stock and option prices. A Canadian study by Halpern and Turnbull[15] examined whether traded stock and call option prices on the TSE, together with the prevailing rates of interest, did satisfy the appropriate conditions in 1978–1979. They found several violations of these restrictions, which should have allowed traders to realize riskless profits. There are, however, indications that these violations were due to the comparative novelty of option trading on the TSE and did not persist in more recent years.

## SUMMARY

**1.** Option values may be viewed as the sum of intrinsic value plus time or "volatility" value. The volatility value is the right to choose not to exercise if the stock price moves against the holder. Thus, option holders cannot lose more than the cost of the option regardless of stock price performance.

[13] M. Rubinstein, "Nonparametric Tests of Alternative Option Pricing Models Using All Reported Trades and Quotes on the 30 Most Active CBOE Option Classes from August 23, 1976, through August 31, 1978," *Journal of Finance* 40 (June 1985).

[14] Mark Rubinstein, "Implied Binomial Trees," *Journal of Finance* 49 (July 1994), pp. 771–818.

[15] Paul Halpern and Stuart Turnbull, "Empirical Tests of Boundary Conditions for Toronto Stock Exchange Options, *Journal of Finance* 40, no. 2 (June 1985).

**2.** Call options are more valuable when the exercise price is lower, when the stock price is higher, when the interest rate is higher, when the time to maturity is greater, when the stock's volatility is greater, and when dividends are lower.

**3.** Call options must sell for at least the stock price less the present value of the exercise price and dividends to be paid before maturity. This implies that a call option on a nondividend-paying stock may be sold for more than the proceeds from immediate exercise. Thus, European calls are worth as much as American calls on stocks that pay no dividends because the right to exercise the American call early has no value.

**4.** The Black-Scholes formula is valid for options on stocks that pay no dividends. Dividend adjustments may be adequate to price European calls on dividend-paying stocks, but the proper treatment of American calls on dividend-paying stocks requires more complex formulas.

**5.** Put options may be exercised early whether the stock pays dividends or not. Therefore, American puts generally are worth more than European puts.

**6.** European put values can be derived from the call value and the put-call parity relationship. This technique cannot be applied to American puts for which early exercise is a possibility.

**7.** The hedge ratio refers to the number of shares of stock required to hedge the price risk involved in writing one option. Hedge ratios are near zero for deep out-of-the-money call options, and approach 1 for deep in-the-money calls.

**8.** Although hedge ratios are less than 1, call options have elasticities greater than 1. The rate of return on a call (as opposed to the dollar return) responds more than one-for-one with stock price movements.

**9.** Portfolio insurance can be obtained by purchasing a protective put option on an equity position. When the appropriate put is not traded, portfolio insurance entails a dynamic hedge strategy in which a fraction of the equity portfolio equal to the desired put option's delta is sold and placed in risk-free securities.

**10.** Many commonly traded securities embody option characteristics. Examples of these securities are callable bonds, convertible bonds, and warrants. Other arrangements, such as collateralized loans and limited-liability borrowing, can be analyzed as conveying implicit options to one or more parties.

**11.** Options may be priced relative to the underlying stock price using a simple two-period, two-state pricing model. As the number of periods increases, we may approximate more realistic stock price distributions. The Black-Scholes formula may be seen as a limiting case of the binomial option model as the holding period is divided into progressively smaller subperiods.

**12.** The simple two-state pricing model is the only model where an exact option price can be derived from the stock and the rate of interest. If there are more than two possible stock prices, then only an upper and a lower bound on admissible option values can be defined. However, both bounds become, at the limit, equal to the Black-Scholes formula, as the holding period is subdivided into progressively finer subintervals.

## Key Terms

Intrinsic value
Black-Scholes pricing formula
Implied volatility
Hedge ratio
Delta
Option elasticity
Portfolio insurance
Dynamic hedging
Binomial model
Incomplete markets

## Selected Readings


*The breakthrough articles in option pricing are:*

Black, Fischer; and Myron Scholes. "The Pricing of Options and Corporate Liabilities." *Journal of Political Economy* 81 (May–June 1973).

Merton, Robert C. "Theory of Rational Option Pricing." *Bell Journal of Economics and Management Science* 4 (Spring 1973).

*Articles on portfolio insurance and replication strategies may be found in:*

McCallum, John S. "On Portfolio Insurance, the Stock Market Crash, and Avoiding a Repeat." *Business Quarterly* 53, no. 2 (Fall 1989).

The January–February 1988 edition of *Financial Analysts Journal* is devoted to issues surrounding portfolio insurance.

*Several applications of option-type analysis to various financial instruments are surveyed in:*

Hull, John; and Alan White. "An Overview of Contingent Claims Pricing," *Canadian Journal of Administrative Sciences* 5, no. 3 (September 1988).

*Other relevant references are:*

Bigger, Nahum; and John Hull. "The Valuation of Currency Options." *Financial Management* 12 (1993).

Boyle, Phelim; and Eric P. Kirzner. "Pricing Complex Options: Echo-Bay Ltd. Gold Purchase Warrants." *Canadian Journal of Administrative Sciences* 2, no. 4 (December 1985).

Hull, John; and Alan White. "Hedging the Risks from Writing Foreign Currency Options." *Journal of International Money and Finance,* June 1987.

Reich, Alan L. "Market Efficiency of IOCC Gold Options Traded on the Montreal Exchange." *International Options Journal* 1, no. 1 (Fall 1984).

*The two-state approach was first suggested in:*

Sharpe, William F. *Investments.* Englewood Cliffs, N.J.: Prentice Hall, 1978.

*The approach was developed more fully in:*

Cox, John C.; Stephen A. Ross; and Mark Rubinstein. "Option Pricing: A Simplified Approach." *Journal of Financial Economics* 7 (September 1979).

Rendleman, Richard J. Jr.; and Brit J. Bartter. "Two-State Option Pricing." *Journal of Finance* 34 (December 1979).

*The extension of the two-state option pricing was introduced in:*

Perrakis, Stylianos; and Peter Ryan. "Option Pricing Bounds in Discrete Time." *Journal of Finance* 39 (June 1984).

Ritchken, Peter. "On Option Pricing Bounds." *Journal of Finance* 40 (September 1985).

*The approach was developed more fully in:*

Perrakis, Stylianos. "Option Pricing Bounds in Discrete Time: Extensions and the Pricing of the American Put." *Journal of Business* 59 (February 1986).

Perrakis, Stylianos. "Preference-Free Option Pricing When the Stock Returns Can Go Up, Go Down, or Stay the Same." *Advances in Futures and Options Research* 3 (1988).

Ritchken, Peter; and S. Kuo. "Option Bounds with Finite Revision Opportunities." *Journal of Finance* 43 (June 1988).

*Empirical work in Canadian option markets is contained in:*

Halpern, Paul; and Stuart Turnbull. "Empirical Tests on Boundary Conditions for Toronto Stock Exchange Options." *Journal of Finance* 40, no. 3 (June 1985).

Mandron, Alix. "Some Empirical Evidence about Canadian Stock Options, Part I: Valuation; and Part II: Market Structure." *Canadian Journal of Administrative Sciences* 5, no. 2 (June 1988).

Gendron, Michel; Nabil Khoury; and Pierre Yourougou. "Probability of Price Reversal and Relative Noise in Stock and Option Markets." *The Journal of Financial Research* 17, no. 2 (Summer 1994).

Ramsey, John. "When is Delta Hedging Rational?"; and Masse, C.; J. Kushner; J. Hanrahun; and R. L. Welch. "The Effect of Option Introduction on the Risk and Return of Canadian Equity Securities for 1975–91." Both articles can be found in *Proceedings of the Annual Conference of the Administrative Sciences Association of Canada, Finance Division* 15, no. 1 (1994).

Gagnon, Louis; and Greg Lypny. "The Benefits of Dynamically Hedging the Toronto 35 Stock Index." *Canadian Journal of Administrative Sciences,* forthcoming (1995).

*The March 1994 issue of the* Canadian Journal of Administrative Sciences *is devoted to Canadian financial markets and institutions. The following articles in that issue contain empirical work on various aspects of Canadian options markets:*

Gagnon, Louis. "Empirical Investigation of the Canadian Government Bond Options Market."

Wei, Jason Z. "Market Efficiency: Experience with Nikkei Put Warrants."

Perrakis, Stylianos; and Peter J. Ryan. "Options on Thinly-Traded Stocks: Theory and Empirical Evidence."

## Problems

1. We showed in the text that the value of a call option increases with the volatility of the stock. Is this also true of put option values? Use the put-call parity theorem as well as a numerical example to prove your answer.
2. In each of the following questions, you are asked to compare two options with parameters as given. The risk-free interest rate for *all* cases should be assumed to be 6 percent. Assume the stocks on which these options are written pay no dividends.

*i.*

| Put | $T$ | $X$ | $\sigma$ | Price of Option |
|---|---|---|---|---|
| A | .5 | 50 | .20 | $10 |
| B | .5 | 50 | .25 | $10 |

Which put option is written on the stock with the lower price?

*a.* A
*b.* B
*c.* Not enough information

*ii.*

| Put | $T$ | $X$ | $\sigma$ | Price of Option |
|---|---|---|---|---|
| A | .5 | 50 | .2 | $10 |
| B | .5 | 50 | .2 | $12 |

Which put option must be written on the stock with the lower price?

*a.* A
*b.* B
*c.* Not enough information

*iii.*

| Call | $S$ | $X$ | $\sigma$ | Price of Option |
|---|---|---|---|---|
| A | 50 | 50 | .20 | $12 |
| B | 55 | 50 | .20 | $10 |

Which call option must have the lower time to maturity?

*a.* A
*b.* B
*c.* Not enough information

*iv.*

| Call | $T$ | $X$ | $S$ | Price of Option |
|---|---|---|---|---|
| A | .5 | 50 | 55 | $10 |
| B | .5 | 50 | 55 | $12 |

Which call option is written on the stock with higher volatility?

*a.* A
*b.* B
*c.* Not enough information

*v.*

| Call | $T$ | $X$ | $S$ | Price of Option |
|---|---|---|---|---|
| A | .5 | 50 | 55 | $10 |
| B | .5 | 55 | 55 | $ 7 |

Which call option is written on the stock with higher volatility?

*a.* A
*b.* B
*c.* Not enough information

3. Reconsider the determination of the hedge ratio in the two-state model (page 850), where we showed that one half share of stock would hedge one option. What is the hedge ratio at the following exercise prices: 115, 100, 75, 50, 25, 10? What do you conclude about the hedge ratio as the option becomes progressively more in the money?
4. Show that Black-Scholes call option hedge ratios also increase as the stock price increases. Consider a one-year option with exercise price $50 on a stock with annual standard deviation of 20 percent. The T-bill rate is 8 percent per year. Find $N(d_1)$ for stock prices $45, $50, and $55.
5. We will derive a two-state put option value in this problem. Data: $S_0 =$ 100; $X = 110$; and $1 + r = 1.1$. The two possibilities for $S_T$ are 130 and 80.
   *a.* Show that the range of $S$ is 50 while that of $P$ is 30 across the two states. What is the hedge ratio of the put?
   *b.* Form a portfolio of three shares of stock and five puts. What is the (nonrandom) payoff to this portfolio? What is the present value of the portfolio?
   *c.* Given that the stock currently is selling at $100, solve for the value of the put.
6. Calculate the value of the call option on the stock in problem (5) with an exercise price of $110. Verify that the put-call parity theorem is satisfied by your answers to problems (5) and (6). (Do not use continuous compounding to calculate the present value of $X$ in this example because we are using a two-state model here, not a continuous-time Black-Scholes model.)
7. Use the Black-Scholes formula to find the value of a call option on the following stock:

| | |
|---|---|
| Time to maturity | = 6 months |
| Standard deviation | = 50 percent per year |
| Exercise price | = 50 |
| Stock price | = 50 |
| Interest rate | = 10 percent |

8. Recalculate the value of the option in problem 7, successively substituting one of the changes below while keeping the other parameters as in problem (7):
   *a.* Time to maturity = 3 months
   *b.* Standard deviation = 25 percent per year
   *c.* Exercise price = $55
   *d.* Stock price = $55
   *e.* Interest rate = 15 percent
   Consider each scenario independently. Confirm that the option value changes in accordance with the prediction of Table 21.1.
9. A call option with $X = \$50$ on a stock currently priced at $S = \$55$ is selling for $10. Using a volatility estimate of $\sigma = .30$, you find that

$N(d_1) = .6$ and $N(d_2) = .5$. The risk-free interest rate is zero. Is the implied volatility based on the option price more or less than .30? Explain.

**10.** Would you expect a $1 increase in a call option's exercise price to lead to a decrease in the option's value of more or less than $1?

**11.** Is a put option on a high-beta stock worth more than one on a low-beta stock? The stocks have identical firm-specific risk.

**12.** All else being equal, is a call option on a stock with a lot of firm-specific risk worth more than one on a stock with little firm-specific risk? The betas of the two stocks are equal.

**13.** All else equal, will a call option with a high exercise price have a higher or lower hedge ratio than one with a low exercise price?

**14.** Should the rate of return of a call option on a long-term Treasury bond be more or less sensitive to changes in interest rates than the rate of return of the underlying bond?

**15.** If the stock price falls and the call price rises, then what has happened to the call option's implied volatility?

**16.** If the time to maturity falls and the put price rises, then what has happened to the put option's implied volatility?

**17.** According to the Black-Scholes formula, what will be the value of the hedge ratio of a call option as the stock price becomes infinitely large? Explain briefly.

**18.** According to the Black-Scholes formula, what will be the value of the hedge ratio of a put option for a very small exercise price?

**19.** The hedge ratio of an at-the-money call option on IBM is 0.4. The hedge ratio of an at-the-money put option is −0.5. What is the hedge ratio of an at-the-money straddle position on IBM?

**20.** A collar is established by buying a share of stock for $50, buying a six-month put option with exercise price $45, and writing a six-month call option with exercise price $55. Based on the volatility of the stock, you calculate that for a strike price of $45 and maturity of six months, $N(d_1) = .60$, while for the exercise price of $55, $N(d_1) = .35$.

*a.* What will be the gain or loss on the collar if the stock price increases by $1?

*b.* What happens to the delta of the portfolio if the stock price becomes very large? Very small?

**21.** These three put options all are written on the same stock. One has a delta of −.9, one a delta of −.5, and one a delta of −.1. Assign deltas to the three puts by filling in this table.

| Put | *X* | Delta |
|---|---|---|
| A | 10 | |
| B | 20 | |
| C | 30 | |

**22.** You are *very* bullish (optimistic) on stock EFG, much more so than the rest of the market. In each question, choose the portfolio strategy that will give you the biggest dollar profit if your bullish forecast turns out to be correct. Explain your answer.

*a.* *Choice A:* \$10,000 invested in calls with $X = 50$.
*Choice B:* \$10,000 invested in EFG stock.

*b.* *Choice A:* 10 call options contracts (for 100 shares each), with $X = 50$.
*Choice B:* 1,000 shares of EFG stock.

**23.** Imagine you are a provider of portfolio insurance. You are establishing a four-year program. The portfolio you manage is currently worth \$100 million, and you hope to provide a minimum return of 0 percent. The equity portfolio has a standard deviation of 25 percent per year, and T-bills pay 5 percent per year. Assume for simplicity that the portfolio pays no dividends (or that all dividends are reinvested).

*a.* What fraction of the portfolio should be placed in bills? What fraction in equity?

*b.* What should the manager do if the stock portfolio falls by 3 percent on the first day of trading?

**24.** You would like to be holding a protective put position on the stock of XYZ Co. to lock in a guaranteed minimum value of \$100 at year-end. XYZ currently sells for \$100. Over the next year, the stock price will increase by 10 percent or decrease by 10 percent. The T-bill rate is 5 percent. Unfortunately, no put options are traded on XYZ Co.

*a.* Suppose the desired put option were traded. How much would it cost to purchase?

*b.* What would have been the cost of the protective put portfolio?

*c.* What portfolio position in stock and T-bills will ensure you a payoff equal to the payoff that would be provided by a protective put with $X = 100$? Show that the payoff to this portfolio and the cost of establishing the portfolio matches that of the desired protective put.

**25.** Suppose that the risk-free interest rate is zero. Would an American put option ever be exercised early? Explain.

**26.** Let $p(S,T,X)$ denote the value of a European put on a stock selling at $S$ dollars, with time to maturity $T$, and with exercise price $X$, and let $P(S,T,X)$ be the value of an American put.

*a.* Evaluate $p(0,T,X)$

*b.* Evaluate $P(0,T,X)$

*c.* Evaluate $p(S,T,0)$

*d.* Evaluate $P(S,T,0)$

*e.* What does your answer to (*b*) tell you about the possibility that American puts may be exercised early?

**27.** Consider an increase in the volatility of the stock in problem (33), below. Suppose that if the stock increases in price, it will increase to \$130, and that if it falls, it will fall to \$70. Show that the value of the call option is now higher than the value derived in problem (33).

**28.** Calculate the value of a put option with exercise price \$100 using the data in problem (33), below. Show that put-call parity is satisfied by your solution.

**29.** XYZ Corp. will pay a \$2 per share dividend in two months. Its stock price currently is \$60 per share. A call option on XYZ has an exercise price of \$55 and three-month time to maturity. The risk-free interest rate is 0.5 percent per month, and the stock's volatility (standard deviation) = 7 percent per month. Find the pseudo-American option value. Hint: Try defining one "period" as a month, rather than as a year.

**30.** "The beta of a call option on General Motors is greater than the beta of a share of General Motors." True or false?

**31.** "The beta of a call option on the S&P 500 index with an exercise price of 330 is greater than the beta of a call on the index with an exercise price of 340." True or false?

**32.** What will happen to the hedge ratio of a convertible bond as the stock price becomes very large?

The following problem is based on a question that appeared in a past CFA examination:

**33.** You are considering the sale of a call option with an exercise price of \$100 and one year to expiration. The underlying stock pays no dividends, its current price is \$100, and you believe it has a 50 percent chance of increasing to \$120 and a 50 percent chance of decreasing to \$80. The risk-free rate of interest is 10 percent.

*a.* Describe the specific steps involved in applying the binomial option-pricing model to calculate the call option's value.

*b.* Compare the binomial option-pricing model to the Black-Scholes option-pricing model.

---

*Chapter* 22

# Futures and Forward Markets

**FUTURES AND FORWARD CONTRACTS ARE SIMILAR TO OPTIONS IN THAT THEY SPECIFY THE PURCHASE OR SALE OF SOME UNDERLYING SECURITY AT SOME FUTURE DATE.** The key difference is that the holder of an option to buy is not compelled to buy and will not do so if it is to his or her disadvantage. A futures or forward contract, on the other hand, carries the obligation to go through with the agreed-upon transaction. To see how futures and forwards work and how they might be useful, consider the portfolio diversification problem facing a farmer of a single crop, for example, wheat. The entire planting season's revenue depends critically upon the highly volatile crop price. The farmer cannot easily diversify his or her position because virtually his or her entire wealth is tied up in the crop.

The miller who must purchase wheat for processing faces a portfolio problem that is the mirror image of the farmer's. He or she is subject to profit uncertainty because of the unpredictable future cost of the wheat.

Both parties can reduce this source of risk if they enter into a **forward contract** requiring the farmer to deliver the wheat when harvested at a price agreed upon now, regardless of the market price at harvest time. No money need change hands at this time. A forward contract is simply a deferred delivery sale of some asset with the sale price agreed upon now. All that is required is that each party be willing to lock in the ultimate price to be paid or received for delivery of the commodity. A forward contract protects each party from future price fluctuations.

A forward contract is not an investment in the strict sense that funds are paid for an asset—it is only a commitment today to transact in the future. Forward arrangements are part of our study of investments, however, because they offer a powerful means to hedge other investments and generally modify portfolio characteristics, as this farming example illustrates.

Forward markets for future delivery of various commodities go back in time at least to ancient Greece. Organized *futures markets,* though, are a relatively modern development, dating only to the nineteenth century. Futures markets replace informal forward contracts with highly standardized, exchange-traded securities.

This chapter describes the workings of futures markets and the mechanics of trading in these markets. We show how futures contracts are useful investment vehicles for both hedgers and speculators and how the futures price relates to the spot price of an asset. This chapter deals with both principles of futures markets in general and specific futures markets in some detail.

## 22.1 The Futures Contract

Futures markets formalize and standardize forward contracting. Buyers and sellers do not have to rely on fortuitous matching of their interests; they can trade in a centralized futures market. The futures exchange standardizes the types of **futures contract** that may be traded; it establishes contract size, the acceptable grade of commodity, contract delivery dates, and so forth. Although standardization eliminates much of the flexibility available in informal forward contracting, it has the offsetting advantage of liquidity. Futures contracts also differ from forward contracts in that they call for a daily settling of any gains or losses on the contract. In contrast, in forward contracts no money is exchanged until the delivery date.

In a centralized market, buyers and sellers can trade through brokers without personally searching for trading partners. The standardization of contracts and the depth of trading in each contract allow futures positions to be easily liquidated through a broker, rather than personally renegotiated with the other party to the contract. Because the exchange guarantees the performance of each party to the contract, costly credit checks on other traders are not necessary. Instead, each trader simply posts a good faith deposit, called the *margin,* to guarantee contract performance.

### The Basics of Futures Contracts

The futures contract calls for delivery of a commodity at a specified delivery or maturity date, for an agreed-upon price (called the **futures price**), to be paid at

**Figure 22.1**
Prices for Canadian commodity futures.

From *The Globe and Mail,* July 12, 1995. Reprinted by permission.

**Winnipeg Commodity Exchange**

**Futures**

| SeaHi | SeaLow | Mth. | Open | High | Low | Settle | Chg. | Opint |
|---|---|---|---|---|---|---|---|---|
| **CANOLA 20 tonnes, can $/tonne** | | | | | | | | |
| 459.5 | 362.0 | Aug95 | 428.8 | 434.7 | 428.8 | 432.8 | +0.6 | 6767 |
| 431.0 | 350.0 | Sep95 | 419.0 | 424.5 | 419.0 | 423.0 | +1.5 | 3910 |
| 426.5 | 119.5 | Nov95 | 412.5 | 417.9 | 412.3 | 416.1 | −0.4 | 23273 |
| 433.0 | 383.0 | Jan96 | 420.5 | 424.9 | 419.0 | 423.4 | +0.4 | 7116 |
| 438.8 | 390.0 | Mar96 | 427.5 | 431.0 | 425.2 | 428.8 | −0.7 | 4502 |
| Est sales | | | Prv Sales | Prv Open Int | | | | Chg. |
| | | | 4997 | 45613 | | | | +1082 |
| **FLAXSEED 20 tonnes, can $/tonne** | | | | | | | | |
| 350.5 | 269.0 | Jul95 | 331.0 | 333.0 | 331.0 | 333.0 | −2.5 | 497 |
| 341.0 | 279.0 | Oct95 | 312.5 | 314.0 | 310.0 | 311.7 | −2.3 | 3230 |
| 340.0 | 282.5 | Dec95 | 313.0 | 317.0 | 313.0 | 314.5 | −1.5 | 2158 |
| 327.0 | 291.9 | Mar96 | 322.0 | 322.5 | 320.5 | 320.5 | −1.5 | 857 |
| Est sales | | | Prv Sales | Prv Open Int | | | | Chg. |
| | | | 323 | 6742 | | | | −35 |
| **OATS 20 tonnes, can $/tonne** | | | | | | | | |
| 153.0 | 109.8 | Oct95 | 152.0 | 153.0 | 152.0 | 152.1 | −0.4 | 1414 |
| 152.0 | 115.5 | Dec95 | 150.9 | 150.9 | 150.2 | 150.2 | −0.8 | 1271 |
| Est sales | | | Prv Sales | Prv Open Int | | | | Chg. |
| | | | 28 | 3255 | | | | +6 |
| **RYE 20 tonnes, can $/tonne** | | | | | | | | |
| 119.5 | 116.0 | Jul95 | | | | 119.0 | | 5 |
| 120.0 | 119.0 | Sep95 | | | | 122.0 | | 15 |
| Est sales | | | Prv Sales | Prv Open Int | | | | Chg. |
| | | | 0 | 20 | | | | |
| **WESTERN BARLEY 20 tonnes,can $/tonne** | | | | | | | | |
| 148.7 | 99.0 | Aug95 | 143.0 | 143.5 | 142.0 | 143.5 | −1.5 | 3134 |
| 135.4 | 111.6 | Nov95 | 129.5 | 130.5 | 129.5 | 130.5 | +1.0 | 4328 |
| 136.5 | 114.5 | Feb96 | 131.0 | 132.0 | 131.0 | 131.7 | −0.3 | 1018 |
| Est sales | | | Prv Sales | Prv Open Int | | | | Chg. |
| | | | 337 | 9086 | | | | +83 |
| **WHEAT 20 tonnes, can $/tonne** | | | | | | | | |
| 186.0 | 101.0 | Jul95 | 174.5 | 175.0 | 174.5 | 175.0 | +0.2 | 1522 |
| 172.0 | 105.9 | Oct95 | 167.5 | 168.0 | 167.5 | 168.0 | | 3377 |
| 170.0 | 134.5 | Dec95 | 166.0 | 166.8 | 166.0 | 166.1 | −0.8 | 2502 |
| 172.0 | 139.6 | Mar96 | 167.8 | 167.9 | 167.7 | 167.9 | | 1803 |
| Est sales | | | Prv Sales | Prv Open Int | | | | Chg. |
| | | | 214 | 9254 | | | | −63 |

contract maturity. The contract specifies precise requirements for the commodity. For agricultural commodities, allowable grades (e.g., No. 2 hard winter wheat, or No. 1 soft red wheat) are set by the exchange. The place or means of delivery of the commodity is specified as well. For agricultural commodities, delivery is made by transfer of warehouse receipts issued by approved warehouses. For financial futures, delivery may be made by wire transfer; in the case of index futures, delivery may be accomplished by a cash settlement procedure similar to those for index options. (Although the futures contract technically calls for delivery of an asset, delivery in fact rarely occurs. Instead, traders much more commonly close out their positions before contract maturity, taking gains or losses in cash. We will examine how this is done shortly.)

Because the futures exchange completely specifies the terms of the contract, the traders need bargain only over the futures prices. The trader taking the **long position** commits to purchasing the commodity on the delivery date, while the trader who takes the **short position** commits to delivering the commodity at contract maturity. The trader in the long position is said to "buy" a contract; the short-side trader "sells" a contract. We are using the words *buy* and *sell* loosely, because a contract is not really bought or sold like a stock or bond, but is entered into by mutual agreement. At the time the contract is entered into, no money changes hands.

Figure 22.1 shows prices for several agricultural futures contracts on the Winnipeg Commodity Exchange as they appear in *The Globe and Mail.* The bold-face lines lists the commodity, the contract size, and the pricing unit. The first contract listed is for canola. Each contract calls for delivery of 20 metric tons, and prices are quoted in dollars per ton. The next several rows detail price data for contracts expiring on various dates. The August 1995 maturity canola contract, for example, opened during the date at a futures price of $428.8 per ton. The highest futures price during the day was $434.7, the lowest was $428.8, and the settlement price (a representative trading price during the last few minutes of trading) was \$432.8. The settlement price increased by 60 cents from the previous trading day. The highest futures price over the contract's life to date was \$459.5, and the lowest was \$362. Finally, open interest, or the number of outstanding contracts, was 3,910. Similar information is given for each maturity date for all six commodities traded on the exchange.

The trader holding the long position, who will purchase the good, profits from price increases. Suppose that in August the price of canola turns out to be \$435 per ton. The long-position trader who entered into the contract at the futures price of \$432.80 on July 11 would pay the agreed-upon \$432.80 per ton to receive canola that, at contract maturity, is worth \$435 per ton in the market. Since each contract calls for delivery of 20 tons, ignoring brokerage fees, the profit to the long position equals 20(\$435 − \$432.8) = \$44. Conversely, the short position must deliver 20 tons of canola, each with value \$435, for the previously agreed-upon futures price of only \$432.80. The short position's loss equals the long position's gain.

To summarize, at maturity:

$$\text{Profit to long} = \text{Spot price at maturity} - \text{Original futures price}$$
$$\text{Profit to short} = \text{Original futures prices} - \text{Spot price at maturity}$$

where the spot price is the actual market price of the commodity at the time of delivery.

---

**CONCEPT CHECK** Question 1. Graph the profit realized by an investor who enters the long side of a futures contract as a function of the price of the asset on the maturity date. Compare this graph to a graph of the profits realized by the purchaser of the asset itself. Next, try the same exercise for a short futures position and a short sale of the asset.

---

The futures contract is therefore a zero-sum game, with losses and gains to all positions netting out to zero. Every long position is offset by a short position. The aggregate profits to futures trading, summing over all investors, also must be zero, as is the net exposure to changes in the commodity price. For this reason, the establishment of a futures market in a commodity should not have a major impact on the spot market for that commodity. That is, a futures market in Canadian Tire stock, were it to be established, should not affect Canadian Tire's ability to raise money in the equity market.

---

**CONCEPT CHECK** Question 2. What is the difference between the futures price and the value of the futures contract?

Question 3. Evaluate the criticism that futures markets siphon off capital from more productive uses.

---

**Table 22.1** Sample of Futures Contracts

| Foreign Currencies | Agricultural | Metals and Energy | Interest Rate Futures | Equity Indices |
|---|---|---|---|---|
| British pound | Corn | Copper | Eurodollars | S&P 500 |
| Canadian dollar | Oats | Aluminum | Euromarks | S&P mid-cap 400 |
| Japanese yen | Soybeans | Gold | Eurolira | NYSE index |
| Swiss franc | Soybean meal | Platinum | Euroswiss | Value Line index |
| French franc | Soybean oil | Palladium | Treasury bonds | Major market index |
| Deutsche mark | Wheat | Silver | Treasury bills | OTC |
| U.S. dollar index | Barley | Crude oil | Treasury notes | Russell 2000 |
| European currency unit | Flaxseed | Heating oil | Municipal bond index | Nikkei 225 |
| Australian dollar | Canola | Gas oil | LIBOR | Eurotop 100 |
| Mark/Yen cross rate | Rye | Natural gas | Short gilt† | FTSE index |
| Sterling/Mark cross rate | Cattle (feeder) | Gasoline | Long gilt† | CAC-40 |
| | Cattle (live) | Propane | Australian government bond | Australia ordinary share |
| | Hogs | CRB index* | German government bond | Toronto 35 |
| | Pork bellies | | Canadian government bond | |
| | Cocoa | | Italian government bond | |
| | Coffee | | Federal funds rate | |
| | Cotton | | | |
| | Orange juice | | | |
| | Sugar | | | |
| | Lumber | | | |
| | Rice | | | |

*The Commodity Research Bureau's index of futures prices of agricultural as well as metal and energy prices.
†Gilts are British government bonds.

## Existing Contracts

Futures and forward contracts are traded in the United States and other financial centres on a wide variety of goods in five broad categories: agricultural commodities, metals and minerals (including energy commodities), foreign currencies, interest rate futures, and stock market indices. The financial futures contracts are recent innovations, for which trading was introduced in 1975. Innovation in financial futures has been quite rapid and is ongoing. Table 22.1 enumerates some of the various contracts trading in the United States in 1995.

In Canada, futures contracts for several major agricultural commodities have been trading for a long time at the Winnipeg Commodity Exchange (WCE). The early 1980s saw the introduction of several precious metal, stock index, and interest rate futures, together with options on stock indices, foreign currencies, and bonds. By the end of the decade, most of these instruments had failed (see the accompanying box). By 1995, apart from the WCE the only active futures trading in Canada was in TSE 35 and TSE 100 contracts in Toronto, and bankers' acceptances, Canada bond futures, and options on Canada bond futures and bankers' acceptances in Montreal. Low liquidity, thin trading, and the ready availability of

## Montreal Exchange to Draw on Past for Futures

Those who believe this country really needs commodity markets find a paradox in an apparent lack of interest by potential customers. After all, Canadians are supposed to be averse to risk.

Ken Broaderip, vice-president and national futures manager out of Toronto for Nesbitt Thomson Deacon, summed it up this way at a conference in Montreal awhile back: "What's happened in Canada is somewhat of an embarrassment to our industry."

When compared with investors and financial managers in other countries, Canadians seem to have been slow to find advantages in commodity markets. Investment dealers will quickly reach this conclusion when they observe how much markets in Chicago and Philadelphia expanded during the 1980s. Meanwhile, Canadian efforts to develop commodity markets have produced extremely limited results.

Mr. Broaderip was delivering his assessment in Montreal because the Montreal Exchange has been the most persistent in trying to establish commodity markets. It used to be called the stock exchange, but the title was shortened to reflect this broader interest. The ME sponsors an annual gathering that attracts a respectable collection of experts in commodity trading from the major centres.

By apologizing before such a group, Mr. Broaderip seemed so, well, Canadian. His point, though, is a good one. Why are Canadians so seemingly slow to adopt a type of market that grew so rapidly elsewhere during the past decade?

Part of the answer is probably in the nature of the growth in commodity markets. The hot items were financial commodities. This was a direct result of the unpegging of convertible currencies.

Interestingly, the Canadian government was a pioneer in allowing the value of its currency to float against those of its trading partners. But such a move became significant to the world economy only when major currencies were set adrift.

Abandoning the fixed-rate system introduced massive uncertainties into world trade. The inevitable result was the development of ways to hedge against currency swings.

Futures or options on currencies quickly became an integral part of most trading arrangements. Strategies to hedge against changes in currency values are commonplace. It's now possible to buy a mutual fund containing securities in one country and a built-in hedge to ease the mind of an investor in another country.

Because currency reasons were the base for the growth in commodity markets, the fast-growing markets were in the major industrial countries. The dominant commodity markets in North America are in Chicago.

The Montreal Exchange tried during the 1980s to develop a futures market in Canadian dollars. Exchanges in Chicago and Philadelphia offered competing products. The U.S. exchanges won hands down. They had a head start in picking off the market on a secondary currency because they already had traders in commodity pits handling large volumes in futures or options on the major currencies.

When trying to develop the market in Canadian dollar futures, the ME made mistakes in design and strategy. Based on that experience, the ME has been much more thorough in its current efforts to develop futures and options contracts on Canadian government bonds.

Simply put, futures and options on bonds are a way of hedging against interest rate swings. This time, the ME is out in front with a contract that is similar to those for other government bonds and the ME's odds for success are greater.

As for the currency markets, the Canadian experience involves the history of the banking system. Canadian bankers had much more experience internationally than most of their American counterparts. With their large branch networks, the Canadian

*(Continued)*

banks were able to deliver foreign exchange expertise to businesses in small towns.

Treasurers at large Canadian companies learned to deal directly with brokers in financial commodities. It used to be common for Canadian companies to report losses on currency transactions, but no more. Institutional fund managers have become equally adept at hedging currency risk.

Somehow, domestic demand was never concentrated enough to get the Canadian financial institutions into the business at home in a big way. Domestic brokers were either not active in financial commodities or became minor players in foreign commodity markets.

Financial commodity markets may have been more efficient in providing currency hedges, but for smaller businesses, the banks were already there with long-established ways of dealing in currencies.

Now that the banks have investment dealer subsidiaries—thus employing about 80 percent of the brokers—they may take a different view of commodity markets.

Source: Bud Jorgensen, *The Globe and Mail,* January 23, 1991. Reprinted by permission.

comparable financial instruments in the United States are major reasons for the relative failure of financial innovations in Canadian futures markets.[1]

Outside the futures markets, a fairly developed network of banks and brokers has established a forward market in foreign exchange. This forward market is not a formal exchange in the sense that the exchange specifies the terms of the traded contract. Instead, participants in a forward contract may negotiate for delivery of any quantity of goods, as distinguished from futures markets where contract size is set by the exchange. In forward arrangements, banks and brokers simply negotiate contracts for clients (or themselves) as needed.

## 22.2 Mechanics of Trading in Futures Markets

### The Clearinghouse and Open Interest

Trading in futures contracts is more complex than making ordinary stock transactions. If you want to make a stock purchase, your broker simply acts as an intermediary to enable you to buy shares from or sell to another individual through the stock exchange. In futures trading, however, the exchange plays a more active role.

When an investor contacts a broker to establish a futures position, the brokerage firm wires the order to the firm's trader on the floor of the futures exchange. In contrast to stock trading, which involves specialists or market makers in each security, futures trades take place among floor traders in the "trading pit" for

[1] A more extensive treatment of the reasons for the failure of many new Canadian futures instruments can be found in E. Kirzner, "The Unfolding Derivative Securities Story: Abroad and in Canada," *Canadian Investment Review* 1, no. 1 (Fall 1988).

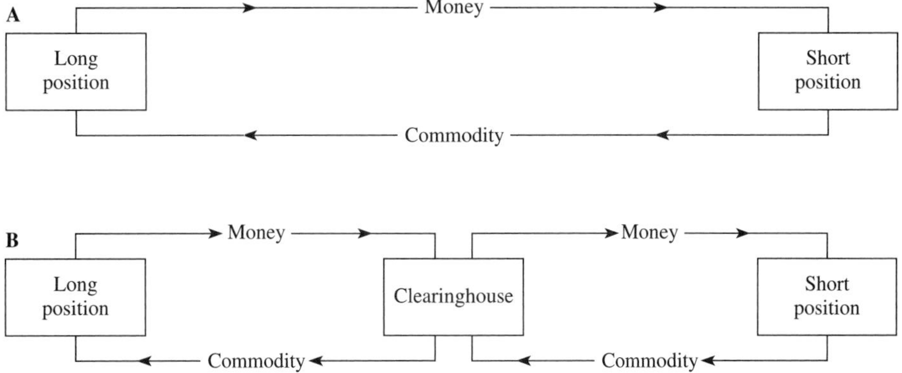


**Figure 22.2**
**A**—Trading without the clearinghouse.
**B**—Trading with the clearinghouse.

each contract. Traders use voice or hand signals to signify their desire to buy or sell. Once a trader willing to accept the opposite side of a trade is located, the trade is recorded and the customer is notified.

At this point, just as is true for options contracts, the **clearinghouse** enters the picture. Rather than having the long and short traders hold contracts with each other, the clearinghouse becomes the seller of the contract for the long position and the buyer of the contract for the short position. The clearinghouse is obligated to deliver the commodity to the long position and to pay for delivery from the short; consequently, the clearinghouse's position nets to zero. This arrangement makes the clearinghouse the trading partner of each trader, both long and short. The clearinghouse, bound to perform on its side of each contract, is the only party that can be hurt by the failure of any trader to fulfill the obligations of the futures contract. This arrangement is necessary, because a futures contract calls for future performance, which cannot be guaranteed as easily as an immediate stock transaction.

Figure 22.2**A** illustrates what would happen in the absence of the clearinghouse. The trader in the long position would be obligated to pay the futures price to the short position trader; the trader in the short position would be obligated to deliver the commodity. Figure 22.2**B** shows how the clearinghouse becomes an intermediary, acting as the trading partner for each side of the contract. The clearinghouse's position is neutral, since it takes a long and a short position for each transaction.

The existence of the clearinghouse enables traders to liquidate positions easily. If you are currently long in a contract and want to undo your position, you simply instruct your broker to enter the short side of a contract to close out your position. This is called a **reversing trade.** The exchange nets out your long and short positions, reducing your net position to zero. Your zero net position with the clearinghouse eliminates the need to fulfill at maturity either the original long or the reversing short position.

The **open interest** on the contract is the number of contracts outstanding. (Long and short positions are not counted separately, meaning that open interest can be defined as the number of either long or short contracts outstanding.) The clearinghouse's position nets out to zero, of course, and so is not counted in the computation of open interest. When contracts begin trading, open interest is zero. As time passes, open interest increases as progressively more contracts are entered. Almost all traders, however, liquidate their positions before the contract maturity date. Instead of actually taking or making delivery of the commodity, virtually all traders enter reversing trades to cancel their original positions, thereby realizing the profits or losses on the contract. Actual deliveries and purchases of commodities are then made via regular channels of supply. The percentage of contracts that result in actual delivery is estimated to range from less than 1 percent to 3 percent, depending on the commodity and the activity in the contract. The image of a trader awakening one delivery date with a hog in the front yard is amusing, but unlikely.

You can see the typical pattern of open interest in Figure 22.1. In the flaxseed contracts, for example, the July delivery contracts are close to maturity and open interest is relatively small; most contracts have been reversed already. The next few maturities have significant open interest. Finally, the most distant maturity contract has little open interest, because the contract has only recently been available for trading.

## Marking to Market and the Margin Account

Anyone who saw the film *Trading Places* knows that Eddie Murphy as a trader in orange juice futures had no intention of purchasing or delivering orange juice. Traders simply bet on the future price of juice. The total profit or loss realized by the long trader who buys a contract at time zero and closes, or reverses, it at time $t$ is just the change in the futures price over the period $F_t - F_0$. Symmetrically, the short trader earns $F_0 - F_t$.

The process by which profits or losses accrue to traders is called **marking to market.** At initial execution of a trade, each trader establishes a margin account. The margin is a security account consisting of cash and/or near-cash securities, such as Treasury bills, which ensure that the trader is able to satisfy the obligations of the futures contract. Because both parties to a futures contract are exposed to losses, both must post margin. This is in contrast to options, where only the option writer has an obligation and thus needs to post margin. Because the margin may be satisfied with interest-earning securities, posting the margin does not impose a significant opportunity cost of funds on the trader. The initial margin usually is set between 5 percent and 10 percent of the total value of the contract. Contracts written on assets with more volatile prices require higher margins.

On any day that futures markets trade, futures prices may rise or fall. An increase in price benefits long positions that agreed to purchase the good at the lower price that was established when the contract was initiated; conversely, a price increase harms short positions that still must deliver the good at the originally agreed-upon futures prices. Instead of waiting until the maturity date for traders to realize all gains and losses, the clearinghouse requires all positions to recognize profits as they accrue daily. If the futures price of wheat at the WCE rises from \$103 to \$105 per ton, the clearinghouse credits the margin account of the long position for 20 tons (which is the standard size of the wheat-futures contract) multiplied by \$2 per ton, or \$40 per contract. Conversely, for the short position the clearinghouse takes this amount from the margin account for each contract held. This daily settling is marking to market.

Therefore, the maturity date of the contract does not govern realization of profit or loss. Marking to market ensures that, as futures prices change, the proceeds accrue to the trader's margin account immediately.

---

**CONCEPT CHECK** Question 4. What must be the net inflow or outlay from marking to market for the clearinghouse? (Hint: What is the net position of the clearinghouse?)

---

If a trader accrues sustained losses from marking to market, the margin account may fall below a critical value called the **maintenance margin** or **variation margin.** Once the value of the account falls below this value, the trader receives a margin call. Either new funds must be transferred into the margin account, or the broker will close out enough of the trader's position to reduce the required margin for that position to a level at or below the trader's remaining margin. This procedure safeguards the position of the clearinghouse. Positions are closed out before the margin account is exhausted—any losses suffered by the trader are thereby covered.

Marking to market is the major way in which futures and forward contracts differ, besides contract standardization. Futures follow a pay- (or receive) as-you-go-method. Forward contracts are simply held until maturity, and no funds are transferred until that date, although the contracts may be traded.

It is important to note that the futures price on the delivery date will equal the spot price of the commodity on that date. Since a maturing contract calls for immediate delivery, the futures price on that day must equal the spot price—the cost of the commodity from the two competing sources is equalized in a competitive market.[2] You may obtain the delivery of the commodity either by purchasing it directly in the spot market or by entering the long side of a futures contract.

A commodity available from two sources (spot or futures market) must be priced identically, or else investors will rush to purchase it from the cheap source in order to sell it in the higher-priced market. Such arbitrage activity could not persist without prices adjusting to eliminate the arbitrage opportunity. Therefore, the futures price and spot price must converge at maturity. This is called the **convergence property.**

Because of convergence, the profits realized over the life of futures and forward contracts are quite similar. Call $f_0$ the forward price at contract inception and $P_T$

---

[2] Small differences between the spot and futures prices at maturity may persist because of transportation costs, but this is a minor factor.

the spot price of the commodity on the maturity date $T$. The profit to the long position of the forward contract is $P_T - f_0$, that is, the difference between the value of the good received and the price that was contracted to be paid for it. The futures contract, by contrast, uses daily marking to market. The sum of all daily settlements will equal $F_T - F_0$, where $F_T$ stands for the futures price at contract maturity. We have noted, however, that the futures price at maturity equals the spot price, so total futures profits also may be expressed as $P_T - F_0$. Summing the daily marking-to-market settlements results in a profit formula identical to that of the forward contract.

Because these payments accrue continually, we should not, strictly speaking, simply add them up to obtain total profits without first adjusting for interest on interim payments. Some empirical evidence, however, suggests that interest earnings on daily settlements have only a small effect on the determination of futures and forward prices. For this reason, we often ignore this fine point and simply take the profits or losses on a futures contract held to maturity to be $P_T - F_0$ for the long position, and $F_0 - P_T$ for the short, Section 22.4 explores this issue in greater detail.

---

**CONCEPT CHECK** Question 5. If futures prices are equally likely to go up as to go down on each trading day, what are the expected proceeds from marking to market? The expected interest earnings on those proceeds?

---

To illustrate the time profile of returns to a futures contract, consider an example for which the current futures price for silver for delivery five days from today is \$7.60 per ounce (in U.S. dollars). Suppose that over the next five days the futures price evolves as follows:

| Day | Futures Price |
|---|---|
| 0 (today) | \$7.60 |
| 1 | \$7.70 |
| 2 | \$7.75 |
| 3 | \$7.68 |
| 4 | \$7.68 |
| 5 (delivery) | \$7.71 |

The spot price of silver on the delivery day is \$7.71: The convergence property implies that the price of silver in the spot market must equal the futures price on delivery day.

The daily marking-to-market settlements for each contract held by the long position will be as follows:

| Day | Profit (Loss) per Ounce | × 5,000 Ounces/Contract = Daily Proceeds |
|---|---|---|
| 1 | 7.70 − 7.60 = .10 | $500 |
| 2 | 7.75 − 7.70 = .05 | 250 |
| 3 | 7.68 − 7.75 = −.07 | −350 |
| 4 | 7.68 − 7.68 = 0 | 0 |
| 5 | 7.71 − 7.68 = .03 | 150 |
| | | $550 |

The profit on day 1 is the increase in the futures price from the previous day, or ($7.70 − $7.60) per ounce. Because each silver contract on the Commodity Exchange (CMX) calls for purchase and delivery of 5,000 ounces, the total profit per contract is 5,000 multiplied by $.10, or $500. On day three, when the futures price falls, the long position's margin account will be debited by $350. By day five, the sum of all daily proceeds is $550. This is exactly equal to 5,000 times the difference between the final futures price of $7.71 and the original futures price of $7.60. Thus the sum of all the daily proceeds (per ounce of silver held long) equals $P_T - F_0$.

## Cash versus Actual Delivery

Most futures markets call for delivery of an actual commodity, such as a particular grade of wheat or a specified amount of foreign currency, if the contract is not reversed before maturity. For agricultural commodities where quality of the delivered good may vary, the exchange sets quality standards as part of the futures contract. In some cases, contracts may be settled with higher- or lower-grade commodities. In these cases, a premium or discount is applied to the delivered commodity to adjust for the quality difference.

Some futures contracts call for **cash delivery.** An example is a stock index futures contract where the underlying asset is an index such as the TSE 35 or the S&P 500 index. Delivery of every stock in the index clearly would be impractical. Hence the contract calls for "delivery" of a cash amount equal to the value that the index attains on the maturity date of the contract. The sum of all the daily settlements from marking to market results in the long position realizing total profits or losses of $S_T - F_0$, where $S_T$ is the value of the stock index on the maturity date $T$, and $F_0$ is the original futures price. Cash settlement closely mimics actual delivery, the only difference being that the cash value of the asset rather than the asset itself is delivered by the short position in exchange for the futures price.

More concretely, the TSE 35 index contract calls for delivery of $500 multiplied by the value of the index. At maturity, the index might list at 200, a market value-weighted index of the prices of all 35 stocks in the index. The cash settlement contract calls for delivery of $500 × 200, or $100,000, in return for 500 times the futures price. This yields exactly the same profit as would result from directly purchasing 500 units of the index for $100,000 and then delivering it for 500 times the original futures price.

## Regulations

Futures markets in Canada are under the jurisdiction of the provincial securities commissions, with the exception of grain futures traded on the WCE, which are subject to federal law. Most futures trading is self-regulated, although some provinces have passed commodity futures acts.

In the United States, futures markets are regulated by the Commodities Futures Trading Commission (CFTC), a federal agency. The CFTC sets capital requirements for member firms of the futures exchanges, authorizes trading in new contracts, and oversees maintenance of daily trading records.

The futures exchange sets limits on the amount by which futures prices may change from one day to the next. For example, the price limit on the TSE 35 futures contract is $4,500, corresponding to a change of 9 ($4500/$500) in the index. This means that if TSE 35 futures close today at 200, trades tomorrow in the TSE 35 index may vary only between 191 and 209. Likewise, the price limit on silver contracts traded on the Chicago Board of Trade is $1, which means that if silver futures close today at $7.40 per ounce, trades in silver tomorrow may vary only between $6.40 and $8.40 per ounce. The exchanges may increase or reduce price limits in response to perceived increases or decreases in price volatility of the contract. Price limits often are eliminated as contracts approach maturity, usually in the last month of trading.

Price limits traditionally are viewed as a means to limit violent price fluctuations. This reasoning seems dubious. Suppose that an international monetary crisis overnight drives up the spot price of silver to $10.50. No one would sell silver futures at prices for future delivery as low as $7.40. Instead, the futures price would rise each day by the $1 limit, although the quoted price would represent only an unfilled bid order—no contracts would trade at the low quoted price. After several days of limit moves of $1 per day, the futures price would finally reach its equilibrium level, and trading would occur again. This process means no one could unload a position until the price reached its equilibrium level. This example shows that price limits offer no real protection against price fluctuation.

## Taxation

Because of the marking-to-market procedure, investors do not have control over the tax year in which they realize gains or losses. Instead, price changes are realized gradually, with each daily settlement. Therefore, taxes are paid at year-end on accumulated profits or losses, regardless of whether the position has been closed out.

## 22.3 Futures Markets Strategies

### Hedging and Speculating

Hedging and speculating are two polar uses of futures markets. A speculator uses a futures contract to profit from movements in futures prices; a hedger, to protect against price movement.

If speculators believe that prices will increase, they will take a long position for expected profits. Conversely, they will exploit expected price declines by taking a short position. As an example of a speculative strategy, suppose someone thinks that silver futures prices, currently at $7.20 U.S. per ounce, will rise to $7.50 by month's end. Each silver contract on the Commodity Exchange (CMX) calls for delivery of 5,000 ounces. If the silver futures price does in fact increase to $7.50, the speculator profits by 5,000 multiplied by $.30, or $1,500 per contract. If the forecast is incorrect and silver prices decline, the investor loses 5,000 times the decrease in the futures price for each contract purchased. Speculators bet on the direction of futures price movements.

Why does a speculator buy a silver futures contract? Why not buy silver directly? One reason lies in transaction costs, which are far smaller in futures markets. Another reason is storage costs. Holding silver in inventory directly and insuring it is needlessly expensive when futures contracts may be used instead. A third reason is the leverage that futures trading provides. Each silver contract calls for delivery of 5,000 ounces of silver, worth about $36,000 in our example. The initial margin required for this account might be only $5,000. The $1,500 per contract gain on the silver translates into a 30 percent ($1,500/$5,000) return, despite the fact that the silver futures price increases only 4.2 percent ($.30/$7.20). Futures margins, therefore, allow speculators to achieve much greater leverage than is available from direct trading in the commodity.

Hedgers, by contrast, use futures markets to immunize themselves from price movements. Holders of silver (e.g., jewelers) might want to protect the value of their inventory against price fluctuations. In this case, they have no desire to bet on price movements in either direction. To achieve such protection, a hedger takes a short position in silver futures, which obligates the hedger to deliver silver at the contract maturity date for the current futures price. This locks in the sale price for the silver and guarantees that the total value (per ounce) of the silver-plus-futures position at the maturity date is the current futures price.

For illustration, suppose that the futures price for delivery next year is $7.80 and that the only three possible year-end prices per ounce are $7.40, $7.80, and $8.20. If investors currently hold 10,000 ounces of silver, they would take short positions in 2 contracts, each for 5,000 ounces. Protecting the value of an asset with short futures positions is called *short hedging*. Note that the futures position requires no current investment. (We can ignore the margin requirement in the initial investment because it is small relative to the size of the contract and because it may be posted in interest-bearing securities and so does not present a time-value or opportunity cost.)

Next year, the profits from the short futures position will be 10,000 times any decrease in the futures price, or the sum of the marking-to-market settlements. At maturity, the final futures price will equal the spot price of silver because of convergence. Hence the futures profit will be 10,000 times $(F_0 - P_T)$, where $P_T$ is the price of silver on the delivery date and $F_0$ is the original futures price, \$7.80. For the three possible price outcomes, the total portfolio value equals:

| | Silver Price at Year-End | | |
|---|---|---|---|
| | **\$7.40** | **\$7.80** | **\$8.20** |
| Silver holdings (Value = 10,000 $P_T$) | \$74,000 | \$78,000 | \$82,000 |
| Futures profits or losses | 4,000 | 0 | −4,000 |
| Total | \$78,000 | \$78,000 | \$78,000 |

Note that the total portfolio value is unaffected by the year-end silver price. The gains or losses on the silver holdings are exactly offset by those on the two contracts held short. For example, if silver prices fall to \$7.40 per ounce, the losses on the silver inventory are offset by the \$4,000 gain on the futures contracts. That profit equals the difference between the futures price on the maturity date (which is the spot price of \$7.40) and the originally contracted futures price of \$7.80. For short contracts, a profit of \$.40 per ounce is realized from the fall in the spot price. Because each contract calls for delivery of 5,000 ounces, this results in a \$4,000 gain that offsets the decline in the value of silver held. A hedger, in contrast to a speculator, is indifferent to the ultimate price of the spot commodity. The short-hedger who has arranged to sell the commodity for an agreed-upon price need not be concerned about further developments in the market price.

To generalize this numerical example, you can note that the silver will be worth $P_T$ at maturity, while the profit on the futures contract is $F_0 - P_T$. The sum of the two positions is therefore $F_0$ dollars, which is independent of the eventual silver price.

A *long hedge* is the analogue to a short hedge for a purchaser of a commodity. A company that will purchase silver at year-end can lock in the total cost of the purchase by entering the long side of a contract, which commits it to purchasing at the currently determined futures price.

Exact futures hedging may be impossible for some goods because the necessary futures contract is not traded. For example, producers of bauxite, the ore from which aluminum is made, might like to trade in bauxite futures but cannot. Because bauxite and aluminum prices are highly correlated, however, a close hedge may be established by shorting aluminum futures. Hedging a position using futures on another commodity is called *cross hedging*.

**CONCEPT CHECK** Question 6. What are the sources of risk to an investor who uses aluminum futures to hedge an inventory of bauxite?

Futures contracts also may be used as general portfolio hedges. Bodie and Rosansky[3] show that commodity futures returns have had a negative correlation with the stock market. Investors may add a diversified portfolio of futures contracts to a diversified stock portfolio to lower the standard deviation of the overall rate of return. Moreover, the average rate of increase in commodity futures prices has been roughly the same as for common stocks, as the following figures show:

| | **1950–1976** | |
|---|---|---|
| | **Average Annual Return (%)** | **Annual Standard Deviation (%)** |
| Portfolio of T-bills and 23 commodity futures | 13.85 | 22.43 |
| S&P 500 index | 13.05 | 18.95 |

The correlation coefficient between the two portfolios during the estimation period was −.24. This implies that long positions in commodity futures would add substantial diversification benefits to a stock portfolio.

To illustrate, suppose that you invest a fraction of your total wealth in stocks and use the remainder to invest in commodity futures contracts, posting 100 percent margin with T-bills. The stock-futures-bills portfolio presents you with substantial reduction in risk and no sacrifice in expected return. Bodie and Rosansky found that a portfolio composed of 60 percent stock and 40 percent T-bills with futures would have had a return of 13.36 percent and standard deviation of only 12.68 percent—virtually an unchanged average return from either portfolio taken alone, but with roughly a one-third reduction in standard deviation.

Commodity futures also are inflation hedges. When commodity prices increase because of unanticipated inflation, returns from long futures positions will increase because the contracts call for delivery of goods for the price agreed upon before the high inflation rate became a reality.

## Basis Risk and Hedging

The **basis** is the difference between the futures price and the spot price. As we have noted, on the maturity date of a contract the basis must be zero: The convergence property implies that $F_T - P_T = 0$. Before maturity, however, the futures price for later delivery may differ substantially from the current spot price.

[3] Zvi Bodie and Victor Rosansky, "Risk and Return in Commodity Futures," *Financial Analysts Journal,* May/June 1980.

We discussed the case of a short hedger who holds an asset and a short position to deliver that asset in the future. If the asset and futures contract are held until maturity, the hedger bears no risk, because the ultimate value of the portfolio on the delivery date is determined completely by the current futures price. Risk is eliminated because the futures price and spot price at contract maturity must be equal: Gains and losses on the futures and the commodity position will exactly cancel. If the contract and asset are to be liquidated early, however, the hedger bears **basis risk,** because the futures price and spot price need not move in perfect lockstep at all times before the delivery date. In this case, gains and losses on the contract and the asset need not exactly offset each other.

Some speculators try to profit from movements in the basis. Rather than betting on the direction of the futures or spot prices per se, they bet on the changes in the difference between the two. A long spot–short futures position will profit when the basis narrows. For example, consider an investor holding 5,000 ounces of silver, who is short one silver futures contract. Silver might sell for $7.20 per ounce, while the futures price for next-year delivery is $7.80. The basis is therefore 60 cents. Tomorrow, the silver spot price might increase to $7.24, while the futures price might increase to $7.81. The basis has narrowed from 60 cents to 57 cents. The investor realizes a capital gain of 4 cents per ounce on her silver holdings and a loss of 1 cent per ounce from the increase in the futures price. The net gain is the decrease in basis, or 3 cents per ounce.

A related strategy is a **spread** position where the investor takes a long position in a futures contract of one maturity and a short position in a contract on the same commodity, but with a different maturity. Profits accrue if the difference in futures prices between the two contracts changes in the hoped-for direction; that is, if the futures price on the contract held long increases by more (or decreases by less) than the futures price on the contract held short.

## 22.4 The Determination of Futures Prices

### The Spot-Futures Parity Theorem

We have seen that a futures contract can be used to hedge changes in the value of the underlying asset. If the hedge is perfect, meaning that the asset-plus-futures portfolio has no risk, then the hedged position must provide a rate of return equal to the rate on other risk-free investments. Otherwise, there will be arbitrage opportunities that investors will exploit until prices are brought back into line. This insight can be used to derive the theoretical relationship between a futures price and the price of its underlying asset.

Suppose, for example, that the TSE 35 index currently is at 250 and an investor who holds $250 in a mutual fund indexed to the TSE 35 wishes to temporarily hedge her exposure to market risk. Assume that the indexed portfolio pays dividends totaling $45 over the course of the year and, for simplicity, that all dividends are paid at year end. Finally, assume that the futures price for year-end delivery on the TSE 35 contract is 258.[4] Let's examine the end-of-year proceeds for various values of the stock index if the investor hedges her portfolio by entering the short side of the futures contract.

| | | | | | | |
|---|---|---|---|---|---|---|
| Value of stock portfolio | $240 | $245 | $250 | $255 | $260 | $265 |
| Payoff from short futures position (equals $F_0 - F_T = \$258 - S_T$) | 18 | 13 | 8 | 3 | −2 | −7 |
| Dividend income | 5 | 5 | 5 | 5 | 5 | 5 |
| Total | $263 | $263 | $263 | $263 | $263 | $263 |

The payoff from the short futures position equals the difference between the original futures price, $258, and the year-end stock price. This is due to convergence: The futures price at contract maturity will equal the stock price at that time.

Notice that the overall position is perfectly hedged. Any increase in the value of the indexed stock portfolio is offset by an equal decrease in the payoff of the short futures position, resulting in a final value independent of the stock price. The $263 payoff is the sum of the current futures price, $F_0 = \$258$, and the $5 dividend. It is as though the investor arranged to sell the stock at year-end for the current futures price, thereby eliminating price risk and locking in total proceeds equal to the sales price plus dividends paid before the sale.

What rate of return is earned on this riskless position? The stock investment requires an initial outlay of $250, while the futures position is established without an initial cash outflow. Therefore, the $250 portfolio grows to a year-end value of $263, providing a rate of return of 5.2 percent. More generally, a total investment of $S_0$, the current stock price, grows to a final value of $F_0 + D$, where $D$ is the dividend payout on the portfolio. The rate of return is therefore

$$\text{Rate of return on perfectly hedged stock portfolio} = \frac{(F_0 + D) - S_0}{S_0}$$

This return is essentially riskless. We observe $F_0$ at the beginning of the period when we enter the futures contract. While dividend payouts are not perfectly riskless, they are highly predictable over short periods, especially for diversified portfolios. Any uncertainty is *extremely* small compared to the uncertainty of stock prices.

Presumably, 5.2 percent must be the rate of return available on other riskless investments. If not, then investors would face two competing risk-free strategies with different rates of return, a situation that could not last. Therefore, we conclude that

$$\frac{(F_0 + D) - S_0}{S_0} = r_f$$

[4] Actually, the futures contract calls for delivery of $500 times the value of the TSE 35 index, so that each contract would be settled for $500 times 258. We will simplify by assuming that you can buy a contract for one unit rather than 500 units of the index. In practice, one contract would hedge about $500 × 250 = $125,000 worth of stock. Of course, institutional investors would consider a stock portfolio of this size to be quite small.

Rearranging, we find that the futures price must be

$$F_0 = S_0(1 + r_f) - D = S_0(1 + r_f - d) \qquad \textbf{(22.1)}$$

where $d$ is the dividend yield on the stock portfolio, defined as $D/S_0$. This result is called the **spot-futures parity theorem.** It gives the normal or theoretically correct relationship between spot and futures prices.

Suppose that parity were violated. For example, suppose the risk-free interest rate in the economy were only 4 percent, so that according to parity, the futures price should be $250(1 + .04) − $5 = $255. The actual futures price, $F_0$ = $258, is $3 higher than its "appropriate" value. This implies that an investor can make arbitrage profits by shorting the relatively overpriced futures contract and buying the relatively underpriced stock portfolio using money borrowed at the 4 percent market interest rate. The proceeds from this strategy would be as follows:

| Action | Initial Cash Flow | Cash Flow in One Year |
|---|---|---|
| Borrow $250, repay with interest in one year | +$250 | −250(1.04) = −$260 |
| Buy stock for $250 | −$250 | $S_T$ + $5 dividend |
| Enter short futures position ($F_0$ = $258) | 0 | $258 − $S_T$ |
| Total | 0 | $3 |

The net initial investment of the strategy is zero. But its cash flow in one year is positive and riskless. The payoff is $3 regardless of the stock price. This payoff is precisely equal to the mispricing of the futures contract relative to its parity value.

When parity is violated, the strategy to exploit the mispricing produces an arbitrage profit—a riskless profit requiring no initial net investment. If such an opportunity existed, all market participants would rush to take advantage of it. The results? The stock price would be bid up, and/or the futures price offered would be bid down until Equation 22.1 was satisfied. A similar analysis applies to the possibility that $F_0$ is less than $255. In this case, you simply reverse the strategy above to earn riskless profits. We conclude, therefore, that in a well-functioning market in which arbitrage opportunities are competed away, $F_0 = S_0(1 + r_f) - D$.

The parity relationship also is called the **cost-of-carry relationship** because it asserts that the futures price is determined by the relative costs of buying a stock with deferred delivery in the futures market versus buying it in the spot market with immediate delivery and "carrying" it in inventory. If you buy the stock now, you tie up your funds and incur a time-value-of-money cost of $r_f$ per period. On the other hand, you receive dividend payments with a current yield of $d$. The net carrying-cost advantage of deferring delivery of the stock is therefore $r_f - d$ per period. This advantage must be offset by a differential between the futures price and the spot price. The price differential just offsets the cost-of-carry advantage when $F_0 = S_0(1 + r_f - d)$.

The parity relationship is easily generalized to multiperiod applications. We simply recognize that the difference between the futures and spot prices will be larger as the maturity of the contract is longer. This reflects the longer period to which we apply the net cost of carry. For contract maturity of $T$ periods, the parity relationship is

$$F_0 = S_0(1 + r_f - d)^T \tag{22.2}$$

While we have described parity in terms of stocks and stock index futures, it should be clear that the logic applies as well to any financial futures contract. For gold futures, for example, we would simply set the dividend yield to zero. For bond contracts, we would let the coupon income on the bond play the role of dividend payments. In both cases, the parity relationship would be essentially the same as Equation 22.2.

The arbitrage strategy described above should convince you that these parity relationships are more than just theoretical results. Any violations of the parity relationship give rise to arbitrage opportunities that can provide large profits to traders.[5] We will see shortly that index arbitrage in the stock market is a tool to exploit violations of the parity relationship for stock index futures contracts.

**CONCEPT CHECK** Question 7. What are the three steps of the arbitrage strategy if $F_0$ is equal to \$253? Work out the cash flows of the strategy now and in one year in a table like the one on page 888.

## Spreads

Just as we can predict the relationship between spot and futures prices, there are similar methods to determine the proper relationships among futures prices for contracts of different maturity dates. These relationships are simple generalizations of the spot-futures parity relationship. We will restrict ourselves to stock futures in this discussion and thus avoid the additional complications that arise from noninterest carrying costs.

Call $F(T_1)$ the current futures price for delivery at date $T_1$, and $F(T_2)$ the futures price for delivery at $T_2$. Let $d$ be the dividend yield of the stock between $T_1$ and $T_2$. We know from the parity Equation 22.2 that

$$F(T_1) = S_0(1 + r_f - d)^{T_1}$$
$$F(T_2) = S_0(1 + r_f - d)^{T_2}$$

As a result,

$$F(T_2)/F(T_1) = (1 + r_f - d)^{(T_2 - T_1)}$$

[5] Our parity relationship was derived without transactions costs and marking-to-market. When there features are present, the parity notations may not produce arbitrage profits. See the discussion at end of this section.

Therefore, the basic parity relationship for spreads is

$$F(T_2) = F(T_1)(1 + r_f - d)^{(T_2 - T_1)} \tag{22.3}$$

Note that Equation 22.3 is quite similar to the spot-futures parity relationship. The major difference is in the substitution of $F(T_1)$ for the current spot price. The intuition also is similar. Delaying delivery from $T_1$ to $T_2$ provides the long position with the knowledge that the stock will be purchased for $F(T_2)$ dollars at $T_2$ but does not require that money be tied up in the stock until $T_2$. The savings realized are the cost of carry between $T_1$ and $T_2$ of the money that would have been paid at $T_1$. Delaying delivery from $T_1$ until $T_2$ frees up $F(T_1)$ dollars, which earn risk-free interest at rate $r_f$. The delayed delivery of the stock also results in the lost dividend yield between $T_1$ and $T_2$. The net cost of carry saved by delaying the delivery is thus $r_f - d$. This gives the proportional increase in the futures price that is required to compensate market participants for the delayed delivery of the stock and postponement of the payment of the futures price. If the parity condition for spreads is violated, arbitrage opportunities will arise. [Problem (5) at the end of the chapter explores this phenomenon.]

To see how to use Equation 22.3, consider the following data for a hypothetical contract:

| Contract Maturity Date | Futures Price |
|---|---|
| January | 105 |
| March | 106 |

Suppose that the effective annual T-bill rate is expected to persist at 10 percent and that the dividend yield is 4 percent per year. The "correct" March futures price relative to the January price is, according to Equation 22.3,

$$105(1 + .1 - .04)^{1/6} = 106.025$$

The actual March futures price is 106, meaning that the March futures contract is slightly underpriced compared to the January futures contract, and that, aside from transaction costs, an arbitrage opportunity seems to be present.

Equation 22.3 shows that futures prices should all move together. Actually, it is not surprising that futures prices for different maturity dates move in unison, because all are linked to the same spot price through the parity relationship. Figure 22.3 plots futures prices on gold for three maturity dates. It is apparent that the prices move in virtual lockstep and that the more distant delivery dates require higher futures prices, as Equation 22.3 predicts.

## Forward versus Futures Pricing

Until now we have paid little attention to the differing time profile of returns of futures and forward contracts. Instead, we have taken the sum of daily marking-to-market proceeds to the long position as $P_T - F_0$ and assumed for convenience

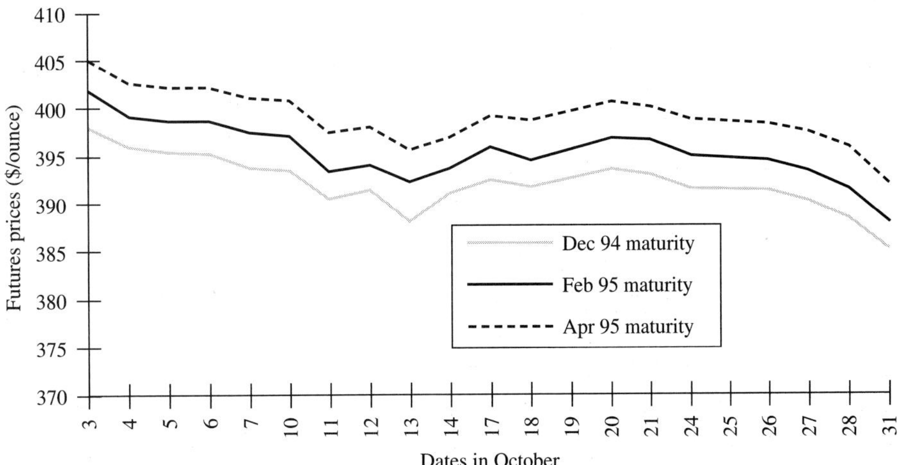


**Figure 22.3**
Gold futures prices, October 1994.

that the entire profit to the futures contract accrues on the delivery date. The parity theorems we have derived apply strictly to forward pricing because they are predicated on the assumption that contract proceeds are realized only on delivery. Although this treatment is appropriate for a forward contract, the actual timing of cash flows influences the determination of the futures price.

Futures prices will deviate from parity values when marking to market gives a systematic advantage to either the long or short position. If marking to market tends to favour the long position, for example, the futures price should exceed the forward price, since the long position will be willing to pay a premium for the advantage of marking to market.

When will marking to market favour either the long or short trader? A trader will benefit if daily settlements are received when the interest rate is high and paid when the interest rate is low. Receiving payments when the interest rate is high allows investment of proceeds at a high rate; traders therefore prefer a high correlation between the level of the interest rate and the payments received from marking to market. The long position will benefit if futures prices tend to rise when interest rates are high. In such circumstances, the long trader will be willing to accept a higher futures price. Whenever there is a positive correlation between interest rates and changes in futures prices, the "fair" futures price will exceed the forward price. Conversely, a negative correlation means that marking to market favours the short position and implies that the equilibrium futures price should be below the forward price.

In practice, however, it appears that the covariance between futures prices and interest rates is low enough so that futures prices and forward prices often differ by negligible amounts. In estimating the theoretically appropriate difference in futures and forward prices on foreign exchange contracts, Cornell and

Reinganum[6] found that the marking-to-market premium is so small that contracts as quoted do not carry enough decimal points to reflect the predicted difference in the two prices.

On the other hand, the difference between futures prices and forward prices also is influenced by transaction costs. For a forward contract, any violation of the spot-futures parity theorem can be exploited by a simple buy-and-hold portfolio strategy. The marking-to-market feature of the futures contract, on the other hand, implies that the corresponding strategy for such contracts must be dynamic, involving many more purchases and sales of the assets in the portfolio. These activities may raise total transaction costs to the point of eliminating the arbitrage profits. In such cases, the parity relationship may be violated, even though no profitable arbitrage may be feasible. For index futures on the S&P 500, MacKinlay and Ramaswamy[7] show that such violation can be serious for long-maturity contracts.

## 22.5 Futures Prices versus Expected Spot Prices

So far we have considered the relationship between futures prices and the current spot price. One of the oldest controversies in the theory of futures pricing concerns the relationship between the futures price and the expected value of the spot price of the commodity at some *future* date. Three traditional theories have been put forth: the expectations hypothesis, normal backwardation, and contango. Today's consensus is that all of these traditional hypotheses are subsumed by the insights provided by modern portfolio theory. Figure 22.4 shows the expected path of futures prices under the three traditional hypotheses.

### Expectations Hypothesis

The *expectations hypothesis* is the simplest theory of futures pricing. It states that the futures price equals the expected value of the future spot price of the asset: $F_0 = E(P_T)$. Under this theory, the expected profit to either position of a futures contract would equal zero: The short position's expected profit is $F_0 - E(P_T)$, while the long's is $E(P_T) - F_0$. With $F_0 = E(P_T)$, the expected profit to either side is zero. This hypothesis relies on a notion of risk neutrality. If all market participants are risk neutral, they should agree on a futures price that provides an expected profit of zero to all parties.

The expectations hypothesis bears a resemblance to market equilibrium in a world with no uncertainty; that is, if prices of goods at all future dates are currently known, then the futures price for delivery at any particular date would

[6] Bradford Cornell and Marc R. Reinganum, "Forward and Futures Prices: Evidence from the Foreign Exchange Markets," *Journal of Finance* 36 (December 1981).

[7] A. Craig MacKinlay and Krishna Ramaswamy, "Index Futures Arbitrage and the Behaviour of Stock Index Futures Prices," *Review of Financial Studies* 1, no. 2 (Summer 1988).

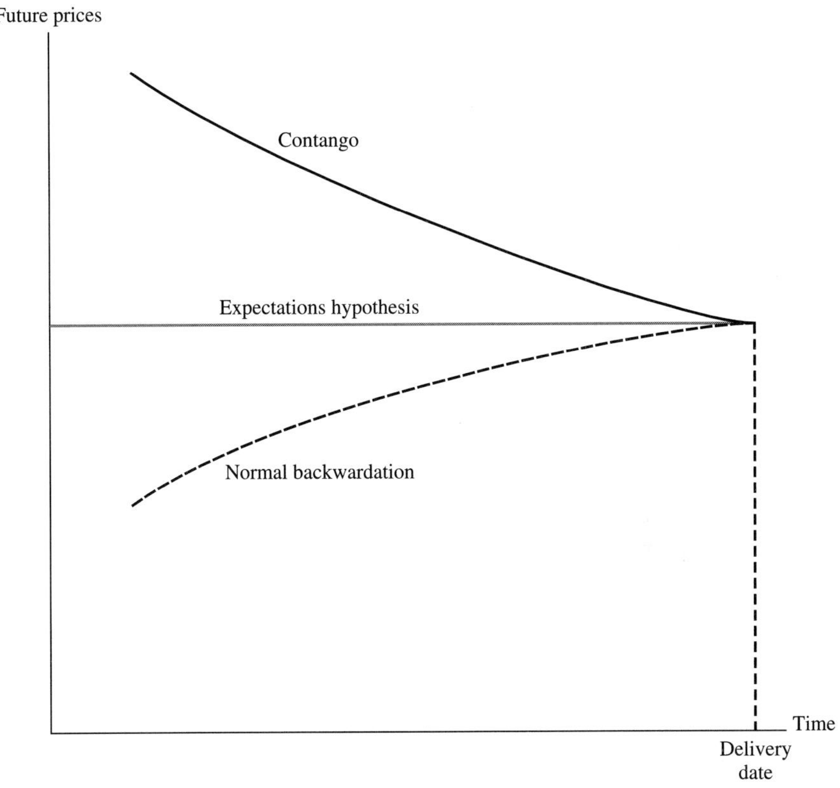


**Figure 22.4**
Futures price for delivery at the end of the harvest, in the special case that the expected spot price remains unchanged.

simply equal the currently known future spot price for that date. It is a tempting but incorrect leap to assert next that under uncertainty the futures price should equal the currently expected spot price. This view ignores the risk premiums that must be built into futures prices when ultimate spot prices are uncertain.

## Normal Backwardation

This theory is associated with the famous British economists, John Maynard Keynes and John Hicks. They argued that for most commodities there are natural hedgers who desire to shed risk. For example, wheat farmers will desire to shed the risk of uncertain wheat prices. These farmers will take short positions to deliver wheat in the future at a guaranteed price; they will short hedge. In order to induce speculators to take the corresponding long positions, the farmers need to offer them an expectation of profit. Speculators will enter the long side of the contract only if the futures price is below the expected spot price of wheat, for an expected profit of $E(P_T) - F_0$. The speculator's expected profit is the farmer's expected loss, but farmers are willing to bear the expected loss on the contract in order to shed the risk of uncertain wheat prices. The theory of *normal backwardation* thus suggests that the futures price will be bid down to a level below the expected spot price and will rise over the life of the contract until the maturity date, at which point $F_T = P_T$.

Although this theory recognizes the important role of risk premiums in futures markets, it is based on total variability rather than on systematic risk. (This is not surprising, as Keynes wrote almost 40 years before the development of modern portfolio theory.) The modern view refines the measure of risk used to determine appropriate risk premiums.

## Contango

The polar hypothesis to backwardation holds that the natural hedgers are the purchasers of a commodity, rather than the suppliers. In the case of wheat, for example, we would view grain processors as willing to pay a premium to lock in the price that they must pay for wheat. These processors hedge by taking a long position in the futures market; they are long hedgers, as opposed to farmers, who are short hedgers. Because long hedgers will agree to pay high futures prices to shed risk, and because speculators must be paid a premium to enter into the short position, the *contango* theory holds that $F_0$ must exceed $E(P_T)$.

It is clear that any commodity will have both natural long hedgers and short hedgers. The compromise traditional view, called the *net hedging hypothesis,* is that $F_0$ will be less than $E(P_T)$ when short hedgers outnumber long hedgers, and vice versa. The strong side of the market will be the side (short or long) that has more natural hedgers. The strong side must pay a premium to induce speculators to enter into enough contracts to balance the "natural" supply of long and short hedgers.

## Modern Portfolio Theory

The three traditional hypotheses all envision a mass of speculators willing to enter either side of the futures market if they are sufficiently compensated for the risk they incur. Modern portfolio theory fine-tunes this approach by refining the notion of risk used in the determination of risk premiums. Simply put, if commodity prices pose positive systematic risk, futures prices must be lower than expected spot prices.

As an example of the use of modern portfolio theory to determine the equilibrium futures price, consider once again a stock paying no dividends. If $E(P_T)$ denotes today's expectation of the time $T$ price of the stock, and $k$ denotes the required rate of return on the stock, then the price of the stock today must equal the present value of its expected future payoff as follows:

$$P_0 = \frac{E(P_T)}{(1 + k)^T} \tag{22.4}$$

We also know from the spot-futures parity relationship that

$$P_0 = \frac{F_0}{(1 + r_f)^T} \qquad \textbf{(22.5)}$$

Therefore, the right-hand sides of Equations 22.4 and 22.5 must be equal. Equating these terms allows us to solve for $F_0$:

$$F_0 = E(P_T)\left(\frac{1 + r_f}{1 + k}\right)^T \qquad \textbf{(22.6)}$$

You can see immediately from equation 22.6 that $F_0$ will be less than the expectation of $P_T$ whenever $k$ is greater than $r_f$, which will be the case for any positive-beta asset. This means that the long side of the contract will make an expected profit [$F_0$ will be lower than $E(P_T)$] when the commodity exhibits positive systematic risk ($k$ is greater than $r_f$).

Why should this be? A long futures position will provide a profit (or loss) of $P_T - F_0$. If the ultimate realization of $P_T$ involves positive systematic or nondiversifiable risk, the profit to the long position also involves such risk. Speculators with well-diversified portfolios will be willing to enter long futures positions only if they receive compensation for bearing that risk in the form of positive expected profits. Their expected profits will be positive only if $E(P_T)$ is greater than $F_0$. The converse is that the short position's profit is the negative of the long's and will have negative systematic risk. Diversified investors in the short position will be willing to suffer an expected loss in order to lower portfolio risk and will be willing to enter the contract even when $F_0$ is less than $E(P_T)$. Therefore, if $P_T$ has positive beta, $F_0$ must be less than the expectation of $P_T$. The analysis is reversed for negative-beta commodities.

**CONCEPT CHECK** Question 8. What must be true of the risk of the spot price of an asset if the futures price is an unbiased estimate of the ultimate spot price?

## 22.6 STOCK INDEX FUTURES

### The Contracts

In contrast to most futures contracts, which call for delivery of a specified commodity, stock index contracts are settled by a cash amount equal to the value of the stock index in question on the contract maturity date times a multiplier that scales the size of the contract. The total profit to the long position is $S_T - F_0$, where $S_T$ is the value of the stock index on the maturity date. Cash settlement avoids the costs that would be incurred if the short trader had to purchase the stocks in the index and deliver them to the long position, and if the long position then had to sell the stock for cash. Instead, the long trader's profit is $S_T - F_0$

**Table 22.2** Stock Index Futures

| Contract | Underlying Market Index | Contract Size | Exchange |
|---|---|---|---|
| S&P 500 | Standard & Poor's 500 index. A value-weighted arithmetic average of 500 stocks. | $500 times the S&P 500 index | Chicago Mercantile Exchange |
| Value Line | Value Line Composite Average. An equally weighted average of about 1,700 firms. | $500 times the Value Line index | Kansas City Board of Trade |
| NYSE | NYSE Composite Index. Value-weighted arithmetic average of all stocks listed on the NYSE. | $500 times the NYSE index | New York Futures Exchange |
| Major market | Price-weighted arithmetic average of 20 blue-chip stocks. Index is designed to track the Dow Jones Industrial Average. | $500 times the Major Market index | Chicago Mercantile Exchange |
| S&P mid-cap | Index of 400 firms of midrange market value. | $500 times the index | Chicago Mercantile Exchange |
| National over-the-counter | Value-weighted arithmetic average of 100 of the largest over-the-counter stocks. | $500 times the OTC index | Philadelphia Board of Trade |
| Nikkei | Nikkei 225 stock average. | $5 times the Nikkei index | Chicago Mercantile Exchange |
| FTSE 100 | Financial Times-Share Exchange Index of 100 U.K. firms. | £25 times the FTSE index | London International Financial Futures Exchange |
| FTSE Eurotrack 100 | Index of 100 non-U.K. European firms. | 50 Deutsche marks times the index | London International Financial Futures Exchange |

dollars, and the short trader's is $F_0 - S_T$ dollars. These profits duplicate those that would arise with actual delivery.

As noted earlier, the only index futures contracts currently trading in Canada are the TSE 35 and the TSE 100, which trade in the Toronto Futures Exchange (TFE) with a multiplier equal to $500. Several other index futures were introduced in the past by the TFE and the Montreal Exchange (ME), but they did not meet with any success. In the United States, however, there are several stock index futures contracts currently traded. Table 22.2 lists the major ones, showing under contract size the multiplier used to calculate contract settlements. An S&P 500 contract, for example, with a futures price of 450 and a final index value of 455 would result in a profit for the long side of $\$500 \times (455 - 450) = \$2{,}500$.

The broad-based U.S. stock market indices are all highly correlated. Table 22.3 presents a correlation matrix for five indices. The only index whose correlation with the others is below .90 is the Value Line index. This index uses an equally weighted geometric average of 1,700 firms, as opposed to the NYSE or S&P indices, which use market value weights. This means that the Value Line contract

**Table 22.3** Correlation Among Major U.S. Stock Market Indices

| Index | DJIA | MMI | S&P 500 | Value Line | NYSE |
|---|---|---|---|---|---|
| DJIA | 1.0000 | .9779 | .9774 | .8880 | .9750 |
| MMI | | 1.0000 | .9497 | .8104 | .9403 |
| S&P 500 | | | 1.0000 | .9137 | .9972 |
| Value Line | | | | 1.0000 | .9337 |
| NYSE | | | | | 1.0000 |

Note: Correlations were computed from weekly percentage rates of price appreciation during calendar year 1989.

Source: Hans R. Stoll and Robert E. Whaley, *Futures and Options: Theory and Applications* (Cincinnati: South-Western Publishing, 1993). Reprinted by permission.

overweights small firms compared to the other indices, which may explain the lower observed correlation.

## Creating Synthetic Stock Positions

One reason why stock index futures are so popular is that they substitute for holdings in the underlying stocks themselves. Index futures let investors participate in broad market movements without actually buying or selling large numbers of stocks.

Because of this, we say futures represent "synthetic" holdings of the market portfolio. Instead of holding the market directly, the investor takes a long futures position in the index. Such a strategy is attractive because the transaction costs involved in establishing and liquidating futures positions are much lower than taking actual spot positions. Investors who wish to frequently buy and sell market positions find it much less costly to play the futures market rather than the underlying spot market. "Market timers," who speculate on broad market moves rather than on individual securities, are large players in stock index futures for this reason.

One means to market time, for example, is to shift between Treasury bills and broad-based stock market holdings. Timers attempt to shift from bills into the market before market upturns and to shift back into bills to avoid market downturns, thereby profiting from broad market movements. Market timing of this sort, however, can result in huge brokerage fees with the frequent purchase and sale of many stocks. An attractive alternative is to invest in Treasury bills and hold varying amounts of market index futures contracts.

The strategy works like this: When timers are bullish, they will establish many long futures positions that they can liquidate quickly and cheaply when expectations turn bearish. Rather than shifting back and forth between T-bills and stocks, they buy and hold T-bills, and adjust only the futures position. This minimizes transaction costs. An advantage of this technique for timing is that investors can implicitly buy or sell the market index in its entirety, whereas market timing in the spot market would require the simultaneous purchase or sale of all the stocks in the index. This is technically difficult to coordinate and can lead to slippage in execution of a timing strategy.

You can construct a T-bill plus index futures position that duplicates the payoff to holding the stock index itself. Here is how:

1. Hold as many market index futures contracts long as you need to purchase your desired stock position. A desired holding of $1,000 multiplied by the TSE 35 index, for example, would require the purchase of two contracts because each contract calls for delivery of $500 multiplied by the index.
2. Invest enough money in T-bills to cover the payment of the futures price at the contract's maturity date. The necessary investment will equal the present value of the futures price that will be paid to satisfy the contracts. The T-bill holdings will grow by the maturity date to a level equal to the futures price.

For example, suppose that an institutional investor wants to invest $25 million in the Canadian equity market for one month and, to minimize trading costs, chooses to buy the TSE 35 futures contract as a substitute for actual stock holdings. If the index is now at 250, the one-month delivery futures price is 252.5, and the T-bill rate is 1 percent per month, the investor would buy 200 contracts. (Each contract controls $500 × 250 = $125,000 worth of stock, and $25 million/ $125,000 = 200.) The institution thus has a long position of 100,000 × the TSE 35 index (200 contracts × the contract multiplier of $500). To cover payment of the futures price, it must invest 100,000 × the present value of the futures price in T-bills. This equals 100,000 × (252.5/1.01) = $25 million market value of bills. Notice that the $25 million outlay in bills is precisely equal to the amount that would have been needed to buy the stock directly. The bills will increase in value in one month to $25.25 million.

This is an artificial, or synthetic, stock position. What is the value of this portfolio at the maturity date? Call $S_T$ the value of the stock index on the maturity date $T$, and, as usual, let $F_0$ be the original futures price:

| | In General (Per Unit of the Index) | Our Numbers |
|---|---|---|
| 1. Profits from contract | $S_T - F_0$ | $100{,}000(S_T - 252.5)$ |
| 2. Value of T-bills | $F_0$ | 25,250,000 |
| Total | $S_T$ | $100{,}000 S_T$ |

The total payoff on the contract maturity date is exactly proportional to the value of the stock index. In other words, adopting this portfolio strategy is equivalent to holding the stock index itself, aside from the issue of interim dividend distributions and tax treatment.

---

**CONCEPT CHECK** Question 9. This result implies something about the relative cost of pursuing this strategy compared to that of purchasing the index directly. As the payoffs are identical, so should be the costs. What does this say about the spot-futures parity relationship?

---

The bills-plus-futures strategy may be viewed as a 100 percent stock strategy. At the other extreme, investing in zero futures results in a 100 percent bills position. Moreover, a short futures position will result in a portfolio equivalent to that obtained by short selling the stock market index, because in both cases the investor gains from decreases in the stock price. Bills-plus-futures mixtures clearly allow for a flexible and low transaction-cost approach to market timing. The futures positions may be established or reversed quickly and cheaply. Also, since the short futures position allows the investor to earn interest on T-bills, it is superior to a conventional short sale of the stock, where the investor typically earns no interest on the proceeds of the short sale.

## Empirical Evidence on Pricing of Stock Index Futures

Recall Equation 22.2, the spot-futures parity relationship between the futures and spot stock price:

$$F_0 = S_0(1 + r_f - d)^T$$

Several investigators have tested this relationship empirically. The general procedure has been to calculate the theoretically appropriate futures price using the current value of the stock index and Equation 22.2. The dividend yield of the index in question is approximated using historical data. Although dividends of individual securities may fluctuate unpredictably, the annualized dividend yield of a broad-based index such as the S&P 500 is fairly stable, usually in the neighbourhood of 3 percent per year. The yield is seasonal with regular and predictable peaks and troughs, however, so the dividend yield for the relevant months must be the one used. Figure 22.5 illustrates the dividend yield of the S&P 500 index since 1991.

If the actual futures price deviates from the value dictated by the parity relationship, then (forgetting transaction costs) an arbitrage opportunity arises. Given an estimate of transaction costs, we can bracket the theoretically correct futures price within a band. If the actual futures price lies within that band, the discrepancy between the actual and the proper futures prices is too small to exploit because of the transaction costs; if the actual price lies outside the no-arbitrage band, profit opportunities are worth exploiting.

Modest and Sundaresan[8] constructed such a test using the April and June 1982 S&P 500 contracts. Figure 22.6 replicates an example of their results. The figure

---

[8] David Modest and Mahadevan Sundaresan, "The Relationship between Spot and Futures Prices in Stock Index Futures Markets: Some Preliminary Evidence," *Journal of Futures Markets* 3 (Spring 1983).

**Figure 22.5** Monthly dividend yield of the S&P 500

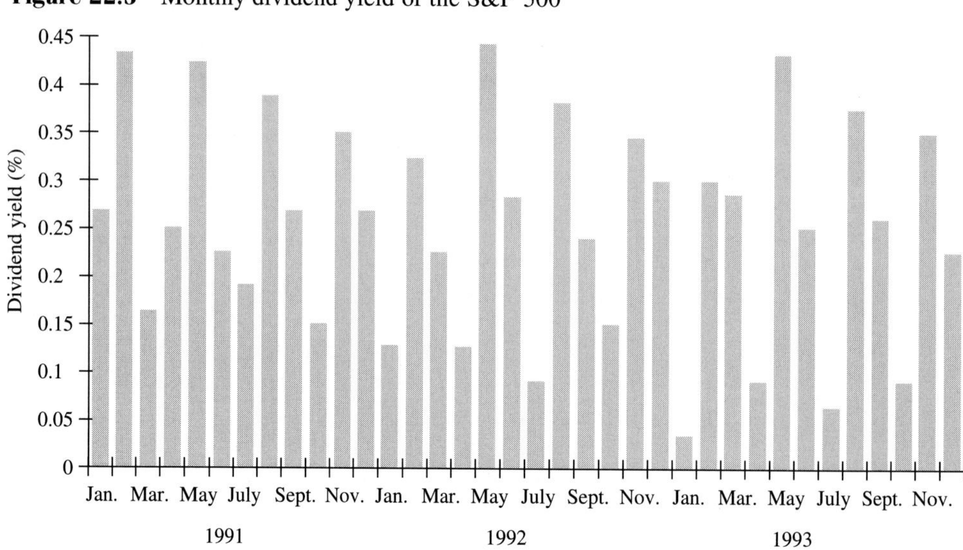


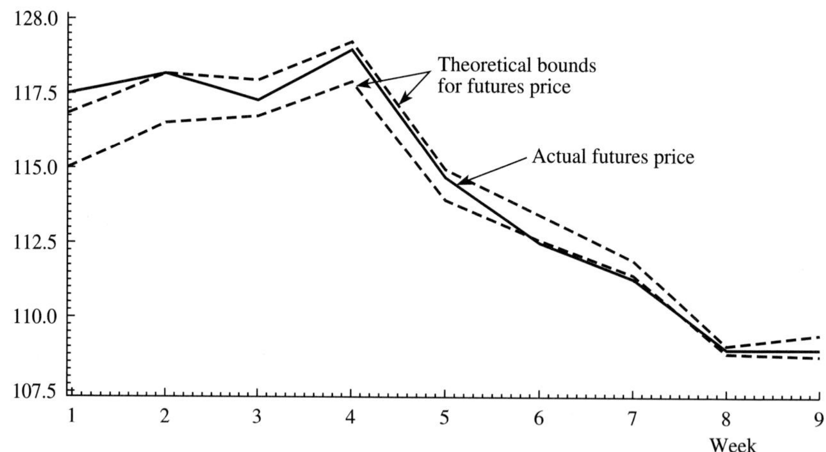


**Figure 22.6** Prices of S&P 500 contracts maturing June 1982. Data plotted for April 21–June 16, 1982.

From David Modest and Mahadevan Sundaresan, "The Relationship between Spot and Futures Prices in Stock Index Futures Markets: Some Preliminary Evidence," *Journal of Futures Markets* 3 (Spring 1983). © John Wiley & Sons, Inc., 1983. Reprinted by permission.

shows that the futures prices generally did lie in the theoretically determined no-arbitrage band, but that profit-opportunities occasionally were possible for low-cost transactors.

Modest and Sundaresan point out that much of the cost of short selling shares is attributable to the investor's inability to invest the entire proceeds from the short sale. Proceeds must be left on margin account, where they do not earn interest. Arbitrage opportunities, or the width of the no-arbitrage band, therefore depend upon assumptions regarding the use of short-sale proceeds. Figure 22.6 assumes that one-half of the proceeds are available to the short seller.

**Concept Check** Question 10. What (if anything) would happen to the top of the no-arbitrage band if short sellers could obtain full use of the proceeds from the short sale? What would happen to the low end of the band? (Hint: when do violations of parity call for a long futures–short stock position versus short futures–long stock position?)

## Index Arbitrage and the Triple Witching Hour

Whenever the actual futures price falls outside the no-arbitrage band, there is an opportunity for profit. This is why the parity relationships are so important. Far from being theoretical academic constructs, they are in fact a guide to trading rules that can generate large profits. One of the most notable developments in trading activity has been the advent of **index arbitrage,** an investment strategy that exploits divergences between the actual futures price and its theoretically correct parity value (see the accompanying box).

In theory, index arbitrage is simple. If the futures price is too high, short the futures contract and buy the stocks in the index. If it is too low, go long in futures and short the stocks. You can perfectly hedge your position and should earn arbitrage profits equal to the mispricing of the contract.

In practice, however, index arbitrage can be difficult to implement. The problem lies in buying "the stocks in the index." Selling or purchasing shares in all stocks in an index is impractical for two reasons. The first is transaction costs, which may outweigh any profits to be made from the arbitrage. Second, it is extremely difficult to buy or sell stock of many different firms simultaneously, and any lags in the execution of such a strategy can destroy the effectiveness of a plan to exploit temporary price discrepancies.

In the real world, most arbitrageurs devise portfolios with a small number of stocks that closely mimic the broader market index. These subportfolios are called *baskets,* and the traders who develop them are called *basket weavers.* Their trades on the spot market are made in this proxy portfolio only, which reduces the execution problems in getting trades off quickly. The substitution, however, creates tracking or basis risk because the futures price on a broad stock index will not correlate as closely with the value of the proxy portfolio as it will with the index itself.

Arbitrageurs need to trade an entire portfolio of stocks quickly and simultaneously if they hope to exploit disparities between the futures price and its corresponding stock index. For this they need a coordinated trading program; hence the term **program trading,** which refers to coordinated purchases or sales of entire portfolios of stocks. The response has been the designated order turnaround (DOT) system, which enables traders to send coordinated buy or sell programs to the floor of the stock exchange via computer.

Index arbitrage seems to have had its own effect on market movements. Four times a year, for example, the TSE 35 futures contract expires at the same time as the TSE 35 index option contract and option contracts on individual stocks.

## Watching the Witching
## A Primer on Program Trading for Investors

Yes, Virginia, there is program trading in Canada—and a double witching hour on the third Friday of each month.

But before elaborating on those statements, it is well to explain what program trading is all about.

A computer trading program is not, repeat not, a complicated formula fed into a computer to enable it to flash buy and sell signals.

It is simply a simultaneous trade of a number of stocks.

The stocks traded are known as a "basket" of stocks.

A basket can be any number of stocks assembled to mimic the performance of a particular stock index.

In most instances, the computer's role is limited to adding up the price of every stock in the basket, which it can do much faster than any human being.

The investor concerned then has control of a basket of stocks that will move up and down in line with a particular stock index.

He can then trade that basket of stocks against a futures contract in that same index, profiting from differences in price between the two.

Program trading got its start as a trading mechanism in the mid-1980s when the New York Stock Exchange first allowed program traders to put through their trades at the close of the day, giving them the leeway to negotiate the prices at which they were going to do a program trade in advance.

Since those early days, program trading has broadened into a whole spectrum of trading strategies that can influence prices on the NYSE at any time of the day.

Program trading is a somewhat less visible feature of the Toronto-market, but, like Everest, it is there and can have some unpredictable effects on stock prices from one hour to another.

It is at its most noticeable on the third Friday of any month when the option (TXO) and futures (TXF) contracts on the TSE 35 index for that month expire.

The TSE 35 index is made up of 35 household-name stocks to be found in just about every major institutional portfolio.

As a result, institutional investors can use the TXO and TXF contracts to sharpen their performance.

For instance, the TXOs or TXFs can be used as an insurance policy against the TSE 35 declining. Or a private investor can buy them as a means of participating in an expected market rally.

Between these two very simple approaches lies a host of more arcane strategies that are often based as much on market mathematics as on expectations of the market moving one way or the other.

Managers of index funds (portfolios limited to all the stocks in one particular stock index) use the futures and options markets to try to beat the performance of that particular index.

Not a few institutions holding the stocks in the TSE 35 index in their basic portfolios seek to improve their return by selling TXO calls, being the right to the cash amount of any increase in the value of a particular TXO option in the period to expiry date.

The selling institution pockets the premium that the buyer pays for the call and can cover any potential loss in a fast-rising market by taking some profits from TSE 35 stocks in its own portfolios.

Whatever the strategy, all the buyers and sellers concerned have to decide how they are going to close out their positions ahead of the expiry of each month's TXO and TXF contracts, which is based on the opening prices of all 35 stocks in the TSE 35 index on expiry Friday.

That is when the trading programs begin to roll in, generally leading to a very significant increase in volume for the first hour of trading.

Thomas Briant, the TSE officer responsible for

(Continued)

options and futures market surveillance, tells this column that trading volumes in the opening hour of an expiry Friday can amount to as much as 40 percent of the total volume of trading that day, compared with a level nearer 20 percent on other days.

There can also be significant difference between the level at which the TSE 35 closes on the Thursday night, and its level for the first five or 10 minutes of trading on expiry Friday morning.

In turn, this also can do some funny things to the value of the TXO options contract, which has become by far the largest option contract traded in Canada.

The sharpest overnight change in the TSE 35 on an expiry Friday in Briant's records is 2.42 (equivalent to 1¼ percent of the index), the Friday the March 1991 contracts closed.

The sharpest overnight change in 1990 was 2.18.

Expiry Friday also can bring significant order imbalances (say, far more orders to buy a particular stock than orders to sell it).

It is a time when an individual investor with market orders to be filled should be keeping a close watch on what is going on.

The TSE requires members firms putting through program trades to notify it in advance.

It then puts out on its tape 20 minutes before the start of trading on an expiry Friday a list of indicated order imbalances.

The basic idea is to alert institutional investors of potential trading opportunities and to encourage them [to] put in orders to lessen these imbalances.

But make sure your broker knows about them, too.

If institutions are going to be given the fortuitous opportunity to get a particularly good deal on a sale of BCE Inc. stock, so should you.

At the very least, check out that your broker is watching the ticker for those imbalances and keeps you briefed.

Source: Patrick Bloomfield, *The Financial Post,* April 2, 1991. Reprinted by permission.

The great volatility of the market at these periods has led people to call the simultaneous expirations the **triple witching hour.**

Expiration-day volatility can be explained by program trading to exploit arbitrage opportunities. Suppose that before a stock index future contract matures, the futures price is a little above its parity value. Arbitrageurs will attempt to lock in superior profits by buying the stocks in the index (the program trading buy order) and taking an offsetting short futures position. If and when the pricing disparity reverses, the position can be unwound at a profit. Alternatively, arbitrageurs can wait until contract maturity day and realize a profit by closing out the offsetting stock and futures positions with "marked-on-close" orders, that is, closing out both positions at prices in the closing range of the day. By waiting until the close of the maturity day, arbitrageurs can be assured that the futures price and stock index price will be aligned—they rely on the convergence property.

Obviously, when many program traders follow such a strategy at market close, a wave of program selling passes over the market. The result? Prices go down. This is the expiration-day effect. If execution of the arbitrage strategy calls for a sale (or short sale) of stocks, unwinding on expiration day requires repurchase of the stocks, with the opposite effect: prices will increase.

The success of these arbitrage positions and associated program trades depends on only two things: the relative levels of spot and futures prices and synchronized trading in the two markets. Because arbitrageurs exploit disparities in futures and spot prices, absolute price levels are unimportant. This means that large buy or sell programs can hit the floor even if stock prices are at "fair" levels, that is, at levels consistent with fundamental information. The markets in individual stocks may not be sufficiently deep to absorb the arbitrage-based program trades without significant price movements, despite the fact that those trades are not informationally motivated.

In an investigation of expiration-day effects, Stoll and Whaley[9] found that the market is in fact more volatile at contract expirations. For example, the standard deviation of the last-hour return on the S&P 500 index is .641 on expirations of the S&P 500 futures contract, whereas it is only .211 on nonexpiration days. Interestingly, the last-hour volatility of non-S&P 500 stocks appears unaffected by expiration days, consistent with the hypothesis that the effect is related to program trading of the stocks in the index. In a subsequent study, however, these same authors found that any expiration-day effects detected in their sample were quite mild. Hence, index arbitrage probably does not have a major impact on stock prices, and any impact it does have appears to be short-lived.

## 22.7 Foreign Exchange Futures

### The Markets

Exchange rates between currencies vary continually and often quite substantially. This variability can be a source of concern for anyone involved in international business. A Canadian exporter who sells goods in England, for example, will be paid in British pounds, and the dollar value of those pounds depends on the exchange rate at the time payment is made. Until that date, the Canadian exporter is exposed to foreign exchange rate risk. This risk, however, is easily hedged through currency futures or forward markets.

The forward market in foreign exchange is fairly informal. It is simply a network of banks and brokers that allows customers to enter forward contracts to purchase or sell currency in the future at a currently agreed-upon rate of exchange. Unlike those in futures markets, these contracts are not standardized in a formal market setting. Instead, each is negotiated separately. Moreover, there is no marking to market as would occur in futures markets. The contracts call only for execution at the maturity date.

[9] Hans R. Stoll and Robert E. Whaley, "Program Trading and Expiration Day Effects," *Financial Analysts Journal*, March–April 1987; and "Expiration-Day Effects: What Has Changed?" *Financial Analysts Journal*, January–February 1991.

For currency futures, however, there are formal markets. As already noted, trading in such futures was introduced by the Montreal Exchange but did not meet with any success; by 1991, it had been eliminated. Elsewhere, however, currency futures markets were established by the Chicago Mercantile Exchange (International Monetary Market), the London International Financial Futures Exchange, and the MidAmerican Commodity Exchange. In these exchanges, contracts are standardized by size, and daily marking to market is observed. Moreover, there are standard clearing arrangements that allow traders to enter or reverse positions easily.

Figure 22.7 reproduces a listing of foreign exchange spot and forward rates from *The Globe and Mail.* The listing gives the number of both Canadian and U.S. dollars required to purchase some unit of foreign currency. Figure 22.8 reproduces futures listings from *The Financial Post,* which show the number of dollars needed to purchase a given unit of foreign currency. In Figure 22.7, both spot and forward exchange rates are listed for various delivery dates for several major currencies. The forward quotations always apply to delivery in 30, 90, 180, or 360 days. Thus, tomorrow's forward listings will apply to a maturity date one day later than today's listing. In contrast, the futures contracts mature in March, June, September, and December, and these four maturity days are the only dates each year when futures contracts settle.

## Interest Rate Parity

As is true of stocks and stock futures, there is a spot-futures exchange rate relationship that will prevail in well-functioning markets. Should this so-called interest rate parity relationship be violated, arbitrageurs will be able to make risk-free profits in foreign exchange markets with zero net investment. Their actions will force futures and spot exchange rates back into alignment.

We can illustrate the **interest rate parity theorem** by using two currencies, the Canadian dollar and the British (U.K.) pound. Call $E_0$ the current exchange rate between the two currencies, that is, $E_0$ dollars are required to purchase one pound. $F_0$, the forward price, is the number of dollars that is agreed to today for purchase of one pound at time $T$ in the future. Call the risk-free interest rates in Canada and the United Kingdom $r_{\text{CAN}}$ and $r_{\text{UK}}$, respectively.

The interest rate parity theorem then states that the proper relationship between $E_0$ and $F_0$ is given as

$$F_0 = E_0\left(\frac{1 + r_{\text{CAN}}}{1 + r_{\text{UK}}}\right)^T \tag{22.7}$$

For example, if $r_{\text{CAN}} = .06$ and $r_{\text{UK}} = .05$ annually, while $E_0 = \$2.10$ per pound, then the proper futures price for a one-year contract would be

$$\$2.10\left(\frac{1.06)}{1.05}\right) = \$2.12 \text{ per pound}$$

**Figure 22.7**
Foreign exchange listing.

From *The Globe and Mail,* July 13, 1995. Reprinted by permission.

# Foreign Exchange

## Cross Rates

| | Canadian dollar | U.S. dollar | British pound | German mark | Japanese yen | Swiss franc | French franc | Dutch guilder | Italian lira |
|---|---|---|---|---|---|---|---|---|---|
| **Canada dollar** | — | 1.3552 | 2.1568 | 0.9665 | 0.015480 | 1.1620 | 0.2779 | 0.8629 | 0.000837 |
| **U.S. dollar** | 0.7379 | — | 1.5915 | 0.7132 | 0.011423 | 0.8574 | 0.2051 | 0.6367 | 0.000618 |
| **British pound** | 0.4636 | 0.6283 | — | 0.4481 | 0.007177 | 0.5388 | 0.1288 | 0.4001 | 0.000388 |
| **German mark** | 1.0347 | 1.4022 | 2.2316 | — | 0.016017 | 1.2023 | 0.2875 | 0.8928 | 0.000866 |
| **Japanese yen** | 64.60 | 87.55 | 139.33 | 62.44 | — | 75.06 | 17.95 | 55.74 | 0.054070 |
| **Swiss franc** | 0.8606 | 1.1663 | 1.8561 | 0.8318 | 0.013322 | — | 0.2392 | 0.7426 | 0.000720 |
| **French franc** | 3.5984 | 4.8766 | 7.7611 | 3.4779 | 0.055703 | 4.1814 | — | 3.1051 | 0.003012 |
| **Dutch guilder** | 1.1589 | 1.5705 | 2.4995 | 1.1201 | 0.017940 | 1.3466 | 0.3221 | — | 0.000970 |
| **Italian lira** | 1194.74 | 1619.12 | 2576.82 | 1154.72 | 18.494624 | 1388.29 | 332.02 | 1030.94 | — |

**Mid-market rates in Toronto at noon, July 12, 1995. Prepared by the Bank of Montreal Treasury Group.**

| | | $1 U.S. in Cdn.$ = | $1 Cdn. in U.S.$ = |
|---|---|---|---|
| U.S./Canada spot | | 1.3552 | 0.7379 |
| 1 month forward | | 1.3561 | 0.7374 |
| 2 months forward | | 1.3568 | 0.7370 |
| 3 months forward | | 1.3572 | 0.7368 |
| 6 months forward | | 1.3596 | 0.7355 |
| 12 months forward | | 1.3658 | 0.7322 |
| 3 years forward | | 1.3972 | 0.7157 |
| 5 years forward | | 1.4472 | 0.6910 |
| 7 years forward | | 1.5082 | 0.6630 |
| 10 years forward | | 1.6152 | 0.6191 |
| Canadian dollar | High | 1.3465 | 0.7427 |
| in 1995: | Low | 1.4267 | 0.7009 |
| | Average | 1.3878 | 0.7206 |

| Country | Currency | Cdn. $ per unit | U.S. $ per unit |
|---|---|---|---|
| Britain | Pound | 2.1568 | 1.5915 |
| 1 month forward | | 2.157u | 1.5906 |
| 2 months forward | | 2.1565 | 1.5894 |
| 3 months forward | | 2.1551 | 1.5879 |
| 6 months forward | | 2.1520 | 1.5828 |
| 12 months forward | | 2.1440 | 1.5698 |
| Germany | Mark | 0.9665 | 0.7132 |
| 1 month forward | | 0.9683 | 0.7140 |
| 3 months forward | | 0.9712 | 0.7156 |
| 6 months forward | | 0.9758 | 0.7177 |
| 12 months forward | | 0.9842 | 0.7206 |
| Japan | Yen | 0.015480 | 0.011423 |
| 1 month forward | | 0.015558 | 0.011472 |
| 3 months forward | | 0.015702 | 0.011569 |
| 6 months forward | | 0.015923 | 0.011712 |
| 12 months forward | | 0.016370 | 0.011985 |
| Algeria | Dinar | 0.0293 | 0.0216 |
| Antigua, Grenada and St. Lucia | E.C.Dollar | 0.5029 | 0.3711 |
| Argentina | Peso | 1.35520 | 1.00000 |
| Australia | Dollar | 0.9780 | 0.7217 |
| Austria | Schilling | 0.13740 | 0.10139 |
| Bahamas | Dollar | 1.3552 | 1.0000 |
| Barbados | Dollar | 0.6810 | 0.5025 |
| Belgium | Franc | 0.04698 | 0.03466 |
| Bermuda | Dollar | 1.3552 | 1.0000 |
| Brazil | Real | 1.4667 | 1.0823 |
| Bulgaria | Lev | 0.0205 | 0.0151 |
| Chile | Peso | 0.003605 | 0.002660 |
| China | Renminbi | 0.1632 | 0.1205 |
| Cyprus | Pound | 3.0626 | 2.2599 |
| Czech Rep | Koruna | 0.0519 | 0.0383 |
| Denmark | Krone | 0.2480 | 0.1830 |
| Egypt | Pound | 0.3984 | 0.2939 |
| Fiji | Dollar | 0.9724 | 0.7175 |
| Finland | Markka | 0.3159 | 0.2331 |
| France | Franc | 0.2779 | 0.2051 |
| Greece | Drachma | 0.00596 | 0.00440 |
| Hong Kong | Dollar | 0.1750 | 0.1292 |
| Hungary | Forint | 0.01066 | 0.00787 |
| Iceland | Krona | 0.02136 | 0.01576 |
| India | Rupee | 0.04316 | 0.03185 |
| Indonesia | Rupiah | 0.000602 | 0.000444 |
| Ireland | Punt | 2.2110 | 1.6315 |
| Israel | N Shekel | 0.4585 | 0.3383 |
| Italy | Lira | 0.000837 | 0.000618 |
| Jamaica | Dollar | 0.04132 | 0.03049 |
| Jordan | Dinar | 1.9415 | 1.4327 |
| Lebanon | Pound | 0.000837 | 0.000618 |
| Luxembourg | Franc | 0.04698 | 0.03466 |
| Malaysia | Ringgit | 0.5527 | 0.4078 |
| Mexico | N Peso | 0.2218 | 0.1637 |
| Netherlands | Guilder | 0.8629 | 0.6367 |
| New Zealand | Dollar | 0.9118 | 0.6728 |
| Norway | Krone | 0.2173 | 0.1604 |
| Pakistan | Rupee | 0.04369 | 0.03224 |
| Philippines | Peso | 0.05302 | 0.03912 |
| Poland | Zloty | 0.5694 | 0.4202 |
| Portugal | Escudo | 0.00919 | 0.00678 |
| Romania | Leu | 0.000683 | 0.000504 |
| Russia | Ruble | 0.000299 | 0.000221 |
| Saudi Arabia | Riyal | 0.3614 | 0.2667 |
| Singapore | Dollar | 0.9690 | 0.7151 |
| Slovakia | Koruna | 0.0465 | 0.0343 |
| South Africa | Rand | 0.3710 | 0.2738 |
| South Korea | Won | 0.001789 | 0.001320 |
| Spain | Peseta | 0.01128 | 0.00832 |
| Sudan | Dinar | 0.0258 | 0.0190 |
| Sweden | Krona | 0.1880 | 0.1387 |
| Switzerland | Franc | 1.1620 | 0.8574 |
| Taiwan | Dollar | 0.0522 | 0.0385 |
| Thailand | Baht | 0.0547 | 0.0404 |
| Trinidad, Tobago | Dollar | 0.2377 | 0.1754 |
| Turkey | Lira | 0.0000303 | 0.0000224 |
| Venezuela | Bolivar | 0.00799 | 0.00590 |
| Zambia | Kwacha | 0.001523 | 0.001124 |
| European Currency Unit | | 1.7914 | 1.3219 |
| Special Drawing Right | | 2.1012 | 1.5505 |

The U.S. dollar closed at $1.3560 in terms of Canadian funds, up $0.0025 from Tuesday. The pound sterling closed at $2.1581, up $0.0081.

In New York, the Canadian dollar closed down $0.0013 at $0.7375 in terms of U.S. funds. The pound sterling was up $0.0030 to $1.5915.

**Figure 22.8**
Foreign exchange futures.

From *The Financial Post,* May 31, 1996. Reprinted by permission.

**42 INVESTING** Friday, May 31, 1996

# Futures Pr

Figures supplied by Star Data Systems Inc.

| — Lifetime — | | | | — Daily — | | | | Open |
|---|---|---|---|---|---|---|---|---|
| High | Low | Month | Open | High | Low | Settle | Chg | interest |
| **Currency** | | | | | | | | |
| **Australian Dollar (IMM)** | | | | | | | | |
| A$100,000, US$ per A$; 0.0001 = $10 per contract | | | | | | | | |
| 0.8028 | 0.7260 | June96 | 0.7970 | 0.7970 | 0.7942 | 0.7952 | −0.0026 | 11,189 |
| 0.7981 | 0.7244 | Sep96 | 0.7923 | 0.7923 | 0.7905 | 0.7912 | −0.0027 | 187 |
| Est. vol. | 703 | | Prev. vol. | | 1,952 | Prev. open int. | | 11,415 |
| **British Pound (IMM)** | | | | | | | | |
| 62,500 pounds, US$ per pound; 0.0002 = $12.50 per contract | | | | | | | | |
| 1.5874 | 1.4880 | June96 | 1.5308 | 1.5396 | 1.5294 | 1.5338 | +0.0034 | 59,749 |
| 1.5840 | 1.4860 | Sep96 | 1.5314 | 1.5380 | 1.5280 | 1.5318 | +0.0034 | 1,786 |
| Est. vol. | 22,913 | | Prev. vol. | | 39,571 | Prev. open int. | | 61,587 |
| **Canadian Dollar (IMM)** | | | | | | | | |
| C$100,000, US$ per C$; 0.0001 = $10 per contract | | | | | | | | |
| 0.7500 | 0.6905 | June96 | 0.7290 | 0.7318 | 0.7284 | 0.7304 | +0.0015 | 43,655 |
| 0.7490 | 0.7135 | Sep96 | 0.7298 | 0.7331 | 0.7295 | 0.7316 | +0.0015 | 5,431 |
| 0.7460 | 0.7130 | Dec96 | 0.7320 | 0.7335 | 0.7320 | 0.7325 | +0.0015 | 2,682 |
| 0.7399 | 0.7117 | Mar97 | 0.7342 | 0.7342 | 0.7332 | 0.7332 | +0.0015 | 452 |
| 0.7395 | 0.7185 | June97 | ... | 0.7335 | ... | 0.7334 | +0.0015 | 267 |
| Est. vol. | 8,220 | | Prev. vol. | | 13,436 | Prev. open int. | | 52,577 |
| **French Franc (IMM)** | | | | | | | | |
| 500,000 francs, US$ per franc; 0.0001 = $5 per contract | | | | | | | | |
| 0.2059 | 0.1911 | June96 | ... | ... | 0.1925 | 0.1925 | −0.0003 | 2,656 |
| Est. vol. | 2 | | Prev. vol. | | 8 | Prev. open int. | | 2,754 |
| **German Mark (IMM)** | | | | | | | | |
| 125,000 marks, US$ per mark; 0.0001 = $12.50 per contract | | | | | | | | |
| 0.7315 | 0.6463 | June96 | 0.6511 | 0.6551 | 0.6511 | 0.6520 | −0.0003 | 78,334 |
| 0.7332 | 0.6485 | Sep96 | 0.6555 | 0.6587 | 0.6551 | 0.6555 | −0.0003 | 6,173 |
| 0.7101 | 0.6537 | Dec96 | 0.6620 | 0.6620 | 0.6595 | 0.6595 | −0.0003 | 1,615 |
| Est. vol. | 22,751 | | Prev. vol. | | 26,837 | Prev. open int. | | 86,144 |
| **Japanese Yen (IMM)** | | | | | | | | |
| 12.5 million yen, US$ per yen (scaled .00); 0.0001 = $12.50 per contract | | | | | | | | |
| 1.3143 | 0.9203 | June96 | 0.9260 | 0.9390 | 0.9255 | 0.9303 | +0.0034 | 76,971 |
| 1.2136 | 0.9320 | Sep96 | 0.9424 | 0.9510 | 0.9415 | 0.9421 | +0.0037 | 6,944 |
| 1.0561 | 0.9432 | Dec96 | 0.9615 | 0.9615 | 0.9540 | 0.9541 | +0.0042 | 2,639 |
| 1.0045 | 0.9549 | Mar97 | ... | 0.9669 | ... | 0.9662 | +0.0048 | 101 |
| Est. vol. | 34,735 | | Prev. vol. | | 27,139 | Prev. open int. | | 86,655 |
| **Mexican Peso (IMM)** | | | | | | | | |
| 500,000 new pesos, US$ per peso; 0.000025 = $12.50 per contract | | | | | | | | |
| 0.1340 | 0.0902 | June96 | 0.1329 | 0.1335 | 0.1328 | 0.1334 | +0.0005 | 7,574 |
| 0.1270 | 0.0841 | Sep96 | 0.1255 | 0.1261 | 0.1252 | 0.1260 | +0.0005 | 5,216 |
| 0.1202 | 0.0970 | Dec96 | 0.1184 | 0.1195 | 0.1182 | 0.1192 | +0.0006 | 2,078 |
| 0.1134 | 0.1007 | Mar97 | 0.1115 | 0.1128 | 0.1115 | 0.1125 | +0.0006 | 978 |
| Est. vol. | 3,994 | | Prev. vol. | | 3,122 | Prev. open int. | | 15,846 |
| **Swiss Franc (IMM)** | | | | | | | | |
| 125,000 francs, US$ per franc; 0.0001 = $12.50 per contract | | | | | | | | |
| 0.9120 | 0.7852 | June96 | 0.7939 | 0.7994 | 0.7928 | 0.7946 | −0.0002 | 42,539 |
| 0.9188 | 0.7917 | Sep96 | 0.8010 | 0.8042 | 0.7998 | 0.8003 | −0.0006 | 3,850 |
| 0.9023 | 0.7976 | Dec96 | 0.8095 | 0.8100 | 0.8064 | 0.8064 | −0.0009 | 857 |
| Est. vol. | 19,292 | | Prev. vol. | | 16,793 | Prev. open int. | | 47,254 |
| **U.S. Dollar Index (FINEX)** | | | | | | | | |
| 1000 x index points and US cents; 0.01 = $10 per contract | | | | | | | | |
| 89.05 | 82.05 | June96 | 88.32 | 88.33 | 87.89 | 88.27 | −0.04 | 10,380 |
| 88.93 | 85.00 | Sep96 | 88.23 | 88.23 | 87.78 | 88.15 | −0.06 | 733 |
| | | | Prev. vol. | | 1,769 | Prev. open int. | | 11,115 |

Consider the intuition behind this result. If $r_{CAN}$ is greater than $r_{UK}$, money invested in Canada will grow at a faster rate than money invested in the United Kingdom. If this is so, why wouldn't all investors decide to invest their money in Canada? One important reason why not is that the dollar may be depreciating relative to the pound. Although dollar investments in Canada grow faster than pound investments in the United Kingdom, each dollar is worth progressively fewer pounds as time passes. Such an effect will exactly offset the advantage of the higher Canadian interest rate.

To complete the argument, we need only determine how a depreciating dollar will show up in Equation 22.7. If the dollar is depreciating, meaning that progressively more dollars are required to purchase each pound, then the forward exchange rate $F_0$ (which equals the dollars required to purchase one pound for delivery in one year) must exceed $E_0$, the current exchange rate. This is exactly what Equation 22.7 tells us: When $r_{CAN}$ exceeds $r_{UK}$, $F_0$ must exceed $E_0$. The depreciation of the dollar embodied in the ratio of $F_0$ to $E_0$ exactly compensates for the difference in interest rates available in the two countries. Of course, the argument also works in reverse; if $r_{CAN}$ is less than $r_{UK}$, then $F_0$ is less than $E_0$.

What if the interest rate parity relationship is violated? For example, suppose the futures price is \$2.11 instead of \$2.12. You could adopt the following strategy to reap arbitrage profits. In this example, let $E_1$ denote the exchange rate that will prevail in one year. $E_1$ is, of course, a random variable from the perspective of today's investors.

| Action | Initial Cash Flow (\$) | CF in One Year (\$) |
|---|---|---|
| 1. Borrow one U.K. pound in London. Convert to dollars. | 2.10 | $-E_1(1.05)$ |
| 2. Lend \$2.10 in Canada. | −2.10 | 2.10(1.06) |
| 3. Enter a contract to purchase 1.05 pounds at a (futures) price of $F_0 = \$2.11$. | 0 | $1.05(E_1 - 2.11)$ |
| Total | 0 | \$.0105 |

In step 1, you exchange the one pound borrowed in the United Kingdom for \$2.10 at the current exchange rate. After one year you must repay the pound borrowed with interest. Since the loan is made in the United Kingdom at the U.K. interest rate, you would repay 1.05 pounds, which would be worth $E_1(1.05)$ dollars. The Canadian loan in step 2 is made at the Canadian interest rate of 6 percent. The futures position in step 3 results in receipt of 1.05 pounds, for which you would first pay $F_0$ dollars each, and then trade into dollars at rate $E_1$.

Note that the exchange rate risk here is exactly offset between the pound obligation in step 1 and the futures position in step 3. The profit from the strategy is therefore risk-free and requires no net investment.

To generalize this strategy:

| Action | Initial CF (\$) | CF in One Year (\$) |
|---|---|---|
| 1. Borrow one U.K. pound in London. Convert to \$. | $\$E_0$ | $-\$E_1(1 + r_{UK})$ |
| 2. Use proceeds of borrowing in London to lend in Canada. | $-\$E_0$ | $\$E_0(1 + r_{CAN})$ |
| 3. Enter $(1 + r_{UK})$ futures positions to purchase one pound for $F_0$ dollars. | 0 | $(1 + r_{UK})(E_1 - F_0)$ |
| Total | 0 | $E_0(1 + r_{CAN}) - F_0(1 + r_{UK})$ |

Let us again review the stages of the arbitrage operation. The first step requires borrowing one pound in the United Kingdom. With a current exchange rate of $E_0$, the one pound is converted into $E_0$ dollars, which is a cash inflow. In one year the British loan must be paid off with interest, requiring a payment in pounds of $(1 + r_{UK})$, or in dollars $E_1(1 + r_{UK})$. In the second step the proceeds of the British loan are invested in Canada. This involves an initial cash outflow of $\$E_0$, and a cash inflow of $\$E_0(1 + r_{CAN})$ in one year. Finally, the exchange risk involved in the British borrowing is hedged in step 3. Here, the $(1 + r_{UK})$ pounds that will need to be delivered to satisfy the British loan are purchased ahead in the futures contract.

The net proceeds to the arbitrage portfolio are risk-free and given by $E_0(1 + r_{CAN}) - F_0(1 + r_{UK})$. If this value is positive, borrow in the United Kingdom, lend in Canada, and enter a long futures position to eliminate foreign exchange risk. If the value is negative, borrow in Canada, lend in the United Kingdom, and take a short position in pound futures. When prices are aligned properly to preclude arbitrage opportunities, the expression must equal zero. If it were positive, investors would pursue the arbitrage portfolio. If it were negative, they would pursue the reverse positions.

Rearranging this expression gives us the relationship

$$F_0 = \frac{1 + r_{CAN}}{1 + r_{UK}} E_0 \tag{22.8}$$

which is the interest rate parity theorem for a one-year horizon, known also as the **covered interest arbitrage relationship.**

**CONCEPT CHECK** Question 11. What are the arbitrage strategy and associated profits if the initial futures price is $F_0 = \$2.14$/pound?

Ample empirical evidence bears out this theoretical relationship. For two other currencies, for example, on July 13, 1995, *The Globe and Mail* listed the six-month U.S. interest rate at 2.76 percent[10] and the six-month Canadian rate at 3.20 percent. The U.S. dollar was then worth 1.3552 Canadian dollars. Substituting these values into Equation 22.8 gives $F_0 = 1.3552(1.032/1.0276) = 1.36100$. The actual forward price at that time for six-month delivery was \$1.3596 per U.S. dollar, so close to the parity value that transaction costs would prevent arbitrageurs from profiting from the discrepancy.

[10] Recall from Chapter 2 that U.S. T-bill rates are quoted as bank discount rates. The actual quote was 5.30%, which translates into a bond equivalent yield rate of 5.52%.

## 22.8 Interest Rate Futures

### The Markets

The late 1970s and 1980s saw a dramatic increase in the volatility of interest rates, leading to investor desire to hedge returns on fixed-income securities against changes in interest rates. Similarly, thrift institutions that had loaned money on home mortgages before 1975 suffered substantial capital losses on those loans when interest rates later increased. An interest rate futures contract could have protected banks against such large swings in yields. Demonstration of these losses has spurred trading in interest rate futures.

As with other futures contracts, several Canadian interest rate futures were introduced by the TFE and Montreal Exchange. Very few of them survive today. Figure 22.9 shows the futures contracts that traded on the Montreal Exchange in July 1995. Only bankers' acceptances and Canada bond futures had survived by that date.

Interest rate futures contracts call for delivery of a bond, bill, or note. Should interest rates rise, the market value of the security at delivery will be less than the original futures price, and the deliverer will profit. Hence, the short position in the interest rate futures contract gains when interest rates rise.

In the United States, the major interest rate contracts currently traded are on Treasury bills, Treasury notes, Treasury bonds, and a municipal bond index. These securities thus provide an opportunity to hedge against a wide spectrum of maturities from very short (T-bills) to long term (T-bonds). In addition, futures contracts tied to Eurodollar rates and to interest rates in Germany and the United Kingdom trade on the London International Financial Futures Exchange and are listed in the major U.S. financial publications.

### Bond Futures Strategies

Bond futures can be useful hedging vehicles for bond dealers or underwriters. Suppose, for instance, that an underwriting syndicate brings out a bond issue on behalf of a corporate client. As is typical in such cases, the syndicate quotes an interest rate at which it guarantees that the bonds can be sold. In essence, the syndicate buys the company's bonds at an agreed-upon price and then takes the responsibility of reselling them in the open market. If interest rates increase before the bonds can be sold to the public, the syndicate, not the issuer, bears the capital loss from the fall in the value of the bonds. This loss can be hedged through bond futures.

How can the underwriter construct the proper hedge ratio, that is, the proper number of futures contracts per bond held in its inventory? Suppose that the Canada bond futures contract nominally calls for delivery of an 8 percent coupon, 20-year maturity federal government bond in return for the futures price. (In practice, other bonds may be substituted for this standard bond to settle the contract, but

**Figure 22.9**
Canadian interest rate futures.

From *The Globe and Mail,* July 12, 1995. Reprinted by permission.

# Cdn. Futures & Options

## Toronto Futures Exchange

### Futures

| SeaHi | SeaLow | Mth. | Open | High | Low | Settle | Chg. | Opint |
|---|---|---|---|---|---|---|---|---|
| TSE 35 $500x, 0.02 pt=$10 | | | | | | | | |
| 245.10 | 0.01 | Jul95 | 243.50 | 245.40 | 243.50 | 245.18 | +0.48 | 649 |
| 246.30 | 228.04 | Sep95 | 244.90 | 246.90 | 244.90 | 246.60 | +0.50 | 4279 |

| Est sales | Prv Sales | Prv Open Int | Chg. |
|---|---|---|---|
| 147 | 660 | 4928 | —88 |

| SeaHi | SeaLow | Mth. | Open | High | Low | Settle | Chg. | Opint |
|---|---|---|---|---|---|---|---|---|
| TSE 100 $500x, 0.05 pt=$25 | | | | | | | | |
| 278.70 | 278.00 | Sep95 | | | | 285.10 | +0.50 | 113 |

| Est sales | Prv Sales | Prv Open Int | Chg. |
|---|---|---|---|
| | 0 | 113 | unch |

## Montreal Exchange

### Futures

| SeaHi | SeaLow | Mth. | Open | High | Low | Settle | Chg. | Opint |
|---|---|---|---|---|---|---|---|---|
| 3-month bankers' acceptances, $1M, pts. of 100% | | | | | | | | |
| 93.94 | 90.42 | Sep95 | 93.81 | 93.81 | 93.74 | 93.74 | –0.13 | 31226 |
| 93.85 | 90.39 | Dec95 | 93.67 | 93.71 | 93.65 | 93.65 | –0.12 | 15860 |
| 93.70 | 89.95 | Mar96 | 93.55 | 93.57 | 93.52 | 93.53 | –0.10 | 17958 |
| 93.55 | 89.92 | Jun96 | 93.40 | 93.43 | 93.38 | 93.38 | –0.10 | 10636 |
| 93.34 | 90.17 | Sep96 | 93.25 | 93.26 | 93.22 | 93.22 | –0.10 | 6393 |
| 93.22 | 90.20 | Dec96 | 93.05 | 93.05 | 93.05 | 93.05 | –0.10 | 2206 |

| Est sales | Prv Sales | Prv Open Int | Chg. |
|---|---|---|---|
| 5466 | 6041 | 85550 | –1836 |

| SeaHi | SeaLow | Mth. | Open | High | Low | Settle | Chg. | Opint |
|---|---|---|---|---|---|---|---|---|
| 1-month bankers' acceptances, $3M, pts. of 100% | | | | | | | | |
| 92.84 | 92.52 | Jul95 | | | | 93.30 | –0.10 | 20 |
| 92.80 | 92.80 | Aug95 | | | | 93.40 | –0.10 | 10 |

| Est sales | Prv Sales | Prv Open Int | Chg. |
|---|---|---|---|
| | 0 | 30 | |

| SeaHi | SeaLow | Mth. | Open | High | Low | Settle | Chg. | Opint |
|---|---|---|---|---|---|---|---|---|
| 10-year Cda bonds, $100K, pts of 100%, 1 pt = $10 | | | | | | | | |
| 108.75 | 102.46 | Sep95 | 107.75 | 107.80 | 107.58 | 107.63 | –0.43 | 21560 |

| Est sales | Prv Sales | Prv Open Int | Chg. |
|---|---|---|---|
| 3208 | 3293 | 21560 | +262 |

| SeaHi | SeaLow | Mth. | Open | High | Low | Settle | Chg. | Opint |
|---|---|---|---|---|---|---|---|---|
| 5-year Cda bonds, $100K, pts of 100% | | | | | | | | |
| 106.55 | 104.70 | Sep95 | 106.30 | 106.35 | 106.25 | 106.25 | –0.30 | 1849 |

| Est sales | Prv Sales | Prv Open Int | Chg. |
|---|---|---|---|
| 293 | 50 | 1849 | –18 |

### Options

| Price | Calls | — | Last | Puts | — | Last |
|---|---|---|---|---|---|---|
| Canada bond futures, $100,000, pts. of 100% | | | | | | |
| | Jul | Aug | Sep | Jul | Aug | Sep |
| 104 | s | 3.66 | s | s | 0.06 | s |
| 105 | s | 2.86 | s | s | 0.50 | s |
| 106 | s | 2.01 | s | s | 0.59 | s |
| 107 | s | 1.28 | s | s | 0.86 | s |
| 108 | 0.24 | 0.77 | s | 0.66 | 1.19 | s |
| 109 | s | 0.42 | s | s | 1.78 | s |
| Prev. day calls vol | | 0 | Open int. | | | 53 |
| Prev. day puts vol | | 0 | Open int. | | | 232 |
| 3-mo. bankers' acceptances futures,$1M,pts of 100% | | | | | | |
| | Sep | Dec | Mar | Sep | Dec | Mar |
| 90.00 | 3.74 | 3.65 | s | r | 0.01 | s |
| 90.50 | 3.24 | 3.15 | s | r | 0.01 | s |
| 91.00 | 2.74 | 2.65 | 2.53 | r | 0.03 | 0.09 |
| 91.50 | 2.24 | 2.15 | 2.08 | r | 0.05 | 0.14 |
| 92.00 | 1.74 | 1.69 | 1.67 | 0.01 | 0.09 | 0.21 |
| 92.50 | 1.27 | 1.28 | 1.30 | 0.03 | 0.16 | 0.31 |
| 93.00 | 0.81 | 0.90 | 0.95 | 0.08 | 0.27 | 0.45 |
| 93.50 | 0.44 | 0.58 | 0.66 | 0.20 | 0.44 | 0.63 |
| 94.00 | 0.19 | 0.33 | 0.42 | 0.44 | 0.68 | 0.87 |
| 94.50 | 0.05 | 0.16 | 0.24 | 0.80 | 1.00 | 1.17 |
| Prev. day calls vol | | 0 | Open int. | | | 6613 |
| Prev. day puts vol | | 0 | Open int. | | | 6721 |

we will use the 8 percent bond for illustration.) Suppose that the market interest rate is 10 percent and that the syndicate is holding $100 million worth of bonds, with a coupon rate of 10 percent, and 20-year time to maturity. The bonds currently sell at par value of $1,000. If the interest rate were to jump to 11 percent, the bonds would fall to a market value of $919.77, a loss of $8.02 million. (We use semiannual compounding in this calculation.)

To hedge this risk, the underwriter would need to short enough futures so that the profits on the futures position would offset the loss on the bonds. The 8 percent 20-year bond of the futures contract would sell for $828.41 if the interest rate were 10 percent. If the interest rate were to jump to 11 percent, the bond price would fall to $759.31, and the fall in the price of the 8 percent bond, $69.10, would approximately equal the profit on the short futures position per bond to be delivered.[11] Because each contract calls for delivery of $100,000 par value of bonds (100 bonds at par value of $1,000), the gain on each short position would equal $6,910. Thus, to offset the $8.02 million loss on the value of the bonds, the syndicate would need to hold $8.02 million/$6,910 = 1,161 contracts short. The total gain on the contracts would offset the loss on the bonds and leave the underwriter unaffected by interest rate swings.

The actual hedging problem is more difficult for several reasons: (1) the syndicate probably would hold more than one issue of bonds in its inventory; (2) interest rates on government and corporate bonds will not be equal and need not move in lockstep (and a corporate bond contract does not exist in Canada); (3) the Canada bond contract may be settled with any of several bonds instead of the 8 percent benchmark bond; and (4) taxes could complicate the picture. Nevertheless, the principles illustrated here underlie all hedging activity.

## 22.9 Commodity Futures Pricing

Commodity futures prices are governed by the same general considerations as stock futures. One difference, however, is that the cost of carrying commodities, especially those subject to spoilage, is greater than the cost of carrying financial assets. Moreover, spot prices for some commodities demonstrate marked seasonal patterns that can affect futures pricing.

### Pricing with Storage Costs

The cost of carrying commodities includes (in addition to interest costs) storage costs, insurance costs, and an allowance for spoilage of goods in storage. To price commodity futures, let us reconsider the earlier arbitrage strategy that calls for holding both the asset and a short position in the futures contract on the asset. In this case, we will denote the price of the commodity at time $T$ as $P_T$, and assume for simplicity that all noninterest carrying costs ($C$) are paid in one lump sum at time $T$, the contract maturity. Carrying costs appear in the final cash flow.

[11] We say "approximately" because the exact figure depends upon the time to maturity of the contract. We assume here that the maturity date is less than a month away, so that the futures price and bond price move in virtual lockstep.

| Action | Initial Cash Flow | CF at Time $T$ |
|---|---|---|
| Buy asset; pay carrying costs at $T$ | $-P_0$ | $P_T - C$ |
| Borrow $P_0$; repay with interest at time $T$ | $P_0$ | $-P_0(1 + r_f)$ |
| Short futures position | $0$ | $F_0 - P_T$ |
| Total | $0$ | $F_0 - P_0(1 + r_f) - C$ |

Because market prices should not allow for arbitrage opportunities, the terminal cash flow of this zero net investment, risk-free strategy should be zero.

If the cash flow were positive, this strategy would yield guaranteed profits for no investment. If the cash flow were negative, the reverse of this strategy also would yield profits. In practice, the reverse strategy would involve a short sale of the commodity. This is unusual but may be done as long as the short sale contract appropriately accounts for storage costs.[12] Thus we conclude that

$$F_0 = P_0(1 + r_f) + C$$

Finally, if we call $c = C/P_0$, and interpret $c$ as the percentage "rate" of carrying costs, we may write

$$F_0 = P_0(1 + r_f + c) \qquad \textbf{(22.9)}$$

which is a (one-year) parity relationship for futures involving storage costs. Compare Equation 22.9 to the first parity relationship for stocks, Equation 22.2, and you will see that they are extremely similar. In fact, if we think of carrying costs as a "negative dividend," the equations are identical. This treatment makes intuitive sense because, instead of receiving a dividend yield of $d$, the storer of the commodity must pay a storage cost of $c$. Obviously, this parity relationship is simply an extension of those we have seen already.

It is vital to note that we derive Equation 22.9 assuming that the asset will be bought and stored; it therefore applies only to goods that currently *are* being stored. Two kinds of commodities cannot be expected to be stored. The first is highly perishable goods, such as strawberries, for which storage is technologically not feasible. The second includes goods that are not stored for economic reasons. For example, it would be foolish to buy wheat now, planning to store it for ultimate use in three years. Instead, it is clearly preferable to delay the purchase of the wheat until after the harvest of the third year. The wheat is then obtained without incurring the storage costs. Moreover, if the wheat harvest in the third year is comparable to this year's, you could obtain it at roughly the same price as you would pay this year. By waiting to purchase, you avoid both interest and storage costs.

In fact, it is generally not reasonable to hold large quantities of agricultural goods across a harvesting period. Why pay to store this year's wheat, when you can purchase next year's wheat when it is harvested? Maintaining large wheat

[12] Robert A. Jarrow and George S. Oldfield, "Forward Contracts and Futures Contracts," *Journal of Financial Economics* 9 (1981).

inventories across harvests makes sense only if such a small wheat crop is forecast that wheat prices will not fall when the new supply is harvested.

---

**CONCEPT CHECK** Question 12. People are willing to buy and "store" shares of stock despite the fact that their purchase ties up capital. Most people, however, are not willing to buy and store wheat. What is the difference in the properties of the expected evolution of stock prices versus wheat prices that accounts for this result?

---

Because storage across harvests is costly, Equation 22.9 should not be expected to apply for holding periods that span harvest times, nor should it apply to perishable goods that are available only "in season." You can see that this is so if you look at the U.S. futures markets page of the newspaper. Figure 22.10, for example, gives futures prices for several times to maturity for corn and for gold. Whereas the futures price for gold, which is a stored commodity, increases steadily with the maturity of the contract, the futures price for corn is seasonal; it rises within a harvest period as Equation 22.9 would predict, but the price then falls across harvests as new supplies become available.

Futures pricing across seasons requires a different approach that is not based on storage across harvest periods. In place of general no-arbitrage restrictions we rely instead on risk premium theory and discounted cash flow (DCF) analysis.

## Discounted Cash Flow Analysis for Commodity Futures

We have said that most agricultural commodities follow seasonal price patterns; prices rise before a harvest and then fall at the harvest when the new crop becomes available for consumption. Figure 22.11 graphs this pattern. The price of the commodity following the harvest must rise at the rate of the total cost of carry (interest plus noninterest carrying costs) to induce holders of the commodity to store it willingly for future sale instead of selling it immediately. Inventories will be run down to near zero just before the next harvest.

Clearly, this pattern differs sharply from financial assets, such as stocks or gold, for which there is no seasonal price movement. For financial assets, the current price is set in market equilibrium at a level that promises an expected rate of capital gains plus dividends equal to the required rate of return on the asset. Financial assets are stored only if their economic rate of return compensates for the cost of carry. In other words, financial assets are priced so that storing them produces a fair return. Agricultural prices, by contrast, are subject to steep periodic drops as each crop is harvested, which makes storage across harvests consequently unprofitable.

Of course, neither the exact size of the harvest nor the demand for the good is known in advance, so the spot price of the commodity cannot be perfectly predicted. As weather forecasts change, for example, the expected size of the crop and the expected future spot price of the commodity are updated continually.

**Figure 22.10**

Futures prices for corn and gold.

*The Financial Post,* May 31, 1996. Reprinted by permission.

| — Lifetime — | | | | — Daily — | | | | Open |
|---|---|---|---|---|---|---|---|---|
| **High** | **Low** | **Month** | **Open** | **High** | **Low** | **Settle** | **Chg** | **interest** |
| **Soybeans (CBOT)** | | | | | | | | |
| 5,000 bushels, US cents per bushel; 1/4 cent = $12.50 per contract | | | | | | | | |
| 847 | 599½ | July96 | 775 | 787 | 771½ | 786½ | +11½ | 63,878 |
| 845 | 626 | Aug96 | 772 | 784 | 770½ | 783¼ | +9¼ | 14,585 |
| 822 | 623 | Sep96 | 759½ | 768 | 759½ | 766¾ | +8¼ | 6,607 |
| 810 | 579 | Nov96 | 751 | 758 | 749½ | 756 | +4 | 85,519 |
| 814 | 650 | Jan97 | 760 | 764½ | 757½ | 763 | +4¾ | 7,225 |
| 816½ | 678 | Mar97 | 766½ | 771 | 764 | 770½ | +7 | 3,047 |
| 818 | 735 | May97 | 767½ | 771½ | 766 | 771½ | +5½ | 3,235 |
| 820 | 601½ | July97 | 767½ | 772 | 766 | 771½ | +5½ | 2,956 |
| 734 | 597½ | Nov97 | 694 | 697 | 692 | 692 | −2 | 1,848 |
| | | | | Prev. vol. | 92,607 | | Prev. open int. | 188,900 |
| **Gold (COMEX)** | | | | | | | | |
| 100 troy ozs., US$ per troy oz.; 10 cents = $10 per contract | | | | | | | | |
| 460.00 | 365.00 | June96 | 391.20 | 391.60 | 390.20 | 390.50 | −0.70 | 27,980 |
| 436.90 | 390.40 | Aug96 | 394.70 | 394.90 | 393.50 | 394.00 | −0.40 | 75,340 |
| 432.20 | 392.80 | Oct96 | 398.00 | 398.00 | 396.80 | 397.00 | −0.40 | 6,070 |
| 456.80 | 373.70 | Dec96 | 400.50 | 401.10 | 399.50 | 400.00 | −0.30 | 36,011 |
| 434.30 | 398.10 | Feb97 | 403.20 | 403.20 | 402.80 | 402.80 | −0.20 | 6,542 |
| 428.00 | 400.50 | Apr97 | 406.40 | 406.40 | 405.40 | 405.40 | −0.10 | 6,478 |
| 466.50 | 385.10 | June97 | 408.50 | 408.50 | 408.10 | 408.10 | ... | 8,248 |
| 431.00 | 405.50 | Aug97 | ... | ... | ... | 410.90 | +0.10 | 1,331 |
| 432.70 | 411.40 | Oct97 | ... | ... | ... | 413.60 | +0.10 | 225 |
| 478.80 | 396.90 | Dec97 | ... | ... | ... | 416.40 | +0.20 | 8,135 |
| 424.00 | 416.30 | Feb98 | ... | ... | ... | 419.30 | +0.30 | 538 |
| 493.60 | 412.30 | June98 | 425.00 | 425.00 | 424.80 | 424.80 | +0.50 | 5,526 |
| 509.90 | 424.00 | Dec98 | ... | ... | ... | 433.40 | +0.80 | 4,829 |
| 521.00 | 429.80 | June99 | ... | ... | ... | 442.00 | +1.10 | 3,886 |
| 521.10 | 435.70 | Dec99 | ... | ... | ... | 450.50 | +1.40 | 3,572 |
| 486.60 | 441.80 | June00 | ... | ... | ... | 459.10 | +1.70 | 3,269 |
| 474.50 | 448.40 | Dec00 | ... | ... | ... | 467.90 | +2.00 | 3,260 |
| | | | | Prev. vol. | 56,977 | | Prev. open int. | 201,240 |

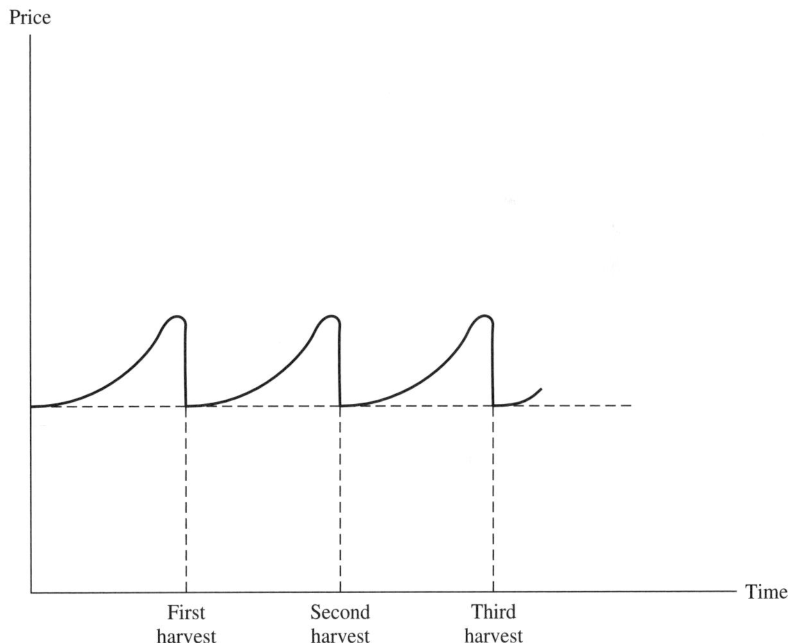


**Figure 22.11**

Typical commodity price pattern over the season. Prices adjusted for inflation.

Given the current expectation of the spot price of the commodity at some future date and a measure of the risk characteristics of that price, we can measure the present value of a claim to receive the commodity at that future date. We simply calculate the appropriate risk premium from a model such as the CAPM

**Table 22.4** Commodity Betas

| Commodity | Beta |
|---|---|
| Wheat | −0.370 |
| Corn | −0.429 |
| Oats | 0.000 |
| Soybeans | −0.266 |
| Soybean oil | −0.650 |
| Soybean meal | 0.239 |
| Broilers | −1.692 |
| Plywood | 0.660 |
| Potatoes | −0.610 |
| Platinum | 0.221 |
| Wool | 0.307 |
| Cotton | −0.015 |
| Orange juice | 0.117 |
| Propane | −3.851 |
| Coca | −0.291 |
| Silver | −0.272 |
| Copper | 0.005 |
| Cattle | 0.365 |
| Hogs | −0.148 |
| Pork bellies | −0.062 |
| Eggs | −0.293 |
| Lumber | −0.131 |
| Sugar | −2.403 |

From Zvi Bodie and Victor Rosansky, "Risk and Return in Commodity Futures," *Financial Analysts Journal* 36 (May–June 1980). Reprinted by permission.

or APT and discount the expected spot price at the appropriate risk-adjusted interest rate.

Table 22.4, which presents betas on a variety of commodities, shows that the beta of orange juice, for example, was estimated to be .117 over the period. If the T-bill rate is currently 7 percent, and the historical market risk premium has been about 8.5 percent, the appropriate discount rate for orange juice would be given by the CAPM as

$$7\% + .117(8.5\%) = 7.99\%$$

If the expected spot price for orange juice six months from now is \$1.75 per pound, the present value of a six-month deferred claim to a pound of orange juice is simply

$$\$1.75/(1.0799)^{1/2} = \$1.68$$

What would the proper futures price for orange juice be? The contract calls for the ultimate exchange of orange juice for the futures price. We have just shown that the present value of the juice is \$1.68. This should equal the present value of the futures price that will be paid for the juice. A commitment to a payment of $F_0$ dollars in six months has a present value of $F_0/(1.07)^{1/2} = .967 \times F_0$. (Note that the discount rate is the risk-free rate of 7 percent, because the promised payment is fixed and therefore independent of market conditions.)

To equate the present values of the promised payment of $R_0$ and the promised receipt of orange juice, we would set

$$.967F_0 = \$1.68$$

or

$$F_0 = \$1.74$$

The general rule, then, to determine the appropriate futures price is to equate the present value of the future payment of $F_0$ and the present value of the commodity to be received. This gives us

$$\frac{F_0}{(1 + r_f)^T} = \frac{E(P_T)}{(1 + k)^T}$$

or

$$F_0 = E(P_T)\left(\frac{1 + r_f}{1 + k}\right)^T \qquad \textbf{(22.10)}$$

where $k$ is the required rate of return on the commodity, which may be obtained from a model of asset market equilibrium such as the CAPM.

Note that Equation 22.10 is perfectly consistent with the spot-futures parity relationship. For example, apply Equation 22.10 to the futures price for a stock paying no dividends. Because the entire return on the stock is in the form of capital gains, the expected rate of capital gains must equal $k$, the required rate of return on the stock. Consequently, the expected price of the stock will be its current price times $(1 + k)^T$, or $E(P_T) = P_0(1 + k)^T$. Substituting this expression into Equation 22.10 results in $F_0 = P_0(1 + r_f)^T$, which is exactly the parity relationship. This equilibrium derivation of the parity relationship simply reinforces the no-arbitrage restrictions we derived earlier. The spot-futures parity relationship may be obtained from the equilibrium condition that all portfolios earn fair expected rates of return.

The advantage of the arbitrage proofs that we have explored is that they do not rely on the validity of any particular model of security market equilibrium. The absence of arbitrage opportunities is a much more robust basis for argument than the CAPM, for example. Moreover, arbitrage proofs clearly demonstrate how an investor can exploit any misalignment in the spot-future relationship. To their disadvantage, arbitrage restrictions may be less precise than desirable in the face of storage costs or costs of short selling.

We can summarize by saying that the actions of arbitrageurs force the futures prices of financial assets to maintain a precise relationship with the price of the underlying financial asset.[13] This relationship is described by the spot-futures parity formula. Opportunities for arbitrage are more limited in the case of commodity futures, because such commodities often are not stored. Hence, to make a precise prediction for the correct relationship between futures and spot prices, we must rely on a model of security market equilibrium, such as the CAPM or APT, and estimate the unobservables, the expected spot price, and the appropriate rate of return. Such models will be perfectly consistent with the parity relationships in the benchmark case where investors willingly store the commodity.

**CONCEPT CHECK** Question 13. Suppose that the systematic risk of orange juice were to increase, holding the expected time $T$ price of juice constant. If the expected spot price is unchanged, would the futures price change? In what direction? What is the intuition behind your answer?

## 22.10 SWAPS

We noted in Chapter 16 that interest rate swaps have become common tools for interest rate risk management. Since their inception in 1981, swaps have grown to a North American market of well over $6 trillion in notional principal. A large and active market of several hundred billion dollars also exists for foreign exchange swaps. Recall that a swap arrangement obligates two counterparties to exchange cash flows at one or more future dates. To illustrate, a **foreign exchange swap** might call for one party to exchange $1.6 million for 1 million British pounds in each of the next five years. An **interest rate swap** with notional principal of $1 million might call for one party to exchange a variable cash flow equal to $1 million times the LIBOR rate for $1 million times a fixed rate of 8 percent. In this way, the two parties exchange the cash flows corresponding to interest payments on a fixed-rate 8 percent coupon bond for those corresponding to payments on a floating-rate bond paying LIBOR.

As we saw in Chapter 16, an interest rate swap agreement is a cheap and quick way to restructure the balance sheet. The swap does not entail trading costs to buy back outstanding bonds or underwriting fees and lengthy registration procedures to issue new debt. In addition, if the firm perceives price advantages in either the fixed or floating rate market, the swap market allows it to issue its debt in the cheaper of the two markets and then "convert" to the financing mode that best suits its business needs.

Foreign exchange swaps also enable the firm to quickly and cheaply restructure its balance sheet. Suppose, for example, that the firm issues $10 million in debt at 8 percent, but it actually prefers that its interest obligations be denominated in British pounds. For example, the issuing firm might be a British corporation that

[13] Recall, however, the qualifications to this statement mentioned at the end of Sections 22.4 and 22.6.

perceives advantageous financing opportunities in Canada but prefers pound-denominated liabilities. Then the firm, whose debt currently obliges it to make dollar-denominated payments of $800,000, can agree to swap a given number of pounds each year for $800,000. By so doing, it effectively covers its dollar obligation and replaces it with a new pound-denominated obligation.

How can the fair swap rate be determined? For example, do we know that an exchange of LIBOR is a fair trade for a fixed rate of 8 percent? Or what is the fair swap rate between dollars and pounds for the foreign exchange swap we considered? To answer these questions we can exploit the analogy between a swap agreement and a forward or futures contract.

Consider a swap agreement to exchange dollars for pounds for one period only. Next year, for example, one might exchange $1 million for £.5 million. This is no more than a simple forward contract in foreign exchange. The dollar-paying party is contracting to buy British pounds in one year for a number of dollars agreed upon today. The forward exchange rate for one year delivery is $F_1$ = $2.00/pound. We know from the interest rate parity relationship that this forward price should be related to the spot exchange rate, $E_0$, by the formula $F_1 = E_0(1 + r_{CAN})/(1 + r_{UK})$. Because a one-period swap is in fact a forward contract, the fair swap rate also is given by the parity relationship.

Now consider an agreement to trade foreign exchange for two periods. This agreement could be structured as a portfolio of two separate forward contracts. If so, the forward price for the exchange of currencies in one year would be $F_1 = E_0(1 + r_{CAN})/(1 + r_{UK})$, while the forward price for the exchange in the second year would be $F_2 = E_0[(1 + r_{CAN})/(1 + r_{UK})]^2$. As an example, suppose that $E_0$ = $2.038/pound, $r_{CAN}$ = 5 percent, and $r_{UK}$ = 7 percent. Then, using the parity relationship, we would have prices for forward delivery of $F_1$ = $2.038/£ × (1.05/1.07) = $2.00/£ and $F_2$ = $2.038/£ × $(1.05/1.07)^2$ = $1.9625/£. Figure 22.12**A** illustrates this sequence of cash exchanges assuming that the swap calls for delivery of one pound in each year. While the dollars to be paid in each of the two years are known today, they vary from year to year.

In contrast, a swap agreement to exchange currency for two years would call for a fixed exchange rate to be used for the duration of the swap. This means that the same number of dollars would be paid per pound in each year, as illustrated in Figure 22.12**B.** Because the forward prices for delivery in each of the next two years are $2.00/£ and $1.9625/£, the fixed exchange rate that makes the two-period swap a fair deal must be between these two values. Therefore, the dollar payer underpays for the pound in the first year (compared to the forward exchange rate) and overpays in the second year. Thus, the swap can be viewed as a portfolio of forward transactions, but instead of each transaction being priced independently, one forward price is applied to all of the transactions.

Given this insight, it is easy to determine the fair swap price. If we were to purchase one pound per year for two years using two independent forward rate agreements, we would pay $F_1$ dollars in one year and $F_2$ dollars in two years. If, instead, we enter a swap, we pay a constant rate of $F^*$ dollars per pound. Because both strategies must be equally costly, we conclude that

**Figure 22.12**
Forward contracts versus swaps.
**A**—Two forward contracts, each priced independently.
**B**—Two-year swap agreement.

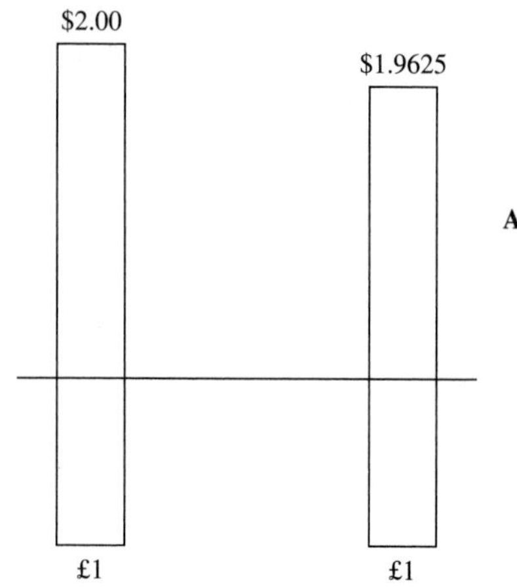


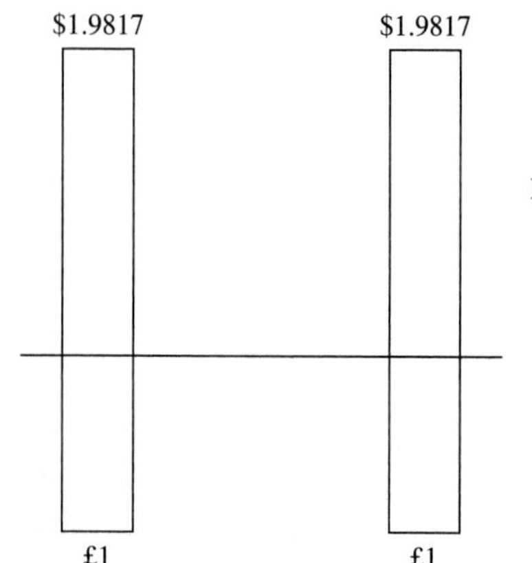


$$\frac{F_1}{1 + y_1} + \frac{F_2}{(1 + y_2)^2} = \frac{F^*}{1 + y_1} + \frac{F^*}{(1 + y_2)^2}$$

where $y_1$ and $y_2$ are the appropriate yields from the yield curve for discounting dollar cash flows of one and two years maturity, respectively. In our example, where we have assumed a flat Canadian yield curve at 5 percent, we would solve

$$\frac{2.00}{1.05} + \frac{1.9625}{1.05^2} = \frac{F^*}{1.05} + \frac{F^*}{1.05^2}$$

which implies that $F^* = 1.9817$. The same principle would apply to a foreign exchange swap of any other maturity. In essence, we need to find the level annuity, $F^*$, with the same present value as the sequence of annual cash flows that would be incurred in a sequence of forward rate agreements.

Interest rate swaps can be subjected to precisely the same analysis. Here, the forward contract is on an interest rate. For example, if you swap LIBOR for an 8 percent fixed rate with notional principal of $100, then you have entered a forward contract for delivery of $100 times $r_{\text{LIBOR}}$ for a fixed "forward" price of $8. If the swap agreement is for many periods, the fair spread will be determined by the entire sequence of interest rate forward prices over the life of the swap.

## 22.11 Other Developments in Futures and Swaps

As it becomes apparent that investors want to speculate on or hedge against a source of uncertainty, the futures exchanges respond by introducing new contracts to satisfy investor demands. The exchanges profit in proportion to the volume of trading on the contract, so it pays for them to seek out new contracts with wide appeal to investors. We have seen that Canadian futures exchanges did not have much success with the introduction of new instruments, but that U.S. exchanges have successfully introduced several new types of contracts in recent years.

The ingredients that contribute to successful futures contracts are the presence of natural hedging demands by investors, a closely related spot market for the commodity and the ability to engage in spot-futures arbitrage strategies, and an easily understood contract design.

Swaps also have given rise to a wide range of spinoff products. Many of these add option features to the basic swap agreement. For example, an *interest rate cap* is an agreement in which the cap buyer makes a payment today in exchange for possible future payments if a "reference" interest rate (usually LIBOR) exceeds a "limit rate" on a series of settlement dates. For example, if the limit rate is 7 percent, then the cap holder receives ($r_{\text{LIBOR}}$ − 0.07) for each dollar of notional principal if the LIBOR rate exceeds 7 percent. The purchaser of the cap in effect has entered a swap agreement to exchange the LIBOR rate for a fixed rate of 7 percent with an option to not execute the swap in any period that the transaction is unprofitable. The payoff to the holder of the cap is

(Reference rate − Limit rate) × Notional principal *if* this value is positive

and zero otherwise. This, of course, is the payoff of an option to purchase a cash flow proportional to the LIBOR rate for an exercise price proportional to the limit rate.

Similar to caps, an *interest rate floor* pays its holder in any period that the reference interest rate falls *below* some limit. This is analogous to a sequence of options to sell the reference rate for a stipulated "strike rate."

A *collar* combines interest rate caps and floors. A collar entails the purchase of a cap with one limit rate and the sale of a floor with a lower limit rate. If a firm starts with a floating-rate liability and buys the cap, it achieves protection against rates rising. If rates do rise, the cap provides a cash flow equal to the reference interest rate for a payment equal to the limit rate. Therefore, the cap places an upper bound equal to the limit rate on the firm's interest rate expense.

The written floor places a limit on how much the firm can benefit from rate declines. Even if interest rates fall dramatically, the firm's savings on its floating-rate obligation will be offset by its obligation to pay the difference between the reference rate and the limit rate. Therefore, the collar limits the firm's net cost of funds to a value between the limit rate on the cap and the limit rate on the floor.

Other option-based variations on the basic swap arrangement are *swaptions.* A swaption is an option on a swap. The buyer of the swaption has the right to enter an interest rate swap on some reference interest rate at a prespecified fixed interest rate on or before some expiration date. A call swaption (often called a payer swaption) is the right to pay the fixed rate in a swap and receive the floating rate. A put swaption is the right to receive the fixed rate and pay the floating rate. An exit option is the right to walk away from a swap without penalty. Swaptions can be European or American.

There also are futures and forward variations on swaps. A forward swap, for example, obligates both traders to enter a swap at some date in the future with terms agreed to today.

## SUMMARY

**1.** Forward contracts are arrangements that call for future delivery of an asset at a currently agreed-upon price. The long trader is obligated to purchase the good, and the short trader is obligated to deliver it. If the price of the asset at the maturity of the contract exceeds the forward price, the long side benefits by virtue of acquiring the good at the contract price.

**2.** A futures contract is similar to a forward contract, differing most importantly in the aspects of standardization and marking to market, which is the process by which gains and losses on futures contract positions are settled daily. In contrast, forward contracts call for no cash transfers until contract maturity.

**3.** Futures contracts are traded on organized exchanges that standardize the size of the contract, the grade of the deliverable asset, the delivery date, and the delivery location. Traders negotiate only over the contract price. This standardization creates increased liquidity in the marketplace and means buyers and sellers can easily find many traders for a desired purchase or sale.

**4.** The clearinghouse represents an intermediary between each pair of traders, acting as the short position for each long, and as the long position for each short. In this way, traders need not be concerned about the performance of the trader on the opposite side of the contract. In turn, traders post margins to guarantee their own performance on the contracts.

**5.** The gain or loss to the long side for a futures contract held between time 0 and $t$ is $F_t - F_0$. Because $F_T - P_T$, the long's profit if the contract is held until maturity is $P_T - F_0$, where $P_T$ is the spot price at time $T$ and $F_0$ is the original futures price. The gain or loss to the short position is $F_0 - P_T$.

**6.** Futures contracts may be used for hedging or speculating. Speculators use the contracts to take a stand on the ultimate price of an asset. Short hedgers take short positions in contracts to offset any gains or losses on the value of an asset already held in inventory. Long hedgers take long positions to offset gains or losses in the purchase price of a good.

**7.** The spot-futures parity relationship states that the equilibrium futures price on an asset providing no services or payments (such as dividends) is $F_0 = P_0(1 + r_f)^T$. If the futures price deviates from this value, then market participants can earn arbitrage profits.

**8.** If the asset provides services or payments with yield *d,* the parity relationship becomes $F_0 = P_0(1 + r_f - d)^T$. This model also is called the cost-of-carry model, because it states that the futures price must exceed the spot price by the net cost of carrying the asset until maturity date *T.*

**9.** The equilibrium futures price will be less than the currently expected time *T* spot price if the spot price exhibits systematic risk. This provides an expected profit for the long position that bears the risk and imposes an expected loss on the short position that is willing to accept that expected loss as a means to shed risk.

**10.** Futures contracts calling for cash settlement are traded on the TSE 35 and TSE 100 in Canada and in various U.S. stock market indices. Stock index contracts may be mixed with Treasury bills to construct artificial equity positions, which makes them potentially valuable tools for market timers. Market index contracts also are used by arbitrageurs who attempt to profit from violations of the parity relationship.

**11.** Foreign exchange futures trade in the U.S. on several foreign currencies, as well as on a European currency index. The interest rate parity relationship for foreign exchange futures is

$$F_0 = E_0\left(\frac{1 + r_{\text{US}}}{1 + r_{\text{foreign}}}\right)^T$$

Deviations of the futures price from this value imply arbitrage opportunity. Empirical evidence, however, suggests that generally the parity relationship is satisfied.

**12.** Interest rate futures allow for hedging against interest rate fluctuations in several different markets. Currently, few of them are actively traded in Canada.

**13.** Commodity futures pricing is complicated by costs for storage of the underlying commodity. When the asset is willingly stored by investors, then the storage costs enter the futures pricing equation as follows:

$$F_0 = P_0(1 + r_f + c)^T$$

The noninterest carrying costs, *c,* play the role of a "negative dividend" in this context.

**14.** When commodities are not stored for investment purposes, the correct futures price must be determined using general risk-return principles. In this event

$$F_0 = E(P_T)\left(\frac{1 + r_f}{1 + k}\right)^T$$

The equilibrium (risk-return) and the no-arbitrage predictions of the proper futures price are consistent with one another.

**15.** Swaps, which call for the exchange of a series of cash flows, may be viewed as portfolios of forward contracts. Each transaction may be viewed as a separate forward agreement. However, instead of pricing each exchange independently, the swap sets one "forward price" that applies to all of the transactions. Therefore, the swap price will be an average of the futures prices that would prevail if each exchange were priced separately.

### Key Terms

Forward contract
Futures contract
Futures price
Long position
Short position
Clearinghouse
Reversing trade
Open interest
Marking to market
Maintenance margin (Variation margin)
Convergence property
Cash delivery
Basis
Basis risk
Spread
Spot-futures parity theorem
Cost-of-carry relationship
Index arbitrage
Program trading
Triple witching hour
Interest rate parity theorem
Covered interest arbitrage relationship
Foreign exchange swap
Interest rate swap

### Selected Readings

*Extensive treatments of the institutional background of several futures markets in the United States and Canada are provided in:*

Hore, John E. *Trading on Canadian Futures Markets,* 3rd edition. The Canadian Securities Institute, 1987.

Kolb, Robert W. *Understanding Futures Markets.* Glenview, Ill.: Scott, Foresman, and Co., 1985.

*Excellent, although challenging, treatments of the differences between futures and forward markets and the pricing of each type of contract are in:*

Black, Fischer. "The Pricing of Commodity Contracts." *Journal of Financial Economics* 3 (January–March 1976).

Cox, John; Jonathan Ingersol; and Stephen A. Ross. "The Relation between Forward Prices and Futures Prices." *Journal of Financial Economics* 9 (December 1981).

Jarrow, Robert; and George Oldfield. "Forward Contracts and Futures Contracts." *Journal of Financial Economics* 9 (December 1981).

*Textbooks covering both theoretical and institutional aspects of U.S. and Canadian futures markets are:*

Khoury, Nabil; and Pierre Laroche. *Options et Contracts à Terme* (in French), 2nd edition. Québec: Les Presses de l'Université Laval, 1995.

Siegel, Daniel R.; and Diane F. Siegel. *Futures Markets.* Hinsdale, Ill.: Dryden Press, 1990.

*For treatments of the backwardation/contango debate, see:*

Cootner, Paul H. "Speculation and Hedging." Standford, Calif.: Food Research Institute Studies, Supplement, 1967.

Hicks, J. R. *Value and Capital,* 2nd ed. London: Oxford University Press, 1946.

Keynes, John Maynard. *Treatise on Money,* 2d ed. London: Macmillan, 1930.

Working, Holbrook. "The Theory of Price of Storage." *American Economic Review* 39 (December 1949).

*The use of futures contracts in risk management is treated in:*

Smith, Clifford W. Jr.; Charles W. Smithson; and D. Sykes Wilford. *Managing Financial Risk.* N.Y.: Harper & Row, 1990.

*Two empirical studies on Canadian index futures markets are:*

Park, Tae H.; and Lorne N. Switzer. "Bivariate GARCH Estimation of the Optimal Hedge Ratios for Stock Index Futures: A Note." *Journal of Futures Markets* 15, no. 1 (1995); and "Index Participation Units and the Performance of the Index Futures Markets: Evidence from the Toronto 35 Index Participation Units Market." *Journal of Futures Markets* 15, no. 2 (1995).

*A useful introduction to foreign exchange markets may be found in:*

Chrystal, K. Alex. "A Guide to Foreign Exchange Markets." *Federal Reserve Bank of St. Louis,* March 1984.

*Canadian studies of the use of financial futures to hedge interest rate risk are:*

Fortin, Michel; and Nabil Khoury. "Hedging Interest Rate Risks with Financial Futures." *Canadian Journal of Administrative Sciences* 1, no. 2 (December 1984).

Gagnon, Louis; Samuel Mensah; and Edward H. Blinder. "Hedging Canadian Corporate Debt: A Comparative Study of the Hedging Effectiveness of Canadian and U.S. Bond Futures." *Journal of Futures Markets* 9, no. 1 (1989).

Gagnon, Louis; and Greg Lypny. "Hedging Short-Term Interest Risk Under Time-Varying Distributions." *Journal of Futures Markets,* forthcoming (1995).

*Analyses of risk and return in commodity futures are in:*

Dusak, Katherine. "Futures Trading and Investor Returns: An Investigation of Commodity Market Risk Premiums." *Journal of Political Economy* 81 (December 1973).

Khoury, Nabil T.; and Jean-Marc Martel. "Optimal Futures Hedging in the Presence of Asymmetric Information." *Journal of Futures Markets* 5, no. 4 (1985).

*The issue of the storage of commodities is treated in:*

Brennan, Michael. "The Supply of Storage." *American Economic Review* 47 (March 1958).

Khoury, Nabil T.; and Jean-Marc Martel. "A Supply of Storage Theory with Asymmetric Information." *Journal of Futures Markets* 9, no. 6 (1989).

*Empirical studies on Canadian Commodity futures markets include:*

Khoury, Nabil T.; and Pierre Yourougou. "Price Discovery Performance and Maturity Effect in the Canadian Feed Wheat Market." *Review of Futures Markets* 8, no. 3 (1989).

______. "The Informational Content of the Basis: Evidence from Canadian Barley, Oats, and Canola Futures Markets." *Journal of Futures Markets* 11, no. 1 (1991).

*A good introduction to swaps is:*

Brown, Keith C.; and Donald J. Smith. *Interest Rate and Currency Swaps: A Tutorial.* Charlottesville: Institute of Chartered Financial Analysts, 1995.

## Problems

**1.** Why is there no futures market in cement?

**2.** Why might an investor choose to purchase futures contracts rather than the underlying asset?

**3.** What is the difference in cash flow between short selling an asset and entering a short futures position?

**4.** Consider a stock that will pay a dividend of $D$ dollars in one year, which is when a futures contract matures. Consider the following strategy: Buy the stock, short a futures contract on the stock, and borrow $S_0$ dollars, where $S_0$ is the current price of the stock.

*a.* What are the cash flows now and in one year?

*b.* Show that the equilibrium futures price must be $F_0 = S_0(1 + r) - D$ to avoid arbitrage.

*c.* Call the dividend yield $d = D/S_0$, and conclude that $F_0 = S_0(1 + r - d)$.

**5.** Consider this arbitrage strategy to derive the parity relationship for spreads: (1) enter a long futures position with maturity date $T_1$ and futures price $F(T_1)$; (2) enter a short position with maturity $T_2$ and futures price $F(T_2)$; and (3) at $T_1$, when the first contract expires, buy the asset and borrow $F(T_1)$ dollars at rate $r_f$ and pay back the loan with interest at time $T_2$.

*a.* What are the total cash flows to this strategy at times 0, $T_1$, and $T_2$?

*b.* Why must profits at time $T_2$ be zero if no arbitrage opportunities are present?

*c.* What must be the relationship between $F(T_1)$ and $F(T_2)$ for the profits at $T_2$ to be equal to zero? This relationship is the parity relationship for spreads.

**6.** Suppose that an investor in a 50 percent tax bracket purchases three soybean futures contracts at a price of $5.40 a bushel and closes them out at a price of $5.80. What are the after-tax profits to the position?

**7.** These questions address stock futures contracts:

*a.* A hypothetical futures contract on a nondividend-paying stock with current price $150 has a maturity of one year. If the T-bill rate is 8 percent, what is the futures price?

*b.* What should be the futures price if the maturity of the contract is three years?

*c.* What if the interest rate is 12 percent and the maturity of the contract is three years?

**8.** You suddenly receive information that indicates to you that the stock market is about to rise substantially. The market is unaware of this information. What should you do?

**9.** Suppose the value of the TSE 35 stock index is currently 250. If the one-year T-bill rate is 8 percent and the expected dividend yield on the TSE 35 is 5 percent, what should the one-year maturity futures price be?

**10.** It is now January. The interest rate is currently 8 percent annually. The June futures price for gold is $346.30, while the December futures price is $360. Is there an arbitrage opportunity here? If so, how would you exploit it?

**11.** The Toronto Futures Exchange has just introduced a new futures contract on Brandex stock, a company that currently pays no dividends. Each contract calls for delivery of 1,000 shares of stock in one year. The T-bill rate is 6 percent per year.

*a.* If Brandex stock now sells at $120 per share, what should be the futures price?

*b.* If Brandex stock immediately decreases by 3 percent, what will be the change in the futures price and the change in the investor's margin account?

*c.* If the margin on the contract is $12,000, what is the percentage return on the investor's position?

**12.** The multiplier for a futures contract on the stock market index is 500. The maturity of the contract is one year, the current level of the index is 400, and the risk-free interest rate is 0.5 percent per month. The dividend yield on the index is .2 percent per month. Suppose that after one month, the level of the stock index is 410.

*a.* Find the cash flow from the marking-to-market proceeds on the contract. Assume that the parity condition always holds exactly.

*b.* Find the holding-period return if the initial margin on the contract is $15,000.

**13.** Consider the futures contract written on the S&P 500 index and maturing in six months. The interest rate is 5 percent per six-month period, and the future value of dividends expected to be paid over the next six months is $8. The current index level is 427.5. Assume that you can short sell the S&P 500 index.

*a.* Suppose the expected rate of return on the market is 10 percent per six-month period. What is the expected level of the index in six months?

*b.* What is the theoretical no-arbitrage price for a six-month futures contract on the S&P 500 stock index?

*c.* Suppose the futures price is 424. Is there an arbitrage opportunity here? If so, how would you exploit it?

14. The one-year futures price on a stock-index portfolio is 406, the level of the stock index currently is 400, the one-year risk-free interest rate is 3 percent, and the year-end dividend that will be paid on a $400 investment in the market index portfolio is $5.
    *a.* By how much is the contract mispriced?
    *b.* Formulate a zero net-investment arbitrage portfolio and show that you can lock in riskless profits equal to the futures mispricing.
    *c.* Now assume (as is true for small investors) that if you short sell the stocks in the market index, the proceeds of the short sale are kept with the broker, and you do not receive any interest income on the funds. Is there still an arbitrage opportunity (assuming you don't already own the shares in the index)? Explain.
    *d.* Given the short-sale rules, what is the no-arbitrage *band* for the stock-futures price relationship? That is, given a stock index level of 400, how high and how low can the futures price be without giving rise to arbitrage opportunities?
15. Consider these futures market data for the June delivery S&P 500 contract, exactly six months hence. The S&P 500 index is at 400, and the June maturity contract is at $F_0 = 401$.
    *a.* If the current interest rate is 2.2 percent semiannually, and the average dividend rate of the stocks in the index is 1.2 percent semiannually, what fraction of the proceeds of stock short sales would need to be available for you to earn arbitrage profits?
    *b.* Suppose that you, in fact, have access to 90 percent of the proceeds from a short sale. What is the lower bound on the futures price that rules out arbitrage opportunities? By how much does the actual futures price fall below the no-arbitrage bound? Formulate the appropriate arbitrage strategy and calculate the profits to that strategy.
16. You manage a $3 million portfolio, currently all invested in equities, and believe that you have extraordinary market timing skills. You believe that the market is on the verge of a big but short-lived downturn; you would move your portfolio temporarily into T-bills, but you do not want to incur the transaction costs of liquidating and reestablishing your equity position. Instead, you decide to temporarily hedge your equity holdings with TSE 35 index futures contracts.
    *a.* Should you be long or short on the contracts? Why?
    *b.* If your equity holdings are invested in a market-index fund, into how many contracts should you enter? The TSE 35 index is now at 300 and the contract multiplier is 500.
    *c.* How does your answer to (*b*) change if the beta of your portfolio is .6?
17. Suppose that the spot price of the Swiss franc is currently 80 cents. The one-year futures price is 84 cents. Is the interest rate higher in Canada or Switzerland?

**18.** Consider the following information:

$$r_{\text{Can}} = 15\%$$
$$r_{\text{UK}} = 17\%$$
$$E_0 = 2.0 \text{ dollars per pound}$$
$$F_0 = 1.97 \text{ (one-year delivery)}$$

where the interest rates are annual yields on Canadian or U.K. bills. Given this information:

*a.* Where would you lend?
*b.* Where would you borrow?
*c.* How could you arbitrage?

**19.** Renée Michaels, CFA, plans to invest $1 million in Canadian government cash equivalents for the next 90 days. Michaels' client has authorized her to use non-Canadian government cash equivalents, but only if the currency risk is hedged to Canadian dollars by using forward currency contracts.

*a.* Calculate the Canadian dollar value of the hedged investment at the end of 90 days for *each* of the two cash equivalents in the table below. Show all calculations.
*b.* Briefly explain the theory that best accounts for your results.
*c.* Based upon this theory, estimate the implied interest rate for a 90-day Canadian government cash equivalent.

| Interest Rates<br>90-Day Cash Equivalents | |
|---|---|
| Japanese government | 7.6% |
| German government | 8.6% |

Exchange Rates
Currency Units per Canadian Dollar

| | Spot | 90-Day Forward |
|---|---|---|
| Japanese yen | 133.05 | 133.47 |
| German deutsche mark | 1.5260 | 1.5348 |

**20.** A trust company is underwriting an issue of 30-year zero-coupon corporate bonds with a face value of $100 million and a current market value of $5.354 million (a yield of 5 percent per six-month period). The firm must hold the bonds for a few days before issuing them to the public, which exposes it to interest rate risk. The company wishes to hedge its position by using T-bond futures contracts. The current T-bond futures price is $90.80 per $100 par value, and the T-bond contract will be settled using a 20-year 8 percent coupon bond paying interest semiannually. The contract is due to expire in a few days, so the T-bond price and the T-bond futures price are virtually identical. The yield implied on the bond is therefore 4.5 percent per six-month period. (Confirm this as a first step.) Assume that the yield curve is flat and that the corporate bond will continue to yield 0.5 percent more than T-bonds per six-month period, even if the general level of interest rates should change. What hedge ratio should the underwriter use to hedge its bond holdings against possible interest rate fluctuations over the next few days?

**21.** If the spot price of gold is $350 per troy ounce, the risk-free interest rate is 10 percent, and storage and insurance costs are zero, what should the forward price of gold be for delivery in one year? Use an arbitrage argument to prove your answer, and include a numerical example showing how you could make risk-free arbitrage profits if the forward price exceeded its upper bound value.

**22.** If the wheat harvest today is poor, would you expect this fact to have any effect on today's futures prices for wheat to be delivered (post-harvest) two years from today? Under what circumstances will there be no effect?

**23.** Suppose that the price of corn is risky, with a beta of .5. The monthly storage cost is $.03, and the current spot price is $2.75, with an expected spot price in three months of $2.94. If the expected rate of return on the market is 1.8 percent per month, with a risk-free rate of 1 percent per month, would you store corn for three months?

**24.** The U.S. yield curve is flat at 5 percent and the German yield curve is flat at 8 percent. The current exchange rate is $0.65 per mark. What will be the swap rate on an agreement to exchange currency over a three-year period? The swap will call for the exchange of one million deutsche marks for a given number of dollars in each year.

**25.** Firm ABC enters a five-year swap with firm XYZ to pay LIBOR in return for a fixed 8 percent rate on notional principal of $10 million. Two years from now, the market rate on three-year swaps is LIBOR for 7 percent; at this time, firm XYZ goes bankrupt and defaults on its swap obligation.

*a.* Why is firm ABC harmed by the default?

*b.* What is the market value of the loss incurred by ABC as a result of the default?

*c.* Suppose instead that ABC had gone bankrupt. How do you think the swap would be treated in the reorganization of the firm?

**26.** At the present time, one can enter five-year swaps that exchange LIBOR for 8 percent. Five-year caps with limit rates of 8 percent sell for $0.30 per dollar of notional principal. What must be the price of five-year floors with a limit rate of 8 percent?

**27.** At the present time, one can enter five-year swaps that exchange LIBOR for 8 percent. An *off-market swap* would then be defined as a swap of LIBOR for a fixed rate other than 8 percent. For example, a firm with

10 percent coupon debt outstanding might like to convert to synthetic floating-rate debt by entering a swap in which it pays LIBOR and receives a fixed rate of 10 percent. What up-front payment will be required to induce a counterparty to take the other side of this swap? Assume notional principal is $10 million.

**28.** In each of the following cases discuss how you, as a portfolio manager, would use financial futures to protect the portfolio.

*a.* You own a large position in a relatively illiquid bond that you want to sell.

*b.* You have a large gain on one of your long Treasuries and want to sell it, but you would like to defer the gain until the next accounting period, which begins in four weeks.

*c.* You will receive a large contribution next month that you hope to invest in long-term corporate bonds on a yield basis as favourable as is now available.

**29.** Your client, for whom you are underwriting a $400 million bond issue, is concerned that market conditions will change before the issue is brought to market. He has heard that it may be possible to reduce the risk exposure by hedging in the Montreal Exchange's Canada bond futures market. Specifically, he asks you to:

*a.* Briefly explain how the hedge works.

*b.* Describe *three* practical problems that would limit the effectiveness of the hedge.

**30.** Futures contracts and options on a futures contract can be used to modify risk. Identify the fundamental distinction between a futures contract and an option on a futures contract, and briefly explain the difference in the manner that futures and options modify *portfolio* risk.

**31.** The United Dominion Co. is considering the sale in February 1983 of $100 million in 10-year debentures that probably will be rated AAA, like the firm's other bond issues. The firm is eager to proceed at today's rate of 10.5 percent. As treasurer, you know that it will take about 12 weeks (until May 1983) to get the issue registered and sold. Therefore, you suggest that the firm hedge the pending bond issue using Canada bond futures contracts. (Each Canada bond contract is for $100,000.) Explain how you would go about hedging the bond issue, and describe the results, assuming that the following two sets of future conditions actually occur. (Ignore commissions and margin costs, and assume a one-to-one hedge ratio.) Show all calculations.

| | Case 1 | Case 2 |
|---|---|---|
| **Current Values—February 1983** | | |
| Bond rate | 10.5% | 10.5% |
| June 1983 Canada bond futures | 78.875 | 78.875 |
| **Estimated Values—May 1983** | | |
| Bond rate | 11.0% | 10.0% |
| June 1983 Canada bond futures | 75.93 | 81.84 |

*Chapter* 23

# Some Recent Developments in Investment Research

**THE MATERIAL IN THE PRECEDING CHAPTERS OF *INVESTMENTS* COMPRISES THE UNDERLYING FOUNDATION OF CONTEMPORARY INVESTMENT MANAGEMENT.** Although the history of science teaches us to expect many further revisions, this material represents our current understanding. On the important issues of the empirical support for asset pricing models (Chapter 10) and the broader question of market efficiency (Chapter 11), we have reported on gaps in our present knowledge, and identified pricing anomalies (such as the January effect) that are yet to be explained.

Obviously, the quest for better understanding of capital markets and for better investment techniques is ongoing. A few thousand scholars and investment professionals regularly publish reports of their research efforts in the area of investments. The purpose of this chapter is to interpret the findings of a small set of these reports. We restrict our scope to acquired knowledge that, in our view, may already be valuable to practitioners in the investment field. We expect that future editions of this text will incorporate this material into the preceding chapters, leaving this chapter for even newer findings. We welcome your comments on our choices in the present exposition, and would appreciate suggestions for developments to be included in the next edition of *Investments.*

In this edition, our choices include time-varying volatility in asset returns, the current assessment of the validity of asset pricing models, and extensions of option pricing theory.

## 23.1 Stochastic Volatility and Asset Returns

The price of a stock may change for two reasons: First, the arrival of new information may lead investors to change their assessment of intrinsic value; second, even in the absence of new information, unexpected changes in investor liquidity needs combined with trading frictions may create temporary buying or selling pressures that cause the price to fluctuate around its intrinsic value. Except for the least liquid assets, however, new information should account for the lion's share of price changes, at least when we examine returns for horizons longer than a few weeks. Therefore, we may associate the variance of the rate of return on the stock with the rate of arrival of new information. As a casual survey of the media would indicate, the rate of revision in predictions of business cycles, industry ascents or descents, and the fortunes of individual enterprises fluctuates regularly; in other words, the rate of arrival of new information is time varying. Consequently, we should expect the variances of the rates of return on stocks (as well as the covariances among them) to be time varying.

In an exploratory study of the volatility of NYSE stocks over more than 150 years (using monthly returns over 1835–1987), Pagan and Schwert[1] compute estimates of the variance of monthly returns. Their results, depicted in Figure 23.1, show just how important it may be to consider time variation in stock variance. The centrality of the risk-return trade-off suggests that once we make sufficient progress in the modeling, estimation, and prediction of the time variation in return variances and covariances, we should expect a significant refinement in understanding expected returns as well.

When we consider a time-varying return distribution, we must refer to the *conditional* mean, variance, and covariance, that is, the mean, variance, or covariance conditional on currently available information. The "conditions" that vary over time are the values of variables that determine the level of these parameters. In contrast, the usual estimate of return variance, the average of squared deviations over the sample period, provides an *unconditional* estimate, because it treats the variance as constant over time.

The most widely used model to estimate the conditional (hence, time varying) variance of stocks and stock index returns is the Generalized AutoRegressive Conditional Heteroskedasticity (GARCH) model, pioneered by Robert F. Engle.[2] Bollerslev, Chou, and Kroner[3] provide an extensive survey of the contribution of this technique to empirical work in finance. The work we present here is illustrative of the issues examined in current lines of research, but is far from exhaustive.

---

[1] Adrian Pagan and G. William Schwert, "Alternative Models for Conditional Stock Volatility," *Journal of Econometrics* 45 (1990), pp. 267–90.

[2] Robert F. Engle, "Autoregressive Conditional Heteroskedasticity with Estimates of the Variance of the U.K. Inflation," *Econometrica* 50 (1982), pp. 987–1008.

[3] Tim Bollerslev, Ray Chou, and Kenneth Kroner, "ARCH Modeling in Finance: A Review of the Theory and Empirical Evidence," *Journal of Econometrics* 52 (1992), pp. 5–59.

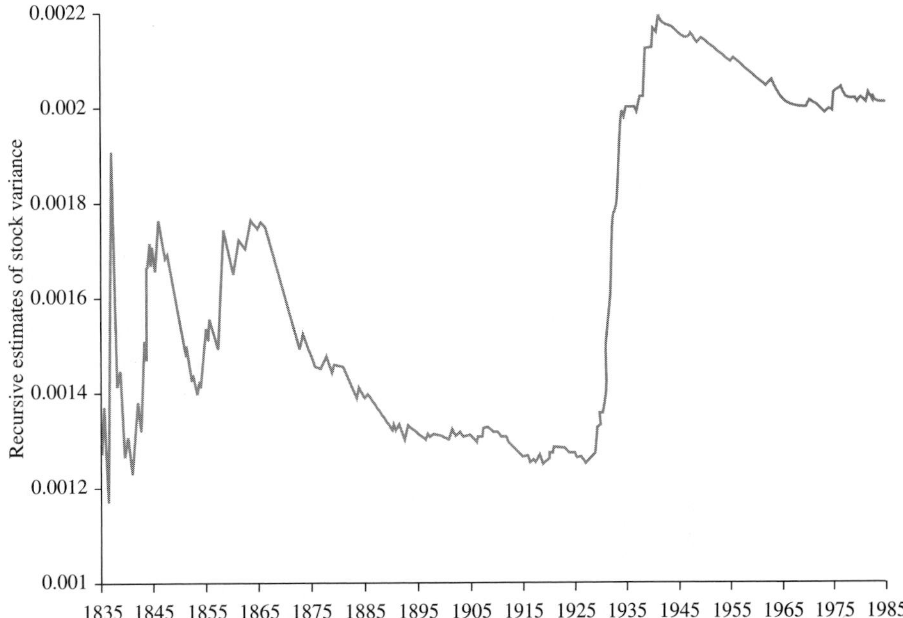


**Figure 23.1**
Estimates of the monthly stock return variance, 1835–1987

Source: Adrian R. Pagan and G. William Schwert, "Alternative Models for Conditional Stock Volatility," *Journal of Econometrics* 45 (1990), pp. 267–90. Reprinted by permission.

The GARCH model uses rate of return history as the information set that conditions our estimates of variance. The model posits that the forecast of market volatility evolves relatively smoothly each period in response to new observations on market returns. The updated estimate of market-return variance in each period depends on both the previous estimate and the most recent squared residual return on the market. The squared residual is an unbiased estimate of variance, so this technique essentially mixes in a statistically efficient manner the previous volatility estimate with an unbiased estimate based on the new observation of market return. The updating formula is:

$$\sigma_t^2 = a_0 + a_1\epsilon_{t-1}^2 + a_2\sigma_{t-1}^2 \quad \textbf{(23.1)}$$

As noted, equation 23.1 asserts that the updated forecast of variance is a function of the most recent variance forecast $\sigma_{t-1}^2$, and the most recent squared prediction error in market return, $\epsilon_{t-1}^2$. The parameters $a_0$, $a_1$, and $a_2$ are estimated from past data.

To estimate the return surprise, $\epsilon_t$, we require an equation for the expected return. One of the extensions of the model, GARCH-Mean, estimates two simultaneous equations for the expected excess return and variance. The first equation is 23.1; the second is an equation for the market excess return:

$$r_t - r_{ft} = b_0 + b_1\sigma_t^2 + \epsilon_t \quad \textbf{(23.2)}$$

Equation 23.2 asserts that the expected market excess return is an increasing function of predicted variance, with slope coefficient $b_1$. Therefore, the expected excess return on the stock index is linear in the predicted variance from equation (23.1).

In testing this model with monthly NYSE data for April 1951 through December 1989, Glosten, Jagannathan, and Runkle[4] find that the model more closely fits the data when the residual (i.e., unexpected) excess return is described by

$$\epsilon_t = \eta_t(1 + \lambda_1 \text{OCT} + \lambda_2 \text{JAN}) \tag{23.2a}$$

The dummy variables, OCT and JAN are set to 1.0 in October or January, respectively, and zero otherwise, allowing for different expected excess returns in those months. In addition to using the better specified residual, $\eta_t$, in the variance equation, they also allow the variance prediction to be different if the previous excess return is negative, and to respond to changes in the risk-free rate. Thus, they generalize equation 23.1 to:

$$\sigma_t^2 = a_0 + a_1\eta_{t-1}^2 + a_2\sigma_{t-1}^2 + a_3 r_{ft} + a_4 I_{t-1} \tag{23.1a}$$

where $I_{t-1}$ is a dummy variable set to 1.0 if $\eta_{t-1}$ is positive and zero otherwise.

The econometric work of Glosten, Jagannathan, and Runkle (as well as many others) demonstrates the importance of allowing for time-varying volatility and expected returns. However, this study, as many others, finds an inverse relationship between the expected return and volatility: The coefficient $b_1$ in equation 23.2 turns out to be significantly negative. This troubling result is hard to square with the notion of risk averse investors.

A possible explanation for the apparent negative correlation between expected return and volatility originates with the impact of the business cycle on predictions of expected return and volatility. Whitelaw[5] incorporates a number of business cycle variables in the simultaneous estimation of the conditional mean and standard deviation of the monthly returns on the CRSP (Center for Research in Security Prices) value-weighted stock index over the period April 1954 through April 1989. Table 23.1 illustrates the role of these variables in the determination of the moments of the return distribution.

The time series of the estimated conditional means and standard deviations of stock returns reveal a nonsynchronous cyclical pattern, as illustrated in Figure 23.2. The correlation patterns implied by these offset cycles differ from those implied by coincident cycles. Because the cycles for expected return and volatility are not synchronous, the correlation between mean return and risk may appear positive in some periods and negative in others. This may explain the puzzling results of earlier studies.

Whitelaw further investigates the relationship between the estimates from month $t - 1$ to month $t$ of the expected excess return ($m_{t-1,t}$) and volatility ($v_{t-1,t}$) by estimating simultaneously the equations

---

[4] Lawrence R. Glosten, Ravi Jagannathan, and David E. Runkle, "On the Relation between the Expected Value and the Volatility of the Nominal Excess Return on Stocks," *Journal of Finance* 48 (1993), pp. 1779–1802.

[5] Robert F. Whitelaw, "Time Variations and Covariations in the Expectation and Volatility of Stock Returns," *Journal of Finance* 49 (1994), pp. 515–42.

**Table 23.1** Estimation of Conditional First and Second Moments of Returns

Regressions of monthly, quarterly, and annual, continuously compounded, excess stock returns and volatilities for the CRSP value-weighted index on lagged explanatory variables for the periods May 1953 to April 1989, July 1953 to April 1989, and April 1954 to April 1989, respectively. The conditioning variables are the Baa-Aaa spread (DEF), the commercial paper-Treasury spread (CP), the one-year Treasury yield (1YR), and the dividend yield (DIV). Heteroscedasticity-consistent standard errors are in parentheses. DW is the Durbin-Watson statistic. The $\chi^2(4)$ statistic tests the hypothesis that all the coefficients except the constant are zero. The number in brackets is the probability that a $\chi^2(4)$ will exceed the value of the statistic.

| Explanatory Variables | | | | | | | | |
|---|---|---|---|---|---|---|---|---|
| **Constant** | **DEF** | **CP** | **1YR** | **DIV** | **Adj. $R^2$** | **$R^2$** | **DW** | **$\chi^2(4)$** |
| | | | | **Mean** | | | | |
| | | | | Monthly | | | | |
| −1.820 | 2.295** | −0.313 | −0.469** | 0.794** | 0.074 | 0.082 | 1.991 | 39 |
| (1.003) | (0.618) | (0.720) | (0.086) | (0.269) | | | | [0.00] |
| | | | | Quarterly | | | | |
| −5.991* | 5.817** | −0.242 | −1.270* | 2.430** | 0.176 | 0.184 | 0.764 | 34 |
| (2.863) | (1.777) | (1.921) | (0.256) | (0.821) | | | | [0.00] |
| | | | | Annual | | | | |
| −28.037** | 9.806 | 3.970 | −3.410** | 10.546** | 0.412 | 0.417 | 0.249 | 26 |
| (10.537) | (5.974) | (3.928) | (0.933) | (2.908) | | | | [0.00] |
| | | | | **Volatility** | | | | |
| | | | | Monthly | | | | |
| 1.884** | −0.044 | 2.070** | 0.104 | −0.029 | 0.099 | 0.107 | 2.071 | 34 |
| (0.734) | (0.500) | (0.476) | (0.067) | (0.217) | | | | [0.00] |
| | | | | Quarterly | | | | |
| 4.979** | −0.364 | 2.466** | 0.274* | −0.378 | 0.059 | 0.067 | 1.263 | 19 |
| (1.777) | (1.007) | (0.793) | (0.136) | (0.579) | | | | [0.00] |
| | | | | Annual | | | | |
| 16.197** | −1.559 | 0.277 | 0.822** | −1.830 | 0.053 | 0.062 | 0.635 | 8.6 |
| (3.340) | (2.435) | (1.548) | (0.332) | (1.110) | | | | [0.07] |

*Significant at the 5% level.
**Significant at the 1% level.

Source: Robert F. Whitelaw, "Time Variations and Covariations in the Expectation and Volatility of Stock Returns," *Journal of Finance* 49 (1994), pp. 515–42. Reprinted by permission.

$$m_{t-1,t} = b_0 + b_1 m_{t-2,t-1} + b_2 v_{t-2,t-1} + \epsilon_{mt} \quad \textbf{(23.3a)}$$

$$v_{t-1,t} = a_0 + a_1 m_{t-2,t-1} + a_2 v_{t-2,t-1} + \epsilon_{vt} \quad \textbf{(23.3b)}$$

The estimates from these equations, which allow for feedback between the levels of the forecasts, are presented in Table 23.2. The table reports coefficient estimates of: $b_1 = .977$ and $a_2 = .824$ in equations 23.3a and 23.3b, confirming that the variables are highly autocorrelated.

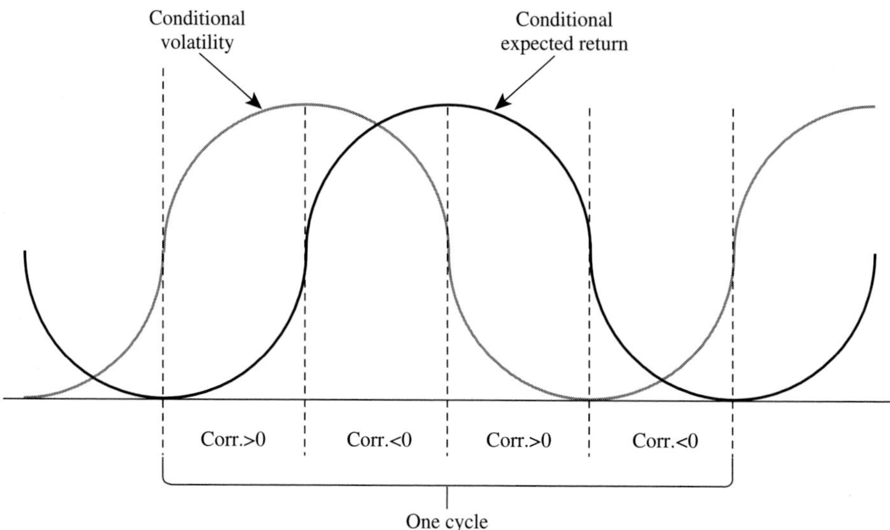


**Figure 23.2** A schematic representation of the cyclical variation in the conditional mean and the conditional volatility of returns and the implied contemporaneous correlations between the moments.

Source: Robert F. Whitelaw, "Time Variations and Covariations in the Expectation and Volatility of Stock Returns," *Journal of Finance* 49 (1994), pp. 515–42. Reprinted by permission.

**Table 23.2** VAR(1) Estimation of the Fitted Conditional Expectation and Volatility of Returns

A VAR(1) estimation of the conditional moments of monthly, continuously compounded, excess returns for the CRSP value-weighted index for the period June 1953 to April 1989. $m_{t-1,t}$ and $v_{t-1,t}$ are the fitted mean and volatility from the estimation of equations 23.3a and 23.3b. Heteroscedasticity-consistent standard errors are in parentheses.

| | Explanatory Variables | | | | |
|---|---|---|---|---|---|
| | **Constant** | $m_{t-2,t-1}$ | $v_{t-2,t-1}$ | **Adj.** $R^2$ | $R^2$ |
| $m_{t-1,t}$ | 0.459 | 0.977** | 0.118* | 0.895 | 0.895 |
| | (0.239) | (0.038) | (0.058) | | |
| $v_{t-1,t}$ | 0.743** | −0.107* | 0.824** | 0.759 | 0.760 |
| | (0.258) | (0.045) | (0.067) | | |

*Significant at the 5% level.
**Significant at the 1% level.

Source: Robert F. Whitelaw, "Time Variations and Covariations in the Expectation and Volatility of Stock Returns," *Journal of Finance* 49 (1994), pp. 515–42. Reprinted by permission.

Whitelaw finds that the coefficient of volatility in the mean equation (equation 23.3a) is positive ($b_2$ = .118) and statistically significant, a finding that is consistent with risk aversion. We also see that the mean has a significantly negative coefficient in the volatility equation, suggesting that volatility decreases when means are high.

Understanding the forces that drive the risk premium on stocks over time is also important to understanding co-movements of expected returns. Evans[6] allows for time varying risk premia and betas, where the latter are identified from the dynamics of the conditional covariances of returns. He estimates a two-factor CAPM using CRSP monthly stock and bond returns over the period 1963–1990. Evans concludes that changes in the risk premiums on the stock and bond factors dominate the effects of changes in beta on the prediction of portfolio returns.

The sum total of applications of time-series techniques to accommodate the time-varying nature of rates of return is still tentative. However, the gathering momentum suggests to us that these techniques will soon find their way into the standard tool kit of practitioners. As we shall see, the ideas discussed so far are relevant to the developments we discuss next.

## 23.2 The Empirical Content of Asset Pricing Models

As Chapter 10 indicated, the search for empirical support for the CAPM and the APT has been frustrating. Study after study has concluded that asset returns do not line up around the hypothesized security market line predicted by the CAPM and APT. Several researchers surmise that even if a positive expected return-beta relationship is valid, a full-blown asset pricing model cannot currently be empirically validated because of a host of statistical problems that, perhaps, can never be fully overcome.

It is not surprising that a study by Fama and French,[7] briefly discussed in Chapter 11, received great attention when it reported that:

"Two easily measured variables, size and book-to-market equity, combine to capture the cross-sectional variation in average stock returns associated with market $\beta$, size, leverage, book-to-market equity, and earnings-price ratios. Moreover, when the tests allow for variation in $\beta$ that is unrelated to size, the relation between market $\beta$ and average returns is flat, even when $\beta$ is the only explanatory variable."

This is a highly disturbing conclusion. If the empirical evidence suggests that systematic risk is unrelated to expected returns, we must relinquish one of the cornerstones of the theory of finance. Indeed, in Fama and French's words: "In short, our tests do not support the central prediction of the [CAPM and APT], that average stock returns are positively related to $\beta$." This conclusion captured the attention of the practitioner as well as academic communities, and was reported in both the *New York Times* and *The Economist.*

The most damning evidence that Fama and French (FF) provide is of the lack of a positive relation between average returns and beta. Table 23.3 best illustrates

[6] Martin D. Evans, "Expected Returns, Time Varying Risk, and Risk Premia," *Journal of Finance* 49 (1994), pp. 655–79.

[7] Eugene F. Fama and Kenneth R. French, "The Cross-Section of Expected Stock Returns," *Journal of Finance* 47 (1992), pp. 427–466.

**Table 23.3** Properties of Portfolios Formed on Size and Pre-Ranking $\beta$: NYSE Stocks Sorted by ME (Down) then Pre-Ranking $\beta$ (Across): 1941–1990

At the end of year $t-1$, the NYSE stocks on CRSP are assigned to 10 size (ME) portfolios. Each size decile is subdivided into 10 $\beta$ portfolios using preranking $\beta$s of individual stocks, estimated with 24 to 60 monthly returns (as available) ending in December of year $t-1$. The equal-weighted monthly returns on the resulting 100 portfolios are then calculated for year $t$. The average returns are the time-series averages of the monthly returns, in percent. The postranking $\beta$s use the full 1941–1990 sample of postranking returns for each portfolio. The pre- and postranking $\beta$s are the sum of the slopes from a regression of monthly returns on the current and prior month's NYSE value-weighted market return. The average size for a portfolio is the time-series average of each month's average value of ln(ME) for stocks in the portfolio. ME is denominated in millions of dollars. There are, on average, about 10 stocks in each size-$\beta$ portfolio each month. The All column shows parameter values for equal-weighted size-decile (ME) portfolios. The All rows show parameter values for equal-weighted portfolios of the stocks in each $\beta$ group.

| | All | Low-β | β-2 | β-3 | β-4 | β-5 | β-6 | β-7 | β-8 | β-9 | High-β |
|---|---|---|---|---|---|---|---|---|---|---|---|
| **Panel A: Average Monthly Return (in percent)** | | | | | | | | | | | |
| All | | 1.22 | 1.30 | 1.32 | 1.35 | 1.36 | 1.34 | 1.29 | 1.34 | 1.14 | 1.10 |
| Small-ME | 1.78 | 1.74 | 1.76 | 2.08 | 1.91 | 1.92 | 1.72 | 1.77 | 1.91 | 1.56 | 1.46 |
| ME-2 | 1.44 | 1.41 | 1.35 | 1.33 | 1.61 | 1.72 | 1.59 | 1.40 | 1.62 | 1.24 | 1.11 |
| ME-3 | 1.36 | 1.21 | 1.40 | 1.22 | 1.47 | 1.34 | 1.51 | 1.33 | 1.57 | 1.33 | 1.21 |
| ME-4 | 1.28 | 1.26 | 1.29 | 1.19 | 1.27 | 1.51 | 1.30 | 1.19 | 1.56 | 1.18 | 1.00 |
| ME-5 | 1.24 | 1.22 | 1.30 | 1.28 | 1.33 | 1.21 | 1.37 | 1.41 | 1.31 | 0.92 | 1.06 |
| ME-6 | 1.23 | 1.21 | 1.32 | 1.37 | 1.09 | 1.34 | 1.10 | 1.40 | 1.21 | 1.22 | 1.08 |
| ME-7 | 1.17 | 1.08 | 1.23 | 1.37 | 1.27 | 1.19 | 1.34 | 1.10 | 1.11 | 0.87 | 1.17 |
| ME-8 | 1.15 | 1.06 | 1.18 | 1.26 | 1.25 | 1.26 | 1.17 | 1.16 | 1.05 | 1.08 | 1.04 |
| ME-9 | 1.13 | 0.99 | 1.13 | 1.00 | 1.24 | 1.28 | 1.31 | 1.15 | 1.11 | 1.09 | 1.05 |
| Large-ME | 0.95 | 0.99 | 1.01 | 1.12 | 1.01 | 0.89 | 0.95 | 0.95 | 1.00 | 0.90 | 0.68 |
| **Panel B: Post-Ranking β** | | | | | | | | | | | |
| All | | 0.76 | 0.95 | 1.05 | 1.14 | 1.22 | 1.26 | 1.34 | 1.38 | 1.49 | 1.69 |
| Small-ME | 1.52 | 1.17 | 1.40 | 1.31 | 1.50 | 1.46 | 1.50 | 1.69 | 1.60 | 1.75 | 1.92 |
| ME-2 | 1.37 | 0.86 | 1.09 | 1.12 | 1.24 | 1.39 | 1.42 | 1.48 | 1.60 | 1.69 | 1.91 |
| ME-3 | 1.32 | 0.88 | 0.96 | 1.18 | 1.19 | 1.33 | 1.40 | 1.43 | 1.56 | 1.64 | 1.74 |
| ME-4 | 1.26 | 0.69 | 0.95 | 1.06 | 1.15 | 1.24 | 1.29 | 1.46 | 1.43 | 1.64 | 1.83 |
| ME-5 | 1.23 | 0.70 | 0.95 | 1.04 | 1.10 | 1.22 | 1.32 | 1.34 | 1.41 | 1.56 | 1.72 |
| ME-6 | 1.19 | 0.68 | 0.86 | 1.04 | 1.13 | 1.20 | 1.20 | 1.35 | 1.36 | 1.48 | 1.70 |
| ME-7 | 1.17 | 0.67 | 0.88 | 0.95 | 1.14 | 1.18 | 1.26 | 1.27 | 1.32 | 1.44 | 1.68 |
| ME-8 | 1.12 | 0.64 | 0.83 | 0.99 | 1.06 | 1.14 | 1.14 | 1.21 | 1.26 | 1.39 | 1.58 |
| ME-9 | 1.06 | 0.68 | 0.81 | 0.94 | 0.96 | 1.06 | 1.11 | 1.18 | 1.22 | 1.25 | 1.46 |
| Large-ME | 0.97 | 0.65 | 0.73 | 0.90 | 0.91 | 0.97 | 1.01 | 1.01 | 1.07 | 1.12 | 1.38 |

this point. FF find that both size and beta are positively correlated with average returns. But because these explanatory variables are highly (negatively) correlated, they seek to isolate the effect of beta. They accomplish this by forming 10 portfolios of different betas *within* each of the 10 size groups.

The top line in Panel B of Table 23.3 shows that the portfolio beta of each beta group, averaged across the 10 size portfolios steadily increases from .76 to 1.69.

**Table 23.3** (Continued)

| | All | Low-β | β-2 | β-3 | β-4 | β-5 | β-6 | β-7 | β-8 | β-9 | High-β |
|---|---|---|---|---|---|---|---|---|---|---|---|
| | | | | | | Panel C: Average Size (ln(ME)) | | | | | |
| All | | 4.39 | 4.39 | 4.40 | 4.40 | 4.39 | 4.40 | 4.38 | 4.37 | 4.37 | 4.34 |
| Small-ME | 1.93 | 2.04 | 1.99 | 2.00 | 1.96 | 1.92 | 1.92 | 1.91 | 1.90 | 1.87 | 1.80 |
| ME-2 | 2.80 | 2.81 | 2.79 | 2.81 | 2.83 | 2.80 | 2.79 | 2.80 | 2.80 | 2.79 | 2.79 |
| ME-3 | 3.27 | 3.28 | 3.27 | 3.28 | 3.27 | 3.27 | 3.28 | 3.29 | 3.27 | 3.27 | 3.26 |
| ME-4 | 3.67 | 3.67 | 3.67 | 3.67 | 3.68 | 3.68 | 3.67 | 3.68 | 3.66 | 3.67 | 3.67 |
| ME-5 | 4.06 | 4.07 | 4.06 | 4.05 | 4.06 | 4.07 | 4.06 | 4.05 | 4.05 | 4.06 | 4.06 |
| ME-6 | 4.45 | 4.45 | 4.44 | 4.46 | 4.45 | 4.45 | 4.45 | 4.45 | 4.44 | 4.45 | 4.45 |
| ME-7 | 4.87 | 4.86 | 4.87 | 4.86 | 4.87 | 4.87 | 4.88 | 4.87 | 4.87 | 4.85 | 4.87 |
| ME-8 | 5.36 | 5.38 | 5.38 | 5.38 | 5.35 | 5.36 | 5.37 | 5.37 | 5.36 | 5.35 | 5.34 |
| ME-9 | 5.98 | 5.96 | 5.98 | 5.99 | 6.00 | 5.98 | 5.98 | 5.97 | 5.95 | 5.96 | 5.96 |
| Large-ME | 7.12 | 7.10 | 7.12 | 7.16 | 7.17 | 7.20 | 7.29 | 7.14 | 7.09 | 7.04 | 6.83 |

Source: Eugene F. Fama and Kenneth R. French, "The Cross-Section of Expected Stock Returns," *Journal of Finance* 47 (1992), pp. 427–66. Reprinted by permission.

The top line in Panel C shows that the average portfolio size within each beta group is almost identical, ranging from 4.34 to 4.40. This allows us to interpret Panel A as a test of the net effect of beta on average returns holding size fixed.

Panel A of the table clearly shows that, for the period 1941–1990, average returns are not positively related to beta. The two highest beta portfolios have the two lowest average returns, and the highest average returns occur in the fourth and fifth beta portfolios. The response to these results has been of three strands: utilizing better econometrics in the test procedures; improving estimates of asset betas; and reconsidering the theoretical sources and implications of the results in the FF and similar studies.

Improving the econometric procedures employed in tests of asset returns seems the most direct response to the FF results. Amihud, Bent, and Mendelson[8] improve on the FF test procedures, using Generalized Least Squares (GLS) and pooling the time-series and cross-section rates of return. For the entire period analyzed by FF, 1941–1990, Amihud, Bent, and Mendelson find a significantly positive relation between average returns and beta, even when controlling for size and book-to-market ratio. The expected return-beta relationship is still not statistically significant for the most recent subperiod 1972–1990. However, in light of the considerable variability of stock returns, it is perhaps not surprising that it is difficult to obtain statistically significant results over shorter sample periods.

Kothari, Shanken, and Sloan[9] concentrate on the measurement of stock betas. They choose annual intervals for the estimation of stock betas to sidestep problems caused by trading frictions, nonsynchronous trading, and seasonality in

[8] Yakov Amihud, Jesper C. Bent, and Haim Mendelson, "Further Evidence on the Risk-Return Relationship," Working Paper, Graduate School of Business, Stanford University (1992).

[9] S. P. Kothari, J. Shanken, and Richard G. Sloan, "Another Look at the Cross-Section of Stock Returns," *Journal of Finance* 50 (1995), pp. 185–224.

monthly returns. As it turns out, this procedure generates results that are more favorable to the expected return-beta hypothesis. Thus, they conclude that there has been substantial compensation for beta risk over the 1941–1990 period, and even more over the 1927–1990 period. Table 23.4 shows the coefficient estimates for the average return-beta relationship with and without the presence of the size variable, for five different ways of grouping portfolios and for two periods.

A different approach is taken by Roll and Ross[10] and Kandel and Stambaugh.[11] Their work expands on the well-known "Roll's Critique" (see Chapter 10 for a review). Essentially, the argument is that tests that reject a positive relationship between average return and beta point to inefficiency of the market proxy used in those tests, rather than a refutation of the theoretical expected return-beta relationship. Put another way, there always exists a portfolio that, if used as market proxy, will produce an exact linear relationship between average return and beta. That portfolio lies on the efficient frontier derived from the realized returns. The FF results imply only that the value-weighted market proxy that they use does not lie on the ex post efficient frontier.

The new wrinkle in the Roll and Ross and Kandel and Stambaugh studies is a demonstration that it is plausible that even well-diversified portfolios (such as the value- or equally weighted portfolios of all stocks in the sample) will fail to produce a significant average return-beta relationship.

Roll and Ross (RR) derive an analytical characterization of indices (proxies for the market portfolio) that produce an *arbitrary* cross-sectional slope coefficient in the regression of asset returns on beta. Their derivation applies to any universe of assets and requires only that the market proxy be constructed from that universe or one of its subsets. They show that the set of indices that produce a zero cross-sectional slope lie within a parabola that is tangent to the efficient frontier at the point corresponding to the global minimum variance portfolio.

One of the properties of the efficient frontier is that the covariance of any asset with the global minimum variance portfolio ($G$) is the same, and equal to the variance of portfolio $G$. Hence, the beta of any asset with respect to Portfolio $G$ is equal to 1.0. Thus, if $G$ were to be used as the market proxy, the covariance of asset returns with their betas would be zero (because all stocks would have an identical beta of 1.0), and so would be the slope coefficient of average return as a function of beta. But, as RR show, $G$ is the only efficient portfolio with this property. All other portfolios that produce a zero slope coefficient must lie inside the efficient frontier.

Figure 23.3 shows one such configuration. In this "plausible" universe (where plausible is taken to mean that the return distribution is not extraordinary), the set

---

[10] Richard Roll and Stephen A. Ross, "On the Cross-Sectional Relation between Expected Return and Betas," *Journal of Finance* 49 (1994), pp. 101–21.

[11] Schmuel Kandel and Robert F. Stambaugh, "Portfolio Inefficiency and the Cross-Section of Expected Returns," *Journal of Finance* 50 (1995), pp. 185–224; "A Mean-Variance Framework for Tests of Asset Pricing Models," *Review of Financial Studies* 2 (1989), pp. 125–56; "On Correlations and Inferences About Mean-Variance Efficiency," *Journal of Financial Economics* 18 (1987), pp. 61–90.

**Table 23.4** Cross-Sectional Regressions of Monthly Returns on Beta and Firm Size: Equally weighted Market Index

Time-series averages of estimated coefficients from the following monthly cross-sectional regressions from 1927 to 1990 (Panel A) and from 1941 to 1990 (Panel B), associated $t$-statistics, and adjusted $R^2$s are reported (with and without Size being included in the regressions).

$$R_{pt} = \gamma_{0t} + \gamma_{1t}\,\beta_p + \gamma_{2t}\,Size_{pt-1} + \epsilon_{pt}$$

where $R_{pt}$ is the buy-and-hold return on portfolio $p$ for one month during the year beginning from July 1 of the year $t$ to June 30 of year $t + 1$; $\beta_p$ is the full-period postranking beta of portfolio $p$ and is the slope coefficient from a time-series regression of annual buy-and-hold postranking portfolio returns on the returns on a equally weighted portfolio of all the beta-size portfolios; $Size_{pt-1}$ is the natural log of the average market capitalization in millions of dollars on June 30 of year $t$ of the stocks in portfolio $p$; $\gamma_{0t}$, $\gamma_{1t}$, and $\gamma_{2t}$ are regression parameters; and $\epsilon_{pt}$ is the regression error. Portfolios are formed in five different ways: (i) 20 portfolios by grouping on beta alone; (ii) 20 portfolios by grouping on size alone; (iii) taking intersections of 10 independent beta or size groupings to obtain 100 portfolios; (iv) ranking stocks first on beta into 10 portfolios and then on size within each beta group into 10 portfolios; and (v) ranking stocks first on size into 10 portfolios and then on beta within each size group into 10 portfolios. When ranking on beta, the beta for an individual stock is estimated by regressing 24 to 60 monthly portfolio returns ending in June of each year on the CRSP equally weighted portfolio. The $t$-statistic below the average $\gamma_0$ value is for the difference between the average $\gamma_0$ and the average risk-free rate of return over the 1927–1990 or 1941–1990 period. The $t$-statistics below $\gamma_1$ and $\gamma_2$ are for their average values from zero.

| Portfolios | $\gamma_0$ $t$-statistic | $\gamma_1$ $t$-statistic | $\gamma_2$ $t$-statistic | Adj. $R^2$ |
|---|---|---|---|---|
| | **Panel A. 1927 to 1990** | | | |
| 20, beta ranked | 0.76 | 0.54 | | 0.32 |
| | 3.25 | 1.94 | | |
| | 1.76 | | −0.16 | 0.27 |
| | 2.48 | | −2.03 | |
| | 1.68 | 0.09 | −0.14 | 0.35 |
| | 3.82 | 0.41 | −2.57 | |
| 20, size ranked | 0.30 | 1.02 | | 0.32 |
| | −0.18 | 3.91 | | |
| | 1.73 | | −0.18 | 0.33 |
| | 3.70 | | −3.50 | |
| | −0.05 | 1.15 | 0.03 | 0.40 |
| | −0.85 | 4.61 | 0.76 | |
| 100, beta and size ranked independently | 0.63 | 0.66 | | 0.07 |
| | 1.67 | 3.65 | | |
| | 1.72 | | −0.17 | 0.09 |
| | 3.92 | | −3.17 | |
| | 1.21 | 0.04 | −0.11 | 0.12 |
| | 3.74 | 2.63 | −2.83 | |
| 100, first beta, then size ranked | 0.57 | 0.73 | | 0.12 |
| | 1.43 | 3.49 | | |
| | 1.73 | | −0.18 | 0.12 |
| | 3.70 | | −3.48 | |
| | 1.12 | 0.45 | −0.10 | 0.16 |
| | 3.43 | 2.83 | −2.65 | |
| 100, first size, then beta ranked | 0.58 | 0.71 | | 0.12 |
| | 1.54 | 3.39 | | |
| | 1.72 | | −0.18 | 0.12 |
| | 3.66 | | −3.43 | |
| | 1.14 | 0.43 | −0.10 | 0.16 |
| | 3.78 | 2.58 | −2.87 | |

**Table 23.4** (Continued)

| Portfolios | $\gamma_0$ t-statistic | $\gamma_1$ t-statistic | $\gamma_2$ t-statistic | Adj. $R^2$ |
|---|---|---|---|---|
| | **Panel B. 1941 to 1990** | | | |
| 20, beta ranked | 0.95 | 0.36 | | 0.33 |
| | 4.69 | 1.63 | | |
| | 1.61 | | −0.10 | 0.28 |
| | 2.31 | | −1.49 | |
| | 1.70 | −0.03 | −0.10 | 0.36 |
| | 3.49 | −0.18 | −2.00 | |
| 20, size ranked | 0.54 | 0.76 | | 0.32 |
| | 0.82 | 3.69 | | |
| | 1.73 | | −0.14 | 0.34 |
| | 4.03 | | −3.28 | |
| | 0.32 | 0.85 | 0.02 | 0.44 |
| | −0.15 | 4.35 | 0.56 | |
| 100, beta and size ranked independently | 0.87 | 0.42 | | 0.07 |
| | 2.95 | 3.33 | | |
| | 1.70 | | −0.13 | 0.10 |
| | 4.29 | | −3.40 | |
| | 1.43 | 0.20 | −0.10 | 0.13 |
| | 4.63 | 2.12 | −2.89 | |
| 100, first beta, then size ranked | 0.82 | 0.49 | | 0.12 |
| | 2.76 | 3.07 | | |
| | 1.73 | | −0.14 | 0.13 |
| | 3.99 | | −3.22 | |
| | 1.35 | 0.26 | −0.09 | 0.17 |
| | 4.35 | 2.20 | −2.78 | |
| 100, first size then beta ranked | 0.81 | 0.49 | | 0.12 |
| | 2.75 | 3.12 | | |
| | 1.71 | | −0.13 | 0.13 |
| | 3.96 | | −3.17 | |
| | 1.32 | 0.27 | −0.09 | 0.17 |
| | 4.39 | 2.38 | −2.77 | |

Source: S. P. Kothari, J. Shanken, and Richard G. Sloan, "Another Look at the Cross-Section of Stock Returns," *Journal of Finance* 50 (1995), pp. 185–224. Reprinted by permission.

of portfolios with zero slope coefficient of the return-beta regression lies near the efficient frontier. Thus, even portfolios that are "nearly efficient" do not necessarily support the expected return-beta relationship.

RR make the point that the slope coefficient in the average return-beta regression cannot be relied on to reject the theoretical expected return-beta relationship. It can only indicate that the market proxy that produces this result is inefficient. But their results are valid only for tests that use Ordinary Least Squares (OLS) regressions, such as those of FF, Kothari et al., and many others. Their result does not apply to results that use Generalized Least Squares (GLS) regressions, such as Amihud et al.

**Figure 23.3**

Market index proxies that produce betas having no relation to expected returns.

These proxies are located within a restricted region of the mean-variance space, a region bounded by a parabola that lies inside the efficient frontier except for a tangency at the global minimum variance point. The market proxy is located on the boundary at a distance of $M = 22$ basis points below the efficient frontier. While betas against this market proxy have zero cross-sectional correlation with expected returns, a market proxy on the efficient frontier just 22 basis points above it would produce betas that are perfectly positively collinear with expected returns.

Source: Richard Roll and Stephen A. Ross, "On the Cross-Sectional Relation between Expected Return and Betas," *Journal of Finance* 49 (1994), pp. 101–21. Reprinted by permission.

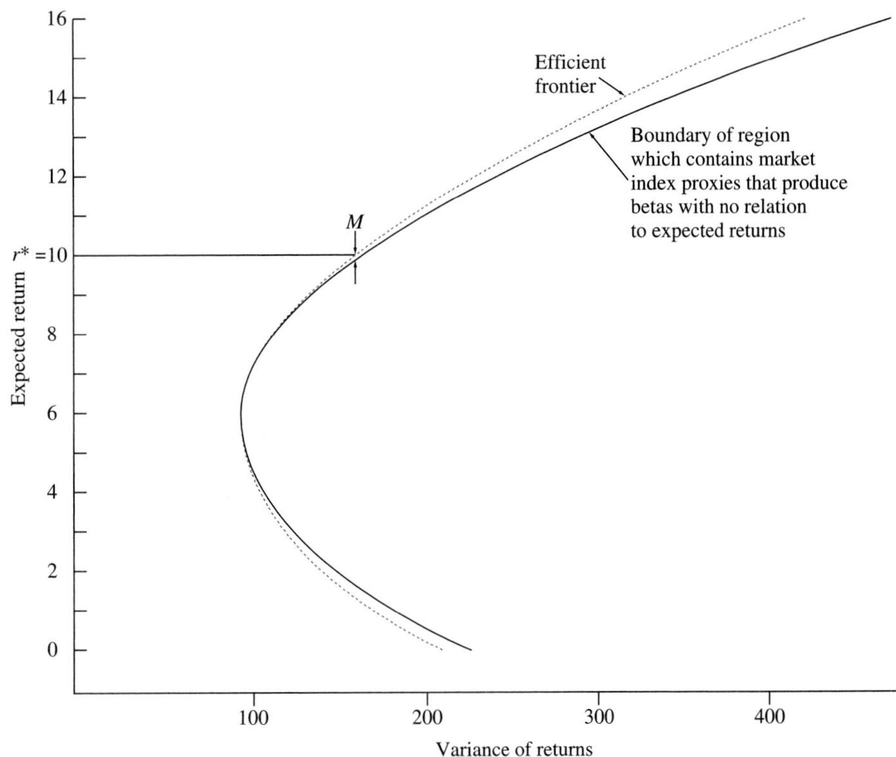


Kandel and Stambaugh (KS) proceed with similar insight to derive a more constructive theory of the relation between the efficiency of a portfolio and the expected return-beta relationship it produces. In doing so, they extend Roll and Ross's conclusions and go further in interpreting the practical implications of "Roll's Critique."

KS derive a measure of *relative efficiency* for any portfolio ($P$). This measure is based on the expected return of Portfolio $P$ ($m_P$), and the expected returns of two unique portfolios: (i) The global minimum variance portfolio ($G$) with mean return $m_G$; and (ii) the efficient frontier portfolio ($X$) with the same variance as $P$, with mean return $m_X$.

Because $P$ and $X$ are equally risky, the relative efficiency of Portfolio $P$ (denoted $RE_P$) is defined in terms of risk premiums over the minimum-variance portfolio $G$ as follows:

$$RE_P = \frac{m_P - m_G}{m_X - m_G}$$

This measure results in values between $-1.0$ and 1.0. When $P$ is efficient, so that $m_P = m_X$, $RE_P = 1.0$. The value $-1.0$ occurs when $P$ lies on the discarded part of the efficient frontier directly below $X$.

When average asset returns are regressed against their betas on $P$ using GLS, the procedure makes use of the entire covariance matrix of the asset asset-returns, unlike OLS which uses only the betas and returns. This results in an intercept ($a_0$) and slope ($a_1$) coefficient that have the properties:

$$a_0 = m_{X0} + (1 - RE_P)(m_X - m_{X0}) \quad \textbf{(23.4a)}$$

$$a_1 = RE_P(m_X - m_{X0}) \quad \textbf{(23.4b)}$$

and the square correlation coefficient of the regression is:

$$R^2_{\text{GLS}} = RE^2_P$$

where $X0$ is the (unique) zero beta portfolio of $X$ with mean return $m_{X0}$. Note that equation 23.4 implies that when $P$ is efficient (so that $RE_P = 1.0$), the CAPM will hold. In this case, the intercept in (23.4a) will be equal to the zero-beta mean return, and the slope coefficient in (23.4b) will equal the risk premium on portfolio $X$ which is identical to that of $P$. Moreover, when, as we expect in practice, Portfolio $P$ is inefficient, the correlation coefficient of the GLS regression reveals the relative efficiency of $P$, $RE_P$.

The RR and KS studies teach us a practical lesson about the implications of the CAPM. We saw in Chapter 8 that the CAPM implies both that: (i) the market portfolio is mean-variance efficient, and (ii) the relation between expected return and beta is linear. Now we know that when the CAPM provides, at best, an approximate description of reality, one of these implications can hold approximately while the other can fail completely. Thus, it is useful to think about each implication separately and concentrate on that which is relevant to the issue at hand.

In the context of performance evaluation, when an index fund is pitted against an alternative portfolio strategy with similar risk, the mean-variance efficiency of the index is the relevant implication. However, we now know that the degree of efficiency of the index has little bearing on the properties of the expected return-beta relationship. In this context, KS caution that using the expected return-beta relationship for capital budgeting purposes may be misleading when the expected return-beta relationship is not exact.

## 23.3 Option Pricing

Research involving contingent claims analysis is probably the most active in the area of finance. The scope and economic importance of applications of contingent claims analysis has spawned a quite distinct professional expertise, usually referred to as financial engineering, which is really a separate field in investment

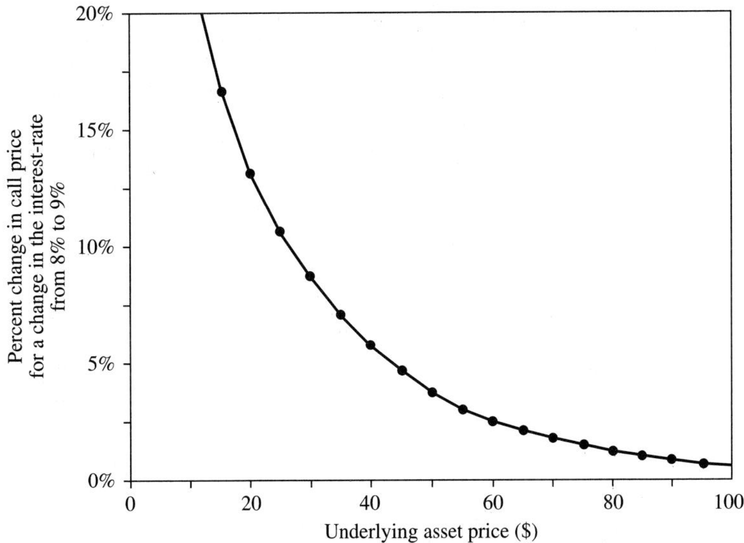


**Figure 23.4**
The percent change in a call price (with $60 exercise price and half a year to expiration, on an underlying asset with price variability of 0.3%/year) for a change in the annual interest rate from 8% to 9%, as a function of the underlying asset price.

management, investment banking, and corporate finance. Several journals (for example, *Derivatives Quarterly* and *The Journal of Derivatives*) are dedicated to research in this area, while a significant part of the space in other finance journals contains articles in this area. Recent advances in this field tend to be highly technical, however, and, for the large part, the marginal contribution of this work to the *conceptual* framework of investments relative to its technical difficulty would put it outside standard courses in investments and the scope of this text. We briefly describe one exception, an article by Bergman[12] that extends option pricing to incorporate differential borrowing and lending rates. This article is a significant departure from other work because it shows that the no-arbitrage option pricing relationships (such as the pricing models based on replication that we developed in Chapter 21) are not necessarily independent across each asset and its derivative securities. In fact, Bergman shows that no-arbitrage bands will depend on the number of securities that are traded.

The Black-Scholes option pricing model assumes a complete market without trading friction and with a uniform borrowing and lending rate. Almost no attention in the literature has been given to the potential implications for option pricing of differences in the borrowing and lending rates. Bergman suggests that the reason is that prices of equity options appear insensitive to changes in interest rates. To motivate his attempt to incorporate differential interest rates into the model, Bergman first demonstrates that for a range of underlying prices and interest rates, call prices will in fact change by a large *proportional* amount when interest rates change. See Figure 23.4 for an example of this analysis.

[12] Yaacov Z. Bergman, "Option Pricing with Differential Interest Rates," *Review of Financial Studies* 8 (1995).

Suppose that at time $t = 0$ a European put and a call written on the same stock, with identical exercise price, $X$, and maturity $T$, are selling for $P$ and $C$, respectively. Then if the borrowing rate, $r_B$ exceeds the lending rate $r_L$, the familiar put-call parity must be replaced with the double inequality,

$$e^{r_L T} \leq \frac{\mathrm{X}}{\mathrm{S} + \mathrm{P} - \mathrm{C}} \leq e^{r_B T} \tag{23.5}$$

It can be seen that when $r_L = r_B$, equation 23.5 reduces to the familiar put-call parity condition. When all other assumptions of the Black-Scholes (BS) model hold, equation 23.5 implies an arbitrage band on the put and call prices, bounded by the BS prices of the put and call evaluated at the appropriate interest rate:

$$C_{BS}(r_L) \leq C \leq C_{BS}(r_B) \tag{23.6a}$$

$$P_{BS}(r_B) \leq P \leq P_{BS}(r_L) \tag{23.6b}$$

where $C_{BS}(r_L)$ in equation 26.6 denotes the Black-Scholes value of a call option evaluated using the interest rate $r_L$, and the notation is similar for put options and borrowing rates.

Now consider two call options on the same stock with the same maturity date but with different exercise prices, $X_1 < X_2$. We can find all price combinations that rule out arbitrage opportunities based on any option position that is long one contract of $C_1$ (the call with $X_1$) and short $\mu$ contracts of $C_2$ (the call with $X_2$). If we repeat this exercise for different values of $\mu$, and combine all the no-arbitrage bands implied by all possible values of $\mu$, we will produce a no-arbitrage oval (i.e., an oval-shaped region of price combinations in which arbitrage opportunities are not present), as depicted in Figure 23.5. This oval links the prices of options with different exercise prices.

Bergman extends this analysis in two ways. First, when short sales are costly, contingent claim pricing is analogous to the case of differential interest rates. Second, the existence of contingent claims on other underlying assets generates no-arbitrage bands on spreads with pairs of contingent claims on two assets, and so on. Thus, no-arbitrage ovals can be constructed for the entire set of contingent claims on a universe of underlying assets. The important conclusion is that trade frictions imply that the option prices that are consistent with the absence of arbitrage opportunities are not unique. The frictions result in entire regions—Bergman's arbitrage ovals—that link the prices of all contingent claims. Moreover, an increase in the number of claims mitigates the cost of the friction (i.e., shrinks the arbitrage ovals).

**Figure 23.5**
The arbitrage oval. Any pair of call prices that lies outside the arbitrage oval represents an arbitrage opportunity.

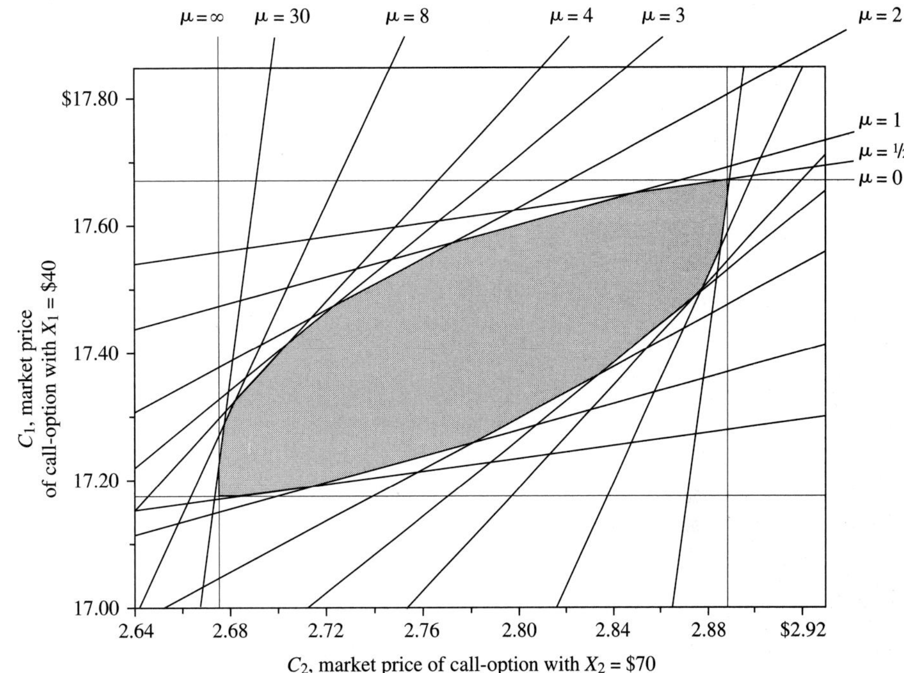

# Appendix

Appendix A

# Quantitative Review

**STUDENTS IN MANAGEMENT AND INVESTMENT COURSES TYPICALLY COME FROM A VARIETY OF BACKGROUNDS.** Some, who have had strong quantitative training, may feel perfectly comfortable with formal mathematical presentation of material. Others, who have had less technical training, may easily be overwhelmed by mathematical formalism.

Most students, however, will benefit from some coaching to make the study of investments easier and more efficient. If you had a good introductory quantitative methods course, and liked the text that was used, you may want to refer to it whenever you feel in need of a refresher. If you feel uncomfortable with standard quantitative texts, this reference is for you. Our aim is to present the essential quantitative concepts and methods in a self-contained, nontechnical, and intuitive way. Our approach is considered structured in line with requirements for the CFA program. The material included is relevant to investment management by the ICFA, the Institute of Chartered Financial Analysts. We hope you find this appendix helpful. Use it to make your venture into investments more enjoyable.

*Note:* If you do not already have a financial calculator, we strongly advise you get one. Most financial calculators have a statistical mode that allows you to compute expected values, standard deviations, and regressions with ease. Actually, working through the user manual is a helpful exercise by itself. If you are interested in investments, you should look at a financial calculator as a good initial investment.

## A.1 Probability Distributions

Statisticians talk about "experiments," or "trials," and refer to possible outcomes as "events." In a roll of a die, for example, the "elementary events" are the numbers 1 through 6. Turning up one side represents the most disaggregate *mutually exclusive* outcome. Other events are *compound,* that is, they consist of more than one elementary event, such as the result "odd number" or "less than 4." In this case "odd" and "less than 4" are not mutually exclusive. Compound events can be mutually exclusive outcomes, however, such as "less than 4" and "equal to or greater than 4."

In decision making, "experiments" are circumstances in which you contemplate a decision that will affect the set of possible events (outcomes) and their likelihood (probabilities). Decision theory calls for you to identify optimal decisions under various sets of circumstances (experiments), which you may do by determining losses from departures from optimal decisions.

When the outcome of a decision (experiment) can be quantified, that is, when a numerical value can be assigned to each elementary event, the decision outcome is called a *random variable.* In the context of investment decision making, the random variable (the payoff to the investment decision) is denominated either in dollars or as a percentage rate of return.

The set or list of all possible values of a random variable, *with* their associated probabilities, is called the *probability distribution* of the random variable. Values that are impossible for the random variable to take on are sometimes listed with probabilities of zero. All possible elementary events are assigned values and probabilities, and thus the probabilities have to sum to 1.0.

Sometimes the values of a random variable are *uncountable,* meaning that you cannot make a list of all possible values. For example, suppose you roll a ball on a line and report the distance it rolls before it comes to a rest. Any distance is possible, and the precision of the report will depend on the need of the roller and/or the quality of the measuring device. Another uncountable random variable is one that describes the weight of a newborn baby. Any positive weight (with some upper bound) is possible.

We call uncountable probability distributions "continuous," for the obvious reason that, at least within a range, the possible outcomes (those with positive probabilities) lie anywhere on a continuum of values. Because there is an infinite number of possible values for the random variable in any continuous distribution, such a probability distribution has to be described by a formula that relates the values of the random variable and their associated probabilities, instead of by a simple list of outcomes and probabilities. We discuss continuous distributions later in this section.

Even countable probability distributions can be complicated. For example, on the New York Stock Exchange stock prices are quoted in eighths. This means the price of a stock at some future date is a *countable* random variable. Probability distributions of countable random variables are called *discrete distributions.* Although a stock price cannot dip below zero, it has no upper bound. Therefore a stock price is a random variable that can take on infinitely many values, even though they are countable, and its discrete probability distribution will have to be given by a formula just like a continuous distribution.

There are random variables that are both discrete and finite. When the probability distribution of the relevant random variable is countable and finite, decision making is tractable and relatively easy to analyze. One example is the decision to call a coin toss "heads" or "tails," with a payoff of zero for guessing wrong and one for guessing right. The random variable of the decision to guess "heads" has a discrete, finite probability distribution. It can be written as

| Event | Value | Probability |
|---|---|---|
| Heads | 1 | .5 |
| Tails | 0 | .5 |

This type of analysis usually is referred to as "scenario analysis." Because scenario analysis is relatively simple, it is used sometimes even when the actual random variable is infinite and uncountable. You can do this by specifying values and probabilities for a set of compound, yet exhaustive and mutually exclusive, events. Because it is simple and has important uses, we handle this case first.

Here is a problem from the 1988 CFA examination.

Mr. Arnold, an Investment Committee member, has confidence in the forecasting ability of the analysts in the firm's research department. However, he is concerned that analysts may not appreciate risk as an important investment consideration. This is especially true in an increasingly volatile investment environment. In addition, he is conservative and risk averse. He asks your risk analysis for Anheuser-Busch stock.

**1.** Using Table A.1, calculate the following measures of dispersion of returns for Anheuser-Busch stock under each of the three outcomes displayed. Show calculations.

*a.* Range.

*b.* Variance: $\Sigma \Pr(i)[r_i - E(r)]^2$

*c.* Standard deviation

*d.* Coefficient of variation: $\text{CV} = \dfrac{\sigma}{E(r)}$

**Table A.1** Anheuser-Busch Companies, Inc., Dispersion of Potential Returns

| Outcome | Probability | Expected Return* |
|---|---|---|
| Number 1 | .20 | 20% |
| Number 2 | .50 | 30% |
| Number 3 | .30 | 50% |

*Assume for the moment that the expected return in each scenario will be realized with certainty. This is the way returns were expressed in the original question.

**2.** Discuss the usefulness of each of the four measures listed in quantifying risk.

The examination questions require very specific answers. We use the questions as a framework for exposition of scenario analysis.

Table A.1 specifies a three-scenario decision problem. The random variable is the rate of return on investing in Anheuser-Busch stock. However, the third column that specifies the value of the random variable does not say simply "Return"—it says "Expected Return." This tells us that the scenario description is a compound event consisting of many elementary events, as is almost always the case. We streamline or simplify reality in order to gain tractability.

Analysts who prepare input lists must decide on the number of scenarios with which to describe the entire probability distribution, as well as the rates of return to allocate to each one. This process calls for determining the probability of occurrence of each scenario *and* the expected rate of return *within* (conditional on) each scenario, which governs the outcome of each scenario. Once you become familiar with scenario analysis, you will be able to build a simple scenario description from any probability distribution.

## Expected Returns

The expected value of a random variable is the answer to the question, "What would be the value of the variable if the 'experiment' (the circumstances and the decision) were repeated infinitely?" In the case of an investment decision, your answer is meant to describe the reward from making the decision.

Note that the question is hypothetical and abstract. It is hypothetical because, practically, the exact circumstances of a decision (the "experiment") often cannot be repeated even once, much less infinitely. It is abstract because, even if the experiment were to be repeated many times (short of infinitely), the *average* rate of return may not be one of the possible outcomes. To demonstrate, suppose that the probability distribution of the rate of return on a proposed investment project is +20 percent or −20 percent, with equal probabilities of .5. Intuition indicates that repeating this investment decision will get us ever closer to an average rate of return of zero. But a one-time investment cannot produce a rate of return of zero. Is the "expected" return still a useful concept when the proposed investment represents a one-time decision?

One argument for using expected return to measure the reward from making investment decisions is that, although a specific investment decision may be made only once, the decision maker will be making many (though different) investment decisions over time. Over time, then, the average rate of return will come close to the average of the expected values of all the individual decisions. Another reason for using the expected value is that admittedly we lack a better measure.[1]

[1] Another case where we use a less-than-ideal measure is the case of yield to maturity on a bond. The YTM measures the rate of return from investing in a bond *if* it is held to maturity and *if* the coupons can be reinvested at the same yield to maturity over the life of the bond.

The probabilities of the scenarios in Table A.1 predict the relative frequencies of the outcomes. If the current investment in Anheuser-Busch could be replicated many times, a 20 percent return would occur 20 percent of the time, a 30 percent return would occur 50 percent of the time, and a 50 percent return would occur the remaining 30 percent of the time. This notion of probabilities and the definition of the expected return tells us how to calculate the expected return:[2]

$$E(r) = .20 \times .20 + .50 \times .30 + .30 \times .50 = .34 \text{ (or 34\%)}$$

Labeling each scenario $i = 1,2,3$, and using the summation sign, $\Sigma$, we can write the formula for the expected return:

$$E(r) = \Pr(1)r_1 + \Pr(2)r_2 + \Pr(3)r_3 \qquad \textbf{(A.1)}$$
$$= \sum_{i=1}^{3} \Pr(i)r_i$$

The definition of the expectation in equation A.1 reveals two important properties of random variables. First, if you add a constant to a random variable, its expectation is also increased by the same constant. If, for example, the return in each scenario in Table A.1 were increased by 5 percent, the expectation would increase to 39 percent. Try this, using equation A.1. If a random variable is multiplied by a constant, its expectation will change by that same proportion. If you multiply the return in each scenario by 1.5, $E(r)$ would change to $1.5 \times .34 = .51$ (or 51 percent).

Second, the deviation of a random variable from its expected value is itself a random variable. Take any rate of return $r_i$ in Table A.1 and define its deviation from the expected value by

$$d_i = r_i - E(r)$$

What is the expected value of $d$? $E(d)$ is the expected deviation from the expected value, and by equation A.1 it is necessarily zero because

$$E(d) = \Sigma \Pr(i)d_i = \Sigma \Pr(i)[r_i - E(r)]$$
$$= \Sigma \Pr(i)r_i - E(r)\Sigma \Pr(i)$$
$$= E(r) - E(r) = 0$$

## Measures of Dispersion: The Range

Assume for a moment that the expected return for each scenario in Table A.1 will be realized with certainty in the event that scenario occurs. Then the set of possible return outcomes is unambiguously 20 percent, 30 percent, and 50 percent. The *range* is the difference between the maximum and the minimum values of the random variable, 50 percent − 20 percent = 30 percent in this case. Range is

---

[2] We will consistently perform calculations in decimal fractions to avoid confusion.

clearly a crude measure of dispersion. Here it is particularly inappropriate because the scenario returns themselves are given as expected values, and therefore the true range is unknown. There is a variant of the range, the *interquartile range,* that we explain in the discussion of descriptive statistics.

## Measures of Dispersion: The Variance

One interpretation of variance is that it measures the "expected surprise." Although that may sound like a contradiction in terms, it really is not. First, think of a surprise as a deviation from expectation. The surprise is not in the *fact* that expectation has not been realized, but rather in the *direction* and *magnitude* of the deviation.

In our example Table A.1 leads us to *expect* a rate of return of 34 percent from investing in Anheuser-Busch stock. A second look at the scenario returns, however, tells us that we should stand ready to be surprised because the probability of earning exactly 34 percent is zero. Being sure that our expectation will not be realized does not mean that we can be sure what the realization is going to be. The element of surprise lies in the direction and magnitude of the deviation of the actual return from expectation, and that is the relevant random variable for the measurement of uncertainty. Its probability distribution adds to our understanding of the nature of the uncertainty that we are facing.

We measure the reward by the expected return. Intuition suggests that we measure uncertainty by the expected *deviation* of the rate of return from expectation. We showed in the previous section, however, that the expected deviation from expectation must be zero. Positive deviations, when weighted by probabilities, are exactly offset by negative deviations. To get around this problem, we replace the random variable "deviation from expectations" (denoted earlier by $d$) with its square, which must be positive even if $d$ itself is negative.

We define the *variance,* our measure of surprise or dispersion, by the *expected squared deviation of the rate of return from its expectation.* With the Greek letter sigma square denoting variance, the formal definition is

$$\sigma^2(r) = E(d^2) = E[r_i - E(r)]^2 = \Sigma \Pr(i)[r_i - E(r)]^2 \qquad \textbf{(A.2)}$$

Squaring each deviation eliminates the sign, which eliminates the offsetting effects of positive and negative deviations.

In the case of Anheuser-Busch, the variance of the rate of return on the stock is

$$\sigma^2(r) = .2(.20 - .34)^2 + .5(.30 - .34)^2 + .3(.50 - .34)^2 = .0124$$

Remember that if you add a constant to a random variable, the variance does not change at all. This is because the expectation also changes by the same constant, and hence deviations from expectation remain unchanged. You can test this by using the data from Table A.1.

Multiplying the random variable by a constant, however, *will* change the variance. Suppose that each return is multiplied by the factor $k$. The new random variable, $kr$, has expectation of $E(kr) = kE(r)$. Therefore the deviation of $kr$ from its expectation is

$$d(kr) = kr - E(kr) = kr - kE(r) = k[r - E(r)] = kd(r)$$

If each deviation is multiplied by $k$, the squared deviations are multiplied by the square of $k$:

$$\sigma^2(kr) = k^2\sigma^2(r)$$

To summarize, adding a constant to a random variable does not affect the variance. Multiplying a random variable by a constant, though, will cause the variance to be multiplied by the square of that constant.

## Measures of Dispersion: The Standard Deviation

A closer look at the variance will reveal that its dimension is different from that of the expected return. Recall that we squared deviations from the expected return in order to make all values positive. This alters the *dimension* (units of measure) of the variance to "square percents." To transform the variance into terms of percentage return, we simply take the square root of the variance. This measure is the *standard deviation*. In the case of Anheuser-Busch's stock return, the standard deviation is

$$\sigma = (\sigma^2)^{1/2} = \sqrt{.0124} = .1114 \text{ (or 11.14\%)} \qquad \textbf{(A.3)}$$

Note that you always need to calculate the variance first before you can get the standard deviation. The standard deviation conveys the same information as the variance but in a different form.

We know already that adding a constant to $r$ will not affect its variance, and it will not affect the standard deviation either. We also know that multiplying a random variable by a constant multiplies the variance by the square of that constant. From the definition of the standard deviation in equation A.3, it should be clear that multiplying a random variable by a constant will multiply the standard deviation by the (absolute value of this) constant. The absolute value is needed because the sign of the constant is lost through squaring the deviations in the computation of the variance. Formally,

$$\sigma(kr) = \text{Abs}(k)\ \sigma(r)$$

Try a transformation of your choice using the data in Table A.1.

## Measures of Dispersion: The Coefficient of Variation

To evaluate the magnitude of dispersion of a random variable, it is useful to compare it to the expected value. The ratio of the standard deviation to the expectation is called the *coefficient of variation*. In the case of returns on Anheuser-Busch stock, it is

$$CV = \frac{\sigma}{E(r)} = \frac{.1114}{.3400} = .3275 \tag{A.4}$$

This standard deviation of the Anheuser-Busch return is about one-third of the expected return (reward). Whether this value for the coefficient of variation represents a big risk depends on what can be obtained with alternative investments.

The coefficient of variation is far from an ideal measure of dispersion. Suppose that a plausible expected value for a random variable is zero. In this case, regardless of the magnitude of the standard deviation, the coefficient of variation will be infinite. Clearly, this measure is not applicable in all cases. Generally, the analyst must choose a measure of dispersion that fits the particular decision at hand. In finance, the standard deviation is the measure of choice in most cases where overall risk is concerned. (For individual assets, the measure $\beta$, explained in the text, is the measure used.)

## Skewness

So far, we have described the measures of dispersion as indicating the size of the average surprise, loosely speaking. The standard deviation is not exactly equal to the average surprise though, because squaring deviations, and then taking the square root of the average square deviation, results in greater weight (emphasis) placed on larger deviations. Other than that, it is simply a measure that tells us how big a deviation from expectation can be expected.

Most decision makers agree that the expected value and standard deviation of a random variable are the most important statistics. However, once we calculate them another question about risk (the nature of the random variable describing deviations from expectations) is pertinent: are the larger deviations (surprises) more likely to be positive? Risk-averse decision makers worry about bad surprises, and the standard deviation does not distinguish good from bad ones. Most risk avoiders are believed to prefer random variables with likely *small negative surprises* and *less* likely *large positive surprises,* to the reverse, likely *small good surprises* and *less* likely *large bad surprises.* More than anything, risk is really defined by the possibility of disaster (large bad surprises).

One measure that distinguishes between the likelihood of large good-versus-bad surprises is the "third moment." It builds on the behaviour of deviations from the expectation, the random variable we have denoted by $d$. Denoting the *third moment* by $M_3$, we define it:

$$M_3 = E(d^3) = E[r_i - E(r)]^3 = \Sigma \Pr(i)[r_i - E(r)]^3 \tag{A.5}$$

Cubing each value of $d$ (taking it to the third power) magnifies larger deviations more than smaller ones. Raising values to an odd power causes them to retain their sign. Recall that the sum of all deviations multiplied by their probabilities is zero because positive deviations weighted by their probabilities exactly offset the negative. When *cubed* deviations are multiplied by their probabilities and then added up, however, large deviations will dominate. The sign will tell us in this case whether *large positive* deviations dominate (positive $M_3$) or whether *large negative* deviations dominate (negative $M_3$).

Incidentally, it is obvious why this measure of skewness is called the third moment; it refers to cubing. Similarly, the variance is often referred to as the second moment, because it requires squaring.

Returning to the investment decision described in Table A.1, with the expected value of 34 percent, the third moment is

$$M_3 = .2(.20 - .34)^3 + .5(.30 - .34)^3 + .3(.50 - .34)^3 = .000648$$

The sign of the third moment tells us that larger *positive* surprises dominate in this case. You might have guessed this by looking at the deviations from expectation and their probabilities; that is, the most likely event is a return of 30 percent, which makes for a small negative surprise. The other negative surprise (20 percent $-$ 34 percent $= -14$ percent) is smaller in magnitude than the positive surprise (50 percent $-$ 34 percent $=$ 16 percent) *and* in also *less* likely (probability .20) relative to the positive surprise, 50 percent (probability .30). The difference appears small, however, and we do not know whether the third moment may be an important issue for the decision to invest in Anheuser-Busch.

It is difficult to judge the importance of the third moment, here .000648, without a benchmark. Following the same reasoning we applied to the standard deviation, we can take the *third root* of $M_3$ (which we denote $m_3$) and compare it to the standard deviation. This yields $m_3 = .0865 = 8.65$ percent, which is not trivial compared with the standard deviation (11.14 percent).

## Another Example: Options on Anheuser-Busch Stock

Suppose that the current price of Anheuser-Busch stock is $30. A call option on the stock is selling for 60 cents, and a put is selling for $4. Both have an exercise price of $42 and maturity date to match the scenarios in Table A.1.

The call option allows you to buy the stock at the exercise price. You will choose to do so if the call ends up "in the money," that is, the stock price is above the exercise price. The profit in this case is the difference between the stock price and the exercise price, less the cost of the call. Even if you exercise the call, your profit may still be negative if the cash flow from the exercise of the call does not cover the initial cost of the call. If the call ends up "out of the money," that is, the stock price is below the exercise price, you will let the call expire worthless and suffer a loss equal to the cost of the call.

The put option allows you to sell the stock at the exercise price. You will choose to do so if the put ends up "in the money," that is, the stock price is below the exercise price. Your profit is then the difference between the exercise price and the stock price, less the initital cost of the put. Here, again, if the cash flow is not sufficient to cover the cost of the put, the investment will show a loss. If the put ends up "out of the money," you again let it expire worthless, taking a loss equal to the initial cost of the put.

**Table A.2** Scenario Analysis for Investment in Options on Anheuser-Busch Stock

| | Scenario 1 | Scenario 2 | Scenario 3 |
|---|---|---|---|
| Probability | .20 | .50 | .30 |
| **EVENT** | | | |
| 1. Return on stock | 20% | 30% | 50% |
| Stock price | $36.00 | $39.00 | $45.00 |
| (initial price = $30) | | | |
| 2. Cash flow from call | 0 | 0 | $3.00 |
| (exercise price = $42) | | | |
| Call profit | −$.60 | −$.60 | $2.40 |
| (initial price = $.60) | | | |
| 3. Call rate of return | −100% | −100% | 400% |
| Cash flow from put | $6.00 | $3.00 | 0 |
| (exercise price = $42) | | | |
| Put profit | $2.00 | −$1.00 | −$4.00 |
| (initial price = $4) | | | |
| Put rate of return | 50% | −25% | −100% |

The scenario analysis of these alternative investments is described in Table A.2.

The expected rates of return on the call and put are

$$E(r_{\text{call}}) = .2(-1) + .5(-1) + .3(4) = .5 \quad \text{(or 50\%)}$$
$$E(r_{\text{put}}) = .2(.5) + .5(-.25) + .3(-1) = -.325 \quad \text{(or } -32.5\%\text{)}$$

The negative expected return on the put may be justified by the fact that it is a hedge asset, in this case an insurance policy against losses from holding Anheuser-Busch stock. The variance and standard deviation of the two investments are

$$\sigma^2_{\text{call}} = .2(-1 - .5)^2 + .5(-1 - .5)^2 + .3(4 - .5)^2 = 5.25$$
$$\sigma^2_{\text{put}} = .2[.5 - (-.325)]^2 + .5[-.25 - (-.325)]^2 + .3[-1 - (-.325)]^2 = .2756$$
$$\sigma_{\text{call}} = \sqrt{5.25} = 2.2913 \text{ (or 229.13\%)}$$
$$\sigma_{\text{put}} = \sqrt{.2756} = .525 \text{ (or 52.5\%)}$$

These are very large standard deviations. Comparing the standard deviation of the call's return to its expected value, we get the coefficient of variation:

$$\text{CV}_{\text{call}} = \frac{2.2913}{.5} = 4.5826$$

Refer back to the coefficient of variation for the stock itself, .3275, and it is clear that these instruments have high standard deviations. This is quite common for stock options. The negative expected return of the put illustrates again the problem in interpreting the magnitude of the "surprise" indicated by the coefficient of variation.

Moving to the third moments of the two probability distributions:

$$M_3(\text{call}) = .2(-1 - .5)^3 + .5(-1 - .5)^3 + .3(4 - .5)^3 = 10.5$$
$$M_3(\text{put}) = .2[.5 - (-.325)]^3 + .5[-.25 - (-.325)]^3 + .3[-1 - (-.325)]^3 = .02025$$

Both instruments are positively skewed, which is typical of options and one part of their attractiveness. In this particular circumstance the call is more skewed than the put. To establish this fact, note the third root of the third moment:

$$m_3(\text{call}) = M_3(\text{call})^{1/3} = 2.1898 \text{ (or } 218.98\%)$$
$$m_3(\text{put}) = .02^{1/3} = .2725 \text{ (or } 27.25\%)$$

Compare these figures to the standard deviations, 229.13 percent for the call and 52.5 percent for put, and you can see that a large part of the standard deviation of the option is driven by the possibility of large good surprises instead of by the more likely, yet smaller, bad surprises.[3]

So far we have described discrete probability distributions using scenario analysis. We shall come back to decision making in a scenario analysis framework in Section A.3 on multivariate statistics.

## Continuous Distributions: Normal and Lognormal Distributions

When a compact scenario analysis is possible and acceptable, decisions may be quite simple. Often, however, so many relevant scenarios must be specified that scenario analysis is impossible for practical reasons. Even in the case of Anheuser-Busch, as we were careful to specify, the individual scenarios considered actually represented compound events.

When many possible values of the rate of return have to be considered, we must use a formula that describes the probability distribution (relates values to probabilities). As we noted earlier, there are two types of probability distributions: discrete and continuous. Scenario analysis involves a discrete distribution. However, the two most useful distributions in investments, the normal and lognormal, are continuous. At the same time they are often used to approximate variables with distributions that are known to be discrete, such as stock prices. The probability distribution of future prices and returns is discrete—prices are quoted in eighths. Yet the industry norm is to approximate these distributions by the normal or lognormal distribution.

---

[3] Note that the expected return of the put is −32.5 percent; hence the worst surprise is −67.5 percent, and the best is 82.5 percent. The middle scenario is also a positive deviation of 7.5 percent (with a high probability of .50). These two elements explain the positive skewness of the put.

**Standard Normal Distribution.** The normal distribution, also known as Gaussian (after the mathematician Gauss) or bell-shaped, describes random variables with the following properties and is shown in Figure A.1:

- The expected value is the mode (the most frequent elementary event) and also the median (the middle value in the sense that half the elementary events are greater and half smaller). Note that the expected value, unlike the median or mode, requires weighting by probabilities to produce the concept of central value.
- The normal probability distribution is symmetric around the expected value. In other words, the likelihood of equal absolute-positive and negative deviations from expectation is equal. Larger deviations from the expected value are less likely than are smaller deviations. In fact, the essence of the normal distribution is that the probability of deviations decreases exponentially with the magnitude of the deviation (positive and negative alike).
- A normal distribution is identified completely by two parameters, the expected value and the standard deviation. The property of the normal distribution that makes it most convenient for portfolio analysis is that any weighted sum of normally distributed random variables produces a random variable that also is normally distributed. This property is called stability. It is also true that if you add a constant to a "normal" random variable (meaning a random variable with a normal probability distribution) or multiply it by a constant, then the transformed random variable also will be normally distributed.

Suppose that $n$ is any random variable (not necessarily normal), with expectation $\mu$ and standard deviation $\sigma$. As we showed earlier, if you add a constant $c$ to $n$, the standard deviation is not affected at all, but the mean will change to $\mu + c$. If you multiply $n$ by a constant $b$, its mean and standard deviation will change by the same proportion to $b\mu$ and $b\sigma$. If $n$ is normal, the transformed variable also will be normal.

Stability, together with the property that a normal variable is completely characterized by its expectation and standard deviation, implies that if we know one

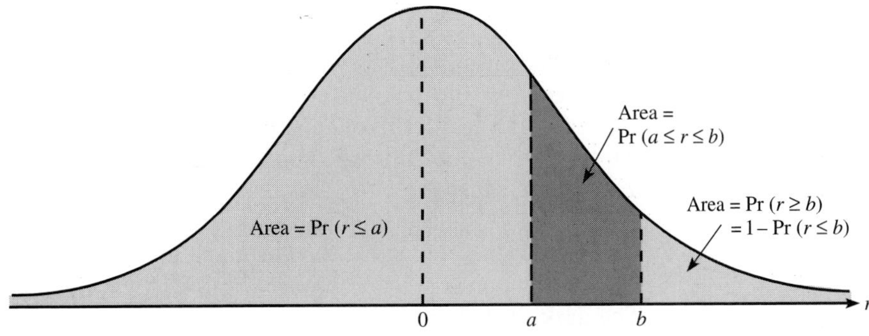


**Figure A.1**
Probabilities under the normal density.

normal probability distribution with a given expectation and standard deviation, we know them all.

Thus, the *standard normal distribution* has an expectation of zero, and both variance and standard deviation equal to 1.0. Formally, the relationship between the value of the standard normal random variable, $z$, and its probability, $f$, is given by

$$f(z) = \frac{1}{\sqrt{2\pi}} \exp\left(\frac{-z^2}{2}\right) \tag{A.6}$$

where "exp" is the quantity $e$ to the power of the expression in the large parenthesis. The quantity $e$ is an important number just like the well-known $\pi$ that also appears in the function. It is important enough to earn a place on the keyboard of your financial calculator, mostly because it is used also in continuous compounding.

Probability functions of continuous distributions are called *densities* and denoted by $f$, rather than by the "Pr" of scenario analysis. The reason is that the probability of any of the infinitely many possible values of $z$ is infinitesimally small. Density is a function that allows us to obtain the probability of a *range of values* by integrating it over a desired range. In other words, whenever we want the probability that a standard normal variate (a random variable) will fall in the range from $z = a$ to $z = b$, we have to add up the density values, $f(z)$ for all $z$s from $a$ to $b$. There are infinitely many $z$s in that range, regardless how close $a$ is to $b$. *Integration* is the mathematical operation that achieves this task.

Consider first the probability that a standard normal variate will take on a value less than or equal to $a$, that is, $z$ is in the range $[-\infty\ a]$. We have to integrate the density from $\infty$ to $a$. The result is called the *cumulative (normal) distribution,* and denoted by $N(a)$. When $a$ approaches infinity, any value is allowed for $z$; hence the probability that $z$ will end up in that range approaches 1.0. It is a property of any density that when it is integrated over the entire range of the random variable, the cumulative distribution is 1.0.

In the same way, the probability that a standard normal variate will take on a value less than or equal to $b$ is $N(b)$. The probability that a standard normal variate will take on a value in the range $[a,b]$ is just the difference between $N(b)$ and $N(a)$. Formally,

$$\Pr(a \leqq z \leqq b) = N(b) - N(a)$$

These concepts are illustrated in Figure A.1. The graph shows the normal density. It demonstrates the symmetry of the normal density around the expected value (zero for the standard normal variate, which is also the mode and the median), and the smaller likelihood of larger deviations from expectation. As is true for any density, the entire area under the density graph adds up to 1.0. The values $a$ and $b$ are chosen to be positive, so they are to the right of the expected value. The left-most shaded area is the proportion of the area under the density for which the value of $z$ is less than or equal to $a$. Thus this area yields the cumulative distribution for $a$, the probability that $z$ will be smaller than or equal to $a$. The dark shaded area is the area under the density graph between $a$ and $b$. If we add that area to the cumulative distribution of $a$, we get the entire area up to $b$, that is, the probability that $z$ will be anywhere to the left of $b$. Thus, the area between $a$ and $b$ has to be the probability that $z$ will fall between $a$ and $b$.

Applying the same logic, we find the probability that $z$ will take on a value greater than $b$. We know already that the probability that $z$ will be smaller than or equal to $b$ is $N(b)$. The compound events "smaller than or equal to $b$" and "greater than $b$" are mutually exclusive *and* "exhaustive," meaning that they include all possible outcomes. Thus, their probabilities sum to 1.0, and the probability that $z$ is greater than $b$ is simply equal to one minus the probability that $z$ is less than or equal to $b$. Formally, $\Pr(z > b) = 1 - N(b)$.

Look again at Figure A.1. The area under the density graph between $b$ and infinity is just the difference between the entire area under the graph (equal to 1.0), and the area between minus infinity and $b$, that is, $N(b)$.

The normal density is sufficiently complex that its cumulative distribution, its integral, does not have an exact formulaic closed-form solution. It must be obtained by numerical (approximation) methods. These values are produced in tables that give the value $N(z)$ for any $z$, such as Table 21.2 of this text.

To illustrate, let us find the following probabilities for a standard normal variate:

$\Pr(z \leqq -.36) = N(-.36) =$ Probability that $z$ is less than or equal to .36
$\Pr(z \leqq .94) = N(.94) =$ Probability that $z$ is less than or equal to .94
$\Pr(-.36 \leqq z \leqq .94) = N(.94) - N(-.36) =$ Probability that $z$ will be in the range $[-.36, .94]$
$\Pr(z > .94) = 1 - N(.94) =$ Probability that $z$ is greater than .94

Use Table 21.2 of the cumulative standard normal (sometimes called the area under the normal density) and Figure A.2. The table shows that

$$N(-.36) = .3594$$
$$N(.94) = .8264$$

In Figure A.2 the area under the graph between $-.36$ and .94 is the probability that $z$ will fall between $-.36$ and .94. Hence,

$$\Pr(-.36 \leqq z \leqq .94) = N(.94) - N(-.36) = .8264 - .3594 = .4670$$

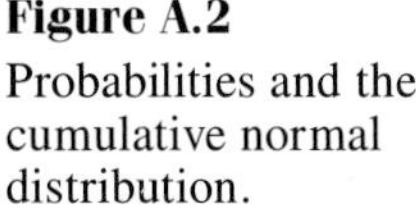

**Figure A.2**
Probabilities and the cumulative normal distribution.

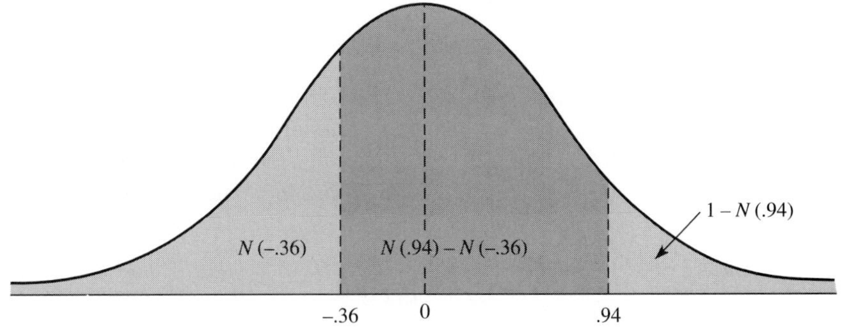

The probability that z is greater than .94 is the area under the graph in Figure A.2, between .94 and infinity. Thus it is equal to the entire area (1.0) less the area from minus infinity to .94. Hence,

$$\Pr(z > .94) = 1 - N(.94) = 1 - .8264 = .1736$$

Finally, one can ask, "what is the value, $a$, so that $z$ will be smaller than or equal to $a$ with probability $P$?" The notion for the function that yields the desired value of $a$ is $\Phi(P)$ so that

$$\text{If } \Phi(P) = a, \text{ then } P = N(a) \tag{A.7}$$

For instance, suppose the question is, "which value has a cumulative density of .50?" A glance at Figure A.2 reminds us that the area between minus infinity and zero (the expected value) is .5. Thus we can write

$$\Phi(.5) = 0, \text{ because } N(0) = .5$$

Similarly,

$$\Phi(.8264) = .94 \text{ because } N(.94) = .8264$$

and

$$\Phi(.3594) = -.36$$

For practice, confirm with Table 21.2 that $\Phi(.6554) = .40$, meaning that the value of $z$ with a cumulative distribution of .6554 is $z = .40$.

**Nonstandard Normal Distributions.** Suppose that the monthly rate of return on a stock is closely approximated by a normal distribution with a mean of .015 (1.5 percent per month), and standard deviation of .127 (12.7 percent per month). What is the probability that the rate of return will fall below zero in a given month? Recall that because the rate is a normal variate, its cumulative density has to be computed by numerical methods. The standard normal table can be used for any normal variate.

Any random variable, $x$, may be transformed into a new standardized variable, $x^*$, by the following rule:

$$x^* = \frac{x - E(x)}{\sigma(x)} \tag{A.8}$$

Note that all that we have done to $x$ was (1) *subtract* its expectation and (2) *multiply* by one over its standard deviation, $1/[\sigma(x)]$. According to our earlier discussion, the effect of transforming a random variable by adding and multiplying by a constant is such that the expectation and standard deviation of the transformed variable are

$$E(x^*) = \frac{E(x) - E(x)}{\sigma(x)} = 0; \; \sigma(x^*) = \frac{\sigma(x)}{\sigma(x)} = 1 \tag{A.9}$$

From the stability property of the normal distribution we also know that if $x$ is normal, so is $x^*$. A normal variate is characterized completely by two parameters: its expectation and standard deviation. For $x^*$, these are zero and 1.0, respectively. When we subtract the expectation and then divide a normal variate by its standard deviation, we standardize it; that is, we transform it to a standard normal variate. This trick is used extensively in working with normal (and approximately normal) random variables.

Returning to our stock, we have learned that if we subtract .15 and then divide the monthly returns by .127, the resultant random variable will be standard normal. We can now determine the probability that the rate of return will be zero or less in a given month. We know that

$$z = \frac{r - .015}{.127}$$

where $z$ is standard normal and $r$ the return on our stock. Thus, if $r$ is zero, $z$ has to be

$$z(r = 0) = \frac{0 - .015}{.127} = -.1181$$

For $r$ to be zero, the corresponding standard normal has to be $-11.81$ percent, a negative number. The event "$r$ will be zero or less" is identical to the event "$z$ will be $-.1181$ or less." Calculating the probability of the latter will solve our problem. That probability is simply $N(-.1181)$. Visit the standard normal table and find that

$$N(-.1181) = \Pr(r \leqq 0) = .5 - .047 = .453$$

The answer makes sense. Recall that the expectation of $r$ is 1.5 percent. Thus, whereas the probability that $r$ will be 1.5 percent or less is .5, the probability that it will be *zero* or less has to be close, but somewhat less.

**Confidence Intervals.** Given the large standard deviation of our stock, it is logical to be concerned about the likelihood of extreme values for the monthly rate of return. One way to quantify this concern is to ask: "What is the interval (range) within which the stock return will fall in a given month, with a probability of .95?" Such an interval is called the *95 percent confidence interval.*

Logic dictates that this interval be centered on the expected value, .015, because $r$ is a normal variate (has a normal distribution), which is symmetric around the expectation. Denote the desired interval by

$$[E(r) - a, E(r) + a] = [.015 - a, .015 + a]$$

which has a length of $2a$. The probability that $r$ will fall within this interval is described by the following expression:

$$\Pr(.015 - a \leqq r \leqq .015 + a) = .95$$

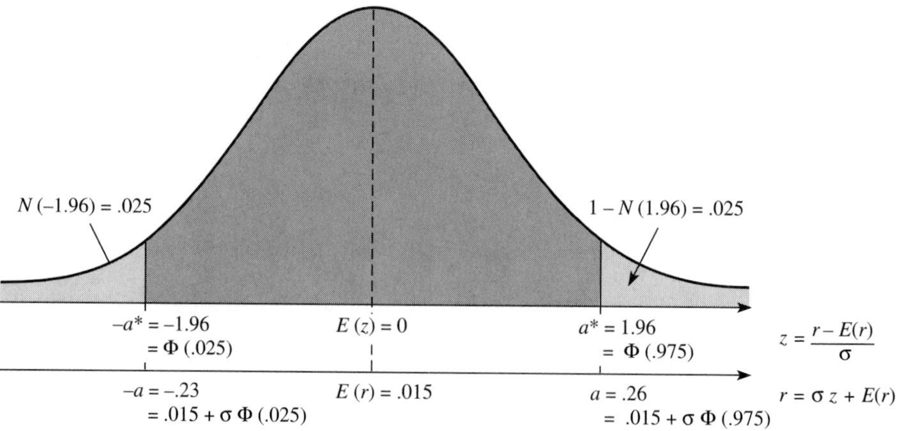


**Figure A.3**
Confidence intervals and the standard normal density.

To find this probability, we start with a simpler problem, involving the standard normal variate, that is, a normal with expectation of zero and standard deviation of 1.0.

What is the 95 percent confidence interval for the standard normal variate, $z$? The variable will be centered on zero, so the expression is

$$\Pr(-a^* \leqq z \leqq a^*) = N(a^*) - N(-a^*) = .95$$

You might best understand the substitution of the difference of the appropriate cumulative distributions for the probability with the aid of Figure A.3. The probability of falling outside of the interval is $1 - .95 = .05$. By the symmetry of the normal distribution, $z$ will be equal to or less than $-a^*$ with probability of .025, and with probability .025, $z$ will be greater than $a^*$. Thus, we solve for $a^*$ using

$$-a^* = \Phi(.025) \text{ which is equivalent to } N(-a^*) = .025$$

We can summarize the chain that we have pursued so far as follows. If we seek a $P = .95$ level confidence interval, we define $\alpha$ as the probability to fall outside the confidence interval. Because of the symmetry, $\alpha$ will be split so that half of it is the probability of falling to the right of the confidence interval, while the other half of $\alpha$ is the probability of falling to the left of the confidence interval. Therefore the relation between $\alpha$ and $P$ is

$$\alpha = 1 - \mathrm{P} = .05; \quad \frac{\alpha}{2} = \frac{1 - P}{2} = .025$$

We use $\alpha/2$ to indicate that the area that is excluded for $r$ is equally divided between the tails of the distributions. Each tail that is excluded for $r$ has an area of $\alpha/2$. The value, $\alpha = 1 - P$, represents the entire value that is excluded for $r$.

To find $z = \Phi(\alpha/2)$, which is the lower boundary of the confidence interval for the standard normal variate, we have to locate the $z$ value for which the standard normal cumulative distribution is .025, finding $z = -1.96$. Thus, we conclude that $-a^* = -1.96$ and $a^* = 1.96$. The confidence interval for $z$ is

$$[E(z) - \Phi(\alpha/2), E(z) + \Phi(\alpha/2) = [\Phi(.025), \Phi(.975)] \\ = [-1.96, 1.96]$$

To get the interval boundaries for the nonstandard normal variate $r$, we transform the boundaries for $z$ by the usual relationship, $r = z\sigma(r) + E(r) = \Phi(\alpha/2)\sigma(r) + E(r)$. Note that all we are doing is setting the expectation at the center of the confidence interval and extending it by a number of standard deviations. The number of standard deviations is determined by the probability that we allow for falling outside the confidence interval ($\alpha$), or equivalently, the probability of falling in it ($P$). Using minus and plus 1.96 for $z = \Phi(.025)$ and $\Phi(.975)$, the distance on each side of the expectation is $\pm 1.96 \times .127 = \pm .249$. Thus, we obtain the confidence interval

$$[E(r) - \sigma(r)\Phi(\alpha/2), E(r) + \sigma(r)\Phi(\alpha/2) = [E(r) - .249, E(r) + .249] \\ = [-.234, .264]$$

so that

$$P = 1 - \alpha = \Pr[E(r) - \sigma(r)\Phi(\alpha/2) \leqq r \leqq E(r) + \sigma(r)\Phi(\alpha/2)$$

which, for our stock (with expectation .015 and standard deviation .127) amounts to

$$\Pr[-.234 \leqq r \leqq .264] = .95$$

Note that, because of the large standard deviation of the rate of return on the stock, the 95 percent confidence interval is 49 percentage points wide.

To reiterate with a variation on this example, suppose we seek a 90 percent confidence interval for the annual rate of return on a portfolio, $r_p$, with a monthly expected return of 1.2 percent and standard deviation of 5.2 percent.

The solution is simply

$$\Pr\left[E(r) - \sigma(r)\Phi\left(\frac{1-P}{2}\right) \leqq r_p \leqq E(r) + \sigma(r)\Phi\left(\frac{1-P}{2}\right)\right] \\ = \Pr[.012 - (.052 \times 1.645) \leqq r_p \leqq .012 + (.052 \times 1.645)] \\ = \Pr[-.0735 \leqq r_p \leqq .0975] = .90$$

Since the portfolio is of low risk this time (and we allow a 90 percent rather than a 95 percent probability of falling within the interval), the 90 percent confidence interval is only 2.4 percentage points wide.

**The Lognormal Distribution.** The normal distribution is not adequate to describe stock prices and returns for two reasons. First, whereas the normal distribution admits any value, including negative values, actual stock prices cannot be negative. Second, the normal distribution does not account for compounding. The lognormal distribution addresses these two problems.

The lognormal distribution describes a random variable that grows, *every instant,* by a rate that is a normal random variable. Thus the progression of a lognormal random variable reflects continuous compounding.

Suppose that the *annual continuously compounded* (ACC) rate of return on a stock is normally distributed with expectation $\mu = .12$ and standard deviation $\sigma = .42$. The stock price at the beginning of the year is $P_0 = \$10$. With continuous compounding (see appendix A to Chapter 5), if the ACC rate of return, $r_C$, turns out to be .23, then the end-of-year price will be

$$P_1 = P_0 \exp(r_C) = 10e^{.23} = \$12.586$$

representing an effective annual rate of return of

$$r = \frac{P_1 - P_0}{P_0} = e^{r_C} - 1 = .2586 \text{ (or 25.86\%)}$$

This is the practical meaning of $r$, the annual rate on the stock, being lognormally distributed. Note that however negative the ACC rate of return ($r_C$) is, the price, $P_1$, cannot become negative.

Two properties of lognormally distributed financial assets are important: their expected return and the allowance for changes in measurement period.

**Expected Return of a Lognormally Distributed Asset.** The expected annual rate of return of a lognormally distributed stock (as in our example) is

$$\begin{aligned} E(r) &= \exp(\mu + \tfrac{1}{2}\sigma^2) - 1 = \exp(.12 + \tfrac{1}{2} \times .42^2) - 1 = e^{.2082} - 1 \\ &= .2315 \text{ (or 23.15\%)} \end{aligned}$$

This is just a statistical property of the distribution. For this reason, a useful statistic is

$$\mu^* = \mu + \tfrac{1}{2}\sigma^2 = .2082$$

Often, when analysts refer to the expected ACC return on a lognormal asset, they are really referring to $\mu^*$. Often, the asset is said to have a normal distribution of the ACC return with expectation $\mu^*$ and standard deviation $\sigma$.

**Change of Frequency of Measured Returns.** The lognormal distribution allows for easy change of the holding period of returns. Suppose that we want to calculate returns monthly instead of annually. We use the parameter $t$ to indicate the fraction of the year that is desired, in the case of monthly periods $t = 1/12$. To transform the annual distribution to a $t$-period (monthly) distribution, it is necessary merely to multiply the expectation and variance of the ACC return by $t$ (in this case, 1/12).

The monthly continuously compounded return on the stock in our example has the expectation and standard deviation of

$$\mu(\text{monthly}) = .12/12 = .01 \text{ (1\% per month)}$$
$$\sigma(\text{monthly}) = .42/\sqrt{12} = .1212 \text{ (or 12.12\% per month)}$$
$$\mu^*(\text{monthly}) = .2082/12 = .01735 \text{ (or 1.735\% per month)}$$

Note that we divide variance by 12 when changing from annual to monthly frequency; the standard deviation therefore is divided by the square root of 12.

Similarly, we can convert a non-annual distribution to an annual distribution by following the same routine. For example, suppose that the weekly continuously compounded rate of return on a stock is normally distributed with $\alpha = .003$ and $\sigma = .07$. Then the ACC return is distributed with

$$\mu^* = 52 \times .003 = .156 \text{ (or 15.6\% per year)}$$
$$\sigma = \sqrt{52} \times .07 = .5048 \text{ (or 50.48\% per year)}$$

In practice, to obtain normally distributed, continuously compounded returns, $R$, we take the log of 1.0 plus the raw returns:

$$r_C = \log(1 + r)$$

For short intervals, raw returns are small, and the continuously compounded returns, $R$, will be practically identical to the raw returns, $r$. The rule of thumb is that this conversion is not necessary for periods of one month or less. That is, approximating stock returns as normal will be accurate enough. For longer intervals, however, the transformation may be necessary.

## A.2 Descriptive Statistics

Our analysis so far has been forward looking, or, as economists like to say, ex ante. We have been concerned with probabilities, expected values, and surprises. We made our analysis more tractable by assuming that decision outcomes are distributed according to relatively simple formulas, and that we know the parameters of these distributions.

Investment managers must satisfy themselves that these assumptions are reasonable, which they do by constantly analyzing observations from relevant random variables that accumulate over time. Distribution of past rates of return on a stock is one element they need to know in order to make optimal decisions. True, the distribution of the rate of return itself changes over time. However, a sample that is not too old does yield information relevant to the next period probability distribution and its parameters. In this section we explain descriptive statistics, or the organization and analysis of such historic samples.

### Histograms, Boxplots, and Time Series Plots

Table A.3 shows the annual excess returns (over the T-bill rate) for two major classes of assets, the S&P 500 index and a portfolio of long-term government bonds, for the period 1926 to 1987.

**Table A.3** Excess Return (Risk Premiums) on Stocks and Long-Term Treasury Bonds (Maturity Premiums)

| Date | Equity Risk Premium | Maturity Premium |
|---|---|---|
| 1926 | 0.0835 | 0.045 |
| 1927 | 0.3437 | 0.0581 |
| 1928 | 0.4037 | −0.0314 |
| 1929 | −0.1317 | −0.0133 |
| 1930 | −0.2731 | 0.0225 |
| 1931 | −0.4441 | −0.0638 |
| 1932 | −0.0915 | 0.1588 |
| 1933 | 0.5369 | −0.0038 |
| 1934 | −0.016 | 0.0986 |
| 1935 | 0.475 | 0.0481 |
| 1936 | 0.3374 | 0.0733 |
| 1937 | −0.3534 | −0.0008 |
| 1938 | 0.3114 | 0.0555 |
| 1939 | −0.0043 | 0.0592 |
| 1940 | −0.0978 | 0.0609 |
| 1941 | −0.1165 | 0.0087 |
| 1942 | 0.2007 | 0.0295 |
| 1943 | 0.2555 | 0.0173 |
| 1944 | 0.1942 | 0.0248 |
| 1945 | 0.3611 | 0.104 |
| 1946 | −0.0842 | −0.0045 |
| 1947 | 0.0521 | −0.0313 |
| 1948 | 0.0469 | 0.0259 |
| 1949 | 0.1769 | 0.0535 |
| 1950 | 0.3051 | −0.0114 |
| 1951 | 0.2253 | −0.0543 |
| 1952 | 0.1671 | −0.005 |
| 1953 | −0.0281 | 0.0181 |
| 1954 | 0.5176 | 0.0633 |
| 1955 | 0.2999 | −0.0287 |
| 1956 | 0.041 | −0.0805 |
| 1957 | −0.1392 | 0.0431 |
| 1958 | 0.4182 | −0.0764 |
| 1959 | 0.0901 | −0.0521 |
| 1960 | −0.0219 | 0.1112 |
| 1961 | 0.2476 | −0.0116 |
| 1962 | −0.1146 | 0.0416 |
| 1963 | 0.1968 | −0.0191 |
| 1964 | 0.1294 | −0.0003 |
| 1965 | 0.0852 | −0.0322 |
| 1966 | −0.1482 | −0.0111 |
| 1967 | 0.1977 | −0.134 |
| 1968 | 0.0585 | −0.0547 |
| 1969 | −0.1508 | −0.1166 |
| 1970 | −0.0252 | 0.0557 |
| 1971 | 0.0992 | 0.0884 |
| 1972 | 0.1514 | 0.0184 |
| 1973 | −0.2159 | −0.0804 |

**Table A.3** Continued

| Date | Equity Risk Premium | Maturity Premium |
|---|---|---|
| 1974 | −0.3447 | −0.0365 |
| 1975 | 0.314 | 0.0339 |
| 1976 | 0.1876 | 0.1167 |
| 1977 | −0.123 | −0.0579 |
| 1978 | −0.0062 | −0.0834 |
| 1979 | 0.0806 | −0.116 |
| 1980 | 0.2118 | −0.1519 |
| 1981 | −0.1962 | −0.1286 |
| 1982 | 0.1087 | 0.2981 |
| 1983 | 0.1371 | −0.0812 |
| 1984 | −0.0358 | 0.0558 |
| 1985 | 0.2444 | 0.2325 |
| 1986 | 0.1231 | 0.1828 |
| 1987 | −0.0024 | −0.0816 |
| Average | 0.0833 | 0.0106 |
| Standard deviation | 0.2106 | 0.0798 |
| Minimum | −0.4441 | −0.1519 |
| Maximum | 0.5369 | 0.2981 |

Source: Data from the Center for Research of Security Prices, University of Chicago, Chicago, Illinois. Reprinted by permission.

One way to understand the data is to present it graphically, commonly in a *histogram* or frequency distribution. Histograms of the 62 observations in Table A.3 are shown in Figure A.4. We construct a histogram according to the following principles:

- The range (of values) of the random variable is divided into a relatively small number of equal-sized intervals. The number of intervals that makes sense depends on the number of available observations. The data in Table A.3 provide 62 observations, and thus deciles (10 intervals) seem adequate.
- A rectangle is drawn over each interval. The height of the rectangle represents the frequency of observations for each interval.
- If the observations are concentrated in one part of the range, the range may be divided into unequal intervals. In that case the rectangles are scaled so that their *area* represents the frequency of the observations for each interval. (This is not the case in our samples, however.)
- If the sample is representative, the shape of the histogram will reveal the probability distribution of the random variable. In our case 62 observations are not a large sample, but a look at the histogram does suggest that the returns may be reasonably approximated by a normal or lognormal distribution.

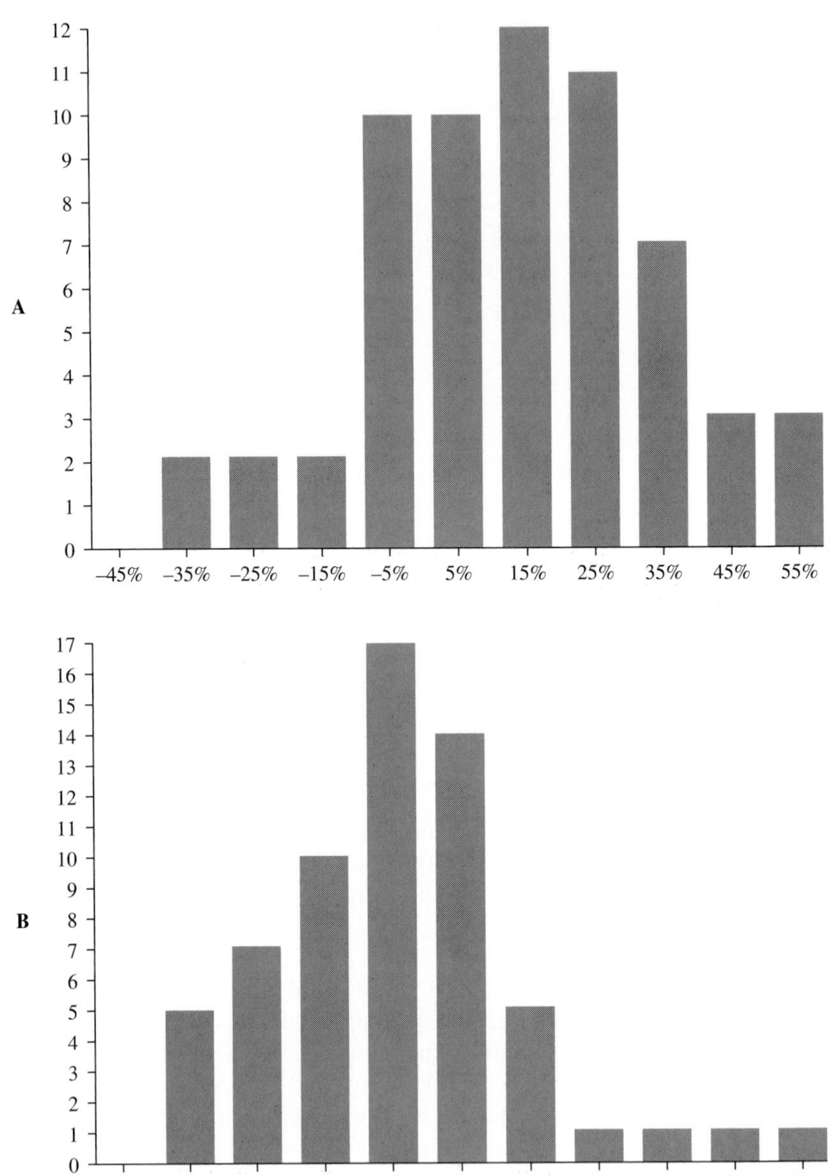


**Figure A.4**
**A,** Histogram of the equity risk premium. **B,** Histogram of the bond maturity premium.

Another way to represent sample information graphically is by *boxplots.* Figure A.5 is an example that uses the same data as in Table A.3. Boxplots are most useful to show the dispersion of the sample distribution. A commonly used measure of dispersion is the *interquartile range.* Recall that the range, a crude measure of dispersion, is defined as the distance between the largest and smallest

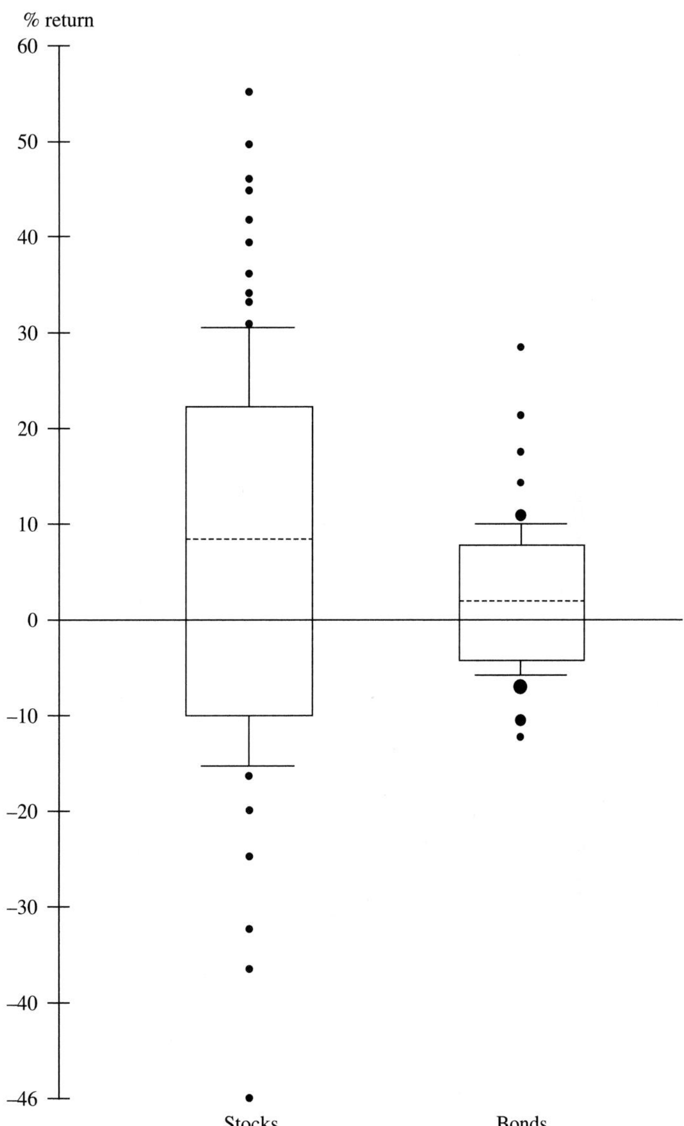


**Figure A.5**
Boxplots of annual equity risk premium and long-term bond (maturity) risk premium (1926–1987).

observations. By its nature, this measure is unreliable because it will be determined by the two most extreme outliers of the sample.

The interquartile range, a more satisfactory variant of the simple range, is defined as the difference between the lower and upper quartiles. Below the *lower* quartile lies 25 percent of the sample; similarly, above the *upper* quartile lies 25 percent of the sample. The interquartile range therefore is confined to the central 50 percent of the sample. The greater the dispersion of a sample, the greater the distance between these two values.

In the boxplot the horizontal broken line represents the median, the box represents the interquartile range, and the vertical lines extending from the box represent the range. The vertical lines representing the range often are restricted (if necessary) to extend only to 1.5 times the interquartile range, so that the more extreme observations can be shown separately (by points) as outliers.

As a concept check, verify from Table A.3 that the points on the boxplot of Figure A.5 correspond to the following list:

| | **Equity Risk Premium** | **Bond (Maturity) Risk Premium** |
|---|---|---|
| Lowest extreme points | −43.94 | −13.66 |
| | −35.23 | −12.85 |
| | −31.92 | −11.21 |
| | −26.66 | −10.94 |
| | −20.19 | −10.50 |
| | −17.10 | −7.85 |
| | | −7.74 |
| | | −7.52 |
| | | −7.52 |
| | | −7.46 |
| Lowest quartile | −8.39 | −5.06 |
| Median | 8.15 | 1.30 |
| Highest quartile | 22.19 | 5.29 |
| Highest extreme points | 31.14 | 9.85 |
| | 33.32 | 10.37 |
| | 33.68 | 10.82 |
| | 35.99 | 11.11 |
| | 39.10 | 15.73 |
| | 41.19 | 17.22 |
| | 47.19 | 21.58 |
| | 47.42 | 26.96 |
| | 51.31 | |
| | 53.53 | |
| Interquartile range | 30.58 | 10.35 |
| 1.5 times the interquartile range | 45.87 | 15.53 |
| From: | −14.79 | −6.46 |
| To: | 31.09 | 9.06 |

Finally, a third form of graphing is time series plots, which are used to convey the behaviour of economic variables over time. Figure A.6 shows a time series plot of the excess returns on stocks and bonds from Table A.3. Even though the human eye is apt to see patterns in randomly generated time series, examining time series evolution over a long period does yield some information. Sometimes, such examination can be as revealing as that provided by formal statistical analysis.

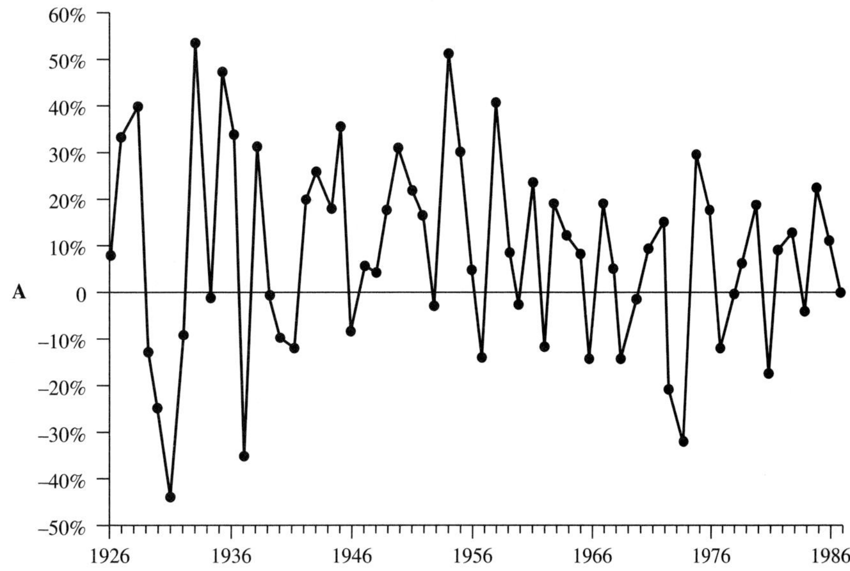


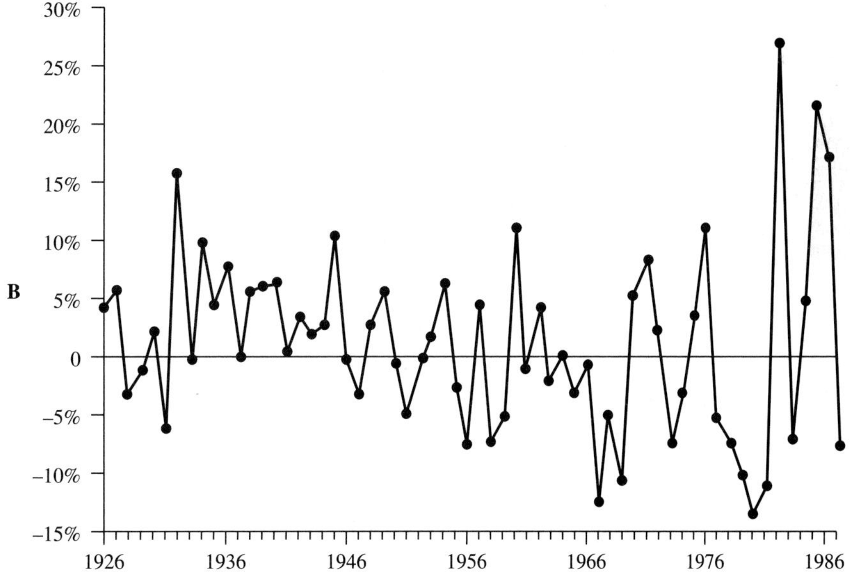


**Figure A.6**
**A,** Equity risk premium, 1926–1987.
**B,** Bond maturity premium, 1926–1987.

## Sample Statistics

Suppose we can assume that the probability distribution of stock returns has not changed over the past 62 years. We wish to draw inferences about the probability distribution of stock returns from the sample of 62 observations of annual stock excess returns in Table A.3.

A central question is whether given observations represent independent observations from the underlying distribution. If they are, statistical analysis is quite straightforward. Our analysis assumes that this is indeed the case. Empiricism in financial markets tends to confirm this assumption in most cases.

**Estimating Expected Returns from the Sample Average.** The definition of expected returns suggests that the sample average be used as an estimate of the expected value. Indeed, one definition of the expected return is the average of a sample when the number of observations tends to infinity.

Denoting the sample returns in Table A.3 by $R_t$, $t = 1, \ldots, T = 62$, the estimate of the annual expected excess rate of return is

$$\bar{r} = \frac{1}{\mathrm{T}} \Sigma R_t = 8.33\%$$

The bar over the $r$ is a common notation for an estimate of the expectation. Intuition suggests that the larger the sample the greater the reliability of the sample average, and the larger the standard deviation of the measured random variable, the less reliable the average. We discuss this property more fully later.

**Estimating Higher Moments.** The principle of estimating expected values from sample averages applies to higher moments as well. Recall that higher moments are defined as expectations of some power of the deviation from expectation. For example, the variance (second moment) is the expectation of the squared deviation from expectation. Accordingly, the sample average of the squared deviation from the average will serve as the estimate of the variance, denoted by $s^2$:

$$s^2 = \frac{1}{T-1} \Sigma(R_t - \bar{R}^2) = \frac{1}{61} \Sigma(R_t - .0833)^2 = .04436 \ (s = 21.06\%)$$

where $\bar{R}$ is the estimate of the sample average. The average of the squared deviation is taken over $T - 1 = 61$ observations for a technical reason. If we were to divide by $T$, the estimate of the variance will be downward-biased by the factor $(T - 1)/T$. Here too, the estimate is more reliable the larger the sample and the smaller the true standard deviation.

## A.3 Multivariate Statistics

Building portfolios requires combining random variables. The rate of return on a portfolio is the weighted average of the individual returns. Hence understanding and quantifying the interdependence of random variables is essential to portfolio analysis. In the first part of this section we return to scenario analysis. Later we return to making inferences from samples.

## The Basic Measure of Association: Covariance

Table A.4 summarizes what we have developed so far for the scenario returns on Anheuser-Busch stock and options. We know already what happens when we add a constant to one of these return variables, or multiply by a constant. But what if we combine any two of them? Suppose that we add the return on the stock to the return on the call. We create a new random variable that we denote by $r(s + c) = r(s) + r(c)$, where $r(s)$ is the return on the stock and $r(c)$ is the return on the call.

From the definition, the expected value of the combination variable is

$$E[r(s + c)] = \Sigma \Pr(i) r_i(s + c) \tag{A.10}$$

Substituting the definition of $r(s + c)$ into equation A.10 we have

$$\begin{aligned} E[r(s + c)] &= \Sigma \Pr(i)[r_i(s) + r_i(c)] = \Sigma \Pr(i) r_i(s) + \Sigma \Pr(i) r_i(c) \\ &= E[r(s)] + E[r(c)] \end{aligned} \tag{A.11}$$

In words, the expectation of the sum of two random variables is just the sum of the expectations of the component random variables. Can the same be true about the variance? The answer is "no," which is, perhaps, the most important fact in portfolio theory. The reason lies in the statistical association between the combined random variables.

As a first step, we introduce the *covariance,* the basic measure of association. Although the expressions that follow may look intimidating, they are merely squares of sums; that is, $(a + b)^2 = a^2 + b^2 + 2ab$, and $(a - b)^2 = a^2 + b^2 - 2ab$, where the *a*s and *b*s might stand for random variables, their expectations, or their deviations from expectations. From the definition of the variance

$$\sigma^2_{s+c} = E[r_{s+c} - E(r_{s+c})]^2 \tag{A.12}$$

To make equations A.12 through A.20 easier to read, we will identify the variables by subscripts *s* and *c* and drop the subscript *i* for scenarios. Substitute the definition of $r(s + c)$ and its expectation into equation A.12:

$$\sigma^2_{s+c} = E[r_s + r_c - E(r_s) - E(r_c)]^2 \tag{A.13}$$

Changing the order of variables within the brackets in equation A.13.

$$\sigma^2_{s+c} = E[r_s - E(r_s) + r_c - E(r_c)]^2$$

Within the square brackets we have the sum of the deviations from expectations of the two variables, which we denote by *d*. Writing this out,

$$\sigma^2_{s+c} = E[(d_s + d_c)^2] \tag{A.14}$$

Equation A.14 is the expectation of a complete square. Taking the square we find

$$\sigma^2_{s+c} = E(d_s^2 + d_c^2 + 2d_s d_c) \tag{A.15}$$

The term in the brackets in equation A.15 is the summation of three random variables. Since the expectation of a sum is the sum of the expectations, we can write equation A.15 as

$$\sigma^2_{s+c} = E(d_s^2) + E(d_c^2) + 2E(d_s d_c) \quad \textbf{(A.16)}$$

In equation A.16 the first two terms are the variance of the stock (the expectation of its squared deviation from expectation) plus the variance of the call. The third term is twice the expression that is the definition of the covariance discussed in equation A.17. (Note that the expectation is multiplied by 2 because expectation of twice a variable is twice the variable's expectation.)

In other words, the variance of a sum of random variables is the sum of the variances, *plus* twice the covariance, which we denote by $\text{Cov}(r_s, r_c)$, or the covariance between the return on $s$ and the return on $c$. Specifically,

$$\text{Cov}(r_s, r_c) = E(d_s d_c) = E\{[r_s - E(r_s)][r_c - E(r_c)]\} \quad \textbf{(A.17)}$$

The sequence of the variables in the expression for the covariance is of no consequence. Since the order of multiplication makes no difference, the definition of the covariance in equation A.17 shows that it will not affect the covariance either.

We use the data in Table A.4 to set up the input table for the calculation of the covariance, as shown in Table A.5.

First, we analyze the covariance between the stock and the call. In scenarios 1 and 2, both assets show *negative* deviations from expectation. This is an indication of *positive co-movement.* When these two negative deviations are multiplied, the product, which eventually contributes to the covariance between the returns, is positive. Multiplying deviations leads to positive covariance when the variables move in the same direction, and negative covariance when they move in the opposite direction. In scenario 3 both assets show *positive* deviations, reinforcing the inference that the co-movement is positive. The magnitude of the products of the deviations, weighted by the probability of each scenario, when

**Table A.4** Probability Distribution of Anheuser-Busch Stock and Options

| | Scenario 1 | Scenario 2 | Scenario 3 |
|---|---|---|---|
| Probability | .20 | .50 | .30 |
| **RATES OF RETURN (%)** | | | |
| Stock | 20 | 30 | 50 |
| Call option | −100 | −100 | 400 |
| Put option | 50 | −25 | −100 |
| | **$E(r)$** | **$\sigma$** | **$\sigma^2$** |
| Stock | .34 | .1114 | .0124 |
| Call option | .50 | 2.2913 | 5.25 |
| Put option | −.325 | .5250 | .2756 |

**Table A.5** Deviations, Squared Deviations, and Weighted Products of Deviations from Expectations of Anheuser-Busch Stock and Options

| | Scenario 1 | Scenario 2 | Scenario 3 | Probability-Weighted Sum |
|---|---|---|---|---|
| Probability | .20 | .50 | .30 | |
| Deviation of stock | −.14 | −.04 | .16 | |
| Squared deviation | .0196 | .0016 | .0256 | .0124 |
| Deviation of call | −1.50 | −1.50 | 3.50 | |
| Squared deviation | 2.25 | 2.25 | 12.25 | 5.25 |
| Deviation of put | .825 | .075 | −.675 | |
| Squared deviation | .680625 | .005625 | .455635 | .275628 |
| Product of deviations ($d_s d_c$) | .21 | .06 | .56 | .24 |
| Product of deviations ($d_s d_p$) | −.1155 | −.003 | −.108 | −.057 |
| Product of deviations ($d_c d_p$) | −1.2375 | −.1125 | −2.3625 | −1.0125 |

added up, results in a covariance that shows not only the direction of the co-movement (by its sign) but also the degree of the co-movement.

The covariance is a variance-like statistic. Whereas the variance shows the degree of the movement of a random variable about its expectation, the covariance shows the degree of the co-movement of two variables about their expectations. It is important for portfolio analysis that the covariance of a variable with itself is equal to its variance. You can see this by substituting the appropriate deviations in equation A.17; the result is the expectation of the variable's squared deviation from expectation.

The first three values in the last column of Table A.5 are the familiar variances of the three assets, the stock, the call, and the put. The last three are the covariances; two of them are negative. Examine the covariance between the stock and the put, for example. In the first two scenarios the stock realizes negative deviations, while the put realizes positive deviations. When we multiply such deviations, the sign becomes negative. The same happens in the third scenario, except that the stock realizes a positive deviation and the put a negative one. Again, the product is negative, adding to the inference of negative co-movement.

With other assets and scenarios the product of the deviations can be negative in some scenarios, in others positive. The *magnitude* of the products, when *weighted* by the probabilities, determines which co-movements dominate. However, whenever the sign of the products varies from scenario to scenario, the results will offset one another, contributing to a small, close-to-zero covariance. In such cases we may conclude that the returns have either a small, or no, average co-movement.

**Covariance Between Transformed Variables.** Since the covariance is the expectation of the product of deviations from expectation of two variables, analyzing the effect of transformations on deviations from expectation will show the effect of the transformation on the covariance.

Suppose that we add a constant to one of the variables. We know already that the expectation of the variable increases by that constant; so deviations from expectation will remain unchanged. Just as adding a constant to a random variable does not affect its variance, it also will not affect its covariance with other variables.

Multiplying a random variable by a constant also multiplies its expectation, as well as its deviation from expectation. Therefore the covariance with any other variable will also be multiplied by that constant. Using the definition of the covariance, check that this summation of the foregoing discussion is true:

$$\text{Cov}[a_1 + b_1 r_s, a_2 + b_2 r_c] = b_1 b_2 \text{Cov}(r_s, r_c) \qquad \textbf{(A.18)}$$

The covariance allows us to calculate the variance of sums of random variables, and eventually the variance of portfolio returns.

## A Pure Measure of Association: The Correlation Coefficient

If we tell you that the covariance between the rates of return of the stock and the call is .24 (see Table A.5), what have you learned? Because the sign is positive, you known that the returns generally move in the same direction. However, the number .24 adds nothing to your knowledge of the degree of co-movement of the stock and the call.

To obtain a measure of association that conveys the degree of intensity of the co-movement, we relate the covariance to the standard deviations of the two variables. Each standard deviation is the square root of the variance. Thus, the product of the standard deviations has the dimension of the variance that is also shared by the covariance. Therefore, we can define the correlation coefficient, denoted by $\rho$, as

$$\rho_{sc} = \frac{\text{Cov}(r_s, r_c)}{\sigma_s \sigma_c} \qquad \textbf{(A.19)}$$

where the subscripts on $\rho$ identify the two variables involved. Since the order of the variables in the expression of the covariance is of no consequence, equation A.19 shows that the order does not affect the correlation coefficient either.

We use the covariances from Table A.5 to show the *correlation matrix* for the three variables:

| | Stock | Call | Put |
|---|---|---|---|
| Stock | 1.0 | .94 | −.97 |
| Call | .94 | 1.0 | −.84 |
| Put | −.97 | −.84 | 1.0 |

The highest (in absolute value) correlation coefficient is between the stock and the put, −.97, although the absolute value of the covariance between them is the lowest by far. The reason is attributable to the effect of the standard deviations.

The following properties of the correlation coefficient are important:

- Because the correlation coefficient, just as the covariance, measures only the degree of association, it tells us nothing about causality. The direction of causality has to come from theory and be supported by specialized tests.
- The correlation coefficient is determined completely by deviations from expectations, as are the components in equation A.19. We expect, therefore, that it is not affected by adding constants to the associated random variables. However, the correlation coefficient is invariant also to multiplying the variables by constants. You can verify this property by referring to the effect of multiplication by a constant on the covariance and standard devation.
- The correlation coefficient can vary from −1.0, perfect negative correlation, to 1.0, perfect positive correlation. This can be seen by calculating the correlation coefficient of a variable with itself. You expect it to be 1.0. Recalling that the covariance of a variable with itself is its own variance, you can verify this using equation A.19. The more ambitious can verify that the correlation between a variable and the negative of itself is equal to −1.0. First, find from equation A.17 that the covariance between a variable and its negative equals the negative of the variance. Then check equation A.19.

Since the correlation between $x$ and $y$ is the same as the correlation between $y$ and $x$, the *correlation matrix is symmetric about the diagonal.* The diagonal consists of 1.0s because it represents the correlation of the returns with themselves. Therefore, it is customary to present only the lower triangle of the correlation matrix.

Reexamine equation A.16. You can invert it so that the covariance is presented in terms of the correlation coefficient and the standard deviations as in equation A.20:

$$\text{Cov}(r_s, r_c) = \rho_{sc}\sigma_s\sigma_c \quad \textbf{(A.20)}$$

This formulation can be useful, because many think in terms of correlations rather than covariances.

**Estimating Correlation Coefficients from Sample Returns.** Assuming that a sample consists of independent observations, we assign equal weights to all observations and use simple averages to estimate expectations. When estimating variances and covariances, we get an average by dividing by the number of observations minus one.

Suppose that you are interested in estimating the correlation between stocks and long-term default-free (government) bonds. Assume that the sample of 62 annual excess returns for the period 1926 to 1987 in Table A.3 is representative.

Using the definition for the correlation coefficient in equation A.19, you estimate the following statistics (using the subscripts $s$ for stocks, $b$ for bonds, and $t$ for time):

$$\bar{R}_s = \frac{1}{62}\sum_{t=1}^{62} R_{s,t} = .08334; \bar{R}_b = \frac{1}{62}\sum R_{b,t} = .01058$$

$$\sigma_s = \left[\frac{1}{61}\sum (R_{s,t} - \bar{R}_s)^2\right]^{1/2} = .21064$$

$$\sigma_b = \left[\frac{1}{61}\sum (R_{b,t} - \bar{R}_b)^2\right]^{1/2} = .07977$$

$$\text{Cov}(R_s, R_b) = \frac{1}{61}\sum [(R_{s,t} - \bar{R}_s)(R_{b,t} - \bar{R}_b)] = .00257$$

$$\rho_{sb} = \frac{\text{Cov}(R_s, R_b)}{\sigma_s \sigma_b} = .15295$$

Here is one example of how problematic estimation can be. Recall that we predicate our use of the sample on the assumption that the probability distributions have not changed over the sample period. To see the problem with this assumption, suppose that we reestimate the correlation between stocks and bonds over a more recent period—for example, beginning in 1965, about the time of onset of government debt financing of both the war in Vietnam and the Great Society programs.

Repeating the previous calculations for the period 1965 to 1987, we find:

$$\bar{R}_s = .0312; \quad \bar{R}_b = -.00317$$

$$\sigma_s = .15565; \; \sigma_b = .11217$$

$$\text{Cov}(R_s, R_b) = .0057; \quad \rho_{sb} = .32647$$

A comparison of the two sets of numbers suggests that it is likely, but by no means certain, that the underlying probability distributions have changed. The variance in the rates of return and the size of the samples are why we cannot be sure. We shall return to the issue of testing the sample statistics shortly.

## Regression Analysis

We will use a problem from the CFA examination (Level I, 1986) to represent the degree of understanding of regression analysis that is required for the ground level. However, first let us develop some background.

In analyzing measures of association so far, we have ignored the question of causality, identifying simply *independent* and *dependent* variables. Suppose that theory (in its most basic form) tells us that all asset excess returns are driven by the same economic force, whose movements are captured by a broad-based market index, such as excess return, on the S&P 500 stock index.

Suppose further that our theory predicts a simple, linear relationship between the excess return of any asset and the market index. A linear relationship, one that can be described by a straight line, takes on this form:

$$R_{j,t} = a_j + b_j R_{M,t} + e_{j,t} \tag{A.21}$$

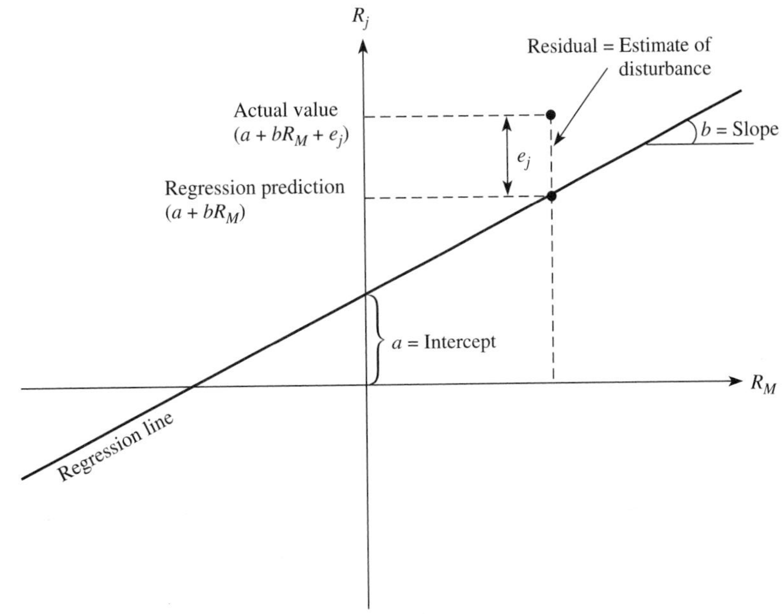


**Figure A.7**
Simple regression estimates and residuals. The intercept and slope are chosen so as to minimize the sum of the squared deviations from the regression line.

where the subscript $j$ represents any asset, $M$ represents the market index (the S&P 500), and $t$ represents variables that change over time. (In the following discussion we omit subscripts when possible.) On the left-hand side of equation A.21 is the dependent variable, the excess return on asset $j$. The right-hand side has two parts, the explained and unexplained (by the relationship) components of the dependent variable.

The explained component of $R_j$ is the $a + bR_M$ part. It is plotted in Figure A.7. The quantity $a$, also called the *intercept,* gives the value of $R_j$ when the *independent* variable is zero. This relationship assumes that it is a constant. The second term in the explained part of the return represents the driving force, $R_M$, times the sensitivity coefficient, $b$, that transmits movements in $R_M$ to movements in $R_j$. The term $b$ is also assumed to be constant. Figure A.7 shows that $b$ is the slope of the regression line.

The unexplained component of $R_j$ is represented by the disturbance term, $e_j$. The disturbance is assumed to be uncorrelated with the explanatory variable, $R_M$, and of zero expectation. Such a variable is also called a noise variable, because it contributes to the variance but not to the expectation of the dependent variable, $R_j$.

A relationship such as that shown in equation A.21 applied to data, with coefficients estimated, is called a *regression equation*. A relationship including only one explanatory variable is called *simple regression*. The parameters $a$ and $b$ are called (simple) *regression coefficients.* Since every value of $R_j$ is explained by the regression, the expectation and variance of $R_j$ are also determined by it. Suppose we use the expectation of the expression in equation A.21:

$$E(R_j) = a + bE(R_M) \qquad \textbf{(A.22)}$$

The constant $a$ has no effect on the variance of $R_j$. Because the variables $r_M$ and $e_j$ are uncorrelated, the variance of the sum, $bR_M + e$, is the sum of the variances. Accounting for the parameter $b$ multiplying $R_M$, the variance of $R_j$ will be

$$\sigma_j^2 = b^2\sigma_M^2 + \sigma_e^2 \qquad \textbf{(A.23)}$$

Equation A.23 tells us that the contribution of the variance of $R_M$ to that of $R_j$ depends on the regression (slope) coefficient $b$. The term $(b\sigma_M)^2$ is called the *explained variance.* The variance of the disturbance makes up the *unexplained variance.*

The covariance between $R_j$ and $R_M$ is also given by the regression equation. Setting up the expression, we have

$$\begin{aligned} \text{Cov}(R_j, R_M) &= \text{Cov}(a + bR_M + e, R_M) \\ &= \text{Cov}(bR_M, R_M) = b\text{Cov}(R_M, R_M) = b\sigma_M^2 \end{aligned} \qquad \textbf{(A.24)}$$

The intercept, $a$, is dropped because a constant added to a random variable does not affect the covariance with any other variable. The disturbance term $e$ is dropped because it is, by assumption, uncorrelated with the market return.

Equation A.24 shows that the slope coefficient of the regression, $b$, is equal to

$$b = \frac{\text{Cov}(R_j, R_M)}{\sigma_M^2}$$

The slope thereby measures the co-movement of $j$ and $M$ as a fraction of the movement of the driving force, the explanatory variable.

One way to measure the explanatory power of the regression is by the fraction of the variance of $R_j$ that it explains. This fraction is called the *coefficient of determination,* and denoted by $\rho^2$.

$$\rho_{jM}^2 = \frac{b^2\sigma_M^2}{\sigma_j^2} = \frac{b^2\sigma_M^2}{b_M^2\sigma_M^2 + \sigma_e^2} \qquad \textbf{(A.25)}$$

Note that the unexplained variance, $\sigma_e^2$, has to make up the difference between the coefficient of determination and 1.0. Therefore, another way to represent the coefficient of determination is by

$$\rho_{jM}^2 = 1 - \frac{\sigma_e^2}{\sigma_j^2}$$

Some algebra shows that the coefficient of determination is the square of the correlation coefficient. Finally, squaring the correlation coefficient tells us what proportion of the variance of the dependent variable is explained by the independent (the explanatory) variable.

Estimation of the regression coefficients $a$ and $b$ is based on minimizing the sum of the square deviation of the observations from the estimated regression line (see Figure A.7). Your calculator, as well as any spreadsheet program, can compute regression estimates.

The CFA 1986 examination for Level I included this question:

*Question.*

Pension plan sponsors place a great deal of emphasis on universe rankings when evaluating money managers. In fact, it appears that sponsors assume implicitly that managers who rank in the top quartile of a representative sample of peer managers are more likely to generate superior relative performance in the future than managers who rank in the bottom quartile.

The validity of this assumption can be tested by regressing percentile rankings of managers in one period on their percentile rankings from the prior period.

1. Given that the implicit assumption of plan sponsors is true to the extent that there is perfect correlation in percentile rankings from one period to the next, list the numerical values you would expect to observe for the slope of the regression, and the *R*-squared of the regression.
2. Given that there is no correlation in percentile rankings from period to period, list the numerical values you would expect to observe for the intercept of the regression, the slope of the regression, and the *R*-squared of the regression.
3. Upon reforming such a regression, you observe an intercept of .51, a slope of $-.05$, and an *R*-squared of .01. Based on this regression, state your best estimate of a manager's percentile ranking next period if his [or her] percentile ranking this period were .15.
4. Some pension plan sponsors have agreed that a good practice is to terminate managers who are in the top quartile and to hire those who are in the bottom quartile. State what those who advocate such a practice expect implicitly about the correlation and slope from a regression of the managers' subsequent ranking on their current ranking.

*Answer.*

1. Intercept $= 0$
   Slope $= 1$
   *R*-squared $= 1$
2. Intercept $= .50$
   Slope $= 0.0$
   *R*-squared $= 0.0$
3. 50th percentile, derived as follows:
   $$\begin{aligned} y &= a + bx \\ &= .51 - 0.05(.15) \\ &= .51 - .0075 \\ &= .5025 \end{aligned}$$
   Given the very low *R*-squared, it would be difficult to estimate what the manager's rank would be.
4. Sponsors who advocate firing top-performing managers and hiring the poorest implicitly expect that both the correlation and slope would be significantly negative.

### Multiple Regression Analysis

In many cases, theory suggests that a number of independent, explanatory variables drive a dependent variable. This concept becomes clear enough when demonstrated by a two-variable case. A real estate analyst offers the following regression equation to explain the return on a nationally diversified real estate portfolio:

$$RE_t = a + b_1 RE_{t-1} + b_2 NVR_t + e_t \quad \textbf{(A.26)}$$

The dependent variable is the period $t$ real estate portfolio return, $RE_t$. The model specifies that the explained part of that return is driven by two independent variables. The first is the previous period return, $RE_{t-1}$ representing persistence or momentum. The second explanatory variable is the current national vacancy rate ($NVR_t$).

As in the simple regression, $a$ is the intercept, representing the value that RE is expected to take when the explanatory variables are zero. The (slope) regression coefficients, $b_1$ and $b_2$, represent the *marginal* effect of the explanatory variables.

The coefficient of determination is defined exactly as before. The ratio of the variance of the disturbance, $e$, to the total variance of RE is 1.0 *minus* the coefficient of determination. The regression coefficients are estimated here, too, by finding coefficients that minimize the sum of squared deviations of the observations from the prediction of the regression.

## A.4 Hypothesis Testing

The central hypothesis of investment theory is that nondiversifiable (systematic) risk is rewarded by a higher *expected* return. But do the data support the theory? Consider the data on the excess return on stocks in Table A.3. The estimate of the expected excess return (the sample average) is 8.33 percent. This appears to be a hefty risk premium, but so is the risk—the estimate of the standard deviation for the same sample is 21.06 percent. Could it be that the positive average is just the luck of the draw? Hypothesis testing supplies probabilistic answers to such concerns.

The first step in hypothesis testing is to state the claim that is to be tested. This is called the *null hypothesis* (or the null for short), denoted by $H_0$. Against the null, an alternative claim (hypothesis) is stated, which is denoted by $H_1$. The objective of hypothesis testing is to decide whether to reject the null in favor of the alternative, while identifying the probabilities of the possible errors in the determination.

A hypothesis is *specified* if it assigns a value to a variable. A claim that the risk premium on stocks is zero is one example of a specified hypothesis. Often, however, a hypothesis is general. A claim that the risk premium on stocks is not zero would be a completely general alternative against the specified hypothesis that the risk premium is zero. It amounts to "anything but the null." The alternative that the risk premium is *positive,* while not completely general, is still unspecified. Although it is sometimes desirable to test two unspecified hypotheses (for instance, the claim that the risk premium is zero or negative, against the claim that it is positive), unspecified hypotheses complicate the task of determining the probabilities of errors in judgment.

What are the possible errors? There are two, called type I and type II errors. Type I is the event that we will *reject* the null when it is *true.* The probability of type I error is called the *significance level.* Type II is the event that we will *accept* the null when it is *false.*

Suppose we set a criterion for acceptance of $H_0$ that is so lax that we know for certain we will accept the null. In doing so we will drive the significance level to zero (which is good). If we will never reject the null, we will also never reject it when it is true. At the same time the probability of type II error will become 1 (which is bad). If we will accept the null for certain, we must also do so when it is false.

The reverse is to set a criterion for acceptance of the null that is so stringent that we know for certain that we will reject it. This drives the probability of type II error to zero (which is good). By never accepting the null, we avoid accepting it when it is false. Now, however, the significance level will go to 1 (which is bad). If we always reject the null, we will reject it even when it is true.

To compromise between the two evils, hypothesis testing fixes the significance level; that is, it limits the probability of type I error. Then, subject to this preset constraint, the ideal test will minimize the probability of type II error. If we *avoid* type II error (accepting the null when it is false) we actually *reject* the null when it is indeed *false.* The probability of doing so is *one minus the probability of type II error,* which is called the *power of the test.* Minimizing the probability of type II error maximizes the power of the test.

Testing the claim that stocks earn a risk premium, we set the hypotheses as

$$H_0: \quad E(R) = 0 \quad \text{The expected return is zero.}$$
$$H_1: \quad E(R) > 0 \quad \text{The expected return is positive.}$$

$H_1$ is an *unspecified alternative.* When a null is tested against a completely general alternative, it is called a *two-tailed test* because you may reject the null in favor of both greater or smaller values.

When both hypotheses are unspecified, the test is difficult because the calculation of the probabilities of type I and II errors is complicated. Usually, at least one hypothesis is simple (specified) and set as the null. In that case it is relatively easy to calculate the significance level of the test. Calculating the power of the test that assumes the *unspecified* alternative is true remains complicated; often it is left unsolved.

As we will show, setting the hypothesis that we wish to reject, $E(R) = 0$ as the null (the "straw man"), makes it harder to accept the alternative that we favor, our theoretical bias, which is appropriate.

In testing $E(R) = 0$, suppose we fix the significance level at 5 percent. This means that we will reject the null (and accept that there is a positive premium)

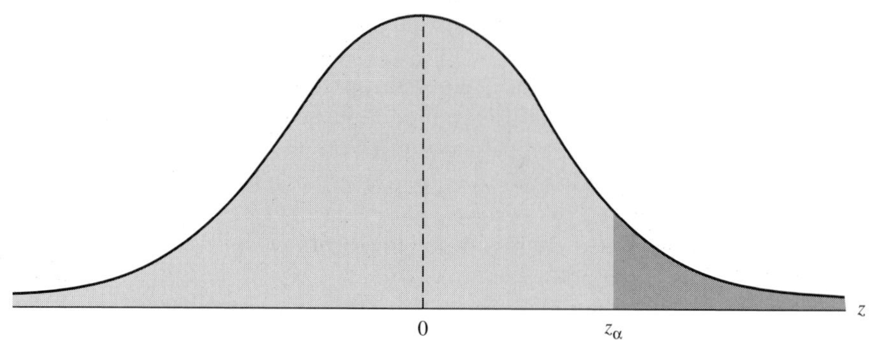


**Figure A.8**
Under the null hypothesis the sample average excess return should be distributed around zero. If the actual average exceeds $z_\alpha$, we conclude that the null hypothesis is false.

*only* when the data suggest that the probability the null is true is 5 percent or less. To do so, we must find a critical value, denoted $z_\alpha$ (or critical values in the case of two-tailed tests) that corresponds to $\alpha = .05$, which will create two regions, an acceptance region and a rejection region. Look at Figure A.8 as an illustration.

If the sample average is to the right of the critical value (in the rejection region), the null is rejected; otherwise, it is accepted. In the latter case it is too likely (e.g., the probability is greater than 5 percent) that the sample average is positive simply because of sampling error. If the sample average is greater than the critical value, we will reject the null in favor of the alternative. The probability that the positive value of the sample average results from sampling error is 5 percent or less.

If the alternative is one-sided (one-tailed), as in our case, the acceptance region covers the entire area from minus infinity to a positive value, above which lies 5 percent of the distribution (see Figure A.8). The critical value is $z_\alpha$ in Figure A.8. When the alternative is two-tailed, the area of 5 percent lies at both extremes of the distribution and is equally divided between them, 25 percent on each side. A two-tailed test is more stringent (it is harder to reject the null). In a one-tailed test the fact that our theory predicts the direction in which the average will deviate from the value under the null is weighted in favor of the alternative. The upshot is that for a significance level of 5 percent, with a one-tailed test, we use a confidence interval of $\alpha = .05$, instead of $\alpha/2 = .025$ as with a two-tailed test.

Hypothesis testing requires assessment of the probabilities of the test statistics, such as the sample average and variance. Therefore, it calls for some assumption about the probability distribution of the underlying variable. Such an assumption becomes an integral part of the null hypothesis, often an implicit one.

In this case we assume that the stock portfolio excess return is normally distributed. The distribution of the test statistic is derived from its mathematical definition and the assumption of the underlying distribution for the random variable: In our case the test statistic is the sample average.

The sample average is obtained by summing all observations ($T = 62$), and then multiplying by $1/T = 1/62$. Each observation is a random variable, drawn independently from the same underlying distribution, with an unknown expectation $\mu$ and standard deviation $\sigma$. The expectation of the sum of all observations is the sum of the $T$ expectations (all equal to $\mu$) divided by $T$, therefore equal to the population expectation. The result is 8.33 percent, which is equal to the true expectation *plus* sampling errors. Under the null hypothesis, the expectation is zero, and the entire 8.33 percent constitutes sampling errors.

To calculate the variance of the sample average, recall that we assume *d* observations were independent, or uncorrelated. Hence the variance of the sum is the sum of the variances, that is, $T$ times the population variance. However, we also transform the sum, multiplying it by $1/T$; therefore we have to divide the variance of the sum $T\sigma^2$ by $T^2$. We end up with the variance of the sample average as the population variance divided by $T$. The standard deviation of the sample average, which is called the *standard error*, is

$$\sigma(\text{average}) = \left(\frac{1}{T^2}\Sigma\sigma^2\right)^{1/2} = \left(\frac{1}{T^2}T\sigma^2\right)^{1/2} = \frac{\sigma}{\sqrt{T}} = \frac{.21064}{\sqrt{62}} = .02675 \quad \textbf{(A.27)}$$

Our test statistic has a standard error of 2.675 percent. It makes sense that the more the number of observations, the *smaller* the *standard error* of the estimate of the expectation. However, note that it is the variance that goes down by the proportion $T = 62$. The standard error goes down by a much smaller proportion, $\sqrt{T} = 7.87$.

Now that we have the sample mean, 8.33 percent, its standard deviation, 2.675 percent, and know that the distribution under the null is normal, we are ready to perform the test. We want to determine whether 8.33 percent is significantly positive. We achieve this by standardizing our statistic, which means that we subtract from its expected value under the null hypothesis and divide by its standard deviation. This standardized statistic can now be compared to $z$ values from the standard normal tables. We ask whether

$$\frac{\overline{R} - E(R)}{\sigma} > z_\alpha$$

We would be finished except for another caveat. The assumption of normality is all right in that the test statistic is a weighted sum of normals (according to our assumption about returns). Therefore it is also normally distributed. However, the analysis also requires that we *know* the variance. Here we are using a sample variance that is only an *estimate* of the true variance.

The solution to this problem turns out to be quite simple. The normal distribution is replaced with the *student-t* (or *t*, for short) *distribution*. Like the normal, the $t$ distribution is symmetric. It depends on degrees of freedom, that is, the number of observations less one. Thus, here we replace $z_\alpha$ with $t_{\alpha,T-1}$.

The test is then

$$\frac{\overline{R} - E(R)}{s} > t_{\alpha,T-1}$$

When we substitute in sample results, the left-hand side is a standardized statistic and the right-hand side is a $t$-value derived from $t$ tables for $\alpha = .05$ and $T - 1 = 62 - 1 = 61$. We ask whether the inequality holds. If it does, we *reject* the null hypothesis with a 5 percent significance level; if it does not we *cannot reject* the null hypothesis. Proceeding, we find that

$$\frac{.0833 - 0}{.02675} = .3114 > 1.671$$

In our sample the inequality holds, and we reject the null hypothesis in favor of the alternative that the risk premium is positive.

A repeat of the test of this hypothesis for the 1965–1987 period may make a skeptic out of you. For that period the sample average is 3.12 percent, the sample standard deviation is 15.57 percent, and there are $23 - 1 = 22$ degrees of freedom. Does that give you second thoughts?

## The *t*-Test of Regression Coefficients

Suppose that we apply the simple regression model (equation A.21), to the relationship between the long-term governmental bond portfolio and the stock market index, using the sample in Table A.3. The estimation result (percent per year) is

$$a = .5668,\ b = .0589,\ R\text{-squared} = .0242$$

We interpret these coefficients as follows. For periods when the excess return on the market index is zero, we expect the bonds to earn an excess return of 56.68 basis points. This is the role of the intercept. As for the slope, for each percentage return of the stock portfolio in any year, the bond portfolio is expected to earn, *additionally,* 5.89 basis points. With the average equity risk premium for the sample period of 8.33 percent, the sample average for bonds is $.5668 + .0589 \times 8.33 = 1.058$ percent. From the squared correlation coefficient you know that the variation in stocks explains 2.42 percent of the variation in bonds.

Can we rely on these statistics? One way to find out is to set up a hypothesis test, presented here for the regression coefficient $b$.

$H_0$: $b = 0$ The regression slope coefficient is zero, meaning that changes in the independent variable do not explain changes in the dependent variable.

$H_1$: $b > 0$ The dependent variable is sensitive to changes in the independent variable (with a *positive* covariance).

Any decent regression software supplies the statistics to test this hypothesis. The regression customarily assumes that the dependent variable and the disturbance are normally distributed, with an unknown variance that is estimated from the sample. Thus, the regression coefficient b is normally distributed. Because once again the null is that $b = 0$, all we need is an estimate of the standard error of this statistic.

The estimated standard error of the regression coefficient is computed from the estimated standard deviation of the disturbance and the standard deviation of the explanatory variable. For the regression at hand, that estimate is, $s(b) = .0479$. Just as in the previous exercise, the critical value of the test is

$$s(b)t_{\alpha,T-1}$$

Compare this value to the value of the estimated coefficient $b$. We will reject the null in favor of $b > 0$ if

$$b > s(b)t_{\alpha,T-1}$$

which, because the standard deviation $s(b)$ is positive, is equivalent to the following condition:

$$\frac{b}{s(b)} > t_{\alpha,T-1}$$

The $t$-test reports the ratio of the estimated coefficient to its estimated standard deviation. Armed with this *t-ratio,* the number of observations, $T$, and a table of the student-$t$ distribution, you can perform the test at the desired significance level.

The $t$-ratio for our example is $.0589/.0479 = 1.2305$. The $t$-table for 61 degrees of freedom shows we cannot reject the null at a significance level of 5 percent, for which the critical value is 1.671.

A question from the CFA 1987 level exam calls for understanding of regression analysis and hypothesis testing.

*Question.*

An academic suggests to you that the returns on common stocks differ based on a company's market capitalization, its historical earnings growth, the stock's current yield, and whether or not the company's employees are unionized. You are skeptical that there are any attributes other than market exposure as measured by beta that explain the differences in returns across a sample of securities.

Nonetheless, you decide to test whether or not these other attributes account for the differences in returns. You select the S&P 500 stocks as your sample, and regress their returns each month for the past 5 years against the company's market capitalization at the beginning of each month, the company's growth in earnings throughout the previous 12 months, the prior year's dividend divided by the stock price at the beginning of each month, and a dummy variable that has a value of 1 if employees are unionized and 0 if not.

1. The average $R$-squared from the regressions is .15, and it varies very little from month-to-month. Discuss the significance of this result.
2. You note that all of the coefficients of the attributes have $t$-statistics greater than 2 in most of the months in which the regressions were run. Discuss the significance of these attributes in terms of explaining differences in common stock returns.
3. You observe in most of the regressions that the coefficient of the dummy variable is $-.14$, and that the $t$-statistic is $-4.74$. Discuss the implication of the coefficient regarding the relationship between unionization and the return on a company's common stock.

*Answer.*

1. Differences in the attributes' values together explain about 15 percent of the differences in return among the stocks in the S&P 500 index. The remaining unexplained differences in return may be attributable to omitted attributes, industry affiliations, or stock-specific factors. This information by itself is not sufficient to form any qualitative conclusions. The fact that the $R$-squared varied little from month-to-month implies that the relationship is stable and the observed results are not sample specific.
2. Given a $t$-statistic greater than 2 in most of the months, one would regard the attribute coefficients as statistically significant. If the attribute coefficients were not significantly different from zero, one would expect $t$-statistics greater than 2 in fewer than 5 percent of the regressions for each attribute coefficient. Since the $t$-statistics are greater than 2 much more frequently, one should conclude that they are definitely significant in terms of explaining differences in stock returns.
3. Since the coefficient for the dummy variable representing unionization has persistently been negative and since it persistently has been statistically significant, one would conclude that disregarding all other factors, unionization lowers a company's common stock return. That is, everything else being equal, non-unionized companies will have higher returns than companies whose employees are unionized. Of course, one would want to test the model further to see if there are omitted variables or other problems that might account for this apparent relationship.

Appendix B

# Solutions to Concept Checks

---

*Part I*

## Introduction

### *Chapter 1*—The Investment Environment

**1.** The real assets are patents, customer relations, and the college education. These assets enable individuals or firms to produce goods or services that yield profits or income. Lease obligations are simply claims to pay or receive income and do not in themselves create new wealth. Similarly, the $5 bill is only a paper claim on the government and does not produce wealth.

**2.** The car loan is a primitive security. Payments on the loan depend only on the solvency of the borrower.

**3.** The borrower has a financial liability, the loan owed to the bank. The bank treats the loan as a financial asset.

**4.** Creative unbundling can separate interest or dividends from capital gains income. Dual funds do just this. In tax regimes where capital gains are taxed at lower rates than other income, or where gains can be deferred, such unbundling may be a way to attract different tax clienteles to a security.

### *Chapter 2*—Markets and Instruments

**1.** The bond equivalent yield is 7.00. Therefore, $P = 10{,}000/[1 + .070 \times (182/365)] = 9{,}662.73$.

**2.** If the bond is selling below par, it is unlikely that the government will find it optimal to call the bond at par, when it can instead buy the bond in the secondary market for less than par. Therefore, it makes sense to assume that the bond will remain alive until its maturity date. In contrast, premium bonds are vulnerable to call because the government can acquire them by paying only par value. Hence it is likely that the bonds will repay principal at the first call date, and the yield to first call is the statistic of interest.

**3.** *a.* You are entitled to a prorated share of dividend payments and to vote in any of Alcan's stockholder meetings.

*b.* Your potential gain is unlimited because Alcan's stock price has no upper bound.

*c*. Your outlay was $\$50 \times 100 = \$5{,}000$. Because of limited liability, this is the most you can lose.

4. The price-weighted index increases from 62.5 [(100 + 25)/2] to 65 [(110 + 20)2], a gain of 4 percent. An investment of one share in each company requires an outlay of $125 that would increase in value to $130, for a return of 4 percent (5/125), which equals the return to the price-weighted index.
5. The market value–weighted index return is calculated by computing the increase in value of the stock portfolio. The portfolio of the two stocks starts with an initial value of $100 million + $500 million = $600 million and falls in value to $110 million + $400 million = $510 million, a loss of 90/600 = .15, or 15 percent. The index portfolio return is a weighted average of the returns on each stock with weights of ⅙ on XYZ and ⅚ on ABC (weights proportional to relative investments). Because the return on XYZ is 10 percent, while that on ABC is −20%, the index portfolio return, is $\frac{1}{6} \times 10\% + \frac{5}{6} \times (-20\%) = -15\%$, equal to the return on the market value–weighted index.
6. The payoff to the option is $2 per share at maturity. The option costs $0.35 per share. The dollar profit is therefore $1.65. The put option expires worthless. Therefore the investor's loss is the cost of the put, or $3.00.

## *Chapter 3*—Investing in Securities

1. *a*. Used cars trade in direct search markets when individuals advertise in local newspapers and in dealer markets at used-car lots or automobile dealers.

   *b*. Paintings trade in broker markets when clients commission brokers to buy or sell art for them, in dealer markets at art galleries, and in auction markets.

   *c*. Rare coins trade mostly in dealer markets in coin shops, but they also trade in auctions and in direct search markets when individuals advertise they want to buy or sell coins.

2. $$\frac{100P - \$4{,}000}{100P} = .4$$
   $$100P - \$4{,}000 = 40P$$
   $$60P = \$4{,}000$$
   $$P = \$66.67 \text{ per share}$$

3. The investor will purchase 150 shares, with a rate of return as follows:

| Year-End Change in Price | Year-End Value of Shares | Repayment of Principal and Interest | Investor's Rate of Return |
|---|---|---|---|
| 30% | 19,500 | $5,450 | 40.5% |
| No change | 15,000 | 5,450 | −4.5% |
| −30% | 10,500 | 5,450 | −49.5% |

4. $$\frac{\$150{,}000 - 1{,}000P}{1{,}000P} = .4$$
$$\$150{,}000 - 1{,}000P = 400P$$
$$1{,}400P = \$150{,}000$$
$$P = \$107.14 \text{ per share}$$

5. Using equation (3.3), we again have \$71,429 against a total asset value of \$125,000; using equation (3.4), the price (*P*) of Alcan is:

$$300P \times 1.3 = \$125{,}000 - \$71{,}429 = \$53{,}571 \text{ or } P = \$137\tfrac{3}{8}$$

If Alcan rises to \$60, margin requires total assets of \$23,400 (for the short sale) plus \$71,429 (again) or \$94,829; since assets are comprised of \$85,000 + 500*P*, for *P* the price of Seagram's, then the minimum price is:

$$500P = \$94{,}829 - \$85{,}000 = \$9{,}829 \text{ or } P = \$19\tfrac{5}{8}$$

## *Chapter 4*—Individuals and Institutional Investors

1. Individual reader's response.

$$C\sum_{t=1}^{55}\frac{1}{1.03^t} = 25{,}000\sum_{t=1}^{55}\frac{1}{1.03^t} + 8{,}000\sum_{t=36}^{55}\frac{1}{1.03^t}$$
$$26.7744C = 25{,}000 \times 21.4872 + 8{,}000 \times 5.2873$$
$$= 537{,}180.50 + 42{,}297.66$$
$$C = \frac{577{,}478.16}{26.7744} = \$21{,}643 \text{ per year}$$

Saving is: $S = 25{,}000 - C = 25{,}000 - 21{,}643 = \$3{,}357$ per year

2. He has accrued an annuity of $.01 \times 15 \times 15{,}000 = \$2{,}250$ per year for 15 years, starting in 25 years. The PV of this annuity is \$2,812.13. PV = 2,250 PA (8%, 15) × PF (8%, 25).
3. If Eloise keeps her present asset allocation, she will have the following amounts to spend after taxes five years from now:

**TAX-QUALIFIED ACCOUNT**

| | | |
|---|---|---|
| Bonds: | $\$50{,}000\ (1.1)^5 \times .72$ | = \$ 57,978.36 |
| Stocks: | $\$50{,}000\ (1.15)^5 \times .72$ | = \$ 72,408.86 |
| | **Subtotal** | **\$130,387.22** |

**NONRETIREMENT ACCOUNT**

| | | |
|---|---|---|
| Bonds: | $\$50{,}000\ (1.072)^5$ | = \$ 70,785.44 |
| Stocks: | $\$50{,}000\ (1.15)^5 - .28 \times [50{,}000(1.15)^5 - 50{,}000]$ | = \$ 86,408.86 |
| | **Subtotal** | **\$157,194.30** |
| | TOTAL | **\$287,581.52** |

If Eloise shifts all of the bonds into the retirement account and all of the stock into the nonretirement account she will have the following amounts to spend after taxes 5 years from now:

**TAX-QUALIFIED ACCOUNT:**

| | | |
|---|---|---|
| Bonds: | $\$100,000\ (1.1)^5 \times .72$ | = \$115,957.00 |

**NONRETIREMENT ACCOUNT:**

| | | |
|---|---|---|
| Stocks: | $\$100,000\ (1.15)^5 - .28[100,000(1.15)^5 - 100,000]$ | = \$172,817.72 |
| | TOTAL | = **\$288,774.72** |

Her spending budget will increase by \$1,193.20.

**4.** $B_0 \times$ PA(4%, 5 years) = 100,000 implies that $B_0$ = \$22,462.71.

| $t$ | $R_t$ | $B_t$ | $A_t$ |
|---|---|---|---|
| 0 | | | \$100,000.00 |
| 1 | 4% | \$22,462.71 | \$ 81,537.29 |
| 2 | 10% | \$23,758.64 | \$ 65,923.38 |
| 3 | −8% | \$21,017.26 | \$ 39,640.53 |
| 4 | 25% | \$25,261.12 | \$ 24,289.54 |
| 5 | 0 | \$24,289.54 | 0 |

## *Part II* Portfolio Theory

### *Chapter 5*—Concepts and Issues: Return, Risk, and Risk Aversion

**1.** *a.*
$$1 + r = (1 + R)(1 + i) = (1.03)(1.08) = 1.1124$$
$$r = 11.24\%$$

*b.*
$$1 + r = (1.03)(1.10) = 1.133$$
$$r = 13.3\%$$

**2.** Average = 6.26%; Standard deviation = 17.00%.

**3.** $R = (.12 - .13)/.13 = -.00885$ or $-.885\%$

When the inflation rate exceeds the nominal interest rate, the real rate of return is negative.

**4.** The expected rate of return on the risky portfolio is \$22,000/\$100,000 = .22, or 22%. The T-bill rate is 5%. The risk premium therefore is 22% − 5% = 17%.

**5.** The investor is taking on exchange rate risk by investing in a pound-denominated asset. If the exchange rate moves in the investor's favor, the investor will benefit and will earn more from the U.K. bill than the Canadian bill. For example, if both the Canadian and U.K. interest rates are 5%, and the current exchange rate is \$2.00 per pound, a \$2.00 investment today can buy one pound, which can be invested in England at a certain rate of 5%, for a year-end value of 1.05 pounds. If the year-end exchange rate is \$2.10 per pound, the 1.05 pounds can be exchanged for 1.05 × \$2.10 = \$2.205 for a rate of return in dollars of $1 + r =$ \$2.205/\$2.00 = 1.1025, or 10.25%, more than is available from Canadian bills. Therefore, if the investor expects favourable exchange rate movements, the U.K. bill is a speculative investment. Otherwise, it is a gamble.

**6.** For the $A = 4$ investor, the utility of the risky portfolio is

$$\begin{aligned} U &= .20 - \tfrac{1}{2} \times 4 \times .2^2 \\ &= .12 \end{aligned}$$

while the utility of bills is

$$\begin{aligned} U &= .07 - \tfrac{1}{2} \times 4 \times 0 \\ &= .07 \end{aligned}$$

The investor will prefer the risky portfolio to bills. (Of course, a mixture of bills and the portfolio might be even better, but that is not a choice here.)

For the $A = 8$ investor, the utility of the risky portfolio is

$$\begin{aligned} U &= .20 - \tfrac{1}{2} \times 8 \times .2^2 \\ &= .04 \end{aligned}$$

while the utility of bills is again .07. The more risk-averse investor therefore prefers the risk-free alternative.

**7.** The less risk-averse investor has a shallower indifference curve. An increase in risk requires less increase in expected return to restore utility to the original level.

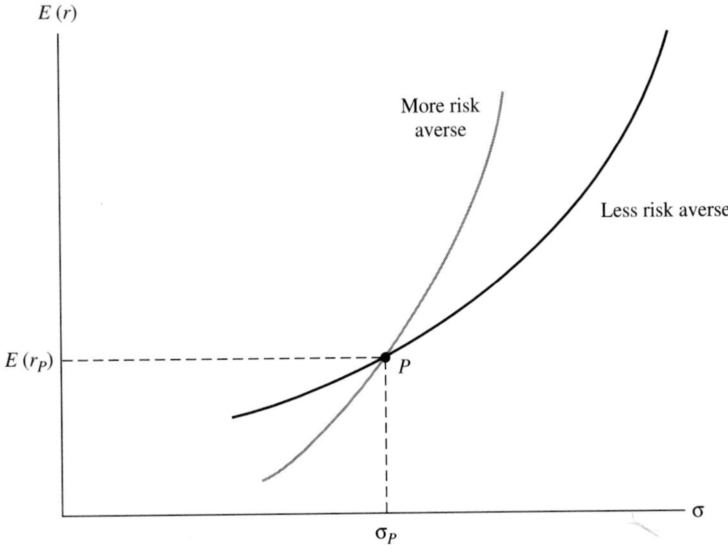

**8.** Despite the fact that gold investments *in isolation* seem dominated by the stock market, gold still might play a useful role in a diversified portfolio. Because gold and stock market returns have very low correlation, stock investors can reduce their portfolio risk by placing part of their portfolios in gold.

**9.** *a.* With the given distribution for SugarBeet, the scenario analysis looks as follows:

| | Normal Year for Sugar | | Abnormal Year |
|---|---|---|---|
| | Bullish Stock Market | Bearish Stock Market | Sugar Crisis |
| Probability | .5 | .3 | .2 |
| | | Rate of Return (%) | |
| Best Candy | .25 | .10 | −.25 |
| SugarBeet | .07 | −.05 | .20 |
| T-bills | .05 | .05 | .05 |

The expected return and standard deviation of SugarBeet is now:

$$E(r_{\text{SugarBeet}}) = .5 \times .07 + .3(-.05) + .2 \times .20$$
$$= .06$$
$$\sigma_{\text{SugarBeet}} = [.5(.07 - .06)^2 + .3(-.05 - .06)^2 + .2(.20 - .06)^2]^{1/2}$$
$$= .0872$$

The covariance between the returns of Best and SugarBeet is:

$$\text{Cov(SugarBeet, Best)} = .5(.07 - .06)(.25 - .105) + .3(-.05 - .06)(.10 - .105) + .2(.20 - .06)(-.25 - .105) = -.00905$$

and the correlation coefficient is:

$$\rho_{\text{(SugarBeet, Best)}} = \frac{\text{Cov(SugarBeet, Best)}}{\sigma_{\text{(SugarBeet)}}\sigma_{\text{(Best)}}} = \frac{-.00905}{.0872 \times .1890} = -.55$$

The correlation is negative but less than before (−.55 instead of −.86), so we expect that SugarBeet will now be a less powerful hedge than before. Investing 50% in SugarBeet and 50% in Best will result in a portfolio probability distribution of

| | | | |
|---|---|---|---|
| Probability | .5 | .3 | .2 |
| Portfolio return | .16 | .025 | −.025 |

resulting in a mean and standard deviation of

$$E(r_{\text{Hedged portfolio}}) = .5 \times .16 + .3 \times .025 + .2(-.025)$$
$$= .0825$$
$$\sigma_{\text{Hedged portfolio}} = [.5(.16 - .0825)^2 + .3(.025 - .0825)^2 + .2(-.025 - .0825)^2]^{1/2}$$
$$= .0794.$$

*b.* It is obvious that even under these circumstances the hedging strategy dominates the risk-reducing strategy that uses T-bills (which results in $E(r) = 7.75\%$, $\sigma = 9.45\%$). At the same time, the standard deviation of the hedged position (7.94%) is not as low as it was using the original data.

*c, d.* Using Rule 5 for portfolio variance, we would find that

$$\sigma^2 = .5^2 \times \sigma^2_{\text{Best}} + .5^2 \times \sigma^2_{\text{Beet}} + 2 \times .5 \times .5 \times \text{Cov(SugarBeet, Best)}$$
$$= .5^2 \times .189^2 + .5^2 \times .0872^2 + 2 \times .5 \times .5 \times (-.00905)$$
$$= .006306$$

which implies that $\sigma = .0794$, precisely the same result that we obtained by analyzing the scenarios directly.

**5B.1.** Investors appear to be more sensitive to extreme outcomes relative to moderate outcomes than variance and higher *even* moments can explain. Casual evidence suggests that investors are eager to insure extreme losses and express great enthusiasm for highly, positively skewed lotteries. This hypothesis is, however, extremely difficult to prove with properly controlled experiments.

**5B.2.** The better diversified the portfolio, the smaller is its standard deviation, as the sample standard deviations of Table 5B.1, p. 199, confirm. When we draw from distributions with smaller standard deviations, the probability of extreme values shrinks. Thus the expected smallest and largest values from a sample get closer to the expected value as the standard deviation gets smaller. This expectation is confirmed by the samples of Table 1 for both the sample maximum and minimum annual rate.

**5C.1.** *a.* $U(W) = \sqrt{W}$

$U(50{,}000) = \sqrt{50{,}000}$

$= 223.61$

$U(150{,}000) = 387.30$

*b.* $E(U) = .5 \times 223.61 + .5 \times 387.30$

$= 305.45$

*c.* We must find $W_{CE}$ that has utility level 305.45. Therefore

$\sqrt{W_{CE}} = 305.45$

$W_{CE} = 305.45^2$

$= \$93{,}301$

*d.* Yes. The certainty equivalent of the risky venture is less than the expected outcome of \$100,000.

*e.* The certainty equivalent of the risky venture to this investor is greater than it was for the log utility investor considered in the text. Hence this utility function displays less risk aversion.

## *Chapter 6*—Capital Allocation Between the Risky Asset and the Risk-Free Asset

**1.** Holding 50% of your invested capital in Ready Assets means that your investment proportion in the risky portfolio is reduced from 70% to 50%.

Your risky portfolio is constructed to invest 54% in VO and 46% in CT. Thus the proportion of VO in your overall portfolio is .5 × .54 = 27%, and the dollar value of your position in VO is $300,000 × .27 = $81,000.

**2.** In the expected return–standard deviation plane, all portfolios that are constructed from the same risky and risk-free funds (with various proportions) lie on a line from the risk-free rate through the risky fund. The slope of this CAL (capital allocation line) is the same everywhere; hence the reward-to-variability ratio is the same for all of these portfolios. Formally, if you invest a proportion, $y$, in a risky fund with expected return, $E(r_P)$, and standard deviation, $\sigma_P$, and the remainder, $1 - y$, in a risk-free asset with a sure rate, $r_f$, then the portfolio's expected return and standard deviation are

$$E(r_C) = r_f + y[E(r_P) - r_f]$$
$$\sigma_C = y\sigma_P$$

and therefore the reward-to-variability ratio of this portfolio is

$$S_C = \frac{E(r_C) - r_f}{\sigma_C} = \frac{y[E(r_P) - r_f]}{y\sigma_P} = \frac{E(r_P) - r_f}{\sigma_P}$$

which is independent of the proportion, $y$.

**3.** The lending and borrowing rates are unchanged at: $r_f = 7\%$. $r_f^B = 9\%$. The standard deviation of the risky portfolio is still 22%, but its expected rate of return shifts from 15% to 17%.

The slope of the two-part CAL is

$$\frac{E(r_P) - r_f}{\sigma_P} \quad \text{for the lending range}$$

$$\frac{E(r_P) - r_f^B}{\sigma_P} \quad \text{for the borrowing range}$$

Thus in both cases the slope increases from 8/22 to 10/22 for the lending range and from 6/22 to 8/22 for the borrowing range.

**4.** *a.* The parameters are: $r_f = .07$, $E(r_P) = .15$, $\sigma_P = .22$. With these parameters, an investor with a degree of risk aversion, $A$, will choose a proportion, $y$, in the risky portfolio of

$$y = \frac{E(r_P) - r_f}{A\sigma_P^2}$$

With $A = 3$ we find that

$$y = \frac{.15 - .07}{3 \times .0484} = .55$$

When the degree of risk aversion decreases from the original value of four to the new value of three, investment in the risky portfolio increases from 41% to 55%. Accordingly, the expected return and standard deviation of the optimal portfolio increase.

$$E(r_C) = .07 + .55 \times .08 = .114 \quad \text{(before: .1028)}$$
$$\sigma_C = .55 \times .22 = .121 \quad \text{(before: .0902)}$$

*b.* All investors whose degree of risk aversion is such that they would hold the risky portfolio in a proportion equal to 100% or less ($y < 1.00$) are lending rather than borrowing and so are unaffected by the borrowing rate. The least risk-averse of these investors hold 100% in the risky portfolio ($y = 1$). We can solve for the degree of risk aversion of these "cut off" investors, from the parameters of the investment opportunities:

$$y = 1 = \frac{E(r_P) - r_f}{A\sigma_P^2} = \frac{.08}{.0484A}$$

which implies

$$A = \frac{.08}{.0484} = 1.65$$

Any investor who is more risk tolerant (that is, with $A$ less than 1.65) would borrow if the borrowing rate were 7%. For borrowers,

$$y = \frac{E(r_P) - r_f^B}{A\sigma_P^2}$$

Suppose, for example, an investor has an $A$ of 1.1. When $r_f = r_f^B = 7\%$, this investor chooses to invest in the risky portfolio

$$y = \frac{.08}{1.1 \times .0484} = 1.50$$

which means that the investor will borrow 50% of the total investment capital. Raise the borrowing rate, in this case to $r_f^B = 9\%$, and the investor will invest less in the risky asset. In that case,

$$y = \frac{.06}{1.1 \times .0484} = 1.13$$

and "only" 13% of his or her investment capital will be borrowed. Graphically, the line from $r_f$ to the risky portfolio shows the CAL for lenders. The dashed part *would* be relevant if the borrowing rate equaled the lending rate. When the borrowing rate exceeds the lending rate, the CAL is kinked at the point corresponding to the risky portfolio.

The following figure shows indifference curves of two investors. The steeper indifference curve portrays the more risk-averse investor, who chooses portfolio $C_0$, which involves lending. This investor's choice is unaffected by the borrowing rate.

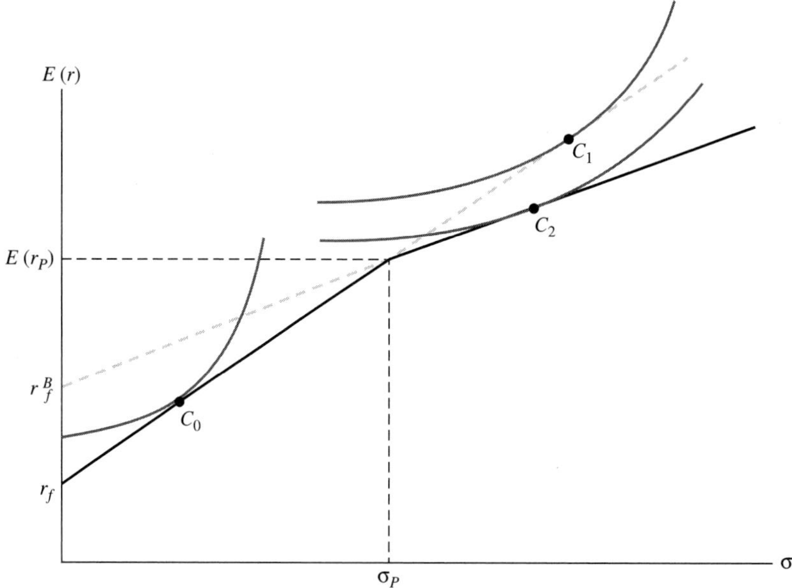


The more risk-tolerant investor is portrayed by the shallower-sloped indifference curves. If the lending rate equaled the borrowing rate, this investor would choose portfolio $C_1$ on the dashed part of the CAL. When the borrowing rate goes up, this investor chooses portfolio $C_2$ (in the borrowing range of the kinked CAL), which involves less borrowing than before. This investor is hurt by the increase in the borrowing rate.

**5.** If all the investment parameters remain unchanged, the only reason for an investor to decrease the investment proportion in the risky asset is an increase in the degree of risk aversion. If you think that this is unlikely, then you have to reconsider your faith in your assumptions. Perhaps the TSE300 is not a good proxy for the optimal risky portfolio. Perhaps investors expect a higher real rate on T-bills (inflation is ignored in this model).

## *Chapter 7*—Optimal Risky Portfolios

**1.** *a.* The first term will be $w_D \times w_D \times \sigma_D^2$, since this is the element in the top corner of the matrix ($\sigma_D^2$) times the term on the column border ($w_D$) times the term on the row border ($w_D$). Applying this rule to each term of the covariance matrix results in the sum $w_D^2\sigma_D^2 + w_D w_E \text{Cov}(r_E,r_D) + w_E w_D \text{Cov}(r_D,r_E) + w_E^2\sigma_E^2$, which is the same as equation 7.2, since $\text{Cov}(r_E,r_D) = \text{Cov}(r_D,r_E)$.

*b.* The bordered covariance matrix is

| | $w_X$ | $w_Y$ | $w_Z$ |
|---|---|---|---|
| $w_X$ | $\sigma_X^2$ | $\text{Cov}(r_X,r_Y)$ | $\text{Cov}(r_X,r_Z)$ |
| $w_Y$ | $\text{Cov}(r_Y,r_X)$ | $\sigma_Y^2$ | $\text{Cov}(r_Y,r_Z)$ |
| $w_Z$ | $\text{Cov}(r_Z,r_X)$ | $\text{Cov}(r_Z,r_Y)$ | $\sigma_Z^2$ |

There are nine terms in the covariance matrix. Portfolio variance is calculated, from these nine terms:

$$\begin{aligned}\sigma_P^2 = {} & w_X^2\sigma_X^2 + w_Y^2\sigma_Y^2 + w_Z^2\sigma_Z^2 \\ & + w_X w_Y \text{Cov}(r_X,r_Y) + w_Y w_X \text{Cov}(r_Y,r_X) \\ & + w_X w_Z \text{Cov}(r_X,r_Z) + w_Z w_X \text{Cov}(r_Z,r_X) \\ & + w_Y w_Z \text{Cov}(r_Y,r_Z) + w_Z w_Y \text{Cov}(r_Z,r_Y) \\ = {} & w_X^2\sigma_X^2 + w_Y^2\sigma_Y^2 + w_Z^2\sigma_Z^2 \\ & + 2w_X w_Y \text{Cov}(r_X,r_Y) + 2w_X w_Z \text{Cov}(r_X,r_Z) + 2w_Y w_Z \text{Cov}(r_Y,r_Z)\end{aligned}$$

**2.** The parameters of the opportunity set are $E(r_D) = .20$, $E(r_E) = .15$, $\sigma_D = .45$, $\sigma_E = .32$, and $\rho(D,E) = .25$. From the standard deviations and the correlation coefficient we generate the covariance matrix:

| Fund | *D* | *E* |
|---|---|---|
| *D* | .2025 | .0360 |
| *E* | .0360 | .1024 |

The *global minimum-variance* portfolio is constructed so that

$$\begin{aligned}w_D &= [\sigma_E^2 - \text{Cov}(r_D,r_E)] \div [\sigma_D^2 + \sigma_E^2 - 2\,\text{Cov}(r_D,r_E)] \\ &= (.1024 - .0360) \div (.2205 + .1024 - 2 \times .0360) = .2851 \\ w_E &= 1 - w_D = .7149\end{aligned}$$

Its expected return and standard deviation are

$$\begin{aligned}E(r_P) &= .2851 \times .20 + .7149 \times .15 = .1643 \\ \sigma_P &= [w_D^2\sigma_D^2 + w_E^2\sigma_E^2 + 2w_D w_E \text{Cov}(r_D,r_E)]^{1/2} \\ &= [.2851^2 \times .2025 + .7149^2 \times .1024 + 2 \times .2851 \times .7149 \times .0360]^{1/2} \\ &= .2889\end{aligned}$$

For the other points we simply increase $w_D$ from .10 to .90 in increments of .10; accordingly, $w_E$ ranges from .90 to .10 in the same increments. We substitute these portfolio proportions in the formulas for expected return and standard deviation. Note that for $w_D$ or $w_E$ equal to 1.0, the portfolio parameters equal those of the fund.

We then generate the following table:

| $w_D$ | $w_E$ | $E(r)$ | $\sigma$ |
|---|---|---|---|
| .00 | 1.00 | .1500 | .3200 |
| .10 | .90 | .1550 | .3024 |
| .20 | .80 | .1600 | .2918 |
| .2851 | .7149 | .1643 | .2889(min) |
| .30 | .70 | .1650 | .2890 |
| .40 | .60 | .1700 | .2942 |
| .50 | .50 | .1750 | .3070 |
| .60 | .40 | .1800 | .3264 |
| .70 | .30 | .1850 | .3515 |
| .80 | .20 | .1900 | .3811 |
| .90 | .10 | .1950 | .4142 |
| 1.00 | .00 | .2000 | .4500 |

You can now draw your graph.

**3.** *a*. The computations of the opportunity set of the two stock funds are like those of Question 2 and will not be shown here. You should perform these computations, however, in order to give a graphical solution to part *a*. Note that the covariance between the funds is

$$\begin{aligned}\text{Cov}(r_A, r_B) &= \rho(A,B) \times \sigma_A \times \sigma_B \\ &= -.2 \times .20 \times .60 = -.0240\end{aligned}$$

*b*. The proportions in the optimal risky portfolio are given by

$$\begin{aligned}w_A &= \frac{(.10 - .05).60^2 - (.30 - .05)(-.0240)}{(.10 - .05).60^2 + (.30 - .05).20^2 - .30(-.0240)} \\ &= .6818 \\ w_B &= 1 - w_A = .3182\end{aligned}$$

The expected return and standard deviation of the optimal risky portfolio are

$$\begin{aligned}E(r_P) &= .6818 \times .10 + .3182 \times .30 = .1636 \\ \sigma_P &= [.6818^2 \times .20^2 + .3182^2 \times .60^2 \\ &\quad + 2 \times .6818 \times .3182(-.0240)]^{1/2} \\ &= .2113\end{aligned}$$

Note that in this case the standard deviation of the optimal risky portfolio is smaller than the standard deviation of fund *A*. Note also that portfolio *P* is not the global minimum-variance portfolio. The proportions of the latter are given by

$$\begin{aligned}w_A &= [.60^2 - (-.0240)] \div [.60^2 + .20^2 - 2(-.0240)] = .8571 \\ w_B &= 1 - w_A = .1429\end{aligned}$$

With these proportions, the standard deviation of the minimum-variance portfolio is

$$\begin{aligned}\sigma(\text{min}) &= [.8571^2 \times .20^2 + .1429^2 \times .60^2 \\ &\quad + 2 \times .8571 \times .1429 \times (-.0240)]^{1/2} \\ &= .1757\end{aligned}$$

which is smaller than that of the optimal risky portfolio.

*c.* The CAL is the line from the risk-free rate through the optimal risky portfolio. This line represents all efficient portfolios that combine T-bills with the optimal risky portfolio. The slope of the CAL is

$$\begin{aligned}S &= [E(r_P) - r_f]/\sigma_P \\ &= (.1636 - .05)/.2113 = .5376\end{aligned}$$

*d.* Given a degree of risk aversion, *A*, an investor will choose a proportion, *y*, in the optimal risky portfolio of

$$\begin{aligned}y &= [E(r_P) - r_f]/(A\sigma_P^2) \\ &= (.1636 - .05)/(5 \times .2113^2) = .5089\end{aligned}$$

This means that the optimal risky portfolio, with the given data, is attractive enough for an investor with $A = 5$ to invest 50.89% of his or her wealth in it. Since fund *A* makes up 68.18% of the risky portfolio and fund *B* 31.82%, the investment proportions for this investor are

| | | |
|---|---|---|
| Fund *A*: | .5089 × 68.18 = | 34.70% |
| Fund *B*: | .5089 × 31.12 = | 16.19% |
| | TOTAL | 50.89% |

**4.** Efficient frontiers derived by portfolio managers depend on forecasts of the rates of return on various securities and estimates of risk, that is, the covariance matrix. The forecasts themselves do not control outcomes. Thus preferring managers with rosier forecasts (northwesterly frontiers) is tantamount to rewarding the bearers of good news and punishing the bearers of bad news. What we should do is reward bearers of *accurate* news. Thus, if you get a glimpse of the frontiers (forecasts) of portfolio managers on a regular basis, what you want to do is develop the track record of their forecasting accuracy and steer your advisees toward the more accurate forecaster. Their portfolio choices will, in the long run, outperform the field.

**5.** Portfolios that lie on the CAL are combinations of the tangency (risky) portfolio and the risk-free asset. Hence they are just as dependent on the accuracy of the efficient frontier as portfolios that are on the frontier itself. If we judge forecasting accuracy by the accuracy of the reward-to-volatility ratio, then all portfolios on a CAL will be exactly as accurate as the tangency portfolio.

**6.** The new estimates are as follows:

| | | Holding Period Return | | |
|---|---|---|---|---|
| **State of Economy** | **Probability** | **Stocks** | **Bonds** | **Cash** |
| Boom with low inflation | .05 | 74% | 4% | 6% |
| Boom with high inflation | .2 | 20% | −10% | 6% |
| Normal growth | .5 | 14% | 9% | 6% |
| Recession with low inflation | .2 | 0 | 35% | 6% |
| Recession with high inflation | .05 | −30% | 0 | 6% |
| Expected return | $E(r)$ | 13.2% | 9.7% | 6% |
| Standard deviation | $\sigma$ | 17.96% | 14.57% | 0 |

The correlation coefficient between stocks and bonds is −.3449.

**7.** To find the composition of the optimal combination of stocks and bonds to be combined with cash we use the following formula:

$$w^* = \frac{[E(r_s) - r_f]\sigma_b^2 - [E(r_b) - r_f]\text{Cov}(r_b, r_s)}{[E(r_s) - r_f]\sigma_b^2 + [E(r_b) - r_f]\sigma_s^2 - [E(r_s) - r_f + E(r_b) - r_f]\text{Cov}(r_b, r_s)}$$

where $w^*$ is the porportion of stocks in portfolio $O^*$ and $1 - w^*$ is the porportion of bonds. Substituting in the formula we get

$$w^* = \frac{(13.2 - 6)212.2849 - (9.7 - 6)(90.2525)}{7.2 \times 212.2849 + 3.7 \times 322.5616 + (7.2 + 3.7)90.2525}$$
$$= \frac{1194.5}{1738.2} = .687$$

So the proportion of stocks in the $O^*$ portfolio changes from 45% to 69%.

**7A.1.** The parameters are $E(r) = .15$, $\sigma = .60$, and the correlation between any pair of stocks is $\rho = .5$.

*a.* The portfolio expected return is invariant to the size of the portfolio because all stocks have identical expected returns. The standard deviation of a portfolio with $n = 25$ stocks is

$$\sigma_P = [\sigma^2(1/n) + \rho \times \sigma^2(n - 1)/n]^{1/2}$$
$$= [.60^2/25 + .5 \times .60^2 \times 24/25]^{1/2} = .4327$$

*b.* Because the stocks are identical, efficient portfolios are equally weighted. To obtain a standard deviation of 43%, we need to solve for $n$:

$$.43^2 = .60^2/n + .5 \times .60^2(n - 1)/n$$
$$.1849n = .3600 + .1800n - .1800$$
$$n = \frac{.1800}{.0049} = 36.73$$

Thus we need 37 stocks and will come in slightly under target.

*c.* As $n$ gets very large, the variance of an efficient (equally weighted) portfolio diminishes, leaving only the variance that comes from the covariances among stocks, that is

$$\sigma_P = \sqrt{\rho \times \sigma^2} = \sqrt{.5 \times .60^2} = .4243$$

Note that with 25 stocks we came within 84 basis points of the systematic risk, that is, the nonsystematic risk of a portfolio of 25 stocks is 84 basis points. With 37 stocks the standard deviation is .4300, of which nonsystematic risk is 57 basis points.

*d.* If the risk-free rate is 10%, then the risk premium on any size portfolio is 15 − 10 = 5%. The standard deviation of a well-diversified portfolio is (practically) 42.43%, hence the slope of the CAL is

$$S = 5/42.43 = .1178$$

---

*Part III*

# Equilibrium in Capital Markets

## *Chapter 8*—The Capital Asset Pricing Model

**1.** We can characterize the entire population by two representative investors. One is the "uninformed" investor, who does not engage in security analysis and holds the market portfolio, whereas the other optimizes using the Markowitz algorithm with input from security analysis. The uninformed investor does not know what input the informed investor uses to make portfolio purchases. The uninformed investor knows, however, that if the other investor is informed the market portfolio proportions will be optimal. Therefore to depart from these proportions would constitute an uninformed bet, which will, on average, reduce the efficiency of diversification with no compensating improvement in expected returns.

**2.** *a.* Substituting the historical mean and standard deviation in equation 8.2 yields a coefficient of risk aversion of

$$\overline{A} = \frac{E(r_m) - r_f}{\sigma_M^2} = \frac{.0303}{.1716^2} = 1.029$$

*b.* This relationship also tells us that for the historical standard deviation and a coefficient of risk aversion of 1.5, the risk premium would be

$$E(r_m) - r_f = \overline{A}\sigma_M^2 = 1.5 \times .1716^2 = .0442(4.42\%)$$

**3.** $\beta_I = \beta_{NUR} = 1.15$. Therefore, whatever the investment proportions, $w_I$, $w_{NUR}$, the portfolio $\beta$, which is

$$B_P = w_I\beta_I + w_{NOR}\beta_{NOR}$$

will equal 1.15.

As the market risk premium, $E(r_m) = r_f$, is .08, the portfolio risk premium will be

$$E(r_P) - r_f = \beta_P[E(r_m) - r_f]$$
$$= 1.15 \times .08 = .092$$

4. The alpha of a stock is its expected return in excess of that required by the CAPM.

$$\alpha = E(r) - [r_f + \beta[E(r_m) - r_f]]$$
$$\alpha_{XYZ} = .12 - [.05 + 1.0(.11 - .05)] = .01$$
$$\alpha_{ABC} = .13 - [.05 + 1.5(.11 - .05)] = -.01$$

*ABC* plots below the SML, while *XYZ* plots above.

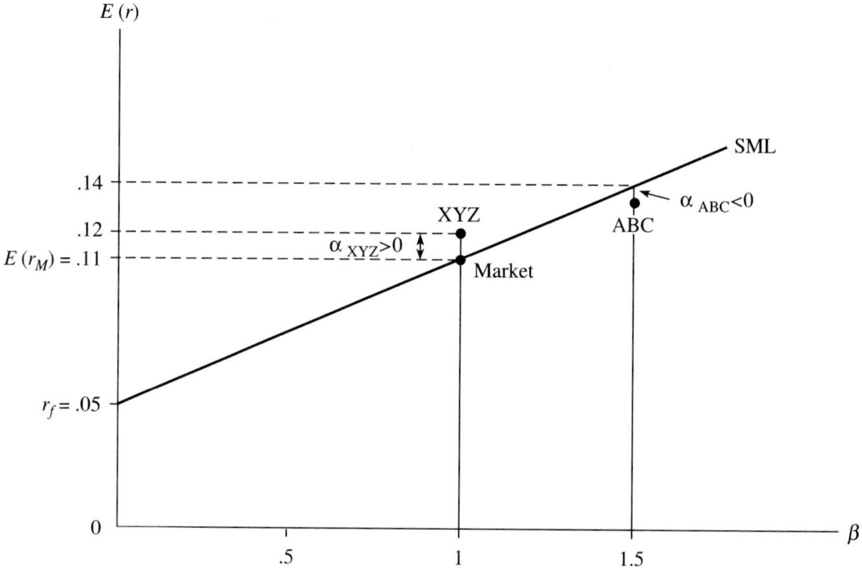


5. The project-specified required expected return is determined by the project beta coupled with the market risk premium and the risk-free rate. The CAPM tells us that an acceptable rate of return for the project is

$$E(r_f) + \beta[E(r_M) - r_f] = 8 + 1.3(12 - 8) = 13.2\%$$

which becomes the project's hurdle rate. If the IRR of the project is 15%, then it is desirable. Any project with an IRR equal to or less than 13.2% should be rejected.

6. If the basic CAPM holds, any zero-beta asset must be expected to earn on average the risk-free rate. Hence the posited performance of the zero-beta portfolio violates the simple CAPM. It does not, however, violate the zero-beta CAPM. Since we know that borrowing restrictions do exist, we expect the zero-beta version of the model is more likely to hold, with the zero-beta rate differing from the virtually risk-free T-bill rate.

## *Chapter 9*—Index Models and the Arbitrage Pricing Theory

**1.** The variance of each stock is $\beta^2\sigma_M^2 + \sigma^2(e)$.
For stock $A$, we obtain

$$\sigma_A^2 = .9^2(.20)^2 + .3^2 = .1224$$
$$\sigma_A = .35$$

For stock $B$,

$$\sigma_B^2 = 1.1^2\,(.20)^2 + .1^2 = .0584$$
$$\sigma_B = .24$$

The covariance is

$$\beta_A\beta_B\sigma_M^2 = .9 \times 1.1 \times .2^2 = .0396$$

**2.**
$$\begin{aligned}\sigma^2(e_P) &= (1/2)^2[\sigma^2(e_A) + \sigma^2(e_B)]\\ &= 1/4(.3^2 + .1^2)\\ &= 1/4(.09 + .01)\\ &= .025\end{aligned}$$

Therefore
$\sigma(e_P) = .158$

**3.** Burns Fry's alpha is related to the CAPM alpha by

$$\alpha_{\text{BF}} = \alpha_{\text{CAPM}} + (1 - \beta)r_f$$

For Seagram, $\alpha_{\text{BF}} = .36\%$, $\beta = .85$, and we are told that $r_f$ was .8%. Thus

$$\begin{aligned}\alpha_{\text{CAPM}} &= .36 - (1 - .85).8\\ &= .24\%\end{aligned}$$

Seagram still performed well relative to the market and the index model. It beat its "benchmark" return by an average of .24% per month.

**4.** The least profitable scenario currently yields a profit of \$10,000 and gross proceeds from the equally weighted portfolio of \$700,000. As the price of Dreck falls, less of the equally weighted portfolio can be purchased from the proceeds of the short sale. When Dreck's price falls by more than a factor of 10,000/700,000, arbitrage no longer will be feasible, because the profits in the worst state will be driven below zero.

To see this, suppose that Dreck's price falls to \$10 × (1 − 1/70). The short sale of 300,000 shares now yields \$2,957,142, which allows dollar investments of only \$985,714 in each of the other shares. In the high real interest rate–low inflation scenario, profits will be driven to zero:

| Stock | Dollar Investment | Rate of Return | Dollar Return |
|---|---|---|---|
| Apex | \$985,714 | .20 | 197,143 |
| Bull | 985,714 | .70 | 690,000 |
| Crush | 985,714 | −.20 | −197,143 |
| Dreck | −2,957,142 | .23 | −690,000 |
| TOTAL | 0 | | 0 |

At any price for Dreck stock *below* \$10 × (1 − 1/70) = \$9.857, profits are negative, which means this arbitrage opportunity is eliminated. *Note:* \$9.857 is not the equilibrium price of Dreck. It is simply the upper bound on Dreck's price that rules out the simple arbitrage opportunity.

**5.** $\sigma(e_P) = \sqrt{\sigma^2(e_i)/n}$

*a.* $\sqrt{30/10} = 1.732\%$

*b.* $\sqrt{30/100} = .548\%$

*c.* $\sqrt{30/1{,}000} = .173\%$

*d.* $\sqrt{30/10{,}000} = .055\%$

We conclude that nonsystematic volatility can be driven to arbitrarily low levels in well-diversified portfolios.

**6.** A portfolio consisting of two-thirds of portfolio *A* and one-third of the risk-free asset will have the same beta as portfolio *E,* but an expected return of (⅓ × 4 + ⅔ × 10) = 8%, less than that of portfolio *E*. Therefore one can earn arbitrage profits by shorting the combination of portfolio *A* and the safe asset and buying portfolio *E*.

**7.** *a.* For portfolio *P,*

$$K = \frac{E(r_P) - r_f}{\beta_P} = \frac{.10 - .05}{.5} = .10$$

For portfolio *Q,*

$$K = \frac{.15 - .05}{1} = .10$$

*b.* The equally weighted portfolio has an expected return of 12.5% and a beta of .75. $K = (.125 - .05)/.75 = .10$.

**8.** *a.* Total market capitalization is 3,000 + 1,940 + 1,360 = 6,300. Therefore the mean excess return of the index portfolio is

$$\frac{3{,}000}{6{,}300} \times .10 + \frac{1{,}940}{6{,}300} \times .02 + \frac{1{,}360}{6{,}300} \times .17 = .10$$

*b.* The covariance between stock *A* and the index portfolio equals

$$\text{Cov}(R_A, R_M) = \beta_A \sigma_M^2 = .1 \times .25^2 = .0625$$

*c.* The variance of *B* equals

$$\sigma_B^2 = \text{Var}(\beta_B R_M + e_B) = \beta_B^2 \sigma_M^2 + \sigma^2(e_B)$$

Thus, the firm specific variance of *B* equals

$$\sigma_B^2 - \beta_B^2 \sigma_M^2 = .30^2 - .2^2 \times .25^2 = .0875$$

**9.** The CAPM is a model that relates expected rates of return to risk. It results in the expected return–beta relationship where the expected excess return on any asset is proportional to the expected excess return on the market portfolio with beta as the proportionality constant. As such, the model is impractical for two reasons: (i) expectations are unobservable, and (ii) the theoretical market portfolio includes every publicly traded risky asset and is in practice unobservable. The next three models incorporate assumptions that overcome these problems.

The single factor APT model assumes that one economic factor, denoted $F$, exerts the only common influence on security returns. Beyond it, security returns are driven by independent, firm-specific factors. Thus, for any security $i$,

$$r_i = a_i + b_i F + e_i$$

The single index model assumes that in the single factor model, the factor, $F$, is perfectly correlated with and therefore can be replaced by a broad-based index of securities that can proxy for the CAPM's theoretical market portfolio.

At this point it should be said that many interchange the meaning of the index and market models. The concept of the market model is that rate of return surprises on a stock are proportional to corresponding surprises on the market index portfolio, again with proportionality constant $\beta$.

**10.** Using equation 9.18, the expected return is

$$.04 + .2(.06) + 1.4(0.8) = .164$$

## *Chapter 10*—Empirical Evidence on Security Returns

**1.** The SCL is estimated for each stock; hence we need to estimate 100 equations. Our sample consists of 60 monthly rates of return for each of the 100 stocks and for the market index. Thus each regression is estimated with 60 observations. Equation 10.1 in the text shows that when stated in excess return form, the SCL should pass through the origin, that is, have a zero intercept.

**2.** When the SML has a positive intercept and its slope is less than the mean excess return on the market portfolio, it is flatter than predicted by the CAPM. Low beta stocks therefore have yielded returns that, on average, were more than they should have been on the basis of their beta. Conversely, high beta stocks were found to have yielded, on average, less than they should have on the basis of their betas.

**3.** The intercept of the SML was .00359 (36 basis points) instead of zero as it should have been according to the simple CAPM. Equation 10.5 in the text shows that if the zero-beta version of the CAPM is valid because of restrictions on borrowing, and the SCL and SML are estimated from excess returns over the risk-free rate (rather than over the zero-beta rate), then the intercept will be the difference between the zero-beta rate and the risk-free rate. Thus, if BJS had found that the average risk premium of the zero-beta portfolio was 36 basis points (per month), the zero-beta version of the CAPM would have been supported. Similarly, the slope of the estimated SML should equal the difference between the market mean return and that of the zero-beta portfolio. The market index risk premium averaged 1.42% per month, and the slope of the SML was estimated as 1.08%. Here, a risk premium of 34 basis points would have supported the zero-beta version of the CAPM.

4. A positive coefficient on beta-squared would indicate that the relationship between risk and return is nonlinear. High beta securities would provide expected returns more than proportional to risk. A positive coefficient on $\sigma(e)$ would indicate that firm-specific risk affects expected return, a direct contradiction of the CAPM and APT.
5. It is very difficult to identify the portfolios that serve to hedge systematic sources of risk to future consumption opportunities. Both lines of research explore the data in search of such portfolios. Factor analysis techniques indicate the portfolios that may be providing hedge services. Researchers can then try to figure out what the source of risk is and show how important it is. The second line of attack attempts to use theoretical arguments to guess at the identity of economic variables that may be correlated with consumption risk and then determine whether these variables do indeed explain rates of return.

*Part IV*

## Active Portfolio Management

### *Chapter 11*—Market Efficiency

1. The information sets that pertain to the weak, semistrong, and strong form of the EMH can be described by the following illustration:

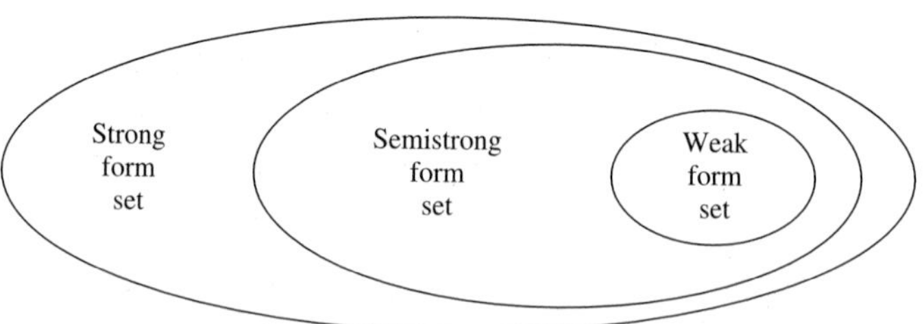


The weak-form information set includes only the history of prices and volumes. The semistrong-form set includes the weak-form set *plus* all publicly available information. In turn, the strong-form set includes the semistrong set *plus* insiders' information. It is illegal to act on the incremental information (insiders' private information). The direction of *valid* implication is

Strong-form EMH ⇒ Semistrong-form ⇒ Weak-form EMH

The reverse direction implication is *not* valid. For example, stock prices may reflect all past price data (weak-form efficiency) but may not reflect revelant fundamental data (semistrong-form inefficiency).

2. If *everyone* follows a passive strategy, sooner or later prices will fail to reflect new information. At this point there are profit opportunities for active investors who uncover mispriced securities. As they buy and sell these assets, prices again will be driven to fair levels.
3. Predictably declining CARs do violate the EMH. If one can predict such a phenomenon, a profit opportunity emerges: sell (or short sell) the affected stocks on an event date just before their prices are predicted to fall.
4. The answer depends on your prior beliefs about market efficiency. Magellan's record has been incredibly strong. On the other hand, with so many funds in existence, it is less surprising that *some* fund would appear to be consistently superior after the fact. The answer really depends more on faith than inference.
5. If profit opportunities can be made, one would expect mutual funds specialising in small stocks to spring into existence. Moreover, one wonders why buyers of small stocks do not compete for those stocks in December and bid up their prices before the January rise.
6. Concern over the deficit was an ongoing issue in 1987. No significant *new* information concering the deficit was released on October 19. Hence this explanation for the crash is not consistent with the EMH.

## *Chapter 12*—Active Portfolio Management and Performance Measurement

1. Sharpe: $(\bar{r} - \bar{r}_f)/\sigma$

$$S_P = (.35 - .06)/.42 = .69$$
$$S_M = (.28 - .06)/.30 = .733$$

Alpha: $\bar{r} - [r_f + \beta(\bar{r}_M - \bar{r}_f)]$

$$\alpha_P = .35 - [.06 + 1.2(.28 - .06)] = .026$$
$$\alpha_M = 0$$

Treynor: $(\bar{r} - \bar{r}_f)/\beta$

$$T_P = (.35 - .06)/1.2 = .242$$
$$T_M = (.28 - .06)/1.0 = .22$$

Appraisal ratio: $\alpha/\sigma(e)$

$$A_P = .026/.18 = .144$$
$$A_M = 0$$

2. We show the answer for the annual compounded rate of return for each strategy and leave you to compute the monthly rate.

Beginning-of-period fund:

$$F_0 = \$1{,}000$$

End-of-period fund for each strategy:

$$F_1 = \begin{cases} 3{,}600 & \text{Strategy = Bills only} \\ 67{,}500 & \text{Strategy = Market only} \\ 5{,}360{,}000{,}000 & \text{Perfect timing} \end{cases}$$

Number of periods: $N$ = 52 years
Annual compounded rate:

$$[1 + r_A]^N = \frac{F_1}{F_0}$$

$$r_A = \left(\frac{F_1}{F_0}\right)^{1/N} - 1$$

$$r_A = \begin{cases} 2.49\% & \text{Strategy = Bills only} \\ 8.44\% & \text{Strategy = Market only} \\ 34.71\% & \text{Strategy = Perfect timing} \end{cases}$$

**3.** The timer will guess bear or bull markets completely randomly. One half of all bull markets will be preceded by a correct forecast, and similarly for bear markets. Hence. $P_1 + P_2 - 1 = \frac{1}{2} + \frac{1}{2} - 1 = 0$.

**4.** *a*. When short positions are prohibited, the analysis is identical except that negative alpha stocks are dropped from the list. In that case the sum of the ratios of alpha to residual variance for the remaining two stocks is .7895. This leads to the new composition of the active portfolio:

$$x_1 = .3457/.7895 = .4379$$
$$x_2 = .4438/.7895 = .5621$$

The alpha, beta, and residual standard deviation of the active portfolio are now:

$$\alpha_A = .4379 \times .07 + .5621 \times .03 = .0475$$
$$\beta_A = .4379 \times 1.6 + .5621 \times .5 = .9817$$
$$\sigma(e_A) = [.4379^2 \times .45^2 + .5621^2 \times .26^2]^{1/2} = .2453$$

The cost of the short sale restriction is already apparent. The alpha has shrunk from 20.56% to 4.75%, while the reduction in the residual risk is more moderate, from 82.62% to 24.53%. In fact, a negative alpha stock is potentially more attractive than a positive alpha one: Since most stocks are positively correlated, the negative position that is required for the negative alpha stock creates a better diversified active portfolio.

The optimal allocation of the new active portfolio is:

$$w_0 = \frac{.0475/.6019}{.08/.04} = .3946$$

$$w^* = \frac{.3946}{1 + (1 - .9817) \times .3946} = .3918$$

Here, too, the beta correction is essentially irrelevant because the portfolio beta is so close to 1.0.

Finally, the performance of the overall risky portfolio is estimated at

$$S_P^2 = .16 + \left[\frac{.0475}{.2453}\right]^2 = .1975; S_P = .44$$

It is clear that in this we have lost about half of the original improvement in the Sharpe measure. Note, however, that this is an artifact of the small coverage of the security analysis division. When more stocks are covered, then a good number of positive alpha stocks will keep the residual risk of the active portfolio low. This is the key to extracting large gains from the active strategy.

*b.* When the forecast for the market index portfolio is more optimistic, the position in the active portfolio will be smaller and the contribution of the active portfolio to the Sharpe measure of the risky portfolio will be of a smaller magnitude. In the original example, the allocation to the active portfolio would be

$$w_0 = \frac{.2056/.6826}{.12/.04} = .1004$$

$$w^* = \frac{.1004}{1 + (1 - .9519) \times .1004} = .0999$$

Although the Sharpe measure of the market is now better, the improvement derived from security analysis is smaller:

$$S_P^2 = \left(\frac{.12}{.20}\right)^2 + \left(\frac{.2056}{.8262}\right)^2 = .4219$$

$$S_P = .65; S_M = .60$$

**12A.1.**

| Time | Action | Cash Flow |
|---|---|---|
| 0 | Buy two shares | −40 |
| 1 | Collect dividends; then sell one of the shares | 4 + 22 |
| 2 | Collect dividend on remaining share, then sell it | 2 + 19 |

*a.* Dollar-weighted return:

$$-40 + \frac{26}{1 + r} + \frac{21}{(1 + r)^2} = 0$$

$$r = .1191 = 11.91\%$$

*b.* Time-weighted return:

The rates of return on the stock in the 2 years were

$$r_1 = \frac{2 + (22 - 20)}{20} = .20$$

$$r_2 = \frac{2 + (19 - 22)}{22} = -.045$$

$$(r_1 + r_2)/2 = .077, \text{ or } 7.7\%$$

**12A.2.** *a.* $E(r_A) = [.15 + (-.05)]/2 = .05$

$E(r_G) = [(1.15)(.95)]^{1/2} - 1 = .045$

*b.* The expected stock price is $(115 + 95)/2 = 105$.

*c.* The expected rate of return on the stock is 5%, equal to $r_A$.

## *Chapter 13*—International Investing

**1.** The graph would asympote to a lower level, as shown in the following figure, reflecting the improved opportunities for diversification. However, there still would remain a positive level of nondiversifiable risk.

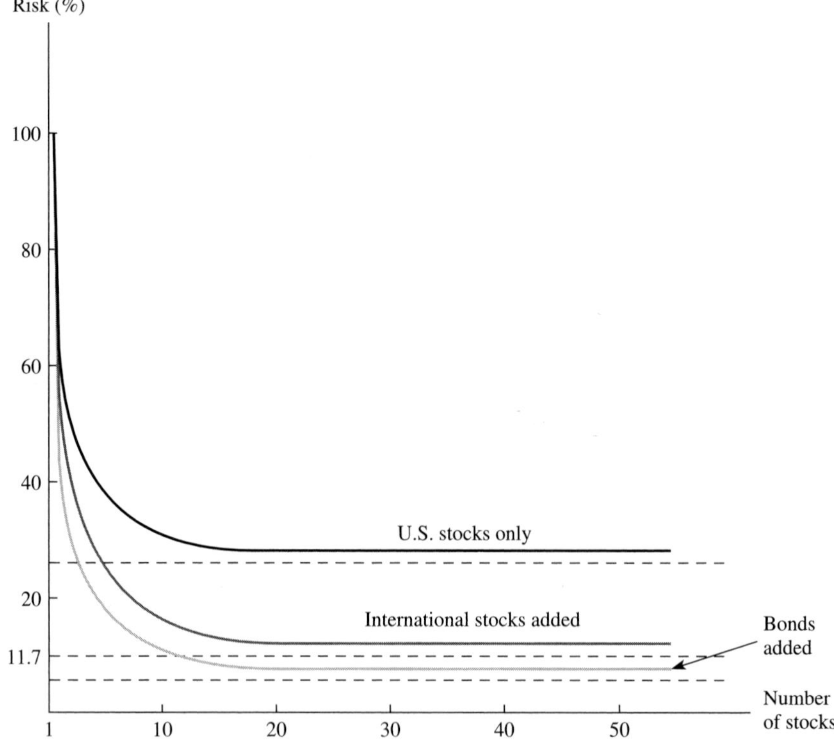

**2.** $1 + r(\text{Cdn}) = [(1 + r_f(\text{UK})] \times (E_1/E_0)$

*a.* $1 + r(\text{Cdn}) = 1.1 \times 1.0 = 1.10 \quad r(\text{Cdn}) = 10\%$

*b.* $1 + r(\text{Cdn}) = 1.1 \times 1.1 = 1.21 \quad r(\text{Cdn}) = 21\%$

**3.** You must sell forward the number of pounds that you will end up with at the end of the year. However, this value cannot be known with certainty unless the rate of return of the pound-denominated investment is known.

*a.* $10{,}000 \times 1.20 = 12{,}000$ pounds

*b.* $10{,}000 \times 1.30 = 13{,}000$ pounds

**4.** *Country selection:*

$$(.40 \times .10) + (.20 \times .05) + (.40 \times .15) = .11$$

This is a loss of .015 (1.5%) relative to the EAFE passive benchmark.

*Currency selection:*

$$(.40 \times 1.10) + (.20 \times .9) + (.40 \times 1.30) = 1.14$$

This is a loss of 6% relative to the EAFE benchmark.

---

*Part V*

## Fixed-Income Securities

### *Chapter 14*—Bond Prices and Yields

1. The callable bond will sell at the *lower* price. Investors will not be willing to pay as much if they know that the firm retains a valuable option to reclaim the bond for the call price if interest rates fall.
2. It should receive a negative coefficient. A high ratio of liabilities is a poor omen for a firm that should lower its credit rating.
3. At a semiannual interest rate of 3%, the bond is worth $40 × *PA*(3%, 60) + $1,000 × *PF*(3%, 60) = $1,276.75, which results in a capital gain of $276.75. This exceeds the capital loss of $189.29 ($1,000 − $810.71) when the interest rate increases to 5%.
4. Yield to maturity exceeds current yield, which exceeds coupon rate. An example is the 8% coupon bond with a yield to maturity of 10% per year (5% per half year). Its price is $810.71, and therefore its current yield is 80/810.77 = .0987 or 9.87%, which is higher than the coupon rate but lower than the yield to maturity.
5. The bond with the 6% coupon rate currently sells for 30 × *PA*(3.5%, 20) + 1,000 × *PF*(3.5%, 20) = $928.94. If the interest rate immediately drops to 6% (3% per half year), the bond price will rise to $1,000, for a capital gain of $71.06, or 7.65%. The 8% coupon bond currently sells for $1,071.06. If the interest rate falls to 6%, the present value of the *scheduled* payments increases to $1,148.77. However, the bond will be called at $1,100, for a capital gain of only $28.94, or 2.70%.
6. The current price of the bond can be derived from the yield to maturity. Using your calculator, set: $n$ = 40 (semiannual periods); payment = $45 per period; Future value = $1,000; interest rate = 4% per semiannual

period. Calculate present value as $1,098.96. Now we can calculate yield to call. The time to call is five years, or 10 semiannual periods. The price at which the bond will be called is $1,050. To find yield to call, we set: $n = 10$ (semiannual periods); payment = $45 per period; Future value = $1,050; present value = $1,098.96. Calculate yield to call as 3.72%.

7. The coupon payment is $45. There are 20 semiannual periods. The final payment is assumed to be $600. The present value of expected cash flows is $750. The yield to maturity is 5.42% semiannual or 10.8%.
8. Price = $70 × PA(8%, 1) + $1,000 × PF(8%, 1) = $990.74

$$\text{Rate of return to investor} = \frac{\$70 + (\$990.74 - \$982.17)}{\$982.17} = .080$$
$$= 8\%$$

9. At the lower yield, the bond price will be $631.67 [$n = 29$, $i = 7\%$, FV = $1000, PMT = $40]. Therefore, total after-tax income is

| | | |
|---|---|---|
| Coupon | $40 × (1 − .36) = | $25.60 |
| Imputed interest | ($553.66 − $549.69) × (1 − .36) = | 2.54 |
| Capital gains | ($631.67 − $553.66) × (1 − .28) = | 56.17 |
| Total income after taxes | | $84.31 |

Rate of return = 84.31/549.69 = .153 = 15.3%

## *Chapter 15*—The Term Structure of Interest Rates

1. The bond sells today for $683.18 (from Table 15.2). Next year, it will sell for $1,000 ÷ [(1.10)(1.11)(1.11)] = $737.84, for a return $1 + r = 737.84/683.18 = 1.08$, or 8%.
2. The data pertaining to the T-bill imply that the 6-month interest rate is $300/$9,700 = .03093, or 3.093%. To obtain the forward rate, we look at the 1-year T-bond. The pricing formula

$$1{,}000 = \frac{40}{1.03093} + \frac{1040}{(1.03093)(1 + f)}$$

implies that $f = .04952$, or 4.952%.
3. 9%.
4. The risk premium will be zero.
5. If issuers wish to issue long-term bonds, they will be willing to accept higher expected interest costs on long bonds over short bonds. This willingness combines with investors' demands for higher rates on long-term bonds to reinforce the tendency toward a positive liquidity premium.
6. If $r_4$ equaled 9.66%, then the 4-year bond would sell for $1,000/[(1.08)(1.10)(1.11)(1.0966)] = $691.53. The yield to maturity would satisfy the equation $691.53(1 + y_4)^4 = 1{,}000$, or $y_4 = 9.66\%$. At a lower value of $r_4$, the bond would sell for a higher price and offer a lower yield. At a higher value of $r_4$, the yield would be greater.

## *Chapter 16*—Fixed-Income Portfolio Management

**1.** *a.*

| (1) Time until Payment | (2) Payment | (3) Payment Discounted at 10% | (4) Weight | (5) Column (1) × Column (4) |
|---|---|---|---|---|
| 1 | $ 90 | $ 81.8182 | .0833 | .0833 |
| 2 | 1,090 | 900.8264 | .9167 | 1.8334 |
| | | $982.6446 | 1.0 | 1.9167 |

Duration is 1.1967 years. Price is $982.6446.

*b.* At an interest rate of 10.05%, the bond's price is

$$90 \times PA(10.05\%, 2) + 1{,}000\ PF(10.05\%, 2) = 981.7891$$

The percentage change in price is −.087%.

*c.* The duration formula would predict a price change of

$$-\frac{1.9167}{1.10} \times .0005 = -.00087 = -.087\%$$

which is the same answer that we obtained from direct computation in (*b*).

**2.** The duration of a level perpetuity is $(1 + y)/y$ or $1 + 1/y$, which clearly falls as $y$ increases. Tabulating duration as a function of $y$ we get

| *y* | *D* |
|---|---|
| .01 | 101 years |
| .02 | 51 |
| .05 | 21 |
| .10 | 11 |
| .20 | 6 |
| .25 | 5 |
| .40 | 3.5 |

**3.** Potential gains and losses are proportional to both duration *and* portfolio size. The dollar loss on a fixed-income portfolio resulting from an increase in the portfolio's yield to maturity is, from equation 16.2, $D \times P \times \Delta y/(1 + y)$, where $P$ is the initial market value of the portfolio. Hence $D \times P$ must be equated for immunisation.

**4.** The perpetuity's duration now would be 1.08/.08 = 13.5. We need to solve the following equation for $w$:

$$w \times 2 + (1 - w) \times 13.5 = 6$$

Therefore $w = .6522$.

**5.** Dedication would be more attractive. Cash flow matching eliminates the need for rebalancing and thus saves transaction costs.

**6.** The 30-year 8% coupon bond will provide a stream of coupons of $40 per half-year, which, invested at the assumed rate of 4% per half-year, will accumulate to \$480.24. The bond will sell in 5 years at a price equal to \$40 × PA(4.25%, 50) + \$1,000 × PF(4.25%, 50), or \$948.52, for a capital gain of \$51.71. The total 5-year income is \$51.71 + \$480.24 = \$531.95, for a 5-year return of \$531.95/\$896.81 = .5932, or 59.32%. Based on this scenario, the 20-year 10% coupon bond offers a higher return for a 5-year horizon.

**7.** The trigger point is $\$10M/(1.12)^3 = \$7.118M$.

**8.** The manager would like to retain the money market securities because of their relative pricing compared to other short-term assets. There is, however, an expectation that rates will fall. The manager can hold this *particular* portfolio of short-term assets and still benefit from the drop in interest rates by entering into a swap to pay a short-term interest rate and receive a fixed-interest rate. The resulting synthetic fixed-rate portfolio will increase in value if rates do fall.

*Part VI*

# Equities

## *Chapter 17*—Security Analysis

**1.** *a.* Dividend yield = \$2.15/50 = 4.3%
Capital gains yield = (59.77 − 50)/50 = 19.54%
Total return = 4.3% + 19.54% = 23.84%

*b.* $k = 6\% + 1.15\,(14\% - 6\%) = 15.2\%$

*c.* $V_0 = (\$2.15 + \$59.77)/1.152 = \$53.75$, which exceeds the market price. This would indicate a "buy" opportunity.

*d.* $P = \$50 = (OI - .08 \times \$20)/(1 \times .152)$; therefore, $OI = .152 \times \$50 + .08 \times \$20 = \$9.2$ (million).

**2.** *a.* $E(D_1)/(k - g) = \$2.15/(.152 - .112) = \$53.75$

*b.* $E(P_1) = P_0(1 + g) = \$53.75(1.112) = \$59.77$

*c.* The expected capital gain equals \$59.77 − \$53.75 = \$6.02, for a percentage gain of 11.2%. The dividend yield is $E(D_1)/P_0 = \$2.15/53.75 = 4\%$, for an HPR of 4% + 11.2% = 15.2%.

**3.** *a.* $g = ROE \times b = .20 \times .60 = .12$
$D_1 = (1 - b)E_1 = (1 - .60) \times \$5 = \$2$
$P_0 = D_1/(k - g) = \$2/(.125 - .12) = \$400$
$PVGO = P_0 - E_1/k = \$400 - \$5/.12 = \$360$

*b.* $g = .10 \times .60 = .06$
$P_0 = \$2/(.15 - .06) = \$22.22$
$PVGO = \$22.22 - \$5/.15 = \$-11.11$
This stock needs new management that will cut the plowback ratio to zero, giving $P_0 = \$5/.15 = \$33.33$.

**4.** $$V_{1993} = \frac{.54}{(1.123)} + \frac{.66}{(1.123)^2} + \frac{.78}{(1.123)^3} + \frac{.90 + P_{1997}}{(1.123)^4}$$

Now compute the sales price in 1997 using the constant growth DDM.

$$P_{1997} = \frac{.90 \times (1+g)}{k-g} = \frac{\$90 \times 1.118}{.123 - .118} = \$201.24$$

Therefore, $V_{1993} = \$128.65$.

**5.** *a*. ROE = 12%

$b = \$.50/\$2 = .25$

$g = \text{ROE} \times b = 12\% \times .25 = 3\%$

$P_0 = D_1/(k-g) = \$1.50/(.10 - .03) = \$21.43$

$P_0/E(E_1) = \$21.43/\$2 = 10.71$

*b*. If $b = .4$, then $.4 \times \$2 = \$.80$ would be reinvested and the remainder of earnings, or \$1.20, paid as dividends.

$$g = 12\% \times .4 = 4.8\%$$
$$P_0 = E(D_1)/(k-g) = \$1.20/(.10 - .048) = \$23.08$$
$$P_0/E(E_1) = \$23.08/\$2.00 = 11.54$$

**6.** *a*. $P_0 = \dfrac{(1-b)E(E_1)}{k-g} = \dfrac{.6 \times \$1}{.1 - .04} = \$10$

*b*. $\dfrac{E(D_1^*)}{P_0} = \dfrac{(1-b)E(E_1^*)}{P_0} = \dfrac{(1-.4) \times \$1}{\$10} = .06$, or 6% per year

The rate of price appreciation $= g^* = b^* \times \text{ROE}^* = 4\%$ per year

*c*. *i*. $g = (1.04)(1.06) - 1 = .1024$, or 10.24%

*ii*. $\dfrac{E(D_1)}{P_0} = \dfrac{E(D_1^*)(1+i)}{P_0} = .06 \times 1.06 = .0636$, or 6.36%

*iii*. ROE = 16.6%

*iv*. $b = \dfrac{g}{\text{ROE}} = \dfrac{.1024}{.166} = .6169$

**7.** With fixed costs of \$2 million and variable costs of \$1.5 million, firm C has variable costs of \$7.5, \$9, and \$10.5 million in each scenario; the corresponding total costs are \$9.5, \$11, and \$12.5 million. Thus, the profits for firm C are \$.5, \$1, and \$1.5 million under recession, normal, and expansion scenarios. We conclude that the higher the operating leverage, the higher is the resulting business risk; operating leverage increases the sensitivity of operating income to economic conditions.

## *Chapter 18*—Financial Statement Analysis

**1.** A debt/equity ratio of 1 implies that Mordett will have \$50 million of debt and \$50 million of equity. Interest expense will be $.09 \times \$50$ million, or \$4.5 million per year. Mordett's net profits and ROE over the business cycle will therefore be

| Scenario | EBIT | Nodett Net Profits | Nodett ROE | Mordett Net Profits[a] | Mordett ROE[b] |
|---|---|---|---|---|---|
| Bad year | $ 5M | $3 million | 3% | $ .3 million | .6% |
| Normal year | 10M | 6 | 6% | 3.3 | 6.6% |
| Good year | 15M | 9 | 9% | 6.3 | 12.6% |

[a]Mordett's after-tax profits are given by: .6(EBIT − $4.5 million).
[b]Mordett's equity is only $50 million.

**2.** Ratio Decomposition Analysis for Mordett Corporation

| | ROE | (1) Net Profit / Pretax Profit | (2) Pretax Profit / EBIT | (3) EBIT / Sales (ROS) | (4) Sales / Assets (ATO) | (5) Assets / Equity | (6) Combined Leverage Factor (2) × (5) |
|---|---|---|---|---|---|---|---|
| ***a.* BAD YEAR** | | | | | | | |
| Nodett | .030 | .6 | 1.000 | .0625 | .800 | 1.000 | 1.000 |
| Somdett | .018 | .6 | .360 | .0625 | .800 | 1.667 | .600 |
| Mordett | .006 | .6 | .100 | .0625 | .800 | 2.000 | .200 |
| ***b.* NORMAL YEAR** | | | | | | | |
| Nodett | .060 | .6 | 1.000 | .100 | 1.000 | 1.000 | 1.000 |
| Somdett | .068 | .6 | .680 | .100 | 1.000 | 1.667 | 1.134 |
| Mordett | .066 | .6 | .550 | .100 | 1.000 | 2.000 | 1.100 |
| ***c.* GOOD YEAR** | | | | | | | |
| Nodett | .090 | .6 | 1.000 | .125 | 1.200 | 1.000 | 1.000 |
| Somdett | .118 | .6 | .787 | .125 | 1.200 | 1.667 | 1.311 |
| Mordett | .126 | .6 | .700 | .125 | 1.200 | 2.000 | 1.400 |

**3.** GI'S ROE in 19X3 was 3.03% computed as follows:

$$\text{ROE} = \frac{\$5{,}285}{.5(\$171{,}843 + 177{,}128)} = .303, \text{ or } 3.03\%$$

Its P/E ratio was $4 = \dfrac{\$21}{\$5.285}$

and its P/B ratio was $.12 = \dfrac{\$21}{\$177}$.

Its earnings yield was 25% compared with an industry average of 12.5%. Note that in our calculations the earnings yield will not equal ROE/(P/B) because we have computed ROE with average shareholders' equity in the denominator and P/B with end-of-year shareholders' equity in the denominator.

**4.** Honeywell Ratio Analysis

| Year | ROE | (1) Net Profit / Pretax Profit | (2) Pretax Profit / EBIT | (3) EBIT / Sales (ROS) | (4) Sales / Assets (ATO) | (5) Assets / Equity | (6) Combined Leverage Factor (2) × (5) | (7) ROA (3) × (4) |
|---|---|---|---|---|---|---|---|---|
| 1987 | 11.4% | .616 | .796 | 7.75% | 1.375 | 2.175 | 1.731 | 10.65% |
| 1984 | 10.2% | .636 | .932 | 8.88% | 1.311 | 1.474 | 1.374 | 11.65% |

ROE went up despite a decline in operating margin and a decline in the tax burden ratio because of increased leverage and turnover. Note that ROA declined from 11.65% in 1984 to 10.65% in 1987.

**5.** LIFO accounting results in lower reported earnings than does FIFO. Fewer assets to depreciate results in lower reported earnings because there is less bias associated with the use of historic cost. More debt results in lower reported earnings because the inflation premium in the interest rate is treated as part of interest expense and not as repayment of principal. If ABC has the same reported earnings as XYZ despite these three sources of downward bias, its real earnings must be greater.

## *Chapter 19*—Technical Analysis

**1.** Suppose a stock had been selling in a narrow trading range around $50 for a substantial period and later increased in price. Now the stock falls back to a price near $50. Potential buyers might recall the price history of the stock and remember that, the last time the stock fell so low, they missed an opportunity for large gains when it later advanced. They might then view $50 as a good opportunity to buy. Therefore, buying pressure will materialize as the stock price falls to $50, which will create a support level.

**2.**

| | | | | | | |
|---|---|---|---|---|---|---|
| 49 | | | | | | |
| 46 | | | X | O | | |
| 43 | X | O | X | O | | |
| 40 | | O | X | O | | |
| 37 | | | | O | | |
| 34 | | | | O | | |

**3.** By the time the news of the recession affects bond yields, it also ought to affect stock prices. The market should fall *before* the confidence index signals that the time is ripe to sell.

*Part VII*

# Derivative Assets

## *Chapter 20*—Options and Other Derivatives: Introduction

**1.** *a.* Proceeds $= S_T - X = S_T - 20$ if this value is positive; otherwise, the call expires worthless.

Profit = Proceeds − Option price = Proceeds − \$0.150.

| | $S_T = 15$ | $S_T = 25$ |
|---|---|---|
| Proceeds | 0 | 5 |
| Profit | −\$0.15 | \$4.85 |

*b.* Proceeds $= X - S_T = 20 - S_T$ if this value is positive; otherwise, the call expires worthless.

Profit = Proceeds − Option price = Proceeds − \$1.70.

| | $S_T = 15$ | $S_T = 25$ |
|---|---|---|
| Proceeds | 5 | 0 |
| Profit | \$3.30 | −\$1.70 |

**2.** Before the split, profits would have been 100 × (\$40 − \$35) = \$500. After the split, profits would be 1,000 × (\$4 − \$3.5) = \$500. Profits would be unaffected.

**3.** *a.* Payoff to put writer $= \begin{cases} 0 & \text{if } S_T > X \\ -(X - S_T) & \text{if } S_T \leq X \end{cases}$

*b.* Profit = Initial premium realized + Ultimate payoff

$$= \begin{cases} P & \text{if } S_T > X \\ P - (X - S_T) & \text{if } S_T \leq X \end{cases}$$

*c.* Put written

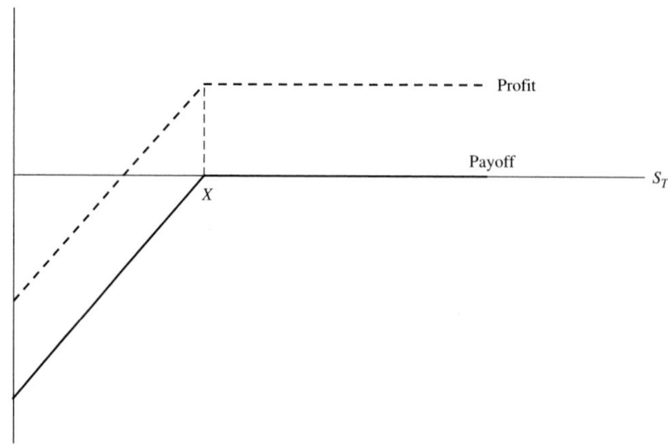

*d.* Put writers do well when the stock price increases and poorly when it falls.

**4.**

Payoff to a Strip

| | $S_T \leq X$ | $S_T > X$ |
|---|---|---|
| 2 Puts | $2(X - S_T)$ | 0 |
| 1 Call | 0 | $S_T - X$ |

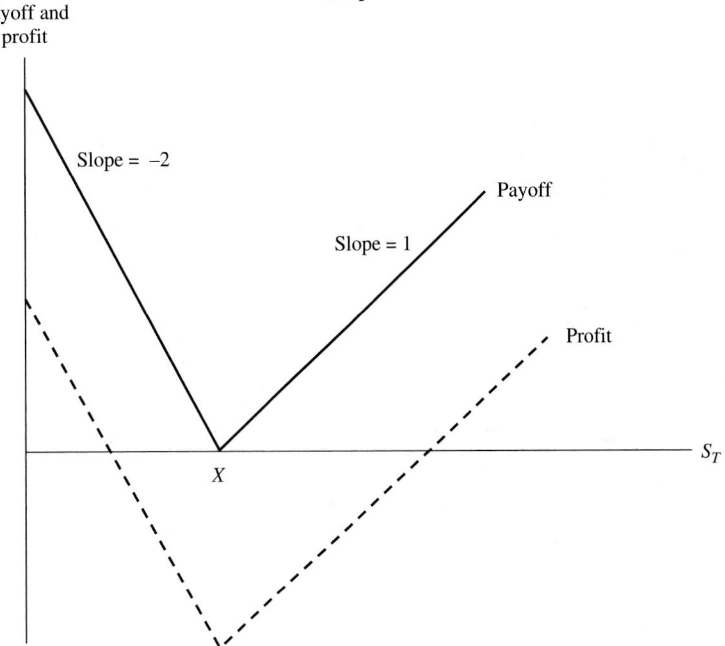

Payoff to a Strap

| | $S_T \leq X$ | $S_T > X$ |
|---|---|---|
| 1 Put | $X - S_T$ | 0 |
| 2 Calls | 0 | $2(S_T - X)$ |

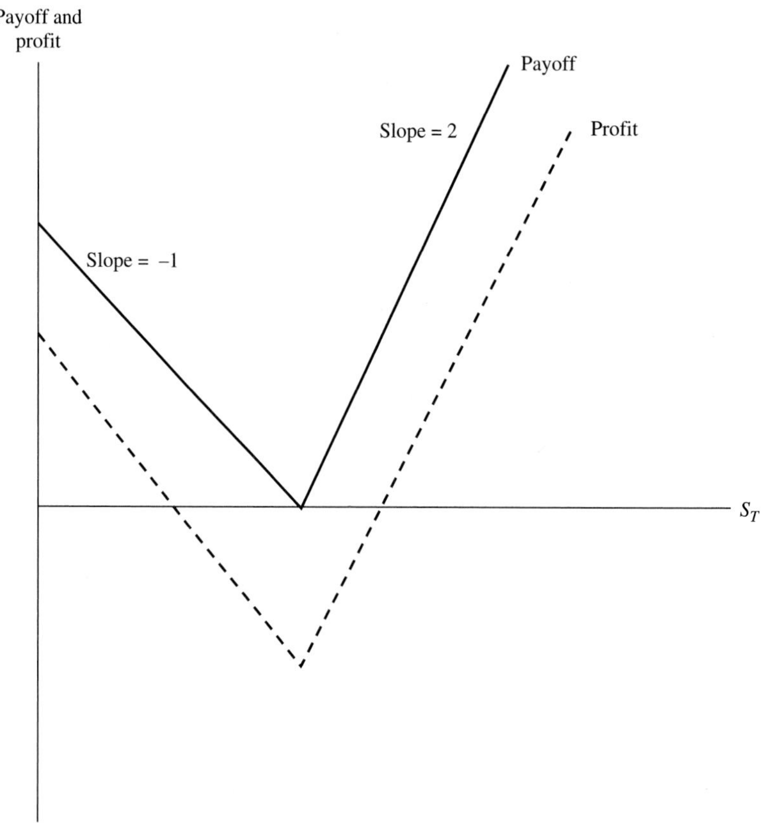


**5.** The covered call strategy would consist of a straight bond with a call written on the bond. The value of the strategy at option expiration as a function of the value of the straight bond is given in the following figure, which is virtually identical to Figure 20.7.

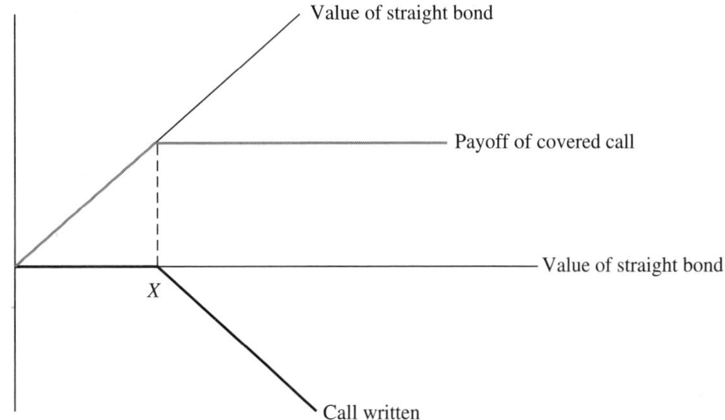


6. The call option is worth less as call protection is expanded. Therefore, the coupon rate need not be as high.
7. Lower. Investors will accept a lower coupon rate in return for the conversion option.
8. The appropriate calls to replicate the bull CDs have exercise prices equal to 1.05 × 240 × 1.005, and the riskless investment is 1.005/1.03. Investing in a portfolio of \$10/(240 × 1.05) in calls and 1.005/1.03 in the riskless asset yields the largest of 1.005 and $(1 + r_M)/1.05$, which corresponds to the bull CD's return per \$ par value. The value of the portfolio is 10/252 + 1.005/1.03 = 1.0154, which is the value of the bull CD per unit par value.

## *Chapter 21*—Option Valuation

1. Yes. Consider the same scenarios as for the call:

| Stock price | \$10 | \$20 | \$30 | \$40 | \$50 |
|---|---|---|---|---|---|
| Put payoff | \$20 | \$10 | \$ 0 | \$ 0 | \$ 0 |

| Stock price | \$20 | \$25 | \$30 | \$35 | \$40 |
|---|---|---|---|---|---|
| Put payoff | \$10 | \$ 5 | \$ 0 | \$ 0 | \$ 0 |

The low volatility scenario yields a lower expected payoff.

2.

| If Variable Increases | The Value of a Put Option |
|---|---|
| $S$ | Decreases |
| $X$ | Increases |
| $\sigma$ | Increases |
| $T$ | Increases |
| $r_f$ | Decreases |
| Dividends | Increases |

3. The parity relationship assumes that all options are held until expiration and that there are no cash flows until expiration. These assumptions are valid only in the special case of European options on nondividend-paying stocks. If the stock pays no dividends, the American and European calls are equally valuable, whereas the American put is worth more than the European put. Therefore, although the parity theorem for European options states that

$$P = C + S_0 - \text{PV}(X)$$

in fact, $P$ will be *greater* than this value if the put is American.
4. Implied volatility exceeds .5. Given a standard deviation of .5, the option value is $13.70. A higher volatility is needed to justify the actual $15 price.
5. A $1 increase in stock price is a percentage increase of 1/122 = .82%. The put option will fall by (.4 × $1) = $.40, a percentage decrease of $.40/$4 = 10%. Elasticity is −10/.82 = −12.2.
6. Higher. For deep out-of-the-money options, an increase in the stock price still leaves the option unlikely to be exercised. Its value increases only fractionally. For deep in-the-money options, exercise is likely, and option holders benefit by a full dollar for each dollar increase in the stock, as though they already own the stock.
7. Because the option now is underpriced, we want to reverse our previous strategy:

| | | Cash Flow in 1 Year for Each Possible Stock Price | |
|---|---|---|---|
| | Initial Cash Flow | $S = 50$ | $S = 200$ |
| Buy 2 options | −48 | 0 | 150 |
| Short-sell 1 share | 100 | −50 | −200 |
| Lend $52 at 8% interest rate | −52 | 56.16 | 56.16 |
| TOTAL | 0 | 6.16 | 6.16 |

## *Chapter 22*—Futures and Forward Markets

**1.** 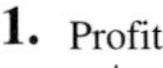

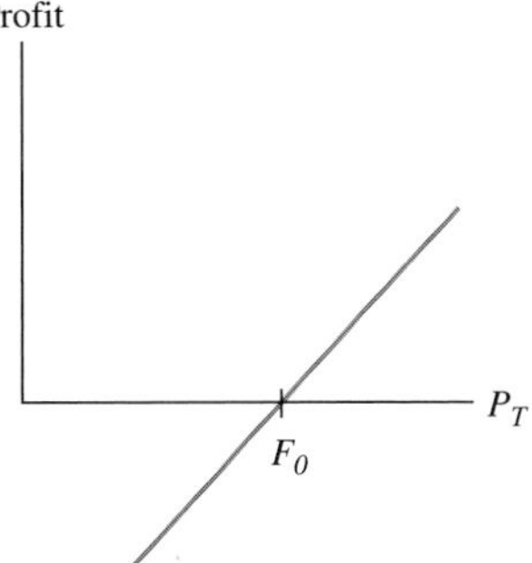


Long futures profit = $P_T - F_0$

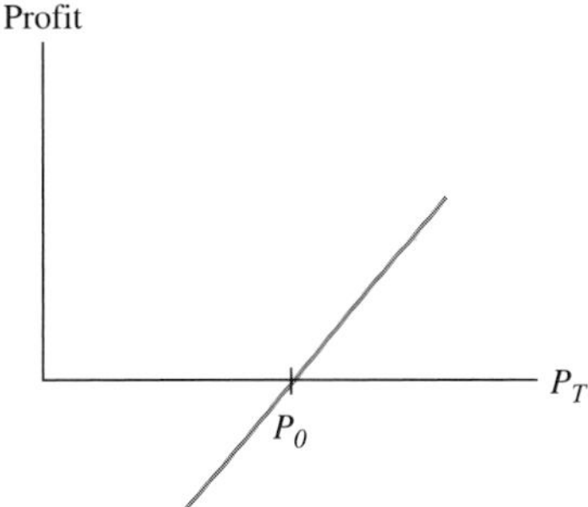


Asset profit = $P_T - P_0$

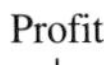

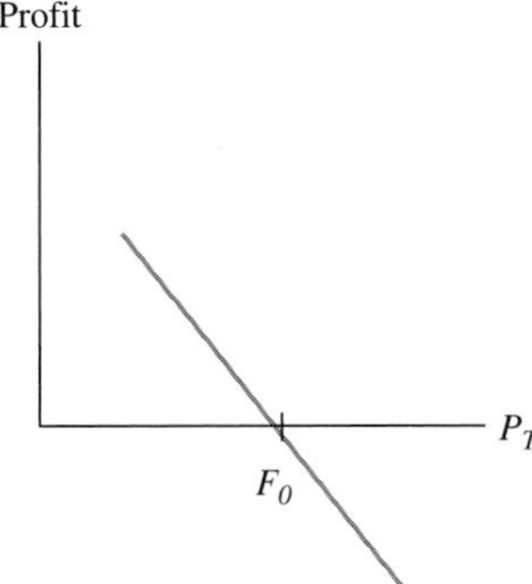


Short futures profit = $F_0 - P_T$

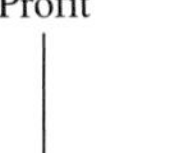

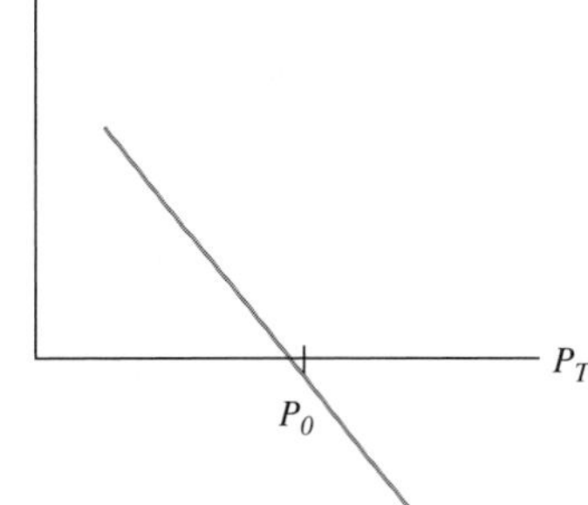


Short sale profit = $P_0 - P_T$

**2.** The futures price is the agreed-upon price for deferred delivery of the asset. If that price is fair, then the *value* of the agreement ought to be zero; that is, the contract will be a zero-NPV agreement for each trader.

**3.** Because long positions equal short positions, futures trading *must* entail a "canceling out" of bets on the asset. Moreover, no cash is transacted at the inception of futures trading. Thus, there should be minimal impact on the spot market for the asset, and futures trading should not be expected to reduce capital available for other uses.

**4.** The clearinghouse has a zero net position in all contracts. Its long and short positions are offsetting, so that net cash flow from marking to market must be zero.

**5.** Zero. Zero.

**6.** The risk would be that aluminum and bauxite prices do not move perfectly together. Thus, basis risk involving the spread between the futures price and bauxite spot prices could persist even if the aluminum futures price were set perfectly relative to aluminum itself.

7.

| Action | Initial CF | Time-$T$ CF |
|---|---|---|
| Lend \$250 | −\$250 | + \$250 × 1.04 = \$260 |
| Short stock | \$250 | $-S_T$ − \$5 |
| Long futures | 0 | $S_T$ − \$253 |
| | 0 | \$2 |

8. It must have zero beta. If the futures price is an unbiased estimator, then we infer that it has a zero risk premium, which means that beta must be zero.
9. As the payoffs to the two strategies are identical, so should be the costs of establishing them. The synthetic stock strategy costs $F_0/(1 + r_f)^T$ to establish, this being the present value of the futures price. The stock index purchased directly costs $S_0$. Therefore we conclude that $S_0 = F_0/(1 + r_f)^T$, or $F_0 = S_0(1 + r_f)^T$, which is the parity relationship.
10. If the futures price were above the parity level, investors would sell futures and buy stocks. Short selling would not be necessary. Therefore the top of the no-arbitrage band would be unaffected by the use of the proceeds. If the futures price were too low, investors would want to short sell stocks and buy futures. Now the costs of short selling are important. If proceeds from the short sale become available, short selling becomes less costly and the bottom of the band moves up.
11. According to interest rate parity, $F_0$ should be \$2.12. Since the futures price is too high, we should reverse the arbitrage strategy just considered.

| | CF Now (\$) | CF in 1 Year |
|---|---|---|
| 1. Borrow \$2.10 in Canada. Convert to one pound. | +2.10 | −2.10(1.06) |
| 2. Lend the one pound in the U.K. | −2.10 | 1.05 $E_1$ |
| 3. Enter a contract to sell 1.05 pounds at a futures price of \$2.14. | 0 | (1.05)(2.14 − $E_1$) |
| TOTAL | 0 | .021 |

12. Stocks offer a total return (capital gain plus dividends) large enough to compensate investors for the time value of the money tied up in the stock. Wheat prices do not necessarily increase over time. In fact, across a harvest, wheat prices will fall. The returns necessary to make storage economically attractive are lacking.
13. If systematic risk were higher, the appropriate discount rate, $k$, would increase. Referring to equation 22.10, we conclude that $F_0$ would fall. Intuitively, the claim to 1 pound of orange juice is worth less today if its expected price is unchanged, but the risk associated with the value of the claim increases. Therefore, the amount investors are willing to pay today for future delivery is lower.

Appendix C

# Glossary

**Abnormal return:** Return on a stock beyond what would be predicted by market movements alone. Cumulative abnormal return (CAR) is the total abnormal return for the period surrounding an announcement or the release of information.

**Accounting earnings:** Earnings of a firm as reported on its income statement.

**Acid test ratio:** See Quick ratio.

**Active management:** Attempts to achieve portfolio returns more than commensurate with risk, either by forecasting broad market trends or by identifying particular mispriced sectors of a market or securities in a market.

**Active portfolio:** In the context of the Treynor-Black model, the portfolio formed by mixing analyzed stocks of perceived non-zero alpha values. This portfolio is ultimately mixed with the passive market index portfolio.

**Adjustable-rate mortgage:** A mortgage whose interest rate varies according to some specified measure of the current market interest rate.

**Advance-decline line:** A graph of the net difference between the number of stock prices advancing and the number declining; a technical indicator of market breadth.

**Agency problem:** Conflicts of interest among stockholders, bondholders, and managers.

**Alpha:** The abnormal rate of return on a security in excess of what would be predicted by an equilibrium model like the CAPM or APT.

**American Depository Receipt (ADR):** The instrument traded on the NYSE which represents an equity interest in a (foreign) company; ADRs are equivalent to a number of shares in the company, as traded in that company's home market, and are entitled to proportional payments of dividends.

**American option, European option:** An American option can be exercised before and up to its expiration date. Compare with a *European option*, which can be exercised only on the expiration date.

**Announcement date:** Date on which particular news concerning a given company is announced to the public. Used in *event studies*, which researchers use to evaluate the economic impact of events of interest.

**Appraisal ratio:** The signal-to-noise ratio of an analyst's forecasts. The ratio of alpha to residual standard deviation.

**Arbitrage:** A zero-risk, zero-net investment strategy that still generates profits.

**Arbitrage pricing theory:** An asset pricing theory that is derived from a factor model, using diversification and arbitrage arguments. The theory describes the relationship between expected returns on securities, given that there are no opportunities to create wealth through risk-free arbitrage investments.

**Asked price:** The price at which a dealer will sell a security.

**Asset allocation decision:** Choosing among broad asset classes such as stocks versus bonds.

**Asset turnover (ATO):** The annual sales generated by each dollar of assets (sales/assets).

**At the money:** When an options exercise price equals its asset value.

**Auction market:** A market where all traders in a good meet at one place to buy or sell an asset. The TSE is an example.

**Average collection period, or days' receivables:** The ratio of accounts receivable to sales, or the total amount of credit extended per dollar of daily sales (average AR/sales × 365).

**Balance sheet:** A financial statement of the assets, liabilities, and net worth of the firm as of a particular date.

**Bank discount yield:** An annualized interest rate assuming simple interest, a 360-day year, and using the face value of the security rather than purchase price to compute return per dollar invested.

**Banker's acceptance:** A money market asset consisting of an order to a bank by a customer to pay a sum of money at a future date.

**Basis:** The difference between the futures price and the spot price.

**Basis risk:** Risk attributable to uncertain movements in the spread between a futures price and a spot price.

**Benchmark error:** Use of an inappropriate proxy for the true market portfolio.

**Beta:** The measure of the systematic risk of a security. The tendency of a security's returns to respond to swings in the broad market.

**Bid price:** The price at which a dealer is willing to purchase a security.

**Bid-asked spread:** The difference between a dealer's bid and asked price.

**Binomial model:** An option valuation model predicated on the assumption that stock prices can move to only two values over any short time period.

**Black-Scholes formula:** An equation to value a call option that uses the stock price, the exercise price, the risk-free interest rate, the time to maturity, and the standard deviation of the stock return.

**Block house:** Brokerage firms that help to find potential buyers or sellers of large block trades.

**Block sale:** A transaction of more than 10,000 shares of stock.

**Block transactions:** Large transactions in which at least 10,000 shares of stock are bought or sold. Brokers or "block houses" often search directly for other large traders rather than bringing the trade to the stock exchange.

**Board lot:** A standard volume of traded securities, generally equal to 100 shares. It can be larger (smaller) for low-priced (high-priced) securities.

**Bogey:** The return an investment manager is compared to for performance evaluation.

**Bond:** A security issued by a borrower that obligates the issuer to make specified payments to the holder over a specified period. A *coupon bond* obligates the issuer to make interest payments called coupon payments over the life of the bond, then to repay the *principal* at maturity.

**Bond equivalent yield:** Bond yield calculated on an annual percentage rate method. Differs from effective annual yield.

**Bond index portfolio:** A portfolio of bonds stratified to include representatives of available grades, coupons, and maturities in weights proportional to the actual bond universe.

**Book value:** An accounting measure describing the net worth of common equity according to a firm's balance sheet.

**Breadth:** A technical indicator measuring the extent to which movement in a market index is reflected in the price movements of all stocks.

**Brokered market:** A market where an intermediary (a broker) offers search services to buyers and sellers.

**Bull CD, bear CD:** A *bull CD* pays its holder a specified percentage of the increase in return on a specified market index while guaranteeing a minimum rate of return. A *bear CD* pays the holder a fraction of any fall in a given market index.

**Bullish, bearish:** Words used to describe investor attitudes. *Bullish* means optimistic; *bearish* means pessimistic. Also used in bull market and bear market.

**Bundling, unbundling:** A trend allowing creation of securities either by combining primitive and derivative securities into one composite hybrid or by separating returns on an asset into classes.

**Business cycle:** The sequence of expansion and contraction of activity in the economy, observable after the fact.

**Call option:** The right to buy an asset at a specified exercise price on or before a specified expiration date.

**Call protection:** An initial period during which a callable bond may not be called.

**Callable bond:** A bond that the issuer may repurchase at a given price in some specified period.

**Capital allocation decision:** The choice of the proportion of the overall portfolio to place in safe money market securities, versus risky but higher-return securities like stocks.

**Capital allocation line (CAL):** A graph showing all feasible risk-return combinations of a risky and risk-free asset.

**Capital gains:** The amount by which the sale price of a security exceeds the purchase price.

**Capital market line (CML):** A capital allocation line provided by the market index portfolio.

**Capital markets:** Includes longer-term, relatively riskier securities.

**Cash delivery:** The provision of some futures contracts that requires no delivery of the underlying assets (as in agricultural futures) but settlement according to the cash value of the asset.

**Cash equivalents:** Short-term money-market securities.

**Cash flow matching:** A form of immunization, matching cash flows from a bond with an obligation.

**Cash/bond selection:** Asset allocation in which the choice is between short-term cash equivalents and longer-term bonds.

**CDN system (COATS):** The automated quotation system for the Canadian OTC market, the equivalent of NASDAQ in the United States.

**Certainty equivalent:** The certain return providing the same utility as a risky portfolio.

**Certificate of deposit:** A bank time deposit.

**Clearinghouse:** Established by exchanges to facilitate transfer of securities resulting from trades. For options and futures contracts, the clearinghouse may interpose itself as a middleman between two traders.

**Closed-end (mutual) fund:** A fund whose shares are traded through brokers at market prices; the fund will not redeem shares at their net asset value. The market price of the fund can differ from the net asset value.

**Collateral:** A specific asset pledged against possible default on a bond. *Mortgage* bonds are backed by claims on property. *Collateral trust bonds* are backed by claims on other securities. *Equipment obligation bonds* are backed by claims on equipment.

**Collateralized mortgage obligation (CMO):** A mortgage pass-through security that partitions cash flows from underlying mortgages into successive maturity groups, called *tranches*, that receive principal payments according to different maturities.

**Commercial paper:** Short-term unsecured debt issued by large corporations.

**Commission broker:** A broker on the floor of the exchange who executes orders for other members.

**Common stock:** Equities, or equity securities, issued as ownership shares in a publicly held corporation. Shareholders have voting rights and may receive dividends based on their proportionate ownership.

**Comparison universe:** The collection of money managers of similar investment style used for assessing relative performance of a portfolio manager.

**Complete portfolio:** The entire portfolio, including risky and risk-free assets.

**Concentration (of control):** The holding by a few individuals of controlling blocks of shares in companies representing a large segment of the Canadian economy.

**Confidence index:** The ratio of the average yield on 10 top-rated corporate bonds divided by the average yield on 10 intermediate-grade corporate bonds; a technical indicator that is bullish when the index approaches 100 percent, implying low risk premiums.

**Constant growth model:** A form of the dividend discount model that assumes dividends will grow at a constant rate.

**Contango theory:** Holds that the futures price must exceed the expected future spot price.

**Contingent claim:** Claim whose value is directly dependent on or is contingent on the value of some underlying assets.

**Contingent immunization:** A mixed passive-active strategy that immunizes a portfolio if necessary to guarantee a minimum acceptable return but otherwise allows active management.

**Convergence property:** The convergence of futures prices and spot prices at the maturity of the futures contract.

**Convertible bond:** A bond with an option allowing the bondholder to exchange the bond for a number of shares. The *market conversion price* is the current value of the shares for which the bond may be exchanged. The *conversion premium* is the excess of the bond's value over the conversion price.

**Convexity:** The property of curvature in the graph which expresses the rate of change in bond value in response to changes in the interest rate; higher coupon bonds have greater convexity than lower or zero-coupon bonds of the same duration.

**Corporate bonds:** Long-term debt issued by private corporations typically paying semiannual coupons and returning the face value of the bond at maturity.

**Correlation coefficient:** A statistic that scales the covariance to a value between minus one (perfect negative correlation) and plus one (perfect positive correlation).

**Cost-of-carry relationship:** See spot-futures parity theorem.

**Country selection:** A type of active international management that measures the contribution to performance attributable to investing in the better-performing stock markets of the world.

**Coupon rate:** A bond's interest payments per dollar of par value.

**Covariance:** A measure of the degree to which returns on two risky assets move in tandem. A positive covariance means that asset returns move together. A negative covariance means they vary inversely.

**Covered call:** A combination of selling a call on a stock together with buying the stock.

**Covered interest arbitrage relationship:** See interest rate parity theorem.

**Credit enhancement:** Purchase of the financial guarantee of a large insurance company to raise funds.

**Cross hedge:** Hedging a position in one asset using futures on another commodity.

**Cross-holdings:** The holding of an equity interest by a corporation in another, independent corporation; this practice artificially inflates the aggregate value of equities.

**Cumulative abnormal return:** See abnormal return.

**Currency selection:** Asset allocation in which the investor chooses among investments denominated in different currencies.

**Current ratio:** A ratio representing the ability of the firm to pay off its current liabilities by liquidating current assets (current assets/current liabilities).

**Day order:** A buy order or a sell order expiring at the close of the trading day.

**Day's receivables:** See average collection period.

**Dealer market:** A market where traders specializing in particular commodities buy and sell assets for their own accounts. The OTC market is an example.

**Debenture or unsecured bond:** A bond not backed by specific collateral.

**Dedication strategy:** Refers to multiperiod cash flow matching.

**Default premium:** A differential in promised yield that compensates the investor for the risk inherent in purchasing a corporate bond that entails some risk of default.

**Deferred annuities:** Tax-advantaged life insurance product. Deferred annuities offer deferral of taxes with the option of withdrawing one's funds in the form of a life annuity.

**Defined benefit plans:** Pension plans in which retirement benefits are set according to a fixed formula.

**Defined contribution plans:** Pension plans in which the corporation is committed to making contributions according to a fixed formula.

**Delta (of option):** See hedge ratio.

**Demand shock:** An event affecting the aggregate demand for goods and services, thereby influencing the state of the economy.

**Derivative asset/contingent claim:** Securities providing payoffs that depend on or are contingent on the values of other assets such as commodity prices, bond and stock prices, or market index values. Examples are futures and options.

**Derivative security:** See primitive security.

**Detachable warrant:** A warrant entitles the holder to buy a given number of shares of stocks at a stipulated price. A detachable warrant is one that may be sold separately from the package it may have originally been issued with (usually a bond).

**Direct search market:** Buyers and sellers seek each other directly and transact directly.

**Discount function:** The discounted value of $1 as a function of time until payment.

**Discounted dividend model (DDM):** A formula to estimate the intrinsic value of a firm by figuring the present value of all expected future dividends.

**Discretionary account:** An account of a customer who gives a broker the authority to make buy and sell decisions on the customer's behalf.

**Diversifiable risk:** Risk attributable to firm-specific risk, or non-market risk. Non-diversifiable risk refers to systematic or market risk.

**Diversification:** Spreading a portfolio over many investments to avoid excessive exposure to any one source of risk.

**Dividend payout ratio:** Percentage of earnings paid out as dividends.

**Dollar-cost averaging:** A strategy for investing by which the same sum of money is invested at regular time intervals; as an alternative to buying the same number of shares, this results in lower average cost for the portfolio.

**Dollar-weighted return:** The internal rate of return on an investment.

**Doubling option:** A sinking fund provision that may allow repurchase of twice the required number of bonds at the sinking fund call price.

**Dow theory:** A long-standing approach to forecasting stock market direction by identification of long-term trends; the Dow Jones Industrial and Transportation Averages were used by Charles Dow to identify and confirm underlying trends.

**Dual funds:** Funds in which income and capital shares on a portfolio of stocks are sold separately.

**Duration:** A measure of the average life of a bond, defined as the weighted average of the times until each payment is made, with weights proportional to the present value of the payment.

**Dynamic hedging:** Constant updating of hedge positions as market conditions change.

**EAFE index:** The European, Australian, Far East index, computed by Morgan, Stanley, is a widely used index of non-U.S. stocks.

**Earnings retention ratio:** Plowback ratio.

**Earnings yield:** The ratio of earnings to price, E/P.

**Economic earnings:** The real flow of cash that a firm could pay out forever in the absence of any change in the firm's productive capacity.

**Effective annual yield:** Annualized interest rate on a security computed using compound interest techniques.

**Efficient diversification:** The organizing principle of modern portfolio theory, which maintains that any risk-averse investor will search for the highest expected return for any level of portfolio risk.

**Efficient frontier:** Graph representing a set of portfolios that maximize expected return at each level of portfolio risk.

**Efficient market hypothesis:** The prices of securities fully reflect available information. Investors buying securities in an efficient market should expect to obtain an equilibrium rate of return. Weak-form EMH asserts that stock prices already reflect all information contained in the history of past prices. The semistrong-form hypothesis asserts that stock prices already reflect all publicly available information. The strong-form hypothesis asserts that stock prices reflect all relevant information including insider information.

**Endowment funds:** Organizations chartered to invest money for specific purposes.

**Eurodollars:** Dollar-denominated deposits at foreign banks or foreign branches of American banks.

**European option:** A European option can be exercised only on the expiration date. Compare with an American option, which can be exercised before, up to, and including its expiration date.

**Event study:** Research methodology designed to measure the impact of an event of interest on stock returns.

**Excess return:** The difference between the actual rate of return on a risk-free asset and the risk-free rate.

**Exchange rate:** Price of a unit of one country's currency in terms of another country's currency.

**Exchanges:** National or regional auction markets providing a facility for members to trade securities. A seat is a membership on an exchange.

**Exercise or strike price:** Price set for calling (buying) an asset or putting (selling) an asset.

**Expectations hypothesis (of interest rates):** Theory that forward interest rates are unbiased estimates of expected future interest rates.

**Expected return:** The probability weighted average of the possible outcomes.

**Expected return-beta relationship:** Implication of the CAPM that security risk premiums (expected excess returns) will be proportional to beta.

**Extendible bond:** A bond that the holder may choose either to redeem for par value at maturity, or to extend for a given number of years; it is known as a put bond in the United States.

**Face value:** See Par value.

**Factor model:** A way of decomposing the factors that influence a security's rate of return into common and firm-specific influences.

**Factor portfolio:** A well-diversified portfolio constructed to have a beta of 1.0 on one factor and a beta of zero on any other factor.

**Fair game:** An investment prospect that has a zero-risk premium.

**FIFO:** The first-in first-out accounting method of inventory valuation.

**Filter rule:** A technical analysis technique stated as a rule for buying or selling stock according to past price movements.

**Financial assets:** Financial assets such as stocks and bonds are claims to the income generated by real assets or claims on income from the government.

**Financial engineering:** Innovative security design and repackaging of investments.

**Financial intermediary:** An institution such as a bank, mutual fund, investment company, or insurance company that serves to connect the household and business sectors so households can invest and businesses can finance production.

**Financial investment:** The investment of capital in financial instruments and asset, rather than in real, physical goods (real investment).

**Firm-specific risk:** See diversifiable risk.

**First-pass regression:** A time series regression to estimate the betas of securities or portfolios.

**Fiscal policy:** The use of taxes and government spending to affect aggregate demand as well as other objectives of macroeconomic policy.

**Fixed annuities:** Annuity contracts in which the insurance company pays a fixed dollar amount of money per period.

**Fixed-charge coverage ratio:** Ratio of earnings to all fixed cash obligations, including lease payments and sinking fund payments.

**Fixed-income security:** A security such as a bond that pays a specified cash flow over a specific period.

**Flight to quality:** Describes the tendency of investors to require larger default premiums on investments under uncertain economic conditions.

**Floating-rate bond:** A bond whose interest rate is reset periodically according to a specified market rate.

**Floor broker:** A member of the exchange who can execute orders for commission brokers.

**Flower bond:** Special Treasury bond (no longer issued) that may be used to settle federal estate taxes at par value under certain conditions.

**Forced conversion:** Use of a firm's call option on a callable convertible bond when the firm knows that bondholders will exercise their option to convert.

**Foreign exchange market:** An informal network of banks and brokers that allows customers to enter forward contracts to purchase or sell currencies in the future at a rate of exchange agreed upon now.

**Foreign exchange swap:** The exchange of cash flows denominated in one currency for cash flows denominated in another currency, in order to manage the foreign exchange risk.

**Forward contract:** An arrangement calling for future delivery of an asset at an agreed-upon price. Also see futures contract.

**Forward interest rate:** Rate of interest for a future period that would equate the total return of a long-term bond with that of a strategy of rolling over shorter-term bonds. The forward rate is inferred from the term structure.

**Fourth market:** Direct trading in exchange-listed securities between one investor and another without the benefit of a broker.

**Fully diluted earnings per share:** Earnings per share expressed as if all outstanding convertible securities and warrants have been exercised.

**Fundamental analysis:** Research to predict stock value that focuses on such determinants as earnings and dividends prospects, expectations for future interest rates, and risk evaluation of the firm.

**Futures contract:** Obliges traders to purchase or sell an asset at an agreed-upon price on a specified future date. The long position is held by the trader who commits to purchase. The short position is held by the trader who commits to sell. Futures differ from forward contracts in their standardization, exchange trading, margin requirements, and daily settling (marking to market).

**Futures option:** The right to enter a specified futures contract at a futures price equal to the stipulated exercise price.

**Futures price:** The price at which a futures trader commits to make or take delivery of the underlying asset.

**Globalization:** Tendency toward a worldwide investment environment, and the integration of national capital markets.

**Growth company:** A company for which the growth rate is greater than the market average due to superior opportunities for reinvestment.

**Guaranteed insurance contract:** A contract promising a stated nominal rate of interest over some specific time period, usually several years.

**Hedge ratio (for an option):** The number of stocks required to hedge against the price risk of holding one option. Also called the option's delta.

**Hedging:** Investing in an asset to reduce the overall risk of a portfolio.

**Holding period return:** The rate of return over a given period.

**Homogenous expectations:** The assumption that all investors use the same expected returns and covariance matrix of security returns as inputs in security analysis.

**Horizon analysis:** Interest rate forecasting that uses a forecast yield curve to predict bond prices.

**Illiquidity premium:** Increase in the expected return of illiquid assets to compensate for their higher transaction costs.

**Immunization:** A strategy that matches durations of assets and liabilities so as to make net worth unaffected by interest rate movements.

**Implied volatility:** The standard deviation of stock returns that is consistent with an option's market value.

**In the money:** In the money describes an option whose exercise would produce profits. Out of the money describes an option where exercise would not be profitable.

**Income fund:** A mutual fund providing for liberal current income from investments.

**Income statement:** A financial statement summarizing the profitability of the firm over a period of time, such as a year; revenues and expenses are listed and their difference is calculated as net income.

**Incomplete markets:** Financial markets in which the number of available independent securities is less than the number of distinct future states of the world.

**Indenture:** The document defining the contract between the bond issuer and the bondholder.

**Index arbitrage:** An investment strategy that exploits divergences between actual futures prices and their theoretically correct parity values to make a profit.

**Index fund:** A mutual fund holding shares in proportion to their representation in a market index such as the S&P 500.

**Index model:** A model of stock returns using a market index such as the S&P 500 to represent common or systematic risk factors.

**Index option:** A call or put option based on a stock market index.

**Indifference curve:** A curve connecting all portfolios with the same utility according to their means and standard deviations.

**Industry life cycle:** The set of stages in the evolution of an industry from innovative development to maturity and decline, which define the expectable returns for member firms.

**Initial public offering:** Stock issued to the public for the first time by a formerly privately owned company.

**Input list:** The set of estimates of expected rates of return and covariances for the securities that will constitute portfolios forming the efficient frontier.

**Inside information:** Non-public knowledge about a corporation possessed by corporate officers, major owners, or other individuals with privileged access to information about a firm.

**Insider trading:** Trading by officers, directors, major stockholders, or others who hold private inside information allowing them to benefit from buying or selling stock.

**Insider transactions:** Transactions by officers, directors, and major stockholders in their firm's securities; these transactions must be reported publicly at regular intervals.

**Insurance principle:** The law of averages. The average outcome for many independent trials of an experiment will approach the expected value of the experiment.

**Insured defined benefit pension:** A firm sponsoring a pension plan enters into a contractual agreement by which an insurance company assumes all liability for the benefits accrued under the plan.

**Integration:** The condition in which two distinct financial markets can be analyzed as if they were a single market.

**Interest coverage ratio, or times interest earned:** A financial leverage measure (EBIT divided by interest expense).

**Interest rate:** The number of dollars earned per dollar invested per period.

**Interest rate parity theorem:** The spot-futures exchange rate relationship that prevails in well-functioning markets.

**Interest rate swaps:** A method to manage interest rate risk where parties trade the cash flows corresponding to different securities without actually exchanging securities directly.

**Intermarket spread swap:** Switching from one segment of the bond market to another (from Treasuries to corporates, for example).

**Intrinsic value (of a firm):** The present value of a firm's expected future net cash flows discounted by the required rate of return.

**Intrinsic value of an option:** Stock price minus exercise price, or the profit that could be attained by immediate exercise of an in-the-money option.

**Investment dealers:** Firms that specialize in the sale of new securities to the public, typically by underwriting the issue; they are known as investment bankers in the United States.

**Investment company:** Firm managing funds for investors. An investment company may manage several mutual funds.

**Investment horizon:** The planned liquidation date of an investment portfolio or part of it; it plays a role in the choice of assets.

**Investment portfolio:** Set of securities chosen by an investor.

**Investment grade bond:** Bond rated BBB and above or Baa and above. Lower-rated bonds are classified as speculative-grade or junk bonds.

**Jensen's measure:** The alpha of an investment.

**Junk bond:** See speculative grade bond.

**Law of one price:** The rule stipulating that equivalent securities or bundles of securities must sell at equal prices to preclude arbitrage opportunities.

**Leading economic indicators:** A collection of economic series shown to precede changes in overall economic activity; these include retail sales, financial, manufacturing, house sales measures, and the U.S. index.

**Leakage:** Release of information to some persons before official public announcement.

**Leverage ratio:** Measure of debt to total capitalization of a firm.

**LIFO:** The last-in first-out accounting method of valuing inventories.

**Limit order:** An order specifying a price at which an investor is willing to buy or sell a security.

**Limited liability:** The fact that shareholders have no personal liability to the creditors of the corporation in the event of failure.

**Liquidation value:** Net amount that could be realized by selling the assets of a firm after paying the debt.

**Liquidity:** The ease with which an asset can be converted to cash.

**Liquidity preference theory:** Theory that the forward rate exceeds expected future interest rates.

**Liquidity premium:** Forward rate minus expected future short interest rate.

**Load fund:** A mutual fund with a sales commission, or load.

**London Interbank Offered Rate (LIBOR):** Rate that most creditworthy banks charge one another for large loans of Eurodollars in the London market.

**Long position or long hedge:** Protecting the future cost of a purchase by taking a long futures position to protect against changes in the price of the asset.

**Maintenance, or variation, margin:** An established value below which a trader's margin cannot fall. Reaching the maintenance margin triggers a margin call.

**Management expense ratio:** The combination of operating expenses and other charges expressed as a ratio of total assets in a mutual fund.

**Margin:** Describes securities purchased with money borrowed from a broker. Current maximum margin is 50 percent.

**Market making:** The act of receiving orders to buy and sell securities and dealing in those securities, thereby establishing market liquidity and a price for the securities.

**Market model:** Another version of the index model that breaks down return uncertainty into systematic and non-systematic components.

**Market or systematic risk, firm-specific risk:** Market risk is risk attributable to common macroeconomic factors. Firm-specific risk reflects risk peculiar to an individual firm that is independent of market risk.

**Market order:** A buy or sell order to be executed immediately at current market prices.

**Market portfolio:** The portfolio for which each security is held in proportion to its market value.

**Market price of risk:** A measure of the extra return, or risk premium, that investors demand to bear risk. The reward-to-risk ratio of the market portfolio.

**Market segmentation or preferred habitat theory:** The theory that long- and short-maturity bonds are traded in essentially distinct or segmented markets and that prices in one market do not affect those in the other.

**Market timing:** Asset allocation in which the investment in the market is increased if one forecasts that the market will outperform T-bills.

**Market value-weighted index:** An index of a group of securities computed by calculating a weighted average of the returns of each security in the index, with weights proportional to outstanding market value.

**Market-book ratio:** Market price of a share divided by book value per share.

**Marking to market:** Describes the daily settlement of obligations on futures positions.

**Mean return:** See Expected return.

**Mean-variance analysis:** Evaluation of risky prospects based on the expected value and variance of possible outcomes.

**Mean-variance criterion:** The selection of portfolios based on the means and variances of their returns. The choice of the higher expected return portfolio for a given level of variance or the lower variance portfolio for a given expected return.

**Measurement error:** Errors in measuring an explanatory variable in a regression that lead to biases in estimated parameters.

**Membership or seat on an exchange:** A limited number of exchange positions that enable the holder to trade for the holder's own accounts and charge clients for the execution of trades for their accounts.

**Minimum–variance frontier:** Graph of the lowest possible portfolio variance that is attainable for a given portfolio expected return.

**Minimum–variance portfolio:** The portfolio of risk assets with lowest variance.

**Modern portfolio theory (MPT):** Principles underlying analysis and evaluation of rational portfolio choices based on risk-return trade-offs and efficient diversification.

**Monetary policy:** The manipulation of the money supply to influence economic activity and the level of interest rates.

**Money market:** Includes short-term, highly liquid, and relatively low-risk debt instruments.

**Mortality tables:** Tables of probabilities that individuals of various ages will die within a year.

**Mortgage-backed security:** Ownership claim in a pool of mortgages or an obligation that is secured by such a pool. Also called a *pass-through*, because payments are passed along from the mortgage originator to the purchaser of the mortgage-backed security.

**Moving average:** A rolling average of stock prices, based on a short, intermediate, or long period, serving as a reference point for the current price; displayed on a chart.

**Multifactor CAPM:** Generalization of the basic CAPM that accounts for extra-market hedging demands.

**Municipal bonds:** Tax-exempt bonds issued by state and local governments in the United States, generally to finance capital improvement projects. General obligation bonds are backed by the general taxing power of the issuer. Revenue bonds are backed by the proceeds from the project or agency they are issued to finance.

**Mutual fund:** A firm pooling and managing funds of investors.

**Mutual fund theorem:** A result associated with the CAPM, asserting that investors will choose to invest their entire risky portfolio in a market-index mutual fund.

**Naked option writing:** Writing an option without an offsetting stock position.

**NASDAQ:** The automated quotation system for the OTC market, showing current bid-asked prices for thousands of stocks.

**Neglected-firm effect:** That investments in stock of less well-known firms have generated abnormal returns.

**No-load fund:** A mutual fund with no sales commission.

**Nondiversifiable risk:** See Systematic risk.

**Nonsystematic risk:** Non-market or firm-specific risk factors that can be eliminated by diversification. Also called unique risk or diversifiable risk. Systematic risk refers to risk factors common to the entire economy.

**Normal backwardation theory:** Holds that the futures price will be bid down to a level below the expected spot price.

**Odd-lot theory:** Assessment of market tops and bottoms by observation of the net buying and selling of odd-lots (shares sold in less than round or board lots); used as a contrarian measure so that odd-lot buying suggests a top.

**Open (good-till-canceled) order:** A buy or sell order remaining in force for up to six months unless canceled.

**Open interest:** The number of futures contracts outstanding.

**Open-end (mutual) fund:** A fund that issues or redeems its own shares at their net asset value (NAV).

**Optimal risky portfolio:** An investor's best combination of risky assets to be mixed with safe assets to form the complete portfolio.

**Option elasticity:** The percentage increase in an option's value given a 1 percent change in the value of the underlying security.

**Original issue discount bond:** A bond issued with a low coupon rate that sells at a discount from par value.

**Out of the money:** Out of the money describes an option where exercise would not be profitable. In the money describes an option where exercise would produce profits.

**Over-the-counter market:** An informal network of brokers and dealers who negotiate sales of securities (not a formal exchange).

**Par value:** The face value of the bond.

**Pass-through security:** Pools of loans (such as home mortgage loans) sold in one package. Owners of pass-throughs receive all principal and interest payments made by the borrowers.

**Passive investment strategy:** See passive management.

**Passive management:** Buying a well-diversified portfolio to represent a broad-based market index without attempting to search out mispriced securities.

**Passive portfolio:** A market index portfolio.

**Passive strategy:** See passive management.

**P/E effect:** That portfolios of low P/E stocks have exhibited higher average risk-adjusted returns than high P/E stocks.

**Personal trust:** An interest in an asset held by a trustee for the benefit of another person.

**Plowback ratio:** The proportion of the firm's earnings that is reinvested in the business (and not paid out as dividends). The plowback ratio equals 1 minus the dividend payout ratio.

**Political risk:** Possibility of the expropriation of assets, changes in tax policy, restrictions on the exchange of foreign currency for domestic currency, or other changes in the business climate of a country.

**Portfolio insurance:** The practice of using options or dynamic hedge strategies to provide protection against investment losses while maintaining upside potential.

**Portfolio management:** Process of combining securities in a portfolio tailored to the investor's preferences and needs, monitoring that portfolio, and evaluating its performance.

**Portfolio opportunity set:** The possible expected return-standard deviation pairs of all portfolios that can be constructed from a given set of assets.

**Preferred habitat theory:** Holds that investors prefer specific maturity ranges but can be induced to switch if premiums are sufficient.

**Preferred stock:** Non-voting shares in a corporation, paying a fixed or variable stream of dividends.

**Premium:** The purchase price of an option.

**Price-earnings multiple:** See Price-earnings ratio.

**Price-earnings ratio:** The ratio of a stock's price to its earnings per share. Also referred to as the P/E multiple.

**Price weighted average:** This is computed by adding the prices of 30 companies and dividing by the divisor.

**Primary market:** New issues of securities are offered to the public here.

**Primitive security, derivative security:** A *primitive security* is an instrument such as a stock or bond for which payments depend only on the financial status of its issuer. A *derivative security* is created from the set of primitive securities to yield returns that depend on factors beyond the characteristics of the issuer and that may be related to prices of other assets.

**Principal:** The outstanding balance on a loan.

**Profit margin:** See Return on sales.

**Program trading:** Coordinated buy orders and sell orders of entire portfolios, usually with the aid of computers, often to achieve index arbitrage objectives.

**Prospectus:** A final and approved registration statement including the price at which the security issue is offered.

**Protective convenant:** A provision specifying requirements of collateral, sinking fund, dividend policy, etc., designed to protect the interests of bondholders.

**Protective put:** Purchase of stock combined with a put option that guarantees minimum proceeds equal to the put's exercise price.

**Proxy:** An instrument empowering an agent to vote in the name of the shareholder.

**Prudent man:** A phrase implying the conduct of conservative investment practices by professional and institutional investors when managing others' funds.

**Public offering, private placement:** A *public offering* consists of bonds sold in the primary market to the general public; a *private placement* is sold directly to a limited number of institutional investors.

**Pure yield pickup swap:** Moving to higher yield bonds.

**Put option:** The right to sell an asset at a specified exercise price on or before a specified expiration date.

**Put-call parity theorem:** An equation representing the proper relationship between put and call prices. Violation of parity allows arbitrage opportunities.

**Quick ratio:** A measure of liquidity similar to the current ratio except for exclusion of inventories (cash plus receivables divided by current liabilities).

**Random walk:** Describes the notion that stock price changes are random and unpredictable.

**Rate anticipation swap:** A switch made in response to forecasts of interest rates.

**Real assets, financial assets:** *Real assets* are land, buildings, and equipment that are used to produce goods and services. *Financial assets* are claims such as securities to the income generated by real assets.

**Real interest rate:** The excess of the interest rate over the inflation rate. The growth rate of purchasing power derived from an investment.

**Real investment:** The investment of capital in physical goods, such as equipment or plant, resulting in expansion of the productive base of the economy.

**Rebalancing:** Realigning the proportion of assets in a portfolio as needed.

**Registered bond:** A bond whose issuer records ownership and interest payments. Differs from a bearer bond, which is traded without record of ownership and whose possession is its only evidence of ownership.

**Registered trader:** A trader who makes a market in the shares of one or more firms and who maintains a "fair and orderly market" by dealing personally in the stock; registered traders are known as specialists in the United States.

**Registration statement:** Required to be filed with the SEC to describe the issue of a new security.

**Regression equation:** An equation that describes the average relationship between a dependent variable and a set of explanatory variables.

**REIT:** Real estate investment trust, which is similar to a closed-end mutual fund. REITs invest in real estate or loans secured by real estate and issue shares in such investments.

**Relative strength:** The ratio of an individual stock price to a price index for the relevant industry; a technical indicator of the out- or underperformance of a company relative to the industry or market.

**Replacement cost:** Cost to replace a firm's assets. "Reproduction" cost.

**Repurchase agreements (repos):** Short-term, often overnight, sales of government securities with an agreement to repurchase the securities at a slightly higher price. A *reverse repo* is a purchase with an agreement to resell at a specified price on a future date.

**Residual claim:** Refers to the fact that shareholders are at the bottom of the list of claimants to assets of a corporation in the event of failure or bankruptcy.

**Residuals:** Parts of stock returns not explained by the explanatory variable (the market-index return). They measure the impact of firm-specific events during a particular period.

**Resistance level:** A price level above which it is supposedly difficult for a stock or stock index to rise.

**Restricted shares:** A special type of shares that have no voting rights, or only limited voting rights, but otherwise participate fully in the financial benefits of share ownership.

**Retractable bond:** A bond that gives the right to the holder to redeem early at par value, instead of holding it till maturity date.

**Return on assets (ROA):** A profitability ratio; earnings before interest and taxes divided by total assets.

**Return on equity (ROE):** An accounting ratio of net profits divided by equity.

**Return on sales (ROS), or profit margin:** The ratio of operating profits per dollar of sales (EBIT divided by sales).

**Reversal effect:** A tendency of stocks that perform unusually poorly or unusually well during one period to follow with the opposite performance during the next period.

**Reversing trade:** Entering the opposite side of a currently held futures position to close out the position.

**Reward-to-volatility ratio:** Ratio of excess return to portfolio standard deviation.

**Riding the yield curve:** Buying long-term bonds in anticipation of capital gains as yields fall with the declining maturity of the bonds.

**Risk arbitrage:** Speculation on perceived mispriced securities, usually in connection with merger and acquisition targets.

**Risk-averse, risk-neutral, risk-lover:** A *risk-averse* investor will consider risky portfolios only if they provide compensation for risk via a risk premium. A *risk-neutral* investor finds the level of risk irrelevant and considers only the expected return of risk prospects. A *risk-lover* is willing to accept lower expected returns on prospects with higher amounts of risk.

**Risk-free asset:** An asset with a certain rate of return; often taken to be short-term T-bills.

**Risk-free rate:** The interest rate that can be earned with certainty.

**Risk lover:** See risk averse.

**Risk–neutral:** See risk averse.

**Risk premium:** An expected return in excess of that on risk-free securities. The premium provides compensation for the risk of an investment.

**Risk-return trade-off:** If an investor is willing to take on risk, there is the reward of higher expected returns.

**Risky asset:** An asset with an uncertain rate of return.

**Seasoned new issue:** Stock issued by companies that already have stock on the market.

**Second-pass regression:** A cross-sectional regression of portfolio returns on betas. The estimated slope is the measurement of the reward for bearing systematic risk during the period.

**Secondary market:** Already existing securities are bought and sold on the exchanges or in the OTC market.

**Securitization:** Pooling loans for various purposes into standardized securities backed by those loans, which can then be traded like any other security.

**Security market line:** Graphical representation of the expected return-beta relationship of the CAPM.

**Security analysis:** Determining correct value of a security in the marketplace.

**Security characteristic line:** A plot of the expected excess return on a security over the risk-free rate as a function of the excess return on the market.

**Security selection:** See security selection decision.

**Security selection decision:** Choosing the particular securities to include in a portfolio.

**Segmentation:** The state of relative independence of different financial markets, as characterized by different responses to specific factors.

**Selectivity:** The ability to select individual stocks that will perform well in particular economic climates.

**Semistrong-form EMH:** See Efficient market hypothesis.

**Separation property:** The property that portfolio choice can be separated into two independent tasks: (1) determination of the optimal risky portfolio, which is a purely technical problem, and (2) the personal choice of the best mix of the risky portfolio and the risk-free asset.

**Serial bond issue:** An issue of bonds with staggered maturity dates that spreads out the principal repayment burden over time.

**Settlement date:** The date at which capital gains are recognized for tax purposes; usually five business days after the actual trade date.

**Sharpe's measure:** Reward-to-volatility ratio; ratio of portfolio excess return to standard deviation.

**Shelf registration:** Advance registration of securities with the SEC for sale up to two years following initial registration.

**Short interest:** The total number of shares of stock held short in the market; considered bullish in that short holdings must be covered by purchases (latent demand), but bearish in that sophisticated traders (who are more likely to short) predict better.

**Short interest rate:** A one-period interest rate.

**Short position or hedge:** Protecting the value of an asset held by taking a short position in a futures contract.

**Short sale:** The sale of shares not owned by the investor but borrowed through a broker and later repurchased to replace the loan. Profit comes from initial sale at a higher price than the repurchase price.

**Simple prospect:** An investment opportunity where a certain initial wealth is placed at risk and only two outcomes are possible.

**Single-country fund:** A mutual fund that invests solely in the securities of a single country.

**Single–index model:** A model of stock returns that decomposes influences on returns into a systematic factor, as measured by the return on a broad market index, and firm-specific factors.

**Sinking fund:** A procedure that allows for the repayment of principal at maturity by calling for the bond issuer to repurchase some proportion of the outstanding bonds either in the open market or at a special call price associated with the sinking fund provision.

**Skip-day settlement:** A convention for calculating yield that assumes a T-bill sale is not settled until two days after quotation of the T-bill price.

**Small-firm effect:** That investments in stocks of small firms appear to have earned abnormal returns.

**Speculation:** Undertaking a risky investment with the objective of earning a positive profit compared with investment in a risk-free alternative (a risk premium).

**Speculative grade bond:** Bond rated Ba or lower by Moody's, or BB or lower by Standard & Poor's, or an unrated bond.

**Split share:** An equity security derived from a common share by splitting it into income and capital shares which return respectively, the original investment plus a stream of dividends and the capital gain portion since the time of splitting.

**Spot rate:** The current interest rate appropriate for discounting a cash flow of some given maturity.

**Spot-futures parity theorem, or cost-of-carry relationship:** Describes the theoretically correct relationship between spot and futures prices. Violation of the parity relationship gives rise to arbitrage opportunities.

**Spread (futures):** Taking a long position in a futures contract of one maturity and a short position in a contract of different maturity, both on the same commodity.

**Spread (options):** A combination of two or more call options or put options on the same stock with differing exercise prices or times to expiration. A vertical or money spread refers to a spread with different exercise price; a horizontal or time spread refers to differing expiration date.

**Squeeze:** The possibility that enough long positions hold their contracts to maturity that supplies of the commodity are not adequate to cover all contracts. A *short squeeze* describes the reverse: short positions threaten to deliver an expensive-to-store commodity.

**Standard deviation:** Square root of the variance.

**Statement of changes in financial position:** A listing of the sources and uses of funds through operations, financing, and investments; over the specific time period, the net addition to the cash position is determined.

**Stock exchanges:** Secondary markets where already issued securities are bought and sold by members.

**Stock selection:** An active portfolio management technique that focuses on advantageous selection of particular stocks rather than on broad asset allocation choices.

**Stock split:** Issue by a corporation of a given number of shares in exchange for the current number of shares held by stockholders. Splits may go in either direction, either increasing or decreasing the number of shares outstanding. A *reverse split* decreases the number outstanding.

**Stop-loss order:** A sell order to be executed if the price of the stock falls below a stipulated level.

**Straddle:** A combination of buying both a call and a put, each with the same exercise price and expiration date. The purpose is to profit from expected volatility in either direction.

**Straight bond:** A bond with no option features such as callability or convertibility.

**Street name:** Describes securities held by a broker on behalf of a client but registered in the name of the firm.

**Strike price:** See Exercise price.

**Strip, strap:** Variants of a straddle. A *strip* is two puts and one call on a stock; a *strap* is two calls and one put, both with the same exercise price and expiration date.

**Stripped of coupons:** Describes the practice of some investment banks that sell "synthetic" zero-coupon bonds by marketing the rights to a single payment backed by a coupon-paying Treasury bond.

**Strong-form EMH:** See Efficient market hypothesis.

**Subordination clause:** A provision in a bond indenture that restricts the issuer's future borrowing by subordinating the new leaders' claims on the firm to those of the existing bond holders. Claims of *subordinated* or *junior* debtholders are not paid until the prior debt is paid.

**Substitution swap:** Exchange of one bond for a bond with similar attributes but more attractively priced.

**Supply shock:** An event affecting the aggregate supply of goods and services, thereby influencing the state of the economy.

**Support level:** A price level below which it is supposedly difficult for a stock or stock index to fall.

**Swaps:** Arrangements between firms to exchange the payments associated with debt contracts (made with other parties), without actually exchanging the underlying contract.

**Swing fund management:** The practice of active portfolio management through the switching of weights for asset classes in response to predictions of economic changes.

**Systematic risk:** Risk factors common to the whole economy, for example non-diversifiable risk; see Market risk.

**Tactical asset allocation:** Active portfolio management achieved by the use of options and derivatives to alter the response of asset classes to economic changes; rapid and cost-effective changes to asset class sensitivity are produced by computer analysis.

**Tax anticipation notes:** Short-term municipal debt to raise funds to pay for expenses before actual collection of taxes.

**Tax swap:** Swapping two similar bonds to receive a tax benefit.

**Tax deferral option:** The feature of the U.S. Internal Revenue Code that the capital gains tax on an asset is payable only when the gain is realized by selling the asset.

**Tax-deferred retirement plans:** Employer-sponsored and other plans that allow contributions and earnings to be made and accumulate tax free until they are paid out as benefits.

**Tax shelters:** Investment opportunities whereby most, if not all, of the investment can be deducted from ordinary income for tax purposes over a years' horizon.

**Tax-timing option:** Describes the investor's ability to shift the realization of investment gains or losses and their tax implications from one period to another.

**Technical analysis:** Research to identify mispriced securities that focuses on recurrent and predictable stock price patterns and on proxies for buy or sell pressure in the market.

**Tender offer:** An offer from an outside investor to shareholders of a company to purchase their shares at a stipulated price, usually substantially above the market price, so that the investor may amass enough shares to obtain control of the company.

**Term insurance:** Provides a death benefit only, no buildup of cash value.

**Term premiums:** Excess of the yields to maturity on long-term bonds over those of short-term bonds.

**Term structure of interest rates:** The pattern of interest rates appropriate for discounting cash flows of various maturities.

**Thin trading:** Persistently infrequent trading, including long intervals without any recorded transactions, for a given security.

**Third market:** Trading of exchange-listed securities on the OTC market.

**Tick:** The net difference between the number of stocks trading higher than their previous trade prices and the number trading lower; a technical indicator of market breadth.

**Time value (of an option):** The part of the value of an option that is due to its positive time to expiration. Not to be confused with present value or the time value of money.

**Time-weighted return:** An average of the period-by-period holding period returns of an investment.

**Times interest earned:** See interest coverage ratio.

**Tobin's *q*:** Ratio of market value of the firm to replacement cost.

**Tranche:** See collateralized mortgage obligation.

**Treasury bill:** Short-term, highly liquid government securities issued at a discount from the face value and returning the face amount at maturity.

**Treasury bond or note:** Debt obligations of the U.S. federal government that make semiannual coupon payments and are sold at or near par value in denominations of $1,000 or more.

**Treynor's measure:** Ratio of excess return to beta.

**Trin:** The ratio of the number of advancing to declining stocks divided by the ratio of volume in advancing versus declining stocks; a technical indicator of market strength that is bullish when the value is less than one.

**Triple-witching hour:** The four times a year that the S&P 500 futures contract expires at the same time as the S&P 100 index option contract and option contracts on individual stocks.

**Unbundling:** See Bundling.

**Underwriting, underwriting syndicate:** Underwriters (investment bankers) purchase securities from the issuing company and resell them. Usually a syndicate of investment bankers is organized behind a lead firm.

**Unique risk:** See Diversifiable risk.

**Unit investment trust:** Money invested in a portfolio whose composition is fixed for the life of the fund. Shares in a unit trust are called redeemable trust certificates, and they are sold at a premium above NAV.

**Universal life policy:** An insurance policy that allows for a varying death benefit and premium level over the term of the policy, with an interest rate on the cash value that changes with market interest rates.

**Uptick, or zero-plus tick:** A trade resulting in a positive change in a stock price, or a trade at a constant price following a preceding price increase.

**Utility value:** The welfare a given investor assigns to an investment with a particular return and risk.

**Utility:** The measure of the welfare or satisfaction of an investor.

**Variable annuities:** Annuity contracts in which the insurance company pays a periodic amount linked to the investment performance of an underlying portfolio.

**Variable life policy:** An insurance policy that provides a fixed death benefit plus a cash value that can be invested in a variety of funds from which the policyholder can choose.

**Variance:** A measure of the dispersion of a random variable. Equals the expected value of the squared deviation from the mean.

**Variation margin:** See Maintenance margin.

**Warrant:** An option issued by the firm to purchase shares of the firm's stock.

**Weak-form EMH:** See Efficient market hypothesis.

**Weekend effect:** The common recurrent negative average return from Friday to Monday in the stock market.

**Well-diversified portfolio:** A portfolio spread out over many securities in such a way that the weight in any security is close to zero.

**Whole-life insurance policy:** Provides a death benefit and a kind of savings plan that builds up cash value for possible future withdrawal.

**Workout period:** Realignment period of a temporary misaligned yield relationship.

**Writing a call:** Selling a call option.

**Yield curve:** A graph of yield to maturity as a function of time to maturity.

**Yield to maturity:** A measure of the average rate of return that will be earned on a bond if held to maturity.

**Zero-beta portfolio:** The minimum-variance portfolio uncorrelated with a chosen efficient portfolio.

**Zero-coupon bond:** A bond paying no coupons that sells at a discount and provides payment of the principal only at maturity.

**Zero-investment portfolio:** A portfolio of zero net value, established by buying and shorting component securities, usually in the context of an arbitrage strategy.

# Name Index

# Subject Index